I am excited and impatient to put this reference volume to use. The reviews – brief, informative and stimulating – help me get engaged with Africa's issues and context.

Daniel Bourdanné (Chad)
General Secretary, International Fellowship of Evangelical Students (IFES)

Readers will find themselves provided here with valuable and comprehensive reflections on theological life in Africa.

Bosela Eale (Congo-DRC)
All Africa Conference of Churches (AACC)

This is a one-stop source for researchers, scholars, libraries, ministry leaders, and all who are interested in Africa and in African Christianity.

Aiah Foday-Khabenje (Sierra Leone)
General Secretary, Association of Evangelicals in Africa (AEA)

These reviews are timely, thoughtful and practical – an immense, well-crafted resource for those wishing to engage meaningfully with the African continent.

Ndaba Mazabane (South Africa)
Chair, World Evangelical Alliance (WEA)

Here is an invaluable tool for discovering important but less known publications in the area of African Christian reflection.

Edward Murphy, S.J. (Zimbabwe)
Librarian, Jesuit Arrupe University, Harare

Christian scholarship in Africa and about Africa has mushroomed over the years, and a reference point has been badly needed. Scholars will welcome this publication as an easily accessible reference point.

Las Newman (Jamaica)
Global Associate Director, Lausanne Movement

This new volume captures the intellectual initiative of the Christian movement in Africa. It contributes useful and provocative perspectives, a record of critical turning points, and stimulus for ongoing study – a work of real merit and service to the cause.

Lamin Sanneh (Gambia)
Professor of History, Yale University, New Haven, CT

For those seeking better understanding of contemporary African trends and issues, this will become an indispensable reference for decades to come.

Frew Tamrat (Ethiopia)
Vice-Principal, Evangelical Theological College, Addis Ababa

Christian Reflection in Africa

Langham
GLOBAL LIBRARY

Christian Reflection in Africa

Review and Engagement

Paul Bowers

Editor

REVIEWS OF CONTEMPORARY AFRICA-RELATED LITERATURE
RELEVANT FOR INFORMED CHRISTIAN REFLECTION IN AFRICA

Langham
GLOBAL LIBRARY

Published 2018 by Langham Global Library
An imprint of Langham Publishing

Langham Partnership
PO Box 296, Carlisle, Cumbria CA3 9WZ, UK
www.langham.org

ISBNs:
978-1-78368-897-5 Print
978-1-78368-445-8 ePub
978-1-78368-446-5 Mobi
978-1-78368-447-2 PDF

British Library Cataloguing-in-Publication Data
A catalogue record for this book is available from the British Library

ISBN: 978-1-78368-897-5

Cover & Book Design: projectluz.com

To Evie

Contents

Preface xi

Abbreviations xv

Authors A–C .... *reviews 1–245* 1

Authors D–G .... *reviews 246–428* 143

Authors H–K .... *reviews 429–615* 251

Authors L–M .... *reviews 616–775* 365

Authors N–P .... *reviews 776–948* 463

Authors Q–T .... *reviews 949–1111* 567

Authors U–Z .... *reviews 1112–1200* 669

Author Index 727

Title Index 740

Subject Index 775

Contributors 783

Preface

Anyone closely familiar with Africa is aware of the almost unmanageable abundance of Africa-related materials being published in recent years both on and off the continent. Amidst this abundance, which books should we be reading if we want to understand modern Africa? What publications should we be taking note of in order to keep conversant with contemporary African Christianity? Where indeed might ministry leaders and academic professionals turn for considered review in the flood of recent studies on Africa, and especially where should they turn for thoughtful assessment of such publications from a Christian perspective?

This Collection

The project upon which this reference collection is based is the review journal *BookNotes for Africa,* a specialist publication which, since 1996, has been bringing to notice just such materials, and offering brief learned reviews of their contributions. The core intention both of the journal and of this compilation has been to encourage and to facilitate informed Christian reflection and engagement in Africa, through thoughtful encounter with the published intellectual life of the continent. And as best possible also to model such informed reflection. Assembled here for ready access is the entire collection of these reviews through the first thirty issues of the journal's history.

Keeping track of recent Africa-related publications can prove daunting. This is true in part because the standard bibliographic resources of global academia still insufficiently service this region. It is also true because of the sometimes still limited patterns of communication within the continent. What is released of worth in Sierra Leone may not gain notice in Ethiopia, and what is produced in South Africa may not be readily accessible in Congo. The unfortunate outcome both within Africa and elsewhere can often be a deficient acquaintance with the remarkable outpouring of Africa-related literature in our day.

In attempting to span the spectrum of literature relevant to this project, the books and other media here selected for review represent a broad cross-section of interests and issues, of qualities and styles, of viewpoints and interpretations. Reviews are a single paragraph in length, academic in tone, and engaged in both description and assessment. The project has been limited from the beginning to titles published from 1986 onward, with emphasis on the more recent. Within those bounds the selection has included the secular as well as the religious, majoring on learned contributions while also providing occasional notice of the inspirational or more popular. Whereas practical realities affecting the project through the years have meant that the titles reviewed are predominantly in English, key contributions in French have also been included, and sometimes also those in German. Selection has been focused almost entirely on sub-Saharan Africa. While not managing to canvass every title of worth within these parameters, the collection does nevertheless provide an exceptional sampling of what might best facilitate thoughtful Christian awareness and engagement in modern Africa. If some of the books reviewed are not well known outside Africa, all of them merit some measure of notice within Africa.

More than a hundred contributors have participated in the project over the journal's lifespan. The reviews here presented were thus composed by a diverse team, at different times and places, and display a variety of styles and outlooks. While the reviews have been lightly re-edited to fit the requirements of this fresh presentation, their individualities have been carefully conserved. The identity of reviewers has been represented in the journal only by initials, as a way of signalling the presence of varied perspectives while maintaining focus on the content of the reviews. All reviews were contributed on a volunteer basis. Virtually all contributors have been either from Africa or have served at length in Africa. Most have been involved in theological education on the continent. Nearly all have earned doctorates. Evaluations have been carried out from a broadly evangelical perspective, as represented by the institutions in Africa that have served as sponsors for the journal. These have included at various times: ECWA Theological Seminary Jos (JETS) in Nigeria; George Whitefield College (GWC) in South Africa; the Theological College of Central Africa (TCCA) in Zambia; and the Evangelical Theological College (ETC) in Ethiopia. A representative list of the contributors appears as an appendix to this publication.

Using This Collection

How might readers make best use of the considerable collection of reviews provided here? The librarian might use this resource for assessments that could support (or discourage) acquisitions. The lecturer might be looking for appropriate Africa-oriented texts in the subjects being taught. The student could be searching for selections best suited for a required essay. Leaders in the African Christian community might be tracking materials for essential reading. Researchers could be discovering otherwise little-noticed sources for their particular inquiry, while academic scholars could be scanning for additional bibliographic information in their fields of expertise. Indeed, alert readers of any sort wishing for a convenient resource relating to modern Africa, and to Christian presence there, should find their interests readily addressed in these pages.

The array of reviews may be easily searched in one of three ways: either (i) by *authors* of the publications under review, or (ii) by *titles* of those publications, or (iii) by *subjects* addressed in such publications. As to authors, the books reviewed in this collection are presented by authors listed in alphabetical order. As an additional convenience, an alphabetized index of all authors is available at the end of this volume. For searches that might relate instead to the titles of publications, a second index provides the titles of all reviewed books in alphabetical order. For many who might rather be consulting this resource for input on specific subjects or topics, the comprehensive subject index, also located at the end of this volume, should prove the best first stop.

These are not, however, the only ways that readers of this reference work could find it useful. There is an additional potential benefit, perhaps even an invaluable one, for the sort of reader to whom it might apply. Let us suppose someone who might welcome a chance to keep somewhat current on what has been published in recent years in and about Africa, someone who would like to keep broadly cognizant of emerging writers and recent intellectual trends, and someone who in the process would also value a measure of thoughtful evaluation from a Christian perspective. Let us recognize that under no circumstances could such a person afford to do all the reading that this might imply. Nor, for that matter, all the purchasing or borrowing. That is where this compilation of concise reviews can become uniquely useful. Exploring such reviews in combination can provide a way of familiarizing the reader with vast landscapes, enlarging one's awareness of what is available, enhanced by a range of viewpoints, and all within a manageable compass. Much is currently being written and published in and about Africa and about African Christianity, much that is well deserving thoughtful notice. Surveys of current literature such as this one exist not least to cater for just such interests and needs.

For the attentive, committed reader, consulting any sequence of pages in this collection could quickly bring the same gratifying discoveries that are the lot of those who rejoice in browsing along the shelves of a quality library or bookshop. To read through any ten or twelve pages here is immediately to experience acquaintance with the diffuse panorama both of Christian presence in Africa, and of the African context itself – a range of acquaintance difficult to encounter by any other means. For those willing not only to use this volume to locate specific resources, but as well to have horizons expanded, one's range of knowledge extended, and all this reviewed with informed Christian sensitivity, merely reading review after review through any section of this volume could prove endlessly enticing and fulfilling.

Everyone using this resource will in due course experience, as I have, an enormous sense of gratitude to those numerous volunteer contributors whose thoughtful reviews make up this collation. Their diligent, generous-hearted self-investment for the benefit of the larger community presents a challenging example for all of us. For me the rewarding collaborations and personal friendships thereby afforded through the years have been a particular joy. While many would deserve mention, the project would not have succeeded without the essential assistance, from the very first days until now, of my very valued colleague Rich Stuebing. Likewise the staff at George Whitefield College in Cape Town, South Africa, have played a crucial role in generously managing the journal's production and distribution over many years. Finally, I wish to express my gratitude to Evie, my wife, my life companion and friend, and my collaborator in this and many other ministry endeavours.

Paul Bowers

May 2018

Abbreviations

AACC	All-Africa Conference of Churches
ACTEA	Association for Christian Theological Education in Africa (formerly Accrediting Council for Theological Education in Africa)
AEA	Association of Evangelicals in Africa
AIC	Africa Inland Church
AICs	African Initiated/Independent/Indigenous Churches
AIM	Africa Inland Mission
AMECEA	Association of Member Episcopal Conferences in Eastern Africa
ANC	African National Congress
ATR	African Traditional Religions
CAR	Central African Republic
CECA	Communauté Evangélique au Centre de l'Afrique
CMS	Church Missionary Society
CUEA	Catholic University of Eastern Africa
DACB	Dictionary of African Christian Biography
DRC	Democratic Republic of Congo
EAR	East African Revival
ECWA	Evangelical Church of West Africa
EECMY	Ethiopian Evangelical Church Mekane Yesus
FPR	Front Patriotique Rwandais (Rwandan Patriotic Front)
ICETE	International Council for Evangelical Theological Education
IFES	International Fellowship of Evangelical Students
IMC	International Missionary Council
KHC	Kale Heywet Church
LMS	London Missionary Society
NLM	Norwegian Lutheran Mission
PROCMURA	Project for Christian-Muslim Relationships in Africa
RPF	Rwandan Patriotic Front
RSA	Republic of South Africa
SIL	Summer Institute of Linguistics (SIL International)

SIM	formerly Sudan Interior Mission, now simply SIM
SUM	Sudan United Mission
TEE	Theological Education by Extension
UMCA	United Missionary Church in Africa
UMS	United Missionary Society
UNESCO	United Nations Educational, Scientific and Cultural Organization
UNIP	United National Independence Party
WCC	World Council of Churches
WEA	World Evangelical Alliance
WHO	World Health Organization
YWCA	Young Women's Christian Association

Authors
A–C

Abarry, Abu S.

see review 72

1.   **Abba, Joe-Barth Chiemeka**

Special Pastoral Formation for Youths in Africa in the 21st Century: The Nigerian Perspective: With Extra Focus on the Socio-Anthropological, Ethical, Theological, Psychological and Societal Problems of Today's Youngsters

Frankfurt: Peter Lang, 2009. 407 pages, ISBN: 9783631584347.

The author is a Roman Catholic theologian from Nigeria who trained in the United States and Germany. The book is a revised version of his PhD thesis in Pastoral Theology from the Ludwig-Maximilians-University in Munich, Germany (2005). As indicated by the subtitle, this is a multidisciplinary work, approaching its topic, youths in Africa, from a number of scholarly perspectives. Its overall aim can nevertheless be summarized in a few words, namely how to "train, control and bring up our youths successfully in life." After a more general introduction, where the concept of youth is being discussed in relation to family, church and modern society, the author moves the focus to Nigeria, where his empirical data are found and his discussion hence is anchored. The role of religion in youth life plays an important role here; mainly in positive, church contexts, but also in more negative, secret cult contexts. Negative experiences such as unemployment, drugs, and corruption are also addressed. And so are positive experiences such as sports and friendship. All these aspects of the life of youths are discussed from pastoral perspectives, discussing how the church can contribute to the formation of the younger generation. One finds it surprising that, amidst all the challenges that modern young people encounter, a book on youths does not find room for a closer discussion of sexuality. There is no reason to think that Nigerian youths do not face the same ethical challenges in this regard as youths everywhere, and this should have been addressed more directly. It should also be mentioned that the book is somewhat verbose. Nevertheless, it is a solid piece of work, and an obvious dialogue partner for those dealing with the relationship between church and youth, not only in Nigeria.

2.   **Abe, Gabriel Oyedele**

History and Theology of Sacrifice in the Old Testament

Benin City, Nigeria: Seevon Prints, 2004. 131 pages.

Abe is a well-known Nigerian scholar in biblical studies, as a previous editor of the *African Journal of Biblical Studies* and Professor of Religious Studies at a university in Nigeria. His present book on sacrifice in the OT tries to combine chronological and systematic approaches to the phenomenon. From chronological perspectives it outlines the development of Israelite sacrifice, from the Ancient Near Eastern background and up to its role in postexilic Judaism. And from systematic perspectives it outlines the various forms of Israelite sacrifice and their religious significance. The book may serve as a textbook for undergraduate students of theology or religious studies, and as such it fills a gap in the Nigerian context. Still, it should be admitted that the book suffers from two major shortcomings. One is an outdated research horizon. This unfortunate situation probably reflects a lack of access to updated sources, a familiar problem for biblical scholarship in Africa. Nevertheless, a book like the present cannot afford to ignore such basic and generally accessible research surveys as G. A. Anderson's article on sacrifice in the *Anchor Bible Dictionary*. A second shortcoming is the absence of any discussion of the relationship between OT and traditional African forms of sacrifice. This comes as a surprise, as assumed parallels between the two have often been discussed by Nigerian biblical scholars, from C. Olowola to J. S. Ukpong. Nevertheless, the book deserves a place in the bookshelves of Nigerian seminary and university libraries.

3.   Abe, Gabriel Oyedele

The Religion of the Exile

Lagos: New Dawn International, 2005. 139 pages.

The author is Professor of Religious Studies at Adekunle Ajasin University in Nigeria. This book is a discussion of the religion of the Jews during the sixth century BC, that is during the so-called Babylonian Captivity. Abe outlines the biblical narrative of the Exile, from deportation and settlement in Babylon to the edict of Cyrus and the reformation of Ezra and Nehemiah. Throughout a chronologically structured presentation he shows particular attention to the religious challenges these experiences created, from the disaster in 586 BC to the reorientation of the exilic and early postexilic prophets. Some attention is also given to possible Babylonian influence. The book may be of use as a textbook for undergraduate students of theology or religious studies in Nigeria, where it is meant to serve in historical sequence to J. O. Akao's *A History of Early Israel* (Ibadan, 1999). It should be noticed that the book suffers from an outdated research horizon, a fact that is very unfortunate, given the current focus of research on the Exile. Still, it offers a presentation of some central aspects of the religious challenges that, according to the OT, faced the Jewish community during exilic times. Universities and seminaries in Nigeria should consider including the book in their library holdings.

4.   Aben, Tersur A.

African Christian Theology: Illusion and Reality

Bukuru, Nigeria: Africa Christian Textbooks, 2008. 197 pages, ISBN: 9789784888844.

This book by the Provost of the Theological College of Northern Nigeria (TCNN) looks at the possibility and desirability of African Christian Theology. Aben explores possible definitions of the topic that are represented by a 1969 statement of the All Africa Conference of Churches held in Abidjan which defines Africa Christian Theology as "a theology based on the biblical faith of Africans, which speaks to the African soul." The author identifies four sub-categories under this definition: syncretism, which fuses African traditional religion with Christianity; enculturation, which fuses African culture with Christianity; liberation theology, which fuses acts that liberate Africans from oppression; and African evangelicalism, which reflects on and expounds Scripture by African thought-forms and semantics. Surprisingly, the author rejects all four types, claiming that all of these types are determined by the African context. Instead, Aben believes that there should be only one global Christian theology. For him, theology is the study of God and his nature. African Christian theology, for him, is "a study of God's nature, words, and deeds." In subsequent chapters the author looks in greater depth at contextualization and enculturation. He believes that all contextualization is syncretism since it involves fusing elements of two separate religions. Enculturation for him is safer, since it is fusing Christianity with a "neutral" culture. But in the end, enculturation and all of current African Christian Theology have yielded few solid results. Most of this so-called theology is simply comparative studies. The author in his conclusion calls on African theologians to engage in serious theological study which will have global significance and which will wrestle with serious theological issues like the nature of God, the problem of sin and the need for salvation. While one may criticize the author's identification of contextualization with syncretism, and his criticism of African evangelicalism, one praises him for calling African theologians back to their primary task.

5.   **Aboagye-Mensah, Robert K.**

Mission and Democracy in Africa: The Role of the Church

Accra: Asempa Publishers, 1994. 164 pages, ISBN: 9789964782269.

The author has been a lecturer at Trinity College, Legon, a director within the Christian Council of Ghana, and a minister within the Methodist Church of Ghana, and brings academic, theological and pastoral experience to bear on his subject. Having clarified principal terms and sketched the historical development of democracy from Athens onward, he explores traditional African socio-political structures, focusing especially on the Akan of Ghana. He seeks to demonstrate that vital elements of democracy have long characterized traditional African politics, especially in the realm of communality. In other words, democracy is not a Western invention imported into Africa. At the same time, he identifies weaknesses within the traditional systems, particularly the lack of freedom for the individual to disagree. It was precisely this missing element, the author argues, that Christian mission brought. It did this through Bible translation of the vernacular, through education, and through missionary proclamation and leadership training. The tension between the individual and the community is further examined, and this in turn leads naturally to a debate about ethnicity and ethnocentrism: what is it that makes the one acceptable and even desirable, and the other insidious and destructive? Contemporary examples of political systems in Africa are considered. The author strives to be balanced, identifying strengths and weaknesses in alternative styles of governance, but the book is an argument and not a coolly detached statement. He strongly advocates the democratic process for Africa (while acknowledging that it will take time and effort), and argues that the Church is strategically placed to help bring it about. Each chapter has numerous footnotes and the final bibliography reveals a commendable breadth of sources, ranging from Plato to modern African politicians with many between. Also to be welcomed is the book's theological and biblical component, which those who know the author would expect, but which is all too often absent in such debates. The book is an important contribution in the field under discussion, and deserves wide notice among those who continue such inquiries in Christian Africa.

6.   **Abogunrin, Samuel O., editor**

Biblical Healing in African Context

Ibadan: Nigerian Association for Biblical Studies, 2004. 350 pages.

In 2003 the Nigerian Association of Biblical Studies (NABIS) held a conference on biblical healing at Babcock University in Nigeria. This book contains 24 papers that were presented at the conference, and thereby offers a useful sampling of the Nigerian mind on the topic. A few papers treat the issue of miracles. While rationalistic Westerners tend to deny miracles, the first paper asserts that "miracles are real and valid." A belief in God and a denial of miracles is a contradiction of terms, says another presenter. A number of essays demonstrate the fact of miraculous healing in the Bible, which is compatible with the African worldview. The NT also shows that faith is essential for healing. But the Nigerian Pentecostal preoccupation with miracles is a theological danger, according to some presenters. One paper calls biblical healing the "craze in contemporary Nigerian society." The author states that this "craze for healing . . . must be accompanied by a genuine spirit of discernment and sincere holiness." Again, in many Pentecostal churches "the importance of physical healing has been overestimated." As one person says, a preoccupation with miracles can lead one to forget the cross: "The Christian strength lies in the cross which is the yardstick of Christianity." But the final paper asserts that "the only intelligible way of preaching the gospel to Nigerians and the whole of Africa is through the performance of miracles." So the discussion continues! Although the papers vary in quality, this book represents a lively discussion on the topic of healing in Africa.

7.   **Abogunrin, Samuel O., editor**

Biblical Studies and Corruption in Africa

Ibadan: Nigerian Association for Biblical Studies, 2007. 667 pages.

Corruption is a critical social problem in much of the world, and not least in Africa. "Corruption has left Africa almost economically barren with untold hardship, hunger, disease and woes." It is thus appropriate that the Nigerian Association for Biblical Studies (NABIS) sponsored a conference on the topic. This book contains the papers presented at that conference. The date and venue of the conference are not stated. This massive book contains 34 papers on corruption. Most are biblical studies, drawing from all parts of Scripture, but especially from the OT prophets and the teachings of Jesus. There are four papers on Amos and two on John the Baptist. A new term, "Gehazism," is coined in honour of Gehazi, the corrupt servant of Elisha. The papers are for the most part very evangelical, taking seriously the biblical text and its relevance today. Many of them are also more in the nature of sermons than in the nature of academic inquiry. Nevertheless, with this volume the biblical scholars have spoken.

8.   **Abogunrin, Samuel O., editor**

Biblical Studies and Women Issues in Africa

Ibadan: Nigerian Association for Biblical Studies, 2003. 260 pages.

In 2001 the Nigerian Association for Biblical Studies (NABIS) held a conference on "Women's Issues in Africa" in Ilorin, Nigeria. This volume contains nineteen papers presented at that conference. The first paper defines the problem: "All over the world the oppression of women is affirmed as a hard and abiding reality of life." So what does Scripture say about the oppression of and discrimination against women? Four papers look at the concept of prophetess and those who are called prophetesses in the Bible: Miriam, Deborah, Huldah and Anna. If these women held such high offices, are we not then to recognize women's talents in our churches? But does this necessarily mean female ordination? An Anglican canon believes that "Paul's teaching in 1 Timothy 2:9–15 is normative." At least three papers look at the important role of women in the NT. If Jesus and others accorded significance to women, then we should do the same. Generally the thrust of the papers is good, whereas the scholarship is sometimes superficial and imprecise. For example, one presenter assumes that since the word "Yahweh" allegedly comes from a masculine form of "to be," then Yahweh's gender is "predominantly masculine." This is remarkable; a word's meaning is not defined by its etymology, and what is one to make of "predominantly"? In general this collection of essays reminds us that in the church in Africa, women are indispensable and their issues deserve sustained attention.

9.   **Abogunrin, Samuel O., editor**

Biblical View of Sex and Sexuality from African Perspective

Ibadan: Nigerian Association for Biblical Studies, 2006. 358 pages.

This volume, containing selected papers from the 2005 conference of the Nigerian Association for Biblical Studies, is certain to raise reactions. Sex and sexuality already engage so much of the human personality, but positions taken by some of the 25 contributors here should provoke response as well. Included are papers variously condemning "masculinity" (otherwise called "patriarchy," Aluko); supporting male "superiority" (his term, Toryough); or blaming "religion" for sex commercialisation (Boje). One writer, relying on OT documentary theories, criticizes the Bible as inconsistent (Akao), while others ignore the Bible (Boje, Esabue), which may seem odd for a biblical studies gathering. Homosexuality per se (not just homosexual practice) is named a sin by nearly every writer who mentions it. Anglicans of the West who uphold homosexual behaviour get no support from a contributing Reverend Professor (Asaju). Another writer claims no one can live a celibate life, so Catholic requirements for priests can only produce hypocrites (Abioje). Still another assumes all Christians agree that "marriage is a sacrament" (Nweke). Nevertheless, NABIS is to be commended for attempting such a wide-ranging discussion on so many aspects of human sexuality. Correctly, the writers agree that African churches have been largely silent on sexual matters and thereby have contributed to problems in church and society. Practically all who comment on the question agree monogamy in marriage is the Bible's intended ideal. One writer urges space for African polygamy in the Church, and another has intriguing suggestions for marriage ceremonies (Ejenobo). There are some good biblical studies here (e.g. Adeniyi, Amalo, Nwaomah, Oguntoyinbo-Atere). The article on sex differentiation by Anthony Ojo from the Major Seminary of SS Peter and Paul, Ibadan, is a model of useful word study and theological reasoning. Ojo also benefitted from a good library, something other contributors apparently lacked. Whereas internet resources make a useful appearance in some papers, others are weakened by citations from outdated reference works or even from elementary school literature. There is disagreement among the papers and much repetition, as may be expected. Nearly all the contributors are or were lecturers in southern Nigerian universities. This collection will be useful as an example of a cross-section of Nigerian Christian academic opinion on the selected topic at the beginning of the twenty-first century.

10.   **Abogunrin, Samuel O., J. O. Akao, and Dorcas Ola Akintunde, editors**

Christology in African Context

Ibadan: Nigerian Association for Biblical Studies, 2003. 411 pages.

This is a collection of papers presented at the annual conference of the Nigerian Association for Biblical Studies (NABIS), held at the University of Port Harcourt in 2002. All except one of the 27 papers are on Christology. The editors of the collection are all lecturers in Christian religion at the University of Ibadan, Nigeria. This book is useful not least because several of the papers survey, compare, and assess the variety of Christological viewpoints in Africa. Thus the lead article by Samuel Abogunrin, Professor of NT at Ibadan, surveys selected approaches to the study of Christology from the earliest period of African Christianity to contemporary times. He suggests that Christology in early North Africa was abstract and philosophical, not contextualized, and thus remained foreign to Africans. Christologies of mission Christianity in the nineteenth and early twentieth centuries were similarly defective. Abogunrin then considers the strengths and weaknesses of five contemporary

African Christological models. He ends with the following suggestions: African Christology should be faithful to the Bible, incarnational, and authentically African and catholic at the same time. The contribution from Eunice Abogunrin, lecturer in ECWA Theological Seminary, Igbaja (with her MA from Wheaton College, and her PhD from Trinity international University) presents the death of Christ as a substitution, sacrifice, propitiation, reconciliation, and redemption, and then uses four myths, all from southwestern Nigeria, to illustrate the atoning work of Christ, pointing out both similarities and differences. The article by Dorcas Akintunde, senior lecturer in OT at Ibadan, on "Christology and the Contemporary Women in Africa," represents feminist theology with a difference. The Christology she advocates is orthodox, with a tilt toward practical implications of the Christ of faith to the particular problems and sufferings of women in Africa. She highlights Christological views of some radical feminist theologians from Latin America and Asia to show how her view differs from them. Examining Christological models propounded by African women, she concludes that both academic and popular formulations of African women show a functional Christology that is not troubled by issues of masculinity. As thus indicated, the articles in the book are rich and varied in standard. A major significance of the book is that it shows the complexity of theological work in Africa. The book is a solid trailblazer.

11. Abogunrin, Samuel O., editor

Decolonization of Biblical Interpretation in Africa

Ibadan: Nigerian Association for Biblical Studies, 2005. 425 pages.

This collection of 26 articles results from a conference of the Nigerian Association for Biblical Studies on the topic of biblical interpretation, held (it seems) in 2004. The title and the first articles claim that biblical studies in Africa have been "colonized." By decolonisation the writers mean the overthrow of a Eurocentric monopoly on the interpretation of Scripture. This book is a plea for an African biblical hermeneutics. Justin Ukpong claims that "inculturation [is] the most fundamental process of decolonization." But the nature of the inculturation hermeneutics on display in this book varies. David Adamo claims that African biblical studies will be "liberational and culturally sensitive." Solomon Taiwo assumes that "liberation is the focus or goal of African Biblical Studies." But other authors focus instead on inculturation. Two essays focus on how the Psalter has been used in the Aladura and Igbo contexts respectively. Two other essays are comparative studies on OT and African customs on death. But inculturation can also be applying Scripture to the African context. Caleb Ogunkunle reflects on Elijah as a model for prophets today. The editor, Samuel Abogunrin, believes that the NT should address issues like oppression, poverty, corrupt African leaders, wars, the debt burden, and the like. A couple of essays deal with women's liberation. The presuppositions of these articles also vary. For some, Scripture is obviously God's infallible word for us. But David Adamo denies that there is one "uniform, unconditional, universal and absolute interpretation or hermeneutic." His article and several others are post-modern, assuming that a single Bible text has many meanings. This can be problematic. When George Folarin tells us that the man who hid his one talent in Matthew 25 was a "hero of the peasants" in the liberation struggle of the oppressed against exploitation, then inculturation hermeneutics has gone too far, since the text clearly condemns this man. Dapo Asaju warns against carrying Afro-centric interpretations too far lest they result in "another form of colonizing" whereby "African culture may impose itself upon the essence of the Bible message." Robinson Ikpen also warns against "the error of substituting culture for the Gospel." This book is useful in representing something of the range of lively discussion in progress on the issue of African biblical interpretation.

12. **Abogunrin, Samuel O.**

The First Letter of Paul to the Corinthians: African Bible Commentaries

Ibadan: Daystar Press, 1991. 193 pages, ISBN: 9789781222054.

This volume was one of the first two volumes of a projected series of Bible commentaries written with the African situation in mind. Abogunrin was head of the Department of Religious Studies at the University of Ibadan in Nigeria, and general editor of the NT part of this series. The basic premise of these commentaries is that Western exegetical methods and insights are simply not enough. The Scriptures must be read and interpreted in the readers' context. 1 Corinthians seems a good place to begin such a project, since here we find the Apostle struggling to incarnate a message about a Jewish Messiah for a church in a Hellenistic city. Some of Paul's concerns are similar to problems which the church in Africa encounters as it seeks to live the gospel in its own culture. Abogunrin does a commendable job in pointing out the many ways in which Paul's answers to problems at Corinth can also provide insight for the church in Africa. Unfortunately the commentary shows little contact with the recent wealth of Pauline scholarship, which has emphasized the social context of Paul's churches, Pauline rhetorical and epistolary structures, and Paul's understanding of the relationship between the new movement of believers in Christ and Israel "according to the flesh." It is to be hoped that African scholars will not abandon the worldwide theological conversation just at a time when Western scholars are beginning to take non-Western scholarship seriously. Nevertheless, this is a book that many theological colleges may wish to use as a textbook or for supplementary reading.

13. **Abraham, Emmanuel**

Reminiscences of My Life

Trenton, NJ: Red Sea Press, 2010. 366 pages, ISBN: 9781569023266.

Born in 1913 in western Ethiopia, the author has here produced a fascinating autobiography which details his humble boyhood, years of education, government positions in London, New Delhi, Rome and Addis Ababa, and involvement with the church. The first section of the book describes his own life story. The next section deals with the Ethiopian Evangelical Church Mekane Yesus (EECMY) and its establishment, relationships with bodies such as the Lutheran World Federation, the Ethiopian Orthodox Church, various Lutheran mission groups and other international organisations. Lastly Abraham deals with the synods within EECMY, their development work and a brief coverage of the confiscation of church property during the Ethiopian revolution. Material for the book is based on his reports, personal memories of conversations, memorandums and official documents. Throughout his outstanding professional life, Abraham was a close confidant of the Emperor Haile Selassie. His long years of service as an Oromo person to an almost entirely Amhara government/church is remarkable. As well, his dual career in government and church is outstanding. He served the EECMY faithfully throughout his life, for many years as President. The book is sponsored by a number of international Lutheran church and mission bodies, and is obviously Lutheran in orientation. The general reader will find interesting nuggets throughout the book, ranging from the author's interpretation of the establishment of the Radio Voice of the Gospel (and its later annexation by the Dergue regime) to personal anecdotes of social engagements with Nkrumah and interactions with the Patriarch of the Ethiopian Orthodox Church. Certainly the book provides a wealth of Ethiopian history. As a personal life story by a modern-day African churchman and statesman, it will prove inspirational for the thoughtful Christian reader in Africa. This autobiography is a model of how an era of political and church history may be captured and gifted to an entire nation.

14.   Abrahams, Samuel P., Jeremy Punt, and David T. Williams, editors

Theology on the Tyume

Alice, South Africa: Lovedale Press, 1997. 177 pages, ISBN: 9781868100439.

The thirteen essays in this collection are all by members of the Faculty of Theology at the University of Fort Hare, located on the banks of the river Tyume in the Eastern Cape of South Africa. The collection serves the double purpose of honouring a long-serving professor at the faculty, Gideon Thom, and also commemorating the eightieth anniversary of the university. The university's history merits commemoration. For the most part of the past century Fort Hare has been the premier institution in South Africa for university-level education for blacks. Many of the most notable names in the anti-apartheid struggle were former students at the university, including Nelson Mandela. An introductory mission statement for this essay collection emphasizes that the university's Faculty of Theology aims to articulate theological perspectives on the totality of human life and knowledge, drawing in particular on the unique insights of the African heritage. This aim is reflected throughout the book, as most essays somehow relate their discussion to the African (and not only South African) context. The essays cover biblical interpretation and hermeneutics, as well as ecumenics and religious dialogue. Of special interest are two contributions on theological education. Reflecting on the central role of biblical studies for theological education, J. Punt especially argues for fostering competency in biblical languages. And D. T. Williams discusses whether the university or seminary is the best place for theological training. Pointing out the central role that theological studies have played in the past in the Western university tradition, Williams argues that the removal of such studies to separate institutions reflects the secularisation process. In the seminaries the students are separated from other academic disciplines, whereas in the universities they are (according to Williams) more likely to be involved in the mainstream of human life, and thereby develop a theology that is contextual. While not everything advocated in this collection of essays will prove convincing, it is a welcome contribution from scholars dedicated to attempting a relevant theology for Africa.

15.   Abubakre, R. D., R. A. Akanmidu, and E. O. Alana, editors

Religion and Politics in Nigeria

Ilorin, Nigeria: Nigerian Association for the Study of Religion, 1993. 200 pages, ISBN: 9789783050822.

How to make politicians "conscious of the sinfulness of their preoccupation with self" (from the preface) is a question that surfaces often in this collection of articles by sixteen scholars of religious studies. Floating on the surface of many articles, however, is the question of how to make religion serve the national interest of nation-building. The writers teach at ten colleges and universities in Nigeria, all but one in the southern part of the country. Two writers take the view of traditional religion, and the rest are divided between Christian and Muslim viewpoints. Although the editors hope that religious leaders will see the importance of the book, they are aiming more at the general reader and students of Religious Studies. This is not a textbook, although it could start lively discussions in any country where religion is a substantial player in public issues. Some of the Muslim contributors advocate clearly Islamic solutions to political problems. An article on religion and character by M. A. Abdu-Raheem stands out as a gracious example of fairness and accuracy in the portrayal of other religions. Many Christian contributors are so neutral as to be confused in their religious identity. The most informative and thought-out articles are by the editors themselves and one or two others. Others are more introductory. Readers may find the book useful in representing the state of discussion in Nigeria on such issues at the time of publication.

16.   Achermann, Eduard

Cry, Beloved Africa!

Munich: African University Studies, 1993. 265 pages, ISBN: 9783530002447.

Achermann was formerly a Catholic Swiss missionary and teacher of theology in Malawi, Uganda, Tanzania and South Africa for 30 years. Here he wishes to examine the results of westernisation and of the missionary enterprise upon the continent. His analysis is that Africa is worse off now than it was before the arrival of Western culture, technology, commercialism and the missionary. As evidence he points to the disintegration of the family structure, culture and morality, with the attendant rise of corruption and materialistic consumerism. Drawing upon the disciplines of sociology, anthropology and human development, Achermann probes the reason for this decline and observes that Western civilisation has been superimposed upon the foundation of African culture. He argues that acquiring life skills within an African context develops from a frame of reference and a worldview that does not equip one to deal with the layer of westernisation that has been superimposed on African life. One is provided neither with the understanding of westernized technology and administration, nor with the resources to maintain the structures now in place. Achermann applies this to the missionary with his resources and technology, and says that the material disparity between the African and the missionary is the source of much of the problem, because it has awakened a desire to pursue "the good life." This pursuit has led the younger generation to abandon traditional family and cultural structures, as well as Christianity, with the paramount goal of attaining material goods, which in turn has led to corruption and moral decline. Achermann's solution is for the missionary to develop a simpler lifestyle, coming down materially to the level of those he is serving, even to the point of abandoning the use of technological resources. He then should teach Africans how they can attain a higher level of material gain until they reach parity with the West. When this is achieved the African will be more likely to believe in a just God and thus be open to follow Christian values and morality. Thus, in Achermann's eyes, the problem and the solution are primarily economic. This is a rather disappointing solution, since corruption and moral decline are spiritual issues. Also the solution seems simplistic because it does not address the fact that Africa is westernising, and that effort needs to be made in formulating a Christian response to this present reality. The overall assessment might well also feel paternalistic, though that is not intended. In any case the everyday realities of African Christianity are today far less centred on the missionary than Achermann's assessment assumes. Those researching discussion on the relationship between the West and African Christianity and culture will find this book a useful example of one perspective.

17.   Ackerman, Denise, Jonathan Draper, and Emma Mashinini, editors

Women Hold Up Half the Sky: Women in the Church in Southern Africa

Pietermaritzburg: Cluster, 1991. 397 pages, ISBN: 9780958314152.

As part of the South African debate about the nature of a transformed society, the main emphasis of this book is the place of women in church and society. The immediate concern is the rightful place of women in the ministry and leadership of the church, with the ordination of women the initial motive for its publication. The very South African (only one author from outside South Africa) and Anglican flavour of the book does not distract from the important issues dealt with, which are also relevant to women all over Africa. The 32 articles are fitted under six main headings: (1) Women and the Bible: A Hermeneutical Problem; (2) Theological Foundations: Towards a Feminist Theology; (3) Spirituality and the Christian Women; (4) Women and the Church: Historical Perspectives; (5) Women and Ministry; (6) Women's Experience of the Struggle for Justice in Southern Africa. As a first publication of its kind for southern Africa, this readable book is an important introduction and orientation to an African view on women's issues at the time of publication.

18. ACTEA

Directory of TEE Programmes in Africa

Nairobi: ACTEA, 1993. 37 pages.

This is the second edition of ACTEA's directory of Africa-based programmes for theological education by extension (TEE). TEE was introduced to Africa in 1969, and by the end of the next decade Africa had more students involved in TEE than any other continent. This *Directory* gives names and addresses for 153 TEE programmes in 31 African countries, and offers details on 122 of these programmes. Where available, this includes information on the year begun, the sponsor, the enrolment per year over the past five years, the languages used, the length of the programmes, and a breakdown of the staff in terms of African/expatriate and full-time/part-time. Total enrolment in all reporting programmes was 33,284 participants; extrapolating from this figure for all documented programmes on the continent would result in an estimate of nearly 38,500 TEE students in Africa. This *Directory* represents the most comprehensive and up-to-date reference source for such information at the time of publication. As such it should be accessible to anyone researching about extension theological education in Africa.

19. Adadevoh, Delanyo, editor

Religion & Government in Africa: A Christian Response

Accra: ILF Publishers, 2009. 433 pages, ISBN: 9781600000058.

The various papers in this compendium emanate from the 2006 African Forum on Religion and Government, held in Abuja, Nigeria, and organized by the International Leadership Foundation, under the leadership of the editor of this volume. Originally from Ghana, Adadevoh also serves in the senior leadership of an international Christian student ministry. The eighteen papers consider the role that religion ought to play in African government. They are classified by areas of concern: Government (four papers – including one by Tokunboh Adeyemo); Leadership (three papers – including one by Adadevoh himself); Education (two papers); Gender (two papers); Development (three papers); and Peace and Reconciliation (four papers). Also included are three plenary addresses (by Olusegun Obasanjo, former president of Nigeria; by Pierre Nkurunziza, president of Burundi; and by the editor), as well as a brief résumé of each article. The conference speakers represented both anglophone and (to a more limited extent) francophone Africa. The papers themselves seem to aim for good communication on important topics rather than getting lost in academic bypaths. Adeyemo's essay encourages African governments to recognize the importance of the Church, and then calls on both institutions to submit to God's sovereign rule, acknowledging their different but intersecting roles in society. Adadevoh's essays and plenary address underscore the importance of a moral vision for all Africans, without which no true leadership can exist. Good leaders are developed through internal transformation to have a moral worldview, informed by their relationship to God. The concept of *ubuntu*, an African philosophy of overall wellbeing for all through right relationships, can serve as a guide for leaders. The values to be sought and inculcated include integrity, freedom, communality, justice, and excellence, at all levels. Another paper examines the possibility of constructing a curriculum for theological education that will train future leaders and implant within them this moral, holistic vision. It advocates biblical education joined with other elements enabling one to minister to the whole person. The educational model must not be merely cognitive. The essays in this volume could readily serve as discussion starters for Christian groups wanting to consider how best to find a way forward in meeting the needs of Africa.

20. **Adamo, David Tuesday**

Africa and Africans in the New Testament

Lanham, MD: University Press of America, 2006. 140 pages, ISBN: 9780761833024.

Adamo has served as head of the Department of Religious Studies at Delta State University, Nigeria. Over the years he has published extensively on African biblical hermeneutics. Adamo is a serious researcher who makes no efforts at hiding his ideological presuppositions. In reaction to what he describes as the generally Eurocentric approach reflected in traditional (Western) biblical scholarship, with its (conscious or unconscious) attempts at de-Africanising the Bible, he offers an alternative, a conscious Afrocentric approach, proceeding from and advocating African experiences and concerns. This 2006 monograph on the role of Africa and Africans in the NT follows up his 1998 monograph on the role of Africa and Africans in the OT. The two show both similarities and differences. The Afrocentric approach is more or less the same in both monographs, but there is development as far as methodological and geographical focus is concerned. Adamo's 1998 monograph is basically an analysis of OT references to the African nation of Cush/Ethiopia, ignoring the large number of references to Egypt as well as more general Afrocentric reading strategies. The present study on the NT offers a broader perspective in two ways. First, it shows sensitivity to all geographical references that somehow can be linked to the African continent, not only Cush/Ethiopia, but also Egypt, Libya, etc. And secondly, Adamo this time focuses not only on explicit references to Africa, but also discusses the (possible) African background of NT authors (Mark and Matthew, possibly even Paul) and early interpreters (such as Clement of Alexandria, Tertullian, Athanasius, Augustine and many others). Many of Adamo's readers will likely remain unconvinced by his arguments. Adamo is able to see traces of Africans and African influence even where other scholars will definitively reject the whole idea. Still, Adamo's underlying concern deserves support. Christianity is indeed an African religion, and the African dimension of Christianity is not something of recent centuries only. It has been there right from the beginning.

21. **Adamo, David Tuesday**

Africa and the Africans in the Old Testament

Eugene, OR: Wipf & Stock, 2001. 220 pages, ISBN: 9781579106584.

Adamo is a university lecturer in religious studies in Nigeria. The book is based on his 1986 PhD dissertation at Baylor University (USA). In this study he seeks to replace a Eurocentric approach to the Bible, that allows no room for African presence and influence in the OT, with an Afrocentric conception of the history and achieve-ment of Africans during the biblical period. Adamo describes his work as a "critical and objective investigation of the presence, the role and the contribution of Africa and Africans in the political, religious and economic history of ancient Israel in the period of the OT." Examining terms used to refer to Africa and Africans in the ancient world, Adamo concludes (from the evidence of Josephus in the first century AD) that the Hebrew word typically translated "Kush" in the OT should rather be translated "Africa." While the study mostly speaks of "Africa" in terms of black Africa, the ancient Egyptians are also treated as part of the inquiry. Chapters attend to the presence of Africa and Africans in the Law, the Prophets, and the Writings respectively. A final chapter summarizes the argument, and the book concludes with a bibliography. In this wide-ranging study covering a vast expanse of time and geography, Adamo does not escape the appearance of building sweeping analyses on relatively narrow foundations. He admits that much work remains to be done on ancient African history, but he believes the results will reinforce his conclusions. Adamo is certainly right in urging greater attention to the presence of Africans and African influence in the OT; whether this particular work proffers the kind of careful research needed to support that task will be up to the reader to judge.

22. Adamo, David Tuesday, editor

Biblical Interpretation in African Perspective

Lanham, MD: University Press of America, 2006. 275 pages, ISBN: 9780761833031.

The editor, a professor at Delta State University, Nigeria, has published extensively on African biblical herme-neutics. The present volume is a collection of essays exploring various aspects of African biblical interpretation, which includes contributions by some of Adamo's scholarly colleagues along with articles by some of Adamo's students. The essays fall generally into two categories, those approaching African biblical interpretation from historical perspectives, and those engaging in contextual interpretations of biblical texts. Adamo opens the collection with a survey of the historical development of OT interpretation in Africa, which also serves to clarify the hermeneutical presuppositions of this prominent African biblical scholar. Then follows an essay by Gerald West (South Africa) on the use of the Bible in South African Black Theology, which includes a valuable description of West's own personal and scholarly development as an African biblical scholar. Grant LeMarquand (Canada) provides a sharply focused comparative analysis of Western and African biblical scholarship. Knut Holter (Norway) surveys chronological and geographical aspects of sub-Saharan doctoral dissertations in OT studies from 1967 to 2000. Other articles, principally from Nigeria, treat variously: Queen Vashti in the Book of Esther; poverty in the OT; the role of Africa and Africans in Acts; biblical and postcolonial Nigerian aspects of chieftaincy institutions; Eph 4:1–6 and Rom 12:3–21, each in African perspective; and a comparison of celibacy in the Bible and in Africa. A second article by Adamo, analysing imprecatory psalms, serves also as an introduction to Adamo's studies of biblical interpretation in African Instituted Churches.

23. Adamo, David Tuesday

Explorations in African Biblical Studies

Eugene, OR: Wipf & Stock, 2001. 172 pages, ISBN: 9781579106829.

Adamo is Professor of Biblical and Religious Studies at Delta State University in Nigeria This is an essay col-lection republishing some of his previous articles that have focused on the so-called African presence in the

OT. Some of the essays analyse African or African-American hermeneutics, others go into biblical themes (e.g. creation, peace, suffering, the African people of Cush) or texts (e.g. Deut 6:4) and interpret them from an African perspective. Adamo has never been afraid of cutting new paths through thick forests, and his constant emphasis on an African presence in the texts could be treated as an incentive to critical engagement both with the author and with the texts and themes under discussion.

24.   Adamo, David Tuesday

Reading and Interpreting the Bible in African Indigenous Churches

Eugene, OR: Wipf & Stock, 2001. 124 pages, ISBN: 9781579107000.

Adamo's research has for many years included attention to issues of African biblical hermeneutics generally, with particular attention to biblical interpretation in African Indigenous Churches (AICs). This monograph presents and analyses various examples of how the Bible is "used" in AICs. After brief introductory chapters presenting African worldviews and some of the relevant (Nigerian) churches, a large number of examples follow of how the Bible is used "therapeutically," "for protection" and "for success." Let one typical case, a "therapeutic" one, the curing of smallpox, exemplify these various uses: "Prophet Adewole recommends Ps 84 to be read ten times over water with the holy name Alojah, Alojah, Alojah to be pronounced 21 times. Or a mixture of fried oil, potash, shear butter, with the reading of Ps 84 to it. The oil is for rubbing the body and the water for bathing." Probably most of Adamo's readers would, both here and in a number of corresponding cases, quite intuitively think in terms of syncretism. But not Adamo. Rather, he emphasizes such uses of the Bible as important examples of a non-westernized biblical interpretation in Africa. In any case, Adamo's general openness towards popular biblical interpretation outside the historical churches does usefully direct attention to this not insignificant dimension of biblical usage in Africa, and invites thoughtful engagement with the resulting implications.

25.   Addai-Mensah, Peter

Mission, Communion and Relationship: A Roman Catholic Response to the Crisis of Male Youths in Africa

Frankfurt: Peter Lang, 2009. 242 pages, ISBN: 9781433104985.

The author is a Roman Catholic theologian from Ghana, and this is a revised version of his doctoral dissertation from Weston Jesuit School of Theology, Cambridge MA. A case study from Ghana is presented, surveying the challenging situation many young males experience, and reflecting on how the churches (plural, not only the Roman Catholic Church) can respond to this. In recent years Ghana has established many programmes for women and girls, often with good results. Young males, however, have not received corresponding attention, in spite of the broad range of problems they face: living on the streets in the cities, being drug addicts and serving as couriers for drug barons, participating in armed robberies and highway assaults, increasingly high unemployment, and a tendency to look down on Ghanaian culture and become enchanted by foreign ones. In response, the author argues that communion and solidarity are a missiological imperative of the Roman Catholic Church, in collaboration with other churches.

26.   **Addo, Ebenezer Obiri**

Kwame Nkrumah: A Case Study of Religion and Politics in Ghana

Lanham, MD: University Press of America, 1999. 250 pages, ISBN: 9780761813187.

Unlike critics of Nkrumah, Addo's intention in this book is "an effort to rehabilitate Nkrumah whose motive and style of leadership have not been fully assessed." The author does a commendable job in that intention. He could have done as well with fewer references to the leadership theories of Max Weber in a book that reads like a reworked doctoral dissertation. Given the diversity of tribes, religions and regional interests in Ghana when Nkrumah became Prime Minister in 1952, and then led the nation into independence in 1957, he faced the daunting task of nation building. As a charismatic leader and a shrewd political theorist, he fashioned a plan that intentionally tapped into the traditional belief system and culture of the population to create legitimacy for his leadership. The author observes that in Ghanaian traditional society leadership "is tinged with sacredness." Religion is a "key variable that fuels Ghanaian politics, guides its direction and generates its successes." How Nkrumah blended, orchestrated, and artfully employed traditional African religion, Islam and Christianity for political purposes is the central theme of Addo's study. Nkrumah also linked his leadership with chieftaincy traditions, "because in this institution, there is a fusion of the sacred and the secular." Nkrumah therefore adopted many of symbols of a chief, and appropriated for himself religious-political titles and honorifics such as "Redeemer" and "Messiah," seeing himself as one who saved his people from imperialism and colonialism. Nkrumah embraced socialism as a system he considered consonant with the communalism of traditional culture. He believed it was necessary to de-colonize the citizens in order to form a new order that would draw upon the traditions of the past and incorporate African socialism. In the process he also pushed for a more syncretistic brand of religion to aid national coherence. Nkrumah was overthrown by a military coup in 1966, owing in part to a failing economy and abuse of the detention laws, plus Nkrumah's increasing dictatorialness and the sense that he was building a personality cult. Addo finds it admirable that Nkrumah had the pulse of the common people and knew the responsive chords to pluck. Whereas other writers may have criticized Nkrumah's messianic pretensions), Addo prefers to treat this as part of what Nkrumah felt it necessary to do as a pioneer in nation building.

Adebo, Tarakegn

see review 607

Adei, Georgina

see review 27

27.   **Adei, Stephen, and Georgina Adei**

The Challenge of Parenting: Principles and Practice of Raising Children

Achimota, Ghana: Africa Christian Press, 1991. 124 pages, ISBN: 9789964878979.

The Ghanaian authors draw on their own experience as children in Ghana and as parents to their four children in various international settings, along with their reading of various Christian authors, in order to illustrate Christian responses to pressures facing parents and children today. Using biblical principles applicable in any setting, they deal with current issues, including many which are especially relevant in the modern, urban African setting. Their intention is that scriptural teaching should correct cultural positions as needed, for example by fathers taking an active role in child care from birth, and parents giving their own children biblically based sex education. While some may differ with their advice to parents to teach their children to read by age four, the authors also differ with "modern theorists" at some points, for example the use of spanking in disciplining children. They avoid extremes by calling parents to make their parenting task a priority in service to God, and also by emphasising the need for parents to maintain their own marriage in light of the children's temporary presence in the home. Their balanced approach includes affirming childless marriages, along with encouraging hard-pressed parents to trust God and their own insights rather than being intimidated by an inability to be "perfect parents." Altogether this is a very helpful treatment of Christian parenting, one that can be used with profit both by parents and by all who minister to them. Since many Christians in Africa are keenly interested in this topic, and since books on this topic written from an African perspective are rare, pastors and churches ought to encourage its use within their membership, bookshops should stock it, and theological colleges should ensure that their students are familiar with its availability.

28.   Adeleye, Femi B.

Preachers of a Different Gospel: A Pilgrim's Reflections on Contemporary Trends in Christianity

Carlisle, UK: HippoBooks, 2011. 160 pages, ISBN: 9789966003157.

Adeleye has been involved in student ministry with the International Fellowship of Evangelical Students (IFES) for 30 years, working to nurture nationally-led Christian student witness that will produce a new generation of leaders for the churches and nations of Africa and beyond. Born in Nigeria, he has been more recently based in Ghana. He was one of the plenary speakers at the Lausanne 2010 Congress in Cape Town. Informed, enlightening, passionate, convincing and correcting – these are the words that come to mind in reading this intended unmasking of the "prosperity gospel." The phrase in the title, "a different gospel," is of course taken from Paul's rebuke of those in the early church who had turned from God's truth to something different (2 Cor 11:4; Gal 1:6). Adeleye does the same for African Christianity today. He cuts deeply into the heart of the "Health and Wealth Gospel" now proclaimed in many parts of Africa, and surgically divides truth from deception. He traces the growth of this different gospel from its birth in North America, to its transfer to Africa, and to its current manifestations on this continent. Using his personal knowledge as well as written resources, he recounts examples of African adaptations of prosperity teaching that may surprise even the well-informed – such as "when blackcurrant juice is added to water and prayed over by the bishop, it becomes the blood of Jesus," which is then to be used as a protective charm against demonic attacks. Throughout the book Adeleye deals as much with Christian character as with Christian ideas. He also tells how Christians' attitudes towards God, worship and the Bible have changed since the charismatic revivals of his youth. His call to African Christians is to return to a thorough study of the Bible as their source of authority. This is a well-written, accessible book, but not exhaustive or technical. Other books will provide more detail, for example, on the history and ideological origins of prosperity theology as well as its misuse of Scripture. This book deserves to be widely used in Africa's churches. It also needs to be familiar reading in pastoral training institutions throughout the continent. Like Osei-Mensah's *Wanted: Servant Leaders*, Adeleye's *Preachers of a Different Gospel* deserves to be used as a standard work in such settings.

29.   Adeso, P., L. Naré, and J. Njoroge, editors

Kingdom of God in the Synoptics: Conversion, Justice and Peace in Africa

Nairobi: Catholic Biblical Centre for Africa and Madagascar, 1997. 168 pages.

This volume represents the "Proceedings of the Sixth Congress of the Pan-African Association of Catholic Exegetes" (PACE), held in Accra, Ghana, in 1993. The Association was established in the early 1980s to promote Africanized biblical studies within the Roman Catholic Church in Africa. Its congresses are intended to meet every second year, each with a specific theme, with membership drawn mainly from lecturers in biblical studies in Catholic seminaries and universities of Africa, but also including some bishops (ex-lecturers in biblical studies). This sixth PACE Congress focused on the Kingdom of God according to the Synoptics. It consists of ten articles, all focusing on texts and topics related to the Synoptic Gospels. The contributors are variously from Burkina Faso, Cameroon, Côte d'Ivoire, Congo (DRC), Nigeria, Burundi and Kenya. They address such topics as: the justice of the Kingdom (Matt 3:15); the Beatitudes and the Kingdom (Matt 5:1–12); Jesus, the Temple, and the universal dimension of God's message of salvation (Mark 11:15); the question of who is the greatest in the Kingdom (Matt 18:1–5); kingship and peace (Luke 19:39); and true justice as compassion (Mark 6:30–44). While some of the essays have a rather elementary profile, others are quite worthy of notice. One example is a discussion of the Beatitudes by Cornelius Esua, now Archbishop in Cameroon and President of PACE. After a survey of questions related to text and genre, he makes a solid exegesis of the verses, emphasising their OT roots, and in conclusion draws some consequences for the African church. Another example is Deogratias Ruhamanyi Bisimwa, professor at the Catholic University in Bukavu, Congo (DRC), who discusses the petition for forgiveness in the Lord's Prayer. Based on a solid exegetical analysis he argues that the Matthew formulation ("our debts") and that in Luke ("our sins") can be reconciled, and he then reflects on the nature of "forgiveness" in the political context of (early 1990s) Congo (DRC). It should be noted that this is a congress volume, hence an uneven collection of essays, and on a limited area in biblical studies, giving particular focus to conversion, justice and peace, and all this from an African perspective. Nevertheless, it is a worthy documentation of how this theme was understood amongst representative Catholic exegetes of Africa in the early 1990s.

30.   Adewuya, J. Ayodeji

A Commentary on 1 and 2 Corinthians

London: SPCK, 2009. 208 pages, ISBN: 9780281061990.

This commentary in SPCK's useful International Study Guide series aims particularly at an international audience of first-year theology students who need the basic information without getting lost in academic English or footnotes. In recent years SPCK has been upgrading the series, adding and replacing more book studies, of which this volume is a good example. The series has also become more intentionally diverse from the "supply side." In this case one notes that, whereas the previous main author was a missionary in the Philippines, the main author this time is Nigerian, and currently teaching in a Pentecostal seminary in the USA. His other publications show a particular interest in the topic of holiness in the NT. The three other contributors in this volume, writing the Applied Theology Essays, are likewise representative of a broad spectrum. Kirsten Kim ("Holy Spirit and Spirituality") has lived in Korea and India and teaches in the UK; Lisa Meo ("Women in Corinthians"), from Fiji originally, has retired to Australia; and Daryl Balia ("Reconciliation") is a South African

Methodist resident in Scotland. Besides the summary, introduction, and interpretation associated with each passage, the SPCK commentaries add special topics (such as "Spiritual Warfare" and "Paul's Thorn in the Flesh"), developed by the author. Study suggestions and discussion questions follow each section, providing fodder not only for the students but also for the lecturers who teach them. This particular contribution on the Corinthian correspondence provides insights beyond the text as the various parts (commentary, essays, and discussion questions) draw the reader into different non-Western examples or practical considerations that force the student to consider an application to his/her local culture. The author demonstrates competence in handling the biblical text and familiarity with the questions raised in academic circles, without going beyond the needs of a first-year theology student.

31.   Adewuya, J. Ayodeji

Holiness and Community in 2 Cor 6:14–7:1: Paul's View of Communal Holiness in the Corinthian Correspondence

Eugene, OR: Wipf & Stock, 2011. 248 pages, ISBN: 9781610971942.

This is a revised version of a PhD dissertation accepted by the University of Manchester in the UK. The author comes from Nigeria, and has served as a missionary in the Philippines, where he also taught at the Asian Seminary of Christian Ministries. The book is an analysis of the relationship between "holiness" and "community" in 2 Corinthians 6:14–7:1. First the socio-historical context of this text is discussed, then follows a close reading of the text with particular attention to its relationship with the Holiness Code in Leviticus, and finally consideration is given to the place of this text within its broader literary context, the Pauline literature. The main thesis is that the concept of holiness in 2 Corinthians 6:14–7:1, as well as in the Pauline corpus as a whole, is not satisfactorily explained in terms of the individual, but only as the individual stands in relation to the community of faith. Taking into account the author's African background, one might have expected that this main thesis would draw on African concepts of communality. However, this is not the case, at least not on an explicit level. Even where Ayewuya talks about "the prevalent individualism that has plagued Western life," references to literature on African communal traditions and experiences are more or less absent. One finds this quite surprising; surely Adewuya's main thesis would have benefited from a more explicit use of African material. In spite of this, the book is a clear-cut and convincing advocacy for a communal understanding of the concept of holiness in the Pauline literature, and as such it will be of interest for NT lecturers and postgraduate students everywhere.

32.   Adeyemi, E. A.

From Seven to Seven Thousand: The Story of the Birth and Growth of SIM/ECWA Church in Ilorin

Ilorin, Nigeria: Okinbaloye Commercial Press, 1995. 163 pages, ISBN: 9789783273245.

This book is on the birth and growth of a particular congregation of the Evangelical Church of West Africa (ECWA) in Ilorin, Nigeria, between 1946 and 1995. Adeyemi is a trained historian with BA, MA, and PhD (University of Ilorin) degrees in history. He was also an elder of the First ECWA Church in Ilorin, and served as its Secretary at the time he wrote the book, which gave him access to records of the church that he would not otherwise have had. The book concludes with nineteen appendices, representing extracts of data from various ECWA assemblies in Ilorin; in addition the bibliographic citations include reference to archival materials available in Nigeria National Archives Library in Kaduna, and minutes of Board of Elders' meetings of First ECWA Church, Ilorin. The Ilorin church originated in the work of the international mission SIM. Adeyemi traces how it eventually grew to represent some ten local assemblies in the Ilorin environs. Also addressed is the crisis that led to the formation of the Second ECWA church in Ilorin in 1973. Adeyemi indicates that the roots of this lie in conflict between two ethnic factions in the church. Time and effort by ECWA leaders at national level contributed to an eventual reconciliation. Other crises dealt with by the church's own leadership through the years included those relating to modes of worship, church traditions, spiritual perceptions, and insubordination of youth. Adeyemi also covers major legal problems that the First ECWA Church had with her neighbours. These are all presented and interpreted from the perspective of the First ECWA Church, with the views of other parties to the issues not reported. The last chapter of the book contains brief profiles of selected founding leaders of the Ilorin church. The entire presentation is somewhat sparse on the larger context; for example, the author devotes very little space to the growth of other ECWA churches in Ilorin. It is also problematic that he uses SIM and ECWA synonymously, rather than differentiating their respective roles. This work is to be valued as an example of a contemporary local African congregation attempting to reckon with its history, detailing how it has grown and developed through the years, how it has dealt with its internal problems, and how and why these efforts failed or succeeded. As such it will be of interest to historical researchers concerned to understand better the life of individual local African churches.

33. Adeyemi, Femi

The New Covenant Torah in Jeremiah and the Law of Christ in Paul

Frankfurt: Peter Lang, 2006. 328 pages, ISBN: 9780820481371.

This is the product of the author's doctoral dissertation at Dallas Theological Seminary in Texas. At the time of publication Adeyemi was a visiting lecturer at ECWA Theological Seminary Igbaja (ETSI) in Nigeria. The study takes up the issue of Paul and the Law. Its purpose "is to set forth the identity of the law that will be written on the hearts of people at the time of the fulfilment of the New Covenant, as prophesied by Jeremiah and later understood by Paul." The author's thesis is that "the prophet Jeremiah intended the Torah of his New Covenant prophecy to be understood as an eschatological Torah of the Messiah, and that Paul understood Jeremiah's prophecy in the same way, designating the new Torah 'the Law of Christ.'" Adeyemi argues that the content of the Mosaic *torah* and the promised *torah* of the new covenant are essentially different, thus stressing discontinuity between the two covenants. The supporting exegesis of Jeremiah 31, however, is sometimes problematic. For example, the author insists that the word *torah* at v.33 cannot refer to the Mosaic covenant stipulations enjoined upon Israel but rather to "a new Torah different from the Torah of Moses." The explicit reference to the *Mosaic* covenant in the immediate context, however, makes such a claim appear as special pleading. The author rightly sees that the Mosaic covenant and the promised new covenant are to be different, but the disjunction that he insists upon between the two is not justified. Jeremiah promises that the *torah* of the failed Mosaic covenant will be brought forward and taken up into the new covenant framework. Not without change, for as Adeyemi himself brilliantly observes, v. 34's promise of a definitive forgiveness renders superfluous "the procedures for atonement and forgiveness of sin" embedded within the failed older covenant. The *torah* of the new covenant age is therefore better understood as a transformed Mosaic *torah* grounded in a definitive atonement that forever redefines that *torah*. It is in the inauguration of Jeremiah's new covenant that an obedient Israel is finally birthed, which can and will finally fulfil Israel's vocation to mediate the Abrahamic blessing to the nations (Gen 12:3; Exod 19:4–6). In contrast to Adeyemi's complete discontinuity model would therefore be an approach that embraces continuity as well as discontinuity. Nevertheless, Adeyemi's monograph is a genuine contribution to the ongoing discussion concerning Paul and the Law. The work is a stimulating and substantial read, and engages most of the relevant secondary literature. More than most contributions in this field, Adeyemi has established the centrality of Jeremiah 31:31–34 to Paul's thought concerning the Mosaic Law and the "Law of Christ." The study deserves to be in theological research libraries both in Africa and abroad.

34.   Adeyemo, Tokunboh, editor

Africa Bible Commentary: A One-Volume Commentary Written by 70 African Scholars

Carlisle, UK: HippoBooks, 2016. 1632 pages, ISBN: 9789966003812.

African pastors, lay leaders and students now have a commentary of their very own. Produced by a team of 69 African evangelicals over the course of five years, this is the first one-volume Bible commentary written by African scholars in Africa for Africa. This monumental achievement was overseen by Tokunboh Adeyemo, then General Secretary of the Association of Evangelicals in Africa (AEA), together with a team of editors and advisors, including Samuel Ngewa, Kwame Bediako and Yusufu Turaki. The commentary includes treatment of every book of the Bible, section by section. Of particular note are the 70 special articles on matters of relevance to the African church, and as well the distinct African voice that can be heard throughout. The special articles range in subject from "Christians in Politics" and "Street Children" to "Widow Inheritance" and "Wealth and Poverty," all topics of daily concern to the church in Africa. The voice of the African church can also be heard in the unique African illustrations used in the commentary itself. An example from the commentary on Matthew regarding the disciple's reward for following Jesus (Matt 19:27–29): "Jesus' answer shows that God is not unmindful of those who sacrifice a lot for him. Family is a big thing to give up. In Africa, we define ourselves by our extended families or clans. To give up one's family is to lose oneself. To be given up by one's family is a terrible tragedy, which often happens when a Muslim becomes a follower of Jesus." It is true that many of the commentators received their training in the West and reflect the hermeneutical training they experienced there. While seeking to speak to African realities, their interpretations of the text are often informative but not unique. Nor is there an attempt to struggle with critical details. At the same time, the commentary does manage to display the variety that is the evangelical church in Africa. The *Africa Bible Commentary* will prove an invaluable resource for African Christians desiring to understand Scripture from within the context of their unique cultures. It will also bring to the global church a fresh perspective on the Bible and a keen insight into the issues with which the African church wrestles.

35. Adeyemo, Tokunboh, editor

A Christian Mind in a Changing Africa

Nairobi: AEA, 1993. 256 pages.

"For decades in Africa evangelism and missionary activities have been directed at getting people saved (i.e. spiritually) but losing their minds." This statement from the foreword constitutes the (somewhat overstated) starting point for this compendium of papers (and some responses) that were given at a Worldview Consultation organized in Kenya in 1988 by the Department on Ethics, Society and Development of the Association of Evangelicals in Africa (AEA), with the laudable intention of overcoming the common criticism of Christianity in Africa as "mindless." The consultation participants were predominantly East African (of the 42 listed participants, only two were from West Africa and one from southern Africa). Following three introductory papers on the Bible and culture, the remaining ten major papers attempt to wrestle in a scholarly way with issues of what it means to be a Christian within the East African context. Four widely divergent areas are addressed: marriage and family life, economics, the judiciary, and two key social concerns, namely the relationship between church and state, and questions of ethnocentricity and tribalism. The common factor among the papers is a varyingly successful attempt to place such issues under the scrutiny of the Bible. Many of the papers are well presented, but their specifically Christian thrust seems largely dependent on somewhat platitudinous quoting from the Bible; one looks in vain for Scripture carefully exegeted and applied to the situation of "A Changing Africa." Instead, the collection generally reflects how biblical references have been used by some Christian professionals in various walks of life, and thus gives some insight into the influence that Christianity may be having on the "mind" of Africa. The volume represents a welcome concern, and one may hope that it will stimulate comparable endeavours even more effectively carried out in future.

36. Adeyemo, Tokunboh

Is Africa Cursed?: A Vision for the Radical Transformation of an Ailing Continent

Nairobi: WordAlive, 2009. 156 pages, ISBN: 9789966805133.

Throughout his tenure as General Secretary of the Association of Evangelicals in Africa (AEA), Adeyemo had his finger on the pulse of the African continent. Here he assesses Africa's predicaments and offers some solutions. The book is divided into two parts of approximately equal length. The first division, entitled "Hope for Africa," focuses on Africa's identity, particularly in the context of biblical revelation. Adeyemo concludes that Africa and her people are not under a divine curse, and in fact are the recipients of God's multiple prophetic blessings. Africa's problem is primarily moral and spiritual in nature. The second part of the book expands the conviction that a faithful and obedient Church should have a prophetic, pastoral, and priestly role in relation to the state and to society. Some readers will question what appears to be a fundamental but unarticulated assumption of the book: that a country's strong economy is a mark of God's blessing and a direct result of the people's obedience and worship of God. In treating the relationship between church and state, Adeyemo embraces "the position of the Roman Catholic and Orthodox Churches in which the church is to be above the state" because it "is more meaningful to the African Christian worldview." It is not clear what features of the African Christian worldview make this construal of church-state relations meaningful. In the final chapter, the focus falls not so much on a call to reconfigure the church-state relationship but on practical matters of authentic Christian life and influence such as "bearing the fruit of the Holy Spirit" and "maintaining the standards of excellence." The book is not intended to be profound or groundbreaking; rather it is aimed at the level of a broad Christian readership, and could prove useful there, as a popular statement by a notable African Christian leader on a topic of much contemporary interest and concern.

37. **Adeyemo, Tokunboh**

The Making of a Servant of God

Nairobi: Christian Learning Material Centre, 1993. 82 pages.

Adeyemo served as General Secretary of the Association of Evangelicals in Africa. The topic of this book is church leadership for Africa, the focus is on the OT prophet Daniel, the basic assumption is that leaders are made not born, and the call is for leaders who have learned to serve, not dominate. This book pleads that, like Daniel, the serving leader must be prepared at all levels, must live an exemplary prayer life, must minister diligently through the power of the Spirit, must expect suffering and persecution, and must be able to handle earthly rewards humbly. Aside from a historical slip in an illustration dealing with John Knox, the book is well presented. This short volume began life as material for leadership seminars in Zimbabwe and Kenya, and the easy-to-understand oratorical style remains in this printed version. Adeyemo punches his points home so fiercely with one fist that one might sometimes think he has left out the other side of the point; but then the other fist rams in that other side just as fiercely, and the author regains the needed balance. This can be a very convicting book! It does not cover identical ground to Gottfried Osei-Mensah's *Wanted: Servant Leaders*, and will not replace it; but Adeyemo's book could be useful as a supplement to Osei-Mensah's in courses on pastoral leadership or for general readers.

38. **Adeyemo, Tokunboh**

Salvation in African Tradition

Nairobi: Evangel, 1997. 124 pages, ISBN: 9789966200631.

Writing from an evangelical perspective, the author has here updated his 1979 book on African traditional religion. The first six chapters deal with the "salvation crisis," knowing God, worship, sin, death and destiny, and conflicting forces. For this new edition two new major chapters have been added. Chapter 7 is titled "Ideas of Salvation," and deals with salvation by correct ritual, by humanism, by asceticism, by moralism, by mysticism, by submission and by grace. Chapter 8 is titled "Questions about Salvation" and deals with pluralism, universalism, second chance, syncretism and humanism. The book would fit in well for courses on African traditional religion or soteriology.

39. **African Rights**

Rwanda: Death, Despair, and Defiance

London: African Rights, 1995. 1234 pages, ISBN: 9781899477036.

This remarkable and disturbing book contains hundreds of first-hand interviews, many of them gathered as the genocide in Rwanda was still going on (April–July 1994). Told by men, women, and children of all ages, the stories were transcribed directly by African Rights personnel. Most had just made it to safety, and many were still in hospital beds, not knowing what had happened to loved ones as the genocide continued in other parts of Rwanda. The stories are told with heart-wrenching honesty. A mother tells how she decided to leave her child to save her own life. Children tell of hiding under dead bodies to avoid the killers. Fathers relate how they were forced to kill family members. The stories are each carefully documented with names and ages and details of where the person was from, or what place they were fleeing to. This revised edition covers events up to 15 September 1994. While the major portion of this book consists of the direct testimonies of individuals, this is interspersed with explanation and narrative, chronicling the construction of the genocide, the lists, the policy of the massacres, the perpetration of the killings in each prefecture, and the attempts to cover the truth. While other titles on Rwanda may give more background into the pathology behind the genocide, this volume's strength lies in its wealth of first-hand accounts of what actually happened. The book conveys at heart level what is inevitably missed in concise news reports. Readers cannot help but see themselves in one of the stories, wondering what they would have done in such a situation, how they would feel now, so that reading must be tackled in small segments. The goal of the human rights organisation African Rights in making this 1200 page compilation was to preserve the truth, so that justice could be done as soon as the area stabilized. The names and faces of the individuals who suffered through such horror or were killed so brutally must not be lost in the statistics, or in the general incomprehensibility of how such a thing could happen. In the circumstances, it is doubtful that these stories will be heard again in such clarity and gut-wrenching detail. This book is a must for anyone who would begin to understand the scope of what the Rwandese experienced, and the complexity of what they have subsequently faced: the struggle to rebuild families, churches, a society, a value system . . . and indeed individual souls.

40. Agang, Sunday Bobai

The Impact of Ethnic, Political, and Religious Violence on Northern Nigeria, and a Theological Reflection on Its Healing

Carlisle, UK: Langham Monographs, 2011. 332 pages, ISBN: 9781907713156.

Agang is the Provost of ECWA Theological Seminary in Kagoro, Nigeria. This is the adaptation of his PhD dissertation in ethics completed in 2007 at Fuller Theological Seminary. The first part deals with the historical causes of violence in northern Nigeria. These come from a combination of factors, starting from the precolonial days when the powerful Muslim Hausa-Fulani groups enslaved minority groups, feeling justified in this because the minority groups were not Muslim. This situation was perpetuated in some ways during the days of indirect rule under Britain. There is still much tension between the former ruling groups, who see their power and Islamic purity being eroded, and rising minority groups combined with immigrants from southern Nigeria who resent being oppressed, who believe in spreading Christianity, and who espouse a more Western way of education and life. Leaders manipulate sentiments to encourage violence, violence that will benefit themselves politically but only brings misery to the masses. Thus the violence has social, ethnic, political, and religious roots. The result of the ongoing violence in Nigeria is that common people are afraid, and this makes them lack compassion and retaliate in kind. Agang gives three major case studies (Kafanchan 1987, Kano 1991, Kaduna 2000) to illustrate his points. He also brings in insights from Moltmann's *Theology of Hope*, from Liberation Theology, and from Walter Wink's analysis of the Powers. He concludes that power is mandated by God for use to help others (as Jesus did), but fallen humanity uses it selfishly. The church as the transformed humanity needs to model using power unselfishly, and people of all faiths in northern Nigeria need to stop the cycle of violence by espousing love and justice. Agang would like to see the system of traditional rulers in Nigeria abolished, and all government only in the hands of elected officials. More legal checks and balances for the use of power in the public sphere need to be created, and officials need to be trained and then monitored in acceptable political ethics so that injustice may be reduced and resentment cooled. The poor of all ethnic and religious groups need to accept each other and band together non-violently to resist the power-grabbing violence of the elite and the rich. Agang gives Tolstoy, Ghandi, Dorothy Day, Martin Luther King Jr., and Desmond Tutu as examples of the success of nonviolent resistance, showing that it is not passivity but actively creating an alternative way of living in community and nation. Agang finishes by describing his own efforts at fostering love and justice among the poor of northern Nigeria through his GAWON (GANTYS Aid for Widows, Orphans, and the Needy) Foundation.

41. **Agang, Sunday Bobai**

When Evil Strikes: Faith and the Politics of Human Hostility

Eugene, OR: Wipf & Stock, 2016. 298 pages, ISBN: 9781498235662.

Nigeria has been plagued in the last few decades by ethnic and religious violence. Most recently it has been the violence of the Boko Haram and some Fulani that has shaken society. This book was written to proffer a solution to Nigeria's problem of violence. Agang, who is Provost of ECWA Theological Seminary in Kagoro, Nigeria, has personally experienced some of this violence. His reflection here begins by offering a biblical perspective under the rubrics of creation, fall and redemption. The human problem is a spiritual one: violence proceeds out of human self-interest and pride. The biblical solution is love and forgiveness. Agang then considers three Christian approaches to violence: pacifism, just war, and just peace-making. He opts for the third option, but with a pacifist slant. How should a Christian respond when violent men attack? Agang says that we should respond peacefully and without violence. He says that the only option for self-defence is that taught by Jesus, namely, "nonviolent just self-defence." He considers a number of Bible passages that speak of peace, including Jesus' words to turn the other cheek. He refers to the Servant Songs in Isaiah, which speak of redemption effected through suffering, not redemptive violence. The cross of Jesus is also an example of a non-violent response to violence. Agang also cites from past and present Nigerian church history examples of peaceful interaction with those of a different religion. Yet too often the church has been distracted from her primary mission. Instead, church and society should respond to Muslim terrorism by engaging in just peace-making and restorative justice. Churches should attempt to transform society and to realize the peaceful eschatological kingdom of God in our present society. In his conclusion, Agang says: "Self-defence is not the primary concern of the Christian community. Rather, love and peace are." This book is a passionate plea for peace and justice. It rejects all forms of violence. But is such strict pacifism perhaps inadequate? Is it really wrong for responsible local persons or members of the Nigerian Army to use force (defensive violence) against Boko Haram? Yet Agang's plea for peace and justice must be heard. Too often the Christian church in Nigeria and elsewhere can be distracted by pride and self-interest. This book is a significant contribution to reflection on a present dilemma of Christianity in Nigeria.

42.   Agbede Afolabi, Ghislain

Vers une doctrine biblique et évangélique sur Marie

Cotonou, Benin: Éditions Foundation Adonai-Yireeh, 2011. 164 pages, ISBN: 9789991939575.

This book, by a pastor from Benin, was first presented as a master's thesis at FATEB, the evangelical post-graduate seminary in the Central African Republic. Agbede presents clearly the origin and development of the worship of Mary by Roman Catholic Christians. He traces the data from the period of the early Church Fathers, through the Church Councils, the Middle Ages, the Reformation, and Vatican II. The author then analyses primary source material: the biblical passages that speak of Mary, the patristic texts and documents from the various Councils, in order to suggest an evangelical response to the question of Mary worship. Documents stemming from Mariology specialists are also cited and examined for their contributions and weaknesses, and the positions maintained by those in different branches of Christianity are explained. Also considered are 'appearances' of Mary, including one reputed to have occurred at Kibeho, a village in Rwanda, where from 1965 to 1993 several young women claimed to have visions of Mary (and Jesus). The author examines these sightings and finds that the objective proof is lacking. He also thinks that a compassionate Mary would have given early warning of the coming genocide had she really transmitted messages to these young women. Agbede underscores the necessity of viewing Scripture as the most important factor in making decisions concerning Mary. His conclusion is that Mary is undoubtedly the human God chose to bear his Son, but this choice was not because Mary was (or became) sinless. Mary herself had a sin nature and needed Jesus as her Saviour. Honouring Mary for her role in the history of salvation is to be recommended, whereas devotion to Mary as though she were in some sense divine is contrary to all that Scripture teaches. All branches of Christendom must avoid this error. The author invites a continuing conversation on this topic, calling on theologians from a variety of Christian confessions. This book is recommended for students, pastors, and lay Christians interested in the question of the place of Mary in Christianity. Although fully documented with a bibliography and end notes, the thesis itself has been reworked to make it more accessible to a wider audience.

43.   Agbeti, J. Kofi

West African Church History Volume 1: Christian Missions and Church Foundations 1482–1919

Leiden: BRILL, 1986. 175 pages, ISBN: 9789004071674.

Agbeti, a lecturer in the University of Cape Coast, Ghana, here offers a history of Christianity in anglophone West Africa up until the end of the First World War. Agbeti does so by providing separate chapters on each of eight overseas Protestant mission societies which had work in West Africa during the period, plus two chapters on Catholic societies similarly engaged. Thus the content is substantially a history of the West African efforts of selected mission agencies. The recounting is based principally on available secondary literature published up to the mid-1970s. Specialists will readily identify gaps in the coverage. Although Agbeti intended his book as a text for "A level" students in West Africa, the price of the book rendered such a use improbable. Some theological libraries may wish to have a copy to increase their holdings in West African mission history.

44.   **Agbeti, J. Kofi**

West African Church History Volume 2: Christian Missions and Theological Training 1842–1970

Leiden: BRILL, 1991. 262 pages, ISBN: 9789004091009.

Agbeti's second volume on West African church history focuses on the histories of seven mission/denominational efforts in ministerial training, and the development of two united training colleges, Trinity College in Legon, Ghana, and Immanuel Theological College, in Ibadan, Nigeria. The bulk of the focus is on institutions in Ghana. The only two not in Ghana are in Nigeria. Surprisingly, the oldest theological training institution in West Africa, Fourah Bay of Sierra Leone, is not treated. Thus, the content is more selective than the title indicates. Agbeti relied heavily on primary sources for his historical reconstructions, and thus the stories he relates are not available elsewhere, and provide a valuable contribution to this aspect of the story of Christianity in West Africa. After setting the scene, Agbeti explores each mission's work in a separate chapter. Closing the book are two chapters, one on analysis and the other offering suggestions for future directions in ministerial training. The analysis chapter is the most significant of the book, and could be profitably read and interacted with by anyone involved in theological education in Africa. Generally the presentation is interesting without getting bogged down in details; the stories flow, and a realistic sense of the focus, energy and frustrations of the pioneers in ministry training comes through. It is interesting to note Agbeti's rightful concern that university-based religious studies programmes are not appropriate places for ministerial training, and his subsequent proposal for the creation of a Christian University of West Africa.

45.   **Ahoua, Raymond**

The Transference of the Three Mediating Institutions of Salvation from Caiaphas to Jesus: A Study of Jn 11:45–54 in the Light of the Akan Myth of the Crossing of a River

Frankfurt: Peter Lang, 2008. 208 pages, ISBN: 9783039114665.

This book is a revision of a doctoral dissertation completed at the University of Eastern Africa in Kenya. The author is a Roman Catholic priest of the Congregation of the Sons of Divine Providence (Don Orione), working as a missionary in Kenya, after some years at the Catholic University of West Africa in Abidjan. The book is a synoptic reading of two texts: (i) the NT narrative about Caiaphas, the high priest who argues in the Sanhedrin that one man should die for the people, rather than allowing the whole nation to perish (John 11:45–54); and (ii) an Akan myth about the sacrifice of the king's niece, here too in order to rescue the whole people. The book focuses on three parallel 'institutions', claimed to be reflected in both texts: priesthood, prophecy and royalty. To each of the three, the author devotes a main chapter, and seems able to justify his claim that both the NT text and the Akan myth circle round these three institutions. The book is a typically Roman Catholic work. For example, the author makes use of relevant current scholarly literature in English, Italian and French, reflecting the Catholic exemplary tendency to equip its clergy in international settings. The book also reflects typically Catholic hermeneutical concerns. The point of departure is the need for inculturation of faith and theology into Africa, and this interpretative perspective is legitimized through references to Catholic church documents. An illustrative example is the author's inclusive usage of the term "God." In some cases one is not certain whether the term "God" refers to Christian or traditional Akan concepts. Thus "the *Komien* [priest/prophet] appears to be the guarantor of this responsibility, since God has chosen him for this purpose." In other cases it is clear that "God" is used with deliberate ambiguity. Thus with reference to Hebrew 1:1, "God has spoken to our ancestors through the prophets," the author argues that the presence of *Komien* in Akan societies "testifies to God's progressive revelation to humankind." This contribution merits attention as a particular example of consciously Africanized biblical interpretation.

46. Ajayi, J. F. Ade, Lameck K. H. Goma, and G. Ampah Johnson

The African Experience with Higher Education

Accra: Association of African Universities, 1996. 288 pages, ISBN: 9780821411612.

Commissioned by the Association of African Universities, this study examines the historical background of universities in Africa and analyses the vital issues facing those universities in the 1990s. Its focus is limited to universities south of the Sahara, but excluding South Africa. Both anglophone and francophone Africa are covered. The authors are all former university vice-chancellors with broad experience in higher education in Africa. The book falls into three parts: historical background, issues and problems in the 1990s, and a look toward the twenty-first century. There are two appendices: a "Handbook on Academic Freedom and University Autonomy," and a "Code of Conduct for Academics." This book is thoroughly researched, well written, and handsomely produced. It seems unlikely that any other single resource covers this subject in such a balanced manner. Those in theological education might overlook this book because its focus on national universities seems extraneous to their concerns. But the issues faced by universities often directly parallel those faced by tertiary theological colleges, such as diminishing financial resources, obstacles to change, perceptions of mission, the quest for excellence, the concern for relevance, the need for leadership, and so forth. Furthermore, while the focus is on national universities, Christian universities have begun to spring up around the continent. How can church-related universities and university colleges deal with the issues that they too must face? Finally, the book concerns itself with the question of what constitutes an African university. How can the university be owned by Africa, becoming relevant to Africa and meeting Africa's needs, not merely mimicking Western models but structured to reflect African values and realities? That is of course a vital concern not only for universities, but as much or more for theological institutions.

47. Ajayi, Joel A. A.

A Biblical Theology of Gerassapience

Frankfurt: Peter Lang, 2010. 267 pages, ISBN: 9781433107856.

This is an investigation of "gerassapience," a term coined by the author, referring in the OT to "old-age wisdom." The author is a Nigerian scholar teaching at Liberty University (in Lynchburg VA), and the book is a revision of his PhD research for Baylor University. The main point of the book is that the ancient Israelites associated wisdom with old age. This point is developed through a systematic investigation of relevant OT texts, with a comparative look at some selected historical (i.e. Israel's neighbours) and contemporary (i.e. Yoruba) traditions expressing similar concepts. The book consists of eight chapters. Chapter 1 addresses introductory matters, with special focus on the research situation. Chapter 2 relates the work to three methodological approaches: linguistics, tradition history, and social anthropology. Chapters 3 and 4 analyse the two key terms, *chokmah* ("wisdom") and *zaken* ("old age"), and their cognates. Chapters 5 through 7 then attempt to draw some chronological lines in the "gerassapience" materials of pre-monarchical, monarchical and post-monarchical wisdom traditions. Chapter 8 offers a brief summary, and the book concludes with a ("select"!) bibliography of around one thousand books and articles. This is a solid piece of work. There are of course questions which could have been discussed more thoroughly (e.g. the relationship between contemporary African and Ancient Near Eastern sources, used for comparative purposes), and instances where alternative solutions could have been tried out (e.g. the chronological approach). Still, it is a well-researched book that can serve as a resource for further research on biblical and African concepts of "old-age" and "wisdom," and on the interaction between the two.

48. Ajulu, Deborah

Holism in Development: An African Perspective on Empowering Communities

Monrovia, CA: MARC, 2001. 206 pages, ISBN: 9781887983150.

The author has managed an indigenous Christian NGO in Uganda while also doing postdoctoral research in Oxford, England, so she writes from both theoretical and practical experience. She writes to assess and to urge, from a biblical perspective, the holistic empowerment of communities as well as individuals for overcoming poverty. Her book is intended as a call to development agencies, both Christian and secular, to strengthen this emphasis in their programmes. After introducing the problems of development and proposals for biblical solutions, she carefully defines each aspect of the issue. She analyses empowerment from three angles, first from a biblical perspective, including issues of human dignity, justice, and stewardship; then from a conceptual perspective, with a strong focus on rural development in developing countries; and finally from an empirical perspective, through a case study of the goals and activities of eight development agencies in East Africa, both Christian and secular. The case study was done through interviews with policy makers in each of the organisations that agreed to participate. She then evaluates the holistic community emphasis of each agency based on their articulation of their goals and their descriptions of their activities. The author states that the rich are also often powerless to change their attitudes toward and treatment of the poor, so that addressing their perceptions of their responsibilities for empowering the poor will also be empowering for them. She notes that this emphasis is lacking in the agencies in her case study, and she calls for it to be included as an important part of empowering the poor. For those working in leadership positions in development agencies, this part of the book will be especially enlightening and challenging. The style overall is highly academic, with citations from a wide range of sources, many quoted at length. Those therefore most likely to benefit from this book would be professionals in the areas treated, or those pursuing research in these areas.

Ajulu, Deborah

see also review 386

Akallo, Grace

see review 699

Akanmidu, R. A.

see review 15

Akao, J. O.

see review 10

49.   **Akinade, Akintunde E., editor**

A New Day: Essays on World Christianity in Honor of Lamin Sanneh

New York: Peter Lang, 2010. 322 pages, ISBN: 9781433104565.

It is indeed not easy to organize a Festschrift that does justice to the broad range of research interests of a multifaceted scholar like Lamin Sanneh (from Gambia, now at Yale, USA). Still, the present volume, a kind of mosaic with contributions from some of Sanneh's colleagues and students, succeeds in developing at least some of Sanneh's key areas. An introduction by the editor, Akintunde Akinade (of Georgetown University, Washington DC) offers both an exploration of the key phrase in the book's title: "World Christianity," and a survey of the contributions in the text. These fall into two parts. The first is entitled "Engaging the faith: issues, dimensions, and movements in world Christianity." Here Andrew Walls writes on world Christianity in the early church, while other presentations consider variously: the meaning of the term "World Christianity"; mission theology in a post-Constantinian era; the last word of the sixteenth-century missionary and social reformer Bartolomé de la Casas; theological education in a transnational context; Christianity and revival in relation to the Rwandan genocide; the response to poverty in African Initiated Churches (AICs); the Axumite empire; leadership in Ghana's new charismatic communities; visions and dreams in an AIC church; and Independent Church Movements in Africa and in the African diaspora. Two of these essays are of particular interest, at least as seen from an African perspective. Philomena Mwaura explores how AICs in Kenya have developed a spirituality of hope and resistance in their response to poverty. Herein they have found resources to transcend their marginal conditions and to be beacons of hope. Kwabena Asamoah-Gyadu analyses leadership concepts in neo-Pentecostal churches in Ghana, emphasising their ability to build sustainable leadership structures that reflect socio-cultural contexts of development, modernisation and globalisation. The second part of the book is entitled "Understanding and embracing the other: cross-cultural and interreligious perspectives." Here one finds papers on: a Pentecostal revival in India in 1905; the Lord's Prayer in interreligious perspective; Rashîd Ridâ's mission seminary; Muslims and Christians in Yorubaland; the relationship between the Christian concept of the Holy Spirit and the Eastern concept of Chi; and the teaching of religion in theological schools. Of particular interest among these, again from an African perspective, is Yushau Sodiq's essay on Muslims and Christians in Yorubaland, written from the perspective that the two are "unavoidable neighbors." Its concluding suggestions for improving the relationship between the two are relevant and useful far beyond the borders of Yorubaland. Finally, as an appendix, is Peter Phan's review of Sanneh's *Disciples of All Nations* (2008). All in all, the collection is a worthy Festschrift for one of the most important theologians of Africa in the late twentieth and early twenty-first centuries.

50.   **Akintunde, Dorcas Ola, editor**

African Culture and the Quest for Women's Rights

Ibadan: Sefer Books, 2001. 139 pages, ISBN: 9789783575318.

This is a collection of papers presented at a workshop held in Ibadan in 2001, under the auspices of the Institute of Women in Religion and Culture (directed by Mercy Oduyoye) and the Circle of Concerned African Women Theologians. All the papers are by African women scholars. They describe cultural practices such as female circumcision, widowhood rituals, inheritance discrimination, violence against women and restriction from leadership positions. They call for a change of attitude among men, and among women themselves who inflict some of these things on other women and often contribute to low female self-esteem. The papers advocate attention to education for females and working for their full human rights. Some of the papers address theological concerns, seeing in Jesus a model for recognition of women, denying that menstruation renders women impure for divine service, rejecting the culture of biblical times as normative on gender issues, using positive female role models in Scripture to condemn churches that forbid full recognition of female leadership, and invoking the biblical mandate to defend the disadvantaged in society. The writers advocate changing African culture where it does not promote female welfare. Although some of the papers speak from a mainly sociological perspective, all are well documented. The book would be a valuable resource for the study of women's issues in Africa and the African church.

51.   **Akintunde, Dorcas Ola, Marcelin S. Dossou, and Fabien Ouamba**

Introduction à la Théologie Sytématique Volume 2: Ethique

Yaoundé: Éditions Clé, 2003. 148 pages, ISBN: 9782723501781.

This is the second in a two-volume work on systematic theology, the first of which, covering dogmatics, was authored by Marcelin Dossou, et al. As with the first volume, this is intended as a manual for teaching theology in theological schools in French-speaking Africa. It consists of a collection of articles of different lengths covering faith and ethics, the history of ethics, the ethics of non-violence, rape and violence against women, the environment, and bioethics in Africa. The content of the book mostly gives more attention to questions arising from within the African context than did the first volume. The authors work largely from within an ecumenical orientation, with the result that evangelicals can learn from the ways in which these authors stress social questions and the social and structural factors touching on the moral lives of individuals. At the same time ecumenical theologians will need to consider the necessity for personal renewal, individual virtue, guidelines for personal living, and the renewal of the smallest social units such as the couple and the family as an essential underpinning for their social projects. The book could serve as a helpful resource on several ethical issues in the African context which it addresses and about which little material is otherwise available. But as it stands, the content of this book is too eclectic to be useful as an ethics course-manual. Questions of personal ethics are almost entirely lacking, and even the social issues reflect more the personal interests of the authors than an even coverage of the contemporary issues.

Akintunde, Dorcas Ola

see also review 10

52. **Akpunonu, Peter Damian**

The Overture of the Book of Consolations (Isaiah 40:1–11)

Frankfurt: Peter Lang, 2004. 166 pages, ISBN: 9780820467788.

Back in 1971 at the Urbanian Pontifical University in Rome, Akpunonu, a Roman Catholic priest from Nigeria, was among the first handful of African scholars to complete a doctorate in OT, with a thesis on Isaiah 40–55. After this he has served in various capacities in Nigerian theological institutions, including nearly a decade as rector of the prestigious Catholic Institute of West Africa in Port Harcourt. Subsequently he has been professor of biblical studies at the University of St. Mary of the Lake, Illinois. Accordingly, Akpunonu is one of the deans of African OT studies, and the present book should be met with interest, as it follows up his more than 35 years of attention to Isaiah 40–55. The book is a detailed analysis of the first eleven verses of Isaiah 40, and its focus is to show how these verses anticipate the major theological lines of Isaiah 40–55. After a brief survey of the historical context (the Babylonian exile), a study of the literary style of Isaiah 40–55 follows. Then comes the more direct focus on the first eleven verses of Isaiah 40, from thematic and exegetical perspectives. The reader will find a number of interesting details in the close reading of this passage. None, however, explicitly addresses the text from an African perspective. The reader will probably also be quite disappointed to find that the presentation is somewhat dated with regard to the scholarly discussion of this text in particular and of Isaiah in general. Although there are a few references to scholarly contributions from the last decade, most of the discussion reflects the research situation in the 1960s and 70s, rather than that of today. And this is a pity, as Isaiah 40:1–11 plays a major role in the more recent acknowledgement of the literary unity of the Book of Isaiah. Nevertheless, the publication of this book should be noticed, as it reflects the growing pattern of African OT scholars publishing research contributions on a monograph level.

53. **Akpunonu, Peter Damian**

The Vine, Israel and the Church

Frankfurt: Peter Lang, 2004. 242 pages, ISBN: 9780820461601.

The author is a Roman Catholic priest from Nigeria who has served in various capacities in Nigerian theological institutions, and subsequently has been a professor of biblical studies at the University of St. Mary of the Lake, Illinois. This book offers a thematic study of the vine motif throughout the OT and NT. After an introductory chapter on vine and viticulture in Israel and the Ancient Near East, chapters follow on the major texts, such as Isaiah 5:1–7 (Canticle of the vine), Psalm 80 (God's vineyard), Matthew 21:33–44 (Parable of the tenants), and John 15:1–8 (Jesus as the true vine). In each case Akpunonu goes meticulously into the textual material, discussing relevant introductory questions as well as making detailed exegetical analysis. In conclusion there are two chapters discussing Israel (OT) and the church (NT) as Vine. The topic is important, not only for exegetical but even more for ecclesiological studies. The book is therefore a welcome contribution from a senior member of the guild of biblical studies in Africa, although a more explicit African perspective would have been welcomed. One might also have wished for more interaction between the analysis of the OT and NT texts. And some readers will probably be somewhat puzzled to see how the author tends to identify the NT church with one particular denomination, namely the Roman Catholic church (see especially the epilogue). Still, the book is recommended for lecturers and researchers in postgraduate contexts.

Alana, E. O.

see review 15

54.   **Alazar Abraha, MCCJ**

Saint Justin de Jacobis: His Missionary Methodology in Eritrea and Ethiopia

Nairobi: Paulines, 1995. 119 pages, ISBN: 9789966211866.

The author, an Eritrean, became a Comboni Missionary in 1987 and at the time of publication was serving as a missionary in Kenya in the Diocese of Eldoret. His topic is a nineteenth-century Italian Catholic missionary to Ethiopia, with the stated purpose "to highlight some significant works of St Justin de Jacobis as a model for our modern missionary work of the church." Born in Italy in 1800, de Jacobis began service as an ordained Vincentian priest. In 1839, Pope Gregory XVI commissioned him "to establish the Catholic church in Abyssinia." De Jacobis served as a missionary to Ethiopia from 1839–1860. He is responsible for successfully planting the Catholic Church in Ethiopia, leaving a legacy of a 12,000-member vicariate behind at his death. De Jacobis was canonized in 1975. Abraha contrasts de Jacobis' success with the failure of a previous Jesuit mission to Ethiopia in the sixteenth and seventeenth centuries. He attributes de Jacobis' achievement to his missional stance of contextualization. Whereas the Jesuits sought to impose European Catholicism upon the Abyssinians, de Jacobis laboured to plant a truly indigenous Catholic Church. At the time of publication, Alazar Abraha held an MA in theology, and the research reflects this level of training. Moreover, sometimes sweeping generalisations are made about a topic, but which lack argument. A few too many of these results in a partial loss of confidence in the work as a true guide into de Jacobis' times, life and work. The book is written in English, which is not the author's first language, and at times this shows; there are sentences throughout that are unclear as to their precise meaning. Nevertheless, Alazar Abraha is to be commended for introducing to a wider audience an otherwise obscure missionary and his story of planting the Catholic Church in Ethiopia. Libraries attempting a full collection in African church history, or in the history of missions in Africa, could consider securing a copy.

55.   **Alkali, Nura, editor**

Islam in Africa: Proceedings of the Islam in Africa Conference

Ibadan: Spectrum Books, 1993. 454 pages, ISBN: 9789782461742.

This is a collection of 28 papers presented by Muslim scholars at the "Islam in Africa" conference held in 1989 in Abuja, Nigeria. A few of the papers are updated to 1993. The conference was sponsored by the Islamic Council, London, and the Nigerian Supreme Council for Islamic Affairs. Nineteen of the authors were based in Nigeria, although some papers address aspects of Islam in East Africa, Senegambia, Africa as a whole, the USA and the Caribbean. The topics relating to Africa include the use of Sharia law, Islam and education, the history of the spread and propagation of Islam, and Islamic economics. Problems frequently addressed are the situation of Muslims in countries where they are in a minority or not under an Islamic government, economic under-development in Islamic and African countries, and the legacy of colonialism. There is also a chapter from a woman's perspective. This is a book by Muslims for Muslims. Its chief value for others will likely be to sensitize them to Muslim viewpoints on the issues discussed. The book could be considered for theological libraries with specialist collections in Islamics.

Altbach, Philip G.

see review 1084

56. Altschul, Paisius, editor

The Unbroken Circle: Linking Ancient African Christianity to the African-American Experience

St Louis: Brotherhood of St. Moses the Black, 1997. 210 pages, ISBN: 9780916700515.

The present work speaks to the longing for Africa in the hearts of many African-Americans by pointing out (and rightly so) that Christianity is not a Western religion, but one that has deep historical roots in African soil. The book is a collection of talks presented at three "Ancient Christianity and Africa-America" conferences held in the USA during the 1990s, hosted by The Joy of All Who Sorrow Eastern Orthodox Church in Indianapolis. The presenters are all from the Orthodox traditions, some are Copts or Ethiopians, most are from The Brotherhood of St. Moses the Black, an Orthodox mission to African-Americans. The book points out that, as Orthodox believers, the presenters are not Afrocentric but rather Christocentric. The articles explore two themes: (1) the ancient African dimension of Christian history (attention is given to the witness of Anthony, Athanasius, Perpetua and Felicity, Cyprian and many others); and (2) the legacy of suffering in the African-American church (especially through the witness of suffering slave Christians). The connection between these two themes appears to be the witness of both groups to a true otherworldliness. The ancient churches of Egypt and Ethiopia were monastic churches who looked beyond this world and its suffering to the God beyond the world. The slave Christianity of America, as is seen in its hymnody, also points beyond itself to a loving and saving God. This is a fascinating book which attempts to bridge the gap between a people (African-Americans) and the gospel by means of the witness of authentically African and authentically Christian lives. The message of the book is that God cares for Africa, and in fact has always cared for African people. Happily, one does not need to be an Orthodox Christian to rejoice in this truth.

57. An-Na'im, Abdullahi Ahmed, editor

Proselytization and Communal Self-Determination in Africa

Eugene, OR: Wipf & Stock, 2009. 328 pages, ISBN: 9781606086711.

This collection of twelve essays by Muslim and Christian scholars from both African and Western countries explores the critical question whether Islam, Christianity, and African religions can peacefully co-exist in pluralistic societies in Africa. In particular, the authors explore the issue of proselytization. In modern societies, increased travel and communication bring religious communities into more frequent contact and thus enhance opportunities both for "proselytizing initiatives" and for possible conflict. The contributors work within a human rights paradigm. In other words, they begin with the notion that communities inherently have the right of self-determination. Thus, as the publisher's blurb states, the question is, "Where does one community's right to commend itself to others leave off, and another community's right to be left alone begin?" The essays explore the subject within the larger context of political, social, economic, ethnic, cultural, and legal realities of several African countries. The result is a rich gathering of first-rate essays on a subject of vital importance. As with any work drawing together several authors approaching a subject in a multidisciplinary fashion, this book defies simple summary. Thus, a sampling of essay topics and authors must suffice to illustrate the variety. Lamin Sanneh, a West African Christian teaching at Yale, writes on "Church and State Relations: Western Norms, Muslim Practice, and the African Experience." The late Hannah Kinoti of the University of Nairobi examines "Religious Fragmentation in Kenya," exploring the social consequences of the religious pluralism found even within major religions in Kenya. Chabha Bouslimani, an Algerian journalist working in France, analyses the problems of inter-Islamic proselytization in Algeria. J. D. van der Vyver, a South African who is now Professor of International Law and Human Rights at Emory University in the United States, provides an overview of "Religious Freedom in African Constitutions." Overall, this collection provides a substantial and fascinating exploration of the intersection of religious movements in modern Africa, carried out from an interdisciplinary perspective.

58. **Ande, Titre**

Leadership and Authority: Bula Matari and Life - Community Ecclesiology in Congo

Oxford: Regnum, 2010. 189 pages, ISBN: 9781870345729.

Ande is Anglican Bishop of Aru, and formerly principal of an Anglican theological school in Bunia, both located in northeastern Congo (DRC). The book emerges from his doctoral research (at the University of Birmingham) and his own observations and leadership experience in Congo. In it he intends to provide "a critical analysis of the theology and exercise of authority in the EAC (Eglise Anglicane du Congo – Anglican Church of Congo)." Ande claims that pre-colonial African leadership had a consensual and democratic character, but that this was lost due to Western colonialism, which introduced a centralized, paternalistic and oppressive model. The Bula Matari of the title is a Kikongo phrase meaning "breaker of rocks," and was the name given by Congolese to Henry Morton Stanley, agent of Leopold of Belgium in his colonisation of the Congo. It then became a metaphor for the despotic colonial state, and Ande suggests that Mobutu's post-colonial government (1965–1997) followed the Bula Matari model in its tyranny, paternalism and concentration of power. Moreover, he argues that leadership in the Congolese church, specifically the EAC, reflects that of the Bula Matari state. In pursuit of a theological response he examines the ecclesiology of some recent African theologians, including Pobee, Sawyerr, Bujo, Dickson and Magesa. Finally he advocates a "life-community" ecclesiology, with leadership characterized by service, consensus and self-criticism, and the ability to bear prophetic witness to the exploitative structures of the state rather than supporting or even mirroring them. The volume has much to offer. Ande's analysis of the Mobutu years is informative, as also his account of the origins of the EAC. His appeal to the church to examine itself in the light of Scripture is timely and widely applicable, while his discussion of abuses of power within the EAC is both prophetic and courageous. Moreover, Ande's critique of some trends in African theology, especially his call for context to be subordinated to Scripture, is highly appropriate: "Theology in Africa must avoid turning more to African traditional religion as a source of theology than to the Scriptures." There are some weaknesses. The flow of thought and clarity of expression are at times problematic. Ande might have offered a fuller biblical grounding for his own theological proposals. And his argument occasionally lacks substance, especially in the general and largely unsupported description of pre-colonial Congolese society. Nevertheless *Leadership and Authority* is a significant source for understanding the church and its leadership in Congo (DRC) during the past century.

59. Anderson, Allan

African Reformation: African Initiated Christianity in the Twentieth Century

Trenton, NJ: Africa World Press, 2001. 282 pages, ISBN: 9780865438842.

Of contemporary literature available on the "AIC" phenomenon in African Christianity (whether the "I" in "AIC" is taken to stand for "independent," "indigenous," or "initiated"), the vast bulk has related to particular movements or the range of movements in a single locale. Anderson has significantly helped the student of AICs by giving us a broad survey that includes a general overview of the movements, brief histories of selected examples from every corner of the continent, and discussion of lessons to be drawn from this segment of African Christianity for the church around the world. Anderson's own scholarly expertise, as well as 24 years association, has been with the Pentecostal varieties of independence found on the south of the continent, and he utilizes this background to advantage. The book is divided into three sections built on the primary thesis that "Africa has had a reformation of the Spirit that has revolutionized the face of Christianity." The first section introduces the reader to the terminology, typologies, concepts, and body of scholarship associated with the AICs. The second section gives brief historical introductions to numerous AICs across the continent, organized geographically, with an introductory chapter on the earliest movements and a final chapter on Pentecostal and charismatic forms. The final section offers lessons drawn from the engagement of AICs and culture, the practical nature of theological convictions within AICs, and a more general discussion of reform and renewal in the African church as a whole. As a survey, the book is well written and engaging. Refusing to fall into the reductionistic trap whether in terminology or analysis, Anderson walks a fine line between generalisation and particularity. Generalisation in this case would involve overstating the commonalities seen in AICs across the continent, whereas particularity would involve being so idiosyncratically focused that general conclusions are deemed impossible to draw. In sum, Anderson has compiled a significant body of research on an extraordinarily complex topic, boiled it down to a readable text, without compromising on the complexity of the movement. It should now serve as a primary text for any type of overview of the AICs, and it also contributes significantly in understanding African church growth and contemporary African Christian history.

60. Anderson, Allan

Moya: The Holy Spirit in an African Context

Pretoria: UNISA Press, 1991. 141 pages, ISBN: 9780869816936.

While admitting that he comes from a Western background, the author defends writing on this theme in its African context by stating that he has spent the last 30 years of his life in Pentecostal and charismatic churches, and has lived most of his life in Africa. In many ways, therefore, the book is written from an apologetic stance, defending the practice of the Pentecostal and charismatic churches in Africa. The book was written as a project of the Institute for Theological Research of the University of South Africa. The topic is of vital interest to any Christian, African or expatriate, working in African churches. While the reader may not always agree with either the theological presuppositions or the conclusions of the author, the issues are too important to be overlooked, and at least the author has tried to come to terms with them. The book focuses on the "Spirit-type" churches of Africa, a broad term which is used here to include the independent churches and the Pentecostal and charismatic churches of Africa. One key point the book seeks to make is that in the past Christian theologians (both African and non-African) have fallen short of fully understanding either the African worldview or the independent churches or both. Writers such as John Taylor, Bendt Sundkler and John Mbiti are criticized, although it must be said that this is done in an objective and non-aggressive manner. On the other hand, there is no doubt that the writer finds a soul mate in Inus Daneel, who is often quoted, and who wrote the foreword to the book. Another point made is that the African "Spirit-type" churches have filled a gap in our thinking and understanding of the person and role of the Holy Spirit, a gap that was formed by the inadequate treatment of the topic in traditional Western pneumatology. The "Spirit-type" churches are said to be in a much better position to answer the prevalent questions asked by Africans concerning the spirit world than are churches which depend on a pneumatology that comes from the West.

61. **Anderson, Allan**

Zion and Pentecost: The Spirituality and Experience of Pentecostal and Zionist/Apostolic Churches in South Africa

Pretoria: UNISA Press, 2000. 349 pages, ISBN: 9781868881437.

Building on his doctoral dissertation and previously published books, Anderson here reflects the rich mixture of his years of experience among Pentecostal churches, and also among independent churches in South Africa, hundreds of field interviews and participant observations in a wide variety of African initiated churches (AICs), and extensive bibliographic research. One would be hard-pressed to find a better-researched text dealing with the segment of the AICs that Anderson presents in *Zion and Pentecost*. He begins with an overview history of the movement, which includes a fascinating account of the indigenous nature of the churches from the beginning, as well as the reality of a racist undercurrent in western-initiated Pentecostal movements in South Africa. Having established the historical context, the remainder of the text focuses on issues related to contextualization. Based on ethnographic research, and integrating findings of other researchers in southern Africa, Anderson explores issues such as the African gospel, ritualized church practices (clothing, liturgy, sacraments), the intersection of the Christian faith with traditional religious perspectives (spirits, ancestors, diviners, divination, burial), and key theological concerns (Christ, the Spirit, salvation, and healing). In his concluding chapter Anderson offers important implications for missiological reflection. The story of these churches, with their beliefs and practices, is told so vividly that the reader will be drawn into the life of the churches described. Anderson throughout lets the church members speak for themselves. He is careful to note that their voices, though generally unified, are hardly uniform. While his conclusion, that "Pentecostal and Zionist churches have now become *the* major force to be reckoned with in Southern African Christianity" (emphasis his), is perhaps overdrawn, the significance of these churches in offering thoroughly indigenous attempts to contextualize the gospel for Africa must not be discounted. In spite of theological aberrations (as documented and explained by Anderson), these churches are part of the Church and have much to offer in terms of lived theology, practical expressions of faith couched in culturally relevant forms, and the dynamic power to change a society. This book is a welcome addition to the ever-expanding body of literature on the AICs, and will be a valuable acquisition for anyone reading or researching about the African-initiated church movement.

62.   Anderson, David M., and Douglas H. Johnson, editors

Revealing Prophets: Prophecy in Eastern African History

Martlesham, UK: James Currey, 1995. 320 pages, ISBN: 9780852557174.

This fascinating compendium about prophets and prophecy within East Africa grew out of a conference of some 40 participants held in 1989 at the University of London. The ten contributors to this volume offer the reader a rich and thorough understanding of seers, prophets and prophecy mainly within the ever fluctuating and dynamic traditional religions of Kenya, Tanzania, and Uganda. Each chapter portrays various prophets engaged in dialogue with their respective communities. The introductory chapter by the editors breaks new ground in its thorough definition of the role of East African prophets. Without undermining the predictive element of the OT prophets, the editors affirm that the mark of a prophet is "his ability to clarify and articulate what the people who follow him have themselves begun to feel about the particular situation." This collection of essays will prove important reading for theological educators and pastors in several respects. For example, it provides a valuable key for better appreciating the pivotal role that prophets play within the burgeoning charismatic churches throughout Africa. It is often difficult to discern whether contemporary so-called Christian prophets who are functioning within these churches are true to the biblical criteria of a prophet or merely dependent upon the traditional religious model of their forbearers. Unfortunately, not all essays affirm the biblical premise that God "has not left himself without testimony" (Acts 14:17). There is ample evidence that traditional religious prophets within Ethiopia predicted the coming of a new religious order. The most significant of these was the pre-Christian prophet Esa, often hailed as the John the Baptist of southern Ethiopia, who preached a message of repentance in the 1920s.

63.   Anderson, Richard

We Felt Like Grasshoppers

Nottingham: CrosswayUK, 1994. 348 pages, ISBN: 9781856841061.

This book is the story of the Africa Inland Mission (AIM), founded in 1895, with its first missionaries going to Kenya that same year. Subsequently AIM also undertook extensive work in Uganda, Sudan, Congo (DRC), Tanzania, and Central African Republic, and more recently other parts of Africa. The author is a medical doctor who served for many years with AIM in Kenya, and in due course was AIM's International Director. The book contains a compelling collection of stories candidly portraying the sometimes painful and sometimes wonderfully encouraging endeavours both of the AIM missionaries and the people with whom they worked in Africa. It is a story of mission – its "principles, puzzles, methods and even mistakes." The book contains history, biography, autobiographical testimonials, the good and bad, tough and difficult, through a century of transition, turmoil and political change. This book is a useful introduction to the history of one of the leading international evangelical mission agencies in Africa.

Anderson, William

see review 1169

64.   **Anglican Church of Kenya**

Our Modern Services: Anglican Church of Kenya 2002

Nairobi: Uzima Press, 2002. 342 pages, ISBN: 9789966855732.

It has often been argued that among the strengths of Anglicanism as a tradition are its clear, biblically-based services of worship enshrined in the Book of Common Prayer (BCP), which emanates from the sixteenth-century English Reformation. This liturgical tradition has certainly provided worldwide Anglicanism not only with orderly forms of worship but also with a doctrinal foundation. On the other hand, the Thirty-Nine Articles of Religion, a thoroughly Reformed theological confession, argues that worship should be done "in a tongue . . . understood of the people" (Art. XXIV), and that rites of the church can change according to what is deemed necessary by any "particular or national Church," so long as the changes are not "repugnant to God's Word" (Art. XXIV). For many member churches of the Anglican Communion these Articles have given impetus to revisions of the BCP or to writing completely new liturgies. Over the last decades most churches which have undertaken such a process have looked to Patristic liturgies to provide exemplars for new forms of worship. The first completely revised prayer book from Africa, however, has looked to different sources. Produced by the Anglican Church of Kenya (formerly known as "The Church of the Province of Kenya"), one of the largest churches in the worldwide Anglican family (with more than 2.5 million members), *Our Modern Services* keeps to the basic structure of worship found in the BCP. It has, however, found inspiration both in African tradition and in the Kenyan church's roots in the East African Revival for fresh prayers and even some new services. For example, at a time when most Western churches were removing sacrificial language from eucharistic prayers, due to Western theological embarrassment about the blood involved, the Kenyan eucharistic liturgy emphasizes Jesus' death as a sacrifice for sins. While Western churches are reviving medieval chanting as part of Anglican worship, the Kenyan book is inserting material from gospel hymns into their liturgy; thus, for example, a stanza from "Rock of Ages" appears in the service of Compline (Late Evening Prayer). Mention of "faithful ancestors in heaven" replaces the familiar "all the company of heaven" found in most Anglican services. This book is to be recommended, not only to other Anglicans inside and outside of Africa, but to Christians of other traditions as a faithful attempt by one church to remain rooted in biblical truth as well as faithful to the call of God to be relevant within African culture.

Anguandia, Enosh A.

see review 1067

65.   **Anonby, John A.**

The Kenyan Epic Novelist Ngugi: His Secular Reconfiguration of Biblical Themes

Lewiston, NY: Edwin Mellen Press, 2006. 236 pages, ISBN: 9780773454965.

Anonby is the retired Professor of English at Trinity Western University in Canada. He has also served on the faculty of Pan Africa Christian University in Nairobi. This book devotes a chapter to each of the widely-read Kenyan author Ngugi wa Thiong'o's first six novels: *The River Between, Weep Not, Child, A Grain of Wheat, Petals of Blood, Devil on the Cross* and *Matigari*, paying particular attention to the biblical motifs and allusions used prolifically in each book (*Wizard of the Crow* was published in 2006, too late to be included). Anonby traces

Ngugi's hardening stance against colonialism and Christianity as he depicts the struggle for independence in the first two novels, and in the last four novels the impact of neo-colonialism and the continued oppression of the poor after the achievement of Uhuru. Anonby maintains that Ngugi rejects institutional Christianity as taking sides with oppressors, and sees forms of Christianity that emphasize individual salvation and heavenly reward as ineffective compared to the socialist-style efforts needed to improve the lot of common people in this life. Ngugi uses biblical images, texts, and allusions freely and fluidly for their emotive power, and subverts them to shock and provoke the reader into realizing how far Christianity has departed from its own ideals and, from his viewpoint, how helpless it is to remedy Africa's ills. Ngugi's perspective on Christianity is not exceptional for many of Africa's educated elite, and vividly reflects an influential dimension of the African intellectual context that African Christianity must yet learn to hear and address. Anonby is to be commended for providing this thoughtful introduction.

66. Appiah, Kwame Anthony, and Henry Louis Gates, editors

Encarta Africana

Redmond, WA: Microsoft Corporation, 1999. ISBN: 9780735601055.

This remarkable 2-disc set represents the first comprehensive multimedia encyclopedia of African history and culture, with over 5,500 articles, photos, videos, audio clips and maps (3361 actual articles) encompassing the African continent and its diaspora. The editors are both associated with Harvard University. The best way into the resources of the encyclopedia is to access the Africana "Find" tool. This function uses 78 "categories" within eight general "areas of interest." Several of the categories appear under more than one area of interest. For example, the category "religion" has 92 associated articles in the "North America: Culture and Sports" area, 51 in "African Culture and Sports," 45 in "Hispanic America and Brazil," and 51 in "Europe, Asia, and Middle East." All told, then, there are some 229 articles on religion in the encyclopedia, providing a broad and fairly comprehensive survey of the religions of Africans both on the continent and in the diaspora. The 51 religion articles in the "African Culture and Sports" area of interest run from Abd al-Qadir (Algerian religious and military leader) to Fulbert Youlou (Catholic priest, nationalist leader, and president of the Republic of the Congo). Between these you will find articles on Edward Blyden, Independent and Charismatic Churches in Africa, Christian missionaries in Africa, Simon Kimbangu, and rites of passage and transition. Within each article, words that have associated articles (e.g. the word "Kenya" in an article on Jomo Kenyatta) are highlighted and linked to the article they reference. Additionally, choosing the option of "More information about this subject" in the title bar for the article gives three choices: (1) a list of related articles; (2) suggestions for further reading; and (3) web links. Thus for the "Rites of Passage and Transition" article, there are nine additional related articles, five books listed as recommended reading (they are not available on the CD), and one web link. In this case, the link was to a web page that no longer exists (overall *Encarta Africana* offers more than 500 web links, which are organized in a web links directory). Altogether *Encarta Africana* provides a powerful tool at a very reasonable price, and is highly recommended for institutions and individuals. While it may not meet the needs of the specialized researcher (e.g. Africa's indigenous churches receive only one major article of 2800 words, and several smaller ones of roughly 500 words each), it will provide accurate general information on a wealth of topics of significance for understanding Africa and its diaspora.

67. **Arén, Gustav**

Envoys of the Gospel in Ethiopia: In the Steps of the Evangelical Pioneers 1898–1936

Stockholm: EFS Förlaget, 1999. 569 pages, ISBN: 9789152626559.

Gustav Arén worked as a missionary in Ethiopia from 1945 onward, and became in 1960 the "founder" of the Mekane Yesus Seminary in Addis. Throughout his years in Ethiopia he collected historical materials and information on the church. The results are two major works on the pre-history of the Ethiopian Evangelical Church Mekane Yesus. The first book, *Evangelical Pioneers in Ethiopia: Origins of the Evangelical Church Mekane Yesus*, appeared in 1978. As indicated by its title, that book described the origins of this church and of the evangelical movement in Ethiopia and Eritrea in total. The present book, published posthumously, continues where the first ended and brings the development forward to the time of the Ethio-Italian war 1935–1941. Both books are detailed studies based on extensive research in Ethiopia as well as in mission archives throughout the world, and at the same time they are written in a manner that makes the reading exciting. The first volume has become a standard text on the evangelical movement in Ethiopia, and it seems obvious that this second volume will fill the same role. The reader meets a number of outstanding persons who followed in the steps of the earliest pioneers. One is reminded over and over of the rich culture that existed in Ethiopia prior to the coming of the evangelical missions, and how indigenous representatives, together with missionaries, established congregations that today form the core of the evangelical churches in the region. Together with the first volume, this book provides many keys towards understanding why the development of Christianity in this region has been different from that in other parts of the continent.

68. **Arenas, Fernando**

Lusophone Africa: Beyond Independence

Minneapolis: University of Minnesota Press, 2011. 368 pages, ISBN: 9780816669844.

This is presented as "a study of the contemporary cultural production of Portuguese-speaking Africa and its critical engagement with the processes of globalization and the aftermath of colonialism." Arenas is a professor at the University of Minnesota, and it is clear that he is very familiar with the language, culture and history of the Lusophone world. His introduction and first two chapters provide excellent background information. It is this information that may be of most value to those wanting to understand the political and social history behind the contemporary (post-1975) realities of Africa's five Portuguese-speaking countries, including their relationships to both Brazil and Portugal. Arenas notes that much of the African continent has remained "suppliers of raw materials (particularly mineral wealth), much like they were under colonialism." He calls this "dependent capitalism" and feels that the benefits of globalisation have tended to fall into the hands of a relatively small group, people he refers to as the new colonialists. The real strength of the book is its social commentary showing the effects of globalisation on whole societies. How does one perceive what life is like for ordinary people? It is through hearing their music, watching their films and reading their novels and short stories. The second half of the book is a rich annotative bibliography of artists, directors and writers – walking through styles of music and plot summaries of films and books. While readers may be unfamiliar with most of the examples treated, it makes sense that one will learn much more about the soul of a people through their cultural expressions. It is unfortunate that Arenas almost completely ignores cultural expressions that are religious, especially given the importance of music and story within the African religious context. Nevertheless, for those seeking to offer answers to the many problems that Africa faces, this book could be a useful reference for knowing whom to listen to or what to watch or read in order to understand the real beliefs and practices of African peoples.

69. Asamoah-Gyadu, J. Kwabena

African Charismatics: Current Developments within Independent Indigenous Pentecostalism in Ghana

Leiden: BRILL, 2005. 284 pages, ISBN: 9789004140899.

This book on Ghanaian Pentecostalism is written by the Professor of African Christianity at Trinity Theological Seminary in Ghana. His thesis is that "Pentecostalism at the moment represents the most cogent, powerful and visible evidence of religious renewal and influence in Ghana." The author distinguishes three historical waves of Ghanaian Pentecostal Christianity. The first wave is the Sunsum sorè movement. Sunsum sorè, meaning spiritual worship or church, refers to the African Independent Church movement in Ghana in the first half of the twentieth century, which arose partly as a result of the William Wadé Harris events. The Musama Disco Christo Church is an example of this movement. Sunsum sorè is an example of African-enculturated spiritual theology. But this movement has been in decline because of its syncretistic tendencies and its lack of serious biblical discipleship. Yet the author believes that this movement is a significant historical influence on modern Ghanaian Pentecostalism. The second wave of Ghanaian Pentecostalism is represented by the churches proceeding out of classical Western Pentecostalism in the 1960s and 1970s. The Church of Pentecost is an example. The third wave is the contemporary Charismatic Ministries or the modern Pentecostal movement which began in the late 1970s. Although influenced from the West, this movement is now African. The author analyses this movement from the perspective of salvation. Salvation for them is based on a Spirit-filled conversion which transforms individual lives. Salvation is also seen as healing and deliverance from the power of the devil. But salvation for them also often means prosperity. Here, the author argues, Pentecostalism goes off track, since it deviates from the message of the cross. Yet Pentecostalism in general has offered renewal for individuals in Ghana. This book is recommended as a good contemporary case study of African charismatic and Pentecostal Christianity in one African country.

70. Asamoah-Gyadu, J. Kwabena

Contemporary Pentecostal Christianity: Interpretations from an African Context

Oxford: Regnum, 2013. 194 pages, ISBN: 9781908355072.

This book offers a knowledgeable, sympathetic analysis of Pentecostalism in Africa, with particular reference to Ghana. The author is a professor at Trinity Theological Seminary in Ghana. He begins by noting the incredible success of Pentecostalism in Africa. He understands Pentecostalism as a powerful movement of the Holy Spirit which necessarily manifests itself in speaking in tongues. Several things characterize African Pentecostalism. First, worship is an experiential and lively activity. Second, prayer is central and dynamic. Third, the ecclesiology tends to have a democratisation of leadership and the spiritual gifts. Fourth, giving is central in Pentecostal worship. But giving tends to be "transactional": if you give, you will be blessed. Fifth, anointing is a central feature, and gives power. Sixth, the Lord's Supper is often central, and this too brings power. Finally, Pentecostals hold to the authority of the Bible, but they also tend to use it as a talisman. The author is impressed by the movement of the Holy Spirit in the Pentecostal churches in Africa, but he is also critical of their movement towards Prosperity Theology. There tends to be a preoccupation with power. Thus tithing, anointing, the Lord's Supper and prayer for the Pentecostals all convey power. But is this the emphasis of Scripture? What of people who faithfully pray and tithe and yet continue to experience misfortunes? The author uses Martin Luther's theology of the cross to remind us that suffering is also a part of the gospel. It was through suffering that Jesus brought salvation to us. We need to focus on the suffering of others and not just on prosperity. While readers of other traditions may disagree with the author on such things as necessary evidences of the fullness of the Holy Spirit, this book is an excellent survey of the strengths and weaknesses of Pentecostalism in Africa.

71. Asamoah-Gyadu, J. Kwabena

Sighs and Signs of the Spirit: Ghanaian Perspectives on Pentecostalism and Renewal in Africa

Oxford: Regnum, 2015. 192 pages, ISBN: 9781908355812.

The author is professor of African theology at Trinity Theological Seminary in Ghana. This book considers Pentecostalism in Africa with particular reference to Ghana. Asamoah-Gyadu argues that the Holy Spirit is "the single most important reason" for the Pentecostal or spiritual renewals in Africa. This supernatural factor is ignored by most Western studies of Pentecostalism. This book focuses on twentieth and twenty-first century spiritual or Pentecostal movements in Africa, and argues that the Holy Spirit is the key to the success of African Pentecostalism. So what does this Pentecostal movement look like? In the first place, it emphasizes "taking territories and raising champions." This is a theology of dominion which accents success or prosperity in this life. Three images symbolize this dominion pneumatology: the dove, the eagle and the globe. Especially the eagle and the globe suggest prosperity and success. Two OT patriarchs are reinterpreted along these lines. Jacob is seen as a successful businessman, while Esau is perceived to be a business failure. Pentecostalism uses modern media successfully, although "the ultimate sacramental material is the Bible." Pentecostalism understands the power of the spoken word. This is evident in their use of microphones and the power of positive confession. Pentecostalism has also understood the traditional African cultic mediator. The Pentecostal preacher functions like the traditional African priest. Part of Pentecostalism's success is its trans-denominational nature as evident in the Full Gospel Businessmen's Fellowship and Women's Aglow. Pentecostalism is also African in its understanding of the spirit world and its use of exorcism. A penultimate chapter warns against the dangers of the prosperity gospel, but a final chapter praises Pentecostalism as a movement of the Holy Spirit which has brought renewal to the stagnant mainline mission churches. But is everything described here actually the work of the Holy Spirit? Is prosperity theology really the work of the Holy Spirit? The Holy Spirit is indeed active in Africa, remarkable things are happening in Africa, but a study like this should be more nuanced in its presentation of the work of the Spirit.

Asamoah-Gyadu, J. Kwabena

see also review 652

72. Asante, Molefi Kete, and Abu S. Abarry, editors

African Intellectual Heritage: A Book of Sources

Philadelphia: Temple University Press, 1996. 848 pages, ISBN: 9781566394031.

The editors of this anthology were both teaching at Temple University in the USA at the time of publication, and the book is a collection of readings used with their students in African American Studies. The readings are presented in six categories: The Creation of the Universe, Religious Ideas, Culture and Identity, Philosophy and Morality, Society and Politics, and Resistance and Renewal. Each part contains readings from ancient Egypt, modern Africa, and the African Diaspora. In the readings from Modern Africa, Creation Stories are given from the San, Khoi, Barozvi, Dogon, Yoruba, and Asante. Religious Ideas come from Jomo Kenyatta (ancestor veneration), Asante (praise poems to Tano River and the earth), Lodagaa (an ancestor libation), Ga (libation oratory), Igbo (invocations), the Ifa corpus (good character traits), and Akan religion. Culture and Identity contains a Yoruba Praise to Ogun, various myths and sagas, the Akan Odwira Festival, Indigenous Institutions of Ghana, the Ga Homowo festival, and Wole Soyinka on "African Classical Concepts of Tragedy." Part 4 includes selections from John Mbiti, Kwame Gyekye, Leopold Senghor, Kwame Nkrumah, and Chinua Achebe, as well as collections of Igbo and Luyia proverbs. Part 5 includes Mensah Sarbah, "On the Fante National Constitution"; Julius Nyerere, "One-Party Government"; Kwame Nkrumah, "Need for a Union Government for Africa"; and C. L. R. James, "The Rise and Fall of Nkrumah." Part 6 has Haile Selassie's address to the League of Nations, and the Charter of the OAU. The book intends to inform African Americans about their cultural heritage, and contains a great amount of material written by people of African descent living in the USA and other parts of the West. At the same time, it is a convenient collection of material on a number of themes in African religion, culture, and history.

73. Aseka, Eric M.

Africa in the 21st Century

Eldoret: Zapf Chancery, 1996. 59 pages, ISBN: 9789966992512.

The author analyses the future of Africa from his perspective as a political economist, and as chair of the history department at Kenyatta University in Nairobi. His position is made evident from the first page of his introduction, when he describes terms such as "black Africa," "sub-Saharan Africa," "the South," "the Third World" and "undeveloped countries" as "racist" and "highly demeaning" – although he himself uses most of these terms subsequently in this little book. His castigation of everything from the United Nations and the USA to the World Bank and the "secret services" of various countries is symptomatic of that type of rhetoric that attributes Africa's ills to external forces. Although Aseka eventually gives brief acknowledgement of some internal factors that contribute to Africa's ills (such as tribalism, nepotism and corruption), the reader is left with a feeling of hopelessness because Africa is seen to have no control over its own fate. Aseka sees little hope of significant change until the twenty-second century. The African Christian community needs to hear what is being said in the secular universities of Africa, even if in this case it is a voice of despair.

74. **Ashforth, Adam**

Witchcraft, Violence, and Democracy in South Africa

Chicago: University of Chicago Press, 2005. 416 pages, ISBN: 9780226029740.

This book is the culmination of ethnographic research conducted in Soweto, South Africa, beginning in the early 1990s. Ashforth explores the "spiritual insecurity" that is integral to life in a society where most believe that witches, motivated by jealousy and malice, are responsible for whatever suffering people happen to experience. Given the realities of poverty, disease, unemployment, homicide, rape, and more, there is a great deal of misfortune crying out for explanation. Witchcraft discourse provides this by attributing such things to the evil powers of other individuals. Because witches act in secret, however, one can never know for sure who might be responsible for this or that misfortune. Various spiritual authorities (diviners, or Christian prophets) may be consulted, and community gossips voice their opinions with conviction, but the various explanations are often contradictory, leaving sufferers confused and fearful. Ashforth argues that, in a very real sense, the recent socio-economic transformations that South African society has undergone have only increased the general level of spiritual insecurity. Under apartheid, the primary social division was between wealthy Whites and poor Blacks – a relatively comprehensible if terribly unjust reality. Now a relatively small number of Blacks has joined the ranks of the prosperous, leaving the vast majority in devastating poverty. Why have some succeeded where so many have not? Again, ideas about witchcraft provide emotionally satisfying answers: the good fortune of the few must be due to their extraordinary occult powers, while one's own failure to advance can be attributed to jealous others who stand in the way. All of this poses enormous problems for a government seeking to be part of the "modern" world, a world that does not readily accommodate such "traditional" conceptions. If judges and legislators seem reluctant to provide redress against accused witches, they give the impression that they are unjustly bent on protecting evil people. Additionally, recent initiatives to incorporate "traditional" forms of healing into the South African health care system, while demonstrating commendable openness to non-western knowledge systems, risk allowing a Trojan horse inside the walls of modernising society. Traditional healers generally understand their skill-set not only in terms of dispensing "herbal remedies" analogous to Western medicine, but also of providing protection against witches. Affirming their competence in the former lends implicit legitimacy to the latter. This is an important background reading for anyone seeking to deal with the problems associated with belief in witchcraft in contemporary Africa, and the challenges that this poses for both church leaders and lay believers.

75. **Association of Evangelicals in Africa**

Training God's Servants: A Compendium

Nairobi: AEA, 1997. 185 pages.

All too frequently, out of concern for edification and ecclesiastical "maintenance," theological college curricula and pedagogy may minimize evangelism and/or cross-cultural mission. And in face of the urgency and the immensity of the task, missions training institutions all too frequently may forget that a grounding in theology and the ecclesiology of evangelism are essential to biblical church-planting. This book is a compilation of the papers and findings of a continent-wide workshop in 1996 sponsored jointly by two units of the Association of Evangelicals in Africa (AEA), namely its Theological and Christian Education Commission and its Evangelism and Missions Commission. Participants came from Nigeria, Kenya, Malawi, Chad, Uganda, Benin Republic, and the UK. The purpose of the workshop was to address the lack of theological input in missionary training and the lack of missionary focus in theological training. The resulting compendium contains papers about curriculum design (Victor Babajide Cole, Lois Fuller and Clare Fuller), training models (Sid Garland, Matthew Collins), missions and church development (Rene Daidanso), and field relationships (Roy and Jan Stafford). The book also reports the findings and recommendations of three working groups, which addressed respectively: the role of the missionary and the theologian in missions in Africa, models of training for missions in Africa, and curricula for missionary training. As with any such collection, the materials display considerable variety in length, documentary support, and thrust. All however make substantive contributions, and despite the date, the book has long-term relevance both for curricular enhancement at theological colleges in Africa and for Africa-based training programmes for cross-cultural mission.

76.   August, Karel T., and Christof Sauer, editors

Christian-Muslim Encounter in Africa

Leiden: BRILL, 2006. 310 pages, ISBN: 9789004152649.

This volume represents a reprint from the journal *Missionalia* vol. 34, with permission from the Southern African Missiological Society. It offers ten papers presented during the 2006 SAMS conference in Stellenbosch by an immensely broad, diverse spectrum of scholars. The reader will be switching from solidly evangelical contributions from such as John Azumah ("Christian Witness to Muslims: Rationale, Approaches and Strategies"), and David Greenlee ("Coming to Faith in Christ: Highlights from Recent Research"); to more ecumenical ones, such as Nico Botha ("Learning Inter-Religious Encounter: A Social Constructivist Perspective"), and George Malek ("The Incarnation of Dialogue"); to controversial political figures like Allan Boesak ("Standing by God in His Hour of Grieving: Christians and Muslims Living Together in South Africa"), and Muslim activist Farid Esack ("Islamic 'Da'wah' and Christian Mission: A Muslim Perspective"). Azumah, as a Muslim convert to Christianity, ably reasons for the right of every Muslim to hear the gospel of Jesus Christ, referring to Article 18 of the Universal Declaration of Human Rights as much as to the Great Commission in Matthew. His article alone repays more than one will spend to obtain the book! Norwegian professor Jan Opsal, in his "Islam and Human Rights: African Voices for Reformation," presents solid research on the theologies of Sudanese reformer Mahmoud Mohamed Taha (executed in 1985 for his radical reinterpretation of the Qur'an), his student Abdullahi Ahmed An-Na'im, and South African Farid Esack, and concludes: "It does not require prophetic skills to assume that some Muslims will perceive Esack's fight for liberation of women as an attack on Islam rather than a renewal of the religion." Malek's paper on the incarnation of dialogue is full of thought-provoking, at times controversial statements. Try to digest these: "Love knows no boundaries and cannot be 'Christianized' or 'Muslimised'"; and "Islam is far more effective in finding accessibility and acceptability in Christian territories than Christianity in Islamic territories." Nicole Ravelo-Hoerson concludes her paper with a quotation from the Islamic scholar Hekmat, who stated that "contrary to orthodox views, Islam can only benefit from a reformation for women, as this will not spell its end but its rejuvenation." Especially useful is the concluding chapter by Christoph Sauer providing demographic data where Muslims live in South Africa, based on results of the most recent two censuses. On the other hand, given that the title suggests a focus on Africa in general, readers might well feel misled in discovering that more than half of the articles are particular to the South African historical context.

77.   **Ault, James**

African Christianity Rising

Northampton, MA: James Ault Productions, 2013.

Ault is a documentary maker, author, and ethnographer who has spent years using video to tell narratives. With a PhD in sociology, along with expertise in African studies, he seeks through video to "bring viewers into different social worlds through intimate, dramatically compelling stories carefully chosen to reveal those worlds." Here he has produced a set of videos that seek to capture the colour, diversity, vibrancy, and animation of Christianity on the African continent. The result is an extraordinary contribution. He and his production team travelled to Ghana and Zimbabwe where they spent hours filming mission-founded churches, older AICs, and newer Pentecostals. The resulting video series comes in four discs: two that deal with a variety of Christian expressions in Ghana and Zimbabwe, and two that provide "educational extras" to help flesh out deeper stories on the continent. In the latter, one finds such rich treasures as candid interviews with Andrew Walls and Kwame Bediako, along with an intimate encounter with a traditional priest and follow-up visits with some of the key characters in the videos. Some might find fault with the limited geographical purview of the study, but these two regions do seem in this case to have provided sufficient breadth to describe much of the richness and variety of Christianity on the continent, without overstretching content. *African Christianity Rising* is critically valuable in several respects. The task of studying something so multifaceted and experiential as African Christianity confounds written description. Unfolding the many nuances requires a tool with greater animation than merely words etched on a page. This video series offers an invaluable teaching resource for courses relating to African Christianity, whether offered in Africa or overseas. It is just that good. It would also greatly benefit all theological libraries that seek credible holdings on African Christianity. The price might seem somewhat disconcerting, but when one factors for the richness of the material, it could be funds well spent.

78.   **Autesserre, Séverine**

The Trouble with the Congo: Local Violence and the Failure of International Peacebuilding

Cambridge: Cambridge University Press, 2010. 334 pages, ISBN: 9780521156011.

This book makes a valuable contribution to the understanding of civil (often ethnically inflected) armed conflict in Africa. The author teaches political science at Columbia University and Barnard College in New York. She refers to popular journalistic explanations that attribute inter-ethnic violence to ancient hatreds that supposedly "boil over" whenever the lid of a strong national state is removed. This "primodialist" understanding of inter-ethnic violence has been debunked by recent scholars, who argue that, most often, local conflict between groups would be manageable were it not that elites who are vying for power at national or provincial levels seek to manipulate existing tensions in order to consolidate loyalty and support among members of their own ethnic group or race. While acknowledging that this type of "top-down" explanation has been a valid corrective to "primodialist" explanations, Autesserre argues convincingly that an exclusive focus on top-down accounts can miss critically important dynamic local factors that must be addressed if conflicts are to be resolved and communities reconciled. Local histories of competition between groups over the resources necessary for survival (especially land) must be understood and addressed. She applies this theoretical framework to an analysis of the UN peace keeping mission in the Democratic Republic of Congo (MONUSCO), contending that this in some ways impressive effort has failed to end violence in eastern Congo because it focused its attention virtually exclusively on national and regional elites (national leadership in Kinshasa, and the political leaders of Uganda and Rwanda, who have played such a significant role in Congo's longstanding civil war). She maintains that MONUSCO, shaped by an organisational culture that defined the task in top-down fashion, wasted valuable time and resources on arranging for national elections, without ensuring that the infrastructure necessary for real democracy was in place (a military and police force capable of and willing to protect its citizens; a working, non-corrupt judicial system; a free press; and, crucially, resolution of local conflicts that have wreaked havoc on national unity). As a result, local tensions among different groups in a complex and shifting array of ethnic loyalties have prevented UN efforts from bringing armed violence to an end. The focus on top-down solutions to what the UN saw as exclusively top-down problems meant that no significant resources were made available for crucial "bottom-up" reconciliation efforts. Autesserre's work provides a challenge to church leaders, who are often ideally situated to work toward reconciliation in situations of local conflict. Christian denominations often have networks of leaders in local churches on all sides of a given context of ethnic tension. This book thus comes with broader potential applicability for those interested in inter-communitarian conflict resolution and the ministries of reconciliation throughout Africa.

79. Awoonor, Kofi Nyidevu

Africa: The Marginalized Continent

Accra: Woeli, 1994. 184 pages, ISBN: 9789964978150.

This volume contains fourteen speeches and previously published essays by Ghana's former ambassador to the United Nations. Written in the midst of the immediate post-Cold War environment of the early 1990s, these contributions attempt to extend the political philosophy of Kwame Nkrumah into the new era brought about by the collapse of Marxism. The fundamental themes that underlie these writings are: (1) democracy is not feasible within nations plagued by inexorable poverty; (2) the wealthy West has an obligation to assist Africa's nations so that escape from poverty becomes possible; (3) an "unholy alliance" against the developing nations exists among Western nations, thereby denying Africa the support necessary for development. This book finds its place in an ongoing debate among scholars about whether Africa's problems today primarily originate internally (e.g. with corrupt leaders) or externally (e.g. with oppressive policies of Western nations and organisations). Obviously Awoonor sides with the externalists. In his view, at the time of independence Africa's former colonies were left without adequate economic structures and social institutions to foster the educational systems and health care necessary to support democratic political structures. The burden, therefore, falls upon wealthy Western nations not only to provide generous aid to Africa's poorer nations, but also to make adjustments in the world trading order so as to create a level playing field for Africa's economies. This book can be usefully compared with the one by another Ghanaian intellectual, George Ayittey, *Africa in Chaos* (2000). Ayittey claims that neither increased financial aid nor changes in the international economic order can help African nations that are run by kleptocrats and stifled by bureaucracy. In other words, unless the internal systems are fixed, no amount of external change will help. Arguments from both poles of the debate need to be heard. Finally, the differences between these authors expose the myth, common to publisher's blurbs and reviewer's rhetoric, that Africa speaks with one voice on these issues. Authentic African voices do not sing the same tune on this or on any number of other crucial issues. For further debate to remain healthy and productive, multiple voices must be heard and evaluated on the merits of their arguments.

Ayanga, Hazel

see reviews 380 and 471

80.   **Ayegboyin, Deji, and S. Ademola Ishola**

African Indigenous Churches: An Historical Perspective

Lagos: Greater Heights Publications, 1997. 174 pages, ISBN: 9789780280383.

This is an undergraduate textbook on African Indigenous Churches (AICs) written by two scholars who teach the subject respectively at the University of Ibadan and the Nigerian Baptist Seminary at Ogbomosho in Nigeria. It contains learning objectives and review/study questions for each chapter. Four chapters are devoted to generalities (terminology, responsible factors, characteristics, future prospects), seven to AICs in Nigeria, three to those in Ghana, and the remaining three to Harris (West Africa), Kimbangu (Central Africa), and Shembe (South Africa). Each movement receives treatment of its history, doctrine and practices. The English is easy to follow and the stance sympathetic but orthodox. The book praises AICs for their attempts to contextualize, attractive worship, evangelism, healing, the prominent place given to women, and the high level of member participation. It also notes common problems such as schisms, church discipline, financial support, autocratic leaders, lack of Bible training, extra-biblical practices, and lack of organisation. The authors conclude that AICs are here to stay, although they are now challenged by the growth of neo-pentecostal churches. This constitutes a good introductory text on AICs, especially those in West Africa.

Ayegboyin, Deji

see also review 506

81.   **Ayittey, George B. N.**

Africa Betrayed

New York: St. Martin's Press, 1992. 412 pages, ISBN: 9780312104009.

Ayittey is a Ghanaian economist teaching at George Washington University in the United States. In this book he offers a withering critique of what he calls "black neo-colonialism." This epithet refers to the oppressive rule of African leaders who assumed political control of Africa's newly independent countries beginning in the 1950s. Ayittey states, "in most parts of Africa independence from oppressive colonial rule was in name only. All that changed was the color of the guards and the masters." Promising freedom, these rulers brought only further oppression. Thus, as the title of the book declares, Africa has been "betrayed" by her own sons. Ayittey traces this devastation topically, chapter by chapter. Well documented, he labours to support his tale as much as possible by using African sources, in order to avoid the charge of employing racially-biased Western sources. He concludes with a call for "The Second Liberation of Africa," proposing governing structures based on indigenous African traditions. Thus, in the debate between those who lay blame for Africa's woes on outsiders and those who locate the causes internally, Ayittey places himself firmly among the internalists. This does not mean that he finds no fault with the West for Africa's current predicament. He documents both the deplorable conditions enforced by the colonialists and the ways in which current Western policies harm Africa. Yet, he asks, "Must we blacks wait for [racism's] end before we take the initiative ourselves to solve our own problems?" In light of the heated nature of this debate, Ayittey's position, however well documented and carefully argued, is controversial. Yet his voice is not one that can be ignored.

82.   Ayittey, George B. N.

Africa in Chaos

London: Palgrave Macmillan, 2000. 416 pages, ISBN: 9780333772348.

Ayittey is a Ghanaian who teaches economics at a university in Washington, DC. In *Africa in Chaos* he examines why Africa remains "intractably mired in poverty." He describes those who approach this problem either as "externalists" (meaning those claiming Africa's problems are caused by the West and the colonial legacy), or as "internalists" (namely those who place the blame on inept political leaders and problematic political and economic systems within Africa itself). Ayittey himself sides almost entirely with the internalists. In Ayittey's view, post-colonial Africa is caught between two Africas, the traditional one and the modern "western" one. The tension between these two has led to havoc. Rather than returning to traditional political systems, post-independent Africa maintained borrowed "modern" colonial governing systems that concentrated power in the hands of a few. As a result Africa since independence has been characterized by the struggle for power, with those few who have it ruthlessly clinging to the same. Ayittey employs a "take no prisoners" approach in his treatment of African heads of state, the "parasitic minority" who rule over what he labels "predatory" and "mafia" states. These people, he argues, are the primary cause of Africa's woes. Ayittey sees the solution in investment, but investment only after what he calls "environmental defects" are remedied. These defects are human creations, including such overlapping factors as the absence of the rule of law, corruption, bad governance, and burgeoning state bureaucracies. Only when these defects are cured, when true reforms take root that disperse power beyond the hands of the kleptocrats, can investment, both foreign and domestic, have its intended impact. This book will thus infuriate some and stimulate others. Yet it is an important contribution to a heated debate. Whether or not its assessments are sound and its solutions realistic, in any case the issues it raises are ones that those concerned with Africa's plight dare not ignore.

Ayuso Guixot, Miguel A.

see review 99

83.   Azumah, John

The Legacy of Arab-Islam in Africa: A Quest for Inter-religious Dialogue

London: OneWorld Publications, 2001. 288 pages, ISBN: 9781851682737.

Azumah is now among Africa's leading Christian scholars of Islam. Ordained in the Presbyterian Church of Ghana, he was earlier a lecturer at the Henry Martyn Institute in Hyderabad, India, and more recently has been on the teaching staff at London School of Theology. This is a revised form of his PhD thesis at the University of Birmingham. The book presents a detailed review and analysis of some of the darker features of Islamic history as it developed in Africa. "Our aim is not to demonstrate how horrible and nasty the Islamic past in Africa has been, but rather to say that it was, as other systems of the time, not glorious." Azumah has two further goals in the process: to correct the somewhat romantic views of Islam in Africa among certain

Western scholars, and to invite African Muslims into honest dialogue with African Christians concerning these issues. After discussing these goals, he looks first at the manner in which Islam developed in Africa, noting especially how the African religious context fostered a "creative and resilient pluralism" in which African Islam incorporated many traditional religious features. Next he deals with the response to this situation by certain Muslim leaders in the form of military jihad. While these often brutal campaigns achieved limited "success" in expanding Islamic identity and influence, they did not eradicate the indigenous African worldview and its resultant practices. The longest chapter reviews the wretched effects of slavery among Africans by Arab and African Muslims, which was justified by a strong anti-pagan sentiment as well as by racial prejudice. Azumah rightly criticizes attempts by both Muslim and Western scholars to minimize the harsh realities of Muslim slavery, claiming that it was just as cruel as its Western counterpart. Azumah ends his book by calling for a fresh Muslim-Christian dialogue which reassesses these historical issues with a view towards more positive relations between Africa's Muslim and Christian communities. While this is certainly a worthy ambition which calls for patient and persistent effort, this book would require Muslims to take a considerable step of critical self-analysis. Unfortunately, current events, along with an increasingly intransigent Muslim stance towards the Christian west, mitigate against this goal. Nevertheless, Azumah's book is an essential text for better understanding the particularities of Islam in Africa.

84. **Azumah, John**

My Neighbour's Faith: Islam Explained for Christians

Carlisle, UK: HippoBooks, 2008. 176 pages, ISBN: 9789966805027.

In this book Azumah again distinguishes himself as an important African Christian scholar of Islam. In this slender volume he offers both an overview of Islam and a mature analysis concerning issues of Christian-Muslim relations which are especially relevant to the African context. Curiously the version of this book available in Africa omits reference to Africa in the subtitle, whereas the version distributed overseas uses the subtitle: *Islam Explained for African Christians* (making the African orientation explicit). Originally from Ghana, Azumah is now a lecturer at London School of Theology, UK. He outlines his approach in this book as one that seeks "to avoid the two extremes of demonising and romanticising Islam." While he generally succeeds in this objective, there is a tendency throughout the book to emphasize the more aggressive side of African Islam. For example, chapter 2 "the Challenges Posed by Islam" presents the expansionist goals of Islam in Africa as the primary impetus for a Christian understanding of Islam. Although the author is concerned about a problem that is undoubtedly valid for numerous African Christians, the book might have been balanced by other more positive examples of Muslim-Christian cooperation, for example in the area of community development. Nevertheless, what follows in the next six chapters is a generally fair summary of Islamic belief and practice, including Islamic history, the Qur'ān and Hadīth, divisions within Islam, Islamic law, and women in Islam. Unfortunately, this material is all too brief, and for a more complete introduction to Islam from a Christian perspective, readers would be better served by Chapman's *Cross and Crescent* or Cooper and Maxwell's *Ishmael My Brother*. However, the last four chapters of Azumah's book are what make it especially worthwhile. Here we find the author at his best as he wrestles with the contentious issues of Christian-Muslim relations. He sets the historical-theological context of the Islamic view of Jews and Christians, and then presents an excellent overview of Jesus in Islam. The final two chapters offer an even-handed Christian approach to practical issues such as the imposition of Islamic law, and theological questions such as whether Muslims and Christians worship the same God. In the end, this book is a very worthy addition to the handful of books dealing with Islam by African Christian scholars.

85. Backeberg, Werner

Fundamentalism: Muslims Differ Widely from Evangelicals

Pretoria: IMER, 2002. 160 pages, ISBN: 9781868544271.

In recent years it has become fashionable in some circles to portray evangelical fundamentalism in the same frame as Islamic terrorism and suicide bombings. Backeberg's treatise is neither naïvely defending the evangelical camp nor stamping all Muslims as terrorists, but rather is describing the phenomena of employing physical violence and terrorism in the service of religion. In an early section he illustrates how fundamentalism shows itself as a global trend, with historic roots in Roman Catholicism, Judaism, Sikhism, Hinduism, Buddhism and Confucianism. He then gives special attention to the worldwide upsurge of "Islamism," namely the conviction that only those are true Muslims who "overcome their inner hesitations and are willing to kill the enemies of Allah" (Hassan al-Banna, founder of the Muslim Brotherhood, Egypt). The development of Islamic radicalism is documented and explained in depth in case studies that include Iran, Iraq, Syria and Lebanon, Saudi Arabia, Egypt, the Sudan, Algeria, Malaysia, Indonesia, and Afghanistan. Backeberg next addresses his conviction that "whereas in Islamic fundamentalism the main issue is political and military power, evangelical fundamentalists' main concern is the commitment to basic doctrines and the proclamation of the message of God's love to all nations." Once again he is very helpful in putting these reflections into historical perspective, explaining the impact of the Enlightenment, Romanticism, Liberal Theology and other philosophical trends, all contributing their part to the challenge of maintaining a biblically-committed Christianity. Backeberg has been teaching theology in South Africa for many years, and particularly helps those readers who do not have access to German-speaking resources. The book will help Christian readers in Africa gain a wider perspective on phenomena they may be experiencing in contact with Islam in their own context. It should also help clarify misrepresentations of evangelicalism in the contemporary secular and religious press. And it should help everyone understand better how biblical commitments differ from a fanatical religious fundamentalism.

86. Bakare, Sebastian

The Drumbeat of Life: Jubilee in an African Context

Geneva: World Council of Churches, 1997. 52 pages, ISBN: 9782825412299.

Using the dynamic image of the drumbeat within African communities, Bakare has made a powerful plea for church participation in the resolution of the intractable problems of Africa. Throughout Africa the sound of the drumbeat is the call to the community to gather together. Such gatherings with their pulsating rhythms express the belonging and solidarity of the members of the community with each other. Such, in its way, was the gathering of Christians from all around the world in Harare in 1998 for the Assembly of the World Council of Churches (WCC). At such a time as this, the world Christian community is invited to gather together in response to the sound of the African drums, for Africa is a continent in crisis. First published as a contribution towards the eighth (or Jubilee) WCC Assembly in Harare in 1998, Zimbabwean theologian Sebastian Bakare's thoughtful booklet explores the meaning of the biblical notion of "Jubilee" for Africa in general, and for Zimbabwe in particular, as one way of creatively responding to the problems of Africa. Tackling such vexed issues as "uprooted peoples," "slavery in Africa," "land and the landless," the "debt crisis," and the "AIDS pandemic," Bakare calls on the world's churches to incorporate the message of the "jubilee" into their understanding of mission. In fact, insists Bakare, so central is this message of "jubilee" that the WCC Assembly gathering with its theme, "Turn to God – Rejoice in Hope," is/was a kairos moment for the churches of the world. Of particular interest would be Bakare's comments on the problem of landlessness in Zimbabwe, and a reference to his earlier publication, *My Right to Land: A Theology of Land in Zimbabwe* (1993).

87.   Bakari, Mohamed, and Saad S. Yahya

Islam in Kenya: Proceedings of the National Seminar on Contemporary Islam in Kenya

Nairobi: Signal Press, 1995. 339 pages.

Bakari serves as Professor of Linguistics at the University of Nairobi. This excellent compendium resulted from a "National Seminar on Islam in Kenya" convened in Nairobi in 1994 by the Kenya-based Muslim Educational and Welfare Association. The 22 authors represent a broad spectrum of specialists, mostly from Kenya and some from abroad, with one-third non-Muslim. Except for Bakari, who provided three articles, the contributors each concentrate on a specific field of specialisation. Seven papers focus on the Muslim community of Kenya from ethnic (Ishmaili, Asian, African, Somali) and geographic perspectives. Other papers examine the perception of Muslims in the wider society, intellectual and cultural traditions, economic developments, social change and the educational sector. Although the subtitle of the book puts the stress on the contemporary status of Islam in Kenya, there are fascinating historical notes. For example, by no means all British colonial administrators were adversely inclined towards Islam; they preferred to enlist Muslims as police and interpreters based on the conviction that "they are the only element with comprehension of politics, justice or government." Unfortunately the value of the book is somewhat affected by some inconsistencies in facts and figures. The attentive reader is constantly challenged to measure Islamic claims against generally accepted statistics (only Muslim writers seem to assume that Muslims constitute between one third and one fourth of the population in Kenya). And the German society for technical cooperation GTZ is most certainly not a missionary organisation as claimed. Also many of the Muslim contributors seem to use their presentations to get back at their Christian compatriots. Thus one finds rather bitter feelings expressed against "the Kenyan bureaucrats" who display "bigotry, abuse and harassment against Muslims." This in turn is blamed on the impact of missionary education, misconceptions about Muslims by other Kenyans, and the lack of basic data about Muslims in general. Despite these shortcomings, this book presents a wealth of information and opinion that will enable a better understanding of Islam in Kenya and a more realistic assessment of Christian-Muslim relations and interaction in that country.

88.   Baker, Kristina, and Honor Ward

AIDS, Sex and Family Planning: A Christian View

Achimota, Ghana: Africa Christian Press, 1989. 92 pages, ISBN: 9789964878962.

This small book by Baker and her mother draws on their many years of Scripture Union service in Africa, and especially in Zambia, where Baker also worked as a medical doctor and AIDS educator. They have used the art of storytelling to excellent advantage in presenting common questions asked by Christians about AIDS, sex and family planning. The stories are engaging and believable, so that interest is easily sustained throughout the book. Many current questions are addressed, including justification for the use of family planning by Christians, the advantages and disadvantages of possible methods, dealing with pressure from relatives over a couple's fertility choices, the God-given purposes of sex within marriage, preparing young people to make healthy, biblical choices in their sexual behaviour, and helping relatives and friends stricken by AIDS. The advice to those dealing with AIDS sufferers is especially compassionate, and points clearly to God's love and the need of salvation through Christ in order for helpers and sufferers alike to experience God's forgiveness and sustaining grace. Lay people will certainly benefit from reading this book, as will students at all levels. For theological students and those in ministry positions it is an especially helpful example of how to talk about these issues simply and clearly, and bookshops should find it a popular book to stock.

89.   Bakke, Johnny

Christian Ministry: Patterns and Functions within the Evangelical Church Mekane Yesus

Oslo: Solum Forlag, 1987. 297 pages, ISBN: 9788256004676.

Bakke served in Ethiopia with the Norwegian Lutheran Mission from the 1960s onward, with most of his energies devoted to the Mekane Yesus Seminary both as principal and as lecturer. The Ethiopian Evangelical Church Mekane Yesus (EECMY) is the oldest and second largest of the Protestant "new" churches in Ethiopia. This study, a published Uppsala University doctoral dissertation, is divided into three sections. Part 1 describes the traditional religious setting in the Sidamo and Wollege areas of Ethiopia, both of which were to become strong centres of the Mekane Yesus church. The Ethiopian Orthodox Church clergy hierarchy and educational system are also described as backdrop. Part 2 deals with the three main Lutheran groups which entered Ethiopia, German, Swedish and Norwegian, and the ensuing interaction between those missions, as well as with traditional religion and with the Orthodox Church, up until the time of the first ordinations in the EECMY. The final section of the book discusses structure, leadership, ministerial training, proclamation and development within the EECMY, and ends with tensions and developments in ministry during the Ethiopian "cultural revolution" (which began in 1974 and continued beyond the writing of this dissertation). Throughout, Bakke attempts to evaluate and compare the EECMY ministerial patterns and functions against the backdrop of indigenous models both in traditional culture and in the Orthodox Church. Bakke identifies several tensions in the development of Christian ministry within the EECMY. For example, the position accorded to evangelists in the ministry of the developing church presented a dilemma. Although the evangelists were crucial to evangelism and the total work of the church, they were not mentioned in the constitution nor configured in the EECMY hierarchy. Finances were another ongoing discussion in EECMY, as outside funding challenged local church stewardship. Also the young educated pastors were weighed down with leadership and administrative responsibilities that prevented them from serving as true "shepherds of the flock," resulting in a rather rigid hierarchy. The spirit of the entire book evidences a deep heart for the church. Although a scholarly thesis, this book is very readable, and has become a handbook within the missions and churches of Ethiopia. Its wider usefulness lies in the universal value of any church history as a case study, and it deserves to be in all theological libraries attempting good coverage of Christian history in Africa.

90.   **Balisky, E. Paul**

Wolaitta Evangelists: A Study of Religious Innovation in Southern Ethiopia, 1937–1975

Eugene, OR: Wipf & Stock, 2009. 410 pages, ISBN: 9781606081570.

The author served with the international mission SIM for nearly 40 years in Ethiopia, and at the time of publication was professor of Church History at the Ethiopian Graduate School of Theology in Addis Ababa. This represents his doctoral work completed at Aberdeen under Andrew Walls. The Wolaitta of the title is a region of southern Ethiopia that was among the first to respond to Protestant missionary outreach. Balisky offers a careful historical reconstruction of the story of how the indigenous evangelists of Wolaitta brought that message to the surrounding regions and beyond, with a passion and dedication that recalls the evangelistic commitment narrated in Acts. At the same time, the book is the story of the birth of the Kale Heywet Church, now the largest indigenous evangelical denomination in Ethiopia, and her missionary extension throughout the south. The result today is a massive geographical triangle of vibrant, society-transforming, evangelical Christianity that embraces the central-southern region of the country. The book includes maps and photos that complement the text. Indigenous worship songs are scattered at appropriate points that enliven the prose, and interesting mini-biographies of several evangelists are sprinkled throughout, giving the work a personal touch. The historical documentation has been meticulously and painstakingly done, much of which stems from personal interviews with eyewitnesses, as well as archived missionary correspondence. The almost dizzying array of personal as well as geographical place names mentioned in the book (all in transliterated Amharic) sometimes loses the reader, but this also adds significant local colour to the myriad of small stories that make up the overall reconstruction. The first four chapters explain the broader historical, sociological and religious factors that prepared Wolaitta for the gospel; while the remaining four relate the belief system of the Wolaitta church and the determined work of some three hundred of its evangelists to bring its message to the outlying regions. Given the rich historical orientation it provides to the context, the book is a must read for all those wanting in-depth understanding of Christian presence in southern Ethiopia. As a model work of church history in its own right, the book should be seriously considered for acquisition by research libraries both within Africa and abroad. As the Christian movement surges forward into this new century as a majority world faith, the preservation of the smaller stories that form the previous century's astounding epic of global expansion must become an essential task of the Church, whose gospel has again "turned the world upside down." Balisky's monograph offers an exemplary model of how such local historical reconstructions should be done.

91.   **Balisky, Lila, editor**

Songs of Tesfaye Gabbiso

Addis Ababa: SIM Press, 2015. 120 pages.

Here presented in an English/Amharic diglot are the 105 songs in Amharic from the seven cassettes of Tesfaye Gabbiso, a well-known Ethiopian Christian musician (no music notation is yet available). The translation is by Ato Haile Jenai. This collection is an attempt to provide songs of the Ethiopian church for a wider audience than just Amharic speakers. As well, this project assists in creating a base for much-needed written archival resources to be available for future research. It is intended that the songs also provide a devotional book for today's older generation, plus a challenge to young singers to compose lyrics rich in spiritual content. The hammer and sickle of Ethiopia's Marxist era shaped the life and music of Tesfaye Gabbiso. His work is full of worship, witness and spiritual teaching. The music is anchored in the omnipotence and high worth of God and the saving grace we have received through Jesus Christ. God's character is repeatedly affirmed, His patience, kindness, mercy, pity, favour, comfort, relief, rescuing, nourishment, strength and sheltering. Like the Psalmist, the lyrics express awe of the Lord and expose personal weakness, temptations and failures. Many songs explore biblical stories and themes with a clear focus. A smaller number are calls to action. They address those who have wandered away or have been tripped up by criticism or the seeming success of unbelievers. Music is both a communal and an individual experience in Ethiopia. There is little distinction between the personal pilgrimage of the songwriter, singer, listener, and the recurring themes that emerge in the theology expressed in the lyrics. This is what creates the resonance and blessing in Tesfaye's music. His songs are well loved not only in Ethiopia but throughout the Ethiopian diaspora and in other religious traditions. Some Tesfaye Gabbiso songs may be found on YouTube.

92. Banana, Canaan S.

Come and Share: An Introduction to Christian Theology

Gweru, Zimbabwe: Mambo Press, 1991. 119 pages, ISBN: 9780869224953.

This is a collection of theological essays from an African perspective. A principal attraction of the book is the author himself. Canaan Banana was an ordained Methodist minister who served as Zimbabwe's first president from 1980 to 1988. In *Come and Share* he covers topics such as: church and state, the legacy of African traditional religion, the classless society and the kingdom of God, the language of African theology, Jesus as a political Messiah, Jesus as "ancestor," and ecclesiology in the African context. The book is a running commentary on these topics. Banana does not divorce politics from religion. He embraces both African traditional religion and the biblical message as complementaries. Although the book abounds in biblical references, it is not an exposition of biblical theology. Jesus Christ is presented as a purely human being. The lack of organisation and the many contradictions in the material suggest that the book was put together either hurriedly or prematurely.

93. Banerjee, Abhijit V., and Esther Duflo

Poor Economics: A Radical Rethinking of the Way to Fight Global Poverty

New York: PublicAffairs, 2011. 320 pages, ISBN: 9781586487980.

This is one of the most important books to come out about development in several years. The authors are economists at the Massachusetts Institute of Technology who seek to determine, by deploying randomized controlled trials, the types of interventions that have been proven to better the lives of poor people in the developing world. They demonstrate that in attempting to alleviate poverty, careful social science research can discover useful things about poor people that can go some way towards policies that can actually improve their lives. The authors write for a popular audience, but do not enter into debates about whether aid is good or bad, nor do they support a particular development technique. As a result their approach is somewhat stripped of the heat and fire that are often apparent in development literature. The first part of the book, on private lives, has chapters on hunger, health, education, and birth control. Chapters in the second part, on institutions, address issues such as insurance, banking, microfinance and business development. There is much to be learned in each of these sections. For example, in Kenya when farmers were offered half-price fertilizer during planting season, few took advantage of the offer, lacking the cash reserves to afford the fertilizer even at a discounted rate. However, when they were given the opportunity to buy a full-cost voucher for fertilizer use just after the harvest when they had cash, many did so, and redeemed the voucher the next planting season. The issue in this case was the timing of the assistance being given. When it changed, there was a 50 percent increase in the use of fertilizer, despite the fact that it was not offered at a discounted rate. Many of the examples running through the book come from Africa, but those from other areas of the developing world are equally instructive. The presentation is fundamentally sympathetic to the poor, and respectful of them, while not endorsing every decision they make. One can thus come to understand why a family might scrimp to buy a TV set, or throw a massive family wedding, while the children do not receive adequate nutrition. For Christian groups seeking to improve the lives of the poor, the research findings and resulting suggestions offer multiple practical lessons. Readers will be encouraged by the fact that providing certain "nudges" can and does lead to improvements in such areas as health, nutrition, and agricultural productivity.

94.   Bangsund, James C.

Reading Biblical Hebrew: A Grammar and Basic Lexicon

Usa River, Tanzania: Makumira University College, 2007. 337 pages, ISBN: 9789987657087.

The author, from America, taught at Makumira University College in Tanzania for more than a decade. The present book represents his legacy as far as Biblical Hebrew is concerned, with BD students as the book's primary target group. The book is not a reference grammar; it does not offer a systematic and research-sensitive survey of Hebrew grammar (cf. the traditional Gesenius-Kautzsch or the more recent van der Merwe et al.). Rather, it is a textbook offering a successive and pedagogically-sensitive entry into Biblical Hebrew (cf. the tradition of Lamdin). Two points may be made in evaluation. First, the strength of the book (and of the genre it belongs to) is its ability to take the student step by step into the language of the OT. The book's 78 chapters present its readers successively with an introduction into sounds and signs, and words and forms, all performed with good textual examples and subsequent exercises. (It is surprising, though, to find a more or less total absence of discussion of syntax at a clause level). Also included are good introductions to Hebrew poetry and to the scientific edition of the Hebrew Bible, the BHS. But secondly it should be remarked that the book shows hardly any traces of being developed in an African context for an African audience. Even though the language of instruction is English, one would have wished that the author had made some references to the advantages many African students of Biblical Hebrew have at their disposal. An obvious example in Tanzania would be the advantages that Kiswahili-speaking students have as far as vocabulary is concerned. Another example could be the fact that some (e.g. Bantu) languages have cases of syntactical structures that are closer to Biblical Hebrew than to anything that English or other European languages are able to provide. A sensitivity to these examples would serve pedagogical purposes, of course, but it would also acknowledge African resources as far as OT studies are concerned.

95. Bangsund, James C.

Understanding the Old Testament: An Introduction and Theological Overview

Usa River, Tanzania: Makumira University College, 2007. 332 pages, ISBN: 9789987657056.

Bangsund taught OT studies and Biblical Hebrew at Makumira University College in Tanzania from the mid-1990s until 2007. The present book, intended as a text primarily for BD students, belongs to the traditional "introduction" genre, with surveys of structure and content of each book in the OT. However, the book also shows some attention to theological and hermeneutical questions related to a Christian interpretation of the OT; hence the title's key term "understanding." As far as methodology is concerned, the author seems to have a predilection for literary approaches, such as when he argues that whether the Pentateuch was written by Moses or is the result of several authors does not matter very much; either option allows us to hear what the Scripture is saying. Still the presentation generally follows mainstream historical-critical interpretation; such as when Isaiah is taken in three distinct parts, in spite of the author's acceptance of the book's literary unity. The author should be commended for his balanced and informed presentation of the material, and the book certainly fills a need in universities and theological seminaries in eastern Africa. Yet it should be noticed that the book makes no references to its African audience. This could have been understandable for a typical "introduction," but for a book aiming at *"understanding* the Old Testament" and written in an African context, one could have wished for more attention to the African readership.

96. Barnett, Tony, and Alan Whiteside

AIDS in the Twenty-First Century: Disease and Globalization

London: Palgrave Macmillan, 2006. 464 pages, ISBN: 9781403997685.

This excellent overview of the AIDS pandemic is both accessible to the general reader as well as relevant for those who already know a considerable amount about both AIDS and the infection that causes it, HIV. The book is divided into three parts. The first is an overview of the disease, complete with definitions, charts and diagrams for the layperson, and discussions of how the virus moves through populations. Of particular interest is a discussion of the origins of the disease which posits a transfer of the virus from the monkey to the human population in the 1930s, and then considers how it was possible for the virus to be latent until the upheaval of postcolonial wars and the impact of modern transport infrastructure created an environment in which the virus could spread. The second section of the book examines the spread of the epidemic and discusses why certain countries have been able to control HIV infection better than others. Here there is a chapter devoted specifically to Africa, in which the authors repeatedly draw the link between poverty, social upheaval and the spread of HIV. The third section of the book addresses vulnerability and impact, and examines how HIV infection clusters in families, killing off the most productive members and leaving the rest to cope as best they can. The book specifically addresses the problem of AIDS orphans and the effect of AIDS on the elderly. In this last section the authors also assess governmental and societal responses to AIDS, noting that the most effective educational techniques regarding HIV infection are those that occur through personal relationships. This book is an outstanding overview of HIV/AIDS and an admirable reference source. It is written by a development specialist (Barnett), and by a professor of public health (Whiteside). The latter grew up in Swaziland and lives and teaches in South Africa, where he is the Director of the Health Economics and HIV/AIDS Research Division at the University of Natal.

97. Barrett, David, and T. John Padwick

Rise Up and Walk!: Conciliarism and the African Indigenous Churches, 1815–1987

Nairobi: Oxford University Press, 1989. 111 pages, ISBN: 9780195726312.

In this short book Barrett and Padwick provide the most concise synopsis available on the development of ecumenical initiatives and frustrations in the African indigenous church (AIC) movement. Intended as a follow-up to Barrett's *Schism and Renewal* (1968), this book chronicles the major events and players in the struggle of the independent churches to gain acceptance in the missionary and mainline communities. Included in that story are the developmental statistics from Barrett's database which trace the numeric growth of the movement through the twentieth century. More than half of the book is given over to appendices and indices, including an event by event account of important AIC initiatives from 1815 to 1987, a bibliography of resources, and a list of regional and national indigenous councils. Within the chronicle of events (arranged around sixteen ecumenical initiatives) are several notable issues, ranging from the designation for the AICs (are they to be called independent, initiated, or indigenous?), to the potential for self-financing continent-wide AIC ecumenical initiatives, to the frustrations of the AICs in seeking to be recognized by any larger church bodies, whether national, regional, continental or mainline, evangelical, or orthodox. This chronicle, however, is not a purely historical account; it comes from a position of advocacy on behalf of the AICs, primarily from Barrett's own work among them and his assessment of them as legitimate churches which need to be acknowledged as such. Though brief, *Rise Up and Walk!* is dense with information on events, key people, statistics, and organisations. Though now beginning to be dated (e.g. the success of the Organization of African Instituted Churches has forced the hand of the WCC to recognize it and, by extension, all AICs affiliated with it, factors that were not yet in place when the book was written), it is still a valuable, basic (and relatively inexpensive) resource for the study of the AIC movement.

98. Barry, Hallen

A Short History of African Philosophy

Bloomington, IN: Indiana University Press, 2009. 208 pages, ISBN: 9780253221230.

Hallen is professor of philosophy at Morehouse College, and a fellow of the W. E. B. DuBois Institute for Afro-American Research at Harvard University. In this book he discusses major ideas, figures, and schools of thought in philosophy in the African context. While drawing out critical issues in the formation of African philosophy, he focuses on modern scholarship and relevant debates that have made African philosophy essential to understanding the rich and complex cultural heritage of the continent. The author builds on connections with Western philosophical traditions to explore African contributions to cultural universalism, cultural relativism, phenomenology, hermeneutics, and Marxism. Among earlier figures discussed are Ptah-hotep (Egypt, c. 2400 BC), Zar'a Ya'aqob (Abyssinia, seventeenth century), and Anton Wilhelm Amo (Ghana, eighteenth century). Figures from the twentieth century include: Paulin Hountindji, V. Y. Mudimbe, Oyeronke Oyewumi, Kwame Anthony Appiah, Kwasi Wiredu, Lucius Outlaw and Lewis Gordon. Hallen also examines critical African challenges to Western conceptions of philosophy by taking on questions such as whether philosophy can exist in cultures that are significantly based on oral tradition, and what may or may not constitute philosophical texts. The book includes a chapter referencing some additional philosophers, plus useful works, journals and websites on African philosophy. Besides offering an excellent initial orientation to African philosophy, the book would serve as a useful reference handbook for any student of African philosophy.

99. **Barsella, Gino, and Miguel A. Ayuso Guixot**

Struggling to be Heard: The Christian Voice in Independent Sudan 1956–1996

Nairobi: Paulines, 1997. 126 pages, ISBN: 9789966213723.

In seven short chapters the authors survey the search of the past 40 years for some form of co-existence between Sudan's Muslim and Christian communities. They conclude that an existing "common natural kindly disposition and tolerance" among ordinary people within the Muslim and Christian communities of Sudan should dispose both communities towards resolution by dialogue. However, this can only occur on condition that successive Sudanese governments resist fundamentalist influences in favour of respect and understanding of differences among Sudan's population. The authors provide a helpful analysis and a desperate plea for a change in the social climate. The situation of course painfully echoes problems faced by Christian communities in other parts of Africa. This is another title in the Faith in Sudan booklet series, which has made available a broad range of fresh reflection on the challenges and prospects of Christian presence in Sudan. The papers collected in the series originated in a major conference on Christianity in Sudan held in Limuru, Kenya, in 1997. The materials from the conference represent often invaluable resources in this largely neglected field, and the series deserves to be widely referenced and used.

100. **Bascom, Kay**

Hidden Triumph in Ethiopia

Pasadena: WCL, 2001. 166 pages, ISBN: 9780878086061.

This is the biography of an Ethiopian Christian, Negussie Kumbi, who suffered for his faith under the Marxist regime in that country (1974–1991). The author served in Ethiopia with the mission SIM. In light of the events of his life and death, Negussie Kumbi was selected as a heroic Christian individual, representative of over a hundred Ethiopian Christians whom the author interviewed. Woven in with the biography is much information on missions (mainly SIM), church communities (mainly the Kale Heywet Church), and the Ethiopian historical-political context, all of this adding breadth to the book. The story covers Negussie's life from birth, through childhood and education, contacts with missionaries, years of persecution, study at Scott Theological College in Kenya, marriage and family, and ends with his rather sudden death. The question of his untimely death looms large. The book is obviously written for a Western readership, with rather extensive coverage given to the expatriate missionary element; an adaptation to carry a stronger Ethiopian orientation and translation into Amharic would be in order. Even so, this is a worthy contribution to a slowly growing body of biographical writing about saints in the evangelical churches of Ethiopia.

101. **Bassey, Michael Edet**

Witnessing in the Acts of the Apostles: A Study of the Communication Strategies and Their Relevance to the Evangelization of Africans Today with Particular Reference to the Efik/Ibibio People of Nigeria

Rome: Urbaniana University Press, 1988. 476 pages, ISBN: 9788840133157.

This book is a doctoral dissertation in biblical studies submitted to the Urbanian University in Rome in 1988. The author, a Catholic priest in Nigeria, proceeds from the observation that the gospel is presented in various ways throughout the NT. Given this background, the book of Acts is analysed from the perspectives of how the witnesses in the early church communicated the gospel to their diversified audiences, what strategies they used, whether their methods were efficacious, and what insights we may draw from Acts as far as the inculturation of the gospel in contemporary Africa is concerned. The book is not a typical exegetical study, following certain key texts in detail; rather, it offers a systematic analysis of central terms and concepts in Acts related to "witness." Its approach to the relationship between Africa and the Bible is symptomatic of the later decades of the twentieth century. The underlying concept is that of application; more recent reader-sensitive approaches are not reflected. The author believes that it is possible, by help of traditional Western critical tools, to extract certain general ideas from the biblical texts, ideas which then eventually can be "applied" to the contemporary evangelisation of Africa.

102. **Bates, Robert H., V. Y. Mudimbe, and Jean F. O'Barr, editors**

Africa and the Disciplines: The Contributions of Research in Africa to the Social Sciences and Humanities

Chicago: University of Chicago Press, 1993. 270 pages, ISBN: 9780226039015.

The editors offer a collection of seven learned articles showing the contributions that African studies can make, or have made, to core disciplines of the modern academic world. If the challenge of past decades for Africa's intellectuals has been to assert a separate African identity, the intellectual challenge of the coming decades will be to articulate Africa's place within the world community. Within that frame of reference, these essays address how Africa can make, and has already made, distinctive contributions to central inquiries of the global academic community. This is recommended reading especially for those seeking to track the frontiers of modern African intellectual life. The articles on anthropology, literature, and especially philosophy also have significant implications for any attempt to understand the inner dynamics of the African Theology movement.

103. **Bates, Robert H.**

When Things Fell Apart: State Failure in Late-Century Africa

Cambridge: Cambridge University Press, 2008. 218 pages, ISBN: 9780521715256.

Bates is one of the leading political scientists studying Africa. This book is a short and accessible summary of a number of complex theoretical arguments, supported by statistical analyses that are relegated to the appendix. Bates examines the short history of African states since independence and asks why political order turned into political conflict in so many places. He is also concerned about the foundations of political order, what makes it flourish and why governments would adopt policies which undermine the wellbeing of their populations. Bates argues that after independence a decline in overall public revenue due to the oil shocks of the 1970s and efforts at political reform led politicians to adopt a strategy of predation, of preying on their populations and the resources of the state rather than seeking to promote wellbeing through the provision of public goods. Political reform, Bates argues, can lead to political disorder as politicians with shortened time horizons for remaining in office seek to line their pockets with as much wealth as they can. If politicians have longer time horizons for staying in office, they realize that this strategy has limited benefits to them, and that they can secure a lower but steadier stream of revenue by providing services to the population and gaining wealth through taxation and other more legitimate means. In states that are failed, namely those that are no longer able to provide to their citizens even the most basic public good, namely safety, people then have a choice to be either wealthy or secure. Poverty becomes a way of assuring personal security in failed states. While Bates has lots of experience living and working in Africa, this book is an abbreviated theoretical argument about why states are the way they are in Africa. He alludes to some of his previous research but does not go into detail regarding any particular countries or contexts. The results may feel illuminating but somewhat incomplete.

104.   Battle, Michael

Reconciliation: The Ubuntu Theology of Desmond Tutu

Cleveland: Pilgrim Press, 2009. 256 pages, ISBN: 9780829818338.

Battle has here provided the first attempt at a full-length treatment of the theology of Desmond Tutu, former Anglican Archbishop of South Africa. The book is not a biography nor a history, but an exposition of Tutu's faith, especially as it has been expressed in his writings, speeches and sermons. Battle's thesis is that Tutu's thought is a synthesis of a traditional African emphasis on God as Creator with an Anglican emphasis on incarnation, that God has interacted with and even entered the creation in Christ. These two streams of thought, the African and the Anglican, find expression especially in Tutu's view of the *imago Dei*, which in turn undergirds Tutu's political action against apartheid and for racial reconciliation. If God is the creator of all, and if all are created in the image of God, and if God is revealed as self-giving love in the incarnation and crucifixion of Jesus, then apartheid must be opposed as a heresy as well as a sin. In contrast to more radical forms of political theology, Tutu's thought is always directed by love of the neighbour. This emphasis owes much, Battle thinks, to "Ubuntu": "the African concept of community embraced by Tutu [which] provides a corrective hermeneutic for Western salvation theology that focuses on the individual." The result is that Christian action must always be directed towards the healing of relationships rather than revenge. Battle was in a good position to produce this study, having served for a year as Tutu's adjutant. Most valuable is the extensive bibliography which lists not only Tutu's published works, but also his speeches and sermons, whether handwritten or typed, whether dated or undated. The foreword to the book is provided by Tutu himself.

105.   Bauckham, Richard J., editor

Bible and Mission: Christian Witness in a Postmodern World

Grand Rapids: Baker, 2004. 126 pages, ISBN: 9780801027710.

In their original form the chapters of this thought-provoking book were first presented in Africa as the 2002 Frumentius Lectures at the Ethiopian Graduate School of Theology in Addis Ababa. Bauckham was the widely-regarded professor of NT studies at the University of St Andrews in Scotland. In this study he argues that though the Bible attempts to make sense of the whole of human reality within a single story or "metanarrative," this does not privilege certain groups or cultures over others, as do such metanarratives as those set forth by Islam and by globalisation, which in fact destroy particularity. Rather, the story of the Bible comes to climax in the universal kingdom of God in which every particular reaches its true destiny. Mission provides the hermeneutic for this universal kingdom of God because, in mission, God's people set out from the particular toward the universal – a universal which is found precisely in other particulars. This book is specifically relevant to Africa for five reasons. First is the fact that its content was originally presented as special lectures at the Ethiopian Graduate School of Theology in Africa. Second, the book contains extended reflection on the way in which biblical geography, not least in its surprisingly frequent references to Ethiopia and northern Africa, contributes to the universal vision of the biblical story. However much the peoples and nations of Ethiopia and the other ends of the earth serve representatively to suggest the reach of God's universal, eschatological lordship, they do not for that reason lose their particularity. Third, the central thesis of the book offers a powerful response to the still often-heard complaint that Christianity destroys local African cultures. Fourth, the effects of globalisation on Africa remain hotly debated. Bauckham argues that the Christian story resists and critiques the metanarrative of globalisation with its definition of development as economic growth, and its aggrandizement of wealth accumulation as the ultimate good. Fifth, in pointing out that mission belongs to the biblical story's movement from the particular to the universal, Bauckham implies that the essential direction of mission is not from the wealthy and powerful to the poor and disenfranchised; rather it is a movement "to all by way of the least." May this central feature of the biblical story shape and motivate the African Church's participation in mission. This is a book to be carefully pondered, not least by those committed to active biblical and theological reflection in Africa.

106.   **Baudena, Peter, and John Gichuhi**

Prayer in an African Context

Nairobi: Paulines, 2002. 120 pages, ISBN: 9789966215505.

Whereas this is a useful book with many helpful and practical insights for a Christian's prayer life, the title is somewhat misleading. The introduction explains that the authors had originally developed a book on prayer in the Kikuyu language, which was later expanded to this English version as an attempt by the authors to respond to a call from the Catholic Synod of Bishops in Africa to "consider inculturation an urgent priority in the life of particular Churches." Also early in the book the authors explain that prayer was a gift of God to Africa even before the message of Christ arrived, and is part and parcel of African culture. Furthermore, an anthology of traditional African prayers is attached at the end of the book. Unfortunately, the authors fail to link either their introductory statement or the appended traditional prayers to the rest of the text on Christian prayer through any type of analysis or thoughtful reflection. As a result, the anticipated African orientation of the text is minimal and unintegrated. The closest the text comes to living up to its title is through several simple statements, such as one highlighting the fact that spontaneous praise, thanksgiving or petition, of the type offered during traditional community gatherings, is a useful example for the modern Christian to avoid formalism in prayer. The Virgin Mary's role in prayer, and a longer section exhorting readers to use the Eucharist as the most precious form of prayer, appear without any background explanation – a disconcerting feature in that one might expect these specific prayers and liturgy (so clearly originating outside of the African context) to be presented with some type of analysis instead of an assumed acceptance. Although the book does not include any substantive contextual discussion of African traditional prayer or of prayer by modern Africans, the text does usefully take the reader through various topics including prayer as God's gift to us, a practical discussion of dealing with distractions, our attitude in approaching God, the role of Christ and the Holy Spirit, the use of Scripture for prayer and the fruits of a prayerful life.

107. Baur, John

2000 Years of Christianity in Africa: An African Church History

Nairobi: Paulines, 2009. 560 pages, ISBN: 9789966211101.

Here is a recent and very welcome text on African church history, which distinguishes itself (i) for being up to date, (ii) for treating African Christian history from its beginnings (not just from the nineteenth century), and (iii) for telling the story from the perspective of Africa (not merely as missions history). Such an approach can furnish a healthy historical contribution to African Christian self-understanding. Baur is a Roman Catholic father from Switzerland, who has served in Tanzania and Kenya since 1956. The principal part of the book traces the history of Christianity on the continent from earliest times to the present. This is followed by a valuable (if sometimes uneven) country-by-country survey of twentieth century African Christianity, covering some 125 pages. The book then concludes with an excellent bibliography, extensive tables and maps, and a comprehensive index. Baur attempts to be ecumenical, giving equal attention to Protestant and Catholic developments, and is substantially successful in this intention, although he evidences a very minimal familiarity with evangelical African Christianity. Nevertheless, this would make a useful basic text for the study of African church history if supplemented with other materials.

108. Baur, John

The Catholic Church in Kenya: A Centenary History

Nairobi: St. Paul Publications, 1990. 256 pages.

This history chronicles the development of the Catholic Church in Kenya, from its inception with the Tana River mission in 1889 by the Holy Ghost Missionaries from Zanzibar, to its position as the largest church in Kenya in 1990. John Baur, who taught church history in seminaries in Tanzania and Kenya for over 30 years, is well acquainted with the cultural and historical setting of Kenya and its effect on the growth of the church. The first part of the book is a regional survey. Each area's story is presented chronologically from the arrival of the first Catholic missionaries to the present status of the church in that region. The accounts relate the contributions not only of the missionaries but also of the local converts who helped to establish the church. This geographical approach enables the Kenyan reader quickly to find material on the history of the Catholic Church in his or her home area. Detailed maps and photographs help the reader to locate missions and identify those personalities discussed in the narrative. The second part of the book is a thematic survey where the author covers topics such as: training of clergy, church institutions (such as schools, hospitals and the media), ecumenism, and the role of the church in Kenya since independence. The final chapter very helpfully addresses some of the difficult and important issues that both Protestants and Catholics face in what Baur describes as "the incarnation of our faith in our African life." He deals openly and honestly with the struggles the church has had as she has wrestled with the development of an African liturgy, an African Christian theology, marriage, morality, urban ministry and ministry to youth. This book is written in a readable style, and will benefit anyone needing to know more about the history and influence of the Catholic Church in Kenya.

109.   Bayart, Jean-François, Stephen Ellis, and Béatrice Hibou

The Criminalization of the State in Africa

Martlesham, UK: James Currey, 1999. 144 pages, ISBN: 9780852558126.

This book is part of the African Issues series published by the International African Institute in London. The writers are all established scholars in African studies. Bayart is director of the Centre d'Etudes et de Recherches Internationales in Paris; Ellis works at the Afrika-Studiecentrum in Leiden, and is co-editor of the journal *African Affairs*; Hibou is a fellow of the Centre National de la Recherche Scientifique in France. Their book is not pleasant reading, as it describes in a comprehensive way how crime is rampant on the African continent. The major thesis of the book is that crime in many African countries is interconnected with politics – that indeed crime is at such a stage of sophistication that the state itself has become a vehicle for organized criminal activity. The term "felonious state" is used to describe such countries that have passed beyond mere corruption. Not just African politicians and leaders are involved, but also criminals from other continents (particularly Asia), especially where drugs and fraud are concerned. The content of the book at times suggests interesting questions for the Christian reader. For example the book details how some of the criminal activity may be interlinked with traditional cultural and ethnic factors – which raises a question how the Christian church in Africa can deal more adequately with the issue of sin as it relates to the continent's cultural contexts. Originally published in French (1997), this English translation can be rather stilted at times, making it difficult to get the meaning. The use of technical and social terms and phrases does not help, especially as they are not always explained (e.g. "kleptocracy," "multilateral institutions"). The book does not offer any solutions to the problem – but that was not its intent. For many the book will simply confirm in more detail what was already supposed. But its significance goes beyond that, by posing a warning which needs to be heeded, namely the strong possibility that parts of sub-Saharan Africa could be sliding backwards into societies that have become economically and politically criminalized. Not a positive perspective, but one that cannot wisely be ignored.

110.   Bayart, Jean-François

The State in Africa: The Politics of the Belly

Cambridge: Polity, 2010. 420 pages, ISBN: 9780745644370.

The author is Director of the Centre d'Études et de Recherches Internationales (CERI) in Paris, and a widely recognized authority on African affairs, with a lengthy list of publications to his credit. Bayart's main argument in this book is that African political realities should be viewed as specifically African in character, and not simply as the products of external (mainly Western) influences. What he refers to as "the politics of the belly" has its roots in pre-colonial modes of political action. African political leaders are not puppets of Western powers (as argued by dependency theorists, for example), but independent actors, who deliberately make use of "strategies of extraversion" as means of accumulating the necessary material foundations of power. Africa's generally low productivity and low population density have made it difficult for its political elites to accumulate the material resources from local sources that would enable them to bring large territories under central authority. Thus they could only exploit whatever externally based sources of wealth were available to them. This pattern already applied during the slave trade, as African leaders accumulated the means of domination (especially firearms) from European slavers, and has continued through the colonial and neo-colonial periods down to the present. According to the optics of African political culture ("the politics of the belly"), only those who can convert relations with the external world (foreign aid, for example) into the kind of personal wealth that enables them to support networks of clients with culturally adequate generosity are really worthy to exercise political power. Patron-client systems of this kind, however, lead to factional politics, most often along ethnic lines (the most natural social field for the development of these networks). This helps to explain the tendency to what is often portrayed in the media as ethnic conflict. Along with other scholars, Bayart criticizes "primordialist" views of such conflicts (the idea that tensions between ethnicities are rooted in ancient and enduring hatreds), arguing that ethnic identity and conflict are better seen as *effects* of political action than as a cause. Bayart develops a number of other significant themes that taken together, he believes, provide a better framework for understanding African political history than the general fare of political science analysis that has been available. This book is not the last word on African political systems (Bayart has been criticized for minimising the impact of the colonial era, for example), but it is nevertheless one of the more important contributions to this topic.

111. Bayley, Anne

One New Humanity: The Challenge of AIDS

London: SPCK, 1996. 330 pages, ISBN: 9780281049233.

The author has produced a detailed and challenging assessment from a Christian perspective of the impact of AIDS worldwide. In doing so she has drawn on her own knowledge and experience gained while serving as a physician in Zambia and Uganda, as well as the input from professional colleagues in Africa and reports by international agencies. She clearly depicts the enormity of the dilemmas AIDS is creating for humanity in general, for national governments and for families in particular, and she gently but firmly addresses the social and behavioural issues that facilitate the spread of AIDS. Using biblical material very effectively, she encourages us all to live out the reality of our faith in Christ in our relationships to one another, whether HIV infected or not. She focuses on the importance of including HIV infected people as full participants in society and of treating them with respect and kindness in their illnesses. In this way she very effectively brings a message of hope to a seemingly hopeless set of problems. Books in this SPCK series (originally sponsored by the World Council of Churches), are "inter-cultural, ecumenical and contextual in approach," and are designed to be used as study guides. The author sometimes seems to reflect this theological orientation, so that an evangelical perspective might somewhat differ on a few points (for example, on the reality of the demonic possession of individuals). The discussion questions at the end of each chapter are excellently framed for encouraging a helpful and practical evaluation of the current situation and implementing helpful responses. This book is particularly recommended for use wherever AIDS is prevalent. Discussion groups in churches with an educated membership would find it very useful, and lecturers at theological colleges caring for courses that include attention to AIDS need to be familiar with it.

112.   **Bediako, Kwame**

Christianity in Africa: The Renewal of a Non-Western Religion

Maryknoll, NY: Orbis, 1996. 284 pages, ISBN: 9781570750489.

The substance of this volume was originally delivered as the Duff Lectures in Edinburgh between 1989 and 1992, where Bediako was a visiting lecturer in African theology at New College. This book responds to the thesis that, given the phenomenal numerical growth of Christianity in the non-Western regions of the world, Christianity's centre of gravity has shifted from the West to the non-Western regions, particularly to Africa. Bediako's response blazes a trail by focusing on how this shift should be reflected in the theology of the Christian faith. The book is divided into three parts. From the Ghanaian context, the first part considers issues deemed significant if Christianity's credentials are to be established in Africa, such as African identity and African languages. From a broader view, the second part explores the possibility of reconceptualising and reformulating the Christian faith in terms of "primal apprehensions of reality." Because he finds anticipations of the gospel in African primal religions, Bediako concludes that Christianity ought to adopt the ancestors of such religions, among whom Christ should be ranked as the Great Ancestor. The third part of this study seeks to identify challenges the African church will face in the twenty-first century, such as the survival of ancestors and the establishment of genuine democracies. Given its expansive scope, this volume would be relevant to students of African theology, African church history, or African missions.

113.   **Bediako, Kwame**

Jesus in Africa: The Christian Gospel in African History and Experience

Oxford: Regnum, 2000. 144 pages, ISBN: 9781870345347.

Bediako was a Ghanaian theologian, and Director of the Akrofi-Christaller Memorial Centre for Mission Research and Applied Theology in Akropong, Ghana. This book is a collection from his writings that reflects the three major areas of his interest: the grassroots experience of Jesus in Africa; the relevance of the struggle by the early Church Fathers to understand and establish Christianity in their own culture to the similar struggle in Africa today; and the history of Christianity in Africa, especially as it relates to African traditional religion and institutions. This book contains journal articles, the entire text of Bediako's booklet *Jesus in African Culture* (1990), portions from his book *Theology and Identity* (1992), abridged sections from *Christianity in Africa* (1995), and one formerly unpublished paper. The book is enhanced by a seven-page biography of Bediako and introduction to his thought, and a Bediako bibliography. Bediako is convinced not only that "translation" of the gospel into all levels of African life and consciousness is imperative, but also that the resulting theology has "universal relevance and far-reaching significance for the global church." The amazing growth of the Church in Africa and its increasing importance in world Christianity make Africa a crucial place for theological reflection. No one concerned with theology in Africa should be unacquainted with Bediako's thought, and this book is a handy introduction.

114.   **Bediako, Kwame**

Jesus in African Culture: A Ghanaian Perspective

Accra: Asempa Publishers, 1990. 49 pages, ISBN: 9789964781804.

In this admirable short study "from a Ghanaian perspective," Kwame Bediako confronts the problem of African Christians "living at two levels – half African and half European," who "are uncertain about how the Jesus of the Church's preaching saves them from the terrors and fears which they experience in their traditional world-view." The key to Bediako's approach to this issue is to "relate Christian understanding and experience to the realm of the ancestors," which he considers to be the cultural focal point of the Akan people of Ghana. Building upon Mbiti's notion of "Christus Victor" (Christ supreme over every spiritual rule and authority), Bediako proposes that by presenting Jesus Christ as sovereignly displacing "the mediatorial function of our natural 'spirit fathers'," the believer can be freed from any "terrorising influence" of traditional beliefs about the ancestors. Bediako also addresses the inherent authority conflict between African Christian presence and the traditional role of the Chief in Akan society as the intermediary between the state and the ancestors. He suggests that an accent on the spiritual nature and "non-dominating" quality of Christ's kingdom could reduce these tensions in a constructive way. Bediako turns to the book of Hebrews to provide an appropriate theological basis for building a context-sensitive Christology, especially the presentation there of Christ's high-priestly mediatorial role. He speaks of the transforming relationship of Christianity to three key aspects of Akan traditional religious belief, namely sacrifice, priestly mediation, and ancestral function. Although the book is dated 1990, the footnotes only reference studies prior to 1981.

115.   **Bediako, Kwame**

Theology and Identity: The Impact of Culture upon Christian Thought in the Second Century and in Modern Africa

Oxford: Regnum, 1999. 507 pages, ISBN: 9781870345101.

This magnificent contribution to African theology has an epochal quality about it, generous in its size and scope, magisterial in its learning, articulate in its presentation, penetrating in its assessments, and even instructive in its limitations. At time of publication Bediako headed a research study centre in his home country, Ghana. With minor editorial revisions, this is his doctoral dissertation submitted in 1983 at the University of Aberdeen. Bediako has increasingly functioned as an African Christian thinker from whom much advanced-level discussion has to take some bearings (as did Mbiti in the past). The impact of this book lies not least in its distinctive interpretive approach. Bediako first offers five chapters on the variety of ways that second-century Christianity evolved its sense of identity in relation to Greco-Roman culture (Tatian, Tertullian, Justin, and Clement of Alexandria). He then uses this as the background interpretive framework for the following five chapters, addressing the quest for Christian identity in relation to traditional culture in twentieth-century Africa (Idowu, Mbiti, Mulago, and Kato). And the limitations? Some will suggest that the question determining Bediako's entire approach may be fundamentally mis-framed, that the defining matrix from which to construct a valid African Christian theology may not be the religious culture of traditional Africa *per se* (as Bediako insists), but rather the present life of the African Christian community (as Tiénou argued in his doctoral thesis, produced the year after Bediako's). Others will wonder if Bediako only answers half of the question that controls his outlook. So deeply exercised to establish the proper relationship of African Christianity to Africa's traditional heritage, does he sufficiently raise and address the other half of the identity question: how should African Christianity relate to its Christian heritage? How is African Christianity to be both authentically African and authentically Christian? Many will also find Bediako's handling of Kato, both in this book and elsewhere in his writings, curiously off-note. Kato was the first African head of the Association of Evangelicals in Africa, and the first from that community to take part in the theological discussions on the continent. Bediako's interpretive grid requires a modern African Tertullian at one extreme: "What hath Jerusalem to do with Athens"; so Kato is commandeered for the role. In Bediako's skilled hands Kato becomes a theological extremist opposed to African culture. Yet whatever Kato's limitations, he cannot be responsibly fitted to that mould. Kato was a main-stream evangelical in his beliefs, and a respected Christian leader both in Africa and internationally. He was also heartily affirming of Africa's cultural heritage; "Let African Christians be Christian Africans!" was the theme of one of his most important addresses. The implications of Bediako's portrait in this case are substantively misleading, and the disdainful tone fits awkwardly in a book otherwise characterized by courteous even-handedness. That apart, this sophisticated and multi-faceted study will richly reward sustained attention for everyone who takes seriously the theological task of African Christianity.

Bediako, Kwame

see also review 1186

116.   Bediwegi, Etienne Ung'eyowun

La vocation du prophète des nations: Une lecture africaine de Jr 1,4–19

Kinshasa: Éditions Le Sénéve, 2003. 234 pages.

A revised doctoral dissertation from the Catholic Faculty in Kinshasa (1999), this book is an interpretation of Jeremiah 1:4–19 (which concerns Jeremiah's call as a prophet "to the nations"), with particular attention to the inculturation potential of this pericope in contemporary Africa. After a brief introduction, with the expected survey of historical research and statement of the problem, the book is divided in two parts. First comes a close reading of the pericope; very close in fact, in the sense that it offers a lexicographic word-by-word analysis. Based on this analysis, the author is able to conclude that the pericope functions as a prologue to Jeremiah as a whole, a prologue that introduces major themes that eventually are to be elaborated throughout the prophetic book. The second part of this study then relates the pericope to various contextual challenges. One is a new translation of the pericope into Lingala. Another is a discussion of Jeremiah's vocation in relation to the phenomenon of prophets in contemporary African Christianity. A third is the question of idolatry (cf. Jer 1:16), which is related to examples of contemporary de-humanisation in Africa. A fourth is the question of war (cf. Jer 1:15), which is a call to the church to speak prophetically in today's society. The publication of a book such as this merits special notice. The number of OT doctoral degrees awarded by African academic institutions remains low, and only a handful of such dissertations written in French get published. Given this situation, and certainly also because of its exegetical and contextual analyses of the Jeremiah text, this contribution and others like it ought to be sought out and acquired by any francophone theological library in Africa.

117. Behrend, Heike

Alice Lakwena and the Holy Spirits: War in Northern Uganda, 1986–1997

Martlesham, UK: James Currey, 1999. 224 pages, ISBN: 9780852552476.

Behrend is professor of anthropology at the University of Cologne. Her analysis of the phenomenon of Alice Lakwena and the Holy Spirit Mobile Forces in Uganda is both fascinating and depressing. In 1985 Alice took the name of Lakwena ("messenger"), said to be the spirit of an Italian engineer who had died in Uganda. Throughout the book Behrend is careful to distinguish between the words of the medium Alice, and those of Lakwena, who possessed her and was the true leader of the movement. This was a predominantly Acholi movement, that resisted the government of Yoweri Museveni from August 1986 until its defeat in November 1987. After her initial possession, Alice focused on healing until Lakwena decided that it was useless to heal people when they ended up dying at the hands of the government soldiers anyway. Thus began one of the most curious armies in Africa, claiming that they were trying to eradicate witchcraft but at the same time being led by spirit mediums in every aspect of their fight. Readers familiar with Africa will not be surprised at Alice's claims that the reasons for death must be discovered. In this case, death was always the result of sin, not enemy bullets, which were useless against "holy" fighters who underwent purification rituals before each battle and often sang rather than shot. (Behrend comments, "God's might was not taken as an absolute power independent of human will, but as manipulable through a number of magical acts"). The author goes to great lengths to explore this movement, even submitting to daily sessions with a medium (despite her professed unbelief in its efficacy!) in order to gain access to key sources. Christian readers will be troubled by many aspects of this book, including how a country so affected by the East African Revival could be a source of such syncretism (the author's sources on the East African Revival are both limited and biased), why the author seems to have no problem with the term Christian holy spirits' (as opposed to the malevolent kind), how a violent movement could list Scripture verses to support its Holy Spirit Safety Precautions, and the disquieting theological similarity to modern prosperity gospel proponents who insist that defeats are always due to a lack of faith. Christian leaders in Africa do well to familiarize themselves with such resources as this for understanding the seldom-discussed attitudes that Christians should have to the many wars and war movements on the African continent.

118. Behrend, Heike, and Ute Luig, editors

Spirit Possession: Modernity and Power in Africa

Martlesham, UK: James Currey, 1999. 192 pages, ISBN: 9780852552582.

The thesis of this book is that what the editors term "spirit possession cults" are proliferating all over the world and are no longer limited to Africa, Asia and the Caribbean. Unfortunately for African Christian readers who may interpret spirits as evil, spirit possession is approvingly defined in the introduction in nebulous (Western?) terms such as "refractions of social realities," "abstract qualities" and "products of imagination." The editors, each of whom contributes an article, are lecturers at German universities. The book covers nine African countries, reasonably distributed throughout the continent. In the chapter from Madagascar, for example, the "dominant paradigm" is that "possession shrouds critique in symbolic gesture and language" so that the spirit (not the person) is blamed for minority opinions. Apparently consulting spirit mediums was banned in the days of French rule but is now a common part of business and political life. One of the most fascinating chapters relates the story of the Lord's Resistance Army in Uganda and the major role that spirit possession played, and continues to play. The chapter from Niger stresses the return to relationships with spirits as part of the modern emphasis on cultural identity, a movement that is probably true in most parts of the continent. This chapter also considers the widespread phenomenon that people often become possessed with spirits after seeking help for an incurable illness. The tone of the book is, ironically, almost completely secular; spirits are to be researched but not really believed. One writer even thanks "the many mediums (and their spirits) for their patience and forthrightness"! Christianity is treated as an institution that interferes with cultural practices and offers no real alternative to spirit possession. Thus the "balokole" (revived ones) of the East African Revival are dismissed as merely a "fundamentalist Christian movement" in Uganda, despite their dramatic impact on the history of that country. Christians in Zambia are said to oppose spirit possession "in order to demonstrate their own power," whereas the possession cults "offer meaningful explanations for the social problems of the time." Despite the occasional willingness of some modern anthropologists to question cultural practices that result in evil, this book makes no such judgements. Insofar as it describes an aspect of Africa's cultural milieu, it can be of use for those researching on the continued role of African traditional religion on the continent.

119.   **Bekele, Girma**

The In-Between People: A Reading of David Bosch through the Lens of Mission History and Contemporary Challenges In Ethiopia

Eugene, OR: Wipf & Stock, 2011. 460 pages, ISBN: 9781608992690.

This published PhD thesis from Wycliffe College (University of Toronto) is a tome which could well be described as magisterial. In this work the author creatively applies missiologist/theologian David Bosch's paradigm systems to Ethiopian Christianity – to the Ethiopian Orthodox Church (EOTC), the Catholic Church and the Evangelical Church movement. Part 1 covers Bosch's socio-theological journey and transformation as a Reformed Afrikaner struggling with state-sanctioned apartheid. Part 2 explains Bosch's key missiological concepts and his understanding of the church as "Alternative Community." In Part 3 Girma focuses on Ethiopia's mission history and, through the lens of Bosch's various missiological paradigms, attempts to understand the unique qualities of the EOTC, the two large "mission churches" (Kale Heywet and Mekane Yesus), and the vital Ethiopian Pentecostal movement which is impacting the entire community of Ethiopian evangelicals. Part 4 expands on how the church as an "Alternative Community" must blend together both mission and social justice. The author chides mission agencies for dichotomising between evangelism and social justice, and sees these two aspects of the gospel as the confluence of two rivers. In Part 5 the author envisions a common ecumenical cooperation within Ethiopia to address issues of ethnic-based federalism, poverty and the impact of globalisation. Given the realities of the Ethiopian situation, one may question whether the aspirations and idealism evident in the book are plausible, but is this not what an academic quest can challenge us about? Girma urges the church to become the "in-between people" (a phrase coined by Bosch) melding proclamation and good deeds together in their mission praxis. Girma is to be commended for his scholarly "double listening." Firstly, listening to Bosch through some 86 articles, essays, letters and books. And secondly, his careful listening to historiographers of the ancient Orthodox Church, as well as to contemporary writers on the emerging evangelical movement. There are numerous examples of a need for more scrutiny and consistency in presentation. An illustration of several minor errors: the Meserete Kristos Church, with Mennonite origins, would not call herself Pentecostal, even though the worship style of all Ethiopian evangelical churches is generally charismatic. Also, the lengthy footnotes tend to derail a reader; more care could have been given to condensing footnote material perhaps by use of appendices. All in all, this is a very significant book both for Ethiopia and for the wider church in its challenge to live beyond a status quo posture. Girma's creative critical interpretation of Ethiopian Christianity through the lens of Bosch's paradigms might prove a worthy model for scholarly studies in other parts of Africa.

120. Belshaw, Deryke, Robert Calderisi, and Christopher Sugden, editors

Faith in Development: Partnership Between the World Bank and the Churches of Africa

Washington DC: World Bank Publications, 2001. 256 pages, ISBN: 9780821348482.

It seems almost impossible that a book would cover the issues of economics and development in Africa alongside issues of Christian faith – but this one does! Some might approach the book with suspicion, thinking "what hath the World Bank to do with Christian faith?" The World Bank supplies the answer: the World Bank has learned that it is fruitless to do economic and social reforms if these do not reflect the views of society at large. The book derives from a conference in Nairobi in 2000, held jointly by the Council of Anglican Provinces of Africa and the World Bank, with the theme: "Alleviating Poverty in Africa." The hope was that the conference would give a basis for closer collaboration at grass roots level on the question of development. The book offers nineteen essays by delegates from each side of the partnership (the World Bank and the Anglican Church). There are some familiar names from the evangelical perspective, such as Tokunboh Adeyemo, Vinay Samuel and Chris Sugden. The foundational notions on which the conference took place were that most Africans are poor, and also most are religious; those closest to the poor are religious workers; therefore help in development must inevitably involve religious people. Unexpectedly, a number of the papers do give a balanced and true picture of the issues. There is little grandstanding or patting on the back. The issues are raised in context, and some solutions given. For example it was generally agreed that churches need to become agents of transformation in economic issues. The principal disappointment would be in the nature of the conference rather than in the book itself. The conference talked of partnership between the World Bank and churches of Africa, whereas it was mainly the Anglican church which was represented. While there were representatives from other Christian groups, they were in the minority. Thus the reference to "the Churches of Africa" in the title is misleading. But at least an attempt was made to get two traditionally diverse groups together to talk about helping Africa. The book gives an encouraging outlook for future cooperation between these groups; let us hope that it proves a first step along that road.

Benson, G. Patrick

see review 407

121. Berinyuu, Abraham Adu

Pastoral Care to the Sick in Africa: An Approach to Transcultural Pastoral Theology

Frankfurt: Peter Lang, 1988. 136 pages, ISBN: 9783820416602.

Berinyuu, a Presbyterian minister in Ghana, writes a thought-provoking book on the pastoral care of the sick in Africa. His aim is to suggest ways that African culture can contribute to the church's care of the sick. He believes that there needs to be a dialogue between African culture and Christian theology, and that such a transcultural approach will enrich the ministry of the church to the sick. One of the themes he develops is viewing the pastor as a Christian "diviner" who listens to the sick and helps them discover the causes behind their sickness. Another theme is the need to take a holistic approach to sickness rather than seeing it simply in Western medical terms. A major focus of the book is on the need for rituals, Christian rituals, to be a part of ministry to the sick. Ritual, he says, is a part of African culture and needs to be used in bringing healing. Another valuable contribution of the book is a comparison of Western and African views of man and their implications for helping the sick. Also valuable is the brief survey of the church's approach to the sick at various stages of its history. Limitations of the book include the following. (1) It is a theoretical contribution, and offers very little in the way of practical guidelines for ministry to the sick. For example, there are no case studies. (2) The book's brevity means that it is more of an introduction to the task of integrating pastoral care with African cultural beliefs than a full-length study on this topic. (3) It is assumed "that the Spirit of God is actively present in what all people do to cope in times of crisis." There is no effort to permit Scripture to sit in judgement on African beliefs. It is rather assumed that both Scripture and African culture are equals in their contribution to the dialogue, which of course raises its own issues. As an early contributor to this field of inquiry, Berinyuu has produced a useful study, which should challenge others to do even better.

122.   **Berinyuu, Abraham Adu**

Towards Theory and Practice of Pastoral Counseling in Africa

Frankfurt: Peter Lang, 1989. 140 pages, ISBN: 9783631421468.

Since relatively little has been written on the practice of pastoral counselling in Africa, this thought-provoking contribution on the subject is all the more welcome. The author, a Presbyterian minister from Ghana, rightly emphasizes the importance of culture and of the theory of personality for the development of an appropriate theory and practice of pastoral counselling. He uses two ethnic groups from Ghana, the Tallensis and the Akans, as background for his inquiry. He sees in the "traditional diviner" a model from which the pastoral counsellor can learn much about healing in the African context. Based on this model he defines the broad lines of an "African Therapy" which focuses on conflict, has a community dimension, and uses ritual in the healing process. He then develops a dialogue between this "African Therapy" and Freudian psychoanalysis, pointing out similarities and differences. Finally he suggests that the pastoral counsellor in Africa could well use African therapeutic resources such as storytelling, myths, dance and music to advance the healing process. The book is more theoretical than practical and lacks case studies to show what "African Therapy" might look like in practice. Another limitation of the book is that the theory of personality out of which "African Therapy" grows is based on traditional culture and beliefs. The study does not seem to take account of the major impact that westernisation has made on the African personality. Finally, there is no dialogue with biblical theology in formulating the proposals, and nothing that would distinguish the counselling here designated as "pastoral" from counselling in general. This book is a must for teachers of pastoral counselling, and for those who care about these hugely relevant issues as they apply within the African Christian community.

123. **Bertsche, Jim**

CIM/AIMM: A Story of Vision, Commitment and Grace

Elkhart, IN: Fairway Press, 1998. 854 pages, ISBN: 9780788014154.

The only fault with this book is its obscure title for anyone outside the Mennonite tradition. The acronym CIM refers to the former Congo Inland Mission, and the acronym AIMM to the Africa Inter-Mennonite Mission, the combined mission outreach to Africa of the various Mennonite Conferences in North America. Bertsche has produced a magisterial account of this outreach and the resulting churches in Congo (DRC), southern, and western Africa. Bertsche is well qualified to write this comprehensive 85-year history for several reasons: academically with advanced degrees, missionally with 25 years of experience in Congo (DRC), and administratively serving as the mission's executive secretary for twelve years in Elkhart, Indiana. This is a comprehensive tome of 74 chapters, easy to read, well organized, with detailed maps, a listing of all inter-Mennonite missionaries, full bibliography, a chronology of dates and events pertaining to Mennonite mission, and even a six-page glossary of acronyms! Bertsche writes in his Preface, "It is my hope, therefore, that this history . . . with its supportive documentation will serve as a valuable source of information for African church leaders and writers of the future." His final chapter contains the ruminations of a wise and experienced missiologist. Bertsche critically evaluates MK education, the ministry of singles, over-built mission stations, the role of missionary wives, the tangled fusion of church and mission, inter-Mennonite Mission's future role among AICs, and Mennonite Churches in Congo (how Anabaptist are they?). This same chapter, with a critical eye to the Mennonite contribution to African Christianity but also healthy optimism for the future, makes for a provocative read.

124. **Biko, Hlumelo**

The Great African Society: A Plan for a Nation Gone Astray

Jeppestown, South Africa: Jonathan Ball Publishers, 2013. 293 pages, ISBN: 9781868425211.

More than two decades have passed since South Africa's remarkable transition from apartheid to democracy. Yet despite sure promise and monumental achievement the ANC administration has overseen the emergence of an immensely unequal, polarized society, marred by continuing poverty, frightening levels of violent crime, and endemic corruption at virtually every stratum of law, order and government. For a vast majority of citizens, genuine transformation in the "Rainbow Nation" remains beyond present experience. A venture capitalist by profession, and the son of Steve Biko, the author aims to address central aspects of South Africa's unfolding peril, proceeding first to freshly analyse and interpret the socio-economic legacy of white Afrikaner rule. World-class infrastructure is reckoned the foremost benefit, with abysmal education the main limitation. Biko believes that history, however, should judge the first twenty years of post-apartheid society almost as harshly. Notwithstanding massive gains in literacy, housing, delivery of running water and electricity, as well as far fuller integration with the global economy, post-liberation South Africa is still one of the world's least fair and most inequitable societies. Whole-scale mismanagement, unstable institutional leadership, and increasing desperation among the labour force combine to a noxious brew, and this condition the central chapters of the book attempt to document (with frequent force and clarity). The author's eye is fixed throughout on the next generation, and Biko's leading recommendation to face down future threat is public-private partnerships. He thinks these should be planned, run and part-funded by the private sector in areas requiring most urgent attention, especially health-care delivery, primary and secondary education, house and town-planning, training in technical skills and professional leadership, and also broader economic development policy. Biko claims that a more deliberate, sensible, transparent collaboration between government and business – beginning with a R500 billion corporate donation – offers the nation real hope for a sustainable and successful process of social re-engineering. Among the book's most obvious virtues are its grip, immediacy and readability. Indeed, the narrative emerges both as a page-turner and something of a tour de force, brave, bold and daring. A palpable concern for human flourishing is displayed, together with an impressive array of statistics, penetrating insights, and audacious proposals. Specialists will wonder about the tendency to generalisation and over-simplification, and there are certainly profound flaws in Biko's treatment of Christianity's role, past, present and prospective. But nonetheless the work is worth consideration, not least for the sensitivity and skill with which it captures the country's contemporary mood of disillusionment and expectation.

125.   Bilinda, Lesley

The Colour of Darkness: A Personal Story of Tragedy and Hope in Rwanda

London: Hodder and Stoughton, 1996. 236 pages, ISBN: 9780340642795.

Bilinda, a physiotherapist, went to Rwanda in 1989 under the auspices of Tear Fund. There she met Charles Bilinda, whom she married in 1992. In her book she tells something of her life and work in Rwanda before the 1994 genocide, but the major part of the book deals with the genocide itself and how it affected the lives of Charles and Lesley, as well as countless other Rwandans. Lesley was actually in Kenya when the killings began, and her descriptions of what she found in the country when she was able to go back into Rwanda are heartbreaking. After one has been exposed to news report upon news report, and read many assessments from various viewpoints, it is helpful to read a personal account of the tragedy that occurred in Rwanda, written from a Christian point of view. One receives a very graphic picture of sorrow, hatred and loss, but also stories of kindness and courage and of God's faithfulness.

126.   Bird, Phyllis, Katharine Doob Sakenfeld, and Sharon H. Ringe, editors

Semeia 78: Reading the Bible as Women: Perspectives from Africa, Asia, and Latin America

Atlanta: SBL, 1997. 165 pages, ISBN: 9781589831858.

This special volume, published by the journal *Semeia*, is a compilation of articles presented at the 1995 sessions of "The Bible in Africa, Asia, and Latin America Group" of the Society of Biblical Literature, held in Philadelphia, USA. Although the editors are Americans, the presenters were all from the two-thirds world. Of particular interest for this reference work are the four essays by African contributors. M. Dube, from Botswana, in her "Toward a Postcolonial Feminist Perspective of the Bible" argues that our critical reading of the Bible should be "multi-cultural" and should allow "women as equal subjects." Her assertion that the Bible has been used as a tool of colonialism must be acknowledged as an issue requiring attention. D. Mbuwayesango, from Zimbabwe, in "Childlessness and Woman-to-Woman Relationships in Genesis and in African Patriarchal Society: Sarah and Hagar from a Zimbabwean Perspective (Gen 16:1–16; 21:8–21)," finds heuristic connections between Shona and Ndebele societies and the Genesis narratives, especially with regard to barrenness and inheritance. Similarly, M. Masenya compares Northern Sotho with biblical proverbs in "Proverbs 31:10–31 in a South African Context: Reading for the Liberation of African (Northern Sotho) Women." M. Sibeko and B. Haddad find insight from ordinary African readers (and hearers) of the Bible in "Reading the Bible 'with' Women in Poor and Marginalized Communities in South Africa (Mark 5:21–6:1)." All of these essays are written from what could be called "liberationist" as well as "feminist" perspectives. The volume is especially useful in providing examples of where some African reading of the Bible may be going in the future.

Bissainthe, Gérard

see review 581

127.   Bissu, Emmanuel

Nouveau Testament: Introduction, texte et contexte

Yaoundé: Éditions Clé, 2002. 264 pages, ISBN: 9782723501668.

Editions Clé of Cameroon has produced several books intended for use in a basic theology programme at first-degree level institutions in francophone Africa. This book replaces two earlier textbooks by Bernard Jay, *Le Monde du NT*, and *Introduction au NT*, published by Editions Clé in the 1970s. Bissu's offering, although not as detailed as Jay's, fits well into Edition Clé's publishing scheme as a useful textbook, at least for institutions whose viewpoint resonates with that of the Cameroonian author, a self-proclaimed liberal theologian. About a third of the text is used to address the usual questions of NT Introduction. In the remainder the author has provided a host of other materials that would perhaps enable any lecturer to teach NT Introduction, even if he or she has little formal training in the field. Preliminary chapters deal with the author's concept of the necessary contours of theological studies, first generally and then specifically for the NT. Additional chapters deal with the literary, historical and cultural backgrounds of the NT world, and briefly with NT textual criticism, followed by longer discussions of canon and the formation of the Gospels. After introductions to the individual books of the NT, the final chapters include discussion of post-NT writings (NT Apocrypha) and some theological themes in the NT. As a resource tool for someone who has to teach a course on the subject, or for a student seeking self-instruction, the book has a bit of everything. The drawback to such an approach is, of course, that the author is unable to go into much detail for what one might expect to constitute the heart of the course, the classical questions of Introduction. Somewhat surprisingly, nothing in the presentation would suggest that use in the African context is particularly in view. Nevertheless, as an affordable French-language textbook, this will fill a definite gap in Africa. And in due course perhaps other African scholars might produce a textbook with a similar format presented from an evangelical perspective, that would meet the need for such a textbook in the lower-level evangelical theological schools throughout francophone Africa.

128.   Bitrus, Daniel

The Extended Family: An African Christian Perspective

Nairobi: Christian Learning Material Centre, 2000. 150 pages.

The author, a Nigerian, was at one time General Secretary of the Association of Evangelicals in Africa (AEA). Previously he worked all across Africa with the United Bible Societies. Bitrus clearly states his intention that this book should be a catalyst for further study on the neglected topic of the African extended family. He first identifies the characteristics of a "Christian family," within which he situates the nuclear family's responsibilities to the extended family. He presents the extended family as: valuable for social stability in Africa; under threat by modernism and urbanization; and an important aspect of being African which needs careful, systematic biblical analysis by African theologians. Bitrus also acknowledges some disadvantages of the extended family system, focusing on conflicts and violence in extended family relationships. Possible solutions he advocates include evangelism among extended family members and developing strong leadership channels in the wider family. Though not explicitly stated, he seems to assume that Christian couples or individuals will make their own decisions on how to respond to needs in the extended family, rather than letting the extended family decide for them. Since extended family conflict is often complicated by the expectation of relatives that they should be able to decide for the couple or individual, with threats of ostracism or even witchcraft if their decisions are not obeyed, this aspect deserves further attention. While the author gives numerous Scripture references in support of sharing in the extended family, those passages calling for Christians to put God's will ahead of family requirements and expectations are not mentioned. Some guidance on a biblical balance of these two emphases in Scripture would be welcome. This book gives valuable guidance on sharing materially and strengthening relationships and bonds in the extended family. Bitrus broadens the definition of extended family to include the whole world, as we encounter needy neighbours, and he calls for special bonds of unity among Christians worldwide as we represent the Kingdom of God. The author's final challenge clearly expresses his heart's desire, that well-trained, godly African theologians, who take Scripture as their base and "adhere to the basic presuppositions of historic Christianity" as called for by Byang Kato, will rise to the challenge of contextualizing Christianity in ways that affirm Africanness while being true to God's word and will for his Kingdom.

129. **Blakely, Thomas D., Walter E. A. van Beek, and Dennis L. Thomson, editors**

Religion in Africa: Experience and Expression

Martlesham, UK: James Currey, 1994. 528 pages, ISBN: 9780852552070.

To treat the amazing diversity of religious belief, expression, and practice in Africa, we have this large eclectic volume of essays stemming from a conference in 1986 at Brigham Young University in Utah, USA. Over twenty scholars from four continents contribute, the great majority from America, Belgium, and the Netherlands. All but two, a retired Nigerian university president and a Catholic priest serving in Ghana, were based in Western universities at the time of publication. The quality of scholarship is high, much is based on field research, and the intended readership would be post-graduate students and specialists in the religions of Africa. The collection covers an extremely broad range of subjects and approaches. Some examples would be: "Cultural Change and Religious Conversion in West Africa" (Ghana); "Christ in African Folk Theology: The Nganga Paradigm" (Malawi); "Women and Power in an Edo Spirit Possession Cult" (Nigeria); "Archaeological and Other Prehistoric Evidence of Traditional African Religious Expression"; "Kimbanguism and the Question of Syncretism in Zaïre"; and "Music Performance among the Kpelle of Liberia." All the contributions focus upon sub-Saharan Africa, but with a relative neglect of East Africa. Among the most instructive papers is one by Lamin Sanneh, "Translatability in Islam and Christianity in Africa." The eminent Yale professor focuses attention upon the disparity of attitudes toward indigenisation in the two religions. Whereas Islam has pursued the "goal of alienating the vernacular" with an emphasis upon the non-translatable Qur'an, Christianity has "adopted these [African] languages as necessary and sufficient channels of biblical revelation and worship."

Notions of religious and social reform in Muslim and Christian communities have been strongly influenced by these attitudes toward the vernacular. Sanneh proposes that "Christian reform . . . constituted the vernacular into a principle of renewal and national pride."

130. Blaschke, Robert C.

Quest for Power: Guidelines for Communicating the Gospel to Animists

Belleville, Canada: Guardian Books, 2001. 173 pages, ISBN: 9781553063278.

Blaschke was a missionary with the international mission SIM in the Benin Republic for 27 years, doing pioneer church planting among the animistic Boko people. The first part of this book analyses the spiritual plight of animists, as being in bondage to evil spiritual powers that inflict illness and catastrophe. Animists most easily understand salvation as deliverance from the influence of these powers, and conversion as a change of allegiance to worship the Creator in Jesus. Encounters that demonstrate the power of Jesus over evil spirits or influences are the most common triggers of conversion. Only after conversion do most animists begin to understand the other main aspect of salvation, deliverance from the power and consequences of personal sin, the point from which Western evangelists usually start. Boko concepts of *alafia* (wellbeing), curses and mediation acted as bridges for Blaschke as he started teaching from Genesis. He makes considerable use of insights from Johannes Warneck's book *The Living Christ and Dying Heathenism* (1954). The second part of the book describes the "Event Oriented Discipling" method used to train emerging Boko church leaders. Blaschke finds this method similar to that of the Apostle Paul and consistent with traditional African educational methods. This is a useful book for anyone seeking to evangelize animists, particularly in Africa. It is also a biblically based defence for this approach.

131. Bloomberg, Charles, and Saul Dubow

Christian-Nationalism and the Rise of the Afrikaner Broederbond in South Africa, 1918–48

London: Palgrave Macmillan, 1990. 280 pages, ISBN: 9780333487068.

Bloomberg was a South African journalist who in 1963 published a series of articles exposing a secret, all-male Afrikaner society called the *Afrikaner Broederbond* (Afrikaner Brotherhood). Bloomberg died in 1985, leaving behind an unwieldy 600,000-word manuscript which has been skilfully edited by South African historian Saul Dubow (currently a professor of history at Sussex University). The Broederbond played a determinative role in all spheres of South African life from its inception in 1918 until the end of apartheid in the early 1990s, promoting Afrikaner nationalism and independence from Great Britain, providing social and economic upliftment for poor Afrikaners, promoting the Afrikaans language and Afrikaner culture, and exercising political power through the National Party. The society achieved this end by recruiting Afrikaner academics, politicians, school teachers, Dutch Reformed ministers, policemen, businessmen and others in influential positions. Bloomberg shows how the Broederbond created its ideology of Afrikaner Christian-Nationalism by drawing upon the neo-Calvinist philosophy developed by Abraham Kuyper and others at the Free University in Amsterdam. It is not coincidental that theologians and church leaders, many of whom trained in Holland, played a key role in the development of Afrikaner Christian-Nationalism. However, the ambivalent role that Calvinism played in South Africa is highlighted by the fact that many of the high-profile Afrikaners who opposed apartheid from the 1960s onwards were Reformed theologians. The editor's preface exposes a number of the book's most important flaws: the view that Afrikaners as a group saw themselves as God's chosen people fulfilling a "messianic destiny" has been discredited; the Broederbond was probably not as influential in the National Party government as Bloomberg and others once thought; and most importantly, the rise of Afrikaner Nationalism had many causes and should not be traced exclusively to neo-Calvinism. Despite these problems, Bloomberg's obsessive research ensures that this book will continue to serve as a valuable supplement to standard works on the Afrikaner people, Afrikaner Nationalism and South African history.

132.   Blum, William

Forms of Marriage: Monogamy Reconsidered

Eldoret: Gaba Publications, 1989. 317 pages, ISBN: 9789966836007.

Blum, in his reworked doctoral dissertation, argues that monogamy is the timeless biblical standard. The book has three parts: (1) a study of African marriage customs and concepts, (2) a theological study of monogamy and polygamy, and (3) the matter of baptising polygamists into the church. Since Blum is Roman Catholic, he faces Catholic issues about the validity of marriages not consecrated by priests and the seriousness of not being baptized. But he addresses many issues that all Christians face: what about converts who have plural wives before they believe, the level of church involvement allowed to polygamous persons, the validity of traditional marriages, and responsibility of polygamous men to their wives and children (past and present). Blum, an American who has worked in Uganda, did his doctoral studies in Rome. The book is of interest to readers who wish to think critically about Christian marriage in Africa, and for libraries serving those who do.

Blyth, Mike

see review 362

133.   Bodunrin, P. O., editor

Philosophy in Africa: Trends and Perspectives

Ile-Ife, Nigeria: Obafemi Awolowo University Press, 1985. 279 pages, ISBN: 9789781360725.

This book contains selected papers from the International Conference on African Philosophy held at the University of Ibadan, Nigeria, in February 1981. The book is divided into four parts, the most important of which is the second, on epistemology, which deals mainly with Kwasi Wiredu's concept of truth in the Akan language. The editor, the late Professor Bodunrin, was professor of philosophy in the University of Ibadan and Obafemi Awolowo University, Ile-Ife. The contributors work in different branches of philosophy and are from Africa, Germany and the United States, but all have sought to relate their disciplines to Africa. The book is fairly technical, and by now rather dated, but it could be useful for those seeking exposure to advanced-level philosophical discussion relating to Africa.

134. Boer, Jan H.

Christians and Muslims: Parameters for Living Together: Studies in Christian-Muslim Relations, Volume 8

Belleville, Canada: Essence Publishing, 2009. 562 pages, ISBN: 9781554524099.

Boer holds a PhD from the Free University of Amsterdam, and served for 30 years in northern Nigeria. This eighth volume of his *Studies in Christian-Muslim Relations* series gives his solution to Nigeria's Muslim-Christian crisis. In short, the solution is true religious pluralism. Boer assumes that all of life is religious. Islam is a religious worldview that impacts all of life. Although some Nigerian Christians favour secularism as an alternative, Boer rejects this option since secularism excludes God from parts of our life. For Boer, rooted in the holistic theological perspective of the Dutch theologian-politician Abraham Kuyper, Christianity in its truest sense is a religious worldview that impacts all of life. So religious pluralism is the only way for Nigeria to accommodate at least two religious worldviews. Democratic pluralism means that every citizen will have full human rights. Thus, for example, Muslims in Jos should have full political rights, and Christians in sharia states should have full religious and political freedoms. Religious democratic pluralism means that women should have equal rights in the country, but it may also mean that federal universities impose dress codes for both male and female students. Religious pluralism will allow the formation of Christian and Muslim political parties and religious banking systems. Boer also believes that there should be two parallel religious legal systems in Nigeria – sharia law and common law, since Boer believes that Nigerian common law is really a Christian law. Boer's proposal for Nigeria is a bold one. His total rejection of secularism is commendable, as is his fundamental assumption of the religious nature of all of life. His proposal of democratic pluralism is a welcome contribution. But there is a danger of polarisation in society. Nigeria has rightly shunned the idea of religious political parties for fear of religious polarisation. Boer's assertion that common law is Christian needs to be questioned. Nigerian common law seems more to be a neutral instrument in a pluralistic society that accommodates people of all religions. Putting sharia law as a parallel legal system to Nigerian common law is a bad idea. Despite such core deficiencies, Boer's analyses and proposals deserve close attention, and can open up fresh, fruitful reflection and interaction on the tangled issues of how to attain workable Christian-Muslim relations not only in Nigeria but also elsewhere.

135. Boer, Jan H.

Christians: Why this Muslim Violence?: Studies in Christian-Muslim Relations, Volume 3

Belleville, Canada: Essence Publishing, 2004. 334 pages, ISBN: 9781553067276.

This third volume in a multi-volume series by Boer on Muslim-Christian relations in Nigeria considers the Christian perception of religious violence in Nigeria, namely that the Muslims are to blame. Nigerian Christians are convinced that interreligious tensions are caused by the Muslims. The Christians adduce many reasons. They are convinced that Muslims in Nigeria and worldwide "have a natural instinct for domination." Boer quotes from a number of prominent Nigerian Christian individuals and organisations to show that this is a "largely unanimous" viewpoint. Related to this is the perceived nature of Islam. Islam, the Christians maintain, is intolerant, totalitarian and manipulative. In addition, Nigerian Christians assume that the Nigerian government is biased in favour of the Muslims. In respect to policies, appointments, grants, education, pilgrimages and the like, Nigerian Christians assume that the government at all levels is partial toward the Muslims. Boer then looks at the Nigerian Christian view of some of the main religious clashes in the last few decades. The Nigerian Christians believe that each disturbance was caused by the Muslims. This book is valuable in setting forth the Christian perspective on the question. The author, who knows Nigeria very well, has consulted a large number of local sources. The bibliography is impressive. But since this volume contains only one perspective, it should be read together with the previous and subsequent volumes.

136.   **Boer, Jan H.**

Christians: Why We Reject Muslim Law: Studies in Christian-Muslim Relations, Volume 4

Belleville, Canada: Essence Publishing, 2008. 528 pages, ISBN: 9781554522170.

Sharia law is a very sensitive issue in Nigeria. The previous volume in Boer's series gave the Muslim perspective on sharia; the present volume offers the Christian perspective. The result is more than 500 pages of negative Christian feelings towards sharia. While the Muslims start with the Islamic *theory* of sharia, the Christians judge sharia on the basis of their *experience* of sharia in Nigeria, and this experience is overwhelmingly negative. At the time of writing, twelve of Nigeria's 36 states had adopted sharia law. But the Christians claimed that this is unconstitutional, since Nigeria is a secular or multi-religious country. Sharia law makes Christians into second-class citizens in these sharia states, and there is systematic discrimination against Christians. Church buildings are sometimes demolished, and it is difficult to get permits to build new churches. Also restrictions on evangelism and conversion occur in these states. Northern Christians (such as among the Hausa, Fulani or Kanuri) are discriminated against and harassed. Sharia law reflects the Islamic "grand plan" to Islamise the nation and the world. Sharia law also discriminates against women, both Muslim and Christian. Two chapters are devoted to the views of two prominent Christian leaders in Nigeria, Wilson Sabiya of the Lutheran Church of Christ in Nigeria (LCCN), and Yusufu Turaki of the Evangelical Church of West Africa (ECWA). A final lively and informative chapter focuses on the stance of the Church of Christ in Nigeria (COCIN) in Plateau State in the last decade. This book will resonate strongly with Christians especially in the north of Nigeria. The author quotes a diversity of well-known Nigerian Christians. But the author's personal views on sharia, and on Christian-Muslim relations in Nigeria, are reserved for the next and final volume. Christians will appreciate this volume, but they should read it together with the previous one giving the Muslim perspective on sharia.

137.   **Boer, Jan H.**

Muslims: Why Muslim Sharia Law: Studies in Christian-Mulsim Relations, Volume 6

Belleville, Canada: Essence Publishing, 2007. 400 pages, ISBN: 9781554520619.

On 27 January 2000, Zamfara State in Nigeria instituted sharia law. Within the decade, twelve of Nigeria's 36 states had done so. Suddenly sharia law became a hot topic in Nigeria. This sixth volume of Boer's series, *Studies in Christian-Muslim Relations*, looks at the Muslim perspective on sharia, while the seventh volume considers the Christian perspective. Boer begins here by describing the Muslim theory of sharia. Sharia is for the Muslim not just a legal system but a way of life. One Muslim source says, "Sharia is simply the complete way of life of a Muslim"; another calls sharia "a complete scheme of life and an all-embracing social order where nothing is superfluous and nothing is lacking." Around AD 1800 Uthman dan Fodio instituted sharia in the northern part of what is now Nigeria. But the colonial and the post-colonial period suppressed it. When sharia was reinstituted in recent decades, Muslims in the north of Nigeria had high hopes of a transformed society. Wealthy Muslims, for example, were now to pay the zakat tithe and avoid corruption. But voices from Muslim villages began to complain that nothing had changed. Also sharia was not being fully implemented in the northern states. The governor of Bauchi State, for example, delayed in approving thirty sentences of amputation in his state. The sharia law also attracted international human rights attention, especially when women were sentenced to death by stoning for committing adultery. (Most of these sentences were not carried out.) A further question is the constitutionality of sharia. How constitutional is it in a multi-religious country? This well-researched book, with 38 pages of bibliography, presents Muslim perspectives on the theory and practice of sharia. The author reserves his opinions until the eighth and final volume. If Christians of Nigeria are to understand the viewpoints of their Muslim neighbours, this book could prove vital reading.

138. Boer, Jan H.

Muslims: Why the Violence?: Studies in Christian-Muslim Relations, Volume 2

Belleville, Canada: Essence Publishing, 2004. 208 pages, ISBN: 9781553067191.

Nigeria has seen a large number of violent clashes between Muslims and Christians in the last three decades. The first volume of Boer's *Studies in Christian-Muslim Relations* series catalogues these riots. This second volume offers the Muslim perspective on this violence, while the third volume gives the Christian view. Here Boer catalogues the deep feeling among Nigerian Muslims that they have been oppressed and discriminated against by secular and Christian forces. In this view the ideal Muslim society was established in northern Nigeria by Usman dan Fodio in the early 1800s. This society was religious in all aspects. But this utopia was destroyed by the British colonialists around 1900, who instead instituted a "Christo-secular government establishment." In the current post-colonial period, Muslims still feel betrayed. Secularism with all of its vices militates against an ideal religious society. So why the violence? Muslims claim religious, political, economic, and other factors to explain their deep discontent. We could call these root causes. This book intends only to portray the Muslim mind; value judgements come in a later volume. As such the book is an invaluable contribution. But it also leaves one with the feeling that while Muslims may have some legitimate grievances against colonialism and present secular Nigerian society, such grievances hardly justify the level of violence that Muslims have perpetuated against Christians so systematically in recent decades in Nigeria. In today's world people of different faiths need to find non-violent ways to coexist.

139. Boer, Jan H.

Muslims: Why We Rejected Secularism

Belleville, Canada: Essence Publishing, 2005. 272 pages, ISBN: 9781553069447.

The issue of secularism constitutes a major stumbling block in Christian-Muslim relations in Africa. Muslims are opposed to secularism; Christians may often seem to support it. This fourth volume of Boer's series on Christian-Muslim relations looks at the Nigerian Muslim view of secularism, while the next volume gives the Nigerian Christian view. Exploring a considerable range of written material, letters, lectures, newspaper articles, and other published and unpublished documents, Boer finds that secularism is a major concern in Nigerian Muslim rhetoric. The reason is that Islam is a world-and-life religion; Islam is understood to impact all of life. As one Nigerian Muslim wrote in a Nigerian newspaper, "Islam is a complete way of life." Secularism is defined by one Nigerian Muslim as "the separation of the worldly from the spiritual." Another Muslim defines secularism as "an attempt to run society on a basis other than religion." Again, "secularism is simply an attempt to reconstruct society without reference to God." Since all of life is religion, Muslims reject secularism. Nigerian Muslims also blame the Christian West for bringing secularism to Africa. The title of chapter 4 sums up their complaint: "The unholy triad: Christianity, colonialism and secularism." As a Calvinistic Christian, the author agrees fully with the Muslim rejection of secularism. If Jesus is the Lord over all of life, then we as Christians cannot support secularism. Of course, the question remains as to how two holistic religions, biblical Christianity and Islam, can coexist in one society. But this is a question for a later volume. This book is recommended as a bold attempt to hear and understand Nigerian Islam in its own voice.

140.   **Boer, Jan H.**

Nigeria's Decades of Blood 1980–2002: Studies in Christian-Muslim Relations, Volume 1

Belleville, Canada: Essence Publishing, 2003. 160 pages, ISBN: 9781553065814.

This book is the first in an intended series dealing with Christian/Muslim relations in northern Nigeria during recent decades. Boer brings at least three things to such a study: 30 years of missionary service in Nigeria; a holistic (non-secular) understanding of Christianity; and respect for and friendship with Muslims based upon many years of interaction with them. The book begins by identifying "secularism" as one of the most difficult issues between Christians and Muslims. The author believes that most Christians, including missionaries who brought Christianity to Africa, have wrongfully promoted "secularism" without realising the full implications of what they were doing. Boer appeals to the perspective of Abraham Kuyper, and believes that an understanding of Kuyper's holistic approach to Christianity and a rejection of secularism as commonly understood in the Western world would help to promote a better understanding between Christians and Muslims. The main part of the book is a survey of the religious riots in Nigeria, starting with the uprising in 1982 over the location of the St. George's Anglican Church in Kano, and continuing with subsequent riots and conflicts, including those in Kaduna, Katsina, Bauchi, Plateau and Borno States. The book contains specific names and dates and therefore provides a useful historical resource for this turbulent time in Nigeria's history. The material for this book comes from newspaper and magazine articles, interviews, emails and journals of those who witnessed various events, as well as from Boer's own personal experience. Boer makes every attempt to be fair and objective, presenting reports from both Christian and Muslim perspectives; he makes no attempt, for example, to cover up or justify the atrocities committed by Christians. Two issues that one could wish might be addressed in subsequent volumes of the series would be: (1) a more thorough explanation of the historical roots of the tension between the Hausa/Fulani and the "Middle Belt" people of Nigeria; and (2) a better understanding of the relation between current Christian/Muslim tensions in Nigeria and the overall tension between Muslims and non-Muslims around the world. In a time of great tension between radical Islam and much of the rest of the world, this book makes a considerable contribution to understanding the issues and events particular to the conflict between Christians and Muslims in one crucial part of Africa.

141. **Boesak, Willa**

God's Wrathful Children: Political Oppression and Christian Ethics

Grand Rapids: Eerdmans, 1995. 264 pages, ISBN: 9780802806215.

A senior lecturer in theological ethics at the University of the Western Cape in South Africa, Boesak challenges the post-apartheid nation's black people to channel their understandable political rage in constructive ways. The book is divided into three sections. Section 1 gives a perspective on the resistance of the indigenous people during the colonial and apartheid eras in South Africa, leading up to the black quest for vengeance. Section 2 moves outside South Africa to examine "the Jewish Zealots of first-century Palestine, the late medieval Christian reformer Thomas Muntzer, and the African-American activist Malcolm X, as they shaped their ethical position on wrath and violence." While the past experiences, passions and motives opt for retaliation, section 3 weighs the quest for vengeance "in the light of traditional theological categories such as love, forgiveness, sacrifice, and peace." In so doing, Boesak tests the understandable political anger against biblical and theological-ethical principles. The long history of abuses against the black people has left deep wounds which cannot be ignored simply because South Africa is now a "post-apartheid" state. Thus Boesak calls for a new comprehensive, interfaith examination of both the positive aspects of vengeance and the hateful aspects of revenge. Boesak's contention is that this will lead to necessary, realistic, and compensatory actions in order to curb post-apartheid black political rage and move South Africa's black people toward genuine emotional healing.

142. **Boge, Paul H.**

Father to the Fatherless: The Charles Mulli Story

Pickering, Canada: Castle Quay, 2005. 240 pages, ISBN: 9781897213025.

The author is a professional engineer and writer who has taught at the Mully Children's Family orphanage in Kenya. This biography of Charles Mulli, the founder of that ministry, shows how Mulli went from abandoned child to rich businessman to a sacrificial servant who has invited over 700 children to join his family. Mulli's story first came to light in Wilbur O'Donovan's *Biblical Christianity in Modern Africa*, though only his first name is given there. The fuller story is in this book. Though this would be classed as an inspirational story, it is also an example of evangelical African Reconstruction Theology in action. The Mulli family, wife and eight children included, and now a great many volunteers like Boge, give street children, abandoned children and HIV/AIDS orphans a new family and a new life, both socially and spiritually. The stories of poverty and dreadful hardship in Mulli's own childhood and those of the children who now call him "father" vividly portray the desperate needs of vulnerable children. To survive they become child prostitutes, thieves, gang members, and drug addicts. The love of God through Mulli demonstrates that Christians who embrace radical obedience can make a miraculous impact in the lives of even these hardened hearts. The book is a biography of a life in process; the reader is left wanting to know more of this ministry, as well as more of the man who founded it. As a result of his own experience in Mulli's ministry, the author is obviously enthralled by Mulli's faith, which gives this book the feel of a particularly well-written modern hagiography. But it is also one of too few books about African Christians who are tackling Africa's mega-problems one relationship at a time.

143.   **Bok, Francis, and Edward Tivnan, editors**

Escape from Slavery: The True Story of My Ten Years in Slavery—and My Journey to Freedom in America

New York: St. Martin's Press, 2003. 298 pages, ISBN: 9780312306243.

When he was seven years old Francis Bok was selling eggs and nuts in the market place of his home village in southern Sudan. On that day his world was demolished. Murahaliin militia, armed by the Sudanese government, invaded his village, slaughtered the men and carried off the cattle and most of the women and children. Francis became a slave. For ten years he lived with a northern Sudanese family who beat him, ridiculed him, and treated him as one of their animals, until he escaped and made his way to Khartoum, then to Cairo, and finally to the United States as a refugee. This narrative of Bok's life is a compelling story of suffering courage – and simple faith in God. Bok more recently works for the Boston-based American Anti-Slavery Group, and has had the opportunity to share his story in a variety of venues. The continuing existence of human slavery in modern Africa is a troubling reality.

144.   **Bond, Bruce, and Norene Bond**

When Spider Webs Unite They Can Tie Up A Lion

Auckland: Self-published by Bruce & Norene Bond, 2005. 280 pages, ISBN: 9780473105921.

The authors, from New Zealand, served under the international mission SIM in Ethiopia from 1953 until 1994. The title of their book is taken from an Ethiopian proverb. They write that, approaching their assignment, they felt "much like spider webs – fragile, weak, and unsuitable for the massive task awaiting us. How could we possibly 'tie up a lion'?" And as the Bonds would soon discover, there was never a shortage of "lions" to be tied up. Bruce had trained in an agricultural college, Norene at a teacher training college. They thus proved a perfect team for the newly opened leprosarium at Shashamane, she as a teacher of lepers' children, he as the resident agriculturalist. Later they served as teachers at the ministry training college in Dilla. When their children reached secondary school age, the Bonds returned to New Zealand for their education, and Bruce found himself appointed the SIM New Zealand home director, in which post he served for fifteen years. They then returned to Ethiopia to head up an ambitious agricultural scheme, but Bruce was soon co-opted by fellow missionaries to be the SIM field director. During this period the Marxist regime fell, a democratic government was elected, freedoms were restored to the people, and the persecuted underground church sprang to life. Bible schools closed by the Marxists were reopened, a new degree-granting theological college was launched in Addis Ababa, and the church began an era of unprecedented growth. This book is an easy and delightful read, giving an excellent personal feel for some contemporary on-the-ground missionary labours in one part of Africa.

Bond, Norene

see review 144

145. **Bone, David S., editor**

Malawi's Muslims: Historical Perspectives

Blantyre: CLAIM, 2000. 220 pages, ISBN: 9789990816150.

While the origins and development of Christianity in Malawi have been comprehensively chronicled, there is as yet very little available about how Islam reached this part of Africa and the ways in which it has developed. This book seeks to redress this neglect by making available, for the first time in some cases, the findings of scholarly research on aspects of Islam in Malawi. The material is divided into three sections. The focus of the first is broadly historical, examining the origins and development of Islam in Malawi and the agents who brought it about. Thus one paper gives an outline history of Islam and charts the rise of a new Muslim elite, another explains how and why the Yao people came to be so closely identified with Islam, and a third accounts for the founding of Malawi's first Muslim community in Nkhotakota. The essays in the second section deal respectively with Muslim Brotherhoods, Muslim-Christian relations, and Islamic education. The third section offers three texts which constitute important historical sources for the study of Islam in Malawi. The first is a report written in 1910 by Rev A. Hofmeyr of the Dutch Reformed Church Mission in Malawi. This is followed by the 1911 response to Hofmeyr's report by Archdeacon William Johnson of the Universities Mission to Central Africa, who worked among the Yao for almost 50 years and was the best informed about them of all the Christian missionaries. The final piece was written in 1979 by Ibrahim Panjawani, a leading member of Malawi's Asian community, and is probably the first published account by a Muslim of the history and status of Islam in Malawi. This book will prove of value to anyone seeking a better understanding of the Islamic presence in different parts of Africa, and of Christian-Muslim relations in such contexts.

146. **Bonnah, George Kwame Agyei**

The Holy Spirit: A Narrative Factor in the Acts of the Apostles

Stuttgart: Katholisches Bibelwerk, 2007. 248 pages, ISBN: 9783460005815.

This published Tübingen doctoral thesis, by a Ghanaian Roman Catholic priest, is an erudite study using narrative criticism to explore the prominent Lukan theme of the Holy Spirit. As one would expect from a German thesis (albeit written in English), the work opens with a long section (60 pages) discussing the *status quaestionis*, after which the author concludes that scholars are too apt to study only one aspect of Lukan Pneumatology, leading to "manifold dogmatic thoughts." As it turns out, Bonnah is not averse to seeing a multitude of themes as he explores Luke's use of the Spirit in Acts. Thus his major chapters elucidate Lukan Spirit-terminology, the "triadic" (though not yet Trinitarian) links between God, Jesus and the Spirit, the role of the Spirit in initiation, the connection between the Spirit and the OT Scriptures, and the Spirit in the church's mission. He concludes that none of the themes can be said to dominate Luke's theology of the Spirit. In fact his summary of his thesis cannot be reduced to a sentence or a paragraph but extends to six major points over four pages, followed by several pages of theological observations. The book is careful, thorough, and well written. There is little that is new here, but Bonnah does manage to put between two covers a massive amount of useful material about the Spirit in the book of Acts. Does this dissertation actually answer a question? Perhaps – if one allows the "question" to be very broad: what are the roles of the Spirit in Acts? The answer to that question does not receive a simple one-sentence answer from Bonnah; neither does he present a novel theory. Perhaps that is not such a bad thing: it is useful to have a single volume which summarizes the basic scholarly consensus. This is a solid piece of scholarship on an important topic. Outside of the acknowledgements, however, there is no mention of Africa, or the way this biblical theme might inform African thinking or practice specifically.

147. Boraine, Alex

A Country Unmasked: Inside South Africa's Truth and Reconciliation Commission

Cape Town: Oxford University Press, 2000. 484 pages, ISBN: 9780195718058.

Boraine was the deputy chairperson of the South African Truth and Reconciliation Commission (TRC), and offers here an insider's view of what went on behind the scenes of what was probably one of the most important events in the recent history of that country. The book begins with a description of the pre-history of the TRC. As South Africa moved towards normalisation, many of its citizens realized the need to deal with the past. After various conferences, much discussion and heated negotiations, the Interim Constitution included a "postamble" which called for a "mechanism" to deal with amnesty, "in order to advance . . . reconciliation and reconstruction." This statement eventually led to the creation of the TRC, which held its first hearing in April 1996, and published its five-volume report in October 1998. While the hearings into human rights violations are over, certain aspects of the Commission's work continued afterward. This is a very personal book: Boraine's respect for Desmond Tutu is clearly expressed, as is his frustration, and sometimes anger, with other commissioners. In two riveting chapters Boraine also discusses the TRC's dealings with P. W. Botha and Winnie Madikizela-Mandela, and his personal antipathy towards them and their behaviour. The Commission's inability to expose the machinations of Botha's State Security Council, or Madikizela-Mandela's "Football Club," highlight the TRC's inability to deal with those who were unwilling participants in the process. Boraine acknowledges the central role that Christianity played in the TRC. The chairperson and two commissioners were ordained ministers. Boraine himself had been elected as the President of the Methodist Church in Southern Africa in 1970, before moving into business and then politics. It is therefore surprising that Boraine admits to being "somewhat critical of the general emphasis on the Christian faith" that characterized the TRC. It might even be argued that the Christian understanding of forgiveness and reconciliation was crucial to the success of the TRC, and that commissions which attempt similar projects without this basis risk failure. Readers who want a philosophical examination of the work of the TRC will have to look elsewhere, but those wishing a basic understanding of the history of the process and the major players involved are advised to start here.

148. Borer, Tristan Anne

Challenging the State: Churches as Political Actors in South Africa, 1980–1994

Notre Dame: University of Notre Dame Press, 1998. 309 pages, ISBN: 9780268008291.

Borer, Assistant Professor of Government at Connecticut College (USA), writes on the changing role played by the South African Council of Churches (SACC) and the Southern African Catholic Bishops Conference (SACBC) in the demise of apartheid in South Africa. She focuses on the way in which these two organisations viewed the South African government's legitimacy and their responses to it. The influences that changing political contexts (increasing oppression, the banning of opposition organisations) and religious contexts (Vatican II, liberation theology) had on the two organisations are described, in an attempt to understand the different approaches they took. The institutional differences between the SACC and SACBC are also shown to have been important factors in determining their respective responses to apartheid. Most studies of the anti-apartheid struggle pay inadequate attention to the role played by Christian groups; this work begins to fill that lacuna. The final chapter raises questions regarding the relationship between church and state in post-apartheid South Africa. While Borer provides a useful summary of the developments in South African theology from the 1960s to the early 1990s, the book is content with description and does not offer a theological analysis or discussion of the church's role in South Africa.

149. Bosch, David J.

Believing in the Future: Toward a Missiology of Western Culture

Leominster, UK: Gracewing, 1998. 80 pages, ISBN: 9780852443330.

This small but dense volume is by the widely-respected South African missiologist David Bosch, and was among the last documents to come from his pen. It was written in the form of an essay in late 1991, and was presented by Bosch to a forum in Paris in January 1992, just a few short months before his tragic death that same year. The book talks about modern Western culture in relation to the gospel. In the first part, Bosch outlines what he believes to be the major aspects of the post-modern world. It reads something like a theology book, but for those who have not studied seriously the present "post-modern" world, this offers a very good outline of the influences and thinking that shape people's ideas and behaviour, particularly in the Western world but increasingly everywhere that Western values penetrate, including Africa. Bosch then offers his ideas on how and why this is the case. Not everyone will agree with his analysis, but in typical Bosch fashion he stirs up the reader's mind. In the second part, Bosch outlines what he calls the "contours" of a missiology for Western culture. Although these "contours" are not explicitly identified in the text, it would seem that Bosch meant to include such topics as: social ethics, the third world, religion (faith in God), and worldview. One of the crucial statements made in this discussion relates to the nature of the Church. While it is not a new thought from Bosch, it does form part of the basis for any appropriate missiology for Western (and westernized) cultures. The statement is: "We are in need of a missiological agenda for theology, not just a theological agenda for mission: for theology, rightly understood, has no reason to exist other than critically to accompany the missio Dei." Finally, Bosch states six other topics needed as less significant ingredients for this "missiology of western culture." They are: the ecological dimension, counter-cultural (i.e. against hedonism), ecumenical, contextual, the laity and the local, and the worshipping community. The book requires concentration when reading, but if this can be deployed, the reader will finish with a greater grasp not only of modern Western and westernized culture, but also of how the Christian gospel can and must address that culture missiologically.

150. Bosch, David J.

Transforming Mission: Paradigm Shifts in Theology of Mission

Maryknoll, NY: Orbis, 2011. 640 pages, ISBN: 9781570759482.

Bosch, an eminent international missiologist, served as professor of missiology and dean of the faculty of theology at the University of South Africa in Pretoria until his untimely death in 1992. In this notable study he contends for three related theses. First, Christian thinking about missionary motives and aims has undergone a major change since the end of World War II. Second, during eras stretching from NT times until the present, several different understandings, or paradigms, of mission have been dominant. An awareness of such differing "theologies of mission," and of the transitions that took place as one understanding gave way to another, are necessary in order to assess the present moment. Finally, the present situation confronts the church both with profound danger as well as with a wonderful opportunity to move forward. The first third of the book analyses the biblical understandings of missions. The second third examines dominant missionary theologies throughout the history of the church. The final third explores the current crisis in the theology of mission, and offers Bosch's proposal for a theology of mission that will allow the church to take advantage of the opportunity currently offered it. While this book is important in several respects, for reasons of space only two will be cited here. First, this book proffers a sweeping yet acute analysis of missions thinking throughout the history of the church. Second, Bosch's appraisal of the current moment, and his missiological proposals, offer valuable food for thought. While the book is too long for any except advanced students, those teaching theology of mission, evangelism, and church history in Africa need to read and digest it. And for the libraries of theological institutions in Africa, having this book is a must.

151.   **Botman, H. Russel, and Robin Petersen, editors**

To Remember and to Heal: Theological and Psychological Reflections on Truth and Reconciliation

Cape Town: Human & Rousseau, 1996. 172 pages, ISBN: 9780798136440.

How does one begin to deal pastorally with the sheer magnitude and trauma of what happened to men and women under South African apartheid? Victims, perpetrators and passive bystanders have all in recent times been compelled to look again at the past, and this process of examination will continue for some time to come. Herein lies the value of this important book, for it is an attempt by theologians and a psychologist to address the vexed pastoral issue of how one deals with the past. Each contributor to this volume has provided considerable food for thought, not least the essays by Willa Boesak ("Truth, Justice and Reconciliation"); Robin Petersen ("The Politics of Grace and the Truth and Reconciliation Commission"); Molefe Tsele ("Kairos and Jubilee"); Wolfram Kistner ("The Biblical Understanding of Reconciliation"); and Dirkie Smit ("Confession-Guilt-Truth-and-Forgiveness in the Christian Tradition"). But pride of place in this collection must go to the utterly compelling testimony of Fr. Michael Lapsley whose body was torn apart and disfigured by a letter bomb that exploded in his face. For Lapsley's testimony alone this book is worth acquiring. His words must surely take their place as one of the great Christian statements of faith in the face of human evil.

152.   **Bouba Mbima, Timothée, editor**

La théologie pratique en milieu africain: Ouvrage d'enseignement dans les Facultés et Instituts de théologie

Yaoundé: Éditions Clé, 2002. 200 pages, ISBN: 9782723501712.

The Cameroon publisher Éditions Clé has established a goal to produce resources for seminary students in French-speaking Africa. The publication of this textbook in practical theology, partly funded by the World Council of Churches, results from the collaborative effort of four francophone authors. Four of the book's five chapters are fresh contributions: two by Célestin Kiki, "Introduction to Practical Theology"; "Christian Liturgy," and one each by Samuel Motsebo, "Catechism" and Timothée Bouba Mbima, "Homiletics." The final chapter, "Sorcery and Counselling," by Masamba ma Mpolo, is a reprint from a paper delivered at a colloquium held in 2000 in Kinshasa, and subsequently published. The authors are imbued with the realities faced in pastoral ministry in Africa, which gives both focus and credibility to the volume. The writing style varies but is generally such that the content could be fairly easily grasped by the audience in view, namely pastoral candidates at a seminary. The volume provides a good starting point for discussions in a course on practical theology at the university level. As one of few such academic resources on practical theology available to francophone African seminaries, professors should consider this book for either the basic textbook or supplemental reading. Certainly all the francophone theological institutions in Africa operating at first-degree level should have this book available to their teaching staff and in their library.

153. Bourdanné, Daniel K., editor

Le Tribalisme en Afrique: et si on en parlait?

Cotonou, Benin: Éditions PBA, 2002. 177 pages, ISBN: 9782911752285.

Appropriately, this book addressing the problem of tribalism in Africa incorporates reflections of African evangelical Christians working in different countries: Daniel Bourdanné ("Avant-Propos") at the time of writing based in Ivory Coast; Antoine Rutayisiré ("Rwanda: Église et génocide") in Rwanda; Emmanuel Ndikumana ("Ministère de la reconciliation dans un contexte de conflit tribal") from Burundi; and Abel Ndjerareou ("Dieu et la tribu") from Chad. The authors from Rwanda and Burundi, having experienced the horrors of such conflict in recent history, exhort the Church to examine the situation, discuss it, and bring about reconciliation. Rutayisiré challenges pastors to rethink their presentation of the biblical message, for their message of the Church being God's channel of love rather than hate did not change the ordinary members in the pews. He therefore urges more participative Bible studies so that the members themselves discover and embrace the Christian ethic. In Burundi, Ndikumana was the national Secretary for the Groupes Bibliques Universitaires (GBU) during the genocide crisis. His article underscores the difficulties of trying to overcome long years of ethnic prejudice. Though the Hutu and Tutsi GBU members prayed fervently for each other, they then necessarily returned to their respective home environments, where traditional values and thinking held sway with family members. Throughout and after the turmoil, GBU leaders and members encouraged and helped each other, with support from other groups interested in reconciliation, such as the Mennonites. In the second half of this essay, Ndikumana sets forth his view of the Church's role in tribal reconciliation. Above all, he says, it must not be silent; it needs to be a voice for the voiceless. The final contribution in the volume comes from an OT scholar whose article supplies the biblical background for future solutions. His three approaches to the problem of tribalism are theological (Creation, Fall, human society structured around tribes and ethnic groupings, and God's ability to transform hearts and minds), missiological (God's plan to reach all the nations with the gospel message), ecclesiastical and ethical (living in love as a family of believers, and acting in love toward neighbours outside that circle). Finally, Ndjerareou calls the Church to repentance and to a strong programme of discipleship training, producing those who will be models of Christian love and ethics in their society. The leadership of the Church is challenged to be prophetic in its outlook, deeply involved in intercession, and fulfilling its role of teaching and shepherding the members. [Ndjerareou has developed his thoughts further in a separate publication, *De Quelle Tribu Es-Tu?* (2007).] This volume deserves wide circulation within Christian communities of francophone Africa, and publication in an English edition for anglophone Africa.

154.   **Bourdanné, Daniel K.**

Trois mariages pour un couple

Abidjan: Presses Bibliques Africaines, 1986. 85 pages.

This slim volume is among the books most frequently checked out of the library at one graduate seminary in Africa. It is by a Chadian long associated with IFES student work in francophone Africa (and now the IFES International General Secretary). Intended as a guide for the perplexed young African who wishes to marry and also be true to the God of the Bible, this book examines customary, civil, and church weddings in Africa. What form of wedding, or what combination of forms, should a Christian choose? The author starts the discussion about contextualized marriages and hopes that others will contribute their ideas. In francophone Africa, following French law, marriage is a civil act and must legally be undertaken before a civil authority, usually the local mayor. Yet this aspect should not, according to the author, overshadow the importance of the joining of two families through the customary marriage traditions, including the exchange of goods and (often) money. After all, the young couple will need the support of the family members in the future. Then there is the question of a church wedding. Can it be a simple, non-costly prayer of benediction by the pastor, or does it need to be an elaborate ceremony, complete with a white wedding gown and veil, and with numerous guests at a nuptial feast afterward? What is right for a Christian couple? In posing these questions, Bourdanné highlights the problems the young face today and attempts to help them think through the implications of their choices. The civil ceremony answers certain legal questions concerning the status of family members. The customary wedding invokes the union of two families. The church community functions as a witness and a support for the newlyweds. Should a young couple have all three types of weddings? This booklet is recommended for Christian youth ministries in francophone Africa, and especially those serving high school and university students. An edition for anglophone Africa would be very welcome.

155.   **Bourdillon, M. F. C.**

Religion and Society: A Textbook for Africa

Gweru, Zimbabwe: Mambo Press, 1990. 406 pages, ISBN: 9780869224922.

This book is intended to serve as an introductory text at university level for the study of African religion from a sociological point of view. Bourdillon is a Zimbabwean citizen who has taught sociology at the University of Zimbabwe for fifteen years and is widely published (eleven of his own articles and books are listed in the bibliography). Leading sociologists are cited and evaluated (e.g. Durkheim, Evans-Pritchard, Malinowski), although distinguished scholars from the author's own southern African perspective (e.g. Colson, Gluckman, Wilson) receive much less attention. Bourdillon uses many examples beyond Africa, including everything from American civil religion to Soviet Marxism. He is at pains to be morally and theologically neutral, "not focusing on whether thoughts are true or false." While this certainly makes the book suitable for a university setting, theological colleges may for that reason find it more useful as a resource than as a class text.

156. Bowen, John, editor

The Missionary Letters of Vincent Donovan: 1957–1973

Eugene, OR: Wipf & Stock, 2010. 252 pages, ISBN: 9781608991174.

Vincent Donovan's *Christianity Rediscovered*, first published in 1978, has become something of a "missionary classic." Many cross-cultural workers, especially but not exclusively those working in Africa, have been challenged and inspired by Donovan's work among the Maasai people of Tanzania. Disillusioned with the tendency of Western missionaries and mission societies to build institutions rather than simply offer the good news of Jesus Christ to those who had never heard the message, Donovan, a Roman Catholic priest of the Spiritan order, asked and received permission of his ecclesiastical superior to do primary evangelism. Along the way Donovan learned important lessons. And although Protestants may be tempted to say that much of what he learned are things that we have always known, it is actually fair to say that Protestants have not been any better at simply preaching the gospel story without Western accretions. Now that we are in an age in which more and more of the missionaries who work in cross-cultural situations are not "Western," it would do the entire missionary world good to take another look at Donovan's story. This recent book, edited by John Bowen of Wycliffe College in Toronto, provides that opportunity. Thanks to help from the Spiritans and from Donovan's sister, Bowen has been able to provide an intimate look at Donovan's thinking and how it progressed during his years working in various communities in northern Tanzania. The letters presented here are the regular correspondence that Donovan provided for his relatives and friends in the United States who supported him in his work. For those familiar with Donovan's famous book there are some surprises – such as that many of the lessons presented in *Christianity Rediscovered* as having been learned through his work with the Maasai were actually reflections on his work with the less well-known Sonjo people. In addition to the letters, Bowen appends reflections on three conversations with missionaries who worked with or took over from Donovan. Their views of what happened and what is now happening among those with whom Donovan worked differ substantially and are certainly worth pondering.

157. Bowers, Paul, editor

Evangelical Theological Education: An International Agenda

Springwood, Australia: ICETE, 1994. 125 pages.

This book is a reissue, under a single cover and with a new title and introduction, of two books previously published by Evangel in Nairobi. In its refurbished form, the book is the first title in the new series, *Evangelical Theological Education Today*, published by the International Council for Evangelical Theological Education (ICETE), which links continental associations of evangelical theological schools around the world (the association for evangelical theological schools in Africa, ACTEA, was a founding member of ICETE). The editor, long associated with theological education in Africa, served as the first general secretary of ICETE. The book consists of the principal papers given at ICETE's first two international consultations, which together set out ICETE's international agenda for excellence and renewal in theological education. At the first consultation in 1980 ICETE was founded; and at the second in 1981, held in Chongoni, Malawi, ICETE's well-known *Manifesto on the Renewal of Evangelical Theological Education* was first proposed. The book's importance lies in the global perspectives given by leading theological educators representing various regions of the world. Of the eight papers given, four are by Africa-based contributors; others represent Korea, India, Hong Kong, and

Brazil. This book will be useful for everyone wishing to understand evangelical theological education globally, and to consider the relevance of such a perspective for their own local contexts.

158.   Brain, Joy, and Philippe Denis, editors

The Catholic Church in Contemporary Southern Africa

Pietermaritzburg: Cluster, 1999. 427 pages, ISBN: 9781875053186.

This book was written by a team of Roman Catholic scholars from different cultural and professional backgrounds in southern Africa, working at the invitation of the Catholic Bishops Conference in the context of preparation for the new millennium. The editors are respectively emeritus professor of history at Durban-Westville University and professor of the history of Christianity at the University of Natal, both in South Africa. The book endeavours to present the history of the Catholic Church in contemporary southern Africa. The year 1951 (when the hierarchy in southern Africa was established) is used as the starting point, with reference to earlier events inserted as necessary, while some chapters deal with events as recent as 1999. The book attends to the entire Catholic community in South Africa, Botswana and Swaziland, and encompasses aspects of church life such as: church growth, clergy training, charitable works, politics, education, sexual ethics, spirituality and ecumenical endeavours. This is an important introduction to the establishment, growth and influence of Catholic Christianity in southern Africa. As such it is also an important contribution to the understanding of Christianity in this part of the world.

Brazelton, T. Berry

see review 638

159.   Bredekamp, Henry, and Robert Ross, editors

Missions and Christianity in South African History

Johannesburg: Witwatersrand University Press, 1995. 260 pages, ISBN: 9781868142903.

This collection of twelve essays makes an important contribution to South African mission historiography. These essays were selected from among papers presented at a conference held in 1992 at the University of Western Cape and Genadendal, entitled "People, Culture and Power: Christianity in South African History, 1792–1992." The essays address the relationship between foreign missionaries and the African (and slave or ex-slave) people whom they hoped to convert, and highlight the spiritual, social, economic and political context in which these communities, groups and individuals found themselves, and how they used the Christian faith as a means of empowerment. The emphasis in most essays is to reflect on the response of the local communities to the gospel, while also paying attention to the effects of the gospel on the liberation of women and the results of missionary intervention in local customs. The essays concentrate on a selected number of communities, groups and individuals (mainly from the Western Cape, Eastern Cape and Natal). The value of the book lies in the fresh approach to historical research, moving away from a concentration on the missionaries' understanding of the gospel and their emphasis on the "planting of churches," to an interpretation of the "growth of the church" from the viewpoint of the local communities themselves. The attempt to address the spiritual, social and cultural context of the new (and not so new) converts from their own viewpoint, and to reflect their experiences and interpretation, is an example well worth following by all those involved in research on African church history. It is clear from these essays that the spread of Christianity in southern Africa was very much the work and burden of African agents of the gospel. Yet they have thus far received little attention. These essays have made an important contribution towards correcting this neglect. The title of the book is rather broader than the content warrants, but the approach is an exemplary challenge for all who study the history of Christianity in Africa.

160.   Breman, Christina M.

The Association of Evangelicals in Africa: Its History, Organization, Members, Projects, External Relations and Message

Zoetermeer, Netherlands: Boekencentrum, 1996. 602 pages, ISBN: 9789023903369.

Here is ground-breaking work on a remarkable scale. In this revision of her PhD dissertation for Utrecht University, Breman has offered a comprehensive compilation of information on the Association of Evangelicals in Africa (AEA), and its continental constituencies. The extended subtitle exactly sets out the scope and structure of the project, and the range of data supplied for these topics is breath-taking. Breman was a researcher from the Netherlands who previously worked in Tanzania. This massive volume will now function as a welcome reference resource for information not otherwise easily obtainable on numerous groups and projects in Africa. It also offers extensive and hitherto inaccessible historical information on the early years of AEA. In addition, it seems likely that this publication could open up a whole new field in missiological inquiry. Although AEA is a vibrant, African-led body representing a major segment of the Christian community on the continent, and now more than 50 years old, the history and scope of its influence have gone largely unnoticed in Western missiological and historical literature. The breadth of detail provided by Breman will, if nothing else, easily invite refining, corrective, or auxiliary studies on individual topics, or suggest whole new themes for research. Not every interpretation provided will go unchallenged. In his foreword, AEA's General Secretary Dr Tokunboh Adeyemo warmly commends the study, but also suggests that the measure of AEA's achievement in the previous two decades has not been sufficiently accented; instead of describing this period in terms of "expansion," he (rightly, it would seem) suggests that "transformation" might be the more suitable word. The more than 120 pages of appendices present numerous valuable documents and listings, including the most comprehensive bibliographies so far published for either Byang Kato or Tokunboh Adeyemo. Most theological colleges in Africa working at degree level or higher should consider it obligatory to secure a copy for their library.

161.   Brockman, Norbert C.

An African Biographical Dictionary

Millerton, NY: Grey House Publishing, 2006. 667 pages, ISBN: 9781592371129.

This second edition of Brockman's reference work has been expanded to include 713 biographical sketches from sub-Saharan Africa. The names are in alphabetical order, with an index by nation, plus a new index showing names of missions, denominations and religious subjects. However, because there is no longer an index by sphere of influence (as in the first edition), it is not as easy to identify the coverage of religious figures. The first edition included 22 African Christian leaders, ten expatriate missionaries, thirteen prophets and leaders of New Religious Movements, sixteen Islamic figures and three leaders of African traditional religion. A sampling would include: S. Crowther, A. Boesak, A. Schwietzer, B. Naude, D. Livingstone, D. Tutu, E. Milingo, Frumentius, J. Krapf, J. Luwum, S. Kimbangu, A. Lenshina, and R. Moffat. The book appears to be meant as a first reference for inexperienced students. The entries are brief and simple, but do give references, including internet resources, for further information. The majority of articles have been revised for this second edition, and whereas there seemed to be a political emphasis in material on religious figures in the first edition, the second edition gives more coverage to their religious beliefs and accomplishments. Since the material offered is almost entirely secondary (abbreviated from elsewhere), this book is not an essential academic resource. However, it is a very handy reference tool, giving all African heads of state since independence, and Africans both famous and notorious in many fields.

162. **Brown, Stuart E., editor**

Seeking an Open Society: Inter-Faith Relations and Dialogue in Sudan Today

Nairobi: Paulines, 1997. 101 pages, ISBN: 9789966213327.

This volume includes seven papers on its theme. A brief introduction attempts to identify some lines of "openness" in Christian-Muslim dialogue. Two papers offer case studies of religious pluralism in Senegal and Nigeria respectively. Other papers (i) recount the spiritual pilgrimage of Abdullahi Sha Eldeen and his extended family from Islam to Christianity, and its implications for evangelism; (ii) consider Mahmud Muhammad Taha and republican movements; (iii) look at some means for progress in Christian-Muslim relationships in Sudanese society; and (iv) describe the growth of understanding in relationships between women of the two faiths. The collection concludes with a very brief attempt to suggest the next few steps. The empirical approach of the material underlines both the urgent need for practical moves in inter-faith relations in present-day Sudan, and the fairly elementary state of much Christian thinking about this topic.

163. **Brubaker, G, I Nankuni, and Grace Holland**

Church History, part 2: Lessons from the Church in Africa

Nairobi: Evangel, 2007. 287 pages.

This book is designed for theological education by extension (TEE) programmes in Africa, as part of the well-known series of TEE textbooks long under the direction of Drs Fred and Grace Holland. The principal author, Brubaker, worked with the Hollands in Zambia, has spent many years in Africa, and continues to lecture for short periods in Malawi. Thus he is familiar with the African context and has wide experience in TEE. This book covers African church history well, both geographically and chronologically, although (perhaps not surprisingly) it includes a larger section on Malawi and Zambia than would be found in books on this topic from other parts of the continent. Since it is designed as a TEE text, the English is simple and the content designed primarily for lower-level training. The sources used for the book are admittedly limited (Falk, Latourette and Shaw). Some assertions may be questioned, such as the "Ethiopian" eunuch taking the gospel to modern Ethiopia (actually it was to Nubia, or northern Sudan), and Simon Kimbangu being the messiah (he takes the place of the Holy Spirit in modern Kimbanguism). Illustrations can be overly positive, such as the British colonialist Lugard helping the Christians in Uganda (he used machine guns for the purpose), or Mobutu promoting church unity in Congo (DRC) by reorganising all churches into three bodies (the motive was political, and the means coercive, because Mobutu feared the churches' influence). In the author's eagerness to derive lessons from history (which is commendable), the net is spread rather wide, including attention to the brain drain, tithing, corruption and the theology of revival! Nevertheless, one must be impressed that he has covered African church history both in sufficient detail and in a very readable way for those with limited English. Use of his book need not be limited to TEE classes.

164. Bryan, Steven M.

Jesus and Israel's Traditions of Judgement and Restoration

Cambridge: Cambridge University Press, 2005. 296 pages, ISBN: 9780521010627.

Bryan previously served for more than two decades as a senior lecturer at the Ethiopian Graduate School of Theology in Addis Ababa, before his appointment as Professor of NT at Trinity Evangelical Divinity School in the United States. This volume is a revision of Bryan's University of Cambridge doctoral dissertation. Scholars largely agree that Jesus held to a realized eschatology. That is, God was restoring Israel in some manner through Jesus' own ministry (rather than at some future moment). Bryan addresses the question of the degree to which Jesus understood Israel's eschatological hopes to be realized in his ministry and the manner in which it was being accomplished. In order to do so, of course, Bryan must examine Jesus' words and actions within the context of Israel's traditions regarding these issues. Bryan contends that in contrast to a pattern found in Israel's prophetic writings whereby Israel is judged for its transgression and then subsequently restored, Jesus proclaimed both steps to be taking place simultaneously during his ministry. In doing so, however, Jesus also transformed Israel's numerous expectations for restoration. With regard to judgement and restoration, for example, Jesus pronounced certain judgement on Israel by referring to the "sign of Jonah" given to "this generation" (Mark 8:11–12; Matt 12:38–39). This theme is also found in Jesus' parables of the workers in the vineyard (Matt 20:1–16) and the eschatological banquet (Matt 22:1–14; Luke 14:16–24). At the same time, Jesus selected twelve disciples, proclaimed the presence of the kingdom of God, and made a triumphal entry into Jerusalem – all signs of Israel's restoration. Bryan makes his way through multiple complex issues in Jesus research, writing with clarity and verve. Students new to scholarly analysis of Jesus will benefit from these features of his work. Scholars will additionally profit from his stimulating, well-argued insights on debated issues such as the controversies over purity in Mark 7 and Luke 10. In particular, those who are teaching on Jesus and the Gospels need to make use of Bryan's thesis in their own classroom work if Christian leaders are to gain a solid understanding of just what it was that Jesus was trying to accomplish in his context. A better understanding of Jesus' aims should result in a more faithful church.

165. Buconyori, Elie A.

The Educational Task of the Church

Nairobi: Christian Learning Material Centre, 1993. 144 pages.

One of the strengths of this book is that the content for each chapter was earlier taught by the author as part of a course at Daystar University in Kenya entitled "Christian Educational Ministry." Class dialogue and suggestions from students then led to this final presentation. The former managing director of the Christian Learning Materials Centre in Nairobi, Buconyori is an experienced African educationalist from Burundi. His main emphasis is to help the church's educationalists understand that they should be teaching their church constituencies (of all age groups) to know that Christianity is a way of living which, to be truly Christian, must permeate every aspect of daily life. The first half of the book clearly defines Christian education. The biblical educational heritage from the OT and NT is briefly traced, because the author feels that this topic provides important educational models for today's Christian educators. Insight is also given (from an evangelical viewpoint) on how education and theology interact, in order to provide correct guidance for the Christian worker's educational efforts in the church. The second half of the book includes suggestions on how these educational concepts can be practised among children, youth, adults, and students of all age groups. Since this book is not meant to be the final authority on the African church's educational task, some topics are not fully amplified. For example, specific educational programmes for the church are covered very briefly. Helpful self-assessment activities at the end of each chapter enable the reader to review the content in an interesting, thought-provoking manner.

166.   **Buconyori, Elie A., editor**

Tribalism and Ethnicity / Tribalisme et Ethnicité

Nairobi: AEA, 1997.

This is a compendium of papers by lecturers and students of the Nairobi Evangelical Graduate School of Theology (NEGST) and the Bangui Evangelical School of Theology (BEST). The first two-thirds of the book offers four essays in English, the last one-third offers five essays in French, while the introduction by the editor is in both English and French. The most comprehensive essay in the collection is by Stanley Mutunga of Kenya (at that time the academic dean at NEGST), titled: "Toward a 'Wa Kwetu' without Strangers." "*Wa kwetu*" is a Kiswahili term for the feeling of ethnic or tribal belonging and solidarity. Mutunga shows that "*wa kwetu*" is inevitable, and good in providing security and guidance for insiders, but bad in rejecting outsiders. Both Jesus and Paul felt special affinity for their own people, but broadened this to include others as well. Jesus' emphasis on the "Jews first" did not exclude "the Gentiles after." Churches must use the biblical metaphors of family, people of God, church, body of Christ and disciples to define themselves and create a new "*wa kwetu*" of believers to transcend, but not replace, the natural "*wa kwetu*." Mutunga closes with discussion of many practical things churches can do to put this into practice. A French article deals with tribalism in the NT, covering part of the same ground. Two articles (one French, one English) trace the role of tribalism in the division of the Israelite monarchy. Unfortunately there is no treatment of other parts of the OT. Two French articles deal with the psychological factors in the existence and persistence of tribalism. Another considers how African tribalism has been affected by the slave trade, colonial policies, the struggle for independence and subsequent struggles for power. Balancing the desire to de-emphasize language and cultural divisions, an English article calls for the use of vernacular scriptures and literacy for women. For one article, on the cognitive shift needed by Muslim converts to Christianity, a link to the theme of the collection is not obvious. Two authors criticize the "people group" missiological approach as potentially dangerous in Africa because of its emphasis on ethnic divisions. This compendium merits notice not least because books treating this particular topic from a Christian perspective within the African context are rare indeed.

167. Bujo, Bénézet

African Christian Morality at the Age of Inculturation

Nairobi: Paulines, 1998. 136 pages.

Bujo is a Roman Catholic priest from Congo (DRC) who did his doctorate in Germany. This is a collection of six articles published in German and French in various journals between 1980 and 1987. Bujo's view of the Christian faith focuses on Christ's love, and His liberating and humanising action for humankind. From this perspective Bujo finds bridges to African tradition, in that life is the central theme of African ethos, and this is compatible with the message of the gospel. He elaborates on Christ as proto-ancestor (based on Paul's and John's Christologies), and thus One who mediates life from God as the origin of humankind. But the gospel of Christ's love also transcends African tradition, for instance in extending love also to a sterile marriage partner (who would traditionally be divorced). Thus the Christian faith can become a basis from which to criticize dehumanising tendencies within genuine and depraved African tradition, for example parasitism eroding traditional hospitality. Self-critically Bujo also addresses clericalism and authoritarian leadership, which he finds contrary both to the Christian faith and to the traditional ancestor cult, where the leaders should dialogue with the people, serve them and promote the life of the whole community, not only their own wellbeing. He also denounces a folkloristic "négritude Christianity" within academic circles where theologians have lost touch with the real problems and misery of the majority of Africa's population. Bujo's goal is to root Christianity deeper into African soil, and his short essays are very worthwhile reading, even if the reader will not agree with each detail.

168. Bujo, Bénézet

African Theology in its Social Context

Oxford: Wiley-Blackwell, 1992. 143 pages, ISBN: 9780883448052.

The author, a Roman Catholic priest originally from the Bunia area of eastern Congo (DRC), has been a professor of theology in Switzerland. In this brief volume he accomplishes the task of summarising the history of African theology, pointing it in a helpful new direction and outlining some of the major implications of that direction. Bujo not only looks back at African culture and religious tradition but also to the present postcolonial context. While the author yearns for the liberation of Africa, in contrast with much "black theology" this is not "some sociopolitical liberation to be achieved through revolution, but a liberation in all its aspects, personal as well as social. People should enjoy the fullness of life at every level." Bujo's model attempts to be both Christocentric and Afrocentric: "I believe that a truly dynamic Christianity will only be possible in Africa when the foundations of the African's whole life is built on Jesus Christ, conceived in specifically African categories." Readers will find the work coloured with a strong Roman hue. Anyone who is serious about African theology will want to be familiar with the perspectives on that project which Bujo here enunciates.

169.   Bujo, Bénézet, and Juvénal Ilunga Muya, editors

African Theology in the 21st Century: The Contribution of the Pioneers (Volume 1)

Nairobi: Paulines, 2003. 200 pages, ISBN: 9789966218834.

This is the English version of *Théologie africaine au XXIe siècle: quelques figures*, published the previous year in Switzerland by Editions Universitaires Fribourg Suisse. The main, and one might say only, problem of the book is its title, which gives the impression that it will present African theology in the twenty-first century, with particular attention to "the pioneers." That, however, is not the case. For all practical purposes this is a book that presents individual Roman Catholic theologians, all coming from francophone Africa. There is little synthesis on "African theology" as such, and there are hardly any references to theologians and theologies that are Protestant or anglophone (even Catholic). A better lead title would therefore have been something like "Francophone Roman Catholic Theologians of Africa." That clarified, it is an altogether welcome contribution. The book is a treasure to all those students of African theology who are somewhat hesitant about whether and where to start with regard to the vast material produced in the (mainly) second half of the twentieth century by Catholic theologians writing in French. The book is organized as an essay collection, where eight contemporary (Catholic) scholars write individual essays on the nine selected "pioneers": Vincent Mulago ("An enthusiast of African theology"), Engelbert Mveng ("A pioneer of African theology"), Tharcisse Tshibangu ("Champion of an 'African-coloured' theology"), Alphonse Ngindu Mushete ("The problem of religious knowledge"), Sidbe Semporé ("Spiritual itinerary of an African theologian"), Oscar Bimwenyi ("End of a period of discussion on the possibility of African theology"), Bénézet Bujo ("The awakening of a systematic and authentically African thought"), Barthélemy Adoukonou ("A pioneer of inculturation in West Africa"), and Elochuqwu Eugen Uzukwu ("An untiring African liturgist"). In addition there is a final section on the debate on African theology, especially focusing on the famous Tshibangu-Vanneste debate in Kinshasa in 1960 on universalism/particularism. Each of the essays includes some biographical material, but the main focus is on their theological development and contribution. The editors, Bénézet Bujo from DRC, teaching in the University of Fribourg, Switzerland, and Juvénal Ilunga Muya also from DRC, teaching at Urbaniana in Rome, have allowed the authors to develop their own form and structure. This is a wise decision, taking into account the many-facetted experiences of the nine pioneers, and the influence of these individual experiences on their particular theological development. Two further volumes have appeared, both in French and in English, which in combination with this volume represent an invaluable resource on the range of personalities and perspectives participant in modern African Christian reflection.

170.   Bujo, Bénézet

Christmas: God Becomes Man in Black Africa

Nairobi: Paulines, 1995. 88 pages, ISBN: 9789966211859.

This particular book arose from the author's observation that Christmas in Europe brings more stress than celebration, due to the fact that materialism has overshadowed the true message of Christmas. Furthermore, such materialism is now affecting Africa, where the media promotes the same attitudes. Bujo's approach is to comment on many of the well-known biblical passages associated with Christmas, attempting to look at this material afresh as an African, without passing through the tradition of European interpretation. Thus in the section on "The Word Became Flesh" he stresses the importance of the spoken word in Africa: words can bring life, or as curses, can bring illness or death, and are considered timeless messengers, just as Christ is God's messenger to all people for all time. In "Christmas in a Brutalized Africa" he notes that Jesus seemed to be weak and without hope, but he triumphed. And indeed can be considered the new "proto" ancestor who unites Africans in a single clan to overcome the present divisions and hostilities. In "Epiphany as Definitive Birth" he complains that Africans blindly adopt Euro-American attitudes that reduce human beings to objects of economic profitability, thereby undermining the traditional African concern for people. At several points Bujo reminds the reader of the essential link between "the crib and the cross." He insists that Christian history began with the death of Christ, that the story of Christmas only makes sense in light of the cross. Unfortunately, the book loses focus toward the end when allegory takes over: the whole of humanity is pregnant with the life of God; we must thwart Herod by transforming ourselves into Joseph; we must leave Bethlehem, which is menacing, in order to discover Egypt, which is a picture of African hospitality; "The River Nile crosses our African countries and should be henceforth a symbol that binds us to Jesus Christ." This book is a creative attempt to look at various Christmas passages through African eyes, and in doing so Bujo raises issues that need our attention. Nevertheless, readers may well experience frustration with the liberty taken by the author when applying such Scriptures to the present situation.

171. Bujo, Bénézet

The Ethical Dimension of Community

Nairobi: Paulines, 2010. 240 pages, ISBN: 9789966213365.

This book, by the well-known Congolese Roman Catholic theologian, attempts to develop a moral theology "which is truly African and truly Christian." It is an African response to the moral theology of Thomas Aquinas, which is the foundation for most Roman Catholic ethics. Bujo notes the central place of natural law in Thomistic morality. Reason then deduces absolute ethical norms from natural law. But Bujo questions the absolute nature of this natural law. Bujo believes that Roman Catholic natural law is in fact very Eurocentric and individualistic. Indeed, Bujo doubts that a single unquestionable moral system can be found. So what is the normative source of African ethics? Bujo thinks it is found in the African community. Bujo proposes "a model of palaver" for African ethics. "Palaver" is the talk or discussion of wise men in an African community. These African men (and women?) should be able to make wise decisions regarding right ethical behaviour. Bujo then applies this model of palaver to concrete ethical issues, avoiding the excessively individualistic and Eurocentric solutions provided by Western discussion. Thus he thinks that marriage should be more than a single contract but rather a dynamic process in stages. He does not favour polygamy but argues for greater understanding of the practice. He thinks that the approach to feminism, liberation theology, human rights and political systems has been too Western and individualistic. In general, the book repeatedly criticizes the alleged shortcomings of Western ethics and proposes an African ethics. But one wonders to what extent Bujo's ethics are Christian. He almost never draws ethical principles from Scripture. Nor does he recognize absolute principles in Scripture. While the book is interesting, it seems to fall too easily into traditional pitfalls both of Roman Catholic theology and of African inculturation theology.

172. **Bujo, Bénézet**

Foundations of an African Ethic: Beyond the Universal Claim of Western Morality

New York: Crossroad, 2001. 214 pages, ISBN: 9780824519056.

Bujo is a Catholic priest from Congo (DRC) who did his doctorate in Germany and has been professor of moral theology and social ethics at Fribourg in Switzerland since 1989. In this book his intention is to challenge Western ethical systems with an African ethic, in order to arrive at a "better understanding and living . . . of the realities connected to the Christian faith." His main dialogue partners are Natural Law (often as presented by Thomas Aquinas, contrasting in part with official contemporary Catholic documents), autonomous moral theology (Alfons Auer and others), communitarianism and discourse ethics. On the one hand, Bujo takes up fundamental ethical concepts of the West (for example anthropology, virtue, autonomy, conscience, responsibility), confronts them with African understandings, and challenges the universal validity of the Western concepts, denying that they have been properly inculturated in the Majority World. On the other hand, Bujo introduces African concepts (for example the African palaver, or anamnetical life – a critical remembering of the ancestors to find new solutions for tomorrow), and expresses them in Western philosophical language, with similarities and differences to Western thought indicated. His intention is to show how an African worldview with its moral concepts is able to receive the gospel into its own framework, both where Africa is fundamentally compatible with Christ (at least as compatible as is the Western philosophical tradition), and where African patterns have to be "cured" in terms of their basic intention to guarantee "life in fullness" – which indeed the proto-ancestor Jesus Christ fully reveals. Bujo's book is certainly quite demanding, since the reader has to know Bujo's dialogue partners in order to understand the arguments. Unfortunately Bujo does not interact with biblical ethics. Also Bujo's theories on African concepts seem in part too generalized and not well enough justified. Nevertheless there are many challenging thoughts, deep insights, and practical avenues suggested for a sound inculturation of Christian ethics in Africa (e.g. with respect to polygamy, sorcery, and parasitism, to mention just a few). Bujo will usefully stretch the mind of anyone in Africa lecturing or researching on Christian ethics.

Bujo, Bénézet

see also review 360

Bukasa, Kabongo J.

see review 529

173. **Bunza, Mukhtar Umar**

Christian Missions among Muslims: Sokoto Province, Nigeria, 1935–1990

Trenton, NJ: Africa World Press, 2007. 268 pages, ISBN: 9781592215232.

A revision of Bunza's doctoral dissertation at Usmanu Danfodiyo University in Sokoto, Nigeria, this book attempts to tell the story of Christian missions in northwestern Nigeria from an Islamic point of view. He begins with the establishment of Islam and an Islamic state in the Sokoto Caliphate from 1804 to 1903. With the advent of colonial rule the British authorities, in order to keep the peace, allowed almost no missionary activity in this part of Nigeria until 1930. Thereafter they favoured Christianity by using missionaries to carry out educational and medical services. Islam was so strongly established, however, that missionaries were able to "trap" only marginal and vulnerable people, such as pagans, lepers, and destitute persons. The book repeatedly states that no Muslim of any status in Northern Nigeria has ever converted to Christianity. Missionaries were racist, and part of the colonial agenda, and Christianity was always seen as a foreign instrument of political domination. Muslims were always tolerant, but also saw it as their sacred duty to maintain a stance against the Christians and their cultural, religious and political agenda. By uniting northern and southern Nigeria in 1914, the colonialists opened the north to an influx of southerners who brought their Christian churches with them. Comprising most of the Christians in Northern Nigeria today, these have mostly given up the hopeless task of winning Muslims to Christianity, and concentrate instead on competing with each other. Bunza has done a commendable amount of research. He interviewed all the prominent Christians of Hausa-Fulani origin, combed the colonial archives for all references to missions, and accessed some mission records. His 43-page bibliography includes contemporary Nigerian Christian writers on the topics that he touches. The book closes with a history of Muslim-Christian relations (things all started to go wrong at the Crusades, a theory that downplays the prior Muslim attempt to conquer Europe), highlighting the Qur'anic verses that recommend good relationships between the two groups. His suggestions for peaceful co-existence between Christians and Muslims in Nigeria are: (1) everyone should respect the differences of others, (2) there should be dialogue and getting to understand each other, (3) religion should not be used for extra-religious goals, such as political, economic and ethnic rivalry, (4) Nigeria should have a more federal system where the northern states can fully implement sharia law and Islamic government and society, and (5) the religion of civil servants should be made public so that everyone can see how many Christians and how many Muslims are privileged with jobs in each state. This is to quell the claims of the Christian Association of Nigeria that Muslims are given more jobs. Bunza longs for the good old days of independent Islamic government in Northern Nigeria with freedom from Christian influence and interference.

174. **Burgess, Richard**

Nigeria's Christian Revolution: The Civil War Revival and Its Pentecostal Progeny (1967–2006)

Oxford: Regnum, 2008. 369 pages, ISBN: 9781870345637.

The author was previously a lecturer at the Theological College of Northern Nigeria (TCNN), Bukuru, and is now a research fellow at the University of Birmingham, UK. This book brings together both his personal experience in Nigeria and the results of his meticulous research, in order to provide an account of what he takes to be one of the significant spiritual movements of the twentieth century. The first part of the book summarizes the situation in Nigeria prior to the 1967 Civil War that brought the Igbo people of southeastern Nigeria into conflict with Nigeria's central government. Burgess provides a detailed account of the spiritual revival that then occurred amongst these Igbo people during and immediately following the Civil War. The key role of Scripture Union is analysed, particularly the training they gave to young Igbo Christians concerning the importance of the Bible. The revival was an unstructured movement, so a separate chapter outlines the emergence of the neo-Pentecostal churches during and following the war. Burgess demonstrates the way the neo-Pentecostal churches were contextualized to the local situation, while simultaneously part of a global movement with their emphasis on the "freedom of the Spirit." This global element was the basis of a growing contact with USA Pentecostalism, particularly in the area of formal training opportunities. Three distinguishing features of the

Civil War Revival are discussed, features that in turn became characteristics of the neo-Pentecostal churches, namely: (1) an emphasis on the reading and teaching of the Bible as the Word of God; (2) an openness to the working of the Spirit that allowed culturally relevant expressions of worship and service; and (3) an orientation to mission. Burgess also notes three weaknesses that have subsequently developed in these churches, namely: (1) much church growth is by transfer and not by conversion; (2) there is no substantial improvement in the level of morality in the churches; and (3) evangelism has become a set of activities with little impact outside of the church community. This is a story that needs to be understood. It opens up issues relating to church planting, contextualization, church growth, leadership development and the impact of training outside the local context.

175.   Burgess, Richard

Times of Refreshing: Revival and the History of Christianity in Africa

Bukuru, Nigeria: Africa Christian Textbooks, 2008. 258 pages, ISBN: 9789784830836.

This is a book about revivals in Africa written by a former expatriate lecturer at two theological colleges in Nigeria. It considers the history of some key revivals especially in South Africa, Eastern Africa, Nigeria and Congo (DRC). This work is academic but also inspirational. The author defines a Christian revival as "a communal event, initiated by the Holy Spirit, which assumes an element of decline, out of which believers are called to renewed heights of spiritual vitality and moral probity . . ." The book sets the stage by looking at the three evangelical awakenings and the Pentecostal revival in Britain and America. Then representative revivals in Africa are considered. Burgess is a good storyteller, offering vivid impressions of how the Holy Spirit has worked in dramatic ways throughout Africa in renewing the church. Sometimes a European missionary presence was involved, but often these revivals were purely indigenous. Usually the revivals began spontaneously with the Holy Spirit convicting people of sin; often there was dramatic evidence of the Holy Spirit; and the revivals usually resulted in a greater commitment to holiness and evangelistic activity. Although revivals often started spontaneously, Burgess emphasizes that persistent and earnest prayer can lead to revival. Although the author recognizes non-Pentecostal movements of the Holy Spirit, the book focuses especially on traditionally charismatic manifestations of the Spirit. For example, a concluding section on power encounter focuses on witchcraft, sickness and personal sin as the problem, without mentioning social injustice or corruption. Nonetheless, this academic book serves to accent the need for revival wherever the church has become characterized by carnal interests.

176.   Burney, Robert S.

The Book of Revelation: African Bible Commentaries

Nairobi: Uzima Press, 1988. 109 pages, ISBN: 9789781222061.

The authors of this commentary series are "African biblical scholars and those who are familiar with the life situation in Africa." They are aware, as stated in the general preface, that theology is not done "in a vacuum" and so they come to the Bible asking what the world of the text might have to say to the (African) world of the reader. In this volume Burney combines a gift for clear exposition with helpful comments on the situation in which the African church finds itself. Burney taught for some years at the Nigerian Baptist Theological Seminary. His method of reading this difficult book is the most helpful of several current approaches. He believes that the book was written out of a context in which the churches of Asia Minor were suffering persecution for their faith because they refused to participate in the worship of the emperor (probably Domitian). The Book of Revelation was written, therefore, not as a prediction of the end of the world but to edify believers at the end of the first century. The unique contribution, following the purpose of the series, comes when Burney turns his attention to the African context. He takes note of common ground between the Biblical worldview and the African worldview, and also uses the Biblical text to warn the African church of danger. The Apocalypse of John called its original Asian readers to deeper commitment to the Lordship of Jesus Christ. The same text is still calling the church, including the church in Africa, to uncompromising dedication. This book is both thoughtful and readable, and would make a uniquely relevant textbook in Africa for courses attending to the last book of the Bible.

177. **Burns, J. Patout**

Christianity in Roman Africa: The Development of Its Practices and Beliefs

Grand Rapids: Eerdmans, 2014. 736 pages, ISBN: 9780802869319.

The authors are a husband and wife team, both having served as professors at Vanderbilt in the USA. Their study covers, not what would today be termed "North Africa" (i.e. the lands of Africa adjacent to the Mediterranean), but rather the area that for the Roman world was designated at one time as *Africa Proconsularis*, namely the area embracing modern-day western Libya across to eastern Algeria (hence not Egypt nor Cyrenaica). The authors treat in depth the Christian presence in that part of the continent from the second to the seventh centuries of the Christian era. In recent years Thomas Oden has accented the significant role played by early African Christians in shaping Christianity for all time since. The areas of early African Christianity were principally Egypt, Ethiopia, Nubia (northern Sudan), and northern Africa. It is this last area, Roman Africa, for which this volume is providing a comprehensive, authoritative treatment, the part of Africa where Christianity flourished with such wide and lasting impact only to collapse during the Islamic conquest. Burns and Jensen make a nuanced, multi-dimensional presentation, correlating a survey of the archaeological and literary remains with a creative interpretation of the course both of Christian belief and of Christian practice throughout the period under review. These pages are not for a casual read before bedtime; here one is treated to academic sophistication supported by a full referencing apparatus. In the process the authors propose that the distinguishing doctrinal preoccupation characteristic of Roman African Christianity was ecclesiological, how so to maintain the unity and purity of the church that it might effectively serve as the conduit of divine blessing to humankind. In this way the authors manage to link Tertullian, Cyprian, Jerome and Augustine – and even the Donatists. Here, should one wish, one can also find discussion of the surviving remains of Hippo, including the foundations of the ancient church complex where Augustine himself likely lived and preached. One wonders if modern African Christian pilgrims to the Holy Land may one day find themselves also on pilgrimage to this other holy ground of African Christianity's heritage. Whereas the authors show no acquaintance with Oden, nor consciousness of the potential importance of their work for modern African Christianity, it is only from the vantage point that Oden has highlighted that one can recognise this fuller significance of what they have achieved.

178.   Burrows, William R., Mark R. Gornik, and Janice A. McLean, editors

Understanding World Christianity: The Vision and Work of Andrew F. Walls

Maryknoll, NY: Orbis, 2011. 240 pages, ISBN: 9781570759499.

This book contributes significant reflection on and engagement with Andrew Walls, in terms of his "life, ideas, institutions, networks, publications, activities, and proposals." The papers are offered by friends and colleagues who are "in one fashion or another, all students of Andrew Walls." Besides an introduction by the editors, a conclusion by Kwame Bediako, and a twenty-page bibliography of Walls' works, the book consists of sixteen chapters, variously providing insight into the man himself and his impact on scholarship, or treating familiar themes and ideas from Walls' work, many of which reflect his particular interest in Africa. Jonathan Bonk writes, "One would be hard-pressed to write a credible history of World Christianity today without using ideas, themes, and orientations traceable to Walls." Bediako opens the book with a tribute to Walls as a mentor, and closes it with an essay on the emergence of World Christianity and the consequent remaking of theology. Gillian Bediako's contribution, "Gospel and Culture: Andrew F. Walls in Africa, Africa in Andrew F. Walls" quotes Walls as saying, "All I know, I learned in Africa." Although trained in Patristics, the teaching of church history in Sierra Leone (beginning in 1957) and interacting with African Christianity turned Walls in a new direction. Allison Howell and Maureen Iheanacho have taught alongside Walls at the Akrofi-Christaller Institute in Ghana, and render a vivid portrait of him as a teacher. Lamin Sanneh's contribution highlights "the role of Bible translation as a catalyst in the rise of World Christianity and, by implication, the role of the Bible in Christian life and practice," interests he shares with Walls. Kwabena Asamoah-Gyadu of Ghana reviews Walls' contributions to understanding African Christianity's past and its present. The role of migration in achieving the globalisation of Christianity, Western missionaries "migrating" to the rest of the world, and now the rest of the world migrating to the West, is the topic of Jehu Hanciles' essay. The essays reflect Walls' own warm, firm Christian faith as the writers interact with Walls' contributions. What this book does not do is attempt to systematize Walls' thought. Walls has yet to do that himself. But he is still writing, so the discussion around his work will continue. This volume is important because it gives additional insights into the man who has changed the course of mission studies and the study of world Christianity, while also contributing to the study of African theology and church history. It is recommended for scholars in church history, missions, world Christianity, and theology, especially in Africa.

179.   Burton, Keith Augustus, editor

The Blessing of Africa: The Bible and African Christianity

Downers Grove: IVP US, 2007. 294 pages, ISBN: 9780830827626.

Burton is an African American scholar of the Seventh Day Adventist tradition, presently serving as President of Life Heritage Ministries and also as adjunct instructor of religion at a college in Florida. He has previously published books in biblical studies and in African American studies. The starting point of the present book is a Western interpretive tradition of Genesis 9, which takes the dark-skinned "sons of Ham" as a "cursed race." Against this tradition, the book aims to demonstrate that far from being cursed, the "sons of Ham" are blessed through their interaction with the Bible. This interaction is then approached from a chronological perspective, following the "sons of Ham" throughout three or four millennia, in six main parts. Part 1 defines "Biblical Africa," that is the land of Ham, according to the Table of Nations in Genesis 10. The latter reference leads the author to include also what we today call the Middle East. Part 2 identifies Africans in the Bible, that is (cf. Genesis 10) Cush, Canaan and Mizrayim. Part 3 analyses the role of the Bible in Africa, here including Palestine, Egypt/North Africa, and Arabia/Ethiopia. Part 4 surveys the influence of the Bible in Islam and in the Qur'an. Part 5 discusses Western attempts at taking control over the "sons of Ham": the Crusades, the struggle to colonize the Ethiopian church, and colonisation in sub-Saharan Africa. Part 6 discusses the role of the Bible in the liberation of Africa in the latter half of the twentieth century. The author has collected considerable material on the interaction between the "sons of Ham" and the Bible, and the book represents an important attempt at giving a historical survey of the role of the Bible in Africa (and beyond). As such it fills a gap in today's literature on the relationship between Africa and the Bible. On the other hand, the book's attempt to link an ancient textual entity such as the "sons of Ham" and a more modern geographical entity such as "Africa" is certainly problematic. The book title focuses on Africa (in a narrow sense, the continent of Africa), whereas the discussion includes not only Africa but also the ancient and modern Near East. The results of this approach cannot help but be complicated and confusing.

180.   **Butler, Carolyn**

Under African Skies: Reflections on Advent and Christmas

Cape Town: Lux Verbi, 2008. 96 pages, ISBN: 9780796308504.

Written to provide a celebration of Christmas that resonates for those living in Africa, *Under African Skies* provides a more relevant set of advent reflections and liturgies than traditional northern materials which link the Christmas story to a very different seasonal calendar. Without following a specific church lectionary, the author weaves in liturgies and prayers from a variety of authors and countries on the continent (including from *An African Prayer Book* by Desmond Tutu), as well as traditional liturgical prayers from *The Sunday Missal* and her own writings. Providing daily readings for four full weeks of Advent and "twelve days of Christmas" leading to Epiphany, the format includes one page of reflection on a short Scripture passage, a set of questions for personal application and meditation, and a prayer for each day. The author draws examples into her meditations from a wide range of issues from various African contexts, including springtime and new growth, herding, connection to ancestors, rural/urban shifts, displacement and insecurity, community and extended family support systems, and power dynamics around excluded or marginalized groups/persons. Those intent on deeper exploration of Scripture may find the quoted passages too brief, but the book's strength lies in its fresh approach to celebrating the Advent season and extremely thought-provoking questions for further personal reflection. Used either for individual devotion or for leading group Advent services/times of group prayer for those in Africa, this volume would also be a welcome contribution to the Advent celebrations of Christians worldwide and a perfect gift for those seeking to re-invigorate their usual Christmas traditions with new themes and perspectives on the mystery and the meaning of the Incarnation. The author served with her husband for 35 years in Congo (DRC). Now retired in Cape Town, South Africa, she continues a volunteer ministry among the terminally ill and their caregivers.

181. **Byamungu, Gosbert**

Stronger than Death: Reading David's Rise for Third Millennium

Rome: Urbaniana University Press, 1996. 323 pages, ISBN: 9788840180595.

A Roman Catholic priest originally from Tanzania, Byamungu presently works at the Ecumenical Institute in Céligny, Switzerland. This book, which is built on his ThD dissertation at the Pontifical Gregorian University in Rome (1996), analyses the narrative about David's rise to power (1 Sam 16 ff), and does so from the perspective of seeing how certain biblical characters (especially David and Saul) can serve as "models for life" for contemporary readers of this narrative. The author divides the textual material into four groups: "born to win" (David vs. Saul), "Michal's pitiful image" (David vs. Michal), "the golden thread of friendship" (David vs. Jonathan), and "triumph of good over evil" (David's triumph). Based on a close reading of the texts, the author is then able to present two "anthropological paradigms": the Saul paradigm of isolation, failure and despair, and the David paradigm of patience and humility, goodness and success. The book is indeed a rare flower in the garden of academic readings of the OT. The author acknowledges the post-modern context of contemporary biblical scholarship which assumes that the traditional vision of a disinterested search for objective truth is an illusion, and he also subscribes to the idea that the question is no longer: what does the text mean, but: what does the text do? In spite of the author's methodological and hermeneutical awareness, this project could easily have ended up in the genres of pre-critical hagiographies or semi-critical "sermons with footnotes." However, it does not. In constant discussion with contemporary literary readings of the OT, and to some extent also with historical critical readings of the OT, the author has succeeded in creating a consistent literary study which probably will manage to challenge its readers.

182. **Byaruhanga, Christopher**

Bishop Alfred Robert Tucker and the Establishment of the African Anglican Church

Nairobi: WordAlive, 2008. 234 pages, ISBN: 9789966805089.

Alfred Tucker (1849–1914) was the first Anglican bishop of Uganda. Byaruhanga's study (a revision of a doctoral thesis) examines Tucker's role in establishing Anglicanism in Uganda, a country where there are now more church-going Anglicans than anywhere in the world outside of Nigeria. The subject of Byaruhanga's study is somewhat surprising because historians of the church in Africa have made a major shift in recent years. The first generation of studies were really of Western missionary activity in Africa (see as an exemplar the multi-volume work by Groves, *The Planting of Christianity in Africa*). More recent research has rightly emphasized the role of Africans in the propagation of the faith; for example, Karanja's *Founding an African Faith: Kikuyu Anglican Christianity 1900–1945*, and *A History of the Church in Africa* by Sundkler and Steed. It seems unusual, therefore, that a Ugandan church historian should choose a Western missionary as his focus of study. Byaruhanga's goal, however, is not a return to a de-Africanized view of Christianity, but rather to explore the origins of Ugandan Anglicanism in the light of a rift in historiography, namely the chasm between what he calls the "traditional" view, in which the missionaries are the heroes, and what he calls the "post-colonial revisionist" view, which takes as axiomatic that missionary work was simply a religious version of colonialism from which Africans need to be liberated. Byaruhanga's book walks carefully and sensitively through these two poles, arguing that Tucker's life and work were more complicated than either historiographical pole has yet grasped. His work was certainly enmeshed with the (British) colonial project; Tucker encouraged Britain to take responsibility for the oversight of political life in Uganda and he worked closely with colonial authorities. On the other hand, Tucker was careful to encourage an authentically African version of Anglicanism to develop, by training, licensing and ordaining African teachers, catechists, and clergy and giving laity (men and women) a real voice in decision-making, even against the wishes of many of the missionaries. The book includes biographical sketches of a number of Africans who emerged as important leaders because of Tucker's policies.

Calderisi, Robert

see review 120

183. Callaghy, Thomas, Ronald Kassimir, and Robert Latham, editors

Intervention and Transnationalism in Africa: Global-Local Networks of Power

Cambridge: Cambridge University Press, 2001. 338 pages, ISBN: 9780521001410.

This edited collection adds further nuance to the already complex issues involving global-local relations. The contributors write from a variety of disciplinary perspectives but with shared concern for how actors – whether state, NGO, private, religious, global, or local – develop "transboundary formations" within African nations. Transnationalism already constitutes a burgeoning field, ripe for analysis; yet, the relative weakness of the African state makes such discussions particularly important for the continent. Contrary to the "myth" of sovereignty, an assortment of "forces" are in constant interplay within every state, making claims, offering order, and developing new structures that borrow, adapt, conflict, and engage with existing entities. For some, this represents a fundamental intrusion upon local actors, while others see these dynamics as expressive of agency, through a process of adaptation to global-local flows of information and authority. The essays deal with a wide variety of themes converging around how such "transboundary formations" come into existence, navigate power, and instil order. The book moves from broad historical and theoretical foundations to specific case studies dealing with topics such as debt, governance, human rights, finally calling for researchers to take up the complex multidisciplinary inquiry represented by the book. Many readers may immediately note the implications for African Christianity. While the authors fail to give much more than tacit mention of the role of religion, it would be easy to see how this study could inform such a topic. For example, all across the continent, churches (or more specifically, individual congregations) are navigating through complex but interconnected global-local networks of power. They develop informal ties with global "partners," invite state agents into their churches, work with NGOs, and fashion new entities, all within a series of fluid movements. What results is a combination of local agency with global input, moving the church along economic, political, and social trajectories. The same would be largely true for theological colleges. The relative inaccessibility of the information to religious domains should not undermine its perceived significance. Transnationalism constitutes an important field of study within the larger province of World Christianity. This book would prove a helpful resource for analysis of such dynamics as they arise on the continent.

184. **Campbell, Mavis C.**

Back to Africa, George Ross and the Maroons: From Nova Scotia to Sierra Leone

Trenton, NJ: Africa World Press, 1995. 116 pages, ISBN: 9780865433847.

The George Ross of the title was a Scottish employee of the Sierra Leone Company from 1795 to 1801. The Maroons were a group of African slaves, many of Akan (Ghana) descent, who had gained their freedom and lived in their own community in Jamaica. After clashes with the British colonial government there, they were deported to Nova Scotia in 1796. They petitioned the British to be moved to a warmer place, and were sent to Freetown under the superintendency of Ross in 1800. Ross lived with them in Nova Scotia, learned their ways and came to respect them. This book is his diary, which begins at sea on the way to Freetown in September 1800 and ends in August 1801. He recounts his labours in preventing the ship's crew from cheating the Maroons, in leading the Maroons to help quell an uprising in Sierra Leone, then in securing and apportioning to the Maroons their supplies, land and other help, while himself struggling with fever and with the failings of British colonial officials. He finally resigned in 1801 as he had no suitable housing and was not permitted to arm the Maroon police. Campbell, a professor of history at a North American college, provides an introduction to both the times and the diary, and refers the reader for more details to her two other books *Dynamics of Change in a Slave Society* (1979) and *The Maroons of Jamaica 1655–1791* (1988). Campbell says that the elder Maroons had not accepted Western religion or culture, though they allowed the younger generation to be taught. Otherwise she appears to regard evangelisation as an imposition of Western values, and generally ignores any religious dimensions in the story. This book is a good resource for one important detail in the fascinating history of Sierra Leone, a land which in due course played such a central role in the spread of Christianity in West Africa.

185. **Carmody, Brendan, editor**

African Conversion

Ndola: Mission Press, 2001. 128 pages, ISBN: 9789982071178.

This interesting little book consists of eleven articles woven around the theme of African conversion, defined as "the movement from traditional African religion to some form of Christianity or Islam." Most of the contributions are responses to a well-known article entitled, "African Conversion," written by Nigeria-based sociologist Robin Horton in 1971. The discussion deals seriously with the question why Africans have turned from traditional religion to one of the so-called "major" religions. Horton's thesis was that rural people continue with what he calls the microcosm of traditional religion (spirits, etc.), while more educated and urban Africans put their stress on a Supreme Being – what Horton calls the macrocosm. The development of this belief in a Supreme Being coincided with the entrance of the major religions, so these religions became catalysts for change to modernity because both religions were monotheistic. Most of the following articles seek to apply Horton's model to various parts of Africa, and in doing so all of them find the model to be over-simplified. Part of the problem is the conflict between a sociologist who espouses causal reasons for religion, and practitioners who express concern at Horton's lack of emphasis on aspects such as truth and power as reasons for changing religions. Horton's model also fails to explain the continuing practice of witchcraft among urban, educated Africans. The editor, a Roman Catholic priest who lectures at the University of Zambia, writes a chapter on conversion at the first Jesuit school in Zambia, in which he faces honestly the likelihood that most early Africans converted for "socio-cultural" reasons such as finding employment or learning English. The main disappointment with the book is that there is only one article written after 1988. Yet the book does bring under one cover contributions on this topic from a variety of scholars, including several well known in African studies, such as T. O. Ranger, Wim van Binsbergen and Richard Gray – and the interplay among them can be very stimulating. A list identifying the contributors would have been helpful; the author does not even identify himself! This book will be of greater help to those interested in the sociology of religion in Africa, as the emphasis is not on personal conversion so much as on social change in society. But it also poses significant insight and challenge for conventional understandings of the growth of the Christian community throughout Africa in the past century.

Carpenter, Joel A.

see review 1003

186.   Carr, Stephen

Surprised by Laughter: Some Good News out of Africa

Durham, UK: The Memoir Club, 2004. 224 pages, ISBN: 9781841041001.

Reading this anecdotal autobiography will bring a smile to one's face and a chuckle to one's heart! "Surprised" is an apposite word for the reader's likely reaction, given conventional media perceptions of contemporary Africa. Trained in agriculture in UK, Carr first worked in Africa with the Church Missionary Society (CMS), and later in both government and World Bank appointments. From over 50 years of first-hand experience as an agriculturalist, educator, church worker and government advisor, in Nigeria, Uganda, Sudan, Tanzania, and now retired in Malawi, Carr recounts the joys along with the difficulties, the laughter in spite of the adverse conditions, of the simple, basic, yet positive African lifestyle. He is clearly, although not overtly, seeing things with the eyes of his Christian faith. Drawing on numerous situations, both heart-warming and tragic, the book witnesses to the initiative, creativeness and resilience of those millions of Africans, in both secular and sacred situations, whether they work in the village or operate in the corridors of power, whose primary concern is for the welfare of their family and the successful functioning of their community. A delightful, positive and encouraging read, giving insights into what makes Africa tick.

187.   Cassidy, Michael

Heal the Land: A National Initiative for Reconciliation in South Africa

Monrovia, CA: MARC, 1987. 97 pages.

The year 1985 was crucial in South Africa. Black anger and white fear had reached such a stage that black and white Christians had stopped talking to each other. However, with the sense that only in the church lay the possibility for dramatic change, 400 leaders representing 48 denominations met during September 1985 in Pietermaritzburg to launch the National Initiative for Reconciliation. As believers worldwide prayed around the clock for the conference, the assembled leaders listened to addresses by Michael Cassidy ("The interface of the South African church and context"), David Bosch ("What must the church do in obedience to God for the healing of the land?"), Bonganjalo Goba ("The South African situation in my view: a black Christian perspective"), Jan Hanekom ("An Afrikaans reflection on 2 Chronicles 7:13–14"), and Desmond Tutu ("The processes of reconciliation and the demand of obedience"). This book is a collection of the NIR conference papers and includes an introductory chapter by Cassidy ("Reconciliation in South Africa"). The collection ends with the NIR Statement of Affirmation which called for particular initiatives from the South African government. The intention of the NIR conference was that reconciliation was to be an ongoing process, not just an ideal to which a one-time conference gave lip-service. The collection is not only an important historical resource, but also offers a credible example of how evangelicals can engage with others in reflectively addressing situations of national crisis.

188. Cassidy, Michael

The Passing Summer: A South African Pilgrimage in the Politics of Love

London: Hodder and Stoughton, 1989. 534 pages, ISBN: 9780340426272.

Written in the dark years of repression and encircling gloom in the South Africa of the 1980s, this is arguably Cassidy's finest book, reflecting as it does an evangelical grappling with a desperate socio-political situation for which there were no easy answers. Cassidy is the founder and leader of Africa Enterprise (AE), and the book's title is taken from Jeremiah 8:20: "The harvest is past, the summer has ended, and we are not saved." This book is a splendid mix of eye-opening experiences, incisive historical analysis, profound theological insight and straightforward calls to more effective Christian discipleship. Cassidy has a fascinating story to tell of dealings with South Africans across the political spectrum of the 1980s. His interactions with the former South African President, P. W. Botha, whilst clearly uneasy, nevertheless underline the levels at which Cassidy was operating, if only to warn the then apartheid government of impending catastrophe. Cassidy's historical understanding of South African history and theology provides readers with an extremely useful introduction to how South Africa reached the political and theological impasse that it did during those dark years. Cassidy would probably not claim to be an academic theologian but he certainly knows how to 'do theology' at the coal face as distinct from the ivory tower. His theology is solidly biblical, evangelical, contemporary and generous to those with whom he might differ. And though events may have overtaken his book, it is hardly out of date; *The Passing Summer* still remains strikingly relevant.

189. Cassidy, Michael

The Politics of Love: Choosing the Christian Way in a Changing South Africa

London: Hodder and Stoughton, 1991. 285 pages, ISBN: 9780340546093.

When Nelson Mandela was released from prison on 11 February 1990, the course of South African history changed forever. This book by the founder and leader of the influential evangelical organisation Africa Enterprise (AE) recounts the events surrounding that remarkable day, and endeavours to set out the challenges that would await Mandela and South Africa. Cassidy is not one to duck issues or to offer trite answers, and in this book he gives a sober account of the "giants" that will have to be "slain" if South Africa is going to make a success of the future. Poverty, violence, AIDS – to name just a few of these "giants" – are going to remain long after the advent of democracy, and it will require considerable wisdom and skill to know how to address them. Cassidy offers an analysis and his solutions are helpful, culminating in a final chapter on "Power for the Task." Cassidy quotes the Black American Christian, Carl Ellis: "True liberation is not the right to do what I want; it is the power to do what is right." Part of the value of this book is that it shows an evangelical doing serious thinking – and praying – about socio-political matters, and coming up with tangible Christian proposals. There is nothing of the "You take the whole world but give me Jesus" approach that evangelicals have in the past all too easily embraced. Cassidy is a Psalm 24 evangelical: "The earth is the Lord's and the fullness thereof," and the Lordship of Christ includes the world of politics and economics. This book gives the impression of having been written in a hurry. It is not Cassidy at his best, but then Cassidy at his most mediocre is still worth reading!

190. **Cassidy, Michael**

A Witness Forever: The Dawning of Democracy in South Africa: Stories Behind the Story

London: Hodder and Stoughton, 1995. 236 pages, ISBN: 9780340630327.

A mere twelve days before the April 1994 elections in South Africa, Henry Kissinger acknowledged his failure to break the deadlock surrounding the participation of the Inkatha Freedom Party (IFP) in the election. South Africa was now staring into the abyss. Civil war looked likely. "I have never been on such a catastrophic mission," said Kissinger, "and its failure now has cataclysmic consequences for South Africa." That the elections took place with the IFP included is testimony to an amazing sequence of events that TIME Magazine could only explain as "an authentic miracle." This book by the respected evangelical leader of Africa Enterprise (AE), Michael Cassidy, tells the story of those dramatic days in South Africa, when disaster was averted through the extraordinary intervention of God using the Kenyan negotiator, Professor Washington Okumu, and the prayers of Christians throughout the world. Cassidy is well qualified to have written this account, having played a key role in these events. His book is the moving story of a broken nation on its knees with nothing left to do except pray. Anyone who doubts that God intervenes in history should read this book.

191. **Chabal, Patrick, and Jean-Pascal Daloz**

Africa Works: Disorder as Political Instrument

Martlesham, UK: James Currey, 1999. 192 pages, ISBN: 9780852558140.

Why doesn't Africa work? Why after a half century of independence is the continent still awash in civil war, political chaos, underdevelopment, corruption, and poverty? The goal of this brief volume was to provide an analytical framework to make sense of these questions, of the crises in which most African nations found themselves at the turn of the millennium. The authors, both Africanists from the West who have lived, worked, and researched in black Africa for the better part of two decades, offer as a paradigm what they call the political instrumentalisation of disorder. By this they mean the process by which political actors on the African scene use the apparent disorder and even chaos in African economic and political systems to their own advantage. With the goal of providing a multi-disciplinary look at the current African situation, Chabal and Daloz apply their paradigm to a wide variety of issues including corruption, witchcraft and religion, crime and violence, foreign aid, and development. Their admittedly depressing conclusion is that because of the political instrumentalisation of disorder, a system which traces its roots back long before colonialism to the vertical patron/client organisation of traditional African societies, development as it is understood in the West is culturally impossible in Africa. If disorder is indeed a resource, there is no incentive to work toward effective formal political organisation. Since it is designed to be an essay explaining the authors' paradigm as opposed to a reference work, the book has only a select and brief bibliography. In terms of explicit religious referencing there is only one chapter, which focuses more on witchcraft and ancestor worship than on Christianity or Islam. This under-representation of the role of the church in current African societies is disappointing, especially for those seeking to reflect on the situation from a Christian perspective. On the other hand, the unorthodox and potentially unfashionable positions the authors take in this work, along with their many and detailed examples, make it thought-provoking reading and great fodder for discussions.

192.   Chaillot, Christine

The Ethiopian Orthodox Tewahedo Church Tradition: A Brief Introduction to Its Life and Spirituality

Paris: Inter-Orthodox Dialogue, 2002. 256 pages, ISBN: 9788385368984.

For years theologians and some church leaders in the Orthodox tradition have been trying to bring a greater unity between the Eastern Orthodox Churches and the Oriental Orthodox Churches. The author is a lay-woman who is part of this movement to bring dialogue and greater understanding between the two Orthodox traditions. The subtitle of her book is an accurate summary of its focus: by unfolding in practical terms the life and spirituality of the Ethiopian Orthodox Church (EOC), she hopes to create better understanding and appreciation of its unique traditions. The book provides a brief but accurate survey of the history of the EOC. At times this survey is so brief as to be almost cryptic, and readers will need to turn to other sources to find a fuller explanation. The book is especially valuable in tracing some of the most significant developments in the EOC since the end of Marxism in Ethiopia in 1991, especially the resurgence of theological education and the development of Sunday School, youth, human need, and missions programmes. The book also excels in introducing readers to the rich field of Ethiopian studies, and provides a particularly helpful explanation of the EOC education system and traditional Ethiopian literature and poetry (qene). The bibliography is exhaustive, but not annotated; the text also lacks footnotes. Readers will find it very difficult to use the bibliography to follow-up on a particular interest. The author devotes her longest chapter to an introduction to Ethiopian monasticism and a survey of the location, history and life of dozens of the most important monasteries. Regrettably the descriptions are too brief to provide the reader with anything more than an awareness of the scope of Ethiopian monastic spiritually. The book is also a valuable reference tool to the EOC liturgy and liturgical calendar. The strength of the book is as an introduction to some areas of EOC spiritual practice; it will disappoint readers who seek to understand EOC theology, which is almost completely ignored. The book is recommended as an update and supplement to more standard works on the EOC, but readers should not expect it to be adequate as a single introduction to the EOC.

193.   Chakanza, J. C., and Kenneth R. Ross, editors

Religion in Malawi: An Annotated Bibliography

Blantyre: CLAIM, 1998. 160 pages, ISBN: 9789990816136.

This text contains the first comprehensive bibliographic survey of religion in Malawi. This will henceforth be an indispensable resource for those, whether student, lecturer or researcher, requiring further knowledge about the wide variety and colourful history of religion in Malawi. Sources regarding Islam, the Roman Catholic Church and African religions are accompanied by references to literature on the Presbyterian Synods of Livingstonia, Nhoma and Blantyre, as well as the Evangelical, Pentecostal and Baptist Churches. Each entry has a short annotation to help readers locate more easily those publications of interest to them. The limitation of the bibliography is made plain from the outset. First it lists secondary literature; strictly speaking it is a bibliography of studies of religion in Malawi. Secondly, the collection is restricted to works which are substantially engaged with some aspect of religious life in Malawi. Within the context of these restrictions and the attempt to be comprehensive, the authors do not claim the collection to be the last word. The bibliography is being published in two forms. The conventional one is this book, representing in this first edition the state of knowledge at the end of 1997. The newer one is a computer database maintained at the Kachere Institute, the research wing of the Department of Theology and Religious Studies at Chancellor College, University of Malawi. This important project should be a worthy example to churches throughout Africa of the sort of research and publication that could be usefully undertaken in their areas.

Chesworth, John

see review 689

194.   Cheza, Maurice, and Gérard van't Spijker, editors

Théologiens et théologiennes dans l'Afrique d'aujourd'hui

Paris: Éditions Karthala, 2010. 276 pages, ISBN: 9782811103835.

This volume, edited in collaboration with the Association Francophone Œcuménique de Missiologie, is a collection of fifteen essays by a variety of African scholars, men and women, Protestant and Catholic, francophones as well as an anglophone and an arabophone, hailing from several nations (Benin, Cameroon, the two Congos, Egypt, Ghana, Madagascar, Nigeria). The book is divided into three major sections, each with the essays organized around a theme and each terminating with a biographical note concerning the author and a short bibliography. The essays in the first section seem to centre around the need for contextualization or inculturation of Christianity in the African setting. Ukwuije discusses his view of the mission of the theologian, who as a believer must find effective ways to communicate the truth about God in the culture. Santendi Kinkupu underscores the need for theology to be constantly in touch with the reality around it. Kiki shines a light on many of the problems faced in modern Africa, and says that the African Christian must be willing to address these if he is to be truly Christian. Rakotoharintsifa, from Madagascar, points out the need to affirm one's own culture but not to the extent of being ethnocentric. For Vibila, the globalisation of the economy needs to be tempered by social maturity and concern for others. Fossouo attempts to see in the African monarchical system a new way to understand the Christian's relation to God. And finally, Yinda, the only woman in this first group, presents her view of mission today, mission going in two directions (centripetal and centrifugal) and maintaining true African values. Section 2 has articles by three women theologians (Togboga, Mbuy-Beya, and Ngalula), considering the contribution of women to the church as well as the challenges, structural and linguistic, which women face in wanting to be fully integrated into the church's ministry. Section 3, entitled "Churches and Communities," is a catch-all for the remaining essays, all by men. One finds articles on the church in Congo (Ndongala), the Church worldwide (Quenum), Jesus and the Samaritan woman in John 4:1–12 (Poucouta), Muslims and Christians working together (by Golta, from Egypt), and a seven-page bibliography for African theology (selected by Cheza). The volume as a whole is indicative of the many-faceted interests of the French Ecumenical Mission Association and its desire to have Africans present their reflections to the world at large.

195.   Chidester, David, Judy Tobler, and Darrel Wratten

Christianity in South Africa: An Annotated Bibliography

Westport, CT: Greenwood, 1997. 489 pages, ISBN: 9780313304736.

The three authors work with the Institute for Comparative Religion in Southern Africa at the University of Cape Town, through which this book was developed by means of a long-term research project. This is the second of a three-volume series on South African religions. The first volume documents African traditional religions, and the third one focuses on religious pluralism, with special attention given to Islam, Hinduism, and Judaism. Since the legacy of Christianity in South Africa is extraordinarily complex in both its history and its diversity, the authors orient their contribution by the basic question, "What is Christianity in South Africa?" They then offer guidance towards an answer by providing detailed reviews of more than 650 selected books, articles, and theses under three categories: (1) European and North American Christian missions (grouped by South African regions); (2) mainstream denominations (e.g. Dutch Reformed, Roman Catholic, Anglican, Methodist); and (3) African initiated churches (Ethiopians, Millenarians, Nazarites, Zionists). Helpful introductory essays for each section are also provided. The book is likely to be considered essential for libraries anywhere intending to support serious research on Christianity in southern Africa.

196.   Chikane, Frank

No Life of My Own: An Autobiography

Maryknoll, NY: Orbis, 1989. 132 pages, ISBN: 9781852870119.

Chikane is somewhat of an anomaly. He is a member of a small, racially divided, politically conservative Pentecostal denomination in South Africa. He is a gifted evangelist. How odd that God would choose such a man to lead the South African Council of Churches, a body which has been at the forefront of the struggle for political liberation in South Africa, a body of which his church is not even a member. This is a book about the struggle to remain faithful to God and responsive to people who are suffering at the hands of a system which claimed biblical justification for racism and violence. The claim of biblical justification meant that racism reached even into the churches. Chikane recounts, for example, how the man who supervised his torture, during a period in which Chikane was detained without trial and without charge, was a deacon in his own Pentecostal denomination. This book cannot be read passively. It may well move the reader to tears, to prayer and to a renewed commitment to serve God in the midst of a suffering world.

197.   Chilver, Alan, editor

Women's Ministry in the Church: An African Perspective

Nairobi: AEA, 1997. 117 pages, ISBN: 9789783266094.

This book consists of papers presented in a conference held in 1995 near Abidjan, Côte d'Ivoire, under the auspices of the Theological & Christian Education Commission, an arm of the Association of Evangelicals in Africa (AEA). Six African theologians (four female and two male) participated. The subject matter was considered from its theological, cultural and practical perspectives. Theologically it is argued that spiritual gifting for service in the church is not based on gender consideration and so negates gender discrimination in church ministry. Pauline restriction on the role of females in the church is blamed on the influence of Jewish and Greco-Roman cultures, which were perceived as contrary to biblical and African views of women. Based largely on various NT word studies the case is made for women's leadership role in the NT church. These conclusions raise more theological, hermeneutical and cultural questions than they actually answer. Nevertheless, the book can be recommended as a springboard for further discussions in Africa on the question of women's role in the church.

198.   Chipenda, Jose B., editor

The Church in Africa, Towards a Theology of Reconstruction

Nairobi: All Africa Conference of Churches, 1991. 63 pages.

This short collection of essays was presented to the General Committee of the All Africa Conference of Churches (AACC), at its meeting in 1990 in Nairobi. The essays are rooted in the theology of liberation, but call for a shift in theological metaphor from liberation to reconstruction. The writers seek to focus the attention and the direction of the African church toward the work that needs to be done in the post-colonial era. They provide a clear analysis of the social, religious and political context of the African continent. Looking back some years later, the reader will realize that many of the issues highlighted are still valid today for the church's response and attention. Social issues include debt relief, hunger, the refugee problem, women's concerns, the disabled, the impact of technology, education and youth. Religious issues include the priority of evangelism, God's presence in Africa before Christianity, ecumenical unity, salvation and contextualization. The political area is addressed in a discussion of the relationship of the church and state. One notable contemporary issue that is not addressed is that of AIDS in Africa and the church's response to the epidemic. Although present in 1990, AIDS had not reached the crisis proportions of later. The book's strength is in its analyses, which are still relevant for the reader today. It would have been helpful if along with its call for the church's involvement, the book could have given more practical and concrete suggestions on how these issues could be addressed. However, this book still points the way forward and could be helpful for anyone wishing to reflect carefully on the church's role and task in contemporary Africa.

199.   Chitando, Ezra

Singing Culture: A Study of Gospel Music in Zimbabwe

Uppsala: Nordic Africa Institute, 2002. 105 pages, ISBN: 9789171064943.

The author, professor of history and religion at the University of Zimbabwe, presents a well-researched study of "gospel music" in Zimbabwe. African music is a subject begging for more scholarly attention, and it is encouraging to note that of the 100 books, conference papers and journal articles included in this book's references, nearly half are by African writers. A list of conducted interviews as well as a "Select Discography" enhance the resources. Although the focus of this research covers only one decade, 1990–2000, Chitando couches the gospel music of that decade in a multidisciplinary study of the broader context and history of Zimbabwe. As to a possible working definition of "gospel music," Chitando agrees with something like a "cultural product," with content of Christian truth created by Christian "cultural workers," and not confined to the church but penetrating all of society. He further reminds any would-be purists that music is never frozen in time. Gospel music has been and is constantly evolving. Some of the topics presented include gospel music in minority languages, growing space for women in the singing industry, enhancement of ecumenism through music, influence of singing youth groups, questions of singers' motivations and influence of economics in the mix. The book leaves the reader desiring continued conversation. For example, how does a singer's interpretation of the Bible influence the theology of listeners? What moral expectations might the public have of a gospel singer's life and character? What political clout does gospel music wield? In the conclusion, Chitando suggests that the Western media's usual gloom and doom portrayal of Africa is powerfully countered by gospel music's foundational message which "chooses life" in the midst of whatever despair or struggle may be at hand. Church musicians, songwriters, and researchers should take note of Zimbabwe's gospel music culture and the format of Chitando's presentation. The book is a model for the country-specific research that should be undertaken (at least in a popular, if not academic, style) to describe the "gospel music" scene across Africa.

200.   Choramo, Mehari, and Brian Fargher

Ethiopian Revivalist: Autobiography of Evangelist Mehari Choramo

Edmonton: Enterprise Publications, 1997. 211 pages, ISBN: 9780968183205.

This book, and the one by Sorsa Sumamo, provide an interesting genre in which Brian Fargher, SIM missionary to Ethiopia from 1957 to 1986, assisted Ethiopian Christian evangelists from the Kale Heywet Church in telling their own stories. Mehari Choramo, who lived into his 80s still faithfully in ministry, represents the great number of evangelists within the Kale Heywet Church who have devoted their lives to the cause of the gospel. The compiler/annotator, who has known Mehari for some 40 years, has himself provided rich missiological insights from his own experience and academic background. The basis of the material is taped interviews with Mehari, with seven additional chapters interspersed by Fargher to provide context for Mehari's life ministry. This book and its companion are both very readable, and their style and composition provide vivid examples of how the lives of contemporary saintly believers in Africa may be captured and presented for the benefit of ordinary Christians, as well as for those in training for Christian leadership roles.

Christiaensen, Luc

see review 908

201.   Christian History Magazine

The African Apostles

Carol Stream, IL: Christianity Today Inc., 2003. 46 pages.

This recent issue of the popular magazine *Christian History* is devoted to Africa, and will prove a helpful resource to anyone interested in the history of the church on the continent, especially in the period from the later 1800s to World War II. Many of the most prominent African church leaders of that era are highlighted: Ajayi Crowther from Nigeria, Joseph Kiwanuka from Uganda, William Wadé Harris from Liberia, Simon Kimbangu from Congo (DRC), plus several others. There are also interesting articles on the leaders of the East

African Revival and the Aladura churches of West Africa. The final section lists a number of resources on this topic, both secular and Christian, and throughout are numerous photographs and other visuals. The magazine's usual "Did you know?" section is unfortunately based on David Barrett's statistics that state numbers of "professing" Christians in places like Congo (DRC) (95.4 percent) and Angola (94.1 percent). This encourages an inaccurate impression that some countries have been evangelized, whereas in fact a number have recently had serious moral and political strife, suggesting that much work often yet remains for the gospel to take deep and effective rootage. Possibly due to the fact that many of the writers used are based in North America rather than Africa, there are occasional factual errors (e.g. Lamin Sanneh is Gambian rather than Nigerian; and the White Fathers were founded in the late 1860s, not the 1840s).

202. Chuba, Bwalya S.

Mbeleshi in a History of the London Missionary Society

Gaborone: Pula Press, 2000. 304 pages, ISBN: 9789991261768.

Chuba is a Zambian and an ordained minister of the United Church in Zambia, who has served as Principal of Kgolagano College of Theological Education by Extension in Botswana. His book offers a historical account of one of the early mission stations established by the London Missionary Society in Zambia. Attention is paid to services rendered by early LMS missionaries at Mbeleshi, and the role played by indigenous Christians in making the missionary work successful. Besides containing a wealth of information, the book challenges the reader to continue the work started by early missionaries, both foreign and local. Making use of archival material from old LMS stations in Zambia, the School of Oriental and African Studies, the National Archives in Zambia, the Council of World Mission office and oral sources, Chuba has contributed a most valuable introduction to the work of the LMS in Zambia and the contribution of local Christians in the development of Mbeleshi Mission station and its work. The first two chapters give an overview of the LMS work, starting with its 1877 expedition into Central Africa from the east coast, the beginning of work among the Mambwe-Lungu people, and the subsequent extension of missionary work among the Bemba people in the northern part of Zambia. After recounting the establishment of the Mbeleshi mission station, Chuba treats the services extended from that centre, including establishing churches, training evangelists, education, medical work, technical training and agricultural work. Special attention is given to the literacy work of the Mission. Finally the author considers obstacles and challenges faced by the Mbeleshi Mission, yesterday and today, before providing a concluding summary. This book is an important contribution to Zambian church historiography in particular and to the history of African Christianity in general. Its value is that much further enhanced by the fact that it is written by a local Zambian scholar.

203. Chukwulozie, Victor

Muslim-Christian Dialogue in Nigeria

Ibadan: Daystar Press, 1986. 201 pages, ISBN: 9789781221927.

This book is a scholarly work by a Nigerian Roman Catholic priest and professor at the Department of Philosophy at the University of Nigeria, Nsukka. Part 1 introduces the social context for inter-faith dialogue (better, "trialogue": Islam, Christianity and African traditional religions), offering a brief but adequate historical overview of the entrance of Islam and Christianity (both Catholic and Protestant) into Nigeria. Part 2 records recent Catholic and Protestant attempts at dialogue with Islam, separately and at times together. Also reported are the very limited lasting results from these attempts, and the major obstacles encountered, particularly from the Muslim fundamentalist element. In part 3 the author endeavours to show the biblical principles and theological basis for dialogue by quoting from the church fathers (Justin, Clement, and Augustine), and the scholastics (Thomas and Nicholas). The Islamic concept of state, and Islamic mysticism, are significant chapters in the last section. This book should be of interest for lecturers and advanced students in Islamics in Africa.

204.   Chukwuocha, A. C.

The War Within: Christians and Inner Conflicts

Carlisle, UK: HippoBooks, 2009. 144 pages, ISBN: 9789966805393.

The author was previously Student National President of the Nigeria Fellowship of Evangelical Students (NIFES), and now serves as an Anglican priest in Nigeria. As such he has been well placed to observe spiritual conflicts in the lives of his parishioners as well as in his own life and Nigeria's national life. He uses examples of ways people try to excuse their inner spiritual conflicts as a springboard to dealing with this issue. He states that "the more intense our desire to walk in step with Christ, the more we face inner conflicts." He addresses questions about why we have these conflicts, how we can deal with them, and the relationship between our salvation and these conflicts, emphasising the necessity of using our minds along with reliance on the Holy Spirit in order to mature in our walk of faith. John Stott affirms the author's effectiveness as follows: "I appreciate your honesty in acknowledging the vulnerability and frailty of us Christians; your insistence that our fallen self-centred nature is not abolished when we are converted; your appeal to your readers to use their minds; and your confidence that the Holy Spirit is able to cause his fruit to ripen in our lives." This book challenges all Christians to evaluate their desires and commit themselves to work at following Jesus above all, by persevering through confession and repentance when they fall into sin, and by seeking to be holy as God is holy. While gently recognising the inner struggles that believers face and the times they may succumb to temptations, the author uses a wide array of scriptural references to assure believers that they cannot lapse into regular or continuous sinning and still claim to be Christ's followers. He shares his own liberating experience of coming to realize that the devil he feared, the force producing the conflicts in his life, is one of the " . . . rulers or authorities over which Jesus Christ my Lord has active supremacy (Col 1:16)." He affirms that since that day he has no longer feared what the devil may do to him. Freedom from this fear is crucial to liberating African Christians, and indeed all Christians, to commit themselves to follow Christ in total obedience as they seek God's holiness in their lives. Coming from an African churchman, this message is especially timely for Christians in Africa who may wonder about the Christian claims made by some leaders whose lives do not reflect God's standards. Christians at all stages of their spiritual journeys will be challenged and encouraged by this book, which is written at a level suitable for readers in secondary school and above.

205.   Chung, Meehyun, editor

Contextual Theology: Voices of West African Women

New Dehli: ISPCK, 2010. 176 pages, ISBN: 9788184651058.

This book is a collection of ten essays by women from the Church of the Brethren (EYN) in Nigeria and the Presbyterian Church of Cameroon (PCC). The editor is head of the Women and Gender Desk at Mission

21 (formerly the Basel Mission) in Switzerland. These are practical essays arguing that women, who are often oppressed in Africa, can be agents of good in our society. For example, Kanadi Gava writes that "women have contributed a lot toward community development in Gava [in Nigeria]." Safiya Doma says that women have an important role to play in HIV prevention. Rebecca Dali argues that women have a vital role to play in the economic development of church and society. Azange Margaret highlights the role of women in reconciliation and transformation. Eta Elvira argues that church and state should care for the poor, many of whom are women. Roseline Vandi and Suzan Zira argue for women's ordination in the EYN church. Koni Patrick highlights the issue of violence against women, while Mary Nyampa thinks polygamy makes women into second-class citizens. Perpetua Fonki warns against fraud in Pentecostal claims of healing. The essays are written at a very practical level.

206. Church of the Province of Kenya

Rabai to Mumias: A Short History of the Church of the Province of Kenya, 1844–1994

Nairobi: Uzima Press, 1994. 203 pages, ISBN: 9789966855329.

This short volume introduces the reader to the story of the church body once known as the Church of the Province of Kenya (CPK) and now known as the Anglican Church in Kenya (ACK), from its beginnings in the missionary work of the Church Missionary Society (CMS) to its present-day existence as a prominent denomination in modern Kenya. The title refers to the first mission station at Rabai near the coast, founded by Johann Ludwig Krapf and Johannes Rebmann in the 1840's, and to the town of Mumias in western Kenya near where Bishop Hannington, the first Anglican bishop of the region, was martyred in 1885. The book was produced under the direction of the ACK's Provincial Unit of Research. At times the book reads more like a chronicle of events than a narrative. It also suffers from the fact that many of the people to whom attention is given in the story are missionaries and bishops. More attention would have been welcome to the lives of ordinary Anglican Christians, many of whom were the most effective bearers of the gospel message. No doubt part of the reason for these deficiencies is that the book was written by a committee. In spite of these shortcomings there is a wealth of valuable material here. It is well researched and should provide a basis for future more specialized studies on the history of Anglicanism in Kenya. The book should spur other denominational bodies to attempt similar projects before too many of the memories of first and second generation Christians are lost.

207. Church, Henry G.

Theological Education That Makes a Difference: Church Growth in the Free Methodist Church in Malawi and Zimbabwe

Blantyre: CLAIM, 2002. 214 pages, ISBN: 9789990816464.

This doctoral dissertation, sponsored by the Department of Theology and Religious Studies of the University of Malawi, is by an American missionary who has worked with the Free Methodists in Malawi and Zimbabwe for more than twenty years. The study is based on interviews with numerous Free Methodist members and pastors throughout Malawi. The thesis is that the outstanding growth of the Free Methodist Church in Malawi, when evaluated against experience in other countries, is best explained by the special model and philosophy of theological education used within the Free Methodist Church in Malawi. Unfortunately, the Free Methodist programme under study is not in fact compared with others elsewhere. Also since the objective of church growth dominates, other issues in theological education receive insufficient consideration; by far the longest chapter consists of a favourable comparison between principles from George Peters' *A Theology of Church Growth* and the growth of the Free Methodists in Malawi. The Free Methodist programme, called "Chilinde," is based on three 4-week course modules offered at Lilongwe, each followed by three months of ministry, so that the student completes the programme in five years, with most of that time spent in the churches rather than in the classroom. Every student must plant three churches as a requirement for graduation. The language of instruction is English, and the entry level is grade eight, despite the fact that the church is predominantly rural and uneducated (an average of 3.25 years of schooling). Costs are heavily subsidized from overseas, and the lecturers listed are almost entirely non-resident. There is an uncomfortable tendency to make exaggerated claims, such as the remarkable statement that all the objectives of the *ICETE Manifesto on the Renewal of Evangelical Theological Education* have been met! Whereas everyone must rejoice that the Free Methodist community in Malawi has grown so rapidly, one cannot avoid the feeling that more interaction with others in the field outside the group under study could have helped avoid the impression given of sometimes uncritical self-congratulation. The challenge of the book is nevertheless for theological educators to reconsider the balance between residential and non-residential study in light of the needs of the churches.

208.   Clarence-Smith, William Gervase

Islam and the Abolition of Slavery

New York: Oxford University Press, 2006. 320 pages, ISBN: 9780195221510.

The author is a professor at the School of Oriental and African Studies in London. This book is interested in Islamic abolitionists and the role they played in suppressing slavery and the slave trade in the Islamic world. Although it was pressure from the West that forced Islamic states to pass anti-slavery laws in modern times, Islamic abolitionists were vital to those laws being enforced. Various views about slavery existed in the Islamic world, but the abolitionists drew on the weak foundations for the institution of slavery in the Qur'an and Islam's strong vision of social equality for all Muslims to argue that slavery was un-Islamic. The first part of the book traces the social and legal history of slavery in Muslim countries, and the second part examines the various responses of Muslims to Western pressure to end the slave trade and slavery itself. The author surveys the entire span of Islamic history, but with concentration on the last two centuries. Africa appears repeatedly, with good coverage of both East and West Africa, as well as North Africa of course. The most important Muslim abolitionists were in Asia, but the text mentions the work of several African Muslim scholars who argued that the Qur'an and Muhammad did not intend slavery to persist in Islam. The most radical African abolitionists mentioned are the Sudanese Mahmud Muhammad Taha (1909–1985), who wrote "The Second Message of Islam" (and was executed for it by the government of Sudan) and his disciples Abdullahi al-Na'im and Muhammad Khalil. The latter is still writing and is the most radical abolitionist of the three. Clarence-Smith concludes, "Although distinctive [Islamic] critiques of slavery emerged in Africa, Southeast Asia, and in the West, their impact on the heartlands of Islam remains uncertain." The last chapter compares Islam's approach to slavery and abolition historically to that of Judaism, Christianity and Far Eastern religions.

209. Clark, Phil, and Zachary Kaufman, editors

After Genocide: Transitional Justice, Post-Conflict Reconstruction and Reconciliation in Rwanda and Beyond

London: Hurst, 2009. 352 pages, ISBN: 9781850659198.

After Genocide is the fruit of three conferences held at Oxford University, and aims to analyse "the political, legal and regional impact of events in post-genocide Rwanda within the broader themes of transitional justice, reconstruction and reconciliation." The authors of the twenty essays that comprise the book (which include genocide survivors, scholars and professional practitioners) do not always speak with the same voice, and one purpose of the collection is to focus points of contention, notably the tension between the demands of justice and the pursuit of reconciliation. An important chapter is Clark's, in which he discusses key themes of transitional justice: reconciliation, peace, justice, healing, forgiveness and truth. The major dilemma which the book confronts is how all six can be satisfied simultaneously. Another significant paper is Buckley-Zistel's "We are Pretending Peace," discussing deliberate memory loss, chosen amnesia, as a strategy for survival, but one which fails to deal with the past and so risks a recurrence of the tragedy of 1994. A major theme of the work is to respond to a growing revisionism which denies the genocide or dwells on relatively peripheral issues – "Genocide-Laundering" as one author calls it. The preface is written by Rwanda's president, Paul Kagamé, who sees the work as "a vital riposte to the cynical rewriters of history," and castigates revisionists, the international community, the UN and France. He takes particular exception to Lemarchand's provocative article, "The Politics of Memory in Post-Genocide Rwanda," which raises pertinent questions about Kagamé's own political movement, its human rights record, and what Lemarchand alleges to be its manipulation of "memory" in the interests of the regime. Clark and Kaufman, as editors, give disproportionate space to the role of international institutions in establishing justice, notably the International Criminal Tribunal for Rwanda (ICTR). More important for justice within Rwanda has been the government's use of the *gacaca* system of community-based courts to deal with the thousands of imprisoned but untried genocide suspects. *Gacaca* has been controversial due to a perceived lack of legal due process, but Clark argues that it facilitates engagement between antagonistic parties and thereby promotes reconciliation. Not everybody would agree. Despite the many churches in Rwanda, there is little reference to Christian responses to the genocide, but the editors note how "the Christian beliefs of many Rwandans have inspired their pursuit of healing and reconciliation." A contribution on "psycho-social healing" summarizes one significant Christian approach which seeks to reconcile members of the rival ethnic groups at the cross. For anybody wishing to understand the genocide and the huge dilemmas involved in dealing with its aftermath, *After Genocide* is essential reading.

210. Clarke, Clifton R.

African Christology: Jesus in Post-Missionary African Christianity

Eugene, OR: Wipf & Stock, 2011. 204 pages, ISBN: 9781608994335.

Clarke is a black British Pentecostal bishop who worked as a mission partner with the CMS in Ghana teaching for ten years at the Good News Theological College and Seminary in Accra. This book is the result of his doctoral research for the University of Birmingham on the Christology of Ghanaian African Independent Churches (AICs). He discovered their Christology by listening to sermons, prayers, songs and testimonies, and by questionnaires and interviews. The book interacts with the views of Pobee, Bediako, Akrong, and others.

AIC Christology is oral and functional, related to what Jesus can do for people in their individual and corporate lives. Jesus is the healer of disease and its underlying spiritual causes, and the conqueror of unseen forces that hinder fullness of life. He is identified with God. AICs make heavy use of the Bible in the vernacular, which has allowed them to relate to Jesus directly. Unlike the trained theologians, AICs make little use of the image of Ancestor for Christ. King and Saviour are more common. AICs inhabit the African world of meaningful symbolism, using cross, water, staff, vestments, oil, candle and Bible as symbols of the unseen. Clarke wonders, then, why AICs make so little use of the sacraments, especially the Lord's Supper, and suggests a clash of the symbolic meaning of water, wine, bread and blood. This needs more exploration. Clarke makes a plea for academic theologians and such grassroots theology to listen to and enhance each other's understanding.

211.　Clarke, Donald S.

AIDS: The Biblical Solution

Nairobi: Evangel, 1994. 137 pages, ISBN: 9789966200532.

This book attempts a comprehensive biblical approach to the AIDS plague, especially as it is being experienced within Africa. The author was on the faculty of Nairobi International School of Theology, and holds a PhD in education. Among topics addressed are: the medical aspects of AIDS, AIDS mis-education, how to avoid AIDS, counselling AIDS patients, and what should the Church do. The book concludes with a list of recommended resources and a glossary. Although now somewhat dated by subsequent developments, the book is significant as a laudably early Christian response to the AIDS crisis in Africa. Also, despite the date of publication, the Christian perspective offered in the book is substantive and remains relevant.

212.　Clarke, Ian

The Man with the Key Has Gone!

London: New Wine Ministries, 1998. 320 pages, ISBN: 9781874367239.

Clarke was a general practice physician in Northern Ireland when in midlife he felt God's call to medical missions in Uganda. This is his account of what followed. He moved to Uganda with his wife and young family in 1988, serving with the Anglican Church Missionary Society (CMS) at Kiwoko, north of Kampala. Apart from herbalists and those dealing in witchcraft, it was an area bereft of medical care. In time he founded and developed a 220-bed hospital there, with surgical facilities, a TB ward, a maternity ward, a laboratory, a laboratory assistant training school, a nurse training school, and an active community-based health care programme. As the hospital administrator, Clarke also gained inevitable experience with government bureaucracy. Being a gifted writer, he treats his frequent visits to government offices with appropriate wit. Often enough business could not be concluded in an expeditious manner because the person with authority was not available – "the man with the key has gone," the office clerk would explain. The HIV pandemic eventually dominates and even overwhelms this narrative, and to a large extent the life of Clarke and his family. His emotional involvement and grief are palpable. Whereas Clarke is never judgemental about how AIDS had been contracted, his Christian views are evident as he advises Ugandans to abstain from sex before marriage and to be faithful in marriage. Given the many merits of this book, it is difficult to be critical, but the narrative does become somewhat over-weighted with so many tragic AIDS cases that are very similar. As the book reaches its end, Clarke is discovered to be gravely ill with a rapidly progressing cancer and has to be medically evacuated back to Ireland for treatment. The story subsequent to this book is that he recovered and returned to play a further leading role in medical ministry in Uganda.

213. Clarke, Peter B., editor

New Trends and Developments in African Religions

Santa Barbara, CA: ABC-CLIO, 1998. 328 pages, ISBN: 9780313301285.

The introduction to this book states, "This book focuses on African and African-derived religions and how these display themselves in the contemporary world, particularly the Americas, the Caribbean and Europe." The book aims to show that African religions are not irrelevant in the modern world, but have something to contribute in the world religious scene as a whole. The editor of this collection of articles is professor emeritus of the history and sociology of religion at the University of London, and formerly an associate professor of history at the University of Ibadan in Nigeria. The seventeen articles included in this collection deal with religions that syncretise African with other religions, including Candomble, African-Brazilian religion, Rastafarians, Macumba, Umbanda, the Earth People, the Nation of Islam, Santeria, Winti, the Malingo cult in Italy, the True Teachings of Christ Temple in Amsterdam, and Caribbean Shakerism, treating them mainly within a psychological and sociological framework. Only the final chapter deals with a phenomenon wholly within Africa: Victor Wan-Tatah's article on conversion into the Nazarene Church of Isaiah Shembe. Among other goals, the book seeks to "make a contribution to the wider and ongoing debate on syncretism that continues to preoccupy those in the anthropology, history, and sociology of religion" fields. This book would be useful to those studying syncretism in any context, but is not particularly focused on Africa itself.

214. Clarke, Peter B.

West Africa and Christianity

London: Edward Arnold, 1986. 271 pages, ISBN: 9780713182637.

This book, a companion to the author's *West Africa and Islam* (1982), attempts to describe and interpret the whole history of the Christian community in West Africa, which for him includes Cameroon and Chad. The content has more detail and personal research than other familiar texts in this field of study. Clarke later became a professor in the history and sociology of religion at the University of London. In the late 1970s and early 1980s he taught at a teachers college in northern Nigeria and also at the University of Ibadan. By the nature of the case, much of the history of Christianity in West Africa is missions history and Clarke reflects that. As a balance, there is a chapter on the "independent" churches and three on church history since 1960. Most chapters look at Christian missionary activity country by country. Clarke tells us that he has focused on "the methods used to spread Christianity, such as the school, the important role played by African and expatriate clergy and laymen and women, particularly that of the catechist." The training of indigenous clergy occupies a large space. Clarke is weak on the activities of the smaller denominational and interdenominational missions, betrayed not least by giving them wrong names (thus the "Christian Missionary Alliance"; the "Worldwide Evangelical Crusade") and associations (Seventh Day Adventists are treated as Pentecostals!). Clarke is a historian and not a missiologist, so he shows little acquaintance with church growth literature, which could have sharpened his interpretation. He does not refer to comity, the Bible Societies or evangelical fellowships, except once for Ghana. Some judgements about state-church relations, the role of charismatic-pentecostal churches and his naiveté concerning Christian-Muslim relations, would need to be modified today.

215.   Clement, Atchenemou Hlama, Raymond Hassan, Moyo Ozodo, and Bill Kornfield

Cross-Cultural Christianity: A Textbook on Cross-Cultural Communication

Jos: Nigeria Evangelical Missionary Institute, 1996. 136 pages, ISBN: 9789782668691.

This is a textbook developed out of the cross-cultural communication course taught by Kornfield, a missionary educator, to the first set of students in the Nigeria Evangelical Missionary Institute. Three of the best students (two Nigerians and one Chadian) wrote up the material as it applied to African missionary trainees. Their work was checked and supplemented by Kornfield to produce the first edition in 1989. Since then the African authors have continued to teach the material, and from their experience have produced this expanded and updated edition, which includes a section of notes for teachers. The book takes students through the steps of accepting oneself, accepting other individuals, and accepting another culture. There is a chapter on the tools of cross-cultural communication and the final chapter gives guidelines on how to present Christ cross-culturally. The topics dealt with in these last chapters include norms, values, culture shock, culture learning, building relationships, identification, syncretism and paternalism. The book ends with twenty case studies grouped by chapter. Each chapter in the text also begins with a case study. The first edition of the book had already proved itself useful in training African missionaries and this second edition is even better. The book is highly recommended as a text for training African evangelists, pastors and missionaries for effective cross-cultural ministry.

216.   Cochrane, J. R., I. W. Henderson, and Gerald O. West, editors

Bibliography in Contextual Theology in Africa: Volume 1

Pietermaritzburg: Cluster, 1993. 60 pages, ISBN: 9780958314114.

A team related to the University of Natal in South Africa was responsible for this bibliography on contextual theology in Africa, which covers theological publications from sub-Saharan Africa as a whole, although with special emphasis on southern Africa. The team pragmatically defined "contextual theology" as "any theological writings from within, or about, the Christian faith and tradition which locate their ideas and arguments in relation to the political, social, cultural and economic contexts which make up the various regions of Africa." Approximately 150 publications are listed, and each entry is annotated for easy exploration, with an abstract and designation of field and key words. Although this booklet was introduced as the first in a series, the bibliography project eventually developed into a journal – the *Bulletin for Contextual Theology in Africa*. Those intending advanced-level research on Christian reflection in Africa will want to secure access to a copy of this bibliography.

217.   Cochrane, J. R., John W. de Gruchy, and Stephen Martin, editors

Facing the Truth: South African Faith Communities and the Truth &
Reconciliation Commission

Athens, OH: Ohio University Press, 1999. 252 pages, ISBN: 9780821413074.

This book consists of two parts. The first is a 62-page report, prepared by the Research Institute on Christianity in South Africa (RICSA), based at the University of Cape Town, entitled "Faith Communities and Apartheid." In this report the editors summarize the testimony given in 1997 during the "faith community hearings" of South Africa's Truth and Reconciliation Commission (TRC). Reflecting South African demographics, these hearings were originally meant to be "church hearings," hence most of the submissions were made by Christian groups, although other faiths were also represented. The report highlights the ways in which various faith communities in South Africa understood themselves in relation to apartheid, and the action or, sadly, inaction, that arose from this. The second part of the book consists of ten essays (two of which form the "Afterword") addressing issues that arose from these hearings. Many of these essays simply refocus on the faith community hearings some standardized arguments about the TRC and reconciliation, and readers who are familiar with the literature will not find anything new here. There are, however, one or two gems. Robin Petersen's essay on "The AICs and the TRC" is excellent, and it is unfortunate that other submissions have not been dealt with in a similar fashion. Most churches in South Africa would agree that reconciliation is important, but the "how" continues to evade them. While this book does not offer any solutions, it will goad the attentive reader into thinking more carefully about these matters. One suspects that the submissions to these hearings will come to be recognized as important documents in South African church history, and certainly this RICSA report provides a good place to start exploring them.

218.   Coetzee, P. H., and A. P. J. Roux, editors

The African Philosophy Reader

Abingdon, UK: Routledge, 2004. 672 pages, ISBN: 9780415968096.

This book is intended for first-degree students of African Philosophy. The editors both served at the University of South Africa. The readings are divided into seven categories: Culture, Trends, Metaphysics, Epistemology, Ethics, Politics, and Aesthetics. Each of the seven categories begins with an introductory essay followed by essays by some African philosophers reprinted from various sources. In the essay that introduces the whole volume, E. Biakolo of Botswana maintains that philosophy is a cultural enterprise, and is thus culture specific. "There is no single philosophical (conceptual) order for all mankind." Therefore, what we have in African Philosophy is mainly description of philosophical concepts specific to certain tribes or regions (e.g. "Eniyan: The Yoruba Concept of a Person" by S. Gbadegesin; "Themes in Chewa Epistemology" by D. Kaphagawani). Ghana, Nigeria, and Uganda are the places where regional philosophies have emerged, but South Africa has mainly worked with European philosophical thought. A few essays explore whether there are philosophical concepts common to all of Africa. Others explore broad concepts such as logic and rationality, truth, morality, and aesthetics from an African viewpoint. A number of the essays work with concepts from ATR, notably "On Decolonizing African Religions" by K. Wiredu. Wiredu argues that Africans, specifically the Akan, do not think of the ancestors and so-called "lesser gods" as supernatural beings but as part of the realm of nature, and treat them in a utilitarian manner, not as something to do with "religion," as Western descriptions would have it. Likewise K. A. Appiah, in "Old Gods, New Worlds," speaking of the Ashante, believes that the ritual behaviour of Africans is more in function like science is in Western societies, but the traditional worldview promotes a communal society that the Western worldview does not. Mbiti is mentioned briefly by several contributors. Whereas the tenor of the remarks is that Mbiti is a bit dated and Western-influenced, and his theory of communal identity of the person in African philosophy is critiqued, he is also acknowledged as a proponent of the idea that a philosophical system and ideology of a tribe can be extracted from its proverbs, folk tales and traditions. This book would be a useful resource for those thinking through the contextualization of Christianity in Africa, though Christian readers would have to draw their own conclusions about how African thought relates to Christianity since this is not a focus of the book.

219.   Cole, Victor Babajide, Ross F. Gaskin, and Ronald J. Sim, editors

Perspectives on Leadership Training

Nairobi: NEGST, 1993. 265 pages, ISBN: 9789966200419.

This book consists of articles relating broadly to Christian leadership training, especially in Africa, contributed by seventeen distinguished individuals who are or have been associated with the Nairobi Evangelical Graduate School of Theology either as lecturers or in other leadership capacities. The book was produced to mark the tenth anniversary of the founding of NEGST. Among the contributors are Tokunboh Adeyemo, Victor Cole, Sam Ngewa, Bill Dyrness, and Tony Wilmot. The articles are grouped under four themes, namely: educational, missiological, theological/biblical, and pastoral perspectives on leadership training. Those interested in theological education in Africa will certainly want to read this stimulating collection of essays, and theological libraries throughout the continent should expect to have it in their holdings.

220.   Collier, Paul

The Bottom Billion: Why the Poorest Countries Are Failing and What Can Be Done About It

New York: Oxford University Press, 2008. 224 pages, ISBN: 9780195374636.

Of the six billion people living in the world today, five billion have seen their quality of life improve over the last half century. This leaves one-sixth living in extreme destitution; or what the Oxford economist Paul Collier describes as the "bottom billion." In this provocative and intellectually stimulating book, he eschews simplistic answers in favour of a multi-faceted approach to the dire problems of poverty in the global economy. Devastatingly, among the fifty-eight countries that make up this category, the large majority are in Africa. Collier never identifies the specific nations that make up this inauspicious grouping, but loosely refers to them as "Africa+," with the + being nations such as Haiti, Bolivia and North Korea. Collier examines the reasons why such countries languish, identifying four common "traps": (1) conflict; (2) natural resources; (3) being landlocked with bad neighbours; and (4) poor governance. He then proceeds to look at possible solutions (what he calls "instruments"): (1) aid; (2) military intervention; (3) laws and charters; and (4) trade policy. These are not all equal, nor do they indiscriminately match the four "traps." The final chapter offers an integrative proposal for how the "instruments" can best serve in addressing the "traps" to help define a way forward for those nations that make up the "bottom billion." This book wrestles with the thorny problems of global economic policy, yet is written in language suited for the everyday reader, with clear explanations and vivid case studies. This may be one of the most formative books on global poverty (or, alternatively, on development) in recent years, and of particular relevance for Africa. While not overtly theological in nature, readers will easily discern ways in which the Church can contribute to the solutions suggested in the book.

221.   Collins, Barbara

Becoming a Trans-Cultural Woman

Nairobi: Evangel, 1999. 197 pages, ISBN: 9789966200952.

This book is intended as an instructional manual for women preparing to minister to women in cultural settings different from their own. The content is organized around topics covered in the Africa Inland Church programme for wives among its cross-cultural missionary trainees in Kenya. Topics move from the foundational issue of a woman's commitment to God through various aspects of mothering such as childbirth, birth control and child development, before proceeding to a woman's cultural adjustment, and to ministry among women and children. Since the educational background of wives in the AIC programme varies widely, the book seeks to address and train a diverse group of women, a difficult task in any culture. The author uses journal entries of women to make each lesson practical, and includes African cultural material, in addition to a strong scriptural grounding, and material from professional sources which are referenced in the bibliography. The feedback and discussion questions at the end of each section will help women learn from Scripture and from each other as they apply the material to situations they face. The presentation of the material seems to mix colloquialisms and some Americanisms with more technical terms in ways that would benefit from additional editing in a subsequent edition. Under the guidance of a skilful leader, however, this book as it stands will provide much helpful material, while stimulating women to evaluate biblically and apply their learning to their lives and ministries. Training programmes in Africa for cross-cultural ministry should certainly secure a copy for evaluation.

Collins, Belinda A.

see review 1199

222.   Colson, Elizabeth

Tonga Religious Life in the Twentieth Century

Lusaka: Bookworld, 2007. 316 pages, ISBN: 9789982240451.

The author is widely known in academic circles and among the Tonga people as the foremost anthropological authority on the Tonga people of southern Zambia, having lived and worked among them for varying lengths of time since 1946. In this her most recent book she draws on her experiences and field notes across her time in Zambia, as well as on her current observations, to describe and evaluate the state of religious life and especially the influences of Christian missions among the Tonga people today. She includes urban dwelling Tongas along with the village people among whom she has worked for many years, providing an anthropologist's assessment of how traditional beliefs and values are persevering and adapting to modern life. In following her subjects across the years, she also reports and analyses the faith positions of Tongas who have converted to Christianity through the role of the various Christian missions that have worked among the Tonga since the early twentieth century. She is thus especially effective at reflecting the degrees of cultural change and syncretism involved in Christian conversion, writing primarily from the perspective of the unconverted Tongas. The study therefore offers a valuable perspective on the influence of Christianity that is not easily accessible to those whose information comes primarily from Christian converts. In addition to valuable insights on syncretism and Christian conversion, the author also gives a clearly articulated description of the Tonga version of African traditional religion today. The majority of her book deals with traditional rituals, officiants of these rituals, manifestations of spirits, shrines and their maintenance, life course rituals, and evil and witchcraft. She writes from what is primarily an "insider" perspective, due to her years of living among her Tonga village friends even though she is not a Tonga by birth. As an anthropologist, she also takes a more value neutral stance when describing aspects of the traditional religion and practice that are being opposed today in the wider society, issues such as incest, abortion and killing of multiple birth babies like twins. Christians will bring biblical moral standards to bear in these situations, and therefore her stance may trouble some readers. This book will be illuminating for Christians ministering in areas of Africa where traditional religion is being practiced along with Christianity, and especially useful for those seeking to formulate appropriate Christian reflection about traditional religion and its interaction with Christianity in contemporary Africa.

223.   Comaroff, Jean, and John L. Comaroff, editors

Modernity and Its Malcontents: Ritual and Power in Postcolonial Africa

Chicago: University of Chicago Press, 1993. 272 pages, ISBN: 9780226114408.

This edited volume brings together the writings of various historical anthropologists associated with the University of Chicago for the purpose of exploring how Africans negotiate ritual for crafting their own modernity. As the title implies, the essayists contend that Africans do so not in one uniform fashion, but by acting, reacting, sometimes accommodating, but more often by reimaging modernity through a rich assortment of rituals and symbols, building upon the past in order to forge a new future. Hence, the book contains chapters dealing with such varied themes as capitalism in marketplaces in Niger, or how the Chewa in Malawi draw upon the secrecy of the Nyau dance in order to reconstitute power in the face of Western agency. However, the majority of essays focus upon witchcraft in contemporary Africa; for, in the words of the editors, witches represent "modernity's prototypical malcontents." The chapters dealing with witchcraft reveal some of the diverse ways it functions in contemporary societies, often involving such things as the acquisition of wealth and/or the power to affect reproduction within women. While the editors repeatedly forewarn that witchcraft in Africa remains eminently real, the essayists tend to focus upon the rise of witchcraft, including fluctuations within the cocoa market in Nigeria, conflations of urban and rural societies, and regional changes in the political economy in Zambia. In all of these, there is the attempt, whether realized or not, to show the variances of witchcraft in Africa in the face of massive socio-cultural change. As one author describes regarding "soul-eating" amongst the Hausa, "Using symbols that reverberate to the very core of human experience – consumption, reproduction, death – soul-eating can be viewed as addressing the threat posed by uncontrollable desire and jealousy in society." In such ways the essayists seek to demonstrate how current forms of witchcraft are largely influenced by massive socio-cultural change. It is likely that many readers may find the chapters dealing with witchcraft unsatisfactory in explaining deeper facets of the spiritual realm. None of the essayists deny the reality of cosmological forces, but they do tend to focus more on the social, political, or economic reasons for witchcraft rather than the substance of evil itself. Despite these concerns, the chapters do provide rich description into the worlds of Africans as they negotiate through a variety of modern and traditional, secular and sacred, individual and collectivist resources, never putting these into simple, easily constructed binaries, but combining them together with imaginative energy to forge new modernities. Such a book will especially interest those actively researching witchcraft in the African context, or African engagement with modernity.

Comaroff, John L.

see review 223

224. Concerned Evangelicals

Evangelical Witness in South Africa: South African Evangelicals Critique Their Own Theology and Practice

Oxford: Regnum, 1986. 40 pages, ISBN: 9781870345002.

Although the book's title indicates a self-appraisal, it is a critique (developed between September 1985 and June 1986), largely by black evangelicals in South Africa, of the theology and practice of white evangelicals, particularly focusing on their failure to take part as a prophetic voice of conscience to the apartheid regime. As a result, the evangelicals (both black and white) lacked an adequate theology to address the crises they were facing. Evangelicals were perceived as not only supporting but even promoting the status quo. Consequently, they lost credibility, making the situation no longer conducive to fulfilling their call to ministry, much less any evangelistic outreach. The critique is, therefore, a call "to all evangelicals here and abroad (to re-examine) our ways, to see whether we are still doing the will of our Father or are consciously or unconsciously busy with somebody's agenda rather than the agenda of the Lord." The critique identifies seven areas of concern: (1) theological problems such as conservatism and dogmatism, (2) theologies which blindly support and maintain existing world systems, (3) the general tendency of the church to conform to the norms and values of society, (4) the impression that Western capitalistic culture and Christianity are one and the same, (5) the lack of inter-fellowship and cooperation among evangelicals across racial and denominational lines, (6) the lack of balance between the dimensions of salvation and social change, and (7) the radical demands of the gospel for repentance, forgiveness, new life, and commitment to our responsibilities. While recognising that the majority in South Africa are black, the impact of the document would doubtless have been even more effective had it been possible to include some additional whites and at least some Asians among its 132 signatories.

225. Connor, Bernard F.

The Difficult Traverse from Amnesty to Reconciliation

Pietermaritzburg: Cluster, 1998. 151 pages, ISBN: 9781875053131.

In this outstanding but neglected book the South African Catholic theologian, Bernard Connor, attempts to go beyond the work of South Africa's Truth and Reconciliation Commission's (TRC) to ask how, far from being a mere "spectator sport," the TRC can prove to be a "saving and life-giving experience." Reconciliation, he acknowledges, is a "difficult traverse." Whilst granting that amnesty is an affair of state, effecting reconciliation is a great deal more complex. Combining mercy with the quest for justice in the search for reconciliation is an extraordinarily delicate task. As Connor observes, introducing mercy too early or excessively can jeopardize justice; too late or not at all can thwart reconciliation altogether. In the final analysis reconciliation is not a state of affairs that can be brought about by human design. Acceptance of former enemies, for instance, is a grace that challenges our old selves and the established pattern of a society, and for that to happen a profound work of grace is needed. Indeed, reconciliation is a working of grace. Drawing from philosophers, social scientists, and Catholic theologians, Connor's book is about how we might keep ourselves within this ambit of grace so that we might become better instruments of reconciliation. It sometimes happens that a new and important book appears on the scene only to be put on the half-price bookstall, since people are either not interested or are afraid that its contents may be too disturbing. The fact that Connor's book has not been given the acclaim that it so richly deserves says something about the condition of the church in post-apartheid South Africa. This is a book waiting to be discovered, not only by the thoughtful Christian in South Africa and also by a wider international readership, since Christians throughout Africa and elsewhere will certainly find insights here that are relevant as well for their own contexts.

226.   Conradie, Ernst M., and Charl E. Fredericks, editors

Mapping Systematic Theology in Africa: An Indexed Bibliography

Stellenbosch: SUN Press, 2004. 186 pages, ISBN: 9781919980294.

This book is the fruit of a project led by Ernst Conradie from the University of the Western Cape. Professor Conradie's team systematically worked their way through large university and college libraries in Africa in order to identify books and articles germane to systematic theology within the African context. The team focused on the three major university libraries in and near Cape Town, and searches were also performed in libraries in other parts of anglophone Africa, including those of Daystar University, Nairobi Evangelical Graduate School of Theology and Scott Theological College in Kenya, and the University of Zimbabwe and Africa University in Zimbabwe. The result of this labour is this highly useful bibliography, containing over 1300 entries that, using African theology as the specific frame of reference, either focus on, or contain substantial sections on, systematic theology and/or ethics. Two indices follow, one for systematic theology and the other for ethics, with entries grouped according to the traditional loci in these fields. Texts that would traditionally fall within the field of "biblical studies" have not been included. Most entries are from the 1960s onward, although a few from earlier years can be found, including at least one from 1899. Only a few doctoral dissertations are referenced. Evangelical scholars have not been ignored; titles by Kato, Tiénou, and Adeyemo, for example, appear in the listings. The most significant limitation is the absence of French texts; this is a bibliography by and for anglophone Africa. The researchers seem to have surveyed several dozen journals, including the *Journal of African Christian Thought*, the *African Theological Journal*, and the *African Journal of Evangelical Theology*, as well as some international journals. The bibliography has a (perhaps unavoidable) bias towards South African titles (although the voluminous literature on the struggle against apartheid and the Truth and Reconciliation Committee has been wisely omitted). Whereas minor errors are inevitable, not all are insignificant for a resource of this nature. Thus one will find Isaac Zokoué referenced in the bibliography as "Zokode" and in the index as "Zokoude." And while the bibliography has managed to incorporate a vast range of materials, it is not so difficult to notice the lacunae. *Mapping* must be taken as but a first step, but nevertheless a very welcome and distinguished first step. Despite its limitations, this is a valuable reference resource for everyone working in the fields of African theology or systematic theology.

227.   Cook, David, and Michael Okenimkpe

Ngugi wa Thiong'o: An Exploration of His Writings

Nairobi: East African Educational Publishers, 1997. 284 pages, ISBN: 9780435911744.

This volume offers a sympathetic critique of the literary and political writings (up to 1997) of Kenya's most famous novelist, Ngugi wa Thiong'o, provided by two highly qualified critics very familiar with pressing African issues. This is therefore not only an excellent introduction to Ngugi's voluminous output but also a penetrating analysis of the social and political context of his works. A major feature of this critique of Ngugi's works is its focus on the struggles Ngugi had with what he regarded as a politicized and hypocritical Christianity. Since Ngugi's writings have for many years been standard texts in secondary and university education in Africa, his take on African Christianity has not been without impact. Cook and Okenimkpe demonstrate that in *The River Between*, Ngugi "presents to us a society divided between Christians and non-Christians" as the tactics of the British colonial government become increasingly intrusive. Nevertheless, Ngugi's depiction of these struggles indicates a "complex religious awareness" based upon his admiration of some aspects of Christian teaching. In *Weep Not, Child*, Ngugi portrays a much darker scene in which the immature protagonist's faith in the Bible is shattered when he endures a beating at the hands of nominally Christian authorities. Both in this novel and in *A Grain of Wheat*, Cook and Okenimkpe find that "Christianity is admired and accepted, and yet is looked at critically and askance, till eventually it loses authority." In a similar vein, *Petals of Blood* is a harsh indictment of the Christian establishment that supports "a social order which protects their selfish comforts and relegates the multitude to perpetual poverty." The next novel, with its seemingly outrageous title, *Devil on the Cross*, employs parody and inversion; it is not intended to be blasphemous. The authors' analysis of this work is perceptive, and seemingly accurate: ". . . we must not imagine that Ngugi is trying to invert morality in placing Satan on the cross in Christ's place. He is not saying that Satan is his Christ, but rather that, whatever they may pretend, it is the Devil whom the capitalistic power magnates and their entourage really worship." Regarding *Matagari*, the authors accurately affirm that "in most of Ngugi's novels there are biblical references, direct and indirect, and Matigari is no exception." But curiously they miss the obvious feature of this semi-allegorical work as a political recasting of the gospel narratives incorporating biblical allusions from beginning to end. In spite of the plethora of Christological references in this novel, this work is a powerful attack on institutionalized Christianity, including its metaphysical beliefs. For Ngugi, social, economic, and political justice must be at the heart and core of true religion. Attentive Christian theological engagement in Africa will do well to take into fuller account the challenges that Ngugi's message and influence represent.

228.   Coomes, Anne

African Harvest: The Captivating Story of Michael Cassidy and African Enterprise

Oxford: Monarch, 2002. 550 pages, ISBN: 9781854245991.

Coomes, a former editor of *The Church of England Newspaper*, here documents the life of the noted founder and director of African Enterprise, Michael Cassidy of South Africa, and the history of the organisation itself. The book is, as its title promises, captivating. The anecdotal writing style mirrors the AE strategy of using story and testimony heavily in its mission. Treating the life of Cassidy first, the author draws out influences that likely shaped the person he came to be: his desire for unity, reconciliation and forgiveness in the face of disrupted relationships; his political and social conscience; his life of prayer; his sense (from boarding school experience) of how it feels to be a victim, and his insistence later on justice and fair play. After conversion to Christianity as a new student at Cambridge University, he added evangelistic zeal to these passions, reacting against nominal Christianity. He also later came to realize the necessity of synthesising the spiritual with the political and social responsibilities of the gospel, emphasising a kingdom gospel that seeks to make Christ Lord of all parts of personal and corporate life. The story of AE, the organisation Cassidy founded in 1962, then follows, including its efforts to intervene, provide relief and bring reconciliation during the Ugandan crises in the late 1970s, the independence struggle in Zimbabwe, the South African journey toward majority rule, and the Rwandan genocide of the 1990s. Also included is an instructive account of the internal crisis in the late 1970s and early 1980s that nearly tore the organisation apart: the humility and repentance required to seek forgiveness from the Lord and one another; the hard work necessary to achieve understanding and reconciliation; the reward of coming out on the other side of the crisis unified. AE's ministry activities beyond the shores of Africa are also reported, including work to bring reconciliation in Ireland and Israel. The book ends with an epilogue by Cassidy, offering his own reflections on 40 years of AE ministry. This is a worthy read for inspiration, challenge and instruction, presenting as it does one of the most active evangelical leaders in southern Africa in recent decades, and the extraordinary ministry that he founded.

229.   Coomes, Anne

Festo Kivengere: The Authorised Biography

Oxford: Monarch, 1990. 478 pages, ISBN: 9781854240217.

Kivengere was undoubtedly one of Africa's best-loved Christian leaders, and his death from leukaemia in 1988 was a great loss to the continent. Fortunately for the readers of this challenging biography, he opened up his heart and life before he died, so that others may continue to gain from his wisdom and his deep love for Christ. Beginning from Kivengere's days as a boy in rural Uganda, the author carefully traces his life as a teacher, pastor and bishop, to the day that Kivengere and his wife escaped Idi Amin's death squads in 1977 by walking into Rwanda ("You will never know fear until you are running at night for your life in your own country"). The book concludes with his international ministry and his return to Uganda as a national hero seeking to heal the wounds left by Amin's years in power. Besides being an excellent biographical resource for modern African church history (Kivengere was converted during the East African Revival), a strength of the book is that it does not try to make Kivengere superhuman. There are several examples of family tension where he humbled himself and asked for forgiveness.

230.   Cooper, Barbara M.

Evangelical Christians in the Muslim Sahel

Bloomington, IN: Indiana University Press, 2010. 480 pages, ISBN: 9780253222336.

A history professor at Rutgers University, Cooper has researched in depth the work of the evangelical mission SIM in and around Maradi, in the Niger Republic. Cooper provides insights and perspectives on SIM's work that likely would not have occurred to SIM insiders. While often complimentary, she faults SIM for its "reluctance to engage in social services for the sake of charity or social uplift (because) the mission's unabashed goal is the conversion of non-Christians to Christianity." Granted SIM's evangelistic goal, the supposed "reluctance" in social services contrasts with the author's later acknowledgement of SIM's extensive involvement in medical, education, agricultural, development, and famine-relief ministries. Most SIM missionaries would doubtless strongly disagree that they had provided these charitable ministries in any sense "reluctantly." Overall, this is a valuable and insightful book that exhibits enormous research. Especially penetrating is Cooper's analysis of the popular and growing Pentecostal movement and her explanation why it is so attractive to Christians in Niger. She also concludes that the leaders of the SIM-related church in Niger have adopted a well-reasoned, culturally and religiously sensitive approach to Muslim evangelism. The book's chief flaw is the author's insistence on viewing the strategies of SIM as based upon its "fundamentalist" beliefs, a word that she defines as a dualism that sees everything as either of God or Satan, good or evil, right or wrong, and by implication unable to deal with ambiguities. This "fundamentalist" characterisation, which seems to arise more from Cooper's own preconceptions than from her data, contributes to a misleading image of SIM. Cooper's analysis would have been more secure had she used more nuanced interpretive categories, ones less freighted with vagueness and potential abuse.

231. **Cooper, Frederick**

Africa since 1940: The Past of the Present

Cambridge: Cambridge University Press, 2002. 230 pages, ISBN: 9780521776004.

Cooper is professor of African history at New York University. In this book he proposes to bridge the gap between the colonial and post-colonial periods of modern African history, by addressing what difference the end of the colonial empires meant, and what kinds of processes continued even as governments changed hands. He frequently notes that Africa's "big men" have continued to exploit their people as much as the colonizers who preceded them did. Yet he adds that even the states that oppress their people have kept the same borders as they had at independence, and that that feat should not be minimized. His primary emphasis is political history, so the church receives little attention; thus the longer references to the church in the index are misleading. He notes that religious movements should be analysed as "attempts to give moral anchorage to people crossing cultural and moral boundaries, and of innovative syntheses of a range of doctrinal and ritual practices," but religion is not seen as a major factor in Africa's history. When Cooper deals with religion he seems to prefer radical movements like the Lenshina crisis that occurred just after Zambia's independence, rather than dealing with the religious groups in the relatively peaceful end to apartheid in South Africa. Perhaps the most helpful aspects of this book is the analysis of proposed solutions to Africa's problems. Among those that he judges to be "false" solutions are: privatize and depend on the market; create an African capitalist class to increase employment; and promote African economies rather than dependence on the rest of the world. He ends by suggesting that governments and outside organisations should take advantage of social organisations that are already in place, such as cocoa producers and market women; governments must also be "social" democracies even if they are not "socialist" (which failed in places like Tanzania); international organisations claiming to help Africa should themselves be willing to reform rather than placing the onus on African states alone; and such organisations should pay more attention to African social critics of their own governments rather than depending on outside analysis only. This book is of limited help to understanding Christianity in modern Africa, but it does give a broader interpretation of the context in which African Christianity has grown and helps in understanding its present context.

232.   **Coquery-Vidrovitch, Catherine**

African Women: A Modern History

Boulder, CO: Westview Press, 1997. 336 pages, ISBN: 9780813323619.

Coquery-Vidrovitch is a recognized historian, and director of a French research centre on Africa. Here she has provided yet another valuable study on sub-Saharan Africa, concentrating this time on the history of women during the past two centuries. The book is well documented, as one would expect of a research historian, with a rich selective bibliography and numerous footnotes. The presentation is divided into four major sections, each of which deals with African women during a general historical period: women in the nineteenth century; the movement from countryside to town; the colonial period up to the time of independence; and the life of women in Africa in the so-called period of "modernity." One of the strengths of this study is the fact that the author has not limited herself to francophone Africa but has searched widely across the continent in order to highlight the variety of situations in which African women have found themselves over the past two centuries. A noticeable weakness of the book is the author's apparent lack of interest in African women as a spiritual force. Only a handful of pages deal with women in religion. In African traditional religions, where anthropological studies have provided little evidence that women had much authority or power, the author wonders whether this lack is owing to general male dominance in anthropological research. The author also mentions some twentieth-century African women as having had visions and then starting their own spiritual movement, often as a splinter group breaking from an established Christian church. Elsewhere she pauses to excoriate the gender bias of missionaries who ran schools that segregated girls from boys and did not train girls for much more than being wives and mothers. Otherwise the author does not mention religion as a factor in an African woman's life. No notice is taken, for example, of the valuable contribution that women's groups in churches have today, both as a spiritual force in Christianity and as a socialisation factor for women who participate. Coquery-Vidrovitch sees two themes undergirding contemporary reflection on the future of women in Africa, namely emancipation and development. She recognizes that the emancipation of the African woman will take a different course than that of the Western woman, simply because African culture (which tends to emphasize the group rather than the individual) works in a different way. She sees development as a viable possibility for women, especially because girls as well as boys have the (legal) right to go to school and thus get an education that prepares them for more than hand-to-mouth existence. There are few studies of this scholarly calibre on women in Africa.

233.   **Corbitt, J. Nathan**

The Sound of the Harvest: Music's Mission in Church and Culture

Grand Rapids: Baker, 1998. 352 pages, ISBN: 9780801058295.

"Music is a universal language." Yet anyone who has tried to understand the message of his teenager's favourite rap group from the standpoint of the music favoured in his own teenage years would surely question the validity of such a statement. And those who struggle to worship in cross-cultural settings would add their query. Corbitt's premise in this book is not that "music is a universal language," but rather that the applications to which music is put make music a universal factor in worship and mission. "Music is always cross-cultural. Its meanings are so bound to the people and cultures who make it, we often fail to see our commonness because of our strangeness. God's song of a redemptive call and purpose are found in every place." In seven chapters

Corbitt makes a case for using music as prophet, priest, proclaimer, healer, preacher and teacher. An additional four chapters deal with the voice, song, instruments, and musicians themselves. Corbitt is currently professor of communications and music at Eastern College in the United States. Before that he spent more than a decade in cross-cultural ministry in East Africa. In each chapter Corbitt uses stories and examples from his ample experience during these years as a musical missionary. These vignettes effectively drive home the points being made, and set this book apart from many other ethnomusicological textbooks. The book will serve excellently as a primary text for any course in Africa on music and the church.

234. Corten, André, and Ruth Marshall-Fratani, editors

Between Babel and Pentecost: Transnational Pentecostalism in Africa and Latin America

London: Hurst, 2001. 317 pages, ISBN: 9781850654384.

This book offers a cross-disciplinary collection of scholarly essays on the international Pentecostal movement. Drawing from the fields of anthropology, sociology, psychology, economics, politics and globalisation, it offers the reader an academic and technical social sciences approach to the study of contemporary transnational Pentecostalism. One weakness of this book is that the technical nature of the discourse in some of the articles is so entrenched in post-modern form that those not already initiated into the discipline will find the reading difficult to follow (not least the essays by the editors themselves). A second weakness parallels the first. In the social science fields it is typically expected that the language of the converts and proponents must be examined psychologically and socially rather than taken at face value, often because the worldview of the social scientist allows little if any room for true interaction between the supernatural realm and humanity. Thus in these essays the dichotomy between sacred and secular tends to be too strongly maintained. Explanatory frames for Pentecostalism found throughout the text are not just largely anthropological or psychological – they can be exclusively so. Certainly Pentecostals themselves could hardly be satisfied with such accounts, and neither should other Christian readers. Desiring to avoid reductionism of one kind, many authors fall into another by not taking the reality of the supernatural into account in their explorations. African students of Pentecostalism will certainly be interested in the essays that focus on movements in the continent, especially the summary chapters by César and Droogers. While libraries with collections emphasizing Pentecostalism will want to have a copy, most others would be advised to search for books in the field that are more accessible.

235. Coulon, Paul, editor

Christianisme et humanisme en Afrique: Mélanges en hommage au cardinal Bernadin Gantin

Paris: Éditions Karthala, 2003. 408 pages, ISBN: 9782845863941.

Cardinal Bernadin Gantin of Benin for many years held senior positions in the Vatican hierarchy. He died in 2008. Published in his honour several years earlier, this Festschrift is a collection of 26 essays, grouped in six categories: Man (three essays); Africa and Its Problems (five); The Church (five); The Bishop (three); Synodal Problems and Perspectives for Involvement (four); and New Perspectives (six). The contributors are from Africa (including several from Benin) as well as others from the Catholic hierarchy in Rome. Among these is the (then) Cardinal Joseph Ratzinger (subsequently Pope Benedict XVI), who wrote on the concepts of Universality and Catholicity. For him, "Catholicity" refers to the "pluriformity" of the Catholic church, and "Universality" underlines the broad scope of the church's labour. The majority of the contributors to this volume are directly related to pastoral ministry or administration in the Catholic church; others hail from the university setting. Two women authors were given a voice. Sister Nicole-Joseph Ballé underscored the necessity of a solid educational base for African children if the society is to move forward. The second, layperson Agnès Adjaho ("La femme: une chance pour l'Église et l'humanité"), reminds the Church that women, too, must be taken into account. Although any Festschrift will be uneven in the value of its contributions, this volume, by its multitude of articles, has much to offer. The contributions that touch Africa most directly are chapters 4–10 and 20–24; some of the other chapters appear to be applicable to any society. Most readers are likely to find something of interest with in the tome.

236. Cowley, Roger W.

Ethiopian Biblical Interpretation: A Study in Exegetical Tradition and Hermeneutics

Cambridge: Cambridge University Press, 1989. 512 pages, ISBN: 9780521352192.

The primary goal of this study is to explore the exegetical traditions that influenced the seventeenth-century *andemta* Amharic commentary (AC), and what processes led to its formation. A secondary goal is to discern the hermeneutical trends and implications of the AC. The author was an Anglican missionary and a scholar in Oriental studies who spent over twenty years collecting manuscripts and researching Ethiopian Orthodox tradition and history. His unfortunate death at the age of forty-eight in 1988 cut short a promising career in his field. Cowley begins this publication by summarising the current state of research on the AC, which in his day was rather scarce. He then carefully analyses several portions of the AC in comparison with patristic, Syriac, Arabic and rabbinic commentaries. Cowley's conclusion on the origins of the AC is rather complex, but the general trend that he traces is in the following order: biblical text, patristic interpretation, Syriac, Arabic and Geez interpretation, and lastly the AC which collects from the Geez or directly from the earlier sources (although not directly from rabbinic sources). In the concluding chapter Cowley summarizes his findings and argues that the AC is in "essential continuity" with Antiochene exegesis and its subsequent developments. He also concludes that there is no set philosophical interpretive system in Ethiopian biblical hermeneutics; rather the exegetical conclusions can be generalized into patterns of interpretation that are not hard and fast rules (this particular conclusion has been challenged in recent scholarship). This book has much merit in that it elucidates non-Western interpretive traditions that were developed in various cultural contexts, and summarizes some of the major methods, trends, themes and theological stances that characterize Ethiopian hermeneutics. During his lifetime the author was widely accepted as a pioneer in his field, and this book exhibits the rigorous attention to detail that characterized his scholarship. The book is very technical and assumes a working knowledge of written Amharic, Geez, Greek, Syriac, Hebrew and Arabic. However, Cowley's arguments can still be followed if one has a rudimentary knowledge of patristic, rabbinic and medieval exegetical history. The book is recommended for advanced-level scholarship, whereas its technical arguments based on original manuscripts and Oriental languages would render it impractical for students below the post-graduate level. General familiarity with the content and conclusions of Cowley's study would, however, be relevant to the history of biblical interpretation in Africa, and in illustrating the role that culture can play in such interpretation.

237. **Cox, James L.**

Expressing the Sacred: An Introduction to the Phenomenology of Religion

Harare: University of Zimbabwe, 1992. 192 pages, ISBN: 9780908307289.

This book principally seeks to explore a methodology for the study of religion. At the time of writing the author was a lecturer in the Department of Religious Studies at the University of Zimbabwe, and later at the Centre for the Study of Christianity in the Non-Western World at the University of Edinburgh. By phenomenology of religion Cox means comparative study of religion and the history of religions. Despite a lack of coherent presentation, the book is a serious scholarly contribution, offering a fresh approach to the study of religion in the African context. It will prove of special interest to students of the spirit world of the African, of African Christianity, or of the psychological aspects of the phenomenology of religion.

238. **Cox, James L., and Gerrie ter Haar, editors**

Uniquely African?: African Christian Identity from Cultural and Historical Perspectives

Trenton, NJ: Africa World Press, 2003. 310 pages, ISBN: 9781592211142.

This volume contains selected essays from conferences conducted under the auspices of the African Christianity Project in 1994 and 1997 in conjunction with the University of Edinburgh and several African universities. As the title indicates, the central theme intended for the collection concerns "What, if anything, can be described as uniquely African?" The context for this question involves the hegemony of Western cultural, religious, and institutional systems that shape identity, including African identity, in the contemporary world. By examining and critiquing structures and ideologies imposed upon Africa by the West, the authors are meant to reflect upon aspects of uniquely African identity. The essays themselves focus primarily on West Africa. Contributions are grouped into sections: Theoretical Perspectives, Culture and Identity, Christianity and African National Identities, and African Christian Identity. Based on the volume's title, one might expect essays addressing issues of identity, asking questions such as "Who are we?" in the midst of a rapidly changing world. The majority of the chapters, however, take a historical approach (as the subtitle partially indicates), examining how Western influences have interacted with and transformed not only African traditional religious concepts and practices, but political and educational systems as well. On the whole one does not find a sharp focus on issues of identity proposed by the volume's title. A promising article by Ogbu Kalu, entitled "'Globecalisation' and Religion: The Pentecostal Model in Contemporary Africa," looks at the place of African Pentecostalism within the context of primal religions and globalisation. Yet, what begins in an intriguing thesis soon disappears behind a barrage of unexplained technical concepts. The collection includes articles that make useful contributions on specific topics reflecting the interests and specialisations of individual authors, but anyone looking for substantive treatment of issues relating to African Christian identity will need to look elsewhere.

Cox, James L.

see also reviews 757 and 921

239. **Craig Harris, Lillian**

In Joy and in Sorrow: Travels among Sudanese Christians, Faith in Sudan, Volume 8

Nairobi: Paulines, 1999. 204 pages, ISBN: 9789966214843.

The stories that Craig Harris tells in volumes 7 and 8 of the "Faith in Sudan" series are not for the faint-hearted. Many of her narratives are stories of suffering in a place where genocidal jihad and Western greed for oil have conspired in the death of millions of Southern Sudanese, many of them Christians. There is also hope in these pages, but it is a hope that is only to be understood in the light of the cross. Whereas volume 7 contained stories about the suffering of women, this volume is somewhat broader in scope, including many stories in which Sudanese men are the main characters. Of special interest is the author's long preface, titled "The Church in Sudan: 'Doubts Without and Fears Within'." Here she spells out the major problems in Sudanese society (confusion over identity, politicized religion, racism, civil war, displacement, slavery, underdevelopment), the major problems in the Sudanese churches (disunity, lack of theological education, corruption, gender inequality), and finally pointers to a way forward (cease-fire, education, unity within the churches, the leadership of women, acceptance of pluralism, dialogue). Her analysis is accurate, but positive signs that a peaceful future may be around the corner are regrettably few and far between. Theological schools in Africa should have a complete set of this attractive and affordable series in their libraries.

240. **Craig Harris, Lillian**

Keeping the Faith: Travels with Sudanese Women. Faith in Sudan, Volume 7

Nairobi: Paulines, 1999. 176 pages, ISBN: 9789966214850.

Most of the volumes of this excellent series "Faith in Sudan" (under the general editorship of Andrew Wheeler and William Anderson) have a strong theological or historical focus. The essays in *Keeping the Faith* are not primarily theological or historical, but narrative. Readers who may not have been to the Sudan will find here a living context in which to place the facts of recent Sudanese church history. The author's photographs and rich descriptive stories provide faces and names of real people struggling for life in the midst of so much death. An American trained in international relations with a doctorate in Chinese History, Craig Harris spent approximately three years in the Sudan while her husband was the British Ambassador. In her diplomatic role she was able to travel throughout the country and observe Sudanese Christians from a wide variety of stations and conditions. The couple was expelled by the Sudanese government in 1998 after the technically "illegal" visit of George Carey, then the Archbishop of Canterbury. The chapters in this volume each deal with one episode in the life of the Sudanese church. Every chapter is dated (chapter 1 is about an incident in Malakal in June 1995, the last chapter deals with a suicide in Omdurman in 1998). As the title of the book indicates, most of the stories found here are primarily about Sudanese women. Much of this book is also about suffering. But it is also about hope. In the midst of devastation are women working for justice and for peace, for understanding and for forgiveness.

241.   Croegaert, Luc

The African Continent: An Insight into Its Earliest History

Nairobi: Paulines, 1999. 336 pages, ISBN: 9789966214416.

Croegaert is a Belgian Jesuit father who served for 32 years as a missionary teacher in Congo (DRC), Burundi and Rwanda. First published in French in 1985, this book is primarily a secular history of the continent before the nineteenth century, with the Christian presence in Africa before modern times only given occasional attention. For example, the conquest of Islam in North Africa is covered well, particularly how it affected the Berbers. Portuguese exploration and discovery receive detailed treatment, and the first entry of Christianity into the interior of Africa (involving King Afonso of the Congo) is covered in depth. There is also a helpful section tracing the origins of the myth of Prester John in the context of early Ethiopian Christianity. Perhaps surprisingly, there is relatively little information on the slave trade, apart from references to the Arab trade and a summary of the abolitionist movement; the Atlantic trade is hardly mentioned. Croegaert's summary of slavery is a succinct quotation from a Cameroonian historian: "Islam opened up the trade in the black man, Europe followed, Africa was the victim and the accomplice." The greatest strength of the book is the astonishing bibliography attached to each chapter (though it may occasionally make tedious reading – too many names, dates and places to digest). Given its focus, this book will be of somewhat limited help to lecturers in African Church History. But it should prove a gold mine for those interested in researching or doing a higher degree in early African history.

Cross, K. E.

see review 476

242.   Cummings, Mary Lou

Surviving without Romance: African Women Tell Their Stories

Scottdale, PA: Herald Press, 1991. 207 pages, ISBN: 9780836135381.

This book offers invaluable insight into the lives of Christian women in east and central Africa. During her husband's sabbatical in 1986–1987, the author visited and did interviews in five countries in that part of Africa, under the auspices of the Mennonite Central Committee. Together with the stories of the many African women she interviewed, Cummings effectively weaves in her own story of her interest in Africa and her family's visit to Africa. Consequently, the book includes insights on culture shock and adjustments to Africa by an American family with adolescent children, told alongside the stories of joy and sorrow narrated to the author by African women. The author's stated intention is to let African women tell their stories so that others can benefit from their experiences and insights. She quickly learned that just by listening to these women, she was affirming their worth as people in a new way that was surprising to many of them. They often felt initially that they had nothing important to say, but as she sensitively listened to them, they shared their stories in considerable detail. While some were glowing stories of lifelong faithfulness to the Lord by both spouses, many stories included early marital happiness followed by trials due to the spiritual decline or death of a husband, or the coming of multiple wives into the home. The author also articulates some of the root assumptions of traditional cultures in Africa as revealed to her by these women, especially the prime importance to women of having children.

And she notes how rapid social change is creating problems in social systems that had a helpful function in the past – systems such as polygamy, levirate marriage, bride price and resistance to the presence of unmarried women in the society. She notes that the closest emotional bond in a family is between mother and children, and that the African women she interviewed did not generally expect romance or partnership with their husbands. The overriding message of this book is one of women's perseverance in trust that God will provide and care for them, and many of them said that Jesus was their husband. The faith of these women amazed the author and will challenge readers also. Since it presents the perspective of an American Christian woman, the book may prove especially helpful for orientation of people coming from overseas to work in Christian ministry in Africa. But the book would also prove an affirmation to African women readers. And it could offer helpful insights to men as well, especially those in church leadership roles, on the struggles faced by many women in Africa.

243. **Cunningham, Scott**

'Through Many Tribulations': The Theology of Persecution in Luke-Acts

London: Bloomsbury, 1997. 376 pages, ISBN: 9781850756613.

The author of this important study is well known in Africa both as a distinguished lecturer in theological schools in West Africa, and also owing to his faithful labours throughout the African continent on behalf of ACTEA, the association working to strengthen evangelical theological education in Africa, and later for Overseas Council in a similar role. This updated and slightly revised version of his doctoral dissertation in the USA has resulted in a clearly written and very accessible study tracing out the theme of suffering persecution as part of Christian discipleship in the two-volume work of Luke-Acts. Cunningham has not only made an important scholarly contribution in NT studies, but has highlighted an issue that, although often ignored in Western biblical scholarship, is very timely for many parts of the non-Western Christian world. Taking its focus principally from the literary and narrative characteristics of Luke-Acts, the core of the study is devoted to a close examination of passages relevant to the theme throughout these two linked NT books. Based on the findings, the concluding chapter then identifies and expounds the leading elements of Luke's persecution theme, and discusses how this theme fits generally within Luke's larger purposes. The strength of the dissertation lies in its consistently solid and dependable scholarly exegesis of the passages in question. The noted missiologist Hiebert has pointed out that in the book of Acts miracles (power encounters) often led not to great conversions but to great persecution. Cunningham has come at the same idea more generally and as a biblical scholar, showing clearly that persecution may indeed result from witnessing, yet also that God's purposes will triumph and that the persecution itself can be seen as a validation of the believer's position as a true disciple of Jesus Christ. Cunningham has made a useful contribution in providing a soundly biblical framework for understanding the relationship between Christian testimony and persecution. It remains for someone now to take what are here identified as biblical principles and demonstrate how to apply them effectively in different African contexts.

244. **Cuthbertson, Greg, Hennie Pretorius, and Dana Robert, editors**

Frontiers of African Christianity: Essays in Honour of Inus Daneel

Pretoria: UNISA Press, 2003. 336 pages, ISBN: 9781868881932.

This collection of essays written by friends, colleagues and former students honours the life and ministry of Marthinus "Inus" L. Daneel. The contributions from South Africa, Zimbabwe, the United Kingdom and the

United States indicate the global reach of Daneel's influence, exercised through his supervision of postgraduate students and his publications. The present volume also contains a thirteen-page bibliography of Daneel's work from 1970–2001. The first half of the book offers eight essays focusing on "The many names of Inus Daneel." Dana Robert, a professor of world mission (Boston University) and Daneel's wife, provides an outline for this section with a brief autobiographical essay. The remaining essays describe his work as a missionary amongst the Shona people, his research into both AICs and traditional African religions, his role in establishing Fambidzano (an ecumenical movement that facilitates theological education in AICs) and his work as an environmentalist with the Zimbabwean Institute of Religious Research and Ecological Conservation (ZIRRCON). The name of this organisation is indicative of the way in which these various elements in Daneel's life were organically integrated. As a professor of missiology at the University of South Africa (UNISA) from 1981 to 1996, his influence in South African missiological circles was superseded only by his senior colleague, David Bosch. The second half of the book contains six essays on "AIC studies" and four on "African religions." None of the essays in this Festschrift stands out as excellent in its own right, yet the whole is greater than the sum of its parts and this collection makes a valuable contribution to our understanding of an important late twentieth-century missiologist.

245. Cutter, Charles H.

Africa 2002: World Today Series

Harpers Ferry, WV: Stryker-Post, 2002. 286 pages, ISBN: 9781887985390.

The distinctive value of this handy reference publication on Africa is that it is released in an updated edition annually. Available year by year is thus an up-to-date survey of each African country, giving basic description, followed by a narrative summary of its recent political and economic history. The presentation usually covers events almost to the immediate present; for example, the edition here reviewed included reference to events that occurred in the first half of 2002, the year of publication. Where else might one go for a quick, reliable briefing on the latest political developments in, for example, São Tomé or Mauritania – not to mention the latest on Nigeria, South Africa, or Congo-Kinshasa? Each country article concludes with a brief but astute assessment of the country's immediate future prospects. Indeed, the entire publication is characterized by sober realism, rendering it all the more useful. The reader is also offered numerous well-selected photographs and maps, and an extended bibliography, with most titles drawn from the past decade. As is true for most reference resources, although religion is mentioned, this particular dimension of contemporary Africa is generally slighted; this is not the place to look for an update on that major component of African realities. Cutter is emeritus professor of political science at San Diego State University in the United States. Libraries and researchers should find this a markedly convenient, repeatedly updated, and reasonably priced basic reference tool on contemporary Africa.

Authors
D–G

246.   **Dali, Rebecca Samuel**

A Biography of Rev. Dr. Musa D. Gotom: A Pastor of Pastors and a Man Seeking after God's Heart

Bukuru, Nigeria: Africa Christian Textbooks, 2007. 106 pages, ISBN: 9789781351976.

Writing biographies of local African church leaders is an important calling, especially as our leaders become older. Hence the significance of this book. In a sense, Musa Gotom's own life story is emblematic of the story of all those church groups that derived from the work of the Sudan United Mission (SUM) in Nigeria. These churches are now linked together as the Fellowship of Christian Churches in Nigeria (TEKAN), comprising thirteen denominations. The SUM came to Nigeria in 1904, and the national churches became independent in 1955. Gotom was born in 1940 in the present-day Plateau State, and was educated in schools of his own church denomination, the Church of Christ in Nigeria (COCIN). He subsequently received his PhD from Claremont University in California, was the first Nigerian lecturer at the well-known Theological College of Northern Nigeria (TCNN), and then the first Nigerian principal of that institution. In addition he became General Secretary and then President of COCIN, and President of TEKAN. Yet, despite all of these titles and positions of authority, Gotom remained a man of God and a humble person. In a time when many church leaders are seen to be chasing after power, according to many interviewees Gotom's main shortcomings as a church leader have been that he is too gentle, too patient and too humble! In short, he is a model of a servant leader. The two chapters on Gotom's early life and his call to ministry are somewhat sketchy in terms of facts; but the two chapters on training pastors and on Gotom as a church administrator have much useful information. The author of this biography, Rebecca Dali, is a lecturer at TCNN, and at the time of publication a PhD candidate at the University of Jos. Her book can serve as a model and inspiration for senior church leaders throughout the continent. It can also serve as a useful challenge in Africa to undertake biographies of other senior church leaders among us.

Daloz, Jean-Pascal

see review 191

247.   **Damap, Justina Karimu**

Widowhood: A Challenge to the Church

Bukuru, Nigeria: Africa Christian Textbooks, 2007. 144 pages.

Damap was the wife of a pastor involved in development work in northern Nigeria. He was an advocate for widows, and she has carried on this work since his death in a plane crash in 2002, leaving her a widow herself. She holds BTh and MTh degrees, and is a lecturer at the Theological College of Northern Nigeria (TCNN). The book arose out of seminars and training she has given in many church settings. Damap writes out of a context where, in addition to suffering the loss of a life partner, a widow is considered part of a deceased man's property to be inherited along with all his other assets by his relatives. She retains nothing and is expected to survive by submitting to levirate marriage, and often to humiliating and harmful mourning customs. Christian widows wishing to avoid harm or marriage to an in-law who may be already married, not a Christian, or otherwise unsuitable for her and her children, have received inconsistent support from churches. Damap outlines the traditional practices and many of the harmful results to widows and their children. She also opposes the common practice in churches of forbidding widows to show grief openly by demonstrating that in both the OT and NT godly people, including Jesus, mourned and wept over death. Another section surveys the biblical material advocating care of widows, and concludes that the age limit of "over 60" in 1 Timothy 5 does not mean neglecting the needs of younger widows. There is also a section discussing the NT teaching allowing remarriage of widows but advising caution. There are practical suggestions for the church's ministry throughout the book, but a chapter at the end brings many of these together. She surveys six Protestant denominations in her area (ECWA, EYN, Baptists, Anglicans, CRCN, COCIN), examining the church constitutions and using interviews, and finds that all give some support to widows but not all take a stand against harmful traditional customs in their written policies. Damap recommends that along with providing counsel, fellowship, training, and gifts for widows, churches should actively oppose widowhood customs that demean women and make it hard for them to follow Christ fully. Churches must have written policies to discipline church members who force these customs on women, provide legal aid to widows being so forced, ensure all members are married under the Marriage Ordinance (so the wives have legal rights) and not just tribal custom, and urge husbands to provide wills and female ownership of assets that can provide for their wives should they die. Churches must then consistently implement these policies, so that the culture in the church, and eventually society, will change.

248.   Daneel, M. L.

African Earthkeepers: Volume 1 Interfaith Mission in Earth-Care

Pretoria: UNISA Press, 1998. 340 pages, ISBN: 9781868880508.

African Earthkeepers: Volume 2 Environmental Mission and Liberation in Christian Perspective

Pretoria: UNISA Press, 2000. 431 pages, ISBN: 9781868881352.

Daneel, at one time Professor of Missiology at the University of South Africa (UNISA), has done extensive research and writing on the traditional and Christian religions of the Shona people of Zimbabwe. With these two volumes he makes further important and original contributions to the study of African religion and of African Initiated Churches (AICs), treating them as social movements, as products of indigenous culture and leadership, and as creators of African theologies. Daneel initiated and became the driving force behind an unusual partnership in "the war of the trees." He recounts the amazing response of African traditional religionists and of the AICs in Zimbabwe to the environmental devastation that had taken place in their country as a result of its War of Independence. The first volume deals with the traditional religious contribution to the earthkeeping struggle, while the second volume describes its Christian counterpart, providing a profile of the emergent AIC theology within the green struggle. Daneel concludes by placing the enacted theologies of the African earthkeepers within the international framework of ecotheology. Readers will be drawn to the detailed descriptions of the newly introduced "clothing the land" (mafukidzanyika) ritual ceremonies, and the "earth healing" (maporesanyika) ceremonies held by the earthkeeping churches. Working in tandem, the traditional chiefs and spirit mediums (the traditional custodians of the land), and the AIC members led by their bishops, represent the largest grassroots environmental and tree-planting movement in southern Africa. The two volumes emphasize the necessity of united action in ecological mission, within a context of multi-religious initiative that need not imply religious relativism nor syncretistic compromise at the expense of Christian witness.

249.   Daneel, M. L.

All Things Hold Together: Holistic Theologies at the African Grassroots. Selected Essays by M. L. Daneel

Pretoria: UNISA Press, 2008. 424 pages, ISBN: 9781868884292.

This is a collection of essays written over a long period (1974–2003) by one who has probably been the leading researcher of independent churches in southern Africa, especially among the Shona in Zimbabwe. Daneel, who had been living among Shona AICs (African Independent/Initiated Churches) for many years, is the founder of Fambidzano, an ecumenical group for these churches, and is a leader in promoting care for the environment among them. Sundkler's familiar categories are used throughout this treatment of AICs: "Ethiopian" (similar to Western churches), "Zionist" (Spirit-type, characterized by tongues, healing and prophecy) and "messianic" (the leader usurps the role of Christ). The foreword notes of Daneel that, "Refusing to be bound by Enlightenment academic standards that demand objective detachment from one's "subjects," he has instead engaged in radical participant observation." Daneel insists that AICs are true missionary churches that have recently moved closer to "dynamic Christian faith." "I have no hesitation in classifying the AICs of southern Africa as Christian churches." The reader may wonder just how reliable such evaluation might be, provided as it is by an assertedly non-neutral observer. For example, he describes both Isaiah Shembe (a "messianic" South African) and Johane Maranke (founder of the VaPostori, a syncretistic and polygamous group originating in Zimbabwe) as Christians; many other observers would disagree. Daneel merely recognizes in such groups an over-realized eschatology (healing has too prominent a place) and a "temporarily weakened Christology," but offers no corrective. He even claims that rampant divisions can lead to "renewed spiritual fervour" and "constructive regrouping." Daneel states that his interest lies in interpreting empirical phenomena, not in questioning scriptural norms. The disappointing result is rich information with little evaluative reflection. Of greater concern is a refusal to condemn the common practice of wizard-finding among AICs, even when they reflect common ATR practices in rewarding jealousy, supporting harsh treatment of old women and intimidating non-members by suggesting they may be wizards if they do not join the AIC. The author complains that others write about AICs too negatively, e.g. Barrett, Sundkler, Beyerhaus and M-L Martin, in contrast, he feels, to David Bosch, who wrote that Christians should take both biblical revelation and the African world seriously. Daneel feels that only the AICs are doing that! The book will prove useful as a compendium of Daneel's reflections on AICs, always provided there is no expectation of balanced evaluation.

250.   Daneel, M. L.

Fambidzano: Ecumenical Movement of Zimbabwean Independent Churches

Gweru, Zimbabwe: Mambo Press, 1989. 643 pages, ISBN: 9780869224656.

As informed observers of Christianity in Africa are well aware, the prolific growth of African Independent Churches (AICs) is a phenomenon not to be ignored, particularly by anyone involved in missiological endeavour or attempting to teach contextually-sensitive theology in sub-Saharan Africa. Daneel has developed a reputation as one of the foremost authorities in the study of AICs. This volume is one among several that he has written in the field. In this one he traces the birth and growth of Fambidzano, the organisation which was founded as an experiment in Zimbabwe in 1972 by Professor Daneel and a number of AIC bishops and church leaders, with the stated purpose of fostering "ecumenical relations, the advancement of theological education and the eventual realisation of ecclesiastical unity among the Shona Independent Churches." While this book is a historical account of particular developments, it does also assist the reader in reflecting on the implications of the larger movement in Africa. Is the AIC movement the ultimate outcome of constructive contextualization, or is it to be considered a set of largely syncretistic initiatives, resulting in the distortion of the gospel message and therefore itself in need of reform? Also, in view of the highly individualistic tendencies among leaders within the movement, is any form of ecumenism possible which might eventually enable the strengthening of these churches? Reading this book with such larger questions in mind can make this volume all the more engaging and instructive.

251.   Daneel, M. L.

Old and New in Southern Shona Independent Churches

Berlin: De Gruyter, 2009. 558 pages, ISBN: 9783110908596.

"Every language is a temple in which the soul of the people who speak it is enshrined . . . For whether one is to teach or govern, one's first duty is to understand the people." These were the insightful words written in 1898 by Edwin Smith, a pioneer scholar-missionary to central Africa. In his multiple publications on the Shona of Zimbabwe, Daneel has fulfiled that summons, by providing those in present-day cross-cultural Christian ministry and outreach with invaluable information and insight on how indigenous Christians express and celebrate their understanding of the Scriptures and Christian faith in an African context. Daneel devotes this sizeable volume to leadership and fission dynamics in the African Independent Churches (AICs). His approach is descriptive, rather than a critique of strengths and weaknesses, or a comparison and contrast with Western views. It is within these contemporary AICs that the style of Christian worship and church leadership reflect more of the African culture than do the Western models for directing the expression and expansion of the Christian faith. In dealing with fission in the AICs, the process of frequent fragmentation of these church groups, the author rightly points out that this pattern is rooted in the "hiving-off of villages" of traditional African rural culture. Daneel was born and raised in Zimbabwe, is well versed in the Shona culture, and has worked extensively with the Shona Independent churches. This is a masterpiece on indigenous African church leadership patterns, and important for anyone serious about understanding African expressions of the Christian faith. It will be an eye-opener not only to those coming from overseas but also to African Christians who are products of Western approaches to Christianity. The book will challenge readers in Christian ministry roles in Africa to review their models for church leadership – and hence also their models for church leadership formation.

252.   Daneel, M. L.

Quest for Belonging: Introduction to a Study of African Independent Churches

Gweru, Zimbabwe: Mambo Press, 1987. 310 pages, ISBN: 9780869224267.

Daneel's work here is one of several that appeared in the mid to late 1980s dealing with the African Independent Church (AIC) movement. *Quest for Belonging* provides an excellent, empathetic overview of the movement as a whole, though the bulk of the work is focused on Shona examples, among which Daneel did his own field work. Several qualities make the book important for the student of the AICs. First, Daneel provides an excellent survey of the models needed to understand independency, and ably critiques them, showing cogently that this movement cannot be reductionistically studied. (It must be noted, as Daneel himself indicates, that his explanation for the rise of the AICs follows David Bosch's outline.) Second, Daneel's description and analysis of the influence of day-to-day village life in the independent churches, and how people live out dual roles (in village and in church), gives a vital perspective on the movement. For example, the discussion of the parallel of leadership structures in village and church provides a wealth of insights on the movement, which would usually elude anyone who has not lived among them. Third, he clearly shows the dangers of stereotyping and armchair research which condemns the AICs wholesale without any attempt at genuine ethnographic research into the emic perspectives. Finally, he provides a rationale for locating the doctrinal ethos of the AICs not in syncretism but in genuine attempts to adapt biblical principles to African realities. Perhaps the biggest weakness of the book comes out of its greatest strength. Daneel is at his best when discussing independency in southern Africa and especially the Shona, but the book is not as broadly conceived as the title would imply.

253.   Dau, Isaiah Majok

Suffering and God: A Theological Reflection on the War in Sudan

Nairobi: Paulines, 2002. 256 pages, ISBN: 9789966218445.

This is a remarkable book for a number of reasons. First, it contains an exceptionally competent overview of Christian reflection on the problems of evil and suffering from a biblical perspective, and a strong analysis of major theological thinkers and schools of thought, especially Augustine, Calvin, Luther, Barth, Moltmann, Berkouwer and liberation theology. Dau's judgements on Scripture and on the Christian tradition on these questions are balanced and judicious. Secondly, Dau explores these central theological questions from the context of one of the more horrendous examples of evil and suffering in the world: the civil war in Sudan. His presentation on the background to the Sudanese conflict, and on the reality of Christian faith in the midst of that conflict, provides an appropriate horizon of vision for asking questions of the meaning of this suffering. Thirdly, Dau rightly and wisely does not provide a Sudanese "answer" to the problem of evil so much as point to God's response in the person of the Crucified One, who comes to share human suffering in His incarnation and His death on the cross. Dau then undergirds this by considering the Sudanese churches' appropriation of the message of Jesus in their community, their character formation, and their amazing hope. In these reflections Dau makes good use of the work of the late Marc Nikkel on Jieng (Dinka) Christian songs. That the churches could endure such suffering as has been endured and continue to grow and be strengthened is indeed one of the great miracles of our time. Finally, this book may be the first published doctoral work in theology by a Jieng Christian, and probably the first by a Sudanese Pentecostal. This book deserves a wide reading.

Davenport, Rodney

see review 307

254.   Davidson, Basil

The Black Man's Burden: Africa and the Curse of the Nation-State

Martlesham, UK: James Currey, 1992. 368 pages, ISBN: 9780852557006.

Davidson's book brings to bear over 40 years of observation and research on the political situation of Africa since independence. As a historian, Davidson looks back to Africa's pre-colonial past when the continent was experiencing a "slow expansion of wealth and self-development." He then examines colonialism's destructive impact upon Africa's culture and politics, and the aftermath of independence when the former colonies were granted nation-statehood. He then examines the causes of the failure of these countries to establish effective democratic governments, drawing lessons and observations from the development of nation-states in Europe. His insights are helpful in understanding the present political scene in many parts of Africa, which are democratic in name but are lacking in practice. The book deals with the issues of tribalism, the failure of the nation-state to provide for and protect its citizens, dictatorial government and the subsequent lost legitimacy of the state in the eyes of the people. In Davidson's estimation, these all demonstrate that the nation-state was a burden placed upon the African which did not fit with the African consensual and relational culture and worldview. Drawing upon different examples from recent history, Davidson proposes that a way of escape from these problems, and a "ground of hope," is through participatory democracy and a devolution of centralized executive power to locally representative bodies in which the people are more directly involved in self-governance. This book will be helpful to those engaged in critical reflection on the political dilemmas of Africa's recent past and its present.

255.   de Gruchy, John W.

Being Human: Confessions of a Christian Humanist

Norwich: SCM, 2006. 228 pages, ISBN: 9780334029793.

This book's subtitle is a deliberate echo of Augustine's *Confessions* and, like Augustine, de Gruchy has produced a work that is not autobiography, while still making its argument autobiographically. In his words, it is "more of a confession, apologia or testimony drawing on selected episodes from my experience mediated by Christian faith." The autobiographical sketch that follows locates the author in twentieth-century South Africa and, more importantly, in the church struggle against apartheid. This struggle provides the essential background against which de Gruchy's thinking developed and explains many of the emphases evident in his theological labours. Throughout the text the reader is introduced to those theologians and writers who have been most influential in forming de Gruchy as a "Christian humanist," a label he prefers to other denominational or ideological labels available to him. While tracing Christian humanism back to the Renaissance recovery of classical tradition and the ensuing Reformation, de Gruchy's main influences come from the twentieth century. It is not surprising to find that his most important interlocutors are Dietrich Bonhoeffer and Karl Barth, whose ecclesiologies de Gruchy studied in his 1971 doctoral dissertation. But the reader is also allowed to see the author in dialogue with the writings of Teilhard de Chardin, Karl Rahner, John Robinson and John Polkinghorne, among many others. Regrettably, substantial engagement with the Bible is almost totally absent, something that would most likely have puzzled many of those to whom de Gruchy looks as Christian humanists. This work cannot therefore be considered a robust theological defence of Christian humanism, but it nonetheless succeeds as a memoir of one of the more important South African theologians of the late twentieth century.

256.   de Gruchy, John W.

Christianity and Democracy: A Theology for a Just World Order

Cambridge: Cambridge University Press, 1995. 308 pages, ISBN: 9780521458412.

This comprehensive and excitingly relevant book is a major contribution to the debate on democracy within the contemporary world order – especially in Africa. De Gruchy was the respected Professor of Christian Studies at the University of Cape Town. In discussing democracy, he distinguishes between the democratic system and the democratic vision. The first refers to those constitutional principles and procedures which have developed over the centuries, and which have become an essential component of any genuine democracy. The second refers to that hope for a society in which all people are truly free, yet where social responsibility rather than individual self-interest prevails; and a society which is truly just, and therefore one in which the gulf between rich and poor has been overcome. This democratic vision de Gruchy traces to the ancient prophets of Israel, and especially to their messianic hope for a society in which the reign of God's shalom would become a reality. De Gruchy then sketches out the complex, multi-layered and ambiguous relationship between Christianity and Western democracy, and not least the secularisation of democracy as it has become the polity of modernity. Next the author offers five case studies of the church's involvement in twentieth century struggles for democracy. These include the civil rights movement in the USA, the struggle for democratic liberation in Nicaragua, democratic reconstruction in East Germany, plus developments in sub-Saharan Africa and in South Africa. In sub-Saharan Africa he finds that the churches were (cautiously) part of the process of liberation at and after independence; thereafter, with important exceptions, their silence seemed to grow as they were co-opted and manipulated by African governments. Latterly their voice seemed to revive in the renewed processes of democratisation of the 1990s. In South Africa the churches played an indispensable role in the democratisation process, although they now face the danger of becoming uncritical legitimators of the new order. De Gruchy is especially concerned to demonstrate the extent to which, in these various cases, ecumenical Christianity has begun to reconnect with democracy and act as its contemporary midwife. He argues that while democracy needs to rediscover its spiritual heritage, Christianity needs to develop a theology adequate for its participation in the realisation of a just democratic world order, and he outlines a way forward in that task. In conclusion the author proposes that there is today a convergence between the democratic system and its vision, and the ecumenical koinonia, its holistic missionary paradigm and its vision of shalom. The two traditions, separated by the distortions of modernity, have rediscovered each other in theory and praxis. This wide-ranging study of exceptional depth and significance is a major contribution to the contemporary debate.

257.   de Gruchy, John W.

Faith for a Time Like This: South African Sermons

Cape Town: Rondebosch United Church, 1992. 131 pages.

Not least among the contributions of Professor John de Gruchy of South Africa has been his work as a preacher. This helpful collation of sermons preached during the difficult years of 1988 to 1992 gives us valuable insights not only into the issues that faced the church in South Africa in those desperate years of crises, but more particularly how a leading South African theologian sought to proclaim the gospel in the midst of such times. Biblically rooted, incisive, searching, and theologically compelling, these sermons remain brilliant in their simplicity, and they provide ample support to de Gruchy's contention set out in his own foreword, that "sermons and preaching, together with the witness of the church, provide the cutting edge of theology." Events in South Africa may have moved on since these sermons were first delivered, but to read them is to have brought home the importance and power of prophetic preaching. Students of preaching will want to read this book as an excellent example of how to set about the task of preaching God's word in the face of political repression and social disintegration, and Christians in similar circumstances will draw encouragement and hope from the strong Christocentric focus.

258.　de Gruchy, John W.

Liberating Reformed Theology: A South African Contribution to an Ecumenical Debate

Grand Rapids: Eerdmans, 1991. 291 pages, ISBN: 9780864862020.

This book is "an expanded and edited version" of the 1990 Warfield Lectures given at Princeton Theological Seminary by de Gruchy, now emeritus professor of Christian studies at the University of Cape Town. The deliberately ambiguous title well summarizes the book's contents: it is both about the liberation of Reformed theology in the South African context from its apartheid past, and about how Reformed theology can be liberating. The book begins by arguing that there is nothing inherent in Reformed theology that led to apartheid: "Calvinism did not lay the foundations for apartheid any more than Catholicism laid the foundation for oppression in Latin America." In subsequent chapters de Gruchy picks up on traditional doctrinal loci within Reformed theology and re-examines them. Calvin's theology is explained in its historical situation, and deviant theologies like those used to encourage and sustain apartheid are critiqued before de Gruchy's own (now-liberated, and thus liberating) Reformed theology is presented. Although he seeks to enter into dialogue with various liberation theologies, this is not where the main thrust of de Gruchy's work lies, and his engagement with them is perhaps less substantial than the introduction would lead one to believe. Rather, this book represents a contextualized Reformed theology for South Africa in the late 1980s. While some aspects of this work therefore speak specifically to white churches in apartheid South Africa, there are many elements within it that will continue to challenge the church throughout Africa.

259.　de Gruchy, John W.

Reconciliation: Restoring Justice

Minneapolis: Fortress Press, 2002. 272 pages, ISBN: 9780800636005.

De Gruchy, doyen of South African theologians, devoted much of his academic life to addressing the relationship between politics and theology. A vocal critic of the apartheid government, de Gruchy was intimately involved in the reconciliation process in South Africa in the 1990s. In 2002, de Gruchy gave the Hulsean Lectures in the UK, and this allowed him the opportunity of further reflection on the process of reconciliation, the fruits of which are gathered together in this book. De Gruchy is concerned with situating reconciliation within a particular context – in his case, post-apartheid South Africa – because there is no such thing as reconciliation in the abstract. De Gruchy is also concerned specifically with reconciliation within the Christian tradition. His discussion engages, amongst others, Anselm, Abelard and Barth, but draws heavily on Bonhoeffer's ecclesiology in his chapter on "Reconciliation Embodied." As the title of the book indicates, de Gruchy argues that reconciliation is ultimately about restoring justice. However, the relationship between justice and reconciliation is complicated, and needs more space than de Gruchy is able to devote to it in the final chapter of his book. De Gruchy provides a fine example of theological engagement and could be profitably read for that reason alone. Christians living within contexts of conflict will also want to pay careful attention to what the author has to say about reconciliation.

260.   de Gruchy, John W.

Theology and Ministry in Context and Crisis: A South African Perspective

Grand Rapids: Eerdmans, 1987. 183 pages, ISBN: 9780802802903.

In this important theological study of the Christian ministry, de Gruchy focuses upon the ordained pastor as a practical theologian. The author makes it clear that all ministry (in this case set against the background of the then apartheid South Africa) is contextualized and set in particular crises. The vital connection between the ordained ministry and a local community of faith has to be affirmed. To fulfil the vocation of ministry, the pastor has to be a practical theologian who is able to discern the meaning of the gospel within the particular context of his or her ministry. The following issues receive attention: what the church is and how it operates; the role of the ordained ministry in relation to the ministry of all the faithful; who articulates theology and how theology speaks to the needs of the church; who listens to theology and how it affects the lives of individuals and the working of the church body; how the life experience of devastating suffering feeds theology and ministry. The book thus goes far beyond the South African apartheid experience and provides important reflection for all who are involved in pastoral ministry. It is especially relevant for all who need to reflect carefully on ministry in present day Africa, whether urban or rural.

de Gruchy, John W.

see also reviews 217 and 1137

261.   de Jong, Albert

The Challenge of Vatican II in East Africa: The Contribution of Dutch Missionaries to the Implementation of Vatican II in Tanzania, Kenya, Uganda and Malawi 1965–1975

Nairobi: Paulines, 2004. 208 pages, ISBN: 9789966219619.

If one should need a careful study of the impact of Vatican II in Catholic Africa, more particularly its impact in East Africa, more particularly in the first decade after the Council, more particularly as experienced by *Dutch* missionaries, then this is exactly the resource to consult. Granted that this very delimited focus may engage only a very narrow readership, nevertheless the author has contributed a richly researched, realistic and highly nuanced interpretation of his chosen subject. At the time of writing de Jong was a lecturer at the Catholic University of Eastern Africa in Nairobi. What we are offered is a specific episode, closely recounted, within the larger story of missionary involvement in the contextualization of the church in Africa – but with a surprising twist. The Dutch Catholic missionary presence in eastern Africa was not negligible, with on average over a thousand missionaries on site during the designated period. As de Jong tells it, this group generally struggled to understand the implications of Vatican II for missionary outreach, but once assimilated they then engaged in extensive inculturation efforts – only, much to their surprise, to find persistent resistance from the church's emerging African leadership. So much so that in de Jong's estimation these efforts to bring the renewal of Vatican II to the eastern African church had lapsed by 1975. It is a curious story, full of wider implications. Would there be similar findings if equivalent research were pursued in other parts of Africa, of failed attempts by Western missionaries, Protestant as well as Catholic, to encourage indigenising practice in African church life, which became blocked by African resistance to missionary-directed contextualizing initiatives? Precisely because this story goes against the flow of accepted interpretation, there may be more examples than one might expect. The author concludes with a sadly emblematic story of an individual missionary's insistence on the use of drums in worship, against the directives of his African superior, which ended in the missionary's resignation and departure from Africa. It is not clear that de Jong himself fully recognizes the lessons to be learned from this Dutch missionary experience, for example that Africanisation of the church is best led by Africans, and that Western notions and African notions of what is or is not most truly African might not always match.

262.   de Jong, Albert

Mission and Politics in Eastern Africa: Dutch Missionaries and African Nationalism in Kenya, Tanzania and Malawi, 1945–1965

Nairobi: Paulines, 2000. 352 pages, ISBN: 9789966214744.

The author was a lecturer in the Catholic University of Eastern Africa. In this book he examines the role and responsibility of missionaries in politics by examining the nationalist movements that led to independence in Kenya, Tanzania and Malawi, in light of the Roman Catholic Church's position that it stands above party politics. The Church affirmed the colonial government as the God-ordained authority on one hand, and recognized the right of every people to self-determination on the other. The different ways in which the Church's position worked out practically for Dutch Catholic missionaries is the burden of this book. The missionaries in Kenya, although sympathetic to those calling for independence, tried to maintain an objective neutrality and criticized Mau Mau freedom fighters and the colonial government equally. In Tanzania, a Catholic newspaper was started which openly supported Julius Nyerere, who was a member of the Church. In Malawi, a third path was followed by some opposed to the nationalist political party, who sought to oppose it actively through the establishment of a Catholic political party. However, it must be noted that there were examples of all three approaches in each of the countries. Although the book has a delimited focus, it illuminates difficulties and challenges for cross-cultural Christian ministry anywhere. For example, the Dutch missionaries had to walk a tight line between being dependent upon the colonial government's good graces in order to continue ministry on the one hand, and seeking on the other hand to be sympathetic to the need of the nationals for independence. What guidelines would adequately address the challenge for cross-cultural workers in maintaining a good relationship with the local government while maintaining a positive witness for truth and justice in society? Secondly, the assumed superiority of Western culture and Christianity kept some of the Dutch missionaries from feeling that the African was politically competent or ready for self-governance, with the result that nationalistic movements were not fully supported. Granted that implicit ethnocentric and paternalistic tendencies can endanger any cross-cultural religious venture, can these be adequately curtailed, while efforts are sufficiently focused on developing self-confident and independent Christians in the receiving context who are able to accept responsibility not only in the church but also in society and politics?

263. de la Haye, Sophie

Byang Kato: Ambassador for Christ

Achimota, Ghana: Africa Christian Press, 1986. 128 pages, ISBN: 9789964875176.

Here is a welcome biographical sketch of the life of the well-known evangelical African leader, Byang Kato, the first African to head the Association of Evangelicals in Africa, who died by accidental drowning in 1975 at the young age of 39. This is not a definitive study of Kato's life and achievements. That has yet to be written. While this little book does outline his various roles and responsibilities, its purpose is not primarily to stress his great accomplishments, but rather to demonstrate his personal struggles to live for Christ as a young man, as a family man, and as a Christian leader. As such it has a very practical message for those in preparation for church leadership roles. Bookshops in Africa should find it a popular title to stock, and it would make an appropriate gift for those graduating from theological colleges.

264. de Visser, Arjan J.

Kyrios and Morena: The Lordship of Christ and African Township Christianity

Pretoria: A. J. De Visser, 2001. 263 pages, ISBN: 9780620276078.

This is a revision of the doctoral dissertation submitted at Potchefstroom University in South Africa. It involved several years of intensive ethnographic research, following a decade of pastoral service in an African township northwest of Pretoria. De Visser's primary concern is expressed in the title: *Kurios* is the Greek word for "Lord," and *Morena* is its closest equivalent in Sotho and Tswana. Thus the central focus of the study is to uncover the views on the lordship of Christ among African Christians. The locus of the research project were three denominational groups in the township, namely the Evangelical Lutheran Church, the Zion Christian Church, and a group of Pentecostal and charismatic churches (chosen to represent the primary groups of Protestant Christianity in South Africa – mainline, independent, and Pentecostal). De Visser concisely summarizes his findings: "This research shows that in the faith of many church members the Lordship of Jesus Christ is a vague notion. It is accepted that Jesus Christ has died for our sins in the past, but it is less clear what He is doing presently. The living Christ is a remote figure in the faith of the majority of church members." De Visser is not portraying African Christianity as weaker in some way than Western Christianity; he wisely notes that a similar study in Western Christianity would likely find an equally remote view of Christ, even if for different reasons. The author attempts in conclusion to offer biblical focus from a Reformed perspective on those aspects of Christology that need strengthening among the groups studied. These include their conceptions of God, salvation, the person of Christ, and the Lordship of Christ both over the life of the individual believer and over the world. With this publication de Visser has added yet another important voice to the expanding body of literature on African expressions of Christianity.

265.   de Waal, Alex, editor

Islamism and Its Enemies in the Horn of Africa

Bloomington, IN: Indiana University Press, 2004. 279 pages, ISBN: 9780253216793.

"Islamism" has been fashioned in recent times as a term differentiating militant Islam from other expressions of the Islamic faith, such as popular Islam. This radical form has developed out of the teaching of people such as Sayyid Qutb from the Muslim Brotherhood in Egypt. De Waal has done a great service in bringing together some very valuable contributions on Islam's involvement with radical elements in the Horn of Africa, a region that has become a "laboratory for political Islam" over many years. The main focus of the book is Sudan and Somalia, but there are also extensive references to the role of Islamists in Ethiopia, Egypt, Djibouti, Eritrea, Kenya and Uganda. The six main articles by Islamic and Western writers focus on the failure and persistence of Jihad, the dubious role played by Islamic NGOs, the politics of destabilisation in the Horn between 1989–2001, and America's role in the region since the 9/11 events. Not everyone might easily agree with some of the writers' conclusions, but it would be hard not to learn from the bulk of vivid observations and analysis. The book is a "must-read" for policymakers, academics and journalists, but also provides valuable orientation for thoughtful Christians needing a clearer understanding of the challenges of contemporary Islam in this part of Africa.

266.   Debela, Birri

Divine Plan Unfolding: The Story of Ethiopian Evangelical Church Bethel

Minneapolis: Lutheran University Press, 2014. 258 pages, ISBN: 9781932688948.

Debela Birri, senior Ethiopian church statesman, has produced a model church history based on his 1995 doctoral dissertation submitted to the Lutheran School of Theology, Chicago. His work on the Ethiopian Evangelical Church Bethel melds together scholarly archival research, pertinent secondary works as well as first-hand oral histories. The story begins in 1919 when a governor in western Ethiopia issued an urgent invitation to an American Presbyterian doctor working in Sudan to come and assist in arresting the Spanish flu that was devastating the Ethiopian population. This was the unlikely convergence of an Ethiopian Orthodox leader inviting a Protestant missionary to his province, and the interaction eventuated in the birth of the Evangelical Church Bethel. The author affirms that this indeed was a significant part of a "Divine Plan Unfolding" for the people of western Ethiopia. Debela sensitively balances stories of initial Presbyterian missionaries in western Ethiopia with those original heroic leaders of the Ethiopian Evangelical Bethel Church such as Gidada Salon and Mamo Chorka. These indigenous leaders endured double persecution, initially from the Italian aggressors in the early 1940s, and subsequently from the Orthodox Church a decade later. This book makes a lasting contribution to Ethiopian historiography in the following ways: (1) The initial chapter briefly but succinctly unpacks the historical context of Christianity in western Ethiopia. (2) The primal religion of the Oromo as well as their complex gada system of social and political structure is explained. (3) The stories of initial conversions to the evangelical faith through to the establishment of local churches in western Ethiopia are accurately recorded from primary sources. (4) The record of church/mission relations is told with empathy and candour. An important concluding chapter, added to the original dissertation, sheds light on the process of the lengthy and intricate merger process of the Ethiopian Evangelical Church Bethel synods, rooted in the Presbyterian Church of America, with the Ethiopian Lutheran churches planted by European Lutherans. This union in 1974 into the Ethiopian Evangelical Church Mekane Yesus has created a dynamic African evangelical body which continues to make a significant contribution to both church and state. This stands as a very readable and scholarly history of a vibrant branch of Ethiopia's evangelical church movement.

267.   Decorvet, Jeanne

Samuel Ajayi Crowther: Un père de l'Église en Afrique noire

St-Légier, Switzerland: Groupes Missionnaires, 1992. 214 pages, ISBN: 9782880500498.

Samuel Crowther was captured as a youth by slave traders in Nigeria, but was rescued by the British and taken to Sierra Leone, where he received his education. After further training in England, Crowther returned to Africa under the Church Missionary Society (CMS) and eventually was the first African to become an Anglican bishop. This fresh biography of Crowther in French helps highlight the leading role he played in the planting of Christianity in West Africa in the nineteenth century, and his efforts to ensure that the church in Africa might be self-sufficient and African. The author offers a dynamic historical narrative that seeks to make the persons and situations come alive, so that readers are inspired and challenged to reflection. The book includes a commendation by Emmanuel Oladipo of Scripture Union. Since very little has ever been published in French on this major figure in African church history, this book deserves a place in all francophone theological libraries.

268.   Decret, François

Early Christianity in North Africa

Cambridge: James Clarke & Co Ltd, 2011. 240 pages, ISBN: 9780227173565.

The author is an authority on early North African Christianity. This translation of his 1996 French-language text on North African church history is effective for its treatment of the historical and cultural context of African church fathers. Individual chapters cover Tertullian, Cyprian and Augustine, set in the wider context of the socio-economic situation of the first five centuries of the church. Tensions between the new church and the surrounding Berber social culture are evaluated, such as traditional burial practices that tended to be absorbed and adopted by the young church. The author includes a helpful analysis of the well-documented differences in how church leaders dealt with "lapsed" brethren during times of persecution, which are described in sufficient detail to be useful as a reference source (the maps and chronology in the appendices are especially useful). Weaknesses of the North African church are well addressed, such as the schisms due to theological divisions. Treatment of the wider religious landscape before the Muslim conquest is helpful for gaining a better understanding of why the church collapsed so quickly in the seventh century; the author notes that some practices laid at the feet of the Muslim invaders had already caused Christians to suffer under both Vandal and Byzantine administrations (e.g. payment of taxes and limitation of worship). The final chapter, which addresses the question "What happened to African Christianity?" is particularly helpful, both for courses in early church history and also for the contextual background of later African Church history. This volume is a welcome addition to the rapidly growing resources available for the study of Christian history on the African continent.

269.   Dedji, Valentin

Reconstruction and Renewal in African Christian Theology

Nairobi: Acton Publishers, 2003. 284 pages, ISBN: 9789966888402.

This path-breaking study of contemporary African Christian theology is the revision of a doctoral dissertation completed at the University of Cambridge. Dedji, a Methodist scholar from Benin, offers an in-depth comparative assessment of four prominent figures in modern African theological discussion, namely: Jesse Mugambi of Kenya; Kä Mana of Congo (DRC), Kwame Bediako of Ghana, and Jean-Marc Ela of Cameroon. Dedji's central thesis is that the cultural identity stream in African theology represented by Bediako, and the liberationist stream represented by Ela, need now to be superseded by the reconstructionist emphasis first launched by Mugambi in the early 1990s, and now best exemplified by Kä Mana. The main body of the book is a presentation and assessment of each of these four theologians. What distinguishes Dedji's project is his attempt to expound each person's contributions complexly, with measured, courteous assessment. Here is an impressive and attractive example of African theology maturely comparing, evaluating, and critiquing itself. The exposition begins with Mugambi, and his 1991 call for a new direction in African theological reflection, away from liberation themes derived from the Exodus motif toward reconstruction themes drawn from Nehemiah. Mugambi argues that addressing Africa's desperate need for social reconstruction should become the defining mission of the African church and of African theology. But in Dedji's view it is Kä Mana who now represents the most promising version of this reconstructionist agenda, in part because Kä Mana is utterly realistic about the crises gripping Africa and about Africa's own accountability in those crises, and in part because Kä Mana deploys a complexly nuanced multi-disciplinary interpretation of these realities and how they may be addressed. Dedji expounds Bediako with much sympathy, but Bediako's preeminent concern with contextual identity both Kä Mana and Dedji himself judge as no longer appropriate amidst the continent's harrowing cultural, economic and political disintegration. In such an Africa a dignified African Christian identity will only become achievable when African Christianity gives full priority to societal transformation. Also Ela's powerful cry for liberating justice is exemplary, but Dedji wants a turn away from a justice always projected in terms of oppressed/oppressor, towards a justice that makes full space for accountability, repentance, forgiveness and reconciliation. It must be admitted that Dedji's exposition sometimes seems overwhelmed by the data, and his obvious rhetorical skills are sometimes allowed to do duty for interpretive skills. Dedji has made a distinguished contribution that merits close attention. Nevertheless, it is nothing less than extraordinary and sobering that the biblical perception of the core human predicament and the Divine redemptive initiative in remedy is virtually undetectable either within the varied theological views expounded or within Dedji's assessments. Here is seemingly a critical challenge to African evangelical Christianity, an absent voice yet needing to be heard.

Delgado, Mariano

see review 597

Demery, Lionel

see review 908

Denis, Philippe

see review 158

270. **Detago, Misgana Mathewos**

The Efficacy of Parental Blessing: A Narrative Critical Study of Gen 27:1–28:9 in Its Context of Gen 25:19–33:20

Münster: LIT Verlag, 2012. 344 pages, ISBN: 9783643900920.

The author is Director of the Ethiopian Graduate School of Theology in Addis Ababa. The book is his PhD thesis from the University of Gloucestershire (UK), supervised by Professor Gordon McConville. It aims to explore how Isaac's blessing of Jacob, obtained through Jacob's deception of his father, is efficacious in spite of its negative context. The key narrative of the investigation is therefore Genesis 27:1–28:9, but it is read in the larger context of Genesis 25:19–33:20. The author proceeds from the observation that "blessing" is a key motif in Genesis (containing almost one fourth of the OT references of the Hebrew root brk), and in particular in the Jacob cycle. Parental blessing forms an important aspect of this, and the present investigation is an attempt at shedding some light on the nature – and in particular the question of efficacy – of a father's blessing. The book is opened by (1) a brief introduction, presenting purpose and defining key terms, and (2) a history of interpretation of blessing and especially parental blessing. Then follow three exegetical chapters, basically utilising tools and interpretive perspectives from narrative criticism; (3) first on the key narrative (Gen 27:1–28:9) in relation to the preceding Gen 25:19–26:35, (4) then on the key narrative itself, (5) and finally on the key narrative in relation to the following Genesis 28:10–33:20. As far as the main question of efficacy vs deception is concerned, (6) it is concluded that " . . . it is God's favourable attitude towards Jacob and his descendants that makes the blessing work for them in a complex manner that entails struggle, conflict, deception, and favouritism." One could guess that the author's interest for parental blessing reflects his African context, but there are no signs of this, and the bibliography contains no references to African colleagues in the field of OT studies. Still, it is a solid piece of work, with a detailed exegetical treatment of the texts.

271. **Deutsch, Jan-George, Peter Probst, and Heike Schmidt, editors**

African Modernities: Entangled Meanings in Current Debate

Portsmouth, NH: Heinemann, 2002. 184 pages, ISBN: 9780325071213.

The chapters in this edited volume present varying perspectives on the complex and sometimes ambiguous topic of modernity in Africa. The book benefits from contributions by scholars of academic distinction within the broader field of African studies. This includes the editors, who shape the course of the discussion by introducing the reader to the various nuances of the topic, establishing an overview of the historical developments related to modernity in Africa, as well as proposing a way forward. All the contributors approach the subject from perspectives of their own disciplines, including historical (Lonsdale), sociological (Behrend), anthropological (Camaroff), and philosophical (Gikandi), in addition to others that help make up this valuable tapestry of interacting and contrasting viewpoints (thus well justifying the subtitle: "entangled meanings in current debate"). Some of the topics include: Jomo Kenyatta's political theology, Prophet Isiah Shembe, "theatre of memory," images from Likoni Ferry photographers, the colonial state in South Africa and its construction of subjects, and the role of reason in African philosophy. A broad panorama of viewpoints on the continent is covered, demonstrating how the topic of modernity may arise concurrently in religion, politics, literature and art. Scholars, practitioners, theologians and pastors alike need to consider these changing dynamics within contemporary African societies, and how Africans themselves, in significant or subtle ways, are responding to global patterns of cultural flow. What is in play is more complex than some mere replication of Western modernity. Africans are altogether active agents within the process, both where resultant forms may appear similar to Western modernism (as in the case of Gikandi's rationalism) or as a critique of Western modernism (Comaroff). Because of their great diversity, the chapters may not appeal to all readers, and the complexity of the subject matter may be a bit laborious at times. But those seeking a deeper understanding of modern Africa, and modern African intellectual life, will want to expose themselves to material of this calibre. And advanced-level libraries should view this as a valuable addition for their library.

272. Dickson, Kwesi A.

Uncompleted Mission: Christianity and Exclusivism

Nairobi: Acton Publishers, 2000. 177 pages, ISBN: 9789966888983.

Dickson was previously professor of theology and religion at the University of Ghana. In this study he asserts that the church's raison d'être as long as it remains in the world is mission. He concedes that much has been achieved, but suggests that there still remains a long way to go, as long as there persists what he calls the exclusivism of Christianity. The author's view is that as long as the missionary has not seriously, meaningfully and practically engaged with the local religio-cultural realities of his target peoples, then his mission is "incomplete." By exclusivism Dickson refers to the attitude that either deliberately or by default leads to taking one's own perspectives as the only legitimate expression of Christianity even in a foreign context. The result is that Christianity ends up with the shape, theology and rituals of the missionary's home culture, with all the foreignness that goes with that. He sees the "Judaisers" as a good illustration of this exclusivism, inasmuch as they could not envisage Christianity in Gentile form and so insisted on Jewish cultural accretions. He suggests that this attitude, which he calls exclusivism, has its roots in the OT, notwithstanding its statements which can be seen as portraying openness to non-Jewish religio-cultural realities. He suggests that this attitude persists into the NT and the early church, even in the practice of Paul who acknowledges God's involvement in other nations, but dismisses them as essentially ignorant. The author's conclusion is that the early church "was unable to face . . . the continuity between the Jewish and Christian traditions and other people's traditions." Is there a way forward, a way to complete the mission of the church? Dickson calls for further reflection on the biblical material that embraces new hermeneutical approaches on the one hand, while also carefully listening to and evaluating the African religio-cultural realities on the other hand, attending to the continuities of those realities with the Christian message and thus leading to a theology and rituals that will be authentically African as well as recognisably Christian. This is a provocative contribution in the ongoing debate on appropriate contextualization. It rightly draws attention to the problems that lie in the way of true indigenisation, and to the need to avoid a transplanted Christianity with no real power to hold its professors in time of crisis. Many may nevertheless take exception to some of the critical presuppositions which underpin the author's proposed solutions. This book will be accessible mainly to more academic audiences.

273.   **Dietrich, Walter, and Ulrich Luz, editors**

The Bible in a World Context: An Experiment in Contextual Hermeneutics

Grand Rapids: Eerdmans, 2002. 96 pages, ISBN: 9780802849885.

The essays in this slim volume are edited versions of papers presented at a symposium sponsored by the Theological Faculty of Bern (Switzerland) in 2000. In addition to an introduction by both editors and a short epilogue by Dietrich, the book presents three programmatic essays on hermeneutics – one from a Latin American (Elsa Tamez), one by an Asian (Seiichi Yagi), and one by an African (Justin Ukpong). The same three scholars then each present an exegetical essay on the same biblical text: Luke 2. As should be expected, the essays vary in quality. The exegetical article by Tamez is a particularly fine study which focuses on the Roman imperial context of the birth of Jesus, especially as found in Luke 2:1–20, in which she finds a stark contrast between the "pax Romana" of Augustus and the peace offered in Jesus of Nazareth. Readers using this reference resource will be most interested in the African essays by Justin Ukpong, a Roman Catholic from Nigeria now recognized as one of the leading biblical scholars on the continent. Ukpong contributes a very fine methodological study in which he explains his approach to African inculturation hermeneutics. As distinct from Western methods (which he refers to as "intellectualist"), he conceives of African hermeneutics as both "pragmatic" and "contextual." Ukpong also makes it clear that biblical studies in Africa are done in the context of the Christian faith, as opposed to the more detached readings of the West which tend to have the academy as the primary audience. His exegetical paper argues that the theme of the Lukan birth narratives is that "in the coming of Jesus God has raised up the weak and the lowly, and simultaneously put down the great and the mighty." Although the essays by Yagi are disappointing, the book as a whole is a valuable contribution. Ukpong's essays will be of great interest to African students of the Bible, but Tamez's contributions should also be read carefully by anyone interested in contextual exegesis.

274.   **Dike, Eugene Ebere**

The Role of Mass Media for the Pastoral Development of the Catholic Church in Nigeria

Münster: LIT Verlag, 2001. 344 pages, ISBN: 9783825853679.

This is the dissertation of a Catholic father from south-eastern Nigeria, submitted for the PhD degree in Germany. His aim is to encourage the use of media in the evangelistic task of the Nigerian church, by which he means the role of the church in inculcating the faith within, and dialoguing with society at large. In particular Dike wishes to encourage the church to use communications media more effectively for teaching its membership to contextualize and to incorporate Christian values into everyday African life, and for dialogue with the state and with society at large, witnessing to gospel values such as peace, freedom and justice, within a context of authoritarianism, Islamisation and continued cultural influence of African traditional religions. The study includes a detailed quantitative analysis and evaluation of a particular Catholic newspaper in Nigeria. Perhaps not surprisingly for a PhD dissertation, the text is tedious to read; the language is quite technical and complex, and no overview summaries are provided. Whereas the perspective is grounded in Catholic perceptions, the content is not irrelevant for readers of other orientations. This could be a useful addition for advanced-level theological libraries in Nigeria, and for post-graduate programmes anywhere focusing on the Christian use of media.

Dikirr, Patrick M.

see review 686

275.   **Dimandja, Eluy'a Kondo, and Mbonyinkebe Sebahire, editors**

Théologie et cultures: Mélanges offerts à Mgr Alfred Vanneste

Ottignies-Louvain-la-Neuve, Belgium: NORAF, 1988. 436 pages, ISBN: 9782871840053.

At the occasion of Monseigneur Vanneste's promotion to an emeritus status, a Festschrift was produced to honour the original Doyen of the first Catholic seminary in Africa, now known as the Faculté de Théologie Catholique de Kinshasa. Since Vanneste was also instrumental in opening up the discussion of African theology (in the celebrated debate between Tshibangu and Vanneste in 1960), this volume produced by former students and associates is a worthy endeavour. The nineteen essays in the volume (plus a preface and postscript) are divided into five sections, beginning with homage to the man himself. The following sections deal more directly with the church on the African continent. Other than a Dutch tribute to Vanneste (which is also translated into French) and one essay in English, all contributions are in French. Three of the selections have been previously published, including an article by the honouree. As with any collection of essays, the quality can vary. An essay concerning the conflict between the gospel and culture (by Juvénal Rutumbu) is itself worth the price of the book. In another article, some heretofore unpublished documents concerning late nineteenth-century church-state relations in the Belgian Congo are made available. An Ethiopian cult and the indigenous healing movements on the fringes of African Christianity also receive notice by different contributors. The spectrum of interests among the authors is vast and thus will appeal to a varied audience. Although the tenor of the writings is Catholic, there is much that can be of use to anyone doing research in the area of African theology or church history. Any seminary where French is used ought to have this book in its library as a valuable contribution to the study of African theology, as should research libraries anywhere intending a solid collection in African theology.

Dixon, Suzanne

see review 638

276.   **Djoeandy, Omar**

Redefining Success: Exchanging Bondage for Blessings

Nairobi: Nairobi Chapel, 2002. 68 pages.

Djoeandy is a medical doctor and a member of the pastoral team at Nairobi Chapel, one of the largest, most active evangelical congregations in Nairobi. Based on a sermon series originally delivered there, this booklet presents a lively and pointed discussion of a modern Christian's definition of success. It is a good example of the kind of preaching that may be heard today in Africa's educated urban churches. The book is also easily applicable for Western Christians; the sermon series was reportedly well received in Australia and the United States (Djoeandy is an Australian of Indonesian background). Djoeandy presents the commonly accepted definition of worldly success, and then uses a compelling combination of Scripture and insights from personal experience to show how Christ radically redefined success in his own generation, and how we in this present age can redefine success through active Christian community. Perhaps the most valuable contribution of this book is its clear presentation of how an unchallenged and unconsciously accepted worldly definition of success leads us into bondage, and not into peace and blessings. Djoeandy provides many practical examples of how to change one's lifestyles to better reflect Christ's definition of success. Along with effective real life examples, Djoeandy also cautions readers against a guilt-based lifestyle change. Instead, we are encouraged to be motivated by Christ's love for us and to use intentional Christian community to help us live by a Kingdom-centred definition of success. Although the booklet is too brief to deal adequately with all aspects of the topic, Djoeandy's ability to make this discussion compelling for a topic that is deeply relevant but rarely addressed within African congregations would make this book a useful resource.

277. Donders, Joseph G.

Non-Bourgeois Theology: An African Experience of Jesus

Maryknoll, NY: Orbis, 1985. 200 pages, ISBN: 9780883443521.

This book by a former professor of philosophy at the University of Nairobi is different from most books relating to mission and theology in Africa. For one thing, it is not merely academic but also anecdotal. Almost every chapter is triggered by something said or done at a significant conference or papal visit somewhere in Africa, or by some telling incident real or imaginary that took place in an African city or village; the remainder of each chapter then explores the wider debate. It is thus firmly earthed in African life, with many real-life examples. For this reason, too, the book is easy to read. Secondly, the chapters represent articles written or lectures delivered at different times and places. It is a collection of reflections, and so, perhaps unavoidably, the author repeats himself, and the book lacks any overall direction. Although much of what Donders writes relates to the African experience of Catholic Christianity, much of the book will be (sometimes uncomfortably) pertinent for Protestant mission and church life as well. Most of the issues discussed will be familiar to those interested in or involved with theology in Africa: holistic healing, spirit world, community, increasing importance of laity as opposed to a clerical elite, the tyranny of imposed ("bourgeois") theology, urban Christianity, polygamy, religious independentism, to name just some. Less predictable themes include the modern phenomenon of fatherless families, the menace of the written word that can "terrorize," and African dialectics (alternative decision-making processes). Evangelical readers may well hesitate about the author's stance on Scripture and his apparent inclusivism. Nevertheless, all will recognize in Donders someone who stands in sympathetic proximity to the African world. His is a plea for African Christianity to be true to itself, and many of his insights have a pertinence beyond the shores of the African continent for every context where the gospel is seeking to become incarnate.

278. Dong, Peter Marubitoba

The History of the United Methodist Church in Nigeria

Nashville: Abingdon, 2000. 112 pages, ISBN: 9780687090143.

This book attempts to recount the history of the United Methodist Church in Nigeria, a denomination that derives from the missionary work in middle-belt Nigeria at the beginning of the twentieth century by the Evangelical United Brethren (EUB) denomination in North America. In the 1970s the resulting churches regrouped themselves under African leadership with the present name, which intends to align it within global

Methodism. The book apparently originates from a committee assigned by the denomination to write its history. The outcome is a collection of often unconnected contributions authored by different members of the committee, apparently composed originally in Hausa and later translated. The results are not entirely successful. The material suffers from lack of good editing, with numerous typographical and grammatical errors, along with inconsistencies in expression and inaccuracy or even contradictions of fact. For example, at one point we are told that "the translation of the NT into the indigenous languages in Nigeria was initiated by the Wycliffe International in the early 1960s"; but elsewhere it is reported that the Gospel of Mark was translated into the local dialect and published by the National Bible Society of Scotland in 1943. More to the point, the book cannot be accurately referred to as a history. Its style is more on the order of a promotional brochure, for in-house use. The text at times even takes on the character of personal appeal: "We need many prayers to establish another hospital where love and the care can be expressed"; or "While these three training centres are extremely helpful, more are needed . . . It is our ardent hope and belief that someone somewhere is listening." The book undoubtedly has a worthy story to tell; the denomination has experienced a remarkable five-fold increase in recent decades, and it is commendable that the denomination wanted this story told. To the credit of the authors, there appears to be a deliberate effort to point to the indispensable contribution of the indigenous missionaries in spreading the gospel. The writers also take time to mention many of these missionaries by name. The photographs in the book add more character to the book. Furthermore, it is refreshing to see that the special role of women in spreading the gospel is not overlooked. But this good story has been regrettably obscured in its presentation. If another edition of this book is published, it will be greatly improved by a comprehensive editing. In its current form it will be most beneficial to members of the United Methodist Church in Nigeria, who can overlook the deficiencies in order to find the gems buried in it.

279. Donham, Donald L.

Marxist Modern: An Ethnographic History of the Ethiopian Revolution

Martlesham, UK: James Currey, 1999. 284 pages, ISBN: 9780852552643.

Donham, Professor of Anthropology at Emory University, attempts to analyse a small faith community, the Maale, in southwestern Ethiopia. His scholarly study focuses on the impact made upon traditionalist Maale society in the 1960s by the SIM mission agency, which within his analytical categories he terms "anti-modernist." He then relates how the Ethiopian Marxist/Leninist Revolution of 1974 to 1991, which he calls "modernist," attempted to radically reshape Maale society. What makes Donham's ethnographic study especially significant is his use of personal narratives of ordinary Maale Ethiopians. Their stories, recorded at intervals from 1974 to 1996, are the "resulting sedimentation" that provides the rich contribution of the book. A conundrum for Donham was to observe what he termed, in the religious sense, "anti-modernist" SIM missionaries from Australia, Canada, New Zealand and the United States, preaching the gospel and inspiring the formation of communities of Maale evangelicals who, in turn, became "an intensely modernist group of converts," involved in the vanguard of education, modern health practices and constructive social interaction. It would appear that Donham's overarching categories of "modernist" versus "anti-modernist" break down with these developments. In his "Afterword/Afterward" Donham acknowledges that by 1991 modernist Marxism within Greater Ethiopia had run its course with no genuine followers. But on the other hand, he observed that during the heyday of the Ethiopian Revolution the Maale evangelical churches began to attract the young in increasing numbers. He concedes in the end that the Maale evangelicals are the new modernists. Donham is to be commended for his willingness to explore a faith community in such depth by means of his particular social anthropological theory. His conclusion, however, suggests that his categories were insufficient to encompass all the dynamics of either church or mission.

Doré, Joseph

see review 529

280.   Dortzbach, Deborah, and Meredith W. Long

The AIDS Crisis: What We Can Do

Downers Grove: IVP US, 2006. 157 pages, ISBN: 9780830833726.

The authors have served with World Relief in helping churches develop strategies to combat AIDS and provide awareness, education and care for those infected and affected. Both authors have lived and worked extensively in Africa, and African case studies feature prominently in this presentation. Their primary focus is on how sufferers and their families can now be helped to experience God's love through His people, the church, and how the spread of the disease can be halted. The motivation offered for writing the book is that "As Christians, none of us can confront AIDS without also confronting core issues that define us." These issues include: our own actions and attitudes on sex and its involvement in AIDS; social and structural evils moulding the environments which allow AIDS to proliferate; the conflict between grace and judgement in our societies and our churches; and the role of the church in bringing God's love into the lives of AIDS sufferers. Revealing case studies from various parts of the world are included to illustrate the immediacy of the need and the redemptive role church people are playing in these situations. The authors forthrightly deal with sensitive issues like promoting condom use to reduce the spread of HIV/AIDS while holding firmly to abstinence as God's way to deal with this disease. The book is clearly a call to action and most chapters end with a section on "Taking the Next Steps," which includes both questions for reflection and questions to promote action by the reader to find ways to help address this crisis. The case studies add immediacy to the call to action and would be expected to help local people be more open about sharing their own situations regarding AIDS. This book would be a valuable asset in the libraries of pastors and church leaders and would also be helpful in institutions training Christian workers. In addition, it would help Christian parents who are seeking a way to communicate with their children about this important issue.

281.   Dortzbach, Deborah

AIDS in Africa: The Church's Opportunity

Nairobi: MAP International, 1996. 48 pages.

More than a hundred and fifty delegates met in Kampala, Uganda, in 1994 for an All-Africa Church and AIDS Consultation. This little booklet summarizes the major findings of that consultation in the distinctive form of a practical study guide, offering information, reflection, suggested lines of action, and references for further study. It seeks to cover in simple style the principal themes which Christian leaders in Africa must address if the Church is to respond appropriately to the current AIDS crisis. This booklet could serve well for organising discussion among concerned Christians anywhere in Africa needing a systematic, effective guide on what must be considered and what must be done. It also includes the challenging "Declaration" by which the delegates expressed their concluding commitments and vision. Readers in Africa seeking basic, sensitive, informed material addressing Christian responsibility in the AIDS epidemic will find this an excellent resource.

282. Dossou, Marcelin S., Fabien Ouamba, and Daniel Zo'o Zo'o

Introduction à la théologie systématique. Volume 1: Dogmatique

Yaoundé: Éditions Clé, 2002. 273 pages.

This is one of the first volumes in a subsidized series of manuals from Editions CLE for teaching theology in seminaries and Bible schools in French-speaking Africa. The three authors teach theology in institutes in Cameroon and Benin. This book consists of six parts covering the main chapters to be taught in Dogmatics. Most chapters place a heavy stress on the historical development of the doctrines considered, as is common in systematic theology in continental Europe. The introduction stresses the need for contextualized manuals for theological education in Africa, but with the exception of the chapter on ecclesiology and the bibliographies, the content of the different chapters has little that relates to Africa and could equally be taught in Europe or North America. The theological positions are not always well balanced. For example, in the first chapter the theological conceptions of Henri Blocher and Paul Tillich are used side by side without noting the tensions between the two approaches. The chapters can be used as supplementary reading for courses taught in French, but as a main support for a course in dogmatics, they will often be too short. Undoubtedly the publishers' intention to develop manuals for theological education in francophone Africa is a welcome forward step.

Dossou, Marcelin S.

see also review 51

283. Draper, Jonathan, editor

The Eye of the Storm: Bishop John William Colenso and the Crisis of Biblical Inspiration

London: Bloomsbury, 2003. 408 pages, ISBN: 9780826470904.

Until recently John William Colenso was not generally regarded as an important figure in South African church history. Found guilty of heresy by the Bishop of Cape Town in 1863, Colenso is probably known to many people only in terms of the title of a 1983 biography, *The Heretic*. But, as this collection of essays shows, such epithets can be misleading. The author of this biography, from the University of Natal, has drawn together a group of biblical scholars, theologians and historians for re-evaluations of Colenso. Published on the occasion of the 150th anniversary of Colenso's consecration as Bishop of Natal, the essays focus on four areas of Colenso's life: Bible, Theology, Ekukhanyeni (his mission station), and Family and Society. In the first part of the book the reader is reminded of Colenso's lexicographical and orthographical work in Zulu that accompanied his Bible translation projects. Colenso anticipated many of the discussions that would become central in twentieth-century African theology. His commentary on Romans, for instance, was written "from a missionary point of view," and this led Colenso to read Romans as a condemnation of settler racial pride. His universalism also led him to reject the doctrines of substitutionary atonement and eternal punishment while emphasising the place of natural religion and conscience. A handful of essays explore reasons for the overwhelmingly negative reaction that Colenso's writing received in nineteenth-century English society, including dissatisfaction with the critical methods he employed, his association with certain scientists who were highly critical of orthodox Christianity, and the fact that he wrote from "out of Africa." The third part of this work focuses on Colenso's mission station, Ekukhanyeni, and on the school he started there. This proved to be one of the more enduring aspects of Colenso's work, as his students remained influential in Natal well into the twentieth-century. The book concludes with a group of essays that focus on Colenso's wife and daughters, and his interaction with colonial and Zulu society. Draper's essay on Colenso's 1863 trial shows that it was procedurally flawed and unjust. It is perhaps for this reason that the Church of the Province of Southern Africa passed a resolution in 2002 to lift the condemnation for heresy that Bishop Gray had passed on Colenso. It is somewhat alarming to note that certain doctrinal points for which Colenso was originally excommunicated are no longer controversial and have instead become acceptable in certain Christian traditions. Especially valuable is the bibliography of works by Colenso and on Colenso, which will now allow interested parties easier access to primary and secondary sources relating to Colenso.

Draper, Jonathan

see also review 17

284.   Dube, Jimmy G., editor

A Socio-Political Agenda for the Twenty-First Century Zimbabwe Church: Empowering the Excluded

Lewiston, NY: Edwin Mellen Press, 2006. 220 pages, ISBN: 9780773455771.

Dube has served on the faculty of the United Theological College, Harare. This book results from his doctoral dissertation at Drew University, USA. It proposes a theological framework which he calls "a social and politically sensitive theology," by which he intends to empower "the *excluded* people and groups" of Zimbabwe, whom he understands as "victims of colonialism and Western imperialistic Christianity." In Dube's unnuanced portrayal, pre-missionary African society was a utopia – socially, politically, and spiritually. Colonial authorities and missionaries were then responsible for "drastically destroying the social structures of African society" through urbanisation and Christianisation. And missionary Christianity also "thoroughly humiliated the indigenous people" by refusing to embrace ATR as part of the heritage of the African people, whose spiritual needs were already well provided for through African traditional belief systems. Dube emphasizes that it was these beliefs, not missionary Christianity, that motivated and empowered the indigenous Africans to stand up against the white man's racial superiority and colonialism during the liberation wars in Zimbabwe in the 1970s. Unfortunately this overall diagnosis, appealing as it may appear within some segments of contemporary Zimbabwe, sits askew at numerous points to established scholarly research. In the second section of his book Dube expounds his assumption that the primary role of the Church in Africa lies in social and political transformation. He blames the African Church for its failure to come up with solutions to Africa's socio-political problems. First, he calls for a new generation of "radical Christians" who can participate in the repossession of the fertile land which white settlers had seized from the defenceless Africans. Second, he calls upon "radical Christians" to topple African dictators. He cites Kenya, Malawi, and Zambia as examples of where the African

Church was instrumental in getting rid of African dictators. It is sometimes difficult to avoid a sense of naivety in the solutions outlined. One will have to look elsewhere for balanced estimation of the history and role of Christianity in Africa, or for sound and constructive alternative Christian solutions to the current spiritual, social and political challenges facing people in Zimbabwe and Africa.

285.   Dube, Musa W., editor

Africa Praying: A Handbook on HIV/AIDS Sensitive Sermon Guidelines and Liturgy

Geneva: World Council of Churches, 2003. 260 pages, ISBN: 9782825414071.

With the support of the Ecumenical HIV/AIDS Initiative of the World Council of Churches (WCC), this resource has been produced to "equip the church leader/worker with strategies to break the silence and stigma surrounding HIV/AIDS, creating a compassionate and healing church." The editor is a lecturer in biblical studies at the University of Botswana and an HIV/AIDS theological consultant for the WCC. Essentially the book provides guidelines for 89 services which could be used in a congregational setting in Africa. Each service provides the text of prayers, words of songs, and sermon guidelines based on a selected biblical passage. The idea is that, with this resource, a church leader could develop an entire service and liturgy focused on issues relating to HIV/AIDS. The topics are organized into five sections, each containing about ten subjects. For instance, the first part, headed "Services for Life Markers," contains topics dealing with: birthdays, confirmation, weddings, anniversaries, graduation and closing ceremonies, death and funerals, tomb unveiling, healing and memorial services, and thanksgiving. Other parts include: Services on the Church Calendar (e.g. Christmas); Themes for General Services (e.g. reconciliation); Services for Specific Groups (e.g. youth); and Services on Social Factors Contributing to HIV/AIDS (e.g. poverty, economic justice). Does the book succeed? Certainly the idea is to be commended. The scope of the HIV/AIDS pandemic in Africa is well known, and churches need to address the crisis more effectively. Providing suggested guidelines for sermons and liturgy may aid ill-equipped pastors in doing so. Nevertheless, a number of factors may limit the use of this resource across the continent and across theological traditions. First, contributors are selected almost exclusively from countries of southern Africa; this results in a text that is not always as helpful to the rest of Africa. Second, the text reflects the ideologies and emphases for which the WCC is known (e.g. gender roles, justice, peace, power, equality, poverty). Whereas evangelicals can be challenged to address these issues as important elements both in the HIV/AIDS crisis and in biblical theology, evangelicals may well wish to speak somewhat differently from the way these issues are addressed in this text, and add other core issues as well. Thirdly, careful biblical expositors will be disappointed in the way Scripture passages are sometimes used as springboards for points of application that seem poorly linked with the referenced text.

286.   Dube, Musa W., editor

Other Ways of Reading: African Women and the Bible

Atlanta: SBL, 2001. 262 pages, ISBN: 9781589830097.

All who are familiar with contemporary trends in African theology will be aware of the important contribution being made by the Circle of Concerned African Women Theologians, a continental network inspired and organized by Mercy Oduyoye. This volume of thirteen essays originated from the Circle and is edited by one of its most prominent biblical scholars. The volume is strongly weighted in the direction of southern Africa; most of the contributors are from no farther north than Botswana (one American, one Ghanaian, and two Kenyans are also involved). Perhaps the social location of the writers in (or from) southern Africa helps somewhat to explain the distinctly postcolonial emphasis of these studies. In much postcolonial rhetoric, biblical texts are identified strongly with the colonial masters (the explorers, settlers and missionaries) who brought the Bible to Africa. For many postcolonial readers, therefore, the Bible is a part of the problem. Especially telling are two essays in the section "Patriarchal and Colonizing Translations" in which the authors complain that the Shona and Tswana traditional religions were effectively hijacked by Bible translations that used African divine names to translate the name of God in the Scriptures. Writing on the Shona, Dora Mbuwayesango concludes her essay, "In the project I propose, the Hebrew names of God would be maintained in order to maintain the differences between Mwari and Yhwh Elohim. The pen should rescue the Shona deity. Writing merged Mwari with the biblical god and it is through writing that the identification of Mwari with the genderless Shona deity will be reclaimed." In effect Mbuwayesango seems to be arguing for a de-evangelisation of the Shona people. These essays leave us with much to ponder – including in what measure some of the Circle's theologians should still be identifying themselves as expressly "Christian" theologians.

287. **Dube, Musa W.**

Postcolonial Feminist Interpretation of the Bible

St Louis: Chalice, 2000. 230 pages, ISBN: 9780827229631.

Musa Dube, professor in biblical studies at the University of Botswana, has produced a work of far-reaching implications which will require an answer. Based on her Vanderbilt University doctoral dissertation, this work attempts to understand the story of the Canaanite woman (Matt 15:21–28) against the background of postcolonial theory. The central thesis of the book is that literature (including the Bible) is a tool often employed by colonial writers in order to justify the subjugation of conquered peoples. She examines texts from the "classical period" and from the modern colonial period in order to reveal a rhetorical pattern to such imperialist literature. Such literature portrays subjugated peoples as in need of the colonizer due to their inferior culture and intellect. Often women in these colonial stories are portrayed as helpless and in need of saving by the superior culture of those who are in reality their oppressors. There is much in this analysis that is true and worthy of reflection. Dube also concludes, however, that the Bible is a colonialist book. She argues that the Exodus, far from being a book sympathetic to the downtrodden (as many liberation readers have argued), is actually deeply implicated in the colonialist project, since the goal of the Exodus from Egypt is the dispossession of the Canaanites through their violent expulsion or extermination. The only survivor of the downfall of Jericho, Dube points out, is Rahab, who betrays her own people in order to save herself. The Rahab pattern is replicated in the story of the Canaanite woman in Matthew 15 who is, in reality, a subject of patriarchal and imperial domination. Dube's work is deeply sceptical of Scripture. "Feminist attempts to reclaim the stories [of the Bible]," she writes, " . . . should also be accompanied by a decolonizing reading. This begins with an acknowledgment that most of the so-called canonical texts are not only patriarchal but also imperial." Even Jesus is considered "an imperial and patriarchal symbol." Most Christian readers in Africa will find this book unacceptable; indeed many will find the arguments to be anti-biblical and anti-Christian. Nevertheless, Dube's work must be taken seriously, for the colonial project has deeply wounded Africa, and if such responses to that wounding as this one are not appropriate, biblically-grounded Christians will need to ensure that more appropriate responses are provided.

Dube, Musa W.

see also reviews 1116, 1171 and 1173

Dube, S. W. D.

see review 873

Dubow, Saul

see review 131

Duflo, Esther

see review 93

288.   Dunn, D. Elwood

A History of the Episcopal Church in Liberia, 1821–1980

Lanham, MD: Scarecrow Press, 1992. 478 pages, ISBN: 9780810825734.

We have here another welcome example of African Christianity undertaking to tell its own story, in this case the story of the small Anglican community positioned in the distinctive historical setting of Liberia, and deriving not from Britain (as with most Anglicanism on the continent) but from the Episcopal Church in America. The author is himself a Liberian, a life-long affiliate of the church he profiles, and presently a published university professor in the United States. More than a third of the book is devoted to an impressive array of supporting materials, including thirteen appendices, 46 historical photographs, and an exceptionally comprehensive bibliography. The book's value is in its rich details, which will serve well the needs of researchers for generations to come. Its chief limitations are in its overall structure and in its interpretive grid. Perhaps owing to available archival materials, Dunn's book is in fact a history not of the Episcopal Church in Liberia (ECL), but of the successive bishops of that church. Also for understanding this history Dunn adopts as his interpretive grid the problematic role of European colonialism and Christian missions in the formation of modern Africa. But whereas the standardized modern assumptions implied by such a framing may be appropriate for other parts of the continent, their imposition on Liberia tends to distort and suppress Liberia's distinctive history, where the "colonial" founders were not expatriate Europeans but freed black slaves from America, where their "colonisation" antedated most European colonial occupation of Africa by at least half a century, and where their efforts resulted in a free black republic well over a century before most of the rest of the continent achieved independence. Dunn also tends to measure the success of the church and its bishops principally in terms of the church's impact on the life of the nation, as seen especially in educational institutions provided and in the frequent presence of its members in higher levels of government. The climax for Dunn is achieved in 1982 when the ECL finally dissolves relations with its mother church in the States and is incorporated into the larger Anglican community's Province of West Africa, thus finally "coming home to Africa." Though published in 1992, the narrative ends prior to Liberia's political upheavals beginning in the early 1980s that have so changed the face of that troubled land. Remarkably, although the prophet William Wadé Harris (c. 1860–1929) was at one time affiliated with the ECL, and is perhaps therefore the best-known member of that community in modern African Christian history, here he surfaces solely in several of the bibliographic entries.

289.   Dyrness, William A., editor

Emerging Voices in Global Christian Theology

Eugene, OR: Wipf & Stock, 2003. 256 pages, ISBN: 9781592444472.

In this short volume, Dyrness (of Fuller Theological Seminary, USA) has reproduced nine essays which are meant to introduce the Western reader to contemporary Christian reflection outside of western Europe and North America. Although the contributors are all evangelical writers, there is little else which holds the volume together. While many of the essays are what one might expect to find in a collection of theological reflections, others have a more narrative quality, reporting something of the context of suffering and political struggle with which most non-western Christians must live. The book is in four sections: Eastern Europe (one essay), Africa (three), Asia (three), Latin America (two). As is common for such collections, the essays are uneven. But readers will be pleased to know that the three African contributions are excellent. The essays by Tony Balcomb ("South Africa: Terrifying Stories of Faith from the Political Boiling Pot of the World"); Cyril Okorocha ("The Meaning of Salvation: An African Perspective"); and Kwame Bediako ("Jesus in African Culture: A Ghanaian Perspective"), provide in combination an excellent introduction to theology in African contexts. But if the book is used as a text for courses on Christianity in Africa, Asia and Latin America, it would need to be supplemented by other readings.

290.   Dyrness, William A.

Learning about Theology from the Third World

Grand Rapids: Zondervan, 1990. 224 pages, ISBN: 9780310209713.

The author, for many years associated with the School of Theology at Fuller Theological Seminary, also taught previously in Asia and from time to time in Africa. In this book he demonstrates the need and benefits of listening to the theologians and cultural concerns of Africa, Asia, and Latin America. Dyrness proposes that these concerns be passed through an "interactional model of contextualization" (adapted from R. Schreiter), which can foster a dynamic interplay between culture and Scripture. The goal of this process is a transformation of life and values in the Christian by the Holy Spirit. Three chapters cover the above mentioned geographical theologies. The chapter on Africa deals with the topics of harmony, God and the powers, the human community, the means of fellowship. The book introduces principal concerns by African theologians, and could therefore be used profitably for classroom discussions on relating biblical theology and basic African values.

291.   Eber, Jochen

Johann Ludwig Krapf: Ein schwäbischer Pionier in Ostafrika

Riehen, Switzerland: ArteMedia Winteler, 2006. 272 pages, ISBN: 9783905290417.

Missiological books that are both missions-motivational and soundly researched biographies are rather the exception. Hagiographical biographies of mission pioneers of the past might often have led readers to discouraging self-comparison with such "spiritual heavyweights," and thus proven a disincentive. This biography of the well-known German nineteenth-century missionary pioneer in East Africa, Johann Ludwig Krapf, is different. The author is a pastor and academic dean of a study centre in Germany. In this biography he presents Krapf in a way that can also acknowledge Krapf's weaknesses. Thus one learns, for example, that the Africa-zealous missionary who later served in the homeland as a promoter of missions experienced phases of reluctance toward mission, and even depression. In the main part of the biography, Eber presents Krapf's adventurous trips to Ethiopia and his subsequent travels in what are today known as Kenya and Tanzania. Here one learns much about the lands and their peoples, as well as about contemporary travel. For example, Eber reports that Krapf travelled with an air mattress, which was considered one of the newest technological achievements, enabling a restful night's sleep in the middle of the African wilderness. Of course, Eber mentions Krapf's famous discovery of Mount Kenya, while Krapf's colleague Johann Rebmann became the first European to see the snows of Kilimanjaro. That was at that time a sensation, since snow-capped mountains at the equator were for Krapf's contemporaries simply unimaginable. Even Krapf's theology is treated by Eber. Krapf's untiring missionary activity and dangerous exploratory journeys were prompted by his intense eschatological expectations. But Krapf was also linked with Johann Michael Hahn, and the resulting question remains unanswered how the enthusiastic missionary Krapf could nonetheless be linked with Hahn's obviously unmissionary "reconciliation of all things" theology. The book is superbly illustrated with many contemporary illustrations, and offers an extensive bibliography. Moreover, it is easy to read. All in all this represents a fresh and valuable contribution to understanding this key figure of African mission history.

292. **Eboussi Boulaga, Fabien**

Christianity without Fetishes: An African Critique and Recapture of Christianity

Maryknoll, NY: Orbis, 1984. 238 pages, ISBN: 9780883444320.

The author is a Cameroonian who left the Jesuit priesthood after intensive self-examination related to his feelings on "the whole Christian project as it encounters a new Africa." He subsequently became a professor of philosophy at the University of Côte d'Ivoire. In the foreword it is noted that though Eboussi Boulaga "is perhaps the leading theologian of francophone West Africa, this is his first book to be translated into English" and that theologians in the "English-speaking world are the poorer for that," since Eboussi is such a brilliant thinker and a leader of francophone theologians. This book is a valuable contribution to the growing debate on inculturation of a Western-oriented Christian faith in non-western cultural contexts. The author seeks to answer major questions related to the relevance of the Christian faith as practised in African culture. While Eboussi criticizes and rejects the imported Christianity which has been imposed on the African people by the Western churches, in his later chapters he offers suggestions for a solution to the problems which he has described. He says first that the power and self-determination of the African people must be rediscovered and rectified and that they must consider themselves "subjects" and not "objects." Second, he says that the reformation must be from within the African churches themselves. Third, he says that if there is to be reformation, the African churches must communicate among themselves. Eboussi's academic specialisation in the disciplines of philosophy and theology is evident throughout, which makes this not an easy book to read. And while Eboussi presents his case well, certainly not all – and especially those of a Western orientation – would agree with his direction or conclusions. It is nevertheless a welcome book for all who are serious about examining from a scholarly perspective problems and solutions relating to the inculturation process, and it would be a valuable addition to any theological library.

Edwards, S. D.

see review 872

293.   Eide, Oyvind M.

Restoring Life in Christ: Dialogues of Care in Christian Communities: An African Perspective

Neuendettelsau, Germany: Erlanger Verlag, 2008. 185 pages, ISBN: 9783872149060.

This book represents the initial results of a research project on pastoral care in Tanzania. The project aims to develop a theology of pastoral care "from below," that is a theology built on the experiences and practice of local pastors. A number of pastors have participated in the project, and their experiences have been discussed through workshops and seminars. The present book offers a theoretical introduction to the project. Two more books will follow, each containing five case studies. These latter books will be translated into Swahili, and written for lay people, evangelists and pastors practicing care in Christian communities. The introduction to the book is written by Eide, then professor in the School of Mission and Theology (MHS), Norway. He relates the project to current paradigms of pastoral care, and emphasizes biblical and African perspectives. Three essays follow by Tanzanian contributors, on the integration of African perspectives, on the importance of female perspectives, and on the necessity of cultural sensitivity. Next come five chapters by Eide and Leif Engedal, professor in the Norwegian School of Theology (MF), in which they outline a theology of pastoral care and counselling, with particular focus on the need for a theological foundation, the function of word and sacrament, and the conversation between theology and culture. The book concludes with four verbatim conversations from the experiences of the participating pastors. The verbatim materials, providing a background for the preceding more theoretical chapters, include the following cases: (i) David (50) is infected by AIDS: counselling on AIDS and the image of God. (ii) Martha (18) is pregnant and the boyfriend has run away: counselling on discipline and grace. (iii) Anna is beaten by her husband: counselling on domestic violence and human dignity. (iv) Esther is a young and pregnant widow: counselling on grief, compassion and hope. The book is an especially valuable contribution to the emerging focus on developing Africanised pastoral care, and certainly deserves to be read and used by those lecturing in pastoral theology and pastoral counselling in Africa.

294.   Eide, Oyvind M.

Revolution and Religion in Ethiopia: The Growth and Persecution of the Mekane Yesus Church, 1974–1985

Martlesham, UK: James Currey, 2000. 320 pages, ISBN: 9780852558416.

Eide was previously professor of practical theology at the Norwegian School of Mission, Stavanger. Prior to that he served in church ministry in Ethiopia. In this book he makes an important contribution to understanding the role of religion in modern Ethiopian history, and in particular the role of evangelical Christianity during the revolutionary years of the Dergue (1974–1985). The author interprets the place of evangelical Christianity in relation to the political and religious centres of traditional Ethiopia, by opting for a centre-periphery perspective on the ethno-political, socio-political and religio-political dynamics of the Ethiopian Empire. He points out that in the time of the emperors, the Ethiopian form of Orthodox Christianity functioned as the most profound expression of the meaning of being Ethiopian. Evangelical Christianity in Ethiopia, most notably the Ethiopian Evangelical Church Mekane Yesus (EECMY), developed in powerful interaction with the local ethnic groups at the periphery of these national political and religious structures and dynamics. When the revolution came, the evangelicals were initially hoping that it would bring in a fairer situation, giving the different ethnic groups and the non-Orthodox churches a recognized place in the society. This did not happen. The Dergue found that it could not govern without the assistance of the traditional centres of power. Eide estimates that the number of closed churches during the persecution by the Dergue regime amounted to at least 2500. As a reason for the persecution he offers the fact that the evangelical churches in general strengthened the periphery, so they were seen as a resistance to the unification process and central control within the ethnic, social and ideological realm. Although this study deals with a specific period of recent Ethiopian church history, its interpretive framework, namely the tensions between centre and periphery in national life, and the potential impact of this for church groups, may well prove applicable to Christian experience in other parts of Africa.

295. Eijk, Ryan van, and Jan van Lin

Africans Reconstructing Africa

Nijmegen, Netherlands: Theologische Faculteit KU-Nijmegen, 1997. 109 pages, ISBN: 9789075934021.

In the final years of the twentieth century a growing number of ecumenical theologians (Kä Mana, Mugambi, Chipenda, Villa-Vicencio) started speaking about a "theology of reconstruction," thereby implying that Africa needs to go beyond a theology of liberation to start reflecting on the contribution the church and theology can make to the many crises of the continent. Additional to the Exodus, the reconstruction of the land by Nehemiah after the Exile is taken as a paradigm for theological reflection and action. It is interesting that this reconstruction theology is much more rooted in African soil than in liberation theology. This collection of essays, representing some of these new developments, resulted from a conference held in the Netherlands in 1996 in association with the Catholic University of Nijmegen. The contributions by Mohammed Salih (Sudan/Netherlands) on "Africa and diversity of images: Communities quest for democracy and local governance," and Basker Vashee (Zimbabwe) on "The economic crises in sub-Saharan Africa" analyse the political and economic crisis of Africa, but without any specific reference to the contribution the church could make as steward of the gospel. Edmund Akordor (Ghana/Netherlands) and the well-known ecumenical theologian Mercy Oduyoye (Ghana) write respectively on the role that African communities and African women play and can play in this reconstruction. The most interesting and by far the longest contribution (40 pages) is from Ryan van Eijk, former Roman Catholic missionary in Ghana and now working as a missiologist in the Netherlands. He gives an overview of the theology of reconstruction (possibly the first in English), dealing with the roots of the African crisis, its recent escalation, the role of the churches and four proposals for a theology of reconstruction (Villa-Vicencio, Kä Mana, Mugambi and Uzukwu). This last contribution alone makes the entire publication a worthwhile addition for any library that wants to offer an adequate introduction to the literature of African theology. Readers from various theological persuasions will want to be taking account of this new theological development, as they also seek to address the modern African crisis. Their contributions may include a salutary warning that addressing the socio-political questions should not entail a reduction of the gospel solely to these issues.

296.   Eitel, Keith E.

Transforming Culture: Developing a Biblical Ethic in an African Context

Nairobi: Evangel, 1986. 185 pages, ISBN: 9789966850034.

Essentially representing a Doctor of Missiology project at Trinity Evangelical Divinity School (USA), this book attempts to develop a paradigm for ethics in the African context, together with an application of the proposed paradigm for the question of polygamy. The model for personal ethics developed has five basic principles, which can be summarized as: (1) Scripture is normative and authoritative; (2) Christians are not to do something which they know would destroy their bodies; (3) questionable acts which risk causing a Christian to stumble are to be avoided; (4) contradicting spiritual authority in making ethical decisions is sin; and (5) everything one does should glorify God. The application to polygamy concludes that it is tolerated rather than favoured in the OT, and that it is not in conformity to biblical norms. Eitel advocates not requiring polygamists to divorce, while restricting the roles they may play in church. The fact that this was initially a DMiss project probably accounts for the overly long prolegomena (80 pages out of 175 pages of text). In contrast, the chapter exploring biblical foundations for personal ethics is a scant twelve pages! Also the discussion is almost exclusively focused on the development of a personal ethic; the whole arena of social ethics is decidedly absent. While this may have been an appropriate delimitation for a DMiss project, it means that both the title and sub-title are seriously misleading, and the parameters of the discussion disappointing on a continent where recent history suggests how much social ethics is in need of solid Christian reflection. While noting this as one example among past discussions of Christian ethics in the African setting, the book's limitations in scope and relevance must also be taken clearly into account.

297.   Ejeh, Theophilus Ugbedeojo

The Servant of Yahweh in Isaiah 52:13–53:12: A Historical Critical and Afro-Cultural Hermeneutical Analysis with the Igalas of Nigeria in View

Münster: LIT Verlag, 2012. 296 pages, ISBN: 9783643901644.

The author is a Roman Catholic priest from Nigeria, and the book is a revised version of his 2010 doctoral dissertation at the Faculty of Theology in Paderhorn, Germany. The main point of the book is to build a bridge between Isaiah 52:13–53:12 – the fourth so-called Servant Song, a key text in the NT reception of the OT – and the life and culture of the Igalas of Nigeria. This aim is achieved through the logical development of the book's six main chapters. Chapter 1 offers a translation (into English; the author's translation of the text into Igala follows as an appendix in the end of the book) and exegetical analysis of the text, arguing that it was authored around the time when the Persian King Cyrus conquered Babylon, at the verge of the return of the exiled Judeans back to Jerusalem. Chapter 2 meticulously goes through the early reception history of the text, first in later OT texts, then in the Apocrypha and in other Jewish literature, and finally in the NT. Chapter 3 briefly studies the theological concern of the text, identified as the compassion of God with his creation, an idea that is then followed through the NT's interpretation of Jesus as the Servant described in the text. Chapter

4 turns attention to the Igalas, with the expected outline of language, culture and traditional religion. This then provides the background for chapter 5's contextual analysis of the text. This is a brief chapter – not even ten percent of the total number of pages. But it is here, one might argue, that we find the main contribution of the book, with its discussions of how the Isaiah text is to be translated and related to the worldview and language of the Igala. One would have wanted to see more of this discussion, but it is at least a beginning. Finally, chapter 6 makes the necessary (from a theological point of view) interpretation of the Isaiah text vs. Igala context from Christological and Roman Catholic perspectives. The book is one of the many contextual studies coming from contemporary African biblical scholars.

298. Ekem, John David Kwamena

Early Scriptures of the Gold Coast (Ghana): The Historical, Linguistic, and Theological Settings of the Gã, Twi, Mfantse, and Ewe Bibles

Rome: Edizioni, 2011. 204 pages, ISBN: 9788863721881.

Ekem has provided us with a model of historical study on nineteenth and early twentieth-century African Bible translations. He is well equipped for this task. Ekem is a Ghanaian NT scholar and ordained Methodist, who has also been a Bible translation consultant, and the Academic Dean of Trinity College, Legon, and director of that institution's Institute of Mother-Tongue Biblical Hermeneutics. Given that much original archival research had to be done in the German-language archives of the Basel and Bremen missionary societies (as well as the English-language archives), the fact that Ekem's doctorate is from Hamburg gives him the needed linguistic tools to complete this study. As the subtitle suggests, the book is a study of Bible translation in the four largest language groups of Ghana. Although the names of European missionaries involved in these first translation projects are fairly well known (Johannes Zimmermann for Gã; Johann Christaller for Twi), little mention has previously been made of their African counterparts who, as native speakers, played an indispensible role in the production of these translations. In fact, as Ekem points out, the very first translators in these languages were native Africans (Jacobus Capitein and Christian Protten), although their production was limited. Ekem introduces us to African translators like Thomas Kwatei (Quartey), Jacob Nikoi, David Asante, Theophilus Opoku, Ludwig Adzaklo, Andreas Aku, Aaron Onipayede and Immanuel Quist, whose contributions deserve our attention and appreciation. Ekem's study is primarily historical; the linguistic and theological settings mentioned in the subtitle are barely touched on and, as Ekem acknowledges, there is much work left to be done. The author himself points to some intriguing topics for further research – for example, Quist apparently produced an entire commentary on Matthew's gospel in Ewe which, although "preserved in the Bremen State Archives" appears no longer to be in print, if it ever was. Surely such resources should be rescued from European archives and made available for African readers! It is wonderful that volumes such as this one on the history of Bible translation are beginning to appear through the work of the Nida Institute for Biblical Scholarship. It is hoped that the quality of future volumes will match the fine standard set by this readable and fascinating work.

299. **Ekwunife, Anthony N. O.**

Christianity and the Challenges of Witchcraft in Contemporary Africa

Enugu, Nigeria: Snaap Press, 2011. 104 pages, ISBN: 9789789100569.

This book is an expanded version of a paper delivered to the National Association of Spiritual Directors of Catholic Major Seminaries in Nigeria. It pursues answers to two questions. First, how are we to understand the nature of witchcraft in the African context? And second, how should this phenomenon be approached in pastoral practice? Unfortunately, the book is too brief for the author to defend his answers adequately. In response to the first of these questions, Ekwunife argues that there are indeed men and women who are witches. Their power is personal, not demonic, and they are therefore morally responsible agents who can be held accountable for the harm that they inflict on others. He thus disagrees strongly with what is probably the majority view among African Christians, that witches are empowered by demons. This majority understanding of witchcraft, he contends, leads to spurious and counter-productive efforts to exorcize demons of witchcraft. It is better to see witches as morally responsible agents, acting on the basis of their own personal power, through their "ethereal bodies," to "suck the ethereal blood of their victims." Witches can be identified by their "excessive individualism," their "taciturn" bearing "during community meetings," their quarrelsome or cantankerous disposition, and/or their exceptional skill in one domain or another of life. He goes on to provide "evidence" for his views garnered from personal experience and from stories that he has heard. This evidence is, however, extremely thin and unconvincing, consisting of a very small number of cases for which very few details are provided. Ekwunife's answer to the second question regarding pastoral responses to witchcraft is equally cursory. He suggests that spiritual directors who are approached by those who believe they are being attacked by witches should recommend intensified prayer, trust in God, possibly a medical check-up, and consultations with those who have expertise in traditional anti-witchcraft techniques or medicines. He also recommends caution in one's social contacts in order to avoid putting oneself in a position where witches might easily attack (through food or physical contact). Although the book has a very short chapter entitled "The Theology of Witchcraft in the African Context," Ekwinife does not discuss the biblical data regarding the nature of supernatural powers in any depth. Many will feel that this book accepts too uncritically the epistemology of African witchcraft discourse. As such, it can serve as a useful illustration of a perhaps not altogether uncommon approach to the problem of witchcraft in the African context. It does not, however, contribute substantially to the kind of careful discussion that is needed in order to meet the theological and pastoral challenges posed by this set of phenomena.

300. **Ela, Jean-Marc**

African Cry

Eugene, OR: Wipf & Stock, 2005. 160 pages, ISBN: 9781597523295.

The *African Cry* of the title is a cry for liberation from the bondage which enslaves Africans to an imported and imposed Christianity. Writing from an African Roman Catholic persuasion, Ela examines the liberation process for the African churches. A Cameroonian theologian who works among the Kirdis in north Cameroon, he begins his book by using the Eucharist as an example of an imported faith which has little meaning for the people of a given culture. Ela shows that the expansion of Christianity coincided with the expansion of empires and that the church in Africa has remained "a testimonial to a colonising West." He points to a new awareness of purpose in missions and says conversion is no longer the only issue at hand, "but also the promotion of the human being in all of the dimensions of his or her existence." Ela calls on the church to redefine itself in its own context since not to do so will render the church continually dependent on the home churches of the West for its success. In a positive light Ela considers that a serious rethinking and reforming of the church in Africa would lead to a faith which would be true to the context of the African people. In the book Ela's "cry" for liberation and self-determination for the African church is clearly heard. It is a cry for a better way for the church in Africa. It is a cry for the African church to participate in the struggle to liberate itself, and to bring others to a true understanding of the gospel in an African context. It is a challenging, well-written and well-translated work which will bring varied reactions depending on one's presuppositions. It should be included on the reading list of all those interested in a fuller understanding of the issues of contextualization of the faith in African society.

301.   Ela, Jean-Marc

Le message de Jean-Baptiste

Yaoundé: Éditions Clé, 1992. 70 pages.

The author's name will be well known to those whose studies have touched on (francophone) African theology. The works of this prolific Cameroonian theologian should find a place in all theological libraries operating at a university level. (Happily, a few of Ela's books have been translated into English.) Yet this monograph under review does not primarily address ivory tower theologians. The author seeks a wider audience, particularly focusing on those involved in active Christian service. Ela wants to bring the example of John the Baptist into the parish church, challenging African pastors to have a similar humble attitude of self-renunciation if they are to experience a manifestation of Christ's presence in their ministry. With abundant use of biblical sources and insights from first-century culture, Ela highlights the various facets of John's ministry: a "baptizer" (a relatively minor aspect of his ministry), an educator, a prophet, an evangelist, a minister of the Word of God. And always his actions and his witness were complementary. His life was not an easy one, going from desert asceticism to prison and finally to decapitation. In a similar vein, the modern servant of the Lord should expect, not the receiving of gifts from others but instead the giving of oneself for others, accomplished in a self-effacing manner, regardless of the personal cost. Ela is concerned that the message and ministry of this precursor of Jesus be understood in Africa today as a model for Christians (and especially for Christian leaders). The pastor, he says, must also be considered a forerunner and a herald, the one who prepares the way for the people to receive Jesus. The word must summon first the speaker, then the listeners, to recognize and follow the true Messiah. Whether or not one agrees with his methods and interpretations, Ela's writings always present a challenge to the reader, and this slim volume is well worth the time it takes to read and reflect on the stimulating ideas that Ela presents.

302.   Ela, Jean-Marc

My Faith as an African

Eugene, OR: Wipf & Stock, 2009. 208 pages, ISBN: 9781606086230.

The author of this thought-provoking book is a Roman Catholic priest from Cameroon. He insists that Christian theology has entered a new era in which "we must give each local church responsibility for its own theological thinking." His main thrust is that, for an Africa encountering the shock of modernity, "liberation of the oppressed must be the primary condition for any authentic inculturation of the Christian message." Ela's own theological formation took place in the midst of practical ministry among the peasants of northern Cameroon, who were faced with famine, drought, sickness, and injustice. There Ela was forced to ask himself how the gospel might most suitably be expressed within an African context of ancestor veneration, harvest events, modern civilisation, liturgy, death, cultural symbols, etc. Readers, especially those who are not Roman Catholic, may find some parts in this book unpersuasive. Several examples will suffice. Ela believes that, rather than attacking African ideas about the ancestors, the church should encourage African Christians to stay in contact with their loved ones who have left this earth, and allow their veneration. That his interpretation of sin is almost exclusively in terms of oppression, misery, poverty, and deprivation is also troubling. Ela rightly recommends that for the African church "good ideas and logical doctrines are no longer sufficient; but must be incorporated into theology, catechesis, and liturgy." He warns us "to stop imposing on young churches solutions that do not respond to their deepest hopes and anxieties." There is no doubt that Ela is addressing important issues; these are the very questions that African theologians have been raising. It is his answers to these questions that will be the bone of contention. When Ela not only states the necessity and urgency of his questions, but goes on boldly to suggest how we can make Christianity more relevant, he certainly succeeds in communicating his ideas. But whether readers should agree with his answers is another matter.

303.   Ela, Jean-Marc

Repenser la théologie africaine: Le Dieu qui libère

Paris: Éditions Karthala, 2003. 448 pages, ISBN: 9782845863743.

This volume concludes with a bibliography of books written by Ela himself and another page of articles, studies, and interviews about him, signs of his influence in the area of African Theology over the decades. His work, always influenced by his Roman Catholicism, his native Cameroon, and his academic interest in sociology, tends to have that "common touch" which makes it accessible to so many. As the subtitle ("The God who liberates") indicates, Ela concerns himself here with the many-sided question of how Africa and Africans can be truly free from not only cultural impositions from the outside but also the oppression that comes from what are perceived as unjust economic and political structures. The book is divided into four sections. Section 1, titled "Gospel and Liberation" includes such representative chapters as: "Speaking God into a Wounded Continent" and "The Motif of Liberation in African Theology." Section 2, under the title: "The Time of Pagans," includes such chapters as: "The New Actors of the Mission" and "Witnesses of the Gospel in a World with Many Faces." Among chapters in section 3, on "Memorialising Jesus Christ in a Church-Family," is: "The Lay Ministries in Christian Communities." Section 4, "The Pope in the Church: An African Appeal," has chapters on: "Service of Peter or Power of Rome?" and "The Bishops of Africa under the Control of the Roman Curia." Ela entitles his conclusion: "Christianity Must Accept Risks," which quickly shows that he is not going to be satisfied with the status quo. Citing earlier appeals, even by Vatican II, that Christianity must be rooted in the local culture, the author stresses anew the fundamental challenge, namely to present Jesus clearly and poignantly in the African culture. The Church (and Ela is thinking primarily of the Roman Catholic Church here) has to take into account the needs of Africa, especially now that such a large proportion of that church body is in fact of African origin. Rome must give full importance to African congregations or pastors. Ela writes clearly, if not very originally, in much of what is found here. The book is a good overview of many aspects of current thinking in African Theology, and a useful synthesis of Ela's work over the years.

304. Ellis, Stephen, editor

Africa Now: People, Policies and Institutions

Martlesham, UK: James Currey, 1996. 320 pages, ISBN: 9780852552315.

This collection of essays analyses issues relating to Africa which are important for Western donors (governments, banks and NGOs). The volume was financed and published by the Dutch Government for the 1995 General Assembly of the Global Coalition for Africa. The editor is a Dutch-based researcher. The fifteen contributors are mostly African academics, with the majority based in Africa (from Stellenbosch and Harare to Tunis and Casablanca). From the time of independence until the late 1980s, economic development was the key word for Africa. But the results of 30 years of foreign effort were sobering. Meanwhile stronger economies had emerged, especially in Asia. With the end of the Cold War, the foreign involvement in Africa motivated by geo-political interests was cut back, and a recession in the West led to a further decrease of foreign aid. Against this background of general "aid fatigue" and international loss of interest in Africa, this book tries to encourage future engagement for development, placing this in a wider theoretical framework that takes into account such issues as good governance and the social attitudes that form the foundation for civic institutions and public culture. The collection is organized in three sections: (1) "States and Citizens" analyses the African states in historical perspective, discusses nationalism, ethnicity and democracy, and describes religious (Christian und Muslim) impacts, as well as the role of morality in the present African political scene; (2) "Institutions and Policies" focuses on economic issues (partly in quite technical language!), especially the effects of the structural adjustment programmes pushed by the Bretton Woods institutions; (3) "Africa in the World" elaborates the crisis of the state in Africa and different endeavours at regional cooperation in Africa. Here is included an excellent essay on aid, its past relative ineffectiveness, different possible policies and pragmatic proposals for the future. Overall the essays are quite diverse. Some present fresh and specific (economic) research for advanced readers, while others use a broad brush to sketch in quite well-known political and social realities. Unfortunately, several relatively positive examples of national development in 1995 have since then taken definitive turns for the worse (e.g. Zimbabwe, Ivory Coast). Together with other recent developments (for instance in debt management), this gives the volume a somewhat outdated feel. The whole question of the impact (or lack thereof!) of religion, with its values and ethics, on good governance is treated only marginally, which should be of great concern for Christian leaders and theological educators. Overall the volume provides a fairly interesting and useful, even if somewhat diffuse and dated, orientation to development issues in Africa.

305. Ellis, Stephen

The Mask of Anarchy: The Destruction of Liberia and the Religious Dimension of an African Civil War

New York: NYU Press, 2006. 336 pages, ISBN: 9780814722381.

Ellis, a scholar of African history based in the Netherlands, here attempts to portray the devastating civil war that has racked Liberia since 1989, using the perspective of Liberians themselves. The author contends that while Western pundits have assigned the origin of the war to the political or social upheavals deriving from the forces of colonialism and modernity, Liberians attribute the conflict to "anarchy" in the realm of deepest reality, the spiritual world. This spiritual disruption stems from the misuse of traditional cultic activities (meant to appease ancestors) by new political leaders descended from Liberia's African American settlers, who employed these practices to increase and consolidate their own power. The war, therefore, has been waged by spirits against human beings. Understood as a reflection of spiritual conflict, participants on all sides thus relied on spiritual practices such as eating the hearts of dead enemies in order to gain their power, or the widespread use of amulets for protection, behaviour inexplicable within the demythologized worldview of Western academics. The bulk of the book consists of two parts. The first chronicles events of the war beginning in 1989, as well as identifying the main actors in the conflict, both Liberian and international. The second section takes a longer-term perspective by examining the history of political control as exercised in the country, and the religious-cultural roots of the war, especially as they relate to the understanding of power in the society. The book includes several useful features including: an index of acronyms (essential for keeping track of the myriad of organisations and movements involved), a list of principal characters, maps depicting major counties and towns as well as ethnic groups, plus an extensive bibliography of unpublished material (some of it from Liberian government archives), of books and articles specifically related to Liberia and its civil war, and of works of comparative nature dealing with Africa. Ellis seems to imply that from the perspective of Liberians themselves, peace will come only through a return to traditional religions whereby peace can be restored among the spirits. Certainly not all Liberians would agree. Nevertheless, whether one agrees with his conclusions either implied or asserted, Ellis has drawn proper attention to an essential but often overlooked dynamic in the ongoing tragedy that is Liberia. This book also bears wider implications for the interpretation of contemporary Africa.

306.   Ellis, Stephen, and Gerrie ter Haar

Worlds of Power: Religious Thought and Political Practice in Africa

Oxford: Oxford University Press, 2004. 263 pages, ISBN: 9780195220162.

Ellis, a political scientist who works for the International Crisis Group, and Ter Haar, a professor of religion, continue in this book their academic study of the political role of religion in Africa. They take as a given, both here and in their previous work, that in the African context power is largely thought to originate in the spirit world, and those in pursuit of power, such as politicians and insurgents, will both hold and make use of this belief. They argue that Africans think about the world through religious ideas and these ideas provide a mechanism for social and political action in Africa. The book is organized by single-word chapter headings such as Words, Spirits, Secrets and Power. In the chapter entitled "Words" Ellis and Ter Haar talk about the role of rumour or radio trottoir in forming people's interpretation of events or understanding of political realities. The authors trace the way in which a traditional understanding of the spirit world has changed through the last century, and the way that Christianity and Islam have accommodated traditional beliefs. An example of this would be spirit possession, which has changed with the advent of Christianity and colonialism, and which instead of remaining animist is now practiced by some syncretistic forms of Christianity. Also religion no longer is the sole mediator between local groups and institutions. Colonial states intervened and began to separate the spheres of religion and governance, but this separation was never completed. So the spirit world remains a source of power and legitimacy for government officials and other leaders. There is a particularly interesting discussion of justice versus law. Ellis and Ter Haar argue that most Africans are more concerned with justice than with its operationalisation in law because of a history of the illegitimacy of law combined with communal demands. Though they examine religion in a purely academic way, the authors believe that spiritual power is real power and should be taken seriously. They argue that religion can be an effective means of regulating not just the transformation of individuals, but also the transformation of society. The book is replete with examples and is richly researched. Exploring the use of power and the perceptions of the spirit world within the church itself would be one avenue of research where the ideas presented by Ellis and Ter Haar might be profitably applied.

Ellis, Stephen

see also review 109

307. Elphick, Richard, and Rodney Davenport, editors

Christianity in South Africa: A Political, Social and Cultural History

Martlesham, UK: James Currey, 1998. 512 pages, ISBN: 9780852557518.

Elphick (Wesleyan University, Connecticut, USA) and Davenport (Rhodes University, Grahamstown, South Africa) here edit the collective effort of 29 authors from four continents, all of whom have worked in South Africa, with the common purpose of demonstrating Christianity's impact on the country's political, social, and cultural history. The book is divided into five parts. Part 1 deals with the introduction of Christianity to South Africa from 1652 to 1910 through the efforts of the earliest missionaries and church groups, and recounts Christian beginnings along regional and ethnic lines – among the Xhosa, Zulu, Tswana, and Sotho groups, as well as the white settlers. Organized along ecclesiastical lines, part 2 includes chapters regarding the Afrikaner and English-speaking churches, along with the Roman Catholic, African-Initiated, and Pentecostal churches. The third part discusses Christianity's expression in various subcultures – e.g. the gold miners, women's Christian organisations, and the Muslim, Jewish, and Hindu groups. Christianity's impact on the creative arts (literature, music, and architecture) is explained in part 4. Finally, part 5 takes a look at Christianity's relationship to politics, thinking through issues of power and race. The aim of the book is to show that, in addition to economic and ideological factors, Christian beliefs have had a pervasive influence on the changes which have taken place within South Africa, as strongly indicated by the fact that more than 72 percent of South Africans now claim to be Christian. Although the authors' coverage is not comprehensive nor their research complete (by their own admission), they have succeeded in their intention of taking "a significant step toward the creation of a comprehensive history of South African Christianity."

308. Engelke, Matthew

A Problem of Presence: Beyond Scripture in an African Church

Oakland, CA: University of California Press, 2007. 321 pages, ISBN: 9780520249042.

This book is an anthropological analysis of an unusual branch of the well-known Zimbabwean independent/indigenous church group known as the Masowe Apostles, which traces back to Johane Masowe and his 1932 vision in what is now Zimbabwe (there is a helpful biographical section on Masowe). The particular group studied here meets on Fridays, not on Saturdays as most of the other groups do, and is therefore known as the

Friday Masowe. The other distinctive of this group, and an important focus of this book, is that they do not read the Bible. This AIC insists on having a "live and direct" faith, not one that depends on a material book, claiming that Jesus and the apostles did not have a Bible either, so biblical truth is greater than the biblical text. They depend on the Holy Spirit alone, and healing is a major emphasis, as with other Masowe groups. Engelke states the main focus of his concern in the concluding chapter: "The problem of presence (i.e. the Holy Spirit) is a problem of representation – of how words, objects and actions get defined as such and, in the process, become significant." The author is an anthropologist of religion at the London School of Economics, and this book won the 2009 Turner Prize for Ethnographic Writing. Engelke provides helpful historical and cultural background, noting that individual dependence on the written word can replace the African traditional emphasis on community. He also outlines how the Friday Masowe outlook relates to that of other Africans such as Desmond Tutu, and political leader Canaan Banana of Zimbabwe (the former said the Bible led to liberation; the latter to exploitation – because the missionaries gave Africans the Bible and took their land). The author also shows familiarity with Zimbabwe church historians Terence Ranger and Clive Dillon-Malone who have both written on the African Apostles. Because it is primarily an ethnographic study and sometimes relies on technical terminology, this is not a book that will have wide interest outside of southern Africa and cultural anthropologists. Readers may well be frustrated that, as an anthropologist, the author hesitates to make moral judgements on issues such as a key contact/leader being convicted of raping the women who came for healing ("for me it is a sociological point, not a religious one"). Most Christians will also be rightly startled and troubled by the group's avoidance of Scripture. The Friday Masowe seem a striking example of how an AIC group that considers itself Christian can depart from basic Christian understanding and practice in its responsiveness to context.

309.   **Englebert, Pierre**

Africa: Unity, Sovereignty and Sorrow

Boulder, CO: Lynne Rienner Publishers, 2009. 360 pages, ISBN: 9781588266231.

The author is a university professor in the United States who specializes in African political and economic development. In this book on the effectiveness of African states he notes that they are characterized by a weak form of sovereignty that is based on their genesis as colonial creations. He refers to this type of sovereignty as juridical sovereignty, or the ability to make laws for a territory. Juridical sovereignty in Africa is imputed on states by external recognition rather than the ability to control territory or people. Given that this is the case, Englebert questions why there are not more secessionist movements in Africa based on the claim of other groups to control territory or provide better public goods such as education and infrastructure. Englebert answers by arguing that it is not in the best interests of elites to break up the state. Control of the state means control over resources so rather than trying to secede, elite groups have a greater interest in dominating the state that exists rather than forming a new one. Highlights of this book are its discussion of citizenship and why it has become so politicized in multiple African contexts, as well as its presentation of detailed research from the Congo (DRC). For those interested in the DRC, the author gives rich and persuasive illustrations of his argument. Moreover, Englebert provides a lens for understanding corruption that will be of interest to many who watch it happen and who wonder what would motivate people to engage in behaviour which seems so counterproductive to civic wellbeing. The book may prove frustrating for those whose interests lie outside of the Congo, Côte d'Ivoire, and a handful of other African countries, since some of the ideas apply less well to more organized states such as Tanzania or Botswana.

310. Englund, Harri, editor

Christianity and Public Culture in Africa

Athens, OH: Ohio University Press, 2011. 240 pages, ISBN: 9780821420225.

With the demise of "secularization" theories much anticipated by sociological prognosticators and the resurgence of religious forms around the world, scholars have begun giving renewed energies to studying the kinds of intersections taking place between religion and public life. This edited collection builds upon such foundations, seeking to understand the myriad of ways that Africans "have variously appropriated Christian idioms beyond the boundaries of religious expression, asserted a cleavage between religions, kept secular and religious concerns separate, and sought moral and material renewal through Christian practice." The editor, a professor of Social Anthropology at Cambridge University, has brought together scholars of African studies for the purposes of exploring such intersections occurring between Christianity and public life, broadening the analysis beyond the reductionistic predilections many scholars have shown to conflate religion with politics. The different essayists represent wide-ranging perspectives on the above-mentioned themes. The book is divided into three parts: missionary and nationalist encounters; patriarchy and public culture; and plurality of Pentecostal publics. As the reader might expect from such diverse sections, the ensuing chapters cover such lively topics as the legitimacy of the secular in Zambian society, reproductive politics in Niger, Luo widow inheritance in Kenya, and Islamophobia in Malawi. Not all chapters are created equal, but the reader will enjoy an array of intellectually-stimulating, well-written, and societally-relevant essays covering the broad sweep of life in sub-Saharan Africa. None of the writers approach their respective subjects from a Christian perspective, nor should this be expected within the field of African studies. But the reader will find balanced evaluations on the various topics, making this a seminal piece of scholarship on the wider theme of how Christianity makes its impact (or, alternatively, is thus impacted) within contemporary African society.

Eric, Walter

see review 786

311. Erlich, Haggai

Saudi Arabia and Ethiopia: Islam, Christianity, and Politics Entwined

Boulder, CO: Lynne Rienner Publishers, 2014. 249 pages, ISBN: 9781626371934.

Israeli scholar Erlich is deservedly recognized as a leading expert on the role of Islam in Ethiopian history and society. His previous works have especially analysed the interaction between Ethiopia and nearby Arab countries such as Egypt. His latest book is a thorough and well-documented account and analysis of the often problematic relations between Saudi Arabia and Ethiopia from the early twentieth century to the present. Given its wealth and regional influence, Saudi Arabia was normally the dominant player. It took special interest in the large number of Muslims in Ethiopia, considered to comprise between one third and one half of the population, who were often treated as second-class citizens within their country. Erlich traces how, on the one hand, the

Saudi regime has tended to ignore the political aspirations of the Ethiopian government, whether it was the Christian reign of Haile Selassie, the communist dictatorship, or the current secular republic. On the other hand, both the political and religious leaders of Saudi Arabia often sought to promote the role of Islam in Ethiopia through pragmatic diplomacy, religious persuasion, and occasional confrontation. The role of Saudi Arabia's Wahhabi elite is especially highlighted, and the often contentious interaction between Wahhabism and traditional Ethiopian Islam is duly noted. Given this chequered relational past, Erlich is unable to predict the direction of future Saudi-Ethiopian relations, but he believes that the competition between religions will continue to be a significant factor. The book is replete with notes on a wide variety of resources, including otherwise inaccessible newspaper articles and communiqués. Although Erlich's book deals with religion and politics between two specific countries, the presentation is paradigmatic of the role of Islamic involvement in much of sub-Saharan Africa.

Erwin, Steve

see review 499

312. Esack, Farid

On Being a Muslim: Finding a Religious Path in the World Today

London: OneWorld Publications, 2009. 224 pages, ISBN: 9781851686919.

Esack is a progressive South African Muslim who participated, and continues to participate, in the struggle for justice and human rights in his native country. This book is a very personal appeal to fellow Muslims, in South Africa and beyond, to embrace the larger socio-political objectives of Islamic faith and practice, without falling into either political or spiritual extremism. He seeks "a path between dehumanising fundamentalism and fossilized traditionalism" that is nevertheless firmly based on Islamic ideals. Esack begins with the individual Muslim's struggle to make sense of Islamic faith within the modern world. In search of an authentic Islamic spirituality, he advocates the development of a personal yet this-worldly relationship with Allah (despite his progressive orientation, he retains the traditional Arabic-Islamic reference to God). He moves on to deal with issues of self-acceptance and relationships with others, but then arrives at his primary concern: social involvement. Islam is an inherently political religion, he claims, but not inherently intolerant. One must seek the objectives of the law more than the law itself. From this enlightened Muslim perspective, he tackles issues of justice, women's rights, religious pluralism, and especially constructive engagement as equal citizens in post-apartheid South Africa. The book is peppered with personal anecdotes and quotations from a variety of people, including the Christian voices of Dietrich Bonhoeffer and Cardinal Newman. Since much of Esack's own religious growth developed through friendship with Christians, there is "space in [his] own theology" for cooperation with non-Muslims who affirm a belief in a loving Creator which is worked out in social action. This book is thus a helpful insight into a less familiar type of Islamic outlook by a remarkable South African personality, one who seems to share a social agenda similar to that of many African Christians, yet from a very different religious tradition.

313. **Esack, Farid**

The Qur'an: A Short Introduction

London: OneWorld Publications, 2002. 214 pages, ISBN: 9781851682317.

Although a number of worthwhile books about the Qur'an by Western scholars are available, very few modern Muslim authors have produced such works for a general audience. Thus Esack has made a valuable contribution to this field. The author is a progressive South African Muslim, known for his involvement in issues of human rights. Although this book is a general introduction rather than contextualized for Africa, Esack incorporates several anecdotes reflective of his South African setting. One of the more helpful features of the book is the manner in which Esack begins: by examining the various approaches to the Qur'an taken by Muslims and non-Muslims, and by considering the function which the Qur'an serves in the lives of ordinary believers. Only then does he move on to deal with the important technical matters: the formation of the Qur'an in the life of Muhammad and its "collection" following his death; its structure and features; theological issues surrounding the text; and its interpretation by Muslim scholars throughout history. The book ends with an excellent but brief presentation of the major doctrinal and social themes of the Qur'an. Throughout the work Esack provides both traditional and modern Muslim perspectives on the issues. The result is a fine introduction for anyone interested to know, from an informed Muslim perspective, not only what the Qur'an says, but also (and perhaps more importantly) the crucial role it plays in the life and faith of Muslim believers, whatever their particular context.

314. **Eshete, Tibebe**

The Evangelical Movement in Ethiopia: Resistance and Resilience

Waco: Baylor, 2009. 494 pages, ISBN: 9781602580022.

The author provides the first full-length English-language history of the evangelical movement in Ethiopia. The work, which began as a doctoral dissertation at Michigan State University, traces the movement from its roots in various outside initiatives to bring renewal within the Ethiopian Orthodox Church, dating back to the seventeenth century and continuing through to the end of Ethiopia's tragic Marxist period in 1991. Drawing on dozens of oral interviews and archival sources, Tibebe [as he would be properly referenced in the Ethiopian context] weaves an engaging and thoroughly credible narrative of the emergence and growth of a Church, which, in the face of severe opposition, has become an influential force in a troubled region. Although Tibebe acknowledges the key role of Western missions in the establishment of Christian churches outside of the Ethiopian Orthodox Church, the major thesis of the book is that Ethiopian evangelicalism can by no means be construed as a "foreign" religion. This has been the major critique levelled by the Ethiopian Orthodox Church against the evangelical churches, a charge picked up with devastating effect by the Marxist Derg regime when it rose to power in 1974. Tibebe accounts for the role of the Western missions by crediting them with impact rather than agency, and depicts the evangelical movement as a reformation movement which grew out of the Orthodox Church and brought to expression "a latent dimension of an already existing faith." Tibebe's case for the primacy of local agency in the growth of evangelicalism is argued in several ways, but three are key. First, he highlights the extent to which Ethiopian evangelicalism has its antecedents in Ethiopian Orthodoxy. Second, Tibebe demonstrates that the two most astonishing periods of growth occurred when the Western missions were mostly absent, i.e. during the Italian occupation of 1936–1941 and during the communist

Revolution of 1974–1991. Third, he argues that much of this local leadership emerged out of an independent Pentecostal movement which erupted in the 1960s among students in urban areas and spread into most of the evangelical denominations during the time of the Revolution. Primarily on the basis of his case for local agency, Tibebe seeks to claim for evangelicals a portion of the space traditionally occupied by the Orthodox as the traditional purveyors and protectors of Ethiopia's national identity. But surely Ethiopian agency alone is not what makes evangelicalism authentically Ethiopian, but rather also the nature of the encounter between evangelical faith and Ethiopian realities. Those realities have meant that the evangelical focus on faithfulness to the gospel and its proclamation has led to extreme persecution. Tibebe's work is a wonderful chronicle of one African community's profound commitment to biblical Christianity and to mission amidst recurring waves of violent opposition. One suspects that this, more than the claim the author makes to an evangelical share in Ethiopia's national identity, will be his greatest contribution to the study of Christianity in Ethiopia.

315.   Etue, Kate, and Recah Theodosiou

Mission: Africa: A Field Guide

Nashville: Thomas Nelson, 2003. 159 pages, ISBN: 9780849944260.

This book seeks to "encourage, equip, and motivate" American Christian youth to participate in mission trips to Africa to help alleviate the AIDS pandemic there. The book's particular innovation is to feature Christian celebrities prominently in order to gain the attention of potentially indifferent American teens. "If well-liked black and white Christian celebrities care enough to help, then what can I do to help?" Popular musicians and famous figures on the American speaking circuit share their personal encounters with suffering Africa, including a moving story by an American adoptive parent of an Ethiopian orphan. Photos of Christian artists or music groups like Michael W. Smith, Jars of Clay, DC Talk, and Out of Eden draw attention, as do the inserted messages advertising web links, quick facts, and Bible verses. Specific global structural inequities are explained. Biblical passages on suffering and compassion are interspersed through the text. The conclusion provides a crash course on social activist strategies for American Christian teens, and includes: a liturgical prayer; strategic instructions on petitioning elected officials; raising local awareness; raising money; researching charitable organisations; and instructions on how to plan personal travel to Africa. The AWAKE Project and World Vision are showcased agencies. The book is a fascinating exemplar of how one might engage and focus contemporary American Christian youth in social outreach. As to relevance for Africa, despite the reference to Africa in the title, that would be better sought elsewhere.

Evers Rosander, Eva

see review 1174

316.   Eze, Emmanuel Chukwudi

African Philosophy: An Anthology

Oxford: Wiley-Blackwell, 1997. 512 pages, ISBN: 9780631203384.

Here is a welcome anthology on African Philosophy, which distinguishes itself for being a very comprehensive introduction and likely to become a standard reference work. The book brings together 56 "canonical" philosophical texts from Africa, African-American, Afro-Caribbean, and Black European thinkers. The texts collected cover an enormous historical range: from traditional to modern, pre-colonial through colonial to postcolonial; from the slave period through the emancipation and the Civil Rights movements to post-modern. Additionally they represent a variety of cultural and ideological viewpoints, including secular, feminist, Christian, Islamic, and animist perspectives. The texts are arranged along lines of traditional thematic divisions in philosophy: part 1 "What is African Philosophy?"; part 2 "Human Nature: Mind, Body, and Self-Identity"; part 3 "Philosophy, Politics, and Society"; part 4 "Ethics"; part 5 "On Knowledge and Science"; part 6 "Philosophy and Colonial Encounter"; part 7 "Philosophy and Race"; part 8 "Philosophy and Gender"; part 9 "Philosophy and Transatlantic African Slavery"; part 10 "Ontology and the Nature of Art"; and part 11 "Philosophy of Religion." This book will be useful for anyone involved with the study of intellectual life in Africa, and especially those involved with African Theology, whether the novice or the experienced philosopher or theologian. The book should also be considered as a reference resource for theological libraries.

317.   Ezeh, Uchenna A.

Jesus Christ the Ancestor: An African Contextual Christology in the Light of the Major Dogmatic Christological Definitions of the Church from the Council of Nicea (325) to Chalcedon (451)

Frankfurt: Peter Lang, 2003. 323 pages, ISBN: 9783906770116.

Ezeh, a Nigerian Roman Catholic priest, has made a fresh contribution to the growing Christological literature seeking to find African images to explain the person and work of Jesus Christ. His book is based on his doctoral work at Leopold-Granzens University in Austria. The strength of his work is his thorough understanding of both the African horizon and the horizon of orthodox Christology as expressed in the ancient creeds of the Church. He begins by laying the foundation for the African horizon with brief but accurate surveys of African traditional religion, African cosmology/worldview, the "Ancestral Cult" in Africa, and the emergence of African theology. In the most deeply developed section of the book, Ezeh clearly explains the history and significance of the early church councils at Nicea, Ephesus, and Chalcedon. This provides a Christian norm by which to compare African Christologies of Jesus as Ancestor. (Curiously, in explaining this early Christological history he fails to mention the non-Chalcedonian movement in Egypt, Nubia and Ethiopia which dominated African Christology for over a thousand years.) The writings of Bujo and Nyamiti are used as principal examples of modern African ancestor Christology. Ezeh does little biblical analysis of these models, but, by using the ancient creeds as a point of comparison, evaluation by a biblical, orthodox standard is ensured. He is not afraid to show the limitations of Christ as Ancestor, but overall judges that "this Christological model is truly Christian and African." Although one might wish there had been more emphasis on biblical assessment, this is a useful contribution to African Christology from a creedal Catholic perspective, one that is sensitive to ensuring that contextual theology be both relevant and Christian. Anyone interested in African Christology should become familiar with Ezeh.

318. Ezigbo, Victor I.

Re-imagining African Christologies: Conversing with the Interpretations and Appropriations of Jesus in Contemporary African Christianity

Eugene, OR: Wipf & Stock, 2010. 356 pages, ISBN: 9781606088227.

A Nigerian theologian who did his MA at Wheaton College and his PhD in Edinburgh, the author here constructs a detailed description and critique of two kinds of African (especially Nigerian) Christology: that of academic theologians, and that of grassroots Christians. The academics' approaches, of seeing Jesus (a) using Western theological formulations or (b) as the fulfilment of some aspect African religion (e.g. Jesus as ancestor), or (c) as liberator (which Ezigbo describes in detail), fail to impact the average Christian African. Ezigbo's interviews with grassroots Christians, on the other hand, reveal a Christology that sees Jesus primarily as a Solution to life's problems and Enabler of people's aspirations. Ezigbo's contention is that African theologians must now move beyond the old paradigm of responding to Western disdain of African traditional religions, and as well the quest suggested by John V. Taylor, in his 1963 classic, *The Primal Vision*, for Jesus as the answer to questions Africans would ask. Africa's context has changed. African theology must impact the church at the grassroots, and have universal relevance. In response, Ezigbo proposes his "Revealer Christology Model." In this model, Jesus is not just the solution for people's perceived needs; he also brings his own agenda and questions. Jesus critiques, remoulds and informs people about what their real problems are and what God's solutions are. Ezigbo gives a chapter each to (1) the idea of revelation in Africa and in theology, (2) how Christ reveals God to people, (3) how Christ reveals the real situation among people, God, and evil spiritual beings, and (4) how Christ reveals the true meaning, identity, and hope of humanity. These revelations require adjustment in thinking and practice, dethroning people's own agendas and conforming to that of Christ. The book is well organized and the argument, though detailed, is easy to follow. Dozens of African theologians from a wide range of positions are discussed. This is a valuable book for anyone doing theological work, especially in Africa, whether academically or at the grassroots. It would be an asset in any theological library.

319. Falk, Peter

The Growth of the Church in Africa

Bukuru, Nigeria: Africa Christian Textbooks, 1997. 554 pages, ISBN: 9789782668738.

One of the difficulties in teaching African church history at first degree level has been the scarcity of suitable textbooks. Books are either too simple, too expensive (if published in the West) or out of print. In an attempt to remedy this situation Africa Christian Textbooks of Jos, Nigeria, has obtained Falk's permission to reprint his book (first published in 1979 by Zondervan). For many years Falk was a missionary lecturing at the Institut Supérieur Théologique de Kinshasa in Congo (DRC). His book is a detailed survey of African church history from the days of the early church up to 1975. The first two chapters recount the history of the early church in northern Africa. Chapter 3 then discusses the rise of Western missionary interest. The next eight chapters survey (mainly on geographical lines) the growth of the church from 1652 to 1975. Chapters 12 and 13 examine the conditions affecting and methods involved in the spread of Christianity. The final chapter surveys the rise of independent churches and the development of ecumenism. The book is designed to be used as a basic textbook at first-degree level, and for this purpose it will prove effective, offering each student a reasonable overview of the history of Christianity in Africa. It will need, however, to be supplemented in two ways.

First, since the original publication was 1979, changes and developments since then would need to be taken into account (e.g. Zaire has become Congo). Secondly, lecturers will probably want to develop some of the main themes of African church history further through supplementary reading. By their nature surveys of such scope have to choose between being selective in their material or being relatively brief in their treatment of important issues. Falk opts for the latter. Evaluative discussion is not entirely lacking; he comments briefly (from an evangelical angle) on different features often enough. But certainly for the post-graduate level the book would not be adequate.

320.   Falola, Toyin, and Christian Jennings, editors

Africanizing Knowledge: African Studies across the Disciplines

Somerset, NJ: Transaction Publishers, 2002. 447 pages, ISBN: 9780765801388.

Whereas the title of this book neatly encapsulates the dominant objective of the African intellectual enterprise of modern times, the content of the book manages to illustrate the ambiguities and tensions implicit in such a venture. If "Africanizing knowledge" means for Africa to take charge of its own intellectual life, that noble quest has been advancing learned thought in and about Africa to good purpose. If "Africanizing knowledge" means, as it so often does, an earnest endeavour to de-westernize each intellectual discipline, then there is a problem, since African scholarship is itself inextricably expressive of modern Africa's already considerable westernisation. As a result, the enterprise inevitably stumbles over the present-day realities of the continent. For example, this book on Africanizing knowledge is published in the west, by editors and contributors largely trained and working in the west, all expressing themselves in a Western language, and all doing so in the standard modes of Western academic discourse. Nevertheless, by thus representing a dominant motivation of African intellectual life, together with its inherent paradoxes, this book deserves notice. The book consists of 26 papers, originally presented at a conference at the University of Texas at Austin in 2001, with the editors and the majority of the contributors coming from that institution. The papers are grouped under categories relating to history, art, literature, and scholarship. Not surprisingly, the quality of contributions various considerably. Also the intentions implied in the attractive subtitle are not achieved, since a full range of disciplines is not encountered. Likewise most of the papers are not addressing the "Africanisation" of a particular discipline but merely represent an individual's own Africa-related research within that discipline. Whereas some of the papers do not avoid a certain stridency, the editors' introduction is refreshingly modest and cautionary: "Rather than running ourselves in circles as we chase the elusive dream of authenticity in our research . . . we would do better to simply approach our profession . . . with a healthy dose of open-minded scepticism, a concerned commitment to the present and future of the continent, and maybe even a trace of humility." An opening paper by the Kenyan scholar Atieno-Odhiambo provides a substantial survey of African historiography that researchers in that discipline will find useful. Otherwise this book may be safely skipped, both by readers and by theological libraries.

321.   **Falola, Toyin**

Nationalism and African Intellectuals

Rochester, NY: University of Rochester Press, 2004. 394 pages, ISBN: 9781580461498.

Evangelical theological reflection in Africa has devoted extensive attention over the years to the issues of contextualization, with much profit. But one important aspect of the African context has largely eluded notice, namely modern Africa's intellectual life. Just as one can hardly hope to understand the Western world of today without some orientation to Western enlightenment modernity (and now post-modernity), so also one can hardly expect to understand the contemporary African context without a basic awareness of modern African intellectual life. This survey is one useful place to begin the acquaintance. Falola, originally from Nigeria, has been a well-published academic historian at the University of Texas. Here he sets himself to sketch out the history of Africa's intelligentsia over the past two centuries. The richly nuanced presentation is supported by an impressive range of reference notes and bibliography. As Falola's survey makes clear, Africa's educated elite have been a principal generative influence in the formation of modern Africa. His story includes the pre-colonial intellectuals of nineteenth-century Africa, the emergence of Pan-Africanism in the African diaspora during the colonial period, and the heady anticipations surrounding African national independence events after World War II. He focuses particular attention on the rise of the modern African universities, whose graduates have largely constituted the intelligentsia of contemporary Africa. He does not flinch from describing as well the painful decline of the universities in recent decades, and the disarray, demoralisation, and even cynicism that increasingly characterized African intellectual circles by the end of the century, in the face of the many seemingly intractable crises that have impacted the continent. Falola's contribution is fresh, elegantly told and thoroughly illuminating. It is also hardly definitive. Whereas Falola intends to consider all of Africa, one cannot escape noticing that the continent is often being viewed from a West African vantage point. Thus Blyden and Nkrumah are well attended, while others from eastern, central and southern Africa, such as Nyerere or Mandela, feature only at the margins. Falola does not treat Christianity as an alien feature in the African context, but he accords it only minimal attention. The African Theology movement receives no notice, even though it represents the dominant intellectual project of modern African Christianity, and even though it deliberately evolved itself as a sub-component of Africa's larger intellectual movement. Only Mbiti is mentioned, once, and that in relation to African philosophy. One can too readily misread the modern African context if one fails to take this essential feature of that context into account, and Christian theological reflection in Africa will hardly find a fruitful way forward without deliberately including this contemporary intellectual tradition within its critical purview.

Falola, Toyin

see also review 1183

322. Fape, Michael D.

Powers in Encounter With Power: Spiritual Warfare in Pagan Cultures

Tain, UK: CFP, 2003. 192 pages, ISBN: 9781857928730.

Fape is an Anglican bishop from Nigeria who completed his doctorate at Aberdeen. In this book, based on post-doctoral research, he discusses Paul's concept of spiritual warfare from an African perspective, with a certain focus on Ephesians 6:10–12. His aim in writing is that Christians, especially African Christians, should understand their deliverance from the forces of darkness. Fape discusses a range of issues including the origin of evil powers, Paul's terminology of 'principalities and powers' and his understanding of spiritual warfare, the cross of Christ as the defeat of the powers, traditional African notions of spiritual warfare, the role of Christ in spiritual warfare, the believer's weapons and the purpose of victory. There is much in the book to stir interest and discussion. Among other things, the author defends the widely held view that an account of Satan's fall can be found in Isaiah 14 and Ezekiel 14, and understands the "war in heaven" of Revelation 12:7–11 in the same way. He shares Cullmann's view that when Paul speaks of the "authorities" in Romans 13:1 he is thinking not only of human rulers but also of spiritual powers "operating in the background." However, the author's approach to the biblical data can be problematic, with exegesis and theological interpretation that are too often speculative and questionable. For example, Fape suggests that Satan's purpose in tempting Adam and Eve was to prevent them "from taking over his exalted position in the plan of God from which he had been expelled," a view for which he offers no support. Some references to possession diminish human moral responsibility: thus, when Herod tried to kill Jesus, "demonic spirits had taken possession of him"; and Paul's epistle to the Colossians was necessary because "a spirit of heresy had taken possession of some of the Colossians." Elsewhere, citing Samson as an example, Fape suggests that some believers "may not finish their God-given assignment before death" due to their own failure in spiritual warfare. He states that Paul's crown of righteousness was waiting for him "if only he fought rightly, finished his race successfully and was able to keep the faith intact as a victorious Christian." And, detaching Romans 1:16 from its context, he argues that "the preaching of the gospel means *power* to various people according to their needs for divine intervention." While Fape explicitly disavows the so-called "prosperity gospel," he nevertheless claims that prosperity is included in "the promise of complete deliverance from the powers of darkness." As an addition to the very limited range of theological literature on spiritual warfare in the African context this book merits attention. However, it does require careful evaluation, and readers should be critically alert.

323. Fargher, Brian

The Origins of the New Churches Movement in Southern Ethiopia, 1927–1944

Leiden: BRILL, 1996. 329 pages, ISBN: 9789004106611.

The international mission SIM (formerly the Sudan Interior Mission) has worked in southern Ethiopia since 1927. This study is focused on SIM's work there with particular reference to the origin and development of the indigenous body, the Kale Heywet Church (KHC), which came into existence as a result of the SIM work. Fargher (who served with SIM in Ethiopia for many years) does not want to write the history of this church as such. Following the principles of non-interference and parallel development of church and mission which SIM adopted from Roland Allen, he wants to write the mission side of the story of how the KHC came into existence, leaving it to Ethiopians themselves to write the history of their own church. Although this scope functions as a limitation, this book will serve as a necessary background for any future studies on the KHC. The book title employs the term, "the New Churches Movement." It would seem that the author has created this phrase in order to describe the Protestant church bodies that grew out of the work of evangelical missions in Ethiopia from about 1920 onward, in distinction from the historic Ethiopian Orthodox Church (EOC). Nevertheless Fargher seems at times in practice to confine the term to the churches planted by the SIM. This is evident, for example, when he claims that such churches insisted on re-baptism of those from an EOC background. This was true for the SIM-related churches but not for those with Lutheran and Presbyterian connections. This usage therefore creates some confusion. Although the SIM, in line with most other Protestant missions, concentrated its work in those areas of the country where the EOC presence was very limited, it is not possible to write studies of missions or churches in Ethiopia without relating to the EOC. This is commendably recognized by the first chapter, on "Ethiopia's National Church." The major part of the study, however, is a thorough examination of the work of the SIM in the designated period. The independence of the "New Churches Movement" in relation to SIM is pointed out in several places. For example, the churches appear today as models of financial self-support. Obviously this result could not have been reached without a clear and firm policy from the mission, and this factor is well researched in this study. The book stands as an interesting and exciting presentation, and because of its thoroughness will remain an outstanding contribution to the study of Ethiopian Evangelical Christianity. The book certainly belongs in all libraries intending to cover the history of missions in Africa.

Fargher, Brian

see also reviews 200 and 1078

324.   Fasokun, T. O., Anne Katahoire, and Akpovire B. Oduaran

The Psychology of Adult Learning in Africa

Cape Town: Pearson, 2005. 172 pages, ISBN: 9789282011171.

This book is part of a new series aimed at training professional adult educators in Africa at undergraduate and graduate levels. The authors of this particular text are linked respectively with Obafemi Awolowo University, Nigeria; Makerere University, Uganda; and the University of Botswana. They treat topics such as: the characteristics of adult learners in Africa; patterns and theories of adult learning (including discussion on how Western theories may or may not be useful in Africa); how "Life Span Development" might apply in Africa; what does and does not motivate learning; learning styles; and assessment. Focusing on the African context, the authors also discuss the indigenous apprenticeship system, cooperative learning, brainstorming, problem-solving, role-play, simulations, group discussions, case studies and dialogues as effective instructional techniques. Each chapter begins with an overview, a list of learning objectives, and definitions of key terms; various activities for readers are interspersed throughout the text; and chapters end with a summary, key points, an activity, further questions and suggested readings (including both Western and African books and articles). The book assumes mostly formal, monolingual community-based adult teaching rather than informal learning or college and university settings. Nevertheless, lecturers in theological colleges in Africa could certainly glean a number of useful concepts for helping their students learn more effectively, concepts that most might otherwise spend years discovering by trial and error. For example, research emphasizes that relationships between teacher and learner, and among fellow learners, are very important. Also whereas problem-based learning is important anywhere, community-based problem-solving is especially relevant for adult learning in Africa.

325. Fatokun, Samson Adetunji

Soteriology: An African Outlook

Warburton, Australia: End Time Publishing, 2010. 232 pages, ISBN: 9789780712594.

This book, written by a University of Ibadan lecturer and Pentecostal pastor in Nigeria, looks at salvation in the African context. The book begins by considering salvation in the OT, in the ministry of Jesus and in the early church. The author concludes that salvation in the OT is primarily material or physical. Salvation in the ministry of Jesus is mainly deliverance from sin, its power and consequences. The author then considers salvation in the early church, which, oddly, includes both Paul and the church fathers through Augustine. The author thinks that salvation in the early church is primarily spiritual. Fatokun then looks at sin, sacrifice, saviour gods and the historical Jesus in traditional African religion and in Christianity. The author stresses the unique role of Jesus Christ in history and theology. In the final chapters he contrasts the idea of salvation in contemporary African churches with that of Scripture. He claims that many modern African churches see salvation as materialistic, while the NT and early church see salvation as being primarily spiritual. This criticism of Prosperity Theology by a Pentecostal pastor is welcome. But it is unfortunate that the biblical survey of salvation at the beginning of the book is superficial and unsystematic. A study of sin, forgiveness, atonement, repentance and covenant will show that spiritual salvation is a central theme of the OT as well. And to treat Paul in the same category with the church fathers is not helpful. While the titles of books such as this might sometimes seem to imply more than is actually delivered, they do also offer a useful sense of the sort of materials now increasingly emerging from within African Christian communities.

Fendall, Lon

see review 718

326. Ferdinando, Keith

The Triumph of Christ in African Perspective: A Study of Demonology and Redemption in the African Context

Carlisle, UK: Paternoster, 1999. 450 pages, ISBN: 9780853648307.

This magnificently conceived and magisterially composed book addresses a complex of topics that are of utmost relevance to African Christianity. And it does so in a manner that displays the best of evangelical biblical scholarship. Ferdinando served for many years in the Congo (DRC), including as head of the distinguished Institut Supérieur Théologique de Bunia, and also subsequently in Uganda and Rwanda. The book's unifying theme is the all-encompassing "triumph of Christ" as a manifestation of the universal sovereignty of God. Written from the perspective of Africa, it seeks to transform a traditional pessimistic religious perspective by means of a Word-illumined focus on the significance of Christ's sinless life and sacrificial work of redemption on the cross. In the light of the Lord's overwhelming victory over all the forces of wickedness, both biblical demonology and African occult are revealed for what they are, and relegated to their temporary, subordinate and subdued place in this world, as they await their ultimate destiny in God's final judgement. Ferdinando supports this fundamentally optimistic and encouraging message through a detailed study of the relevant materials of Scripture for the proper biblical response to an ever-threatening dominion of darkness. No controversial issues are ignored. For Christians anywhere facing the culturally-conditioned attacks of Satan in their lives, as well as temporal suffering or oppression, Ferdinando shows that syncretism or accommodation to ancestral beliefs, practices, values, and/or perspectives is not the answer. Only an ever-deeper, personally applied understanding of what God has already done and will do for us in and through Jesus the Christ will do. No compromise is possible – only a fuller, faith-founded commitment to knowing and living Christ more completely. Ferdinando's glowing vision of Christ's supreme triumph confidently puts Scripture in the forefront (where it rightly belongs) in the life-and-death battle of the Christian community with diabolical deception of all forms, whether traditional or modern. Church leaders, pastors, theological educators, theological students, and educated lay Christians in Africa would find this a highly relevant text to read and study. The biblically-based optimism it offers is as spiritually educative as it is personally contagious.

327.   **Ferguson, James**

Global Shadows: Africa in the Neoliberal World Order

Durham, NC: Duke University Press, 2006. 268 pages, ISBN: 9780822337171.

The author is Professor of Cultural and Social Anthropology at Stanford University. He begins this study by pointing to the startling fact that most scholarly descriptions of globalisation have little or nothing to say about Africa. Africa does not fit either the optimistic narrative of globalisation's proponents, nor the critique of those contending that globalisation has made it easier for capitalism to exploit cheap labour around the globe (where are the African "sweat shops"?). Not fitting into either of these major analytical story lines, Africa is simply ignored in the literature. This is not to say, however, that the continent is therefore totally disconnected from global markets. In fact, foreign direct investment has significantly increased in recent years. The problem is that this global input has for many countries been mainly limited to economic "enclaves," especially in mineral extraction and export. This type of investment does not usually benefit anyone but outside investors and a very limited number of African elites. Ferguson is primarily an anthropologist, so this book includes ethnographic treatments of Africans' subjective responses to this set of circumstances. For example, he describes the rise and fall of a Zambian online magazine, *Chrysalis*, which began its short career trumpeting the potential glories of an African Renaissance that Thabo Mbeki had said would result from "liberalized" economies (under the guidance of "structural adjustment programs" imposed by World Bank and the International Monetary Fund officials). He goes on to describe the sense of disillusionment and despair that quickly set in as it became clear that few but the elites would benefit from these initiatives. Ferguson contrasts the outlook of World Bank and IMF officialdom – according to whom structural adjustment policies were simply based on morally-neutral scientific principle – with local judgements that economic decisions are always moral ones. He concludes, "The African insight that markets, prices, and wages are always human products is a powerful one." This book would be particularly helpful to anyone interested in the ethnography of modernisation in Africa, and to those wrestling with the question of how biblical teaching on economic and social justice applies to the relationship between Africa and its global neighbours. It would also make very useful reading for advanced thinking on contextualization, thinking that seeks to move beyond contextualizing the gospel in terms of traditional African cultures in order also to engage theologically with contemporary African realities within their global contexts.

328.   **Fiedler, Klaus**

Christianity and African Culture: Conservative German Protestant Missionaries in Tanzania, 1900–1940

Leiden: BRILL, 1996. 238 pages, ISBN: 9789004104976.

The author, originally from Germany, has served in Malawi from the early 1990s onward. This study, the fruit of part of his doctoral research, selectively covers the important era of German mission work in Africa from the beginning of the twentieth century until World War II. Fiedler carefully paints a picture of missionaries who were culturally conservative, in that they stressed the need to maintain indigenous structures within the church during the height of the colonial era. A central purpose of this book is to dispel the myth that all missionaries during the colonial era were concerned only with civilisation, commerce, and Christianity. Many were deeply concerned that the African social structures be part of the local churches which developed out of the missionary work. Fiedler is not trying to suggest that all missionaries were "cultural conservatives" of this type, but he wants us to see that common stereotypes of colonial-era missionaries are not as objective as we may think them to be. Perhaps the most significant contribution of the book is to put the well-known Bruno Gutmann in the historical context of German contemporary thinking, and to see how he struggled in working out his theoretical paradigms in the complex interplay of missionaries, mission agencies, world-wide issues (e.g. Word War I), and the national church itself. This book is especially welcome in that it makes a historical slice of German missiological theory and practice accessible to the English-speaking world. It would be important for libraries focusing on African mission history.

329.   **Fiedler, Klaus**

The Story of Faith Missions: From Hudson Taylor to Present Day Africa

Oxford: Regnum, 1994. 428 pages, ISBN: 9781870345187.

Faith missions (such as SIM and AIM) have had a lasting influence in Africa. Fiedler's doctoral dissertation (done at Heidelberg under Professor Sundermeier in 1991) traces the history, practice, and ecclesiology of this movement, especially in Africa. Chapters cover the work of faith missions in Africa; the concept of unity in African faith missions; and the catholicity and apostolicity of the church in Africa. Ample footnotes contribute interesting details, or provide information, for example on theological schools and accreditation. Fiedler's contribution is first of all his historical research into the faith mission movement, including its roots, which are mainly in England, and his typology of mission societies, among which he distinguishes pre-classical, classical, and post-classical mission societies. Secondly, Fiedler analyses the practice of these groups in ecclesiological terms of the Nicene and Reformation creeds, which gives a critical point of view that can be helpful for self-evaluation among such groups, but also provides a grid for others to understand them and recognize that they are not as marginal as mission history has seemed to imply, but form a whole stream in many groups and organisations. This book fills an important gap in the study of mission history in Africa, and deserves the attention of any advanced-level theological library in Africa.

330. Fiedler, Klaus, editor

Theology Cooked in an African Pot

Blantyre: CLAIM, 2000. 188 pages, ISBN: 9789990816655.

This useful collection of essays was selected from the proceedings of a conference of the Association of Theological Institutions of Southern and Central Africa (ATISCA), held in Mbabane, Swaziland in 1996. The overall aim is to present various aspects of the process of theological "contextualization" as it is being carried out in the region. As the preface explains, the metaphor of "African pots" in the title refers to "the African worldview, traditions, anthropology, and indeed African epistemology." In the first of the book's three major parts, two substantial essays call attention to the vital need for Christian theology to be more fully and perceptively contextualized in the region, and suggest ways in which such a programme might be carried out. Part 2 consists of "case studies" that illustrate contextualization "in action" in southern and central Africa. Among the topics treated are faith healing, relationships between the living and their ancestors, burial customs, traditional healers, syncretism, and the practice of giving "names" to children. In all of these the growing influence and novel practices of African Initiated Churches (AICs) are noted and at times described in more detail. Part 3 features comparative studies by two non-African theologians who examine the process of contextualization as it was carried out in Medieval Europe and among the Hindu in Bengal in the late eighteenth century. The book concludes with a practical essay on the need for publications done in Africa by Africans on the related fields of oral and written theology and church history.

331. Finneran, Niall

The Archaeology of Christianity in Africa

Stroud, UK: History Press, 2002. 192 pages, ISBN: 9780752425108.

Finneran has a PhD in the prehistoric archaeology of northern Ethiopia, and wrote this book while a research fellow in archaeology at the School of Oriental and African Studies in London. Here he offers a pioneering attempt to survey and interpret the archaeological evidence for African Christianity, covering sites in North Africa, Egypt, Nubia, Ethiopia, and from the early stages of European colonial-related missions in East, West and Southern Africa. From the available evidence Finneran explores what the process of conversion might have been like, how much syncretism there was, indications of competing forms of Christianity, and the social, economic and political changes that Christianity brought. Finally he looks at contemporary Christian art and architecture in Africa as an outcome of the interaction of the Christian and African worldviews. The book has 85 drawings and photos, plus eighteen colour plates, and a bibliography for each chapter. Finneran attempts to construct cultural history as seen from an African viewpoint. Unfortunately, in his conclusion that Africans were motivated to embrace Christianity by a perception of economic advancement and political gains, he has missed the deep spirituality which is one of the hallmarks of an African worldview. He sees conversion as a purely sociological phenomenon, and syncretism as a positive development. The book is an excellent introduction to its topic, is beautifully printed and relatively inexpensive.

332. Fish, Burnette C., and Gerald W. Fish

The Kalenjiin Heritage: Traditional Religious and Social Practices

Pasadena: WCL, 1996. 400 pages, ISBN: 9780878087693.

The Kalenjin are a cluster of related ethnic sub-groups in Kenya, including the Kipsigis, Nandi, Marakwet, and others. The Fishes were approached by the Africa Gospel Church (AGC) in Kenya to put into writing the traditional religious values and social practices of the Kipsigis, and to identify "redemptive analogies" which pastors and others could use as points of entry for the presentation of the Christian message. Although their research is largely limited to the Kipsigis sub-group, ceremonies and cultural practices are similar across the Kalenjin grouping. Discussing the deity of the Kalenjins, Asiis, the authors find that "many of the names and titles attributed to Asiis . . . are similar to titles for Jehovah God of Abraham." Other topics covered include rites of passage and related ceremonies; occult connections; defilement, cleansings, and uses of blood; beliefs regarding death, murder; other miscellaneous ceremonies such as anointing, adoption, thanksgiving, sainthood and taboos. The Fishes have generally evaluated these aspects of traditional culture positively. The book provides a helpful orientation for those seeking ways more effectively to present the gospel among the Kalenjin. It could also be of interest for anyone researching potential "redemptive analogies" in traditional African culture.

333. Fish, Burnette C., and Gerald W. Fish

The Place of Songs: A History of the World Gospel Mission and the Africa Gospel Church in Kenya

Marion, IN: World Gospel Mission, 1989. 581 pages, ISBN: 9780962040634.

The authors spent more than 40 years serving with World Gospel Mission in Kenya. After the Fishes' retirement, the leaders of the Africa Gospel Church (the Kenyan church started by WGM in Kenya) felt that this couple was uniquely qualified to write the history of the mission and the church. *A Place of Songs* is the first comprehensive history of these two organisations in Kenya. It gives a great deal of background, and then looks at the various ministries which developed through the efforts of the missionaries and the church leaders. The history of such institutions as Tenwek Hospital and Kenya Highlands Bible College is given in much detail. Theological colleges attempting a library collection of church history and missions history in Kenya might consider adding this book to their holdings.

Fish, Gerald W.

see reviews 332 and 333

334. Fisher, Humphrey J.

Slavery in the History of Muslim Black Africa

London: Hurst, 2001. 410 pages, ISBN: 9781850655244.

While countless books have been written about the triangular slave trade between Africa, Europe and the Americas in the seventeenth and eighteenth centuries, much less is known about slavery within Africa itself. Fisher has written a substantial specialist book concentrating on patterns of slavery and slave trade within

Africa generally and within Muslim Africa in particular. Qu'ranic and historical Muslim attitudes towards the enslavement of Muslims and non-Muslims are explained and illustrated. The reader will be struck by the scale of the trade, both in terms of time (spanning a thousand years from the tenth to nineteenth and even into the twentieth century), and in terms of geographic and numerical extent (for instance, some scholars estimate that as much as half of the Hausa population towards the end of the 19th century was of slave status). Fisher, formerly Reader in African History at London University's School of Oriental and African Studies, has made extensive use of a recently translated magisterial record by a German physician, Gustav Nachtigal, who travelled widely during the mid-nineteenth century in Islamic Africa of the Sahara and the Sahel. Of greater importance than the external demand for slaves in the New World, was the internal, domestic demand, a demand fuelled by the many different values put on slaves as, variously: cooks, concubines, tillers of soil, tenders of horses, craftsmen, sailors, builders, soldiers, eunuchs, and as human diplomatic gifts and tribute. It is an intriguing story. In his even-handed treatment of the subject, Fisher notes that in some instances the enslaved felt loyalty and even affection for their masters, but far more often it is the appalling suffering and degradation in human terms that shows through in the book. This millennium-long episode represents a long, ugly scar in the history of the continent, and one not very widely explored in contemporary discussion.

335.   **Folarin, George O.**

The Gospel of John in African Perspective

Ilorin, Nigeria: His Love Publishers, 2001. 160 pages.

Folarin is a minister of the Christ Apostolic Church in Nigeria, with degrees from ECWA and Baptist theological colleges, as well as from several Nigerian universities. He has taught the course on John's Gospel at Amadu Bello University in Zaria, and at the UMCA Theological College in Ilorin, and this book is a course text for the post-secondary level. After dealing with the historical setting and matters of literary introduction, Folarin analyses key words and concepts in John, and surveys John's eschatology, Christology, soteriology and pneumatology. There is a section on implications for African Theology at the end of each topic, and a final chapter titled "Reflections on the Christology of African Pentecostal Churches." The bibliography includes a number of African authors. This book interacts competently and intelligibly with a wide range of views, while itself working from a conservative and African viewpoint.

336.   **Folarin, George O.**

Studies in Old Testament Prophecy

Kaduna: Adewale Printing Works, 1994. 88 pages.

This book grew out of lecture notes for an undergraduate course in "Old Testament Prophecy and Apocalyptic Literature" offered at Ahmadu Bello University in Zaria, Nigeria. After a definition of prophets and prophecy, and a history of prophetism in Israel, the author analyses the work and message of OT prophets. There are summaries of the work of all the writing prophets, and chapters on the Son of Man, Jewish Apocalyptic and Prophecy in Africa. The book interacts throughout with major OT scholars, weighing conservative and liberal views, but supporting conservative conclusions. Particularly relevant and insightful are the comparison of OT "sons of the prophets" and the schools of the prophets of Nigeria's Christ Apostolic Church, and the comparison of African and OT prophets. The book could well serve as a textbook at the degree level. If out of print, it would deserve to be reprinted.

Fon, Wilfred

see review 418

337.   Forslund, Eskil

The Word of God in Ethiopian Tongues: Rhetorical Features in the Preaching of the Ethiopian Evangelical Church Mekane Yesus

Uppsala: Swedish Institute of Mission Research, 1993. 274 pages, ISBN: 9789185424351.

The aim of Forslund's study is to "define and describe some rhetorical features in the preaching in the EECMY" (Ethiopian Evangelical Church Mekane Yesus), showing how "preachers use the language, style and structure of their sermons as rhetorical strategies" in order to make the message relevant to various situations. The book's four major parts introduce successively (i) the broad features of the national background relevant to the discussion of the rhetorical use of language, (ii) the characteristics of the sample texts and the methodology applied, (iii) the "rhetorical situation" or specific context in which each sermon was used, and (iv) the features of style and structure which can be identified as deliberate attempts by the preacher to engage his audience. The EECMY, of predominantly Lutheran heritage, is one of the oldest Protestant church bodies in Ethiopia. The analysis makes use of a corpus of 196 sermons, preached by 72 EECMY preachers, and gathered over a period of years. G. A. Kennedy's application of the classical model of rhetoric to the writings of the NT forms the methodology of Forslund's approach. The book is a doctoral dissertation, and while that will mainly restrict its readership to academia, its contribution is central to hermeneutic, homiletic and contextualizing studies, and should be read by those teaching, studying or writing in these fields in Africa. Many of the features noted in EECMY sermons are widely found elsewhere in the African church, and homiletics teâchers might do well to recognize and build on them.

338.   Foulkes, James, and Joe Lacy

To Africa with Love: A Bush Doc's Story

Franklin, TN: Providence House Publishers, 2005. 238 pages, ISBN: 9781577363507.

This is the biography of a medical missionary who served for 37 years in Zambia. Like many books of this genre, it is a mixture of medical practice in a mission hospital deep in the African bush, evangelism, establishing churches, dealing with demon possession, all interspersed with exciting tales of rogue elephants, man-eating lions, and encounters with the dreaded black mamba snake. The book is a cut above the average because it has been professionally written and edited. Foulkes entered enthusiastically into life in central Africa, becoming, of necessity, a big-game hunter and a fisherman, in order to provide meat for the hospital patients. Along with many high adventures and good times enjoyed while camping with his family, he also had his share of heartaches. During his first year in Africa his eighteen-month old son died, and years later his sixteen-year old daughter also died, followed shortly thereafter by the death of his first wife. The account progresses sequentially, with a good amount of suspense pulling the reader along. It does, however, tend to bog down at times with rather intricate medical technicalities, and the background information about the hospital's original founder is more extensive and detailed than is needed. Although Foulkes had not set out to be a medical researcher, he became an acknowledged expert in the African sleeping sickness disease and wrote several articles on it for tropical medicine journals. The reader comes away impressed by Foulkes' strong Christian commitment, his significant contribution to the spiritual formation of the churches in Zambia, his compassionate medical service rendered in a particularly remote area of Africa, and his contribution to the nation of Zambia by the medical education provided in his hospital's school of nursing.

339.   **Fowler, Stuart**

The Oppression and Liberation of Modern Africa

Melbourne: Antithesis Educational Services, 1995. 117 pages, ISBN: 9781868222223.

This is a balanced critical study of the major forces that displaced and reshaped what we now know as modern Africa, with special attention to political and religious forces of the colonial period. Fowler has spent many years lecturing in African and Western institutions. Here he provides modern scholars of African history and African Christianity with a fresh and thought-provoking analysis of the European conquest and partition of Africa, and of the views of European powers about Africa and its people that shaped the policies by which they then sought to "establish law and order among the pagans" of Africa. By 1914 the whole of Africa (with the exception of Ethiopia and Liberia) had been divided among the European powers, who paid little attention to the existing social and authority structures of the African peoples. Thus Africa was reshaped culturally, politically and morally. The African social accountability system, which had kept people together for centuries, was overlooked and became a thing of the past. The new subjects now had to report to the new masters, and learn to please not their neighbours and communities but their owners. In that context, how should missionaries have presented the Christian message of liberation in Christ? And as subjugated people, how did Africans view missionaries and view Christianity, in both the pre-colonial and post-colonial periods? This well-researched book is an unusual exposition of European activities in Africa, and provides a challenging assessment for any Christian engaged in ministry in former colonial states.

340.   **Fraser, Eileen**

The Doctor Comes to Lui: A Story of Beginnings in the Sudan

Cape Town: Frontline Fellowship, 2000. 83 pages.

This biographical sketch of the missionary work of Dr Kenneth Grant Fraser in the Sudan in the early part of the twentieth century was first published in 1938. This new edition is a welcome contribution to the growing corpus of books on Christianity in the Sudan now in print. The book retains the original introduction by Llewellyn Gwynne, who in 1938 was the Anglican "Bishop in Cairo and the Sudan." The preface added for this new edition is by Bullen Dolli, Bishop of Lui, which is one of the 24 dioceses in the Episcopal Church of the Sudan today – striking testimony to the tremendous growth of the church in the Sudan in the intervening years. Also included is a helpful foreword by Peter Hammond of Frontline Fellowship. Fraser, originally from Scotland, arrived in the Sudan in 1920 and died there in 1935. His work was remarkable both for its vision and for its success. As a medical doctor, Fraser was able not only to provide medical treatment, but also to train many Sudanese in basic medical skills that were put to the test in out-clinics. The Frasers also began schools for boys and for girls, and engaged in primary evangelism, church planting and Bible translation, which met with a remarkable response in the Lui area. We are told that when the church in Lui was found to be too small to hold all those wanting to attend Christmas worship in 1923, services were held under "Laro," the old "slave tree" where Arabic slave traders had had their headquarters. A measure of Fraser's impact is that the Cathedral in the diocese of Lui was named after him, the Kenneth Fraser Memorial Cathedral. Sadly, shortly after re-publication of this small book in the year 2000, an Antonov bomber of Sudan's national Islamic government destroyed the Cathedral. The people of Lui commenced to make bricks for the rebuilding.

Fredericks, Charl E.

see review 226

341.   French, Howard

China's Second Continent: How a Million Migrants Are Building a New Empire in Africa

New York: Vintage, 2015. 304 pages, ISBN: 9780307946652.

It only takes simple observation to see the growing influence of China in contemporary Africa. The author has had experience as a journalist in both Africa and China and has written about both, so this book comes out of a familiarity with life and work in both places. It is written to help people understand what is happening in the relationship between China and countries in Africa. French describes his encounters with various individuals while travelling through Africa, both Chinese and African. He captures their thoughts and attitudes about the involvement of China and Chinese individuals in Africa. He also tries to understand and explore what the consequences are for both countries as the relationship between them grows and develops. Many people are beginning now to wonder about that, and especially about the considerable influx of Chinese into Africa. Indeed, it seems that almost every corner of Africa is touched or will be touched by Chinese presence in the near future. And far from coming merely as temporary expatriates, many Chinese are actually migrating to Africa to take up long-term residence. They are coming as farmers, tradesmen, business entrepreneurs, doctors, teachers – and, as the book's subtitle suggests, perhaps a million or more in numbers already. There is nothing much included in this book that would relate to religion, either in China or in Africa. But Africa's Christian communities might well ponder what their attitude should be towards these new migrants, and what opportunities and challenges these emerging developments might suggest.

342.   French, Howard

A Continent for the Taking: The Tragedy and Hope of Africa

New York: Random House, 2005. 280 pages, ISBN: 9781400030279.

It is sad when Western journalists are sent to Africa only to cover the continent's crises. The result can too readily be a highly distorted view of the continent. French is an African American journalist who was sent by the *New York Times* in the 1990s to report on Africa. He covered Abacha's Nigeria, Mobutu's Congo (DRC), Taylor's Liberia and the war in Rwanda. Most of his time was spent in cities like Lagos and Kinshasa. So of course his view of the continent is negative and cynical. French's African experience awakened him "to the selfishness and short-sightedness of the rich and the dignity of the poor in their suffering, and to the uses and abuses of power." It is important to be reminded of the corruption in Africa and the Big Man complex that plagues this continent. But there is more to Africa than this. What is lacking in this survey are ordinary Africans, farmers, teachers, school children and market women. Such people may not be rich but are often adequately responsible and happy. One also misses Africans who have sincere religious purpose and meaning in their lives. Africa has problems that should not be overlooked; but there is also a huge field of good that was missed by this particular journalist.

343.   **Freston, Paul**

Evangelicals and Politics in Asia, Africa and Latin America

Cambridge: Cambridge University Press, 2004. 360 pages, ISBN: 9780521604291.

A graduate of the University of Cambridge in England, Freston has been a university lecturer in sociology in Brazil, and has authored six books on the sociology of Protestantism in Latin America. In this book he uses his intimate knowledge of the situation in Brazil to establish a benchmark for his wider review of the issues and approaches pursued by evangelicals with regard to politics in Asia, Africa and Latin America in general. Approximately a quarter of the book deals with the situation in Africa, taking into account both mission-planted churches and African independent churches. The section on Africa is well researched, and the author writes about the churches from a sympathetic yet balanced perspective. At least for Africa this book is in pioneer territory; there is almost no other scholarly treatment with this scope available on this theme. Freston offers a lot of detail, but the style of writing makes the material easy to read and assimilate. The fullest coverage is given to Nigeria, Kenya, Zambia and South Africa, while Sudan, Angola, Mozambique, Zimbabwe, Malawi, Rwanda, Uganda and Ghana are covered in a few pages each. In each case the author focuses on the second half of the twentieth century and explores the different ways that evangelicals have become involved in the political arena. Each area of involvement and its effectiveness or otherwise is briefly but sensitively evaluated and, where appropriate, compared with similar situations in Latin America. While it would be good to have an entire book on this theme devoted to Africa alone, the amount of material contained in the section on Africa, together with its clarity, depth and reliability, makes this a unique contribution. With its concise and accessible summary of the recent history of African evangelicals and politics, it will prove an invaluable resource.

344.   **Froise, Marjorie**

South African Christian Handbook 1999–2000

Welkom, South Africa: Christian Info, 1999. 405 pages, ISBN: 9780620240246.

When Froise released this fifth edition of her *South African Christian Handbook*, she had already been producing handy reference tools for Christianity in southern Africa for more than fifteen years. Past editions of this particular resource were already in wide use by Christian and secular leaders, agencies, and researchers in southern Africa and internationally. She said that this edition would be her last. If so, then it must be said that she saved the best for last! This is a vast, rich trove of useful information on Christianity in the new post-apartheid South Africa at the beginning of the new millennium. Here one is provided with basic data on some 2500 Christian organisations and ministry entities in modern South Africa, classified under six major categories and 44 sub-categories. Included are: church bodies (denominations and similar groupings); missions and teaching ministries (e.g. student, youth and children's ministries), Christian education (including 102 seminaries and theological colleges) media ministries (such as bookshops, publishers, radio ministries); service agencies (social services, adult education, counselling); and accommodation (conference centres, children's homes, hospice care). As a sign of the times, this new edition added sub-categories for homes for street children, AIDS ministries, and websites (205 websites are listed). For the exhausted researcher there is even a section on Christian retreat centres in South Africa! All this wealth of data is served by two marvellous indices, one giving alphabetical access to all the organisational entities for which information is provided, and the other doing so for the 2479 individuals referenced in the data. But this reference resource does more than serve as a directory; it also furnishes fulsome materials for a closely informed perspective on the religious data of the country. The first 109 pages present detailed analysis and assessment of the status of Christianity in South Africa, based especially on the findings of the 1996 government census. Professor H. J. Hendriks of Stellenbosch University offers the basic data of that census, and then contributes a key chapter on "Religion in South Africa: Census '96'." Froise herself adds two chapters on "The Church in Context" and "The Church in Action." The data reported in this major part of the *Handbook* is supported by a remarkable set of 61 tables, charts and graphics. Granted that the material is now increasingly dated, nevertheless because of the range of information recorded for so many entities, it will remain a valuable resource for researchers on Christian presence in modern South Africa for some time. Would that Christian communities in other major African countries had similar expansive, up-to-date resources to use.

345. **Froise, Marjorie, editor**

Swaziland Christian Handbook 1994

London: IVP-UK, 1994. 125 pages, ISBN: 9780620167123.

This handbook offers the reader basic information about the country of Swaziland at the time of its publication, both in terms of its history, people, and present economic and social situation, and especially in terms of the Christian churches, mission agencies, colleges, media, and service agencies that are operational there. Furthermore, the book gives an indication of several phases of church outreach and growth in that country, and what would be needed for the church to be grounded in the faith and less fragmented. The book's value lies not only in the comprehensive overview of the country of Swaziland, but also in the author's attempted interpretation of the tasks before the Christian church there. The latter is well worth considering, especially if one is working or thinking of working with the church in Swaziland, or needs to know in more detail about the Christian presence there.

346. **Froise, Marjorie, editor**

World Christianity: South Central Africa

Monrovia, CA: MARC, 1991. 164 pages, ISBN: 9780912552767.

This book is intended to provide "a factual portrait" of Christianity in South Central Africa. Marjorie Froise is an experienced researcher, who was also editor of the *South Africa Christian Handbook*. The countries dealt with in this book are: Angola, Comoros, Madagascar, Malawi, Mauritius, Mozambique, Reunion, Seychelles, St. Helena, Ascension, Tristan da Cunha, Zambia, and Zimbabwe. A chapter is devoted to each country, usually employing the following outline: historical background, socioeconomic conditions, the people, status of

Christianity, national churches, foreign missionaries, unreached peoples, Christian activities, and needs in the country. Inevitably, books of this nature can become dated very quickly, especially when one considers the political and social changes within Africa as a whole. Nevertheless, this book can serve as a useful resource for any researcher needing concise orientation to Christianity at the time of publication in the countries listed.

347. **Froise, Marjorie**

World Christianity: Southern Africa: A Factual Portrait of the Christian Church in South Africa, Botswana, Lesotho, Namibia and Swaziland

Monrovia, CA: MARC, 1989. 127 pages, ISBN: 9780912552637.

This title is part of the World Christianity series which MARC has been publishing since 1971. The books in the series contain "country profiles" and "country portraits" in an effort to keep the "freshest possible information before those who plan and strategize for evangelism and mission." This volume in the series presents a "factual portrait" of the Christian church in the countries of South Africa, Botswana, Lesotho, Namibia and Swaziland current to 1989. There is a chapter devoted to each country, giving information on the history, people, socioeconomic conditions, status of Christianity and the church, unreached peoples, and needs of the country. Tables give helpful facts on each country. This is a useful reference source for researchers, provided one keeps in mind that many of the facts were collected in the 1980s. Subsequent publications by Froise updated material on South Africa and Swaziland but not on the other three countries.

348. **Fuller, Clare**

Banfield, Nupe, and the UMCA

Ilorin, Nigeria: World Partners, 2001. 119 pages, ISBN: 9789783537477.

This book is about the ministry of Canadian missionary Alexander Banfield. During the first three decades of the twentieth century, Banfield played a key role in the planting of the church in northern Nigeria, linking three strategic organisations through his ministry: the SIM, the United Missionary Church in Africa (UMCA), and the British and Foreign Bible Society. In 1902 he was a pioneer in founding a mission station at Patigi on the Niger River, the first station in Africa of what later became known as the Sudan Interior Mission (SIM). Several years later, as a missionary of the Mennonite Brethren in Christ, he was instrumental in founding the United Missionary Church in Africa, now an important denomination in Nigeria. He also devoted himself with passion to learning and documenting the Nupe language, and became the main translator of the Bible in that language. And, perhaps most importantly, through establishing the Niger Press, he played a leading role in publishing vernacular Bibles and other Christian literature for northern Nigeria. For those interested in the ministry of Banfield, this book will become the single most accessible introduction. It is brief, written in simple English, yet neither superficial nor cursory. At several points Fuller corrects previous accounts and popular misconceptions through a close reading of primary sources. The material is moderately documented, averaging about one endnote per page of text, including a wide variety of primary and secondary sources, many little known. Though Fuller's intended audience is his UMCA denomination and mission, this book will make a solid contribution to any library intending strong holdings on the planting of the Church in West Africa. Fuller was a lecturer at the UMCA Bible College in Niger State, Nigeria.

349. **Fuller, Lois**

Faith of our Fathers: Life Stories of Some UMCA Elders

Ilorin, Nigeria: Indemac, 1999. 128 pages, ISBN: 9789783228580.

The author, a former missionary in Nigeria with the United Missionary Society, and now Dr Lois Dow, here presents the life stories of thirteen Nigerian pioneer church leaders who served in various capacities within the United Missionary Church of Africa (UMCA). The biographies cover the period from about 1920 to the mid-1990s. These primary accounts are rich in local Nigerian colour, depicting first generation struggles between ATR and Christianity. From these stories it is evident that the quest for education among Nigerian youth was a major factor which attracted them to Christianity. Another factor was that the traditional gods were failing the local population. Rev Ibrahim Alkali relates how a violent struggle erupted between two cults among the Kambari traditionalists, the fallout being that a spiritual vacuum was created which was filled by the preaching of the gospel. These thirteen indigenous pastors and church administrators acknowledge that the expatriate UMS missionaries played a distinct role in laying the groundwork for the subsequent growth of the UMCA in Nigeria, but they also confirm that the local Christians were more adept and skilful in handling the machinations of juju. These biographies also describe how the gospel liberated Nigerian women. For example, of Rev Simon Adedokun's five daughters, one is serving as a politician, two are pastors and two are evangelists. The general impact of Scripture and the ministry of the UMS wives and single missionaries no doubt provided a strong impetus for "women in ministry." In this account, Lois Fuller has made a significant contribution to the history of the church in Nigeria, and offers a template of how the history of other African denominations could be documented. A book like this does not offer objective missiological critique; rather it adds to a store of resources for further research. Mission libraries are replete with the biographies of expatriate missionaries. However, the web-based *Dictionary of African Christian Biography* (DACB) now provides a corrective where the lives of Africans are foregrounded. Thankfully, these thirteen stories are already available online at DACB.

350. **Fuller, Lois**

Going to the Nations: An Introduction to Cross-Cultural Missions

Jos: Nigeria Evangelical Missionary Institute, 1993. 112 pages, ISBN: 9789782668035.

The author is the former Dean of the Nigeria Evangelical Missionary Institute (NEMI), a former lecturer at the United Missionary Church of Africa Theological College, Ilorin, and more recently has been instructor in NT Greek at McMaster Divinity College in Canada. With African Christian readers in mind, this book introduces the biblical basis for and history of cross-cultural missions, together with its theory and strategy. It also discusses the call and preparation of a missionary from Africa. The book is written in a clear, concise style, for those with secondary education or better, and does not presuppose theological training. This book is a strong challenge to those African congregations and denominations that do not yet engage in significant missions work. Fuller says, "A church without a missionary outreach is unknown in the NT, and cannot be considered a church in the true sense of the word." She surveys missions in the various regions of Africa from 1800 onward, including both expatriate and indigenous missionaries. Among the latter she includes Simon Kimbangu and William Wade Harris. West Africa receives more attention than other regions since the book was originally designed for Nigeria. The fact is acknowledged that the vast majority of African converts were and are the fruit of African Christian witness, rather than owing to expatriate missionaries. Discussing the call and preparation of a missionary, the book considers spiritual, physical, educational, character and family qualifications, hindrances to a missionary call from a perspective applicable in Africa, and training to be a missionary. Also addressed are topics such as: contextualization, church growth theory, how much of Africa is unreached, steps to evangelizing unreached people groups, saturation evangelism, TEE, chronological Bible story teaching, the roles of the local church in missions, and the place of missionary societies. A list of places to receive missionary training in Nigeria is included. The book reflects but is not captive to a Nigerian audience; it would serve excellently in any Bible college or seminary missions course anywhere in Africa. Local churches, mission committees, and mission agencies in Africa will want to be aware of this important text. And theological libraries in sub-Saharan Africa would benefit from having a copy on their shelves.

351.   **Fuller, Lois**

The Missionary and His Work

Jos: Nigeria Evangelical Missionary Institute, 1996. 145 pages, ISBN: 9789782668219.

This volume, now in its second edition, is an introduction to missionary life and work for African Christians working in cross-cultural outreach. It is eminently practical, drawing deeply from the author's long-term involvement in the training of missionaries at the Nigeria Evangelical Missionary Institute. The book has 44 chapters, pointing both perhaps to its origin and to its primary usefulness, namely as lecture notes or a textbook for an introductory course for African Christians on missionary life and work. The chapters follow a logical progression: the biblical theology of missions; becoming a missionary; evangelism; church planting; missionary life; miscellaneous topics. Each chapter follows the same pattern: a brief exposition of the topic, an illustration or case study normally drawn from the actual experiences of Nigerian missionaries, and three to five excellent discussion questions. While the book would be quite appropriate for use anywhere in Africa, it would be particularly relevant for the Nigerian missionary, as most illustrations and resources are drawn from the Nigerian context. The book appears to cover the essential topics well in terms of breadth, but one notices the brevity of the individual treatments: the exposition of each topic averages only 700 words total. While this results in an inexpensive, handbook-sized volume, it may seem too brief at points. For example, the chapter on the theology of missions in the early church almost completely neglects the Cornelius episode, surely the most important programmatic text for this purpose in Acts. The English used is simple, and would be understandable by those using English as a non-native language. This book would be suitable for use in missionary training institutes throughout Africa, and would prove an excellent orientation for any African contemplating or engaged in cross-cultural missionary service.

352.   **Fuller, Lois**

A Missionary Handbook on African Traditional Religion

Jos: Nigeria Evangelical Missionary Institute, 1994. 130 pages, ISBN: 9789782668400.

The author, now Dr Lois Dow, worked for many years in Nigeria, including service as Dean of the Nigeria Evangelical Missionary Institute (NEMI), where she helped train Africans preparing to be cross-cultural missionaries. This little book on traditional religion in Africa is well adapted for use as a classroom text. Because it is designed as a "missionary handbook," it goes a step further than (and is thereby an excellent supplement to) many of the more descriptive studies of African traditional religions. Thus in each chapter, Fuller discusses the evangelistic dimensions of the encounter between Christianity and ATR. The issues raised in this handbook are of vital importance not only for missionaries (from whatever continent), but also for anyone ministering in Africa. It offers an excellent model of how to communicate the gospel to those with an animistic worldview. The level of English is suitable for O Level and upwards. Many theological colleges in Africa are already using it in their courses.

353. Fuller, Lois

The Pentateuch: Foundation of God's Message to the World

Bukuru, Nigeria: Africa Christian Textbooks, 1996. 143 pages, ISBN: 9789789050468.

This introduction to the Pentateuch is written by a seasoned educator for the diploma or Bible School student. The language is lucid and the questions at the end of each chapter are useful for the classroom. The book is written from a conservative evangelical viewpoint, presupposing the Mosaic authorship of the Pentateuch and rejecting the documentary hypothesis. The book makes the Pentateuch relevant to the African situation. The main thrust of the book is to remind the believer today how to live before God. Attention is focused especially on the lives of the Patriarchs, Moses and Israel as examples of right living. The bulk of the book looks at Genesis and Exodus; the treatment of the other three books of the Pentateuch is briefer. Fuller calls the book of Exodus "the salvation book of the Old Testament", but she does not fully define salvation as represented in Exodus. Instead, salvation is defined from the NT as forgiveness of sins and being right with God. In Leviticus she focuses on ceremonial issues like priesthood, offerings and feasts. In Numbers she looks at the journey of Israel through the desert. Deuteronomy is summarized in six pages. This book makes the Pentateuch living and relevant for Christians in the African context. The work would be stronger if the theological underpinnings were more developed. The purpose of creation was fellowship with God. This relationship was broken by the Fall, but was renewed by covenant with the Patriarchs and with Israel at Sinai. These covenants give structure to the Pentateuch and the OT. The place of the law could then be made clearer. The law guides people who are in a covenant relation with God. The book might also be strengthened if greater attention were given to the social dimensions of the law. Finally, the question of salvation in the OT is unresolved. The OT words for salvation strongly emphasize the physical side of salvation, but the spiritual dimension of salvation emerges in the covenant concept. This book would be very useful for the diploma level, whereas degree students will likely need something more.

354. Fuller, Lois

You Can Learn New Testament Greek

Bukuru, Nigeria: Africa Christian Textbooks, 1993. ISBN: 9789789050659.

Fuller has many years of experience in teaching Greek, mainly in Nigeria, but also in the United States and Canada, and this is reflected in this excellent beginners guide to NT Greek, which has already been in wide use in Nigeria. The title reflects the positive and encouraging tone of the book throughout. It is more user-friendly than Machen, whilst being equally thorough; and it is more systematic than Dobson. One particular strength of this book is that it takes into account the needs of those whose mother tongue is not English. Greek grammar is simply and clearly explained. Where appropriate, the author explains and tests English grammar before transferring this knowledge to the Greek. Students have, for example, found her explanation of the cases, and the passive and middle voices, particularly helpful. The author also gives illustrations from Nigerian languages, a handy but not major feature of the book. Each lesson ends with several exercises. Most lessons also end with short stories or scripture passages to translate, which students find enjoyable and encouraging, as what they have learned is reinforced. The book also has several useful appendices, as well as Greek-to-English and English-to-Greek vocabularies. This very welcome tool can be used either as a class text, or by individuals studying Greek with minimal guidance from a teacher.

355.   **Fulljames, Peter**

God and Creation in Intercultural Perspective: Dialogue between the Theologies of Barth, Dickson, Pobee, Nyamiti, and Pannenberg

Frankfurt: Peter Lang, 1993. 190 pages, ISBN: 9783631456095.

Can Christian theologies formulated in one cultural context provide important insights for theologians in another? Traditionally such an exchange has tended to happen only in ways that bolstered the dominant culture. But in this suggestive study, Fulljames, a theologian with international experience now based in Birmingham, England, argues that African theology can supplement and correct the insights of two major European thinkers, Barth and Pannenberg. Careful analyses of the method and the doctrine of God's relation to creation for Barth, Pannenberg, Dickson, Pobee, and Nyamiti form the core of this work. These figures are well chosen, representing contrasting methods and cultural contexts. Throughout his intercultural comparison Fulljames argues that the African emphasis on the community of all creation (the interdependence of humans and other created things), life as a symbol for God's relationship to creation (in contrast to God's revelation in Jesus Christ), and human co-creativity provide new directions for theological development which might resolve contemporary European challenges in the areas of ecology and theodicy. While Fulljames' excellent overview of these major theologians fully warrants its addition to African libraries, his bold intercultural evaluations also raise important questions. He does not clearly develop the basis for supplementing and correcting Barth and Pannenberg. In theory, Pannenberg's theological method, which attempts to coordinate Christian revelation with contemporary cultural norms, should be open to correction from other cultures. But the author fails to develop the African theological insights so that they would convince those in other cultures. Nyamiti's understanding of the interrelatedness of creation, for example, is derived from the African concept of ancestors and correlated with the Roman Catholic notion of saints and purgatory. Why would European Protestants find this argument persuasive? Moreover, the ground for supplementing Barth's theology, which deliberately attempts to reverse the accommodation to culture by steadfastly holding to a Christological norm, is not clear. Like trying to create a single whole out of two jigsaw puzzles, Fulljames' intercultural conclusions appear confused and poorly fitting. It is ironic that this study, which recognizes the contextuality of all thought, does not develop these implications for intercultural dialogue. While Fulljames' attempt at intercultural theological analysis points toward a new type of inquiry with fruitful possibilities, to be more adequately effective such analyses should in future perhaps be less ambitious, for example by focusing on only two theologians and allowing them to probe each other's weaknesses and strengths.

356. Fyfe, Christopher, and Andrew F. Walls, editors

Christianity in Africa in the 1990s

Edinburgh: Centre of African Studies, 1996. 163 pages.

This is a collection of papers read at a conference in Edinburgh in 1992. There are thirteen papers covering a range of subjects. Walls introduces the collection with "African Christianity in the History of Religions." He argues that traditional African religion continues within Christianity, in terms of the use of indigenous names for God and "African maps of the universe," while also recognising significant reordering of the "maps" as well as new elements. His conclusion is that "Christianity is at home in African religion; it is African religion." Adrian Hastings briefly extends his History of African Christianity 1950–1975 up to 1990. Three studies of "the missionary legacy" in Africa look at: the Catholic church (Aylward Shorter), Pentecostal missions (Edith Blumhoffer), and the influence of the Church of Scotland on some African churches (James Wilkie). Kwame Bediako discusses "types of African theology," largely going over well-trodden ground. Lamin Sanneh briefly considers Muslim and Christian attitudes to the state. Louise Pirouet considers the churches' involvement with a number of refugee crises in Uganda and Kenya. Zac Niringiye focuses on Africa Evangelistic Enterprise (AEE) and the International Fellowship of Evangelical Students (IFES) within the larger African Christian context. Stan Nussbaum discusses "African Bible Guides," a project bringing together African scholars from both mission-founded and independent churches (including, for example, Kimbanguists and Catholics) to write Bible guides for use by Christian leaders. Walls concludes with "A Summary and Reflection." An appendix contains an article on "The Brotherhood of the Cross and Star," a Nigerian sect whose leader has pretensions to divinity. The book is a useful survey of some central aspects of African Christianity, although obviously now somewhat dated. Also the focus on the 1990s to which the title refers is not consistently maintained. Inevitably in such a collection the quality of the contributions varies, and some may be a little too brief to be very useful. Among the highlights is Shorter's study of the African Catholic church, at seventeen pages one of the longer contributions, which offers a very useful overview of a vast and complex area.

357. Gachiri, Ephigenia W.

Female Circumcision

Nairobi: Paulines, 2007. 136 pages, ISBN: 9789966215772.

The Kenyan author is well qualified to address her subject, since she initiated and currently directs a Catholic educational project focused on the termination of female genital mutilation (FGM) in the Kikuyu area of Kenya, where she has collected much data on the practice. She states that she prefers the term FGM rather than circumcision since biblical references to circumcision, albeit for men rather than women, prompt some to claim biblical support for the practice while the term 'mutilation' highlights the damage it does. She begins with God's creation of woman, and His declaration that His creation was very good, in order to affirm the wholeness of the human body as God created it and the wrongness of mutilating what God called very good. This is followed by personal accounts by circumcised women, and by definitions, descriptions and consequences of FGM, which make for emotionally difficult reading. Using a careful description of the Kikuyu rites of passage for girls, Gachiri studies the significance of female circumcision as part of holistic cultural education in the life cycle of Kikuyu women, while noting that its current practice has lost much of that emphasis because it must be done secretly and quickly to avoid conviction for law breaking. She also documents the connections between FGM and spiritual forces, witchcraft and curses, which still give it power today despite opposition by the church and the state. She notes that Christian pastors are taking the lead in refusing to have their daughters undergo FGM, and that Kenyan law currently forbids it (although historically it was Jomo Kenyatta's support for this practice, in his *Facing Mount Kenya*, that played a major role in perpetuating it for so long in Kenya). The author also documents the practice in 65 African countries, Islamic countries of the Middle East, and in Asia. She concludes by giving specific strategies for convincing various segments of the community of the damage done by FGM, and also strategies for working with these same people to design alternative rites that are wholesome and Christian while still meeting community goals. The book is written to be read by lay people, and Gachiri does a masterful job of being sensitive to people's cultural feelings and values while forthrightly opposing this deeply rooted cultural practice. Her book will be extremely helpful to Christians working in areas where FGM is practiced.

358.   Gaidzanwa, Rudo B.

Images of Women in Zimbabwean Literature

Gweru, Zimbabwe: Mambo Press, 1985. 103 pages, ISBN: 9780869255841.

In this volume the author, a sociology lecturer at the University of Zimbabwe, critically analyses the depiction of women, both rural and urban, in popular local literature. The author argues that women in developing countries like Zimbabwe are sociologically and economically disadvantaged, and that this is reflected in popular indigenous writing. *Images of Women* is an in-depth analysis of Zimbabwean literature, showing that in spite of their key roles in society – as mothers, wives, singles, widows – women are marginalized. Although most of the books the author evaluates are in the local vernacular, the examples discussed will be of interest to anyone concerned with current gender issues. The writer feels that in most African cultures an ideal wife is one who is hardworking and bears a son to her husband. However, she says, such wives are usually brutalized and harassed in spite of such admired characteristics. There are no tangible rewards for belonging to an ideal-woman category. Therefore African women in different societies have no practical methods of articulating, defending and promoting their rights. Although Gaidzanwa decries this stereotypical projection of women within local Zimbabwean literature, she admits that this is not a far-fetched portrait. This is a worthy book, because it gives the reader a woman's point of view of how traditional societies handle women, and how women themselves have accepted their "ideal roles" at the expense of voicing their concerns and rights.

359.   Gaiya, Musa A. B.

A Portrait of a Saint: The Life and Times of Pa Yohanna Gowon (d. 1973)

Jos: Fab Education Books, 1998. 103 pages, ISBN: 9789782023438.

This is the story of the father of General Yakubu Gowon, Nigeria's former Head of State. Yohanna Gowon was born around 1880 on the Jos Plateau in Nigeria (in the Angas or Ngas tribe). The book details his conversion in the first generation of the Angas to hear the gospel, his ministry as an evangelist among the Angas, his migration to the early Christian village of Wusasa seven years after it was founded, his work as an evangelist among the Hausa-Fulani, and his raising of a large family by a committed Christian example. The story is of interest not only because of Pa Gowon's famous son, but also for the light it sheds on the early days of the CMS work among the Angas and in the Zaria and Wusasa mission. There is also an epilogue describing the desecration of his grave in the religious riots of 1987. The book is useful as well for its extensive bibliography. It originated as the thesis for the author's MA in Church History. Gaiya has subsequently been Senior Lecturer in Church History at the University of Jos, and a pastor in the Evangelical Church of West Africa (ECWA). While the content may be faulted in some specifics, this book is significant not least in representing the fact that African Christians are now "doing" their own church history for themselves; and in highlighting the sterling quality and impact of earlier generations of African Christians, so often under-recognized today.

Gaiya, Musa A. B.

see also review 482

Galgalo, Joseph D.

see review 635

360.   Galvan, Maria, and Bénézet Bujo

An African Journey through Mark's Gospel: A Tool for Small Christian Communities

Nairobi: Paulines, 2000. 160 pages, ISBN: 9789966215284.

The authors were Catholic missionaries serving in Kenya when this little devotional guide was first composed and published in the Pokot language. It aims to achieve two main goals, first identification ("Who is that Jesus who challenges us?"), and then application ("How can we follow Jesus in our daily lives?"). The book creatively welds traditional Pokot life and culture with the good news of Jesus as narrated in the Gospel of Mark. The authors follow what they call the "See-Judge-Act" method of instruction. Each of the 103 brief meditations begins with a succinct local case study, drawn from everyday Pokot life, which seeks to introduce the primary theme of the lesson. Several questions follow as a means of stimulating some significant group discussion of the story, which normally poses a special moral or spiritual problem, controversy, or challenge. This leads to a short reading from Mark's Gospel which focuses upon a particular action, instruction, or event in the life of Jesus. Another set of questions brings out the principal truth, teaching, or life-application identified for that lesson. This simple, easy-to-follow format is continued throughout the book. The concise, local case-study and question method is a very effective pedagogical technique anywhere. As deployed here it would prove a good model for other areas of Africa where church leaders have similar didactic and edificational goals. The book is intended not for personal reading but for interactive group Bible study, and the technique it models would be best put to use with one or more competent discussion leaders ("animators") present to provoke and stimulate the discussion. Among minor problems would be that some of the local case studies are so situation specific that they are a little hard for the outsider to grasp. Another potential problem is that of sequence and continuity; each lesson is completely independent and able to stand on its own. While that may be of some benefit when using the book, the running narrative of Mark tends to be broken up in the process, with texts left unrelated no matter how similar in topic or close in textual space. All in all this is a valuable little model of ongoing efforts in Africa to find a more appropriate, contextualized method for effective group Bible study.

361.   **Gamley, Anthony M., editor**

Denis Hurley: A Portrait by Friends

Pietermaritzburg: Cluster, 2001. 193 pages, ISBN: 9781875053292.

When the history of the Catholic Church in South Africa in the twentieth century comes to be written, and in particular that Church's opposition to the immoral political system of apartheid, the name of Denis Hurley will occupy an especially honoured place. Appointed in 1946 at the age of 31 as Bishop and Vicar Apostolic of Natal by Pope Pius XII, and elevated four years later to Archbishop of Durban, Denis Hurley was the youngest Catholic Archbishop in the world. When he retired in 1990 at the age of 75, Hurley was the Catholic Church's longest-serving bishop. He died in 2004. In this collection of 28 essays, religious leaders, theologians, politicians, lawyers, journalists, trade unionists and academics pay tribute to a distinguished pastor, theologian, anti-apartheid activist, liturgist, ecumenist, but above all humble servant of Christ. The foreword is by Desmond Tutu. Whilst many of the tributes are of a personal nature, several are of particular interest, including two biographical essays. Also *Time Magazine*'s prize-winning correspondent at the Second Vatican Council and now contributing editor for *Newsweek* in Rome, Robert Blair Kaiser, offers an article on Hurley and the Vatican Council. Similarly, Professor Phillipe Denis OP considers the decisive influence of Vatican II on a young Hurley. The world-renowned scholar Philip Tobias FRS reflects not only on his friendship with Hurley, but also their mutual regard for the controversial Catholic palaeontologist Teilhard de Chardin SJ, who, Tobias reminds us, visited South Africa on several occasions. Ian Linden of the School of Oriental and African Studies in London concludes his contribution with the observation that through "vision, leadership and courage," Denis Hurley "more than anyone, "saved" the spiritual integrity of the Catholic Church in South Africa." It is not an exaggerated assessment. But it also begs the question – nowhere answered in this interesting book – why the Vatican never gave Hurley a cardinal's hat.

362.   **Garland, Jean, and Mike Blyth**

AIDS Is Real and It's in Our Church

Bukuru, Nigeria: Africa Christian Textbooks, 2005. 326 pages, ISBN: 9781594520266.

The massive impact of the HIV/AIDS pandemic across Africa can hardly be denied – except, that is, in churches. There it has been too regularly ignored or readily dismissed. But for Africa, as the title announces, "AIDS is real, and it's in our church." For many African Christian communities, HIV/AIDS may be the most significant challenge in this generation, and this may be the best book available in addressing the crisis. The book is comprehensive, with seventeen chapters covering in a balanced and readable fashion issues relating to awareness, prevention, and care. Co-written by a physician and a nurse with years of experience in Africa, the book is up-to-date and accurate, citing recent medical studies and referencing cutting-edge best practice. It is also an eminently practical handbook, providing sound advice on prevention and care, and calling for the transformation of attitudes which lead to stigmatisation and a lack of compassion. The book is punctuated throughout with stories and illustrations drawn from the African context. Insightful chapters on "Social Reasons for the Fast Spread of AIDS" and "False Beliefs and Practices about Sex and Childbearing" particularly demonstrate the book's ability to speak into the African context. The authors' evangelical Christian commitment is evidenced by their clear call for abstinence outside of marriage, for faithfulness in marriage, and for the church's compassionate response to people living with AIDS. While the first edition of the book focused upon the Nigerian context, this revised edition is intended to make the book relevant for readers throughout the continent. Given its exceptional quality, this is a book that deserves to be purchased in bulk for wide distribution among churches. It has already proven its usefulness as the primary textbook for courses on HIV/AIDS in African theological schools.

Gaskin, Ross F.

see review 219

363. Gaskiyane, I.

Polygamy: A Cultural and Biblical Perspective

Carlisle, UK: Piquant Editions, 2000. 63 pages, ISBN: 9780953575794.

The confusing variety of responses to polygamy by Christian denominations across Africa is evidence enough of the need for careful reflection on this important subject. The author, though not himself African, writes from a background of over 30 years of ministry in the continent. While the topic will be of interest beyond the bounds of Africa (according to the author, 75 percent of the world's societies permit polygamy and only 16 percent prescribe monogamy), the examples and case studies in the book are from Africa. The approach in this slender publication is practical rather than academic. The chapters address in turn the difficult dilemmas that many Christian churches grapple with in societies where polygamy is widespread, namely: How should Christians view polygamy in non-Christian cultures today which have been polygamous for a long time? How should the church handle new converts who come from a background of traditional polygamy? What is the biblical perspective on the policy of some churches to require polygamists to put away all but one wife? According to Scripture, should polygamists who retain their multiple wives be baptized? Should polygamists be permitted to take Holy Communion? Should polygamists be permitted to be pastors and elders in the local church? In a controversial subject where opinions quickly polarize, one of the strengths of the book is its studied even-handedness. Polygamy is not caricatured as being entirely evil; of the twenty and more factors listed as lying behind the practice, the majority have strong moral and social dimensions such as concern for the extended family, support and care, work-share, coping with childlessness, etc. Less noble factors (lust, power, wealth) are acknowledged as potentially present, too. Islamic attitudes and practices are also fairly considered. The biblical evidence is examined, leading to a general conclusion that while monogamy is undoubtedly God's plan for marriage, polygamy is a human cultural creation, and the Church needs much cultural sensitivity, patience, and pastoral skill in handling the complex human situations that are related to polygamy, as she seeks to lead people further into God's will. The author insists, for instance, that for a Christian polygamist to have to divorce all but one wife would replace one "sin" by another which is far more clearly denounced in Scripture. There is an increasing body of literature by Africans and Africanists relating to marriage in Africa. Perhaps one of the weaknesses of the present book is that it makes no reference to that literature. That apart, and despite the limitations of its size, this booklet is a helpful survey and assessment of the issues affecting a Christian response to polygamy.

364.   **Gates, Henry Louis**

Wonders of the African World

Alexandria, VA: PBS Home Video, 1999. ISBN: 9780780628656.

This series on three DVD discs (six hours) is a six-episode exploration of aspects of African history and culture narrated by Gates, who has been Professor of African American History at Harvard University. On the video Gates travels to the remains of ancient Nubian kingdoms and the ruins of Great Zimbabwe. He investigates the diverse cultures of Timbuktu, the Swahili coast and the slave kingdoms of West Africa. Throughout the series Gates, a descendent of American slaves, struggles with issues of African American identity. He wonders how Africans could have been involved in enslaving fellow Africans. And he highlights how European historians ignored or even denied the existence of great cultures and civilisations in Africa, simply because they assumed that such civilisations could not have been created by black people. Of special interest to the Christian reader is the episode entitled "The Holy Land." In this segment Gates takes the viewer on a tour of Ethiopia in quest for the Ark of the Covenant. Although he is frustrated in his attempts to find the elusive Ark, he does introduce viewers to the colourful world of the Ethiopian Orthodox Church.

Gates Jr., Henry Louis

see also review 66

365.   **Gatti, Nicoletta, and George Ossom-Batsa**

Journeying with the Old Testament

Bern: Peter Lang, 2011. 189 pages, ISBN: 9783034310062.

The authors are Roman Catholic biblical scholars trained in Rome, and they both currently teach OT in Ghana, Gatti in the Central University College (Dansoman) and Ossom-Batsa in the University of Ghana (Legon). The book is a textbook for seminary and undergraduate students, aiming to build a bridge between two genres of introductions to the OT, the highly scientific one on the one hand and the more popular ones on the other. The book also aims to speak a word into the inter-religious environment of Ghanaian universities, where Christian and Muslim students study the Bible and the Qur'an together, "sharing in the common fatherhood of Abraham." The six main chapters of the book follow a traditional pattern of this textbook genre (with the exception of the last chapter), exposing the readers to a relatively updated version of historical-critical scholarship: "the world of the OT," "the canon of the OT," then "the structure and content of the *Torah*," "the *Nebi'im*," and "the *Ketubim*." The final chapter is on "Studying the OT in Africa." The latter does not challenge the hermeneutics or epistemology of the former five, but its subsections: (a) Africa in the OT, (b) interpreting the OT from an African perspective, and (c) reading the OT with African eyes, provide a necessary addition to the rather traditional, Western approaches elsewhere in the book. Considered as a textbook, this is a contribution characterized by pedagogical skills and experience, with summaries, study questions, and brief bibliographies to each chapter.

366. Gatumu, Kabiro wa

The Pauline Concept of Supernatural Powers: A Reading from the African Worldview

Carlisle, UK: Paternoster, 2008. 326 pages, ISBN: 9781842275320.

The author has been a senior lecturer in NT studies at St Paul's University in Limuru, Kenya. This book is the published version of his PhD dissertation, written under the direction of James Dunn at the University of Durham. Gatumu seeks to appropriate the Pauline language of "the powers" in order to address ideas about the spirit world that continue to undermine the faith of African believers. He traces the genesis of this problem in part to the failure of Western missionaries to take these issues seriously (chapters 1 and 2). He then examines African perceptions of the spirit world, though in a surprisingly superficial way, e.g. spending only about one page on the immensely complex topic of beliefs about witchcraft. In the same chapter (chapter 3) he also looks at anthropological (western, naturalistic) interpretations of these belief systems. Next is a helpful overview of Jewish and Greco-Roman ideas about spiritual powers, beliefs that were to one degree or another in the background of Paul's theology (chapter 4). He goes on to discuss the Pauline references to the powers (chapter 5), emphasizing the Apostle's desire to foster confident faith in Christ's victory over them all. Gatumu challenges the tendency of some Western scholars, Rudolf Bultmann and Walter Wink in particular, to "demythologize" what Paul has to say. He proposes instead that we see Paul's language as "metaphorical," though he fails to explain sufficiently what he means by this (chapter 6). He concludes by calling African church leaders to emphasize the supremacy of Christ over every spiritual power, to contextualize Paul's message to the specific realities of African experience, and to think through the relationship between supernatural powers on the one hand and "the (psychological, cultural, economic, political . . .) structures of human existence" on the other. On this last point he is clearly influenced by Wink's description of life-destroying social structures as "demonic." For Wink, use of this term is deliberately metaphorical; he admits that as a modern man, he cannot believe in real evil spirits. Gatumu of course does believe in the reality of supernatural powers, but at times expresses himself in ways that sound much like Wink. At multiple points through his study the author interacts with the significant earlier contribution by Keith Ferdinando, *The Triumph of Christ in African Perspective*. While Gatumu's inquiry will not prove the last word on these matters, it is still worthy of serious attention in ongoing discussions regarding the contextualization of the gospel for the African church.

367. Gatwa, Tharcisse

The Churches and Ethnic Ideology in the Rwandan Crises 1900–1994

Oxford: Regnum, 2005. 300 pages, ISBN: 9781870345248.

The author, originally from Rwanda, served as Director of Clé Publications, Yaoundé, Cameroon. This is the fruit of his doctoral research carried out at Edinburgh. It is "an attempt to analyse the development of the racial ideology [in Rwanda], and in particular the role played by Christian churches." The early chapters consider Rwandan history and argue that the development of ethnic division was a result of "the racial ideology planted, watered and maintained by both the colonial powers and the church." Gatwa thus rejects the views of those, such as Pottier, who claim that ethnic division and tension predated colonisation. Gatwa goes on to argue that during the colonial period the church promoted racial ideology, and then in the post-independence period largely failed to challenge the resulting ethnic animosity and violence. This was due in great measure to the proximity of its leaders to the governing elite, as well as to a lack of serious theological reflection on issues of ethnicity and violence. Finally he looks at moves by some churches since 1994 towards repentance, and reflects on the need for justice, the healing of memories and renewed harmony. What is needed now, he says, is the creation of a "democratic and moral culture" so that society can overcome "the legacy of years of violence." Some chapters, but not all, end with conclusions summarising the content, while the final "Epilogue" is a little thin. Nor will everyone agree with Gatwa's perception of pre-colonial Rwandan history. Nevertheless, the work is an important contribution to our understanding of the genocide, and particularly of the disastrous failure of the church to engage with manifest injustice and evil.

368.   Gatwa, Tharcisse, and Georgine Tsala-Clémençon, editors

Dictionnaire des personnalités célèbres du monde négro-africain

Yaoundé: Éditions Clé, 2004. 273 pages, ISBN: 9782723501866.

This dictionary from the religious publisher Editions Clé has 406 entries on different personalities from the world of African art (including music and film), history and politics, literature, religion (40 pages), the sciences and sports. Entries in this African *Who's Who* vary between one paragraph to a few columns and are generally matter-of-fact. Whereas most entries are black Africans, a few are of European decent, including a few missionaries, and some African Americans are included. Attention seems to be well spread among the different regions of sub-Saharan Africa and between English-speaking and French-speaking countries. By far the most entries are from the twentieth century. One finds Augustine and Origen, Livingstone and Stanley, as well as Crowther, Tutu and Luwum (along with Bill Cosby, Michael Jackson, Chinua Achebe, and Zinedine Zidane!). The wide coverage of the book may help to gain more attention for the role of religious personalities in the past and present of Africa. It is a pity that the book looks less professional than it could, owing to the low quality of the illustrations. Because it brings together much detailed information that is otherwise often difficult to acquire, this could be a useful reference work for francophone theological libraries.

369.   Gaudeul, Jean-Marie

Called from Islam to Christ: Why Muslims Become Christians

Oxford: Monarch, 1999. 313 pages, ISBN: 9781854244277.

By some accounts it may seem only a matter of time until Africa becomes a Muslim continent altogether. This book gives a much needed balance and should come as a clarifying encouragement to Christian readers in Africa. Here are offered the stories of 164 converts from Islam to Christianity, and of these fully two-thirds are drawn from sub-Saharan Africa (in addition, 24 are from the Middle East, 21 from the Indian sub-continent, 2 from Southeast Asia and 9 from Europe). To those with a special commitment to ministry among Muslims, the names of those like Bilquis Sheikh, Esther Gulshan, Sultan Mohammed Khan, Bishop Dehqani-Tafti or Lamin Sanneh will be indicative that the author has not relied on hearsay sources, but has done considerable research in the relevant literature. What then draws Muslims to the Christian faith? Gaudeul carefully evaluates each case and groups the responses under five categories: (1) those who feel drawn by Jesus' personality; (2) those with a thirst for the truth; (3) those who desire to join the Christian community; (4) those who are seeking forgiveness; and (5) those who hunger for a personal experience with a loving God in prayer. The author is neither so naïve as to take every conversion as a genuine change of heart, nor does he adopt a triumphalistic attitude. As one who has worked for many years with the White Fathers in Tanzania, Gaudeul's comments about Islam are fair and well informed. While his Catholic stance occasionally comes through, at the same time he is self-critical enough to say that "forgiveness in Christ is a more Protestant emphasis," while the Catholic Church places more stress on works, so that, as he observes: "To outsiders the result can easily appear to be a religious system very like Islam." Certainly this is a resourceful book, and not least for its excellent bibliography of both English and French titles.

370.   Gbade, Niyi, editor

The Final Harvest: Mobilizing Indigenous Missions

Jos: Nigeria Evangelical Missions Association, 1988. 150 pages, ISBN: 9789782668028.

In 1985 the Nigeria Evangelical Missions Association (NEMA), together with the Missions Commission of the World Evangelical Alliance (WEA), held a consultation on missions in Jos, Nigeria. About 70 delegates attended, mostly from Nigeria but also from North America and some other countries. The concern of the conference was to encourage the development of indigenous mission outreach by African churches. About fourteen papers were presented, both by Nigerians and by expatriates. The papers reflect the sense of urgency affecting the participants in 1985 about cross-cultural witness. Particular attention was focused on the 75 or 80 still unreached ethnic groups in Nigeria at that date. The papers emphasized the need for proper strategies for mission, well-organized mission agencies, good cooperation between foreign missions and national organisations, and biblical ecclesiologies. A special concern was to motivate Nigerian churches and believers to assume the responsibility of evangelising their own country. Thus this collection of essays is of historical interest. Some decades later it is clear that Nigerian churches and mission agencies are pro-active in reaching their own country. Yet, there still remain about 70 or 80 unreached ethnic groups in Nigeria; and the challenge of evangelizing the Muslim populations is even greater. Indeed, it is ironic to wonder now precisely *where* the "Final Harvest" of the title will need to take place. As Europe and North America become ever more secular, it appears that African missions will need increasingly to include the West in their sense of calling.

371.   Gehman, Richard J.

African Traditional Religion in Biblical Perspective

Kijabe, Kenya: Kesho Publications, 1989. 310 pages, ISBN: 9789966860071.

This book is an evangelical exposition of African traditional religion (ATR), in which the author surveys ATR beliefs and practices, using the Akamba people of eastern Kenya as a principal example. The author was involved in theological education in Kenya for many years, during which time he developed a good understanding of ATR. He approaches ATR with the conviction that if we throw everything away in ATR, we lose something for Christian faith, and if we accept everything in ATR we do injustice to that faith. Therefore, his goal is to preserve what is true and good in ATR and to reject error, on the basis of biblical standards. He thus avoids common errors made in the study of ATR: by refusing to compromise the truth of Scripture; and (despite being a Westerner) by rejecting a judgement of ATR based on Western culture, and instead using Scripture alone. This makes his contribution exceptional, offering a fair and sympathetic yet critical analysis of ATR. This book has been in wide use at theological colleges throughout the continent.

372.   Gehman, Richard J.

African Traditional Religion in the Light of the Bible

Bukuru, Nigeria: Africa Christian Textbooks, 2001. 237 pages, ISBN: 9789781350665.

This is a fresh contribution based on Gehman's widely used 1989 textbook *African Traditional Religion in Biblical Perspective*. Although the outline and content of the two books are basically the same, the text has been completely rewritten, extensively abbreviated, and with simpler English used throughout. Gehman was formerly principal of Scott Theological College in Kenya, and subsequently editor of the *Africa Journal of Evangelical Theology*. He treats ATR in terms of basic issues: ATR studies, origins of ATR, human beings in ATR, mystical powers, the spirit world, the supreme being, and final thoughts relating to the Bible and ATR. A case study of the Akamba people of Kenya is also included, and a bibliography, but the appendices of the earlier book have been omitted. The new book is solidly bound with an attractive, colourful cover. This simplified, more accessible version of Gehman's ATR text is very welcome, and should prove widely useful for Christians throughout Africa. It is designed for easy use as a classroom text, with review and discussion questions at the end of each chapter, and at the same time helpfully addresses issues essential for responsible Christian reflection in Africa.

373.   Gehman, Richard J.

Doing African Christian Theology: An Evangelical Perspective

Nairobi: Evangel, 1987. 130 pages, ISBN: 9789966850133.

This book is intended as a survey of the origins of African Christian theology, an evaluation of the basic methodological approach of African Christian theology, and a proposal for the African evangelical church to develop its own African Christian theology. The author lists and explains nine helpful guidelines for this purpose. He centres these guidelines around the theme of contextualization. An extensive bibliography on African Christian theology is an added strength of the book. Gehman was on the faculty of Scott Theological College, Machakos, Kenya. While there he also worked closely with the "Theological Advisory Group" of the Africa Inland Church (AIC). In much of Africa this book is considered a core evangelical contribution to discussions on African Christian theology.

374.   Gehman, Richard J.

Learning to Lead: The Making of a Christian Leader in Africa

Wheaton, IL: Oasis International, 2008. 341 pages, ISBN: 9781594520907.

Gehman trained church leaders in Kenya for 36 years. At the end of that time he visited and interviewed 175 of his former students, in seven African countries, about their experience and advice concerning church leadership. Their insights mentioned throughout the book, as well as liberal use of African proverbs, give credibility and relevance to the whole. In the first part of the book Gehman reports the findings from his extensive interviews. Most taking part reported that they did not enjoy leadership because of: boring meetings, power struggles, administrative duties that take one away from involvement with grassroots people, criticism and infighting. The challenges they identified included: being too poorly paid, jealousy by other leaders, leadership struggles, gossip, false accusations, divisions, tribalism. Women leaders complained of discrimination. Pastors complained that rigid elders wouldn't accept innovation. Participants felt that preparation for their particular roles should certainly include attention to management and leadership skills. But character development was considered even more essential than skills training. About three-quarters of the book is then devoted to discussion of character development, as the area that causes most leaders to fail, with remaining sections dealing with management issues. In fact, the book might have been called "Discipleship for Christian Leaders." It deals with topics such as: the spiritual disciplines, having a forgiving spirit, perseverance, problems of pride, servant leadership, self-esteem, jealousy, anger, integrity, purity, and honesty. Discussion about management includes attention to: leaders as change agents, planning, decision making, organising, delegating, motivating, self-discipline, time management, shepherding, maintaining balance, and cultivating unity. This would be an excellent text for a course in Christian leadership and ministry in Africa. One can tell that the interactions of the book took place in East Africa, but the resulting material is likely to be relevant anywhere in Africa. The chapters are short enough to be used one per session even in less formal settings; the exegesis of biblical passages is competent and relevant; and each chapter ends with application questions.

375. Gehman, Richard J.

Who Are the Living Dead?

Nairobi: Evangel, 1999. 350 pages, ISBN: 9789966200884.

One should not be put off by the somewhat "popular" cover and illustrations of this book. This is a serious study by an experienced scholar on the religious and social issues relating to the traditional African approach to death and to the after-life. Gehman's work, from a conservative evangelical perspective, essentially concludes that the Christian should have nothing to do with the ancestors, and that whenever genuine spirits are involved they are demons or evil spirits rather than the departed. Gehman carefully presents biblical and cultural considerations, explains the approaches taken towards the ancestors by various camps (from Catholic to more liberal Protestant to evangelical), and shows why the position he takes is both biblical and in accord with at least one major segment of the contemporary African church. His concluding section presents basic discipleship-oriented teaching on theological issues germane to the topic (namely death and the afterlife, Christ's victory over death, the blessed hope of Christians, and the fate of the ancestors). For those who might want to use this as a textbook, each section begins with a summary and concludes with questions for review and reflection. The latter are among the special strengths of the book, as readers are challenged to review the evidence, compare what Gehman presents with their own contemporary context, and draw conclusions that are biblically informed and culturally sensitive. Perhaps the most significant disappointment with the text is that the review of other scholars' positions on the ancestral debate ends in 1974, with the comment that little more of real importance has been written since then. Whether that assessment is true or not, it does leave this part of the book looking limited and dated. Whatever the reader's position on the issues addressed, Gehman's text is an important one to have in hand when working through these issues. Even those who disagree with him will benefit from a text that carefully lays out a conservative evangelical position and its practical implications.

376. **Gelfand, Michael**

Godly Medicine in Zimbabwe: A History of Its Medical Missions

Gweru, Zimbabwe: Mambo Press, 1988. 302 pages, ISBN: 9780869224335.

Gelfand traces in detail the beginning and development of mission hospitals in Zimbabwe, against the backdrop of a nation that has undergone significant change over the past century: first the European settlement, then colonialization, the war of liberation, and finally independence in 1980. His account shows clearly the importance of the mission hospitals to the country, since they developed in places where there was little or no Christian witness and where the government of each era has found it difficult to persuade employees to live. The author also makes the suggestion that having some sort of ministry of healing as an integral part of the mission strategy helped the mission cause by providing treatment not only for the spirit but also for the body and mind. From the earliest days, missionaries in Zimbabwe showed an interest in the whole person and this brought great credibility to the Christian message they were seeking to proclaim. While this book is country specific, and many readers may not be interested in the content details, it is a book that substantively underlines the impact missions in Africa have had and can have when their approach is holistic.

377. **Gerloff, Roswith, and Klaus Hock, editors**

*Christianity in Africa and the African Diaspora: The Appropriation of a
    Scattered Heritage*

New York: Bloomsbury Professional, 2011. 370 pages, ISBN: 9781441123305.

We have here 26 papers deriving from an academic conference held outside Berlin in 2003. As can happen in such gatherings, many of the learned participants seemingly chose to address their own lines of interest rather than explore within a common theme, in this case an already fairly capacious one. The "scattered" in the subtitle may say as much about the collection itself as about the heritage under review. Thus one set of papers attends to historical aspects of Christian presence in Africa; a second addresses gender issues in African Christianity; a third concentrates on charismatic Christianity on the continent; while a final set considers manifestations of Christianity in the African diaspora. Most contributors are academics in university positions, roughly half based in Africa and half in Europe or North America. As usual, the quality of presentation differs widely. A number represent substantive inquiries, whereas others may appear to readers, sadly enough, as little more than summaries of preferences and opinions. A brief sampling may illustrate both the variety and the potentialities. Thus Deji Ayegboyin offers a thoughtful assessment of the impact of Western colonialism, positive as well as negative, on the shape of contemporary Nigerian Christianity. Jonathan Bonk provides an introduction to and rationale for the web-based *Dictionary of African Christian Biography*, first launched in 1995. An interesting if too abbreviated survey of the varieties of Anglican Christianity in Africa titled "The Empire Fights Back" is furnished by Kevin Ward. From Andreas Heuser comes a somewhat assertive reinterpretation of the sudden expansion of Christianity among indigenous populations of Natal in southern Africa in the earliest part of the twentieth century. Deidre Crumbley presents a unique report on Aladura gender practice in cyberspace, as seen from the African diaspora. Expanding on previous academic studies in the field, Matthews Ojo highlights how indigenous Pentecostal outreach has spread in coastal West Africa through use of trans-national networks. Philomena Mwaura contributes a survey on the rise of charismatic Christianity in Kenya, as does Kwabena Asamoah-Gyadu for Ghana. Several studies variously interpret the role and status of African Christian diaspora communities in Germany, the Netherlands, and Britain. Of special interest is the reflection offered by Aurélien Gamnpiot on challenges faced by Kimbanguists in adjusting to their immigrant settings within secular European society. While specialist researchers will want to be aware of potentially useful resources within this collection, all but the most advanced libraries can safely devote their acquisition budget elsewhere.

378. Geschiere, Peter

The Modernity of Witchcraft: Politics and the Occult in Postcolonial Africa

Charlottesville, VA: University of Virginia Press, 1997. 311 pages, ISBN: 9780813917030.

Geschiere has spent a number of years in anthropological research in Cameroon. Here he provides a useful study of the character and impact of witchcraft discourse in that country and beyond. His primary thesis, as indicated by the English title, is that beliefs about witchcraft in contemporary Africa should not be viewed simply as a holdover of ancient and mysterious African traditions. Rather we need to understand that they have developed and been transformed over time as a result of Africa's involvement in a globalising economic and political environment. New forms of witchcraft have emerged in response to new economic and political realities. Witchcraft discourse is therefore an aspect of Africa's experience of *modernity*, and it remains a dynamic resource that people often use as they seek to understand the rapidly changing world around them. This world is often confusing, full of uncertainty and danger. Life seems to reflect a struggle against invisible malicious forces, and witchcraft discourse seems to offer both a reasonable explanation for and a set of resources for navigating oneself through this dark world. This is particularly true of the mysteries of political life and economic fortunes. Why do some people grow politically powerful, and then sometimes suddenly fall from grace? How is it that others amass huge fortunes so quickly, leaving others in the miseries of their poverty? The mysterious workings of global political and economic systems can seem for many to be evidence of the reality of witches and their powers. In his analysis, Geschiere (thankfully) distances himself from an older functionalist anthropology, with its idea that all aspects of culture can be seen to contribute to the overall balance of society. He argues that witchcraft discourse is often highly destabilising and destructive of social relationships, fostering suspicion, harmful gossip, and violence against those suspected of witchcraft. This book proves very useful in providing a background perspective for discussions within the African Christian community concerning problems stemming from beliefs about witchcraft. This is certainly a live issue for many believers. Whereas one might have thought witchcraft discourse to be evidence merely of the persistence of old "traditional" systems of belief and practice, Geschiere helps us understand why it is that this framework for interpreting social reality continues to be so persuasive for so many, despite (Geschiere would say at least in part *because of*) the forces of "modernity" at work in Africa today.

Gestrin, Phyllis

see review 966

379.   **Getachew, Haile, Aasulv Lande, and Samuel Rubenson, editors**

The Missionary Factor in Ethiopia

Frankfurt: Peter Lang, 1998. 215 pages, ISBN: 9783631332597.

This book contains the thirteen papers given at a symposium held in 1996 at Lund University, Sweden, addressing the impact of European missions on Ethiopian society. The book is dedicated to Professor Sven Rubenson, missionary and Ethiopian studies scholar, who himself presents one of the papers in the collection: "The Missionary Factor in Ethiopia: Consequences of a Colonial Context." The fact that Orthodox, Catholic and Protestant gathered together for such a meeting is an ecumenical statement in itself. International scholars such as Donald Crummey and Richard Gray are among the contributors, as are Ethiopian and Scandinavian church historians. Three of the articles are written about the Catholic impact, while the articles on Protestant mission deal substantially with Scandinavian Lutheran issues – naturally enough, in light of the background of the contributors. Ethiopia, with its long history of Christianity, provides a unique context in which to study the effects of foreign mission. European missions originally intended to work within the ancient church for renewal and revitalisation. However, as one of the papers concludes, there was a paradigm shift at work that made the original evangelical goal in Ethiopia an "ecumenical failure." Forces of modernisation, the radical emphases of the more recent missions, and the conservatism of the Orthodox church were all too influential. Thus discontinuity occurred. The question of why "Christians came to convert Christians" and whether it was a "good cause" continues to be a point of debate, and parts of the discussion here on what constitutes proselytism may irritate some readers. This scholarly yet readable set of papers is a commendable contribution to discussion on Christian presence in Africa, especially in terms of African church history and missiology.

380.   **Getui, Mary N., and Hazel Ayanga, editors**

Conflicts in Africa: A Women Response

Nairobi: Faith Institute of Counselling, 2002. 176 pages, ISBN: 9789966988843.

The book grows out of the work of the Kenya chapter of the Circle of Concerned African Women Theologians. The editors as well as most of the contributors taught at various Kenyan universities, Getui at Kenyatta University and Ayanga at Moi University. The book aims at discussing two aspects of conflict; one is conflict from the perspective of women, the other is conflict as it affects women. The essays go into important aspects of how religion can live up to what it entails: recognition of human dignity and the call to live in fullness. They address various topics: conflict as a consequence of secularisation; some NT themes with regard to apparent conflicts for women; socio-economic and cultural conflicts in the Muslim family; the impact of war on African women; the effect of ethnic conflicts on development in Africa, with special emphasis on women; and conflicts facing African women during elections. The essays by Josephine Gitome and Grace Wamue would seem of special importance, as they challenge church and theology with regard to how a particularly vulnerable group is treated, namely single mothers. Gitome surveys the position of single mothers in traditional culture, and challenges the church to acknowledge their position. Wamue gives a strong but balanced testimony of how she personally experienced rejection and stigmatisation as a single mother, not only by traditional society, but even more by church and family. Her essay should be compulsory for all students of counselling and pastoral care. The same is the case with Pauline Otieno's essay on disabled women, a marginalized and often forgotten group in church and society. As a whole this essay collection shows that the Circle of Concerned

African Women Theologians is able to address issues of major relevance, not only for women (or men!), but even more for church and society, and not least for theological training institutions aiming to promote the dignity of all human beings.

381.   Getui, Mary N., and Peter M. Kanyadago, editors

From Violence to Peace: A Challenge for African Christianity

Nairobi: Acton Publishers, 1999. 186 pages, ISBN: 9789966888136.

book attempts to challenge Christians regarding a variety of forms of violence. One cannot avoid disappointment, however, with the minimal Christian content of the book. Most of the contributions are limited to sociological surveys of the problem areas to be confronted, and few writers have anything to say about specifically Christian solutions. The opening chapter by Kanyandago is almost totally secular, blaming most of Africa's problems on Christianity, which he claims is synonymous with imperialism and colonialism. He calls for the church to make public apology for "the wrong interpretation and application of the Gospel," and then he suggests payment of reparations. The quality of argument improves with Mugambi's paper on the Christian ideal of peace. His query on how a divided church can be an agent of peace on a divided continent certainly deserves the church's attention (pacifists should beware: he has no problem saying that the Bible supports armed conflict!). Several papers follow on the violence associated with, for example, refugees, children and traffic accidents, but few have any significant Christian content. The final chapter by Houle, one of the editors of the series, quotes Kanyandago favourably, but fails to apologize as called for. Overall, the orientation suggested by the subtitle is not represented by the contributions. The reader is also left with the impression that this book was put together hurriedly.

382.   Getui, Mary N., Tinyiko Maluleke, and Justin Ukpong, editors

Interpreting the New Testament in Africa

Nairobi: Acton Publishers, 2001. 311 pages, ISBN: 9789966888020.

This volume brings together essays from a conference on "African Hermeneutics and Theology" held in South Africa in 1999. The title of the book is in fact misleading; the contents reflect the broader concerns indicated by the title for the *conference*. The contributors represent all corners of sub-Saharan Africa, supplemented by a sprinkling of European and American scholars. The nineteen essays are organized under such categories as: Introductory Remarks, Scholarly and Popular Readings, Contextual Readings, Secular Challenges, and Postscripts. Topics addressed are quite diverse: examination of both academic and popular readings of the Bible (readings often contrasted with one another), a proposal for a biblical response to Africa's debt crisis, African women's hermeneutical concerns, an attempt to "map" biblical interpretation on the continent, a comparison of Paul's Areopagus speech with motifs from an Igbo folk narrative, and an overview of Africa in the NT. The quality of the essays varies as much as the topics. For example, in "Mapping African Biblical Interpretation," West helpfully compares and contrasts black African readings of the Bible with those of white South African scholars and white Western scholars, offering a cogent analysis of the context and resulting manner in which the Bible is read on the continent. Maluleke proposes a useful heuristic grid for categorising the ways in which different African Christian theologies relate to the Bible. In addition, Mijoga analyses the manner in which the Bible is used "pre-critically" in African sermons in Malawi, a timely subject indeed. On the other hand, when

Ntreh describes the role of Africa in the life of Jesus, the purpose of this essay, and the reason for his attempt to link this matter to the issue of methodology, never become clear. In addition, Dube pens a scathing response to a Westerner's criticism of one of her published articles; however such issues are to be adjudicated, the tone of the response leaves cause for concern. Yet scholars on the continent, or those from outside, can fruitfully consult this volume for a sampling of how the Bible is sometimes read in Africa.

383.   Getui, Mary N., Knut Holter, and Victor Zinkuratire, editors

Interpreting the Old Testament in Africa

Frankfurt: Peter Lang, 2001. 246 pages, ISBN: 9781453910108.

Here we are offered a collection of 23 papers presented at a conference on the same topic as the title of this book, held in Kenya in 1999. The contributors come from: Kenya, Nigeria, South Africa, Uganda, Tanzania, and Norway, and represent Catholic, ecumenical, evangelical, feminist, charismatic, AIC, and Coptic perspectives. The editors have grouped the material into five categories: Mapping the Context of OT Studies in Africa, Finding Africa in the OT, Using Africa to Interpret the OT, Using the OT to Interpret Africa, and Translating the OT in Africa. As one expects with a collection of writings by so many authors, the length and quality of the pieces vary considerably. Although the volume contains several essays of significant quality, others have the feel of a graduate student's research paper, or summaries of such papers. A representative sampling could include the following: Holter of Norway provides a valuable and succinct overview of the current state of OT scholarship on the continent. Mjola of the Bible Society of Tanzania draws attention to the cultural bias in OT studies brought to the table in social-scientific criticism, arguing that African scholars have much to offer to a discipline conducted almost exclusively under Western cultural auspices. Shisanya's comparison of feminist interests in the Hagar narratives of Genesis with similar issues in Abaluhya culture in Kenya succeeds in some places, but fails at other points where the biblical content is misread. Jonker of the University of Stellenbosch describes a "communal" approach for reading the Bible in Africa, whereby different reading "publics" (e.g. academy, church, society) contribute to the discussion of the text. And Adamo, referencing criticisms that his use of OT texts relating to Africa lacks critical reflection, responds not by arguing for the viability of his interpretations, but by vigorously asserting (not demonstrating) that his critics are wrong. Several papers refer to an "African hermeneutic." From a careful reading it seems apparent that this term is used in this collection to refer not to a particular method of interpretation (indeed all methods are usually approved), but rather to the idea that the Bible ought to be read with Africa and her needs in mind. That is an attitude, not a methodology.

384.   Getui, Mary N., editor

Theological Method and Aspects of Worship in African Christianity

Nairobi: Acton Publishers, 1998. 131 pages, ISBN: 9789966888969.

The contributors to this volume are all from either ecumenical or Roman Catholic backgrounds, all are or have been linked with university departments of religion, and all but one are from eastern Africa (the exception, from Ghana, has taught at a university in Kenya). The editor has been chair of the Department of Religious Studies at Kenyatta University in Kenya. The six articles in this collection are divided into two parts. In the first part the contributors offer critical theological reflection on making the gospel relevant in Africa's local situations and cultures. They call on African theologians to begin interacting introspectively among themselves, rather than just consuming theological packages and curricula originating from the West. And by employing "Reconstruction Theology" they call upon theologians to be more accountable to the ordinary people, e.g. by serving the disabled and upholding the dignity of women. Examples are drawn from various African communities. One of the writers is particularly pronounced in his view: "It is an absurdity in our contemporary post-modern world to believe that truth is the monopoly of a particular religious tradition or culture. Truth cannot be reached by one point of view trying to convince all others that it alone is correct." The articles in the second part of the volume focus on aspects of worship in African Christianity. Akurinu Churches of Kenya are cited which strive to "remove foreignness in Christian worship, by making their liturgy spiritually attuned to the cultural and religious heritage." Also the role of proverbs in society is considered, and it is noted that proverbs can serve as building blocks for the gospel of Christ in Africa. In another article the writer compares initiation rites with ecclesial sacraments, and says "the African Christian can rediscover God's presence" through such rites. But how this is to happen is not elaborated. Generally the writers are calling on Africa to become more self-critical and rely on its own resources before turning to others for loans and grants. Although some of the material will not invite agreement, the book can provoke one to think critically on the topics addressed. And it can familiarize the reader with how some scholars of ecumenical or Catholic orientation are attempting to do so within the context of eastern African.

385. Getui, Mary N., and Emmanuel A. Obeng, editors

Theology of Reconstruction: Exploratory Essays

Nairobi: Acton Publishers, 2003. 265 pages, ISBN: 9789966888013.

The Theology of Reconstruction is a relatively recent African theological movement that has arisen in the post-cold war era. Differing from previous African theological trends such as African cultural identity and African liberationist theology, this movement adapts Nehemiah's ministry as a metaphor for rebuilding African society towards a future of self-esteem, integrity and global contribution. The present volume is a collection of sixteen essays from African theologians who share this commitment to reconstruction. Each essay follows roughly the same pattern, describing a particular societal problem, diagnosing the source or sources of the problem, crafting a genuinely African theological response to the problem, and offering practical steps that the Church should take in order to be an agent of societal transformation. The issues addressed are: care for the natural environment, women's rights, child abuse, HIV/AIDS, the food crisis, poverty, political pluralism, and the recovery of African identity. The essays are intensely practical and prophetic, calling the Church to repent where it has ignored or contributed to systems of injustice. However, while all the authors argue that the gospel must bring about societal transformation, most of them hold that transformation is primarily a task for the Church to accomplish. In terms of the *theological* reflection suggested in the title, it might have been more helpful had the authors centred transformation not in human effort but in the salvation accomplished by the unique work of Christ's incarnation, life, death and resurrection. Also a few of the authors cast Western theology as predominantly dualistic, patriarchal and rationalistic. They offer alternative paradigms that are more akin to panentheism, appealing to medieval Christian mysticism and process theology. In so doing, these particular authors replace one Western theological system with another, and the replacement has significant shortcomings. For example, Gecaga suggests that we abandon the Augustinian creation-fall-redemption worldview, because it encourages the exploitation of the environment, and replace it with "Creation-centred Spirituality." Unfortunately this disregards the robust theological tradition beginning with Irenaeus that has viewed history as a story leading to the summation of all creation under Christ. The contribution from Obeng does in fact advocate just this worldview. This volume represents a significant fresh stream in recent African theological reflection, and addresses some of the most pressing issues facing African society today.

Getui, Mary N.

see also review 1150

386.   Gibbs, Sara, and Deborah Ajulu

The Role of the Church in Advocacy: Case Studies from Southern and Eastern Africa

Oxford: INTRAC, 1999. 102 pages, ISBN: 9781897748510.

The focus of this publication is on the sometimes-overlooked role that churches have played in Africa in advocating for human rights. Gibbs is a consultant on public health, who previously worked in the international section of the UK Department of Health. Ajulu is a development and research consultant in the UK, who has previously written on holistic development in biblical perspective. INTRAC is an organisation located in Oxford that provides training, consultancy and research services to international development and relief organisations. Though some argue that missions paved the way for colonialism in Africa, less is known of their advocacy for human rights, against social injustice and for alleviation of poverty. While there were missionaries of the past who spoke out against government policies that exploited African people, in present times it is African church leaders who have been the critical voice to governments that ignore injustice and to donor agencies that unduly influence policy. After detailing the methodology of the study, the authors describe the development of the churches in Africa (Catholic, Anglican, Presbyterian and Lutheran). Next explored are issues related to the advocacy work of European NGOs in Africa, and the views of European development workers on the role and capacity of churches in Africa to advocate effectively. Separate chapters are then devoted to each of three examples of church involvement: the National Council of Churches in Kenya advocating for human rights and democracy; churches in Malawi engaging in that country's transition to multi-party democracy; and Zambian churches' advocacy on economic issues to alleviate poverty and improve the basic standard of living. The authors contend that churches have often been overlooked in donor efforts to promote civil society. Also churches have tended to work in isolation from other groups. They assert that collaboration leads to more effective interventions and advocacy. While this paper is somewhat dated, it yet retains value for study of the historical trajectory of churches' involvement in advocacy work in Africa. It is also valuable both for understanding perceived strengths and weaknesses in the churches' ability to advocate, and for generating ideas and vision of what may be helpful and possible in future for church groups in Africa engaging in advocacy. An extensive listing of sources at the end is another helpful element.

387.   Gibellini, Rosino, editor

Paths of African Theology

Norwich: SCM, 1994. 176 pages, ISBN: 9780334025689.

This collection of writings on African theology includes such familiar names as Mbiti, Nyamiti, and Ela, joined by such lesser-known contributors as Lumbala and Maimela. The first part of the book focuses on the relationship between Christianity and African culture. This is the usual arena for most African Christian theology. The second part examines liberation theology in the African context – a shift, that is, away from cultural matters linked with the past towards political and social issues affecting the present and future. This includes a chapter by the Ghanaian theologian Mercy Oduyoye on feminist theology in an African perspective. Theological literature in Africa has traditionally been doubly divided: between French (and mainly Catholic), and English (and mainly Protestant). So this anthology with its eleven contributors coming from both anglophone and francophone Africa, Protestant and Catholic, is to be welcomed. At the time of writing the editor was literary director of Editrice Queriniana in Brescia, Italy. According to the book's introduction, the contributions he has brought together were prepared expressly for this volume.

388. Gibson, James L.

Overcoming Apartheid: Can Truth Reconcile a Divided Nation?

New York: Russell Sage, 2006. 488 pages, ISBN: 9780871543134.

Gibson uses survey data taken in 2000 and 2001 to examine the effects of the Truth and Reconciliation Commission (TRC) in South Africa. He argues that one of the clear benefits of the TRC for South Africa is that it established a common and moderated view of the apartheid era, specifically that the anti-apartheid struggle was just, though flawed, and that those defending apartheid did terrible things. This common perspective on the truth of the past, however, has not led to a common experience of reconciliation. Unquestionably the most interesting finding from the surveys was the degree of variation among groups in terms of how reconciled they felt. All of the groups exhibit some degree of reconciliation, but there is not the deep, cross-cutting result that one would hope to see. Blacks are significantly less reconciled than Whites, Asians or Coloureds. The percentages of groups that are at least somewhat reconciled are 33 percent of "Africans," 56 percent of Whites, 59 percent of Coloured and 48 percent of Asians. Least reconciled of all sub-groups were blacks who were frequent church attenders, although Gibson is unable, based on the survey data alone, to say why. Gibson argues that racial isolation is a significant cause of irreconciliation. Those reporting fewer contacts outside of work with people from other racial groups were less reconciled. Among blacks, the least reconciled group, four out of five reported that they have never had a meal with a white person. He argues that for blacks, truth has not led to reconciliation. A read through *Overcoming Apartheid* leads one to a healthy cautiousness as to whether establishing truth commissions can actually lead to reconciliation.

389. Gichinga, Emmy M.

Basic Counselling Skills

Nairobi: Gem Counselling, 2003. 110 pages, ISBN: 9789966981516.

The author is a clinical psychologist in Nairobi who both lectures in the field and has her own counselling practice. She is also a wife and mother. Gichinga describes this book as a manual on basic counselling skills. She has used the material presented in the book extensively for counselling training in the Kenyan context. The book does not attempt to re-invent the wheel; rather it distils familiar counselling material from a number of well-known Western authors and re-presents this in brief, usable compass. Those acquainted with Adams, Collins, Crabb, Egan, Rogers, and Wright will be on familiar territory. In the opening chapters the author describes counselling and introduces interpersonal communication and helping skills. Following chapters discuss the qualities of a helper (basically Rogerian), some specific counselling helps (such as those in Egan's *The Skilled Helper*), and some of the processes in counselling. An additional chapter offers some case studies which help earth the teaching in the African context. The last chapter has an appendix with diagrams from various authors which might be used for taking records, picturing the counselling situation and assessing counselling needs. While the book is a helpful outline that can be used in training programmes, it is (as the author warns) not meant as a stand-alone self-help manual. It does need to be used in a teaching context where it can be elaborated and discussed in a learning environment. One interesting, practical touch is the inclusion of a vocabulary builder of useful feeling words, which can help the counsellor get a better grip on the problem situation through labelling feelings more precisely beyond merely feeling bad or good.

Gichuhi, John

see review 106

390.   Gichure, Peter Ignatius

Contextual Theology: Its Meaning, Scope and Urgency

Nairobi: Catholic University of Eastern Africa, 2008. 183 pages, ISBN: 9789966909602.

Gichure is Senior Lecturer of Dogmatic Theology at the Catholic University of Eastern Africa in Kenya, and a member of the Ecumenical Symposium of East African Theologians. In this scholarly (490 footnotes) and well-written Roman Catholic explanation and recommendation of what Protestants call "contextualization," Gichure defines "contextual theology" as "the process of making the Word of God incarnate in a given community." For him, theology is faith seeking understanding, and all theology, including Roman Catholic theology, has always been contextual, even when that fact has not been recognized. Although he refers to Protestant writers (including Hesselgrave and Rommen's *Contextualization*), Gichure places contextual theology firmly within RC ecclesiastical structures and carefully carves out a place for it as an aspect of RC theology. He sets out the need for this theological approach; traces how RC theology has developed in response to the culture it was interacting with; examines how contextual theology has emerged out of the world's inescapable cultural diversity and resulting theological pluralism (pluralism being defined as multiple theological positions within the RC tradition); defines the scope and limits of contextual theology as it uses the best aspects of other theological approaches (such as inculturation, incarnation, liberation theology, political theology, feminist theology and ecological theology); and concludes that contextual theology, while connected to existing RC theology and answerable to various Roman teaching authorities, should happen at the local level where the bishop and the theologians in his diocese, and the voices of the laity, discuss the issues in their area. Doing contextual theology is not a choice; it is an imperative. Contextualization "is the desire to hear the universal message and make it relevant within a given context. It is the actualisation of the gospel of Christ in a given context." If there is an unexpected aspect to this distinguished contribution, it would be that the book deals with the theory of contextual theology without giving concrete examples of it in Africa. Nevertheless, one could wish for a book with equivalent scope and depth from an African evangelical Protestant perspective. This book should prove significant for anyone reflecting on theological contextualization in Africa.

391. **Gifford, Paul**

African Christianity: Its Public Role

Bloomington, IN: Indiana University Press, 1998. 384 pages, ISBN: 9780253212047.

This book will inform, disturb and challenge. Gifford sets out to examine Christianity as it has responded to and in turn influenced the political and social life of Africa. Four countries (Ghana, Uganda, Zambia and Cameroon) are selected as case studies because of the geographical spread they represent across the continent, and because they are roughly comparable in population and importance. The author is at pains to allow the distinctiveness of each to emerge, so that while there are some similarities, there are also marked contrasts. However, before embarking on the detailed case studies, Gifford paints the canvas with broad brushstrokes, helpfully setting the context not only of the colonial period but also of post-colonial mega-trends right up to the present. Africa is quickly changing, and the insights Gifford provides in conceptualising these changes are most helpful. Terms such as "neo-patrimonialism," "clientelism," and "externality" might need some mental adjustment, but they help the reader to understand the contemporary dynamics at work in Africa. A picture emerges of great diversity both between the different countries and also between Christian bodies and groupings within each country (ranging from Roman Catholic to Protestant main-line to Pentecostal and AICs) and their respective public roles (or lack of such). Certain recurring themes point to significant patterns in the continent: the pervasive growth of "Faith-Gospel" (prosperity and deliverance) teaching, the upsurge in charismatic influences less concerned with local contextualization and more with international or global Christianity, and "extraversion" (the importance of international links). Based on field research and wide reading, the book is written with often uncomfortable honesty, but it also provides insights into how the Christian Church in Africa has often impacted society for good, and still can. While the book would of course be of particular interest within the four case-study countries, the implications are transferable and deserve serious consideration by a much wider readership. The author teaches at the School of Oriental and African Studies in London.

392. **Gifford, Paul, editor**

The Christian Churches and the Democratisation of Africa

Leiden: BRILL, 1995. 301 pages, ISBN: 9789004103245.

This book contains a report on and the papers of a conference by the same name held in Leeds, England, in 1993. The contributors are either academics who study politics and religion in Africa, or African mainline church officials. They address questions on why the churches were not much involved in the struggle to escape colonialism, why liberation from colonialism did not result in democracy, and the roles the churches are playing now in the new efforts to achieve democracy and to sustain it. They note that mainline churches (like Anglican, Catholic, Methodist, Lutheran) have become vocal and critical of non-democratic governments, while evangelicals, Pentecostals, and independents tend to avoid politics or support any government that gives them recognition. However, some participants felt that with their emphasis on personal spiritual liberation the independent, evangelical and Pentecostal churches may be preparing people to be the kind of citizens that can sustain democracy. Case study papers from South Africa, Malawi, Zimbabwe, Mozambique, Congo (DRC), Cameroon, Rwanda, Uganda, Nigeria, Ghana, Liberia and Madagascar are included. Contributors included Desmond Tutu, Kwesi Dickson and Adrian Hastings. This book will prove a worthy resource for anyone studying Christianity and politics in Africa.

393.   Gifford, Paul

Christianity and Politics in Doe's Liberia

Cambridge: Cambridge University Press, 2002. 368 pages, ISBN: 9780521520102.

Gifford writes in broad sympathy with African theologies of liberation. No church or school of thought is spared from his close scrutiny in this important and fascinating book. With half a page of footnotes on many pages, the depth of Gifford's research is there for all to see. He did not restrict himself to written sources. For example, Gifford tells us that in his research he attended as many as five different services on a Sunday, beginning about 6 am and ending about 9 pm. Though limited to one small country, the writer intends his study to shed light on what is happening in other African countries. After a survey of Liberia's history and politics up to the beginning of the recent civil war, Gifford examines four branches of Christianity: (1) the mainline or historical or mission churches, (2) the evangelical churches, (3) the (pentecostal) faith gospel groups of health and wealth, and (4) the independent churches–whom he found to be increasingly influenced by the American Christianity described in (2) and (3). Gifford argues that the form of Christianity prevailing in Liberia promoted American interests, and also "served essentially to divert attention from the social situation and to leave Doe unchallenged in his mismanagement and corruption." Although Gifford is generally unsympathetic to evangelical Christianity, evangelicals will do well to ponder his points on spiritual warfare, biblical fatalism, the world, the human person, patience in affliction, and obedience to the authorities. Generally he finds that evangelicals (with a few praise-worthy exceptions), and even more so Pentecostals, failed to offer a prophetic critique of the structural evils (internal and external) under which Liberians were suffering. He also admits that the churches linked to the WCC were not meeting the existential spiritual needs of the people. With a regular supply of overseas funds, they no longer needed theology, "were losing their spiritual authority . . ., and were turning into NGOs." And increasingly their development projects served only the elite. As usual with liberation theology, the horizontal (relationship with neighbour) gets more emphasis than the vertical (relationship with God). But perhaps Gifford contributes needed motivation towards a more biblical balance. Christian theologians, church leaders, leaders of Christian NGOs, and Christian politicians in many parts of Africa could read this book with profit.

394.   Gifford, Paul

Christianity, Politics and Public Life in Kenya

London: Hurst, 2009. 256 pages, ISBN: 9781850659358.

In this study Gifford deals with themes common to his previous writings, where he accuses African society (in this case, Kenyan Christianity) with conspiracy to "clientelism and corruption," by perpetuating elements of neo-patrimonialism. This, Gifford believes, lies at the heart of many of Africa's problems, in which elite agents serve as gate-keepers by which the rest of the country accesses (or, more commonly, is restricted from) fundamental resources. Here he provides "rich description" for a variety of forms of Christianity in Kenya, based upon empirical analysis, but done somewhat loosely, and hardly theologically, with a range of categories, sometimes lumping Catholics together with mainline Protestant Christians, and other times placing non-Pentecostal churches together with distinctly Pentecostal varieties, based upon what he perceives to be common characteristics. The various chapters are illustrated by colourful examples garnered from a wide range of sources: sermons, theological material, various church-related paraphernalia, and newspaper editorials. Gifford pays attention to implicit and explicit messages arising from ecclesiastical agents, and furnishes astute analysis into the predominant themes coming out of the churches. Yet too often the text focuses upon leading ecclesiastical agents, such as popular preachers, with less attention given to the *washiriki* [literally, "fellowshippers," or laity]. Upon his own admission, Gifford's latest treatment of African Christianity is hardly exhaustive, and some will find it misses subtle yet important dynamics of local initiative and creativity in the face of global flows of meaning. Yet, his central diagnosis of faulting Kenyan Christianity for all too often becoming "an integral part of a dysfunctional system," rather than drawing upon the gospel of Jesus Christ to stand against societal abuse, can hardly be dismissed. Whether one agrees or not with Gifford's interpretations, it is difficult to find fault with his plea for African Christianity to contribute a greater prophetic role to the nature of social life and politics. Taking the findings of this book seriously could not help but enhance the quality of realistic Christian reflection in Africa.

395.   Gifford, Paul

Ghana's New Christianity: Pentecostalism in a Globalizing African Economy

Bloomington, IN: Indiana University Press, 2004. 216 pages, ISBN: 9780253217233.

Gifford has been Professor of African Christianity at the School of Oriental and African Studies (SOAS) in London. He has established a reputation as a chronicler of African Christianity with multiple publications in recent years. In telling the story of Ghana's "New Christianity," Gifford limited his investigation to six charismatic denominational leaders and their churches within the greater Accra area, which represents about one-fourth of the Ghanaian population of eighteen million. From 2000 to 2002 Gifford lectured at Accra's Central University College, and researched charismatic Ghanaian Christianity by attending Sunday services, crusades, conventions, conferences and prayer meetings, listening to their media, reading their published material (over half the book's bibliographical entries were published in Ghana), and pursuing conversations with Ghanaians from diverse walks of life. Gifford attempts to answer two questions: (1) What kind of Christianity is evolving in greater Accra? and (2) What are the socio-political as well as economic roles this new Christianity is playing in Ghanaian society to enable her to join the world market? His chapters explore a variety of topics such as: prosperity theology, a literal approach to biblical preaching, healing, charismatic Christianity with a strong emphasis on the prophetic, extolling a Christian work ethic, financial transparency, morality, deliverance theology, and spiritualizing politics. Gifford concludes his book by affirming that "the charismatic churches, or Pentecostals generally, meet the needs of Africans." He assumes that these kinds of churches will proliferate within Africa. But he is less than convinced that these churches foster much socio-political or economic reform. They seem instead to catapult their pastors into the role of the "big man" in Africa, rather than empowering the rank and file. This study is especially helpful in that it critically explores an emerging stream of African Christianity which does not fit former familiar categories such as the AIC, evangelical, ecumenical, Roman Catholic, or even traditional charismatic streams.

396. **Gifford, Paul**

The New Crusaders: Christianity and the New Right in Southern Africa

London: Pluto Press, 1991. 131 pages, ISBN: 9780745304564.

This is a revised edition of the author's 1988 publication titled: *The Religious Right in South Africa*. Gifford's focus in this study was decidedly on "the New Right," with any reference to the African context almost incidental. In discussing the "New Right" (a somewhat outdated term), Gifford begins with a summary of the movement in America before examining the movement's influence outside the US (primarily in Latin America and South Africa). In the third chapter the author surveys some conservative organisations within Zimbabwe. The author admits that the "New Right" is a "broad term which encompasses all sort of disparate groups." Just how "disparate" becomes evident when he groups Campus Crusade with Jimmy Swaggart Ministries and the Unification Church (Moonies). The unnuanced, almost naive presentation has more the feel of a harangue, an off-loading of personal frustrations, than of serious scholarship. The author's analysis of the "Two Types of Christianity" in chapter 4 is typically dualistic and lacks any shading or subtlety. While the growth of all types of conservative Christianity in Africa is an important area for scholarship, the endeavour is not furthered by such one-dimensional studies. Gifford has done somewhat better in later publications. This one is more revealing of Gifford than either of the "New Right" or of Africa, and can be safely bypassed.

397. **Gifford, Paul, editor**

New Dimensions in African Christianity

Nairobi: All Africa Conference of Churches, 1992. 213 pages, ISBN: 9789966987907.

This collection of essays represents an attempt to explore the recent growth of African independent (or initiated, or indigenous) churches (AICs) and Pentecostal/charismatic churches across the continent since the 1980s. Individual authors, although mostly Western, are experts in their specialized fields of religious studies, and cover a well-representative (though not comprehensive) cross-section of African studies. Among countries treated are Nigeria, Liberia, Kenya, Congo (DRC), Malawi, and Mozambique. One common concern that arises within many of the chapters is how Christianity enables congregants to engage in political and/or socio-economic affairs. Therefore, the focus of this book is less theological and more sociological – yet with the acknowledgement that, in Africa, Christian churches utilize theological resources to position themselves within the contemporary world. Some of the essayists place emphasis upon imaginative responses of African churches to contemporary realities, while others are more derisive toward Western agents for negatively impacting African Christianity and/or societal affairs (such as Reinhard Bonnke in Kenya). This book constitutes a valuable resource for individuals or institutions interested in post-1980 research dealing with AICs, and particularly those wanting to explore individual case studies of Pentecostalism in Africa. The various chapters express many currents affecting broader concerns of African Christianity, but future research should pay closer attention to elements of continuity and discontinuity with global patterns of Christianity, as the authors sometimes give the impression that these ecclesiastical communities are sourced either from within Africa or from within the West (rather than a combination of the two).

Gilbert, Lela

see review 674

Gilbert, Marvin

see review 840

Gilbreath, Edward

see review 521

398. Gilchrist, John

Facing the Muslim Challenge: A Handbook of Christian-Muslim Apologetics

Benoni, South Africa: MERCSA, 1999. 171 pages.

The South African attorney John Gilchrist has provided a useful apologetic handbook for sensitive and informed Christian witness in Muslim contexts. In six concise chapters Gilchrist takes the reader through the four major areas of objection in Muslim-Christian encounter: the Integrity of the Bible, the Trinity, the Sonship of Jesus Christ, and the Crucifixion and Atonement. Then he adds two extras: the Muslim claim that Muhammad was prophesied in the Bible, and Muslim claims about the Gospel of Barnabas. Each section opens with a true-to-life presentation of the specific Muslim objection (the author has visited Muslim homes in his country for close to 30 years), and the objection is then answered with precision and insight from both biblical and Islamic sources. This handbook not only provides valuable guidance for Christian witness among Muslims, but also offers challenge and discovery for anyone seeking to apply Christian doctrine to flesh-and-blood representatives of other religious persuasions. Because Gilchrist's concern goes well beyond creating another library textbook on Islam, he has especially invested himself in a comprehensive introductory section that brings out the importance of right attitudes and approaches in interacting with Muslims. Those directly involved in Christian witness among Muslims might wish that Gilchrist had been able to include other common objections such as: "Was Christianity invented by Paul?," "Science, the Qur'an and the Bible," "Why are there so many different churches?," and "Muslims follow biblical forms of worship more than today's Christians."

399. Gilchrist, John

Sharing the Gospel with Muslims: A Handbook for Bible-Based Muslim Evangelism

Cape Town: Life Challenge Africa, 2003. 160 pages, ISBN: 9781594521065.

In this companion volume to his apologetics handbook, *Facing the Muslim Challenge*, Gilchrist seeks to enable the reader to take the initiative in presenting biblical concepts to his or her Islamic friend. Gilchrist writes from long experience in personal outreach to Muslims in South Africa, and out of the conviction that the most effective way of presenting Muslims with the gospel is to base one's witness on Scripture. Starting from Adam and Eve, and progressing with Noah and Abraham and other OT individuals, the author demonstrates how both Quranic and biblical portrayals of these prominent people of God can be used to show the uniqueness of the Messiah. This material is followed by chapters using the NT to address the uniqueness of Jesus, his

Sonship, Messiahship, and Second Coming, as well as the love of God. Here the author underlines Christ's "methodology of evangelism," namely speaking directly into the context of each person by use of common ground, while at the same time displacing the grip of religious heritage. Gilchrist does not intend to slight other forms of witness to Muslims, such as friendship evangelism, relational evangelism, contextualization, or approaches through felt-needs. But he maintains that it is the Word of God that penetrates the human heart, and he therefore offers guidance on how to share Scripture with Muslims with clarity and understanding.

Gillespie, Carol

see review 442

400.   Gilliland, Dean S.

African Religion Meets Islam: Religious Change in Northern Nigeria

Lanham, MD: University Press of America, 1986. 241 pages, ISBN: 9780819156358.

Gilliland was a United Methodist missionary in Nigeria for over twenty years, and served there as principal of the Theological College of Northern Nigeria (TCNN). Later he moved to Fuller School of World Missions. The book asks why some ethnic groups respond favourably to Islam, and to Christianity, while others remain resistant. More fundamentally it explains why in the encounter with Islam and Christianity many Nigerians have never really abandoned their pre-Islamic or pre-Christian worldview. The author believes that to a large extent the propensity of a people group to respond to one or other of these two religions depends on the level of congruity between the tribal self-identity and the belief systems of the new religion. He thus begins by analysing African tribal religions and how they have responded to Islam. He then deals with differing aspects of the interaction between Islam and the tribal religions. Next he examines more recent religious changes linked to the massive growth of Christianity in central Nigeria since 1960, as well as the religious politics of Nigeria in the 1960s and 1970s. The final chapter highlights how some groups have been able to divorce their religious beliefs from their political allegiances. Much of the material in the book seems to have been completed in the 1970s, although the final chapters include materials updated to the time of publication in the 1980s. The book is a very useful study of the processes by which various ethnic groups have adjusted to religious change, and have yet in many ways remained quite constant in their worldview. It thus offers help in understanding contexts where the fundamental challenge for the Christian faith is how to bring about real change in people's worldviews.

401.   Gilmore, Alec, editor

An International Directory of Theological Colleges 1997

Norwich: SCM, 1996. 380 pages, ISBN: 9780334026648.

For Africa this international directory proved to be something of a disappointment. It lists only 388 theological schools on the continent, offering full details for a mere 163 of these, and only names and addresses for the rest. One must sympathize with the considerable difficulties in securing data on theological education in Africa. But for comparison, the *ACTEA Directory of Theological Schools in Africa* already in 1985 had documented at least 742 schools on the continent, and provided details on 524 of these. This 1997 Directory does usefully include some new or updated data not available from the 1985 *ACTEA Directory*. But even so, one is left with a measure of uncertainty to find the Institut Supérieur Théologique de Bunia listed both in Congo (DRC) and in Kenya (and there as an *Anglican* school), or to find Namibia Evangelical Theological Seminary positioned in Windhoek, *South Africa*! At least for Africa, this Directory needed a good deal more work before publication. And, indeed, the same must apparently apply for other parts of the world. The reference of its promotional blurb to "comprehensive" coverage translates into a claimed documentation for "over 2000 institutions"; but in 1994 Bong Ro of Korea had already published a *World Directory of Theological Institutions* (included, in fact, in this Directory's bibliography), which documents some 4000 institutions worldwide. So, despite the title and the promotional materials, perhaps this is one of those titles that should mostly interest only the occasional research specialist.

402.   Gitari, David, editor

Anglican Liturgical Inculturation in Africa: The Kanamai Statement with Introduction, Papers from Kanamai and a First Response

Piscataway, NJ: Gorgias Press, 2010. 56 pages, ISBN: 9781607243809.

When the first wave of Anglican missionaries came to Africa, they brought not only their Bibles but also their copies of the *Book of Common Prayer*, that standard of and resource for worship compiled and edited by the sixteenth-century Reformer Thomas Cranmer. The first generation of African Anglicans accepted this book as part of the package for those becoming part of the worldwide Anglican Communion. However that same book, in its *Thirty-Nine Articles of the Christian Religion*, calls for the liturgy to be led "in a tongue . . . understood of the people" (Article 24). Although this was of course a polemic against the Latin Mass, at another level to have worship in a culture somewhat removed from the people seems also to be (as the Article says) "repugnant." The "Kanamai Statement" presented in this booklet, together with other papers associated with that document, explore the issue of the inculturation of Anglican liturgy in African contexts, taking as their text Resolution 22 of the 1988 Lambeth Conference of African bishops which affirms that the Church everywhere must "work at expressing the unchanging gospel of Christ in words, actions, names, customs, liturgies, which communicate relevantly in each contemporary society." The booklet contains a brief introduction by the editor, at that time the Archbishop of the Anglican Church in Kenya; an article presenting principles of liturgical inculturation by one of the foremost of the Communion's liturgists, Colin Buchanan; an essay by Elisha Mbonigaba of Uganda which explores specifically African issues of liturgical indigenisation; the Statement itself; and a response by Solomon Amusan of Nigeria. The use of African music, art and architecture is affirmed. It is clear to the writers that on some issues the gospel must judge African traditional practices. Although some initiation rites are judged to be neutral, the practice of female circumcision should be addressed by teaching "with a view to end the practice." Interesting suggestions concerning funerals include suggested prayers at the funeral of one who has committed suicide, and prayers for a person who has died without marrying. Both of these circumstances can prove to be very difficult pastoral situations for many African clergy. Some issues are given surprisingly little attention in this booklet: the relationship between eucharist and sacrifice, the place of the ancestors in Christian prayer and worship, and the use of African music in liturgical musical settings as well as hymnody. No doubt these issues can be explored in greater depth at future meetings of African Anglican liturgists.

403.   **Gitari, David**

In Season and Out of Season: Sermons to a Nation

Oxford: Regnum, 1996. 155 pages, ISBN: 9781870345118.

This is a book with a passion. It brings to light Bishop David Gitari's love and concern for his home country, Kenya. The book is a collection of sermons which the Anglican bishop preached from 1975 to 1994. Each sermon has a text and a context. Indeed Gitari acknowledges that he is endeavouring to bring God's Word to bear on the contemporary world, in this case the country of Kenya. He skilfully exegetes the passage, gleaning the major principles addressed. He then applies those principles to the particular context within the country at the time. A helpful part of the book is the description of the setting of each sermon – the event(s) which prompted Gitari to preach the sermon – and also at times the impact of the sermon on various people or decisions made at political or ecclesiastical level. The book shows that Gitari is not afraid to address the evils of society from a Christian perspective. He runs a risk in doing so but believes a prophetic voice needs to be heard. This book should motivate others to speak out from God's Word against injustice and wrong-doing in Africa's public arenas.

404.   **Gitari, David**

Let the Bishop Speak

Nairobi: Uzima Press, 1988. 64 pages.

David Gitari, Archbishop of the Anglican Church of Kenya, was an evangelical who believed in expository preaching. He also believed that if the Word of God is rightly proclaimed it will address the social and political realities affecting the lives of ordinary people, as well as the religious dimensions of their existence. This brief book contains four sermons, all preached in the month of June 1987, while Kenya was in the midst of a political crisis over constitutional changes relating to the electoral process. Gitari sought through his Sunday preaching to bring scriptural insight into the political debate. What resulted was a turbulent attack from politicians who fiercely condemned Gitari and his views. The row was only ended when the Kenyan President stated that Gitari was free to air his opinions; the wording of this intervention supplies the title of the book: "Let the Bishop Speak." The sermons and the press reports of the political reactions are all contained in this volume. A provocative read, and an excellent modern example of African Christian proclamation amidst political upheaval!

405.   **Gitari, David**

Responsible Church Leadership

Nairobi: Acton Publishers, 2005. 221 pages, ISBN: 9789966888648.

This book is a collection of materials stemming from the ministry of Gitari, former Archbishop of the Anglican Church of Kenya, in which he addresses issues of church leadership in the African (or Kenyan) context. Gitari first rehearses several leadership models from the OT and NT, including Ezekiel, Nehemiah and Jesus himself. According to Gitari, servanthood is the essence of biblical leadership. "In the world the great man is the one who controls others. But in the Christian assessment, service alone is the badge of greatness." Next Gitari applies the servant-leader model to the reality of the Christian church in Africa. Using the Anglican Church in Kenya as a case study, he emphasizes the role of the church leader (the bishop in his case) as a person who serves by teaching the truth of the gospel to those placed under his care. It is only when the bishop trains both the clergy and the laity that the church becomes a strong witness of the saving power of Christ within the social and political life of the world. Using his experience in evangelism among nomadic tribes in northern Kenya, Gitari challenges church leaders to find new cultural ways, not contradictory to the Scriptures, to indigenise the gospel and make it more relevant to the African masses. The book closes on the thorny issue of the relationship between the church and the state in Africa. Against both those who try to silence the church from within and those who threaten it from outside, Gitari argues for a more balanced approach. According to him, the church should not side with those in power, nor should it oppose them needlessly. Instead, the church should follow a "constructive and creative participation." Gitari contends that the church participates constructively and creatively in the political life of the country when it becomes a setting for education and formation for basic human rights, development, justice and equality. Although the book is at times a difficult read because of its composite nature, its content is rich in biblical teaching and practical wisdom on how to lead God's people in Africa effectively.

406. Gitari, David

Troubled but Not Destroyed: The Autobiography of Archbishop David Gitari, Retired Archbishop of the Anglican Church of Kenya

McLean, VA: Isaac Publishing, 2014. 361 pages, ISBN: 9780991614547.

This autobiography of Gitari appeared in print one year after his death in 2013. In common with many of the mainline leaders of the African churches after colonialism, Gitari was a leader in both "ecumenical" and "evangelical" circles, as well as in his own denomination. As bishop and then as archbishop of the Anglican Church in Kenya, Gitari was able to carry out his ministry giving appropriate attention to issues of social justice and the political life of his nation, while at the same time stressing the centrality of scriptural authority, the importance of a personal relationship with Christ, and (especially important for global Anglicanism in the postmodern world) biblically-based morality. Each one of these theological commitments, combined with his fearlessness in opposing what he saw to be injustice, untruth or immorality, landed Gitari in an adversarial position with other leaders, both political and ecclesiastical. Details of Gitari's career have appeared in print before (e.g. J. K. Karigia, *Eight Great Years 1994–2002*), but this volume fills in many details not previously known, many facts emerging in public now because Gitari kept detailed journals throughout his working life. The sheer number of details makes this volume a hard read – the narrative is not always smooth. In addition, no one ever accused Gitari of being self-effacing, and the reader may get the feeling at times that the author thought rather highly of himself. On the other hand, Gitari was certainly a man of great vision and courage, an important leader in the development of the post-colonial African church. This book will be a useful accession for any theological library attempting a solid collection on African Christianity, and should be a required addition for Anglican theological libraries globally.

407.   Gitari, David, and G. Patrick Benson, editors

Witnessing to the Living God in Contemporary Africa

Nairobi: Uzima Press, 1986.

This important collection makes available the papers of the first meeting of the Africa Theological Fraternity, held in Kerugoya, Kenya, in 1985. Gitari was at the time the Anglican Bishop of Mt. Kenya East, and later Archbishop of the Anglican Church of Kenya; Benson was at the time Gitari's assistant, and subsequently a parish priest in England. Here they have brought together an attractive volume reflecting on the meaning of God in the African context from an evangelical Christian perspective. Although the volume title refers to the "Living" God, most of the papers contain the phrase "God the Father." These two images, God as a caring Father and God as living and active, are set against the enormous problems of Africa. The issue of human suffering rings through almost every essay. Of special note is the contribution of Cyril Okorocha (later an Anglican bishop in Nigeria) who warns that if Christians are committed to praying the Lord's Prayer, which asks for daily bread, they must also be willing to work to ensure that everyone has access to food. The essay by Wambutda argues that God must prove Himself stronger than other gods in Africa, just as the gods of Canaan were defeated by Yahweh. Bediako's trinitarian reflections and Gitari's story of seeking justice within Kenyan society are also noteworthy.

408.   Gitau, Samson K.

The Environmental Crisis: A Challenge for African Christianity

Nairobi: Acton Publishers, 2000. 187 pages, ISBN: 9789996688861.

This book started life as a doctoral thesis by the author in 1997. Going beyond the accumulation of scientific and statistical data that continually describes and updates the way we are destroying our planet, Gitau attempts "to develop an African Christian theological basis for conservation in Kenya." The author investigates how Africans traditionally understand nature, humanity and deity; what the Bible has to say about creation; and what the churches are doing with respect to environmental conservation. All this is with a view to developing a theological model which will inform an appropriate relationship to our environment. Gitau argues that the religious dimension cannot be ignored in the battle to preserve our God-given planet; the job cannot be left to scientists, governments and NGO's alone; the church needs to recognize that her mission includes responsible stewardship over the creation, which we are to care for and use rather than exploit and destroy. Although the author acknowledges the scientific contribution to environmental conservation, he bemoans the lack of robust theologising on the part of the church. He challenges African Christians not only to hear again the biblical insights for guiding our relationship with nature, but also to learn something from our African traditional heritage which has helpful things to say regarding the "nature-human" relationship. The contribution of African wisdom is developed by way of comparing the concepts of the Maasai and the Kikuyu with biblical teaching. Gitau then proposes an African theological basis for environmental conservation before presenting his conclusions and recommendations. The book is a useful contribution to a spirituality that is thoughtful, integrated and holistic rather than dichotomistic, truncated and syncretistic. It is a helpful book for thinking ethically and practically about living in the environment in which God has placed us as caretakers. Since the topic of environmental responsibility is thus far only rarely addressed in African Christian discourse, this book is commended for all those seeking to think and live in a Christian manner with respect to Africa's environmental challenges.

409. Gittins, Anthony J., editor

Life and Death Matters: The Practice of Inculturation in Africa

Nettetal, Germany: Steyler Verlag, 2000. 175 pages, ISBN: 9783805004435.

This book is based on a consultation held in Tamale, Ghana, in 1997, where some twenty Roman Catholic missionary anthropologists, mainly European and American, came together to discuss various experiences with inculturation. The editor is professor of missiology at the Catholic Theological Union in Chicago. Ten papers from the consultation have been reworked and equipped with discussion questions for this volume, which is intended to serve as a textbook for church workers involved in inculturation. The first chapter, written by the editor, discusses theoretical aspects of inculturation, offering definitions of central theological and anthropological terminology. The Roman Catholic background and context is reflected in the discussion; still, most theologians and missiologists would probably find that its concept of the possibilities and limitations of inculturation is balanced and relevant: "the harvest of inculturation is ripe when the Gospel has become relevant to, yet not compromised by a culture." The theory chapter discusses the basic issues of inculturation, and the remaining nine chapters are case-studies that attempt to identify and respond to these issues in contemporary African life (e.g. Western vs. African family models in ecclesiology, and traditional religious rituals vs. Christian rituals). The strength of the book lies in its combination of (some) theory and (various) case studies, and as a whole it demonstrates central concepts of contemporary Roman Catholic inculturation hermeneutics.

410. GMI

The World of Islam: Resources for Understanding

Colorado Springs: GMI, 2000.

Global Mapping has added to their catalogue yet another massive library reference tool encompassed on a single CD. A cooperative venture among the Institute for the Study of Islam and Christianity, Fuller Seminary School of World Mission, the Lausanne Committee for World Evangelization, and Global Mapping International, this CD resource incorporates 45 books and articles, seven sets of full course materials, an 850-page survey of Islam by the Institute for the Study of Islam and Christianity (available only on this CD), maps, photographs, and an annotated bibliography. The compilers note certain guidelines that have governed their selection of materials to be included: avoiding more offensive and confrontational materials, concentrating on English resources, indicating some Muslim sources, avoiding duplication of materials already on CD, being broadly evangelical, representing options rather than positions, favouring practical materials that are also academically reliable, and surfacing some of the diversity in Islam. As would be expected given the topic, this remarkable fresh resource has extensive inclusions relating directly to Africa. A search on the word "Africa" yields 945 hits. Among the materials that such a search would link to are: Dretke's *A Christian Approach to Muslims: Reflections from West Africa*; Malek's *Islam: Challenge and Mandate*; Nehls' *Christians Answer Muslims* and *Christians Ask Muslims*; and an ISIC research paper on "Community Development in Islam and Christianity, with special reference to Africa." In addition, the CD's centrepiece "Survey of Islam" incorporates specific discussion of Islam in the African context; Addison's *The Christian Approach to the Moslem* has historical discussion of Africa and lists many African-related resources in the bibliography; Braswell's *Islam: Its Prophet, Peoples, Politics and Power* has a section on Africa; as does Goldsmith's *Islam and Christian Witness*. Of special interest is the formal report of the consultation "Ministry in Islamic Contexts" that was sponsored by the Lausanne Committee for World Evangelization and the Association of Evangelicals in Africa. The richness of resources available relating to Africa can be seen not least in the number of hits that would result from searching per country: Egypt (986), Sudan (184), South Africa (175), Morocco (161), Nigeria (128), Algeria (109), Libya (75) Kenya (69) Tanzania (18), and Chad (11). All of the CD content is searchable. The annotated bibliography includes nine sections, with links directly to all of the books on the CD. This is a must have resource for those ministering in Islamic contexts in Africa. Global Mapping International and its partners in this project are to be heartily commended.

411. Gofwen, Rotgaf

Religious Conflicts in Northern Nigeria and Nation Building: The Throes of Two Decades 1980–2000

Kaduna: Human Rights Monitor, 2004. 209 pages, ISBN: 9789783607453.

Nigeria has been plagued by numerous religious conflicts in recent decades. For the period from 1980 to 2000 the author is able to list seventeen riots, many of them serious, resulting in considerable human and material loss. The question addressed by the author, a lecturer at the University of Jos, is why these happen. Significant blame is put on the British colonial power which, in creating Nigeria, included very diverse ethnic groups in one country. In this respect "the Nigerian state is an artificial creation," which means that the process of nation-building is very difficult. The loyalty of most Nigerians is first of all to their ethnic group and only secondarily to their nation. But this does not in itself explain the violent religious conflicts in this country. Quoting many respected sources, the author suggests that there are economic, political, religious, ethnic and other reasons for these riots, but among these causes religious intolerance must be seen as the major source of such conflict. Three case studies are presented: the Kafanchan riots of 1987, the Kano conflict of 1991, and the Kaduna riot of 2000. Although the conclusion is not flatly stated, in all three cases it was the Muslims who started the riots. Muslim intolerance is one of the main reasons for religious riots in Nigeria. This is related to the Muslim worldview that all of society should be governed by the sharia law of the Qur'an. Such a comprehensive worldview is hard to fit with the democratic idea of a secular state. Coupled with this is the fact that many of the riots, such as in Kafanchan and Kaduna, occurred in the "Middle Belt" of Nigeria. This is an area where many smaller ethnic groups were historically ruled by the Hausa-Fulani Muslims of northern Nigeria. For these ethnic groups, Christianity has been a means of liberation from the Hausa-Fulani overlords, who in turn did not appreciate the loss of power. The book concludes with a plea for love and tolerance; but there is also recognition that the problems are very deeply rooted and that a solution is not easily found.

412. Golka, Friedemann W.

The Leopard's Spots: Biblical and African Wisdom in Proverbs

London: T & T Clark, 2004. 160 pages, ISBN: 9780567082886.

Golka is professor of OT at the University of Oldenburg in Germany. Throughout the 1980s he published a series of articles on OT proverbs, and these articles constitute the major bulk of the present book. Golka criticizes the traditional claim that OT proverbs originated as literary works in official circles (schools, court) during the monarchy, under the influence of international (Egyptian Mesopotamian) wisdom literature. By comparing OT proverbs to proverbial materials of traditional Africa, Golka concludes that OT proverbs derive rather from a tribal society, namely that of Israel in the period of the Judges. This enables him to refute three assumptions which have dominated traditional interpretation of OT proverbs; (i) that there were schools in ancient Israel, (ii) that a professional class of wise men taught in these schools, and (iii) that their teaching consisted of the moral standards of the civil service. Golka's book is of interest for two reasons. First, its general emphasis on OT proverbs as indigenous Israelite wisdom deserves attention, although most OT scholars probably will find that Golka is too negative towards the theories of wisdom schools and international influence. Secondly, its use of African proverbial material provides some methodological models that would be of interest for others working with the OT in the context of Africa.

Goma, Lameck K. H.

see review 46

413.   Gordon, April A., and Donald L. Gordon, editors

Understanding Contemporary Africa

Boulder, CO: Lynne Rienner Publishers, 2001. 477 pages, ISBN: 9781555878504.

Intended for introductory courses on Africa in North American undergraduate programmes, *Understanding Contemporary Africa* consists of useful survey articles written for the book by university lecturers on Africa. The topics covered include: geography, history, politics since independence, economics and international relations, population studies (with a new section on HIV/AIDS), women and development, family and kinship, literature, and the special case of South Africa. While most of the writers are North American, at least two are African (for the articles on the environment and on religion). The publishers are to be commended for routinely updating this resource with new editions. Each chapter is accompanied by two to three pages of bibliography, listing both popular and expert literature. Generally these lists have been thoroughly revised with each edition. One wonders, however, how accessible these materials would be for most readers in Africa. The photographs help increase the book's appeal; many were supplied by the World Bank, which elsewhere in the book gets a lot of criticism. The article on religion in Africa gives equal space to the three religions that one would expect, and follows the usual descriptions coming from university departments of religion. The only really new point A. Moyo makes about Christianity is that new charismatic evangelical (pentecostal) churches are "growing in popularity in many countries." The map of Islam in Africa is wrong in its details, e.g. about Nigeria. Through many of the articles the question recurs whether there are signs of improvement in the things that trouble Africa. The editors try to be optimistic, but indicators do not encourage any easy optimism while the rest of the world protects its advantages.

Gordon, Donald L.

see review 413

414. **Gordon, Murray**

Slavery in the Arab World

New York: New Amsterdam Books, 1990. 275 pages, ISBN: 9781561310234.

Gordon worked for the United Nations for twenty years, and is a specialist in the socioeconomic problems of Africa and the Middle East. In this book he describes the Arab trade in and use of slaves. He estimates that eleven million black Africans were enslaved by the Arabs, about the same number that went into the New World, but over a much longer period of time. The Arabs also enslaved people of European and Asian descent. Although slaves and their descendants were eventually absorbed into Muslim society, the capture, transport and socialisation of slaves, especially of black Africans, resulted in horrendous suffering. Gordon treats the attitudes of Islam to slavery, the occupations and status of slaves in the Islamic world, especially that of concubines, and the acquisition and castration of boys for eunuchs. There are sections on the history of the Islamic slave trade, especially along the trans-Saharan route and down the Nile. Gordon argues that only European colonisation of Africa put an end to this trade. Interestingly, he suggests that the British colonialist Lord Lugard supported the Islamisation of traditionalist tribes in northern Nigeria in hopes that once they were Muslims, it would be illegal under Islamic law for such groups to be enslaved. Although the last Muslim states made slavery illegal in the 1960s and 1970s, Gordon is concerned about the continued enslavement of black Africans by Arabs in Mauritania and Sudan.

Gornik, Mark R.

see review 178

415. **Gourevitch, Philip**

We Wish to Inform You That Tomorrow We Will Be Killed with Our Families: Stories from Rwanda

London: Pan Macmillan, 2000. 368 pages, ISBN: 9780330371216.

Gourevitch, a staff writer with *The New Yorker*, gives a sober and disturbing account of the 1994 genocide in Rwanda against the Tutsi minority and Hutu moderates. The title of the book is taken from a statement written by a Tutsi pastor to his Hutu pastor overseer. Reading the book will give rise to horror, surprise, anger, grief, and even shame. The author travelled extensively throughout Rwanda and in neighbouring countries both immediately after the genocide and in succeeding years, interviewing survivors, attackers, prisoners, and individuals from school children up to senior government figures. His narrative method is to tell the story of these encounters. In the process Gourevitch addresses how historical, theological, and colonial mentalities have affected, and continue to affect, the Rwandan psyche. He tackles such issues as mob mentality, the human bent to blame others and justify self, the international community's shameless refusal to be involved as it focused on its own interests, ethical issues related both to the mandates and to the actions of humanitarian aid groups working with refugees, the atmosphere and conditions in refugee camps, the surprising response of churches and clergy (e.g. Hutu pastors who were complicit in the death of parishioners and Tutsi fellow clergy), and the catastrophic and inevitable results of such a tragedy – all of which contradict the post-Holocaust claim, Never Again! Rwanda is left with the task of dealing with the colossal psychological repercussions, the massive task of justice and retribution, and the rebuilding of its economy and social structures. Theological colleges in Africa should review their curricula to ensure that the implications of this aspect of the continent's modern history are not being bypassed or ignored.

Govinden, Betty

see review 920

416. Gray, Richard

Black Christians and White Missionaries

New Haven: Yale University Press, 1990. 134 pages, ISBN: 9780300102130.

This slim volume sets out to examine past and present African appropriations of Christianity. The earlier chapters include attention to papal attitudes towards the Atlantic slave trade, as well as to the impact of the early (seventeenth century) penetration by Catholic Capuchin missionaries into Lower Congo, and show how political, geographic and economic factors can all hinder or facilitate the effectiveness of the missionary endeavour. Later chapters survey the colonial and post-colonial period in Africa. Gray here is willing to take to task some of the currently popular reductionist and "Christianity = imperialism" theories. He argues, for instance, that in areas relating to sickness and healing, evil and exorcism, death and eschatology, Christianity's penetration and influence have been deep and radical. A final chapter discusses concepts of evil in sub-Saharan Africa, and includes a discussion about syncretism and pluralism. Evangelicals will probably not agree with some of Gray's views here, but the debate is a live one, and evangelicals should be able to contribute to it.

Gray, Richard

see also review 445

417. Graybill, Lyn S.

Truth and Reconciliation in South Africa: Miracle or Model?

Boulder, CO: Lynne Rienner Publishers, 2002. 231 pages, ISBN: 9781588260574.

Graybill intends to provide not only the facts about South Africa's Truth and Reconciliation Commission (TRC) but also insight into the broader South African context in which it operated. The 26-page bibliography bears witness to the author's attempts to allow a multitude of voices to speak. The reader is introduced to the main characters of the TRC through numerous quotations from books, newspaper articles, academic analyses, and TRC transcripts. After a brief historical introduction, Graybill begins the body of her book with two chapters devoted to Nelson Mandela and Desmond Tutu respectively. These are followed by analyses of forgiveness, amnesty, the role of story, women's testimony, the question of white guilt, and the hearings that explored the role of the media and churches in apartheid. While the book doesn't quite provide all the facts and the entire context for the TRC (multiple volumes this length would be needed for that), it is a user-friendly introduction to the Commission and the important issues surrounding it. Graybill is presently a lecturer at the School of International Affairs of Georgia Institute of Technology. Her theological background is frequently glimpsed and, given the centrality of Christian ideas in the TRC process, she provides a welcome balance to many of the non-theological analyses of the TRC. It is thus unfortunate that Graybill's own voice and analysis are often hidden by numerous quotations which sometimes obscure her argument. Nevertheless, this volume will be an ideal introductory guide to anyone exploring issues of forgiveness and reconciliation in post-apartheid South African history.

418.   Grebe, Karl, and Wilfred Fon

African Traditional Religion and Christian Counseling

Wheaton, IL: Oasis International, 2007. 64 pages, ISBN: 9781594520754.

This useful booklet seeks to suggest an approach to counselling people in an African context with respect to particular spiritual problems. It starts by describing the typical worldview that goes with so-called African traditional religion (ATR). Though this picture is based on the Cameroon setting, the description of the African view of reality would be recognized in most parts of Africa. The authors then examine the conflict that African Christians often face in living in their world, where they often find themselves forbidden to respond according to the familiar formulae provided by ATR, by their African worldview or by communal pressure. Sometimes these prohibitions seem like Western cultural impositions, in which the suppression of traditional African solutions is not matched with an offer of viable biblical ones. The authors are concerned that in such situations Christianity in Africa should not resort merely to "backing off," either from fear of being a foreign influence, or else from fear of encouraging a careless embracing of ATR features which merely look like Christianity. They suggest that, although ATR might have elements of truth, there are real differences that are not removed simply by adding a little more Christian light to ATR. For example, though ATR acknowledges God, He is not sovereign or reliable. One cannot be sure what will be pleasing to Him nor be sure of victory by trusting Him. The implications from this examination of the interface between Christianity and ATR are then applied specifically to counselling those who are troubled by spiritual oppression. Thus the "counselling" in the title of the booklet is not general but specific: the authors intend to provide some suggestions for helping those troubled by demonic forces. This is of special value, since consideration of this dimension of counselling is rare, and is usually missing from counselling strategies developed in the West. Provided that one does not become mechanical or superstitious in the application of such, the suggestions offered are practical and helpful. While anyone looking for a general text on counselling in the African context will need to look elsewhere, this booklet does provide those who are going to counsel in the African context with a useful description of ATR in brief compass, and helpful consideration of struggles that need to be overcome if Christianity is to be truly rooted in African soil with neither syncretism nor a superficial adoption of an ill-fitting Western dress.

419.   Grenstedt, Steffan

Ambaricho and Shonkolla: From Local Independent Church to the Evangelical Mainstream in Ethiopia: The Origins of the Mekane Yesus Church in Kambata Hadiya

Uppsala: Uppsala University, 2000. 316 pages, ISBN: 9789185424603.

Submitted to the Faculty of Theology of Uppsala University in 2000, this PhD thesis evaluates the origin of the Kambata Synod of the Ethiopian Evangelical Church Mekane Yesus in southern Ethiopia. The result is a fascinating, moving and sometimes heartbreaking story of religious change in what has become a part of the evangelical heartland of Ethiopia. The evangelical movement in Kambata-Hadiya had its origins in the pioneer work of missionaries from the Sudan Interior Mission (SIM) who entered the area in 1929. The names Ambaricho and Shonkolla in the title refer to two prominent mountains of the region. The Kambata Evangelical Church (KEC) which emerged from the SIM work grew rapidly during the Italian occupation (1936–1941) when the missionaries were absent, but it then underwent a split in 1951 that proved resistant to numerous efforts on several fronts to bring reconciliation. The chief reason for the split was that from around 1949 SIM leadership insisted that the KEC enforce a ban on the consumption of all alcohol, including the mildly alcoholic cultural drink, *borde*. Prior to this, the drinking of *borde* was such an integral part of the culture that it was even served at meetings of church elders. From Grenstedt's point of view, the ban represented a departure from SIM's strong adherence to indigenous principles which, among other things, were reflected in the adaptation of a culturally traditional elder-led system of governance, locally supported church workers, and the formation of congregations marked by freedom from central control. The split would eventually contribute to the disintegration of Ethiopian evangelical solidarity which had kept denominationalism at bay until the 1950s. The breakaway churches in Kambata Hadiya eventually found a more limited solidarity with the Ethiopian Evangelical Church Mekane Yesus (EECMY), which formed in 1962. EECMY established a "home mission" to Kambata Hadiya. It also decided to integrate the work of the foreign missions into the EECMY, based on indigenous principles whereby the institutions and projects of the foreign missions had full Ethiopian ownership from the very beginning. This framework then allowed the Finnish Mission Society to begin work in Kambata Hadiya as part of the EECMY home mission. While this arrangement created an opportunity to assist an indigenous "independent Church," it also led this Church to become "financially much more dependent" than it ever had been and to abandon much of its indigenous character. The integration of foreign missions within the EECMY formed a striking contrast to the "parallel structure" adopted by SIM in which the mission and the Church remained "two separate self-governing entities." Ironically, both forms of relationship between local churches and foreign missions were based on indigenous principles. Both forms continue to be a significant feature of current Church-mission relations in Ethiopia and Africa. Grenstedt's work is thus an important case study for those wrestling with appropriate ways to structure fruitful partnerships between Church and mission.

Grignon, François

see review 787

420.   Groves, Jonathan D.

Reading Romans at Ground Level: A Contemporary Rural African Perspective

Carlisle, UK: LGL, 2015. 126 pages, ISBN: 9781783689200.

This slim but significant volume is by the Mission Director of the UK-based Kerusso Trust, which supports education in rural Malawi. With years of experience in Bible teaching in Malawi, Groves explores the use of Paul's *Letter to the Romans* by preachers in selected rural areas of that country. Groves' field research used questionnaires among some 200 delegates at two interdenominational conferences for church leaders in Malawi. Each respondent was invited to give their personal profile and comment on the major issues or challenges in their ministry-context, and then indicate their use of Romans in their sermons, what texts or passages were used and what major points were made. The results were correlated and assessed (the questionnaires and the responses are helpfully detailed in tables and charts), and conclusions were drawn. Not surprisingly, the data reveals preferred clusters of texts (for evangelism and discipleship) on the one hand, and on the other hand parts of Romans that are "fallow." The discussion of the data is enriched by consideration of the three horizons important for the hermeneutical process. Two of the horizons have long been recognised: the ancient context within which the text was first communicated, and the contemporary socio-cultural context within which that text "speaks" today. Groves acknowledges the importance of these two horizons, but recognises the significance ("interference") of a third "hermeneutical layer," that of the understanding of the text by the preacher/teacher acquired from a training often received in an academic context far removed from the context in which the eventual teaching/preaching is done. Drawing on Oakes' research on the first century context of Pompeii not far from Rome, Groves suggests that some aspects of present-day life in rural Malawi share much with the first century Roman context, and that this fact could reduce the "gap" between the two horizons and allow Romans to speak powerfully and relevantly to the contemporary issues of twenty-first century Malawi. Groves' previous roles in scientific research and information technology have undoubtedly helped in producing a well-researched piece of work, and the data is presented succinctly and clearly. All who are concerned for preaching/teaching which is, at one and the same time, faithful to the biblical text and incisive for the contemporary context, will benefit from this book. It could also form the basis for a very productive conference for African church leaders where the results of this research could be explored and discussed with a view to enriching and deepening the preaching that goes out from thousands of pulpits week by week.

421. **Guest, Emma**

Children of AIDS: Africa's Orphan Crisis

London: Pluto Press, 2003. 200 pages, ISBN: 9780745320755.

Guest, former communications manager for the British charity The Samaritans, has lived in South Africa and travelled extensively in Africa. In this book she examines how and why the globe's poorest continent has been so badly affected, and explores how families, charities and governments are responding to the next wave of the crisis – millions of orphans. Her contention is that AIDS orphans have received far less attention from governments, scientists and funding sources than they deserve. A clear and concise introduction on why the infection is so widely prevalent in Africa is followed by a collection of true stories revealing the experiences of orphans, street children, grandparents, aunts, foster parents, charity and social workers and foreign donors across South Africa, Uganda and Zambia. In conclusion the book questions what will happen to the minds of a generation that grows up alone, poor and shamed by the stigma of the disease that killed their parents. The question as to what can be done also receives attention. The result is a moving, hard hitting, and realistic review of what is happening to AIDS orphans in parts of Africa, and the challenges to be faced. At the same time it provides a message of hope. As a welcome complement to formal presentations in lecture rooms and policy boardrooms, the book should be read by all who are concerned with the children of Africa.

422. Guest, Robert

The Shackled Continent: Africa's Past, Present and Future

London: Pan Macmillan, 2005. 304 pages, ISBN: 9780330419727.

The author is the Africa editor of *The Economist*, and draws on his experiences around Africa during the course of his work. His basic question is: "Why is Africa so poor?" and he acknowledges therefore leaving out a lot of good things about Africa. But one good thing that amazed him is the way extended family members are stretching themselves and their resources to care for AIDS orphans. He also notes Africa's exceptional resources of land, water, minerals and people. He predicts that Africa will eventually achieve a peaceful and prosperous life for its people following the same path that Europe and other wealthy regions have followed: "by making things and providing services that other people want to buy" under a system of good governance that provides a basis for security and trust. This took centuries to develop in Europe, and Asia and Latin America are now at various stages of developing this. So his main focus is on the present barriers to this development in Africa. These include dictatorial leaders who enrich themselves at the people's expense; lack of title deeds to land, thus removing it and the structures built on it as usable assets for developing businesses; AIDS; tribalism; trade barriers; and lack of infrastructure. Woven through all the above is the debilitating effects of rampant corruption at all levels. He does not discuss spiritual issues apart from a few references to witchcraft, so he sees economic development as Africa's only real hope. Being a journalist, the author writes in an interesting and readable style, and includes many instructive and easily understood statistics, comparisons and case studies to illustrate his points. Since he worked from South Africa for a few years, his examples tend to reflect issues in southern Africa more than other parts, but the whole of sub-Saharan Africa is included in his coverage. He acknowledges that his is an outsider's perspective; yet a major strength of this book is that an outsider can sometimes see things that are so familiar as to be unnoticed by insiders. African Christians will view their situations with more insight than he possesses, especially on the effects of spiritual issues on poverty alleviation. But his perspective provides an insightful and well-informed challenge to all who are concerned with overcoming poverty in Africa.

423. Guillebaud, Meg

After the Locusts: How Costly Forgiveness Is Restoring Rwanda's Stolen Years

Oxford: Monarch, 2006. 207 pages, ISBN: 9780825460913.

How does a society recover from genocide? Guillebaud's book discusses the role of forgiveness and reconciliation in bringing healing to genocide survivors and perpetrators through the work of Christian parachurch organisations in Rwanda. The book recounts individual stories of genocide survivors and how they were able to forgive those who killed family members, neighbours and friends. The focus of the book is on the work of Rhiannon Lloyd and African Enterprise. The development of the AE system for bringing traumatized people to the point where they can forgive and sometimes reconcile is detailed. Guillebaud devotes chapters to the AE techniques of "standing in the gap" or asking forgiveness on behalf of others, and the "cross workshop" wherein people are assisted in identifying their suffering with that of Jesus and finding new hope. The book is grounded in biblical truths about costly forgiveness, shame, sorrow and the power of the Crucifixion. Guillebaud is a CMS mission partner who has worked in Rwanda. She does well in this book by tackling hard issues such as rape, residual anger and legal consequences in a practical and Christian way. This is a book that will be of great interest to Christians in Rwanda, or to those anywhere working to lead individuals from trauma to healing and forgiveness.

424.   Guillebaud, Meg

Rwanda: The Land God Forgot? Revival, Genocide and Hope

Oxford: Monarch, 2002. 368 pages, ISBN: 9781854245762.

Although there seems to be no end to the books written on Rwanda since the genocide of 1994, any book that is recommended by George Carey (former archbishop of Canterbury) and Richard Bewes (former rector of All Souls, London) merits some attention. The immediate question, of course, is how this book is any different than the others. The answer lies in the fact that the author, who has served in church leadership training in Rwanda, is a third-generation missionary to Rwanda, so she writes from an inside perspective (her grandfather translated the NT into Kinyarwanda). At the outset she insists that her objective is not so much to evaluate the history and politics of the country as to explore (through her family's experience of 70 years in Rwanda) the East African Revival and the aftermath of the 1994 tragedy in light of how these events affected people she knew. At some points the reader wishes that she had written two books, one biographical and the other analytical, because it is so difficult to combine the two. On the other hand, this book is partly therapy for the author, who lost so many friends in the events of 1994, so for her the two issues are inseparable. Thus the history of both the East African Revival and the genocide are told more through personal stories than by a listing of events. Alongside the Guillebaud family history there is helpful analysis of the problems leading up to the events of 1994, later followed by "Afterthoughts." Although this final chapter is not too well organized, the author attempts to come to terms with many of the common questions posed about how genocide could happen in a so-called Christian country. Some of her observations are: nominal Christians were often guilty, but few genuine Christians took part in the killing, often defending those from other ethnic groups; people did not accept that there should be consequences for sin if they repented; some sought the power of the Holy Spirit for personal gain, not holiness; the gospel that was preached was too often limited to conversion without sufficient emphasis on discipleship; there was an inadequate view of sin; and demonic influence was accepted under the guise of keeping African traditional values. It is helpful to have a book written not only by an insider but by someone who brings theological insights to one of the thorniest issues for African Christianity in modern times.

425.   Guma, Mongezi, and Leslie Milton, editors

An African Challenge to the Church in the Twenty-First Century

Johannesburg: South African Council of Churches, 1997. 146 pages, ISBN: 9780620219242.

Once the euphoria of the 1994 democratic elections in South Africa evaporated, the church in that land struggled to articulate its role. This collection of twelve essays by South African scholars was an attempt to point the way forward. The essays are divided into four sections: African Culture; Land; Morality and Values; and Reconciliation and Koinonia. Together they focus on critical issues facing South Africa as it entered the twenty-first century. The result is a mixed bag of very good and rather disappointing papers. Highlights are the essays by Bonganjolo Goba ("Choosing Who We Are: A Christian Perspective on the Moral Crisis Confronting the South African Society"); Takatso Mofokeng ("Land Is Our Mother: A Black Theology of Land"); and Wolfram Kistner ("Koinonia: The Church Creating Community"). Goba's essay seems particularly appropriate at this juncture in South African history, concerned as it is with the oft neglected theme of moral renewal and the need for a new heart and a new spirit (Ezekiel 36:26, 27). Mofokeng's contribution is no mere academic exercise on the vexed issue of land but is, rather, a passionate biblical reflection on the question of land in the light of his own family's loss of its traditional lands during the course of the twentieth century. Kistner's thoughts on the decisiveness of koinonia for the witness of the church in the new South Africa is an important recovery of a neglected NT theme. As to the remaining essays, suffice it to say that South African theology is showing some signs of fatigue.

426.   Gunda, Masiiwa Ragies, editor

From Text to Practice: The Role of the Bible in Daily Living of African People Today

Bamberg: University of Bamberg Press, 2011. 200 pages, ISBN: 9783863090043.

The book derives from a conference on 'the Bible and Practice' held in 2009 in Bamberg, Germany. After the conference the organizers decided to collect in a special volume those papers that especially focused on Africa. As part of the University of Bamberg's very laudable and newly launched online book project 'Bible in Africa Studies', the conference volume is available to anyone with internet access. The book starts with an introduction by the editor, who teaches OT at the University of Zimbabwe. He emphasizes that reading the Bible should lead to certain practices in the lives of its readers. The obvious questions are then which aspects of the Bible are to be selected and what kinds of practices are to be encouraged. The contributions that follow attempt to respond to this through case studies and reflection. For example, Lovemore Togarasei (Botswana) presents research on the use of the Bible in relation to HIV/AIDS in some Pentecostal churches in Botswana, demonstrating the key role of the Bible with regard to HIV prevention, but also with regard to healing, care and support. Solomon Ademiluka (Nigeria) suggests that the perspective of eighth century BC prophets in Israel, reacting against injustice and economic stratification in ancient Israel, is very relevant in Nigeria's oil-producing Niger delta today. Francis Machingura (Zimbabwe) makes a contextual analysis of the role of Acts 2 within the Apostolic Faith Mission in Zimbabwe, arguing that their strong focus on glossolalia as the sign of the Holy Spirit exaggerates the meaning of Acts 2. Briefly introducing the main areas of research of the biblical scholar Musa Dube of Botswana, Stephanie Feder (Germany) highlights Dube's characteristic focus on relevance and on the potential of contributions from ordinary readers. Obvious Vengeyi (Zimbabwe) presents a solid, interesting comparison between the Bible and the *gona*, an animal horn (or the like) used as a kind of fetish among the Shona for healing purposes. He suggests that some Pentecostal churches in Zimbabwe have developed notions of the Bible that to some extent are influenced by traditional concepts of the *gona*. Masiiwa Gunda (the book's editor) points out the key role of the Bible, and not least the OT, as a kind of manual for daily life in certain AICs in Zimbabwe. The book indeed keeps its promise: some glimpses of the role of the Bible in the daily life of African people today, as seen through the academia's critical lenses.

Guy, Michael R.

see review 748

427.   Gwamna, Je'adayibe Dogara

Perspectives in African Theology

Bukuru, Nigeria: Africa Christian Textbooks, 2008. 261 pages, ISBN: 9789781352119.

Gwamna is a lecturer in NT at the University of Jos in Nigeria. This book contains thirteen essays on mostly NT themes in relation to the Nigerian context. The essays are evangelical and contextual. The book's title, however, could be confusing. What is intended is African Christian theology, and more particularly biblical African theology. Only one lengthy essay addresses the theoretical side of African inculturation. Gwamna is cautious towards contextualization, pointing out past excesses and reminding us that "culture . . . should not be superimposed in an attempt at doing theology in Africa." He insists that "the Bible in its original setting remains the main source of any biblical interpretation anywhere." Yet "if African theologians are able to interpret scriptures that make sense to the African, the Bible will remain a major source of life in Africa." Most of the essays take practical NT themes and relate them to the Nigerian or African contexts. A survey of the poor in the Bible urges practical compassion for the needy. An essay on tongues warns against attitudes of superiority among the charismatics. On feminism Gwamna tries to steer a middle course between the two sides, arguing for a proper role for women in the church. An article on popular prosperity theology warns against the use of magic slogans in prayers, and makes a plea for a return to true biblical theology. A chapter on the kingdom of God and one on John the Baptist are reminders of the Bible's teachings on righteousness and corruption. Other chapters address issues relating to wealth, marriage and sex, obedience to the government and the like. This volume is refreshing in that it repeatedly brings one back to Scripture as the final authority in cultural issues.

428.   Gyekye, Kwame

Tradition and Modernity: Philosophical Reflections on the African Experience

New York: Oxford University Press, 1997. 360 pages, ISBN: 9780195112269.

A Ghanaian-born and Harvard-educated philosopher, Gyekye takes on weighty issues related to cultural interpretation in African societies as they navigate into modernity through their own means or resources. A simple review of content reveals the relevance of such a study for contemporary contexts, as the author provides an overview of philosophy, deals with interconnected themes of person and community, delves into the convoluted terrain of ethnicity, identity, and nationhood, proceeds into chapters that engage political issues, such as traditional political values, socialism, quandaries of political power, and corruption, before concluding with an examination into the multifaceted relationship between tradition and modernity. Not only does Gyekye provide nuance where others are prone to romanticize traditional elements or censure all things modernity-related; he also demonstrates how the pathway to modernity involves active mechanisms of reinterpreting values, ideas, concepts, and institutions, whether from the African past, or from Western contexts. The heart of the matter for Gyekye relates not only to cultural transmission (which remains foregrounded in his discussion), but also how Africans think about their own traditional resources, or how Africa and the West are viewed as separated by an ideological divide. In the end, the author calls upon Africans to critically evaluate all ideas or values, whether sourced from its past or emanating from other cultural contexts. This study provides a deeply engaging, intellectual examination into important topics found within African societies. Christian theological discourse in the African context needs to take more energetic account of the issues advanced by Gyekye. Those committed to disciplined theological reflection should expect to engage with the resources it provides for exploring the convoluted terrain that is societal change in modern Africa.

Authors
H–K

429. **Haar, Gerrie ter**

African Christians in Europe

Nairobi: Acton Publishers, 2001. 308 pages, ISBN: 9789966888266.

Europe is now home to tens of thousands of migrants from tropical Africa. This book focuses on this phenomenon: the causes of this population movement, the main countries of origin, the principal countries of settlement, the self-perception, the struggle for survival – and also the considerable contribution that African Christians have made in Europe. The book is a companion volume to the more wide-ranging one edited by ter Haar on *Religious Communities in the Diaspora*. After linking her present study to that broader canvass, she focuses in on one particular context, that of the Amsterdam suburb of Bijlmer where many Africans have settled. The True Teachings of Christ's Temple community provides a sort of case study. She argues that in practical as well as psychological terms, such Christian communities help create the necessary conditions for their members to acquire a sustainable position within Western society. Their central concerns of Bible, self-help, mutual assistance, worship and healing are examined. Ter Haar's research reveals little in the way of a "longing to return" to the various countries of origin, and there is evidence that the new Christian communities act almost like surrogate extended families for Africans far from their original contexts. A chapter on "Fortress Europe" discusses the increasingly stringent immigration laws in Europe, and the sometimes extreme lengths Africans will go to in order to enter the "Fortress." The reception given to the immigrants varies from country to country and from church to church, but often is less than warm and welcoming. In contrast, the contribution made by such Christians to the life of the church in Europe is often marked by vitality and enthusiasm. This is a fascinating book, on a rarely treated topic, sometimes disturbing but also often heart-warming. The book helpfully underscores African Christianity's "extended" presence and reach in today's world.

430. **Haar, Gerrie ter**

Halfway to Paradise: African Christians in Europe

Cardiff: Cardiff Academic Press, 1998. 226 pages, ISBN: 9781899025039.

Between the 1960s and the 1980s the Bijlmer district of southeast Amsterdam, originally designed to be a modern utopia, was transformed into a postmodern dystopia. The result was that low-cost social housing eventually became home to thousands of immigrants whose religious beliefs often stood in stark contrast to an increasingly secular Dutch society. Over a period of four years, from 1992 to 1996, the author (a professor at the International Institute for Social Studies in Rotterdam) visited social, cultural and religious organisations in the Bijlmer in order to study the way in which African Christians adapted to this context. Although this is essentially a sociological study, a salutary mark of all ter Haar's scholarship is her insistence on taking seriously the religious beliefs of those being studied, refusing to explain these beliefs as mere symbols or social constructions. A description of the development of, and distinction between, mainline/traditional, evangelical, pentecostal and charismatic groups serves to place the churches being studied in a broad theological context. The study focuses primarily on the True Teachings of Christ's Temple, the oldest AIC church in the Netherlands. Ter Haar reinterprets the AIC acronym to refer to an "African international church." This title is a pointer to the book's central thesis, that while these churches have their origins in African Christianity (itself transformed by African cultures and traditional religions), they take their place within the much larger context of global Christianity. The European influences on these churches are primarily those brought about by the legal and social struggles faced by African immigrants and refugees. Both the European and African sides of this migration phenomenon are explored as part of this study. Ter Haar notes, amongst other things, that a number of African Christians, casting their migration in the mould of reverse missions, see themselves as a chosen people with a God-given task of evangelising Europe. It is unclear, however, to what extent these represent cases of prophecy-after-the-migration-event. Ter Haar concludes by noting how the secular Dutch government has, in limited ways, begun to respond positively to religious communities in immigrant populations. Although dated (Islam has certainly changed the way secular European governments view immigrants with strong religious feelings), this informative study should still be read by those interested in the history and prospects of African Christianity in Europe.

431. Haar, Gerrie ter

How God Became African: African Spirituality and Western Secular Thought

Philadelphia: Penn Press, 2009. 136 pages, ISBN: 9780812241730.

This book developed from the Cunningham Lectures which the author, Professor of Religion and Development at the Institute of Social Studies (The Hague), delivered in 2006 in the Faculty of Divinity at the University of Edinburgh. Ter Haar's thesis is that the centrality of spirituality in African thought and life, now expressed primarily through Christianity and Islam, should not be ignored by the West. The subtitle of the book accurately captures the tension between the African and Western worldviews that ter Haar seeks to describe. Beginning with the important role that religious ideas play in Africa, she shows how this tension has often led to an inadequate understanding and misinterpretation of Africa by the West. This fundamental difference in worldview, in turn, continues to complicate the engagement between Africa and the West. Many of the topics addressed by ter Haar elsewhere are touched upon in this book: development in Africa; the relationship between religion and human rights; the role of spirituality in African politics; and Christianity in the African Diaspora. The reification of both "Africa" and "the West" is perhaps the book's major weakness. When ter Haar speaks of "the West," she seems to be referring only to secular Europe, and does so in order to draw her contrasts more starkly. However, much of what is true of African Christian spirituality is also true of Western Christian spirituality. So, too, when discussing African and Western Christianity, the author's example of the latter seems to be European traditional/mainline churches. The differences between African and Western charismatic churches in their respective understanding of the miraculous, for instance, are not as profound as those sketched by the author in terms of "African" and "Western" Christianity. This weakness might be attributed to the book's origin: a series of lectures addressing such a diverse range of topics does not afford a scholar of ter Haar's abilities the opportunity to fine-tune arguments or present nuanced data. While this book serves as an adequate introduction for those unfamiliar with the broad discussion surrounding the issues mentioned above, advanced-level researchers will need to look elsewhere for more detailed scholarship on these issues.

432. Haar, Gerrie ter, editor

Imagining Evil: Witchcraft Beliefs and Accusations in Contemporary Africa

Trenton, NJ: Africa World Press, 2006. 298 pages, ISBN: 9781592214853.

According to ter Haar, a professor at the Institute of Social Studies in The Hague, this collection is different from other studies of witchcraft in that it offers a specifically religious studies perspective, is written by scholars living and working in Africa, and focuses on the personal tragedies that witchcraft accusations produce. Most of the thirteen essays in the book study the witchcraft beliefs of particular African peoples. A major concern is how to respond to the violence that such beliefs frequently engender, especially in view of the increase in witchcraft accusation which some of the contributors identify. Also noted is the poverty that witchcraft belief fosters due to the fear that material prosperity will rouse hostile accusations. Among solutions suggested are scientific education, poverty reduction, development of civil society, education in healthy human relationships, and inculcation of human rights awareness. While some contributors also recognize the necessity of worldview change, they do little to identify the shape a transformed worldview might take. There is some criticism of the alleged failure of the churches to develop an adequate Christian theological response to witchcraft, but again none of the contributors makes up for the deficiency. Nevertheless, one expresses concern that charismatic demonologies which identify the witch with Satan tend only to make matters worse, while another claims that the "triumphalist" missionary proclamation of the supremacy of Christ in the African context has failed to deal with African fears. Among the more stimulating contributions, Ellis examines the decline of witchcraft persecution in early modern Europe, which apparently took place ahead of a decline in witchcraft belief; nor was the decline of the latter a consequence of the rise of scientific thought which subsisted alongside witchcraft belief. Van Beek points out that also in the African context witchcraft belief does not necessarily lead to violence against suspected witches, and discusses the social and religious factors that cause some peoples to move from suspicion to physical violence. Hinfelar discusses certain social, political and legal factors which have allowed witch hunters and others in Zambia to manipulate witchcraft accusations to their own material advantage, and outlines ways in which the Catholic Church has tried to respond. And Danfulani gives a detailed insight into the meaning of anger among the Mupun of Nigeria, with supporting case studies. While the quality of the contributions to this collection is uneven, some of the essays constitute a useful addition to the literature on witchcraft in Africa.

433.   **Haar, Gerrie ter, editor**

Religious Communities in the Diaspora

Nairobi: Acton Publishers, 2001. 276 pages, ISBN: 9789966888389.

In this collection nine scholars provide papers that were either given at an international conference on the subject at Leiden in 1995 or contributed separately. Ter Haar helpfully summarizes the collection in an introduction. Although there is some far-ranging consideration of the general topic of "diaspora" (including ancient Jewish diaspora, third-century Palmyrene diaspora, Hindu and Muslim minorities in Europe), the overall focus is on African religious communities in Europe. The topic has gained in contemporary significance as international mobility increases across the world, and as governments respond with tighter legislation. Interesting comparisons and contrasts are drawn between the Afro-American present-day perception on the one hand, with its distant collective experience of slavery in earlier centuries, coupled with the romantic desire on the part of many to recover their African roots, and the Afro-European perception on the other hand, with its very unromantic post-colonial collective experience of oppression or economic misery. Ter Haar, writing about African religious communities in the Netherlands, notes the significant religious contribution of African communities as they bring missionary zeal and enthusiasm to a European Christianity which is in decline. Patrick Kalilombe of Malawi writes about African communities in Britain where racial and structural exclusion has meant that Black Christianity is a political response to the situation of Blacks in the UK. The Congolese Beya writing of the francophone African diaspora experience in Europe agrees with Kalilombe that Africans in Europe have encountered discrimination; he finds that only by acknowledging God as the author of the play performed on the world stage have francophone African congregations in Britain been able to make their way in the world. This book is a welcome contribution, not only because the African diaspora is a fundamental element of African presence in the modern world, but also because the realities of an African religious diaspora in Europe have only recently begun to receive scholarly attention.

434.   Haar, Gerrie ter

Spirit of Africa: The Healing Ministry of Archbishop Milingo of Zambia

Trenton, NJ: Africa World Press, 1992. 300 pages, ISBN: 9781850651178.

Here is a scholarly but readable book about one of Africa's most controversial Roman Catholic leaders. The author traces the background and training of Milingo, his meteoric rise from radio priest to Archbishop of Lusaka at the early age of 39, the circumstances surrounding his discovery of his healing gift, his increasingly controversial exercise of it to meet the almost overwhelming public response, the growing opposition to his hugely popular ministry which even compelled him to renounce it for periods, his clashes with influential political and religious figures, and the mysterious summons to relocate to Rome in 1982. This put an end to his ministry in Zambia but, amazingly, started it up again in Italy where his healing services soon attracted wide response, and he continued to function from a position within the Vatican. So the story of the man is intriguing enough in itself to make the book fascinating. But ter Haar, at time of publication a lecturer at the Catholic University of Utrecht, goes beyond the biographical to explore wider issues that lie behind both Milingo's ministry and the context in which he exercised this ministry – issues such as African concepts of evil, the spirit world (the "world in-between," to use Milingo's preferred term), African spirituality, African theology, power structures both ecclesial and political, and the influence of the global charismatic community in which Milingo gladly discovered endorsement in the midst of widespread opposition and suspicion. Ter Haar's research draws on archival letters and pamphlets, conversations, newspaper clippings, films, interviews, tape recordings, as well as learned journals and books relating to the wider issues. The book is also an instructive research model, in that the author seeks to make the investigation "emic" (i.e. from the point of view of believers), as well as "etic" (i.e. having an "outside" perspective). Viewpoints will differ in whether Milingo's contextualisation in Zambia was in danger of going too far. Milingo has also had much additional life and ministry since departing Zambia and since this study was published.

Haar, Gerrie ter

see also reviews 238 and 306

435.   Hackett, Rosalind I. J.

Art and Religion in Africa

London: Bloomsbury, 1998. 248 pages, ISBN: 9780304704248.

For anyone needing a learned, authoritative orientation to the interrelationship of art and religion in traditional Africa, this is the book. Hackett, Professor of Religious Studies at the University of Tennessee in the USA, is a widely read and judicious guide to the fascinating intricacies of this subject. But it is *traditional* Africa that she is concerned with; only in a final chapter, on the impact of modernity, does Hackett sketch in briefly the status of Christian or Islamic art in Africa. While she references such academics as Mbiti and Idowu, her interpretive framework for understanding African religion is directed by the sensibilities of more recent scholars such as Mudimbe and Westerlund. In doing so she deploys a sophisticated, welcome sensitivity to the multiformity of traditional African religion. Most readers would find the opening chapter, with its notes, a uniquely illuminating introduction to the subject. Beyond that, this book is best suited to the requirements and capacities of those doing advanced-level research on African religions, who will find much profit from its interdisciplinary approach, and from innumerable clarifying details that would rarely surface in more conventional discussions of ATR. The pages incorporate a large number of photographs and drawings.

436.   Haile, Ahmed Ali

Teatime in Mogadishu: My Journey as a Peace Ambassador in the World of Islam

Scottdale, PA: Herald Press, 2011. 140 pages, ISBN: 9780836195576.

"As a Muslim I really wanted to know God. In Jesus I met God as my loving heavenly father. I yearned for the assurance that my sins were forgiven. In Jesus I knew my sins were forgiven. I am grateful for the ways Islam prepared me to hear and believe in Christ." Haile's story is remarkable in many ways. He is open and generous when he expresses the many positive qualities he inherited from his Islamic upbringing. But he leaves no doubt that the gospel and the Qur'an, the church and the mosque, cannot be mixed. "Although my Muslim roots prepared me to seek the gospel, my Muslim heritage is not the gospel. Neither is the mosque the church." After his bold embrace of the truth, and a daring public confession, he leaves his shattered homeland and travels into neighbouring Kenya, where he becomes a trusted co-worker of David Shenk at the Mennonite Center in Nairobi. When God opens the door for him to embark upon years of biblical and peace studies in the USA, he eagerly takes this opportunity, yet never forgets his family. In the early 1980s he returns to his wounded, bleeding home country where he is fully committed to being a peacemaker amidst myriads of warring parties. A rocket attack in 1992 in bloodstained Mogadishu costs him one of his legs. For his remaining twenty years he becomes a global ambassador of peace. Finally cancer takes him in 2011, yet not before he can tell his story to his dear friends David and Grace Shenk. There are few autobiographies of former Muslims that can tell the story from beginning to end. And there is no other Somali believer who has shared this more compellingly than Haile.

437.   Halbert, Jim, and Viola Halbert

Ivory in Our Hearts: The Special Work of God in Our Lives

Morrisville, NC: Lulu Press, 2006. 448 pages, ISBN: 9781411670365.

The Halberts were an American missionary couple who served for nearly three decades in Africa with the Conservative Baptist Foreign Mission Society (now WorldVenture), mostly in Côte d'Ivoire, but at the end of their ministry also in Kenya. This is their autobiography, recounted principally by Viola, based on saved correspondence, and organized largely in the form of a life chronology, with chapters titled "First-Term," "First Furlough," "Second Term," "Second Furlough," etc. The text is an easy, comfortable read. The couple first met while attending Biola in southern California. Arriving in Côte d'Ivoire for missionary service in 1951, they worked initially in pioneer evangelism and church planting, and later at the Bible Institute in Yamoussukro. The narrative follows the familiar pattern of this genre, recounting family life, travel, health challenges, cross-cultural experiences, and ministry events. What distinguishes this book, and for which it merits special notice, is that in 1974 the Halberts were seconded by their mission to the work of the Association of Evangelicals in Africa (AEA) in Nairobi, under the direction of the then AEA General Secretary, Byang Kato. Jim Halbert served as Kato's personal assistant for the final eighteen months of Kato's life, and then stayed on to help hold AEA operations together until the appointment of Kato's successor in 1977. In this role Halbert handled office correspondence, edited and typed Kato's manuscripts and articles, oversaw publication of AEA's *Afroscope*, organized Kato's travel logistics, helped process the earliest AEA steps toward the eventual founding of FATEB in Bangui and NEGST in Nairobi, managed arrangements for various AEA conferences and workshops, and managed AEA's finances. The chapter devoted to the Halberts' years in Kenya, and their friendship with the Kato family, includes a rare first-hand account of the tragic events surrounding the death of Kato in 1975, including details that have not hitherto appeared in print. The Halberts retired from Africa in 1977. During a return visit in 1997 to locations of ministry in Côte d'Ivoire, Jim was knighted by the Ivorian government with the Chevalier de l'Ordre National "for eminent services rendered to Côte d'Ivoire."

Halbert, Viola

see review 437

Hallencreutz, Carl F.

see review 937

438.   Hamlin, Catherine, and John Little

The Hospital by the River

Oxford: Monarch, 2004. 320 pages, ISBN: 9781854246738.

This is both biography and historical record. On the one hand, it is the story of two remarkable Australian doctors, Reg and Catherine Hamlin, who invested their lives in ministry to women in Ethiopia needing specialist fistula surgery. On the other hand, it is a record of the development of today's remarkable Fistula Hospital in Addis Ababa, with all the bureaucratic, political and economic hurdles that were encountered along the way. Both doctors came from families that had been immersed for generations in various aspects of Christian mission, and this particular medical ministry was undertaken with the desire to see complete transformation through an encounter with Jesus Christ. Thanks in part to the involvement of a professional writer, this is a well-researched and well-written book. The stories of a number of Ethiopians are included alongside those of the Hamlins, and the book both emphasizes and demonstrates the critical need for including a training program as early as possible in the development of such institutional ministry. The book also gives some valuable insights into life during the seventeen years of oppression under the Mengistu regime, since the Hamlins remained in the country during that period. This book should be of particular relevance for those attending to the development of ministries in specialized medical fields on the African continent.

439.   Hanciles, Jehu

Euthanasia of a Mission: African Church Autonomy in a Colonial Context

Santa Barbara, CA: Praeger, 2002. 296 pages, ISBN: 9780275975708.

Originally from Sierra Leone, Hanciles is Associate Professor of World Christianity at Candler School of Theology in the United States. His book is a revision of his Edinburgh PhD thesis. The title "Euthanasia of a Mission" is a quotation from Henry Venn, Church Missionary Society (CMS) secretary for part of the period under review. It is the other side of the coin of Venn's famous three-self formula, that the goal of missions is a self-supporting, self-propagating and self-governing national church. This includes that the mission organisation makes itself superfluous, thus organising its own euthanasia. Hanciles sketches out the historical implementation of Venn's strategy in Sierra Leone in the second half of the nineteenth century, from the beginnings of CMS work in Sierra Leone through the growth of the church and to the final departure of the CMS (except for medical and educational work). A chapter on "ethiopianism," a flare-up of African self-assertion in Sierra Leone in the 1870s, interprets the movement as an unintended reinterpretation of Venn's vision, resulting in the many African Independent Churches all over the continent (albeit with only slight direct consequences for the CMS/Anglican Church in Sierra Leone at the time). In his summation Hanciles names the main problems in the "euthanasia process": (1) miscalculation by Venn of the financial possibilities of the Sierra Leone church and of Sierra Leone as a colony; (2) bad leadership by the appointed (white) bishops; and (3) especially the hostility and opposition of the European CMS missionaries towards Venn's strategy (due to paternalistic and racist attitudes). Self-propagation (and not self-support!) is identified as the main weakness of the emerging national church. A short discussion of critical voices towards Venn's three-self formula (Neill, Yates, Verkuyl) closes the volume. Hanciles writes his history not merely from the mission society point of view, but also tries to include as far as possible the African "agents" and their perspectives. Although the topic is centred on a mission society (as per the title), the book does not focus on CMS decisions or actions which influenced the process of the "euthanasia," but rather describes developments and results in the church (under a white bishop). The author is very much in favour of Venn's vision and implicitly laments that the CMS only succeeded in exiting, not in building a national church truly exercising the three-self principles. While the book is a useful case study of mission strategy and implementation in the nineteenth century, the interpretive issues it embodies are still very relevant at the beginning of the twenty-first century.

Hannon, Paul

see review 1069

440.   Hansen, Len D., editor

The Legacy of Beyers Naudé

Stellenbosch: SUN Press, 2005. 170 pages, ISBN: 9781919980980.

The Beyers Naudé Centre for Public Theology at Stellenbosch University in South Africa was opened in 2002 to honour one of the most famous of the University's graduates, the Afrikaner theologian and opponent of Apartheid, Beyers Naudé. This collection of essays was intended as the first in a series to be published by the Centre, and it fittingly celebrates the legacy of Naudé. Although he has had a number of volumes produced in his honour, this one is different in that it contains nine chapters from Naudé himself, including two famous sermons he preached to his congregation in Johannesburg during the fateful year of 1963 when he started the Christian Institute and was subsequently forced to resign from his church. Interspersed between his contributions are ten essays from well-known theologians (John de Gruchy, Denise Ackermann), South African church leaders (Desmond Tutu, Alan Boesak) and others who would consider Naudé to have been a colleague, friend or significant influence. A number of these essays were presented as part of Naudé's 89th birthday celebrations in 2004 (a few months before his death) and, as might be expected, are characterized by a certain degree of biographical repetition and hagiography.

441.   Harden, Blaine

Africa: Dispatches from a Fragile Continent

London: HarperCollins UK, 1992. 334 pages, ISBN: 9780006378563.

As a bureau chief for the *Washington Post* in sub-Saharan Africa from 1985 to 1989, Harden came face to face with the daunting realities facing Africa. In his introduction Harden offers a glimpse of the range of problems that can very well give reason to despair for the continent. But this book is no cold statistical cataloguing of Africa's immense challenges. While the book contains statistics, its main contribution is to put a human face to the situation, by providing dramatic narratives surrounding people whom Harden met in his travels. For example, we are introduced to a westernized lawyer in Kenya who demonstrates that even in death a man cannot escape tribal requirements. We also meet a professor of family studies in Ghana who is overwhelmed by the demands of his kinfolk. The heart of the book considers "Big Man Disease," the search for leaders in countries that lack national identities. In his final chapter Harden attempts to show where the best hope for the continent might lie, albeit from a secularist standpoint. This is a fascinating book that could be read with profit by any Christian wanting to have a deeper understanding of the complex sociological, economic, and political issues affecting the peoples of Africa.

442.   Hardwick, Lorna, and Carol Gillespie, editors

Classics in Post-Colonial Worlds

Oxford: Oxford University Press, 2010. 440 pages, ISBN: 9780199591329.

This volume of nineteen essays grew out of a conference held at the Open University in Birmingham UK in 2004. Both the editors are associated with the Open University. The "Classics" designation in the title refers to the classical literature of Greco-Roman antiquity. While this special focus might initially seem to be of little interest to users of this reference resource, postcolonial theory cannot be ignored by those interested in the intellectual life of Africa in the twenty-first century. Moreover, as a sociological, text-focused discipline, postcolonial analysis like this can suggest scholarly avenues that biblical and theological scholars might need to explore, and indicate others that are best avoided. The presence of postcolonial theory in biblical studies is already familiar in Africa. The first six essays in this collection focus on Greek tragedy as it has been received and used in modern African theatre. The next two essays explore classical influences in sculpture at Heroes Acre in Harare, Zimbabwe, and in architecture at the Voortrekker Monument in Pretoria, South Africa. These are followed by three essays on literature from the Caribbean and its diaspora, and two more on African appropriations of Greek drama. The final six essays are more theoretical in nature, suggesting some further questions that postcolonial theory might explore, and others that need answering if the discipline is to mature. One of the questions not raised in this collection is its own lack of "postcolonial" representation. Of the nineteen contributors, only three held academic positions outside of Great Britain and America at the time of publication. Nonetheless, advanced-level students not only of classical literature, but also of modern Africa, and of postcolonial interpretations of Africa, will want to be familiar with such texts.

443.   Harries, Patrick, and David Maxwell, editors

The Spiritual in the Secular: Missionaries and Knowledge about Africa

Grand Rapids: Eerdmans, 2012. 355 pages, ISBN: 9780802866349.

Long gone are the caricatures of early missionaries as culture-destroying, naïve simpletons, stumbling into Africa with destructive effect. Contemporary scholarship has more recently nuanced the contribution of expatriate missionaries, looking at the dynamic interplay between faith convictions, Enlightenment heritage, cultural predilections, and the many diverse ways missionaries interacted with and learned from Africans in the process of socio-religious engagement. This edited book offers compelling insight into some of these themes, drawing upon the interplay of spiritual and secular interests to show how Western ecclesiastical agents made critical contribution to the fields of botany, linguistics, anthropology, and medicine, to name just a few, while promoting local fields of knowledge. The contributors largely write from a historical perspective and are among some of the top scholars in the field. The different essays paint a picture of a variety of missionaries, from distinguished churchmen, such as John V. Taylor, to missionary doctors, to the more humble American evangelists. Women took part in these secular endeavours as much as men. The chapters further boast a range of ecclesiastical traditions, including the role of Pentecostal missionaries in the twentieth century as they engaged in spiritual and material affairs. What stands out is that missionaries drew heavily upon indigenous knowledge, assimilating African thought with their own Enlightenment heritage to produce "new ways of understanding their situation, and in the process they brought African ways of ordering and understanding the human and natural environment to the attention of the world." For example, what we know about the fields of anthropology or linguistics today stands on the shoulders of early missionary pioneers. None of the writers romanticize the missionaries. This edited collection simply fills in a gap in African studies, helping the reader appreciate the many, nuanced ways that Western missionaries went about their work with a combination of sacred and secular interests.

Hartin, P. J.

see review 914

444.   Harvey, Charles H.

Ndoki: Trapped in the Web of Witchcraft

Maitland, FL: Xulon Press, 2007. 364 pages, ISBN: 9781604770742.

Based on actual events and the lives of real people, Ndoki recounts the fictionalized story of a young woman growing up in a rural setting in northwestern Angola, near the border with the Congo (DRC). The book is rich in its detailed ethnographic account of many aspects of village life, and compassionate and respectful in its treatment of the local pre-Christian culture. It also gives us a window into the devastating consequences of the long Angolan civil war in the lives of ordinary people. The author, who served as a Canadian Baptist missionary for many years in this part of Africa, weaves into this story his careful analysis of the pervasive local discourse on witchcraft ("ndoki" is the word used in the local language to refer to those believed to be "witches"), and of the many ways in which this approach to explaining sickness and death plays itself out in village life. From a very young age, Titi (the girl who is the primary subject of the story), struggles with the ambivalence of having a grandmother who is generally very kind to her, but who is nevertheless suspected by others in her family of being a witch, responsible for the death of her baby siblings. As Titi grows into a young woman, the terrifying possibilities inherent in this way of understanding misfortune continue to play themselves out in her life, until she finally begins to understand the power of God's love embodied in the lives of followers of Christ. Based as it is on a true story and years of thoroughgoing cultural study by the author, this account rings true. One only wishes that the story were better told. For example, too much descriptive detail, which could better have been given in narrative form, is loaded into dialogue. In spite of this type of weakness, the book is a very valuable example of careful ethnographic research and of strong theological and pastoral reflection on one particular troubling aspect of indigenous African culture. It could contribute significantly to reflection on African traditional religion, contextualization discussions, or studies in pastoral theology.

445. Hasan, Yusuf Fadi, and Richard Gray, editors

Religion and Conflict in Sudan: Papers from an International Conference at Yale, May 1999

Nairobi: Paulines, 2002. 208 pages, ISBN: 9789966218315.

This volume, a helpful addition to the important publication series "Faith in Sudan," consists of papers from an international conference held at Yale University in 1999. The thirteen chapters (plus an important Preface, Introduction, and Epilogue) provide various perspectives on the interface in the Sudan between war and faith, between violence and religious communities. The civil war in Sudan before its 2011 division into two countries cannot be fully understood by reference only to oil, water, land, and race issues, crucial as these are. The conflict was *also* (some would say *primarily*) about religion. As Lamin Sanneh muses in the Preface, "It is often difficult to say which precedes which, religious incitement or political manipulation." Or, as the editors tell us in the Introduction, whereas the war involved various types of power, this book is "primarily interested in trying to assess the religious and ideological components." The first two chapters attempt to put the war in the Sudan into historical context. Following this are two detailed studies of Shari'a written by two Sudanese lawyers. Subsequent chapters include a clear condemnation of the notion of *jihad* as the government of the Sudan has used it in gaining public support for the struggle against the south. The remainder of the contributions focus attention on particular groups (the people of the Nuba Mountains, the Kuku, the Nuer, the Jieng, the people of northern Uganda) and the various ways in which they have been affected by the years of conflict. The volume can contribute to greater understanding not only of the continuing trauma of the Sudan regions, but also of the role that religion can have in Africa's internal conflicts.

446.   Hasenhüttl, Gotthold

Schwarz Bin Ich und Schön

Darmstadt, Germany: Wissenschaftliche Buchgesellschaft, 1991. 177 pages, ISBN: 9783534800544.

Hasenhüttl is professor for Catholic theology at a German university, and has travelled widely in Africa. As the title for his book he has chosen a text from the Song of Songs 1:5: "I am black and lovely." With this phrasing he wants to communicate to the Western reader the African way of thinking, and to encourage dialogue between African thought and Christianity. Western Christianity could be liberated from its tendency to understand God as object, and could re-think the Trinity as "being in relationship." The African worldview focussing on "*Lebenskraft*" (vitality, life force) could be enriched by the Christian concept of love, which also values suffering as well as aspects of life with "inferior strength" (for example disabled life). Hasenhüttl analyses his African experiences from the standpoint of Heidegger's existentialism, and the concept of truth in permanent dialogue without hierarchies. He "demythologizes" African thought from its myths and magic distortions to a pure symbolism, which becomes the partner in dialogue with a demythologized Christianity (from the perspective of liberal theology). Throughout the book Hasenhüttl advocates mission as dialogue, in contrast to two other approaches: "*Tabula rasa*" (everything African is bad and has to be removed as unChristian) and "paternalism" (Africa is prepared for Christianity as nature can be perfected by grace [Aquinas]). Even if one is unpersuaded by the ideological position of the author, and therefore in part with his description of African reality, as well as with his theological and missiological implications, the reader should not dismiss this type of book altogether – because it challenges Christianity in Africa to be relevant at a deeper level of human life (and society!), and it stimulates thought on how this could be so. It also uncovers and criticizes missionary methods that are not confined to the Catholic tradition. Hasenhüttl offers stimulating advanced-level reading for thoughtful theological reflection that is grappling with issues of traditional culture and Christianity.

Hassan, Raymond

see review 215

447.   Hassett, Miranda K.

Anglican Communion in Crisis: How Episcopal Dissidents and Their African Allies Are Reshaping Anglicanism

Princeton: Princeton University Press, 2007. 320 pages, ISBN: 9780691125183.

In a remarkable study Hassett's revised doctoral dissertation in anthropology from Princeton has demonstrated that the emergence of an articulate and confident African Christianity has begun to transform one of the largest of the world's Christian traditions. The Anglican Communion, long centred in England, controlled by white leaders and Western money, is now facing the reality of being a predominantly African church. At the same moment that African Anglicanism has emerged as a force to be reckoned with, theologically conservative Anglicans in the US have found these African Christians to be useful allies in their struggle against the liberal hegemony of their own national church. Nor is this alliance an accident. Hassett traces the recent encounters and developing relations, especially through her field work conducted in two places: in an American parish which is part of an Anglican jurisdiction under the authority of the Archbishop of Rwanda, and at the Uganda

Christian University. In the process of tracing this emerging global movement, Hassett draws on anthropological studies of other globalisation movements, showing how this conservative form of Anglicanism across national and jurisdictional boundaries is a challenge to the hegemonic, monocultural expression of Christianity found in the Christendom model of Anglicanism. This is a seminal work of great timeliness, sensitivity and insight, an important reading of a trend which is bound to affect most so-called mainline denominations in the future.

448. Hastings, Adrian

African Catholicism: Essays in Discovery

Norwich: SCM, 2012. 224 pages, ISBN: 9780334000198.

Hastings' long experience in Africa, combined with extensive and detailed research for his several books and many articles on Africa, has given him an encyclopaedic and sympathetic knowledge of matters African. He is also well placed to write on Catholicism, being himself Catholic and an author of major works on Catholicism. However, the fact that he himself is not an African and that he is also no longer a priest, means that for both of the fields indicated by the title Hastings is able to distance himself critically from that about which he writes. This present book is a collection of twelve essays, some of them originally delivered as lectures in different parts of the world. They range from the historical (e.g. "Mission, Church and State in Southern Africa: The First 150 Years") to theological (e.g. "African Theology"), and from linguistic (e.g. "The Choice of Words for Christian Meanings in Eastern Africa") to pastoral (e.g. "Emmanuel Milingo as Christian Healer"). Some of the essays, like "Ganda Catholic Spirituality," are personal and graphically anecdotal. Others are closely reasoned and more academic. The writing style is sometimes complex, and often hard-hitting (especially when critical of his own Catholicism, as in the last essay, "Our Daily Bread"). But it is informative and stimulating stuff, and time and again one finds oneself exclaiming "I must read that again; Hastings expresses that point so well!" It is not only Catholic readers who will benefit from reading it; many of the essays cover material that is just as pertinent for Protestants. In any case it is salutary for everyone to gain insight into the background, changes and challenges of what is the largest single confessional Christian body in Africa.

449. Hastings, Adrian

The Church in Africa, 1450–1950

Oxford: Clarendon Press, 1996. 720 pages, ISBN: 9780198263999.

This is a comprehensive account of African Christianity from medieval times up to the end of the colonial period. The author draws on his wide familiarity with the books, theses and journal articles which have illumined our understanding of different periods and different aspects of the theme. The book reads therefore rather like the "edited highlights" of the previous 40 years of scholarship on Christianity in Africa. This means that it tends to concentrate on the more well-known and celebrated areas, such as Nigeria and Uganda, rather than breaking new ground by drawing attention to hitherto little noticed movements. What will be exceedingly helpful to students are Hastings' attempts to summarize, with a few well-chosen phrases, the character of a particular movement or the key elements in a particular period. Three examples must suffice: "Overwhelmingly the impression that a careful observer would have gained of the Africa of the 1820s was that Islam was substantially a missionary religion, and an effective one, while Christianity was not." "Collectively African Christianity simply did not make up its mind between missionary and traditional requirements. For the most part it did its best, somewhat unquestioningly, to embrace both." "If the mission churches came to look more and more like a network of schools, the independent prophetic churches came to look more like a network of hospitals and health clinics. And many an African found both attractive." Such broad historical judgments, given after a careful sifting of evidence, will crystallize for many readers an understanding of key characteristics of Christianity in Africa. To attempt to survey five centuries is of course ambitious, but it also provides its own advantages, e.g. the opportunity to treat the European missionary movement as one episode in an African story rather than as the definitive event, as is the case in much of the earlier historiography. Hastings has also succeeded in giving balanced treatment to the Orthodox, Catholic, Protestant and Independent traditions of Christian faith, although he does not take much conscious account of the evangelical contribution to African church history. The themes which are stressed are not new ones – the abiding influence of African traditional religion, the importance of vernacular translation, the centrality of "African agency," the urgency of indigenisation, the interplay of religion and politics – but they are presented here on a broader canvas than has hitherto been available. Without any doubt Hasting's work will stand as a benchmark in the advance of scholarship related to the history of Christianity in Africa.

450. Hay, Margaret J., and Sharon Stichter, editors

African Women South of the Sahara

London: Longman, 1995. 240 pages, ISBN: 9780582643734.

Here is a comprehensive survey of the economic, social, cultural and political roles of women in sub-Saharan Africa. This is the second edition of a work that first appeared in 1984. It combines well-researched descriptions of the state of affairs, case studies, commentaries and comparisons, and insightful conclusions, all contributed by women scholars. Written from the perspective of a range of disciplines, the book sets the role of women in Africa in its historical context and covers all the major sub-Saharan nations and peoples. Each chapter is written by an acknowledged expert, and the authors have tried to translate theoretical perspectives into practical transformation methods. Because the literature both on the past and on the contemporary situation of African women has been consulted and critically evaluated, the volume is a mine of bibliographic information on the subject. The project also evidences good teamwork; with eighteen authors, it nevertheless displays unity of purpose and outline throughout. This is an essential reference work on the topic it so well addresses.

451. Haynes, Jeffrey

Religion and Politics in Africa

London: Zed Books, 1996. 256 pages, ISBN: 9781856493925.

The author, a political scientist with no obvious religious allegiance, leaves the spiritual side of religion to the theologians, and concentrates on an Africa-wide analysis of the social and political aspects of religion. This book is a challenge to theologians to see aspects of religion in Africa that they otherwise might not so easily see, namely how religious groups interact with politics – which is what they do indeed do. The book is strong on theory, and that is where both its strengths and its problems lie. The author offers interesting interpretations of religious phenomena, and (different from authors like Gifford) he allows for complicated facts, for (seeming) contradictions, and for multiple causation of religious phenomena. Yet the rich collection of examples sometimes does not really fit the theories, and that makes the reading a challenge. Haynes puts much emphasis on the role of "popular religion" serving as a "community expression of a group desire to achieve a religious satisfaction which is not forthcoming from a mainstream religion." But the first group he mentions, the "basic Christian communities," hardly developed along those lines in Africa, and the African Instituted Churches (AICs), often seen as vehicles of political discontent in colonial times, happily multiplied even after colonialism had gone. Of much interest to the author are the fundamentalist Christian groups in Africa. His definition is as diffuse as usual, lumping together Radio ELWA, Charismatics, Pentecostals and Seventh-Day Adventists. But against Gifford he accepts that fundamentalism (for him mostly the charismatic movement) is as genuinely an (adapted) African phenomenon as are mainstream Christianity and Islam. He stresses that fundamentalism (i.e. charismatic churches) fulfils real needs, and that it is not necessarily apolitical, but that its "increasing popularity . . . can be accounted for by the combined effects of social, economic and political disruptions associated with the process of modernisation." This seems too simple. Was there not (maybe even more) modernisation in Africa when the mainstream churches established themselves? As a whole this is a book to be read critically as well as self-critically by theologians. (And when reading, one should be sure to check its details against known facts; for example, the well-known figure from mission history in Malawi, Joseph Booth, was not a black American but a white Englishman – and he had no pentecostalist leanings.)

452. Hays, J. Daniel, editor

From Every People and Nation: A Biblical Theology of Race

London: Apollos, 2003. 240 pages, ISBN: 9780851112909.

According to Hays the Western world has tended to impose its own characteristics on its depiction of biblical characters, thereby overlooking or misinterpreting important biblical data for a sound theology of race. Hays examines the pertinent biblical texts. For example, the "Table of Nations" in Genesis 10 is theological grounding for the common origin of all races; all fall equally under the judgment of God, and therefore are equally eligible for the promise of divine blessing that is made to Abraham in Genesis 12. The Prophets and the Psalms present an eschatological vision of Yahweh bringing all peoples together in worship in fulfilment of the promise to Abraham. It is a vision whose fulfilment in Christ is emphasized by such NT authors as Luke and Paul. And the book of Revelation looks forward to the eschatological realisation of the people of God as multi-ethnic and multi-cultural, drawn from every nation upon earth, united in their worship of God and of the Lamb. One emphasis of Hays' presentation is the important part played by Black Africa in the biblical story. For example, Hays notes the 54 references to Cush/Cushites in the Hebrew OT (for example, Ebed-Melech, who helped Jeremiah out of the cistern). In fact, readers could get the impression that the book gives a less than balanced prominence to the role of Cush and Black Africa in the OT text. Hays served for a number of years in Ethiopia (broadly associated with ancient Cush), but his interest in Black Africa is also due to his perception that some of the ugliest expressions of racism have been and are directed towards Black African races. Hayes carefully examines the so-called "curse of Ham" (Gen 9) and exposes what he considers to be a widespread misrepresentation. He is also seeking to redress the widespread opinion in Africa that the biblical world only engaged with Africa with the recent coming of Western missionaries, and that Christianity is a "white man's religion." If some of Hays' arguments are speculative, they are nevertheless based on careful scholarship. And not far beneath the surface of academic rigour are the author's pastoral and contemporary concerns. His theology is one of engagement; he argues passionately not for the obliteration of ethnic differences, but for their theological and spiritual irrelevance within the transforming unity of the family of God in Christ.

453.   **Healey, Joseph**

African Stories for Preachers and Teachers

Nairobi: Paulines, 2005. 152 pages, ISBN: 9789966219497.

Oral literatures – such as proverbs, sayings, riddles, stories, plays, myths, songs – play important roles in the research and publishing of the author, an American Maryknoll priest who has served in East Africa since the late 1960s. Healey's focus on oral literature has a strong ethnographic aspect, but it also reflects his theological setting, arguing that African culture should serve as a basis of an African narrative inculturation theology. The present collection of "stories" is then meant as a help for preachers and teachers who need contextual illustrations, and it includes chapters on topics such as AIDS, community, culture, education, faith, family, life, prayer, etc. The collection is in many ways a treasure chest for everyone engaged in preaching and teaching – even if some users may not share every aspect of Healey's theological framework, summarized as: "The proverbs and myths of the African people reveal that the Holy Spirit sowed the seeds of the Good News in African cultures long before the African people ever heard Jesus' words and teachings."

454.   **Healey, Joseph, and Donald Sybertz**

Towards an African Narrative Theology

Maryknoll, NY: Orbis, 1997. 397 pages, ISBN: 9781570751219.

Both authors are long-serving Catholic missionary priests in East Africa (mainly Tanzania). In this helpful volume they deal with the ever-relevant subject of the contextualization (or to use their preferred term, inculturation) of the gospel message in Africa. The title of the book could be misleading. The phrase "African narrative theology" might suggest a discussion either of the use of "African narrative" in the formulation of Christian theology or of a distinctive "narrative theology" in and for Africa. But the authors clearly explain what they have in mind, namely "to make a correlation between African oral literature . . . and Christianity, and to express this in pastoral theological reflections that concretely speak to people's everyday life." Thus the African narrative theology being proposed is meant to take its starting point from forms of African oral literature such as: "proverbs, sayings, riddles, stories, myths, plays and songs." (Hence "traditional art forms" might better express the approach being recommended than does "narrative.") This approach to theological reflection and message transmission is discussed at length and abundantly illustrated with reference to: the nature of God/Christology, the Church/community of God, hospitality, death and life, meal fellowship, healing, and mission work. Proverbs are the verbal art form that is privileged in the authors' treatment, as is Roman Catholic theology (the authors do, however, offer criticisms of "traditional" Catholic teaching and practice in relation to an African setting). Every chapter includes a final section in which the authors illustrate how their proposed method may be applied. Readers may well disagree with certain aspects of this presentation, for example on the role of the "living dead" in ancestral mediation; the metaphor of the "fifth gospel"; potential sources of theology; traditional and modern "Christ-like saviour figures"; or the notion that "praxis is prior to theology." These do not constitute a reason to avoid this book, but will rather serve to initiate a more specific debate on the various problems and potentials in the practice of contextualization.

Hebga, Meinrad

see review 581

455. Hefling, Charles, and Cynthia Shattuck, editors

The Oxford Guide to the Book of Common Prayer: A Worldwide Survey

New York: Oxford University Press, 2008. 640 pages, ISBN: 9780195297621.

Although this massive volume of studies (73 essays) has some deficiencies, it will likely be regarded as the standard volume on Anglican liturgy for some years to come. Whereas it purports to be a "worldwide" survey, it is clear that it is a western-based volume that considers Europe and North America to be the centre of Anglicanism, with Africa, Asia and Latin America on the margins. The structure of the volume betrays this orientation since parts 1 and 2 deal with the Book of Common Prayer (BCP) within England, and even when part 3 broadens the horizon somewhat to look at the BCP "Outside England," the geographical focus is on Scotland, Ireland, the USA, and Canada. It is only when we reach part 5 "Family Portraits: Prayer Books Today" that we finally have substantial discussion of Anglican worship outside of the West, which includes seven essays on Anglican liturgy in Africa: "Anglican Liturgies in Eastern Africa"; "The Anglican Church of Kenya"; "The Church of Nigeria: The Book of Common Prayer"; "The Church of Nigeria: Occasional Services"; "Central African Prayer Books"; "The Province of Southern Africa"; and "Other Anglican Provinces: Burundi, Rwanda, and Congo." Although most church-going Anglicans in the world live in Africa, this volume gives only a fraction of its space to a discussion of Africa. Of course one reason for this is the much longer history of Anglicanism in the West. Indeed ten years earlier such a volume would likely have overlooked Africa altogether, so in that light this book does represent an important advance.

456. Hege, Nathan B.

Beyond Our Prayers: Anabaptist Church Growth in Ethiopia, 1948–1998

Scottdale, PA: Herald Press, 1998. 256 pages, ISBN: 9780836190854.

Believers in Ethiopia suffered greatly under the Marxist government from the mid-1970s to the early 1990s. This is one of the books about their trials and victories during that era. The Meserete Kristos Church (MKC) of Ethiopia was officially closed by the communist government in 1982 and all its properties seized. When that government was deposed in 1991, the church that emerged from "underground" was ten times larger. This book is a story of God's miraculous work and faithfulness. The first chapters focus on the early missionaries, while the latter chapters focus on the Ethiopian believers who compose the MKC. The beginning of the Mennonite work in Ethiopia was very much related to "development" work, medical and educational. When the government seized schools and hospitals, this forced the church to concentrate on evangelism and discipleship. A large network of house churches and small groups allowed them to survive persecution. The Mennonite missionaries seem historically to have exercised less control over the church than did many other missions in Ethiopia. This has resulted in a strong national leadership, but also in patterns of worship and practice that are significantly different from what missionaries brought. MKC today has few ordained clergy, but lively programmes of worship that include exuberant local hymns, healings, and speaking in tongues.

What many in the West might assume to be Mennonite distinctives are not part of MKC life. "Mennonite" is not even in the church's official name, though MKC has strong links with the Mennonite World Council.

457.   Hegeman, Benjamin L.

Between Glory and Shame: A Historical and Systematic Study of Education and Leadership Training Models among the Baatonu in North Benin

Zoetermeer, Netherlands: Boekencentrum, 2001. 556 pages, ISBN: 9789023911524.

This study focuses on traditional educational patterns among the Baatonu, a people group in Benin, West Africa, as this may be relevant for pastoral training within the Baatonu Christian community. Hegeman, a veteran SIM missionary to Benin, gives a historical overview of this group, addresses the Baatonu traditional religion known as *Deeman Saaru*, and then assesses the educational and leadership methodologies of *Deeman Saaru*, together with those of Islam, secularism, and Christianity. With the defeat of Baatonu forces by the French military in 1897, this once proud community spiralled into poverty and insignificance. Even after independence in the 1960s, the Baatonu "have not regained cultural liberty, political autonomy, or prosperity." These people live today between the glory that their ancestors once knew and the cultural shame and decay of the present. The question the author seeks to answer is, what type of leaders would "such a proud, yet dishonoured, dying culture produce?" The author takes note that most Baatonu pastors are not pleased with their school training, which "fails to prepare them for offering strategic influence in their communities. Of all the religious practitioners, the Baatonu pastors are generally the least esteemed." Being a Protestant pastor "costs too much and offers too little." For this state of affairs Hegeman indicts, perhaps somewhat unfairly, both missionaries and their methods. The "founding missionaries did not succeed in making zealous Baatonu disciples for Christ, but instead formed admiring disciples of their Western lifestyle." Hegeman also indicts the secularisation that missionary theological educators perpetuated, albeit unintentionally. While missionary educators intended to use modern pedagogy as a secular means to a Christian end, to the Baatonu the educational means became the end to a better goal: material promotion, thus leaving the church "impoverished of fully consecrated disciples." Some generalisations and applications from Hegeman's findings may well seem relevant to readers in other parts of Africa, and his perspective on what this can entail for theological education is intriguing. Nevertheless, the assessments in this study are not always measured, nor is the study always as strong in proposing better ways to address the highlighted failures.

458.   Helgesson, Alf

Church, State and People in Mozambique: A Historical Study with Special Emphasis on Developments in the Inhambane Region

Uppsala: Studia Missionalia Upsaliensia, 1994. 442 pages, ISBN: 9789185424283.

This is a well-researched and readable doctoral thesis, drawing on the author's ministry in southern Africa. Those who have worked in Lusophone Africa are aware of not only the tensions with Mozambique's Marxist government both for Catholics and for Protestants, but also the extent to which the Catholic Church was often a part of the largely oppressive Portuguese colonial structures. Until well after Vatican II, Protestantism was often seen as the "enemy." Both Protestant and Catholic churches have changed, as have attitudes within the government. Helgesson's work presents this complicated history of church and state, and church and church. His focus is on the Methodist work in the Inhambane region of southern Mozambique. He presents internal and external conflicts, often involving strong personalities, in some cases resulting in African independent churches. The author also notes the development of excellent schools and medical work, despite much opposition. Some of those who studied in mission schools became key figures during the struggle for independence. Unfortunately this work contains relatively little about the actual growth, beliefs, structures or worship practices of the Methodist church as it developed in Mozambique. Helgesson gives his perspective on the struggles of Mozambique's Catholic Church as well. Catholic missions were actually prohibited in Mozambique for a number of years after 1834. A strong anticlerical feeling in Portugal continued to 1910 and only began to change as the Catholic Church was seen as a "civilising" force worthy of government support. Yet the Catholic Church didn't see itself primarily as an administrative arm of Portugal. It considered its work as spiritual: to create "men" with dignity who knew how to work. Being civilized not only meant learning to speak and live like the Portuguese; it tended to mean becoming Catholic. This was unacceptable to many Mozambicans, especially Protestants. And knowing "how to work" too often involved forced labour without pay. The magnificent Roman Catholic cathedral in Maputo was largely built by such unpaid, forced labour. This work is an important documentation in the history of the church in Mozambique.

Henderson, I. W.

see review 216

459.   Henderson, Lawrence

The Church in Angola: A River of Many Currents

Cleveland: Pilgrim Press, 1992. 448 pages, ISBN: 9780829809381.

Originally published as *A Igreja em Angola: Um rio com várias correntes* in 1990, this is a comprehensive survey of Angolan church history from 1866 to 1989, including the Catholic, Protestant, Pentecostal and Apostolic churches. Given the struggles that Protestant missions had under a Portuguese colonial regime that often worked hand-in-hand with the leadership of a pre-Vatican II church, it is significant that this book was originally published by a Catholic publishing house in Portugal. Henderson does not lose himself in all the details, but paints with broad strokes the development of the Christian community. By the mid-nineteenth century any Catholic mission efforts in earlier centuries had left few traces. Henderson therefore begins his account with the renewal of Catholic outreach in 1866. For the colonial period 1866–1961 he organizes the material according to methods of work (schools, medical work) and various themes (church–government relation, internal organisation, worship), using examples from the various missions and churches throughout Angola. With 1961 comes a new part of the story, as the painful Angolan struggle for political independence impacts the churches (1961–1974). Finally the church in an independent and marxist Angola, ravaged by civil war, is described (1975–1989). The scope of the book is ecumenical, and the tendency is to emphasize similarities over differences (as the subtitle suggests). The author was himself a missionary in Angola from 1947 to 1969. He suggests that the growth and resilience of the church in Angola comes from an existing African spirituality that has much in common with Christianity. He acknowledges that the book might be too much a missionary reflection for the professional historian, while being too "historical" for those wanting stories. But readers may be left appreciating both aspects. Henderson does presuppose a lot of knowledge of Angola that an average reader outside Angola probably would not have. For use of this text outside Angola a general history of Angola would be a helpful complement, to furnish general political, social and economic background. When Henderson concluded his history, the civil war in Angola was still unresolved. By now there is a whole new phase of Angolan Christian history, and many additional stories that need to be told.

460.   Hendriks, H. Jurgens

Studying Congregations in Africa

Cape Town: Lux Verbi, 2003. 244 pages, ISBN: 9780796301994.

Intended as a textbook for a course in Practical Theology, this contribution deals in particular with evaluating and nurturing church congregational life in Africa. Two foundational chapters address theology and ecclesiology. Theology is explained as a process of knowing God rather than as systematic knowledge of God, with a focus on "doing theology" in a contextual way. Ecclesiology is expounded in terms of types and models of different churches, and systems that derive from worldviews. Next the author explains four ways of analysing a local congregation: contextual analysis, identity analysis, process analysis and resources analysis. To improve a church, one should be able to reflect on the context, identity, process and resources of a congregation. Hendriks offers a wealth of paradigms, case studies and advice in support of such analysis. Finally he explains why leadership should be change-oriented, and he explains research methodology. The book provides a mine of information that can be used in analysing and strengthening congregations in Africa. Its chief limitation is that it tends to fail in putting all the pieces together. The presentation can be very technical, and lacks proper introductions and conclusions. As one reads it, one feels that one is entering a great, deep forest: one admires all the wonderful trees but misses the overall view of the forest. Granted the importance of the topic, and the valuable content, for effective use as a student textbook it would need to be more accessible and user-friendly. Lecturers in practical theology in Africa, on the other hand, could find it uniquely useful.

461.   Henkel, Reinhard

Christian Missions in Africa: A Social Geographical Study of the Impact of Their Activities in Zambia

Berlin: Dietrich Reimer Verlag, 1989. 236 pages, ISBN: 9783496009344.

Despite the main title, this book is about Christian missions in Zambia, as the subtitle indicates. The author is a university lecturer in geography who spent two years in Zambia in the 1980s, lecturing at the University of Zambia and researching the impact of Christian missions there. After providing a broad context for his study, he proceeds to describe the growth of Christianity by documenting the establishment (and occasional failure) of mission stations throughout the country. He breaks down the roughly one hundred years of Christianity in Zambia by mapping existing mission stations every ten years from 1895. Then he analyses the character of the various denominations in terms of how urbanized they were/are, and how much their membership is based on ethnic identity, by presenting helpful statistics, tables and graphs to buttress his findings. The graph correlating these two factors, urbanisation and ethnicity, is very creative. Thus he is able to quantify what many observers "felt" was true of Zambian church life, and this may be the best contribution of the book. There are short sections describing most of the denominations in Zambia, often accompanied by data illustrating the distribution of the denomination in the country. Ironically, the one major church for which he was unable to find sufficient data is the New Apostolic Church, which is based in his native Germany. The rest of the book covers such useful topics as the church's relationship to rural life, education, medical care and the economy. Despite the fact that the book's statistics are now decades old (e.g. urbanisation is now well above his figure of 33 percent), there is much helpful material for any researcher in the history of the Zambian church. Its wider significance would be in demonstrating a model worthy of replication for research and publication projects in other parts of the continent.

462. Henry, Helga Bender

Cameroon on a Clear Day: A Pioneer Missionary in Colonial Africa

Pasadena: WCL, 1999. 194 pages, ISBN: 9780878082933.

The author here tells the story of her father, Carl Jacob Bender, an early missionary in western Cameroon. An American of German origin, Bender served in Cameroon with the German Baptists from 1899 to 1919, and then again from 1929 until his death in 1935. Bender, who receives entries in both *The New International Dictionary of the Christian Church* and the *Biographical Dictionary of Christian Missions*, was noted not least for the friendly respect he showed toward Africans and their culture in his evangelistic and educational endeavours, and his efforts to encourage and equip African leadership. Bender was fluent in the local language, composed booklets and hymns for local use, and wrote a study on African songs, riddles, proverbs and fables. He also worked to foster good relations among the various Protestant groups in the Cameroon, and in 1914 was secretary to the first inter-mission conference in Cameroon. The narrative especially highlights the severe disruptions caused to missions by World War I, when British and French forces seized Cameroon from Germany. The occupying powers acted harshly towards missionaries, who were mostly interned and deported. Bender avoided this fate by asserting his American citizenship, and stayed on throughout the war years, not without considerable difficulty. This is a daughter's loving memorial to her father, researched over a number of years, including visits to mission archives in Britain, Germany, and Switzerland, and at least one trip back to Cameroon. The bibliography will be of use to anyone doing further research in this field. The author's husband is the well-known North American theologian Carl Henry, who contributed the foreword (and who himself wrote a brief biography of Bender, *Bender in the Cameroon*, in the early 1940s – a contribution that is missing from the bibliography).

463. Herbst, Jeffrey

States and Power in Africa: Comparative Lessons in Authority and Control

Princeton: Princeton University Press, 2014. 312 pages, ISBN: 9780691010281.

Herbst is Professor of Politics and International Affairs at Princeton University, and author of two previous books on politics in Africa. He begins this study with the recognition that theories of international relations derived from European models have proven unable to explain the creation and development of states in Africa. He therefore sets himself to provide a comparative analysis of state-development in Africa and in Europe. He argues that the differences between the processes on the two continents stem from the divergent topography of the two land masses. Quoting the dictum of Robert Bates, Herbst contends that "the higher the population density, the greater the level of political centralization." Thus, unlike densely populated Europe where governments are highly centralized, only the Ethiopian highlands and the Great Lakes region of eastern Africa feature the kind of environment that allows for high populations densities. In contrast to their European counterparts, African leaders must confront the problems (e.g. the higher costs incurred) of how to consolidate power over widespread, sparsely settled lands. How African authorities have sought to extend power over distance constitutes the central concern of the book. Herbst examines the problems of state consolidation during the pre-colonial era, in the relatively brief but turbulent years of colonialism, and in the recent period of modern independent states. He examines approaches taken by various African leaders for centralising power and evaluates policy options for tackling present problems. Contrary to prevailing assumptions that colonialism obliterated all factors involved in pre-colonial state-building, the author contends that contemporary challenges differ little from those operative before the arrival of the Europeans, since the problem of extending power over distance remains. Herbst offers an original, thought-provoking analysis of the troubled effort at state-formation in Africa. His overriding focus on problems presented by geography, however, runs the risk of a reductionistic thesis. Can so many difficulties trace their origins to topography alone? Nevertheless, by identifying and scrutinising this important and easily overlooked dynamic of the political process in Africa, his study suggests to the thoughtful reader the often unacknowledged complexities of the issues affecting that process. If Herbst's own solution risks oversimplification, even more so perhaps do other more familiar and favoured assumptions on the difficulties of nation-state formation in Africa.

Hexham, Irving

see reviews 872 and 874

Hibou, Béatrice

see review 109

464.   Hiebert, Paul G., R. Daniel Shaw, and Tite Tiénou

Understanding Folk Religion: A Christian Response to Popular Beliefs and Practices

Grand Rapids: Baker, 2000. 414 pages, ISBN: 9780801022197.

This is a comprehensive introduction to the missiological study of popular religions from an evangelical perspective, from the hand of three widely known missiologists. The three combine several decades of experience in cross-cultural study and ministry, representing Asia (Hiebert), Oceania (Shaw) and Africa (Tiénou). Hiebert's well-known thinking on contextualization forms the paradigm for the text. The approach is to see popular or folk religions from a systemic perspective, integrating culture, spiritual, social, personal and biophysical systems through insights from anthropology, sociology, psychology, theology, and religious studies. At least one of the goals is to lay out a paradigm for a missiological analysis and response to a folk religious movement on a local level, and this is breaking new ground for evangelical missions. The first section sets out the model, and this is followed by consideration of the methodology. The bulk of the methodological section presents a bewildering array of phenomenological issues that must be understood if one is to relate to folk religious practitioners. Folk religious beliefs, including the meaning of life and death, human wellbeing and misfortune, guidance in facing the unknown, and the ethics of right and wrong are presented first. Then folk religious practices, including symbolism, myth, rituals, leadership, and religious movements are explored. The reader must bear in mind that this text is intended as a survey, and the authors note that full book-length treatments are needed of each of the folk religions discussed throughout the text. The final sections focus on theological and missiological responses. Though the book is over 400 pages long, fleshing out the last two sections would strengthen an already excellent foundational treatment. As a primer on popular religious movements from around the world, treated from a distinctly Christian perspective, this is the finest book available on the market. It will be especially useful in providing clarifying comparisons and contrasts with Africa's traditional religions and revitalisation movements, in relation to other religious movements around the world, a dimension that can often be lacking in contemporary presentations of ATR.

465.   Hildebrandt, Jonathan

Eldoret Missionary College: From Vision to Reality, The First Ten Years

Minneola, FL: AIM Media Books, 2012. 164 pages.

One noteworthy feature of modern-day Christian mission has been the emergence of cross-cultural mission outreach from the rapidly growing church communities of the non-western world. And one important component of that movement has been the eventual emergence of specialized training institutions for majority-world cross-cultural missionaries. This is the story of the founding and initial years of one of the earliest such institutions in modern-day Africa, Eldoret Missionary College in central Kenya, as recounted by the institution's founding principal. Hildebrandt served for more than 35 years in eastern Africa with the international mission AIM. His name is familiar to African theological schools as the author of the much-used textbook, *History of the Church in Africa: A Survey*. The Eldoret institution was established by the Africa Inland Church (AIC), one of Kenya's largest church bodies. Having founded its own mission board in 1959, and dispatched cross-cultural missionaries thereafter to Kenya's northwestern and coastal regions, AIC leadership eventually recognized an urgent need for providing its missionary candidates with preparatory training in cross-cultural mission. Among principal promoters of the vision were two men, the AIC Bishop, Ezekiel Birech, and an AIC lay member prominent in East African Revival circles, Edward Timo, who with his wife donated choice land near Eldoret for the college. Hildebrandt was appointed to lead the endeavour in 1982, the first classes commenced in 1986, and Hildebrandt handed over leadership to others in 1992. If the account does not always make a captivating read, institutional histories rarely do. One has the sense of a gifted, instinctive entrepreneur, with hands-on technical interests accompanying academic and managerial skills, a combination which exactly suited the needs. Overall one gains a vivid sense of the practical challenges of establishing such a pioneering venture. At times the narrative seems almost lifted from a sequence of personal newsletters; thus some chapter headings are simply: 1986, 1987, 1988. The report can also at times prove quite candid, as when the author acknowledges leadership and staffing disarray subsequent to his departure. The book will be of most interest to those engaged in similar endeavours, and also certainly for those seeking a comprehensive record of this important feature in modern African Christianity.

466.   **Hill, Graham**

Global Church: Reshaping Our Conversations, Renewing Our Mission, Revitalizing Our Churches

Downers Grove: IVP US, 2016. 512 pages, ISBN: 9780830840854.

The author is an Australian theologian teaching practical theology at Morling College in Sydney. In a previous book he developed a missional theology in dialogue with twelve theologians from four major Christian traditions. The present volume continues this dialogical approach, but now engaging with "more than one hundred high profile Majority World Christian leaders" (in Hill's definition the term "Majority World" includes Africa, Asia, the Caribbean, Eastern Europe, Latin America, the Middle East, and Oceania). The purpose of the dialogue is to find out "what they can teach the West about mission, leadership, hospitality, creation care, education, worship and more." The book is organised according to Matthew 5:13–16, with three parts: (1) "Salt": Reshaping our Conversations, (2) "Light": Renewing our Mission, and (3) "City": Revitalizing our Churches. Dialogue partners include 28 Africans (seven Nigerians, six South Africans, five Ghanaians, and then one or two from a number of other countries throughout the continent). Many are critical scholars of theology and biblical studies (such as Kwame Bediako, Justin Ukpong, Musa Dube, Lamin Sanneh, Mercy Oduyoye), but there are also some church leaders (such as Desmond Tutu and William Folorunso Kumuyi). The basic idea of the book, that of developing theological insights in Western contexts through dialogue with Christian leaders in the Majority World, is of course good and laudable, but also difficult. It is good, in the sense that it expresses an explicit will to let Majority World concerns challenge theological thinking and practices in the West. This is a much-needed perspective, frequently voiced, but mainly on a rhetorical level. However, it is not an easy task to accomplish, and in the present attempt to do so the author faces the danger of reducing the many Majority World voices to mere illustrations of his Australian/Western concerns. One example pointing in this direction is his discussion of liberation theology. Acknowledging its potentials, he still rejects key aspects, for example claiming that "Liberationists refuse to spiritualize the biblical idea of 'the poor'. Yet the poor in the Bible are those who are not only oppressed but who also remain faithful to God and seek his deliverance." Another example is his use of Sugirtharajah to present postcolonial biblical interpretation, faithfully quoting Sugirtharajah that colonial power is embodied in "biblical texts and interpretations," but then immediately ignoring Sugirtharajah's concern about the texts themselves, and not only their interpretations. In sum, this does not mean that the book fails to raise important concerns. But it does mean that the reader encounters the "more than one hundred" voices from the Majority World through an already established Western interpretive grid, that of the author.

467.   **Hilliard, Constance B., editor**

Intellectual Traditions of Pre-Colonial Africa

Columbus, OH: McGraw Hill, 1997. 480 pages, ISBN: 9780070288980.

The editor of this collection, a professor of African history in a North American university, begins by outlining the guidelines she followed. Affirming that intellectual traditions take many forms, Hilliard has chosen to limit this collection to verbal productions, whether oral (and now recorded) or written. Also in order to qualify as "African" for this book, a work must have been done by someone fulfilling two conditions: having lived on the African continent and belonging to an indigenous African ethnic group. The contents of the work are arranged both historically and geographically, according to the following order: Pharaonic Egypt; Ancient Nubia; Hellenised Egypt and Nubia; Byzantine and Romanised Carthage; Byzantine, Coptic, and Islamic North Africa; Ethiopia and Somalia; West Africa; Central Africa; East Africa; Southern Africa. Within each section one finds from five to thirteen different literary offerings, encompassing different countries, subjects, and genres. A short introduction helps to set the piece in its context. Helpfully, the editor has also provided a secondary index noting whether the reading qualifies as Historical, Political, Religious, Philosophical, Scientific, or *Belles Lettres*. Thus one could conceivably read only those pieces that were religious in orientation. The wealth of resources not otherwise readily available makes this book extremely valuable. Part of the goal of the book is to demonstrate the rich intellectual history of the African continent, and certainly Hilliard has succeeded in achieving that goal. From the spiritual insights of Christian Church Fathers, such as Augustine and Tertullian, to the poetry of the Berbers, and on to the mathematical principles of Heron of Alexandria, everything seems to find its way into this demonstration of the African intellectual tradition before the colonial era.

468. Hillman, Eugene

Towards an African Christianity: Inculturation Applied

Mahweh, NJ: Paulist Press, 1993. 101 pages, ISBN: 9780809133819.

Hillman, perhaps best known for his *Polygamy Reconsidered* (1975), served for many years among the Maasai people in Kenya and Tanzania. Though a member of the Holy Ghost Fathers, Hillman calls for dropping many elements of traditional Catholicism which he describes as western. These include the church's authoritarian paternalism, imposition of foreign names, exaltation of Mary, rosary beads, adoration of the sacrament, and cluttering the eucharistic liturgy with such "culture-specific accoutrements as imported food, drink, linen, table, chairs, candles, chalice, ciborium, cruets and vestments." However, Hillman does not so much see these as wrong, but merely as applied in the wrong culture. In place of these he is ready to incorporate into Christianity many elements of the traditional Maasai culture and religion, including the ritual slaughtering of animals. One may begin to feel wary of Hillman's philosophical pluralism and universalism which lead to the acceptance of everything in the traditional culture. To such a "wider ecumenism" it seems that there is no longer anything best avoided. At one point he attributes the difference between the Protestant and Catholic perspectives to "the definitive significance attributed to the words of the Bible in the Protestant tradition." And rightly so, evangelicals might respond. Nevertheless, Hillman's challenge to reduce the foreignness of Christianity and to use not only the language but also symbols and rituals of the culture are to be welcomed.

469. Himbaza, Innocent

Le Décalogue et l'histoire du texte: Etudes des formes textuelles du Décalogue et leurs implications dans l'histoire du texte de l'Ancien Testament

Fribourg: Academic Press, 2004. 362 pages, ISBN: 9783525530658.

Himbaza comes from Rwanda, but lives in Fribourg, Switzerland. He has been working for the *Biblia Hebraica Quinta* Project, which is preparing a new scientific edition of the Hebrew Bible, eventually to replace the *Biblia Hebraica Stuttgartensia*. In addition to articles in (mostly Western-based) scholarly journals, Himbaza has previously published a monograph (his Fribourg doctoral thesis) on Bible translation in Rwanda. The present work, a Fribourg *Habilitationsschrift*, is an analysis of the textual history of the Decalogue. It must be pointed out at once that this is the most detailed analysis ever published on the textual history of the Decalogue, and a work that will be a standard reference for decades. Although the Decalogue has indeed received its share of scholarly attention in recent years, including attention to its textual criticism, Himbaza goes both more broadly and more deeply into the material than his predecessors. More broadly, in the sense that he not only analyses the two Masoretic versions of the Decalogue (Exod 20:2–17 and Deut 5:6–22), but also includes a more or less complete spectrum of non-Masoretic Hebrew manuscripts as well as ancient translations. And more deeply, in the sense that he not only surveys these other sources – such as (1) the Qumran, Samaritan and Nash Papyrus Hebrew manuscripts, (2) the Greek, Aramaic, Syriac and Latin translations, and (3) the Jewish (Philo, Josephus, Talmud, etc.) and Christian (NT, Church fathers) sources – but also open-mindedly draws them into the discussion. It is obviously difficult to summarize a book whose *raison d'etre* is to provide the guild of textual critics and Decalogue interpreters with such a variety of details. Nevertheless, three results from Himbaza's research may be briefly mentioned. First, he argues that it is possible to see a difference between Egyptian (Hebrew: Nash Papyrus, Greek: Septuagint) and Palestinian (Masoretic and Samaritan) sources; this is a difference that leads him to suggest that the Decalogue actually experienced cases of local textual evolution. Secondly, he is critical of the various modern attempts at reconstructing a possible original Decalogue consisting of ten short prohibitions; he argues that this can hardly be more than quite vague speculation. And thirdly, he claims that it is impossible to explain the textual variety of the Decalogue from the perspective of translation difficulties; rather, he holds that different versions of the Decalogue must have existed even before the first translation. This singular contribution from Africa is obviously a book for specialists.

470.   Himbaza, Innocent

Transmettre la Bible: Une critique exégétique de la traduction de l'AT: le cas du Rwanda

Rome: Urbaniana University Press, 2001. 624 pages, ISBN: 9788840137803.

Himbaza is a Rwandan theologian based in Switzerland, where he has taught at the Faculty of Theology, University of Fribourg. The book is a revised version of his dissertation accepted by the same university in 1998. Himbaza's major focus is the relationship between biblical text and translation context, and two Rwandan translations are used as case studies: the Protestant *Biblia Yera* (1957, rev. 1993) and the Catholic *Bibiliya Ntagatifu* (1990). After brief introductory chapters presenting the project and outlining the historical background of the two translations, the major bulk of the book is a close reading of a selection of texts taken from Exodus, Samuel, Kings, Isaiah, Hosea, Malachi, Psalms, Esther, and Nehemiah. In each case the two target translations are discussed in relation to the Masoretic Text and to possible influence from English (King James Version, Revised Version) and French (Bible de Jérusalem) translations. It is here noticed that the Catholic translation follows the Bible de Jérusalem in choosing some variants from the Septuagint. Further, for each text Himbaza discusses how, and to what extent, the target translations manage to express the message of the Hebrew texts in language that is sensitive to Rwandan traditional culture. This case study of the relationship between biblical text and translation context will be of interest to translators of course, but exegetes doing contextual interpretation of the OT in Africa will also benefit.

471.   **Hinga, T. M., A. N. Kubai, P. Mwaura, and Hazel Ayanga, editors**

Women, Religion and HIV/AIDS in Africa: Responding to Ethical and Theological Challenges

Pietermaritzburg: Cluster, 2008. 205 pages, ISBN: 9781875053698.

The ten contributors to this book are all African women with wide experience in research on the effects of HIV/AIDS on women in Africa, and significant involvement in service to those infected and affected. The book arises from their collaboration in the Circle of Concerned African Women Theologians, which they describe as "a Pan-African organization of women doing theology, practically, academically and institutionally." The essays are divided into three parts focusing on: factors that render African women vulnerable to HIV/AIDS; ethical and theological issues raised by HIV/AIDS; and a "call to action" through practical responses. One of the great strengths of this book is the research on which it is based, including the stories told by many women of how they were infected and of their situations as people living with HIV/AIDS. Factors identified as increasing women's vulnerability to the virus include extreme poverty, the very low and powerless status of women culturally and sometimes religiously, leading to rape especially in times of war and genocide, and the cultural acceptance of infidelity by husbands/partners that requires silence and a learned helplessness by their wives and lovers. Churches are especially faulted for failing to provide a safe place for women to expose and deal with their pain, and in some cases for using Scripture to perpetuate the abuse and degradation of women who do turn to them for help. While the main focus of the book is on documenting the dire situation facing African women, some specific suggestions are made for practical response. Churches need urgently to take the lead, following the example of Jesus, by standing against the deep stigma which pervades society. Cultural beliefs and practices that increase women's vulnerability to the virus also need to be exposed and replaced by the acceptance of women as fully human and deserving of human rights. Some proposals in the book include redefinitions, however, that may well raise questions among readers, as in the statement that "the sexually chaste person is not necessarily the most celibate. Rather it is recognition of the dignity of sex and obligation towards responsible stewardship of sex and sexuality that marks one as chaste." The writers have responded to the oppression they have witnessed with anger, as did Jesus when he faced clear oppression of the powerless, and the tone of the recommendations reflect their strong feelings. In a future edition, more emphasis on the healthy and joyful benefits to men as well as to women of overcoming patriarchy might be helpfully included.

472.   **Hinton, Mark**

Ministering among Muslims in Africa: An Annotated List of Practical Materials

Nairobi: ACTEA, 1992. 30 pages.

This is a uniquely practical document, offering information that at its time of publication was available nowhere else in just this form. The booklet, produced in simple format, gives details on 38 sources within Africa for materials useful for ministry in Muslim contexts in Africa, including materials designed for outreach, for discipleship, and for ministry training. The booklet catalogues everything available from each of the listed sources, and provides descriptive comment per item. A second part offers the same for 22 sources outside Africa. A third section lists useful materials available from Islamic sources. The material was compiled by Mark Hinton while he was coordinating the ACTEA Islamics Project. Those involved in ministry in Islamic contexts, and those teaching Islamics in theological colleges, will find this document especially valuable.

473. **Hiskett, Mervyn**

The Course of Islam in Africa

Edinburgh: Edinburgh University Press, 1994. 224 pages, ISBN: 9780748604616.

This book provides an updated overview of Islam in Africa from its first incursions in the seventh century into the 1990s. Given the enormity of the task, Hiskett has done a commendable job in identifying the major movements, players and events through history that represent the development of Islam in the various regions of Africa. Hiskett identifies North Africa, Egypt, the Nilotic Sudan, West Africa, Ethiopia and the Horn, and East and South Africa as basic regional entities. The particulars of individual countries are briefly treated within their respective regions. In addition to these historical descriptions, the author also includes a chapter on African Islamic literature, and concludes with a chapter that reviews predominant aspects of the study and poses questions about what he sees at the time as the uncertain future of Islam in the face of democratic aspirations, African unity and secular literacy. As a former British colonial official and a professor of Hausa Studies at the University of Sokoto, the author brings to the discussion a unique lifetime of experience, study, and non-liberal but secular views. This book's necessarily scanty but intriguing sketch of Islamic history will have readers digging for more detail elsewhere. Indeed, recognising the limitations of a survey such as this, Hiskett provides a bibliographic essay in addition to a select bibliography, in order to assist inquirers in the task of augmenting their knowledge of Islam in Africa.

474. **Hochschild, Adam**

King Leopold's Ghost: A Story of Greed, Terror, and Heroism in Colonial Africa

London: Pan Macmillan, 2012. 356 pages, ISBN: 9781447211358.

The world is well aware of the Holocaust during World War II, the Rwandan genocide and the plight of the Christians in Sudan. Few have ever heard about the forced enslavement and slaughter of the people of the Congo River basin under King Leopold of Belgium. Hochschild's work on the Congo in the late nineteenth and early twentieth centuries is a well-researched and clearly written account of the worst side of colonialism in Africa. Hochschild shows how Leopold actively searched for a colony, which he could exploit for financial gain. When Henry Morton Stanley traversed central Africa by way of the Congo, Leopold seized the opportunity and, in the guise of a philanthropist, set about the task of harvesting the Congo for its ivory and rubber. Most of the rubber was harvested by the forced labour of African men whose wives and children were held for ransom until the required amount of rubber was delivered. Those who did not deliver sufficient quantities were whipped or killed – and Leopold's forces accounted for every bullet used with the severed hand of the victims. Hochschild estimates that the population of the Congo basin before Leopold was approximately twenty million, but that by the end of the devastation there were only ten million Africans left. The church through her missionaries played an ambiguous role in this period. Some remained blissfully ignorant. Some attempted to remain "neutral" and so did not speak out. Some however, like the black American Presbyterian William Sheppard, were instrumental in drawing the world's attention to the evil being perpetrated in the Congo. Hochschild teaches at the Graduate School of Journalism at the University of California at Berkeley. The book serves to highlight one of the most horrific examples of the Western colonial impact in Africa. That impact remains among the dominant themes of African intellectual reflection today. Those responsible for teaching church history in African theological colleges should ensure that they are familiar with this tragic story.

Hock, Klaus

see review 377

475. Hoekstra, Harvey Thomas

Honey, We're Going to Africa!

Enumclaw, WA: Winepress Publishing, 1995. 376 pages, ISBN: 9781883893286.

One should not be put off by the title. Hoekstra wrote his autobiography for missionaries and friends, but scholars can glean much of solid worth from this book. Hoekstra recounts his work among the Anuak, Murle, and Majangir (also known as "Mesengo") people of southeastern Sudan and southwestern Ethiopia from 1948 until 1976. Hoekstra lived and worked in these three groups when many aspects of their respective traditional societies were still functioning; but he also lived there long enough to see many changes. Hoekstra was the person primarily responsible for the translation of the Anuak NT. He then went on to translate and publish large portions of the NT in Murle, producing separate volumes printed in Arabic and Roman scripts. His discussion of the translation process in Anuak gives interesting insights into the worldview through the vocabulary of these peoples, such as the Anuak word *jwok*, which he defined as including "God, spirit, luck, illness." Hoekstra gives us the first published descriptions of many aspects of Majangir culture, which are an important supplement to the ethnographic writings of Stauder and Tippett. Hoekstra's description of hiding with his family from an enraged, spear-wielding Majangir man, his account of his long-term personal interaction with the great *tapa'd* (shaman, priest) Balti, the visit of the Ethiopian crown prince and princess to the Godare mission station, are all charged with first person authenticity. For those who study church history, Hoekstra tells of the early, and in many cases very first, Christian missionary work among the Anuak, Murle, Majangir, and also the Sheko. The book will be of obvious interest to any who want to study the cultures mentioned (including cultural changes), the initial growth of churches in these areas, and the activities of the American Mission (Presbyterian). Many academics will skip past the family stories, the accounts of a more personal nature, and the many anecdotes about friends and colleagues – although in skipping these sections, they will miss the motivation, energy, and joy of the author.

476. Hofmeyr, J. W., and K. E. Cross, editors

History of the Church in Southern Africa: A Select Bibliography of Published Material to 1980

Pretoria: UNISA Press, 1986. 809 pages, ISBN: 9780869814352.

Here is an indispensable reference tool for every researcher dealing with church history in southern Africa. This volume and its two successor volumes represent a project started in 1975 by the Institute for Theological Research at the University of South Africa (UNISA) in collaboration with the Department of Church History. The volumes are intended as a contribution in a field which had not received much scholarly attention. The material is divided into four main classes, viz. general, denominational, mission and topical. Each of these four main classes is divided under various headings, thus making it easy for the researcher to gain access to specific available material. A further aid is the comprehensive author and subject indices at the end of each volume. The volumes do not presume to be complete. They do demonstrate a wealth of published material in some areas and the obvious lack of publications in other areas. The bibliographies are limited to published material mainly in the form of books, pamphlets and analytical entries from composite works. Academic theses on masters and doctoral level are included, whether published or unpublished. Sermons, liturgies, church laws and regulations are also included in so far as they contribute to a historical assessment of the relevant church or mission society. Successor volumes include materials dated into the later 1980s. The value of these volumes lies in offering the researcher a reliable introduction to available resource material on church history in southern Africa.

Hofmeyr, J. W.

see also review 926

Hogendorn, Jan S.

see review 650

477. Holland, Grace

T.E.E. Study Materials – Which Way for a Changing Africa?

Nairobi: Evangel, 1992. 50 pages.

In this book the author reviews the history of the TEXT-Africa series, which at the time of publication were the materials most widely used in Africa by theological education by extension programmes (TEE). She also reports on research done in 1982, and repeated a decade later, into the effectiveness of these materials. She surveys the evolving leadership needs of the church in light of social changes on the continent. And she concludes with suggestions for the modification of current TEE materials, and recommendations for the production of new materials at secondary and university level. The significance of the book stems especially from the key role that Holland has played as a pioneer of TEE in Africa, and as principal editor of the TEXT-Africa materials. The study represents her project report submitted for her Doctor of Missiology degree at Trinity Evangelical Divinity School, USA. The book should be essential reading for those investigating the history of TEE in Africa.

Holland, Grace

see also reviews 163 and 783

Holland, Scott

see review 718

Hollyday, Joyce

see review 1146

Holmes, Peter

see review 592

478. Holter, Knut, editor

Let My People Stay!: Researching the Old Testament in Africa. Report from a Research Project on Africanization of Old Testament Studies

Nairobi: Acton Publishers, 2006. 218 pages, ISBN: 9789966888303.

Holter, based in Norway, is one of the world's most prolific advocates for and analysts of African OT studies. This book is essentially a report on three doctoral dissertations. Such a document would appear at first glance to be a dry academic exercise. On the contrary, however, this study is a rather exciting description of contextual exegesis. Following an introductory chapter describing the project in the context of African biblical studies, the book is divided into three major sections. In each section the work of a doctoral student is introduced by that student's supervisor (or "promoter"). Each student then contributes two chapters, using their doctoral research as a starting point for describing the relevance of OT studies for the African situation. In each section these essays are then followed with a chapter by another scholar who points to further dimensions of research and application. The book is pioneering, creative and engaging, and provides an interesting model for cooperative research and scholarship. Especially to be congratulated are the three doctoral students, Lechion Peter Kimilike, Georges Razafindrakoto, and Philip Lokel, whose efforts (on Proverbs, on the Malagasy use of the OT outside of the church, and on Cush) provide the basis for the text. Holter has once again made an exceptional contribution in facilitating and publicising the achievements of African biblical scholarship. All lecturers in OT at theological schools in Africa will want to be familiar with this work, as will African students pursuing doctoral research in biblical studies.

479. Holter, Knut

Old Testament Research for Africa: A Critical Analysis and Annotated Bibliography of African Old Testament Dissertations, 1967–2000

Frankfurt: Peter Lang, 2002. 143 pages, ISBN: 9780820457888.

The ever-growing guild of African OT scholars has probably no better friend and encourager than Knut Holter, currently Director of the Center for Mission and Global Studies at VID University in Stavanger, Norway. Holter launched the *Newsletter on African Old Testament Scholarship* in 1996, and has served as editor of both the journal *Bulletin for Old Testament Studies in Africa* and the *Bible & Theology in Africa* monograph series from the publisher Peter Lang. Here he analyses nearly ninety doctoral dissertations written in French or English and submitted at African and Western institutions by African scholars (excluding South Africans). Holter believes that "a better knowledge of African doctoral dissertations in the Old Testament may . . . deepen our understanding of the variety of interpretative approaches to the Old Testament in Africa." To understand this variety, the author examines the data from three perspectives: (i) students' thematic interests or topics; (ii) the guiding influence of institutions which nurture the scholarship; and (iii) the interpretive contexts or contextualization concerns reflected in the students' research (e.g. using OT insights to interpret Africa and vice versa). His attention to the development and role of institutions, academic networks, and publishers in building African OT scholarship is a highlight of this volume. The book addresses itself to three audiences. First, African OT scholars will be glad to learn of one another's projects and areas of expertise. We may hope that Holter's work will promote a greater sense of community and new lines of communication within sub-Saharan OT scholarship. Secondly, this book provides many leads for those studying in the more general area of African theology, especially in the 41 pages of abstracts. Thirdly, this bibliography may provide some "diversity-training" for scholars and scholarly societies in the West, who have heretofore been largely ignorant of African work on the OT (Holter wisely notes that this is not entirely the fault of Westerners). The book will naturally be of greatest interest to lecturers and graduate students in OT in Africa, and may help spark the emergence of a fresh generation of OT scholarship that is "rooted in African experiences and needs."

480.   Holter, Knut

Tropical Africa and the Old Testament: A Select and Annotated Bibliography

Oslo: University of Oslo, 1996. 106 pages, ISBN: 9788299191371.

According to the introduction which delimits its scope, this bibliography covers scholarly literature which deliberately relates two entities, namely tropical Africa (excluding the northern and southern parts of the continent) and the OT. The bibliography gives a brief annotation for each of 232 items, which are listed alphabetically by author. Each entry is also described by at least one key word, the relevant OT reference(s), and (if applicable) a geographical/language designation. These three categories are then indexed so that one can find all the items relating, for instance, to the key word "adultery," or to the geographical/language designation "Akan," or to "Genesis 1–3" in the OT. These indexes make the contents easily accessible. The selected items are written primarily in English (with a few French and other European language items represented), and the large majority are journal articles (with some books and articles in edited volumes included). Most items were published in the 1980s and 1990s. This bibliography should be considered an essential tool for post-graduate level research on topics within its scope. Ironically and unfortunately, it seems likely that researchers located in the West will have more convenient access to the books and journals here listed than will most of those located in Africa.

481.   Holter, Knut

Yahweh in Africa: Essays on Africa and the Old Testament

Bern: Peter Lang, 2001. 162 pages, ISBN: 9780820458403.

It may sometimes have appeared that the majority of African scholars with advanced degrees were lecturing or doing research in church history, ATR, or theology, rather than in biblical studies. In recent times, however, a wealth of material has in fact been published by African scholars in the field of biblical studies. The purpose of this collection of Holter's essays (most of them previously published) is to analyse some of the important themes and trends in African OT scholarship. Holter lectures in OT at the VID University in Stravanger, Norway. He was also editor of the journal *Bulletin for Old Testament Studies in Africa*. This book is divided into two parts. Part 1 contains several studies of how the OT is read in Africa. Among Holter's insights is that there is a distinction to be made between two approaches taken in Africa. One is "an exegetical approach, where African experience provides some help for the interpretation of the Old Testament." The other is "a hermeneutical approach, where the Old Testament provides some help for the interpretation of the lives of its contemporary African readers." Very few examples of academic biblical scholarship in Africa exist that are content to leave the text unrelated to the African context. In part 2: "Africa in the Old Testament," Holter contributes three articles to a lively and growing discussion about the place of Africa and Africans found in the biblical text itself. This discussion, including Holter's part in the debate, should help to correct the Eurocentric tendencies that have for too long been a part of the global scholarly *Zeitgeist*. At the same time Holter avoids those orientations and claims associated with some more extreme Afrocentric contributions. Throughout the book Holter is a balanced, fair and very sympathetic observer. One of his hopes is that African scholarship can be better known, appreciated and studied in the non-African world.

Holter, Knut

see also review 383

482. Hopkins, Mark, and Musa A. B. Gaiya, editors

Churches in Fellowship: The Story of TEKAN

Bukuru, Nigeria: Africa Christian Textbooks, 2005. 189 pages, ISBN: 9789781351365.

In 1904, four missionaries from the new Sudan United Mission (SUM) arrived in the town of Wase in Nigeria. Their aim was to plant churches in the north of Nigeria and to halt the southward spread of Islam. Today between five and ten million Africans belong to the thirteen daughter or sister church bodies of the SUM. These churches are part of a fellowship called TEKAN (Tarayyar Ekklesiyar Kristi a Nigeria, or the Fellowship of Churches of Christ in Nigeria). This book marks the 50th anniversary of TEKAN's founding in 1955. With twelve chapters by six different authors, it tells the story of the SUM origins, the TEKAN organisation, and the individual churches who are members of TEKAN. Two facts stand out in this book. First is the significant presence of these Christian churches in Nigeria's Middle Belt and Northern regions, areas often considered to be Muslim. But secondly is the weakness of this ecclesiastical union. The churches in this fellowship include Methodists, Lutherans, Reformed and those from the Free Church tradition. But each particular denomination is almost always in practice more important than the broader TEKAN fellowship. The strongest manifestation of this fellowship is the Theological College of Northern Nigeria (TCNN), which is owned by this fellowship of churches. This book fills an important gap in West African church history.

483. Horton, Robin

Patterns of Thought in Africa and the West: Essays on Magic, Religion and Science

Cambridge: Cambridge University Press, 1997. 484 pages, ISBN: 9780521369268.

Horton was a British anthropologist who taught African religion and philosophy at the University of Port Harcourt in Nigeria. He did his fieldwork on the Igbo and Kalabari people. This book is a collection of previously published essays, with an Introduction that outlines all the papers, and a Postscript that refines his views. His major interest is a theoretical framework for interpreting African traditional religion (ATR). On the one hand, he battles anthropologists who try to place ATR in the realm of symbols for psychological and sociological conditions. He thinks ATR is really, like Western science, a logical system for explaining, predicting and controlling the human environment. Whereas the West has a theory of impersonal forces (natural laws) for this, Africans have a theory of personal forces (gods, ancestors etc.), but the logic is the same. On the other hand he attacks ATR scholars like Turner and Idowu who try to make ATR sound too much like modern Western Christianity with its emphasis not on explanation and control but on communion with deity. This book is an important cautionary text for interpretations of ATR, and should be familiar among researchers and lecturers in that field of study.

484.   Hostetler, Marian

They Loved Their Enemies: True Stories of African Christians

Scottdale, PA: Herald Press, 1990. 104 pages, ISBN: 9780836134568.

The author taught for several years in Africa and also spent time in Africa collecting the data for this book on assignment with the Mennonite Board of Missions. Her goal is to inspire readers through the stories of African Christians who loved their enemies in order to follow "Jesus' way of love, non-violence, and forgiveness." Her conclusion is that "only through his way can we find lasting peace and hope for the human family." She begins with those persecuted and killed for their faith during the early years of the church in North Africa, and continues through the development of the Coptic Church and persecution accompanying the rise of Islam. She then moves to the coming of Christianity to sub-Saharan Africa, with testimonies from Madagascar, Uganda, Nigeria, Ivory Coast, Ghana, Cameroon and Congo. Her subjects include well-known personalities like William Wadé Harris and Simon Kimbangu, and also laypeople who were faithful to God's call to respond with his love to those who threatened or persecuted them. She continues with examples from war-torn areas such as Angola, Kenya, Ethiopia, Somalia, Rwanda, Burundi, Sierra Leone, Algeria and South Africa. Each story powerfully illustrates the faithfulness of African Christians who stood firm for their faith while showing God's love to their persecutors. Each story is short and easy to read, and dialogue is often used to make the stories personal. The reader feels part of the setting as the Christian is witnessing to his or her faith, and the effect is powerful.

485.   Howell, Allison M.

A Daily Guide for Culture and Language Learning

Jos: Nigeria Evangelical Missionary Institute, 1990. 190 pages, ISBN: 9789782668172.

Howell has experience in Ghana and Nigeria in helping African (and western) missionaries learn the language and culture of the people to whom they are being sent. These are companion titles born from that role. The *Daily Guide* was developed as a handbook for missionaries in the field. Part 1 covers reasons for learning culture and language, tools for doing so, and the place of linguistics, cultural anthropology and human geography in such study. It also covers hindrances to such learning. Part 2 presents the self-directed GLUE method for language and culture learning developed by Donald Larson. Part 3 gives five stages in 118 situations (conversation topics) to guide the study of culture, vocabulary and expression. Using a situation per day, a student should be able to work through the stages in twelve to eighteen months. Part 4 gives suggestions for going further. There is a companion volume, also by Howell, *Encouraging Language and Culture Learners* (1997), intended as a handbook for supervisors of missionaries using the *Daily Guide*. It gives advice on how to evaluate and encourage language and culture learning. Included are numerous evaluation sheets, checklists, samples of kinds of things people should be able to express at each stage, and a helpful bibliography. The two books are especially designed for Africans preparing for cross-cultural ministry in Africa.

486.   Howell, Allison M.

The Religious Itinerary of a Ghanaian People: The Kasena and the Christian Gospel

Achimota, Ghana: Africa Christian Press, 2002. 416 pages, ISBN: 9789964877071.

As an anthropologist serving on the SIM team in northern Ghana, Howell researched the cultural, social and religious background of the local peoples in order to help missionaries, church leaders and others avoid unnecessary misunderstandings. This book is a condensed form of her work on the Kasena people, used for her PhD thesis at the University of Edinburgh. It is especially valuable as an example of how to go about doing research into the cultural, social and religious background of an African people, and shows how this information can be used to good purpose in Christian mission. For example, such information can be an aid in discerning whether local people are really making Christianity their own. As such research also helps in understanding the usual process of conversion among a people, it can offer guidance in designing effective evangelistic strategies. Knowing the background also helps to plan teaching that addresses the discipleship problems people inherit from their background and worldview. Howell describes the Kasena environment and history, family structure, belief system, major problems and issues, and the interaction of the traditional worldview with Christianity. She compares traditional religious ideas and problem-solving methods with those of Kasena Christian converts, and concludes with some implications from the Kasena experience for theology, and some lessons for missionary work elsewhere. Her research methods are described in detail and much of the data is found in the tables and appendices.

487.   Howell, Allison M.

The Slave Trade and Reconciliation: A Northern Ghanaian Perspective

Accra: Bible Church of Africa, 1998. 86 pages, ISBN: LANG255418.

The editor served in Ghana as a researcher with the international mission SIM. This book is a compilation of presentations made at a seminar on "The Slave Trade and the Gospel" held in northern Ghana in 1998. The book falls into four sections. The first contains fascinating oral stories and songs about the slave trade that the presenters collected from their respective ethnic groups. Each presentation also contains practical application linking the presentation to biblical principles related to slavery. The second part is a scholarly, well-documented presentation by Howell of the history of slavery. She starts with an overview of slavery in the Bible, and briefly sketches the African slave trade up to the end of the nineteenth century. She then especially emphasizes the slave trade within West Africa and particularly in northern Ghana. Next is a homily by Jay Moon entitled "Forgiveness and Reconciliation," which compares the centuries-old problem of slavery to an open sore that continues to weaken its victim until cleansed and healed. Moon uses the account of Saul's mistreatment of the Gibeonites in 2 Samuel 21 as a biblical parallel to the African slave trade. This story teaches that problems of the past affect our lives today, and also that "when the leaders sin and the people do not resist it, then the whole nation is guilty." The presentation appeals for the descendants of all involved in the slave trade to seek forgiveness and reconciliation. This section closes with a description of a foot washing ceremony among the expatriate missionaries and the African Christian leaders present, along with the extemporaneous comments of several who participated. The book concludes with a Bible study related to slavery, as well as a list of practical suggestions that arose from the seminar. This book can prove useful in at least the following ways: (1) It should inspire others in Africa to collect those oral traditions still alive among their people that relate to slavery. (2) The book models a balanced understanding of the African slave trade, and makes clear that both expatriates and Africans were involved both in the development and in the destruction of the slave trade. (3) The book also encourages and models reconciliation and the cleansing of the "deep sore" which slavery created and which still remains sensitive today.

488.   Hudson, John

A Time to Mourn: A Personal Account of the 1964 Lumpa Church Revolt in Zambia

Lusaka: Bookworld, 1999. 160 pages, ISBN: 9789982240123.

There have been numerous articles in books and journals about the conflicts surrounding the Lumpa church of Alice "Lenshina" just before and after Zambia gained independence in 1963–1964. This book, and Kampamba Mulenga's *Blood on Their Hands*, claim to be the first full-length books offering first-hand reports on the regrettable events. The background context was pre-independent Zambia, and the visions that Alice "Lenshina" (from the Latin *regina*, for "queen") had in 1953, in which she claimed to have gone to heaven and been raised from the dead. Within a decade Lenshina's growing Lumpa church had become a threat to the outgoing colonial government, the government-in-waiting of Kenneth Kaunda, and the missionaries (Free Church of Scotland), who were rapidly losing members to the new sect. The Lumpas were put down forcibly in 1963–1964 with considerable loss of life, after an until-then relatively peaceful path to independence. Hudson was a former District Commissioner in a region directly affected by the Lumpa movement, and he writes from a perspective of defending the Northern Rhodesian Regiment's eventual use of force. Both he and Mulenga agree that less force should have been used sooner, but from that point their analyses diverge widely. Consequently, one sometimes wonders if the authors are describing the same events. For example, Hudson quotes the standard government casualty figure of roughly a thousand lives lost, but Mulenga begins with reference to "scores of thousands" in his preface, and then escalates the figure to "hundreds of thousands" by the end of the book. There is no doubt that the Lumpa church made a significant impact on the Zambian church scene with its emphasis on vernacular hymns and its tough stance against witchcraft, alcohol and adultery. One is often reminded of the similar ministries of Harris in the Ivory Coast and Kimbangu in the Congo (DRC). The difference is that Lenshina's activities coincided with political changes that put her and her followers on a collision course with fellow Africans – both local chiefs and national leaders. Unfortunately, both Hudson's and Mulenga's books are so biased that the church in Africa will still need a book that deals accurately with the theological issues raised, such as Lenshina's frequent revelations. The historical events described in these books may have been limited to Central Africa, but they link directly to much wider issues in the history of Christianity on the continent.

489.   Hull, Richard

Jews and Judaism in African History

Princeton: Markus Wiener, 2009. 200 pages, ISBN: 9781558764965.

The author of this survey of Jewish history in the context of Africa is a history professor at New York University. His publication history indicates that Africa has long been a research interest. Here he provides a reasonable overview of the presence of Jews in Africa from the classical period to the present day, a topic otherwise often overlooked except in the context of biblical studies. Allowing that the term "Jew" has had various connotations, he notes that he applies it in this study to those "who either possess the faith or who are of Jewish heritage, whether or not they may actually adhere to the religion of Judaism." The chapter headings clearly indicate the outline in terms of chronology and geography: Jews in Africa in Classical Antiquity; Jews and Muslims in North Africa to the 17th Century; Jews and Conversos in the Formative Years of the West and Central African Atlantic Slave Trade; Jews and the Rise of South Africa; Jews and Judaism in Central and Eastern Africa; North African Jewry since the 17th Century. Each chapter contains thematic sub-sections. Three rough-sketch maps, each tied to a period of history, indicate the location of significant Jewish settlements. For example, on the map of Africa in AD 1500 one can note settlements near Timbuktu (in modern Mali), which do not show on either the map of Jewish settlements prior to AD 400 nor on the map of AD 1600. Those settlements had been pushed elsewhere, primarily to the coastal regions. Hull also notes that the pogroms in Europe, especially those against the Sephardic Jews in Spain, brought an influx of diaspora Jews to Africa in the seventeenth century. Nevertheless, anti-Semitic sentiment was not limited to Europe. Though Jewish groups had been present in Africa for many centuries, their integration was never complete. Muslims and Christians often used them as intermediaries, since the Jews were a group apart. By black Africans they were considered outsiders, because of their racial heritage, their faith, and often their prosperity. The Ethiopian Jews, who traced their Jewish and African roots back to biblical times, called themselves "the house of Israel," but the surrounding population referred to them as *Falasha*, "strangers." Feeling the effects of both drought and insecurity where they lived, this group petitioned Israel in the 1970s and 1980s to help them immigrate to their "Promised Land." Yet even today Judaism continues in certain pockets on the continent, primarily in larger cities along the coast. This book is of interest to the study of religion in Africa, since it touches a neglected aspect of that history. This book highlights as well a group that has little constructive contact today with the Christian church in Africa.

490. Hulley, Leonard, Louise Kretzschmar, and Luke Pato, editors

Archbishop Tutu: Prophetic Witness in South Africa

Cape Town: Human & Rousseau, 1997. 264 pages, ISBN: 9780798136075.

In this volume of 22 essays, South African theologians and churchmen honour the remarkable ministry of the then recently retired Archbishop of Cape Town, Desmond Tutu. As is noted in the foreword, "Archbishop Desmond Tutu has been a towering figure in South African church and political life for over twenty years." The book is divided into three main sections, the first being biographical. Francis Cull's essay "Desmond Tutu: Man of Prayer" is a particularly helpful contribution, showing as it does the profound spirituality of Tutu that underpinned his ministry. It is a spirituality rooted in the Benedictine tradition of "rest, prayer and work, and in that order." The best essays in this Festschrift come from the second section, headed "Life and Faith in an African Context." Simon Maimela contributes an essay on "Culture and ethnic diversity as sources of curse and blessing in the promotion of democratic change." Michael Battle addresses "The Ubuntu Theology of Desmond Tutu." Janet Hodgson tackles the question of the inculturation of Anglicanism on the African continent in her essay, "African and Anglican," while in his contribution entitled "Why Christian ethics needs Africa" Neville Richardson shows why he thinks "the time is ripe for Africa to make a rich contribution to Christian ethics." The final section of the book, "Morality, Religion and Society," is not as good as the previous sections. It tackles, among other things, women issues, theological education, and living in a multifaith South Africa. All in all, this is a helpful volume, although (with some exceptions) by no means an outstanding one.

491.   Hunwick, John, and Eve Troutt Powell

The African Diaspora in the Mediterranean Lands of Islam

Princeton: Markus Wiener, 2002. 220 pages, ISBN: 9781558762756.

Hunwick is an expert in the history of West African Islam, and Powell is a specialist in Middle Eastern studies. Each of them has written an introductory chapter, and the rest of the book is a collection of primary source materials about the Islamic African slave trade, given with a bit of context but no evaluation. The readings are meant to stimulate discussion on the subject. Some are written by Muslims, and others by non-Muslim observers. Most of them come from the last three centuries. According to the authors, the Islamic slave trade has received little attention so far because of possible adverse effects on Arab-African relations, the lack of a unified constituency in Arab lands to press for the study (those with slave ancestry being unwilling to admit it), the lack of interest from Western scholars (Africanist scholars lacking expertise in Islam and Arabic), and Arab sensitivity to criticism of Islam. The readings demonstrate the milder conditions of slavery in the Muslim world than in the plantations of the new world. They also show the severe cruelty of the capture and transport of Africans into the Muslim world, and the practice of castrating boys to serve as eunuchs in the harems of the rich. Almost all slaves became Muslims, though the Hausa *bori* cult continued to be common among them. The readings demonstrate the sad plight of many Africans liberated from slavery who had to stay on in the Arab world. There are also readings from Muslim leaders who decried or helped to abolish slavery in North Africa. Christianity is seldom mentioned, but here too there are heroes and villains. We hear of Christian Abyssinian slave girls who refused to give up their faith, and Coptic monks who made a business of the cruel castration of boys. The book ends with a useful bibliography on the subject. This is an important book on a rarely studied topic.

492.   Hydén, Göran

African Politics in Comparative Perspective

Cambridge: Cambridge University Press, 2012. 236 pages, ISBN: 9781107651418.

This short textbook on African politics is an excellent resource for academic and religious professionals needing a readable, reliable overview of African political and economic development. The book reviews fifty years of research on the independent states in Africa. Hydén, a distinguished professor of political science in the United States, has been studying Africa for well over three decades, and brings to his analysis both a wealth of knowledge and a deep concern and respect for African culture. He tackles topics such as Big Man Rule, agrarian reform, gender, ethnicity and the effectiveness of aid and development programmes. Hydén argues that sub-Saharan Africa operates on the basis of an "economy of affection," webs of relationships which blur distinctions between the public and private realms and tie people together both politically and economically. He also challenges Western understandings of development and the manner in which they are carried out, arguing that African peoples and governments have too little say in development efforts across the continent. The book is a useful recent summary of the state of social science research on economic and political progress in Africa.

493. **Hylson-Smith, Kenneth**

To the Ends of the Earth: The Globalization of Christianity

Carlisle, UK: Paternoster, 2007. 240 pages, ISBN: 9781842274750.

In Europe and America it is often assumed that Christianity is on the decline. But this book reminds us of the astounding growth of global Christianity especially in the last two centuries. The author, a historian of British church history, was a fellow of St Cross College, Oxford. His theme is that "since 1700 Christianity has undergone its greatest period of expansion ever, and is currently more vigorous, healthy and widely embraced than at any previous time." The current worldwide strength of the church is traced to the evangelical revivals in Britain and America in the eighteenth and nineteenth centuries, and the Pentecostal movement in the twentieth century. Whereas there is much truth in Hylson-Smith's theme, much of what he says has already been stated by Philip Jenkins. What is offered here is an optimistic, Anglo-centric and Pentecostal presentation of the facts, leading to a sometimes uneven survey. The chapter devoted to the Western world in the twentieth century gives a disproportionate amount of space to the Pentecostal movement. The chapter on Africa oddly begins with the "prophets and independent churches" instead of the mainline mission churches from which they often derived. In respect to Europe, the author suggests that while it is increasingly unchurched, it is not necessarily secular. While the state of Christianity today is probably not as bad as what the Western media suggest, it is probably not as good as what Hylson-Smith tells us either.

494. **IAPCHE**

Christian Education in the African Context: Proceedings of the African Regional Conference of IAPCHE, Harare, 4–9 March 1991

Grand Rapids: IAPCHE, 1992. 200 pages.

This book contains the papers delivered at the first regional conference of the International Association for the Promotion of Christian Higher Education (IAPCHE), held at Harare, Zimbabwe, in 1991. The book is divided into six sections. Section one deals with the relevance of a Christian approach. The second section gives an introduction to three institutions in Africa aiming at Christian education on post-secondary level. A panorama of Christian scientific endeavour is given in section three. Section four includes the Bible studies held during the conference, while section five concentrates on the task of Christian higher education in the African context and presents conclusions and resolutions of the conference. Section six presents the history, basis and purpose of IAPCHE. The concern of IAPCHE is that academic work be recognized as an expression of life commitment to God the Creator, through Jesus Christ, in the power of the Spirit. Science and scholarship cannot have a neutral, uncommitted character, but should be pursued from a biblical perspective. These matters received attention at the conference in papers of varying quality by scholars from Africa, North America and South Korea. Arising from the papers is the perspective that if Christian higher education in Africa is to fulfil its responsibility, it must be aware of and sensitive to the African context. Furthermore, a Christian worldview should determine our view especially of the African world. Integration on two levels are of importance: (a) faith and science – a Christian perspective on all of the sciences must be developed; (b) education and life – Christian higher education may not be abstract but must reflect and prepare students for life in today's African society. The book could be of interest to anyone concerned with a Christian approach to higher education in Africa.

495.   Ibewuike, Victoria Oluomachukwu

African Women and Religious Change: A Study of the Western Igbo of Nigeria, with a Special Focus on Asaba Town

Uppsala: Uppsala University, 2006. 353 pages, ISBN: 9789150618389.

The author is Nigerian, and the book is a doctoral dissertation accepted by Uppsala University in 2006. It offers an analysis of the religious and socio-political role of women in Asaba, located in the western part of Igboland, Nigeria, with particular reference to how that role has changed throughout the nineteenth and twentieth centuries as a result of colonialism, modernisation, Western education and Christianity. The book successively: surveys the role of women in traditional Igbo society (kinship, politics, economy, religion and life cycle rituals); deals with the changes that came as a result of mission work and colonialism, and the Igbo response, from the 1830s till 2000; and offers a detailed study of the role of women in the Roman Catholic Church in Asaba. This is obviously a narrow study, of special interest for universities and theological seminaries in Nigeria. Still, some of the findings will prove of interest for a broader readership. A notable example would be the claim that the introduction of Christianity led to very different results as far as the position of women is concerned. On the one hand, the Anglican Church Missionary Society (CMS) neglected a traditional system allowing men and women to operate in parallel structures in society. Instead they created institutions where men and women were present simultaneously, with the result that women lost their previous power to speak for themselves. On the other hand, the Roman Catholic Church recruited a number of members of slave origin. These people used to be excluded from the structures of the freeborn, and for them the new and egalitarian faith represented an emancipation.

496.   Ijatuyi-Morphé, Randee

Africa's Social and Religious Quest

Lanham, MD: University Press of America, 2014. 646 pages, ISBN: 9780761862673.

This massive volume is by the Provost of ECWA Theological Seminary Jos (JETS) in Nigeria. Its purpose is to define and analyse Africa's social and religious quest. The author does this by dialoguing with an enormous amount of literature on Africa, Scripture and the contemporary world. At the start he says that "Africa's quest is essentially a search for life and wholeness." The author then describes this quest from four perspectives. First, he looks at culture and religion in African society. Traditionally, and even today, African culture and religion provide protection and power for the African. African religion offered salvation and security in a hostile environment. The second section looks at political, economic and social development. The African, and the OT, emphasize human dignity more than human rights. This is the essence of the image of God concept in Genesis. In our world there is much social oppression. A holistic response would emphasize the cultural mandate (Gen 1:28) and the social mandate. The first teaches the value of work; the second teaches the value of security. The third section of the book looks at religion, social history and ethics. Religion is important because it offers a worldview. The biblical worldview is focussed on the "inaugurated reign of God" or the kingdom of God. The kingdom of God will provide a basis for ethical living, which will lead to the good life. The fourth section is on God, humanity and the world. Humanity craves salvation, but the Bible offers "a selfhood based on and ultimately derived from the personhood of God." In conclusion, the author thinks "the end of Africa's quest is supremely seen as achieving a liberated life." The process is "God's inaugurated rule, so that the true end or goal of the human quest for meaning and destiny may be realized." This book is ambitious and demanding but also rich. The author has interacted with a vast amount of important literature, but in the journey through this literature it is easy to get lost.

497. Ijezie, Luke Emehiele

The Interpretation of the Hebrew Word 'am (People) in Samuel-Kings

Frankfurt: Peter Lang, 2007. 342 pages, ISBN: 9780820483764.

Born in Nigeria, Ijezie did his licence at Biblicum (1995) and his doctorate at Gregoriana (2005), both in Rome, and currently teaches Sacred Scriptures at the Catholic Institute of West Africa in Port Harcourt, Nigeria. The book is a revised version of his 2005 doctoral dissertation on the Hebrew word 'am, in most cases rendered "people." The main point of this investigation is that the semantic range of 'am is not always the same as that of "people" in modern use of the term in English. Rather, the identity of 'am is linked to the organisational structure of the type of society projected in the literary context. The book approaches the function of 'am from three broad perspectives. First, kin-related relations, such as clan and tribe. Secondly, political relations, such as political structures, participants in warfare and participants in governance. And thirdly, religious relations, such as 'am as a community of Yahweh's subjects, and Yahweh's 'am in relation to the monarchy. It is pointed out that the word is not specifically a kinship or military term, as often argued; rather it is used about various functional representatives of society. Ijezie's book is an example of the increased number of monographs published by African scholars within the field of biblical studies. Some have a contextual focus, allowing biblical texts and contemporary African contexts explicitly to interact. Others have a more exegetical focus, analysing the biblical texts from (assumed) "pure" historical perspectives. Still, one may sometimes wonder in such cases whether contemporary contextual concerns may play a role too, under the surface. So would seem to be the case here. The book is an exegetical analysis of the manifold meanings of 'am in Samuel-Kings, but at the same time its focus on the relationship between political and religious aspects of the word has important parallels in the relationship between ethnicity, politics and religion in many parts of contemporary Africa. Let it therefore be recommended as an example of the calibre of relevant biblical research now originating on the continent.

498. Ikenga-Metuh, Imefie

African Religions in Western Conceptual Schemes: The Problem of Interpretation. Studies in Igbo Religion

Jos: IMICO, 1991. 183 pages, ISBN: 9789783095717.

Ikenga-Metuh is a Catholic priest and senior lecturer in religious studies at the University of Jos, Nigeria. His introduction points to the distortions that occur when Western-trained scholars (even if themselves Africans) try to describe African religions in the categories of the alien thought-world of modern academia. Being aware of the dangers, and having full indigenous access to the Igbo language and worldview, Ikenga-Metuh sets out to give a more adequate description of Igbo religion. He says, "The purpose of this book is to enable a Westerner or anybody with a Western worldview to understand Igbo religious beliefs as the Igbo understand them." Although the book is actually a collection of the author's articles on Igbo religion previously published in a number of journals, the treatment of Igbo worldview and beliefs is fairly complete. There is heavy emphasis on beliefs about the Supreme God, but leaner sections specifically on subjects like deities and evil are scattered throughout the book. There is no index to help one locate material on topics not reflected in the table of contents. The author often interacts with scholars' generalisations about African religions, which would make the book a useful resource in the study of African traditional religion.

499.   Ilibagiza, Immaculée, and Steve Erwin

Left to Tell: Discovering God amidst the Rwandan Holocaust

London: Hay House, 2014. 325 pages, ISBN: 9781781802953.

This is not the only personal account of the 1994 genocide in Rwanda, but possibly among the more gripping. By way of background, the reader learns that the Germans were Rwanda's first colonial masters, followed after World War I by the Belgians. Both, the author asserts, "converted Rwanda's existing social structure – a monarchy that under a Tutsi king had provided Rwanda with centuries of peace and harmony – into a discriminatory, race-based class system." After the Belgians quit Rwanda in 1962, "a Hutu government was firmly in place and Tutsis had become second-class citizens facing persecution, violence, and death at the hands of Hutu extremists." The author, one of four children of teachers in Catholic schools, never knew she was Tutsi until the eighth grade, when her Hutu teacher started a weekly roll call requiring every Tutsi, Hutu, or Twa child to identify themselves. This practice, the government claimed, was to achieve ethnic balance in awarding scholarships and allocating well-paid jobs. Despite her excellent grades, Immaculée and her family had to struggle to get her a decent education. Eventually she won a scholarship at the national university. It was while home on holiday during her third year that the holocaust began in earnest. At her father's urging she fled to a Hutu Protestant pastor's home for refuge, and was hidden for three months along with seven other Tutsi women in a small bathroom. Food was scanty and sanitation non-existent. The worst, however, was the repeated searching of the pastor's home by the marauding, murdering gangs, known as the Interahamwe, armed with guns, knives, and machetes chanting, "Kill them all! Kill them big and small! Kill them all!" While she was in hiding, Immaculée's parents and three brothers were brutally murdered. When French troops came into the area, the pastor arranged for the women's transfer to a French refugee camp. Being an educated woman and fluent in French, she became a trusted assistant to the commandant. Eventually the author married an American UN worker and now lives in the United States with her husband and two children, while working for the UN. The tenor of this narrative is how Immaculée came to know God in a deeper way, and how God enabled her to overcome her anger and hatred for her Hutu pursuers. The professional writing style that makes this book an arresting read at the same time tends to blunt the unrelenting visceral fear and terror the victims must have felt.

500.   Iliffe, John

The African AIDS Epidemic: A History

Athens, OH: Ohio University Press, 2005. 210 pages, ISBN: 9780821416891.

The author has produced an extremely thorough and well-documented analysis of Africa's experience with HIV/AIDS, from its beginning through into the early years of the new millennium. For those interested in detail, the author provides 50 pages of notes to support the facts laid out in the text. His intention is to bring together the huge body of literature and make it accessible to professionals as well as general readers. He achieves this objective admirably. He moves systematically through what is known about the origins of the disease to follow the spread of the virus to the east, south and west of the continent, in order to provide a synthesis of the data of the causation of the disease. He notes circumstances that have facilitated the severity of the disease's impact, and documents the responses of governments, international organisations and NGOs, along with the moral and political controversies being dealt with by each. Using medical, anthropological and eyewitness sources, he also describes the effects of the epidemic on households, social systems and economies, and traces the development of care of the infected, the search for cures and vaccines, and the impact of antiretroviral treatments. This book is an excellent resource for all who need a closer familiarity with Africa's AIDS epidemic. The book assumes no prior knowledge or medical or statistical expertise. The author is Professor of African History at the University of Cambridge.

501. Iliffe, John

Africans: The History of a Continent

Cambridge: Cambridge University Press, 2007. 384 pages, ISBN: 9780521682978.

Iliffe is professor of African history at Cambridge University in England. Here he has provided a one-volume history of the continent, beginning with the "homo habilis" two million years ago and carrying through to Nelson Mandela's election in 1994. As a historical overview of the whole continent, written in brief compass and accessible language by an authority in the field, this volume can have few peers. From the quick, broad orientation it affords, the reader is equipped to move towards more specific historical studies on individual countries, periods, or people groups. The particular focus of Iliffe's grand presentation is the demographic development of the continent, as African peoples settle throughout a hostile environment, as a sparse population thinly spread over a vast continent. This larger theme embraces two sub-themes which surface throughout the history: the relation of this relatively isolated continent to Eurasia, and the issue of suffering (under nature and man, with the consequences of courage, endurance and an important sense of honour). Even with admittedly sketchy sources for some times and regions, the author synthesizes centuries and regions into 20 to 40 pages per chapter, highlighting the main processes and dynamics of the history of the people: the establishment of food producing communities, the importance of metals, Christianity and Islam, pioneers in West, East and South Africa, the transatlantic slave trade, regional diversity in the nineteenth century, colonialism and independence. Given the size of the volume and the breadth of the subject, the style is in part generalising, in part exemplifying. While the overall picture painted by Iliffe is impressive and coherent, one cannot help wondering at the feasibility of the entire enterprise. Can the diversity of so many people groups over 5000+ years really be captured in such a neat picture, given the methodological constraints (the scarcity of written sources, the high dependency on linguistic extrapolations and on archaeological interpretation)? One could have wished for greater weight to be placed on religious and cultural aspects, as driving forces and explanatory sources for the course of African history, and not merely as consequences of demographic, political, economic and environmental developments (as the author presents them). Also the international influences since independence seem to be quite sparsely noted, and the focus on population development inevitably decreases the role of personal responsibility. This is an exceptionally handy resource for general orientation to the history of the continent.

502. **Imasogie, Osadolor**

Guidelines for Christian Theology in Africa

Achimota, Ghana: Africa Christian Press, 1993. 92 pages, ISBN: 9789964877996.

How can Christian faith in Africa become integral to life? The perceived ambivalence of Christian commitment across Africa led the former principal of the Nigerian Baptist Theological Seminary to take up this study, here in its second edition. To help analyse this problem, Imasogie appropriates the two most important Western critiques of orthodox theology today: (1) the liberationist's hermeneutic of suspicion (Juan Segundo); and (2) the revisionist's charge that since orthodoxy has absolutised its own culture, it is incapable of reconciling the basic Christian message with dissimilar cultures (David Tracy). The result is an incisive indictment of orthodoxy, especially "the missionary's theology," and a call for a new theological method that values a people's self-understanding. The root of the problem, Imasogie claims, is an uncontextualized theology. Conditioned by the West's quasi-scientific worldview, the missionaries snubbed African spiritual realities; consequently, the Word did not speak to the existential needs of the people and did not "become flesh" in this culture. The monograph begins with a commendatory preface from Charles Kraft, and concludes with some helpful recommendations for relating the gospel to the African life situation. Certainly one should agree that Christians must become more aware of their own involvement in sinful power structures, whether cultural, political, ethnic or gender. A hermeneutic of suspicion is a helpful prod in this task. But the revisionists' critique strikes at the heart of our understanding of the gospel, for David Tracy assumes that the Christian message must be subsumed to universal existential understandings. Yet is not the Gospel of Jesus Christ known only through the historical revelation, which must therefore remain an irreducible authority? Imasogie's goal of an existentially relevant Gospel is laudable, but can this be safely achieved by use of the revisionist's critique, with its subversion of Christ's uniqueness? Christian realities must indeed be redescribed for the contemporary world, but not at the expense of the Gospel's own integrity. Because it forcefully presses key issues in the contextualization debate, this work can function as a useful resource for advanced reflection and discussion.

503. **Imberg, Rune**

A Door Opened by the Lord: The History of the Evangelical Lutheran Church in Kenya

Gothenburg: Församlingsförlaget, 2008. 181 pages, ISBN: 9789172710559.

The author is a Swedish church historian who grew up in Kenya as the son of missionaries and later served in Kenya as a seminary lecturer. He was asked by the leadership of the Evangelical Lutheran Church in Kenya (ELCK) to write the history of the church, as part of the celebration of its sixtieth anniversary in 2008. To accomplish this task, the author has mainly made use of Swedish missionary sources, although some interviews were made as well with Kenyan church members. The book falls in four major parts. (i) The general background of mission work in Kenya and Eastern Africa, with an emphasis on Krapf (1840s–1880s), and on Swedish missionary work in Ethiopia and Eritrea from the 1860s, but also some attention to earlier attempts even back to sixteenth century Portuguese mission. (ii) A detailed exposition of the development of the Swedish Lutheran Mission (SLM) in establishing a mission field in Kenya (1920–1957). (iii) The process from mission to church (1958–1968), with particular focus on the crises around the independence of the nation and the church in the 1960s. (iv) Some elements of the ELCK's development during the last four decades (1968–2008), with a thematic discussion of such topics as leadership issues, church/mission relations, theology and theological education. The book's principal problem is that it is not what the subtitle claims for it; it is not a history of the ELCK. It is rather a history of SLM's work in Kenya. Indeed, only a brief ten pages of the book are devoted to ELCK's history from 1968 to 2008, while the story of other mission agencies working with the ELCK, from Finland, Norway and the USA, is also marginalized. Nevertheless, as long as it is acknowledged that the book is not a history of the ELCK, but a presentation of SLM's early history in Kenya, it is a useful contribution to the history of Christian missions in eastern Africa.

504.   Insoll, Timothy

The Archaeology of Islam in Sub-Saharan Africa

Cambridge: Cambridge University Press, 2003. 488 pages, ISBN: 9780521657020.

Insoll, professor of archaeology at the University of Manchester, UK, has written a series of texts on Islamic archaeology, including *The Archaeology of Islam* (1999). Here he offers the first-ever comprehensive survey of archaeological research relating to Islam in sub-Saharan Africa, accompanied by a massive bibliography. As such this volume will prove an important reference resource in this field for some years to come. Insoll's presentation covers all regions of the continent relevant for such an inquiry, and engages continuously with the most recent research. Insoll attempts a running interpretive synthesis of the vast range of data being presented, asking questions such as why Islam spread, how conversion took place, what forms of Islam have been evident on the continent, and to what extent traditional religion has influenced Islamic practice. Given the sweep of the material presented, one must presume that expert assessment will eventually identify gaps and errors. Indeed at times the material does appear cursory, as though being gleaned hastily in a library (as in the treatment of Islam among the Yoruba). Insoll does not avoid an exaggerated notion of the role of Islam in Africa, stating baldly that "Islam is surely the *leitmotiv* of African history over the last millennium." He also claims that his book is presenting the archaeological record "across almost the whole of the continent south of the Sahara." In fact, with the exception of the east coast as far as Mozambique, the continent from Congo and Kenya southward – that is to say, a major part of sub-Saharan Africa – has lacked any established Islamic presence before modern times, and hence presents almost no material for Insoll's archaeological survey. While granting these limitations, nevertheless this is a valuable contribution to the study of Islam in Africa.

505.   International Association of Universities

Guide to Higher Education in Africa

London: Palgrave Macmillan, 2013. 720 pages, ISBN: 9780230369603.

The 2nd edition of this very handy guide contains by far the most complete, up-to-date information available at time of publication about higher education in Africa. More than 600 institutions in forty-six countries throughout the continent are presented, together with details of national education systems. However, no articles analysing higher education in Africa from more general perspectives are offered, nor any general statistics. Each national entry has the same structure: (i) the institutional context of higher education: institution types and credentials, structure of educational system, national bodies, admission regulations, student life, grading systems; and (ii) the individual institutions: universities (public and private) and other institutions (public and private). Each institution is presented with name, postal address, telephone, fax, e-mail, website, list of faculties and institutes, information on academic year and admission regulations, degrees that are offered, size of academic staff, student enrolment, principal academic and administration officers. Whereas the data does indicate a number of departments of religious studies in state universities in anglophone Africa (not least in Nigeria), from the perspective of tertiary theological education in Africa this reference tool is a disappointment. As it is edited and published by African and international university associations, only those very few theological institutions that are members of these associations are included. In Kenya, for example, the Catholic University of Eastern Africa and Daystar University are presented, as is also (but this is an exception from the general tendency) Scott Theological College, whereas Nairobi Evangelical Graduate School of Theology is not included. The publication of this guide, therefore, demonstrates the current need for a corresponding guide to theological institutions in Africa, for example an updated edition of the *ACTEA Directory of Theological Schools in Africa* (1985).

506.   Ishola, S. Ademola, and Deji Ayegboyin, editors

Rediscovering and Fostering Unity in the Body of Christ: The Nigerian Experience

Akropong, Ghana: African Theological Fellowship, 2000. 199 pages, ISBN: 9789782993359.

This is a compilation of papers presented at a conference of the same title, held by the Nigerian branch of the African Theological Fellowship. ATF describes itself as "a network of African Christian theologians, mission practitioners and Christian intellectuals of evangelical persuasion." The papers are introduced by a foreword (Professor S. O. Abogunrin of the University of Ibadan), a preface (the editors) and the welcome address by Kola Ejiwunmi, the convenor of the Nigerian ATF. Then follow three papers on the biblical material, three more of historical and theological overview, and then papers on denominational perspectives from Roman Catholic, Anglican, Methodist, Baptist, NKST (Reformed), Foursquare, and Christ Apostolic Church representatives. The last two papers are from representatives of the Nigerian Evangelical Fellowship and the Project for Christian–Muslim Relations in Africa. Participants felt that church unity is important because Jesus desires it, and because disunity is a scandal to the unbelieving world. Ejiwunmi notes that, ironically, those keen on unity (the ecumenical movement) tend to be weak on witness to salvation, and those keen on the gospel (the evangelicals) tend to ignore matters of unity. Some papers outline the causes of disunity, and some give the history of church union efforts in Nigeria, particularly the failed attempt in the 1960s to unite the Methodist, Anglicans and Presbyterians. The history of the WCC and the Christian Council of Nigeria are treated, together with such other joint bodies as the Fellowship of Churches of Christ in Nigeria (TEKAN) and the Nigerian Evangelical Fellowship (NEF). Also noted are bodies such as the Pentecostal Fellowship of Nigeria (PFN), the Organisation of African Instituted Churches (OAIC), the Nigerian Association of Aladura Churches (NAAC), and the Christian Association of Nigeria (CAN). Some papers advocate organisational unity, while others see it as impossible and want to work toward spiritual unity through fellowship and co-operation. Many supply concrete recommendations. This volume represents a unique collection of thoughtful contemporary African Christian reflection on Christian unity.

Ishola, S. Ademola

see also review 80

507. Isichei, Elizabeth

A History of Christianity in Africa: From Antiquity to the Present

Grand Rapids: Eerdmans, 1995. 432 pages, ISBN: 9780802808431.

This readable book gives a broad coverage of the development of Christianity in Africa, as the subtitle says: "from Antiquity to the Present." It allows a student of African Christianity to put events in perspective. It also balances missionary activity with indigenous African development and understanding. The reader begins to appreciate the thought and work of Africans in their relationship to political and religious developments in their respective countries. This is done in such a way that the book is more than simply "history" – it is a resource that could be used to test one's own views of the African Christian past and present. The book would be most useful for those who have already studied some history of Africa because, although the treatment is relatively extensive, some details have been assumed. Isichei has been interested in Christianity in Africa for most of her life. She spent sixteen years in Africa, and has kept informed of developments since moving to the University of Otago in New Zealand, where she holds the Chair of Religious Studies. One of the refreshing aspects of her book is the frankness with which Isichei comes to such a vast topic. She recognizes that her views on the subject have changed since her initial interest and this book is an attempt to explain her latest opinions.

508. Isichei, Elizabeth

The Religious Traditions of Africa: A History

Portsmouth, NH: Heinemann, 2004. 432 pages, ISBN: 9780325071145.

Isichei has here made the ambitious attempt to write in one volume a comprehensive history of religion in Africa, which she does by summarising the history of Africa's three major religious traditions: Islam, Christianity, and African traditional religions. Her method is to study each tradition separately and to use a multitude of case studies to examine specific topics within broad time periods. She handles the three religious traditions in very different ways. Thus Islam is dealt with primarily in terms of political movements. While she recognizes that "at the heart of Islam is the soul's relationship to God," there is little discussion of the doctrinal and/or ritual differences between the different Islamic groups that competed for power in Africa. She offers a very good survey of the history of Christianity in Africa. Her section on African traditional religions is the most difficult because of the overwhelming variety of traditional religions and the scarcity of historical sources on these religions. Therefore the presentation is like an ethnographic survey organized around religious topics (divinities, ancestors, rituals, religious practitioners, etc.), with historical change noted almost as a minor theme. Isichei takes a comparative religions approach that the inherent validity of each of these religions makes them equally genuine means of relating to God. She does not let this approach lead her to romanticize Islam and African traditional religions, as is often the case. But she does exhibit her bias against efforts aimed at the conversion of people from one religion to another. While she does not express the same hostility to Western Christian missions that she showed in her earlier *A History of Christianity in Africa* (1995), she still shows her bias against African evangelicalism, by disparaging portrayals of evangelical beliefs and movements. For example: "A Nigerian Evangelical [i.e. Byang Kato] defended the viewpoint that Africans who never heard the Christian message are in Hell. But in general, succeeding generations of missionaries came to believe that there are many different paths to God. . . ." Isichei regards African Initiated Churches as the most authentically African forms of Christianity, and the African Pentecostal movement as "in some ways part of an Americanized global culture." She writes: "Most of those who study [the AICs], including the present writer, regard the prophetic churches as profoundly acculturated expressions of Christian faith. Both black and white Evangelicals were often critical of them . . . In the words of a Nigerian Evangelical, Ogbu Kalu: 'There has been a tendency to glorify the Independent Churches. Most of them are neo-pagan, engaged in non-Christian rituals'." Relying far too heavily on Paul Gifford, Isichei does not present a history of the African Pentecostal movement or attempt a serious account of its growth. Because this book tends to be tedious in detail, it would not be ideal as a textbook. On the other hand, because of much valuable material, it would be a useful resource in any professional study of Africa's three religions.

509.   Iwe, John Chijioke

Jesus in the Synagogue of Capernaum: The Pericope and Its Programmatic Character for the Gospel of Mark. An Exegetico-Theological Study of Mk 1:21–28

Rome: Gregorian & Biblical Press, 1999. 364 pages, ISBN: 9788876528460.

In this published version of his doctoral dissertation, Iwe argues that Mark 1:21–28 is programmatic for Mark's gospel. That is to say, the central themes of Jesus' ministry are found already here in this text, namely: Jesus' teaching and exorcism, his Sonship, the amazement of the crowd, Sabbath and synagogue, Jesus' authority, and the dispute with Jewish authorities. This foundational text, therefore, signals what is to come. The suggestion is not a new one, and Iwe dutifully indicates his sources for this in his introduction. What is new is the thoroughness with which the case is made. Iwe does not explain how Jesus' non-exorcism miracles fit into this scheme. More seriously, Iwe does not deal in any depth with the passion narrative of Mark 11–16, and how Jesus' Galilean ministry relates to the cross. These questions aside, Iwe does demonstrate his case that the main themes of the Capernaum passage also become central for Jesus' ministry. One interesting feature of this book is that Africa is not mentioned. The author is a Nigerian Roman Catholic priest who has taught in Nigerian seminaries. Given the overwhelming tendency of African biblical scholarship to engage in at least some hermeneutical reflection and application, this work is somewhat of an exception. This lacuna may simply be due to the demands put on the author by a Western academic model, which seeks to separate investigation from application. If this is so, we may hope that further publication by the author may seek to show the relevance of this text for Africa. Sadly the book is marred by an abundance of typographical errors.

510.   Izekwe, Augustus Chukwuma

The Future of Christian Marriage among the Igbo vis-à-vis Childlessness: A Canonical cum Pastoral Study of Canon 1055 par.1

Berlin: Logos Verlag Berlin, 2015. 230 pages, ISBN: 9783832540371.

The author, of Igbo ethnic background in Nigeria, is a Roman Catholic priest. This book is his doctoral thesis, finished at the Julius Maximilian University in Würzburg, Germany in 2014. Here he addresses the problem that many Igbo Catholics attempt to conceive before consenting to marriage, or may resort to divorce and remarriage, polygamy, or affairs, if their primary marriage does not produce children, particularly a male heir. One chapter outlines the traditional Igbo view of marriage, noting that a marriage is not regarded as established until a child, especially a son, arrives. Izekwe examines Catholic canon law regarding reasons for annulment of a Catholic marriage related to childlessness, and concludes that a marriage could be annulled if at the time of the wedding a partner was unwilling to have children, or if there was fraud (a partner hid a known fact of impotency or sterility before the wedding). However, mere failure to produce a son when no intent or deceit was present is not grounds for annulment. He then examines canon law about the nature and goal of marriage, and sees significant change between the 1917 law and what was handed down by Vatican II. on Canon 1005 par. 1, namely that children are no longer the main goal of marriage, but only a parallel goal alongside the welfare of the partners. Clergy are mandated to provide adequate marriage preparation for intending couples so that they can have a good Christian marriage. Izekwe recommends that this pastoral preparation must include teaching on the equal value of females, both as children and as wives, and that the wife must not be solely blamed when there is no son. Couples must be taught the Church's doctrines about the indissolubility and goals of marriage. Childless couples should be encouraged to adopt an heir, but probably a child of their relatives who can be accepted as a member of the clan and thus granted inheritance rights by the community. The main drawback of this study may be that the worldview issue underlying the situation is never addressed. Men with no sons are said to have "their names obliterated at death and lose their patrimony." The closest the book comes to acknowledging this problem is a passage near the end, "Although the Igbo has embraced Christianity, he has not thrown away his culture. This means that Christianity has to be fully incarnated into the cultures of people, especially the Igbo . . ." Izekwe's solution is to mitigate the effects of childlessness by the adoption of near kin (together with increased respect for women), rather than by attempting to reshape a worldview that depends on male heirs for valid and enduring identity.

Jacobs, Donald

see review 657

511. Jaeschke, Ernst

Bruno Gutmann: His Life, His Thoughts, and His Work: An Early Attempt at a Theology in an African Context

Arusha, Tanzania: Makumira, 1985. 466 pages, ISBN: 9783872142030.

This book developed from a series of lectures given by Jaeschke at the Lutheran Theological College Makumira in Tanzania. When Jaeschke initially arrived in Moshi he was mentored by Gutmann, and he eventually replaced this man whom he had come to admire so deeply. His personal relationship with Gutmann makes the book very readable. While some objectivity may be lost in the process, Jaeschke's clear desire is to ensure that Gutmann's life and reflections are properly interpreted in light of the times and contexts in which they arose. In addition to the lecture material, the book includes Jaeschke's summarisations and critiques of assessments of Gutmann by several other scholars (primarily African and German). Gutmann's influence on missiology and ecclesiology was at one time considerable. He laid the theoretical foundation for a mission methodology aimed at perfecting existing social structures as a means of "Christianising" whole cultures, which led to what many have found a troubling exaltation of ethnic identity. Jaeschke is a vigorous defender of Gutmann's thinking, so that the book is a blending of personal apologetic and academic treatise. The book thus provides a unique perspective on one of the most interesting German missionaries to serve in Africa. However, to balance this presentation, one should consult Klaus Fielder's excellent *Christianity and African Culture: Conservative German Protestant Missionaries in Tanzania, 1900–1940*.

512.   James, Wendy

The Listening Ebony: Moral Knowledge, Religion, and Power among the Uduk of Sudan

Oxford: Oxford University Press, 1999. 420 pages, ISBN: 9780198234166.

This important study of the Uduk people of southern Sudan well represents those anthropological works which may be of relevance for Christian outreach and theological reflection in Africa. James' work is not, however, the kind of anthropology that treats the culture of an indigenous people as if it were fixed for all time. Now retired, James was previously Professor of Social Anthropology at the University of Oxford. She is deeply aware of the social changes forced upon this traditional hunting people by their proximity to the modern border between Sudan and Ethiopia, and near the division between southern Sudan and the Muslim north. Most importantly for Christian readers, James is aware of the upheaval caused by the presence of American evangelical missionaries. Much of the book is taken up with the "Ebony Men," the traditional diviners of the Uduk people, and their role in interpreting reality and protecting society from the *arum*, evil powers. The growth of the Christian church among the Uduk, and the role of the Bible in this new movement, are a special focus. These sections are highly critical of the missionary enterprise. James is quick to point out perceived missionary blunders, especially a lack of sensitivity to the Uduk culture in the missionary translation of the NT, and the imposition of American conservative cultural values. Many of her criticisms are well taken; Bible translators would benefit from a careful reading of her criticisms of the Uduk NT. She is no expert in Christian theology however (for example, she assumes, wrongly, that the "original sin" in Genesis is sex). She is more sympathetic to the indigenous Christian movement which has grown almost exponentially since the missionaries left, largely due to the leadership of Pastor Paul Rasha Angwo and the serendipitous arrival of a shipment of Uduk New Testaments which corresponded with the missionary expulsions. The anthropologist does not see the hand of God in all this; the Christian reader will. It should be noted that this paperback edition is actually more valuable since it includes an important 9-page preface written ten years after the hardcover edition.

513.   Janvier, George

Biblical Preaching in Africa: A Textbook for Christian Preachers

Bukuru, Nigeria: Africa Christian Textbooks, 2002. 179 pages, ISBN: 9789781350894.

Janvier taught at the ECWA Theological Seminary in Jos, Nigeria, for more than two decades. He speaks of preaching as a spiritual experience, using the term "Power Preaching" and meaning the sort of preaching that transforms the spiritual lives of the hearers. He examines the preaching of Jesus and Paul as examples, and surveys the main themes of Scripture which act powerfully when expounded. The book also covers basic concepts of hermeneutics, detailed instructions on use of reference tools, use of topical vs. expository sermons and other types of sermons, crafting the introduction, the body and the conclusion of the sermon, giving invitations, doing follow up, and the use of notes, illustrations, voice and body language. In the section on sermon layout, Janvier helpfully explains two major preaching styles: linear layout, with a more deductive approach, and circular (spiral) layout with an inductive approach. The latter works well with holistic thinkers and is well adapted to Africa. In this layout, a topic is approached from various angles with examples, illustrations, case studies, proverbs, and concludes with the main point and application. The book is intended as a class text on preaching and succeeds admirably. Courses in Africa in preaching should find it very handy.

514. Janvier, George

Evangelism and Discipleship: Training for Africa

Bukuru, Nigeria: Africa Christian Textbooks, 1999. 104 pages, ISBN: 9789781350559.

Janvier is a former lecturer at ECWA Theological Seminary Jos (JETS) in Nigeria. This is a text for a course in evangelism and discipleship that is intended as a guide for interactive discussions. Rather than giving detailed methods, the book focuses on biblical concepts and principles, and examines the practice of Jesus and Paul. There are also sections on evangelising traditionalists and Muslims, discipleship problems in the African context, and the pastor's role in discipling, especially with youth. A chapter written by Bitrus Thaba shows that the traditional African method of education is by observation and imitation, and the book encourages small group discipling. There are discussion questions for two levels of students at the end of each chapter. Although brief, the book is suitable for what it sets out to do, and would be an effective resource in the hands of a competent teacher.

515. Janvier, George, and Bitrus Thaba

Understanding Leadership: An African Christian Model

Bukuru, Nigeria: Africa Christian Textbooks, 1997. 175 pages, ISBN: 9789781350436.

This is two short books in one, both by lecturers at ECWA Theological Seminary in Jos, Nigeria. Janvier, from the US, at time of publication had been in ministry in Nigeria for more than a decade. He had served in various leadership positions at the seminary and taught courses in leadership, research, and church planting. Pastor Thaba is a Nigerian who has worked as a pastor and was Dean of Student Affairs at the seminary. Janvier provides an extensive list of insights on leadership in the first part of the book. A survey of 106 Nigerian pastors and leaders supplied some of the material. Several chapters address concerns specific to Africa. These include historical and cultural influences on leadership patterns and the resulting models of leadership emerging in Africa. Biblical teaching on leadership is then offered, together with a list of qualities and characteristics of godly leaders. In the second part of the book, Thaba focuses on servant-leadership. He provides biblical material and practical advice on how to be a servant leader. For example, he deals with anger and how to deal with difficult people. He concludes by considering the cultural forces that work against the servant leader. The book does not provide one single model of leadership but helpfully addresses many issues and gives a lot of practical advice. The book is well written, and the material throughout is reinforced by short case studies and relevant cartoons, along with study questions for students. This book will thus be useful in any context seeking to reflect on effective models for Christian leadership in Africa.

516.   **Jeal, Tim**

Stanley: The Impossible Life of Africa's Greatest Explorer

London: Faber & Faber, 2008. 592 pages, ISBN: 9780571221035.

The subtitle is the first clue that this author of a groundbreaking biography of Livingstone in 1973 will here also be challenging many common assumptions. Most readers might expect the accolade of "greatest" to be attached to David Livingstone. Yet in this carefully researched book the author advances evidence that Henry Stanley, long vilified for opening up the Congo to Leopold's atrocities, has been misunderstood. He proposes that Stanley should be considered to be as significant as the "lost" man he "found" in 1871, the one he famously greeted as "Dr Livingstone, I presume?." Jeal's claims rest on material only recently made available in a Belgian museum that in 2002 received much of Stanley's previously classified correspondence. Thus the author is able to document many of the "errors" on Stanley that biographers have simply copied from earlier books. Among many examples are that John Rowlands was probably not Stanley's father (a well-known barrister paid off Rowlands to cover an affair); Stanley was never adopted by an American (he invented the story later); and he cannot be blamed for Leopold's vicious rape of the Congo in the 1890s (Stanley left Africa for good in 1884, having been duped by Leopold as to Leoopold's real reasons for opening up the interior). Yet Jeal does not whitewash his subject either, frequently complaining that it was Stanley's *How I Found Livingstone* that established the good doctor as a saint in the minds of the British public despite Livingstone's many faults. Stanley is portrayed as one who never recovered from his childhood experience of being abandoned to a workhouse by his mother. Yet he was deeply influenced by Livingstone, who became the father he never knew. His relationships with Africans were also very close, whereas his relationships with whites were often tense. But why know about this book, apart from the fact that it is extremely well written? Perhaps as another reminder of the rich complexity of the Christian story in Africa. Although Stanley was not a Christian, he admired and supported the work of missionaries. So it was Stanley who convinced King Mutesa of Uganda to receive the first CMS missionaries to that land, and thus in his own way made a strategic contribution to Africa's Christian narrative.

517.   **Jenkins, Paul, editor**

The Recovery of the West African Past: African Pastors and African History in the Nineteenth Century, C.C. Reindorf & Samuel Johnson

Basel: Basler Afrika Bibliographien, 1998. 212 pages, ISBN: 9783905141702.

Archivist of the Basel Mission and lecturer in African history at the University of Basel, Jenkins was from 1963 to 1972 on the staff of the University of Ghana. This book is a collection of papers from an international seminar held at the University of Basel in 1995 to celebrate the centenary of the publication of Reindorf's *History of the Gold Coast and Asante*. Reindorf was the first African to write a substantial history of a region of Africa. The centenary seminar set out to do justice to this forgotten figure who was proud of African history, who was convinced that only Africans can work accurately on that history, and whose research methodology showed an astonishingly modern blending of written information with indigenous oral sources (which Reindorf himself started collecting in the 1860s). Like his Yoruba counterpart Samuel Johnson (*History of the Yorubas*, ms 1897, published in a reconstructed version in 1921), Reindorf was an indigenous pastor, but neither of their publications was an evangelistic tract. These were serious, balanced histories which deserved and deserve wide attention. The authors of this collection of papers not only assess Reindorf and Johnson as historians.

They also reflect on the forgotten quality of the dialogue achieved in the second half of the nineteenth century by people like Reindorf and Johnson with the practitioners of local and regional tradition. This is an interesting, well-researched and well-reflected resource that should be considered a must for advanced study of West African history and of West African Christian history.

518.   Jenkins, Philip

The Lost History of Christianity: The Thousand-Year Golden Age of the Church in the Middle East, Africa, and Asia–and How It Died

San Francisco: HarperOne, 2010. 315 pages, ISBN: 9780061472817.

In this book Jenkins sets himself to explore what he regards as a thousand years of lost Christian history in the Middle East, Africa, and most especially Asia, documenting in often striking detail the extent and intellectual vibrancy of these forms of Christianity whose scope dwarfed that of European Christianity for nearly a millennium. Jenkins' admiration turns to lament in recording how by the early fourteenth century Christianity was reduced to remnant communities in these regions in the face of Islamic advance and persecution, before succumbing to extinction in a series of violent, sometimes genocidal episodes in the nineteenth and early twentieth centuries. Despite the subtitle, the history of Christianity in Africa is a relatively minor emphasis. The fact that modern Ethiopian Christianity fits rather poorly into Jenkins' theme of extinct communities suggests that the broad strokes needed for his larger story may at times lead to a measure of distortion, especially in his treatment of early African Christianity. He argues that the reason that Christianity in North Africa collapsed so quickly with the arrival of Islam was that it never really became rooted in local languages and cultures. Christianity in North Africa remained a "colonists' religion." This may be usefully compared to Thomas Oden's *How Africa Shaped the Christian Mind*, which shows more evidence than Jenkins acknowledges for early Christian penetration into the African interior, for greater dissemination of Christian faith in African languages, and for an enduring Christian presence, even after the Islamic incursions of the eighth century. Furthermore, while helpfully highlighting the social and political pressures which led to the collapse of Christianity in the parts of the world being surveyed, Jenkins is less inclined to ask whether particular instances of decline may be connected in part with theological commitments. Might, for instance, a loss of missionary zeal have been not simply a consequence but a cause of retraction? For all the merits of Jenkins' study, might his own perspective lead to a similar loss in our own day? Jenkins asks whether Christians might "someday accept that Islam fulfils a positive role, and that its growth in history represents another form of divine revelation, one that complements but does not replace the Christian message." Jenkins' work admirably recovers a Christian history which he fears has been lost. But if the Christians whose mission gave birth to that history had believed that Christ was but one of several complementary revelations, that history would truly have been lost, for it would never have happened.

519.   Jenkins, Philip

The New Faces of Christianity: Believing the Bible in the Global South

Oxford: Oxford University Press, 2008. 272 pages, ISBN: 9780195368512.

This book can be viewed as something of a companion to Jenkins' earlier work, *The Next Christendom*, published in 2002, and acclaimed as a prophetic appraisal of the future of Christianity. Essentially, Jenkins predicted a dramatic shift of the faith's centre of gravity towards the "global South." In *The New Faces*, Jenkins argues that one of the factors underpinning this trend is the tendency for the Bible to be read in the global South with an "authenticity and immediacy" that has become rare in Europe and North America, where Scripture does not resonate with everyday life to the same extent. His basic point, that the Bible finds a "congenial home" in the global South (where people can identify with Scripture's social and economic realities), is then developed into a more nuanced apologetic for the ability of "Southern voices" to challenge "Western" assumptions and prejudices. In a stimulating discussion on hermeneutics, he argues that the literal approach to interpreting the Bible generally favoured by the African Church, far from being "primitive" or representing a lapse into "fundamentalism" (as often portrayed by the media), is actually more advanced than the historical criticism employed by Western liberals, in the sense that it is not dissimilar to postmodern techniques in which the identity of the reader does much to determine the meaning of the text. This dynamic, Jenkins argues, can lead to readings that are both faithful to Scripture and radical in their critique of aspects of life in the global South, such as the oppression of certain ethnic groups or of women. At times Jenkins is politically correct, and at times he is provocative. What is one to make of his suggestion that the Christianity of Africa can be "closer to Islam than to the Christianity of the advanced West"? Although he is clearly not evangelical in his outlook, he does wear his beliefs and his prejudices fairly lightly, and his occasional barbs are generally thought-provoking rather than offensive. A high proportion of Jenkins' examples in *The New Faces* comes from the African context. One finds extensive treatment of crucial subjects such as "good and evil," "poor and rich" and "persecution and vindication," as well as key questions such as whether or not African traditional religion can be regarded as the continent's "Old Testament." There is material here that would be useful to anyone preparing a lecture on the prosperity gospel, or wondering about the correlation of Scripture with some views in Africa on tithing. Those engaged in advanced-level reflection on Christian presence in Africa would likely find this book a very worthwhile read.

Jennings, Christian

see review 320

Johnson, Dean

see review 718

Johnson, Douglas H.

see review 62

Johnson, G. Ampah

see review 46

520.　Joinet, Bernard

The Challenge of Modernity in Africa

Nairobi: Paulines, 2000. 72 pages, ISBN: 9789966213884.

Despite the author's early claim that "modernity is a complex reality," in this short book he manages to provide a basic assessment of modernity in Africa. Joinet is a Roman Catholic priest who writes with the aim of explicating specifically for the continent of Africa both the hazards and the hopes of Western forms of modernity. He begins with a fairly balanced critique of six characteristics of modernity, including industrialisation (technology), global free trade, scientific method, secularism, democracy and individualisation. In each of these, Joinet outlines positive and negative aspects, showing both the perils and the promises, while ultimately advocating the importance of viewing modernity as ambivalent, as neither the enemy nor the saviour of the contemporary world. Despite his proclivities to oversimplify these characteristics, he avoids dichotomies that are so pervasive in studies dealing with modernity on the continent. He also underscores the importance for the Church to actively engage in contemporary social issues such as we find with modernity, even though he offers virtually no theological appraisal other than simply telling the Church that it cannot afford to neglect these matters. Neither does he say anything about how African worldviews may contribute to global forms of modernity. Due to the balanced and simple approach, readers will find this book helpful as a basic introduction to issues of "modernity" for the African context.

521.　Jones, Howard O., and Edward Gilbreath

Gospel Trailblazer: An African-American Preacher's Historic Journey across Racial Lines

Chicago: Moody, 2003. 220 pages, ISBN: 9781593280697.

Jones was an African-American who trailblazed in Christian ministry across racial divides not only in North America but in Africa as well. In this autobiography he tells his story. His great-grandmother had been born into slavery on a Virginia plantation before the American Civil War. He himself was born in 1921 to church-going, working class parents in Cleveland, Ohio. Jones became a believer through the ministry of an integrated Christian & Missionary Alliance (CMA) church, and attended what is now Nyack College in New York. He planned on missionary service, but at that time could not find a mission agency that would accept African-American applicants. Jones became an ordained CMA pastor, planted a church in Harlem, began a racially-integrated youth camp, and had a popular radio ministry in New York City. However, when listeners learned that their radio pastor was black, they discontinued financial support. Then and subsequently Jones surmounted acts of discrimination by moving on with a positive attitude on life and ministry. While pastoring a church in Cleveland, he learned of the Christian radio station ELWA in Liberia, sponsored by SIM. At ELWA's request he and his church choir began a ministry of supplying the radio station with music and preaching tapes. ELWA and SIM then invited Jones to come to Africa to hold evangelistic campaigns. Jones had large crowds and a great response to his messages wherever he held mass meetings in Liberia, Ghana, and Nigeria. Then in

1957 Billy Graham personally invited Jones to join his evangelistic team, and Jones assisted with the Graham crusade that year in New York City. Jones then returned to Africa to continue both a ministry with the Billy Graham team as an Associate Evangelist, and a ministry at ELWA. In that capacity he then set up crusades for Billy Graham all across Africa. Later the family returned to the States, where Jones continued both to travel with Graham around the world and to hold his own campaigns. He retired from this ministry in 2001. In all these roles Jones was not spared from experiences of racial discrimination, as this autobiography makes clear, but he succeeded in pioneering a role for African-Americans in global Christian ministry across racial lines and in encouraging others to follow his example.

522.   Jones, L. Gregory, and Célestin Musekura

Forgiving as We've Been Forgiven: Community Practices for Making Peace

Downers Grove: IVP US, 2010. 140 pages, ISBN: 9780830834556.

This helpful book is co-written by an American from Duke University and a Hutu from Rwanda. The latter as a child was dedicated to become a traditional priest but converted to Christianity and consequently was rejected by his family. The authors alternate chapters rather than attempting to merge their different styles and perspectives, and this format works well. Musekura was a student at NEGST/AIU in Nairobi when the Rwandan genocide occurred in April 1994, and later returned to Nairobi to begin a ministry to Rwandese refugees. Musekura weaves his personal history into the chapters he writes, including the fact that many of his family members were killed in 1997 when he was away doing doctoral studies in the USA. He found that the curricular emphasis on forgiveness received little attention, was too theological and individualistic, and did not deal with communal aspects. It was extremely difficult for him to forgive the nameless killers, but he eventually met some of them who became Christians and are now caring for his widowed mother. He stresses the importance of Christian forgiveness, not a self-help programme, because only divinely forgiven people have the strength to forgive others. Jones builds on this chapter by noting North America's "therapeutic culture" that dispenses cheap forgiveness that "moves on" rather than seeking restoration. His six steps for learning how to "embody" forgiveness are helpful. Then Musekura discusses several case studies where Africans needed to extend forgiveness; the pastor who "invited God to side with him" in his hatred is especially moving, as is the list of places around Africa where reconciliation is in such short supply. Jones follows with a chapter on the relationship between forgiveness and memory, noting that healing memories is not the same as erasing them. In the final chapter Musekura applies the message of reconciliation to practical problems that churches in Africa and North America both face, such as racism and tribalism in our denominations. He asks how un-forgiveness among church leaders affects the wider society, such as in the arena of politics. That is one reason why he founded ALARM (African Leadership and Reconciliation Ministries), a ministry that has spread to a number of African countries. This book is a recommended resource for studies in conflict resolution or just for personal challenge.

523. Jung, Albert de, editor

Ethnicity: Blessing or Curse?

Nairobi: Paulines, 1999. 87 pages, ISBN: 9789966214577.

This booklet includes six papers mostly relating to the broad question of ethnicity and ethnocentrism. The early articles are especially helpful in defining the issues to be addressed. Mary Getui first stresses the advantages of ethnic identity, and then notes the necessity of coexistence through trade, intermarriage and sharing in times of difficulty such as famine. Much of her article is based on and illustrated by Chinua Achebe's novel, Things Fall Apart. Peter Gichure then tries to "have his cake and eat it too." He complains that most ethnic groups have not "updated" themselves to cope with the new realities of urbanisation, industrialisation and westernisation. His solution is first to know one's own culture, then to set up councils of elders in each community who will "produce a revisionist version of the culture taking into account the latest developments." Yet in the same breath he insists that "we must revert to the traditional method and content of teaching," and that rites of passage must be "revived" in order to communicate values. In the next article, Aylward Shorter complains that African bishops too easily dismiss the often close relationship between ethnicity and ethnocentrism; he approvingly quotes a Nigerian bishop who feared that in Rwanda in 1994 "the blood of tribe was thicker than the water of baptism." In order to overcome ethnic tension, he pleads for a dialogue that "means looking for what is held in common, but it also means not being afraid to confront differences." Not surprisingly, Shorter's article is among the best. But the following one, by Pierli, Presbitero and Muko, also makes a helpful contribution. They claim that ethnocentrism (defined as "to absolutise one's culture . . . with a strong sense of superiority") is the leading cause of many social problems: nationhood and gender balance cannot be maintained, and parasitism and corruption are rife. Their selection of quotations is particularly effective. The remaining articles, however, have little connection with the rest of the book. One paper deals with parish concerns and liturgy in Nigeria, another with missions and politics in Tanzania, but neither is really tied to the blessings and curses of ethnicity. This book provides some helpful Roman Catholic analyses of this critical modern African issue.

524. Kabasele Mukenge, André

Lire la Bible dans une société en crise: Etudes d'herméneutique interculturelle

Montreal: EDITIONS Médiaspaul, 2005. 160 pages, ISBN: 2741402035.

Professor of OT at the Catholic Faculty in Kinshasa, Congo (DRC), the author has been one of the key OT scholars in francophone Africa. Within a few years he has published several important studies, exegetical (cf. his 1998 *Habilitationsschrift* for the University of Louvain, *L'unité littéraire du livre de Baruch*), as well as hermeneutical (cf. *La Parole se fait chair et sang*). The present book reflects his interest in African biblical hermeneutics, and explores how the Bible can be read in a context of crisis, like that of the Congo. The book starts with a discussion of the phenomenon of fundamentalism. The author emphasizes that fundamentalism is found not only in Muslim contexts, but indeed also within the Judeo-Christian tradition. In response to the latter, the author advocates the need for "an informed reading" of the Bible. In dialogue with current theological and biblical hermeneutics – not least Gadamer and Ela – he then addresses three areas. The first is the current return of fundamentalism. Here he investigates the context of Christian fundamentalism and responds to some of the questions it raises. The second is the challenge facing the church to act prophetically in contemporary societies in crisis, like the Congo. Here he proceeds from the observation that various human rights groups among others make use of the names of OT prophets, and as an example analyses the potential of addressing Jeremiah's message to a society such as in today's Congo. His third area of reflection is the challenge of interpreting the sufferings of Job in Africa today. Kabasele is a productive and solid author, and his books deserve careful attention not only in francophone Africa but elsewhere as well.

525.   Kabasele Mukenge, André

La Parole se fait chair et sang: Lectures de la Bible dans le contexte africain

Montreal: EDITIONS Médiaspaul, 2003. 176 pages, ISBN: 2741401770.

The subtitle of this book clarifies its background; it is a collection of essays whose common denominator is the challenge of establishing an Africanised interpretation of the Bible. The author is Professor of OT at the Catholic Faculty in Kinshasa. He has previously published heavy exegetical material, as well as more popularized biblical interpretation. The essays of this collection include surveys of African theology and African biblical interpretation, as well as studies of the use of the Bible in Negro Spirituals and of the biblical concept of solidarity. Of particular interest is an essay on how to read the narrative about Cain and Abel in Genesis 4 from an African perspective. The author presents a reading which proceeds from the famous liberation hermeneutical dialogue, based on this text, between Itumeleng Mosala and Allan Boesak in South Africa. However, by relating the narrative to traditional Congolese folklore, he is able to show that this text has a wider contextualized interpretive potential. As a whole, the book offers fascinating glimpses into important inculturation hermeneutical questions. Since there is a scarcity of such books, this contribution is indeed to be welcomed. Clearly, it reflects the author's Roman Catholic context, where the Roman Catholic documents play a more important role as dialogue partners than what readers from other traditions may be accustomed to. Nevertheless the book certainly deserves a place in any advanced-level theological library in francophone Africa.

526.   Kabasele Mukenge, André

L'unité littéraire du livre de Baruch

Paris: J. Gabalda et Cie, 1998. 504 pages, ISBN: LANG255222.

Kabasele Mukenge established himself as a specialist on the book of Baruch with his 1992 doctoral dissertation for the Université Catholique de Louvain in Belgium. The present monumental study, accepted as a *Habilitationsschrift* at the University of Louvain in 1998, demonstrates that Kabasele Mukenge has continued his Baruch studies with much success. He sets out to examine the literary unity of this well-known work of intertestamental Jewish literature. The bulk of the book is made up of a detailed analysis of the various parts of Baruch, with particular attention to structural and lexical features. From this background it is argued that Baruch is the product of a scribe whose aim was to re-read and actualize the book of Jeremiah to a Jerusalem audience in the second century BC. The literary peculiarities of the different parts of the book are said to reflect literary features in the different Jeremiah texts that are being re-read, rather than different stages in the development of the book. This study is indeed a book for specialists. However, as an example of African academic scholarship at a distinguished international level, it will certainly deserve a place in research libraries.

527. **Kabasele-Lumbala, François**

Alliances avec le Christ en Afrique: Inculturation des rites religieux au Zaïre

Paris: Éditions Karthala, 1994. 392 pages, ISBN: 9782865374748.

Kabasele is from what was earlier known as Zaire (as in the subtitle), and now as the Democratic Republic of Congo (DRC). Here he has presented the essence of his doctoral thesis, defended in 1983 at the Sorbonne. The process of enculturation for the Catholic Church in Africa has been a sustained interest for the author, as demonstrated by his subsequent books on the same subject, both in English and French. This study begins by describing the cultural environment of the Bantu, including their fundamental ideas concerning religion. Kabasele's specific contribution is the presentation and analysis of four induction rites used by feminine Catholic religious orders, as practiced in four areas of the Congo. Each community of nuns, with the approval of the Catholic hierarchy, had developed a liturgy which included elements corresponding to ritual deeds and concepts in their own Bantu culture. One order's ceremony had similarities to a pact signed in blood, a strong uniting factor in Bantu culture. Another order of Catholic sisters devised a ceremony very similar to a wedding ritual, with a ring given as a token of the nun's union to Christ. Some elements from the Western liturgy inherited from the Belgian Catholics were retained in the new formulations. The author has attempted to show how both continuity and discontinuity could be discerned in the religious rites he studied. Although the work, first published in 1987, is somewhat dated by now, even with the few pages of postface added for this 1994 edition, it provides a good historical background for understanding how the Catholic Church, after Vatican II, was open to the possibility of putting aside certain aspects of its tradition, such as the Latin service, and of incorporating African symbols and ritual acts in an attempt to identify with the African culture.

528. **Kabasele-Lumbala, François**

Celebrating Jesus Christ in Africa: Liturgy and Inculturation

Maryknoll, NY: Orbis, 1998. 128 pages, ISBN: 9780883449714.

This book explores the Africanisation of Roman Catholic worship in Congo (DRC) and, in particular, several indigenous liturgical initiatives which the author sees as "African ritual celebrations of the salvation through Jesus Christ." Kabasele first presents the importance of what he calls the "human imprint on liturgy." He discusses the traditional African view of the natural and supernatural being present in the human body, and seeks to compare it favourably with Scriptures such as Genesis 1:27, John 1:14, 2 Peter 1:4 and 2 Corinthians 3:3. He contends that these two views, the African and the biblical, are in harmony in asserting that "the human is in the sacred and the sacred in the human." He then moves to the traditional Roman Catholic teachings on the sacraments and develops them in accordance with a Vatican II decision to permit the introduction to the sacraments of symbolic elements that "are native to a people." The ensuing chapters move through each of the Roman Catholic sacraments, outlining the traditional meaning and form, and then giving examples of how local African customs and symbols can be introduced. The book assumes a commitment to Roman Catholic dogma, particularly with regard to the sacraments, and to the place and meaning of symbols. These assumptions limit the value of the book for anyone of a different theological background, although the book is still useful in provoking reflection on the use of African traditional practices and symbols in the life of the Christian community.

529. Kabasele-Lumbala, François, Joseph Doré, René Luneau, and Kabongo J. Bukasa, editors

Chemins de la christologie africaine

Paris: Éditions Desclée de Brouwer, 1986. 317 pages, ISBN: 9782718902951.

This is a collection of essays by thirteen Africans, dealing with several aspects of the African understanding of Jesus. Twelve of the authors are Catholic, generally priests and/or professors; two contributors are women (one of whom is the only Protestant representative in the book). Two of the editors (Doré and Luneau) are based in Paris, while the other contributors reside in francophone countries of central and western Africa. There is, however, one article that attempts to evaluate the perspective of South Africans on the question of Christology. These essays tend not to consider more evangelical interpretations of the evidence. The privileged interpretive position is given to African traditions, to which Christological understandings can or should conform. The essays can be divided into three genres: (i) evaluation of interpretations of Jesus based on African models, such as the Ancestor; (ii) analyses of the writings of African theologians who speak of Christology (Beti, Ela); and (iii) perspectives from specific groups, such as the youth.

530. Kabasele-Lumbala, François

Le Christianisme et l'Afrique: Une chance réciproque

Paris: Éditions Karthala, 1993. 127 pages, ISBN: 9782865374229.

This offering in African theology by a Congolese (DRC) Catholic priest consists of three chapters of roughly equal length, with a brief introduction and conclusion. The title indicates the author's interest, namely to show that Christianity and African life are not at enmity but can instead strengthen each other. Kabasele, apparently intending to address the educated laity, would very much like to motivate his readers to embrace enthusiastically a combination of traditional culture (in its more current forms) and Christian theology. The first chapter attempts a hasty overview of key elements of African culture. The other two chapters highlight in turn the opportunities that Christianity presents for Africa, and the contribution African traditions can make to the understanding of Christian theology. Kabasele makes the point that the orality of the traditional culture makes the ritual aspects of the church tradition "natural" for the communication of spiritual truth in Africa, and should be exploited as such. Christianity, he says, offers a better eschatological hope and a better synthesis for the present. But African culture also makes its contribution through different images that help the African comprehend who Jesus is: chief, (proto-)ancestor, deliverer. Little in the book is new in terms of the expression of African theology, but there are refreshing insights and personal perspectives (such as the author's opinion of the Yamoussoukro cathedral).

531. Kafang, Zamani B.

The Psalms: An Introduction to Their Poetry

Kaduna: Baraka Press, 2008. 186 pages, ISBN: 9789781350948.

The author is principal of a theological college in Nigeria, and holds a PhD in OT studies from Trinity Deerfield in the United States. This is a good example of the sort of basic home-grown texts that are now proliferating within Christian communities across the continent, as African Christianity increasingly assumes responsibility for meeting its own particular needs in biblical awareness at grass-roots levels. The author in this case is offering a simple introduction to the poetry of the Psalms. As he says, he does so to meet the needs of pastors, Bible teachers, and theological students, who otherwise can find difficulty in using the Psalms in preaching and teaching, owing especially to their poetic nature. Kafang states that in his experience it is very rare to hear an African pastor preach from the Psalms. Although Kafang's technical training in OT studies and Hebrew grammar is sometimes on view (and the bibliography is rather advanced for the book's purpose), the content of the book is fairly elementary. After an overview of the Psalms, and modern study on the Psalms, he offers a basic introduction to Hebrew poetry, with extended treatment on figures of speech, such as metaphor, simile, hyperbole, personification, acrostics, euphemism, etc. The longest section of the book treats the metaphors for God in the Psalms (the focus of Kafang's doctoral work). A later chapter surveys the use of the Psalms in temple, synagogue, and church, as well as in personal devotions and in human life. This is followed by a helpful sketch of the theology of the Psalms, and a brief discussion of the relevance of the Psalms for the African church (which does not break much new ground). The author has also published an *Introduction to the Intertestamental Period*.

532.   **Kahl, Werner**

Jesus als Lebensretter: Westafrikanische Bibelinterpretationen und ihre Relevanz für die neutestamentliche Wissenschaft

Frankfurt: Peter Lang, 2007. 532 pages, ISBN: 9783631551400.

This landmark study deals with popular and scholarly interpretation of the NT in Ghana, and its relevance for NT scholarship in the Western world. Kahl was Director of Studies in the Missionsakademie at the University of Hamburg. Previously he took a PhD in NT studies at Emory University in the US, and taught NT in the University of Ghana from 2002 to 2004. This book is based on his *Habilitationsschrift* accepted at the University of Frankfurt am Main in 2004. Kahl is to be congratulated for a unique contribution. His book consists of four major parts. Part 1 discusses the research situation and methodological challenges. Part 2 analyses popular NT interpretation in Ghana. Songs, prayers, Bible studies, sermons, popular pastoral literature, posters and stickers are among the main sources, and interpretive accents in this material are pointed out. Part 3 analyses scholarly NT interpretation in Ghana, starting with a survey of the academic framework, and then pointing out major themes and hermeneutical concerns. Part 4 discusses the major findings of the research project in relation to NT scholarship and theology in Western contexts. The decision to include both academic and popular interpretation enables the author to draw quite general lines as far as NT interpretation in Ghana is concerned, and these lines are then related to major streams in African history, theology and biblical hermeneutics. The decision to single out Ghana is also good, as Ghana is able to offer much useful material, with several profiled NT scholars, and with church contexts offering relevant examples of popular NT interpretation. The major problem with this book is that it is written in German. The author's intentions are entirely laudable: he wants to introduce African NT interpretation to his German colleagues. He rightly feels that Western biblical scholarship will benefit from familiarisation with the interpretive strategies in play in Africa. Still, an unfortunate consequence is that many African scholars and lecturers, who would have benefited from the book if it were written in English, are effectively prevented from reading it. Kahl has himself expressed a wish that it might appear in English in some form. In sum, this is a book that deserves attention among biblical scholars not only in Ghana but all over Africa – as well as in Germany and the rest of the Western world. The book also blazes a trail for other biblical scholars to follow in other African contexts besides Ghana.

533. Kalilombe, Patrick A.

Doing Theology at the Grassroots: Theological Essays from Malawi

Gweru, Zimbabwe: Mambo Press, 1999. 244 pages, ISBN: 9780869227336.

The Catholic Bishop of the Diocese of Lilongwe in Malawi, Kalilombe has been distinguished as a pioneering theologian and ecclesiologist. Circumstances have determined that much of his work has been produced and published outside Malawi. This book collects nine of his essays, preceded by an introduction to the man himself and his life. The essays are varied in origin and subject. The first is a pastoral letter written in 1973 that addresses the challenges that Vatican II represents for the local church. In the second essay the author is reflecting on evangelisation and the Holy Spirit, after attending the 1974 Synod of Bishops in Rome. Other essays attend to "The Salvific Value of African Religions," and "Lessons from African Religion: Unity from Below." Another considers differences between the Black theologies of North America and South Africa and African Theology, as well as the common root, the experience of being black. "Doing Theology at the Grassroots: A Challenge for Professional Theologians" explores the thesis that theology is not a monopoly of a few but a joint enterprise that should include ordinary men and women with no formal training in the scientific handling of God's Word. In the last paper, "Spirituality in the African Perspective," Kalilombe suggests that the important question needing to be answered is whether Christian spirituality recognized African spirituality as a potential ally. The main recurrent themes of the collection highlight the author's missionary vocation, his pastoral concern, the critical role of the "grassroots" in theological construction, the integrity of Chewa traditional belief, and the combination of Catholic commitment with radical openness to all religious and cultural traditions. By highlighting issues of concern in one denomination in one country, this book can become a useful resource for those struggling to come to terms with the contextualization of Christianity in Africa.

534. Kalu, Ogbu U., editor

African Christianity: An African Story

Trenton, NJ: Africa World Press, 2007. 480 pages, ISBN: 9781592215812.

This is an important book, because it is the first attempt by African historians and theologians to tell the whole story of African Christianity themselves. The editor is a widely respected scholar who, before his death, was a professor at McCormick Theological Seminary in Chicago. Before that he was for more than 25 years professor of church history at the University of Nsukka in Nigeria. The perspective of the book is mainstream ecumenical, and is designed as a response to the African nationalist accusations of the 1960s and 1970s that Christianity is a foreign intrusion into Africa that has only had a destructive and oppressive effect on the continent. It attempts to answer this characterisation by showing that there exists a uniquely "African" Christianity that is rooted in African traditional culture and that can transform Africa. The presentation does this by "intentionally privileging the patterns of African agency" in the African Christian story, and by emphasising the social and political role of Christianity in Africa. The privileging of African initiatives results in an over-emphasis on African Independent Churches (Ethiopian, Zionist, Aladura, Roho, etc.), creating considerable duplication of material and the impression that these churches rather than the "mission" churches have constituted the vast bulk of African Christianity. A sociological rather than a theological interpretation of Christianity pervades the book. As an example of current ecumenical African historiography, it is absolutely indispensable, and every theologian and historian interested in African religion should expect to benefit from it. Nevertheless, it does have some serious drawbacks. The first is that because the book is a cooperative effort of nineteen different authors, the quality of writing varies enormously from chapter to chapter. Furthermore, most of the writers presuppose that the reader is already familiar with African church history. In some cases the contributor writes like a specialist writing for other specialists. Readers without a strong background in African history and theology might find themselves struggling. Also the topical and thematic arrangement of the book (it is only very broadly chronological) leaves the reader with only a vague notion of the chronological contours of African Christian history. Oddly enough, no information is provided about any of the contributors apart from the editor; a brief biographical sketch of each would have been helpful. Even so, scholars and lecturers will find this a significant resource, and it should be considered a necessary acquisition by theological libraries.

535. Kalu, Ogbu U.

African Pentecostalism: An Introduction

New York: Oxford University Press, 2008. 376 pages, ISBN: 9780195339994.

In a richly detailed and engaging text, Kalu offers a sweeping discussion of Pentecostalism as seen within the African context. A primary focus of Kalu's argument is that African Pentecostalism cannot be characterized as simply derivative of American (or European) Pentecostalism, since from the very beginning indigenous elements were at the core of its expansion and have continued to play the primary role in shaping its success. He offers convincing evidence of this contention, paying careful attention to the indigenous impulses in developing a composite picture of the people, events, and circumstances that spawned what is now among the largest movements within African Christianity. Kalu first explores the foundations for Pentecostalism in various parts of the continent from the 1900s to the 1960s. He then focuses on the modern Pentecostal movement throughout the continent from the 1970s to the 1990s, exploring the varieties of the movement and their uses of media, models of leadership, and how gender roles played out within them. Next he addresses how Pentecostalism is perceived and plays out in the public space, including its relationship to African worldviews, systemic and political ethics, political theology and the relationship with Islam. Finally Kalu examines the theological frames of Pentecostalism and the roles it is playing in sending out African missionaries to the rest of the world. Bringing together insights and critiques from the disciplines of sociology, anthropology, historiography and theology, and drawing from historical, cultural, instrumentalist, and religious discourses, Kalu weaves together the fascinating story. He does this both in the broad scale as seen across the continent and in the small scale of local settings driven by local leaders and the aspirations, circumstances, and hopes of their followers. In the resulting set of "thick" pictures it is clear to the reader that Kalu is more focused on presenting the movement phenomenologically than in critiquing it, which could be seen as a strength of the book. On the other hand, Kalu clearly intends to correct those who use simplistic or reductionistic approaches to characterize the complex story of Pentecostalism in sub-Saharan Africa.

536. Kalu, Ogbu U.

The Embattled Gods: Christianization of Igboland, 1841–1991

Trenton, NJ: Africa World Press, 2004. 360 pages, ISBN: 9781592211166.

Originally from Nigeria, in his later years Kalu was Professor of World Christianity at McCormick Theological Seminary in the USA. This book offers a history of Igbo Christianity from 1841 to 1991. The Igbos of south-eastern Nigeria, one of the largest ethnic groups in the country, have been very responsive to the gospel. So how should one do Igbo church history? The traditional approach was often missionary historiography. Despite its value, this did not always show enough awareness of the African culture. In reaction to this the nationalist approach developed, stressing African cultural issues, but often at the expense of religious or theological matters. Kalu is highly critical of this approach. Like Nebuchadnezzar's statue, "nationalist historiography had its own feet of clay"; the obsession with cultural matters blinded such scholarship to basic religious issues. Kalu boldly suggests a third approach, namely, "Christo-centric historiography." Igbo church history should ask: "to what extent has the power of the gospel challenged the covenants with the gods of Igboland?" "Church history is the memory of the people of God about the meaning of the gospel in their midst." With this basic methodology in hand, Kalu reviews Igbo church history. He covers familiar ground, but as an Igbo he does so in depth, beginning with the Niger expedition of 1841. The introduction of Christianity into Igboland entailed a clash of gods and of covenant allegiances. The believers who entered into a new covenant were rejecting the old covenant with the traditional gods. Thus in doing church history, "the affirmation of Jesus Christ as Lord . . . is the litmus test." Kalu looks at the growth of Christianity in the northern, southern, central and eastern regions of Igboland. There was significant church growth but also nominalism. Education was an important medium of evangelisation. The Nigerian-Biafran civil war of 1967–1970 was a time of crisis for the Igbos, but "from the ashes of the civil war" Pentecostalism arose and is a dominant force up to the present. Historians may look for sociological reasons for this movement, but Kalu suggests that it is the wind of God or the finger of God in history. "Thus, in spite of our explanations, the Christian presence has grown among the Igbo . . . with an inexplicable and mysterious power." Might this important book by a well-respected Nigerian professor represent a new phase in the writing of African church history?

537. Kalu, Ogbu U., and Alaine Low, editors

Interpreting Contemporary Christianity: Global Processes and Local Identities

Grand Rapids: Eerdmans, 2008. 384 pages, ISBN: 9780802862426.

This edited collection brings together diverse perspectives on how global and local identities interrelate to represent some of the different faces of global Christianity. To accomplish this, the book draws upon the work of historians and theologians, with a few social scientists (all experts in their respective fields) to tackle the complex issues related to globalisation and how it appears within heterogeneous landscapes, such as Africa, Latin America, Europe, Asia and North America. Discourse on globalisation often entails a pejorative reading of a singular, cultural phenomenon, which (many contend), finding its genesis in Western (and usually American) societies, has proceeded to impact people everywhere. The actual dynamics of globalisation, as attested to in this collection, raise awareness of the vibrant imagination of non-Western, local identities against – or at other times, acting within – the outstretched arms of Western culture. Kalu, the noted Nigerian Christian historian and co-editor of this volume, makes these intentions explicit, highlighting how the various authors "locate the key dynamics of change in the internal processes and the initiatives of indigenous players." There are four contributions from Africa, variously on: female leaders of African Initiated Churches in Kenya (Philomena Mwaura); African New Religious Movements in Europe (Afe Adogame); African Christianity, globalisation and mission (Jehu Hanciles); and portraits of Christ in Africa today (Diane Stinton). The merits of this book relate to a kaleidoscopic array of perspectives on Christianity that show how indigenous agents around the world are engaging in globalising currents to articulate Christian faith. As is often the case with any edited collection, readers will be attracted to particular chapters depending upon their interests and/or contexts. The different authors provide a rich tapestry of diverse phenomena of Christian faith around the world, resulting in a valuable contribution to the study of global Christianity, and of African Christianity within that larger framing.

538. Kalu, Ogbu U.

Power, Poverty and Prayer: The Challenges of Poverty and Pluralism in African Christianity, 1960–1996

Trenton, NJ: Africa Research and Publications, 2006. 224 pages, ISBN: 9781592213948.

In this wide-ranging book, Kalu examines the role that Christianity plays in the unfolding story of post-colonial and present-day Africa. He does so from a variety of angles: political, economic, socio-cultural, and religious. An entire chapter is given to considering gender issues; another to Pentecostalism in Africa. In each of these fields Kalu draws on recent scholarly analysis and theory. Of particular interest to him are the forces and dynamics that have contributed to the "on-going pauperisation" of Africa. These include internal factors such as nepotism and autocracy in many states, and the weakening effect of too many NGOs, as well as external factors such as the marginalisation of Africa in the post-Cold War era. Kalu concludes that the failure of the state in many cases is not economic but ethical, and argues that the challenge facing Africa is to address the problem of dysfunction by reaching back to Africa's oldest values of community and responsibility. Indeed, one significant emphasis in Kalu's book, featuring both in the preface and in the very last pages, is that Africa has outgrown the "fad of missionary-bashing" and instead must show its maturity by self-critique. Kalu urges the Church to exercise a prophetic ministry in asserting its distinctive values in the exercise of power in the continent. While the prose is sometimes very involved, there is much in this book to stimulate fresh thinking, debate, and action.

Kalu, Wilhelmina

see review 678

539. Kane, Thomas A.

Dancing Church Around the World

Mahweh, NJ: Paulist Press, 2010. ISBN: 9780809180998.

The saying that "in Africa, to dance is to breathe" exudes throughout this exceptional video production, which depicts church dance in representative Catholic contexts of Ethiopia, Malawi, Kenya, Zaire, Cameroon and Ghana. Kane, a Paulist priest and lecturer with a doctorate in ritual communication, has obviously taken great delight in collecting these examples of dancing and art forms across Africa. Nothing was staged for camera;

it is simply the church at worship in a variety of ways. Many of the prayers and dances have been created by members of local parishes. Rituals and celebrations illustrated include the eucharist, thanks for harvest, preparation for the reading of the Word, morning devotions, processionals, the collection of gifts from the people, Corpus Christi, and the passion of Christ. For example, the enactment of the death of Christ mingles the church with the town in Turbo, Kenya, when the drama proceeds from the church, via stations of the cross, to the town square. The nuns of Poor Clare Monastery in Lilongwe incorporate the sounds and actions of grinding grain in their liturgy and choreography as they pray for their community in the early morning. It is pointed out that the women and children of all ages have opportunity to become involved in church life when it comes to dancing. The Catholic church in many areas of the world, especially since Vatican II, has succeeded in adapting its rites and liturgies to local culture, using the languages and dances of a specific context. The video is in colour, and the script is read deliberately so that the message comes across clearly. This video is certainly a useful tool for worship and music seminars throughout Africa. Non-liturgical churches could be inspired by the planning and care that is put into the act of corporate worship.

540.   Kanyadago, Peter M.

Evangelising Polygamous Families: Canonical and African Approaches

Eldoret: Gaba Publications, 1991. 230 pages, ISBN: 9789966836052.

Kanyadago's reworked dissertation is a discussion of Roman Catholic Canon Law applied to African marriages, which nevertheless contains much that is of interest to any Christian dealing with polygamy. He gives a long study of past struggles and church policies on polygamy. Though he raises some questions for which he does not provide definitive answers, he does squarely address the matter of marriages which were not performed by a priest: he believes that marriages are indissoluble, even if celebrated only by traditional ceremonies. He urges a careful study of local traditions regarding marriage, so that the matters of bride wealth and childlessness are addressed with understanding, not simplistically. Kanyadago, a Ugandan, did his doctoral studies at Louvain. While some may find this book of limited interest because of the focus on Canon Law, it does make a useful contribution to the larger discussion on polygamy.

Kanyadago, Peter M.

see also review 381

541.   Kanyoro, Musimbi R. A.

Introducing Feminist Cultural Hermeneutics: An African Perspective

Cleveland: Pilgrim Press, 2002. 109 pages, ISBN: 9780826460547.

The author is a Kenyan who has served in Switzerland as general secretary of the global YWCA; previously she held an executive post with the Lutheran World Federation. Her book is one in a series of short introductions to issues and topics in feminist theology. This particular contribution to the series is a brief, interesting and balanced presentation of issues of concern to many African Christian women, and the ways in which Christians have or possibly should reflect on and interact with these issues. One strength of the book is its honesty. Kanyoro admits that her education, westernisation and urbanisation have distanced her to a large degree from the world of the village in which she was raised. And, although clearly writing as a "feminist," Kanyoro is not uncritical of much Western feminism, which she judges to be too individualistic. The book contains many insights which should be of value for African theology generally. For example, Kanyoro notes that African women theologians and biblical exegetes are not as quick as many male African scholars to consider African culture as necessarily positive: "Using their lives as examples, African women question the premises that celebrate all cultural practices regardless of their negative impact on women." Perhaps the most valuable part of the book is the section which tells the story of Kanyoro's "research project" in her home village. The project itself involved a three-day retreat/Bible study of the book of Ruth, which took place in 1996 with 150 women, virtually all the women of her western Kenya town. The report reflects on a creative process of Bible study which enables the text of the Bible and the real life experience of rural African women to interact. This section itself is worth the price of the book. Kanyoro has provided an introduction, not so much to what has been done in African feminist hermeneutics (although there is some of that), but to what can be done by and for African Christian women. This can serve as a readable, and in most cases a non-threatening, introduction to an important dimension of biblical exegesis in Africa.

Kanyoro, Musimbi R. A.

see also review 846

542.   Kapolyo, Joe M.

The Human Condition: Christian Perspectives Through African Eyes

Carlisle, UK: LGL, 2013. 140 pages, ISBN: 9781907713040.

Kapolyo is from Zambia, a former principal of the Theological College of Central Africa in Ndola, and later of All Nations Christian College in Britain. His book appears in the *Global Christian Library* series, which intends to reflect the changing centre of gravity of world Christianity by publishing books from non-western authors that reflect their cultures while also speaking to Western readers, thereby facilitating a multi-directional flow of biblical understanding. This book therefore offers a biblical approach to the understanding of humanity, but in the context of the traditional understanding of the author's own people, the Bemba of Zambia. Kapolyo first asks what it means to be human, looking briefly at a number of approaches – Darwinian, Marxist, African – as well as the Christian view. A fuller examination of biblical perspectives follows, including a substantial and helpful discussion of the meaning of the image of God in human beings, elaborated in terms of structural and functional dimensions. A particularly lengthy section treats the stewardship of creation as first of the functional attributes of humanity as divine image-bearer. Here the author makes considerable use of the African context; here too he discusses gender relationships which he views in largely egalitarian terms. Kapolyo next discusses sin, which he defines in terms of both condition and act, before explaining its origins in the fall described in Genesis. He goes on to speak of its consequences and universal scope, and spends some time discussing bondage to the world, the devil and the flesh, drawing very helpfully on illustrations from the Zambian context. The next section concentrates on African culture, explaining Bemba anthropology through a number of core values which touch on the whole of life: spirituality, spiritual activities, group solidarity, exploitation of whatever circumstances to personal/family advantage, belief in the afterlife, distinctive concept of time, and social definition of truth. Finally, the author discusses the communication of the gospel in terms that will make sense in the cultural context. With its African perspective the book is a creative contribution to a hugely discussed area, in itself a valuable achievement. Certainly it is those sections in which Kapolyo draws on insights from his cultural heritage that are most original. Also in his treatment of African culture there is no idealisation or nostalgia; throughout the author is willing to be critical of aspects of his culture and to identify areas that must be transformed. His underlying concern is that the truth of the gospel be effectively communicated within such settings. The volume is to be welcomed in opening up fresh approaches to the writing and teaching of theology in Africa.

543.   Kapteina, Detlef

Afrikanische Evangelikale Theologie: Plädoyer für das ganze Evangelium im Kontext Afrikas

Nürnberg, Germany: VTR, 2001. 335 pages, ISBN: 9783933372444.

Kapteina, a German Baptist minister, previously taught theology at the Baptist College in Sierra Leone, and worked as Africa secretary of the European Baptist Mission. This dissertation on African evangelical theology was written under the supervision of Professor Peter Beyerhaus, and was accepted in 1999 by the Evangelical Theological Faculty at Heverlee/Leuven in Belgium. Kapteina offers a historical overview of the Association of Evangelicals in Africa (AEA), with special accent on the founding years in the 1960s and 1970s and the theological outcome of conferences and declarations up to the present. The principal part of the book is dedicated to the work of evangelical theologians in Africa, especially Byang Kato, Tokunboh Adeyemo, Tite Tiénou, Kwame Bediako, Gottried Osei-Mensah, René Daidanso, David Gitari, and Osadolor Imasogie. Their contribution to the development of an African theology, but also their differences in emphasis to other African theologians, are shown. A chapter each is devoted to the topics of hermeneutics, soteriology, and Christology, each time drawing from the exemplary contribution of one of the above mentioned theologians. Since until recently most leading theological reference works fail to mention evangelical theologies in Africa, Kapteina helps fill a gap. He presents the development and essential teaching of African evangelical theologians, and his bibliography helps to access their dispersed writings. A ten-page English summary is included.

544.   Karamaga, André

L'Évangile en Afrique: Ruptures et continuité

Bière, Switzerland: Cabédita, 1990. 294 pages, ISBN: 9782882950390.

Originally produced as a doctoral thesis at the University of Lausanne (entitled: *Evangile et culture: ruptures et continuité: point de vue d'un Africain*), Karamaga's study is an ambitious undertaking. A Rwandan of Presbyterian background, the author is interested to see how culture and the gospel interact. He is frequently driven to speak in generalities, given the vast nature of his subject. The first chapter attempts to lay the groundwork globally, both in terms of setting out definitions and in terms of looking at the church universal. Chapter two highlights the situation in Africa as a whole when the missionaries arrived, and the impact – positive and negative – that the gospel had as it encountered the cultural and theological context of the Africans. The following chapter looks more specifically at the traditional beliefs held by Rwandans and the results of different mission activities there. The final chapter seeks to bring about some sort of synthesis between African culture and Christian identity. The author's overall conclusion regarding the possibility of fusing the two is reflected in the subtitle of his work: ruptures and continuity. One cannot avoid wondering what direction the book would have taken had it been written after the genocide that took place in Rwanda a few years later.

545. Karamaga, André

Problems and Promises of Africa: Towards and Beyond the Year 2000: A summary of the proceedings of the symposium convened by the AACC in Mombasa in November, 1991: A proposal for reflection

Nairobi: All Africa Conference of Churches, 1993. 90 pages, ISBN: 9789966987983.

In 1991 the All Africa Conference of Churches (AACC) organized a symposium in Mombasa, Kenya, devoted to the theme reproduced in the title of this short book. The book seeks to summarize the symposium proceedings. As the AACC looked towards the year 2000 it sensed that the church in Africa needed to look at itself, at Africa, and at the world as a whole, and to engage in a process of self-criticism in order to plan creatively and deliberately for the future. Although not explicitly stated, the symposium was wrestling with the issue of increasing globalisation and the impact this would have on the church in Africa and on the continent as a whole. Therefore, the symposium's working groups sought to determine what the church of the future should look like, and how it could deal with social issues such as the disintegration of the traditional African family, culture and education. It also grappled with political and economic issues such as democracy in Africa, problems of post-colonialism, security and human rights, debt relief, and the refugee phenomenon. The discussion included on the shift in Africa towards secularity and religious pluralism is helpful in understanding the context in which the AACC church communities found themselves as the final decade of the twentieth century was commencing. The book ends with a consideration of unity both within the church and among humankind, along with a discussion of how to carry out a credible communication of the gospel through various media. The author calls this book "a proposal for reflection."

546. Karanja, John

Founding an African Faith: Kikuyu Anglican Christianity 1900–1945

Nairobi: Uzima Press, 1999. 304 pages, ISBN: 9789966855534.

This carefully researched and clearly written study began life as a Cambridge doctoral dissertation. Its purpose is to trace how a mission effort of the Church Missionary Society became, within less than half a century, a fully African church. The book argues that Anglicanism in central Kenya was a "Kikuyu response to, and appropriation of, Christianity, [which] derived its force and vitality from indigenous models and experiences." Karanja takes the reader from the early missionary period in which education was the dominant mode of evangelism, through the period of rapid growth after World War I, to the major events of conflict and consolidation between the wars, in which the female circumcision crisis and the East Africa Revival were major sources of conflict and consolidation. Karanja argues effectively throughout that it was African Christians acting out of the ethos of their Kikuyu heritage who were the major makers of the history of the church in central Kenya. The missionaries were important catalysts in this process, but the mission would not have been successful without the wisdom imparted by Africans steeped in Kikuyu culture. Of special importance is Karanja's chapter on the translation of the Bible into Kikuyu. Here he shows not only that the translation of Scripture aided

Kikuyu society in general by contributing to the standardisation and enrichment of the language, but also that the availability of the Bible promoted religious independency by providing "an independent standard of reference outside of missionary control." Karanja's research makes meticulous use of information gained from oral interviews with at least 84 informants, as well as that gained from a thorough investigation of archival material found in a number of institutions in both Kenya and Britain. This is a piece of superb scholarship, illustrating a theme that is applicable for many parts of African Christianity. Karanja's book deserves a place in any library intending good coverage of African Christian history.

547.   Kariuki, Obadiah

A Bishop Facing Mount Kenya: An Autobiography, 1902–1978

Nairobi: Uzima Press, 1985. 125 pages, ISBN: LANG255422.

The story of Obadiah Kariuki spans almost the entire history of the Anglican Church in Central Kenya. Kariuki was a boy when the first missionaries of the Church Missionary Society arrived in Kikuyuland. At the time of his death in 1978 the Anglican Church was fully under indigenous leadership. The book tells the story of his early education at the mission school in Kabete, which allowed him to read the Bible, and of his formative experience of the Holy Spirit in the first days of the East Africa Revival. As one of the first indigenous clergy in East Africa, Kariuki played an important role as a bridge between Europeans and Africans in a time of great tension leading up to Kenyan independence. In 1955 he was consecrated as one of the first two African Anglican Bishops (along with Festo Olang') and served in various episcopal roles as the church expanded at an amazing rate through the next quarter century. This book is a useful model for historical research in Africa, being largely a transcription of taped material recorded under the guidance of George Mathu of the University of Nairobi, and edited by Paul Kariuki, working for the Anglican Church in Kenya (then called the Church of the Province of Kenya). Photographs, a chronology of Kariuki's life and times, and an index increase the usefulness of this small volume. At times the text of the book leads off on tangents that seem less than significant, but for the most part the story provides a fascinating insider perspective on the life of one part of the African church in the twentieth century.

Kassimir, Ronald

see review 183

548.   Kastfelt, Niels, editor

Religion and African Civil Wars

London: Hurst, 2005. 288 pages, ISBN: 9781850654551.

The papers in this book were originally presented at a conference on "Religion and Social Upheaval in Africa," sponsored in 1999 by the University of Copenhagen. The seven papers focus primarily on Southern Sudan, Central Africa, Southern Africa and the Sierra Leone/Liberia/Gambia region, although occasional reference is made to other areas of conflict on the continent. Some of the authors have limited personal experience of Africa, with all of them currently holding academic positions in either Europe or North America. Two of the papers deal with Southern Sudan. The one by Sharon Hutchinson focuses on the interplay between militarism,

Christianity and indigenous prophets during the 1991 to 1999 period. The other by Andrew Wheeler majors on the development of the Christian church in the period of military chaos from 1974 to 1999. The paper on Rwanda and Burundi by Timothy Longman initially explores the impact of early Catholic missionaries on the political leadership and policies in both countries. It then pursues the changing role of the Catholic Church in the developing conflict between Hutu and Tutsi. Based on personal involvement over a number of years, René Devisch describes and analyses how local communities in the city of Kinshasa have responded to rampant violence through local activities, such as local healing communes. Paul Richards reviews the activity of the Revolutionary United Front in Sierra Leone, focusing particularly on their forest camps and the religious aspects of their movement and practices. With the border area between Guinea and Liberia as the focus, Christian Højbjerg looks at the relationship between ethnic violence and religious symbols, notably religious masks and their associated rituals. David Maxwell concludes the book with a paper that considers political and religious change in Zimbabwe during the period 1980–1999, particularly with regard to Pentecostalism. He does this by studying in detail the situation in the Katarere chiefdom, rather than the whole country. All of the contributors interpret the term "Christian" in its broadest sense, but they do so clearly, such that any variation of interpretation between authors does not detract from their contribution. The papers have been well researched and are very detailed.

549.   **Kastfelt, Niels**

Religion and Politics in Nigeria: A Study in Middle Belt Christianity

London: I. B. Tauris, 1994. 176 pages, ISBN: 9781850437802.

The Danish branch of the Sudan United Mission (DSUM) began missionary work in Adamawa Province in northeast Nigeria in 1913. Today the Lutheran Church of Christ in Nigeria (LCCN) is the result of the DSUM work. The author is a lecturer in church history and African studies at the University of Copenhagen. Here he looks at the political impact of this mission and this church in this part of Nigeria between 1940 and 1960. The Adamawa Province is home to a number of minority ethnic groups. The British used the Hausa-Fulani emirate system to govern these non-Muslim ethnic groups through the system of indirect rule. The DSUM's provision of Western education resulted in the emergence locally of a political elite, who sought not only to secure their independence from Hausa/Fulani political hegemony, but also to make Christianity a unifying factor in their resistance. An interesting dimension is the support the DSUM missionaries gave to these Christian political elite. Whereas colonial authorities tried to prevent missionary involvement in local politics, it was at times impossible to keep missionaries out of politics when, rightly or wrongly, they felt they were protecting their converts from ill-treatment. Thus from the 1940s onward these Adamawa Christians became deeply involved in attempts to evolve a Christian political culture and cultural identity. This explains why in the early 1950s they linked with the Middle-Zone League, a quasi-Christian political party. Unfortunately the political unity they sought, with its common denominator of Christianity, did not lead to cultural unity among the Adamawa ethnic groups. Much emphasis on ethnic differences affected the Christian unity, and this in turn affected the political unity. Be that as it may, there is no doubt that this book has provided very useful insights into the relationship between Christianity and colonialism in Northern Nigeria. It will especially interest those who specialize in the social and political impact of Christian missions in Africa, not least since the historical experience of Middle-Belt Christian communities in Nigeria cannot always be easily correlated with conventional assumptions about colonialism and missions in Africa.

550.   **Kastfelt, Niels, editor**

Scriptural Politics: The Bible and the Koran as Political Models in the Middle East and Africa

London: Hurst, 2004. 236 pages, ISBN: 9781850654445.

The title of this book is intriguing enough, but even more so is the considerable variety of issues and geographical foci presented in this compendium deriving from a conference held in Copenhagen in 1998. The contributors are mostly from Europe and the Middle East, but they bring along a wealth of insight into the religious climate of Africa as well. Five opening essays on the role of the Bible and the Qur'an as political models in Africa, and (less so) in the Middle East, lay a good foundation. Coverage includes issues of sharia law and sunna practice, as well as Islamic finance both in written texts and contemporary practice. Included is a typically provocative contribution from Paul Gifford on "The Bible as a Political Document in Africa," which treats as the dominant motif of African preaching a prosperity and deliverance gospel. He pays special attention to Mensah Otabil of Ghana, both here and in a later essay on "Pentecostalism and the Politics of Prophetic Power: Religious Modernity in Ghana." Otabil's International Central Gospel church, with its "massive middle class, literate membership," its commitment to boosting black self-confidence, and its "overriding emphasis on the modern individual," is described as having a social and political impact "beyond comparison." Other chapters offer geographical focus on the Sudan, Zambia, Egypt, Uganda, Ghana, Northern Cameroon, and the "Nigerian Bible Belt." Discussing the plight of the Southern Sudanese cause, Mohamed Salih's fairness and open criticism are impressive: "Although Islam has made clear provisions on the treatment of non-Muslims, the prevailing situation in the Sudan and elsewhere illustrates that political Islam's intent to conflate *umma* and state would lead to gruesome abuse of the political and civil rights of non-Muslims." Although readers will certainly not go along with every critical contribution to this book, it is well worth attention for the valuable insights it provides deriving from both Christian and Islamic perspectives.

Katahoire, Anne

see review 324

551.   **Kateregga, Badru D., and David W. Shenk**

A Muslim and a Christian in Dialogue

Harrisonburg, VA: Mennomedia, 2011. 234 pages, ISBN: 9780836196191.

This is an updated version of a book originally published in 1980 by Uzima Press (Kenya), under the title *Islam and Christianity: A Muslim and a Christian in Dialogue* (and also published by Eerdmans in 1981). The authors are a Muslim scholar/diplomat from Uganda and a Christian Mennonite missionary from America but raised in Tanzania. The two had taught comparative religion together at Kenyatta University College in Nairobi. It was an experience in which "often the team-teaching was a dialogue, a witness from one faith to another in the presence of our students." This book is the written expression of their mutual commitment to such interfaith dialogue. The updated version is virtually identical to the original in content and organisation. Some of the wording has been changed for the sake of clarity or courtesy. The pagination is different, some footnotes have been added, and the bibliography has been expanded to include more recent works. The book is divided into two parts, with each author presenting the basic teachings of his faith. Both parts include chapters covering a similar range of topics, including the concept of God, creation, sin, divine guidance/salvation, right conduct and mission. At the end of each chapter a response is given by the other author. In this way, readers are able easily to compare the doctrines of each religion on a given subject. The authors write with appreciation for their common beliefs, but also with honesty concerning where they differ. They together conclude that the most important point of convergence between Islam and Christianity is the conviction that God has revealed his Word to humanity, while the crucial difference is whether "the Word of revelation [is] pre-eminently a book or supremely evident in a person." The book is limited in that it deals almost exclusively with orthodox religious belief rather than religious practice (although there is a chapter in each part devoted to worship). As a result, the African (or any other) context is lacking. Nevertheless, this book remains a remarkable and worthwhile contribution.

552. Kato, Byang H.

Biblical Christianity in Africa

Achimota, Ghana: Africa Christian Press, 1985. 64 pages, ISBN: 9789964877934.

This little book presents five major papers and addresses from the ministry of Byang Kato, who could well be called the "father of evangelical African theology." The first African to head the Association of Evangelicals in Africa (AEA), Kato's untimely death in 1975, at the age of 39, has meant that his written contributions to the field of evangelical theology in Africa are few – which is what makes this booklet especially valuable. Tite Tiénou has provided an introductory preface for this selection. The first paper, "Theological Anemia in Africa," was delivered to the Third General Assembly of the AEA in 1973. Kato warns here of the threats of theological syncretism, universalism and Christo-paganism, and calls for increased higher theological education, scholarship programmes, and published materials by and for evangelicals in Africa. The second paper, presented to an AEA theological consultation at Limuru, Kenya, in 1974, pleads for a return to a biblical view of man's need and of Christ as the only way to find eternal salvation, in contrast with proposals at the time for alternate ways of salvation in dialogue with African traditional religions. The third paper, entitled "Contextualization and Religious Syncretism in Africa" was delivered to the International Congress on World Evangelisation at Lausanne in 1974. In this paper Kato offers an early evangelical understanding of contextualization, emphasising relevant communication of the truth of God. He goes on to discuss ten significant conditions in Africa which encourage syncretism and universalism. In the fourth paper, "Christianity as an African Religion," presented at the University of Ile-Ife in Nigeria in 1975, Kato skilfully challenges the common anti-colonial argument that Christianity is a Western religion, by emphasising that Africa's connections with the Gospel reach back far earlier than recent Western colonialism. He concludes that, with a two-thousand year presence on the continent, Christianity is historically entitled to be termed an African religion. In the fifth paper, given at the University of Nairobi in 1975, Kato discusses African cultural revolution and African theology, and then addresses unbiblical aspects of ecumenical theology and Black Theology. This booklet is highly recommended for anyone interested in the history of modern evangelical theology in Africa.

553.   Kato, Byang H.

Perspectives of an African Theologian: The Writings of Byang H. Kato Th.D.

Ndola: ACTEA, 2007.

This exceptional new resource on CD contains virtually all the papers, articles and books written by that states-man of African evangelicalism of a past generation, the Nigerian Byang Kato (1936–1975). At Kato's untimely death at age 39, he was General Secretary of the Association of Evangelicals in Africa (AEA), and Chair of the World Evangelical Alliance's Theological Commission. Much of the material on this CD has never previously been publicly accessible. The collection is based on the research of the Dutch scholar Christine Breman for her doctoral dissertation on the AEA. Following Breman's early death, the Canadian George Foxall, early coordinator of the Association for Christian Theological Education in Africa (ACTEA), devoted several years of his retirement to scanning all this material onto CD on ACTEA's behalf. Presented are altogether 93 documents, filling nearly 20 MB, from brief articles and typescripts to the entire text of Kato's masters and doctoral theses, all in PDF format. The collection begins with Breman's comprehensive Kato bibliography, which references both his own writings and selected materials about Kato up until 1996. The CD also includes the 1986 biography of Kato by Sophie de la Haye, *Byang Kato: Ambassador for Christ*, as well as the invaluable 1996 article by Breman herself, titled "A Portrait of Dr Byang H. Kato." Not only is Kato's well-known *Theological Pitfalls in Africa* presented, but also several of his less accessible books or booklets, namely: *Biblical Christianity in Africa*; *The Spirits: What the Bible Teaches*; and *African Cultural Revolution and the Christian Faith*. Not included are the French version of *Pitfalls* (1981), and those of Kato's articles that appeared in the French edition of AEA's *Perception*. The CD is of interest not least because at multiple points the content plainly invalidates misrepresentations of Kato that persist in some current academic literature, for example that he rejected the relevance of African culture. This remarkable contribution will now prove an essential resource for all research into the history and thought of modern African evangelical Christianity.

554.   Katongole, Emmanuel M., editor

African Theology Today

Scranton, PA: University of Scranton Press, 2002. 240 pages, ISBN: 9781589660120.

This collection of twelve essays, some already published elsewhere, is intended to make current debates in African theology accessible to readers outside Africa. Many of the authors are well known, including, for example, Mercy Oduyoye, Gerald West, Tinyiko Maluleke and Jesse Mugambe. There is no single theme uniting the collection; indeed the purpose of the book is to "demonstrate the range and depth of concerns that characterize African theological discussion." Nevertheless, "liberation" themes of one sort or another are frequently to the fore. Vähäkangas' essay, "African Approaches to the Trinity" along with Msafiri's "The Church as a Family Model: Its Strengths and Weaknesses," are relatively rare discussions of traditional theological concerns from an African perspective. Some contributions are a little lightweight. In contrast, the editor himself provides two especially worthy articles. The first, "Mission and Social Formation: Searching for an Alternative to King Leopold's Ghost," is a high spot, discussing the tension between "distressed and distressing Africa" on the one hand, and Africa as "a massively Christian continent" on the other. Katongole seeks to explain the distress in terms of the failure of the nation state, and argues that the church should "embody a different (better) narrative of social existence." In his second article Katongole challenges the notion of an African renaissance as it has been put forward by Museveni and Mbeki. An intriguing question arises from reading some of the other articles, namely: why are writers who advocate ideologies of African socio-political liberation so often eager to advance their position through ostensibly Christian theological discourse. One quoted writer explains that the seeming preoccupation of Black Theology in South Africa with Christian discourse was "on account of Christianity's apparent appeal to the black masses." In other words, because the "masses" of South Africa still believe in the Bible and Christianity, it is Christian discourse that must be deployed to mobilize them in pursuit of the revolutionary struggle. In this paradoxical reversal of Marx, the Bible and Christian faith have apparently been manipulated as "the intoxicant of the people" by liberationist black theologians. This book would be a useful resource for anyone looking for examples of modern African theological preoccupations. It is noticeable that the book contains no specifically *evangelical* contribution. One might wonder whether this reflects the state of evangelical theological engagement in Africa, or the fact that evangelicals are rarely invited to the table, or both.

555. Katongole, Emmanuel M.

A Future for Africa: Critical Essays in Christian Social Imagination

Chicago: University of Chicago Press, 2005. 300 pages, ISBN: 9781589661028.

Katongole has been Associate Research Professor at Duke Divinity School in the USA, and a Catholic priest of the Kampala Archdiocese, Uganda. This collection of essays argues for rethinking Christian social ethics as currently employed in Africa so that it may more effectively address persistent social crises afflicting the continent. Katongole presents a twofold argument. First, he contends that customary approaches treat issues in a surface manner, proposing pragmatic solutions without addressing underlying narratives and practices that perpetuate harmful patterns of behaviour. Secondly, those destructive practices and stories can only be effectively dealt with through communities of Christians who embody practices rooted in the narrative of the gospel. His argument is best explicated through an understanding of the three interrelated concepts around which he organizes the essays: *memory*, *performance*, and *imagination*. Memory is more than just mental activity. Past experience shapes our vision of the world, our understanding of who we are in that world, and the habits and patterns of life we adopt to live within such a society. In one of the most powerful chapters of the book, Katongole recalls how he came to understand memory in this way through the manner in which Uganda's experience under Idi Amin shapes social patterns and customs of Ugandan society today. Memory thus creates expectations and norms rooted in these narratives that in turn shape performance (i.e. the patterns in which a society conducts its life). Finally, Katongole contends that Christian social ethics must begin by addressing the issue of imagination. Imagination consists in the ability to think outside of the troubled memory and resulting harmful performances that dominate our societies, to conceive of and embody new patterns of life rooted in the gospel. Behind Katongole's arguments looms the shadow of Stanley Hauerwas (and, unacknowledged, John Howard Yoder). Katongole faults Mugambi of Kenya for holding that Africa's reconstruction should come through government structures in a "new world order." According to Katongole, Mugambi has uncritically adopted a narrative that expects governments in Africa, however dysfunctional they have proven in the past, to be the locus of solutions to social problem on the continent. Katongole finds Bediako of Ghana to be over-concerned with a disembodied African Christian identity at the expense of an embodied church concerned with how people will feed and educate their children. As with most collections of essays, the final product is a bit uneven in quality. Nevertheless, Katongole offers much that will provoke critical engagement on issues of Christian social ethics in Africa.

556.   Katongole, Emmanuel M., and Jonathan Wilson-Hartgrove

Mirror to the Church: Resurrecting Faith after Genocide in Rwanda

Grand Rapids: Zondervan, 2009. 176 pages, ISBN: 9780310284895.

One might wonder if yet another book on the Rwanda genocide of 1994 is necessary. In this case the answer is in the affirmative, because of the author's concern to apply the lessons from Rwanda to the wider world. Katongole is a Rwandan by background but was raised in Uganda by a Tutsi father and a Hutu mother. He is a Roman Catholic priest who serves as associate research professor of theology and world Christianity at Duke Divinity School. As an African Christian, he asserts that evil spiritual forces (from a biblical, not an animistic perspective) were at the heart of the genocide and sees other factors such as tribalism, socio-economic tension, politics and colonialism as the outworking of that evil. He laments that it was unprecedented for church members to kill fellow Christians in their places of worship ("the blood of tribalism was deeper than the waters of baptism") and fears that current (mainly American) expressions of concern "miss the fact that Christian mission is not so much about delivering aid or services as it is about the transformation of identity." Nevertheless, he blames the colonialists for dividing a common culture into separate ethnic groups that had not previously seen each other as enemies. The declaration of Rwanda as a Christian nation in 1945 receives special attention because the East African Revival of the early twentieth century showed that "sincerity and passion were not enough to ensure faithful social engagement" (and thus prevent genocide). After evaluating reasons for the genocide, Katongole addresses "Christian" nations, where he fears that lessons from Rwanda have not yet been learned. For example, many Christians fail to differentiate between patriotism and biblical values and thus fall into the same trap as Rwandans did; loyalty for or against the government of the day is stronger than faith. His continual question is what difference Christianity actually makes in a national crisis, whether it occurs in Africa or in the West. His summary is that Christians must take seriously the memory of the tragic history of Rwanda and the church's failure to act, use Rwanda as a mirror to see where we need to change patterns that are assumed to be normal, and be involved in a mission to question our allegiance to national, tribal, ethnic or racial identities that may come before the gospel. This is a courageous book that raises issues needing attention not only in Africa, where the idea of a "Christian nation" is popular, but also in places from which missionaries have been sent to Africa.

557.   Katongole, Emmanuel M., and Chris Rice

Reconciling All Things: A Christian Vision for Justice, Peace and Healing

Downers Grove: IVP US, 2008. 167 pages, ISBN: 9780830834518.

The authors, one a Roman Catholic priest from Uganda and the other a white American Protestant, are the founding co-directors of the Center for Reconciliation at Duke Divinity School in the USA. What makes this book stand out is the clear emphasis on God's redemptive story that must not be ignored when trying to reconcile seemingly hopeless situations and relationships ("we are too broken to fix it ourselves"). A biblical emphasis on time is also essential, in that we must not forget history (and its pain), nor must we lose hope of a future community that is reconciled. The authors' admirable conviction is that: "while never neglecting works of mercy and justice in a broken world, theology matters." Reconciliation is first of all God's idea, and that is the reason that the church is not just another social agency; it provides accountability when organisations do not. So true reconciliation is not a human achievement, strategy or programme, but a journey with God, and the outcome is unknown because faith is involved. Here the authors use Hebrews 11 to assert that reconciliation needs to reshape the present based on the future, not predict the future based on the present. Reconciliation must begin with lament, so we may have to "unlearn" our attempts to have speedy solutions, distance ourselves from pain and deny our own guilt – so that we may learn the opposites, which are pilgrimage, relocation and confession. African illustrations are regularly employed, especially Nelson Mandela ("leaders are ones who learn to absorb pain without passing it on to others or to themselves") and the Rwanda genocide. The final chapter on heart, spirit and life goes deeper into the reasons that the church is essential to lasting reconciliation because otherwise pragmatism may take over (merely asking, "what works?"). The summary at the end of the book lists ten theses for recovering reconciliation as the mission of God, and is a very useful outline of why the church is so important to reconciliation both within and outside the church. Those concerned for theological reflection and engagement in contemporary Africa will certainly want to read and interact with this book's reflections on reconciliation in the African context.

558. Katongole, Emmanuel M.

The Sacrifice of Africa: A Political Theology for Africa

Grand Rapids: Eerdmans, 2010. 224 pages, ISBN: 9780802862686.

Katongole is a Catholic priest from Uganda who has stories to tell. He grew up in Idi Amin's Uganda and in proximity to the Rwandan genocide. For him the cross and the coffin are two symbols of Africa. Africa's churches continue to grow; yet social violence and injustice characterize Africa. So the question is: Can Christianity save Africa? The big problem in Africa is the nation-state. Katongole speaks of "the madness of nation-state performances in Africa." Like King Leopold II's ruthless rule of the Belgian Congo, greed and plunder characterize too many contemporary African nation-states. So how should the church respond? The old paradigms of reticence (abstaining from politics), frantic activism (of the social gospel people) and co-option (with the government) do not seem to work. Instead, Katongole says, we must "dare to invent the future." These are the words of Thomas Sankara, who tried a Marxist experiment in Burkina Faso in the 1980s. But this experiment failed because of its lack of *telos* (a goal), and a compelling story. Appealing to Jean-Marc Ela, the author says that we must re-imagine the church in Africa. To do this he tells three stories. The first story is of Bishop Paride Taban who fought tribalism in southern Sudan by establishing the Kuron Peace Village. The second story is of Angelina Atyam who dared to practice radical love and forgiveness toward the Lord's Resistance Army in Uganda. The third story is of Maggy Barankitse who fought against tribalism in Burundi by establishing a community called the Shalom House. These redemptive communities at the micro-level are for Katongole the hope for Africa. These people made constructive sacrifices for Africa. This is a deeply moving book. One does wonder, nevertheless, whether one must completely give up on the nation-state in Africa. Must it be an either/or judgement? Are some reforms for African nation-states not also possible?

Kaufman, Zachary

see review 209

559.   **Kauta, John**

Analysis and Assessment of the Concept of Revelation in Karl Rahner's Theology: Its Application and Relationship to African Traditional Religions

Ann Arbor, MI: University Microfilms International, 1992. 480 pages, ISBN: LANG255135.

Karl Rahner's transcendental theology has revolutionized Catholicism in the twentieth century, as Vatican II illustrated. Kauta is a Ugandan Catholic priest resident in the United States. In this doctoral dissertation completed for Fordham University, he explores the implications of Rahner's system for evangelisation and contextualization in an African context. Rahner's central thesis is that God offers salvation to all people at all times through the experiential reality of love, as well as also objectively revealing Himself in the history of Israel culminating in Jesus Christ. Consequently, all creation constitutes the history of salvation; and Jesus Christ, the summit and culmination of creation, is a sign of what all persons can become even without knowing Him. So Rahner concludes that anonymous Christians exist in other religions. Since Jesus is the fulfilment of all non-Christian religions, the missionary's task is to awaken and make explicit the faith that is now only implicitly known. Kauta uses this implicit-explicit relationship or "continuity" model to show that the African traditional religions are compatible with Christianity. Among his many proposals dealing with inculturalisation, he suggests that baptism be adapted with ATR initiation rites, and the Catholic sacrament of penance be modified with African rites of reconciliation. Unfortunately, this study is short on critique. While referencing Clifford Geertz and George Lindbeck, the author fails to understand that they conceive the religions as resembling a culture with its own distinctive meaning system, a view that contradicts Rahner's thesis that religions are non-informational systems expressing the human existential orientation of love. It is Rahner's experiential-expressive view that allows him to homogenize the religions and conceal their distinctive conceptions of reality. For example, how can love be Christian, if it ignores the irreplaceability of Jesus Christ and His cross? Nevertheless this work is a helpful window on some contemporary African Catholic thought.

560.   **Kayanga, Samuel F., and Andrew C. Wheeler, editors**

"But God Is Not Defeated": Celebrating the Centenary of the Episcopal Church of the Sudan 1899–1999

Nairobi: Paulines, 1999. 288 pages, ISBN: 9789966214706.

This important volume of Sudanese Anglican church history is not a continuous narrative. Rather it is a collage of historical studies, theological sketches, poetry, and essays on a diverse range of issues facing the Episcopal Church of the Sudan, one of the member churches of the worldwide Anglican Communion. Especially enlightening are the essays which describe aspects of Sudanese church life: reconciliation and peace-making, worship and music, revival and miracles, the ministry of women, and theological education. The picture painted here does not focus exclusively on war and devastation, those realities which the Sudanese know too well, but on the presence of God reflected in the life of God's people. The title itself, "But God is Not Defeated," reflects both the reality of war and the deep faith of Sudanese Christians that God is present with them in the midst of their suffering. The phrase is attributed to a much revered saint of the Sudanese church, Canon Ezra Baya Lawiri, for many years a priest and Bible translator, who was killed in crossfire in 1990. For the historian, the section "Sowing the Seed, Taking Root 1899–1964" will be most of interest. The year 1899 was when Llewellyn

Gwynne, the first CMS missionary to Sudan, arrived there. In 1964 the Sudanese government expelled foreign missionaries from Sudan. Between these two events, this section argues, the church took root and grew to such an extent that, when the missionaries were forced out, the Sudanese Christians themselves were not only able to lead the Church but to bring it into a period of unprecedented growth. As Abe Enosa writes, ". . . like a repeat of the 'Feeding of the 5000,' the expulsion of the missionaries led to a multiplication in the Church. Pastors, lay readers, women leaders and evangelists took responsibility for doing the work of God. This led to a dramatic growth in the Church." The book is made the more valuable by its inclusion of two to three page profiles of every diocese of the ECS in 1999 (more have been added since the publication of the book), a list of major events in the history of Sudanese Anglicanism, an annotated bibliography, and many photographs.

561. Kebede, Messay

Africa's Quest for a Philosophy of Decolonization

New York: Rodopi, 2004. 256 pages, ISBN: 9789042008106.

Those motivated to understand the inner dynamics of modern Africa's intellectual life, and especially its philosophical sub-strata, should consider starting with this book. Kebede here offers an authoritative exposition and critique of successive competing trends within the discipline of African philosophy over more than half a century. He concurs in that discipline's perspective that the European colonial ideology, with its denigrating representation of Africa's past, remains still too often embedded in the mindset of Africa's educated elite, and thereby lies near the root of whatever has been impeding Africa's progress toward modernity. Kebede taught philosophy at Addis Ababa University from 1976 to 1993; more recently he has been a university professor of philosophy in the United States. He holds a PhD from the University of Grenoble, France. Kebede evaluates in succession: African ethnophilosophy, which asserts African otherness (e.g. Temples, Senghor, Mbiti); professional African philosophy, which denies African otherness (e.g. Hountondji, Towa, Wiredu); followed by the deconstructionists, who instead favour unmasking and relativizing the Western colonial discourse (especially Mudimbe). Numerous other participants in the ongoing debate are also referenced. For his part Kebede wants to argue for a refined and redirected ethnophilosophy, one that can wed the energising power of ideology to rational scientific commitment, as the way through to a reconstructed identity for Africa. While Kebede's own proposals merit attention, it is the overview and assessment of African philosophy's principal players and dominant issues, and their interplay, which is this study's impressive contribution. The density of technical analysis might sometimes overwhelm, framed as it is by philosophic vocabulary and conceptuality. But the excellent summary introductions and conclusions section by section throughout help maintain clarity and coherency. Although the "African Theology" movement can be readily characterized as at root but a sub-set of the task set by the larger African intellectual quest being profiled here, nowhere does it make an appearance in this presentation. Only Mbiti comes to notice, treated for his early input on African philosophy. Nevertheless, any critical understanding of African theology would seem to require a close acquaintance with the larger intellectual debate surveyed in this book. And insofar as evangelical theology anywhere in the world is tasked by inherent commitments to engage with its context, and insofar as such contexts are in part conditioned by dominant worldviews, African evangelical theological discourse can hardly fulfil its proper role absent some meaningful engagement with African intellectual modernity as represented in this book. This is the sort of book that needs to be put to use by those venturing to make contributions in African Christian theological discourse.

Keefer, Constance

see review 638

562.   Keese, Alexander, editor

Ethnicity and the Long-Term Perspective: The African Experience

Frankfurt: Peter Lang, 2010. 215 pages, ISBN: 9783034303378.

The book is the first volume in a new series, linked to the Centre of African Studies at the University of Porto, Portugal, where the editor of both the book and the series is Assistant Professor of African History. The series is a welcome addition to the current flora of Africanist publishing channels, hopefully proving able to voice Lusophone experiences and concerns. This first book proceeds from the observation that violence between ethnic groups constitutes a severe threat to contemporary Africa. However, whereas historians, anthropologists and political scientists previously argued that (supposedly) ethnic conflicts to a large extent are results of colonial constructions, it is now acknowledged that group violence in sub-Saharan Africa, even under ethnic labels, is a far more complex phenomenon. A hermeneutical key concept here is that of having long-term perspectives, meaning basically to take pre-colonial material seriously. The essays of the present book are part of the last two decades' attempt at developing alternatives to the constructivist paradigm. Parts of two major geographical regions, namely East and South-East Africa, and Coastal West Africa, are approached by the book's six long-term studies, which fall into two main sections. In the first, which covers the area of southern Tanzania and northern Mozambique, Eduardo Medeiros and José Capela trace processes of identity-building in the Zambezi Valley; Malyn Newitt looks at ethnic identity in the Zambezi Valley, here from the perspectives of kinship, religion, language and political control; and Felicitas Becker analyses vernacular ethnic stereotypes in southeast Tanzania, 1890–2003. In the book's second main section, covering Senegambia, Guinea-Bissau and Sierra Leone, Paul Nugent looks at the historicity of ethnicity, with the Mandinka/Jola in the Senegambia and the Ewe/Agotime in the trans-Volta as cases; Philip Havik analyses colonial governance, appointed chiefs and political change in Portuguese Guinea; and Alexander Keese looks at identity markers of being "Temne," "Mandinka" or "Susu" in early nineteenth-century Sierra Leone. All in all, the book offers interesting examples and perspectives from contemporary sub-Saharan African, and in particular Lusophone, ethnicity discourse. One would, however, have liked to see a stronger focus on the roles of religion. It gets some attention in the essays by Newitt (Portuguese focus on religious identity in the Zambezi Valley) and Nugent (the rapid conversion of the Jola to Islam), and missionaries are often mentioned *en passant*. But religion could warrant a stronger focus in a discussion of ethnicity in Africa.

Kelley, Robin D. G.

see review 636

563.   Kelly, Robert

Calming the Storm: Christian Reflections on AIDS

Gweru, Zimbabwe: Mambo Press, 1998. 59 pages, ISBN: 9780869226131.

This little booklet is addressed to people who are HIV positive, and especially to those who have recently learned of their status. Kelly is a Jesuit father working in Zambia. He uses Jesus' calming of the storm that had badly frightened his disciples as the framework within which: to give information on AIDS and on the benefits of healthy living; to reflect on biblical love and the place of abstinence; to offer encouragement from Scripture and the life of Jesus to those infected; to call the reader to walk with Jesus; and to encourage helpful care-giving for those who are ill. Father Kelly's call to faith is warm and genuine, although not framed in the way that many evangelical Christians would present it. The author is careful to be inclusive in advising sufferers to visit their minister or priest. The book is written in a style that will make it easily understood by the general public, and so it should be a helpful tool in pastoral ministry, especially to those who are HIV carriers.

564.   Kemdirim, Protus O., and Mercy Amba Oduyoye, editors

Women, Culture and Theological Education

Enugu, Nigeria: Snaap Press, 1998. 191 pages, ISBN: 9789782952042.

Adding to the number of publications on women's issues increasingly coming from within Africa, this compilation of papers from a 1996 conference of the West African Association of Theological Institutions (WAATI) sets out to deal with its topic under three stated sub-themes: African Culture and Women; The Place of Women in the Church, and Theological Education and Women. Only two of the nine main presenters were women, and this constituted the total female contingent among the participants. Nevertheless, the significance of the contribution of women in traditional West African society is acknowledged as being far beyond that of their permitted role in theological education. The first two papers set out the importance of women in modern African culture and nation building, and touch on some biblical reflections in these areas. The next five papers address women's theological education, women's ordination, and women's ministry in church, society and the home in relation to theological education. Another paper presents one specific example of the enormous contribution to the Church's mission made by women throughout the African churches. The final paper is "A Feminist Reading" – written by a man! – of two passages from the OT and one from the NT. This is a loosely connected collection of papers with no other clearly unifying thread than that provided by the title. As is inevitable in such a compendium, the papers vary in depth and value. In general the presentations provide little that is new in dealing with the position of women in the African church. At the same time there are several extensive and highly valuable bibliographies.

565.   Kennedy, Pagan

Black Livingstone: A True Tale of Adventure in the Nineteenth-Century Congo

Santa Fe, NM: Santa Fe Writers Project, 2013. 144 pages, ISBN: 9780988225268.

The subject of this book is William Henry Sheppard, an African American born in 1865 in Virginia, USA, as the American Civil War was ending. At the age of nine, while looking at a map of Africa, he declared that he would go to central Africa when he grew up. In his early twenties he was assigned by the Southern Presbyterian Church to parishes in Alabama and then in Georgia, but his longing for Africa persisted – as did his applications to the Presbyterian Foreign Missions Board for this purpose. Finally he was told he could go, but only in the unlikely event that he found a white colleague to go with him. He set sail for Africa with Sam Lapsley in 1890. The book deals very little with Sheppard's missionary work and mostly with his determined explorations into the interior of the then Belgian Congo, earning him the title "Black Livingstone." The narrative sees Sheppard as "an anthropologist, photographer, big-game hunter, and art collector," as well as an entertainer and orator. He was particularly interested in the unknown and forbidden Kuba Kingdom of the Kasai region, into which he eventually trekked. He learned the Kuba customs, became fluent in the language, and established a Presbyterian mission station operated entirely by black staff. Although he never addressed the racism of the American South, he tackled the violence perpetrated by the African leaders, and was even eventually caught up in a trial in Leopoldville in which he testified against the atrocities of King Leopold and the Belgians for their slaughter of hundreds in their drive to get rich with the rubber harvests. Sheppard's years in the Congo ended in 1910 when he was dismissed from the mission for adultery and for fathering an illegitimate son. The final seventeen years of his life were spent in the USA with his wife and two legitimate children, undertaking children's ministries and itinerant speaking opportunities concerning his African adventures. *Black Livingstone* is more about an explorer than a missionary, but nevertheless does relate to an otherwise little-known component of African Christian history during the colonial period.

566. **Kiaziku, Vicente Carlos**

Culture and Inculturation: A Bantu Viewpoint

Nairobi: Paulines, 2009. 144 pages, ISBN: 9789966084316.

The author is a Roman Catholic theologian from Angola, trained in Venice and Rome, and now serving as a bishop in Mbaza-Congo, Angola. With a focus on experiences gained from the Christianisation of Africa, the book surveys various historical approaches to the encounter between gospel and culture. These range from that of a mere acknowledgement of certain points of similarities, to more systematically analysed concepts, such as "accommodation" and "acculturation." Still, the emphasis of the book is on today's main concept of "inculturation," which is anchored theologically in the incarnation, the life and death of Jesus. Two points should be made. First, the book is a typically Roman Catholic piece of work, in the sense that official Catholic documents play a central role throughout the discussion. Nevertheless, self-critical questions vis-à-vis the Catholic tradition are by no means absent, such as for example the problem caused by a "Westernized" indigenous clergy, a clergy trained in the West, that is, and in many cases estranged from the parishes and dioceses in which service is being given. Second, although the book is written in English, all scholarly references (except one to A. Shorter) are to Portuguese, Spanish and French literature. As such it may serve as an introduction to theological traditions and literature that may be somewhat unfamiliar in more anglophone circles.

567.   Kibor, Jacob

Christian Response to Female Circumcision

Nairobi: Evangel, 2007. 152 pages, ISBN: 9789966201379.

Kibor was formerly principal of Scott Theological College in Kenya. His book is based on his doctoral research at Trinity Deerfield in the USA. Whereas the book focuses on the Marakwet, a Kalenjin people from western Kenya, what Kibor says about female circumcision would seem to have much wider applicability, in that apparently over 80 million African women are affected by this practice. Kibor believes that female circumcision began among the Marakwet not as an expression of male domination but out of the desire of women to have a rite of passage parallel to male initiation into adulthood. Legislative attempts to eliminate the practice have particularly failed. In consequence most Marakwet girls still go through the procedure. In contrast, among Kikuyu Christians female circumcision was largely abandoned as a result of the East African Revival of the 1940s. Kibor argues that the practice persists partly because of peer pressure, but also on account of what it offers in terms of tribal solidarity, the construction of personal identity, the maintenance of premarital chastity, and education for adulthood and marriage. Kibor argues strongly for abolition of the practice, mainly on health grounds: it is excruciatingly painful, it can lead to infection and death, it causes later difficulty in childbearing due to the inelasticity of scar tissue, it results in a loss of sexual fulfilment, and it can leave major psychological scars. Kibor believes that if churches simply prohibit female circumcision they will leave "an educational void in Christian society," which would simply cause the practice to go underground. What is required is a recognition of the meaning of the female rite within Marakwet society, and its replacement by a "functional substitute" that would fulfil the purpose of the rite while eliminating its practice. Quite correctly, but contrary to some other scholars, Kibor rejects the idea that baptism might take the place of female initiation, since its meaning is quite different and it should be limited to those who trust in Christ. Instead he suggests the introduction of a special youth camp for those of the appropriate age, with a significant programme of education for adulthood based on the Bible, and using songs and drama as in the old rite of passage. He concludes by urging Christians to take a firm stand against female circumcision. This is an excellent study, and given the paucity of material from a Christian perspective on this topic, Kibor's book would be a valuable asset for Christian communities and leaders in parts of Africa where this practice remains entrenched.

Kidula, Jean N.

see review 577

568.   Kiel, Christel

Christians in Máasailand: A Study of the History of Mission among the Máasai in the North Eastern Diocese of the Evangelical Lutheran Church in Tanzania

Erlangen: Verlag der Ev.-Luth. Mission, 1997. 315 pages, ISBN: 9783872142863.

This is a slightly abbreviated translation of: *Christen in der Steppe. Die Masai-Mission der Nord-Ost-Diözese in der Lutherischen Kirche Tansanias* (1996). Kiel worked for six years as a missionary among the Maasai in Northern Tanzania. Here she offers her 1994 Berlin dissertation as a missiological study, which is impressive not least for its combination of scholarly distance and personal involvement. In part one, Kiel describes the life of the Maasai in a sympathetic way, making use of previous writings. She presents Maasai religion as largely lacking ancestral veneration, witchcraft and spirit possession cults, but involving a very direct veneration of God, under the female personality of Enkai. In part two, she relates the history of Lutheran work among these pastoralist Maasai. This work was always done, if done at all, as the missionary outreach of the agriculturalist Lutheran neighbours (including their German missionaries). Given so much talk today about "majority-world cross-cultural missionaries," it is refreshing to read the stories of such real-life African missionaries of the past as Hermann Kanafunzi, Ismael and Sara Guga, or Yakobo Kimbei, missionaries who appear in none of the modern statistics but who really existed. After some time German missionaries, though not resident among the Maasai, also began to participate in the work. The pastoralist Maasai remained aloof towards the Christian faith much longer than their agriculturalist neighbours, and when the breakthrough came, it was the women who made it. Many started to suffer from the pepo (spirit) illness, which could not be healed by any Maasai treatment, but by Christian baptism (after due instruction in the Christian faith!). "The Maasai women knew no rituals and no spirits, they had no songs or drums to ward off the danger. They only had their own persons, with body, soul and spirit, and that tipped the scales." It is an interesting case of inculturation that the Lutherans were the only church that accepted the women's approach to conversion and proved the healing faculties of the sacrament of baptism. In part three Kiel reflects on missiological aspects. She analyses the change from a "mission = school" approach to an approach which took the Maasai seriously in their pastoral culture, including the tacit and not so tacit acceptance of Christian polygamy. In perceiving missionary reality and in reflecting on it, Kiel profited from influences of the charismatic movement, just as almost all of her black and white colleagues and predecessors profited from their "Pietistic" leanings in understanding Maasai conversion. The book is characterized by a strong sense of realism. Personal experience and reflection give it more depth, and if one considers conversion to be part of the church's mission, then this book is an important contribution to missiology.

569.   Kiiru, MacMillan

How to Develop Resources for Christian Ministries

Nairobi: Uzima Press, 2004. 144 pages, ISBN: 9789966855879.

The author, a Kenyan, has worked in the field of developing financial resources, including many years with World Vision. This book is a condensed version of his doctoral thesis at Fuller Theological Seminary. Kiiru begins with an overview of biblical teaching on ownership and wealth before stressing his main theme, which is good stewardship of material resources. His short section on the purposes and principles of tithing is especially helpful, although unfortunately he glosses over passages on the dangers of wealth (e.g. 1 Tim 6). He then moves on to assessing leadership principles that relate to stewardship, using Jesus and Paul as examples. Throughout the book too much is made of lists and tables from Western authors (however good they may be), which seems to be at the expense of creative contextualized material that is so much needed in Africa. When African issues are addressed, much is made of "the missionaries never taught us" approach (e.g. the offering bags should have been larger, to communicate expectation of a larger offering, and using a larger opening would not have implied a lack of trust). The Kenyan Harambee approach to communal projects is used as a model, but is not developed in much detail, and the author admits that politicians (and even Christian leaders) have often hijacked this model for personal gain. Kiiru can sometimes surprise, for example with positive references to making a will, support for Ron Sider's approach to meeting the needs of the poor, and criticism of the "three-self" movement popularized by Henry Venn and others. The middle section of the book accurately assesses the need for change in attitudes toward accountability and gratitude, so this part will be helpful for anyone dealing with financial management in church and parachurch entities in Africa. Kiiru ends the book with a section on communication (with supporters, within the organisation, etc.), based mainly on Engel's well-known work. All in all this book is a helpful addition to the growing number of books on the responsible use of resources in developing African projects, although the reader will desire more contextualized illustrations and greater depth in regard to the African situation.

570.   Kiki, Célestin Gb.

La Réforme du Culte: Une nécessité pour les Églises d'Afrique

Yaoundé: Éditions Clé, 2001. 330 pages, ISBN: 2723501299.

This is the slightly reworked doctoral thesis by Pastor Célestin Kiki of the Methodist Church in Benin. The thesis was directed by Professor Henry Mottu of Geneva and written for the Faculté de Théologie Protestante de Yaoundé in Cameroon. The author's principal concern is to encourage the Protestant churches in Africa to develop their own contextualized liturgies, in order to enable Africans to worship in a way that makes sense to them. With that concern is coupled the conviction that orderliness needs to mark the worship services of the church. With these two thoughts in mind, the author surveys worship and liturgy in (1) traditional Africa, (2) the Bible, and (3) current Protestant worship services with which the author is familiar. He attempts to delineate the basic elements of each worship service and explain who the actors are in each case. Of necessity the descriptions are brief; but because the work is a doctoral thesis, footnotes open up the possibility of exploring certain topics further. Having criticized the current situation and some of the cultural "baggage" inherited from missionaries who may have been insensitive to cultural issues, Kiki goes on to suggest a possible way forward. He retains some traditional elements from some Protestant services (such as special ministerial attire and lectionary readings), cautions against putting too much emphasis on a merely rational approach to worship, and highlights the importance of symbolism for the African. Finally, the author suggests what he believes could be the appropriate format of a typical Protestant liturgy for Africa and explains it in detail. Very little of this type of sustained effort is available to French-speaking Africa, and seminaries should be encouraged to have the book in their library everywhere that French is used.

571.   Kilby, Stella E.

No Cross Marks the Spot

Southend on Sea, UK: Galamena, 2001. 300 pages, ISBN: 9780954101602.

Only a brave author will research the history of her own family and try to remain a disinterested party in the evaluation, especially when that family history is so closely related to a well-known personality such as David Livingstone. Born and brought up in South Africa but now resident in England, Kilby is a descendant of Holloway and Anne Helmore, missionaries with the London Missionary Society who spent almost twenty years in Africa before dying in a place to which Livingstone had persuaded them to go. The author sets out to answer principal questions over the reason for their deaths at Linyanti (in northern Botswana), and Livingstone's responsibility in the matter. The LMS archives and Holloway Helmore's personal journals are the main sources for the book, which seems to be researched well, although almost inevitably some personal bias is evident. Livingstone comes in for harsh criticism at several points that are already well known, such as his poor relationships with fellow missionaries and his lack of concern for his family, but Helmore's own tension with others gets off lightly. The author insists that the Helmores need not have died if Livingstone had been at Linyanti (as he had promised) before the exhausted travellers arrived (asserting that Livingstone was more concerned with exploration, his Makololo companions and other mission outreach). Unfortunately, Kilby attributes motives to Livingstone's mistakes, referring to him as deceitful and proud. She is especially angry that he defended his friend the Makololo chief, Sekeletu, who was apparently very unhelpful to the missionaries at Linyanti, possibly because Livingstone was not present. In 1999 the author retraced the steps of the Helmores' last journey and interviewed anyone who knew anything about the failed mission; she was assured by most that Sekeletu had poisoned the missionaries in order to steal their goods. The source of the poison was identified as the Euphorbia (Candelabra) tree, but a botanist claimed such poison could not kill an adult. Nevertheless, the author insists that although most of the party who died probably had malaria, poison was also a factor. Thus a book that is useful in filling in the historical details of a tragic journey becomes less convincing as a polemic against Livingstone, whose weaknesses are already well attested.

Kilman, Scott

see review 1095

572. Kim, Caleb Chul-Soo

Islam among the Swahili in East Africa

Nairobi: Acton Publishers, 2004. 224 pages, ISBN: 9789966888501.

"Islam is in the books and Muslims are in the grave" was the famous response a Sufi saint once gave to the question of true Islam and genuine Muslims. Kim's detailed anthropological study of the Swahili people along the coast of East Africa is neither from books nor from "dead Muslims," nor does it confine itself to general observations about popular Islam. Rather it describes Islamic phenomena at the heartland of Islam's presence in East Africa over the past 1000 years, namely on the island of Zanzibar. Kim is a Korean who has lived and worked for many years in East Africa and served as a lecturer in Islamics at the Nairobi Evangelical Graduate School of Theology. The book is divided into two interrelated parts. The first part deals with the historical background that has given birth to today's Swahili Islam and its dynamic cultural complexity. The second part focuses on Swahili-Muslim beliefs and practices relating to the jinn-possession cults. To the "enlightened" westernized reader the dominance of spirit-jinn possession and spirit cults within some African Islamic cultures may come as a shock, while to others the prevalence of such "therapeutic cults" (Kim) may serve as an eye-opener. Through extensive field research the author has become convinced that these therapeutic cults represent the complex nature of Swahili-Islam and its religio-cultural synthesis in a very colourful, dramatic way. For those new to Islamic teaching the author has added a useful chapter on Islamic belief in Jinns from the Qur'an and Hadith sources. A table comparing the vocation of priest and shaman in terms of authority, function, spirituality and other criteria is likewise stimulating. Every chapter is generously enriched with notes from many personal interviews with Muslim informants, and offers a rich field of bibliographic references. Although in his foreword Professor Mugambi gives credit to the author "that his own views do not overshadow those of the community he has described in this book," other readers might have appreciated having the author's keen observations accompanied by some sense of his personal convictions about such spiritism beliefs.

573. Kimaro, Lucy R.

The Role of Religious Education in Promoting Christian-Muslim Dialogue in Africa

Nairobi: Catholic University of Eastern Africa, 2011. 141 pages, ISBN: 9789966909855.

"Interreligious dialogue is an urgent priority in this age, especially in Africa." The author, from Tanzania, has harvested the fruits of her PhD studies completed at the Catholic University of Eastern Africa (CUEA) in Kenya, combined with ministry experience at the foot of Mount Kilimanjaro, to examine how religious education can aid dialogue between Christians and Muslims in Africa. The continental scope projected for this study is somewhat over-ambitious; the author quotes from an enormous wealth of divergent, often contradictory sources, which may leave the reader at times confused and exhausted. After a rather brief introduction to the historical development of Islamic and Christian Religious Education (IRE and CRE), she focuses on Christian-Muslim dialogue from the Christian and Islamic perspectives, before presenting the findings of her primary research in the Catholic Diocese of Moshi, Tanzania. This is perhaps the clearest, most substantive section of the book. As a member of the mystic Catholic group of Grail Sisters, for whom "spirituality as the Center of Life Together" is key, the author seems to agree that "dialogue does not mean trying to reconcile the irreconcilable, seeking to suppress or to find some common denominator that would reconcile opposition at the price of truth," while stating a few lines later: "Theological investigations have helped Christians to discover that the Qur'an inspires well-springs of life, Oneness and Transcendence of God, conception of life and death . . ." Is the author embracing all sides as helpful tributaries to the river of peace? Not quite. Some limits appear. At various points in her book she is quite explicit about evangelical activities in East Africa, listing by name several "Christian fundamentalists . . . that have jeopardized peace in Tanzania." All in all, this is an important contribution in regard to the value of Religious Education in Tanzania (and to a lesser extent Kenya). It also offers some rather shocking research findings showing how poorly and superficially Religious Education is being handled in the Tanzanian school system, when it could fulfil such a crucial role in the forming of character and interfaith relations. But will it amount to more than wishful thinking when she presents her ideals: "Christian and Muslim teachers should be scripturally (biblically and Qur'anically) informed, godly in their thinking, constructive in critical religious debates, and original in their ideas; ready to understand the signs of the time and knowing what must be done (1 Chr 12:32; Dan 9:1–2)"?

574. Kimilike, Lechion Peter

Poverty in the Book of Proverbs: An African Transformational Hermeneutic of Proverbs on Poverty

New York: Peter Lang, 2010. 314 pages, ISBN: 9781433103278.

Kimilike is a Tanzanian scholar who took his doctoral degree from the University of South Africa, and has served on the teaching staff of Makumira University College in Tanzania. In this study he proposes to deploy "an African transformational hermeneutic" which is alive to the concerns of the African interpretive context, and utilizes African proverbs on poverty to this end. He first reviews existing scholarship on his theme, concluding that Western scholars should be found wanting for assuming that the origin of the biblical proverbs on poverty lies within those who could write and collect these maxims, that is to say within the Israelite elite. Viewed from this perspective, these proverbs can, for example, function "as a form of propaganda to console the poor in their poverty." Kimilike sees such scholarly opinions as having their origins in such Western values as individualism and consumerism. Western interpretation is also faulted for viewing Proverbs as a "secular" rather than a "religious" text, arguing that such binary opposites are foreign to both the biblical and the African worldview. Kimilike is also critical of the way in which some African biblical scholars have dealt with the issue of poverty in the Bible and their understanding of Proverbs in particular. That is to say, he does not believe that "being African" automatically gives a reader an infallible interpretation of the text. Like most African scholars, Kimilike is not writing in his first language; and in his case, neither of his dissertation supervisors is a native English speaker either. The published version could certainly have benefitted from some editorial assistance with stylistic issues. This book is recommended not only as a useful study of poverty in Proverbs, but as an example of how an appropriately critical stance to previous scholarship (not only Western but African!), and an appropriately receptive attitude to an African worldview, can illuminate biblical texts.

575.   Kimuhu, Johnson M.

Leviticus: The Priestly Laws and Prohibitions from the Perspective of Ancient Near East and Africa

New York: Peter Lang, 2008. 434 pages, ISBN: 9781433102004.

The author is a Kenyan scholar, originally trained at St. Paul's United Theological College in Limuru. Subsequently he taught at a Presbyterian college and worked as a Bible translator in Kenya. Currently he is a counsellor in a child and family service in California. The present book is a revision of a PhD thesis in OT accepted by Claremont Graduate University in 2007. The book title is quite misleading. The main title makes the reader expect a kind of commentary on Leviticus, while the subtitle seems to relate the text of Leviticus to the contexts of the Ancient Near East and contemporary or traditional Africa. In reality, the book has a more narrow focus, circling around the family laws of Leviticus 18. The opening chapter reviews family laws and especially the question of incest from anthropological, sociological and exegetical perspectives. The next chapter offers an exegetical interpretation of Leviticus 18. Then follow six chapters analysing scholarly literature on incest and family laws in Egyptian, Ugaritic, Hittite and Canaanite literature. Finally, the last quarter of the book relates some issues in Leviticus 18 to African – in particular Kikuyu – cultural traditions, with special emphasis on how certain key terms expressing taboos have been translated in the Kikuyu OT. Unfortunately, this last quarter does not keep the same academic standard as the rest of the book. The book is not a traditional thesis building up a consistent discourse to a clear conclusion. Rather, it is more a collection of quite independent discussions of family laws in ancient Israel and its surroundings, focused especially around questions raised by Leviticus 18. Nevertheless, in offering a collection of OT and Ancient Near Eastern material related to family laws in Leviticus 18, it makes a useful contribution.

576.   King, Noel Q.

African Cosmos: An Introduction to Religion in Africa

Belmont, CA: Wadsworth, 1985. 192 pages, ISBN: 9780534053345.

When this book was written, King was professor of the history of religions at the University of California Santa Cruz. In *African Cosmos* he concisely overviews religious orientations found across Africa. While the bulk of his focus is on religious elements found traditionally on the continent, he also provides sketches of Christianity and Islam and their interaction in the religious scene. Drawing on his thirteen years of living and working in Africa, and 30 years of research and study, he weaves an interesting account enlivened by stories of personal encounter and experience. King first gives an overview of African traditional religious attitudes towards God, the spirits, the ancestors, humans, and other powers as found in six ethnolinguistic groups divided into three related pairs: Yoruba and Akan, Ganda and Swahili; and Dinka and Acholi. This discussion is followed by a chapter on communicating with the Divine and issues of witchcraft and possession. The entries of Christianity and of Islam into Africa are the concerns of the next chapter, and the devastation of colonialism, with some resulting contemporary issues, provides the principal focus of the final chapter. One primary criticism of the book is that King's phenomenology tends to be limited to an inappropriately positive description of all religions. The assumption that all religions have equal access to ultimate truth undergirds the discussion, and the inherent contradictions among the religions (e.g. the Islamic view on the deity of Christ versus the Christian view) are not developed in any significant way. If anything they are glossed over rather than ignored. One is tempted to attribute this to naiveté, but King's long experience on the continent and his academic specialisation would seem to indicate that the orientation is intentional rather than accidental. The very real tensions among and within the religions (not just doctrinal, but social and political) also tend to be glossed over at best, and the overall impression given is that there are no animosities across the continent. The exception to this is the colonialists, of whom very little positive is said. While this approach might be helpful in avoiding adding fuel to religious fires which may already be burning, it still falls short of the actual encounters people have had over the last several decades in Nigeria, Sudan, Ethiopia, and Uganda. This is an engaging and highly readable book. However, as King notes in his introduction, this is a survey rather than an in-depth discussion. With that in mind, as well as the agenda driving the presentation, the book can be considered a useful example of how some in the academy would want to describe religion in the African context.

577.   King, Roberta R., Jean N. Kidula, James R. Krabill, and Thomas A. Oduro

Music in the Life of the African Church

Waco: Baylor, 2008. 205 pages, ISBN: 9781602580220.

King is Associate Professor of Communication and Ethnomusicology at Fuller Theological Seminary. She has collaborated in producing this book with historian Thomas Oduro, principal of Good News Theological College and Seminary in Ghana, plus James Krabill and Jean Kidula, both experienced ethnomusicologists. Together they produce eight essays on the history and present musical landscape of song in the African church. Both King and Krabill have mission careers and earned doctorates on aspects of music/hymnody in Cote d'Ivoire. Kidula presents scholarly insights from an East African viewpoint, while Oduro colours in a church historian's perspective. King introduces the setting with maps, language considerations and a survey of the rapid growth of the church in Africa, with its accompanying challenges. She then presents a historical overview of how the songs of Euro-American Christianity made their way into African churches. Kidula follows with a description of the music of African life and such issues as the oft-discussed dichotomy between sacred and secular, followed with consideration of some of the intricacies of "Making and Managing Music in African Christian Life." Krabill then speaks to the dynamics of what happens to music when divergent cultures not only meet but collide. Oduro, with his historical expertise, contributes to the collection an overview of church music in the life of African Christian communities. King concludes with the importance of the Bible (Word) in African church music and offers "Global Church: Lessons from Africa" – not least of which is *lex canendi, lex credendi*:

how one sings is how one believes." The major emphasis of the book is to probe the intertwining dynamics of music, culture, church and mission in the exploding spiritual song scene in Africa today. The book is valuable for all academic libraries with its offering of discussion topics at the end of each essay, plus over 50 maps, side-bars, charts and photos. Africa seems set to hold rights to a major section of the choir which features in the Book of Revelation's multi-cultural scene.

578. King, Roberta R.

A Time to Sing: A Manual for the African Church

Nairobi: Evangel, 1999. 183 pages, ISBN: 9789966200990.

This manual for church musicians in Africa is a summation of much of what King has been teaching and modelling during her many years of ministry in Africa. Based mostly at Daystar University in Kenya during that time, she has also served as an ethnomusicologist consultant in Côte d'Ivoire, Senegal, Mali, Ghana, the Congo (DRC), Rwanda, Malawi, and Uganda. King has also served as Associate Professor of Ethnomusicology and Intercultural Communication at Fuller Theological Seminary in the United States. Her book is designed for church musicians of various levels of expertise. It combines sound ethno-musicological principles with practical exercises, and seldom if ever will go "over the head" of the reader. King uses the concept of "New Song Fellowships" as the basis for much of her work. These are small groups that gather together for the express purpose of developing new songs for use in the church. The participants are not trained musicians, though some understanding of music theory and/or ability to play an instrument is helpful. King outlines a system in which the end result is the inspiration, composition, and dissemination of new songs through the medium of these fellowships. This aim can be accomplished in as little as one week, or over the course of two or more months. She includes suggested timetables for either of these approaches. A notable feature of this book is the section of "True Stories," in which King shares experiences of musicians across Africa who have successfully used some of the principles outlined in the book. Reading the book, one cannot help recalling the struggles of indigenous Christians over the years in so many parts of Africa, trying to worship with songs, instruments, and music systems foreign to the local culture. This is a resource that answers directly to the need of African Christian communities for effectively contextual music and worship. As such, and especially given its very practical orientation, this book is an almost unique contribution, and should be widely welcomed and utilized.

579. Kings, Graham, and Geoff Morgan

Offerings from Kenya to Anglicanism: Liturgical Texts and Contexts Including 'A Kenyan Service of Holy Communion'

Cambridge: Grove Books, 2001. 56 pages, ISBN: 9781851744770.

Kings and Morgan have done the Anglican world (and perhaps the wider Christian community) a great service by publishing this small book which serves essentially as a commentary on the historical background and theological and cultural significance of liturgical revision within the Anglican Church of Kenya. The focus of much of this book is King's commentary on selected portions of the Eucharistic rite, but other services are also discussed. Since Kings was the secretary for the committee that produced this rite, his comments are very helpful in providing some of the background into the thinking of this group. Also interesting are

Morgan's insights into the interplay between top-down liturgics (the Bishop says we ought to do this) and grassroots liturgics (this is what we have done here, would it be useful to others?). The picture painted is of an Archbishop (David Gitari) who is aware of the worship needs of his people, but willing to allow the laity to have real involvement in the Church's worship texts. Kings and Morgan mention that the Kenyan Rite has been appreciated and used outside of Kenya – they mention its regular use in the UK. One finds that it is also widely used and appreciated in parts of Canada and the United States as well. As a theologically and biblically sound liturgical text, it is a breath of fresh air for many. This study should be read by anyone interested in the African inculturation of Christian worship.

580.   Kinkupu, Léonard Santedi

Les défis de l'évangélisation dans l'Afrique contemporaine

Paris: Éditions Karthala, 2005. 168 pages, ISBN: 9782845867215.

The author, from the Congo (DRC), presides over the Faculté de Théologie Catholique de Kinshasa. His interest lies in having an evangelistic message and an approach which address the current circumstances of African life. After an introduction, there are four chapters, moving from theory to practice. Chapter 1 deals with terminology related to evangelisation. Kinkupu wants to make sure that his vocabulary is understood in post-Vatican II terms, the Council by which the value of other religions was recognized. Chapter 2 is the most significant of the four, highlighting the challenges to evangelistic outreach in Africa: cults and new religious movements; sickness and the "Health and Wealth Gospel"; ethnic divisions; the socio-economic crisis, including poverty, urbanisation and AIDS; political crises; the ethical challenge; and means of communication that are not adapted to or even available in Africa. Chapter 3 poses the logical question: in light of all these problems and challenges, what is the best way to approach evangelisation in Africa? What new elements need to be included? The author's response is that evangelisation must be a dialogue, one that is both creative and prophetic in nature. Finally, in chapter 4, the actual practice of evangelism is in view. The author identifies three groups as good targets for evangelism: the family, the base communities of the church, and the youth groups. The analysis and conclusions given in this volume are neither overwhelmingly academic nor particularly innovative but are a decent rendering of several aspects of African reality.

581.   Kinkupu, Léonard Santedi, Gérard Bissainthe, and Meinrad Hebga

Des prêtres noirs s'interrogent cinquante ans après

Paris: Éditions Karthala, 2006. 328 pages, ISBN: 9782845868106.

Rarely in Africa does a book maintain enough of an impact that publishers are willing to reissue it. Yet this volume, recognized as a historic foundation-stone for the development of African theology, has been taken up by the French publisher Karthala, in its series *Mémoire d'Églises*, to celebrate the 50th anniversary of the volume's original publication by Cerf and *Présence Africaine*. A new generation of scholars and theologians can thus be introduced to the ideas of African (and Haitian) Roman Catholic priests who in 1956 expressed, in the original publication of this title, a desire for the Christian faith to become firmly part of the everyday lives of their parishioners. Rather than following what they perceived and condemned as the missionary approach of making *tabula rasa* of the African culture, these authors insist that the presentation of the Christian faith must be deeply rooted within that culture, using concepts already in place ("stepping-stones") for such contextualisation. When African culture is given its legitimate value, the priests claim, Christianity can then be understood through comparisons with what is already known in that culture. Furthermore, the consensus among the various essayists is that local church services should reflect an African rather than Western approach to worship. Although these ideas of inculturation are now standard fare in discussing African theology, this volume represents the beginnings of that movement.

582.   Kinoti, George

Hope for Africa and What the Christians Can Do

Nairobi: AISRED, 1994. 99 pages, ISBN: 9789966992208.

Kinoti was provoked to write this small but informative and challenging book from personal experiences of the "widespread economic, social, and political problems" facing Africa. At the time of writing, Kinoti was professor of zoology at the University of Nairobi. He writes however as a serious and concerned Christian (rather than as a zoologist), with the aim of awakening the sleeping African church to the "wretchedness" so widespread on the continent despite the reported rapid growth of the church. The author seeks (i) to alert us to the extent and causes of the crisis, because without proper information we cannot respond as we should; and (ii) to challenge African Christians to play their part which he sees as essential. After describing the problems in the political and economic arenas and examining their causes, he goes on to propose some steps for making a real change in society. Kinoti argues with conviction for the involvement of the Christian in the social, political, and economic arenas so that Africans for a change might know "dignity, justice and material well-being." The book is not a theological volume, but one to be recommended to anyone wishing to explore where hope might be found for an Africa that seems to be enveloped in gloom and doom. Christians in positions of responsibility and influence in Africa need to consider the challenges set forth in this book. The book would also make an excellent gift to friends or acquaintances in such positions.

583.   Kinoti, Hannah W., and John M. Waliggo, editors

The Bible in African Christianity: Essays in Biblical Theology

Nairobi: Acton Publishers, 209. 1997 pages, ISBN: 9789966888365.

This wide-ranging collection of twelve essays includes eight that, in keeping with the volume title, focus on "the impact the Bible has had on African societies, cultures and peoples," how the Bible is invoked, alluded to, applied, and otherwise used in the context of African realities (or, in one case, within the anglophone Black Diaspora). This includes such themes as: how the Bible has been or should be interpreted in African contexts (e.g. Emmanuel Obeng, "The Use of Biblical Critical Methods in Rooting the Scriptures in Africa"; Zablon Nthamburi and Douglas Waruta, "Biblical Hermeneutics in African Instituted Churches"); the Bible's potential positive and negative relation to ecumenism (e.g. Jesse Mugambi, "The Bible and Ecumenism in African Christianity"); and the complementary roles of the Bible itself and other (vernacular) literature in Christian evangelism and discipleship (John Walligo, "Bible and Catechism in Uganda"). The remaining four papers compare, at varying degrees of depth and scholarship, some concepts found in the Bible with concepts found in some African cultures (e.g. David Adamo, "Peace in the Old Testament and in the African Heritage"; Hannah Kinoti, "Well-being in African Society and the Bible"). Although the contributors write for the most part from a broadly ecumenical perspective, Christian readers of any theological persuasion will find here stimulus to careful thought about the use of the Bible in theology and in daily practice, worthwhile challenges to cherished assumptions, encouragement toward more substantial relationships with those of other persuasions, an implicit apologetic for putting the Bible into the languages of the peoples of Africa, and numerous bibliographical pointers to further reading on the important questions scrutinized.

Kinoti, Hannah W.

see also review 1155

584. Kinyua, Johnson Kiriaku

Introducing Ordinary African Readers' Hermeneutics: A Case Study of the Agikuyu Encounter with the Bible

Bern: Peter Lang, 2011. 371 pages, ISBN: 9783034302890.

Let it be said right from the beginning that this is a well-researched and well-written analysis of the Agikuyu (Kikuyu) encounter with the Bible, from a postcolonial perspective. Kinyua is a Kenyan biblical scholar, and the book is based on a University of Birmingham (UK) PhD thesis, supervised by Rasiah Sugirtharajah and Deryn Guest. The influence from Sugirtharajah is particularly clear. Kinyua has a firm grip on current postcolonial discourses, and he is not only able to guide the reader through rather heavy theoretical discussions, but then also to use the insights gained from these discussions in an illuminating way on his Kenyan material. Kinyua's postcolonial concerns are then related to the focus of Gerald West (South Africa) on "ordinary readers" of the Bible and the role of their interpretive strategies in a more general African biblical hermeneutics. The combination of the two is a successful one; the former (postcolonial theory/Sugirtharajah) enables the author to reveal colonial concerns and expressions in church work and Bible translation in early twentieth-century Kenya, whereas the latter ("ordinary reader"/West) enables him to develop some key perspectives of an African biblical hermeneutics that involves a fusion of "ordinary" as well as "scholarly" readers. Two cases of "ordinary readers" of the Bible going against their colonial context should serve to exemplify this. One is the Mau-Mau uprising, where the fight for freedom offers a discourse of resistance that allows an anti-colonial interpretation of the Bible. Another is the revival movement, whose biblical interpretation reflects a totally different discourse of resistance, nevertheless undermining the colonial context. According to Kinyua, both examples are of importance in the development of a postcolonial biblical hermeneutics in Africa. This research contribution ought to be of interest far beyond circles focusing on twentieth-century Kenyan history.

Kirk-Greene, Anthony

see review 967

585.   **Kirwen, Michael C.**

The Missionary and the Diviner: Contending Theologies of Christian and African Religions

Maryknoll, NY: Orbis, 1996. 160 pages, ISBN: 9780883445846.

Kirwen arrived in East Africa as a Maryknoll missionary in 1963, and later served as Director of the Maryknoll Institute of African Studies in Nairobi. This book is driven by Kirwen's assumption that "Christianity . . . has barely touched on the central beliefs, values, ideals and visions rooted in the heart of the African peoples." His findings are communicated in a series of imagined conversations between a missionary (Kirwen himself) and a diviner, in which the differences between Christianity and African traditional religion are explored and debated. The diviner in question is a "composite figure," but the conversations are based on actual discussions. The book is particularly helpful as an introduction to significant themes of African thought as described by an insider. These include African cosmologies and notions of God; the sources of evil and the role of the diviner in dealing with them; marriage customs, and particularly the role of levirate marriage within African culture; spirit possession and the practice of divination; and, finally, life after death and the ancestors. Kirwen develops the dialogues in the context of life – on a pastoral visitation, after ministry at an outstation, an unexpected meeting at a teahouse, and a funeral. He also provides helpful background material and follow-up discussion to engage the reader more fully in the cultural background of the events and perspectives offered. Those parts of the conversation in which the "missionary" responds to the "diviner" are less effective. Descriptions of Christianity are at times simplistic. In his discussion of death and the afterlife, grace is strikingly absent when he says that "those who have loved and lived good lives are rewarded with the sight of God and are welcomed into the community of the saints in a place called 'heaven'." In the discussion of marriage customs he contrasts African tradition not with the biblical vision but rather with the practices of modern Western societies. Kirwen's evaluation of African tradition is also at times dubious. Thus he suggests that the African creation stories should be seen "as the 'Old Testament' preparation for the gospel"; the diviner is identified as "the 'Jesus' figure of traditional religion"; and a generally idealized conception of traditional religion is communicated. As an articulation of central themes of the African traditional worldview by an insider (the diviner), this study is definitely useful. As a coherent and well-argued Christian *response* to that worldview, its value is certainly limited and readers will need to look elsewhere.

Kisangani, Emizet F.

see review 787

586.   **Kisembo, Benezeri, Laurenti Magesa, and Aylward Shorter, editors**

African Christian Marriage

Nairobi: Paulines, 2010. 256 pages, ISBN: 9789966213822.

This is the second edition (the first edition was published in 1977) of a report on a major ecumenical study project that addressed African Christian marriage from sociological, theological and pastoral perspectives. Kisembo, a Ugandan Anglican, was a lecturer of biblical studies at Makerere University and General Secretary of the Bible Society of Uganda. Magesa, a Tanzanian Roman Catholic priest, was dean of the Catholic University of Eastern Africa in Nairobi. Shorter, oldest of the three authors, has been a well-known Africa-based British Catholic missionary scholar and writer. The original five-year study covered most of the anglophone countries of eastern and southern Africa. Among church bodies involved in the project were: Anglican, Church of God, United Church of Zambia, Congregationalist, Dutch Reformed, Greek Orthodox, Lutheran, Mennonite, Methodist, Moravian, Presbyterian, Roman Catholic, Friends, and various Independent and Zionist churches. The eight chapters cover: contrasting concepts of marriage, marriage rites, divorce and remarriage, polygamy, the care of widows, husband-wife relationships, parent-children relations, sex education, "mixed" marriages, population growth and responsible parenthood, and marriage and community. Each chapter is divided into three main sections, namely, (i) case materials, which present facts and documentation of current thinking on the issues within the contemporary African context; (b) theological reflection, which provides the reader with various theological positions on the issues under discussion; and (c) models for pastoral action, which includes concrete recommendations/proposals. Since some of the theological reflection draws heavily on Roman Catholic dogma, the reader may find some concepts and vocabulary to be unfamiliar. Regarding those who have divorced and remarried, the authors affirm the indissolubility of marriage as a binding precept, but propose that such persons who are living in good faith should be accepted in the church. On polygamy, the authors uphold monogamy as the normative form of marriage for Christians, but recommend a limited toleration of polygamy, and consideration for Christians who have lapsed into levirate unions because of economic pressure or the burden of childlessness. The reader will find that the study clearly addresses most of the concrete problems affecting African Christian marriage, and carefully articulates the various theological positions on these questions, while the authors have generally opted for sympathetic solutions to the problems addressed.

Kitoko-Nsiku, Edouward

see review 759

587. Kitshoff, M. C., editor

African Independent Churches Today: Kaleidoscope of Afro-Christianity

Lewiston, NY: Edwin Mellen Press, 1996. 324 pages, ISBN: 9780773487826.

This is a collection of papers presented in tribute to G. C. Oosthuizen, the well-known South African researcher whose career focus has been the indigenous/independent church movements in Africa. The essays cover a broad variety of issues divided into five sections, all relating to the AIC Afro-Christian context, namely issues of history; healing; religious communication; understanding, self-understanding, and mutual sharing; and orality. The authors range from indigenous participant researchers to expatriate academics, though they all share in common an acquaintance with Oosthuizen in some capacity. Averaging roughly 15 double-spaced typewritten pages per paper, the essays tend to be brief rather than deep. The subjects range from broad countrywide panoramas (Pauw) to case studies of individual churches (Boschman, van der Spuy), persons (Shank, Kitschoff), practices (Becken, Mkhize), and modes of expression (Xulu, Mfusi) or indigenous constructs (van Zyl, van Niekerk). Generally the essays are phenomenological in approach rather than ontological, though some move beyond analysis to evaluation (Kitshoff). The more helpful contributions are those presented on: relatively unique ideas (such as van Niekerk on the symbolism of fire and how it plays out in tradition and church), lesser known people (Kuzwayo on Simungu Bafazini Shibe); or oral traditions unknown outside of local contexts (as in Loubser's analysis of sermons preached by Londa Shembe). As an example of ongoing field-based research on AICs, the book is useful, though perhaps not important.

Kitshoff, M. C.

see also review 873

588.   Kivuti, N. A., and Jesse N. K. Mugambi

A Church Come of Age: Fifty Years of Revival in the CPK Diocese of Embu 1942–1992

Nairobi: Acton Publishers, 1992. 69 pages, ISBN: 9789966888006.

This interesting local history of the Anglican Church in the Embu area of central Kenya actually spans the entire history of Embu Anglicanism, from the time of the arrival of the first British missionaries in the first decade of the twentieth century, until 1992, the fiftieth anniversary of the Revival Movement in the area and the occasion which gave rise to this publication. (The acronym "CPK" in the title stands for the Church of the Province of Kenya, which has now been officially renamed the Anglican Church in Kenya.) The booklet includes discussion of historical issues such as the use of education as a tool for evangelism, the female circumcision crisis, the indigenisation of church leadership, and the rise of African nationalism, as well as the coming of the East Africa Revival Movement to the Embu area. Although primarily a telling of local history based largely on oral sources, this small book also highlights the pastoral and theological issues facing the church in Embu in the coming years (and by extension the Anglican communities throughout Kenya). Although these issues are raised throughout the text, they are helpfully summarized and discussed at the end of the book by Mugambi. Especially important are critical questions about legalism within the Revival brethren, the gap between the older generation who were converted within the Revival and the younger generation which is seeking other ways to express their love for God, and the tendency of the Revival to look down on African culture. It is a significant sign of health that this study is at once grateful for the ancestors in the faith who brought the gospel and who spread the message of the Revival, and at the same time looking carefully at problems within the church and the Revival Movement in order to be more faithful followers of Christ in the future. The book contains a map, suggestions for further reading, and photos of some key figures. A list of interviewees with pertinent information about them would have been helpful. This booklet can serve as a useful example of an African Christian community taking action to preserve its own history as a resource for reflection on its place in the mission of Christ in the world.

589.   Knibb, Michael A.

Translating the Bible: The Ethiopic Version of the Old Testament

Oxford: Oxford University Press, 2000. 146 pages, ISBN: 9780197261941.

In 1967 the British Academy's Schweich Lectures were given by Edward Ullendorff and published under the title *Ethiopia and the Bible*. In the 1995 Schweich Lectures, Michael Knibb, Professor of OT at King's College London, and one of the few remaining Ethiopic scholars in the English-speaking world, revisited this topic, focussing particularly on the translation of the OT into Ge'ez (Ethiopic). This book is a revision of those lectures and provides a thorough and highly informative evaluation of this neglected issue. Knibb brings to the task a lifetime of work in Second Temple Jewish texts, particularly those such as 1 Enoch which have been preserved in their entirety only in Ethiopic. In this work he turns his attention to the Ethiopic Scriptures. Knibb argues that the Ethiopic OT was translated from the Greek alone during the Aksumite period which ended in the early seventh century. Unlike Ullendorff, he allows for no influence from Syriac or Hebrew at the time of the original translation. Knibb disputes the widely held belief that the OT translation was undertaken by a group of fifth and early sixth-century Syrian missionaries known as the Nine Saints, and argues that Syriac influence was mediated through the Arabic in the medieval period. Likewise Hebraic elements are isolated in manuscripts which are no earlier than the sixteenth century. During this period, the Ethiopic OT was subjected to a systematic revision, resulting in what is called the "academic recension." The original Ethiopic translation is generally literal, sometimes to the point of being unintelligible. There are, however, many places at which the translators yielded to the demands of the Ethiopic language and produced a "faithful" rather than "literal" translation. Though he does not directly address the issue, Knibb's work will be of interest to those who are involved in text criticism of the Septuagint. His work also raises but does not address questions regarding the earliest form of the Ethiopian OT canon, which in its present form includes such works as 1 Enoch and Jubilees, and thus exceeds the limits of the Septuagint. The work will also be of interest to those concerned with issues of translation technique, especially as reflected in one of the earliest African versions of the Bible. Knibb helps open up a wide but largely untrod field of textual research that should be of particular interest to Ethiopian biblical scholars. More fundamentally, this book illustrates the way in which, in the earliest stages of the Christian era, Christianity came to have a distinctly African identity, through the translation of the Scriptures into an African vernacular language.

590. Knighton, Ben, editor

Religion and Politics in Kenya: Essays in Honor of a Meddlesome Priest

London: Palgrave Macmillan, 2010. 316 pages, ISBN: 9780230106635.

This collection of essays examines interweaving religious and political threads in Kenya through the life of the Anglican Bishop, David Gatari. Most of the chapters discuss, in one way or another, the herculean efforts of this man, who, along with Henry Okullu, Timothy Njoya and Alexander Muge, opposed the oppressive single-party politics of the Moi regime during the 1970s and 1980s, with prophetic ministry continuing to the present. The papers contained in this book enrich the way we understand the multi-faceted interplay between religious ideas (Christian and Muslim) and political practice. Knighton's introduction explores some of the uneasy relationship between the two, chronicling how Bishop Gitari discovered and articulated his prophetic ministry: "depending more upon the power of story than of command." John Lonsdale's chapter suggests that versions of an "emancipation theology" exist in the churches, operating in "a cyclical tendency to worship the state before examining it critically." Other sections take up more specific issues, including the alarming lack of theological engagement in interethnic relations (Paddy Benson); the role of Islamic leaders in the development of the political state in Kenya (John Chesworth); the nuanced relationships between spiritual and material affairs (Galia Sabar); ways in which Christianity has been co-opted by the neopatrimonial state (Paul Gifford); as well as the religious motivations of the Muingiki, including an analysis into how they have been portrayed by the media (Ben Knighton). Not all of the chapters in this valuable collection provide the same degree of clarity toward the discussion, but together they show the diverse interaction between religious and political ideas in the country. Within this whole, Bishop Gitari's lifework provides one important exemplar of how religion can confront, inform, and strengthen socio-political affairs in Africa. While the themes in this book are specific to the Kenyan context, it would nevertheless be an invaluable resource for anyone researching Christianity and politics in Africa.

591. **Kobia, Samuel**

The Courage to Hope: A Challenge for Churches in Africa

Nairobi: Acton Publishers, 2003. 189 pages, ISBN: 9789966888167.

Kobia, a Methodist from Kenya, was General Secretary of the World Council of Churches in Geneva. In this book, written at Harvard Divinity School during a study leave, he borrows from the philosophy and theology of Paul Tillich in order to help Africans to be "open to the future." In Kobia's view, such hope will enable Africans to transcend those ills such as tribalism and corruption that hold back the continent. Central to this task is a return to traditional African values. Kobia writes, "The ancestors teach us that we must listen to the earth, feel its pulse, if we are to recognize our connection to the sacred." Communal values must be returned to a central role in society, since "private ownership is a form of greed and stands in opposition to hospitality." The bulk of the book examines the roots of Africa's present predicament – colonialism and its after-effects, such as corruption – and calls for reconstruction and renaissance on the continent. Two comments will accurately summarize the book's approach. First, Kobia admirably draws upon African cultural traditions and values in order to promote authentic renewal for the continent. Genuine renaissance in Africa must be *African*. Along these lines, he cites numerous examples of African groups and organisations making a difference at ground level on the continent. This is helpful and informative. Secondly, although Kobia draws substantially upon the concept of God as Creator, and also mentions the Holy Spirit, one wonders what happened to Jesus Christ. Other than Jesus' vision for a society of "inclusion and caring," and that Jesus died "pursuing the highest good for humanity," a reader may well wonder who really needs Jesus to enact what Kobia calls for. Or, given Kobia's call for a just society, would not one expect (from a highly visible Christian leader such as the General Secretary of the WCC) a depiction of the central role that the Kingdom of God plays in a Christian vision for such a society? In other words, is there anything genuinely Christian in this call to hope? If so, it is difficult to locate. In summary, Kobia rightly identifies and critiques Western cultural and economic hegemony and its historical effects upon Africa. Yet, in spite of his wariness of the West, one wonders if he has not innocently swallowed a thoroughly Western ecumenical paradigm that talks generically about God but voids the term "Christian" of substance.

592. **Kolini, Emmanuel M., and Peter Holmes**

Rethinking Life: What the Church Can Learn from Africa

Downers Grove: IVP US, 2010. 200 pages, ISBN: 9780830857470.

This book is written for a North American audience that has minimal knowledge of Africa. It is co-authored by a well-known retired African Anglican archbishop (a leader in the Fellowship of Confessing Anglicans), together with a westerner who spent many years in Africa. Kolini contributes most of the material, while the structure and background are from Holmes. The book covers a wide variety of topics and only addresses the subtitle in the last chapter. Thus there are chapters on African traditional religion (ATR), African community, the similarities of OT and African cultures, North African church history, mistakes missionaries made, and the East African Revival (EAR) and its impact. Although the treatment of ATR attempts a balance between what was good and what was bad, sometimes the reader will feel as if the authors are trying to be politically correct beyond what the topic can bear (e.g. ATR respected the earth more than Westerners did, men were despised if they harmed their wife or sisters, the creator God of African belief "loved" his creation). Similarly, there is little distinction between the problems caused by missionaries and those caused by colonialists. Yet many useful points are discussed, such as the loss of community to Western individualism, the rationalistic missionaries' lack of understanding of evil, and the positive aspects of African spirituality. On the other hand, appreciation for missionaries bringing the gospel to Africa is an oft-repeated theme, despite the inevitable misunderstandings that occurred. The chapters on the EAR and its impact form the basis for the last chapter and for the subtitle, the assumption being that it was only the EAR that brought genuine Christianity to East Africa because the EAR finally made ATR redundant (African spirituality was valued, and there was a solution to the problem of evil). Treatment of the EAR is balanced, noting both the excesses and the blessings. It is somewhat unfortunate that the last chapter, being the key to the book, is not laid out in a more helpful way. The points are made rather vaguely as "suggestions" in paragraph form, whereas listing them would have been clearer. They include loving those who are different, listening better, avoiding simplistic judgments, appreciating the spiritual world and dealing specifically with sin (as "walking in the light" in the EAR). The last plea is for the Western church to apologize for (1) ruling over Africans and treating them as second-class citizens; and (2) exporting colonialism, even though the colonial system continued after African independence. This book might serve as a sampler of African perspectives on the various topics addressed.

593. Kombo, James Henry Owino

The Doctrine of God in African Christian Thought: The Holy Trinity, Theological Hermeneutics, and the African Intellectual Culture

Leiden: BRILL, 2007. 298 pages. ISBN: 9789004158047.

Written by a Kenyan who has served as Deputy Vice-Chancellor at Daystar University in Kenya, this book is an evangelical attempt to contextualize the doctrine of God into the African context. If every African society has a name for and an idea of God, how does contextualization proceed? Kombo insists that the starting point "is faith itself." Kombo attempts to "Christianize the African concepts of God and use African metaphysics to explain the new meaning to the African audience." Foundational for his understanding of God is the doctrine of the Trinity. The first chapters look at this doctrine in Scripture and in the early church fathers. The culmination of the first half-millennium of reflection is the so-called Athanasian Creed. Kombo argues that this neglected creed is vital for our faith. But through much of history the Trinity has been presented in European categories. Kombo now wants to present this doctrine in African categories. Drawing especially from the school of Placide Tempels, Kombo concludes that in the African context being is defined especially in terms of force. God is the greatest force. God is the chief force at the top of the hierarchy of being. African inculturation theologians have taken note of this, but they have failed to Christianize the doctrine of God. They have spent too much time in comparative theology, showing the similarities and not the differences between the traditional idea of God and the biblical idea. In the end, professional African theologians have not "helped the African Christian population to articulate an understanding of the God that we encounter in Christ." Kombo says that "African ideas about God pale in comparison to the truth seen in the scripture." He then offers his biblical inculturated theology. For him, God is the "great Muntu manifested by the Son and the

Holy Spirit." "Ntu" in eastern Africa is being; "muntu" is person; God is the Great Muntu. Yet there are not three muntus. The Son and Holy Spirit share the being or essence of the Father. This book is a bold attempt at evangelical inculturation theology.

594. **Komolafe, Sunday Jide**

The Transformation of African Christianity: Development and Change in the Nigerian Church

Carlisle, UK: Langham Monographs, 2013. 474 pages, ISBN: 9781907713590.

The author grew up in the Apostolic Church of Nigeria, earned his PhD at Fuller Theological Seminary, and has served on the teaching staff of the West African Theological Seminary in Lagos. Using a thematic history of the church in Nigeria, this book proposes an appropriate contextual ecclesiology for that country. Such an ecclesiology seeks to take seriously Nigerian culture, Nigerian church history and Scripture. Historically, three main types of churches have existed in Nigeria: mission-planted churches, African independent churches and neo-charismatic churches. All three types of churches are a product of the dynamic interaction between Scripture and culture. The more negative view of culture by the mission churches led to the reaction of the African independent churches. The neo-charismatic churches rose in the last few decades in the context of modern Nigeria. All three types are examples of distinctive Nigerian ecclesiology, with strong and weak points. But how do we move forward in developing a contextual ecclesiology? The author first considers the ecclesiology of the NT, noting that it is profoundly Christocentric. He then asks: "What on earth is the church?" His response is that "the church is *true* to the extent that it functions in obedience to Christ." The author concludes with five challenges for the churches in Nigeria's contemporary society: the doxological challenge affirms the centrality of the kingdom of God; the leadership challenge affirms empowering, servant leadership; the discipleship challenge reminds us that conversion without discipleship is inadequate; the theological challenge warns against anti-intellectualism; and the ethical challenge warns against the danger of materialism. These challenges are relevant to Nigeria's churches which are sorely tempted by the prosperity gospel. The book is highly recommended as a stimulating and clarifying tool for developing a biblically-governed ecclesiology in Nigeria and beyond.

595. **Kore, Danfulani**

Culture and the Christian Home: Evaluating Cultural Marriage and Family in the Light of Scripture

Bukuru, Nigeria: Africa Christian Textbooks, 1995. 126 pages, ISBN: 9789781350382.

A former head of Jos ECWA Theological Seminary in Nigeria, Kore has given the church in Africa a valuable gift in this very helpful handbook on Christian marriage. In order to highlight the many challenges of Christian marriages in Africa today, Kore undertook an unusual but relevant approach: he surveyed 34 Nigerian ethnic groups concerning their beliefs, customs, traditions, social patterns and religious practices in relation to marriage. The book presents the results of this research topically, in chapters concerning (for example) the concept of marriage, choosing a marriage partner, the wedding itself, communication, sexual intimacy, parent-child relationships, family finances and other areas. By this means Kore brings to the fore the realities of what takes place in many African Christian marriages and why. He then compares the cultural beliefs and practices affecting marriage patterns with the clear teaching of the Word of God concerning Christian marriage for all cultures. This book could be very helpful to a great number of married couples throughout Africa, especially if they want the full blessing of God on their marriages and family. Deeply rooted as it is both in a careful inquiry into the African cultural context and in the Scriptural witness on the issues raised, this book deserves attention from those on the continent writing or lecturing in pastoral theology, and also those engaged in Christian marital counselling in Africa.

596. **Kore, Danfulani**

Truths for Healthy Churches

Bukuru, Nigeria: Africa Christian Textbooks, 2006. 187 pages, ISBN: 9789789050604.

Kore, a lecturer at ECWA Theological Seminary Jos (JETS) in Nigeria, has done the African church a favour by writing this book. He has addressed issues which other church leaders have ignored for far too long. No fewer than eighteen practical topics are covered, including the nature of the church, low salaries for Christian workers, generational and ethnic relationships, relationships between African churches and missionaries, African traditional religion and the challenge of Islam. It is refreshing to read this honest, and sometimes confronting, analysis of such a wide range of issues, issues that have challenged the church in Africa from its inception and which have sometimes resulted in wrong ideas and actions, many of which are still insufficiently addressed by church leaders. This is not a theological treatise. Kore is attempting rather to discuss each issue from a biblical standpoint, and then offer a suggested way forward and some practical options. Due to the limited length of the book, readers may be somewhat disappointed that the issues are not dealt with in any great depth. For example, Kore offers his own view on each issue, using biblical references, without acknowledging other possible evangelical interpretations or traditions. Thus on the issue of baptism the author strongly advocates water baptism for believers immediately after conversion, dismissing the need for teaching prior to baptism. While for many evangelicals this might be advisable, for others there may be good reason to handle things differently. To be fair, the purpose of the book is not to debate each issue at length or from different points of view. What Kore has done is provide a helpful basis for further discussion and action on each of the issues. This is enhanced by the incisive questions for discussion at the end of each chapter designed for use in small groups. For those who use the questions in this way, the book could become an instrument of change both in attitude and practice. As Kore himself emphasizes, for much of the church in Africa this is sorely needed.

Kornfield, Bill

see review 215

597.   Koschorke, Klaus, Frieder Ludwig, and Mariano Delgado, editors

A History of Christianity in Asia, Africa, and Latin America, 1450–1990:
   A Documentary Sourcebook

Grand Rapids: Eerdmans, 2007. 464 pages, ISBN: 9780802828897.

The editors have taken us another major step forward in the study of Christianity as a worldwide movement, by providing an excellent anthology of documentary excerpts illustrating the development of Christianity in the non-Western world. Divided equally between the three major non-European regions of the world, Asia, Africa, and Latin America, each section is further subdivided into five historical periods: 1450–1600, 1600–1800, 1800–1890, 1890–1945, and 1945–1990. The text selections are grouped topically within each time period. Designed for students in church history classes, each text is a short excerpt from a larger historical document, designed to illustrate one aspect of the history of Christianity at that time in that region. Each text is introduced with a short commentary putting the selection in its historical context. Coming from an ecumenical point of view, the authors explain that their purpose is "to give voice to the multitude of local initiatives, specific experiences and varieties of Christianity in very diverse cultural contexts," and also to represent "the denominational and contextual plurality of these 'non-Western' churches." While this laudatory purpose produces an excellent collection, certainly in relation to Africa, it has also resulted in certain distinct limitations. For example, while the emphasis on local initiatives and indigenous voices is proper, certain missionary initiatives and voices that were vitally important in the development of non-Western Christianity have been left out, such as Henry Venn's "three-selfs" missiology, or the Kikuyu church union movement in Kenya, to mention two. The ecumenical emphasis on political issues, such as colonialism, slavery, and independence, has been at the expense of important spiritual movements such as the East African Revival. Finally, the attempt to illustrate the "denominational and contextual plurality of these 'non-Western' churches" extends only to churches founded by historic European denominations and African Initiated Churches, but not churches or movements that dissented from or were merely outside of the ecumenical establishment, such as those represented by the Association of Evangelicals in Africa, Byang Kato, or the Lausanne Movement.

598.   Koudouguéret, David

Poétique et traduction biblique: Les récits de la Genèse dans le système
   littéraire sango

Leiden: Leiden University Press, 2000. 236 pages, ISBN: 9789057890468.

Bible translation taken as a task of putting centuries-old documents into a form that captivates the attention of people today presents enormous challenges. This doctoral dissertation was presented to the Research School of Asian, African and Amerindian Studies at the University of Leiden in the Netherlands. The author was Academic Dean at the Bangui Evangelical School of Theology (FATEB) in the Central African Republic (CAR). Before doctoral studies Koudouguéret had already had experience in translating the Bible into contemporary Sango in the CAR, and those years of work awakened in him a desire to find even more effective ways of communicating biblical truth to his own people. His thesis is that the tales told around the fire at night in a village have a form that can be instructive for Bible translators in the CAR, particularly with respect to the narrative portions of Genesis. After a literary analysis of the biblical accounts of creation, Cain and Abel, the Tower of Babel, and Rebecca, the author undertakes a parallel analysis of three Sango story-cycles. In the final third of the thesis, he demonstrates how certain literary devices in Hebrew can be "translated" into cultural forms common to Sango speakers. He does so by drawing on analogous devices occurring in the Sango tales that he studied earlier. Seeing how a literary device has functioned in one context (Hebrew) enables the translator to identify a similar device in the target language (Sango). The result should be a highly readable (or audible, in the case of oral/aural cultures) rendition of the narrative in question. Although the project has a basic similarity to dynamic equivalence theories, it goes far beyond what is generally understood by that term. The starting point for applying Koudougueret's approach would need to be a patient gathering and analysis of local folktales. Next would come the work of locating the links between the two literary systems. When these literary similarities are then put to use, the result should be a translation with which the target-language reader/auditor can immediately identify, because it is expressed in an easily recognisable form. The methodology proposed has much to recommend it. Although the work has been done only on isolated aspects of a few narratives in Genesis, one can envision complementary studies that would correlate other literary forms in the Bible and a receptor language.

599. Koulagna, Jean

L'Ancien Testament, pour commencer

Stavanger, Norway: Misjonshøgskolen, 2010. 130 pages, ISBN: 9788277211169.

The young and very productive author has taught OT and served as Dean at the Institut Luthérien de Théologie, Meiganga, Cameroun. As a member of the "Oxford Hebrew Bible Project," he is responsible, together with his previous *Doktorvater* in Strasbourg, Professor Jan Joosten, for the text of 1 Kings. In 2010 he published two textbooks in OT studies. The one reviewed here is presented as a textbook for first year students of theology. It belongs to the traditional genre of "introduction," with chapters on the physical milieu of Canaan/Palestine, the cultural and religious milieu, the history of Israel, the literary genres and the canon of the OT, the Pentateuch and historical literature, the poetic and wisdom literature, and the prophetic and apocalyptic literature. The book mainly presents rather traditional, historical-critical perspectives on the OT, although newer perspectives, such as a moderate critique of the Wellhausen paradigm of Pentateuch source criticism, are also voiced. A brief section on African OT studies is also included. The book is a welcome contribution to the academic discipline of OT studies in francophone Africa.

600. Koulagna, Jean

Dire l'histoire dans la bible hébraïque: Perspectives exégétiques et herméneutiques

Stavanger, Norway: Misjonshøgskolen, 2010. 216 pages, ISBN: 9788277211152.

Koulagna, based in Cameroon, has previously published his PhD dissertation on Josephus, a couple of textbooks in church history, and one on the history of religions. This is his second published text in OT studies. The book is aimed at second and third year students of theology. However, its value goes beyond that; the book in fact has the profile and academic level of a scholarly monograph. The topic that is investigated is OT historiography, with special attention to the role of narrative texts. First, the different "historical" genres are investigated: myths, legends, etiologies, novels, epics, and genealogies. Then, narrative historiographical sources are analysed: Pentateuch, Deuteronomistic Narrative, and Chronistic Narrative. Finally, the question of an OT "theology of history" is discussed and related to the African context, from inculturation as well as liberation hermeneutical perspectives. The book is a valuable contribution to the academic discipline of OT studies in francophone Africa. The author is well informed about the scholarly debate, and he is not only able to present and participate in the debate in a convincing way, but also to relate it to the African context of his students and colleagues.

601.   Krabill, James R., editor

Nos racines racontées: récits historiques sur l'Église en Afrique de l'Ouest

Cotonou, Benin: Éditions PBA, 1996. 372 pages, ISBN: 9782911752001.

The nature of this publication accounts for its strengths and limitations. As explained in the preface, the major part of the book was contributed by students in West Africa who did reports on the churches with which they were associated. This means that the coverage is selective, and while several churches are thereby presented that might not otherwise be included in a historical study, this is hardly a complete history of the church in West Africa. Also the treatment of each church is selective. For example, the reports supply a good idea of much that has taken place, as divisions, schisms, and claimed revelations have led to the proliferation of churches representing various beliefs and practices. Although some of the accounts do include doctrinal distinctives, in many cases there is no indication of the doctrinal orientation of the church being presented. And major figures in West African church history are not included because they did not come from churches represented by the participating students. Those interested in the history of Christianity in Côte d'Ivoire, Benin and Burkina Faso will profit most from this book, but even they should not expect a complete history.

Krabill, James R.

see also review 577

602.   Krätli, Graziano, and Ghislaine Lydon, editors

The Trans-Saharan Book Trade: Manuscript Culture, Arabic Literacy and Intellectual History in Muslim Africa

Leiden: BRILL, 2010. 424 pages, ISBN: 9789004187429.

This book is a collection of essays about the hundreds of handwritten Arabic manuscript collections to be found in West Africa. Books of this kind were imported as early as the eleventh century into areas like Mauritania and Mali, and into northern Nigeria from the mid-1400s, as they followed the spread of Islam (there are photos of manuscripts from as far south as Ilorin). The editors thereby contribute valuable awareness of a little known but impressive literate culture in parts of West Africa for the past half millennium and more. In the twelfth century, North Africa produced the best paper (before this technology shifted to southern Europe) and gum Arabic, essential to ink production, as well as the best-tanned hides for binding, all of which came from the Saharan region. The books most in demand in this part of Africa were the Qur'an, and books on recitation, exegesis, the Arabic language, rhetoric, literature, life of Muhammad, hadith, history, law, theology, Islamic textbooks, and Sufism. Paper and literacy were also used for business and government transactions. Most manuscripts in collections that exist today (mostly private libraries) were copied between 1625 and 1775 (since paper lasts about 200 years in these regions). The works themselves are often older, and mostly from North Africa, especially Egypt. During the colonial era, many of these libraries were hidden away because Europeans would seize manuscripts and put them in museums in Europe. Today scholars are working to identify, catalogue, study and preserve, and even digitalize these manuscripts. The book discusses preservation efforts in Timbuktu, Morocco, Mauritania and Algeria. Those who read this book will gain an appreciation for the Muslim intellectual heritage in West Africa, which will be useful for a better Christian understanding of and interaction today with the Muslim elite of West Africa.

603.   Kretzschmar, Louise, and Moss Ntlha, editors

Looking Back, Moving Forward: Reflections by South African Evangelicals

Johannesburg: The Evangelical Alliance of South Africa, 2005. 261 pages, ISBN: 9780620353199.

This collection of seventeen essays was compiled in 2005 to celebrate the tenth anniversary of The Evangelical Alliance of South Africa (TEASA). Arising out of the amalgamation of the predominantly black Concerned Evangelicals (CE) and the predominantly white Evangelical Fellowship of South Africa (EFSA), TEASA is made up of a broad cross-section of Christians who seek to identify themselves as evangelicals. While TEASA represents the entire evangelical spectrum (from "fundamentalists" to "radical evangelicals," to use the book's terminology), the contributors seem to have been drawn largely from the latter end of that spectrum. The first part of the book (consisting of four essays) examines the theological and biblical foundations of this evangelical identity by focusing on the history of evangelicalism. The worldwide history of evangelicalism will not be unfamiliar to the informed reader, whereas its history in South Africa might be. Unfortunately, the sections here that focus on South Africa are too brief to be of substantive assistance. A thorough history of this movement in South Africa must still be written. The second part of the book (twelve essays) is concerned with "evangelical witness and challenges facing evangelicals in South Africa today." Matters raised include church growth, evangelism, discipleship, the environment, reconciliation, the African Renaissance, prayer, HIV/AIDS, patriarchy, sexuality, children, and poverty. With the exception of the first three, none of these are of interest solely to Christians. They reflect, rather, the engagement of evangelicals with issues that are current within South Africa's contemporary social, political and economic milieu. It is interesting to note that the theological tensions apparent in the first half of the book are not considered one of the challenges facing evangelicals. While this collection is of interest in so far as it presents a "snapshot" of the concerns of TEASA, it will principally be those living in South Africa, or with an interest in South Africa, who may want to peruse a copy.

604.   Kretzschmar, Louise

The Voice of Black Theology in South Africa

Johannesburg: Ravan Press, 1986. 136 pages, ISBN: 9780869752692.

Using "Black Theology" as an umbrella term to include the various concerns of black South Africans, Kretschmar provides an overview on the South African version of Black Theology that emerged especially during the late 1960s and 1970s. Setting the background for later developments, the first chapter gives attention to some black leaders who as Christians spoke out about a society which, whilst so often calling itself Christian, failed to live up to the Gospel it preached. Chapter 2 indicates the broader international theological context of South African Black Theology. The theology from the African continent is briefly discussed, together with the Black Theology of the USA and Latin American Liberation Theology. Chapter 3 examines the Africanisation of Christianity, with special emphasis on Christianity, African traditional religion, African ancestors, African culture, African theology and political issues. The fourth chapter pays special attention to African Independent Churches, their origins, growth and their role in social transformation. The next two chapters discuss the political implications of the Christian faith in the South African context. Attention is paid to the rise of Black Consciousness in South Africa, its relationship with Black Theology, Black nationalism and liberation. In chapter 7 various responses to South African Black Theology are described and analysed. Apart from its interest for the study of theology, and the history of theology in Africa, this study will interest the non-specialist reader wishing better to understand the inter-relationship between religion and politics in South Africa before the end of the apartheid era.

Kretzschmar, Louise

see also review 490

Kriel, Jacques

see review 991

605. Kritzinger, J. N. J., and W. A. Saayman, editors

Mission in Creative Tension: A Dialogue with David Bosch

Pretoria: S.A. Missiological Society, 1990. 269 pages, ISBN: 9780620148986.

David Bosch was professor and head of the department of missiology at the University of South Africa (UNISA) until his untimely death in 1992, and achieved international distinction for his contributions to the field of missiology. Among his other roles, Bosch played an essential part in the life of the South African Missiological Society from its founding in 1968 onward. To mark the occasion of his sixtieth birthday that Society decided to honour him by dedicating its 1990 congress to interaction with his missiological thought. Assigning to the congress the theme "A Missiology of the Road: In Dialogue with David Bosch," the organizers invited seventeen scholars – one American, one Netherlander, one German, and fourteen South Africans – to present papers in analysis of, interpretation of, and interaction with Bosch's missiology. Presenters spoke to such issues as Bosch's missiological thought, his use of biblical passages, his views on mission and evangelism, his theology of religions, how he tried to bridge the gap between ecumenical and evangelical polarisation, and his use of paradigms in reading Christian history. The papers were then presented in published form in this book (with two more South African scholars adding chapters). It is clear that the values, ideals, and beliefs here in dialogue have been profoundly shaped by social, political, and denominational forces. This book is recommended for all who desire a caution about equating their "religious beliefs and social actions with the will of God," but who nevertheless want to move forward in their missiological endeavours and understandings, with a bold and humble dependence upon God and an openness to learn from the insights of others.

606. Kritzinger, J. N. J., editor

No Quick Fixes: The Challenge of Mission in a Changing South Africa

Pretoria: IMER, 2002. 215 pages, ISBN: 9781868544714.

This collection of essays results from a cooperative project of the Missions Research Network of South Africa. Rather than explore the usual cultural, religious and racial lines along which missions have conventionally been discussed in South Africa, these essays explore concerns in South African society that intersect with or span these traditional groupings. After several essays describing the South African religious context, the larger portion of material is devoted to exploring socio-economic and politico-cultural dimensions of the context, such as human rights, community development, poverty, health, education, crime, and ecology. The final chapter summarizes the book through a collection of short statements that range from the banal ("Solutions to poverty cannot be found before the real problems and their causes are identified. This can only be done through a thorough process of inquiry") to others that warrant further reflection ("the final test for church unity lies not in the theological realm, but in the cultural. The missionary witness of the church depends on the witness of its unity across cultural boundaries"). The editor asserts that "Mission is the church at work in the world. . . . The wellbeing of the total community is the goal of mission." Given that the nature of the church's mission is contested, one would have expected a more careful defence of this position. The book certainly alerts its readers to the numerous issues facing churches in South Africa today, but it fails to provide a sophisticated analysis of those problems or to suggest practical approaches to solutions. Most of the contributions touch on significant aspects within their respective fields, but their discussions lack the depth and careful analysis that these difficult problems demand. Both the aim of this volume and many of the sentiments expressed by its contributors are to be applauded. However, the execution of the project is disappointing, and one awaits a South African equivalent of John Stott's *Issues Facing Christians Today*, with its achievement of both accessibility and depth.

Kritzinger, Klippies

see review 994

607. Kubai, A. N., and Tarakegn Adebo, editors

Striving in Faith: Christians and Muslims in Africa

Nairobi: Life and Peace, 2008. 126 pages, ISBN: 9789187748868.

This is a small collection of essays dealing with Christian-Muslim relations in Africa, especially focusing on practical efforts of peace and reconciliation amidst regional religious conflicts. The authors are almost all Africans (the one European contributor has spent many years in Africa). All write from a scholarly Christian or non-confessional perspective. The chapters, representing the results of research initiated by the Life and Peace Institute in Sweden, were presented in various seminars throughout Africa. The two introductory chapters emphasize the important role of peacemakers among religious communities at the local level. The main part of the book involves four case studies: Sudan, Tanzania, Ethiopia and Nigeria, each covered by one or two chapters. Both chapters on Sudan, by Awet and Wasara/Komey, emphasize that religion is only one factor in the complex ongoing conflict, and that religion is often exploited to support state policies of subjugation. The result is that official attempts to resolve the conflict have largely failed. Tanzania is the one country among the four studied where religious conflict has been minimal; Masudi and Mwakabana point out that this is largely due to unifying factors such as a common culture, the Swahili language and generally good governance. In the chapter on Nigeria, Lateju and Adebayo discuss how the central role of religion in the north upholds a social cohesion where the Christian minority feels excluded, often leading to conflict which has been difficult to stem. Arsano's chapter on conflict in the Ethiopian Rift Valley is disappointing, since it deals only with socio-economic rather than religious factors. Fortunately it is offset by Østebø's excellent overview of the historical and contemporary "asymmetric relationship" between Christians and Muslims in Ethiopia, where Christians have had the upper hand. A common theme throughout the book is that positive Christian-Muslim relations in Africa do take place at the community level, often despite tensions and conflicts in the public arena, and that it is at this level where hope for resolution and reconciliation are to be found. This book, then, is a helpful reminder to the African churches of the need to better enable their congregations to reach out to their Muslim neighbours with the love of Christ.

Kubai, A. N.

see also review 471

608.   Kukah, Matthew Hassan

Religion, Politics and Power in Northern Nigeria

Ibadan: Spectrum Books, 1994. 280 pages, ISBN: 9789782461964.

Kukah has served as the Deputy Secretary-General of the Nigerian Catholic Bishops Conference. He comes from Kaduna State in Central Nigeria, the centre of much of the religio-political struggles which he discusses. He holds a PhD from the University of London's School of Oriental and African Studies. For a number of years the competition between Islam and Christianity has been one of the key features of the Nigerian political process. When British colonial rule arrived in Northern Nigeria, it confirmed the Hausa-Fulani Islamic hegemony which it found in place there, accommodating this within its system of "indirect rule." In the process the colonial government also extended this Islamic hegemony into many parts of central Nigeria (or the Middle Belt), which had never been under Islamic rule before. In due course the rise of political self-consciousness among these Middle Belt peoples, through the evangelistic and educational work of Christian missions, began to threaten the continued dominance of the traditional Hausa-Fulani ruling classes. The resulting struggle was evidenced in various religious riots in most major cities of Central and Northern Nigeria during the 1980s and early 1990s. Kukah traces the development of the Hausa-Fulani hegemony from the jihad of Uthman dan Fodio to the present day. He then discusses the manipulation of the media, the bitter quarrels in various Constituent Assemblies over the role of Sharia law in the Nigerian legal system, the role of religion in the politics of the Second Republic (1979–1983), the religious riots in Kaduna State between 1984 and 1987, and finally the Babangida regime's ambivalent use of religion as part of its political agenda. Kukah's basic thesis is that the Hausa-Fulani ruling classes have used religion, when it suited them, to maintain their traditional political and economic power. This has provoked not only Christians eager to assert their civil and political rights, but also Muslim fundamentalists, usually members of the Izala brotherhood, who have felt that the form of Islam being practiced is far from the ideals of the Qur'an. Kukah effectively traces the various twists and turns of the political issues involved, often quoting from personal interviews with some of the major participants. The book is well researched, and the bibliography and footnotes alone are of exceptional value.

This represents an excellent academic contribution to the study of church-state relations in modern Africa, and Muslim-Christian relations as well.

Kumar, P. Pratap

see review 1055

609.   Kunhiyop, Samuel Waje

African Christian Ethics

Carlisle, UK: HippoBooks, 2008. 416 pages, ISBN: 9789966805362.

Kunhiyop was formerly the Provost of ECWA Theological Seminary Jos (JETS) in Nigeria, and subsequently head of postgraduate studies at the South African Theological Seminary (SATS) near Johannesburg. More recently he has served as the General Secretary of the Nigeria-based Evangelical Church of West Africa (ECWA). Here he provides an important contribution on Christian ethics in the African context. His presentation is worked out from within the evangelical Christian tradition, closely attends to his African cultural background, and offers appropriate interaction with Western academic discourse. Kunhiyop begins by accenting the primacy of social ethics over personal ethics for African Christian reflection. Any tendency to give priority to personal ethics he attributes to Western individualism, which is "unacceptable in Africa." The strength of African Christian ethics, he declares, is the community aspect. Kunhiyop then offers individual treatment of two dozen ethical issues germane to the African context, such as religious conflict, strikes, poverty, AIDS, fundraising, corruption, reproductive technologies, witchcraft, and polygamy, topics that might not appear in a Western text on ethics. At times the author's Western training may seem to have affected his assessments unduly. For example, he seems almost to rationalize witchcraft into non-existence. In dealing with marriage, Kunhiyop examines issues of particular concern to Africans, such as barrenness, impotence, divorce and re-marriage. He notes that procreation is the primary purpose of marriage in Africa, so much so that families without their own biological offspring are under perpetual pressure from relatives to divorce their spouses and re-marry. Kunhiyop takes time to examine some possible causes of infertility, and suggests guidelines for dealing with the problem. In tackling the problem of polygamy, Kunhiyop notes that polygamy is not the perfect will of God for mankind, but that it also is not adultery. His call that a person who is a polygamist before conversion to Christianity should be accepted into full church membership (but not to leadership positions) is bold and fair. In discussing church and state the author shows unquestioning acceptance of the popular notion that there were "strong links between the missionaries and the colonial powers, [so that] it is not surprising that missionary organizations discouraged believers from participating in politics." Archival evidence expounded by Kunhiyop's scholarly colleague Yusufu Turaki demonstrates to the contrary that at least in Nigeria the mission organisations, while civil in their relationship with colonial authorities, were by no means in collaboration with them, and indeed at times were confrontational. All in all, Kunhiyop tackles major ethical issues relevant to the African setting with both biblical sensitivity and cultural insight in a manner that makes this a distinguished contribution to the discussion of Christian ethics in Africa.

610.   **Kunhiyop, Samuel Waje**

African Christian Theology

Carlisle, UK: HippoBooks, 2012. 272 pages, ISBN: 9789966003164.

This is a full-scale systematic theology by a senior evangelical African scholar. Not only is it written by an African, not only does it cover many of the usual topics found in a traditional systematic theology, but it also does so with the African flavour that we have been waiting for. The author holds a PhD from Trinity Deerfield in the United States, and was formerly Professor and Provost at ECWA Theological Seminary Jos (JETS). Presently he is the chief executive officer of ECWA, one of Nigeria's largest denominations. In constructing his systematic theology Kunhiyop does not react against Western theologies, nor label African theology as inevitably liberal or syncretistic, nor does he take a comparative religion approach. His goal is "to articulate a theology that originates from an authentic search for the meaning of Scripture in order to apply it to African life today." His approach is to place his topics (the foundations of African Christian theology; general and special revelation; God and the spirits; creation and the fall; Christ and salvation; the Holy Spirit and salvation; salvation's relationship to the Christian life; the Church as the community of God; the beliefs and practices of the community of God; death; judgement and eternity) within the African context, including ideas from a full range of African theologians and from ATR. He also includes discussion of the topic from selected Western theologians from many traditions. And he is cognisant of post-missionary Western imports to Africa such as Pentecostalism, prosperity theology and secularism. Kunhiyop uses the Bible to assess these other efforts, with conclusions that are generally conservative and traditional. At the same time he conveys a broadness of vision that opens his stance to truth from other traditions. Thus, when speaking of salvation, he gives equal stress to, and ably defends the need for, spiritual, physical, and emotional salvation. Though the book is too brief to give full scholarly attention to all aspects of the topics he treats, it is the right length for his intended purpose. It will make an excellent textbook for theological colleges and Christian universities in Africa from the diploma level up, including the post-graduate level. Theological libraries in Africa will necessarily need a copy, and those elsewhere will want to include this title in their holdings in order to have a well-rounded representation of contemporary African Christian theology.

611.   **Kunhiyop, Samuel Waje**

Christian Conversion in Africa: The Bajju Experience

Jos: JETS, 2005. 198 pages, ISBN: LANG256877.

The Bajju are a small ethnic group in the Middle Belt of Nigeria. Christianity was brought to the Bajju in the twentieth century especially by the international mission SIM and the Roman Catholics. This book, which is Kunhiyop's PhD thesis at Trinity Deerfield, examines Christian conversion in the context of the Bajju people. He first offers a biblical and theological discussion of conversion, defining it as "a turning to God through commitment to Christ." He also notes that conversion can be a single event or a process. Kunhiyop next describes traditional Bajju religion and culture. The traditional Bajju people knew God faintly, but Christianity reveals God more fully. The gospel first came to the Bajju through the pioneering ministry of Thomas Archibald of the SIM. The first two conversions were in 1929; others followed in the next years. The new converts were to abandon adultery, ancestor worship, local wine, dancing, polygamy, and the like. Those who could not make such a break often joined the Roman Catholic or African Independent churches. The author distinguishes between different types of conversions. First-generation Bajju conversions usually involved a radical break with the past; the first converts from 1929, Dogo and Bakut Bityong, are examples of such a conversion. They renounced local wine and polygamy, and they made a public confession of faith. But second generation conversions consisted of two types: the radical conversion of those who came from outside the church; and the gradual conversion of the person who grew up in the church. Finally Kunhiyop reflects on how radical a Christian conversion should be. How much of the traditional culture should be jettisoned? He says that contextualization is necessary but it must be biblical: there should be both continuity and discontinuity. Overall this study would have been strengthened had Roman Catholic and African Independent experience among the Bajju been given greater attention. The study is principally developed from the standpoint of the Evangelical Church of West Africa (ECWA), which derives from the work of SIM. But that acknowledged, this book is a useful addition to historical case studies of Christian conversion in particular African contexts.

612. Kuperus, Tracy

State, Civil Society and Apartheid in South Africa: An Examination of Dutch Reformed Church-State Relations

London: Palgrave Macmillan, 1999. 232 pages, ISBN: 9780333726495.

Apartheid in South Africa was built upon the foundations of neo-Kuyperian theology and Afrikaner nationalism, represented in large measure respectively by the Dutch Reformed Church (DRC) and (in the second half of the twentieth century) the National Party. Set within the larger discussion of state-civil society relations, Kuperus' book focuses on the changing relationship between the South African state and the DRC from 1934 to 1994. This 60-year period is divided into four epochs delimited by significant political events within the country. Each of the main chapters consists of a description of the state's policy during these periods, followed by an investigation into the DRC response. The author, a professor in the international development studies program at Calvin College (USA), situates the relationship between these two entities within a two-dimensional typology describing official interaction and policy collusion. She shows how the two entities moved from "coexisting conflict" (1934–1947) to "mutual engagement" (1948–1961), followed by "collaboration or cooptation" during the height of Apartheid (1962–1978), and, finally back to "mutual engagement" (1979–1994) as Apartheid was gradually dismantled. Kuperus' careful research is supplemented by forty interviews with South African clergyman, politicians and academics conducted in 1993. She shows that church leaders were often more concerned with Afrikaner nationalism and concomitant church unity than with issues of social justice. This meant, sadly, that the church (with notable exceptions) often lagged behind the state when it came to racial policy. The author's concerns are not primarily historical; this book will be of most interest to those engaged in political studies and questions of the relationship between church and state.

613. Kurewa, John Wesley Zwomunondiita

Preaching & Cultural Identity: Proclaiming the Gospel in Africa

Nashville: Abingdon, 2000. 236 pages, ISBN: 9780687090310.

A book on such an important topic by a professor of evangelism at Africa University in Mutare, Zimbabwe, is to be welcomed. The title and subtitle of the book promise much, and the opening chapter laments the lack of indigenisation of much of Christianity in Africa, urging a new generation to preach in such a way that the Gospel truly engages with African identity. So far so good, but the rest of the book does not quite deliver. Much space is spent on the history of preaching, going back to the earliest times of ancient rhetoric, then the preaching of Jesus, the apostles, the early church, the Middle Ages and the Reformation. Rather surprisingly, the historical overview stops abruptly with Luther and Calvin and then turns to preaching in the African context. But even here much of what is said relates more to general principles of preaching equally applicable anywhere in the world, dealing with such admittedly vital topics as the authority of the Word and types of sermon. The author has many challenging things to say about the passion and calling of the preacher, his/her own preparation, and the need for a heart of love for people. All very true and helpful, although hardly Africa-specific. Of greater interest may be the sections on participatory preaching, addressing the whole person according to the holistic, integrated perception of life common in Africa, and the way that national holidays can be creatively used for preaching. The book merits two cheers. Three cheers would be due the author if in a subsequent book he were to explore exegetical and homiletical principles that would help to "narrow the distance" between the voice of God in Scripture and the African context.

614.   Kyomo, Andrew A., and Sahaya G. Selvan, editors

Marriage and Family in African Christianity

Nairobi: Acton Publishers, 2004. 259 pages, ISBN: 9789966888525.

This volume contains ten papers that were presented at a session of the Tanzanian Theological Colloquium in 2002. An ecumenical group, the colloquium includes both academic theologians and pastors. The result is that this book deals with Christian marriage from both the doctrinal and the pastoral perspectives (the final chapter is a lecture that was presented at a 2003 Kenya workshop on female genital mutilation). Using as a springboard the 1994 African Synod in Rome "where it was decided that 'family' as an image of the Church would be the particular African Christian theological contribution to the Church universal in the new millennium," the pressing question becomes: with the family in crisis, how valid is this model, how helpful the contribution? Topics covered include the current crisis in Christian marriage, globalisation/urbanisation/westernisation, developing a cultural approach to a Christian theology of marriage, divorce, church discipline, and leadership. Some rather startling assertions are made, such as: "Marriage is a human institution, developed by human beings for the purpose of satisfying human needs." But even though a thoughtful reader may not agree with every view expressed in these papers, there is much food for thought and discussion: what are the biblical principles for marriage, and what are appropriate cultural expressions of such principles; marriage as process vs event; marriage for procreation vs for relationship; polygamy vs divorce. The chapters on "Pastoral Care and Counselling to Families," and "Preparing Young People for Marriage in Africa" are worth the price of the whole book. As in any collection of papers, the writing is uneven. Also a brief biographical paragraph on each of the contributors would have been a good addition.

Kyomo, Andrew A.

see also review 1122

615. Kyomya, Michael

A Guide to Interpreting Scripture: Context, Harmony, and Application

Carlisle, UK: HippoBooks, 2010. 128 pages, ISBN: 9789966003089.

Kyomya was Academic Dean and taught NT Studies at Nairobi International School of Theology (NIST) in Kenya. He is now bishop of the Busoga Diocese in the Church of Uganda. He also serves as chairman of the Bible Society of Uganda, the Uganda Christian University Council, and the Council for Higher Education. Kyomya's stated intent in this book is to empower African believers "to read the Bible and read it wholesomely," people who, like the NT Bereans, can evaluate the preaching and teaching they hear. He accomplishes this by making the foundational principles of evangelical interpretation clear and relevant to Africa. He covers the need and importance of biblical interpretation, various methods of interpretation, some pitfalls to avoid, the harmony of Scripture, and its application. He places great importance on the context of a Scripture passage, not only its historical context, but especially its literary context. In fact he maintains an almost continuous emphasis on context throughout the book, which may not seem inappropriate in Africa, where (as elsewhere) a great many preachers atomise the biblical text. This may be because that is the pattern of preaching they grew up hearing, or because it is convenient in making a point unsupported by the literary context of the passage. Kyomya illustrates his interpretive principles with well-chosen African examples, especially ones he has experienced. He also works through some specific biblical passages to illustrate how interpretation should be done. He includes three appendices: Interpreting Wisdom Literature, Interpreting Figures of Speech, and Resources for Interpretation, the latter mentioning some of the standard evangelical Bible translations, Bible dictionaries, commentaries and other resources. This is not a technical manual in interpretation, and is not meant to be. Kyomya could have added more detail about inadequate methods of interpretation (he mentions only the allegorical and historical-critical methods), and also for almost any of the principles he deals with, especially principles of application. But he is not attempting anything exhaustive. This book is a valuable, reliable, and easily comprehendible book. Not only could it serve as a suitable text for diploma and first-degree students in theological colleges. It could also be used profitably to train elders, other church leaders, and educated laypeople in the basics of biblical interpretation.

Authors
L–M

Lacy, Joe

see review 338

616.   Lademann-Priemer, Gabriele, editor

Traditionelle Religion und christlicher Glaube: Widerspruch und Wandel

Ammersbek, Germany: Verlag an der Lottbek P. Jensen, 1993. 312 pages, ISBN: 9783861300403.

This volume is a Festschrift honouring the German scholar Hans-Jürgen Becken on his 70th birthday. Becken was a missionary in South Africa among the Zulu people. He worked as a pastor for white and black populations in the 1950s, and after his doctoral research on African Independent Churches (only available in German: *Theologie der Heilung*) he served as a lecturer and director of the Lutheran Theological College Umpumulo in Natal, RSA. The book contains a wide variety of essays, between 5 and 30 pages, from European and South African university professors, evangelists of African Independent Churches (AICs), and mission-related Westerners. Nine articles are in English, and ten in German. The majority focus on South Africa (mainly the Zulu), and especially on the African Independent Churches (AICs), covering in a sociological or contextual perspective such topics as typology, theological education, pneumatology, preaching, and healing. Especially worthwhile are the papers by James Cochrane (on power and the social role of AICs), Gerardus Oosthuizen (on the dynamic of the AICs), and Hennie Pretorius (on the typology of AICs). Three contributions are general missiology: a stimulating paper of Niels-Peter Moritzen on the concept of "Volk" and of homogenous units; plus two critical analyses of the so-called internationalisation of Western mission societies, including the probing question of an African: "What would be your interest in us, if you wouldn't have any money?" The last three contributions are not Africa-related. Offering a diverse and easy to read introduction to AICs in South Africa before 1994, the collection would prove a useful addition for advanced-level theological libraries in South Africa.

617.   Lagerwerf, Leny

Witchcraft, Sorcery and Spirit Possession: Pastoral Responses in Africa

Gweru, Zimbabwe: Mambo Press, 1987. 82 pages, ISBN: 9780869224380.

Lagerwerf seeks to show the theological and pastoral struggle facing the church in responding to traditional African beliefs of the spirit realm. He blends a careful presentation of the thinking of Catholics and selected Protestants from around the continent, giving special attention to the reality of the belief systems and the difficulty of deciding to what extent those systems may be utilized in responding to the spiritual problems that people face. One senses an attempt to steer a middle course, as Lagerwerf acknowledges the deeply held traditional beliefs but desires to call people away from those beliefs towards a more psycho-social orientation in facing issues of witchcraft, sorcery, and possession phenomena. Generally speaking, this work is not so much a presentation of Lagerwerf's own synthesis as it is a survey of what prominent Roman Catholic figures are saying. For those needing to understand the issues affecting the church's response to the spirit realm, as reflected in Catholic discussion, Lagerwerf's book will be a welcome aid.

618. Lamle, Elias Nankap

Cultural Revival and Church Planting: A Nigerian Case Study

Jos: CAPRO, 1995. 196 pages, ISBN: 9789782668509.

The author is a Tarok pastor from Plateau State in Nigeria who has studied at the Theological College of Northern Nigeria. In the first five chapters of this book, he describes the Tarok people, including their history, culture and social structure, traditional religion, and the coming of Christianity. The last three chapters attempt to analyse what happened in the interaction of the Tarok with the missionaries, to find out why there is now a demand for cultural revival, and what this means for the church. Lamle concludes that the missionaries failed to contextualize the gospel and downgraded Tarok culture. A Christian worldview was not absorbed. While almost the entire group embraced Christianity outwardly, aspects of Tarok culture and religion were driven underground. Educated Tarok today wish to reinstate these things as an affirmation of Tarok worth, and men whom the traditional system favoured wish to regain lost power. However, any cultural revival will affirm ancestor worship, and the drunkenness and immorality associated with traditional practices. The author suggests some techniques of contextualized evangelism and deeper discipleship as remedies.

619. Landau, Paul Stuart

The Realm of the Word: Language, Gender and Christianity in a Southern African Kingdom

Martlesham, UK: James Currey, 1995. 249 pages, ISBN: 9780435089658.

This book, from a series entitled "Social History of Africa," offers an analysis of Christian presence in pre-independent Botswana from the 1850s to the 1940s, interweaving attention to church-state relationships with such other factors as the impact of Bible translation on local culture, and the church's empowerment of women in the midst of a male-dominated hierarchy. The author, a lecturer at Yale, waits until the epilogue to state that he does not share the Christians' "experiences and expressions," although that perspective is evident long before the epilogue. Yet there is rich history here, especially as it relates to Khama, who is the best-known early example of a "Christian chief" in southern Africa. The author's analysis of the church-state relationship between the London Missionary Society and Khama's kingdom is of particular interest in light of recent debates in southern Africa regarding the idea of a "Christian nation." Landau quotes an LMS source, that "Khama is head of the Church as well as head of the State," as a summary of his own assessment that "Christian pluralism was the greatest treachery"; to oppose the leader was to oppose the church. Despite its focus on a single country and during an earlier era, this book gives serious consideration to issues that continue to cause major debate in many parts of Africa, and thus represents the sort of inquiry that should be noticed and encouraged continentally.

Lande, Aasulv

see review 379

620.   **Langworthy, Harry**

Africa for the African: The Life of Joseph Booth

Blantyre: CLAIM, 1996. 524 pages, ISBN: 9789990816037.

The more than five hundred pages of this extensive monograph cover in detail the life and times of Joseph Booth, who came to Malawi from Australia in 1892 and "was instrumental in the founding of seven major denominations in that country." Written by Booth's great-grandson, the monograph delves deeply not only into historical records and church archives, but particularly into memorabilia and correspondence preserved by Booth and his family. This gives a personal touch to the varied activities of a man generally considered a "maverick" among missionary legends, who advocated "Africa for the African" long before this idea became popular in religious and political circles. That Booth switched from denomination to denomination in an attempt to gain support and to promote his projects might raise questions about his theological convictions. But one can hardly question Booth's constant concern for evangelising Africans and at the same time equipping them to be self-sufficient through involvement in the industrial and agricultural projects which he promoted. Unfortunately none of his efforts over a period of several decades fully materialized. Financial problems, difficulties with colleagues and unrealistic ideals led to one breakdown after the other. Booth's avid promotions of African independence were suspected of having been "at the bottom" of the notorious Chilembwe Rising in Malawi, leading to his eventual deportation from the African continent in 1915. Most of the remainder of his life was spent in England, where he had been born and where he died in 1932. Langworthy is to be credited with producing as comprehensive a biography of a controversial missionary as could possibly have been written, "warts and all." He does not try to cover up his great-grandfather's weaknesses. Although at times the reader can get lost in the book's minutiae, it is a valuable addition to the complex history of Christianity in Africa.

621.   **Lapp, John, and C. Arnold Snyder, editors**

Anabaptist Songs in African Hearts

Intercourse, PA: Good Books, 2006. 300 pages, ISBN: 9781561485499.

This team effort of various African Mennonite-related authors from around the continent is another laudable example of Africans assuming the task of writing their own church history. Despite the fact that Mennonites are not a large denomination in Africa, their impact as a "peace" church (meaning non-involvement in war) has sometimes been significant in times of conflict, such as in Congo (DRC) and Rwanda. Most Mennonite groups in Africa are found in the southern region (where the Brethren in Christ are most numerous in Zambia and Zimbabwe), and eastern Africa (mainly Ethiopia and Tanzania), but there are also smaller groups in West Africa. All such areas are covered in this collective work, with the southern section being treated in most detail. Most contributors are refreshingly honest in dealing with problems such as disagreements with missionaries over cultural practices, divisions arising from the charismatic movement, the prosperity gospel, and leadership wrangles. Cameos of significant African church leaders are an attractive feature. Perhaps in an attempt to right the imbalance of previous histories of the church in Africa, missionary leaders are not as well covered. One disappointment is the relative lack of emphasis on the development of higher theological education, perhaps because most contributors did not have such training themselves. The "Afterword" gives a welcome challenge to Mennonites in Africa to apply their theology of peace to the continuing crises in Congo (DRC) and Zimbabwe. This book is noteworthy for its African presentation of denominational history at continental level, and should spur other denominations to consider similar projects.

622. Larom, Margaret S., editor

Claiming the Promise: African Churches Speak

New York: Friendship Press, 1994. 120 pages, ISBN: 9780377002678.

This book contains a selection of documents written by some fifteen African church leaders, theologians, and scholars, reflecting on personal histories, reporting on continental ecumenical gatherings (mainly AACC), or analysing religious trends. Among the general topics discussed are: problems and promises of Africa; the Mombasa Symposium; abundant life in Jesus Christ; the AACC Sixth Assembly; women's perspectives; the challenges of governance; and African religious traditions. Some of the contributors are: Andre Karamaga, Modupe Oduyoye, Musimbi Kanyoro, Edna Maluma, Tokunboh Adeyemo ("Church and State in African Perspective"), and Desmond Tutu. The book is of interest in reflecting some of the issues that concern the church in Africa, presented by various prominent religious leaders on the continent.

623. Larom, Peter

Pastor: A Practical Guide for Church Leaders

Achimota, Ghana: Africa Christian Press, 1989. 192 pages, ISBN: 9789964877019.

This practical guide for pastors is written from a general perspective, but because the author's experience has taken place in Africa, there are many African illustrations. Also, because the author is Anglican, the presentation would especially apply for most Anglican contexts. Starting from the premise that the local church is the place of primary nurture for most Christians and that the pastor is their primary spiritual guide, the author sets out to share practical insights with those who bear this responsibility. Drawing on his own experience as a church leader and as a lecturer in a theological college in Uganda, Larom deals with a wide range of responsibilities (which most pastors would probably find too extensive for one person). The book offers helpful guidance in the usual areas of teaching, preaching, evangelism, leading worship, and pastoral care. It also includes practical suggestions in organisation and administration, including the handling of finances and the raising of funds. One often neglected aspect of the church's ministry is brought as a challenge – that of having a deliberate policy of reaching out to society's needy with compassion, imagination and wisdom. The book ends with a focus on "The Pastor as a Man of God," in which the pastor's own walk with God is addressed. Though the local church that forms the context of the discussion is Anglican, the book's usefulness is certainly not limited to that tradition; anyone in pastoral ministry, or in training for such a role, would benefit from the insights offered – provided that the range of work is seen as applicable to a plurality of workers and not just to a solo pastor!

624.   Larsson, Brigitta

Conversion to Greater Freedom?: Women, Church and Social Change in North-Western Tanzania under Colonial Rule

Stockholm: Almqvist & Wiksell International, 1991. 234 pages, ISBN: 9789155426842.

That the majority of Christians in Africa are women is often not adequately taken into account, either in theology or in research. This book illustrates the sort of research that can help to remedy that deficiency. It presents a careful study of the role of women among the Buhaya of Tanzania and their history in relation to Christianity. The first section (up to 1916) shows many Haya girls and women using the *busirika* (place of protection) of the Roman Catholic White Sisters to escape from arranged marriages to old polygamous men or to young men they did not want to marry. The White Sisters soon became a power in the land, and in the majority of cases managed to protect the girls, who stayed for baptismal instruction, and for whom Christian marriages were often arranged. Others stayed permanently and worked as catechists, and some formed the nucleus of the indigenous sisterhood. The second section deals with the time after the First World War when a sharp increase in venereal diseases, and the control by older men of the increasing profits from coffee production, made marriages more difficult. Haya women in turn began "travelling" to Nairobi or Mombasa for prostitution as a major means to become mistresses of their own destiny, an innovation which society largely accepted. Back in Bukoba they would support their families, and buy from the men the land that they could not inherit. A good number found their way back into the church, and being accustomed to independence often attained leadership positions. The third section deals with the role of Haya women in the East African Revival Movement, which came to the area in the 1930s and brought both spiritual and social change. A number of returned prostitutes were saved and often achieved leadership positions in the movement or in the church. More far-reaching were new marriage patterns among those of the Revival, in which husband and wife would treat each other as much more equal, and sometimes even daughters would inherit land, while strict morals produced social improvement. The fourth section shows Haya women making use of education as a tool for their own advancement. The Lutherans provided the first school for girls in the 1930s, and the women trained there became prominent. Then in the 1950s education of girls really took off. In this book women are shown as agents of their own destiny, and more often than not the church paved the way for them to achieve their quest. With her research Larsson offers a good pattern, and shows the potential fruitfulness, for similar research into the history and role of women elsewhere in African Christianity.

625.   Lartey, Emmanuel Y., Daisy Nwachuku, and Kasonga Wa Kasonga, editors

The Church and Healing: Echoes from Africa

New York: Peter Lang, 1994. 157 pages, ISBN: 9783631472279.

This collection of essays written by ten African scholars addresses the subject of spiritual healing in an African context. Its purpose is to suggest ways of making pastoral care and the restoration of the individual and the community more effective in Africa, by learning principles of healing exemplified in traditional healing practice. Subjects addressed include traditional beliefs and practices of healing, a comparison of traditional healing and healing in African independent churches, rituals and symbols in the healing of infertility, Christianising the African palaver as a way of moving towards a Christian kind of group therapy, etc. The authors believe that western-based pastoral counselling does not take seriously the African context and that the Christian pastoral counsellor needs to develop a theory and practice of healing that is African. These essays are consistently high in quality. Nine of the ten authors are actually teaching in schools of higher learning in Africa or practising psychiatry in Africa. The material is thought-provoking and invaluable for any Christian African counsellor who is trying to develop a practice of counselling which is truly African. The authors appear to represent a wide range of theological positions, some conservative and some more liberal. Some of the essays seem to assume that what is traditional is automatically "good," and thus fail to evaluate traditional beliefs and practices critically in the light of Scripture. This book should be a must for lecturers or practitioners in pastoral counselling in Africa.

626.   Lartey, Emmanuel Y.

In Living Colour: An Intercultural Approach to Pastoral Care and Counselling

London: Jessica Kingsley Publishers, 2003. 192 pages, ISBN: 9781843107507.

This is a truly ambitious effort to propose principles for adapting "pastoral care and counselling" to the diversity of cultural and religious settings represented in many world cities today. The author has lectured on pastoral care and counselling at the University of Ghana and thereafter was a Lecturer at the University of Birmingham. He proposes a holistic approach, informed by diverse cultures and religious traditions as well as by liberation theology, for a global context. He has a broad command of his subject and writes in a readable style. The author comes to his subject from an ecumenical standpoint. The meaning of the word "pastoral" is not used in a particularly Christian sense but in the broad sense of religious care offered to people of diverse religious convictions to enable them to realize their full potential. The Bible is not given an authoritative role for informing and evaluating forms of pastoral care and counselling, but is treated as one religious document among many. Pastoral care is viewed as broader than the "spiritual," and includes empowering and liberating the politically oppressed. This book would be important for professors of pastoral care and counselling as well as advanced theological students and educated church leaders. It will force them to face some hard questions related to the scope of pastoral care in Africa, and encourage them to take the cultural context more seriously.

627.   Lartey, Emmanuel Y.

Pastoral Counseling in Inter-Cultural Perspective: A Study of Some African (Ghanaian) and Anglo-American Views on Human Existence and Counseling

Frankfurt: Peter Lang, 1987. 242 pages, ISBN: 9783820498295.

There are two major themes running through this study. One is that pastoral counselling is an inter-disciplinary task involving theological understandings, psychological insights, and the cultural setting. The author maintains that it is this third element that is often neglected. Pastoral counselling in order to be effective must be contextualized, in the sense that it must take seriously the needs, perspectives and worldview of the people for whom it is designed. Secondly, this cultural perspective permits a dialogue on pastoral counselling between Western approaches and African approaches, in which each can be enriched as well as corrected by the other. The book also offers a sort of model of how this can be done. The author begins by trying to develop a view of man which is informed both by theology and by culture. He uses the culture of the Ga and the Akan tribes in Ghana as his source. He then interacts with two schools of psychotherapy, Gestalt and Family Therapy, from an African Christian perspective. Finally he gives two case studies of pastoral counselling, one of an African

Independent Church in Ghana, and the other of a church-based counselling centre in England, and draws conclusions. The study is from a liberal Protestant perspective, where it appears that both the Bible and the cultural context carry equal authority in their contribution to one's view of people and healing. However, it is a serious effort to wrestle with an important question, how the church in Africa can develop forms of pastoral counselling which are at once Christian, take advantage of Western psychological studies, and are also sensitive to the cultural context of Africa.

628.   Last, Murray, and Paul Richards, editors

Sierra Leone 1787–1987: Two Centuries of Intellectual Life

Manchester: Manchester University Press, 1988. 176 pages, ISBN: 9780719027918.

This is a collection of essays in celebration of the bicentennial of the Sierra Leone settlement on the West African coast. The thirteen studies, some quite brief, relate to history, politics, technology, culture, and language. All are by persons presently or previously associated with Sierra Leone. Regrettably, those who may be attracted by the intriguing subtitle will almost certainly be disappointed; nothing within the collection answers readily to such a theme. Also, as is common with such collections, the calibre of the various contributions is uneven. Students of Sierra Leone history will likely find several of the essays of interest, and some advanced libraries seeking ample holdings in the field may wish to consider the book, especially since the price is reasonable.

Latham, Robert

see review 183

629.   Laukkanen, Pauli

Rough Road to Dynamism: Bible Translating in Northern Namibia, 1954–1987: Kwanyama, Kwangali and Ngonga

Helsinki: Luther-Agricola-Society, 2002. 296 pages, ISBN: 9789519047614.

Bible translation is a long, painstaking, sometimes even tedious process. For most it is a labour of love. However, the process and struggle to render God's Word into a new language too often goes unrecorded and unappreciated. Most of those who read the Bible in their own language will be unaware of those who invested themselves so fully to produce the text. The stories of some of those who translated the Scriptures into the languages of Africa are quite well known: Samuel Crowther (Yoruba), Johann Ludwig Krapf (Kiswahili), and John Colenso (Zulu) readily come to mind. A few nineteenth or early twentieth-century translations list the European translator on the title page, but only rarely are the Africans who worked with them recorded. Ype Schaaf has written a very general overview of the history of the translation of the Bible into African languages, but very few scholarly studies of particular translation projects have as yet appeared. Laukkanen has authored a careful yet readable study of the translation of the Bible into three Namibian languages which took place between 1954 and 1987. Not only was this a period in which Namibia was going through immense political turmoil, but it was also a time in which Bible translation itself was undergoing a paradigm shift in which "dynamic equivalence" translation was being developed and put into practice, and in which translation projects became more ecumenical endeavours. The translation projects in Namibia were spearheaded by Finish

Lutherans, but Roman Catholics and Anglicans were also involved. And of course the African members of the projects were full participants. Although the ideals of dynamic equivalence translation are a major theme of the book, Laukkanen does not avoid some of the political intrigue that surfaced – such as when two of the Namibian translators were arrested on the grounds of being SWAPO sympathizers. This study is valuable not merely for those interested in the processes of Bible translation or those interested in Namibian Christianity; it should also be seen as a model for what one might hope could be numerous similar studies on the history of African Bible translation.

630. Launhardt, Johannes

Evangelicals in Addis Ababa (1919–1991): With Special Reference to the Ethiopian Evangelical Church Mekane Yesus and the Addis Ababa Synod

Münster: LIT Verlag, 2005. 347 pages, ISBN: 9783825877910.

In this published form of his 2004 University of Hamburg dissertation, Launhardt offers a richly detailed and fascinating account of the growth and development of the Evangelical movement in the capital city of Ethiopia between 1919 and 1991. Although early twentieth-century Addis Ababa was religiously diverse, the Ethiopian Orthodox Church (EOC) remained dominant, and Evangelicals formed only a slim minority – an estimated 100 Ethiopians publicly professed Protestant faith in 1910. Some of these early Evangelicals had been influenced by a small reform group within the EOC, which had its roots in seventeenth-century German Lutheran influence. Protestant missions entering Ethiopia did not attempt to form Evangelical churches in Addis, but instead sought to nurture renewal within the EOC, or engaged in evangelistic outreach in areas which the government deemed non-Christian outside the capital, primarily in the South. This situation changed with the formation of the first Evangelical congregation in Addis Ababa in 1921, based on the arrival of a number of believers from Eritrea who had been forced out of the Orthodox Church there. Nevertheless by the time of the Italian occupation in 1935, there were scarcely more than 1,000 Ethiopians who openly professed Evangelical faith, and only 200 in Addis Ababa. During the occupation, however, the Evangelical community grew exponentially, owing to indigenous outreach initiatives of believers. By the end of the occupation the number of Evangelicals had increased to 20,000, and by the early 1950s this number had reached 100,000. Evangelical congregations that emerged in the capital during the occupation exercised close cooperation. Nevertheless, movement towards forming a single united evangelical national church for Ethiopia was never fully implemented, as evangelical Christians became increasingly conscious of their confessional and polity differences, and after the Italian occupation were drawn into differing overseas ecclesial relationships and identities. The original Addis Ababa evangelical congregation had evolved by 1958 into the Ethiopian Evangelical Church Mekane Yesus (EECMY), which increasingly identified with the worldwide family represented by the Lutheran World Federation. The rest of Launhardt's book focuses on the EECMY. As the population of Addis Ababa reached more than a million people, the resulting urban problems became a pronounced focus for the EECMY, as it undertook a multitude of social programmes, including schools, orphanages and literacy programmes. During the Marxist period beginning in 1974 the EECMY experienced severe repression and persecution, but the period also proved to be a time in which the Church grew and matured. Granted its altogether unique elements, the remarkable development of the Evangelical community in Ethiopia during the twentieth century remains a particularly notable example of the wider growth of Christianity in Africa.

631.	**Lawrence, Carl**

Rwanda: A Walk through Darkness into Light

Bucks, UK: SP Trust, 1995. 190 pages, ISBN: 9781885305343.

Lawrence's book represents a sincere attempt to give some Christian perspective on the Rwandan genocide, and to raise some of the hard questions that concerned Christians wish to ask. However, the presentation is often impressionistic and the organisation and coverage haphazard, leaving the reader unsure of the book's ultimate purpose, and which parts of it are fact, fiction or opinion. The book is a collection of stories, reflections and quotations, based on the author's inquiries and contacts soon after the events. As such it does not work from an adequate overview of the larger situation – major aspects of what happened in 1994, and of the resulting issues, do not surface. The book does attempt to address the very important question of how the Rwandan events could happen in a country estimated at the time to be 80 percent Christian. Lawrence quotes the simple but significant comment of the American ambassador to Rwanda: "We underestimated the power of evil." The book states that there are "no verifiable cases of believers killing other believers." Whether one takes this as credible, the chapter that deals with this issue is well worth reading. However, when the author engages the very important question of how the church will participate in the rebuilding process, he spends only two pages on the problems of Rwandese church leadership and then more than six pages on the role of the Western missionary, including a summary of the missionary movement in general. Obviously this leaves the real question of the churches' contemporary role today in Rwanda completely unaddressed, even though a chapter has been dedicated to the subject. Part of the problem is that this book was published in 1995, and the situation has evolved well beyond the perspective that this book was able to bring to bear so close on the heels of the events. The book does offer a good picture of the well-orchestrated plan for carrying out the genocide. And interspersed are some thought-provoking analyses, such as: "in the end it has little to do with one's tribe, but much to do with the satanic hunger for raw-power disguised as ethnicity."

Lawrie, Ingrid

see review 685

632.	**Lefkowitz, Mary**

Not Out of Africa: How Afrocentrism Became an Excuse to Teach Myth as History

New York: The Perseus Books Group, 1997. 320 pages, ISBN: 9780465098385.

Given the distorting cultural arrogance of much European historical interpretation in the past, any movement toward a more non-Eurocentric interpretation of global history must be welcomed, not least in Africa. On the other hand, a healthy caution is ever in order toward the perennial tendency of ethnic or sectarian groups to generate self-promoting myths as history. Such pseudo-history can become not only empowering, but also destructive (witness e.g. South Africa or Rwanda). Lefkowitz is a respected professor of classical studies in the United States. In this controversial book she takes on the "Afrocentric" movement within North American academia, intending a scholarly exposé of the historical claims that that movement has been deploying on behalf of African peoples. One of the more extreme contentions made within that movement has been that the principal philosophical and cultural contributions of ancient classical Greece to modern Western culture were actually pilfered from black Egyptian civilization in Africa. Lefkowitz subjects this now widely-disseminated claim to detailed critical assessment, and concludes that it represents nothing less than a credulous falsification of history. Her study is responding most particularly to Martin Bernal's *Black Athena* (1987, 1991) and G. G. M. James' *Stolen Legacy* (1954). The latter she considers a primary source of many contemporary Afrocentric historical assumptions. She finds that James' representation of ancient Egypt was drawn, curiously enough, chiefly from the lore of international Freemasonry, with its fascination for all things Egyptian – material which derived in turn not from any historical sources but from a popular European novel of 1732! As Lefkowitz sleuths her way through the back corridors of history, the fascinating discussion takes in not only Homer, Socrates, and Cleopatra, but also the Septuagint, Philo, Clement of Alexandria, and Augustine, not to mention Edward Blyden, W. E. B. Du Bois, and Marcus Garvey. The material is equipped with fulsome learned endnotes and bibliography (this 1997 edition comes with a further 33 pages of "Epilogue" and supplementary notes responding to issues raised by reviewers). While Afrocentrism may principally be a movement within the African American community, the needs it attempts to address directly reflect those issues of African identity that have dominated African intellectual life for more than a century, and which infuse the concerns of African theology, and of African Christian self-understanding. Mbiti once claimed, very rightly, that given a two-thousand-year presence on the African continent, African Christianity deserves to be recognized as one of Africa's traditional religions. The reminder is both salutary and historically justifiable. This book, and the controversy it represents, are also a reminder that such historical self-affirmations are best pursued with a greater regard for historical credibility than has at times characterized the Afrocentric movement. To counterpoint European myth-making about Africa with what is hardly more plausible myth-making does not serve Africa's best interests.

Leiderman, P. Herbert

see review 638

633. Lemarchand, René

The Dynamics of Violence in Central Africa: National and Ethnic Conflict in the 21st Century

Philadelphia: Penn Press, 2009. 344 pages, ISBN: 9780812220902.

Lemarchand is Professor Emeritus of Political Science at the University of Florida. In this book he has collected a series of his own essays, written over the past two decades, giving his analysis of the tragically intertwined histories of Rwanda, Burundi and Congo (DRC). In Part 1 he sets the stage by examining some of the misconceptions about the causes of the recent violence in these three countries. No, this is not simply an African problem. The various ways in which Western governments and corporations have been involved in this region from the time of the Congo Free State down to the present must be included as critically important causal factors. Neither can these wars be understood simply as conflicts over resources. Complex questions of identity, and of exclusion from meaningful political roles based on historically shaped and yet constantly shifting socio-political constructions of identity (e.g. "Hutu," "Tutsi," "Munyamulenge," "Rwandophone," etc.), have played a disastrous role in all three countries. Moreover, the author demonstrates convincingly that contemporary events cannot be understood without a deep knowledge of historical struggles over land-ownership rights and citizenship, and the ways in which the different histories of these three countries are inseparably intertwined.

Part 2 takes a more detailed look at the ways in which these themes have played out in the mutually reinforcing genocidal histories of Rwanda and Burundi, in the context of a "mythology" of ethnic identities and histories. Part 3 is made up of a number of essays devoted to analysing the possible (though feeble) prospects for peace that seemed to be emerging out of the Great African War in Congo – a war whose final outcome has yet to be fully determined. Despite the fact that the book is a collection of essays written over two decades, there is substantial unity to the overall presentation. Nevertheless, the essays can feel repetitious at times, as earlier material has to be revisited as background in later material. Also earlier essays are inevitably somewhat dated. But this is still a very strong contribution, and is highly recommended for anyone seeking a better understanding of this conflicted region.

634.   LeMarquand, Grant

An Issue of Relevance: A Comparative Study of the Story of the Bleeding Woman (Mk 5:25–34; Mt 9:20–22; Lk 8:43–48) in North Atlantic and African Contexts

New York: Peter Lang, 2004. 284 pages, ISBN: 9780820469287.

What is the relationship between biblical exegesis and application? This book shows that African scholarship tries to keep the two together while European and North American scholarship tends to make a sharp disjunction between the two. For North Atlantic scholarship, exegesis is a highly scientific enterprise, often utilising higher critical methods to discover the original meaning of a text. But in Africa the text is more readily understood in the present-day context. This is illustrated by the story of the healing of the bleeding woman, recounted in all three Synoptic gospels. The author approaches this story from three angles, in respect of miracle, women and blood. On miracles, we discover that the Western interpreter is uncomfortable with miracles. Exegesis of this text characteristically uses source criticism, form criticism, and redaction criticism to address the original setting of the text. But for most of these scholars "the miraculous is perceived to be an embarrassment" and the practical relevance is often suppressed. African interpreters in contrast believe that miracles happen and that God heals. Thus for the African the story is real and relevant; the text is related to their present situation. On the woman issue, before 1980 most North Atlantic scholars paid little attention to the woman in the story. But the rise of feminism in the 1980s relates the story to the female situation but with "a high degree of caution." The African, however, sees the woman's plight and her response as typical for African women today. As for the issue of blood, before 1980 in the North Atlantic situation the blood was either ignored or scientifically objectified; but feminism and Jewish interests began to focus on the issue of ritual cleanness. Africans, on the other hand, see the immediate relevance of the story to the social situation of a woman who is menstruating. This case study reveals different attitudes to exegesis and hermeneutics. North Atlantic exegesis tends to be scientific and sterile. But for the African the text becomes alive and relevant. Maybe Africa can point the way for a more living understanding of the text.

635. LeMarquand, Grant, and Joseph D. Galgalo, editors

Theological Education in Contemporary Africa

Eldoret: Zapf Chancery, 2004. 264 pages, ISBN: 9789966974266.

This collection of essays stems from papers presented at a consultation on theological education held in 2003 at St. Paul's United Theological College (now St. Paul's University) in Limuru, Kenya. A sampling of a few essays must suffice for providing the flavour of the whole. Musa Dube, in her "Current Issues in Biblical Interpretation," focuses attention on feminist biblical studies on the continent (which she believes to represent the "cutting edge" at that moment). The unique contribution of this sector has been in applying innovative theories and methods such as, "storytelling, divination, post-colonial, bosade/womanhood, post-apartheid Black feminist readings and in addressing issues of gender and colonialism in African biblical translations." Godfrey Nguru helpfully compares and contrasts residential and distance approaches to theological education, especially tracking the variety of delivery systems that have gone beyond the traditional residential model, beginning with TEE programmes and now (at time of publication, that is) with the initial forays into online formats. Online delivery is giving African students much greater access to theological education originating from beyond Africa's borders, for good or ill. Peter Mageto attempts to place the HIV/AIDS crisis within a constructive pastoral theology framework, contending that the immense suffering presented by the AIDS pandemic offers the church an opportunity to take up its role as an instrument of healing rather than one of condemnation. Additional essays include: "The Teaching of Theology in Africa: Some Reflections on Sources, Methods and Curriculum"; "Christian Theological Education in the Context of the Religiously Pluralistic Continent of Africa"; "Approaches to Teaching Islam in the Twenty First Century"; and "Theological Education and the Youth in the Family, Church, and School." As usual, a collection of fairly brief contributions means that content will remain fairly general, and that quality will be somewhat uneven. Nevertheless, this volume contains enough thoughtful reflection on the task of theological education in Africa to warrant notice.

LeMarquand, Grant

see also review 802

636. Lemelle, Sidney J., and Robin D. G. Kelley, editors

Imagining Home: Class, Culture and Nationalism in the African Diaspora

London: Verso Books, 1994. 384 pages, ISBN: 9780860915850.

Most of the essays in this volume grew out of a 1988 conference held at Pomona College in the United States under the title "Pan-Africanism Revisited." As one of the Haymarket Series, the book represents views from American left-wing intellectuals on the history and development of Pan-Africanist thought, with considerable emphasis on the influence of class consciousness, and gender to a lesser extent, in the construction of cultural identities and the formation of diaspora/Black nationalist political organisations. *Imagining Home* is an effort to rethink the history of Pan-Africanism and to document the varying ways in which people of the African diaspora have continually reinvented and imagined the home of their ancestors. The first section examines the cultural politics of Pan-Africanism; the second reconsiders some of the intellectuals who were influential in its development; part three deals primarily with Southern African influences on US politics and economics; and the fourth part critiques the scope and vision of Pan-Africanism. The ambivalent place of Africa in the imaginations, cultures and politics of its New World descendants becomes apparent, as the influence of grassroots religious and cultural movements is investigated, and the historical, ideological and institutional connections between South Africa and Afro-Americans. This is a specialist book for the student of Black American ideologies, and is focussed more on North America than on Africa.

637. Leonard, David K., and Scott Strauss

Africa's Stalled Development: International Causes and Cures

Boulder, CO: Lynne Rienner Publishers, 2003. 159 pages, ISBN: 9781588261168.

The authors of this very helpful book begin by noting the strong consensus among scholars that African political systems manifest a marked tendency toward what has variously been referred to as "personal" or "patronage" politics, or "(neo-) patrimonialism." They contend that while such descriptions are accurate enough, what is needed is an account of the historical causes and/or structural supports for such systems. Is this consistency primarily due to primordial tendencies within African cultures and ancient ethnic loyalties, or is it attributable to Africa's historical place in a set of international relationships? The book's subtitle betrays the authors' basic answer to this question. They maintain that, while we ought not to ignore cultural factors, Africa's political systems trace back to and are sustained by "enclave" economic realities. "Enclave production entails export of primary products (usually extractive) that are generated in a small area." This type of economic system had its initial manifestation in the slave trade (product: labour; clearly extractive; generated at certain slave ports), and the same essential pattern has continued to characterize Africa's connection to the outside world ever since. With notable exceptions, African states have developed in contexts where their primary source of revenue has been linked to the extraction of resources for external consumption. Enclave economies generate income for state officials in the form of taxes on exports and constitute "the foundation for personal rule." Given this kind of economic structure, political elites have little or no incentive to promote the kind of local economic development that would be beneficial to the broader population. More controversially, perhaps, the authors also argue that too often overseas development aid has functioned somewhat like an enclave economy, providing state officials with a possible source of income (*détournement*) that is once again independent of the productivity of the local economy. On the basis of their analysis, the authors make a number of recommendations for changes in international policy that they feel could break the cycle that has prevented development from taking off in many African countries. Studies such as this one suggest, among other things, why discussions on contextualizing the gospel in Africa need to move beyond issues relating primarily to traditional culture, and attend as well to major non-traditional factors that affect modern Africa.

LeRoux, J.

see review 885

638. **LeVine, Robert A., Sarah LeVine, Suzanne Dixon, Amy Richman, P. Herbert Leiderman, Constance Keefer, and T. Berry Brazelton**

Child Care and Culture: Lessons from Africa

Cambridge: Cambridge University Press, 1997. 380 pages, ISBN: 9780521575461.

This is a research study of the child rearing goals, assumptions, and behaviour of the Gusii people of south-western Kenya. It was carried out by a distinguished group of anthropologists and physicians, under the direction of Robert LeVine of Harvard University. The study documents changes within Gusii society over several decades, and also compares the results of detailed observations of Gusii mothers with corresponding observations of middle-class American mothers on current child-rearing behaviours. The differences that emerge in both maternal behaviour and infant development are discussed within Robert LeVine's cultural mediation model, illustrating the effects of cultural models and goals of parenthood on the behaviour of mothers in their respective cultures. The book richly documents how universal human traits are filtered through ecological and cultural conditions, resulting in varying goals and assumptions regarding childcare across cultural groups. One of the lessons, therefore, is a warning against seeking for a universal pattern for healthy childcare. Although this study was scientific in nature, it takes helpful notice of relationships between family practices and the religious beliefs of the parents. This comparative study of childcare will help both Western and African parents to define their current goals for their children, evaluate how situations and parental goals have changed in their societies, and then adapt their practices to suit their goals in ways that are healthful for their children. The book is written for university-level readers, and thus would be especially useful for those reflecting on or teaching about aspects of family living and child rearing in Africa.

LeVine, Sarah

see review 638

639. **Levison, John R., and Priscilla Pope-Levison, editors**

Return to Babel: Global Perspectives on the Bible

Louisvillle: WJK, 1999. ISBN: 9780664258238.

This book is an exciting experiment! Ten biblical texts are interpreted: Genesis 11:1–9, Exodus 20:1–17, Psalm 23:1–6, Ecclesiastes 3:1–8, Isaiah 52:13–53:12, Matthew 5:1–12, John 1:1–18, Acts 2:1–42, 1 Corinthians 15:1–58, and Revelation 21:1–22:5. Each text is given three interpretations, reflecting Latin American, Asian, and African perspectives respectively, and each interpretation follows the same structure: context, text, and reflection. The result is a collection of 30 essays, none previously published. Some of the essays are brilliant, others are probably included simply to complete the pattern of the book. Nevertheless, as a whole the essay collection is very valuable, as it provides the reader with relevant comparable material. In a time focussing on contextual theology and biblical interpretation it is most useful to have one single volume offering ten such sets of interpretations, each set reflecting the same three geographical and sociological perspectives. The African contributors – Solomon Avotri (Ghana), Hannah Kinoti (Kenya), Timothy Kiogora (Kenya), Francois Kabasele Lumbala (Congo-DRC), and Patrice Siyemeto (Zambia) – succeed in letting African experiences encounter the biblical texts. Thus, as just one example, Kinoti's interpretation of Psalm 23 manages to find a good balance between traditional and current African experiences. The metaphor of the shepherd certainly appeals to people living close to their domestic animals, sometimes having to protect their flock against hyenas and lions, but it also serves as a source of comfort in the face of current insecurity in Africa. The editors are both professors at Duke University Divinity School in the United States. They have provided a valuable source book for researchers, lecturers and graduate students concerned with contextual biblical interpretation, whether in Africa or elsewhere.

640.   Levtzion, Nehemia, and Randall L. Pouwels, editors

The History of Islam in Africa

Athens, OH: Ohio University Press, 2000. 591 pages, ISBN: 9780821412978.

This excellent volume represents a pioneering approach in treating the history of Islam in Africa on a continent-wide scale. During a conference sponsored by the Van Leer Jerusalem Institute in 1997, some 24 scholars from Israel, Germany, France, USA, South Africa and Kenya interacted at two complementary levels, bringing together the ideas of those who wrote on consecutive periods with those who wrote regional chapters or general thematic chapters. The book opens with an overview by the editors of the diverse patterns of Islamisation in Africa. After a brief survey on the progress of Islam in the major geographical regions, it focuses on state-driven reforms, the role of brotherhoods (predominantly of Sufi origin) for the development of Islam especially in West Africa, the perception of jihad (commonly understood as "holy war" in Islam) by various Islamic proponents across the continent, and how Islam fared under colonial rule, as well as Muslim political ambitions after colonialism up to the mid-nineties (especially in South Africa). This introductory article is quite fascinating reading in itself. In the next section the two gateways used by Islam to enter the African continent are considered, namely from the east and the north. "From both directions the carriers of Islam navigated across vast empty spaces, the waters of the Indian Ocean, and the desert sands of the Sahara," finding excellent transmitters of religious and cultural influence, and encountering filters that slowed down the process of infiltration. The area articles follow, and are well balanced between West Africa with Sudan (eight chapters) and Eastern and Southern Africa (six chapters). Here the article by Jean-Louis Triaud on "Islam in Africa under French Colonial Rule" deserves special attention in pointing out the stark contrasts between the French and British colonial policies. Thus while Britain was quite willing to delegate jurisdictional powers to local Islamic rulers in applying its policy of indirect rule, the French were constantly afraid of conspiracies from the Islamic brotherhoods and imposed a strong authoritarian system on Muslims and non-Muslims alike. The concluding section gives excellent introductions to matters of Law, Women, Education, Islamic Brotherhoods, Folk Islam, Art and Culture, Literature, and Music. With as many as 100 entries in the bibliographies of each article, the reader finds a rich stimulus for further exploration. Possibly a separate article in this section on the practice and effects of slavery would have been justified, as it affected the lives of Africans in both East and West in a significant way. Even so, this is indeed a uniquely valuable volume bringing together the best of scholarship to introduce the student to a comprehensive approach to Islam on the African continent.

Lewis, Damien

see review 779

641. Lewis, Donald M., editor

Christianity Reborn: The Global Expansion of Evangelicalism in the Twentieth Century

Grand Rapids: Eerdmans, 2004. 334 pages, ISBN: 9780802824837.

The chapters that comprise *Christianity Reborn* were originally delivered at a 1999 consultation of the "Currents in World Christianity Project" at St. Catherine's College, Oxford. The focus of the project was the transformation of Christianity in the twentieth century, especially Protestantism in its various forms. At this consultation, and in this text, the focus is more on the evangelical side of the Protestant movement, including Pentecostalism. The editor of the collection has been professor of church history at Regent College, Vancouver, and is editor of the *Blackwell Dictionary of Evangelical Biography, 1730–1860*. Rather than attempt a global sweep (as did Philip Jenkins), this text offers narrower slices as representations of the larger picture. However, those slices are still quite large, as demonstrated by the treatments of Oceania, West Africa, and Latin America in single chapters. The apology for the fact that there is no chapter on Korean Christianity, however, is one indicator of the scope necessary to seriously explore twentieth-century global evangelical Protestantism. Each author is a recognized expert in the geographic area being explored. The reader is left with a sense of the vast breadth of impact of Protestantism around the globe during the twentieth century. Indeed, the vibrancy of conservative Christian faith in the majority world comes through clearly. Regrettably, despite the focus indicated in its subtitle, mainstream African evangelical Christianity is not addressed in this collection of essays. Treatment is provided instead on specific examples of Pentecostalism and African Independent Churches on the continent. Hanciles brings the reader up to date on some of the more recent contours of West African Pentecostalism and provides a nuanced treatment of the processes of conversion seen through a sociological lens. Daneel explores the phenomena of AIC growth in Zimbabwe, wrestling with typologies and digging out insider explanations of the praxis of AICs. In this way the book makes a useful, if also only partial, contribution to framing modern African Christianity within the larger frame of Protestant Christianity globally.

642. Leys, Colin

The Rise and Fall of Development Theory

Bloomington, IN: Indiana University Press, 1996. 216 pages, ISBN: 9780253210166.

This volume contains nine essays originally published between 1977 and 1996, thus covering the period that made the exponents of "development theory" (based on the idea of "autonomous national development") painfully aware that the theory did not in fact work. Leys is convinced that "neo-liberalism," which leaves everything to the free interplay of global market forces, is no solution either. He is convinced that Socialist theory can still contribute a lot to development thinking, especially using Socialist insights on capitalist production and class relations (and not stressing the Socialism which comes after that). Five essays deal directly with Africa and provide much food for thought, showing not least that development theory often has been just that: theory which is struggling to come to terms with reality and trying (!) to improve that reality. Theological assessment of the African situation must learn how to correlate such reflection to rapidly evolving economic realities, and to go beyond the easy slogans of "the church's option for the poor" to find out how that could be worked out – if at all – in an actual economy. Although this is not a book that directly addresses Christian issues, the issues raised merit serious reflection among all those wishing to relate the Christian faith to Africa's developing economic realities.

Libawing, Benjamin L.

see review 771

643. Lierop, Peter van

Christian Education: Principles and Practice

Nairobi: Christian Churches Educational Association, 1992. 231 pages.

The author was a missionary for many years in Korea, with much experience in the field of Christian Education. He was consequently invited to lead seminars in Kenya on that topic, and was then asked by the Christian Churches Educational Association in Kenya to publish the material. The author has attempted to cover most areas of this important subject in this one book. The book is divided into five main sections, covering respectively the history and philosophy of Christian Education, applicable principles and methods, working with various age groups, special techniques, and the organisation and administration of the Sunday School. At the end of every section is a practical summary. The author is to be commended for presenting the material in an easy, systematic way, with many practical insights, so that any reader can understand and profit. Among other things, he points out that music used properly in the Church can achieve the objectives of Christian Education, that counselling is needed for Christian service in the Church and in schools, and what it takes to have a good Sunday School programme. Given the author's extensive cross-cultural experience, it would have been more helpful had he attempted more contextualisation of the material. African readers will agree with the general ideas presented about Christian Education, but might consider some of the practical suggestions very Western and hard to implement in the African context. The book would be a useful resource for lecturers in Christian Education in Africa.

644. Lierop, Peter van

Pastoral Counseling: A Comprehensive Text for Pastors, Counselors, Teachers

Nairobi: CCEA, 1996. 142 pages, ISBN: LANG255430.

This book had its genesis in the teaching ministry of the author in South Korea. Following seminars he was invited to give in Kenya, the Christian Churches Educational Association in Kenya arranged to publish his material for use in Africa. The book represents a distillation of contributions from Western writers, theorists and practitioners in the field of counselling and psychotherapy. Its usefulness lies in the access it provides to many thinkers and practitioners in the area of counselling, material which is either not easily available to the student or pastor in Africa or which is beyond their means. In his introduction Lierop makes a case for the necessity of counselling that has a spiritual dimension, and he gives a useful definition of counselling which moves to the goal of God-honouring wholeness. Part 1 of the book introduces some of the older theorists, such as Freud, Jung, Rank, Sullivan, Horney, Fromm, and Rogers, as well as some schools of psychotherapy. Part 2 of the book deals with some of the basic requirements wherever one might do the counselling and whatever one's orientation, reminding about the importance of the counsellor's personality, the quality of relationship with the counselees, and the role of communication skills. Lierop then deals with Depth Counselling, Crisis Counselling, Confrontational Counselling (in which he presents the approaches of Glasser, Mowrer and his disciples, Frankl and Perls' Gestalt Therapy), and an approach to Marriage Counselling. The rest of the book (more than half) gives help in counselling a variety of common problems including fear and anxiety, anger and hostility, guilt, grief, and depression. He also gives help in dealing with those facing loneliness and pain, and a helpful chapter on death and dying (which draws on the research of Kubler-Ross). Pastors will also find the chapter on visiting the sick useful. The extensive bibliography includes titles authored 30 to even 60 years ago. Nevertheless this particular book will be welcome to many because it is much more affordable and readily available in Africa than other resources.

Lind, Tim

see review 1101

645. Linn, Stella, Maarten Mous, and Marianne Vogel, editors

Translation and Interculturality: Africa and the West

Frankfurt: Peter Lang, 2008. 156 pages, ISBN: 9783631576427.

This volume, consisting of eleven papers presented at a 2004 conference at the University of Groningen in the Netherlands, offers an eclectic set of ideas and studies, which all revolve around positive and negative aspects of translation work, especially at the interface between Western and African cultures. The subjects treated are diverse, from the translation of medical textbooks to translation as an aspect of nation-building in post-apartheid South Africa. Ten of the essays are in English and one in French. Only three are on Bible translation in Africa, and these are themselves extremely different. One, by Emilie Sanon-Ouattara, investigates a sermon on the death of Jesus in Matthew's gospel preached by a Roman Catholic Archbishop at a Mass in Burkina Faso on Good Friday in 2003. At that service the Archbishop preached the "same" sermon twice, first in French and then in the local language, Jula. The similarities and differences between the two presentations, analysed according to what was added and what was omitted when the preacher turned from French to Jula, are a fascinating glimpse into how the rhetorical style of presentations may shift depending on the perceived needs and abilities of the target audience. Harriet Hill investigates how the Adioukrou translation of the Bible (from the Ivory Coast) has shaped the worldview of the Christians of that language group by traditional terminology being filled with biblical content. She notes also that terms from the culture which were not used in the translation of the Bible have not been transformed by the Bible's message. Gerrit van Steenbergen contrasts the worldview of the book of Isaiah with the worldview of the Pokot of northwestern Kenya, concluding that the faith communities who initiate translation projects would do well to note that translation is only the beginning of the interpretative process. While these three essays are relevant for those involved in Bible translation and interpretation in Africa, the volume as a whole is too specialized to be recommended for general attention.

646. Linz, Johanna, editor

Kirchen und Demokratisierung in Afrika: Neuere Entwicklungen im afrikanischen Christentum

Hamburg: Evangelisches Missionswerk in Deutschland, 1995. 63 pages, ISBN: LANG255444.

This booklet on the church and democratisation in Africa is made up of two articles: Paul Gifford's "Neuere Entwicklungen im afrikanischen Christentum" (a translation of: "Some Recent Developments in African Christianity," first published in *African Affairs* [93 (1994) 513–534]); and Nicolas Otieno's "Afrikas Kampf um Selbstbestimmung" ["Africa's Struggle for Self-Determination"]. Gifford is a New Zealander with African experience, who was a professor at the School of Oriental and African Studies in London. Here he is summarising overall church developments in Africa in the 1980s (excluding South Africa, on the grounds that it is already covered by many other studies). He treats respectively: the rise of new prosperity gospel churches and merely evangelistic movements without social/political elements, the weakness of the traditional Protestant churches, and the foreignness of the Catholic Church. The study is descriptive, but the undertone is rather critical towards American influences and new charismatic-pentecostal churches. Also the description is very generalising, supporting the main thesis with scant examples. Otieno is Director of the Civic Resource and Information Centre in Nairobi. He covers the modern history of Africa in broad strokes: colonialism, "négritude," panafricanism, and the Cold War in Africa. He advocates "négritude" and a stronger Africanisation of the church, and criticizes not only (neo-)colonialism but also African leadership. Following Africa's liberation from foreign domination in the 1960s, it now needs a second liberation from oppressive internal structures. The Church could and should play a positive role in this process, avoiding tribalism and authoritarian structures. The article is a very basic summary of well-known positions. The booklet intends to provide a brief, generalising overview for public readership in the churches of Europe.

Little, John

see review 438

Lo, Jim

see review 783

647. Loba-Mkole, Jean-Claude, and Ernst R. Wendland, editors

Interacting with Scriptures in Africa

Nairobi: Acton Publishers, 2005. 206 pages, ISBN: 9789966888532.

The essays in this volume, highly varied in method and focus, consider the diverse ways in which the Scriptures are presented in African translations today. Most contributions stem from papers presented at conferences. Three of them examine Bible translation and scholarly research. Three further ones look at Bible study notes in particular translations (Kikongo, Chichewa, Akan). The final four studies investigate Scripture in non-print media such as audio-cassette and the performing arts. Here only a sampling is possible, but this sampling helps to portray the variety of materials covered. Gerald West of the University of Natal contends that the post-colonial context which remembers the way in which the Bible was used against Africans by "missionaries and colonial agents" is "the background to all African biblical hermeneutics." Aloo Osotsi Mojola examines the difficulties involved in translating names for deities into African languages. One essay forcefully makes the case for theological lexicons written in African languages. Another presents a thorough study of Scripture produced in audio form for teenagers in Yaoundé, Cameroon. Ernst Wendland offers notes on a "lyricized version of the Lord's Prayer in Chichewa." The difficulty in assessing this collection stems from the sheer variety of its content, involving as it does materials that are appropriately addressed to different audiences. For example, the three articles related specifically to individual languages contain material translated into those languages. Anyone not understanding those languages would of course have difficulty comprehending the arguments presented. At the same time, an essay such as Kathleen Jenabu Noss on "Communicating Scriptures through African Performing Arts" is a unique contribution to understanding what is certainly almost unexplored territory. The nature of this book inevitably delimits its usefulness. But since the essays are broadly linked by the topic of the Bible in Africa, the book could have value as a reference work at advanced theological libraries on the continent.

Loba-Mkole, Jean-Claude

see also review 759

648. Logan, Willis H., editor

The Kairos Covenant: Standing with South African Christians

New York: Friendship Press, 1988. 184 pages, ISBN: 9780377001893.

The *Kairos Document* was written by a group of (primarily black) South African theologians at the height of the political conflict in that country in the mid-1980s. The intention was to jolt the church in general from a neutral position to a pro-liberation position. The Document declared, "The time has come. It is the *kairos*, or moment of truth, not only for apartheid but also for the church." This book presents the original *Kairos Document* along with other supporting materials. Logan was director of the Africa Committee in the Division of Overseas Ministries of the National Council of Churches, USA. In his preface to this volume, he states, "The *Kairos Document* is a prophetic statement that presents a direct challenge to all Christians inside and outside South Africa. . . . It is a profound appeal for reflection and action." The book is divided into six sections: the *Kairos Document*, State Theology, Church Theology, Prophetic Theology, *The Kairos Covenant* (an expression of solidarity with South African Christians by USA Christians), and a discussion guide. Beliefs held by many Christians concerning such themes as the authority of God versus the state, law and order, violence, suffering, reconciliation, justice, and hope are critiqued and challenged theologically. Perhaps because the *Kairos Document* came from a largely non-evangelical grouping, it came under heavy criticism by conservative and evangelical groups, a few of which called for its banning. Although the reader may not agree with everything in the book, yet given the political and social conflicts raging throughout Africa, Christian reflection in Africa would do well to wrestle with some of the issues here surfaced, which seem relevant beyond the South African context.

649.   **Long, Meredith W.**

Health, Healing and God's Kingdom: New Pathways to Christian Health Ministry in Africa

Oxford: Regnum, 2000. 288 pages, ISBN: 9781870345361.

Long is Director of International Health Programs for the agency World Relief. Drawing on the comment from an African, "The doctor treats my disease; the nganga heals me," he sets out in this study to identify a biblical pathway that incorporates the strengths and redeems the weaknesses of both modern scientific medicine and traditional African health practices. His work for over two decades in international health, including seven years in Kenya, combined with his wide reading and reflections on Scripture and professional literature, enable Long to illustrate freely with stories, proverbs and insights on how the two pathways reflected in the comment above can be transformed into the holistic health brought by "the one true Healer." Long begins with a careful study of the biblical concept of shalom as it is developed first in the OT and then in its fullness through Christ in the NT. He notes close ties between the OT understanding of health and African traditional views, especially on the causes of suffering in people as well as in the environment, and he identifies the importance to health in both traditions of right relationships within the community. He then identifies specific ways in which biblical shalom reveals the distant God of African tradition to be our loving Father, replaces fatalism with God's love and power, and transforms the ambivalent pressures of African community relationships with the reconciliation and compassionate service of God's healing kingdom. He concludes with specific suggestions on how Christian medical practitioners might incorporate these insights into their work, together with Bible studies designed to guide Christian ministers and communities into God's shalom. This well-written book can be read with understanding by lay people as well as by medical and theological professionals, and will be a valuable resource for anyone engaged in Christian ministry to alleviate suffering in Africa.

Long, Meredith W.

see also review 280

650.   **Lovejoy, Paul E., and Jan S. Hogendorn**

Slow Death for Slavery: The Course of Abolition in Northern Nigeria, 1897–1936

Cambridge: Cambridge University Press, 1993. 412 pages, ISBN: 9780521447027.

In 1897 there were large slave plantations in Northern Nigeria owned by officials and merchants of the Sokoto Caliphate. Slave owning, raiding and trading were common. As the British conquered this area, colonial officials needed to comply with British law prohibiting slavery, but also prevent chaos if social and economic patterns were suddenly overthrown. They also needed to keep on the good side of the slave owners so that they could rule without too much opposition. The book outlines Lord Lugard's strategy. First, slave raiding and selling were outlawed, and anyone born after March 31, 1901 was declared automatically free. People recently captured who wanted to go back home were allowed. Then by a series of policies and decrees it was made very difficult for runaway slaves to find any land to farm outside their own community. Instead, slave owners were required to let any slave buy his own freedom who wanted to. The price was set by the British, and owners had to let slaves have time off and land to earn their own money, even if they charged a fee for the privilege. The British imposed taxation policies that made it cheaper for slave owners to free slaves and rent land to them, and so on. The policies did result in the gradual end of slavery without much disruption to the country. All slavery was outlawed by 1936. The early policies did not help female slaves who were used as concubines, however, and secret slave raiding, especially of children, continued on a small scale. The book says little about missions and Christianity in Nigeria except to note that one of the reasons Lugard did not allow missionaries in many places was that he did not want them to interfere with his strategy. He remembered his experience in East Africa where missions had encouraged slaves to run away from their masters and gave them refuge. The missionaries in Nigeria, however, did not seem very interested in doing this; it was too expensive for them to maintain the fugitives. Dr Walter Miller of the CMS was the most outspoken, but he largely supported the colonial government policy, as did most missionaries. The slave population was so huge that the missionaries also were afraid of chaos if the system changed too suddenly. This book explains much about the social structure in Northern Nigeria that affects evangelism and church planting even today. And all over Africa one may ponder, were the missionaries right to wait for a gradual end to slavery or should they have supported a more direct route?

651.   Lovejoy, Paul E.

Transformations in Slavery: A History of Slavery in Africa

Cambridge: Cambridge University Press, 2012. 412 pages, ISBN: 9780521176187.

A professor at York University in Canada, Lovejoy has spent his career studying African history and slavery. This book examines indigenous African slavery from the fifteenth century to the early twentieth century. Lovejoy uses Marxist and other models to examine the role that slaves had in the economy and society of different regions of Africa, how the external trade in slaves to the Muslim world and the Americas affected this role, greatly increasing the use of slaves by Africans, and the effects of the ending of the three aspects of slavery, namely of enslavement, distribution and use. The capture of fresh slaves continued after abolition of the external trade, so that slaves were retained in Africa by African masters to produce the "legitimate" trade goods required by the Europeans. Both colonialists and missionaries used anti-slavery rhetoric, but were cautious in practice to prevent attacks by African slave owners. Nevertheless, the Christian message, the actions of many mission personnel who disobeyed the official policies of their missions in harbouring runaway slaves, the change to a capitalist economy brought with colonialism, the official anti-slavery stance of the colonial powers, and the actions of slaves themselves who deserted their masters en masse when conditions permitted, all led to the end of institutionalized slavery in Africa by 1930. Lovejoy suggests that writers of African history have overlooked the legacy of slavery that could explain various relationships in the military, economic and political life of African societies. One would think that such considerations should also inform evangelisation and discipling strategies. This book is interesting in that a scholar using Marxist economic categories is ready to credit missions and the gospel with significant impact in ending slavery in Africa.

Low, Alaine

see review 537

652.   Ludwig, Frieder, and J. Kwabena Asamoah-Gyadu, editors

African Christian Presence in the West: New Immigrant Congregations and Transnational Networks in North America and Europe

Trenton, NJ: Africa World Press, 2011. 472 pages, ISBN: 9781592218073.

The editors, respectively from Hermannsburg Mission Seminary, Germany, and from Trinity Theological Seminary, Ghana, are to be congratulated for having compiled this most valuable survey of how the phenomenon of African immigrant churches is developing in Europe and USA. Their book results from a conference at Luther Seminary, St. Paul MN, in 2007, where the organizers succeeded in bringing together key researchers in this emerging field. The book consists of 23 articles organized into five parts (in addition to four appendices filled with further information and surveys). Part I addresses "the African Christian presence in the West and discourses on migration." In the introductory article, the two editors give a very concise survey of research into various aspects of African immigrant churches in Europe and North America. Another contribution is Ogbu Kalu's analysis of "mission in reverse," pointing out that the concept has played an important role in African missiological discourses back to the 1970s. Part II addresses "North American case studies." An interesting example here is Kwabena Asamoah-Gyadu's article on the presence of the Ghanaian Church of Pentecost in the US; this denomination now has churches in nearly half of the US states, and these – being organized by an Overseas Mission office back in Ghana – are able to channel Ghanaian Pentecostal spirituality into a North American context. Part III addresses "Comparisons and interactions." Here Jehu Hancile's article on the relationship between African (immigrant) churches in the US and more traditional African-American churches is particularly interesting. It is argued that collaboration between the two is difficult, due to a wide spectrum of cultural differences. In part IV, addressing "European case studies," Katrin Langewiesche's article on African Roman Catholic missionary networks between Africa and Europe refers to two congregations that are based in Burkina Faso but operate in Europe too. She discuss the fact that African religious brothers and sisters play an increasing role in Europe, whereas their European counterparts play decreasing roles in Africa. Part V addresses "Migrant theologies and theologies of migration." Here Andrew Walls, discussing migration as a biblical motif, points out two broad categories of migration in the OT: an "Adamic," involuntary and punitive migration, and an "Abrahamic" voluntary and hope-driven migration, both finding echoes in contemporary African migration to Europe and the US, thus both being relevant for the development of theologies of migration. This well-informed contribution in a rapidly emerging field of inquiry is both interesting and valuable.

Ludwig, Frieder

see also review 597

Luig, Ute

see review 118

653. Lund, Gregory

Theological Education in Africa: An Annotated Bibliography

Wheaton, IL: Billy Graham Center Archives, 1992. 50 pages.

This is a listing of publications relating to theological education in Africa. The principal section catalogues articles on this topic, organized (oddly enough) according to the journals in which they appeared. In most cases the articles are accompanied by one-paragraph descriptions, perhaps the most valuable aspect of this document. The final seven pages offer a listing of books and dissertations on the topic, with occasional annotations. No index of authors or titles is provided. Without that, and given the scheme of organisation, locating any individual article or book in the bibliography can be awkward. Also the coverage is uneven and incomplete. For example, while the preface states that the bibliography includes materials from 1921 to 1990, the mere fact that nothing is cited from the *International Review of Mission* prior to 1954 renders the significance of this claim uncertain. Nevertheless, absent the availability of something better organized and more comprehensive, a researcher might find this bibliography partially useful.

Luneau, René

see review 529

654. Lutz, Lorry

Sword and Scalpel: A Surgeon's Story of Faith and Courage

Orange, CA: Promise Publishing, 1990. 219 pages, ISBN: 9780939497218.

This is the life story of Robert Foster, a veteran medical missionary doctor in southern Africa. Foster was born in Zambia to pioneer missionary parents serving under the South African General Mission (SAGM). As was then the custom, at age five he was left at a missionary children's home in Canada when his parents returned to Africa. It would be eight years before his parents returned. Foster adjusted well, flourished, and felt called to be a missionary doctor. He was an academically gifted, self-assured, independent young man with leadership qualities. After graduation from the University of Toronto Medical School, he and his wife departed for service in Zambia. Foster was a man of focused determination, ever-expanding vision, and boundless energy. Among other things he built and staffed two hospitals in Zambia, and then another one in Angola. With a civil war raging, Angola was especially challenging, yet the Fosters considered their experience there the highlight of their missionary career. Despite an obvious love for the people of Africa, Foster was initially adamant in his refusal to let his missionary-nurse daughter marry a godly Angolan Christian worker. Ultimately he relented and warmly welcomed his Angolan brother in Christ and son-in-law into the family. In later years he became the International Director of the African Evangelical Fellowship (AEF), the new name for the SAGM. Under his visionary leadership new missionaries were recruited and new fields opened, so that the mandate of Andrew Murray for the SAGM, "Go Forward," was given new impetus. AEF subsequently merged with the international mission SIM. The author of the biography is a former AEF missionary. While learning a great deal about Foster and his medical and mission leadership roles, the reader of this account will gain little in terms of a better understanding of the political and social dynamics in play in southern Africa during the period under discussion.

Luz, Ulrich

see review 273

Lydon, Ghislaine

see review 602

655.   **Mabuntana, Phillipina, and Huibrecht McDonald**

Helping People to Good Health

Nairobi: Evangel, 1987. 257 pages, ISBN: LANG255365.

This programmed learning text has been written by two experienced South African health educationalists in collaboration with several doctors. Its purpose is to help people in general, as well as health care providers, to understand the basis for good health from a biblical perspective. Traditional beliefs regarding illness, as well as the scientific understanding of illness and health, are explored and compared with biblical teaching on health, especially on healthy relationships with God, oneself, others, and nature. The chapters deal with causes of ill health arising from disharmony in these areas, and use Scripture to teach how to restore harmony for healthful living. This is not a handbook on specific physical illnesses, treatments or preventions. Rather it deals extensively with spiritual, emotional and social aspects of illness and health. It uses many realistic vignettes with which African readers can easily identify. It forthrightly addresses harmful practices such as favouring one's own relatives or ethnic group in treatment, desire for revenge, and lack of concern for environmental damage. And it clearly guides readers to assurance of salvation through Christ rather than reliance on witchcraft to protect against the power of ancestral spirits. The last chapter deals with specific traditional causes for fear regarding illness, as well as the problems associated with some "prophet-healing churches" to which traditional people may be drawn for protection. Since it is a Theological Education by Extension (TEE) text, this book is designed to be understandable to people who have achieved three years of secondary school. It gives very clear instructions to readers on using the text as their daily teacher over a ten-week period, with the expectation that they will meet weekly in groups with a TEE facilitator for discussion, following the usual TEE pattern. The style is therefore repetitive in order to ensure that the lessons are learned by those for whom the book was designed. As a result the more accomplished reader may find the format and pace a bit tedious. The book has been tested widely and would be effective in communicating much helpful information on health care, along with the encouragement to trust the Lord and obey His directives regarding health. The text might well be useful not only in standard TEE programmes, but also for courses in community health at secondary-level Bible colleges, and for workshops and refresher courses for Christian health workers. Given its specialized focus, pastors should certainly be aware of its availability and usefulness.

Macharia, Paul

see review 686

656. Mackenzie, Rob

David Livingstone: The Truth behind the Legend

Tain, UK: CFP, 2002. 400 pages, ISBN: 9781857926156.

David Livingstone remains one of the respected figures of African history. Published at a time when the major biographies of Livingstone have been out of print, Mackenzie's book is a welcome addition to the study of this extraordinary man of Africa. Himself an Assemblies of God pastor in Zimbabwe, Mackenzie writes as an evangelist, church planter and theological educator. Writing from this perspective enables him to craft a sympathetic though by no means uncritical account of the life and work of Livingstone, paying particular attention to the motivation and inspiration behind his work and travel – something earlier biographies have either played down or not properly understood. For Livingstone it was the atonement of Christ that lay at the root of his burden and vision for Africa. Far from assuming it to be an obsolete doctrine for students of historical theology, Livingstone retrieved the atonement from the domain of privatized Christianity and set it to work in Africa. The life of Livingstone is the story of a staggering commitment and perseverance in the face of unimaginable hardships. Everything was sacrificed for the sake of the people of Africa – his own physical wellbeing; his relationships; his wife Mary who sought solace in alcohol; his children who hardly knew their missionary-explorer father. Africa may have good cause to rise up and call David Livingstone "blessed," but it is doubtful if any of his children ever did the same. Livingstone was a "driven" man of terrifying proportions, and it is not surprising that few could keep up with him and that his relationships with others faltered as a result. Mackenzie has told a gripping story. Occasionally he lapses into a style that might be more appropriate for a Victorian Sunday School class (also including a closing chapter on the ministry of Reinhard Bonnke is decidedly awkward). But once he gets going, Mackenzie knows how to keep the pages turning. For anyone wanting to study the secondary material on Livingstone, this book could be a good place to begin.

657. MacMaster, Richard, and Donald Jacobs

A Gentle Wind of God: The Influence of the East African Revival

Scottdale, PA: Herald Press, 2006. 404 pages, ISBN: 9780836193183.

This book, by a retired Mennonite academic, assisted by a former missionary in East Africa, is written primarily for the Mennonite community. Yet it is a very helpful addition to the resources now available on the East African Revival (henceforth EAR). The preface and first three chapters of the book deal with the history of the EAR, and include accurate details of the main leaders such as Blasio Kigozi, Simeon Nsibambi, William Nagenda, Yosiya Kinuka, Joe Church, and (later) Festo Kivengere and the multi-racial African Evangelistic Enterprise. The author has taken great care to document his historical record, so that the endnotes are another helpful resource available to the reader. One of the early links of the EAR with the Mennonites is Don Jacobs (who later lectured at the University of Nairobi and spoke at Festo Kivengere's funeral in 1988). Jacobs wrote soon after his arrival in East Africa in 1954 that, "I have met the Anabaptists and they are Africans!" (He was impressed with the pacifism of EAR leaders during the Mau Mau tension in Kenya). The book then develops the ongoing relationship of the Mennonite church in the USA to the EAR, following various missionaries in their US travels, sometimes accompanied by EAR leaders. One of the strengths of the book is its willingness to examine the practical results (and failings) of the EAR, such as Jacobs' claim that he never knew of any irregularities when he was intimately involved in EAR's finances. The author openly discusses the tension between the North American Mennonite insistence on conservative dress codes and the more flexible perspective of the EAR brethren at that time; there was difficulty later on this same issue within the Revival Brethren. The threatened division over the use of charismatic gifts is also addressed carefully. The latter chapters will be of greater interest to Mennonites than to other students of the EAR – especially the long sections listing who spoke where in the USA! Also, the 37 pages of testimonies at the end of the book are limited to North American Mennonites, so the subtitle should probably have added "on the Mennonites." Yet the reflections on the EAR toward the end of the book are especially thoughtful and explicit. This book is a well-researched contribution to African missions history as well as EAR history.

658.   **Magesa, Laurenti**

African Religion: The Moral Traditions of Abundant Life

Maryknoll, NY: Orbis, 2001. 304 pages, ISBN: 9781570751059.

This respected African Catholic theologian has here produced a wide-ranging, well-written and scholarly survey of indigenous African religion. He adopts a comprehensive, synchronic moral and ethical perspective that operates on the assumption that "from beginning to end, from birth to death, African religion stresses and orients its adherents, directly or symbolically, toward the 'abundance of life' motif." This crucial notion of "vital force" is manifested in multiple ways among virtually all African cultures in their system of beliefs, values, and norms (worldview); social institutions; rituals and traditions; marriage and kinship relations; concepts of good and evil; methods of personal or communal protection and self-preservation; as well as modes of socio-political interaction. These topics are discussed in a closely-knit sequence of chapters, each of which develops the author's central thesis, namely: the pre-eminent and pervasive influence of "life" in all its fullness in relation to: (1) the concept of "religion" itself (African religion vis-à-vis other "world religions"); (2) the moral universe (ancestral, spiritual, human, natural powers); (3) the mystique of life (its dynamic, multifaceted communal cycle); (4) transmitting the vital force (marriage, sexuality, procreation, protection); (5) the enemies of life (wrongdoing, witchcraft and affliction); (6) restoring the force of life (prayer, sacrifices & offerings, medicine, divination, protection specialists); (7) and "political" ethics (law, social order, conflict resolution). The concluding chapter helpfully summarizes the author's thesis and his main purpose in writing this book. As might be expected from a book attempting a panoramic overview of such a complex subject, there are inevitably a number of questionable generalisations, i.e. descriptions and assertions that apply to some African societies but certainly not to all (e.g. concerning incarnation, age-sets, blood brotherhood, and bride-wealth). Magesa's treatment is also rather idealized in places, either overly optimistic in its assessment of the resilience and value of certain religious principles and practices, or too strongly "traditional" in its outlook (giving us "the way things once were" rather than the disparate reality that we find all around us in Africa today). The author's positive, generally uncritical approach to his subject is perhaps motivated by his conclusion that, in its status as a great world religion "African Religion has a unique moral contribution to offer to the universal human quest for the Truth." This may leave readers with a fundamental question: can biblically-based Christianity offer the people of Africa anything better than what they already have (or at least had)? This is an impressive and worthwhile study of African traditional religion that lecturers on African religion and on African theology will need to read and reflect upon.

659. **Magesa, Laurenti**

African Religion in the Dialogue Debate: From Intolerance to Coexistence

Münster: LIT Verlag, 2010. 208 pages, ISBN: 9783643900180.

The author is a leading expert on African Christian theology and African traditional religion (ATR). Originally from Tanzania, Magesa holds a PhD from the University of Ottawa in Canada, and has been a lecturer at the Catholic University in Nairobi. Here he allows the reader to learn from the insights and concerns of one who has been working with the relationship between ATR and Christianity for decades. The book starts with a claim that might come as a surprise to some readers, namely that very little has been written on the role of ATR (Magesa prefers "AR," African Religion) from interreligious dialogue perspectives. This is probably correct, as far as institutionalized interreligious dialogue is concerned, and as such the book fills an unfortunate lacuna in the current discourse on ATR in relationship to other world religions, in particular to Christianity and Islam. At the same time, however, the relationship between ATR and Christianity has been a key concern of African Christian theology, and the author is therefore able to build on his own experiences and expertise when approaching this lacuna. The prologue and the first two chapters define some key concepts and argue for the necessity of the project. Chapter 3 offers a survey of ATR as a cultural and social factor. Chapter 4 raises the key question of whether a coexistence of ATR and Christianity is possible. Different models are discussed, and it is concluded that a coexistence presupposes the acceptance of the right of ATR to exist, and to avoid any form of Christian domination over it. Chapter 5 discusses some issues from dialogue experiences between Christianity and ATR, such as interpretive and hermeneutical models and the practical question of who might serve as spokespersons for ATR. Chapters 6 and 7 look at the role of ATR in contemporary African society and in academic studies of religion. Chapters 8 and 9 discuss the role of ATR vis-à-vis religious life, now and in the time ahead. And the epilogue concludes the book by relating the dialogue between ATR and Christianity to society's needs for justice, peace, and care for Mother Earth. The book reflects the author's Catholic (inculturation theological) background, and has less focus on ATR in relation to Islam than one would have expected from the title and introduction. Nevertheless, it is a useful orientation to the study of ATR in relation to other religions.

660. **Magesa, Laurenti**

Anatomy of Inculturation: Transforming the Church in Africa

Maryknoll, NY: Orbis, 2004. 286 pages, ISBN: 9781570755293.

Magesa is a Roman Catholic priest from Tanzania who has pursued a distinguished academic career. The present volume is a lengthy treatment of inculturation, which the author defines as "the process whereby the faith already embodied in one culture encounters another culture." Magesa says that such inculturation involves risk, and vital aspects of the message may be lost, but the process is nevertheless essential to effective communication. The assessment is primarily from a Catholic perspective. In terms of the biblical witness, Magesa finds evidence in the OT that Israel "intuitively incorporated" elements of the neighbouring religions into their worship of Yahweh. Biblical monotheism itself he sees as the culmination of such a process, suggesting a somewhat evolutionary approach to biblical revelation. In the same way the "current process of cultural-historical re-evaluation in Africa" may be seen as a "faithful response to God's continuing self-revelation in the African historical experience." Magesa goes on to claim that "both the African identity and the gospel identity possess within them an irreducible divine character because both enjoy divine origin," thereby rejecting the notion that culture is essentially human and therefore contingent. He refers to "the Word in the gospel" and "the Word in a culture." The revelation of God in the Christian scriptures meets the God who is "already present in the values of a culture." It is no surprise then that he can equate the Bible and African traditional religion (ATR) as both "more or less imperfect expressions of the unfathomable mystery of God." This allows Magesa to present syncretism in a positive light, for example in the case of a "staunch Catholic" who along with family and friends, and "in the context of their Christian faith," offered a sacrifice to appease a deceased wife who was troubling his dreams. The book serves to familiarize readers with core perspectives of this prominent African Catholic theologian on the relation of ATR and Christianity.

661.   Magesa, Laurenti, and Zablon Nthamburi, editors

Democracy and Reconciliation: A Challenge for African Christianity

Nairobi: Acton Publishers, 1999. 242 pages, ISBN: 9789966888259.

Winston Churchill reportedly once said that democracy is a terrible system of government – except when compared with all others. The contributors to this examination of democracy in Africa today would agree. The contributors are all from East Africa, with the exception of one from Ghana and one from South Africa, and represent both Protestant and Catholic traditions. In their introduction the editors state, "The general aim of the volume is to document the fact that although in practice 'democracy' may not be perfect or easily attainable, its tenets are worth promoting in every society and nation." In particular, they look at the church's responsibility not only to embrace democratic principles, but also to help foster these practices through its example to society at large. The need for such an inquiry arises of course from contemporary political history on the continent, whereby losers in the political arena refuse to accept defeat while winners determine to punish the vanquished. Yet democracy requires practices such as negotiation, compromise, and civility. In such an environment and in light of the demands of democracy, the church has the responsibility to act as an agent of reconciliation (hence the wording of the book's title). The book embodies two kinds of essays. Some essays focus on the subject matter in differing countries. Hence one finds essays on: "Civic Education for Democracy in Kenya," "The Church and Democratic Liberties in Uganda," and "The South African Truth and Reconciliation Discourse." Other essays focus on broader thematic issues with topics such as: "Women in the Democratization Process," "Religion and Democracy in Africa," and "Theology and Politics in Africa." In perhaps the most significant essay, Kanyandago of Uganda addresses a vital but too often overlooked issue in his "Management of Power and the Challenge of Democracy in the African Church." He contrasts the traditional African use of power to benefit the community with examples of contemporary practices within the church that fly in the face of such customs. In another helpful essay, Magesa constructs a "Theology of Democracy" from an African perspective. He proposes the clan as a useful model for the church in Africa. Interestingly, the first criterion to which such a model must adhere is, "Respect for the inalienable rights of an individual." Yet the concept of "inalienable rights" per individual is a thoroughly Western concept, based on an understanding of human nature that emerged only in the Enlightenment period of European history. In fact, the modern concept of "democracy" as a means of political organisation of the nation-state first emerges in the same context on the same theological basis. These underpinnings to the entire democratic enterprise in Africa warrant much deeper analysis. Overall, this is a useful volume on issues vital to what is happening on the ground in Africa today.

Magesa, Laurenti

see also reviews 586, 746 and 752

662. **Maier, Karl**

Into the House of the Ancestors: Inside the New Africa

Oxford: Wiley-Blackwell, 1999. 288 pages, ISBN: 9780470348284.

Here is another informed journalistic assessment of the state of modern Africa, in the style of David Lamb's *The Africans* (1987) and Blaine Harden's *Dispatches from a Fragile Continent* (1990) – an assessment which represents once again both the limitations and the usefulness of this genre. Maier was Africa correspondent for one of Britain's leading newspapers from 1986 to 1995. As is common to the genre, Maier proceeds by anecdote interwoven with factual summaries and with generalized assessment. The anecdotal material is richly authentic and impressive, and the factual data is realistic and clarifying, whereas Maier's attempted evaluative framing often seems derivative and perfunctory. Indeed Maier's stories repeatedly transcend the thematic agenda he has attempted to construct for them. One distinguishing theme that does succeed admirably is Maier's upbeat emphasis on the heroic quality of ordinary Africans in the midst of an increasingly chaotic and dysfunctional continent. If it is a fragile continent, Maier argues, it is not inhabited by fragile people! The book intends to celebrate the resilience of the African individual, and does so effectively. Another distinguishing but not so persuasive theme is the need to bring the values of Africa's pre-colonial heritage to bear on its problematic future. In expounding this, Maier especially wishes to accent the constructive role that African traditional religion might assume in solving the continent's predicaments. This possibility he expounds with an affirming pluralism worthy of a post-modern appraiser. African Christianity in contrast is only marginal to the overt themes of the book. Yet it is testament to the realism of Maier's stories that in many of them Christianity makes an unavoidable and often wholesome appearance in the background. Especially for everyone deeply immersed in the life of the continent, this book would prove a rewarding read. Maier's narratives luxuriantly expand horizons and enhance sensitivities to African realities. Also contemporary overviews of African Christianity might well take a bearing from Maier's emphases on the manifest resilience of individual Africans. Even as the African Christian community struggles to cope with the escalating instabilities of the continent, so that even its characteristic proliferation and exuberance seem increasingly impeded, nevertheless without a doubt the continent continues to be plentifully populated with heroic examples of individual African Christian believers functioning with courage amidst so much deprivation and tragedy. This may indeed be a fundamental (if also under-recognized) aspect of African Christian realities at the commencement of the twenty-first century.

663. **Maillu, David G.**

Our Kind of Polygamy

Nairobi: East African Educational Publishers, 2000. 204 pages, ISBN: 9789966463814.

This book presents a defence of polygamy in modern Africa as the solution to various marital problems including childlessness, widowhood, poor health and sexual incompatibility. The author appeals for a return to traditional African understandings of marriage, and offers suggestions for adapting the practice of polygamy to the current situation. This is presented as the appropriate African answer to problems being imported from

Western countries, problems such as frequent divorce and remarriage (serial polygamy), secret lovers, illegitimate children, prostitution, and single women, all of which are said to result from legally mandating monogamy in marriage. The author's stated assumptions include the necessity for all women to be married in order to be fulfilled as women, the impossibility of sexual abstinence for normal human beings, and the unrealistic idealism of expecting sexual faithfulness of men within monogamous marriage. The author deals with the Christian perspective by including a chapter on "Objections based on Christian religion," along with commentary on selected biblical passages. The book is an example of the thinking of a modern African man who is seeking indigenous authenticity on this issue, but its glorification of polygamous marriage does not deal with current research linking polygamy with family problems including child neglect and juvenile delinquency.

664.   Makower, Katharine

The Coming of the Rain: The Biography of a Pioneering Missionary in Rwanda

Carlisle, UK: Paternoster, 2002. 244 pages, ISBN: 9780853649687.

Joe Church (1899–1989) is the best-known missionary figure of the East African Revival. His personal account of this remarkable movement, *Quest for the Highest* (1981), is necessary reading for any student of that revival. Makower's biography gives the reader a deeper look at the personal life of this Cambridge-educated medical doctor who became better known for his Bible teaching than for his healing ministry. Church went to Rwanda in 1927 and finally left in 1961, just before Rwanda received its independence from Belgium. He also spent significant years in Uganda both during that period and after he was unable to return to Rwanda. One of his most important contributions to the spread of the gospel was his insistence on working on the basis of equality with leading Africans such as Yosiya Kinuka, Simeon Nsibambi, William Nagenda and Festo Kivengere. Makower's book is honest about the strengths and weaknesses of this man who insisted on racial equality ahead of his time and yet could ignore his family's needs because of his commitment to revival activities. His wife and five children were often left behind as he travelled about with the revival message. Overall, the reader is impressed with Church's continual concern to keep the revival balanced and based on scriptural teaching, despite his apparent failure to help new believers cope with wider issues such as tribalism, bringing painful reflections on the terrible events in 1961 and 1994. Perhaps the author may be pardoned for going beyond the biographical aspects of her task to examine the genocide of 1994, even though it occurred after Church's death. The book will not serve as a resource for that event; other literature has dealt with it more adequately. This book's contribution is made as an important missionary biography, to be read along with *Quest for the Highest*.

Maluleke, Tynyiko

see review 382

665. **Mamdani, Mahmood**

Citizen and Subject: Contemporary Africa and the Legacy of Late Colonialism

Princeton: Princeton University Press, 1996. 398 pages, ISBN: 9780691027937.

There is little agreement among scholars seeking to explain the causes of Africa's contemporary woes. Some see the abandonment of traditional political forms by African leaders as a primary reason for current state failure, while others suggest to the contrary that it is a revival of traditional ways that is to blame. Mamdani sides with another prominent group, arguing that above all we need to look for explanation to the distortions introduced into African political systems by colonial governments. He locates the primary contribution of the colonial legacy not simply in its coercive violence, but in the specific form through which this coercion was implemented: the institutions of indirect rule. It was, he argues, the "decentralized despotism" of indirect rule that established a framework from which Africa has yet to liberate itself. Indirect rule provided colonial governments with relatively inexpensive means for controlling local populations. Rather than establishing an extended European-style bureaucracy paid for from central coffers, colonial governments empowered local chiefs to rule on their behalf. In so doing, however, they transformed the character of local political authority. Traditional political systems were characterized by various forms of accountability, checks and balances, and even at times lively forms of democracy. Colonial rule swept this away, establishing "customary" chiefs as autocratic tyrants, accountable to the demands of the colonial state and to a developing system of clientelist patronage politics. This also ensured that Africans remained divided along tribal lines; relatively fluid ethnic categories became more rigid and more central to people's identities. Mamdani contends that this colonially tribalised political field, with its decentralized despotism and clientelism, continues in many cases to disrupt the possibility of developing the national political identities and national civil societies that are ultimately necessary for national democratic institutions. Mamdani grew up in Uganda, did his doctoral work at Harvard, and has been a well-regarded professor at Columbia University. Colonial regimes were not all equally characterized by indirect rule in the way implied by Mamdani; his treatment might need to be supplemented by other scholarly voices. But even if Mamdani's presentation may not be the *sufficient* explanation, he nevertheless makes a *significant* contribution toward interpreting the historical background for current political troubles in Africa.

666. **Mamdani, Mahmood**

When Victims Become Killers: Colonialism, Nativism, and the Genocide in Rwanda

Princeton: Princeton University Press, 2002. 384 pages, ISBN: 9780691102801.

With this book Mamdani tries to make the 1994 Rwandan genocide "thinkable," by explaining it in the light of the Rwandan colonial legacy, and thus illustrating some of the ideas presented in his book *Citizen and Subject*. He argues that in pre-colonial times the social categories Hutu and Tutsi were primarily *ethnic* identities. Hutu ethnicity was defined by an expanding Tutsi state as it assimilated various groups. The possibility of social mobility, however, remained open: Hutu who accumulated enough wealth could be assimilated into Tutsi ranks. Moreover there were certain checks on Tutsi power. For at least part of this period, Hutu ritual experts held a certain amount of authority in decision-making. Colonial rulers, however, operating on the basis of racist assumptions, fixed and hardened these relatively fluid social categories. For the Belgians, Tutsis were not simply a different ethnic group; they were a superior race, closer to the European racial type. Tutsis were therefore provided with better educational opportunities and privileged positions in the colonial administration, while the Hutu had to carry the onerous burdens of forced labour. Perhaps predictably, postcolonial Rwanda failed to transcend these colonially racialized identities. Mamdani carefully traces the history of missteps, misunderstandings, and manipulations that fuelled the ultimately tragic conflict between Hutu and Tutsi communities. Tutsis, disenfranchised and persecuted in the postcolonial period by the Hutu majority, struggled for a political home. Hutus, fearing a return to a situation of Tutsi political dominance, were increasingly radicalized by proponents of Hutu Power. The end result of this unfolding dynamic is well known. Mamdani closes this book with helpful reflections on the possibilities of justice in the post-genocide context, arguing that "victor's justice" must give way to "survivor's justice." Anyone who has survived the genocide, Hutu or Tutsi, should be offered the opportunity of striving for reconciliation. This form of justice implies a recognition that neither side has been innocent and that both sides must engage in the pursuit of peace. This is an important case study. Even though most ethnic conflicts in Africa have not descended to the depths of genocidal madness that caught the world's attention in 1994, there are lessons here for pastors and theologians who long to pursue peace and reconciliation between communities in conflict, whether outside or inside the body of Christ.

667.   **Mana, Kä**

Christians and Churches of Africa Envisioning the Future: Salvation in Jesus Christ and the Building of a New African Society

Yaoundé: Clé, 2000. 109 pages, ISBN: 9781870345279.

The author was born in the Congo (DRC), and has worked at the Institut Protestant de Théologie de Porto-Novo in Benin. The subtitle identifies the book's purpose, namely to examine the implications of the gospel for contemporary Africa. Kä Mana understands salvation largely in this-worldly, humanistic terms as "the construction of an African society reconciled to its history." Evangelism is consequently "to organize people and to teach them to organize themselves so as to prepare for the advent of a society worthy of God's plan." He discusses the origins of the social, political and economic malaise of modern Africa, and suggests that a profound integration of the gospel with traditional African values provides the solution: "We intend to integrate the spirit of Africa's founding myths and that of the Christian faith into a new spiritual understanding of our present history." The meaning of the gospel for Africans can only be understood in dialogue with African tradition, but Christ brings to that tradition new meaning and renewal, particularly in terms of a richer appreciation of human solidarity and fraternity. However, Kä Mana seems to understand the Christian story as simply another myth (as distinct from objective historical truth), the role of which is to transform human consciousness. There is indeed a profound subjectivism in the author's approach to the gospel; thus he writes of "the foundational myths through which Jesus Christ gives himself as the meaning in all the areas of significance that we have conferred on him." Similarly, in rejecting Western approaches to Christianity, he insists on "an inventive hermeneutics" which acknowledges Africa's founding myths as "the true path of humanity . . . on which Christ has chosen to march towards God's future in Africa." Although brief, this book is not an easy read; the language is at time opaque and tortuous, in part perhaps the result of translation. Its usefulness is in showing the direction some African theologians are taking. Kä Mana demonstrates an appropriate concern to bring the gospel to bear on the trauma of much of present-day Africa, but in so doing he has largely lost touch with the objective and historical, supernatural and transforming gospel of the NT.

668. Mana, Kä

Foi chrétienne, crise africaine et reconstruction de l'Afrique: Sens et enjeux des théologies africaines contemporaines

Nairobi: CETA, 1992. 220 pages, ISBN: 9789966987921.

This book is useful both as a basic survey of developments in African theology, and as a presentation of the essential concepts of reconstruction theology. The first part of the book gives the historical background of African theology. Numerous African theologians from various perspectives are cited, illustrating that African theology has always been related to the political and historical developments of the time. Kä Mana's attachment to the All-Africa Conference of Churches (AACC) and the ecumenical movement is clear throughout. While his description of the main tenants of "evangelical theology" may be generally correct, he does not provide an even-handed presentation of African evangelicalism. Theologians such as Byang Kato do not fare well under his pen. Nevertheless, this part of the book helps greatly to put the developments of African theology into historical perspective. The second part of the book builds on declarations about the task of the church made by various synods and church bodies throughout francophone Africa. This serves to make clear that Kä Mana's own perspective is not just a personal theology, but one held by many churches committed to the vision of constructing a utopic society. The author also makes a considerable effort to tie his theology into a study of how God dealt with crisis in the Bible. His approach may sometimes leave readers with the impression that the theological perspective more often determines the interpretative outcome than results from it, but there are illuminating points nevertheless made. Those who feel that the principal purpose of the church is social enhancement will find the book especially helpful. It would make a worthwhile addition to any advanced-level theological library in francophone Africa. (The identical text is also published under the title: *Théologie africaine pour temps de crise: Christianisme et reconstruction de l'Afrique* [Paris: Editions Karthala, 1993].)

Mana, Kä

see also review 1191

669. Manaranche, André

Le monothéisme chrétien

Paris: Cerf, 1985. 255 pages, ISBN: 9782204023696.

Manaranche is a Jesuit priest with long experience in teaching both in France and in Senegal. In this study in dogmatics he deals with the specific character of Christian monotheism. The main question is whether Christian trinitarian monotheism should be conceived as one variation within the larger family of monotheisms, including European Deism, Islam, Judaism, and the monotheism of African traditional religions. In confrontation with the idea often heard in African circles that "monotheists of all countries should unite," Manaranche argues perceptively that the trinitarian character of Christian monotheism distinguishes it profoundly from strict monotheisms. Manaranche's interaction with European deism will be less interesting for readers in the African context, but he also returns again and again to the relationship, both present and historical, with alternative African monotheisms. He also discusses and criticizes the approach to the issues which aims at a rapprochement between Christianity and Islam. In treating the biblical basis of the doctrine, the author argues that already the OT belief in the one Creator who relates to the world reflects a structure which is more in accord with the Trinitarian faith into which it developed in the NT than it is with other forms of strict monotheism. Although Manaranche is generally orthodox in his doctrinal conclusions, evangelicals will generally have a problem with the way in which he uses the historical-critical method in his biblical presentation. Manaranche concludes by describing the Trinity as essentially mutual love, and he shows that it is central to the Christian understanding of creation and redemption. This book is valuable because of its clarifications on an issue of crucial apologetical and doctrinal importance, and it would be difficult to find any other book which does this as profoundly in relation to the African context. This book is not easy to read, and even advanced students may not be able to handle it on their own. The Roman Catholic background is not a major problem. This book would be a very worthwhile acquisition for advanced libraries, and for lecturers in systematic theology able to use French.

670.   **Manning, Patrick**

Slavery and African Life: Occidental, Oriental, and African Slave Trades

Cambridge: Cambridge University Press, 1990. 252 pages, ISBN: 9780521348676.

Notions about Africa-related slavery and the slave trade might be limited for many to the number of victims (to the nearest million), the identity of the chief perpetrators (the Dutch, Portuguese, British, and French), and the approximate date (or dates) of abolition. This book by the Associate Professor of History at Northeastern University, USA, reveals how long, how complex and how varied the tragic chapter of slavery actually was. Although slavery is an ancient institution common to many societies, it is its modernity that distinguishes the phenomenon in Africa. Statistics indicate that from the sixteenth to nineteenth centuries Africa lost a staggering eighteen million people by the export of slaves. The Occidental (Atlantic) slave trade accounted for most of these, but Manning's detailed research reveals a second major but less familiar dimension of the slave trade, the Oriental (to North Africa and the Middle East), and a third, namely the market within Africa itself. Dynamic associations between regional sources and regional destinations are traced. Graph charts compute the historical, demographic, and economic trends over the three or four centuries involved. Several ironies emerge from the study. First, the slave trade created pressures and opportunities which, in the course of time, drew in a considerable number of African merchants and traders in slaves, so that Africa cannot simplistically be seen as only "victim." While the surge in demand for slaves was triggered undoubtedly by the need for cheap labour in the plantation economies of the New World, European slave buyers were able to make African merchants an offer they could not refuse, a means of acquiring wealth and power which continued under its own momentum even when the Atlantic slave trade was prohibited and external demand waned. Second, in the course of the nineteenth century the European colonial powers, the very ones who had propagated the slave trade, moved to prosecute it. Indeed the eradication of the slave trade and slavery in Africa was sometimes given (with duplicity, many would argue) as one justification for the scramble for Africa by the European powers following the Berlin Congress in 1884–1885. Manning succeeds in showing how involved and tragic the story of slavery in Africa is. Tragic, not just in terms of the human suffering of bygone centuries but in the enduring legacy of racism, some of whose roots reach back to slavery. Because of the importance of this subject for understanding Africa's past, and also for understanding foundational aspects of modern African intellectual life, it is helpful to have this comprehensive scholarly reassessment available. The topic is also of interest because of the documented Christian contribution both within Africa and beyond towards the eventual abolition of the African slave trade and slavery.

671.   Manus, Ukachukwu

Christ, the African King: New Testament Christology

Frankfurt: Peter Lang, 1993. 280 pages, ISBN: 9783631452110.

Manus is a Roman Catholic lay scholar with a long list of publications in NT studies. The present work surveys contributions to Christological thinking in Africa, concluding that most previous studies show "little awareness of recent developments in New Testament exegesis and research." After a discussion of some African concepts of kingship in pre-colonial periods amongst the Yoruba, Baganda, Shilluk and Zulu peoples, Manus turns to the NT material to argue that Jesus' preaching of the kingdom, as well as the evangelists' portrayal of his ministry as a humble king, have multiple implications for an African Christology. The work is marred by dozens of typographical errors, gender-exclusive language and frequent use of slang. This book may be of interest to theologians, and to NT scholars with an interest in Christology.

672.   Manus, Ukachukwu

Intercultural Hermeneutics in Africa: Methods and Approaches

Nairobi: Acton Publishers, 2003. 225 pages, ISBN: 9789966888044.

Manus is Professor of NT Studies at Obafemi Awolowo University in Nigeria, and has been a visiting professor at the Catholic University of Eastern Africa in Kenya. In this book Manus develops and demonstrates a made-in-Africa hermeneutical theory that he hopes will free the Bible to be more relevant in Africa. He frequently compares his methods to those of Justin Ukpong, also from Nigeria. He does not jettison Western scholarship, but seeks to contextualize his exegesis by making the conscious analysis of the African context an integral part of the hermeneutical process. His approach is very much an academic and scientific effort. Although, like Gerald West of South Africa, Manus wants to "read the scripture with a community of ordinary readers and from the perspective of the ordinary Africans," in this contribution it is not so evident that he "reads with" ordinary Africans. The detail into which Manus goes in explaining his theory can be helpful, but at times it can also be frustrating and even confusing. For example, in one place he references five steps to his method, elsewhere he agrees with Ukpong's four steps, later he details ten steps, and finally in describing a similar method he mentions seven steps. His application of the method to particular texts, such as Galatians 6:1–6, Acts 17:22–34, and Mark 11:15–19, is especially helpful, as he attempts to use his intercultural approach to relate African insights and issues to the biblical passages. This is not an easy book to read. Part of the difficulty is poor proofreading by the publisher. Mistakes of all kinds abound. Perhaps another part of the problem is that the book makes such an effort at maintaining an academic approach. Furthermore, the book accepts historical-critical methods typical of Western liberal scholars, while maintaining the higher regard for Scripture common to Africa. Nevertheless the serious attempt at an African hermeneutic will make this a thought-provoking study for theologians and biblical scholars, even if they find some underlying assumptions unhelpful.

673.   **Maranz, David**

African Friends and Money Matters: Observations from Africa

Dallas: SIL, 2002. 238 pages, ISBN: 9781556711176.

One of the greatest sources of practical cross-cultural frustration and misunderstanding between Africans and expatriates can be in the area of personal finances. Each uses money and other resources in sometimes very different ways, and these cultural differences, experienced almost daily by many, can easily result in misinterpretation and friction. This book focuses on the micro-economics of Africa, attempting to provide a cultural context for understanding personal financial practice in areas such as budgeting, loans, bargaining, saving, the role of money in friendships, gifts, sharing, and debt. The bulk of the presentation is arranged around 90 observations, each supported by fuller descriptions, explanations, illustrations, and often providing Western counterpoints. A typical example reads: "Africans do not budget for special events; rather, they spend as much money and other resources as they can marshal for each one." The presentation is based on Maranz's 25 years of ministry in Africa. While his examples appear to be drawn largely from western francophone Africa, the observations can usually be generalized to the rest of continent while making allowance for local variations. This book is recommended as a unique and practical resource for Africans and expatriates who are living and working together. Westerners, even those who have considerable exposure to African financial practices, will benefit from the author's close observations. Africans on the other hand will gain a better understanding both of Western financial expectations, values, and practices, and as well a clearer surfacing of their own perspectives, sometimes obscured by familiarity. The range of coverage is commendable, but some issues would perhaps deserve greater attention, such as bribery, insurance, and tips. Also while one must acknowledge the continued influence of traditional African values so well described by Maranz, the pervasive influence of urbanisation and westernisation in Africa has often resulted in modifications that would have to qualify some of Maranz's observations. While the author sincerely attempts a non-judgmental approach, nonetheless in a few cases the reader will detect an unfortunate tone of personal frustration. Perhaps this also further illustrates how sensitive the issues involved are, the importance of a clearer understanding of the cultural differences between Africa and the West in these matters, and hence the benefit of having a book like this.

Marshall-Fratani, Ruth

see review 234

674.   **Marshall, Paul, and Lela Gilbert**

Their Blood Cries Out: The Untold Story of Persecution against Christians in the Modern World

Dallas: W Publishing Group, 1997. 335 pages, ISBN: 9780849914188.

Although this important work is not specifically about Africa, several African countries feature prominently in its pages. The book is a comprehensive and perceptive account of Christian persecution around the world. It is divided into two sections. The first is a detailed report on situations of suffering, especially (although not limited to) the persecution of Christians in Islamic and communist countries. The second section elucidates the complex political, philosophical and theological reasons that this issue has not been treated seriously by the governments or even the churches of the Western world. Of special interest to African readers will be the stories of discrimination against evangelical Christians at the hands of some Orthodox Christians in Ethiopia, accounts of various levels of persecution against Christians by Muslims in parts of West and East Africa, and especially the detailed reports of the genocidal activities of the Islamic governments against Christians (and others) in the southern part of Sudan before the division of that country. Especially interesting is Marshall's assessment of the blind spots of both liberal and evangelical Christianity in America. Concerning evangelicals, Marshall is critical of a view of the international arena which is obsessed with discovering fulfilment of biblical prophecy in current events, while passively and fatalistically ignoring the suffering of so many thousands of fellow believers. Marshall, a committed Christian, holds a PhD in political science from York University in Canada, and has held professorships at the University of Toronto and the Free University of Amsterdam.

675. Marshall, Ruth

Political Spiritualities: The Pentecostal Revolution in Nigeria

Chicago: University of Chicago Press, 2009. 368 pages, ISBN: 9780226507132.

This book, by a University of Toronto professor, seeks to understand the political spirituality of Nigerian Pentecostalism. At the start, two facts stand out: first, Nigeria is home to enormous corruption and economic problems; second, Pentecostalism is "the single most important sociocultural force in southern Nigeria," and has great influence in the whole country. Yet the *political* influence of Pentecostalism in Nigeria has seemed negligible. Marshall's focus is primarily on the "new wave" of Pentecostalism which began to be prominent in the 1980s. The prosperity gospel is a significant part of this new wave. Marshall sees conversion as a central part of this Pentecostalism or "Born-Again" movement. Conversion constitutes a "complete break with the past." She assumes that such a rupture would also be a break with the sordid political and economic culture, but this seems not to be the case. Marshall suggests a few reasons for the negligible influence of this movement on Nigerian politics. First, conversion in the evangelical and Pentecostal traditions is usually individual and not social. Second, the leaders of the prosperity churches have adopted the money-oriented lifestyle of the "big men" of politics. Third, there is a preoccupation with seeing the enemy as a spiritual, unseen force. The focus is on Satanic and demonic powers instead of the socio-political forces of our contemporary society. Finally, the Muslims of Nigeria are often featured as one of the main problems of the country. Thus the great potential influence of Pentecostalism on the political system is squandered. While there is merit in the author's analysis, she ignores the nature-grace dualism that characterizes much of evangelicalism and Pentecostalism. If the sphere of grace is only "spiritual" or ecclesiastical, then one's attention will be diverted from the secular or social sphere. Marshall is obviously not Pentecostal nor evangelical. She minimizes the importance of individual conversion. She also neglects the positive community that Pentecostalism offers the marginalized in our society. But her main point stands: the churches in Nigeria should be changing corrupt society in a more forceful way.

676. Martey, Emmanuel

African Theology: Inculturation and Liberation

Eugene, OR: Wipf & Stock, 2009. 190 pages, ISBN: 9781608991259.

Martey is a theologian and ordained minister within the Presbyterian Church of Ghana, and this book is a revision of his 1992 PhD thesis from Union Theological Seminary in New York, directed by James H. Cone.

Martey sets out to analyse the two major strands of African theology, namely the strand that has emphasized inculturation and the strand that has emphasized liberation. He is especially concerned with the relationship between the two. Inculturation theology, on the one hand, responds to Western cultural domination by developing a theology that proceeds from African religio-cultural experiences. Liberation theology, on the other hand, especially in the form of black theology in South Africa, responds to Western socio-political domination by developing a theology that participates in the struggle against the various oppressive exponents of this domination. Over against the traditional tension between these two strands of African theology, Martey argues that a more holistic concept of African culture is necessary, a concept of culture that encompasses socio-political and economic dimensions as well as more religio-cultural dimensions, thereby enabling a synthetic interpretation of the two. Martey's book is an important contribution to the analysis and further development of African theology. Its historical analysis of the various expressions of the two strands of African theology is clear-cut and convincing, and the book's own emphasis, that the two strands complement rather than contradict each other, has become increasingly relevant since its publication in 1993, not least owing to the developments in South Africa. The book needs to be taken into account by those writing or lecturing on African theology.

Martin, Stephen

see review 217

677.   Masamba ma Mpolo, Jean, and Daisy Nwachuku, editors

Pastoral Care and Counseling in Africa Today

Frankfurt: Peter Lang, 1991. 194 pages, ISBN: 9783631441312.

This series of eleven essays was sponsored by the African Association for Pastoral Studies and Counselling (founded in 1985) and is their first major publication. The theme of the book is the contextualization of pastoral counselling in the African context. The book rightly assumes that culture and worldview necessarily affect pastoral counselling, both as to its focus and as to its methods. Most of the ten contributors are professionals in religion and psychology in African universities or theological schools. The essays are all of high quality, and most would be readable by the non-professional. Four of the essays deal with marriage and family related subjects. An important essay by Masambo ma Mpolo of Kinshasa addresses a counselling approach to witchcraft. This book is ecumenical in flavour and contains a broad theological spectrum, all the way from those who do not believe that the Bible is a source of authoritative truth to those who hold that the Bible is the only source of truly Christian counselling. It is recommended for the libraries of advanced-level theological schools in Africa that include an emphasis on pastoral counselling. It is unfortunate that this book on counselling does not include more case studies than it does.

678.   Masamba ma Mpolo, Jean, and Wilhelmina Kalu, editors

The Risks of Growth: Counselling and Pastoral Theology in the African Context

Nairobi: Uzima Press, 1985. 209 pages, ISBN: LANG255125.

This book is a collection of six diverse articles, followed by case studies contributed by the editors. Masamba is from Congo (DRC), a Baptist minister, and headed the Office of Family Education of the World Council of Churches in Geneva. Kalu of Nigeria was a senior lecturer in educational psychology at the University of Nigeria, Nsukka. Masamba begins with a call for pastoral counselling that takes into account the African worldview. Olu Makinde of Nigeria describes the counselling work of traditional diviners, especially among the Yoruba. Jabulani Nxumalo from South Africa talks about confession, witchcraft oppression, the use of symbols, laying on of hands and the use of holy water from traditional and Roman Catholic perspectives. Howard Clinebell of the USA is represented by an article on "Growth Counselling" (from which the title of the book is taken), which does not mention Africa but contributes to the conceptual framework of the book. Kalu of Nigeria provides a practical article and case studies on counselling disabled people and their families in Africa. Bonganjalo Goba of South Africa talks of how the psychological healing of individuals must go hand in hand with the healing of social structures. The extensive final article and case studies by Masamba deal with the psychological roles of ancestors, traditional myths, and beliefs in witchcraft in the lives of Africans, and how these can be dealt with in the counselling situation. After an explanation of the psychological basis of the belief that one is bewitched, he ends by wondering if there might be evil spirits after all. Much in this book is helpful, though there are places where the reader may feel that too much unreflected accommodation has been made to a traditional African worldview. Since professional literature on pastoral counselling in Africa is not plentiful, this book would be an asset for those researching, lecturing or practicing in this field.

679. Masamba ma Mpolo, Jean

Le Saint-Esprit interroge les esprits: Essai de relecture et pistes psychopastorales de la spiritualité en Afrique: Cas de la République Démocratique du Congo

Yaoundé: Éditions Clé, 2002. 218 pages, ISBN: 9789966886743.

Masamba is a Baptist pastor in Congo and has taught pastoral theology at the Protestant Theological Faculty in Yaoundé and at the Protestant University of Kimpese, of which he was the first president. In this study he touches on an area which deeply influences the church in Africa, namely the tendency to interpret large areas of life, especially dreams and illnesses, as caused by demonic forces and therefore calling for deliverance. Particular attention is given to dreams and spiritual visitations at night. Masamba takes the reality of Satan and demons seriously, but at the same time wants to fight the "inflation of spirits" found in many sects, and the fatalistic and irresponsible attitude to life which it provokes. He points to social and psychological causes at the root of all sorts of phenomena attributed to demons, and emphasizes the need to take these areas seriously in the mission of the church. The book is particularly valuable because it addresses this often-neglected area, because of the intermediate theological position it sets out, and because it presents many challenging case studies. However, it is not easy reading, owing to lack of structure and to the way it often leaves the reader wondering precisely what position has been taken regarding the relationship between the psychological and spiritual dimensions of life. This study should be essential reading for lecturers in pastoral theology in francophone Africa.

Mashinini, Emma

see review 17

680.   Masolo, Dismas A.

African Philosophy in Search of Identity

Bloomington, IN: Indiana University Press, 1994. 316 pages, ISBN: 9780748604968.

The birth of the debate on African philosophy is historically associated with two factors: Western discourse on Africa and the African response to that discourse. At the centre of the debate, according to the author, is the concept of reason, a value which is believed to stand as the great divide between the civilized and the un-civilized, the logical and the mystic. Masolo traces the history of the major themes, debates, and participants since the 1940s, and argues that African thinkers have used philosophy as the primary vehicle for theoretical articulation of their identities and as the means for contesting identities imposed by outsiders. The history of African philosophy is therefore the history of Africa in a very special way. It is the history of Africanism in its critical experience and articulation. This intellectual quest precedes and forms the foundation for the diversified attempts to deconstruct the old colonial sciences. For this reason, the author concludes, African philosophy must be born out of its own peculiar cultural circumstances, combined with a living and constructive zeal amongst individual African intellectuals to understand and explain the world around us. Topics include Placide Tempels and the setting of ethnophilosophy; language and reality in the thought of Alexis Kagame; John Mbiti's religious ethnology; the view of Africa in Western discourse as analysed by Fabien Eboussi-Boulaga, Marcien Towa and V. Y. Mudimbe; and the role of reason in the thought of Paulin Hountondji, Kwasi Wiredu and H. Odera Oruka. Since the African theology movement is a direct derivative of this larger African intellectual quest, this book is important reading for all involved with understanding African philosophy and African theology. Originally from Kenya, Masolo earned a doctorate in philosophy at the Università Gregoriana in Rome, and holds a professorship in philosophy at a university in the United States.

681.   Matadi, Ghislain Tshikendwa

Suffering, Belief and Hope: The Wisdom of Job in an AIDS-Stricken Africa

Nairobi: Paulines, 2007. 176 pages, ISBN: 9789966082374.

The author is a Jesuit theologian from Congo (DRC), trained in Rome (Gregorian University) and Berkeley (Jesuit School of Theology), and now serving as a priest and publisher in Kinshasa. The book is a revised version of his Berkeley licence dissertation, addressing the AIDS pandemic in Africa from a biblical perspective. The book starts with a survey of how suffering and death are conceptualized in traditional Africa, and the questions that arise from the current AIDS pandemic. Traditional concepts are then contrasted with Job's theology, as expressed in the Job dialogues. Matadi makes a close reading of some selected texts (Job 3:1–26, 40:3–5, 42:1–6) and is able to demonstrate how Job criticizes a traditional theology of retribution. A contemporary reading of Job's theology, in an AIDS-stricken Africa and with Job as a model, would then mean a rejection of the concept that AIDS is a punishment from God. Rather, the texts about Job's suffering may serve to deepen the faith of contemporary sufferers. The book is well written, and can be useful in reflection and discussion in Africa about AIDS and the Bible.

682. Mawanzi Ndombe, César

Das symbolische Denken als Schlüssel zum Verständnis der negro-afrikanischen (Bantu-) Weltanschauung: eine religionsphilosophische Deutung im Anschluss an die Kulturphilosophie Ernst Cassirers

Frankfurt: Peter Lang, 2008. 420 pages, ISBN: 9783631585313.

The author is a Roman Catholic theologian from Congo (DRC), trained in Congo and Germany. The book is a revised version of a doctoral dissertation in philosophy from St Georgen, Frankfurt. The topic addressed is the concept of "symbolic thinking." It is argued that this concept is an important key to understanding Bantu/African thought, worldview, religion and culture. The philosophy and symbol theory of the German/Jewish philosopher Ernst Cassirers (1874–1945) is used as a hermeneutical frame, and the concept of "symbolic thinking" is understood as a substratum of culture and religion, accessed through symbolic constructs such as myths, rites, and proverbs. The book is organized in three major parts. First, a sketch of an African philosophy of religion, based on Cassirer's thought. Second, some basic features of Bantu religion, with particular attention to "symbolic thinking." And third, the merger between African culture and Christian faith, pointing out how Bantu religion provides a fertile breeding ground for the Christian message. The book is a heavy piece of work, written in a not too easy German. As such it will hardly find a large readership in Africa, not even amongst philosophers and systematic theologians. This is a pity, as it is an important contribution not only with regard to African philosophy, but also as an example of a fruitful dialogue between African and traditional Western philosophy.

683. Maxey, Gary S.

Capturing a Lost Vision: Can Nigeria's Greatest Revival Live Again?

Lagos: WATS Publications, 2016. 300 pages, ISBN: 9789789532872.

Maxey is the founder of the West Africa Theological Seminary (WATS) in Lagos, Nigeria. He holds a doctoral degree from Trinity Deerfield in the United States, and has served in Nigeria for more than three decades. This book provides an in-depth study of Nigeria's remarkable "Civil War Revival." The Nigerian Civil War (the "Biafran War") raged from 1967 to 1970. During this disastrous period a remarkable spiritual revival occurred especially in the nation's student population. Individuals became convicted of sin, repented and committed themselves to Jesus Christ. Whole campuses were affected. Maxey argues that Christian student groups were key to the historical origins of this revival. In particular the British-based Scripture Union laid an evangelical foundation for the revival. "The Scripture Union conditioned a whole generation of secondary students to move onto university campuses with a passion for the reading and study of the Bible, spiritual life, spiritual renewal and evangelism." Two men stand out in their association with Scripture Union: Sydney Elton and Mike Oye. The book proceeds to offer biographical profiles of 13 of the early "foot soldiers" of the Revival, including Oye. Maxey makes frequent reference to the 2008 study by Richard Burgess, *Nigeria's Christian Revolution*, which treats both this revival during and immediately after Nigeria's civil war, and as well its "Pentecostal Progeny" in the decades following. Maxey's focus is on the earlier movement with its more traditional revival characteristics, including emphasis on: (1) repentance and new birth; (2) holiness; (3) evangelism; and (4) love of the Bible and prayer. In other words, this earlier revival was truly evangelical but not necessarily Pentecostal. Maxey argues that "the gifts of the Spirit and the occurrence of the miraculous were characteristically secondary issues." He suggests that the eventual ebbing of this renewal movement developed from: (1) false teaching; (2) routinization of worship; (3) vying for leadership and loss of integrity; (4) the materialism of the prosperity gospel; (5) denominationalism. Maxey argues passionately for the need of a new revival in Nigeria, one that would return to a focus on the Word of God, prayer, the new birth, and sanctification. This is a significant book for the Nigerian Christian community, highlighting as it does this little-known but consequential episode in that community's modern history, and calling it to a renewal of such biblically grounded vitality.

684.   Maxwell, David

African Gifts of the Spirit: Pentecostalism and the Rise of a Zimbabwean Transnational Religious Movement

Martlesham, UK: James Currey, 2006. 320 pages, ISBN: 9780852559666.

The African studies scholar Terence Ranger speaks of this book as the "most illuminating account ever written of an African initiated church . . . a remarkable work of scholarship." Maxwell is a UK university professor who edited the *Journal of Religion in Africa* from 1998 to 2005. His depth and quality of research are indeed impressive. The introduction/overview and conclusion are alone worth the cost of the book. The focus of Maxwell's study is the head of the Zimbabwe Assemblies of God Africa (ZAOGA), which claimed a membership of up to 400,000 in 2000. Its leader, a former Apostolic Faith Mission preacher named "Archbishop" Ezekiel Guti, has become a very wealthy man, but not always for the right reasons. Maxwell writes in detail about Guti's relentless drive for control, often at the expense of others who might threaten his dominance of the organisation. Guti's rise to power illustrates nearly all of the weaknesses commonly associated with AICs, such as nepotism, constant splits, worship of its top leaders (opposition was considered blasphemy), mismanagement of funds, eagerness for titles, theological aberrancy and exaggeration. (Referring to the Guti's hagiography entitled *The Sacred History*, Maxwell's British understatement is, "somewhat economical with the truth.") Yet the author manages to maintain balance in discussing how Guti was able to stress his African heritage (even borrowing from Zimbabwean Vapostori leaders Maranke and Masowe) while obtaining significant funding from impressed (and wealthy) American Pentecostals. Students of African Christianity will certainly benefit from this book's evaluative sections on the independent/indigenous church movement, even if the rather long biographical material on Guti will be of less interest to those outside of the region. How Guti has fared in the more recent economic disintegration of Zimbabwe is not addressed in the book.

685.   Maxwell, David, and Ingrid Lawrie, editors

Christianity and the African Imagination: Essays in Honour of Adrian Hastings

Leiden: BRILL, 2013. 422 pages, ISBN: 9789004245105.

This collection of ten essays honours Adrian Hastings, late professor for theology and religious studies at the University of Leeds, UK, and well known as an authority on the history of African Christianity. Hastings served as a Catholic priest in Uganda from 1958 to 1965, and later also in Zimbabwe. From 1976 onward he maintained an academic career in the UK. The principal editor of this volume is Hastings' successor as editor of the *Journal of Religion in Africa*. Assisting him was Hastings' secretary for over fifteen years, who is now writing a biography of Hastings. Hastings focussed his historical and theological studies of the church in Africa on "popular Christianity," which he felt was more important than ecclesial structures and policies. These essays in his honour also want to chart the role of Africans in the advance of Christianity on the continent, complementing descriptions which have centred more on the perspective and activities of missionaries. The individual essays open windows into specific aspects of African church history, and are mostly by senior specialists. Thus R. Gray describes the role of the Kongo ambassadors to the Pope in the sixteenth century, which eventually led to a direct link between Kongo and Rome, thus by-passing the Portuguese. A. Walls highlights the engagement of Samuel Crowther with Muslim rulers in Nigeria, as he sought common ground in order to reach the Islamised peasantry with the gospel. J. Waliggo shows the important role of African chiefs as catechists in the history of the Catholic Church in Uganda. T. Ranger discusses the role of three leading African Christians in Zimbabwe in the 1930s, who in the wake of the earliest missionaries sparked new mass movements within the Catholic, Anglican and Methodist churches. One essay treats the history of Kikuyu Christianity from 1900 to 1980; another does the same for a district in southern Malawi; and a third presents the history of the Zimbabwean Assemblies of God Africa under its charismatic leader Ezekiel Guti. One essay portrays the Anglican Archbishop Jamani Luwum, who died as martyr under Idi Amin in Uganda; another considers Vincent Damuah of Ghana, who started off as a Catholic priest but then founded a movement in 1982 to revive and reform African traditional religion as an alternative to Christianity and Islam; and a third essay treats Wole Soyinka's book *Ìsarà*, and demonstrates the Christian roots of the modern Nigerian nationalism there promoted. Also included are an academic-literary biography of Hastings (1922–2001), and an exhaustive 40-page bibliography of his writings. The contributions of this volume are of a high calibre. Any advanced researcher in African Christianity will need to be familiar with them, and individual articles will also now be fundamental for serious study of the specific region or topic that they cover.

Maxwell, David

see also review 443

686. **Mazrui, Ali A., Patrick M. Dikirr, Robert, Ostergard, Michael Toler, and Paul Macharia, editors**

Africa's Islamic Experience: History, Culture and Politics

New Delhi: Sterling Publishers, 2009. 268 pages, ISBN: 9788120740853.

The lead editor of this collection, Ali Mazrui, is the well-known academic, originally from Kenya, and now Albert Schweitzer professor in the humanities at the State University of New York. The book makes a strong case for a conceptual linkage between Africa and the Arabian Peninsula, arguing that the linguistic and religious similarities create natural bonds between the two areas. It has several sections: An Overview of Africa's Religious Canvas; The History and Spread of Islam in Africa; Political Islam and African Politics; and Islam and Comparative Culture. Whereas readers will approach these topics with interest, they are actually covered only in a cursory fashion and will be disappointing. For example, Mazrui's introduction to the section on History and Islam in Africa devolves into a critique of US foreign policy in the post-9/11 era, leaving the weighty topic of the History of Islam in Africa only addressed superficially, and often through assertion rather than a review of the rich historical documentation. Chapter topics are diverse, addressing architecture and literature as well as the Muslim communities in specific countries such as Kenya and Niger. Unfortunately, many of the authors treat the Muslim communities in these countries as if they are monolithic, using language such as "the Umma thinks . . ." or "the Umma wants . . ." Not only does this usage undermine the credibility of the authors' conclusions; it is also a missed opportunity to discuss the variety of Islamic points of view on contemporary religious expression and politics. Regretfully, most of the book proceeds in a similar vein, falling short of expectations for good scholarship. That it is disjointed and repetitive is particularly disappointing given the importance of this topic and the wealth of sources available. There is one notable exception to the overall poor quality of the book. Goolam Vahed has an excellent chapter on Indian Muslims in South Africa, which addresses their history, identity development, and challenges they face in faithful practice in an increasingly secular South Africa.

687. Mazrui, Ali A., and Christophe Wondji, editors

General History of Africa: Africa since 1935 (Volume 8)

Martlesham, UK: James Currey, 1999. 1072 pages, ISBN: 9780852550984.

This is the eighth and final volume in the extraordinary UNESCO General History of Africa series, which addresses the entire scope of African history from pre-historic times to the present. Largely the product of African academic scholarship, the series is available unabridged in both English and French, and also in low-cost abridged editions in these and additional languages (including Hausa and Swahili). The final volume was published unabridged in hardback in 1993; this 1999 paperback edition, also unabridged, includes a few updating additions. Apart from those additions, the coverage of the essays and bibliographic entries does not reach beyond the later 1980s; AIDS only barely achieves notice, while Mandela and the end of apartheid not at all. Opening and closing essays are provided by the well-known Kenyan scholar Ali Mazrui, Muslim in background, who (somewhat ironically) holds the Albert Schweitzer professorial chair at a leading American university. The structure admirably supports the comprehensive intentions, addressing principal aspects of the decade of world conflict (1935–1945), the struggle for independence (1945–1960), and the period since independence (1960–). Along the way learned topical chapters survey, for example, economic and social change, developments in education, philosophy, and the arts, pan-Africanism, and Africa within world affairs. The quality of the contributions necessarily varies, but whereas most essays may not be definitive, most are adequate, resulting in a vast wealth of information on modern Africa within one set of covers. The tone throughout is usually realistic. Thus with respect to Nkrumah's famous dictum: "Seek ye first the political kingdom, and all these things shall be added," one guiding question of this volume is why for modern Africa "all these things" have not in fact followed. Familiar themes of modern Africa's Christian history are presented, including the African Independent Churches (AICs) and the emergence of the African Theology movement, but the phenomenal growth of African Christianity does not gain attention. Indeed African Christianity is interpreted as having played a problematic and even contradictory role in the social development of modern Africa. The volume is valuable not least because it interprets throughout from the perspective of the post-colonial African intelligentsia, a perspective which pervasively determines the structures, ambitions, discontinuities and frustrations of modern Africa, and a perspective still normally assumed rather than evaluated or critiqued by Africa's educated elite. One contribution of this work is that it articulates just this perspective, and represents its implications, across the entire range of African development in modern times, thereby providing eloquent primary examples of the dominant intellectual assumptions of modern Africa.

688. **Mbanda, Laurent**

Committed to Conflict: The Destruction of the Church in Rwanda

London: SPCK, 1997. 248 pages, ISBN: 9780281050161.

The author of this interesting book has written out of his life experience, giving many personal reminiscences. Though born in Rwanda, he was raised in Burundi and the USA. He did his PhD at Trinity Evangelical Divinity School, and served with Compassion International. He went to northern Rwanda in 1994, entering Kigali right after the take-over of the capital by the FPR army. He describes the people and situations he found. Looking back into history, he highlights and criticizes the involvement of the Catholic Church in the politics of Rwanda in colonial times as well as after independence up to 1994. But he also recognizes that "the Rwandan political society has successfully used the Church for its political agenda." The Church should now take a lead in true reconciliation. Donors must be careful in their giving not to "contribute to the rebuilding of power struggles in churches and to deeper divisions." "Rehabilitation funds available to certain church leaders are being used to manipulate people and buy votes." Mbanda exposes the danger of a church's leadership that does not keep itself sufficiently independent of the state and its ideology. As this is a vital topic, his book raises important questions about the need for self-examination among church leaders not only in Rwanda but also elsewhere. The author also underlines the need for church leaders to be accountable to the church, especially in financial matters. He emphasizes a servant leadership model, repentance, forgiveness, healing of trauma, discipleship, reconciliation and justice, and the need to overcome the acquired feeling of being guilty by associating with people of another group (a feeling the author sensed in himself). Written in a personal way and with a vivid style, the author transmits his vision of a renewed church that puts the Kingdom of God first, bridges ethnic divides, and restores people to wholeness and unity. "Rwandan Christians have to seek the Kingdom of God first, and then build their nation on Christian principles and foundations." The lessons that the author draws from the Rwandan crisis make this a useful book for people who plan for ministry and church development anywhere.

689. **Mbilah, Johnson A., and John Chesworth, editors**

From the Cross to the Crescent

Nairobi: Project for Christian-Muslim Relations in Africa, 2004. 115 pages.

This in-house publication draws on a 2002 conference held in Accra, Ghana, that brought together over twenty associated staff of PROCMURA (Project for Christian-Muslim Relationships in Africa). The theme of the conference, and of this collection of seven papers, is the *sharia* and its implications in the African context. Contributors are from Kenya, Nigeria, Gambia, Sudan and the Netherlands. One of the overriding goals of this organisation is "to extend a hand of friendship and peace to our Muslim neighbours across Africa and the world at large with the hope that they will reciprocate such good will so that together we may live in peace." This collection begins with a paper by Johnson Mbillah (Ghanaian Presbyterian Church) on "Interfaith Relations in Africa," which sets the stage for other papers to follow. Bishop Josiah Idowu-Fearon and Emmanuel Oyelade in their papers on the *sharia* application in the Nigerian context show the complexities of the situation in that country. Samuel Ador's paper on "Sharia: Historical and Contemporary Perspectives in the Sudan" gives some excellent insights on the historical developments of the *sharia* concept there over the centuries, as well as highlighting some of the very serious consequences for both freedom of religion and freedom of conscience for non-Muslim and non-Arab citizens. He concludes: "Such policies can only lead to disharmony and lack of trust and placing an obstruction on the path of achieving true peace and reconciliation in this nation of the Sudan." John Chesworth (St. Paul's United Theological College, Limuru, Kenya) sums up his research: "It is the contention of this paper that a logical outworking of the introduction of *sharia* will be the activating of *dhimmi* status in order to 'protect' the non-Muslims, especially the Christians. It is hoped that this paper has adequately demonstrated the form of 'protection' that will ensue if this happens." Catherine Jarra, approaching from a Catholic perspective, in her "Dialogue for Peaceful Co-Existence" paper encourages ordinary Christians to promote dialogue in their context of neighbourhood, workplace, and society, and "where inter-faith marriages occur, providing support and understanding." Not everyone would want to go along with some of the ideals portrayed in this article. A concluding Communique calls the reader to "follow the example of Jesus Christ who is himself the 'Prince of Peace,' and by his death on the cross entrusted to us a ministry of reconciliation."

690.   **Mbiti, John S.**

Bible and Theology in African Christianity

Nairobi: Oxford University Press, 1987. 264 pages, ISBN: 9780195725933.

The well-known Kenyan theologian, John Mbiti, is the author of many books on African religion and theology, and renowned as the "father" of African theology. In this book he investigates the meaning of Christianity in the context of Africa and the impact of the Bible upon African Christianity. Mbiti is an advocate for neo-African Christianity – a brand of Christianity which is rooted in the culture of the African people, sensitive to the cries and aspirations of its people, and promotes the tenets of ecumenism and universalism. This kind of Christianity is deepening its presence in Africa and is in the process of formation. According to Mbiti, now is the golden opportunity for African Christians to make Christianity indigenous. He attributes the explosion of Christianity on the continent to the following factors: the work of overseas missionaries, the work of African Christian workers themselves, the presence of African traditional religion (which prepared the religious and spiritual ground for Africans to be receptive to the gospel), and the impact of the Bible. However, Mbiti must be found wanting in his own treatment of the Bible, which he uses to support and advance his cultural and theological convictions without allowing it to challenge these views. Nevertheless, this book does contain helpful insights on contextualizing the Christian message in Africa, and can be recommended for those studying theology and church growth in the context of Africa.

691.   **Mbiti, John S.**

Introduction to African Religion

Portsmouth, NH: Heinemann, 1991. 224 pages, ISBN: 9780435940027.

The first edition of this book has been for some years a required text in many secondary schools and universities across anglophone Africa. Mbiti has often been termed the "father of African Christian theology," and in all events he has been among the most prolific Christian writers on the continent, with more than 400 books and articles to his name. This classic text, first published in 1975, has become very popular as a basic, authoritative introduction to the subject of African religion. According to its preface, this second edition provides an enlarged and updated list of books for further reading, additional appendices, some changes to the text in light of new knowledge, and more photographs (which, regrettably, are poorly reproduced). However, this new edition is really an altogether different book, presenting a distinctly more upbeat outlook on African religion and culture. Thus the first three chapters of this edition are entirely new, explaining the rich African religious heritage, what African religion is and where African religion is found (art, music, dance, myths, shrines, etc.). The opening chapter of the first edition used sources from Tylor, Evans-Pritchard, Spencer, Parrinder, Frazer and others to describe early approaches to African religion as animistic, ancestor worship, magic, etc. In this second edition all the anthropological sources are referenced as "wrong approaches" and dropped. The chapter in the earlier edition containing Mbiti's much-disputed theory on African time (implying that traditional Africa did not think in terms of the future) has here disappeared completely. And whereas the "Table of Contents" of the first edition reads like a theology book, in the new edition the name of God has been dropped from the title of nearly every chapter. So if one already owns the first edition, should it now be replaced with the second edition? The answer is that one should certainly secure a copy of the new edition, but should probably still hold on to the first edition. The first edition remains useful for the good anthropological sources found in its first chapter, and also because of the much-discussed theory of time in the second chapter. Also the changes evident between the two editions will probably over time attract the interest of scholarly study tracking patterns of development in Mbiti's thought. Mbiti's presentation does not escape the danger of over-generalising, to the point of masking the extensive religious variety found among the many ethnic groups in Africa. Nevertheless, this newly updated introduction to Africa's traditional religion will likely remain an established standard for some years to come.

692. **Mbugguss, Martha**

Same Gender Unions: A Critical Analysis

Nairobi: Uzima Press, 2004. 148 pages, ISBN: 9789966855916

This book, written entirely by Africans residing in Nairobi, is a response to the tensions in the worldwide Anglican Communion regarding homosexuality. The summary statement notes, "This book seeks to analyse same gender unions from a traditional, societal, legal, medical and biblical perspective through a balanced and objective approach, while clearly showing that, whichever way you approach it, homosexuality has seriously damaging consequences." The authors include journalists, lecturers and church workers who write on their areas of expertise with clarity and depth. This is no right wing diatribe but is rather a thoughtful analysis of a pressing issue that is increasingly affecting the African church. The preamble, written by the Anglican archbishop of Kenya, gives a historical overview of recent developments in Canada, the US and the UK, and documents decisions of the 1998 Lambeth Conference, showing that some Western communions defied the worldwide church's earlier position that practicing homosexuals must not be ordained as priests. Several authors blame the Western media for making homosexuality such an issue in Africa because it is almost unknown in African society (a Kenyan study is cited). The courage of African Anglicans is also underlined because some African communions have already lost Western financial support as a result of their stand. Every section is done well, including a survey of African literature that quotes widely from African writers and political leaders. The legal chapter develops a response based on Kenyan law and notes that human rights are for all, not particular groups; the author also insists that African societal values should be the basis for its legal code, rather than the individual approach that is common in Western societies. The final chapter outlines a biblical basis for the writers' position and gives a solid interpretative framework for the book. This book is an important and timely addition to the debate over Christian attitudes toward homosexuality because the African Anglican communion, led by Nigeria's Archbishop Peter Akinola, has been leading the struggle for Anglicans to remain biblical in their approach.

693.   **Mbugua, Judy, editor**

Our Time Has Come: African Christian Women Address the Issues of Today

Grand Rapids: Baker, 1995. 151 pages, ISBN: 9780801020186.

This book records the major presentations, together with the resolutions and covenant, of the first conference of the Pan African Christian Women's Assembly (PACWA), held in Nairobi in August 1989. The editor's introduction traces the development of PACWA under the sponsorship of the Association of Evangelicals in Africa (AEA). The first chapter is the keynote address to the conference by the general secretary of AEA, Tokunboh Adeyemo. Following this are 21 short chapters, organized under four headings: the woman God uses; family issues; social issues; and women in ministry. Although the current position and training of the contributors are not stated, they generally present their topics very well and appear to be knowledgeable in their specific areas, which include many of the issues facing women and the church in Africa today. The book does not address theological differences in gender issues, but rather encourages Christian women to be led by the Holy Spirit through Scripture into ways of addressing problem areas in society, and ministering to those affected. It draws attention to difficult issues that are often avoided by the church, issues such as social injustice for women, battered women, sexual abuse and child abuse, along with acknowledged problem areas such as AIDS, divorce, polygamy and illiteracy, and it challenges women to be instrumental in church ministries to people facing these problems.

694.   **Mbuy-Beya, Marie-Bernadette**

Woman, Who Are You?: A Challenge

Nairobi: Paulines, 1998. 158 pages, ISBN: 9789966214102.

This book, written by a Congolese (DRC) Catholic Sister, aims to address the modern plight of the African woman, especially as this relates to the Roman Catholic Church in Congo. The author calls on women to see that they must not passively submit to the status quo. Instead they must pray and actively seek to bring about changes so that African women in the church, and in secular society, can know greater dignity and freedom, and together with others seek practical ways of being liberated in Jesus Christ. This should not be with the aim of lording it over men; instead, this liberation of women should help the downtrodden, the abused, the intimidated, and the social outcast to be able to live with dignity by using one's relationship with Jesus Christ to destroy the barriers that separate the members of society. This in turn will help to build a church that is a true family of God, so that justice and righteousness can be promoted. The author addresses some of the basic problems that African women still face, such as oppression, violence in the home, and sexual harassment. In regard to the church she pinpoints the problem of male domination in service and leadership roles. Women's ordination to the priesthood is not however promoted. A chapter on African women's spirituality covers traditional African spirituality, the spiritual crisis of modern Africa, and the emergence of new spiritualities especially as they relate to the charismatic movement within the Catholic Church. Some of the topics addressed, such as the role of the celibate, the Catholic Sister, the Mother Superior and the Catholic Synod, would not be relevant for the non-Catholic reader. The author's original research included interviewing prostitutes to find out the causes, consequences, and remedies for this increasing problem. Other in-depth research, based on real life situations, was done on the topic of women and violence. These findings are uniquely valuable. The analysis includes: the specific violent actions used against women, who the agents are, who the specific victims are (widows, young girls, old women, etc.), situations that may encourage this type of violence, repercussions, possible solutions, who should sponsor implementation of the solutions, and the timing of the solutions. Despite its Catholic orientation, this would be a valuable resource for those in women's ministries in Africa. It would also be useful in sensitising those in pastoral leadership in Africa to the needs so effectively addressed.

695. McCain, Danny

Tough Tests for Top Leaders: God's Strategy for Preparing Africans to Lead Global Christianity

Jos: MoreBooks, 2005. 196 pages, ISBN: 9789783794900.

McCain has been a long-time lecturer at the University of Jos in Nigeria, and a popular author of Christian books. Here he highlights thirteen key qualities that Christian leaders must have in order to be effective, and therefore promoted by God to more leadership responsibilities in the Kingdom. These qualities are presented with particular application for Christian leaders in the African context. All are undeniable virtues, needing to be developed in the life and ministries of leaders who want to be used effectively by God in Africa or any-where: obedience to God, sincere humility, Christian unity, relevance, unselfishness, suffering, openness to correction, courage, patience, cooperation, specialisation, morality and intimacy. McCain correctly emphasizes the pitfalls of cronyism and tribalism that ensnare African leaders in general and African Christian leaders in particular. He is right to contend that churches in Africa will not grow in a healthy way without the presence of faithful and effective leaders who will instil in them these Christian qualities. Readers may feel, however, that this relevant teaching is presented within a strange theological framework. According to McCain, God tests leaders, and promotes or demotes them if they pass or fail each of the thirteen highlighted challenges. For example, he proposes that the Apostle Peter was disqualified by God for worldwide ministry because he failed the test of unity. So Peter was replaced by Paul, who was more culturally sensitive. This worrisome schema is maintained throughout the presentation. McCain is doubtless reaching for an effective motivational approach. But one does not obey God out of fear of being demoted; rather one obeys out of love and submission. Various biblical leaders failed one or other of these test, but were not "demoted" by God. What of the shortcomings of biblical leaders such as Abraham, Jacob and David? This is an important study, with relevant emphases, but its usefulness feels partially marred by an approach that seems hermeneutically questionable.

696. McCain, Danny

We Believe: An Introduction to Christian Doctrine (Volume 2)

Bukuru, Nigeria: Africa Christian Textbooks, 1996. 208 pages, ISBN: 9789782668684.

An American teaching in the Department of Religious Studies at the University of Jos in Nigeria, McCain has written this two-volume systematic theology out of more than twenty years of experience in Nigeria. His treatment fits the main theological traditions of classic evangelicalism, which in part also matches the experience of the majority of Nigerian Christian university students. McCain also develops various issues on which there is no single evangelical position, such as on the sovereignty of God and the possibility of resisting grace, on baptism, and on church organisation. He admits enjoying the freedom in Nigeria's public universities to pursue biblical theology where it has led him. He shows appreciation for various Methodist and Church of the Nazarene theologians. Only one African writer (a Nigerian Baptist) and two anthologies of African Christian theologians appear in the select bibliography. Otherwise the references are dominated by Reformed writers available through ACTS in Nigeria. This second edition has been moderately re-organized, and adds a few new chapters. The order of topics is roughly built on the Apostles Creed, except that "revelation" comes first, after the manner of Reformation articles of faith. McCain has a popular style that will be pleasing and easily understood by Nigerian undergraduates, and even diploma students. It is not written for fellow scholars, nor is it attempting any innovations in theology. Each chapter has study questions. As for contextualization, McCain sprinkles illustrations from contemporary Nigerian urban life throughout the text; other illustrations come from his pastoral work in the USA. He rarely probes into traditional religion or worldview for illustration or topics, nor is there interaction with Islam. Nevertheless, he is quite aware that topics loved by some Western evangelicals are non-issues in much of Africa (e.g. age of the universe or origin of life). Under cosmology, he stresses God's ownership, our stewardship, and the evil of polluting the earth. Given the importance of the spirit world for African Christian reflection, he has separate chapters on angels, spirits and Satan. His eschatology is as simple as the Apostles Creed, although all the millennial views are explained fairly. *We Believe* has been a useful text for many seminaries in Nigeria. Many pastors, teachers and students will want their own copy.

697.   McCracken, John

Politics and Christianity in Malawi: 1875–1940: The Impact of the Livingstonia Mission in the Northern Province

Blantyre: CLAIM, 2008. 376 pages, ISBN: 9789990887501.

McCracken, a lecturer at the University of Stirling in Scotland, was in 1980–1983 Professor of History at Chancellor College in the University of Malawi. Since the publication of the first edition of this book in 1977 by Cambridge University Press, it has been recognized as one of the most successful studies to be made of the impact of a Christian mission in Africa. This revised third edition includes a new introduction, an updated bibliography covering publications from 1977, and a number of corrections in the text. After a survey of the economy and society of Malawi in the mid-nineteenth century, the text examines the home background of the Livingstonia Mission of the Free Church of Scotland, and the influence of David Livingstone upon it. It then attends to the failure of "commerce and Christianity" around the south end of Lake Malawi, and the subsequent positive response which the mission evoked among the peoples of northern Malawi. The character and function of the Overtoun Institute – possibly the most influential mission in south central Africa – is described in detail. African responses to Christianity and the relationship between Christianity and politics dominate the second half of the book. Also included is a comparative account of missionary attitudes in Malawi, and a comprehensive reassessment of the origins of the Watch Tower Movement. Finally McCracken deals with Church and School between 1914 and 1940, and considers the impact of the First World War, the educational debate and the first steps toward self-government in the young established church. This is a valuable updated contribution to the historiography of the church in Malawi.

698. McCullum, Hugh

The Angels Have Left Us: The Rwanda Tragedy and the Churches

Geneva: World Council of Churches, 2004. 132 pages, ISBN: 9782825411544.

The author, a journalist and Christian, is a staff worker for the All Africa Conference of Churches (AACC). This book is a graphic account of the tragedies which occurred in Rwanda in 1994, which the author describes as inexplicable and horrific. It is a moving book which combines factual information and personal evaluation in a very readable style. The tragic stories of individuals and communities are told as they happened. The horror speaks for itself. The author's intention is to get behind the public face of the tragedy and find the real reason for it. Regularly there is reference to the failure of the international community (including governments and aid agencies) to see the war for what it was (a deliberately and carefully planned operation of genocide) and therefore to act decisively. While there were many acts of heroism by church leaders in saving people from the atrocities, many others have blood on their hands through collaboration in the killing. There are lessons to be learned – the principal one being the need to pursue justice in the biblical sense. For anyone desiring to understand more fully the events in Rwanda of 1994 and beyond, this is essential reading. One hopes that all kinds of people including politicians, aid workers and Christian leaders will not only read such books but will learn from them for the future. [This book is also published as: *Dieu était-Il au Rwanda? La faillite des Églises* (1996).]

McDonald, Huibrecht

see review 655

699. McDonnell, Faith J. H., and Grace Akallo

Girl Soldier: A Story of Hope for Northern Uganda's Children

Grand Rapids: Baker, 2007. 240 pages, ISBN: 9780800794217.

The authors of this book believe that the story of the thousands of African children kidnapped by the Lord's Resistance Army of northern Uganda over the last three decades has not received sufficient attention by the world press or in the Christian community. This presentation seeks to redress this imbalance in two ways – by telling the story of one girl (Grace Akallo) who was victim of Joseph Kony's movement and escaped; and by providing the background information necessary to put this horrific story into context (McDonnell does an admirable job of providing the context). The book is written in chapters which alternate between McDonnell and Akallo. The advantage of this approach is that the reader is not completely overwhelmed by the ghastly detail of the ordeal of one young girl's seven months in hell, and at the same time is reminded constantly both that real lives are at stake and that there are political and religious factors which have given rise to the horror that the Acholi people have endured. McDonnell, an Anglican evangelical activist who has worked for years to alleviate the suffering of persecuted Christians, includes the stories of those (mostly young) Americans who have taken up the task of advocating for the people of northern Uganda. The book is useful in providing documentation of a situation which demands the attention of church leaders as well as politicians in Africa and beyond.

700.   **McGarry, Cecil, and Patrick Ryan, editors**

Inculturating the Church in Africa: Theological and Practical Perspectives

Nairobi: Paulines, 2001. 272 pages, ISBN: 9789966216007.

This work falls into two distinct sections. The first reprints the document from the Second Vatican Council, *Lumen Gentium: Dogmatic Constitution of the Church*. The second contains seven essays exploring the inculturation of the church in Africa based on *Lumen Gentium*. Four of these essays use the metaphor of the "family" as a focal point for examining issues such as peace and justice, spiritual formation, the Trinity and the church. Ryan also provides a helpful introduction to the purpose and content of the volume. The editors provide no information on the contributors, though the names indicate that the authors come both from within and without the continent. As an exploration of the implications of *Lumen Gentium* for the African context, this book by its very nature will be most useful to Roman Catholic readers. For example, the two longest sections of *Lumen* deal with the hierarchical nature of the church (especially the episcopate) and the role of the Blessed Virgin Mary in the church. Both subjects echo through many of the essays. Thus, when an author talks about creating a church that is both genuinely African and authentically Christian, "church" is thought of in Roman Catholic categories. Nevertheless, Protestants remain notoriously weak when it comes to ecclesiology, and in Africa books on this theme from a Protestant perspective are noticeably few. As a result, essays such as "A Community of Disciples to Witness to the Kingdom," "Spiritual Formation of God's Family," and "The Church as Family and the Quest for Justice and Peace in Africa" offer thoughtful reflection for Protestant and Catholic alike in Africa. Since the time of Abraham, God has been calling out a people of His own. How those people understand themselves, and what it means to be faithful to that identity in contemporary Africa, represent vital topics meriting further reflection. This book, in spite of its particular slant, offers useful reflection on the subject.

701.   **McKenna, Joseph C.**

Finding a Social Voice: The Church and Marxism in Africa

New York: Fordham University Press, 1999. 255 pages, ISBN: 9780823217137.

For roughly twenty years, from the mid-1960s to the mid-1980s, Marxist influence increased on the African continent. McKenna scrutinizes the impact of Marxism on the Roman Catholic Church in Africa. Two components of this statement warrant emphasis. First, Protestant churches remain outside the scope of his study. Secondly, McKenna's concern lies with the impact of Marxism on the Catholic Church in Africa, not with Roman Catholic influence on Marxism. After describing the theory and practice of Marxism, McKenna narrates Marxism's influence in Africa in general and the encounter between the Catholic Church and Marxism in particular. This is followed by four case studies of this encounter in Mozambique, Madagascar, Zimbabwe, and Zambia. McKenna concludes by comparing and contrasting the findings of his four country-by-country studies, and then offers summary reflections about the Catholic experience. He notes that Catholic engagement with Marxism in Africa took place during its movement from missionary leadership to indigenous control. Marxism directly addressed social, economic, and political issues – all matters that fall within scope of the Church's pastoral concern. Thus, at a crucial time of transition in the Church's life, this new leadership was forced to address challenges close to the heart of its mission. As a result, the questions presented by Marxism contributed to the development of the Catholic Church's maturity under African leadership. For example, the Roman Catholic community was drawn into issues of social justice, broadening its vision for social welfare in a manner that would not have occurred apart from the presence of Marxist government policies. Although others have investigated the economic, political and social impact of Marxism on the continent, this study analyses the largely unexamined subject of the influence of Marxism on the Roman Catholic Church, successfully demonstrating the role played by social context in the development of the Church. We still await studies looking at this encounter upon other churches.

McLean, Janice A.

see review 178

702.   McLellan, Dick

Warriors of Ethiopia: Ethiopian National Missionaries: Heroes of the Gospel in the Omo River Valley

Eastwood, Australia: Kingsgrove Press, 2006. 240 pages, ISBN: 9780646468709.

Lamin Sanneh has written of the often overlooked role of "local agents" in the propagation of the gospel, particularly in Africa. For Ethiopia this oversight has been exacerbated by the tendency to reserve the term "missionary" for Western expatriate agents of the gospel. Even when engaged in intentional cross-cultural church planting, Ethiopian agents have traditionally been called "evangelists." As the first of McLellan's two subtitles intimates, the dichotomy is false, and the great value of his work is to highlight the primary role of *Ethiopian* missionaries in the advancement of the gospel through southern Ethiopia. All but the last of the book's 28 chapters are entitled with the names of Ethiopian missionaries, and provide brief vignettes which illustrate their faith, courage and sacrifice for the sake of the gospel. McLellan, who served in Ethiopia for 23 years with SIM, writes from personal experience with most if not all of the missionaries he names. One does not come away from the book with a strong sense of any human failings or foibles of these local agents – they remain very much untarnished "heroes" in McLellan's presentation. Nor does McLellan reflect at length on the significance of the partnerships between local and expatriate agents which many of the stories he recounts imply. But few will finish the book without a dramatically heightened awareness of the critical role of *African* missionaries in the spread of Christianity on the continent.

703.   Meier, Inge

Quand Dieu a parlé... au Nigeria: Une traductrice de la Bible raconte

Valence, France: Éditions A.T.B., 1997. 264 pages, ISBN: 9782950939807.

Originally published in German as *Gott spricht jede Sprache* (2nd ed., 1987), this is a book to reward the reader at several levels. (i) Like many "missionary books," its accounts of God's working in the lives of the author and her family, and of their many Nigerian colleagues, are greatly encouraging and faith-building. (ii) Its frank accounts of the problems of cultural adjustment, loneliness, despair, and God's grace in overcoming such difficulties provide realistic instruction for anyone considering cross-cultural ministry. (iii) The description of how the Meiers went about engaging Nigerians in producing effective translations of the NT in three closely related languages (Izi, Ezaa, and Ikwo) gives a good overview of all that can be involved in a Bible translation project. But pastors, trainers, missiologists, and other leaders of the church in Africa will find much more in this third aspect. The Meiers went to Nigeria expecting to provide God's Word for one people group; God used them to provide His Word for three. How and why this came about provides a concrete answer to the dilemma of multilingualism in the life of the Church. We may give intellectual assent to the notion that God's glory is best enhanced when all peoples worship and know Him in their own language rather than a trade or national language; yet we may still balk at the practical difficulties, or fear that such thorough vernacularisation of the Gospel will militate against Christian unity. The Meiers' experience argues forcibly for the inadequacy of attempting Christian nurture, and often even evangelism, using a people group's second or third language (Ibo and English, in this case). As their story testifies, having the Scriptures in the heart language of different people groups helps build, rather than destroy, Christian unity. And it demonstrates clearly the benefits of teamwork between expatriates and nationals, rather than leaving a Bible translation project almost entirely in expatriate hands.

704.   Meinardus, Otto F. A.

Two Thousand Years of Coptic Christianity

Cairo: American University in Cairo Press, 2002. 368 pages, ISBN: 9789774247576.

Meinardus is well known for his learned research on the history and theology of Coptic Christianity. His publications on various aspects of the church in Egypt fill several volumes. This book may be the most important, as it attempts to provide not only a history of Coptic Christianity but an examination of its theology as this is incarnated in some of its most important institutions, especially its churches and monasteries. The volume begins with a fascinating review of the Coptic traditions concerning the Holy Family in Egypt. Here Meinardus has edited and condensed his 1986 *The Holy Family in Egypt*, smoothing out a few of the problems of that earlier publication. There is really no other comparable study of the traditions of the "flight into Egypt" available. From this beginning Meinardus proceeds to discuss the traditions of the founding of the church in Egypt by St. Mark, before continuing on more solid historical ground with a good discussion of the contributions of the early Alexandrian theologians and the founding of monasticism, a subject which occupies a fair amount of the book. Two things would have strengthened this part of the book: discussion is lacking concerning the probable Jewish matrix of earliest Christianity in Egypt, and about the presence of Gnostic Christianity in Egypt, made clear by the discovery of the Nag Hammadi documents. In the later sections of the book it would have been good to hear more about the Coptic Church's relationship with non-Coptic churches. Even the story of the relationship with Ethiopian Christianity receives only minimal treatment. Meinardus also gives scant attention to the current struggles of the Church with the state and with militant Islam – perhaps this is too difficult a subject for a book published in Cairo. The book is strong, however, in its details concerning historically significant places and its very helpful appendices and bibliography.

705.   Meiring, Piet, editor

A World of Religions: A South African Perspective

Pretoria: Kagiso Publishers, 1996. 244 pages, ISBN: 9780798639347.

Whereas in South Africa in the past only Christians were given the opportunity to practise their religion by means of radio and television, the situation changed in 1995. From that date air-time was apportioned to Christians, Muslims, Hindus, the traditional religions of Africa and the Jewish religion. The lack of suitable textbooks for students who had never before been in close contact with "other" religions was considered by the South African Association of Teachers of Mission (ATOM). It became clear that there was need for a publication in which each of the major religions was described as it existed in South Africa. This book resulted, with contributors drawn mainly from the Reformed tradition in South Africa. Chapters on African traditional religions, Hinduism, Buddhism, Judaism, Christianity, Islam, and the New Age are followed by a chapter on the theology of religions. Being specialists in their different fields, the authors give, in uniform format, access to the central facts of each of the major religions. These include the history of the religion, the founder(s), holy scriptures (with interesting extracts), the most important religious truths, ceremonies and rites, as well as a description of the everyday life of a typical family. The authors contend that there is an intense need for dialogue between religions, and notes to this effect conclude each chapter. These notes include guidelines for dialogue and sometimes also practical instruction. The difficult question of the relationship between religions is discussed at the end of the book. Church leaders and members, especially in the South African context, can use the book fruitfully to avoid unnecessary misunderstandings, and theological students in that part of Africa will find it to be a useful and reliable textbook.

706. Meja, Markina

Unbroken Covenant with God

Belleville, Canada: Essence Publishing, 2008. 420 pages, ISBN: 9781554524532.

This is the autobiography of Markina Meja, an Ethiopian born in the early 1920s who died in 2007. In the foreword the missionary scholar Paul Balisky notes that Markina Meja was one of the few educated men of the Wolaitta Kale Heywet Church in southern Ethiopia who had a nearly continuous ministry in the KHC from its founding before the 1935 Italian occupation of Ethiopia to recent times. He served as a teacher in elementary and Bible schools, pastor, evangelist, Bible translator, and secretary and chairman of the church's governing board. For a time as a young man he also taught and pastored with the Norwegian Lutherans. Markina Meja's account includes descriptions of cultural practices both of his people traditionally and of the churches that were founded among them. Stories of events in his own life illustrate these customs. Markina Meja recounts the experience of the churches during the Italian occupation, under Haile Selassie, and under the Marxist Dergue regime, including the establishment of the Evangelical Churches Fellowship of Ethiopia. He also describes his impression of journeys to Tanzania, Europe and North America. This book offers an exceptional first-hand resource for research on the history of the Kale Heywet Church in Ethiopia, or for understanding the life experience of senior first-generation African church leaders.

707. Mejia, Rodrigo

The Conscience of Society

Nairobi: Paulines, 1995. 240 pages, ISBN: LANG255211.

"The Church is the conscience of society, and today a society needs a conscience. Do not be afraid to speak." These words were spoken by Jomo Kenyatta of Kenya in July 1976 to the plenary assembly of AMECEA, the association of Roman Catholic bishops in eastern Africa. This task of being the conscience of society has been taken seriously by the Catholic Bishops of Kenya. In a series of Pastoral Letters dating from 1960 to 1995 the Church leadership has provided excellent biblical reflection, guidance and teaching as they have spoken out on various social, economic, moral and political issues that have arisen in Kenya. These letters have protested against violence, defended human rights, spoken out against corruption and injustice on all levels of society, supported family values, and called for national reconciliation. The tone of the letters is balanced, patriotic and courageous in speaking the truth. This book is a valuable resource for all those interested in the prophetic role of the church in society. Non-Catholic readers may not agree with some minor aspects of Catholic teaching but for the most part will benefit from the clear thinking and carefully crafted statements on the issues that are addressed. Each chapter contains an introduction with an explanation of the historical context, a summary of contents, the text of the letter and questions for reflection; and the book concludes with valuable indices for easy reference.

Melady, Margaret Badum

see review 708

708.   Melady, Thomas Patrick, and Margaret Badum Melady

Ten African Heroes: The Sweep of Independence in Black Africa

Maryknoll, NY: Orbis, 2011. 196 pages, ISBN: 9781570759291.

The Melady husband and wife team has jointly written an insightful easy-to-read saga of ten influential African leaders who played key roles in leveraging their countries into independence in the 1960s. The Meladys are well qualified to write these biographies. Academically they both have earned PhDs and are published authors. A two-year assignment in Ethiopia in 1956–1957 whetted Melady's appetite for things African. Subsequently, he headed up a Catholic organisation based in New York which provided friendship and hospitality to a new generation of African diplomats and leaders during their various diplomatic tours in New York. Through this means he became personally acquainted with these ten leaders. Later he served as US ambassador to both Burundi and Uganda, and in several other Africa-related diplomatic assignments. The Meladys are Catholic but write in a bipartisan manner about four Protestants leaders (Khama of Botswana, Roberto of Angola, Mondlane of Mozambique, Tubman of Liberia), as well as five Catholic leaders (Senghor of Senegal, Nyerere of Tanzania, Kaunda of Zambia, Mboya of Kenya and Olympio of Togo). The one Muslim leader in this compendium is Ahmadou Ahidjo of Cameroon. Throughout the stories of these African leaders, the role of Christianity and faith is a predominant theme. For a variety of reasons this book is significant for Africanists who are focussed on religion. The Christian virtues, such as freedom and the dignity of humankind, are exemplified in the narratives of these ten African heroes. The generous Christian qualities of friendship and care shown by the Meladys to African leaders shine through the pages of each narrative. Through their persuasion, Fordham University of New York agreed to honour Senghor of Senegal, Kwama of Botswana, and Olympio of Togo, each with the distinguished honorary degree of LLD. It would appear that through their influence the Meladys played a significant role in "soft diplomacy" during the dramatic years of African independence. The epilogue, "Africa's New Leaders," notes each of the following in a paragraph or two: Nelson Mandela of South Africa, Sam Nujoma of Namibia, Yoweri Museveni of Uganda, Paul Kagame of Rwanda and Jakaya Kikwete of Tanzania.

709. **Melvern, Linda R.**

A People Betrayed: The Role of the West in Rwanda's Genocide

London: Zed Books, 2009. 384 pages, ISBN: 9781848132450.

Although it may be painful to read yet another analysis of the 1994 Rwanda genocide when close to a million people were killed, new information continues to come to light. Such is the case with this well-researched book by an investigative journalist who also serves as a visiting fellow in the Department of International Politics at the University of Wales. She has done a remarkable job of collating numerous UN official documents from the General Assembly and Security Council, plus personal interviews and significant articles. One of her key themes is that the UN failed to act partly due to a claim by many that the strife in Rwanda was a civil war (the UN could not be involved in "outside intervention"), not genocide (which would have demanded action according to the UN charter). The foreign policies of many countries are condemned: Egypt and France for arms sales, France for helping armed French-speaking members of the Interahamwe to escape to Zaire, Belgium for evacuating its troops after Belgian nationals had been rescued, and the USA for resisting efforts to increase the size of the UN peacekeeping force. The importance of historical context is presented well: UN attention was more focussed on Serbian aggression in Bosnia and the debacle in Somalia, where eighteen Americans were killed just two days before a critical vote to expand the UN force in Rwanda. Hard evidence is given of the well-planned nature of the genocide that began only hours after President Habyarimana was killed in a plane crash. One of the few bright spots in this otherwise depressing book is the role of Major-General Dallaire, a French Canadian who headed the UN peacekeeping force; his courage in the face of terror around him and little support from his superiors is laudatory. Former UN Secretary-General Boutros Boutros-Ghali is portrayed as a weak leader too close to his French friends, whereas Kofi Annan comes off reasonably well. The summary of Rwanda's history will disappoint Christian readers, for the East African Revival is not even mentioned – a reminder of the haunting question why genuine revival 60 years before had so little preventative influence amidst the carnage. On the other hand, Rwanda's history will long be a lesson in the dangers of too close a relationship between church and state (the Hutu archbishop of Rwanda was serving on the government's central committee when the genocide began in April, and he was killed by Tutsi troops in June). As with so many books and articles on Rwanda, there are no real answers here as to what the church should have done to prevent this awful human tragedy.

710. **Meredith, Martin**

The State of Africa: A History of Fifty Years of Independence

London: Simon & Schuster, 2013. 784 pages, ISBN: 9780857203885.

Meredith is a journalist historian, based in Britain, who has written widely on Africa, including biographies of Nelson Mandela and Robert Mugabe. This book covers the political and economic history of the continent from the 1950s until the present, chronicling the painful passage from the high hopes at independence to the gutting of so many African economies today. Meredith tries to answer the question, "How did Harold Macmillan's 'wind of change' become Tony Blair's 'scar on the conscience of the world'?" He attempts the big picture, and it is not always a pretty picture. Botswana, which has bucked the general trend towards dictatorship and corruption and maintained multi-party democracy and good government, is, worldwide, the country hardest hit by AIDS. The corruption of Africa's "Big Men," with their insatiable lust for power and personal wealth at any cost; the meddling of outside powers; the failed secular economic and political theories that disregard the basic fallen nature of humankind; drought and famine; war and AIDS – the commonly recognized culprits are all there. But woven into the fabric of these stories is also man's inhumanity to man. Meredith's canvas is so big and his brush strokes so broad that the lack of footnotes can be discomfiting. Yet it would seem that he has done his homework, if some 665 bibliographic references at the end are any indication. Not every country is given equal space; social history is not allocated as much weight as economic history; foreign relations lacks the fuller treatment it would warrant; but the general effect is of a worthy continent-wide treatment. The particular contribution of this book is that the reader finishes it knowing more about Africa as a whole, as well as many details of specific people and countries. Though Meredith does not treat Christianity in Africa negatively (except when it deserves it, as in Rwanda and South Africa), he does not look for hope there. Yet the book does have implications for Christian Africa. If so much of the problem is rooted in mankind's heart of darkness, as Meredith so vividly demonstrates, hope for Africa can arise from those of its citizens enabled to demonstrate other-centred love through the transforming power of the Gospel.

711.   Messi Metogo, Éloi

Dieu peut-il mourir en Afrique?: Essai sur l'indifférence religieuse et l'incroyance en Afrique noire

Paris: Éditions Karthala, 1997. 249 pages, ISBN: 9782865376926.

In this ground-breaking study, Messi Metogo, professor at the Catholic University of Central Africa in Yaoundé, studies the phenomena of atheism and religious indifference in Africa in order to scrutinize the often-heard idea that Africans are "incurably religious." The first two parts of this study analyse the traditional and contemporary religious situation in Africa and bring to the fore many indicators of indifference or hostility towards religion. As far as Africa's pre-colonial traditions are concerned, he points to the often discussed ideas of the remoteness of the Creator-God and the anthropocentric character of religion, which are reflected in the fact that in contemporary Africa the magic side of traditional religion seems the part which survives most easily. Furthermore, even in ATR some criticism of the gods and religious practices could be found. In his analysis of contemporary Africa he points to sociological research, philosophical criticism and the attitude of the post-colonial African states to show how religion can be pushed to the margins of life, or from an anthropocentric perspective can be put to the service of other aspects of life. In the third part of his study Messi Metogo offers his own theological response, in which he rightly criticizes the tendency of African anthropological research and African theology to tie Africa to its past, while it should in fact respond to today's challenges, including religious indifference. Yet his proposals for inter-religious dialogue pose more problems than they resolve. This book and the bibliography at the end show how regrettable it is that the anglophone and francophone discussions on Christianity in Africa lack serious interaction. It is to be hoped that anglophone libraries will have readers who can profit from this book. Lecturers in ATR and in African Theology will need more adequately to take into account the realities addressed in this major study, and learn to relate their teaching to the challenges not only of African religions but also of religious indifference in modern Africa. If we continue approaching Africa with romantic ideas of the incurably religious African soul, we may not only misconstrue Africa's religious past, but also completely miss what is coming or already present, particularly in urban settings.

712.   Meyer, Gabriel

War and Faith in Sudan

Grand Rapids: Eerdmans, 2005. 236 pages, ISBN: 9780802829337.

The title of this volume is potentially misleading. One might expect a book marketed by a publisher like Eerdmans, and with a title like *War and Faith in Sudan*, to contain, first of all, a theological discussion of the significance of Christian faith in the midst of suffering. One might also expect the book perhaps to focus on the twenty-year civil war between Sudan's north and south. This volume does not attempt either to answer theological questions or to give an account of the Sudanese conflict. Meyer is not a theologian, but a journalist, and his focus here is on the effect of the war on one region, the Nuba Mountains, presenting us with extended vignettes on some important moments and events there. His strength as a writer is in seeing the heartache, the irony, the tragedy and the beauty of the Nuba people as they have lived through such a terrible period of history – all enhanced by 44 photographs. Although the entire book is useful in filling a gap in our knowledge of Sudanese Christian history, two sections are especially helpful. Most moving is the chapter entitled "Songs on the Death of Children" which documents the horrific events surrounding the bombing of Holy Cross School in February 2000. Most illuminating is the concise foreword by Francis Deng, who manages in thirteen pages to draw out the mysterious links among the war between the government and the south (the population of the south being mostly Christian and traditional), the conflict between the government and the Nuba (the Nuba Mountains are technically in northern Sudan, with a mixed Christian, Muslim and traditional population), and the then on-going conflict in Darfur between the government and the almost entirely Muslim population of western Sudan.

Mfumbusa, Bernardin

see review 1180

713.   Michael, Matthew

Christian Theology and African Traditions

Cambridge: Lutterworth Press, 2013. 260 pages, ISBN: 9780718892944.

The author is Academic Dean at ECWA Theological Seminary Kagoro in Nigeria. He holds a PhD in OT studies from ECWA Theological Seminary Jos (JETS). Here he opens up discussion specifically on the interface between Christian theology and African traditions. In doing so Michael is not engaging the modern African context as such, but more specifically the still vibrant presence of traditional Africa within that modern context. He frames his perspective primarily through the discipline of systematic theology, structuring the book by the familiar categories of that discipline. In each category Michael explores ways in which traditional Africa can still affect the theological sensibilities of African Christian believers. The passages devoted to illustrating this constitute some of the most fruitfully practical contributions of the whole. The book throughout gives evidence of a lively, bold, and expansive mind at work, based on wide reading in the literature, with a fulsome apparatus of notes and bibliography deployed. Readers may nevertheless experience the book as in measure perplexing. Partly this is because it remains unclear throughout for whom the publication may be meant. Michael wishes to offer "a contribution to the ongoing quest for an African systematic Christian theology." Is this then intended as a textbook for seminary courses in Africa? Yet the text can be noticeably uneven in the sections of theology covered, with expansive complex treatment in some earlier chapters contrasting with minimalist and even cursory coverage in some later chapters. Is the intention then perhaps not to provide a student textbook but to advance academic discussion of the theme stated in the title? That theme is well worthy of attention; as Michael says, without African Christian thought engaging African traditions, African Christianity is at risk of becoming "incapable and incompetent." He wishes to "reposition" Christian systematic theology away from its Western obsessions to address the questions affecting African believers. But by pursuing this larger task solely in terms of *traditional* Africa, Michel has immediately constricted the pool of questions relevant to his stated project. While traditional Africa is pervasively present in modern Africa, it also remains only one aspect of modern African reality. There is much else vigorously in play in today's Africa that, while lacking derivative links with traditional Africa, significantly impacts the life and thought of present-day African believers, and thereby requires the attention of Africa's aspiring theologians. A project to reorient systematic theology to the relevant needs of Africa's contemporary Christian community remains incomplete absent this larger framing. Perhaps a sequel will enable the project to achieve its fuller promise.

714.　Michel, Thomas S. J.

What Muslims Should Know about Christianity

Nairobi: Paulines, 2003. 167 pages, ISBN: 9789966218964.

Paulines Publications Africa, the prolific publisher of quality literature for the Catholic community in Africa, has released a two-part series to enhance Christian-Muslim understanding. The other title in this series is *What Christians Should Know about Islam* (edited by Ronzani and Onyango-Ajus). Here the publishers have secured a Catholic international specialist in Islamics to provide a very coherent and convincing description of the Christian faith, designed for the Muslim inquirer, or for the Christian needing to know how to respond to Muslim questions about Christianity. Michel has not only spent the last 23 years of his life in Lebanon, Indonesia, Turkey and other places, studied Arabic and acquired a comprehensive understanding of Islamic thinking, but he has also lectured on Christian theology as part of the programme in history of religions at the University of Ankara. The book is a refined presentation of his lectures, covering the Bible, basic doctrines of the Christian faith, historical development of Christianity, and an introduction to Christian philosophy and spirituality. The breadth and depth of his treatment is quite impressive, even including the Anabaptist movements in his presentation of the Reformation period, pietism in the Lutheran church in Germany, and the Pentecostal movement. He well understands and addresses Islamic allegations against the Christian faith, such as why there are four Gospels, and issues relating to the Trinity and Redemption. The brief passage on Mary covers less than a page and starts with the emphatic statement: "Christians never regard Mary as the wife of God." He also concludes: "It is important to remember that all Christians know that the eternal God has no mother, and that God has never physically generated a son." The book concludes with "Suggested Readings from the Bible," recommending some one hundred chapters from Genesis to Revelation (but no reference to the OT apocryphal writings). Certainly this is a book that would assist Muslims in Africa in better understanding Christianity, and assist Christians in Africa to know how better to share their faith with Muslims. It would probably also help many Christian readers to learn more about their own faith!

715. Middleton, John, and Joseph C. Miller, editors

New Encyclopedia of Africa: 5 Volume Set

Detroit: Gale, Cengage Learning, 2007. 3082 pages, ISBN: 9780684315577.

This encyclopedia devoted to Africa has a wealth of information in an accessible style with numerous photos and illustrations. Of particular interest is the amount of material included on Christianity and religion, all written from an African viewpoint (e.g. few expatriate missionaries are named, spirituality is taken seriously, and African agency in the spread of the gospel is highlighted). The 38-page article on Christianity includes an overview, Africa and world Christianity, African Initiated Churches and Neo-Pentecostals, the missionary enterprise, and the Coptic and Ethiopian churches. Each section also directs the reader to related articles on individuals (Augustine of Hippo, Crowther, Equiano, Harris, Johnson, Kimbangu, Shembe, Oshitelu, Tutu, etc.), prophetic movements, religious ritual, archaeology of Christianity in Africa, and so forth. Numerous aspects of African traditional religion (e.g. religion, fetish, witchcraft) and of Islam have their own articles, as do social issues such as the Truth Commission and Child Soldiers. The articles are all in alphabetical order, and the last volume has an extensive index to help the reader find information on any topic mentioned in the five volumes. It is important for those engaged in advanced research to know that this exceptional resource exists, even if they may only be able to gain access through libraries at more prestigious universities in Africa or overseas.

716. Mijoga, Hilary B. P.

Separate but the Same Gospel: Preaching in African Instituted Churches in Southern Malawi

Blantyre: CLAIM, 2000. 208 pages, ISBN: LANG255502.

Mijoga, Professor of Theology and Religious Studies at Chancellor College in the University of Malawi, has an interest in how the Bible is read and interpreted, which has led him to study sermons. For this study he draws from sermons of African Instituted Churches (AICs) in Malawi, and seeks to understand the interpretative techniques which are used in those communities. In an overview of the modes of preaching, accompanied by samples of actual sermons, the author concludes: (i) that the whole Bible is used in choice of passages for sermons; (ii) that a thematic approach with preference for narrative texts is used, with *retelling* and paraphrasing of the biblical text an important process; (iii) that most of the sermons delivered are in the imperative mood – exhortations are the mark of sermons; and (iv) that with regard to the audience addressed, sermons are characterized by endearment, revealing the closeness existing amongst members in these churches. In his next section Mijoga goes on to show that the channels for offering interpretation include: prayers, stories, proverbs, quotations, rhetorical questions, exclamations and references to local situations. In reviewing what the local exegetes preach, the question is whether AIC preachers act as vanguards of African culture or if they rather pay attention to issues like Christology, pneumatology, Satan/devil, eschatology, illness, death, women, legalism, Bible and family. The author finds that what the AIC preachers address is not different from what is addressed by the mainstream church preachers. He suggests that the claim that AICs are "vanguards of African culture" is possibly based on the observance of their rituals rather than on a study of their sermons. Mijoga's conclusion is that, so far as the content of their sermons is concerned, AICs in Malawi do not represent a Christianity that is peculiar or distinct from the Christianity represented by the mainstream churches. He establishes that although the AICs are "separate," they preach the same gospel as the mainstream churches. This book is recommended to all those interested in how the Bible is read and interpreted in Africa, as well as those interested in the African Instituted Churches.

717.   Millard, J. A.

Malihambe: Let the Word Spread

Pretoria: UNISA Press, 1999. 88 pages, ISBN: 9781868880522.

The author holds a doctorate in church history from the University of South Africa (UNISA), and until her retirement was a senior lecturer at that university. Millard produced this little booklet as a result of a research grant that enabled her to profile thirty African Christian leaders in southern Africa. The profiles (each one to three pages in length) are written for the average church member wanting a better awareness of how Christianity spread through southern Africa (the word *malihambe* in the title is translated by the subtitle: "let the word spread"). Millard intends to show through these profiles "how, to a large extent, it was through African voices that the Word spread." Despite its brevity, this book helps the reader to become more aware of the role of African church leaders in an era when many church history texts continue to stress the role of the expatriate missionary. Many of the leaders profiled have Methodist ties, but also included are other well-known figures such as Africaner (the renegade chief who was befriended and converted by Robert Moffat), William Duma (a prominent Baptist who preached widely outside of South Africa) and Tiyo Soga (a Presbyterian who was one of the earliest Africans to be educated in Scotland). Not surprisingly, many of those noted were politically involved in the days of the anti-apartheid struggle. The interest of this particular work may be primarily limited to the southern part of the continent, but it serves to illustrate the valuable contribution now available through the continent-wide resource, the web-based *Dictionary of African Christian Biography*.

718.   Miller, Donald, Scott Holland, Lon Fendall, and Dean Johnson, editors

Seeking Peace in Africa: Stories from African Peacemakers

Telford, PA: Cascadia, 2007. 248 pages, ISBN: 9782825415085.

Published in cooperation with the World Council of Churches, this book is a compilation of presentations given at the *Watu Wa Amani* (People of Peace) Conference in Nairobi in 2004, one of the special activities of WCC to highlight its "Decade to Overcome Violence" (2001–2010). Members of Historic Peace Churches (Friends, Mennonites, Church of the Brethren, Brethren in Christ) primarily from Africa were invited to share experiences and insights on what it means for a church to be a people of peace. Nearly all of the presentations are in the form of personal narrative, with little in the way of academic tone. Part I sets the stage, comparing the conference to a marketplace with a free exchange of ideas. Part II gives history and heritage from several church contexts that have fleshed out a theology of peace making. Part III is a series of personal stories about experiencing violence. Part IV gives stories of Christian peace making: how have churches and Christians responded to violence? Part V takes the challenge to a broader sphere: how is the church addressing problems of conflict and violence with public officials and governments for the common good? The book ends with a section of meditations on peace making and prayers for peace that were given at the conference. Four appendices give details of the conference. The value of this book is less in the details of its content than in its power to stimulate discussion, discipleship and possibility thinking with regard to violence and peace making within the African context. This may be new territory for many, but ground that sorely needs to be addressed.

719.   Miller, Gerald L., and Shari Miller Wagner

A Hundred Camels: A Mission Doctor's Sojourn and Murder Trial in Somalia

Telford, PA: Cascadia, 2009. 228 pages, ISBN: 9781931038546.

In Somalia the blood price paid to the family of a murdered man is 100 camels. That harsh reality hit Gerald Miller, MD, within a few months of his arrival in the Horn of Africa. Miller was an American Mennonite missionary doctor filling in for a year at the Mennonite hospital at Jamama in southern Somalia 40 years ago. He had done his best to save the life of Hussien Sadad Hassan, a government official, who had been severely injured by a drunk driver in a highway collision the night before Miller and his family arrived in Somalia. The Jamama Hospital was not equipped to do the orthopaedic surgery Hassan's fractured femur required, so Miller recommended that he be sent to Nairobi, Kenya. The Somali government refused Hassan an exit permit and ordered Miller to perform the surgery at Jamama. This despite the doctor's concerns, not least of which were Hassan's heart condition and tenuous general health. Miller enlisted the help of another nearby doctor, Dr Urquhart, who actually did the surgery. Following surgery, the patient went into shock and died. The government charged Miller with murder. The murder trial lasted just one day, and was complicated by the use of four languages: Somali, Arabic, Italian, and English. Three people were tried simultaneously, the driver responsible for the collision, Dr Urquhart the surgeon, and Dr Miller who had overall care of the patient. Both the driver (whose inebriated condition was never discussed at the trial) and Urquhart were found not guilty. Miller was found guilty of the patient's death because, according to the judge, he had had the care of the patient before and after the surgery. Although Miller's three-month prison sentence was suspended so that he could continue practising medicine at the hospital, he was ordered to recompense the family with the cash equivalent of 100 camels, and to remain in the country for five years during which he would "do nothing wrong." The most worrisome aspect was the five-year requirement. Miller had only a few months remaining in his one-year commitment and his medical practice back in Indiana beckoned him. The happy ending to this nightmarish story is that the charges were dropped and the doctor and his family were free to leave Somalia. To shelter the Mennonite Mission from retribution, Miller refused to publish his story. However, with the demise of the dictatorial reign of Mohamed Siad Barre, and with the urging of friends, Miller and his daughter decided the time was right to tell this story.

720.   Miller, Helen

The Hardest Place: The Biography of Warren and Dorothy Modricker

Belleville, Canada: Essence Publishing, 2006. 272 pages, ISBN: 9781553069966.

This is the life story of an intrepid pioneer missionary couple to the Somali people, written by a colleague. Warren and Dorothy first met when attending their local church youth group near Boston in the United States. Later during training for missionary service, Dorothy felt that God was calling her to Somalia. Warren thought that the Horn of Africa had been in contact with civilisation for centuries, and wanted to go to a harder place, in fact, *the* hardest place. Little did he know about Somalia! After marriage they departed for Somalia, going as independent missionaries because no mission society was then working in Somalia. Arriving off the coast of British Somaliland in 1933, they were surprised when the British administration, fearing unrest, denied them entrance, even though the Modrickers had been issued a visa. The young couple had to be content with settling, temporarily at least, in the nearby British colony of Aden. There they began to learn the Somali language and make contacts in the Somali community. Back in the States during World War II they met Rowland Bingham of the then Sudan Interior Mission (SIM), and learned that SIM was contemplating opening a field in Somalia. So the Modrickers joined SIM in 1943. Returning to Aden they continued to attempt access to Somalia. Dorothy also undertook a project to translate the Bible into the Somali language, and on their next furlough returned to college to study Hebrew. Finally in 1954 the couple was able to move to Mogadishu, Somalia. Warren was a man of vision and passion who thought expansively, prayed fervently, and worked tirelessly. He was a capable and no-nonsense administrator, able to negotiate effectively with government officials, and a successful fundraiser. But relations with colleagues were not always a strong point. As a good biographer, Miller does not gloss over imperfections. She writes that Warren, "being made of sterner stuff himself, was not too tolerant of what he felt might be lack of determination or courage when difficulties arose." From 1963 onward the work of missions in Somalia became more and more restricted by the newly independent Somali government, and in 1973 SIM was expelled. The Modrickers continued working with Somali people and doing translation work in Addis Ababa, and later in Nairobi. Finally in 1977 the translation of the entire Bible into the Somali language was completed and published, an accomplishment of monumental proportions. During his retirement years Warren had planned to write a book about their experience as missionaries, but he never did. Thankfully, Helen Miller has chronicled the lives of this remarkable couple, and has thus enriched the annals of missionary biography.

721. **Miller, James C.**

The Obedience of Faith, the Eschatological People of God, and the Purpose of Romans

Atlanta: SBL, 2000. 252 pages, ISBN: 9781589837669.

Miller previously taught in biblical studies at Daystar University in Kenya, subsequently at Nairobi Evangelical Graduate School of Theology, and more recently at Asbury Theological Seminary in the USA. This is a revision of his PhD dissertation completed at Union Theological Seminary in Richmond VA. For anyone working in NT studies, Miller here offered a valuable up-to-date orientation to the "Romans Debate," the vibrant ongoing discussion on Paul's purpose in writing that letter. Miller summarizes the relevant questions as follows: why did Paul write *this* letter to *these* Christians at *this* time in his ministry? Unlike many previous attempts to answer these questions, Miller suggests a coherent solution which attempts to explain the entire letter along with the historical context of the Roman Christians. Paul is not concerned to provide a summary of his theology, but writes to a specific group of Christians in the Roman Empire who are struggling with certain gospel issues. Miller's conclusion is that Paul writes to shape "a community of the new age," which Miller also calls the "eschatological people of God." This aim, summarized as the "obedience of faith," will be achieved as the Roman Christians accept Paul's description of how the gospel should work itself out in their ethnically mixed community. Those who work in NT studies will want to take note of this study, not only for the fresh solutions it offers, but also because Miller provides the uninitiated with handy orientation to the scholarly debate on the purpose of Romans.

Miller, Joseph C.

see review 715

722. **Miller, Norman**

Encounters with Witchcraft: Field Notes from Africa

Albany, NY: SUNY Press, 2012. 240 pages, ISBN: 9781438443584.

This is not a theological book, nor even a religious book. But witchcraft fear remains a widespread phenomenon in Africa, and this book is useful as a background guide to some of its social foundations and manifestations. The author is one of America's early African specialists, living in East Africa intermittently since 1960, first as a correspondent, and later working as a university teacher, researcher, documentary filmmaker, and as an advisor to African governments and UN agencies. His experience includes extended periods in Kenya, Tanzania, Uganda and Congo, spread over 40 years. He holds a PhD from Indiana University in political science and African studies. For his inquiries over many years into witchcraft Miller consulted academics, government officers, policemen, politicians, even a judge. He did field research living in a village and also interviewed traditional healers, witch-finders, and self-proclaimed witches. As Miller explores witchcraft fears and responses, he struggles with basic questions: Do witchcraft powers actually exist? He and his Western educated informants say no, but for many Africans the answer is obviously yes. Why does witchcraft persist in modern Africa? Children are informally taught about it from the time they are toddlers. What are its historic roots here? Why is witchcraft-based violence so often found amongst family members? Does witchcraft serve as a hidden legal and political system, a mafia-like under-government in modern Africa? Miller investigates witch-hunters and witch-cleansers, he learns about witchcraft as a political tool, the role secret societies play in witchcraft, that pastoralists don't have witchcraft beliefs and problems while agriculturalists do. He learns about "Christian witchcraft," that is, how various AICs combat, cleanse, and convert witches. Miller's dim view of missionaries and his thoroughly secular point of view challenge us with different ways of thinking, both when we agree with him and when we don't. If the author's own views may colour the steadfastly anti-supernatural feelings of the African professionals he interviews, still he certainly tries to give authentic voices to the many Africans who believe in and greatly fear witchcraft power. The book's narrative style makes for enjoyable reading, and it contains many useful photos, maps and drawings. It is recommended for anyone needing to think more deeply and broadly about this topic.

Mills, DiAnn

see review 794

Milton, Leslie

see review 425

723.   **Mkandawire, Orison Ian**

Chiswakhata Mkandawire of Livingstonia

Blantyre: CLAIM, 2002. 84 pages, ISBN: 9789990816396.

Few people in Malawi are unaware of Livingstonia Mission, and Dr Laws is still a household name in that land. But much of the writing of Livingstonia history is concentrated on the part missionaries from Scotland played, and on the exciting period of the beginnings and the work done into the early twentieth century. Here is offered the welcome biography of a life that spanned from the early years of the twentieth century to the present, the life of Chiswakhata Mkandawire, who was born in 1903 and died in 1998. In this book his son has written a loving tribute to his father. During his long life Mkandawire not only experienced but also participated in many of the crucial events in the history of the Presbyterian Church in Malawi. He knew personally most of the pioneer missionaries and local Christians who together laid the foundations for Christianity in northern Malawi. His career of service to the church lasted for more than 40 years. He worked his way up from office junior in 1922, to Treasurer of the Livingstonia Presbytery, and then of the whole Livingstonia Mission. By the time Livingstonia celebrated its centenary in 1975 he was Principal of the Overtoun Institution, and a key figure in the ethos of Livingstonia. His continuous service to church and mission lasted through the sluggish years of the 1930s, the War years, and the years of gaining independence for both state and church. His was a life of dedication to the service of God (not damaged when his first wife died of a lightning strike out of the blue sky) and the church (even after his unceremonious retirement in 1976, and the witchcraft accusations when his successor died in December of the same year). His advice to his son was: "Always trust in God. He has a purpose for every one of us as long as we obey His orders and commandments." His life forms a unique link between the beginning of Christianity in northern Malawi and the church of the present day. This book is a valuable contribution to the writing of more recent Malawian church history.

724.   **Mogensen, Mogens S.**

Fulbe Muslims Encounter Christ: Contextual Communication of the Gospel to Pastoral Fulbe in Northern Nigeria

Jos: Intercultural Consulting Services, 449. 2002 pages, ISBN: 9789783668751.

This book is a publication of the author's PhD dissertation for Fuller Theological Seminary. Mogensen spent nine years in Nigeria; for four of those years he was in charge of the Lutheran Church of Nigeria's mission project to Fulbe (more commonly known as Fulani). While the book is an academic contribution, it is not encumbered by erudite technical jargon. It takes the people-group approach to missiology that has been popularized by Fuller Theological Seminary, the US Center for World Missions, and especially the Perspectives on the World Christian Movement course, and applies it to the situation of the nomadic Muslim Fulbe people in Northern Nigeria. Mogensen wishes to develop guidelines for the selection of mission approaches among this group that will lead "to contextual conversions and to the establishment of contextual local congregations." Mogensen has accurately analysed the successes and failures of recent mission approaches to reaching the Fulani and has compiled nineteen recommendations for effective communication. He advocates separate Fulbe contextual house fellowships that are connected to the larger body of Christ. He also advocates a presentation of the gospel message that recognizes the importance of dreams and visions, relates to the pre-Islamic Fulbe religious system of Pulaaku, and uses contact points found in the Qur'an (the Isa passages). This text is a must-read for those working with Fulani and other pastoralists in Africa.

725. Mojola, Aloo Osotsi

150 Years of Bible Translation in Kenya, 1844–1994: An Overview and Appraisal

Nairobi: Bible Society of Kenya, 1996. 74 pages.

This booklet responds to the realisation that African Christian communities lack familiarity with the story of Bible translation in Africa, and with the status and prospects for what remains to be done in this ministry, so that their interest and support can be awakened for its completion. Mojola begins his story with the relocation of Johann Ludwig Krapf from Ethiopia to Kenya in 1844, in his attempt to evangelize the Galla (now Oromo), and with his pioneering linguistic and translation efforts in Kiswahili, Kiduruma and Kikamba. Krapf's deserved reputation is owing to his passionate drive and the pioneering nature of his researches rather than to the enduring quality of his translation. The final chapter summarizes current trends: (1) the change in the balance of power ("When the United Bible Societies began [in 1948], fully 90 percent of Bible translations in the Third World were being made by missionaries with the help of informants or translation helpers. Now in 90 percent of the projects the translators are nationals, and missionaries have become the resource persons" [E. A. Nida]); (2) the changing philosophy away from "Union" versions (which seek to represent several dialects within a single version), as a result of practical experience over recent decades; and (3) a growing cooperation among the major Bible translation agencies (United Bible Societies, Summer Institute of Linguistics, national translation agencies and national Bible Societies).

726. Molyneux, K. Gordon

African Christian Theology: The Quest for Selfhood

Lewiston, NY: Edwin Mellen Press, 1993. 432 pages, ISBN: 9780773419469.

This is among the most significant and fascinating books on African theology to appear within the last several decades. As Adrian Hastings himself says in a foreword, "No other work I know of has attempted to understand African theology in this way." The author grew up in the Congo (DRC) and served there for many years in theological education, including as the head of the Institut Supérieur Théologique de Bunia. He holds an MA from Oxford University, and this book represents his PhD research at the School of Oriental and African Studies in London. The originality of Molyneux's project was his attempt to understand African theology as a living process, which he did by means of a detailed description and evaluation of three different examples of "doing" theology in the African context. All three examples were drawn from the Congo. The first was the ongoing scholarly publications enterprise at the prestigious Faculté de Théologie Catholique in Kinshasa (where at a seminar in 1960 the very term "African theology" first came into public use). The second example was the vibrant evolving hymnology of the independent Kimbanguist Church in Congo, through which it consciously expresses its theological perspectives. The third example was the notable series of "Gospel and Culture" seminars organized in the early 1980s by the large evangelical church body CECA in northeastern Congo, through which that community sought contextually-sensitive theological reflection on the felt needs of its membership. In a masterful introductory chapter (well worth reading on its own), Molyneux traces the quest for African Christian theology in the twentieth century as a framework for his three examples. In his concluding chapter Molyneux summarizes his findings, especially as they may apply to theological education in Africa. The book is elegantly readable throughout, and at the same time weighty with insights and implications that will well repay the thoughtful reader. It also shows an admirable familiarity with the range of relevant literature both in French and in English. Most postgraduate theological libraries in Africa will want to own a copy, and those teaching or researching in African Christian theology at advanced levels will want to be familiar with its contributions.

727. Moon, W. Jay

African Proverbs Reveal Christianity in Culture: A Narrative Portrayal of Builsa Proverbs Contextualizing Christianity in Ghana

Eugene, OR: Wipf & Stock, 2009. 234 pages, ISBN: 9781606085530.

Moon was previously a missionary in Ghana, and later associate professor at Sioux Falls Seminary in the United States. Here he offers a fascinating exploration of proverbs and their use in the work of contextualization, most notably the way that they open up the Bible for oral people, and the way they can be integrated into contextualized life and thinking. This is Moon's PhD dissertation for Asbury Theological Seminary. He orients his inquiry around the critical contextualization model of Paul Hiebert, with specific focus on an anthropological approach to signs and symbols in light of constitutive communication theory. Ultimately his goal is to enable people from oral cultures to see how their traditions speak values that parallel those found in the Bible, and also to enable them to see how biblical truths affirm and critique cultural values. Moon convincingly posits that this will enable the development of contextualized communities of Christians who are still within their own cultures but who can anchor themselves in the Scriptures. Among the greatest strengths of this book is the narrative approach in presenting the findings. Moon invents four composite characters, supplemented by field notes and ethnographic interviews carried on over the course of several years. These characters are a lay Christian whose son has just died, two pastors representing opposite approaches to culture and Scripture, and a missionary who wants to learn not just the language but the culture as well. Moon weaves stories of what they go through as they learn how their own proverbs (and songs and stories) help them articulate what their culture values, so that they can understand it better in light of biblical truths. After each story, he presents a short analysis of what has happened in light of the theoretical discussion in the first section of the book. This is an exceptional book, relevant for those engaged in critical reflection on contextualization and its implementation, and as well for lecturers and students at theological colleges seeking how best to engage their own cultures with the Scriptures.

728. Moore, Henrietta L., and Todd Sanders, editors

Magical Interpretations, Material Realities: Modernity, Witchcraft and the Occult in Postcolonial Africa

Abingdon, UK: Routledge, 2001. 272 pages, ISBN: 9780415258678.

This is a collection of anthropological essays on beliefs about witchcraft and occult power in modern Africa. In the introduction the editors give a brief but helpful review of the various theoretical approaches taken by anthropologists to witchcraft beliefs in Africa, going back to Evans-Pritchard's 1937 *Witchcraft, Oracles and*

Magic among the Azande, and including the recent resurgence of interest in this topic that began with Peter Geschiere's *The Modernity of Witchcraft: Politics and the Occult in Postcolonial Africa* (1997). The anthropological perspective represented here sees African discourses on occult power as reflecting not primarily the persistence of ancient traditions, or functional elements of closed static societies (as in older anthropology), but rather as constantly changing ways of perceiving and interacting with Africa's painful experience of modernity and the forces of globalisation. The essays collected in this book are all written from this latter theoretical perspective. A sampling of the articles would include: "Cannibal Transformations: Colonialism and Commodification in the Sierra Leone Hinterland"; "Vulture Men, Campus Cultists and Teenaged Witches: Modern Magics in Nigerian Popular Media"; "Black Market, Free Market: Anti-Witchcraft Shrines and Fetishes among the Akan"; "Save Our Skins: Structural Adjustment, Morality and the Occult in Tanzania"; and "On Living in a World with Witches: Everyday Epistemology and Spiritual Insecurity in a Modern African City." This book provides useful background studies for theological and pastoral discussions on the persistence of witchcraft discourse and its impact in the lives of contemporary African believers. It is fairly technical and assumes a good background in anthropology. As such it would be useful for more advanced libraries expecting to provide resources for lecturers and researchers interested in contextually-sensitive pastoral and theological reflection in this field.

729. Moreau, A. Scott

The World of the Spirits: A Biblical Study in the African Context

Nairobi: Evangel, 1990. 221 pages, ISBN: 9789966850911.

The author first carefully develops a biblical worldview of the spirit realm by reviewing all the relevant passages on angels and demons in the OT and NT. He then presents the traditional African worldview of the spirit realm as represented in many sub-Saharan African groups. The purpose of this two-fold review is both informative and practical. Realising that Africa abounds with beliefs and practices related to the spirit realm, and that many people struggle with problems of demonic affliction, Moreau develops a balanced practical theology for dealing with such experience. He also presents a helpful method for evaluating alleged personal supernatural phenomena, especially in the African context. This book will be very useful for Christians who must deal with pastoral issues relating to the spirit world and the demonic, and will prove a valuable ministry handbook for pastors, elders, counsellors, teachers and church planters. It is biblically reliable, and also includes much practical information from the fields of psychology and pastoral counselling. Also it is exceptionally well referenced with an extensive bibliography. Moreau lectured at Nairobi International School of Theology for some years, and now teaches at Wheaton College Graduate School in the United States.

Morgan, Geoff

see review 579

730. **Morrison, Philip E.**

The Multi-Church Pastor: A Manual for Training Leadership in a Multi-Church Setting

Allentown, PA: Gratia Veritas, 2004. 113 pages, ISBN: 9780970028488.

Morrison was a lecturer at Moffat Bible College in Kenya, where for a long time he taught a course called "The Multi-Church Pastor." Here he deals with a question that relates to pastoral ministry in most parts of Africa: how can pastors in Africa cope with their responsibilities to two, three, or sometimes twenty churches? According to 2 Timothy 2:2, the answer is simple: train the local church leaders. But do ministerial training institutions adequately train pastors to train elders, deacons or other lay people, so that the numerous churches under their oversight have some care when the pastor is absent? Often the answer would have to be "Not at all," and otherwise "Not enough." *The Multi-Church Pastor* was written to help the African pastor of more than one church equip local leadership teams to minister to the congregations when he is not there. This is designed as a working manual. The first section provides theoretical foundations, dealing with the pastor's personal life as defined by what African pastors actually do, administration, principles for training experienced (and usually older) African elders, servant leadership (Osei-Mensah's *Wanted: Servant Leaders* is referenced frequently), and team ministry in the African context. The second section offers practical training sessions in servant leadership, preaching, leading and planning worship, visitation and counselling. Each session in this section is based on self-discovery and the "learning by doing" method. Introducing change in African churches is not always easy, but various difficulties are taken into account with solutions that have succeeded in local African churches. Respect for local and denominational leaders is encouraged throughout. The content of the book has been developed in conjunction with working African pastors and as a result of their experiences in multi-church situations while using earlier forms of the material. That is to say, it is field-tested in Africa and it works. It may not be the last word in helping the multi-church pastor in Africa, but it is an effective first word for an important but hitherto largely neglected category of pastoral ministry in Africa.

731. **Mosala, Itumeleng J.**

Biblical Hermeneutics and Black Theology in South Africa

Grand Rapids: Eerdmans, 1990. 218 pages, ISBN: 9780802803726.

Mosala's explicitly Marxist analysis of selected biblical texts (Micah and the Lucan birth narratives) is an attempt to criticize what he considers the uncritical use of the Bible by black theologians in the United States and in South Africa. James Cone, Desmond Tutu and Alan Boesak are all taken to task for assuming the Bible to be the "Word of God." Mosala himself sees the Bible as reflecting a class struggle which gave rise to the text as we now have it. Mosala does not believe that all biblical texts are useful for the black struggle in South Africa, and argues that the Bible must be "liberated." That is to say, apparently, that the Bible must be unmasked as a bourgeois document before it can be used in liberating ways. Although the reader may disagree both with the presuppositions and with the conclusions of Mosala's work, the book has found a wide readership, and must not be ignored by scholars working in hermeneutics and theology in Africa.

Mosala, Itumeleng J.

see also review 1098

732. Mossai, Sanguma T., editor

Réconciliation: Gage pour la reconstruction

Kinshasa: Éditions CEDI, 2006. 104 pages, ISBN: 9782751500077.

This slender volume is a collection of essays written by five men who are involved in academics and in church ministry in Kinshasa, Congo (DRC). The aim of the editor is to be able to put into the hands of Christian leaders throughout his country the tools they need to understand the crisis the country has been going through and how to react in a Christian manner, aiming for reconciliation rather than broken relationships. The articles are well researched but also aim to be practical, and the authors' investment in the process of reconciliation is obvious as one reads their articles. The three articles by the editor, based on his doctoral dissertation in Missiology at Fuller Theological Seminary in the United States, consider: tribal tensions as an obstacle for evangelisation and mission; tribal identity as a threat or as an opportunity for demonstrating Christian unity and for addressing national reconstruction; and fundamental principles of reconciliation in resolution of tribal conflicts. As can be seen, Sanguma has focused primarily on ethnic tensions. The other writers look more broadly at solving conflicts in the Congolese setting. Doronzo Bunza Yugia considers language as the basis of human relations. Masiala ma Solo focuses on the importance of personal transformation for national reconstruction. Jean-Luc Kuye-meo Mulemera reflects on the potential role of a post-conflict Truth and Reconciliation Commission, and the church's place in any such initiative. Finally, Martinez Kilandamoko explores the rational management of conflicts in the multifaceted crises affecting the Church. One wishes that publications with similar intentions could become available among Christians not only in the Congo but in many other areas of the continent experiencing ethnic or other conflicts.

Mous, Maarten

see review 645

733. Moyo, Ambrose

Zimbabwe: The Risk of Incarnation

Geneva: World Council of Churches, 1996. 49 pages, ISBN: 9782825411964.

This helpful booklet examines the relation between gospel and culture specifically within Zimbabwe. It also provides a fine introduction to those wanting to understand Shona culture and the role of the church in Zimbabwe. Moyo lectured in the Department of Religious Studies at the University of Zimbabwe. It is to his credit that in 49 concise pages Moyo has not only reviewed the history of the encounter between the Christian gospel and the indigenous culture of Zimbabwe, but has endeavoured to make his own contribution to the debate. Moyo's fundamental question is, "What does Christ look like to African Christians?" Using symbols and images from Zimbabwean culture, he answers in terms of Christ as the Saviour of the African world. Moyo's booklet is a pleasure to read and his conclusion is thought-provoking. The incarnation, he says, was a great risk that God took to communicate His love for the world. That risk has to be repeated wherever the gospel of Christ is proclaimed. This means, he says, that we must allow the gospel "to die in culture that it may bring to life with itself a new culture and a new people."

734.   **Moyo, Dambisa**

Dead Aid: Why Aid Is Not Working and How There Is a Better Way for Africa

New York: Farrar, Straus and Giroux, 2010. 208 pages, ISBN: 9780374532123.

This book has gotten a lot of publicity, some of it for what the author says – that foreign aid is harmful, but more because of who Moyo is – an extremely well-educated African woman economist who thinks that foreign assistance to Africa should be cut off completely. Moyo argues that instead of taking foreign aid, governments should seek money through the international financial markets, pursue ties with China, press for freer trade in agricultural commodities and develop microfinance. Since regular people are not benefitting from aid, she believes they will not suffer from its cessation. Aid is so harmful to Africa that Moyo claims it does not just fail to alleviate poverty, it *causes* poverty. Suggesting that aid causes poverty sets a high threshold for proof, proof which this book, targeted at a popular audience, does not provide. Moreover, the strength of Moyo's thesis lies in her narrow definition of aid, which excludes all humanitarian and charitable aid and focuses only on government or development bank direct transfers to governments, what she refers to as systemic aid. Narrowing the definition to systemic aid allows her to discount assistance that goes from governments to NGOs and that which is transferred through religious organisations. This happens to be one of the most effective areas of foreign assistance. Once one accepts that Moyo is only talking about a piece of the whole foreign assistance pie, the book becomes much more interesting. The writing is compelling. She gives a very concise and helpful overview of aid policies through the post-Cold-War era and she criticizes "aid culture." For example, she ridicules what she refers to as "glamour aid," and asks why a musician like Bono has more influence on aid than African policy-makers. Why, indeed? Moyo is just one voice from the host of African intellectuals at the International Monetary Fund, World Bank and major international firms who could also offer their opinions, but do not have public platforms from which to be heard. Moyo also addresses the interests of the many people who are involved in the provision of humanitarian assistance and development aid, noting that they realize "in their heart of hearts, that aid doesn't work, hasn't worked and won't work." Given her focus on systemic aid, this criticism appears to be levelled at the World Bank and some government programmes. Yet, the call to honesty is necessary across the board in the private as well as the public sectors.

735.   **Mpindi, Paul Mbunga**

Manuel de morale chrétienne en Afrique: Vivre la foi chrétienne au quotidien

Cotonou, Benin: Éditions PBA, 2014. 332 pages, ISBN: 9789991918921.

This substantial tome on Christian ethics by an African author is a welcome addition to francophone resources. Mpindi is from Congo (DRC), has taught in Bangui (FATEB) and in Grand Rapids (Calvin Theological Seminary). Mpindi firstly explores convergences and divergences between the respective cosmologies of the African traditional world and the Judeo-Christian biblical world. In some ways the 60+ pages of this section constitute the most important part of the book, informing and explaining much of what follows. Mpindi cautions against naïve generalisation, recognising that there are regional and ethnic variations within the African scene, but concurs with many other scholars that there is a recognisable commonality to African traditional religion. African traditional cosmology and biblical cosmology share a belief in one Supreme Being. However the Supreme Being of the former is considered to have withdrawn from the world and has no concern for relationship with humans, whereas the God of the Bible longs to relate in love and holiness with those who are separated from Him. Consequent on this, ethics within the African traditional world tends to be "utilitarian" (serving communal and personal harmony), whereas within the biblical perspective ethics is first and foremost theocentric (and only after that personal and social). The title of the book speaks of a "Manual," which implies an instructive practical guide, and this is indeed what it is. Practical moral issues explored include: marriage, birth control, divorce, sexuality, work, wealth, finance, politics, science and medicine, abortion, alcohol and tobacco, suicide and euthanasia. But several sections reflect the deliberate positioning of the project within the African context. Thus there are sections on polygamy, on "infallible and absolute authority" in African traditional society, and on tribalism. In all these chapters Mpindi first outlines existing traditional African perceptions, values, and practices, and then brings them into engagement with the distinctively Judeo-Christian biblical understanding. Some readers may wish that other ethical issues had been included, while others might not see eye to eye with every detail of the treatment. But pastors, counsellors, and teachers engaged in forming Christian leaders in francophone Africa will find in this book a valuable resource.

736. Msiska, Stephen Kauta

Golden Buttons: Christianity and Traditional Religion among the Tumbuka

Blantyre: CLAIM, 1998. 62 pages, ISBN: 9781573092296.

"The African has rightly thrown down his dirty, torn old shirt, but he has at the same time lost his golden buttons with it." This is the picturesque way in which the author describes the relationship between traditional Tumbuka religious culture and Christianity. Much of the old indeed had/has to be put aside, but not everything. There are a number of vital beliefs and practices that could do much to enlighten and enliven the Christian faith and way of life. Msiska (born c. 1914) was a prominent clergyman and educator in Malawi's Church of Central Africa Presbyterian (CCAP) for many years until he ran into a conflict with the (then) ruling Malawi Congress Party and was forced into premature retirement. He was one of the first Malawian theologians to make a significant contribution to the contextualization of Christianity in writing, and two of his most influential essays are reproduced in this slim volume. In both we detect (as the editors put it in their preface) "a profound, though not uncritical, sympathy with the traditional religion of his people combined with a passionate concern for authentic Christian discipleship." In addition to an excellent survey of the ancient belief system and way of worship, Msiska presents a thoughtful summary of how the "certainty of Christianity" enables ordinary believers to deal with some of the most pressing issues of their everyday lives, such as fear, disease, customs, marriage, death, the future, and inter-church relations. These essays are preceded by a helpful historical introduction to the life and times of Msiska by a longstanding colleague, Rev Fergus Macpherson. The Kachere Text series is to be congratulated for making these essential insights available to theological educators, their students, the Christian clergy and the Christian laity of Africa today.

737. Muchimba, Felix

Liberating the African Soul: Comparing African and Western Christian Music and Worship Styles

Colorado Springs: Authentic USA, 2008. 148 pages, ISBN: 9781934068427.

The author, a Zambian with wide experience in Christian leadership within and outside Africa, states that he is writing for "all Africans who want to be authentically African in their worship style as well as for others who desire to respect the uniqueness of African Christianity." It becomes clear as the author progresses that he has experienced worship in settings in which Christian missionaries and church leaders have required certain Western styles of worship for Zambian congregations, while viewing use of indigenous music and instruments as being unbiblical. He therefore starts with a fervent plea for indigenous Christians in all settings around the world to develop biblical styles of worship that express their identity as a people. Beginning with a study of the use of music in the OT and NT, and a brief analysis of music in worship throughout Christian history, he moves on to evaluate relationships between missionaries and African culture. From this background, he seeks to demonstrate that the early tendency of many missions toward "noncontextualization" in style of worship and church structure generally has led to Christianity being considered a foreign religion, with consequences that are still felt in the African church today. The author therefore encourages readers to understand the special qualities of African indigenous worship styles and music in contrast to those from the West. He gives specific guidelines on biblical contextualization and calls the African church to express the richness of its culture in worship in authentic biblical ways. He especially encourages the creation of new materials such as songs and dances that engage the African mind and soul. Throughout, the author guards against the pitfalls of syncretism while calling all Christians in Africa to work together in love to use the best of all traditions to worship God through music. The book is written in an easily readable style with many helpful illustrations. While it is intended for lay people, church leaders as well as those in theological training institutions will benefit from considering the ideas presented.

738. Mudenge, S. I. G.

Christian Education at the Mutapa Court: A Portuguese Strategy to Influence Events in the Empire of Munhumutapa

Harare: Zimbabwe Publishing House, 1986. 268 pages, ISBN: 9780949932693.

At the time of writing the author was Zimbabwe's permanent representative to the United Nations in New York. In this little booklet he re-tells the intriguing and little known story of Africans from what is now Zimbabwe who, mostly in the seventeenth century, trained under the Portuguese for Christian ministry and then served in various religious posts in India and further east. At least one was awarded a Master of Theology degree by the Dominicans (in 1670). This booklet was occasioned by the visit made by President Mugabe of Zimbabwe in 1983 to an obscure Christian chapel in India just outside Goa, where one of these Africans had served as priest more than three centuries earlier. This booklet is a reminder that there are many fascinating byways in the history of African Christianity yet awaiting adequate scholarly attention. The booklet is also a reminder to academics that such accounts, properly handled, can attract popular African Christian interest.

739.   Mudimbe, V. Y.

The Idea of Africa

Martlesham, UK: James Currey, 1995. 240 pages, ISBN: 9780852552346.

This is yet another gem in what is fast becoming Mudimbe's signature tradition. It is dense in style, interdisciplinary in approach, and wide-ranging in the sources and issues it tackles. A sequel to the much acclaimed *The Invention of Africa*, this book makes a significant contribution to African postcolonial studies as a masterful critique of the very idea of Africa. Moreover, it also is a project and a construct of an idea of Africa. Employing approaches from both the history of ideas and the sociology of knowledge, and using Foucault as a conceptual and methodological guide, Mudimbe brings together a variety of sources (literature, anthropology, sociology, philosophy, and the arts) which bear witness to the idea of Africa "as expounded within the Western tradition." His consistent thesis is that the idea of Africa is a product of the West. The colonialist association of Africa with primitivist and evolutionist myths became current as a consequence of the rise of anthropology as a science. It is indeed this anthropology, "the most compromised discipline," which invented the idea of Africa that colonialism would elaborate. Mudimbe argues that nowadays we are witnessing a reversal of perspective, as culture has come to be viewed within the social sciences as plural and relative. It is in this context that Mudimbe himself explores the periphery and margins of Western discourse on Africa and its *reprise* by Africans, providing the material with which he constructs his own African universe, a political project for Africa, which he presents in filigree by way of four stories that he tells his "Americanized" children. *The Idea of Africa* is an excellent sample of the best that Africa has to offer. However, to benefit from Mudimbe's insights several hurdles must be overcome. On the one hand is the structuring of the book; the four main chapters are essentially stand-alone studies, and the impression of disconnect is intensified by a sequencing that does not follow a linear logic. The more serious hurdle is the writer's style. At times the sheer volume of information drawn from such a wide variety of disciplines overwhelms the presentation. For Christian readers Mudimbe's work is relevant on two counts. First, Mudimbe remains one of the sharpest critics of the Christian presence in Africa. As in his entire work up to this point, Mudimbe sees Christianity through the prism of its main carrier in Africa, namely modernity. And it is precisely here that one can challenge him. Certainly there is more to Christianity than its undeniable association with the project of modernity; it needs to be appreciated on its own merits. Secondly, Mudimbe exemplifies the quest for identity that is prevalent in African philosophy and literature. He represents a generation of Africans who are not uncritically shackled to past traditions but have instead learned to "bargain" and "improvise" in their construction of their subjective identities. The challenge for Christianity is whether or not it will succeed in playing a formative role in shaping the idea of the Africa of tomorrow.

740.   Mudimbe, V. Y.

The Invention of Africa: Gnosis, Philosophy, and the Order of Knowledge

Martlesham, UK: James Currey, 1990. 256 pages, ISBN: 9780852552032.

This highly acclaimed book provides a deep, scholarly discussion of the development of "Africa" as a category of thought using the grid of Foucault's sociology of knowledge. A combination of philosophy, historiography, anthropology, and sociology, Mudimbe's bibliography exceeds 800 works, and he appears to interweave them all throughout this text. This examination of the historical construction of the idea of "Africa" offers intriguing insights into the enterprise, which combined the efforts of explorer, missionary, and colonial government. The resulting struggle of the African to be able to forge his or her own identity is clearly seen throughout the text. One of the refreshing elements of this book is Mudimbe's willingness to place the missionary task in its own sociological framework rather than simply castigating mission efforts as hidden colonialism. As what might be termed a mild deconstructionist, the author is willing to take the whole Western enterprise on and does not single out a particular element for attack. Another refreshing element is his extended discussion of the work of E. W. Blyden, an early forerunner of those seeking to forge an understanding of what it means to be African from the inside. Finally, the reader should note that Mudimbe's arguments parallel the broader work of Johannes Fabian *Time and the Other: How Anthropology Makes Its Object* (1983). This is especially intriguing in that the connection between the two is not openly acknowledged anywhere by Mudimbe, even though Fabian wrote before Mudimbe and acknowledged the influence of Mudimbe's thinking in his book. Mudimbe is obviously familiar with Fabian, listing Fabian's 1969 article "An African Gnosis" in the bibliography. Why *Time and the Other* is not even listed remains puzzling. Finally, a word of warning is in order. While rich in insights, this book is extremely difficult to read. The reading experience can be made more coherent if one is somewhat familiar with Foucault's work. Additionally, to put Mudimbe in context, Fabian's far more accessible book could profitably be read first. Generally speaking, this text is helpful more for lecturers and researchers who are working in African history, philosophy, or theology than for students. Advanced-level libraries will consider it essential.

741. Mudimbe, V. Y.

Parables and Fables: Exegesis, Textuality, and Politics in Central Africa

Madison, WI: University of Wisconsin Press, 1992. 264 pages, ISBN: 9780299130640.

One of Africa's leading thinkers, Mudimbe has been professor of romance studies and comparative literature at Duke University in the United States. *Parables and Fables*, together with *The Invention of Africa* (1988), and *The Idea of Africa* (1994), form a trilogy and need to be read together. Following Foucault, Mudimbe's main claim is that scientific discourses on Africa are in fact constructions that obey laws and interests alien to Africa. "Until now Western interpreters as well as African analysts have been using categories and conceptual systems which depend on a Western epistemological order." As a result, what we have on Africa are discourses of power and knowledge of otherness. These are discourses where Africa and the Africans are "invented" as the "other" of the West and the Western. They create a fictive subject, which does not coincide with any living reality. Mudimbe labels as "colonial library" all these discourses on Africa which are produced by the colonizers, the anthropologist, and the missionary. *Parables and Fables* makes a special contribution to Mudimbe's larger project. Here too he is "obsessed" with the subordination of the other to the same. He raises two essential questions: (1) "How does one think about and comment upon alterity without essentializing its features?" And (2) "In African contexts can one speak and write about a tradition or its contemporary practice without taking into account the authority of the colonial library that has invented African identities?" In answer to these two questions, Mudimbe starts out by suggesting a complete break with the colonial library. He denounces the smell of the abusive father from which Africa must escape in order to free up an authentic discursive space. Yet by the time of *Parables and Fables* he has come to concede that it is in this very colonial library that African worlds have been established as realities for knowledge. He therefore recommends that African scholars should appropriate the data therein through critical exegesis, employing the same attitude that they have to adopt towards the myths and parables of traditional Africa. The book deserves notice for at least three reasons. First, it not only suggests a theory about the colonial library but also effectively engages that library. Secondly, Mudimbe's re-reading of the Genesis myth of his own tribe, the Luba Katanga, is a creative example of the structural analysis of African myths. Finally, the book offers insightful criticism of anthropological discourse on Africa. In this book Mudimbe has furthered his reputation of an encyclopaedic knowledge. Unfortunately, he has also lived up to his other reputation, that he is at his best when he criticizes. For example, his treatment here of theological issues, such as revelation, displays a certain degree of naiveté. All the same, those attempting responsible theological reflection in the African context will find it essential to familiarize themselves with Mudimbe's growing corpus, and the challenges and insights it represents.

Mudimbe, V. Y.

see also review 102

742.   Mugambi, Jesse N. K.

African Christian Theology: An Introduction

Nairobi: East African Educational Publishers, 1989. 152 pages, ISBN: 9789966468291.

Mugambi's readable text explores issues of significance for a theology that is both Christian and of relevance to the African context. His stated orientation is a holism in which liberation and salvation are two sides of the same coin. Discussion is in four sections: (1) Definition; (2) African Christian Missiology; (3) Christology and Ecclesiology; and (4) Eschatology. With liberation as his overarching goal, his proposed methodology involves seven modes of investigation, ranging from reading and interviewing contemporary African theologians to consultations for community reflection to encouraging a new generation of Africans to join in the process. The missiology section reviews African political history, church history and contemporary African realities. The Christology and Ecclesiology section considers the Kingdom of God, the cross as a Christian symbol, poverty, education, and political power in relation to the power of the cross. The final section, dealing with eschatology, is perhaps the most provocative. Mugambi maintains that there is no unified view of the biblical teaching on our destiny, and that Paul and John borrowed heavily from Greek categories to develop their eschatology. He therefore proposes that we cannot limit human destiny to exclusively Christian or Judaic beliefs, and that traditional African orientations may be profitably examined for insights into the issue of human destiny. Three general comments may be made. First, in spite of his advocacy for a holistic approach, Mugambi devotes considerable attention to liberation issues, while salvation is left in the background for most sections of the book. Second, in comparison to his strident criticism of and call for a liberation from the West, his silence on the oppression within the African scene is its own commentary. Finally, while Mugambi argues that Christianity is foundationally a biblical faith, he calls for greater openness to the validity of non-Christian religions (following Hicks). Awareness of such orientations may aid readers as they decide whether to read or to buy or how otherwise to use this example of African Christian theological reflection.

743.   **Mugambi, Jesse N. K.**

African Heritage and Contemporary Christianity

Nairobi: Longman Kenya Ltd, 1989. 218 pages, ISBN: 9789966496188.

Though somewhat dated, especially in its bibliography, this collection of essays on the relationship between the African heritage and contemporary Christianity is still well worth reading. Mugambi, professor of philosophy and religious studies in the Department of Religious Studies at the University of Nairobi, has been a well-known Kenyan scholar and a prolific author and editor. Here he presents "the revised version of lectures delivered at various seminars for religious education teachers and tutors in Kenya over many years." This results in a certain amount of redundancy in presentation (e.g. the chapter titled "Concluding Remarks" largely duplicates chapter 8). Mugambi begins with a four-chapter historical overview of Christianity's contacts with various cultural settings from the time of Christ to the modern missionary movement in East Africa. While this is a helpful introduction, the persistently negative tone on expatriate missionary motives and methods eventually feels excessive. Mugambi seems to have a problem not just with missionaries; at one point we are told: "At best, the publications by foreign researchers remain suspect to most sensitive African researchers of the contemporary period." The bulk of the book (seven chapters) surveys principal aspects of the African (religious) heritage, e.g. concerning God, the ancestors, rites of passage, and symbolism, with particular reference to how the author believes these elements might serve to enrich the faith and practice (in living, teaching, preaching) of Christianity in East Africa. Mugambi's overview is interesting and at times innovative, e.g. his proposed corrective to Mbiti's notion of the African concept of time. But one detects a certain degree of idealisation in his approach. Thus the fear and suspicion that is commonly generated by witchcraft and sorcery, or the misunderstandings fostered by the varied practices of divination and magic, are virtually ignored. This is coupled with an uncomfortable number of assertions that might seem to run counter to the basic norms of biblical Christianity, regarding universalism, contemporary "salvation," a normative Scripture, work-righteousness, the Trinity (all of chapter 7), synergism, and the personhood of God. In short, instead of seeking "to see how the Christian message might deepen and enrich the African heritage," the author would seem to have contented himself with the inverse of that endeavour. The final chapters include useful comments on the true significance of the rite of baptism, and the current over-emphasis on the celebration of Christmas.

744.   **Mugambi, Jesse N. K.**

The Biblical Basis for Evangelization: Theological Reflections Based on an African Experience

Nairobi: Oxford University Press, 1995. 148 pages, ISBN: 9780195727005.

In this book we are offered eleven theological reflections on Christianity in the African context by Jesse Mugambi, professor of religious studies at the University of Nairobi. Every chapter was initially a paper given at a consultation or to a visiting group, and the book inevitably lacks some coherence as a result. In this respect, the subtitle more accurately reflects the contents than does the title. Mugambi works within ecumenical circles and his reflections follow that orientation. He advocates a holistic approach to mission, defining it as "healing in wholeness," maintaining that salvation is one side of the coin and liberation the other. He is rightly critical of certain elements of the historic missionary enterprise in Africa, but the sharpness of his critique does not always correlate very well with his call for charity towards alternative views. Several elements of interest may be mentioned. Mugambi argues that early missions followed what he calls the orientation of Jewish proselytising rather than the orientation of Jerusalem Council evangelism (Acts 15) – although it is not clear how he would then deal with the prescriptions that the Jerusalem Council placed on new Gentile converts. Second, Mugambi offers a particularly refreshing discussion on the issue of new names being given at baptism. Third, he urges the development of higher-level degrees for those preparing for church ministries, but then curiously omits to mention that Nairobi itself has more church-related graduate-level programmes available than any other urban centre on the continent! One is left to ponder how ecumenical commitments may sometimes function with unexpected delimitations at the local level. Overall this very readable book addresses multiple significant issues.

745.   Mugambi, Jesse N. K.

Christian Theology and Social Reconstruction

Nairobi: Acton Publishers, 2003. 225 pages, ISBN: 9789966888761.

Mugambi, the productive professor of Religious Studies at the University of Nairobi, is well known to anyone dealing with African Christian theology. Back in 1995 Mugambi published what turned out to become an epoch-making monograph, *From Liberation to Reconstruction*, in which he emphasizes *reconstruction*, rather than *liberation*, as the most relevant paradigm for contemporary African Christian theology. The book was met with much enthusiasm and soon became an important discussion partner, not only for theologians, but also for historians and biblical critics. But it also met with some criticism, and in the present book Mugambi has collected some of his responses to his critics. The book should therefore be read as the author's commentary on his own book of 1995, a commentary where he is able to develop and clarify some of the points of view expressed nearly a decade earlier. An illustrative example is a chapter where the author responds to the challenge of some of his critics to clarify the relationship between liberation and reconstruction. The processes of liberation and reconstruction are not mutually exclusive, he argues; rather, they are complementary in the sense that liberation is followed by reconstruction. Further, both are socio-political processes within specific cultural contexts, which means that they are both open to human failures and manipulation. In consequence, the distinction between theology and ideology is often blurred in the processes of liberation and reconstruction, not least because the oppressors use religion to justify their oppressive regimes. Mugambi's new book is important to students of African theology, and it should be read together with his 1995 volume.

746.   Mugambi, Jesse N. K., and Laurenti Magesa, editors

The Church in African Christianity: Innovative Essays in Ecclesiology

Nairobi: Acton Publishers, 1998. 205 pages, ISBN: 9789966420183.

The essays in this collection are of mixed quality, and the authors largely reflect a Roman Catholic and/or ecumenical background. Nevertheless this is a valuable work for anyone, regardless of theological perspective, who wishes to reflect on ecclesiology in the African context. Mugambi surveys contributions to ecumenism in East Africa, and proposes that a stronger ecumenical movement would be both biblical and compatible with evangelism and Pentecostalism. Waruta describes four types of churches in Africa, arguing that dynamism in the church has given way to statism. He then asks how African churches can recapture the dynamic that they had at the time of national independence. In a very useful article, Nthamburi surveys the ecclesiology of the African Independent Churches, highlighting what all African churches can learn in this respect from the AICs, and can usefully incorporate into their own practical ecclesiologies. Nasimiyu-Wasike presents creative ideas on the role of African women in the church's ministry, but she is perhaps overly affirming of the role that Africa's traditional religion can play in suggesting such roles. Getui offers an outstanding essay on "The Family, the Church, and the Development of Youth," with a penetrating look at youth, society and the church, and with many practical suggestions for pastoral workers. Speaking specifically to a Catholic context, Magesa calls for the voice of local churches to be heard by the church hierarchy in an African-wide conference of churches, and for more opportunity for individual non-clerical participation in the church. Walio feels that the African church needs to throw off Western models of the church and adopt African models, especially the clan, as images for what the Body of Christ should be. In an extended and wide-ranging essay, Nyamiti thoroughly develops the implications of God the Father and Jesus Christ as the Church's "divine ancestors." The church and its ritual are the means of the divine ancestors' mediation. Honour of human ancestors must be Christianized and strongly controlled. Nyamiti suggests that the contribution of distinctively African ecclesiology to the universal church is a respect for ancestral authority and tradition. Finally, Kanyandao challenges African ecclesiologies to be built around liberation from suffering as a reflection of the kingdom of God. Anyone teaching ecclesiology in the African context will want to read this book. Most of the essays will include at least some useful insights, and several (such as those by Nthamburi and Getui) are valuable in their entirety.

747.   **Mugambi, Jesse N. K., editor**

A Comparative Study of Religions

Nairobi: University of Nairobi Press, 2010. 389 pages, ISBN: 9789966846891.

This handy reference text for the comparative study of some of the world's major religions is a joint effort of six members of the Department of Religious Studies at the University of Nairobi in Kenya. The work is well researched and thoroughly documented. Although not intending to be comprehensive in its treatment of each religion, it provides excellent basic information about the origin, beliefs and practices of the religions covered. Of special significance is that within its larger scope this survey includes treatment of the religions of preliterate peoples, and in particular of African religion. Other religions under consideration include the religions of India, the religions of the Far East, and the religions of the Near East. The book culminates with a comparative study of some major themes, as well as the present state of religion and its future prospects. Perhaps central to this study is the understanding that religion as a system of beliefs and practices is "directed towards the ultimate concern of society." Each society has values, and these values are protected by the "sacred" or supernatural power which stands behind those values. Themes taken as common among various religions are: the creative act of God, forms of theism, models of relationship (between God and the world), the nature and destiny of man, good and evil, salvation, death, and immortality of the soul. While readers may wish to dissent from some of the viewpoints expressed, the value of a book like this lies in its attempt to study religions comparatively. An African proverb says, "If you have not travelled, you think that your mother is the best cook." One might say that people who have knowledge only of their own religion may not be able to make intelligent judgment of others' beliefs and practices. There is need in Africa for responsible Christian awareness of, reflection on, and intellectual interaction with other faiths, and this book will aid in that task.

748. Mugambi, Jesse N. K., and Michael R. Guy

Contextual Theology across Cultures

Nairobi: Acton Publishers, 2009. 342 pages, ISBN: 9789966888075.

This unusual book is an edited exchange of emails between a Kenyan, Jesse Mugambi, Professor of Philosophy and Religious Studies at the University of Nairobi, and an Englishman, Dr Michael Guy, whose first career after attaining a PhD in Computing was as a chartered engineer creating computer systems software. After early retirement Guy earned a BD and an MPhil at Birmingham University, and he is now a Methodist lay preacher. Mugambi's son married Guy's daughter, thus bringing into contact two men from very different backgrounds. The young Mugambi witnessed the worst aspects of colonial rule while the youthful Guy was unaware of these aspects of the fading British Empire. This book draws the reader into the authors' serious discussion of theology and culture in both the British and African settings. The theological topics are wide-ranging, from polygamy to politics, and from Christmas to contextual theology. Both men agree that the disagreement over ordaining homosexually-oriented bishops within the Anglican Communion is more muddled than managed, but vigorously debate certain aspects of the situation as they bring to one another's attention relevant documents and reports on it. For them contextual theology is based on Guy's principle as quoted by Mugambi, "If the Bible and Experience disagree then we have not found the truth and we have to continue looking until we do. Yes, I agree that the Contextual Approach is much more 'constructive' than the emotionally charged 'conservative' and 'liberal' approaches." For Mugambi and Guy, the Bible is important in doing contextual theology, but the ministry/cultural context, not the Bible, is the determining factor when drawing theological conclusions. It is not possible to place Mugambi or Guy squarely within a single traditional theological category, which is exactly what they intend, but the book is stimulating. Whether readers agree or disagree with the authors' statements on how Africa is affected by globalisation, reconstruction theology, feminism, marriage, politics, intercultural hermeneutics, customary law, multi-faith prayer, poverty, sin and evil, they will often feel like jumping into the discussion by firing off an email in support or dissent. This is not systematic or cerebral theology, but theology in the making, theology under construction.

749. Mugambi, Jesse N. K., editor

Critiques of Christianity in African Literature, with Particular Reference to the East African Context

Nairobi: East African Educational Publishers, 1943. 166 pages, ISBN: 9789966465801.

After considering what is termed the "missionary view" of African Christianity, the author devotes separate chapters to the views of seven East African writers, including prominent novelists (Ngugi wa Thiog'o, Taban Lo Liyong), churchmen (Henry Okullu, John Mbiti), and academics (Okot p'Bitek). Mugambi, professor of religious studies at the University of Nairobi, has published a stream of books over the years. Although some readers may have found his approach at times lacking in critical balance, too much an echo of accepted fashions in secular African academia, here Mugambi has done something exceptional by focussing attention on the critical interface between African Christianity and modern African literature and thought. Mugambi's materials seem mainly to have been collected and assessed in the 1970s, but they remain an authentic representation of issues still pressing upon African Christian thinking decades later – and all too rarely noticed by theologians or theological educators. The book should be of interest to all serious students of the intellectual challenges facing African Christianity in our day.

750.   Mugambi, Jesse N. K., editor

Democracy and Development in Africa: The Role of Churches

Nairobi: All Africa Conference of Churches, 1997. 196 pages, ISBN: 9789966886149.

This volume represents the formal substance of a 1994 consultation on the theme of the book, sponsored by the All Africa Council of Churches (AACC), in collaboration with the World Council of Churches. The first quarter of the book, with three papers, provides the background for the conference, beginning with an updated version of a previously published article by Mugambi on "African Churches in Social Transformation." He notes the particular challenges of democratisation, underscoring the problems he sees coming from those whose perspective is different from that of the AACC, including evangelical churches (which he, following Gifford's *The Religious Right in Southern Africa*, sees as ideological and fundamentalist, causing people to become "docile, submissive and fatalistic"), and Islam. The second paper is a simple summary of the conference proceedings, ending in an appeal for greater ecumenism. The third paper, delivered by Chipenda, the AACC General Secretary, is the opening address of the conference. Noting the difficulties posed by poverty in Africa, the author states the need to value people and to develop leadership among the women and the youth of the continent. The following eight papers are the heart of the volume and touch on different issues related to democratisation and the need for development. Following each address, one finds additional comments from the audience. These papers include: Nation-Building and Constitution-Making in Eritrea; Democratization Development and Christian Councils in Africa Today; Capacity Building, the Church and Development; Cultural and Ethnic Diversity in Promotion of Democratic Change; Social Integration and Development in Contemporary Africa; and The Depth of Democratic Change in Africa. The book's third major section includes recommendations from two working groups and final statements to close the conference. The book ends with a summary of the Morning Meditations and a list of the participants and their ecclesiastic affiliation. This volume offers a helpful snapshot for researchers of the concerns of groups associated with AACC in 1994, as the AACC sought to highlight the need for the church in Africa to reach beyond its church structures to have an impact on the larger society.

751.   Mugambi, Jesse N. K.

From Liberation to Reconstruction: Christian Theology in Africa after the Cold War

Nairobi: East African Educational Publishers, 1995. 258 pages, ISBN: 9789966465245.

The author explores the role of Christian theology in the reconstruction of Africa. The book introduces reconstruction as a new paradigm for African Christian theology under the "New World Order," in succession to the earlier theological accent on liberation. The new theme of reconstruction is attractive because it highlights the necessity of creating a new society within the same geographical space but in relation to different historical moments. The different challenges posed to Africa by the past missionary and colonial inheritance and by the "New World Order" are highlighted. In the process of Africa's transformation the Church has an important role to play, although the task of reconstruction is not restricted to theologians. This book can be profitably read not only by those concerned with theology, but also by persons involved in the humanities and social sciences.

752. Mugambi, Jesse N. K., and Laurenti Magesa, editors

Jesus Christ in African Christianity: Experimentation and Diversity in African Christology

Nairobi: Acton Publishers, 1998. 164 pages, ISBN: 9789966888846.

This collection of essays on Christology is the product of a joint Protestant-Catholic symposium held in Nairobi in 1989, with the expressed purpose to answer the question: "Who and what is Jesus the Christ in and for the Africa of today?" The two editors, both well-known Kenyan religious scholars, intended to present "as wide a spectrum of theological views as possible" on the subject of Christology, in order to promote "creative theological reflection amongst African scholars." Unfortunately, the result is rather *too* creative, at least from an evangelical hermeneutical perspective. On the other hand, it is also rather *uncreative*, in that much of what is presented repeats the tired jargon and conceptualisation of liberation theology. Granted that the setting for the various authors' reflections is African, to that extent the presentation has been "contextualized," and a number of helpful observations do emerge in the discussion. But *theologically*, the viewpoint is all too constricted. Apart from the articles by Hannah Kinoti and by Peter Kanyandogo, the rest of the contributions maintain a narrow emphasis on a secularized, human "Christ" who serves as an exemplary model for solving all of society's current political, economic, cultural, and even religious ills. Given these deficiencies, it is not inconceivable that some lecturers in theological institutions will find this volume useful, by and large, for showing students how *not* to contextualize Christology in Africa.

753. Mugambi, Jesse N. K., and Anne Nasimiyu-Wasike, editors

Moral and Ethical Issues in African Christianity

Nairobi: Acton Publishers, 1999. 233 pages, ISBN: 9789966888372.

Mugambi is the much-published professor in religious studies in Kenya. His co-editor is Anne Nasimiyu-Wasike, who previously headed a Catholic sisterhood in Uganda, and is now an associate professor in religious studies at Kenyatta University in Kenya. This collection of fourteen essays is mostly by East African scholars (five of them women), with Roman Catholic, Lutheran, Methodist and Baptist backgrounds. The essays, between 8 and 24 pages in length, cover a variety of practical issues, such as AIDS, refugees, child abuse, tribalism and amnesty. Others present an African liberation theology, or discuss the change in morality from traditional African life to the post-colonial times. While the methodology of the contributors is not homogeneous, there is a noticeable tendency: (1) to rely strongly and positively on traditional African values based on traditional worldviews (the clear exception is the essay on women and their oppression in traditional Africa), and to correlate these with teachings of the Bible and/or the (Catholic) Church; (2) to view the West quite critically, as well as current western-originated Christianity and churches in Africa; (3) to integrate social, political and economic analysis with cultural and religious factors; (4) to use more a theological approach (i.e. biblically comprehensive) than a biblistic approach (relying on specific texts); and (5) at least in some essays to criticize Scripture. The strength of this collection lies in the analysis of the issues, and in the link made between these and traditional African views. Although many of the essays contribute new insights or usefully summarize the relevant aspects of the topic, it would be wrong to expect profound ethical discussion or biblically balanced solutions from this collection.

754.   Mugambi, Jesse N. K., and Johannes A. Smit, editors

Text and Context in New Testament Hermeneutics

Nairobi: Acton Publishers, 2004. 210 pages, ISBN: 9789966888174.

Mugambi is Professor of Religious Studies at the University of Nairobi, while Smit is Lecturer in Religious Studies at the University of Durban Westville, South Africa. In an introduction and seven articles, this recent collection reveals the current state of the hermeneutical debate in the religious faculties of African universities. The greatest potential value of the book is that it challenges readers to evaluate their assumptions, methods and aims for interpreting the Bible in Africa. A great shortcoming is that of poor proofreading, leaving many distracting errors, both large and small. The contributors are named, but nothing is said about them. Some, such as Justin Ukpong, are well known; others are not at all. Ukpong's article, "Contextual Hermeneutics: Challenges and Possibilities," is worth the price of the book. Among the variety of authors several similar attitudes are evident. There is a passionate concern to interpret the Bible from a specifically African point of view and for the African context. There is usually a high respect for the Bible, though evangelicals will applaud some statements and tear their hair out at others. For example, Mugambi, in his opposition to evangelical Western missionaries, inexplicably links literal interpretation of the Bible with the dictation theory of inspiration. The hermeneutical approach in the articles is usually post-modern, reader-response oriented, focussed on the African context, community oriented, assumes cultural equality and plurality (as opposed to considering Western forms of Christianity as the norm), and dedicated to application in Africa as well as interested in reliable exegesis. A discerning reader will benefit greatly, but even postgraduate students may need guidance in picking the wheat from the chaff.

Mugambi, Jesse N. K.

see also review 588

755.   Mukendi, Félix Mutombo

La Christologie des pères apostoliques

Quiévrain, Belgium: Éditions BANTU, 1998. 201 pages.

This offering from Mutombo Mukendi once again highlights the author's interest in Christology. Printed in a fairly large typeface (about 200 words on a full page), this is an introduction to the Apostolic Fathers, useful for French-speaking institutions at a secondary level or at the beginning of a degree programme. The author does not assume any prior knowledge of the post-apostolic age (c. AD 90–150) on the part of the readers, but instead introduces relevant vocabulary, gives a brief overview of the ante- and post-Nicene fathers and then discusses Clement of Rome, Ignatius, Polycarp, Papias, Hermas, Barnabas, and the Didache in somewhat more detail. Mutombo Mukendi then turns to the ante-Nicene Fathers to discover what they had to say about Jesus Christ. He is particularly interested in the titles the patristic documents associated with Jesus (e.g. Son of David, Son of Man, Son of God, Christ, God, Lord, Saviour). Next the author briefly examines the Apostles Creed, comparing it with the Nicene Creed and the writings of the Apostolic Fathers. Discussion of the titles of Jesus is then resumed, but this time in light of relevant NT texts. Some echoes of the author's previous book reverberate here, but the material is used in a different context and at a different academic level. The author concludes his treatise with the observation that the Apostolic Fathers encourage all leaders to exemplify the same humility, service and sacrifice as Christ did. The bibliography provides a good basic list (about twenty relevant books) for a francophone library seeking to establish its patristics section. Mutombo Mukendi is with the Ligue pour la lecture de la Bible (Scripture Union) in Belgium. Given the limited number of French-speaking Africans who are able to find the time to produce academic books from an evangelical perspective, it is encouraging to see that he has continued to provide material for francophone Bible schools and seminaries.

756. Mukendi, Félix Mutombo

Herméneutique athée et exégèses modernes. A propos d'un thème capital de la foi chrétienne: Le Fils de l'Homme

Kinshasa: Ligue pour la lecture de la Bible, 1997. 190 pages.

Mukendi is a graduate of the Bangui Evangelical School of Theology (FATEB) in the Central African Republic (CAR), and has served in the leadership of Scripture Union in Africa. In part 1 of this book he offers to an informed readership some insights into various exegetical approaches to Scripture. The traditional critical approaches to biblical studies are well represented: form, tradition, and redaction criticism; also treated are materialism, structuralism, psychoanalysis, and various literary approaches. Parts 2 and 3 of Mukendi's presentation concern the theme of the Son of Man (the subject of a previous study by the author). Part 2 outlines an atheistic hermeneutical approach to the Son of Man theme, namely that of Ernst Bloch. Part 3 is an attempt to exegete (briefly) the Johannine Son of Man sayings, with a short theological synthesis at the end. In the book's conclusion, Mukendi argues that hermeneutics and exegesis cannot be divorced from one another, and that one must also be open about the presuppositions with which one approaches a text. While it is possible to use a variety of methods, the bottom line must be accuracy, academic honesty, and genuine communication. Good hermeneutics must inform good exegesis. The bibliography and footnotes seldom mention any text more recent than twenty years old, which leaves an impression that the book was produced much later than the author's original research. For example, the issues raised by the contemporary Jesus Seminar do not enter into the discussion at all. This drawback, however, may seem a slight one when dealing with classical lines of interpretation, as the author is doing here. Given the lack of any comparable text by a francophone African, francophone theological libraries at post-secondary level and higher should attempt to incorporate this affordable volume.

757. Mukonyora, Isabel, James L. Cox, and F. J. Verstraelen, editors

Rewriting the Bible: The Real Issues

Gweru, Zimbabwe: Mambo Press, 1993. 309 pages, ISBN: 9780869225387.

This book was prompted by a number of controversial statements made about the Bible in 1991 by Canaan Banana, a noted figure in political and church life in Zimbabwe and beyond. His thesis was that the Bible as we know it today should be rewritten in order to make it relevant to times and peoples living under circumstances different from the biblical ones. Since his retirement from active politics in 1988, Banana has been lecturing in the Department of Religious Studies at the University of Zimbabwe. In 1991 he read a paper at the United Theological College, Harare (where earlier he had been a part-time lecturer), calling upon Christian scholars to consider the rewriting of the Bible. He suggested that a new "Bible" might help produce peace in the Middle East. Because of his political sympathy for the Palestine Liberation Organization, Banana seriously questioned the claim made by Israel on biblical grounds to be the God-appointed owners of the holy land of Palestine, at the cost of the Palestinian people. Members of staff in the Department of Religious Studies began to interact with him on the issues involved, and this volume represents that interaction. For these academic colleagues the real issue is *interpretation* of the Bible, not the need to rewrite it. This book will be of interest to those wishing to learn how such issues are addressed in the setting of a modern African university.

758.   Mulenga, Kampamba

Blood on Their Hands

Lusaka: Zambia Educational Publishing House, 1998. 225 pages, ISBN: LANG255214.

Together with the book by Hudson, *A Time to Mourn* (1999), this claims to be among the first full-length studies of the "Lenshina" uprising in Zambia, and its bloody suppression, just before and after that country gained its independence in 1963–1964. The movement arose from the visions of Alice "Lenshina" in 1953. A decade later Lenshina's Lumpa Church had grown to such an extent that it was perceived as a threat to public order, and in particular as a challenge to UNIP, the political party of Kenneth Kaunda. UNIP youths insisted that all people carry party membership cards, but Lenshina claimed final authority among her followers and refused use of the UNIP cards. Scuffles led to violence and retaliation on both sides, which then got out of hand. In addition the Lumpa movement formed its own villages (supposedly in reaction to persecution from UNIP), but without permission from local chiefs, and thus became a threat to their traditional role. Mulenga has worked as a personnel officer in a private company in Zambia, and has done a degree by correspondence. This is not an academic book, but Mulenga has certainly accessed a number of good sources, including government archives. He met Lenshina as a child, and members of his family died in the fighting. The book is designed to defend the Lumpas, but regrettably the presentation often lacks balance and plausibility. For example, Mulenga claims that the Lumpas had two million members in 1964, when in fact the total population of Zambia at the time was just over four million. Mulenga favourably compares Lenshina with rejected religious leaders Jesus and Muhammad, and claims that three-quarters of the church members in Zambia were converted by her. He also supports some bizarre claims such as that dead Lumpas sang from their graves after their execution. A general pattern of exaggeration and bias undermines the impact of this otherwise well-researched book. Nevertheless the tragic events that resulted in violent government suppression of this religious movement remain relevant for understanding the larger patterns of African Christianity in colonial and post-colonial times.

759.   Mulholland, Dewey, Jean-Claude Loba-Mkole, and Edouward Kitoko-Nsiku

Philemon: Fellowship in God's Family

Pretoria: Sapientia Press, 2009. 86 pages, ISBN: 9780620437431.

This short commentary on Paul's letter to Philemon, by Mulholland (formerly the director of the Baptist Theological Seminary of Brasília), Loba-Mkole (United Bible Society translation consultant in Kenya) and Kitoko-Nsiku (UBS translation consultant in Mozambique), is presented as the inaugural number in the "Intercultural Commentary Series." Although the volume's subtitle might lead readers to expect *koinonia* to be the main theme expounded by the authors, the introduction will quickly disabuse them of that notion. After referencing the continuing presence of slavery across the globe, the authors assert that "legalism, liberalism, sorcery and fetishism" are also forms of bondage. The introduction ends with a description of elements in Alan Paton's 1948 novel, *Cry, the Beloved Country*, which are used to illustrate bondage to fear. The penultimate chapter also includes a section on "the journey from bondage to freedom," making it clear that the authors regard this as an important theme in Philemon. In the brief "historical-rhetorical study" of the letter the authors apparently deny Pauline authorship of Colossians, yet continue to use that letter in their historical reconstruction of the situation addressed in Philemon. The actual commentary (26 pages) works steadily through the NIV text without explicitly engaging recent scholarship on the letter. Coming as it does at the head of the new "Intercultural Commentary Series," one might have hoped for sustained reflection on the relationship between Philemon and African realities. While the letter is shown to address these realities in one or two places (*koinonia* in v. 6, for instance, is discussed in connection with *ubuntu* and *ujaama*), even the chapter entitled "Messages for Our Generation" focuses on broad (dare one say, "universal") Christian applications such as "a profile of a godly person," "characteristics of an authentic church" and "an example of effective ministry." Misspellings and grammatical errors occur on almost every page of the book to a degree that is distracting. Even publishers of modest capacities owe it to authors and readers to have manuscripts proofread.

760.   Mullen, Roderic L.

The Expansion of Christianity: A Gazetteer of Its First Three Centuries

Leiden: BRILL, 2004. 414 pages, ISBN: 9789004131354.

In this unusual work, the author, Research Fellow at the University of Birmingham, provides a catalogue of locations for which there is archaeological, inscriptional, or literary evidence for the existence of Christian communities prior to AD 325. Mullen's purpose is not to derive a thesis regarding the early expansion of Christianity but rather to provide meticulous documentation of evidence for the proliferation of Christian communities in Asia, Europe and Africa before the Council of Nicea. In Africa alone, Mullen has collected evidence for Christian communities at some 250 sites, providing yet further substantiation for the idea that Christianity is not a recent import to Africa but dates to the earliest period of Christian expansion. This is striking in view of the likelihood that the number of early Christian communities for which no evidence survives may have been much higher. Lamin Sanneh has suggested that the expansion of Christianity in Africa over the past century may provide a window onto the early expansion of Christianity, not least because the early expansion was mediated informally through local agents rather than through organized missionary activity. Mullen's introduction reinforces this perception with the observation that after Paul, "there does not seem to have been an organized Christian mission." He notes Gerd Theissen's study of early wandering charismatic teachers but also the lack of "an overarching or centralized organization behind their work." Whether or not the parallels between contemporary and early Christian expansion are precise, or the inferences regarding the relationship between Christian expansion and missionary activity germane, Mullen has done the church in Africa and elsewhere a great service by gathering the data to substantiate wide-spread Christian presence in Africa at the earliest stages. Unhappily, the cost will mean that, like most of the primary source material to which it points, the book will not be found on the shelves of many African libraries. If that is so, it is important nevertheless to be aware of the book and its findings.

761.   Mundele, Albert Ngengi

A Handbook of African Approaches to Biblical Interpretation

Limuru, Kenya: Kolbe Press, 2012. 125 pages, ISBN: LANG257025.

The author is a Catholic priest from DR Congo who received his training in biblical studies in Rome (Licentiate) and Munich (PhD on symbolism in Second Isaiah), and presently has been serving as Professor of OT, biblical methodology and African approaches to the Bible at the Catholic University of Eastern Africa, Nairobi. The book has a logical structure, introducing the reader to traditional and contextual approaches to biblical interpretation in five main chapters. Chapter 1 gives an overview of the history of biblical interpretations, from those of early Jewish and Christian times and up to those of our own time. Chapter 2 offers some background theory "towards an African biblical approach," arguing that the interpretation should be made in three consecutive steps: analysis of the biblical text, analysis of the African context, and interaction between the two. The next three chapters are then devoted to these three steps respectively. Chapter 3 offers an introduction to a "literary analysis" (in a wide sense of the expression) of the biblical texts, including aspects such as delimitation, textual criticism, structure, genre, style, etc. Chapter 4 focuses on the African context of the interpretation, first in surveying thematic preferences of African biblical interpreters, and then by offering some human sciences theory and methodology with regard to the description of the African context. Finally, chapter 5 lets text and context interact, offering examples of how such interaction has been interpreted within African biblical scholarship. The book is in many ways what the title promises it to be, a pedagogically well-structured handbook of approaches to biblical interpretation. It should probably be added that the perspective of the interpretative approaches is that of a Roman Catholic scholar, who makes extensive use of texts from the Pontifical Biblical Commission to illustrate (and legitimize) his concerns.

762.   Mungazi, Dickson A.

The Honoured Crusade: Ralph Dodge's Theology of Liberation and Initiative for Social Change in Zimbabwe

Gweru, Zimbabwe: Mambo Press, 1991. 142 pages, ISBN: 9780869225073.

This book describes the central role played by Ralph Dodge in the emergence in Zimbabwe of an African church prepared to meet the needs of African people. Dodge served as an American missionary in Angola from 1936 to 1950, and then as episcopal leader of the Methodist Church in Zimbabwe from 1956 to 1964. His leadership was governed by the concept of social change under influence of the church. To him social change was interlinked with the practice of the Christian religion, and social justice within the structure of the colonial society was virtually impossible. His profound commitment to sound, unsegregated education and to higher education for blacks, his rejection of racism in all its forms, his insistence upon the participation of black Africans in the political process, his view of the Church as a servant Church and his courageous willingness to confront the Ian Smith government led to his deportation from Rhodesia in 1964. This study is an interpretative analysis of the work that Dodge did in Africa as a crusader for social change along the lines that he defined. The study begins with a brief outline of the development of the Methodist Church in Africa since 1897. It then moves to show in ten chapters that the events in Africa from 1956 to 1980 were such that the fundamental social change that Dodge worked for was inevitable, and that his deportation only helped to accelerate the revolutionary process that he started. This work is not a biography; rather it is a conceptual analysis of Dodge's work in Africa, a discussion of the meaning and implications of what he tried to accomplish as a Christian responding to a Christian call. It focuses on his ideas of society, the reasons for believing what he did, the outcome of his actions, the ideals he lived by, and the legacy that he left for both the Methodist Church and the Africans. To read these pages is to study a personal testimony and witness of a man whose vision for the people he served, and whose commitment to his Lord, were more important than the risks involved.

763.   Munro-Hay, Stuart

The Quest for the Ark of the Covenant: The True History of the Tablets of Moses

London: I. B. Tauris, 2006. 288 pages, ISBN: 9781845112486.

The author is a British scholar of international merit and a recognized authority on the history and culture of Ethiopia. In this book he attempts to unravel fact from fiction, legend from verified history, as to the present location of the biblical gold-covered Ark of the Covenant placed in Solomon's temple c. 1000 BC. Is the Ark of the Covenant really hidden away in a church in Axum, Ethiopia? Munro-Hay took on a massive task in his detective work, which occupied him from 1995–2005. He investigated all available ancient manuscripts that made reference to the Ark of the Covenant. In his search he contacted scholars and experts in dating various ancient Ethiopian manuscripts. He himself had to become a specialist in the Ge'ez, Coptic and Arabic languages. He visited libraries in London, Oxford, Paris, Berlin and Rome. He was no stranger to Axum, since he joined a British archaeology expedition in Axum during 1973–1974. After completing his painstaking research, he states: "All the obvious avenues of approach to the true story of the Ark of Aksum have been explored." In writing up his findings, Munro-Hay has to tackle head-on the Ethiopian royal and national epic, the Kibra Nagast (KN) which was initially drafted in the thirteenth century. The KN retells the biblical story of the visit of the Queen of Sheba to see the glories of Solomon's temple and palace (1 Kings 10:1–10). But the mythic account goes on to describe Menelik, the son of Solomon and the Queen of Sheba, as a young man returning to Jerusalem and secretly making off with the Ark of the Covenant and installing this talisman in Axum, where it supposedly resides to this very day. It appears that Munro-Hay was vexed by Graham Hancock's *The Sign and the Seal* (1992), and his misinterpretation of significant facts about the Ark of the Covenant. Munro-Hay counters Hancock's amateur and misinformed ideas in some 22 citations within the book, and concludes, "Hancock . . . depends more on drama and ingenuity than fact." The book concludes with a reference to a sixteenth-century manuscript gifted to Louis Philippe, King of France (1830–1848) from Sahela Sellasie, King of Shoa: "Until c. 1579 we hear in other documents only of the altar stone of Zion, not of the Ark." This expresses the conclusion to which Munro-Hay arrives. That which ". . . exists at Maryam Seyon church at Axum, [is] in the form of a stone tablet or slab of some sort."

764.   Murphy, Conor

The New Testament: The African Bible

Nairobi: Paulines, 1995. 706 pages, ISBN: 9789966211200.

While the reference to Africa in the title of this new version of the NT attracts quick interest, the translation is sadly disappointing, nor is it clear what is distinctively "African" about it. A translator must not only know two languages (and cultures) but also have a range of additional knowledge and expertise having to do with the translation process itself. Unfortunately, this translation does not display this range of capacities. For example, it sticks closely to the surface sentence structure of the Greek, translating participial clauses literally. It uses archaisms like "begot," "behoove," "lo" (ubiquitous), "maid-servant," "bondsman" and "swaddling-bands." It shows no evidence of the translator's conscious reflection on idioms and tropes; chiasmus, litotes, metonymy, hendiadys, and euphemism are all rendered literally. The English word "scandalize" (Mark 9:42ff) does not communicate what the original means. The artwork, which is attributed to an individual, looks remarkably similar at times to illustrations published by the United Bible Societies. Footnotes are fairly good, although some devotional comments have an odd flavour. And because of the catechismal notes, this must also be described as a sectarian version.

765.   Murphy, Edward J.

A History of the Jesuits in Zambia

Nairobi: Paulines, 2003. 504 pages, ISBN: 9789966219022.

Father Murphy was formerly librarian at Hekima College in Nairobi (one of the premier theological libraries of Africa). Here he has done church historians a great favour by heading a team of writers to address the history of the Jesuits in Zambia. Beginning at Chikuni in 1905, the Jesuits were a significant factor in the educational development of pre-independent Northern Rhodesia, and this book covers both the secular history of Zambia and how the Jesuits were involved as a religious order that gave particular emphasis to education. The book does not avoid the early tension with the Seventh Day Adventists, whose mission was founded only a few days before the Jesuits came to the same area; competition for Chief Monze's support is a well-known story in Zambian church history. While attempting to represent the wider story, the various authors understandably stress the role of Roman Catholic individuals and their activities, so that at times the Protestant element is overlooked. For example, there is no mention of the very significant cooperation of the three main church groupings (Roman Catholic, mainline Protestant and Evangelical) in the 1980s (opposing Marxism being introduced in the secondary schools) and in 2001 (when former President Chiluba attempted to run for a third term). Yet this does not take away from a fascinating story of one Catholic order's educational and political involvement in the development of a modern African nation. The short biographies of leaders at the end of each chapter are often helpful, although the Polish priests' experience in World War II concentration camps was somewhat outside the main focus. This book adds important insight into one church group's role in Zambia's history, and should serve as a model for other church groups in Zambia and elsewhere in Africa to produce similar volumes. If such church histories are not written soon, much valuable material from the older generation may be lost.

Musekura, Célestin

see review 522

766. **Museveni, Yoweri K.**

What Is Africa's Problem?

Minneapolis: University of Minnesota Press, 2000. 290 pages, ISBN: 9780816632787.

The writer is the current President of Uganda, who came to power in January 1986, after a five-year guerrilla war to overthrow the Obote regime. Museveni takes his country as a microcosm of the currently critical African condition, and he examines the socio-economic, political, and psychological factors that are contributing to the seemingly perpetual state of crisis. He attempts to answer why Africa is plagued with disease, drought, debt, famine, civil war, human rights abuses and lack of democracy – problems which many other societies have somehow managed to alleviate to a considerable degree. He examines the pre-colonial, colonial, and post-colonial causes of the problems, and Africa's inadequate post-independence response to that legacy. In a nutshell, Museveni says, Africa's problem is that it is backward. Why is it backward? First, the natural obstacles of Africa such as deserts and tropical forests prevented the easy spread of ideas and commerce. Second, the climatic conditions are too comfortable, hindering innovation propelled by the need to survive. Third, foreign involvement (from the colonial period and since) has distorted African structures, especially economic ones. And although Museveni is not opposed to the church and religion, and acknowledges the positive role they can play, he believes that religion has contributed to divisiveness in Africa and has hindered progress, especially as it has served the selfish interests of various leaders. He proposes a 10-Point Programme to address Africa's perpetual state of crisis. This includes: better implementation of democracy; fostering greater national unity; striving for greater independence from outside powers; developing an independent, integrated, self-sustaining national economy; fighting corruption; and working towards greater cooperation among African countries. In view of Museveni's analysis of why Africa is backward, the questions to be pondered are: (i) will the implementation of his proposed way forward see Africa out of its present state of crisis? And (ii) what perspective should African Christianity take, and what role should it play, with respect to these issues?

767. **Musolo W'Isuka, Kamuha**

En mission comme le Seigneur

Goma: Éditions UZIMA TELE, 1999. 161 pages.

This is the first offering in a new theological series sponsored by the Protestant School of Theology of the Free University of the Great Lakes, in Goma in the Congo (DRC). The material, here reworked, began as a master's thesis presented at the Bangui Evangelical School of Theology (FATEB) in the Central African Republic. The author is currently enrolled in doctoral studies in missiology at the Free University in Goma. Believing that Jesus Christ represents the best model for missionaries to follow, the author begins with two exegetical studies. First he attends to John 1 and the incarnation of Jesus, where Jesus is sent to earth as a missionary; and secondly he treats John 20, where Jesus commissions his disciples to follow his example and to take the good news everywhere. The author then highlights what he sees as the missionary implications of these two texts, including characteristics such as compassion, sociability, and holiness. Musolo W'Isuka follows this with a theological examination of what he terms the "missionary incarnation." He asks (and responds to) several questions relating to the concept, including whether it is a realistic long-term solution to what he views as the failure of many Western missionaries to relate well to the African context. The chapter concludes with a brief description of the necessary character traits (humility, sacrifice, fellowship) of a successful missionary.

The third major section deals with practical implications. Here the author seeks to address problems that he has encountered in his dealings with the Western missionary community. He stresses, for example, the need for the missionary to be totally integrated as a member of the local church and avoid all hints of paternalism. He notes that material and financial resources have often been a source of misunderstanding and offers his own insights as to how the missionary needs to approach these issues. Finally, Musolo W'Isuka has several suggestions for national Christians that are aimed at helping them to be responsible leaders, able to understand their missionary colleagues and work with them. As a resource for francòphone theological schools, this book should not be overlooked as a discussion-generator or as a bibliographic source for missions study. Although the principles are promulgated with Western missionaries as the background, anyone in cross-cultural ministry in Africa could profit from a thoughtful, self-critiquing perusal of the volume.

768. Musopole, Augustine C.

Being Human in Africa: Toward an African Christian Anthropology

New York: Peter Lang, 1994. 261 pages, ISBN: 9780820423043.

At the time of publication the author, originally from Malawi, was assistant professor at Colgate University in the USA. More recently he has served as secretary general of the Malawi Council of Churches. While not clear from the title or its description on the back cover, the book is primarily a summary and then brief critique of John Mbiti's approach to African theology, which is the subject of six of the seven chapters. Musopole generally endorses Mbiti's approach, and supports his criticisms of the harmful effect of the alleged imposition of Western theology on African Christianity. It is in chapter six that he challenges aspects of Mbiti's thought, while claiming that he does not want "to overthrow Mbiti's interpretative paradigm but rather to rearrange it in order to strengthen it at the points I consider weak." He critiques Mbiti's understanding of African conceptions of time, his rejection of ideologies and theologies that stressed "black" identity (such as Senghor's notion of *négritude* and Cone's black theology), and his use of Western categories in his analysis of African religious thinking. According to Musopole the latter failing led Mbiti wrongly to deny the presence of salvation history and of a teleological dimension in African religions and history. At last, in chapter seven, Musopole makes his own contribution to the question of *being human in Africa*, developing his approach in terms of the image of God, relationality, a single humanity, growth in humanness, freedom, liberation and so on. Musopole argues finally that in the African consciousness of human "dignity and integrity" there is a *praeparatio evangelica*, but that the full reality of humanness "remains hidden until one encounters Jesus." Taken as an introduction to Mbiti's thought, with a brief critique, the book will be useful to some. The author's own contribution in the eighteen pages of the final chapter raises a number of already familiar issues in summary form.

Muya, Juvénal Ilunga

see review 169

769. Muzorewa, Gwinyai Henry

An African Theology of Mission

Lewiston, NY: Edwin Mellen Press, 1990. 256 pages, ISBN: 9780889460737.

Perhaps a more appropriate title for this book would have been "*Towards* an African Theology of Mission," since Muzorewa's survey of theological issues relating to mission is much more an outline of those issues than an in-depth treatment of them. The seven chapters of the book range from a survey of Western mission theologies (almost exclusively ecumenical perspectives) to a discussion of the positive values of syncretism. Also included are preliminary definitions of theology of mission and all too brief presentations on evangelism, conversion, salvation, the church, liberation, and the evangelical movement. While calling for an African approach to the issues, and providing some discussion along these lines, a leading feature of Muzorewa's study throughout is a constant critique of Western mission efforts and theology of mission in Africa. The book would have been truer to its title and stated purpose had it devoted itself more fulsomely to the formulation of a positive African theology of mission. The genre and many of the positions of *An African Theology of Mission* are familiar to those acquainted with contemporary ecumenical theological discussions. Syncretism, when defined as the intermingling of gospel and culture, takes on a positive hue. A modified pluralism (and a corresponding approach to salvation outside of the Church) is based on the concept that God is already at work everywhere in the world revealing Himself, and while He does not do so apart from Christ, the people who receive His revelation may not know Christ's name or work. Thus there is room for inclusive orientations towards the salvific work of other religions, especially Islam, Judaism, and African traditional religions. Notably missing for a theology of mission is engagement with the realities of human sin (both personal and structural) and its impact on cultures.

770. Mveng, Engelbert, editor

Spiritualité et libération en Afrique

Paris: l'Harmattan, 1987. 123 pages, ISBN: 9782858029273.

This is a report on the Pan-African meeting of the Ecumenical Association of Third World Theologians (EATWOT) held in Cairo in 1985. The editor, Bishop Mveng of the Catholic Church in the Cameroon, was the African coordinator of EATWOT. Of the seventeen participants, fifteen were of African origin, with one from Sri Lanka and one from the Philippines. In addition to the Catholic participants, Coptic Orthodox were also present (since the meeting was in Cairo). Ten participants presented the papers included in this book, covering two general themes (five papers each): (1) spirituality as it relates to liberation; and (2) the role of women in the church. Three women (Roman Catholic) contributed to the articles on women. The papers on the first theme generally call for a more realistic concept of spirituality that does indeed affect all Christians in all areas of life, but that does not envision the creation of a utopic society. The emphasis is on the necessity of a spirituality that is lived out in community. Bishop Kalilombe appropriately notes that it is difficult for the church to break away from the old Catholic idea that only those who are priests or who belong to a religious order can be truly spiritual. All of the papers were quite brief, some too brief to be substantive. One would expect in a theological colloquium more in-depth study, with a more thorough examination of Scripture. This weakness may be due to the emphasis on "experience" as a source of revelation, rather than on searching the Scriptures. When dealing with the value of women, Genesis 5:2 and passages from Paul which show the value of women are appropriately cited, but there is little effort to deal with what we might call the difficult passages from Paul that are often used to minimize women. Recommendations are presented based on the themes treated, followed by recommendations for EATWOT in order to enhance its future in Africa. This book has value in representing some of the discussion in Africa on liberation theology and on the role of women in the church. However, it cannot be said that it makes a significant original contribution to either of these discussions.

771.   Mveng, Engelbert, and Benjamin L. Libawing

Théologie, libération et culture africaines: Dialogue sur l'anthropologie négro-africaine

Yaoundé: Éditions Clé, 1996. 232 pages, ISBN: 9782708706118.

This very readable book represents several fascinating conversations between two Cameroonians, a Jesuit professor of history and a non-Catholic journalist working in the area of the social sciences. The conversations have the form of interviews, but they really represent a one-on-one teaching situation, with the priest (deceased in 1995) acting as the teacher that he was. The conversations were not recorded but were later reproduced by the student and then edited by the professor. The journalist has obviously considered several aspects of the relation between culture and religion with respect to the African continent, but his formal training is not in the area of theology. Thus Mveng often needs to fill in the gaps in terms of the historical development of different concepts. For example, he challenges the idea that liberation theology had its birth in Latin America. Rather he sees its debut in religious liberation movements exemplified, for example, in certain AICs and in the birth of African theology, with Latin America following on from these. Nevertheless, the Marxist ideas of liberation do not, Mveng claims, fit well with the African context. Some of the various topics discussed over a period of eight years include the necessity of enculturation for the church in Africa, the cultural identity of the African, the similarities and differences between African and Christian eschatology and their view of death, art and literature in Africa, and the challenges of modernity with respect to what Mveng terms "the multiple fragilities of Africa." The book helpfully provides the mature perspectives of a modern African Catholic churchman on issues of culture and theology in the African setting.

772.   Mvumbi, Frederic Ntedika

The Identity of Christ in Islam: From the Perspective of Thomas Aquinas

Nairobi: Paulines, 2008. 191 pages, ISBN: 9789966083135.

The author is a Dominican priest from the Congo (DRC), with teaching experience in other parts of Africa. Aside from this, there is no particular African character to the book. Rather it is a distinctly Roman Catholic contribution to Christian theological analysis of the Islamic perspective on Jesus. In an earlier study, *Journey into Islam*, Mvumbi included a lengthy chapter on "Qur'ānic Christology," i.e. the Qur'ān's understanding of Jesus as seen in numerous passages that mention him. This book is an expansion of that chapter. Mvumbi asserts that the Qur'ān maintains a genuine Christological perspective of Jesus which should not be regarded as a distortion of the orthodox Christian view, but which is nevertheless incomplete when compared with what Christianity advocates. His first chapter reviews the various Christological heresies that pre-date Islam in order to show how some of the ideas they promoted found their way into the Qur'ānic view of Jesus. The book goes on to offer a theological analysis of Qur'ānic Christology which the author appropriately finds to be closely tied to the Qur'ān's perspective of God. His analysis draws heavily from Thomas Aquinas' major treatise, the *Summa Theologica*. The *Summa's* orthodox exposition of the nature of God offers a corrective to Qur'ānic theology which in turn provides a more complete understanding of the nature and work of Christ. Mvumbi thus seeks to be appreciative of the Qur'ānic view of Jesus while simultaneously critical of its limitations in light of the Christian gospel. To some degree his book is a Catholic version of Kenneth Cragg's *Jesus and the Muslim* (1985). Mvumbi's work is, however, less erudite. Although he includes numerous references to important resources such as Parrinder's *Jesus in the Qur'ān*, he surprisingly makes no mention of Cragg's book, among others. It is, nevertheless, an interesting addition to the few works which dare to discuss this important theme.

773.   Mvumbi, Frederic Ntedika

Journey into Islam: An Attempt to Awaken Christians in Africa

Nairobi: Paulines, 2008. 176 pages, ISBN: 9789966083197.

This is a short introduction to Islam for African Christians from a Roman Catholic perspective. The author is a Dominican priest from Congo (DRC). He has taught Islamic studies in both Nigeria and Kenya, thus bringing a broad range of experience in sub-Saharan Africa to his task. Islam, along with its various African expressions, is a vast subject, so it is not surprising to find certain topics covered well while others are barely mentioned. The result is that some sections of this book are very helpful while others are less so. Readers will especially appreciate the opening section offering a basic description of Islamic beliefs and practices given in question/answer format. Also worthwhile is the section providing an overview of the diversity of Islam and of Christian-Muslim relations in Africa. In his extensive discussion of monotheism in Islam, Mvumbi dwells too long on the pre-Islamic religions of the Semitic world. In his treatment of Qur'ānic Christology, he not surprisingly also gives special attention to Mary in the Qur'ān. The closing sections and appendices deal with issues especially relevant to Catholics: the lack of official leadership in Islam; how congregational preaching can help Christians better understand Islam (here a few examples would have been helpful); and the nature of Christian-Muslim dialogue, based on documents both from Vatican II and from official African Catholic statements. Throughout the work Mvumbi seeks to find common ground on which to build positive Christian-Muslim relations, emphasising that Christians need to learn about Islam in both its ideal and contextual realities, and to love and seek peaceful relations with Muslim neighbours. Overall, this is a semi-scholarly introduction with a prominent Catholic slant. While there are more balanced and reliable Christian introductions to Islam available, Mvumbi's contribution can be welcomed, given the dearth of such works written by and for Africans.

774.   Mwakimako, Hassan

Mosques in Kenya: Muslim Opinions on Religion, Politics and Development

Berlin: Klaus-Schwarz-Verlag, 2011. 84 pages, ISBN: 9783879976430.

In countries where Muslims form a significant minority, Christians often remain unaware of Muslims as neighbours and fellow citizens. There are a few books for Africans which help to dispel this ignorance with regard to Muslim belief and practice (e.g. John Azumah, *My Neighbour's Faith* [2008]). Also needed are books dealing with the social, economic and political dimensions of the Muslim community within a particular region or country. Mwakimako's slender book provides significant information in this regard for Kenya, where Muslims form a sizeable minority of the population. The author is a moderate Muslim scholar who teaches Islam at the University of Nairobi. His book is the product of an extensive survey among Kenyan Muslims which brings together their own opinions on their status and role within Kenyan society. It covers much more than simply mosques as religious and social institutions. Included are issues dealing with education, economics, political involvement, Muslim organisations and women within the Muslim community. Generally, Mwakimako finds that Muslims in Kenya feel marginalized and even discriminated against, without equal access to education, medical facilities, the political process, etc. Of special interest to Christians are Muslims' overwhelming resentment toward Christian opposition to the Kadhi Courts (a provision of the Kenyan Constitution which allows for the settlement of family legal issues according to Islamic sharī'ah), and Muslims' generally negative perceptions of the West. The book ends with several case studies of Muslims within a particular locality which highlight the tensions between traditional Sufi-oriented Muslims and those coming from a strict Wahhabi persuasion; the examples given are mostly drawn from western Kenya. The book includes several charts depicting multiple statistics from various regions of Kenya, which happen to be confusing and sometimes inaccurate. Overall, however, the data and analysis found in this book are very helpful in providing an insider's view of the Muslim community of Kenya.

Mwaura, P.

see review 471

775.   Mwiti, Gladys

Young Lives at Risk

Nairobi: Evangel, 1997. 154 pages, ISBN: 9789966200709.

The author states in her introduction that the book "is written from a Christian counselling perspective and seeks to awaken the awareness of the reader to the confused, embittered world of the abused child," with the intention of encouraging and guiding constructive responses from readers. While referencing both secular and Christian sources generally, the book clearly focuses on the situation in Africa, and especially in Kenya. As such it is a pioneering contribution on an otherwise still largely neglected topic for Christian concern in Africa. The author deals with the difficulties in defining abusive behaviour, and with culturally sanctioned forms of abuse, as well as with the stresses of modern urban living that are associated with escalating abuse levels. Among factors contributing to abuse she points to the effects of filmed violence, especially on TV, which makes violence appear normal, and to the family isolation of urban living. While clearly stipulating that counsellors of abuse victims must be professionally trained Christians, the author also gives helpful suggestions to church leaders and laypeople on ways to prevent, identify and intervene in abuse situations. Parts of the book are fairly clinical, but this would be a useful reference in equipping pastors and others in church ministry roles in dealing with child abuse.

Myers, Bryant L.

see review 1186

Authors
N–P

Nadar, Sarojini

see reviews 918 and 920

Nankuni, I

see review 163

Naré, L.

see review 29

776.   Nash, Peter T.

Reading Race, Reading the Bible

Minneapolis: Fortress Press, 2003. 84 pages, ISBN: 9780800636333.

The major point of this booklet is that race is an anthropological construct rather than a biological reality, and that race in spite of this, or better because of this, really matters in biblical interpretation. The author has for a couple of decades taught Biblical Hebrew and OT studies in universities, seminaries and colleges in the US and in Brazil, and has also been a visiting lecturer in Mozambique, South Africa, and Zimbabwe. This booklet reflects his journey – as an African American – into the relationship between race and biblical interpretation. After a general discussion of the growth and decline of race treated as a biological category, this insight is related to OT interpretation. Nash argues that the traditional historical-critical preference for searching for interpretive parallels to the OT in Arabia and in (a de-Africanised!) Egypt, rather than in Africa, historically speaking reflects racial assumptions. Nash then points out that the recent development of African OT scholarship changes the field of OT studies for the better. The booklet reflects the author's American (US and Brazilian) context. Still, when it challenges biblical scholarship to take the race question seriously, and as part of this discusses Africa's role in biblical interpretation, it obviously touches a concern of African biblical scholarship too.

777.   Nasimiyu-Wasike, Anne, and Douglas W. Waruta, editors

Mission in African Christianity: Critical Essays in Missiology

Nairobi: Acton Publishers, 1993. 191 pages, ISBN: 9789966888495.

This book presents papers delivered at a conference convened by the Eastern African Ecumenical Theological Symposium in Kenya in 1992. The essays cover a broad variety of issues, including ecological concerns, the growing influence of new age orientations, urbanisation, and women's liberation in Africa. The authors represent a significant range of contemporary African ecumenical and Catholic scholarship, though they fall within the broad parameters typically found in critical ecumenical discussion. In general the authors sharply criticize the colonial enterprise and the missionary attachments to that enterprise. In some essays one is left with the impression that the missionaries could do no right except by accident (e.g. Waruta, "The Educational Mission of the Church in Africa: An African Perspective"). Others give a more nuanced and responsible critique of the negatives of missionary work in Africa (e.g. Magesa, "The Mission of the Church in Africa and the Post-Cold-War International Order"). The book is useful for presenting examples of contemporary ecumenical thinking about mission engagement with Africa. The strongest essays are by Mukamba, Magesa and Mugambi. Mukamba provides a solid survey of the historical changes taking place in mission thinking, in light of the larger shifts in intellectual life, which thereby offers a backdrop for developing a missiology of environment and ecology. Magesa provides a reliable, nuanced and relevant analysis of the ramifications of the West's increasing inattention towards Africa since the demise of Communism. Mugambi provides a sensible discussion on urbanisation, modernisation, and post-modernisation in Africa. Apart from these three, it is hard to identify any really new formative ground that has been covered. The collection functions as a sampler of intellectual reflection in African ecumenical circles.

Nasimiyu-Wasike, Anne

see also review 753

778. Naudé, Jacobus A., editor

The Bible and Its Translations: Colonial and Postcolonial Encounters with the Indigenous

Stellenbosch: SUN Press, 2009. 233 pages.

The editor is a professor at the University of the Free State, Bloemfontein, South Africa. The thirteen essays in this volume go back to three conferences on Bible interpretation and translation held in 2006–2008, plus some additional contributions on Bible translation and training of translators. Accordingly, rather than being a unified whole with a clear-cut topic and logical progression, it is a collection of individual essays that only to some extent have a common thematic focus, i.e. that of past and present challenges facing the translation of the Bible, primarily in southern African contexts. Almost all contributors hold university posts in South Africa. The collection opens with an essay using the metaphor of an African fetish mask to describe and interpret power aspects of the translation process. The fetish, be it a mask or a biblical text, encapsulates power by pulling together into one form of expression what lies beyond human control, but it also endows power, as it exerts influence over those who are presented with it. Then follow essays related to the first Bible in Setswana, Robert Moffat's translation of 1857, which was the first in an African language in sub-Saharan Africa. One paper asks what made Moffat's translation so popular, and suggests that an answer might be found in the impression made by Mary and Robert Moffat's nearly 50 years of caring service in Kuruman; they lived out the texts. A second paper focuses on power questions, noticing that the first encounters with the Bible in southern Africa did not take place under colonialism but under African territorial and political control. The next set of essays analyses various contextual challenges. Two of these offer case studies of colonial interference in Bible translation projects in southern Africa. One, from a Zulu context, argues that the original concepts of the Supreme Being – Nkulunkulu – changed and were cast into a Christian mould. And from a Southern Sotho context, a second paper shows examples of Afrikaans influence in a 1909 translation. A third contribution addresses the challenges facing the translators of the first Bible in Afrikaans (1933), before the standardisation of the language. The last set of essays addresses Bible translation and training of Bible translators, for example the role of participation in the translation process by the receptor community, or the biblical concept of wisdom in relation to training of Bible translators. The volume constitutes a welcome contribution in the fields of Bible translation and reception historical studies in colonial and postcolonial southern African contexts.

779.   **Nazer, Mende, and Damien Lewis**

Slave: My True Story

New York: PublicAffairs, 2005. 368 pages, ISBN: 9781586483180.

Nazer is a young Sudanese Muslim woman from the Nuba Mountains. In 1993, at about the age of twelve, she and a dozen other girls were taken by force from their families and villages during a late-night attack by Arab raiders. She was taken by horseback and then truck to Khartoum. She was sold to a family for whom she worked as a slave for the next seven years. Eventually she was sent to London to be a slave in the family of an official serving in the Sudanese Embassy. With the help of other Sudanese in London she escaped from her captivity in 2000 and now lives in England. Her story is one which could be repeated over and over, if only those Sudanese who have been and are still enslaved had the voice and the opportunity to speak. The Nuba, both Muslim and Christian, are among those groups who have suffered most grievously because of the Sudan civil war fought during the 1980s and 1990s. It is worth noting that, although she is a Muslim, Nazer has been aided by Christians since her escape (see especially the mention of the Christian social activist Baroness Caroline Cox). Nazer's story is told simply yet eloquently and provides helpful background for understanding the recent history of the Sudan.

780.   **Ncozana, Silas S.**

Sangaya: A Leader in the Synod of Blantyre Church of Central Africa Presbyterian

Blantyre: CLAIM, 2001. 76 pages, ISBN: 9789990816174.

This is the second title published in the Kachere Texts series, which intends to make available to the general public shorter documents and essays that are of special value as sources for the study of religion in Malawi. In the present booklet the former General Secretary of Malawi's Church of Central Africa Presbyterian (CCAP) Blantyre Synod (1985–1995), Rev S. S. Ncozana, fondly reflects back upon the achievements of his former mentor, Rev Jonathan Sangaya, who was one of the leading Protestant clergymen in Malawi during the 1960s and 1970s. This ministry-oriented biography highlights Sangaya's role as a key transitional figure in the development of an African-led and administered church. In 1962 he became the first Malawian General Secretary for the Blantyre Synod and Moderator of the General Synod of the CCAP. To Sangaya fell the unenviable task of integrating national church and expatriate mission, and thus he "served as a test case of the African's ability to lead the church into the future." Sangaya's considerable success in this regard in many fields of endeavour is recounted in a brief but interesting way, as is his vision for a more ecumenically-minded approach to inter-church relations. Several short theological writings by Sangaya are included in an appendix; one wishes that there could have been more of these, perhaps replacing the section, "Selected Letters and Telegrams of Condolence" (received at his death). While this easy-to-read text may be of primary importance to readers in Malawi, the story of this dynamic leader of the early post-missionary era is of value to all students of African church history.

781. Ndjérareou, Abel

De quelle tribu es-tu?

Cotonou, Benin: Éditions PBA, 2007. 143 pages, ISBN: 9782911752469.

Ndjérareou, originally from Chad, was formerly Dean of the Faculté de Théologie Evangélique de Bangui (FATEB) in the Central African Republic. This is a reworking and development of his contribution to the 2002 book *Le Tribalisme en Afrique… et si on en parlait*, edited by Daniel Bourdanné. In *De quelle tribu es-tu?* Ndjérareou aims to bring a theological, missiological and ethical approach to bear on the problem of tribalism, in brief to answer the question, "What does God say?" The book consists of four chapters: God's Reply, Jesus' Reply, The Church's Reply and The Church Leaders' Reply. Ndjérareou considers the biblical approach to ethnicity, particularly emphasising the implications of the creation of all human beings in God's image, and the malignant effects of the Fall on every human relationship, including ethnic difference. In "Jesus' Reply" he argues from the Great Commission that the great purpose of Christ's work was to create one great new family out of all the nations, such that the church is a new and unique tribe. In the last two sections he applies the biblical teaching to the church and its leadership, where too often the blood of tribe carries greater weight than the blood of Jesus. Accordingly, he calls on the church and its members to recognize their transformed identity and to live it out; and on its leaders to fulfil their prophetic, intercessory and teaching roles with respect to tribal difference, and themselves to be an example to those they lead. The book is clear and easy to read, and it communicates the author's own passion and conviction. It is much enriched by anecdotes drawn from Ndjérareou's personal experiences of tribal tensions and conflict in Chad, and of the way in which Christians and churches have responded. Ndjérareou might perhaps have given more detailed attention to the nature of ethnic or tribal identity, which tends simply to be accepted as a given. There is also very little discussion of the positive value of ethnic difference in the purpose of a God who has so obviously made a world of rich and teeming variety and diversity. The problem with ethnicity, or tribe, is not so much ethnic difference as such, which has immense potential for the mutual enrichment of human beings, but that of the too frequently hostile human response to those who are "other." This book is a courageous contribution to evangelical African reflection on a critical issue, where professing Christian believers, including evangelicals, have so often lost their way with disastrous consequences.

782. Ndletyana, Mcebisi, editor

African Intellectuals in 19th and Early 20th Century South Africa

Cape Town: HSRC Press, 2008. 80 pages, ISBN: 9780796922076.

This slim volume presents short biographical sketches of five influential Xhosa intellectuals from the nineteenth and early twentieth centuries. In his youth Ntsikana (c. 1780–1821) had encountered the missionary Johannes van der Kemp, but was only later converted through a vision. Vuyani Booi describes Ntsikana as a Christian prophet who engaged in what would today be called inculturation. Ntsikana is also known for the hymns he composed, some of which are still sung today. Tiyo Soga (1829–1871) studied theology in Glasgow and became the first black South African clergyman when he was ordained in 1856 by the United Presbyterian Church. He returned to South Africa with his Scottish wife and served as a pastor, missionary and hymn-writer. In addition to this essay, the editor also writes about John Tengo Jabavu (1859–1921), journalist, political activist and educator. Vilified by many for his support of the Afrikaner Boers and his refusal to join the South African Native National Congress (SANNC, which became the African National Congress) because of its (then) racial exclusivity, Jabavu is also remembered for his involvement in establishing what would become the very influential University of Fort Hare. Jabavu's biography reminds us that reality usually moves beyond the dualistic categories so foundational to much postcolonial historiography. Mpilo Walter Benson Rubusana (1858–1936) engaged in similar activities to Jabavu, notes Songezo Joel Ngqongqo, but often from the opposite perspective. Most significantly, Rubusana joined others in founding the SANNC in 1912. Finally, Mncedisi Qangule writes about the poetry of Samuel Edward Krune Mqhayi (1875–1945). In addition to writing poetry, Mqhayi worked as a journalist and is also credited with having produced the first Xhosa novel. The concentration of intellectual activity in the Eastern Cape in this period can be traced to missionary activity in this area. The fact that all these men excepting Mqhayi have entries in the *Dictionary of African Christian Biography* (www.dacb.org) bears witness to the influential role that Christianity played in the intellectual foundations of modern South Africa. Although full-length biographies for most of these figures have been written, some of these are quite dated. This book, suitable for those with secondary education and above, might introduce these important thinkers to a future generation of African historians who could fruitfully explore the themes touched upon in this work.

783.   Ndlovu, Danisa, Jim Lo, and Grace Holland

Ephesians and Philippians

Nairobi: Evangel, 1998. 241 pages, ISBN: 9789966200839.

This is a worthy example of the well-established and popular Text-Africa TEE series of texts. The study-books in this series are designed for students in theological education by extension (TEE) or other non-formal training programmes, but could also be useful in residential courses, especially at the secondary level or lower, e.g. for preparatory assignments. As with all these books, the ten lessons of this study are in linear, programmed format. Each lesson is focussed on the primary themes of one chapter in the biblical text. Ndlovu is a Zimbabwean who studied at Daystar University in Kenya, has lectured at Ekuphileni Bible Institute in Zimbabwe, and coordinated the TEE programme of the Brethren in Christ there. Lo served thirteen years as a missionary doing church planting, teaching, and editing and directing the TEE programme of the Wesleyan Church in Southern Africa. He also taught at Indiana University. Grace Holland, who edited this title, helped to lay the foundation for the Text-Africa project with her husband, Fred, in 1971. She holds a doctorate from Trinity Evangelical Divinity School in the USA, has served as a missionary with the Brethren in Christ in Zimbabwe and Zambia, and did extensive editorial work with the Text-Africa Project. As with the other books in this series, this one is written in simple English (approximately grade 5 level). The programmed format and easy-to-understand language is an intentional device to help adult learners in Africa. The approach is perhaps more devotional than interpretative, intending to stimulate application of the Scriptures to life. The Text-Africa series seeks to avoid denominational distinctives while maintaining a conservative evangelical approach. TEE programmes across Africa will be putting this title to use, and the many theological libraries that collect the Text-Africa series will be adding it to their collection.

784. Ndubuisi, Luke

Paul's Concept of Charisma in 1 Corinthians 12: With Emphasis on Nigerian Charismatic Movement

Bern: Peter Lang, 2003. 274 pages, ISBN: 9783631505847.

Originally from Nigeria, Ndubuisi earned his doctorate from the University of Munich with this thesis, a thorough exegetical treatment of 1 Corinthians 12, with focus on the vocabulary Paul used to discuss spiritual gifts. Whole chapters are devoted to word studies of "charis," "charisma," and "pneuma." Ndubuisi then turns to a discussion of the historical situation in the Corinthian church which gave rise to Paul's treatment of spiritual gifts in 1 Corinthians 12–14, and to a comparison of the teaching on gifts in 1 Corinthians 12 with that in 1 Corinthians 14. Finally there are two chapters on the relevance of this biblical material for the Nigerian (Roman Catholic) charismatic movement. This pastoral application is quite balanced. Ndubuisi has no desire to "quench the Spirit" by calling a halt to the charismatic movement, but he is certainly aware that the movement has some problems and dangers. Discussing the gift of prophecy, for example, he speaks of "the danger of absolutizing the relative," of paying so much attention to a word of prophetic inspiration that other sources of revelation are given a back seat. However, Ndubuisi does not spend much energy complaining about misuses of spiritual gifts, but rather relies on statements made by leaders of the charismatic movement itself to show how their actual teaching is usually very wholesome and balanced. If a complaint about the book is warranted, it would be that the subtitle is inaccurate, as is also the stated intent of the book. Although the book claims to speak of the "Nigerian Charismatic Movement," it is really about the charismatic movement in the Roman Catholic Church. There seems to be little awareness of charismatic movements in other churches in Nigeria. Ndubuisi does occasionally speak of Pentecostals, but when speaking of charismatics he seems to mean only Roman Catholics. Those doing specialist research on Paul, or on charismatic movements in Africa, will want to refer to this text.

785. Neckebrouck, Valeer

Resistant Peoples: The Case of the Pastoral Maasai of East Africa

Rome: Gregorian & Biblical Press, 1993. 86 pages, ISBN: 9788876526633.

David Barrett and others have long noted the general receptivity of the peoples of sub-Saharan Africa to the gospel. Nevertheless while Africans as a whole have been receptive, there have been significant pockets of resistance. Among the more notable pockets have been the Maasai whose traditional territory spans Kenya and Tanzania. The resistance of these pastoral nomads has generated significant discussion over the past several decades. Why have they been resistant when so many of their near neighbours were more receptive? That is the question that Neckebrouck wrestles with in this small book. His approach is to survey several theories – anthropological, missiological, and sociological – to understand Maasai resistance more clearly. Rejecting each of the theories in turn, largely because each one is reductionistic in its own fashion, Neckebrouck offers his own explanation. He posits that Maasai resistance to the gospel derives from a socialisation process that prepares them for their nomadic, pastoral life. This process incorporates an exceptionally strong motivational dynamic through harsh discipline that is necessary for the young Maasai to be able to survive the rigors of nomadic life on the African plains. It is so harsh that it instils a strong ethnocentric bias and an orientation that sees all other ways of life as inferior. This bias has been at the core of Maasai resistance towards all outside influences, including Christian witness. The author does acknowledge that other theories help nuance his argument, and he notes how his explanation avoids the reductionism of a single cause inherent in the other theories he has examined. However, the brevity of the arguments leaves the reader questioning the extent to which the author's own theory is successful where the others have failed. This brief but dense book presents an interesting exercise in anthropological puzzle-solving and discovery. Interestingly, at no point does Neckebrouck attempt to bring in spiritual reasoning. His entire focus is the anthropological, psychological, and sociological frames of analysis. One is left wondering how much richer the discussion could be with the addition of appropriate spiritual components in the argument. The author is a Belgium priest with doctorates in theology and anthropology, who has served extensively in various parts of eastern Africa and Latin America, and is on the faculty of the Catholic University of Louvain.

786.   Nehls, Gerhard, and Walter Eric

Islam: As It Sees Itself, as Others See It, as It Is (Volume 1)

Cape Town: Life Challenge Africa, 1996. 167 pages, ISBN: 9789966895165.

This and its two associated volumes offer extensive reference material for those teaching Islamics or preparing students for ministry in Muslim contexts. The first introduces Islam; the second considers Islamic objections to Christianity; while the third offers practical guidance in outreach to Muslims. A student handbook and a video are also available. The presentation is geared for practical rather than for academic use. Although written in Africa, by authors with extensive experience in Africa, and for use in Africa, the presentation is usually generalized, without particular orientation to the African context. The intentionally pragmatic "on the street" approach throughout may prove off-putting for some, but that same approach probably represents the distinctive contribution of these texts. Much of the content is obviously based on extensive face-to-face experience in ministry, and this in turn results in content not commonly available from more academic resources. These texts would therefore be especially useful for those in Muslim-related ministry, or in preparation for such ministry. And theological libraries will likely want to include them in holdings on Islamics.

787.   Nest, Michael, François Grignon, and Emizet F. Kisangani

The Democratic Republic of Congo: Economic Dimensions of War and Peace

Boulder, CO: Lynne Rienner Publishers, 2006. 164 pages, ISBN: 9781588262332.

This book, funded in large part by the International Peace Academy, seeks to explore the extent to which the recent war in eastern Congo, the "deadliest conflict since World War II," has been driven or enabled by economic motives – in particular by the goal of gaining control over some of the Congo's vast natural resources for exploitation and export to foreign markets. The authors helpfully distinguish between economic, political, and security concerns, arguing that all three of these perspectives must be kept in mind if we are to understand the Congo war. Their conclusion is that the various international actors that have been party to the war (in particular Angola, Rwanda, Uganda, and Zimbabwe) were, in the first place, motivated not by specific economic goals (e.g. control of coltan or diamond export), but rather by political and security interests. Once the war was underway, however, commercial exploitation of resources helped them finance their involvement in the ongoing conflict, and became a reason to remain engaged. At the local level, meanwhile, "grievances related to economic opportunities have long caused tensions," contributing very significantly and directly to the outbreak and conduct of the multiple armed conflicts that have ravaged this country for over a decade. Not content simply to describe, the authors also explore policy proposals that they believe could contribute to a lasting peace. They are convinced that political and security issues must be front and centre in negotiations, even as questions of transparent management of economic resources must also be dealt with in a manner that answers the local grievances mentioned above. While not directly addressing issues of Christian presence in Africa, this book does make a contribution to understanding the social and political context in which Congolese believers are called to live and bear witness to the King of Peace. Its findings are also relevant for a realistic assessment of political and economic issues in the broader African context.

788.   Neuhaus, Richard John

Dispensations: The Future of South Africa as South Africans See It

Grand Rapids: Eerdmans, 1986. 317 pages, ISBN: 9780802836274.

Revisiting the 1980s apartheid era in South Africa will certainly always remain a painful experience for all who stood at the line of divide. Neuhaus' book is an important orientation for those who would like to obtain some insight into the dynamics of that period. This book deals with the oddities, wrongs and fears peculiar to South Africa during the 1980s, but as a study in "micro-history" it is also an introduction to the debate about the future of our life together on this small planet – about relations between rich and poor, between races and among ideologies, indeed about the meaning of freedom, peace and justice and the integrity of creation in a deeply disordered world. Neuhaus is author of *The Naked Public Square: Religion and Democracy in America*, and at the time of writing this book was Director of the Center on Religion and Society in New York. Here he introduces the reader to a wide range of opinions from a wide range of South African individuals of that time. The voices are heard of conservative and liberal whites (conservative and liberal broadly defined in the South African context as either pro- or anti-apartheid), both Afrikaans and English, black and white women in the midst of the struggle, clergymen, academics, business people, farmers, politicians, Allan Boesak, Bishop Tutu, and those from the ANC who saw no alternative to the armed struggle. The complexities of South African society of the time are captured in a compelling narrative. Neuhaus succeeded in putting the diversity and seemingly irreconcilable differences of opinion on the table at a time when the struggle for freedom for everyone was poised on the threshold of a full-scale war. This book is compelling reading for anyone who wishes to grasp something of the diversity of opinion of a people involved in an intense struggle that eventually, by the grace of God, did not lead to full scale war but to constructive steps towards building a new nation.

789.   Ngara, Emmanuel

Christian Leadership: A Challenge to the African Church

Nairobi: Paulines, 2004. 96 pages, ISBN: 9789966217967.

The preface is by Desmond Tutu, and the author is a university lecturer from Zimbabwe. Perhaps the most frustrating aspect of the book is that, despite its title, it is neither very African nor specifically Christian. It is more of a brief secular overview of various aspects of leadership that can have relevance for Christians in Africa. One therefore looks in vain for specific coverage of issues like the pressures of the extended family, hierarchy or corruption. One of Ngara's main concerns is the lack of professional training for pastors. He likens much pastoral training to training teachers to teach but not training them also to be headmasters. He also complains that there is too little emphasis on values and community in modern education. His solution is to provide leadership training as described in the chapter entitled, "Key aspects of leadership: a secular perspective." That is perhaps the best chapter, but unfortunately there is little attempt to integrate this material with a Christian perspective, which is treated separately in a later chapter. His section on "exit outcomes" covers the kind of objectives that should concern theological educators in Africa, although such outcomes, once again, are not specifically Christian nor specifically African. The section on world leadership urges Christians to be salt and light, accepting the fact that Christian principles cannot be forced on secular society. Finally, there are several surprises, such as the positive references to Martin Luther (by a Catholic author) and the note that Vatican II's "brother among brothers" is sexist language! Granted that the title is misleading, as a little book simply on leadership in general it may prove useable and interesting.

790.   **Ngewa, Samuel**

1 & 2 Timothy and Titus

Carlisle, UK: HippoBooks, 2009. 496 pages, ISBN: 9789966805386.

This is the first volume in a series designed to supplement the one-volume *Africa Bible Commentary* by offering much expanded treatment for individual books of the Bible. Ngewa (PhD, Westminster Theological Seminary) has served as professor of NT Studies at Nairobi Evangelical Graduate School of Theology (NEGST). Besides authoring this volume, he is the series editor for the NT volumes generally. The text is divided into preaching/teaching units. Each unit starts with an illustration from African life, continues with an exegesis of the text, makes application to African Christian life and churches, and concludes with discussion questions. Thus it should be useful for small group study as well as being a resource for preachers preparing sermons. The extensive endnotes contain the more technical material, including a discussion of the Greek text (some of the comments about the Greek language are out of date in terms of contemporary scholarship, especially in the use of Greek tenses). The endnotes also offer documentation of references to various Bible versions and academic resources, making the book useful for scholars. Ngewa interacts with 28 other commentaries on the Pastoral Epistles. Thus there is no effort to be "African" by separating the work from the insights and tradition of research of scholars from the West. Rather, the African (especially East African) nature of this book comes out clearly in the illustrations, applications, and occasionally the insights into meaning that come from the African context. This commentary is recommended as a resource for anyone reading or teaching the Pastoral Epistles in an African context.

791.   **Ngewa, Samuel**

Galatians

Carlisle, UK: HippoBooks, 2010. 208 pages, ISBN: 9789966805416.

This is the second volume in the Africa Bible Commentary Series, a series that expands on the one-volume *Africa Bible Commentary*. Ngewa is professor of NT Studies at Nairobi Evangelical Graduate School of Theology in Kenya. The commentary is set up in teaching/preaching units (15 for Galatians), each containing a story from African life, exegesis of the text with application to African Christian/church life, and discussion questions. Endnotes document sources and discuss technical aspects of the exegesis, including alternate interpretations. For example, Ngewa interprets "the Israel of God" as believing Jews, but gives alternate views in the endnotes.

The African nature of the commentary comes out most clearly in the African (especially *East* African) quality of the illustrations, applications and insights. This book is recommended for use in the classroom, advanced Bible study groups, and for sermon preparation. Ngewa's work is also a good model for others in Africa who aspire to write biblical commentary.

792. Ngewa, Samuel, editor

The Gospel of John: A Commentary for Pastors, Teachers and Preachers

Nairobi: Evangel, 2003. 524 pages, ISBN: 9789966201140.

This volume is one of the first, if not *the* first, full-length commentary on a single biblical book by an African evangelical scholar, and thereby represents a pace-setting model for others to follow. Ngewa is a long-time lecturer at Nairobi Evangelical Graduate School of Theology. In keeping with its subtitle, Ngewa states as the aim of his commentary: "to ease the pastor's work in preparing the preaching of expository sermons . . . " on John's Gospel in the African context. It is at this level in particular that this work succeeds. The text of the Gospel is divided into 54 units, each forming the basis of one chapter of the commentary and each intended to provide the material for a sermon on this text. Each chapter follows the same format, beginning with a suggested sermon outline, followed by an explanation of the text, and then concluding with a number of points for application or discussion (some specifically oriented to the African context). More academic concerns are reserved for the last fifth of the book, which contains eleven brief appendices (e.g. "John's relationship to the Synoptics") and 93 pages of notes, mostly discussing problems of interpretation, textual variants, cultural background, and insights from Greek grammar. The three-page bibliography primarily references older, classic commentaries. The exposition is fairly straightforward and is consistent with an evangelical position. The exposition could have been strengthened by making more frequent reference to the Gospel's OT background. Also in interpreting a Johannine text, it would have been helpful to refer more frequently to similar passages in the same book or in related Johannine literature. While the notes contain a wealth of helpful material, for close research in technical matters the user should expect to compare Ngewa's observations with other modern commentaries. In all events, with this contribution Ngewa has opened a new chapter in African evangelical biblical studies. His audience and aim for this commentary are clear, and within that framework he has certainly succeeded. This volume should be warmly welcomed by African pastors preaching their next series in John's Gospel.

793. Ngewa, Samuel, Mark Shaw, and Tite Tiénou

Issues in African Christian Theology

Nairobi: East African Educational Publishers, 1998. 344 pages, ISBN: 9789966467799.

In this exceptional collection of 23 articles by a list of distinguished contributors we are offered (as the preface states) "an interim picture of what African Christian theology looks like from an evangelical perspective." The overall quality of the material and the range of topics addressed demonstrate, as perhaps never before, the coming of age of evangelical scholarship in Africa. The articles are divided into four sections: the task of African Christian theology; the foundations of African Christian theology; Christ and salvation in African Christian theology; and the Spirit, the Church, and the future in African Christian theology. All but three of the articles are by African contributors. Of the three editors, Ngewa and Shaw were lecturers at Nairobi Evangelical Graduate School of Theology, while Tiénou was at Trinity International University in the United

States. The collection speaks well for what has become the premier journal of serious evangelical African reflection, the *Africa Journal of Evangelical Theology* (*AJET*), from which most of the articles have been taken. The selection seeks to cover the standard spread of themes in systematic theology, so that the book might serve as a regular theology text in Africa. However the coverage is limited by the articles that were available, so that treatment of some prominent themes of theology is thin or sketchy at best. While most of the articles maintain a classic evangelical perspective, the contribution from Bediako (not taken from *AJET*) would seem to place him somewhat at odds with this larger orientation on the role and status of African traditional religions. Despite the singular significance of this publication, one must acknowledge limitations as well. Of the sixteen contributors, eleven are from either Kenya or Nigeria. There is only one francophone contributor (Tiénou), and none from southern or central Africa. And surely such a groundbreaking book deserves a more careful presentation. Page after page contains misspellings and editorial lapses. Anyone wishing to reference the articles will be disappointed that the original publication information is almost never provided. Still, this book is a notable and welcome achievement.

794.   **Nhial, Abraham, and DiAnn Mills**

Lost Boy No More: A True Story of Survival and Salvation

Nashville: B&H, 2004. 208 pages, ISBN: 9780805431865.

This is the story of one of the so-called "Lost Boys," a group of adolescent and child refugees, perhaps as many as 35,000, who were forced from their homes in southern Sudan by the genocidal raids of the late 1980s. Large groups of unaccompanied minors made their way on foot to refugee camps in Ethiopia where they stayed until 1991. A change of government in that country in 1991 forced them back into Sudan, and they once again had to escape to a neighbouring country, this time to the refugee camp beside the Kenyan town of Kakuma. Thousands of these boys died of starvation, at the hands of government Sudanese or Ethiopian soldiers or devoured by lions, hyenas or crocodiles. Their stories appeared in the American press since the United States government decided to give refuge to several thousand of these young men. This is the first time their story has been told in a book-length treatment. The narrative centres around one of the "boys," Abraham Nhial, from the town of Aweil and from the Jieng (Dinka) ethnic group. Interviews with several other boys are scattered throughout the book. The book also attempts to set the story against the backdrop of the religious and political conflict in the Sudan. Brief lessons in Sudanese history, the face of radical Islam, and descriptions of organisations which attempted to assist southern Sudan help to give Abraham's story a context. This is not by any means a scholarly treatment. One must hope that one day a more complete account of the journeys of these unaccompanied minors may be told, but for now this book fills a great need.

795.   **Niang, Aliou Cissé**

Faith and Freedom in Galatia and Senegal: The Apostle Paul, Colonists and Sending Gods

Leiden: BRILL, 2009. 182 pages, ISBN: 9789004175228.

This reworked PhD dissertation is by a scholar from the Diola ethnic group in Senegal who now teaches at Memphis Theological Seminary in the USA. Niang compares the situation of the Galatians at Paul's time with the Diola in our time. Both people groups were oppressed by an imperial power. The Galatians, whom Niang connects with the Celtic Gauls, were considered to be uncivilized barbarians by the Greeks and the Romans. The Diola, together with other Africans, were seen by the French colonizers as savages. Yet the Galatians (or Asian Gauls), who were oppressed by the Romans, had a traditional belief in divine justice. And the Diola, who were oppressed by the French, believed that the High God (*Ata*) also guaranteed justice. A traditional prophetess, Aline Sitoé, spoke out for justice and against the French colonizers. For Niang, then, the Apostle Paul in his letter to the Galatians stands out as a "sociopostcolonial hermeneut and countercolonist sent by Jesus Christ/God to create new and inclusive communities." Niang arrives at this conclusion from his own liberation presuppositions which led him to reflect on Galatians 2:11–14 and 3:2–29. It is generous of Niang to put the Apostle on the "right side" of current social questions; many feminists and postcolonialists have put him on the other side. Certainly Paul's message does include people from every tribe and language. But Niang goes off the track when he reduces Paul's message to the social questions. The heart of Paul's message in Galatians is justification before God by faith in Jesus Christ; and the communities that Paul founded were grounded in this faith and union with Jesus. In the end, despite some stimulating discussions, Niang has reduced the Gospel to a social construct and has missed the true liberation for believing communities that comes through faith in Jesus Christ.

796.   Niccum, Curt

The Bible in Ethiopia: The Book of Acts

Eugene, OR: Wipf & Stock, 2014. 366 pages, ISBN: 9781610977357.

This published dissertation argues that the original Ethiopic text of Acts – termed the "A-text" – is a faithful witness to a Greek Vorlage (source text) that was present in eastern Africa in the late fourth century. The author completed his doctorate at the University of Notre Dame and currently is Associate Professor of NT at Abilene Christian University. Niccum first assesses the transmission history of the earliest Ethiopic version of Acts. He debunks the theories of previous scholars who suggested that the original Ethiopic text of Acts had a Semitic Vorlage – whether directly from Syriac or through an intermediary Arabic translation. Niccum mentions references from Chrysostom (fourth century CE), Synesius (ca. 407 CE), and the Caleb Inscriptions (ca. 525 CE), which describe an active Ethiopian textual community working with Greek biblical texts as early as the mid-fourth century. Niccum also lists numerous examples of Ethiopic mistranslations that betray a misreading of Greek *scriptura continua* – a key feature of fourth century Greek texts. Because Ethiopian interaction with the Greek church was scarce after 600 CE, he concludes that the Ethiopic translation of Acts from a Greek Vorlage very likely occurred between 350 and 525 CE. Niccum next analyses the fidelity of the A-text to its Greek Vorlage. He examines numerous instances where the Ethiopic translation closely follows the Greek text while the Coptic and Syriac translations clearly diverge. This further confirms Niccum's hypothesis of a Greek Vorlage and demonstrates that the Ethiopic translator is generally faithful to the Greek text. Niccum then attempts to identify the text type of the Greek Vorlage. He employs Quantitative Analysis, the "Wilcoxon" test, the Comprehensive Profile Method, and also identifies singular and subsingular readings. He concludes that the A-text is Alexandrian in text type, with limited Byzantine influence and only a few outlying variants in the Western text type. Also, by the Aland Teststellen standards, Niccum calculates that the A-text is a Category I ("strict") text, with 46 percent in Category II ("semi-strict"). He finishes his work with a critical Ethiopic text of Acts and an apparatus. For this he compiles all manuscripts from before the seventeenth century, along with useful later manuscripts. Then, through a critical methodology, he isolates the earliest stratum of the Ethiopic transmission history. The result is a reconstructed "A-text." Niccum concludes with an appeal for text critics to reconsider the immense value of early translations. His findings also provide impressive testimony to the sophisticated activity of the African Church in early Christianity. This book is highly technical and requires proficiency in Greek, Ethiopic, and textual criticism. It is recommended only for advanced libraries or for those working at advanced levels in NT textual criticism.

797.   **Nicolson, Ron**

A Black Future? Jesus and Salvation in South Africa

Norwich: SCM, 1990. 288 pages, ISBN: 9780334001201.

In this lively book from the pen of a professor of theology at the University of Natal, the traditional models of salvation are examined within a South African context, and each in turn is assigned to the theological rubbish bin. We are introduced to Sipho, a young black lad living amidst appalling poverty and violence. Sipho is no fictional character. He represents the lives of thousands of black people in South Africa before (and after) the demise of apartheid. As each model of salvation/atonement (substitutionary, victory, exemplarist, etc.) is examined, Nicolson asks how this particular model/theory helps Sipho? By the end of his overview not much remains. Nicolson reserves his most vehement criticisms for the notion of substitutionary atonement, which he links to the rise of apartheid. Substitutionary salvation is dismissed as theology for the bourgeoisie, offering forgiveness to Sipho's oppressors but cold comfort to the oppressed. The views of Liberation Theology and Black Theology on salvation are also examined, and whilst they are given more sympathetic treatment, their inadequacies are highlighted. Nicolson labels his own proposal as an "auto-salvation theory" in terms of which "the saving work of Jesus is to encourage and enable us to make our own history. He is a catalyst in a process of autosoteriology, of self-salvation." This book is the stuff of which heated seminars and tutorials are made! It is controversial, and whilst readers may disagree with Nicolson's critique as well as his proposals, the book does raise an important question: How are we to understand the saving power of Jesus on a continent that seems to lurch from one crisis to another? We still await a significant African text on the atonement.

798.   **Nicolson, Ron**

God in AIDS?: A Theological Enquiry

Norwich: SCM, 1996. 256 pages, ISBN: 9780334026419.

Any work that encourages the Church to take AIDS seriously should find its way not only into theological libraries in Africa, but into the hands of African pastors (if only they could afford it!). This study originates from the same country of Africa from which a serious challenge to the accepted understanding of HIV/AIDS was raised at the highest governmental levels. Nicolson's contribution to the debate is timely for churches where a full-orbed theodicy still needs to be worked out. Perhaps the most significant part of the title of this book is the question mark. From evidence he has collected in Uganda, Tanzania and Zimbabwe, as well as South Africa, Nicolson (Professor in Religious Studies at the University of Natal) raises important questions for Christians. What effect does the existence of AIDS have on our understanding of God? What does the Bible have to say about such phenomena? How can Scripture be applied both didactically and sensitively in pastoral counselling, in study groups and from the pulpit? What implications are there for the teaching of the churches on sex? How are Christian communities to react rightly and care properly both for their members and for those outside who are HIV positive? While the author's pointers towards Christian responses may not always satisfy, he is raising important questions that should stimulate some serious theological reflection among pastors, church leaders and educators in Africa. This book can help towards a more realistic and thoughtfully Christian response to the ravaging impact of this epidemic.

Niehaus, C.

see review 1138

Nielsen, Ann

see review 963

799.   Niemeyer, Larry L.

Discipling: A Kingdom Necessity in the African City

Nairobi: Harvest Heralds, 1999. 268 pages, ISBN: 9780977823604.

This book is a helpful introduction to the challenges of discipling believers in the context of African's ever-growing cities. This particular combination of themes, on the discipleship of urban believers in Africa, makes the book exceptional if not unique. The book arose from the author's interaction with students and pastors while teaching a short course at a theological college in Zambia in 1996. Drawing on his experience as a Christian anthropologist who has worked for more than 30 years in Africa, Niemeyer includes numerous illustrations both from his students and from his ongoing ministry in Kenya. Christians who are concerned for the city but not so familiar with basic anthropology will benefit most from the fast-paced presentation, which is laid out according to what the author calls "14 characteristics of modernity," and which uses the Gospel of Luke as its biblical foundation. The study questions provided at the end of each chapter are especially helpful for implementing what has been covered. The book's main weakness is that it seems to have been produced hurriedly; an outside editor might have caught some of the errors that remain. The style of using boxes for quotations, much like in a magazine article, needs refinement, because one must often turn the page to find the quotation in its context. While many sources are cited, both secular and Christian, this book is not so academic that its usefulness would be limited to theological institutions; lay readers will also benefit from its broad appeal.

800.   Nihinlola, Emiola, and Mojisola Olaniyan, editors

Discovering the Other Side: Challenges of Other Religions

Ibadan: Flourish Books Ltd, 2004. 127 pages.

Nihinlola holds a PhD degree from the Nigerian Baptist Theological Seminary, Ogbomoso, where he is now President; Olaniyan holds a master's degree in communication from the University of Ibadan. Fifteen Baptist writers contributed articles to this book. The writers are diverse in background. For example, one is a missionary, another is a seminary lecturer, a third is a church pastor, and a fourth is a university lecturer. Among the "other religions" dealt with in the text are: Islam, African traditional religions (ATR), Brotherhood of Cross and Stars (BCS), The Grail Movement, Enckanker, Baha'i Faith, Hare Krishna, and Guru Maharaj Ji (GMJ). It is strange, however, that the book also deals with the Roman Catholic Church, The Church of the Lord (Aladura) (CLA), and the Seventh Day Adventist Church (SDA) as "other religions." Each "religion" is treated in terms of History, Beliefs and Teachings, and Christian Attitude. All the articles are brief and simple, many are too brief, and most are not fully documented. While many of them are products of serious academic study, a few are definitely not. Articles on ATR, CLA, BCS, and GMJ reflect African concerns. Articles like that on Islam need further editorial work. The chapter on SDA needs to be re-written. Despite these weaknesses, the book is attending to a definite need that may not otherwise be sufficiently addressed for many African Christian communities. The publication also contains some important information that is difficult to access through other resources (particularly true, for example, for GMJ). For which reasons readers may want to consider whether to secure a copy, or else to replicate its good intentions with a parallel publication for their own context.

801.   Nikkel, Marc R.

Dinka Christianity: The Origins and Development of Christianity among the Dinka of Sudan with Special Reference to the Songs of Dinka Christians

Nairobi: Paulines, 2001. 383 pages, ISBN: 9789966216175.

This full-length study of Christianity among the Dinka people of Sudan was the author's doctoral thesis completed at Edinburgh under the direction of Andrew Walls. A few editorial changes were made before publication but, tragically, Nikkel died of cancer at the age of 50, several months before the book's appearance in print. The study accomplishes several worthy goals. First of all it tells of the reception of the Christian faith by the Jieng (Dinka) people of southern Sudan through work of both Anglican and Roman Catholic missionaries. While the history of missionary outreach through such westerners as Daniel Comboni and Archibald Shaw is not neglected, the focus of the book is on reception history: the stories of early Dinka Christian leaders. These include Roman Catholics like Caterina Zenab (the first evangelist), Daniel Sorur Farim Deng (the first Roman priest), Salim Charles Wilson (author and former slave), and Anglicans such as Jon Arure Thor (the first baptized Anglican) and Daniel Deng Atong (the first Anglican Sudanese Bishop). Also highlighted is the cultural and religious context of the Dinka who received the gospel message, and the ways in which that culture has both been transformed and has given a distinctive shape to Christianity among the Dinka. Of special importance is Nikkel's translation and analysis of Dinka hymnody from every period of their Christian history, but especially of the hymns which have given expression to the joy and sorrow of the Dinka churches through their recent times of civil war, persecution and genocide. This is a model of careful scholarship that at the same time highlights a faith in the cross and resurrection that point beyond the sufferings of this present evil age.

802.   Nikkel, Marc R., and Grant LeMarquand

Why Haven't You Left?: Letters from the Sudan

New York: Church Publishing Inc, 2006. 200 pages, ISBN: 9780898694727.

The beautifully crafted letters included in this collection poignantly describe the life of an American Episcopal missionary among the Dinka (they prefer the name "Jieng") in war-torn southern Sudan from 1981 to 2000. The letters paint a graphic picture of southern Sudan's suffering people harassed by war, disease, slavery and starvation. The editor is Grant LeMarquand, a friend of Nikkel, then academic dean at Trinity School for

Ministry in the USA, and now Anglican Area Bishop for the Horn of Africa. With Nikkel's permission, he has skilfully organized the letters chronologically into five parts with appropriate introductory comments and footnotes. Part 1, "Life in the Village of God" presents the "upbeat" letters of a young instructor at an Anglican theological college in southern Sudan. Life was good to Nikkel as he became ensconced into the rhythms of African spirituality. Part 2, "Is This My Pain?" contains letters written in the midst of war and uncertainty. Nikkel struggles with the reality of faith in a God who understands suffering yet does not seem to intervene in the suffering of His people. Part 3, "Pilgrims and Refugees" represents the letters of a pilgrim reflecting theologically on his own forced march by the Southern People's Liberation Army (SPLA) for nearly two months. Part 4, "God Has Not Deserted You" provides a series of letters depicting the devastation of southern Sudan. A decade of war brought death, loss of cattle and a massive displacement of people. As indigenous social and religious institutions were uprooted, Nikkel struggles with the Sudanese interpretation of Isaiah 18, that God is now judging Cush. Part 5, "My Times Are in His Hands" presents reflective letters about Nikkel's own impending death from cancer. The last two years of Nikkel's life, 1998–2000, paralleled in an unusual manner the situation of the devastated Sudanese community to which he had bonded physically as well as spiritually. Alongside Nikkel's artistic prose are nine translated Jieng hymns, and two rather lengthy translated Jieng prayers addressed to the God of a homeless people. At one point there appears to be a disconnect in Nikkel's writing. Along with three colleagues at the Bishop Gwynne College, he was advised by the friendly SPLA to leave southern Sudan immediately because of impending war. But Nikkel made the decision to stay. As a result these four were eventually escorted on a two-month arduous trek to safety and finally flown out of southern Sudan. Nikkel describes this event as being taken hostage by belligerent soldiers. Did he purposely "become a sojourner among a suffering sojourner people?" Is this why he did not leave?

803.   Niringiye, David Zac

The Church in the World: A Historical-Ecclesiological Study of the Church of Uganda with Particular Reference to Post-Independence Uganda, 1962–1992

Carlisle, UK: Langham Monographs, 2016. 456 pages, ISBN: 9781783681198.

This well-documented book is the author's doctoral thesis, which analyses the relationship between church (meaning Anglican) and state in Uganda, from the first arrival of Christianity in the late nineteenth century onward. Chapters cover the historical context well, beginning with Kabaka Mutesa's attitude toward Muslims, Protestants and Roman Catholics, continuing through the challenges of the Church in dealing with the colonial period, and then with leaders since independence: Milton Obote (who was president twice), Idi Amin, and finally the current president, Yoweri Museveni (who is treated in an updated final chapter added about twenty years after the thesis was presented at New College, Edinburgh). Niringiye has previously served as IFES regional secretary for anglophone Africa, as CMS regional director for Africa, and later as an assistant Anglican bishop in Uganda. His access to personal contacts and church documents makes this book very much worth reading. His intention is to answer the question, "What did it mean to be the 'church' in the historical socio-cultural-political context of Uganda?" (The reader must become accustomed to his frequent use of hyphens!). He shows that religious affiliation quickly became the "basis of group identity and therefore the new way of ascending the ladder of political power." Unfortunately, this assertion often proved to be true throughout Uganda's turbulent history as Church leaders claimed that both rebel efforts and coups were "the will of God." Nominalism became normal, and there was little differentiation between church and state in society, partly because the church educated many of Uganda's political elite. The book includes a good overview of the East African Revival, which the author sees as a major influence on early Ugandan archbishops like Erica Sabiti and Janani Luwum. There are also, as expected, shocking stories from the Amin era (Luwum was martyred under Amin in 1977). Much of the book relates how bishops dealt with ethnic tension and church unity when the national leader supported one geographical group. The long analysis begins with Sabiti's summary of the Church's contributions (1970): service to the suffering, unity of the people, and the knowledge of God. Then Niringiye moves on to comment on "four features" of the church, namely authenticity, identity, sacramental presence and paradox. The author is challenged, however, to fit Uganda's disparate history into such a simple framework. In particular, he seems anxious to avoid citing the ethnic tension that was often at the root of the church leadership's inability to address national problems, preferring to lay the blame on politics. About all he acknowledges in this respect is the church's vulnerability to "the politics of patronage and clientelism." There are few books that address in such detail the varied situations affecting church-state issues in Africa.

Njiru, Joseph N.

see review 1045

Njoroge, J.

see review 29

804.   Njoroge, Lawrence M.

A Century of Catholic Endeavour: Holy Ghost and Consolata Missions in Kenya

Nairobi: Paulines, 1999. 240 pages, ISBN: 9789966214607.

This adaptation of the author's doctoral thesis at the University of Notre Dame in the USA is a historical study of the Holy Ghost and Consolata missionary orders in Kenya since their arrival one hundred years ago. Njoroge was secretary to the Kenyan Archbishop Ndingi Nzeki, and had a teaching ministry based at the Holy Family Basilica in Nairobi. Though the book is focussed primarily on Kenyan Catholic history, the author begins with a helpful overview of the religious history of the East African coast, with an evaluation of the reasons for the popularity of Islam in this region. An informative chapter on the Mau Mau period follows, where it is apparent that the author is a careful researcher, quoting numerous documents. The final chapter raises such issues as the relationship of education and evangelism in mission schools. This is a well-written book that should prove especially helpful to the Roman Catholic community in East Africa, but also will be welcomed in advanced-level libraries anywhere seeking good coverage of African church history.

805. Njoroge, Nyambura J., and Páraic Réamonn, editors

Partnership in God's Mission in Africa Today: The Papers and Reports of the Consultation of African Women and Men of Reformed Tradition, 9–15 March 1994, Limuru, Kenya

Geneva: World Alliance of Reformed Churches, 1994. 94 pages, ISBN: 9789290750185.

The subtitle of this slim volume links the content of this book to a consultation held in 1994 in Limuru, Kenya, which brought together 42 participants from Africa and North America. The consultation was focused on the inclusion of women with men in church and ministry roles. The papers "urged African churches to value the ministries and gifts of all, . . . in order to transform the oppressive church structures and male leadership styles which discriminate against women." The book contains four essays on the relationship of women and men in ministry, a summary report of Bible studies conducted at the conference, the recommendations of working groups, and a list of participants. Readers will find that the book has a distinctly ecumenical tone, and that the essays work from a liberation theology perspective. The greatest shortcoming of this book is that its discussions and recommendations are formulated in such broad terms that they become practically meaningless. For example, the World Alliance of Reformed Churches (WARC) is exhorted to monitor further progress in enabling partnership in ministry. Other recommendations make equally vague calls for issues to be addressed by women's organisations. No further specifics or intended outcomes are provided, and one is left to wonder how achievement of such recommendations could be recognized. For those involved in the WARC or similar ecumenical organs, or for those committed to liberation theology as their primary paradigm for doing theology, this book may prove useful; others not so inclined may not find it so.

806. Nkemnkia, Martin Nkafu

African Vitalogy: A Step Forward in African Thinking

Nairobi: Paulines, 1999. 239 pages, ISBN: 9789966214515.

Nkemnkia is a Cameroonian who took his doctorate in philosophy at the Pontifical Lateran University in Rome in 1993. Much of the bibliographic reference is to literature in French, and the African terms used for discussion are usually those of the Bangwa community of western Cameroon. The author asks if there is such a thing as "African culture," or a distinct way of thinking that can be described as African, when the continent is home to such heterogeneous ethnicities? Is there "cultural unity of the African people"? Is there a peculiarly African way of conceptualising, reflecting on and articulating the African perspective on reality. Nkemnkia suggests that there is. He tackles the task of demonstrating this by outlining a number of strands that contribute to an articulation of the African view of reality. This, he suggests, is long overdue. The book reflects on the limitation of always hearing reality articulated in Western categories even when these realities are African. The neologism "vitalogy" is intended to express the approach to thinking about reality from the African perspective. The author calls it the "science of reflecting on life." The book is a useful contribution to a self-understanding of the African in African thought categories contributed to by ideologists, liberationists, nationalists as well as theologians. Nkemnkia examines the contribution of people like Senghor (*Négritude*), Nyerere (*Ujama* – African socialism Tanzanian-style), Nkrumah, Kaunda, Kagamé, Kwasi, Mbiti, to name only some of the contributions. The book is a work of philosophy which explores a way the African confronts and thinks about reality. The author suggests that the point of departure for the African is concrete reality experienced in relationship rather than through abstract conceptualisations. When African Christians are seeking to make a contribution to an understanding and application of the Bible's message to the continent and the world, it is worth asking the question: What will make such a contribution truly African other than the fact that it is authored by people from Africa? To discover who we are will lead to true fellowship and mutual enrichment. To fail to know what makes us who we are is to allow others to stamp us with their own identity because that is all they know. Alternatively, they will articulate for us some romantic, exotic identity which is characterized by strangeness and differentness without truly portraying the soul of the African. As one African's attempt to unveil the inner workings of African thinking this is an instructive and fascinating book.

807.   Nkurunziza, Deusdedit R. K.

Bantu Philosophy of Life in the Light of the Christian Message: A Basis for an African Vitalistic Theology

Frankfurt: Peter Lang, 1989. 307 pages, ISBN: 9783631422281.

Accepted as a doctoral dissertation by the Catholic Faculty of Theology at Tübingen in 1989, this study incorporates three primary foci: an overview and evaluation of the Bantu philosophy of life, an exploration of continuities and discontinuities between this approach to life and that found in the OT, and an examination of the relationship between the Bantu philosophy of life and the gospel. One should note that the designation "Bantu" in this study refers to five related ethnic groups in the lake region of southwestern Uganda and northwest Tanzania, one of which is the author's home culture. In this philosophy, life is highly valued and becomes sustained in community. Such an outlook is fundamentally "organic." No divisions exist between the spiritual, physical and social realms, and the individual and community are inseparable. God is the source of all life and power. Nkurunziza concludes that the "Bantu life-thought system is a type of the *praeparatio evangelica*," meaning that it is valuable but incomplete. The Bantu and the Israelites of the OT share a similar outlook on God and on life: God is life-giver and creator; all life belongs to God; as a threat to life, death does not come from God. In Jesus Christ, God has both made the fullness of life available, and has overcome death. From the perspective of the Bantu, this is good news indeed. The Bantu thus awaited "a more perfect faith," like those people of OT times. Nkurunziza concludes with a survey of NT teaching regarding Jesus' life, death and message, identifying areas where the gospel challenges a Bantu outlook on life, as well as ways in which the gospel can be inculturated within that same philosophy. As one would expect in a dissertation by a Catholic scholar, many of these issues, such as the eucharist and baptism, betray a distinctively Catholic stance. Unlike many highly-refined dissertations that focus on one little aspect of a topic, this work examines a Bantu culture and the gospel in broad strokes, resulting in a more readable and enjoyable book. Although now somewhat dated, the book also contains useful bibliographies on Bantu Philosophy, African "Weltanschauung," and African Theology. It belongs on theological library shelves as a thoroughgoing examination of the perennial "Christ and Culture" problem within an African setting.

808. Nolan, Albert

God in South Africa: The Challenge of the Gospel

Grand Rapids: Eerdmans, 1988. 244 pages, ISBN: 9781852870102.

Nolan's concern in this book is to arrive at clarity with regard to the question about the role of God (and therefore Christ and the Spirit) in the crisis and conflict experienced in South Africa during the late 1980s. This concern was for him not merely a theoretical construct but a concern developed out of his active ministry as a Dominican priest in various places throughout the country, especially among the disadvantaged youth and as an employee of the Institute for Contextual Theology in Johannesburg. In a simple, straightforward, prophetically uncompromising and thoroughly contextual manner he presents the gospel as the good news that is hopeful and challenging – hopeful and challenging for the poor and oppressed in South Africa, and good news for many people throughout Africa and the world. In the process of eleven chapters (dealing with such topics as: what is the Gospel, sin in the Bible, salvation in the Bible, the good news of salvation, and the role of the church) an emerging theology is presented, a theology born out of the experience and practice of the poor and oppressed Christians of South Africa. This emerging theology affects all who have recognized the cause of the oppressed as the cause of God. The South African experience, amongst others, has taught us how intolerable it is for God's church anywhere to practice a theology of exclusive self-satisfaction. Even though one might not agree with Nolan on some issues raised, his book could be a useful resource for Christian reflection among pastors and concerned Christians anywhere on the continent.

809. Nolen, Stephanie

28 Stories of AIDS in Africa

London: Portobello Books, 2008. 416 pages, ISBN: 9781846270383.

The author is the Africa correspondent for Toronto's *Globe and Mail*. She deftly weaves the stories of 28 real people, one for every million AIDS sufferers in Africa, with facts and statistics, policies, practices and attitudes in the country of residence of each of the persons. From the Kenyan long-haul truck driver to the Malawian nurse to the son of Nelson Mandela, we read captivating stories of the ways people are contracting, living with and dealing with AIDS. The lifestyles and attitudes depicted are sometimes shocking and disheartening. Though her focus is largely on government policies and aid organisations, Christians read beyond what is written to ask how Christians and churches have been involved and need to continue to be involved. While the author writes much about treatment and little about prevention, the question of a Christian response to the crisis remains crucial. One can become weary and discouraged with story after story of hardship and suffering. How do we keep from becoming weary and discouraged (or callous) when these people are our people and our responsibility? A recounting such as this of the real lives of particular individuals can become a springboard for healthy and open discussion of this ongoing crisis. The book includes an epilogue telling what has happened to most of the 28 persons since their stories were written. This readable and resource-rich book also includes a listing of AIDS treatment and care organisations in Africa, along with those who provide advocacy and education.

810.   Noll, Mark A.

Clouds of Witnesses: Christian Voices from Africa and Asia

Downers Grove: IVP US, 2011. 286 pages, ISBN: 9780830838349.

Noll is a well-known evangelical professor of history at the University of Notre Dame in the USA; Nystrom is a widely-published freelance writer. Here they offer interpretive biographies of seventeen Christian leaders from Africa and Asia during the nineteenth and twentieth centuries. Seven of these are from Africa and ten from Asia. The authors intend to supplement the scholarly study of non-western Christianity by portraying specific individuals from those regions, in order to exemplify the tenacious vitality of the Christian faith in parts of the world that have increasingly become principal centres of global Christianity. The seventeen individuals profiled seem selected especially to represent a range of Christian personalities and experiences, from a diversity of Christian traditions and cultural contexts. Among the seven Africans are: Bernard Mizeki, an Anglican missionary catechist martyred in what is now Zimbabwe in 1896; John Chilembwe, an ordained Baptist minister from Malawi who led a bloody rebellion against colonial rule in 1915; and Albert Luthuli, a staunch Christian who was for many years president of the African National Congress in South Africa, and the first African recipient of the Nobel Peace Prize. The presentations of the prophet William Wadé Harris of Liberia, and of the theologian Byang Kato of Nigeria, are especially nuanced and well informed. Kato's visionary contribution to the African evangelical community is well told, and some of the material offered is not otherwise available. Also treated are Simeon Nsibambi, a leader in the East African Revival; and Janani Luwum, the Anglican archbishop of Uganda who was martyred under Idi Amin in 1977. The individual narratives are meant to be primarily descriptive rather than evaluative, in order to facilitate sympathetic engagement more than critical assessment. At the same time, the presentations are carefully realistic, and are grounded wherever possible in original sources. Whereas the book is written for a Western Christian readership, to widen their horizons, and does an effective job of that, it can readily assist that same good purpose for Christian readers in Africa.

811.   Norlén, Gunnar

Islam and Its World

Usa River, Tanzania: Makumira University College, 2001. 275 pages, ISBN: 9789987657025.

The author, from Sweden, spent six years in the Arab world before taking up a lectureship at Makumira University College, an institution of the Evangelical Lutheran Church of Tanzania. Here he has provided a monograph on Islam that covers some familiar ground: Islam's history, beliefs and practices, a survey of the most important groups and sects, and a final chapter on the interrelations between Muslims and Christians. The treatment is not altogether balanced, however. By far the greatest space of this textbook is given to the historical development of the world of Islam (over 50 percent), plus an in-depth presentation of "Islam after Muhammad." Much less concern is displayed for a thorough understanding of the Qur'an and its teaching. Even less is offered in a comparison of Christian and Muslim doctrine. Assistance for Christian witness among Muslim neighbours, or an intentional sharing of the Good News with Islamic people groups remain unattended. The reason for these limitations is not hard to find: the author's hope for his students and readers is aimed at a dialogue prioritising "respect for the creation and for human life, for peace among nations, or for building a better and more equal world for human beings to live in." The author has amassed a considerable amount of information on Islam, but much more on the historical aspects rather than contemporary issues and trends affecting Islam worldwide today. One also cannot help noting the selective way in which certain topics are presented. For example, verses reflecting Christian-Muslim interaction in the Qur'an are only represented by the well-known Sura 5:82 "Nearest to the believers (Muslims) are those who say 'We are Christians'," while all "verses of the sword" are omitted. Although Norlén expresses his desire to write primarily for the East African context, most works referred to come from familiar Western writers. Perhaps this should not be the first book to reach for if seeking a Christian acquaintance with Islam in the African context.

812. Northrup, David

Africa's Discovery of Europe 1450–1850

New York: Oxford University Press, 2013. 240 pages, ISBN: 9780199941216.

Northrup is Professor of History at Boston College in the United States. This is the story of encounters between Africans from south of the Sahara and Europeans in the era before colonialism, told as much as possible from the viewpoint of Africans. The chapters are entitled: First Sights – Lasting Impressions (early Portuguese contacts and others); Politics and Religion; Commerce and Culture; Atlantic Imports and Technology; Passages in Slavery; and Africans in Europe 1650–1850. Northrup challenges a number of popular assumptions, both Western and African. For example, Africans were not gullible, simplistic people duped by the whites. Their sophisticated kings viewed the first white men who came as their inferiors. The Africans were astute in trading and political relations, and generally got what they wanted out of the trade. Second, in only a few places did a guns-for-slaves cycle appear. Africans almost never made war purposely to get slaves. Taking captives was only a by-product of wars made for other political and commercial reasons, so they did not want guns to take slaves but for other ends. Africans wanted a lot of other international goods as well. Slaves were a useful trade item, and African rulers had been using them long before whites appeared. However, the high European demand for slaves to run New World plantations did create artificial conditions and resulted in inexpressible hardship. Third, in early Christian outreach in Africa Northrup believes that both the missionaries and the African converts were sincerely motivated. He prefers to believe the testimonies of Christian Africans who give thanks for their new relationship to God, over against the sceptical comments of historians who think they only converted for economic and political advantages. Some of the Christian Africans highlighted are King Afonso of Kongo, J. A. U. Gronniosaw, Owosu Ansa, J. E. J. Capitein, Philip Quaque, David Boilat, Ajayi Crowther and Tiyo Soga. Readers would find this a useful source of less-familiar biographical and historical detail for African and European interaction before the colonial period.

813. Ntamushobora, Faustin

From Trials to Triumphs: The Voice of Habakkuk to the Suffering African Christian

Eugene, OR: Wipf & Stock, 2010. 96 pages, ISBN: 9781606086315.

This is a light book, light to carry and light to read. But it discusses a theologically weighty question: why are people suffering, despite living lives assumed to please God? The question is obviously not an African one only. It is frequently raised in the biblical texts themselves and even more in the subsequent reception history of these texts. Nevertheless, the question is indeed alive in contemporary Africa too, and this calls for the kind of attention the question gets in this book, an attention that combines counselling concerns with theological and exegetical perspectives. The author is an ordained Baptist minister from Rwanda, currently teaching at

Biola University in the United States. His starting point is the experiences of so many Christian brothers and sisters in places such as Rwanda, Uganda, South Sudan, Sierra Leone, Liberia, and the Congo (DRC), who daily suffer due to political and social unrest, violence, ethnic and religious discrimination, corruption, and chronic diseases, all which experiences can affect their faith. He then proposes that the OT book of Habakkuk has a message that fits their situation. Habakkuk lived in a vicious society where the religious and civil leaders had become corrupt, a society where the poor were suffering, not being considered full members of the community. In response to this, Habakkuk calls for God's justice to be manifest, and here, Ntamushobora argues, the ancient prophetic book has a message to all those who are suffering in Africa today. The book is divided into three main parts, preceded by a general introduction raising the main questions and presenting the book of Habakkuk from a more general perspective. Part 1, "The message of Habakkuk explained," offers an exegetical analysis of the brief prophetic book, without explicit references to the African interpretive context. Part 2, "The message of Habakkuk lived," reads the results of the exegetical analysis in relation to various African experiences of suffering, with special attention to the theological questions they raise. Part 3, "Hope in Africa despite trials and complaints," concludes the reading of Habakkuk with a glimpse of hope, claiming that God has a plan for Africa. All in all, this is a valuable contribution, allowing its readers to relate daily experiences of suffering to an often neglected OT prophetic book.

814. **Nthamburi, Zablon**

The African Church at the Crossroads: A Strategy for Indigenization

Nairobi: Uzima Press, 1991. 151 pages, ISBN: 9789966855152.

Nthamburi has been a lecturer in theology and church history at Kenyatta University in Kenya. In this well-documented book he wrestles with the effect of Western culture on African theology, and how the church must learn to communicate the gospel in metaphors that can be understood and appreciated by Africans. Nthamburi approaches the issue of indigenisation by identifying three sources for African theology, namely African traditional religion and culture, the Bible, and African modern history and development. From this framework he touches briefly on the issues of Christology, the communion of the saints, ecumenism, the role of women in the church, priestly celibacy, and moratorium in missions and evangelism. The strength of this book is that Nthamburi raises important issues with which the African church must come to grips in striving to relate biblical truth to indigenous culture. The weakness is that biblical standards are too often dismissed merely as Western culture. Although the author disavows syncretism, he drifts into it in the application of his principle that "African theology must take more seriously its most important source, African religion and culture." This is evidenced most clearly in his discussion of the ancestors in relation to the person of Christ, who is identified as "the supreme universal spirit ancestor"; and in his discussion of the communion of saints "where we are one communion of the living and the living dead." This book will be useful for those wishing to trace some patterns of theological reflection in Africa in recent decades.

815. Nthamburi, Zablon, editor

From Mission to Church: A Handbook of Christianity in East Africa

Nairobi: Uzima Press, 1991. 144 pages, ISBN: 9789966855138.

In three essays this volume surveys the development of Christianity from its beginnings through the late 1980s in Kenya, Sudan and Uganda. A fourth essay examines the Balokole Revival Movement in Uganda. Refusing to focus on any one denomination or individual, the contributions are intentionally ecumenical. The treatments of the particular countries also contain sections on church-state relations and helpful bibliographies. A Kenyan Methodist, Nthamburi surveys the history of Christianity in Kenya. Andrew Wheeler, a British Anglican, traces Christianity in Sudan from its ancient beginnings to the present. And Kevin Ward, another Anglican, contributes the chapters on Uganda and the Balokole movement. For those unfamiliar with the history of Christianity in these areas, this book will serve as a helpful introductory overview. Essays on Tanzania and Ethiopia are curiously proposed for a separate book; their inclusion here would have made this collection much more useful, and its title more appropriate.

Nthamburi, Zablon

see also review 661

Ntlha, Moss

see review 603

816. Nupanga, Weanzana wa, editor

Le Chrétien et la Politique: Actes du Colloque Interdisciplinaire 06–10 janvier

Bangui: FATEB, 2004. 58 pages.

This slender booklet brings to the wider public the proceedings of the annual interdisciplinary symposium in 2004 of the Faculté de Théologie Evangélique de Bangui (FATEB), Central African Republic. Three of the addresses are included, all given by members of FATEB's faculty. All engage with the issue of the Christian and politics. The first, by Benno van den Torren of the Netherlands, is the longest and most developed, exploring the biblical basis for Christian involvement in the political process and in particular the political significance of Jesus himself. Of the many relevant texts, two are examined in greater detail, "Render to Caesar . . .," and "My kingdom is not of this world. . . ." Van den Torren observes that Jesus' role was greater than a purely political one, but it did have and continues to have major political implications. He then examines the repercussions of this for today's African Christians in relation to the young democracies of the continent, speaking affirmingly of the democratic process but also relativizing it, recognising that it too can be abused. He concludes by advocating four positive ways in which the Church can be more committed to the political process: behavioural example, prophetic pronouncement, distinct identity, and priority of Gospel proclamation. In the second contribution, Enoch Tompte-Tom approaches the topic more from the angle of systematic theology. He catalogues definitions and various theological and political approaches down through history, listing such names as Calvin, Luther, Barth, Bonhoeffer, Tillich and Moltmann, Aristotle and Machiavelli. Regrettably, the brief article does not afford much reflection or discussion, other than to conclude that a contextualized theology that grapples with the real situation within a country will inevitably engage with the political realities of that context. In the final contribution the volume editor, Nupanga, examines the notion of the so-called "secular state." Many African countries, he observes, have taken the model of France as their own, without sharing the particular historical situation that brought about the radical separation of Church and State in that European nation. He regrets that sometimes this divorce has permitted political figures in Africa to be no longer accountable to ethical and moral principles. Within traditional African society there was no dichotomy of spiritual and political authority. Though even briefer than the second paper, it is a thoughtful contribution. The FATEB initiative of annual interdisciplinary symposia whose proceedings are then published for wider consideration is to be warmly applauded, and could serve as a model to other tertiary theological centres in Africa.

817.   Nürnberger, Klaus, and John Tooke, editors

The Cost of Reconciliation in South Africa

Cape Town: Methodist Publishing House, 1988. 216 pages, ISBN: 9780949942968.

The National Initiative for Reconciliation (NIR) was a South Africa Christian initiative born in 1985 amidst the escalating conflict within the country, which sought to make a positive contribution towards the resolution of that crisis. This helpful book was published in 1988 as an "NIR Reader" in order to provide relevant material for study and action groups on justice and reconciliation. Included are essays by David Bosch ("Processes of reconciliation and demands of obedience: Twelve theses"); Frank Chikane ("Integrity of a prophet"); John de Gruchy ("The struggle for Justice and Ministry of Reconciliation"); Klaus Nurnberger ("By grace alone: The significance of the core doctrine of the Reformation for the present crisis in South Africa"); Michael Cassidy ("Reconciliation in South Africa"); and others. In addition the book contains significant excerpts from some of the most important theological statements produced by South African churches in the fight against apartheid. Here one notes the "Kairos Document," the "Evangelical Witness," and the "Letter of the Baptist Union to the State President" – to name just a few that are included. This book serves a twofold purpose: it is instructive in terms of its insights into the vexed issue of reconciliation; but, secondly, it is a useful resource for going back to the church statements that captured the headlines in South Africa when they were first made. As always Bosch's and Nurnberger's contributions deserve special mention. These two men were enormously influential in giving a theological direction to the church in South Africa during the turbulent 1980s.

818.   Nürnberger, Klaus, editor

A Democratic Vision for South Africa: Political Realism and Christian Responsibility

Pietermaritzburg: Encounter Publications, 1991. 624 pages, ISBN: 9780620146814.

Though published three years before the advent of democracy in South Africa, this invaluable volume of essays remains relevant not only for South Africa but for the entire continent. Here theologians, politicians, political scientists, educationalists, and economists reflect on the challenge of democracy. The book is divided into nine parts, each dealing with a different aspect of democracy; for example, we have sections on "The democratic ideal in theological perspective," "Democracy, ideology and propaganda," "Democracy in the African context," and "Prospects of democracy in South Africa." The 45 contributors are mainly though not exclusively South Africans. In a volume where each essay is worth studying, it might seem unfair to highlight particular contributions. However, the six essays by Lutheran Professor Klaus Nurnberger are worthy of special note.

Nurnberger, who teaches theology at Natal University, was a leading theological figure in South Africa, having come strongly to the fore in the troubled years of the 1980s. For evangelicals the joint essay from Caesar Molebatsi, Moss Ntlha and Tony Balcomb on "Six theses concerning Evangelicalism and democracy in the South African situation" is a helpful contribution. Molebatsi has a further essay on "The role of the church in the formation of democratic assumptions and behaviour." Commenting on this excellent volume, the renowned South African missiologist, Professor David Bosch said, "This will undoubtedly enrich and illuminate the ethical imperative of the Church's mission and its struggle to relate to a penultimate and flawed world of political power and ideology."

819.   Nürnberger, Klaus

Making Ends Meet: Personal Money Management in a Christian Perspective

Pietermaritzburg: Cluster, 2008. 84 pages, ISBN: 9781875053704.

The author, a retired professor from the University of KwaZulu-Natal in South Africa, has previously written works on the relation between faith and economics. The aim of this small booklet is to assist people at grass roots level to do something about their financial situation by living within their means. He addresses Christians from the very poor to the very wealthy with the assumption that "avarice" is "the root of all evil," and is thus a spiritual problem. Although his translation may be debated (1 Tim 6:10 in the NIV reads, "The love of money is a root of all kinds of evil"), all would agree with his assertion that money is a major source of tension for individuals, families and churches. His context is South Africa, where the education system does not provide any training in personal money management, so this book is meant to help fill that gap. The first chapter is a theological basis for what follows, and discusses why Christians should control money rather than be controlled by it, using it beneficially and not destructively. This initial chapter ranges widely, covering environmental concerns, poverty, limited resources and population growth, making the reader question the accuracy of the title, despite the helpful nature of the arguments. He then evaluates four groups by devoting a chapter to each one – absolute poverty, relative deprivation, relative privilege and absolute affluence. The priority in each category is to limit expenditure, whatever the economic level. He includes numerous practical examples that readers will find useful. The African context is often noted, such as his concern over the large amounts of money spent on celebrations like weddings and graduations, which can become more worldly than Christian and result in serious debt for the family. His advice to live simply, whatever one's income level, is timely in light of present African realities, and those who follow his suggestions will surely ease the tensions that limited finances so often bring. If there is to be any criticism of this little book, it has to do with the range and depth of the material. Whereas the book presents itself as primarily addressed to the needs of the laity, it is occasionally too heavy on socioeconomic analysis for a reader whose concern is only in "making ends meet." Nevertheless, this would be a useful resource for any reflection or discussion among Christians regarding personal financial management in Africa.

820.   **Nussbaum, Stan, editor**

The African Proverbs Project

Colorado Springs: GMI, 1996.

The African Proverbs Project is one of the most innovative and integrative tools in cross-cultural research available. Taking advantage of the ability to squeeze huge amounts of information onto a single CD, and the ability to quickly read and store information, the resulting resource comprises a virtual library. On this single CD there are 23 books (nine previously unpublished), over 27,000 African proverbs (in many cases accompanied by the English explanation necessary for better understanding the proverb), 42 maps, a directory of over 1500 African languages, two annotated (and computer-searchable) bibliographies covering 1079 articles and proverb collections, and even a biographical directory of people who are researching and collecting the proverbs. Putting this in perspective, this single resource contains more material on African proverbs than most libraries on the continent have in their entire collections. Not only that, but the material is relevant, timely, and offers remarkable insights into a broad variety of African cultures. And it is all searchable in ways that make a vast amount of information readily accessible to the user. This extraordinary research tool will be immensely and immediately helpful (if not downright addictive!) to students of African culture, as well as pastors, scholars, teachers, and students.

821.   **Nussbaum, Stan, editor**

Turner Collection on Religious Movements 1492–1992: Index to the Microfiche, Volume 2: Africa

Birmingham, UK: INTERACT, 1993. 45 pages.

Professor Harold Turner was a religious studies scholar who from 1957 to 1987 collected material about primal new religious movements. These are movements that emerged in primal societies through the interaction of a primal religion with Christianity or other major world religions. With this material Turner established the Interact Research Centre at the Selly Oak Colleges. The collection was subsequently duplicated on microfiche and sold as regional sets. One of those sets was for Africa, which some libraries on the continent may already have in their holdings. Stan Nussbaum, who worked with Turner at the Centre, compiled this inexpensive index series. The volume on Africa contains 396 items in the microfiche set and an additional 150 items in the Centre collection. While most useful for those who have access to the microfiche collection, the index does provide an author/title list of resources on young churches and religious movements in Africa. The limitation is that full bibliographic information is not included, and one would need to have a way to complete the information and obtain items one wishes to use. The index would be useful for research institutions that are able to provide some access to such collections for their students and faculty.

822. Nuttall, Michael

Number Two to Tutu: A Memoir

Pietermaritzburg: Cluster, 2003. 178 pages, ISBN: 9781875053346.

Although the name Michael Nuttall may not be widely known outside of South Africa, this gracious and scholarly bishop of the Anglican Church exercised a quiet yet important role throughout the church in that country. In the run-up to the election of Desmond Tutu as Archbishop of Cape Town in 1986, Nuttall, then Bishop of Natal, was widely tipped to assume the senior position within the Anglican Church in South Africa. The vote however went the way of Desmond Tutu, and Nuttall was appointed "Dean of the Province," or more colloquially, "Number Two to Tutu." He became a supporter, close friend and confidant of the new Archbishop, and together Tutu and Nuttall guided the Anglican Church through the desperate years of political repression and violence and into the new era of democracy. This book tells the story of that relationship; what Tutu in his foreword describes as the "extraordinary partnership" between the two men. Far from being a series of light-hearted memoirs of Nuttall's interactions with the irrepressible Tutu, this book contains fascinating behind-the-scenes accounts and thoughtful reflections of an influential bishop on his close association with Tutu and the role of the Anglican Church in the crisis years leading up to South Africa's first democratic elections in 1994. Few could be better placed to write about this period of South African history than the erudite and wise Nuttall. The book will function as an important source for anyone seeking to understand the extraordinary ministry of Desmond Tutu, as well as introducing readers to the self-effacing Nuttall (who in retirement spent a term as acting Dean of Gonville & Caius at Cambridge University in the UK).

Nwachuku, Daisy

see reviews 625 and 677

823. Nwachukwu, Mary Sylvia C.

Creation-Covenant Scheme and Justification by Faith: A Canonical Study of the God-Human Drama in the Pentateuch and the Letter to the Romans

Rome: Gregorian & Biblical Press, 2002. 372 pages, ISBN: 9788876529412.

By far the majority of published studies on the NT by modern African biblical scholars has been on the Gospels, while the most neglected area of research until recently has been the letters of Paul. This doctoral thesis by Nwachukwu, completed at the Pontifical Gregorian University in Rome, is a worthy contribution which not only begins to address a lacuna in African biblical research, but also contributes to an important modern discussion on Paul which has been taking place in Europe and North America. Indeed where African scholars have written about Paul in recent years, the lack of ready access to quality up-to-date library resources has been too often evident. This lack has meant, sadly, that Africans have not been able to participate in a very lively discussion about Pauline theology. Nwachukwu breaks this pattern. She provides us with a careful and thorough study of Romans 9–11 against the background of the Abrahamic covenant in the book of Genesis. In doing so she takes full account of the recent literature on Paul, especially that literature which has emerged since E. P. Sanders opened up what has been called the "New Perspective on Paul." Especially helpful is that Nwachukwu reads Paul's theology not as abstract theological ideas but as emerging from a narrative about

God's concern for the world. Her reading of Paul is therefore profoundly missiological – God's love for mankind flows from his concern for all of his world, and God's salvation of humanity in Christ is a part of God's eschatological plan to save not just humanity but the whole creation. This is a fine study.

824.   Nwafor, John Chidi

Church and State: The Nigerian Experience

Frankfurt: IKO–Verlag für Interkulturelle Kommunikation, 2002. 436 pages, ISBN: 9783889396327.

This book is a PhD thesis completed at the University of Frankfurt by an Igbo Catholic from the Diocese of Enugu in Nigeria. The additional subtitle of the book is: *The Relationship between the Church and the State in Nigeria in the Areas of Human Rights, Education, Religious Freedom and Religious Tolerance.* The title and subtitles suggest that the topic of the thesis is the relation between church and state in Nigeria. In fact, the author only considers the Roman Catholic Church in Nigeria, with hardly any reference to the numerous Protestant churches there. Nwafor's stated aim is to expound the elements listed in the expanded subtitle. But the thesis largely fails to achieve this objective. Instead, the first chapter gives a lengthy survey of traditional Nigerian polity without an in-depth consideration of modern Nigerian polity (government). The bulk of the thesis, in the second and fourth chapters, analyses Vatican and Nigerian Catholic encyclicals and pronouncements on human rights, religious freedom and the like. But these pronouncements are tangential to the stated aim of the thesis. The third chapter describes what the author thinks is a practical solution to the needs implied, namely the Catholic Institute for Development, Justice and Peace (CIDJAP). This Institute was established in 1986 by the Catholic diocese of Enugu. Very likely this research institute has done some good in the eastern part of Nigeria, but it is doubtful that this is a significant answer to the problem of church and state in Nigeria. This book does provide some Catholic pronouncements on human rights and religious freedom, but it fails to achieve its stated aim.

825.   Nyamiti, Charles

Christ as Our Ancestor

Gweru, Zimbabwe: Mambo Press, 1984. 151 pages, ISBN: 9780869223451.

Nyamiti, originally from Tanzania, has been head of the Department of Doctrinal Theology at the Catholic Higher Institute of East Africa in Nairobi. He has two doctorates and is the author of several books on African Christian theology. The chief aim of this book is to give a complementary contribution to the current theological discussion in Africa on Christ as "Ancestor." Nyamiti finds the approaches employed in constructing ancestral Christology too general and deficient. Their inadequacy, according to him, is that: (1) they lack deep analysis of the African ancestral beliefs and practices; (2) they fail to discover more similarities and differences between the traditional ancestral beliefs and Christian teaching on Christ's relationship to mankind; (3) they do not profitably employ their findings for theological purposes. Nyamiti uses a different methodology to arrive at the Christology he calls "Christ as Our Ancestor." From the African ancestral beliefs and practices, he draws an analogy which he calls the traditional Brother-Ancestor. In his opinion this kind of Ancestor is the closest analogy to Christ. He reasons that through adoption and grace Christ has become our Brother-Ancestor. Hence, he is our Ancestor. While Nyamiti's treatment is certainly creative, he has spiritualised the whole concept of

"Christ as our Ancestor." Nevertheless, this book helps to offer an answer to the question: Who do African theologians say Christ is?, and thereby raises important Christological issues for the African context.

826. Nyamiti, Charles

Some Contemporary Models of African Ecclesiology: A Critical Assessment in the Light of Biblical and Church Teaching

Nairobi: Catholic University of Eastern Africa, 2008. 276 pages, ISBN: 9789966909480.

This third and final volume of Nyamiti's African systematic theology deals with ecclesiology. The initial 60 pages set forth first the biblical and then the Roman Catholic doctrine of the church. The rest of the book presents and critiques fifteen African ecclesiologies, including Nyamiti's own. Nyamiti says that most of these ecclesiologies are either shallow or reductionistic. Nyamiti's own ecclesiology is summed up in 26 pages. It is, of course, ancestral, as is to be expected from the earlier volumes in this series. He sees the Church as being "the living organ of the extension of this divine Ancestorship into human beings." He terms his ancestral ecclesiology as an "African family ecclesiology." The sacraments of baptism, confirmation and eucharist make a person part of this ancestral family of Jesus Christ. For him the Eucharist is the "primary end and determining factor of [the Church's] inner mode of being." Nyamiti's three-volume systematic theology is an interesting experiment in African Christian theology. But one wonders whether the concept of ancestor is really useful in doing Christian theology. Are God the Father and the Son really ancestors in the traditional African sense? Does the concept of ancestor really speak to today's youth in modern Africa? One should also not overlook the harmful effects of the traditional ancestral cult. This does not seem a helpful paradigm for the uses to which Nyamiti has deployed it. On the other hand, his identification of fifteen different African ecclesiologies might well prove suggestive for some future doctoral research projects.

827. Nyamiti, Charles

Studies in African Christian Theology, Volume 1: Jesus Christ, the Ancestor of Humankind: Methodological and Trinitarian Foundations

Nairobi: Catholic University of Eastern Africa, 2006. 286 pages, ISBN: 9789966909350.

Nyamiti has been professor of theology at the Catholic University of Eastern Africa (CUEA) in Nairobi. His three-volume theology is a rare example of African Christian systematic theology. This first volume begins with methodology. Nyamiti indicates that he is a representative of inculturation theology, not liberation theology. African theology, according to him, is a scientific effort guided by reason and faith "to understand and present Christian faith in accordance with African needs and mentality." The sources for African theology are twofold: "Christian sources" (the Bible and church tradition) and "the African socio-cultural situation." Nevertheless, he rejects syncretism: "The primary criterion for judging what is good or not good in the African socio-cultural situation is the Biblical and Church teaching. Whatever is incompatible with that teaching has to be judged as false and inacceptable." But Nyamiti then takes the African concept of ancestor as a paradigm for understanding the Christian faith. He attempts to do so without compromising his Catholic Christian faith. He defines ancestorship as "a sacred kin relationship which establishes a right or title to regular sacred communication with one's own kind through prayer and ritual offering." Nyamiti then claims that ancestorship is crucial for understanding the being of God. God the Father is the Ancestor of the Logos or Son; the Logos is the Descendant of the Ancestor; and the Holy Spirit is "reciprocal ancestral Gift and Oblation of the Father and Son." Then, proceeding from the principle of *analogia entis* (analogy of being), Nyamiti concludes that "ancestral relationship is ultimately an essential dimension of being itself." This helps us to see the sacred dimension of all of life. While Nyamiti offers an interesting experiment in African Christian theology, can his controlling paradigm be faithful to the fundamentals of the biblical witness and church traditions? Whereas Nyamiti's doctrine of God is deeply Augustinian, one wonders whether the concept of Ancestor is appropriate to the Trinity, since the Father never died like other ancestors.

828.   Nyamiti, Charles

Studies in African Christian Theology, Volume 2: Jesus Christ, the Ancestor of Humankind: An Essay on African Christology

Nairobi: Catholic University of Eastern Africa, 2006. 286 pages, ISBN: 9789966909411.

In the first volume of his three-volume African systematic theology, Nyamiti claimed that God the Father is the Ancestor of the Son and also of humankind. In this second volume, he claims that Jesus Christ is the Ancestor of humankind. This for him is primarily through the Son's incarnation. Through his incarnation, Jesus is ancestor both as God and as man. As the divine Logos and as part of the Trinity, Jesus is our ancestor. But as human (and divine) mediator, Jesus is our ancestor through his mediatory work. Strangely though, Nyamiti emphasizes the incarnation more than the cross in his understanding of Christ's mediatorial work. In other words, his theology approaches classic incarnation theology. The ministry of Jesus is summed up in his threefold office, that of prophet, pastoral (king) and priest. Unfortunately, Christ's atoning sacrifice is not properly developed here. Instead, the focus is on the Mass or Eucharist as the "highest and supreme goal" of Christ's life and ministry. It is in the Mass that a person encounters God. But in the Mass, one also encounters ancestors: African ancestors, Catholic saints, and Jesus Christ himself. For Nyamiti, African ancestors and Catholic saints, both in purgatory and in heaven, qualify to be our ancestors. Indeed, they can also intercede for us. Thus, Nyamiti advocates a baptism or Christianisation of the African ancestral cult. Ideally, for him, "the Mass is the supreme accomplishment of the African ancestral cult." Elements of the ancestral cult can now be brought into the Catholic liturgy. But is this not the syncretism that he explicitly rejected in his first volume? Nyamiti's project began with great potential but unfortunately ends up in an African cult of ancestors enacted within a traditional Roman Catholic theology of the Mass and the saints.

829.   Nyirongo, Lenard

Dealing with Darkness: A Christian Novel on the Confrontation with African Witchcraft

Potchefstroom, South Africa: Potchefstroom University, 1999. 125 pages, ISBN: 9781868223466.

Nyirongo has been a managing consultant of a business and training firm in Kitwe, Zambia. He is also an active Christian writer, with several publications to his name. In a sense this novel is a creative dramatisation of the argument of his earlier book, *The Gods of Africa or the God of the Bible*, which is a formal theological and apologetic treatment of the confrontation between Christianity and traditional African religion. This novel tells the early life story of an intelligent young man in eastern Zambia who is forced to leave secondary school because of a family-arranged marriage. This provokes a crisis in his life that eventually leads to his conversion. The rest of the book chronicles the various trials that he encounters while struggling to preserve his childless marriage, and also to find gainful employment in the face of many obstacles. Most of his problems arise as a result of the conflict between his newly found faith and traditional religious beliefs and customary practices. An amazing diversity of these are briefly dealt with: witchcraft, sorcery, evil omens, sacrifices to the ancestral spirits, the use of protective or self-enhancing charms, dreams of "ghosts," cures for barrenness, divination practices, curses, and witch-cleansing procedures. It is a bit unrealistic for so many of these trials to strike in such a relatively short space of time. Nevertheless, the individual vignettes are interestingly presented, and the account's rapid movement serves to preserve the reader's attention. Another major theme involves the young man's confrontation with "dead Christianity" in the lives of many of those whom he encounters on a daily basis, most notably his own parents, who believe that they are "saved" because they belong to a particular church, but whose behaviour in fact differs little from non-Christian neighbours. The young man's faith is also tested in such secular situations as maintaining honesty and integrity at school and in employment, or in response to foreign beliefs such as astrology. The author clearly reveals his evangelical theological convictions. Occasionally this intrudes quite strongly into the storyline, though never enough to detract from the whole. The author's style is generally clear and flowing, while the book's content is engaging and highly relevant to all those who live in Africa. Once started, it is hard to put this book down.

830. Nyirongo, Lenard

The Gods of Africa or the God of the Bible: The Snares of African Traditional Religion in Biblical Perspective

Potchefstroom, South Africa: Potchefstroom University, 1997. 212 pages, ISBN: 9781868222933.

The author boldly sets forth the central motif of his book at the very outset: "What worries me . . . is the denial of the cardinal truths of the Gospel by some well-known African theologians. . . . The denial can be briefly summarized in one proposition: that the African religious beliefs should be regarded as a foundation for faith in Christ." The book is published by the Institute for Reformational Studies at Potchefstroom University in South Africa. The eighteen informative chapters are grouped into four main divisions: knowing God and worshipping Him aright; man's state and destiny; man's identity in the community; and suffering, health and prosperity. Each chapter leads off with a helpful outline of the main ideas and issues to be discussed. This is followed by "the [traditional] African's view" of the subject, a perspective that is often adopted by sympathetic contemporary theologians. Then "the biblical view" is presented and supported by a wide selection of Scripture references. The book has many noteworthy features: a clearly developed, contrastive outline approach to the various topics discussed; an easy, non-technical style of writing; many citations from prominent African theologians from all over the continent (allowing them to "speak for themselves"); a number of useful summary outlines and charts (e.g. on different concepts of "time," or matrilineality vs. patrilineality); and a well-balanced, broadly evangelical theological position. Nyirongo incisively and succinctly calls attention to the insidious danger of syncretism that threatens the vitality and progress of biblically-based Christianity virtually everywhere in Africa. Along the way, he does not hesitate to criticize certain anti-biblical Western influences as well, (e.g. its notion of "progress"). Nyirongo is from Zambia, where he works as a management consultant. He holds a first degree in science education, and a post-graduate diploma in productivity improvement. When one reads his perceptive treatment of such a wide variety of crucial religious issues, it is hard to believe that he has received no formal theological training. Readers may not always agree with Nyirongo's theological position, but they will certainly admire the clarity and conviction with which he has presented it in terms of African traditional religion, biblical texts, and certain deviant contemporary viewpoints.

831.   Nzunda, Matembo S., and Kenneth R. Ross, editors

Church, Law and Political Transition in Malawi 1992–1994

Gweru, Zimbabwe: Mambo Press, 1995. 170 pages, ISBN: 9780869226025.

This collection of essays gives some account of the contributions made by the church and by the law to the transformation of Malawian political life during the years 1992–1994. The two-year span between the issue of the Catholic bishops' pastoral letter of 1992 and the general election of 1994 was marked by a process of rapid political change in Malawi, and resources from both theology and law proved to be of decisive significance in the country's 'peaceful revolution'. Ignited by the pastoral letter of the Catholic bishops, it was in the context of the church (Catholic and Protestant) that people found the courage to raise their voices in protest. And it was in the context of administrative law and the courts that the Malawi public discovered that it had become possible not to be punished without first being tried for mounting political protests, and that the law could actually help in the process of change. In order to take account of these important developments the Department of Law and the Department of Theology and Religious Studies at the University of Malawi joined forces to organize a series of seminars to examine different aspects of this transition. The end result is an illuminating collection of twelve essays, dealing variously with issues such as: Malawi's sedition laws in terms of social contract theory; the Catholic bishops' pastoral letter in the context of Catholic social witness; the experience of women under the one-party state and the key contribution they can make to political transition; the justification of violence from the standpoint of Christian ethics; a critical look at the social witness of the renowned Livingstonia Synod of the Church of Central Africa Presbyterian; and a final essay on the witness of 'smaller' churches in this process of social transformation. In many ways the book reflects the cautious euphoria of a newly found freedom from a totalitarian system – an experience not uncommon in other countries of Africa. This reflection provides valuable insights for Christians concerned with the proper development of democracy in Africa.

O'Barr, Jean F.

see review 102

832.   O'Donovan, Wilber

Biblical Christianity in African Perspective

Carlisle, UK: Paternoster, 1996. 368 pages, ISBN: 9780853647119.

Here we have a basic evangelical theology textbook designed specifically for Africa. The author has spent some thirty years in theological education in Africa, mostly in Nigeria but also in Kenya and Ethiopia. The first edition of this book came out in 1992. Subsequently the book has been put through extensive field testing, and as a result the text has been completely rewritten for this second edition. It now reflects even more fulsomely the range of traditional cultural issues that African Christians face. The distinctive strength of the book is that it approaches theology from the perspective of Africa. It raises and addresses the issues and problems that African Christians face, whether or not these are part of the traditional Western theological agenda. For example, topics addressed include: ancestors, traditional initiation, magic and divination; guidance, false prophets, syncretism and mediators; cultural prejudice and the church; marriage, family, sex, polygamy and divorce; suffering, sickness, curses and bribery; and the church as the extended family of God. Every chapter begins with a story from Africa, and throughout the text are references and applications to the African setting. Each chapter ends with a summary, a list of discussion questions, and suggestions for further reading. The book has been carefully field-tested for clarity of expression. It is evangelical in its perspective without being narrow or sectarian. Thus it focuses on basic biblical truth with practical application to Africa, while omitting discussion of those issues which have been a source of extended disagreement within the evangelical Christian community. Many theological colleges in Africa make this a standard text in core theology courses.

833. O'Donovan, Wilbur

Biblical Christianity in Modern Africa

Carlisle, UK: Paternoster, 2000. 263 pages, ISBN: 9781842270196.

O'Donovan was a missionary in West and East Africa for over 30 years, and taught at six theological colleges on the continent. This is very different in subject matter from O'Donovan's earlier and now widely-used *Biblical Christianity in African Perspective.* That volume dealt with a variety of theological topics, some familiar to traditional Western theology (such as Christology and Eschatology), and others important to Christianity in a traditional African setting (such as the Bible's perspective on beliefs and practices of African traditional religions, sorcery and witchcraft). This new title focuses instead on issues most often associated with urbanized Africa. Both books are characterized by a thoughtful evangelical outlook, a deep appreciation for Africa, her people, her church and her issues, and both are written in simple, clear English. Both books are aimed at helping African Christians deal biblically with African issues, and both frequently use brief case studies of actual people and events to illustrate problems and solutions. In some ways this book seems like the evangelical version of what some ecumenical African theologians are calling "Reconstruction Theology," in which the reconstruction of Jerusalem's walls under Nehemiah becomes an organising theological theme for addressing the continent's needs. Nehemiah is seen as a biblical figure who can represent the aspirations and contradictions of Africa's needed social reconstruction at this time in its history. It is easy to see some overlap between this approach and the contribution of O'Donovan's book. O'Donovan addresses the problems and effects of westernisation and urbanization, such as poverty, pornography, prostitution, AIDS, abortion, materialism, politics, power and corruption, women in the church, abuse of women, the needs of youth, including street children, nominalism, healing and prosperity theology. O'Donovan also suggests ways to deal with these issues and problems, often giving true life examples. Like his previous book, this one deserves to be widely used as a convenient, timely text in theological colleges throughout the continent. It is a call to the evangelical churches of Africa to realize that God wants to use them not only to evangelize but also to reconstruct the continent, as Nehemiah rebuilt the walls of Jerusalem.

Obeng, Emmanuel A.

see review 385

834.   **Obinwa, Ignatius M. C.**

Yahweh My Refuge: A Critical Analysis of Psalm 71

Frankfurt: Peter Lang, 2006. 221 pages, ISBN: 9783631559031.

This book is a revised version of a doctoral dissertation defended in 2001 at the Philosophisch-Theologische Hochschule Sankt Gorgen, Frankfurt, Germany. The author, Rector of Blessed Iwene Tansi Major Seminary in Onitsha, Nigeria, has previously published several books in biblical and theological studies. The present book is an exegetical analysis of Psalm 71, consisting of three parts. The first offers a survey of literature and a translation of the psalm based on a solid textual critical analysis. The second part makes a literary analysis of the psalm, discussing its supposedly anthological character and the questions of order and coherence. Finally, the third part analyses the main theological issues of the psalm. The book is an exegetical study, in a traditional sense of the word. Its strength lies in an extensive use of dictionaries and concordances, an approach which enables the author to identify a broad spectrum of intertextual connections with other parts of Psalms. Still, the book would have benefited from stronger interaction with the current methodological debate, for example as far as intertextuality is concerned. Even though the book is an exegetical study, the author acknowledges that Psalm 71 has a message also to contemporary readers, and his African context is visible in a few places. The book is of general interest for exegetes working with Psalms and for anyone following the development of African exegetical studies.

835.   **Ochieng'-Odhiambo, Frederick**

Trends and Issues in African Philosophy

Frankfurt: Peter Lang, 2010. 237 pages, ISBN: 9781433107504.

Ochieng'-Odhiambo has taught African philosophy in various Kenyan and Southern African universities, and has headed the Department of History and Philosophy at the University of the West Indies in Barbados. The present book is a historical introduction to the main area of his teaching and research; historical, not only in the sense that the discussion relates to changing interpretive contexts, but also in that the main approaches to philosophy in Africa throughout the twentieth and early twenty-first centuries are seen as dialoguing with each other, creating a historically sensitive African discourse. The book has six main chapters. Chapter 1 outlines what is called the historical phase, pointing out traditional Western discourses on Africa on the one hand and Afrocentric responses on the other. Chapter 2 discusses African philosophy as ethnophilosophy, from Tempels and Mbiti onward, with its aim of countering Western intellectual arrogance vis-à-vis Africa. Chapter 3 discusses the so-called professional approach, arguing that its universalist conceptions of African philosophy are still founded on Western paradigms. Chapter 4 presents philosophic sagacity, acknowledging that it addresses specific philosophic issues and concepts, rather than discussing the mere possibility of an African philosophy. Chapter 5 presents nationalist-ideological philosophy, from Nyerere and Senghor to Mandela. Finally, chapter 6 addresses more recent hermeneutical approaches, which, like ethnophilosophy and philosophical sagacity, emphasize that African philosophy should be based on Africa's own experiences and concerns; still, here with a more critical distance both to Western and to African philosophical presuppositions. The book's pedagogical way of organising problems and approaches makes it a valuable addition to the current flora of introductions to African philosophy.

836. Oden, Thomas C.

The African Memory of Mark: Reassessing Early Church Tradition

Downers Grove: IVP US, 2011. 279 pages, ISBN: 9780830839339.

The author has been Director of the Center for Early African Christianity at Eastern University in the United States, and general editor of the landmark 29-volume *Ancient Christian Commentary on Scripture* series. The purpose of this book is "to show the greater plausibility of the African memory of Mark than of its modern [Western] mythic alternatives." The intended audience is ordinary readers, especially "youthful Christian believers on the African continent." The book is the first in decades to reassess the historicity of the African traditions concerning St. Mark, his African origins, his relationship to the apostle Peter, and his African ministry. Oden presents the rich and venerated African church tradition that is virtually unknown outside of Africa. In this "African memory of Mark," St. Mark was born in Cyrene of Africa, was related to the apostle Peter, and – upon Peter's death in Rome and the completion of his gospel – journeyed from Rome to Alexandria and established the apostolic church. There he also died a martyr's death. Oden believes his subject holds significance for helping to bring modern Africa out of its colonization-induced depression. He desires to retell to Christian Africa its own apostolic epic, in the hope that it will create in her a sense of place and destiny among the nations of the world as an intellectual and spiritual equal. Oden therefore invites the reader to reconsider the evidence against what he understands as Western historicist scepticism on "steroids," which in his view refuses to take seriously the African memory of Mark. The work therefore passionately bids the reader to reassess these venerable and powerful traditions and story. More importantly, however, the author challenges the rising generation of African Christians to discover and embrace their own ancient – and distinctly African – Christian heritage. The African memory of Mark arises out of the Coptic (and less directly, the Ethiopian) Orthodox Church, but the vast younger movements south and west of these great Sees are included, because the African memory of Mark is the founding charter of all Christian Africa. While Western historical methods should now revisit the tradition, African memory continues by liturgy and tradition to tell the story of Mark as the apostolic father of African Christianity. The African memory of Mark has inspired and shaped countless thousands of African disciples and just might, because of Oden's energetic labour, inspire and shape many more.

837. Oden, Thomas C.

Early Libyan Christianity: Uncovering a North African Tradition

Downers Grove: IVP US, 2011. 334 pages, ISBN: 9780830839438.

This is the third book in Oden's argument that Africa was the crucial nursery for the nascent Christian movement. Here Oden advances his thesis further by arguing for the importance of the long neglected church in Libya. For students of church history both Egypt and Carthage are familiar centres of early Christianity. But Libya is largely neglected territory in the study of early church history. This is not owing to an absence of information, but to the fact, as Oden points out, that such information is not easily accessed. "Readers seeking to study this area will learn that it has an inaccessible bibliography that requires vast linguistic skills to master." In order to write this first attempt at a history of the early Libyan church, Oden had to bring together studies of highly specific aspects of Libyan Christianity, mining information from research in cognate fields that made passing references to the Libyan church, with the bulk of this material in French or Italian. Oden shows us the geo-political and economic significance of Libya in both the OT and the NT worlds. He then traces the important place that Libyan Christians had in the leadership and mission of the NT church. He demonstrates the consequential role Libya played in the post-apostolic church as a place of intellectual ferment producing famous orthodox theologians (Tertullian), popes (Victor), and heretics (Arias). He devotes considerable space to Synesius of Cyrene, perhaps Libya's most distinguished intellectual. Oden also surveys, city by city, the major Christian sites, all in desperate need of archaeological excavation. Oden finishes with a plea for the value of the study of ancient Christian sources for African Christian identity and for genuine Christian-Muslim dialogue. Though Oden's literary style is a bit rambling and repetitive, and (as he admits) some of his conclusions concerning earliest Libyan Christianity push the evidence to the limit and rely heavily on inference and conjecture, this is a vitally important book, first of all because this is the first effort to build a history of early Libyan Christianity. For most students of early Christianity it will contribute awareness for the first time of the importance of this part of African Christianity. Secondly, the book is a plea for sustained, scholarly research of all kinds into the history of the ancient Libyan church.

838.   Oden, Thomas C.

How Africa Shaped the Christian Mind: Rediscovering the African Seedbed of Western Christianity

Downers Grove: IVP US, 2010. 204 pages, ISBN: 9780830837052.

Amid growing global interest in African Christianity, Oden's book deserves special notice. Oden sets forth the stirring thesis that the Christian thought and theology which proved formative for the development of early Christianity and Christian culture was distinctively African. The common perception is that Christianity in Africa is a relatively recent arrival from the West; Oden asserts the opposite: Christianity in Africa is ancient, and it moved south to north out of Africa. The support for this thesis is not so much an argument as it is an outline of an argument, one which he *calls* on African scholars to make, and to substantiate by extensive research into the early African origins of Christianity. Oden's interests in early African Christianity emerged out of his work over much of the past two decades as editor of the *Ancient Christian Commentary on Scripture* series. Oden states that he and the other editors "were astonished to find such a large percentage of texts from Africa or influenced by African writers among the patristic comments on verse after verse of Scripture." The title and thrust of the book reflects Oden's sense, solidified through years of working in primary texts, of the profound extent to which writers on the African continent played a decisive role in shaping fundamental features of Christian thought and theology. Some readers may question whether a shared geography will be a sufficient basis for African Christians to embrace as their own heritage the work of the early fathers of northern Africa. But Oden calls on young African Christian scholars to do the hard textual, linguistic, and archaeological work necessary to recover this early witness to apostolic truth. "The rising charismatic and Pentecostal energies are stronger emotively than intellectually" and "may not sustain African Christians through the Islamic challenge." Oden argues that the necessary resources to meet the challenge are abundantly available within early African Christianity. It is the task of African scholars to deliver this "unreceived gift" of an early "African orthodoxy" which is both authentically African and faithful to apostolic truth. In doing so, African scholarship may also once more play a decisive role in shaping the global Christian mind. One key question, however, is whether leaders of the Church in Africa will embrace this vision, and therefore release young African scholars from the task of leading institutions in order to take up this more sweeping task?

839.   **Oden, Thomas C.**

The Rebirth of African Orthodoxy: Return to Foundations

Nashville: Abingdon, 2016. 176 pages, ISBN: 9781501819094.

In an earlier work Oden argued the thesis that many Western Christians across a gamut of traditions are experiencing revitalisation through a rediscovery of the Christian tradition that emerged in the early centuries of the Christian era. The fact that this "paleo-orthodoxy" had deep roots in early Christian Africa was not lost on Oden, who subsequently wrote *How Africa Shaped the Christian Mind* (2010), in which he called on a new generation of African scholars to re-engage with the early roots of African Christianity as the basis for African Christian identity today. In this new book Oden seeks to make practical that summons to African Christian scholarship, by serving up a curriculum of ten "seminars," re-packaged now to be digested in group interaction. Three emphases of Oden require appraisal. First, Oden writes out of an urgent concern that Christian theology in Africa eschew originality in favour of rootedness. His explicit concern relates to the inherent taste for originality that characterizes Western theological liberalism, which has now gained a footing in some quarters of the continent. Yet for many Christians in Africa the threat of theological originality comes less from modernism and its theologies than from the myriad of self-styled prophets, apostles, and "wise men" now seducing vast crowds with claims of unique or anointed access to truth. Perhaps participants in these seminars would have been well served had this latter threat been specified. Second, though Oden's commendation of the early African fathers is a welcome emphasis, their theological views were by no means equal in quality. Certainly if the choice is between Augustine and Athanasius on the one hand and T. B. Joshua and David Oyedepo on the other, the preferred influence goes without saying. But perhaps the intended readers could benefit from some direction in avoiding the theological blind alleys that may be found in the early fathers. Third, doing theology did not stop after AD 500, and subsequent developments cannot be safely disregarded. For example, evangelical Christianity of the sort that is flourishing on the continent today is profoundly indebted to the theological emphases of the Reformation. Evangelicals would not be well served to de-emphasize these in favour of a more exclusive focus on the ecumenical Councils. There are many riches to be gained from early African Christianity, but those riches mostly lie in the fields that were contested at that time, such as Trinitarianism and Christology. Shall we not also mine riches from other fields that were contested in other times? Despite such qualifications, Oden is certainly on to something wholesome and promising. If, as Oden hopes, contemporary African Christian scholarship sinks some deep roots into the fertile soil of early African Christianity, it may yet flourish for many centuries to come.

Oduaran, Akpovire B.

see review 324

840.   **Odunze, Don, and Marvin Gilbert**

Successful Family Living

Nairobi: Evangel, 1993. 200 pages, ISBN: 9789966200464.

This overview of issues important for successful family living draws on Odunze's work in family ministries in Nigeria and throughout Africa. The book is a very wise and helpful application of biblical principles to the situations facing families in modern Africa, and topics such as polygamy, family morality, financial manage-ment, and extended family relationships. The author is clearly aware of modern research on family relationships and he uses this material effectively, yet the text (adapted by Marvin Gilbert) is also highly readable. Already in wide use in theological colleges as a text for family life courses, it could also function as an effective study guide for church groups. The book well represents the increasing prevalence of popular Africa-based Christian literature throughout the continent.

Oduro, Thomas A.

see review 577

841.   Oduyoye, Mercy Amba

Beads and Strands: Reflections of an African Woman on Christianity in Africa

Oxford: Regnum, 2002. 114 pages, ISBN: 9781570755439.

To anyone acquainted with Christian theology from the perspective of African women, the name Mercy Oduyoye is already known. Her written contributions have been numerous. The volume itself presents eleven selected papers, some abridged, from the author's previous works. These are placed in three loose groupings – part 1: Africa and Redemption; part 2: Global Issues in African Perspective; and part 3: Women, Tradition and the Gospel in Africa. Chapters in this third section (abridged from *Will to Arise* and *Daughters of Anowa* are perhaps the most distinctive, where themes that are not only African but overtly feminist are concentrated. An introductory autobiography notes various influences on the author's thinking: a Christian family of several generations (with her father in pastoral ministry), and her upbringing in a matrilineal society of Ghana. Her background further includes living in Europe and participating widely in global ecumenical activities and leadership. In a later chapter the author relates her personal experience of oppression, when life as a wife in the patrilineal Yoruba culture of Nigeria deprived her of any decision-making authority, on the sole basis of her gender. The chapter calls for the liberation of African women from structures and mind-sets that (attempt to) make women subservient to men. The essay "Women and Ritual in Africa" looks at rituals for the various stages of a woman's life: birth, puberty, marriage, birthing, death, and mourning (widowhood), within the framework of traditional beliefs and practices. Oduyoye expects that further research along these lines, from the perspective of the woman, would help broaden the church's understanding of how men and women can and should relate to one another in Africa. Oduyoye has directed the Institute of African Women in Religion and Culture (Legon, Ghana).

842.   Oduyoye, Mercy Amba

Daughters of Anowa: African Women and Patriarchy

Maryknoll, NY: Orbis, 1998. 226 pages, ISBN: 9780883449998.

Oduyoye grew up in the Akan society of Ghana and, in writing of her own pilgrimage, aims to "examine the church's attitude to the growth of women into Christ-like persons." The book is well crafted, in some instances almost poetic, and filled with images and rich descriptions of culture. Coming from a Methodist background, she seeks to understand how the "daughters of Anowa" (women of Akan) see themselves today, and what influence the church (broadly defined) has, both negatively and positively, on the experience of women. Divided into "cycles," the book's first section, "Language," deals with images, folktales, and proverbs. The second cycle, "Culture," deals with culture, religion, marriage and patriarchy. And the third, "Dreams," offers chapters on justice for women, challenge to the church and a call to women themselves. Oduyoye deals with issues critically and in a balanced way, looking at them from within the contexts of cultural history, traditional religion and the Christian church. While some may evaluate the book as too disturbing of long-cherished dogma and practice, this book is an essential milestone along the slow road that leads to diminishing the curse and promoting the blessing originally intended for women and men together in home, church, and society. In its African depth and particularity, this book offers challenges and insights at a universal level.

843. **Oduyoye, Mercy Amba**

Hearing and Knowing: Theological Reflections on Christianity in Africa

Eugene, OR: Wipf & Stock, 2009. 176 pages, ISBN: 9781606088616.

Oduyoye, a respected Ghanaian theologian, has been senior lecturer in the Department of Religious Studies at Ibadan University. She holds a master's degree in theology from Cambridge University. In this book Oduyoye reflects theologically on Christianity in Africa in the light of her personal experience with the gospel. Her central motif is that theology is for living, and she draws living lessons from traditional doctrines. For example, the doctrine of the Trinity, she says, is important for understanding reconciliation and redemption and for the fulfilment of our humanity after the shape of the Godhead. She upholds ecumenical principles in her interpretation of theology. She gives some impetus toward the articulation of Christian faith in Africa and looks forward to a day when Christians in Africa will creatively talk about God. Her theological concern lies in this question: How can the Church in Africa play a transforming role and be an instrument of justice? She feels the survival of Christianity in Africa lies in what Christians of Africa can do: (1) To re-read the Bible to hear God speaking to them; (2) To examine books of Western missionary theology in order to unmask their ideological component, draw out the ecumenical truth they embody, and interpret, restate and uncover aspects of truth that may have remained concealed to the Western mind. We must never think that Western Christian theology is unchangeable and adequate for all times and places; (3) To be producers of theology, and not consumers only; (4) To do African Christian theology by taking into account all of Africa's background, because both content and method of one's work are influenced by it; (5) To learn to respect and tap into Africa's hidden resources. Those teaching African theology could find this book highly useful.

844. **Oduyoye, Mercy Amba**

Introducing African Women's Theology

London: Sheffield Academic Press, 2001. 132 pages, ISBN: 9781841271439.

Oduyoye is an independent scholar living in Ghana. She has been active in the Ecumenical Movement, including service as Deputy General Secretary of the World Council of Churches. The book is based on the author's experience between 1976 and 1996 when she was developing what became in 1989 "The Circle of Concerned African Women Theologians." Much of her own work is grouped here with that of others in "The Circle." Although Oduyoye says that much of the theological reflection by African women is done through their own stories and is therefore narrative theology, she presents almost none of her theology here in narrative form.

Consequently this is a dense and at times opaque analysis of certain themes in African Feminist Theology. Oduyoye draws what she wants from African culture and religion, and also draws what she wants from the Bible. "Any interpretation of the Bible is unacceptable if it does harm to women, the vulnerable and the voiceless." A frequent target is the hierarchical and patriarchal structures of most African cultures and of the African church. These structures must go if women and other marginalized groups are to attain true humanity and equal use of their gifts in the church. Oduyoye is not anti-male as some Western feminists are, but men should respect the full humanity of women and not treat them as possessions, as "goats that have been taught to talk." These ideas come out repeatedly in the sections on theology proper, Christology, anthropology, ecclesiology and eschatology, as does her essentially liberal approach. Her use of African religion in Christianity includes a place for the ancestors (though this place is not defined in the book), so she takes Africa's past seriously. She also takes biblical texts seriously and refers to the Bible repeatedly. Her passion, compassion, intelligence and resistance to what she sees as injustice come through clearly throughout the book. She makes several points which should be attended. First, theology should not be just talk about God; it should result in a better church and world. Second, Africa is losing its sense of community and hospitality, both of which are based on the extended family, which is also under attack. Oduyoye is determined to stop the erosion of these crucial African values and institutions if she can. Third, African society and the church need to reassess their attitudes and actions towards women so that woman can contribute what God wants them to contribute.

845. Oduyoye, Mercy Amba

Who Will Roll the Stone Away?: The Ecumenical Decade of the Churches in Solidarity with Women

Geneva: World Council of Churches, 1991. 69 pages, ISBN: 9782825410189.

This slim and easily read book by Oduyoye, founder of the "Circle of Concerned African Woman Theologians," describes the World Council of Churches Decade 1988–1998, which was devoted to churches in solidarity with women. The five chapters are entitled: The Beginnings, The Launching, Promoting the Decade, The Meaning and the Signs of Solidarity, and Ten Years Hence? As the title of the book indicates, the Easter story provides the theme, and this book was written as a progress report for the 1991 Canberra Australia WCC meetings. Colourful descriptions of the Decade efforts around the world are recorded: pilgrimages, art, workshops, drama and declarations, cleaning up graveyards, processions and seminars, worship, literacy programs, social action initiatives, evangelism and curriculum committees, and challenging quotes such as "Sister, can you tell me your name? Your own name, not that of your child or husband." Oduyoye points out how local congregations are slow to respond to higher organisational calls to action. How is forward movement actually to be accomplished? The challenge goes beyond increasing the numbers of women on roll calls, to enabling them to be energized for both "celebration and struggle." Women's self-identity, the unity of humanity bearing the image of God, biblical "solidarity," are all issues which need theological reflection and understanding by both women and men together. The book is well crafted and almost poetic in its style. Oduyoye offers the hope that "the Decade will also touch churches which are not members of the WCC." Readers may find that the book's larger themes frequently reflect their own struggles, dreams and prayers for many African women who have yet to see the stone rolled away.

846. **Oduyoye, Mercy Amba, and Musimbi R. A. Kanyoro, editors**

The Will to Arise: Women, Tradition, and the Church in Africa

Eugene, OR: Wipf & Stock, 2005. 238 pages, ISBN: 9781597524742.

In this collection of essays, African women theologians present their views, in their capacity as women as well in their capacity as scholars, by critiquing the varying ways in which churches relate to traditions affecting women – and especially to practices that are oppressive of women. Their goal is to inject a female perspective into the study of these subjects, since study up to this point has been predominantly done by men. They also hope to challenge women to rise up and find ways of affirming helpful traditions that are compatible with the gospel, while overcoming and healing harmful practices, especially in the areas of polygamy, treatment of widows and prostitution. The level of scholarly insight and presentation is generally high, and the theological perspectives include Catholic and Protestant as well as one Muslim theologian. Scripture undergirds the arguments of most of the writers, with some presenting a more feminist argument while others use a more evangelical or devotional approach. The book should be enlightening to those involved in the contextualization of the gospel in Africa, since scholarly women's voices were until recently not widely heard in this area.

Oduyoye, Mercy Amba

see also review 564

847. **Oduyoye, Modupe**

The Churches' Responsibility for Understanding Islam and the Muslims in Africa: A Short Bibliography

Nairobi: Project for Christian-Muslim Relations in Africa, 1995. 73 pages.

The compiler of this bibliography admits that although the materials were prepared in 1992, "counsels of perfection" put off publication until it was decided that publishing something was better than publishing nothing. African Islam surely needs understanding. Even a moderate selection of the materials listed in this publication would help balance the dominance of attention to the Middle East in texts on Islamics. Anything at all would help Christians who may live near Muslims but who can remain ignorant of Islam apart from stereotypes. Oduyoye was the editor for many years of the *Nigerian Christian* magazine and editor-manager of the remarkable Daystar Press, Ibadan, Nigeria. He is the husband of the well-known theologian, Mercy Amba Oduyoye. The bibliography is organized in two main parts: a survey of Islam and the history and practices of Islam in Africa (North Africa is not much represented), and then the state and history of Christian-Muslim relations. Dialogue is well represented with over 20 pages, in keeping with the aims of PROCMURA. The entries are mostly unannotated. The book ends with four pages of addresses for organisations, publishers and journals related to Christian-Muslim relations. You won't find missions or evangelistic organisations – that is another story. Oduyoye knew of Mark Hinton's *Ministering among Muslims in Africa: An Annotated List of Practical Materials*, and notes that the two lists overlap less than 10 percent. Oduyoye's bibliography bears the signs of being a labour of love, with a bias (inevitably) towards Ibadan, and with an evident limitation of access to resources. There are many intriguing references, to individual chapters in books, to dissertations in British universities, and to papers delivered in conferences years ago and never published. Not all references are to works in English or other European languages. Teachers of Islamics and librarians in Africa would find a copy of this bibliography helpful as a supplementary checklist and guide for searches.

848.   **Oduyoye, Modupe**

The Longest Psalm: The Prayers of a Student of Moral Instruction

Ibadan: Sefer Books, 1994. 118 pages, ISBN: 9789783245433.

The Alphabetical Psalms: Systematic Instruction for a Life of Faith and Trust

Ibadan: Sefer Books, 1995. 59 pages, ISBN: 9789783245440.

Le-mah sabach-tha-niy?: Lament and Entreaty in the Psalms

Ibadan: Sefer Books, 1995. 99 pages, ISBN: 9789783245464.

The Psalms of Satan

Ibadan: Sefer Books, 1997. 65 pages, ISBN: 9789783119598.

The Nigerian author and publisher Modupe Oduyoye gained international attention with his *Sons of God, Daughters of Men: An Afro-Asiatic Commentary on Genesis 1–11* (1984). Throughout the 1990s he has followed this up with a series of brief commentaries on the Psalms, beginning with this one in 1994, and continuing with *The Alphabetical Psalms: Systematic Instruction for a Life of Faith and Trust* (1995); *Le-mah sabach-tha-niy?: Lament and Entreaty in the Psalms* (1995); *The Psalms of Satan* (1997). Over the years Oduyoye has developed his own peculiar approach. As do most commentators, he tries to find a balance between historical insight and pastoral awareness, but this is then combined with a strong focus on linguistic questions. Being trained as a linguist, Oduyoye is able to draw on his impressive knowledge of West African, Indo-European, and Semitic languages. And he uses this knowledge to draw lines from the Hebrew text of the Psalms to various translations of the OT and even to various other oral and literary traditions. However, this exciting approach is also Oduyoye's major problem. One is not always sure on what premises he draws such lines. When he goes from the Hebrew to the Arabic (and Quranic), it is of course possible to find a historical link. And the same is probably also the case when similar links are drawn between certain words in Hebrew and in Hausa (via Arabic). But not all of Oduyoye's examples are that clear. Some seem rather to be a play with consonants or on words. In spite of these methodological problems, Oduyoye's commentaries represent a fresh approach to the Psalms. Their focus on the relationship between biblical Hebrew and certain West African languages (and cultures) makes them a valuable tool for further reflection on what it means to interpret the Psalms within an African context.

849.   **Oduyoye, Modupe**

The Shariy'ah Debate in Nigeria: October 1999–October 2000

Ibadan: Sefer Books, 2000. 130 pages, ISBN: 9789783464575.

Oduyoye is a Nigerian exegete and philologist who has been involved with the Christian Council of Nigeria and the Project for Christian-Muslim Relations in Africa (PROCMURA). The expansion of Muslim Sharia law in some northern states of Nigeria after the return to elected civilian government in 1999 sparked a series of protests from Christians and from advocates of secular government, with violence and loss of life in some areas. This book is a defence of the view that Sharia is beneficial to society and that Christian protest is misguided. Oduyoye faults his fellow Christians for ignorance of Sharia, for refusing to believe Muslim assurances that Sharia will not be applied to non-Muslims, and for resorting to public demonstrations rather than dialogue and the courts. He says that secularism has failed Western society, resulting in such de-civilizing effects as loss of chastity and charity. To him, Sharia is a system that seeks the will of God as the rule of society, and aims to eliminate alcohol consumption, prostitution and usury, all for society's good. Oduyoye buttresses his view by many references to the Arabic and Hausa translations of the Bible where "sharia" is the word used to translate "law." He then takes biblical injunctions to honour the law of God and applies them to honouring the Sharia law being advocated in Nigeria today. The book is rather one-sided, depicting Muslims as sincere and most Christians as hypocritical, and comparing the practice of the adherents of one religion (Christianity) with the doctrine of another (Islam). If the only objections of Nigerian Christians to Sharia were that it threatens their alcohol-related businesses, their freedom to commit sexual immorality and their right to charge usury, Oduyoye may be right. But the deeper issues are Sharia's attitude to non-Muslims, and fear that Sharia will be further expanded to render non-Muslims second-class citizens in states where it is already difficult for them to get land for church buildings, or government jobs and contracts. This book can also be heard, however, as a plea from an African Christian that secularism is less acceptable than Sharia. The book would be of most interest for those studying Christian-Muslim relations, and attitudes towards secularism in Africa.

850. Oehrig, Robert J., Rhena Taylor, and Diane Omondi, editors

Crossing Cultures for Christ

Nairobi: Daystar University, 1987. 110 pages.

This book will interest all those concerned with African-implemented cross-cultural Christian witness. It presents a dozen papers given at an "African Missionary Seminar" held in 1987 in Nairobi, which focused on the challenges of cross-cultural mission done in Africa, by Africans, in an African way. The significance of this book lies especially in its pioneering role on this theme when published. Topics treated include the challenge of missions in Africa, emerging missions in Africa, mission models for the African church, designing an African missionary structure, and funding an African missionary movement. Reports from discussion units within the seminar are also included, with practical recommendations. While the book may not cover everything important to the subject, it does treat many of the most relevant questions. It is task oriented, it gives a bibliography for further reading, it gives topics for group discussion, and it is affordable. As a report on an actual event, it also retains a certain liveliness that a normal text might lack. Certainly those African church bodies already engaged in cross-cultural mission, and especially those individuals responsible for directing such outreach, will find much in this book of benefit as they reflect on their task and assess their efforts. Also those anywhere who are interested in the cross-cultural mission of the African church will discover uniquely valuable materials here in a still too-neglected field.

851.   Ogbannaya, A. Okechukwu

On Communitarian Divinity: An African Interpretation of the Trinity

St. Paul, MN: Paragon House, 1999. 144 pages, ISBN: 9781557787040.

This slender volume, originally a dissertation at Claremont (USA), argues that the African worldview, especially its understanding of community, illuminates Tertullian's concept of the Trinity. The work begins by developing the African idea of community, where individuals are defined first and foremost by the community and therefore reflect its unity, and its impact on the understanding of divinity. This section is perhaps the most important and enduring contribution of this study, because the author rejects the conventional depictions of African traditional religions as either monotheistic or polytheistic. Ogbonnaya challenges Idowu's and Mbiti's view that African religions are fundamentally monotheistic, since this ignores the common ATR theme of the gods' progeny. Ogbannaya also quickly dismisses a polytheistic notion of divinity, where the gods are involved in antagonistic and competing activities. By contrast he interprets the ATR divinities as united in their activities by a singular power or force. This communitarian view is very similar to what Imasogie labels "bureaucratic monotheism." Unfortunately, counter-evidence such as the belief in evil spirits or instances where the divinities compete and thus do not reflect one single power is ignored. And to illustrate this concept of communotheism, Ogbannaya chooses not a traditional African religion but ancient Egyptian religion. Next the author argues that Tertullian employed this communitarian view of divinity to articulate the Trinity as three individual gods united by a common force and power. This is the weakest part of the book. No historical evidence is ever presented to support his assertion that Tertullian converted from African traditional religion. The author studiously ignores the possibility that Scripture is Tertullian's source for the Trinity, instead positing the Western liberal thesis that human subjectivity and not God's revelation is the source of humanity's conception of the divine. Ogbannaya's proposal cannot explain why there are only three persons in the Christian Godhead. Nor does his proposal interact with the consensus of historical scholarship, which interprets Tertullian's use of *persona* as masks rather than as individual personalities. Historical evidence apparently holds little importance for this imaginative project.

852.   Ogola, Margaret, and Margaret Roche

Cardinal Otunga: A Gift of Grace

Nairobi: Paulines, 2013. 303 pages, ISBN: 9789966214263.

This biography of Maurice Michael Cardinal Otunga, Archbishop Emeritus of Nairobi, is written in a popular and readable style. Although somewhat uncritical, it gives a good picture of the emerging Roman Catholic Church in Kenya during the past century while tracing the life of the Church's first national bishop. Cardinal Otunga was born in colonial Kenya as the son of a chief and was chosen by his father to succeed him. However, after being sent to Catholic schools he felt called to serve God, declined to succeed his father, and instead went to Rome to study for the priesthood. Returning to Kenya after his ordination, his desire was to serve as parish priest but he was posted instead to teach at a local seminary, and then was assigned as private secretary to the archbishop. Though this was not his wish, it proved a valuable experience, for at the age of 33 he was appointed Auxiliary Bishop of Kisumu. He had to overcome objections both to his age and to his race, but did so with patience and graciousness. During the transitional years from colonial rule to independence Otunga had a calming influence upon the nation. From 1969 until his retirement in 1997 Cardinal Otunga served in the See of Nairobi. Though brief, this book gives good insights into the cultural, religious and historical context of Kenya in the last half of the twentieth century. It also contains some useful pastoral counsel from the Cardinal in his role as religious leader.

853.   Oguejiofor, Josephat Obi, and Tobias Wendl, editors

Exploring the Occult and Paranormal in West Africa

Münster: LIT Verlag, 2012. 280 pages, ISBN: 9783643901835.

The book is the result of a research project on "the return of the religious," in light of the recent increase in the spread and reinforcement of occult and paranormal phenomena in West Africa. The project was organized through a series of seminars in Germany and Nigeria from 2005 to 2009. Scholars from different academic disciplines (philosophy, religious studies, sociology, anthropology) and countries (Germany, Nigeria, Ivory Coast, Benin, Burkina Faso) worked together in the project. The book includes fourteen essays, covering areas such as the principles and causes of occult and paranormal phenomena, specific manifestations of these phenomena, the logic and processes of the belief, and the place of the phenomena in today's world. Let two essays illustrate the collection as a whole. The first is E. S. Nwauche's analysis of the roles of occult and paranormal phenomena in the legal system in Nigeria. It is argued that the system is contradictory, in the sense that on the one hand it criminalizes these phenomena, whereas on the other it acknowledges the efficacy and use of, for example, juju and oracles in relation to oath taking. The second is J. Harnischfeger's analysis of Ngozi, a local prophetess in the Nsukka (Nigeria) area, who in the mid-1990s initiated a crusade against paganism, destroying the shrine of the local god and putting on display in the public market charms and other sorts of mysterious objects. Ngozi and her followers saw the crusade from the perspective of Christianity as a means and exponent of modernism, whereas the essay argues that there are no clear-cut boundaries between tradition and modernity. To some extent the traditionalists and crusaders inhabited the same spiritual universe, and Ngozi seems to have taken over many of the functions of the shrine of the local god. The book would have benefitted from more stringent editing. Apart from a very brief introduction, there is no attempt at seeing the different cases together – i.e. interpreting the "occult and paranormal phenomena" as such. One would also have wanted to see some information about the institutional context of the authors (nationality, university, academic background); only the two editors are briefly presented: Oguejiofor is professor at the Department of Philosophy at Nnamdi Azikiwe University (Nigeria) and Wendl is professor at the Department of Art History, Free University of Berlin (Germany). Nevertheless, the book offers an interesting collection of case studies on the increasing role of occult and paranormal phenomena in contemporary West Africa, and as such it fills a gap in the current literature.

854.   Ojo, Matthews A.

The End-Time Army: Charismatic Movements in Modern Nigeria

Trenton, NJ: Africa World Press, 2006. 314 pages, ISBN: 9781592213658.

This book, by a professor at Obafemi Awolowo University in Nigeria, looks at the charismatic movement in contemporary Nigeria and especially in the western part of this country. The term "charismatic" for the author is defined by belief in the baptism of the Holy Spirit, and speaking in tongues as the distinctive mark of this baptism. Antecedents of the contemporary charismatic movement go back to the revival of Garrick Braide in the Niger Delta in the 1910s and the Aladura churches. Antecedents also include campus ministries like the Student Christian Movement and Scripture Union. But "it was in 1970 that the Charismatic revival really emerged." Ojo places this beginning especially in the University of Ibadan. He traces the growth of this movement in the 1970s and 1980s amidst social and economic turmoil. This growth was especially strong among the youth in the cities and university campuses. Initially this revival occurred outside of established churches in the form of non-denominational charismatic organisations like the Christian Corpers Fellowship and the Christian Students' Social Movement of Nigeria. But in the 1980s the charismatic movement formed many of its own denominations. The Deeper Life Ministry of William Kumuyi began holding Sunday services in 1982; the Living Faith Church, or Winners' Chapel, of David Oyedepo started in the same year. Ojo highlights distinctive beliefs and practices of this movement. Evangelism is one such belief. "Through evangelism, Charismatics hope that the economic, social and political situation of Nigeria will be transformed into a better one." Generally Ojo praises the charismatic movement as a vital revival of Nigerian Christianity. It is unfortunate, though, that he does not provide a critical evaluation of the prosperity teaching and practice of some Nigerian Pentecostalism. One also wonders whether individual conversion is enough to transform the dismal economic and political culture of Nigeria. It is also a pity that more attention is not given to the eastern part of Nigeria. But this book will be a standard reference book on Nigerian Pentecostalism.

Okenimkpe, Michael

see review 227

855.   Okorocha, Cyril C.

The Meaning of Religious Conversion in Africa: The Case of the Igbo of Nigeria

London: Ashgate, 1987. 354 pages, ISBN: 9780566050305.

Andrew Walls, who supervised this work as a PhD thesis at the University of Aberdeen (1982), says in the foreword that it is "a study of wide interest and considerable importance." The Igbo of southeastern Nigeria are a Christianized people, but most of them still live in two worlds religiously. Many features of the old traditional religion are gone, but some have reappeared under modern guise and are still very influential. This gives us insight into the contemporary African worldview. And it is a people's worldview that determines what understanding they have of the gospel. Okorocha says Igbo conversion is best understood as power encounter where people accept a more powerful system for solving their felt needs. This is important pastorally, because the new faith, to be retained, must meet the needs met by the old religion and more. In Igbo thought, salvation is total wellbeing of life in this world. It comes ultimately from God but is mainly achieved by human effort. Although this falls short of the Bible's vision of salvation by grace, any presentation of the gospel which does not deal with the issue of prosperity in this life will always leave Igbo believers searching elsewhere for this prosperity. The challenge for Igbo Christian theologians is to develop theology that makes sense to the Igbo in that it recognizes that religion is about power, with the goal as enhancement of life, yet is biblical, Christocentric and contributes to the thinking of the world Church. The state of the Igbo is paralleled by many Christianized ethnic groups in Africa, and this book should therefore be widely useful in thinking about the development of indigenous theology and about discipling strategy. There are numerous endnotes for those who want to go further, and many case studies of adherents of various denominations.

856.   Okoye, James Chukwuma

Israel and the Nations: A Mission Theology of the Old Testament

Maryknoll, NY: Orbis, 2006. 224 pages, ISBN: 9781570756542.

Educated in Nigeria, Rome and England, and subsequently teaching at the Catholic Theological Union in Chicago, Okoye here provides a helpful contribution to the theology of mission as reflected in the OT. After briefly surveying the limited literature that is available, he goes on to organize his own study around a number of very important OT texts with significant missional overtones. These he has arranged under four different themes or "faces" of mission in the OT: (1) the universal relevance of God's self-revelation to Israel (Gen 1, Ps 8, and Gen 12:1–3); (2) Israel as a community in mission (Exod 19:1–5, Amos and Jonah); (3) Israel's mission as centripetal, drawing the nations in to Zion (Ps 96 and Isa 2:2–5); and (4) Israel's mission as centrifugal movement outward in witness to the nations (Isa 19:16–25, Zech 14, Isa 56:1–8, Isa 45:22–25, Isa 55:1–5, and elements of the Servant songs in Isaiah). His treatment of these passages demonstrates clearly that Israel was chosen and called by God not simply to be his people, but also to mediate God's salvation to the surrounding nations. The book is not without its weaknesses. For one, Okoye relies too heavily on speculative, critical reconstructions of alleged "layers of tradition" and the work of different "editors" with (as he believes) conflicting views. A more sensitive reading of the text as a unified whole would recognize a higher unity, and find resolutions for these supposed "tensions." For another, Okoye's contention that the religious experience mediated through non-Christian religions is "an effect of the Spirit of truth operating outside the confines of [Christian faith]" seems to ignore the thrust of the OT's condemnation of idolatry. Despite issues like these, however, Okoye's treatment of the various passages is often stimulating, and can contribute to a better understanding of God's heart for the nations as revealed in the OT scriptures.

857.   Okuma, Peter Chidi

Towards an African Theology: The Igbo Context in Nigeria

Frankfurt: Peter Lang, 2002. 135 pages, ISBN: 9789052019758.

Okuma is a Roman Catholic priest from Nigeria, who has studied in Nigeria, England and Belgium. He laments the lack of contextualization in the Catholic church among the Igbo. He says that there is "an urgent need for a contextual theology that is uniquely 'Igbo'." But the problem is that Okuma fails to set forth a clear methodology or example of Igbo Christian theology. The first chapter is an extended summary of official Catholic statements supporting the need for inculturation. The rest of the book has interesting observations about inculturation but no clear definition of theology or the process of inculturation of theology. The brief chapter entitled "Understanding the Igbo" gives no systematic survey of the traditional or modern Igbo. The chapter entitled "Developing the Hermeneutics of Igbo Theology" fails to do that. At one point Okuma emphasizes the importance of using the Igbo language in doing contextual theology and says that "one may not use a foreign language to articulate a meaningful theology for its [sic] own people," despite the fact that he himself is writing in English and not in Igbo. This may not be a priority read.

858.   Okure, Teresa, and Paul van Thiel, editors

Inculturation of Christianity in Africa

Eldoret: Gaba Publications, 1990. 259 pages.

The thirty-two articles collected in this book evaluate the subject of inculturation of Christianity in Africa from the viewpoint of the Roman Catholic Church. The first section consists of excerpts from various papal writings and addresses, which encourage Africans, in the words of Pope Paul VI, "to remain sincerely African, even in your own interpretation of the Christian life." In some sense what follows in the rest of the book works out implications of that admonition. The second and largest section of the book deals with biblical, theological, cultural and missiological bases for inculturation. Okure in her key essay encompasses the whole issue when she says, "inculturation does not simply . . . mean finding suitable expressions for our Christian faith; . . . rather inculturation has to do with the incarnational union between Christ and the peoples of a given culture." Drawing from both the NT and Early Church sources she seeks to show practical ways in which inculturation can be done, as well as some of the dangers and hindrances the church may face. Other articles in this section flesh out and expand her work. The final three sections address the practical issues of inculturation, in music, art and prayer. Van Thiel's articles provide valuable insights into the function and structure of African music, which would be of help to those who are only familiar with Western musical theory. The articles on art and the discussion of how Christ should be represented ethnically are valuable, although the articles which deal more specifically with issues of liturgy will be less helpful for those from a non-liturgical background. This book could be useful for the reader who wants to wrestle with making Christianity culturally relevant without compromising Scriptural standards.

859.   Okure, Teresa

The Johannine Approach to Mission: A Contextual Study of John 4:1–42

Tübingen, Germany: Mohr-Siebeck, 1988. 362 pages, ISBN: 9783161450495.

This work represents a minor revision of the author's PhD dissertation at Fordham University in 1984. Okure, for many years teaching at the Catholic Institute of West Africa in Port Harcourt, Nigeria, here provides one of the best studies of the subject to date. She notes in the preface that her interest in mission reaches back to her childhood days, and that she was inspired by her living experiences of mission in the African context. After a most helpful opening chapter summarising scholarship on mission in John, Okure focuses her study of mission in John on Jesus' interaction with the Samaritan woman in chapter 4. The author's contention that this pericope is a "microcosm" of the entire gospel has been questioned by several reviewers. Her method is rather eclectic, utilising ancient rhetoric, literary criticism, and a "contextual approach" (where one's reading of the whole informs the exegesis of an individual textual unit and vice versa). Okure also subscribes to a form of the "Johannine community hypothesis," conjecturing that the gospel was written to stir the community to renewed missionary zeal which it had lost. This extrapolation from mission texts in John to a presumed setting in the life of the "Johannine community" constitutes the greatest weakness of this work; it is unclear on what basis Okure concludes that the "Johannine community" had lost its missionary zeal. The idiosyncratic methodology likewise limits the value of the work. Nevertheless, this is among the most helpful studies available on the topic.

860. Oladipo, Caleb Oluremi

The Development of the Doctrine of the Holy Spirit in the Yoruba (African) Indigenous Christian Movement

New York: Peter Lang, 1996. 192 pages, ISBN: 9780820427089.

If, owing to the title, readers of this book expect a descriptive or documented account of doctrinal development in any African Indigenous Church or Christian movement, they will be disappointed. The book is instead a defence of ancestor veneration as practiced by the author's Yoruba people of Nigeria, and a proposal that Christianity be transformed by cross-fertilization with Yoruba religion to incorporate ancestor veneration in the same functional category as the Holy Spirit. Oladipo defends religious pluralism, and cross-fertilization is his special proposal for the interaction of all religions. He notes that many African theologians have seen Jesus as the Great Ancestor, whereas he proposes that the Holy Spirit be acknowledged in this role. Curiously enough, when he then mentions objections that might be raised to putting the Holy Spirit in such a role, he does not seem able satisfactorily to answer them. The book has an extensive and useful bibliography, but integration of materials is not its strength, and interaction with scholars like Kwame Bediako is noticeably absent. Oladipo has taught African Studies at Baylor University in Texas. He appears to be most familiar with the Aladura movement in Nigeria, but this movement is described only in very general terms. The book could be of interest to someone studying religious syncretism in Africa, African ancestor veneration or Yoruba Traditional Religion.

861. Olang', Festo

Festo Olang': An Autobiography

Nairobi: Uzima Press, 1991. 58 pages, ISBN: 9789966855114.

This booklet is the autobiography of the first African Archbishop of the Anglican Church of Kenya. Born in 1914 in western Kenya, Olang' was already in childhood someone who learned about bridging between cultures. He was raised in a Luyia family who lived in a Luo district, so that his family was fluent in both languages and cultures. He came to faith in Christ while he was a student in an Anglican school in Maseno through the witness of English missionaries. He became a teacher and then a pastor. Together with another Kenyan, a Sudanese and a Tanzanian, Olang' was one of the first four Africans consecrated as Anglican bishops for East Africa. He served first as an assistant bishop, then as a diocesan, and finally as the first African Archbishop. Three themes stand out in this story. The first is the impact of the East Africa Revival Movement as the formative spiritual ethos in Olang's life and ministry. His trust in Christ as Saviour and Lord in the context of the supportive community of the Revival fellowship is evident. He is not uncritical of some of the tendencies of the Revival, but he is clearly grateful for its faithful witness. The second important theme is Olang's ability to cross cultural boundaries. He did so within Kenya as a teacher, Bible translator and church leader who needed frequently to be a bridge between various peoples, and he also did so internationally in his mission visits to India, Australia and the United States. Third, Olang' witnesses to the tension which existed within most African Christians as Kenya approached independence. Although longing for "Uhuru," Christians, especially members of the Revival, were unwilling to participate in violence as a means to achieve independence. Olang's reflections are a valuable examples of African Christians seeking to tell their own story and preserve their own history.

Olaniyan, Mojisola

see review 800

862. Olowola, Cornelius

African Traditional Religion and the Christian Faith

Achimota, Ghana: Africa Christian Press, 1993. 72 pages, ISBN: 9789964877989.

How are we to deal sensitively with the issues of religion, Christian revelation and the communication of the truths of Christ in African traditional contexts? This question forms a central foundation for Olowola, at one time head of ECWA Theological Seminary in Igbaja, Nigeria, chair of the Association for Christian Theological Education in Africa (ACTEA), and subsequently president of the Evangelical Church of West Africa (ECWA) in Nigeria. Olowola here focuses on three theological topics which he posits as central to the African: God, the spirit world, and sacrifice. On each of these he treats both traditional beliefs and biblical teachings, using the Yoruba of southwestern Nigeria as his example. As such, Olowola's work is useful primarily as a case study, demonstrating one method of exploring central ideas of an African religious tradition in light of biblical teaching. There is no intention to be exhaustive; instead the stated goal is to build a foundation necessary for ongoing study and discussion. In his presentation Olowola notes that early Western descriptions of Africa suggested either a total lack of religion or that God was somehow so distant for the African as practically to be removed from life. He reminds us that these were indeed nothing more than stereotypes. He helps the reader appreciate the traditional African awareness and acknowledgement of God as the Creator of the world. This book is to be valued as an introductory approach to the theme written by a leading African evangelical.

863. Olowola, Cornelius

Christian Pilgrims in Nigeria

Jos: Konsei Commercial Press, 2000. 141 pages.

Olowola was previously head of ECWA Theological Seminary Igbaja in Nigeria, and subsequently held leadership roles at national and continental levels. He earned a ThD from Dallas Theological Seminary (USA). Olowola wishes here "to examine the life of the Israelites in Egypt and make some comparisons with the life of the Nigeria Christians." His theme is that, as the Israelites were pilgrims in Egypt, so Nigerian Christians are pilgrims today. He begins with the Israelites enslaved and oppressed in Egypt, and the victory of the true God and His messenger Moses over the Pharaoh of Egypt and his gods. He then traces out the life of Moses as an example of pilgrim leadership, including the capacity to delegate and to share responsibility, how to face critical decisions, and the meaning of humility. Finally Olowola considers reactions of the people of Israel to Moses, and of Moses to them. Throughout his study Olowola begins by expositing the passage itself. He then addresses interpretive issues (e.g. were the miracles performed by the Egyptian magicians real? Did Pharaoh harden his heart or did God harden Pharaoh's heart?). He then proceeds to applications, considering for example religious oppression and intolerance in Nigeria (those who have killed people in the name of religion will have to answer before God); the kind of leaders to be found in public services and in the churches (those "who trust in charms, amulets and magical powers will not bother about the sufferings of the people"); God's judgment that will come on all that stands against the gospel (whether it be from political, military or church leadership);

the necessity for Nigerian Christians to be involved in both church and state ("Christian pilgrims are not only light, they are salt as well"); and the importance of avoiding an unjust, over-critical spirit (both toward those in church leadership and those in government). This book demonstrates the diverse qualities of the author, his gifts and considerable experience as a pastor, a teacher, an exegete, and a church leader. His patriotism as a Nigerian is also clearly evident. Especially admirable is his ability to treat the biblical text responsibly, as a basis for addressing contemporary issues with relevance and practical application.

864. Olupona, Jacob K., editor

African Spirituality: Forms, Meanings and Expressions

New York: Crossroad, 2001. 512 pages, ISBN: 9780824507800.

This is the third volume in the 25-volume series entitled *World Spirituality: An Encyclopedic History of the Religious Quest*. The twenty chapters by various authors seek to probe "the core spiritual values and the cultural complexities" of African religions. These chapters are organized into four broad topics: Cosmologies and Sacred Knowledge; Authority, Agencies and Performance; Africans' Encounter with Other Religions; and African Spirituality in the Americas. Each article is accompanied by a long citation of sources and references, which together with the index, make this a helpful resource for researchers. However, the coverage is not comprehensive, since the bulk of the research comes from West Africa. The chapter on the evolution of early Christianity in North Africa is especially interesting, as well as other parts that give light on the ways Christianity has impacted or influenced traditional religious belief and practice (e.g. the role of the Holy Spirit in replacing the shrine as a channel of communication and discerning spiritual truth). Several articles relating to Christianity seem to hint at the triumph of African tradition over Western theology. One reflects on AICs in South Africa as expressions of indigenous Christianity in the wake of the alienation and identity crisis that resulted from the introduction of "mission Christianity." Another considers Asante Catholicism as an African appropriation of Catholic religion, effectively redrawing boundaries both of Catholicism and of Asante culture. A well-contextualized evangelical Christian church is not covered. Three of the articles deal specifically with African Muslim spirituality, including one on Sufism in Africa, and another (written by a Jesuit) which traces the "peaceful penetration of Islam into West Africa" through commercial and missionary endeavour. This is not a book one would want to read through cover to cover to gain a body of general knowledge; the various chapters are very diverse, detailed and specific. Rather this could be a helpful resource for researchers concerned with religious traditions of particular groups of African people, practices in certain geographic areas of Africa, or information about a certain type of African religious belief or expression.

865. Olupona, Jacob K., editor

African Traditional Religions in Contemporary Society

St. Paul, MN: Paragon House, 1999. 204 pages, ISBN: 9780892260799.

This collection represents papers originally given at a conference on "The Place of African Traditional Religion in Contemporary Africa", held in 1987 in Nairobi, under sponsorship of the Council for World Religions. Consisting of an introduction and fourteen chapters of roughly twelve pages each, the collection represents both a series of case studies (e.g., Abimbola, Isola) as well as brief, focused analytic essays (e.g., Olupona, Mulago, Zeusse). The whole is edited by Olupona, Professor of African Studies at Harvard. The primary purpose of the conference and of the book is to reflect on the fact that there is a general lack of acceptance and proper understanding of ATRs, even though they continue to play significant roles across the continent today. This lack of acceptance and understanding can be traced in large measure to the fact that both Islam and Christianity have been inherently hostile. The essays include reflections on methodology (Westerlund), women's roles (Mbiti, Omoyajowo), the relationship to Christianity (Mulago; Awolalu), revitalization (Hackett) and new religions movements (Jules-Rosette). Three essays explore elements of the traditions of the Yoruba of Nigeria (Abimbola, Omoyajowo, and Isola), while two others also are Nigeria focused (Mbon, Awolalu). As a whole, the essays are intended to examine ATRs as dynamic and adaptive to contemporary settings, while not losing their essential core in the process. Questions receiving focus in the book include: (1) What role might ATRs play in national development? (2) How might social change impact ATRs in the future? (3) What deep religious structures do ATRs address? and (4) What are appropriate methods for understanding ATRs? Though dated, the book is still available and relatively inexpensive. As part of the growing literature on ATRs, and given the partial focus on the relationship between them and Christianity and Islam, this is a useful contribution.

866.   Olupona, Jacob K., editor

Beyond Primitivism: Indigenous Religious Traditions and Modernity

Abingdon, UK: Routledge, 2003. 364 pages, ISBN: 9780415273206.

The chapters of the book are papers presented at a 1996 conference on indigenous religions, which grew out of a study group under the American Academy of Religion. The first part of the book has five essays discussing modernity, the study of indigenous religions, and how these religions have been marginalized by Western bias in academic study. The remainder of the book has seventeen essays on topics concerning indigenous religions from around the world. While the editor is African, and the topic of the collection is germane to Africa, only one essay is specifically about Africa, "Understanding Sacrifice and Sanctity in Benin Indigenous Religion, Nigeria: A Case Study," by Flora Edouwaye Kaplan. The theme of the collection as a whole is how indigenous religions are both affecting and being affected by the modern world, but many other aspects of indigenous religions are also treated. While this book could be a useful resource for someone studying indigenous religions generally, it would not be especially helpful on particularities of African traditional religions.

867.   Olupona, Jacob K., and S. Nyang Sulayman

Religious Plurality in Africa: Essays in Honour of John S. Mbiti

Berlin: De Gruyter, 1993. 455 pages, ISBN: 9783111788036.

Although the nineteen essays in this collection are of a noticeably mixed quality (as is commonplace for Festschriften), nevertheless many are well worth reading, including several of the highest calibre. Within the framework suggested by the title the coverage is broad, including articles on Islam, Judaism, and Indian religions in Africa. The comprehensive bibliography of Mbiti's writings is uniquely valuable, with 197 scholarly items listed through 1987 (omitting book reviews). Bediako provides a characteristically learned and attractive "appreciation" of Mbiti's theological contribution to African Christianity, not least in Mbiti's treatment of African traditional religion (ATR) as a *praeparatio evangelica* (those familiar with Bediako will not be surprised that he terms this to be Mbiti's "most enduring contribution to African theology"). How fascinating and instructive, then, that another of the more distinguished contributions to this collection, by David Westerlund of Sweden, outlines the rising tide of criticism being directed at the deficiencies not only of secular Western anthropological treatment of ATR, but also of the treatment of ATR by African scholars with theological intentions, including Mbiti himself. Referencing scholars such as Parrinder, Tempels, Mbiti, Idowu and Mulago, Westerlund speaks of the "Christianisation" of African religion by such interpreters, and aligns himself with those now calling for a more responsible and corrective "Africanisation" of the understanding of ATR. Some may well take this as a courteous yet fundamental challenge not only to the work of Mbiti, but also to that of Bediako. Other articles worthy of special notice are an assessment (by Mercy Oduyoye) of Mbiti's views on love and marriage in Africa; and an assessment of Mbiti's contribution to African philosophy. Also of considerable interest is the biographical sketch of Mbiti by Jacob Olupona of Nigeria. Most advanced-level libraries will want to secure a copy.

Omondi, Diane

see review 850

868.　Omoyajowo, Joseph Akinyele, editor

Makers of the Church in Nigeria

Lagos: CSS Bookshops, 1995. 193 pages, ISBN: 9789783229266.

This rich book offers biographical essays on eleven key figures in the history of mission and church in Nigeria. The individuals include five pioneers from the first phase of Nigerian church history. Thomas Birch Freeman (Methodist), who first set foot in Nigeria in 1842, was half-African, having been born in England to an African father and an English mother. The Anglican Bishop Samuel Ajayi Crowther was a Nigerian freed slave who had been educated in Sierra Leone and England. Prominent among early European missionaries who followed were Henry Townsend (CMS, Anglican), Hope Masterton Waddell (Presbyterian), and Father Joseph Shanahan (Roman Catholic). A generation later the domineering approach of European missionaries resulted in the formation of breakaway churches under indigenous African leadership, thus constituting a second phase in Nigerian church history. These churches continued to use the same liturgy, prayer books and ministerial orders as their parent bodies, but allowed for such African practices as polygamy. For this second phase two leaders are selected for treatment: Moses Ladejo Stone (who broke from the Baptists), and J. K. Coker (who broke from the Anglicans). A third phase of Nigerian church history came in the early decades of the twentieth century, with the emergence of several vigorous independent indigenous churches, usually founded and advanced under the leadership of prophets and wonder-workers. Among the most prominent were M. O. Tunolase (of the Cherubim and Seraphim Church), Joseph Ayo Babalola (of the Christ Apostolic Church), Josiah Ositelu (of the Church of the Lord Aladura), and Samuel Oschoffa (of the Celestial Church of Christ). The editor, an Anglican bishop, is to be commended for this valuable effort. His eight fellow-Nigerian authors handle their subjects in a scholarly yet sympathetic manner. The biographies are mostly well footnoted or conclude with a short bibliography, which should open the way for further research. This unique collection of essays should function as a useful model for similar needed publications in other parts of Africa.

869.   **Ondeng, Pete**

Africa's Moment

Nairobi: Asset Capital, 2008. 108 pages, ISBN: 9780615221908.

The author is a Kenyan development officer who has headed the East Africa office of NEPAD, the economic development programme of the African Union. This slim volume is a welcome addition to the recent body of literature that critically assesses Africa's future in a realistic yet positive way. For example, Ondeng states in the introduction that "our history is sealed" – meaning that reparations will never happen. He notes Africans' involvement in slavery and insists that modern African leaders' attitudes toward their people is little different from colonial attitudes of the past. He takes some personal responsibility for Africa's crisis, identifying himself as probably a part of the problem as well as hopefully a part of the solution, and acknowledges that he worked in development for twenty years before asking what it meant! He asserts that the main reason that development programmes fail is the assumption that "someone from outside the box can somehow transform the lives of people in the box without actually stepping in the box." Then he insists that "it is not the lack of resources or the lack of human capacity, but rather the inherent limitations of human nature that keep Africa bound in the dungeons of deprivation." His answer is to change Africa's negative self-image of hopelessness, so he deals head on with issues like widespread corruption, stating, "if there is no accountability, you cannot stop corruption, and if you cannot stop corruption, you cannot have development." (His main case study, the Democratic Republic of Congo, makes for depressing reading, however). He adds that the solution to the debt problem is not solely debt forgiveness but "empowering ordinary Africans to take responsibility for their own future." At the same time, he takes on Structural Adjustment Programmes and asks how poor, mostly illiterate Africans with little capital can enter the global economic marketplace merely by changing macroeconomic policy. Although his approach is not specifically Christian, his faith is clearly the basis for what he says, so Christians will appreciate this contribution. For example, he rejects violence in favour of "transforming the hearts of the people" by practicing forgiveness and repentance, and he ends the book by quoting 1 Corinthians 13.

870.   **Onyancha, Edwin, and Aylward Shorter**

The Church and AIDS in Africa: A Case Study: Nairobi City

Nairobi: Paulines, 1998. 141 pages.

In this helpful book two well-known Catholic writers in Kenya give a comprehensive overview of the AIDS situation in Nairobi, which is taken to be representative of urban areas in Sub-Saharan Africa generally. The authors present their detailed research on the dimensions of the pandemic, and the responses of NGOs, churches and the government. They note the general inertia of government programmes, and document the many church-related programmes and resources that are ministering both to the AIDS-infected and to the AIDS-affected. They thus refute the accusation that churches are not responding to the pandemic. While their list of available resources is a bit tedious to read, it contains a wealth of information and suggestions on effective methods of addressing AIDS in the community. The authors' analyses of church response to issues of stigmatisation, care of the infected and of orphans, behaviour change education, and especially the way poverty undergirds the pandemic make challenging reading. They give special attention to the situation for women whose vulnerability in male-dominated societies has been dramatically exposed by the pandemic. They do not shrink from taking clear positions on controversial issues; their Catholic orientation obviously informs some of these positions. This book serves as a model for the sort of study one could wish to find for other major urban centres in Africa.

Onyancha, Edwin

see also reviews 1046 and 1047

Onyango-Ajus, Peter

see review 974

871. Onyinah, Opoku

Pentecostal Exorcism: Witchcraft and Demonology in Ghana

Blandford Forum, UK: Deo Publishing, 2012. 370 pages, ISBN: 9781905679065.

This slightly revised version of Onyinah's PhD dissertation at the University of Birmingham makes a very significant contribution to the search for an appropriately contextualized pastoral theology of "witchcraft" and "deliverance." Key to the author's analysis is the term "witchdemonology," referring to a set of beliefs and practices that combine elements of traditional culture (especially the notion of the agency of "witches" in causing suffering in other people's lives) and a demonology derived from the Bible, but mediated through missionaries and (more recently) various evangelists from North America. From this perspective, "witches" are believed to be empowered by demons that can be dealt with through rituals of Christian exorcism. A number of Christian "prophets" have developed prayer-camp ministries in Ghana that identify the spiritual causes of suffering in the lives of those who come to them for help. In the process they often identify the "witches" or other types of spiritual powers that are to blame, and offer deliverance to both witches and those they have allegedly harmed. Onyinah argues that these ministries are contemporary Christianized manifestations of the divinatory consultations done by traditional priests of pre-Christian society, and that the prayer camps that have proliferated, especially in loose affiliation with the Church of Pentecost, function in ways similar to older "antiwitchcraft shrines" that were popular in Ghana at some points in its history. He is, moreover, wary of the syncretism implied in this heritage. Onyinah has done extensive historical, anthropological, psychological, ethnographic and biblical research, and thus brings a wealth of material to his discussion. This is no surface-level treatment, but a serious effort to grapple with the realities faced by Christians and church leaders in Ghana. While obviously seeking to present a fair assessment of the prayer camps, the author is ultimately critical of these ministries, identifying abuses in the light of good pastoral practice, failures in terms of ecclesiological principles, and deviation from sound biblical teaching regarding the demonic world. The book is not without its weaknesses. Onyinah's arguments are sometimes difficult to follow, and his presentation of the ethnographic data is at times confusing. One is often left wishing for fuller accounts. The book would also have been strengthened by a more consistent critique of the causal link that "witchdemonlogy" makes between suffering on the one hand and those human beings identified as witches on the other. But its strengths far outweigh its weaknesses. This contribution would be a very useful resource for anyone seeking to understand and respond to the issues of witchcraft and demonology that continue to impact the lives of African Christian believers.

872. **Oosthuizen, Gerhardus C., S. D. Edwards, W. H. Wessels, and Irving Hexham, editors**

Afro-Christian Religion and Healing in Southern Africa

Lewiston, NY: Edwin Mellen Press, 1989. 450 pages, ISBN: 9780889462823.

This volume presents discussion on concepts of health, healing, and African Independent Churches (AICs) in South Africa, in light of social, psychological, and anthropological analysis. The nineteen papers are drawn primarily from two conferences held in 1986 and 1987. Key foci include the definitions of health in African perspective, the process of attaining health within the African worldview, and the types of players who provide relevant forms of health care (both traditional and AIC-related). Several of the papers that present the results of initial qualitative field research raise as many questions as they answer. From a historical viewpoint, the work presented in this volume all took place during the era of apartheid in South Africa. The social tensions generated by apartheid's marginalisation of South African blacks played a significant role in the discussion, and it would be interesting to know if and/or how the belief systems have changed in light of the new political realities there. Finally, almost without exception the analysis centres on the social, psychological, and cultural frames for health and healing. While the spirit-world beliefs of the subjects under study are readily discussed, the reality of spirits they believe in, and the possibility that they are active, is not raised in the discussion until the final essay, and then only tentatively. The reader is left with the impression that while the worldview of the AICs takes spiritual realities into holistic account, those analysing this important topic in this book are some-how unable to take seriously that this belief system may be based on the actual existence and activities of what the Bible clearly identifies as evil spirits. Two essays deserve special mention. (1) Oosthuizen provides a wide-ranging discussion of baptism in light of theology, church history, and African cultural realities. His insightful comparisons with both the NT accounts and practices found throughout church history are significant and deserve wide reading both for the analysis and for the methodology. (2) B. N. Mthethwa offers analysis of Zulu music and dance in the Church of the Nazarites (founded by Isaiah Shembe). The significance of indigenous hymnody and dance and their role in Christian faith in Africa has been by and large neglected in theological circles, and Mthethwa's chapter clearly demonstrates why this oversight must be corrected. Though prohibitive in price, this book is highly recommended for institutions which collect resources on African Independent Churches, counselling, or the spirit world in the African context.

873. **Oosthuizen, Gerhardus C., M. C. Kitshoff, and S. W. D. Dube, editors**

Afro-Christianity at the Grassroots

Leiden: BRILL, 1994. 260 pages, ISBN: 9789004100350.

This collection offers a range of papers on the African Independent Churches (AICs) in southern African, grouped into five sections. The first section (eight papers) provides historical perspectives on several AICs in South Africa, Swaziland, Malawi, and Botswana. The second section (two papers) explores values and ethics in AICs through ritual and symbol. The third (four papers) presents changing patterns and socio-cultural experiences. Section four (three papers) focuses on women in ministry, and section five (two papers) on personal and social transformation. As with the other collections that Oosthuizen has helped compile over the years, these essays range in quality. Mzizi's portrayal of the connection of Swazi Zionism to the royal family provides a fascinating exploration of the socio-cultural elements that help explain both the strength of the Zionists in

Swaziland and the means by which the royal family has been able to live the creative tension of maintaining traditional political orientations while embracing elements of the Christian faith. In the second section both papers merit close reading. Xulu's discussion of the Amahubo songs as means of building and maintaining social and personal power to live, and Dube's semiotic examination of ritual, both shed significant light on the living symbols that pervade the Zionist churches. For readers who might prefer to step back and explore the movement as a whole, Maboea's description of eight broad categories of causes is recommended. De Wet's analysis of Babomvu worldview change and the resulting rise of Zionism in one area of Transkei, and Johnson's delineation of the roles of *insangoma* (traditional healer) versus AIC prophet, both provide helpful insights into the socio-cultural dynamics in play. The contributions in the section on women in ministry begin to fill in an important gap in AIC studies. Hostetter's essay, a marvellous collection of testimonies of AIC members demonstrating the real faith they have and how God has met their needs, was a fitting concluding chapter. Perhaps the biggest frustration with the text is that each essay appears to be designed to stand independently from the others, which means that basic definitions of Zionism and the early history of AIC development in South Africa are rehearsed repeatedly throughout the book. When read as a whole, the repetition is frustrating. But researchers who can manage access to the book might well find that several of the papers suggest helpful lines of inquiry for their own projects.

874. Oosthuizen, Gerhardus C., and Irving Hexham, editors

Empirical Studies of African Independent/Indigenous Churches

Lewiston, NY: Edwin Mellen Press, 1992. 356 pages, ISBN: 9780773495883.

Empirical Studies presents field-research based studies that explore the African Independent Churches (AICs) in the southern African context from a variety of perspectives. The collection consists of thirteen essays divided into four sections. While each section has a theme, the essays within each section typically focus on case studies, which illustrate the theme rather than offer overviews of the issues involved. No indication is given in the text of a common source for the original papers (e.g. a conference or consultation), and as a whole the collection suffers from a lack of coherent vision. At the same time several essays stand out. In the first section, which is roughly devoted to historical works, Becken's paper on his oral research among the Nazaretha is worthy of mention. In the second section, which concentrates on theological issues, Ngobese's theological examination of the Trinity in Shembe's Zulu-oriented thought merits careful reading. The third section, in which case studies related to healing are presented, is the strongest in the book. All three studies in this section are well done, with Daneel's exploration of the role of exorcism perhaps the best study in the entire volume. The fourth section focuses on development. Kritzinger's analysis of how the major AIC researchers (Turner, Oosthuizen, and Daneel) understand the role of development issues within the AICs deserves careful consideration (notwithstanding the negative introduction given to this by the editors!). Altogether this collection presents interesting and important snapshots of several AICs in southern Africa. Of major concern would be the lack of coherent purpose undergirding the whole. Specialist researchers in AICs with access to the volume will certainly find valuable materials within the individual essays.

875.   **Oosthuizen, Gerhardus C.**

The Healer-Prophet in Afro-Christian Churches

Leiden: BRILL, 1992. 202 pages, ISBN: 9789004094680.

In this study Oosthuizen presents the results of interviews he and his researchers conducted with healers and prophets in African Independent Churches (AICs). Most of the initial contacts were made in the Soweto area and on the beaches north of Durban in South Africa. The study as a whole makes a significant contribution to understanding the world of the AICs, and especially the roles of the healer and the prophet, and the ways in which those roles are amalgams of traditional worldviews and Christian practice. The strength of this study is its extended examination of the thinking which undergirds both worldviews. Oosthuizen combines this perspective on the contemporary scene in South Africa with a historical perspective on the role of prophets in the first several centuries of the church. He demonstrates parallels between the social situations and worldviews then and now. And he shows how much of the activities of the AICs are responses to the desire to discover authentic ways for expressing Christian faith without losing track of the traditions that still drive much of African life. Insights range from the role of flags in warding off attacks from lightening and spirits, to the parallels between traditional healers and contemporary prophets. His cataloguing of illnesses as seen through the eyes of the prophets provides wonderful insights into the range of issues faced by the church. Oosthuizen presents the material phenomenologically, arguing that understanding is the key need of the moment. At the same time, he appears to reduce almost all spiritual phenomena to the level of the psychological and socio-cultural. This is troubling in a book which seeks understanding, for in spite of the sensitivity which Oosthuizen displays, his constant use of psychological and sociological terminology to explain issues such as spirit possession and prophecy may leave the worldview of AICs effectively trivialized for the reader. The book is relevant for those interested in both the AICs and the conflation of spirit realm and social realm issues, as well as for those interested in traditional healers and Christian healing in contemporary southern Africa.

876.   **Orgu, Cletus C.**

Prophets as Social Critics: The Role of Prophets in Nation Building

Lagos: Promark Communications, 2015. 90 pages.

Readers of this resource will appreciate that the reviews provided cover a considerable variety of Africa-related publications, thereby aiding not least a consciousness of the vast body of such literature currently being produced. Whereas reviews in this journal usually attend to the more specialised contributions, it is worthwhile to take notice as well on occasion of the more popular offerings arising from within the African Christian community, which seem everywhere increasingly to proliferate. Here is a worthy example from this latter category, a practical presentation on the OT prophets meant for the lay reader. Orgu is provost of LIFE Theological Seminary in Nigeria, with a PhD in biblical studies from Lagos State University. His focus in this booklet is on the applicational relevance of the OT prophets, especially Amos, to the challenges of nation building, especially as seen within an African context such as Nigeria. He compares the social evils of OT Israel with similar evils pervasive in Nigerian society of today, such as corruption, exploitation, oppression of the poor, materialism, injustice, infidelity, luxurious lifestyles, and devaluation of human life. Orgu proposes that, like the prophets of Israel, nations of today need those who are offering prophetic social critique. He not only affirms such a constructive role for pastors, but also applauds that of human rights activists and other social critics in general.

In a fascinating section Orgu highlights specific individuals and initiatives of this sort within contemporary Nigeria. He believes that such examples have emerged in part because the church has not sufficiently addressed its rightful job within society. "Any claim to personal relationship with the God of the Bible which does not translate into social and political righteousness is incomprehensible". The text is sprinkled with quotations and footnotes relating to more academic literature, including the *Africa Bible Commentary*. This is a practical word that much needs to be heard not only in Nigeria.

877. Orobator, Agbonkhianmeghe E.

Theology Brewed in an African Pot

Maryknoll, NY: Orbis, 2008. 176 pages, ISBN: 9781570757952.

Orobator is a Jesuit priest from Nigeria, who has served as rector at Hekima College Jesuit School of Theology in Nairobi. This book is based on courses he taught on theology to Jesuit novices, and is designed to introduce the subject to "non-professional Christians" in Africa and to invite them to do theology. It does not set out to be an exhaustive systematic study but is rather "an attempt to offer a quick sip." However, reflecting the author's Catholicism, there is a chapter on the Virgin Mary; and, reflecting his African background, another on the ancestors. There are questions for reflection and discussion at the end of each chapter, as well as prayers, litanies, and a very thin bibliography at the end. A persistent theme is Orobator's concern that theology be appropriately embedded in the African context, and at many points he draws on Achebe's *Things Fall Apart* to illustrate his exposition. He argues strongly for the presence of truth in African traditional religion, seeing inculturation as "an affirmation of complementary truths present in each tradition's attempts to represent the face of God." There is, he says, little support for an "exclusivist attitude towards other religions in the New Testament"; nor does he see traditional religion as "merely preparatory" for the coming of Christian faith. Orobator's understanding of the person of Christ betrays an Apollinarian tendency; he explains the Trinity in terms that favour a modalistic and economic interpretation; and he attributes feminine gender to the "Creator-Spirit." The argument tends at times to be simplistic, evident in idealized descriptions of traditional African life and religion. The book serves as one particular example of Catholic theological reflection in contemporary Africa.

878. Osborn, H. H.

Fire in the Hills

Crowburough, UK: Highland Books, 1991. 288 pages, ISBN: 9780946616794.

This fascinating book tells the story of the "Ruanda Mission" (now "Mid-Africa Ministries") within the Anglican CMS, and of the revival which spread from Rwanda in the mid-1930s. The author was himself a missionary and a chairman of the Ruanda Mission council. He collected his material from published sources, letters, diaries, and recorded memories of former missionaries. He pays special tribute also to Africans who played a large part in the spreading of the gospel and in missionary work in schools and hospitals. The author begins his narrative with the revival that started at Gahini in the 1930s, turns back to tell how the mission was begun in 1908, on biblical and Keswick lines, and then carries his narrative forward to the Episcopal Church of Rwanda in the 1980s. A last chapter relates the character or even theology of the Rwanda revival, with strong accents on repentance, public confession of sin, reconciliation, and a new filling with the Spirit. The author relates well the atmosphere of this movement, aided by quotations of participants. The book is easy to read, edifying, and stimulates ideas for present church work. Even though it does not claim an academic status, it is full of precise historical details. The author does not suppress differences in viewpoint, e.g. on the role of the laity in the church, or on the revival itself, of which he also mentions negative traits. Since the book was written and published before the terrible genocide of 1994, those events are of course not referenced in this presentation. The revival preached that the ground under the cross is levelled; that is, there are neither whites nor blacks, but they are one in Christ. This led at the time to more unity among missionaries, between missionaries and Africans, and among Africans. Yet within the larger narrative it is also mentioned that at Gahini in 1973 the school had to be closed because secondary school students started to terrorize the Tutsi on the hill, in both the school and the hospital. This book represents valuable first-hand material for those researching the history of Christianity in eastern Africa.

879. Osborn, H. H.

Pioneers in the East African Revival

Winchester, UK: Apologia Publications, 2000. 270 pages, ISBN: 9781901566079.

This book, written by a former missionary to Rwanda and Burundi, is different from other books on the East African Revival (hereafter EAR). It is not so much an analysis of the strengths and weaknesses of the EAR as an introduction to the personal lives of its main leaders. As EAR veteran Zebulon Kabaza notes on the back cover, "One of the reasons there has not been a book focusing on these people until now has been the fear of making an idol of any of them." Six well-known couples are included: Simeoni and Eva Nsimbambi, Joe and Decie Church, William and Sala Nagenda, Lawrence and Julia Barham, Yosiya and Dorokasi Kinuka and Erica and Geraldine Sabiti. Their commitment to the basic elements of the EAR (the cross, repentance, forgiveness, walking in the light, etc.) is a common thread, but the impact of true revival is also illustrated by frequent references to family life – these leaders were not just gifted teachers and preachers but were equally dedicated to their children. There are many stories of the significant moral influence on the society, both within the privacy of families and in the public sphere, such as the destruction of fetishes, the return of stolen goods, public confession, and so forth. Many of these men were highly educated at Cambridge or Makerere and became denominational leaders in the Anglican Communion – despite some of them being encouraged to leave it (by an Anglican missionary!) rather than reform it from the inside. Several of them share openly regarding the division that the EAR caused among missionaries and of occasional tension over unusual behaviour and experiences (they sought to counter these by focusing on God, not on human conduct). The close working relationships among English and African leaders was remarkable for that day (one Ugandan was the best man at an Englishman's wedding in Kampala), but there seemed to be little concern for the problem of tribalism in the wider society. Rwanda paid a heavy price for that in 1959 and 1994. Only Erica Sabiti seems to have been directly involved in such "political" issues, and since Idi Amin assassinated his successor as archbishop (Janani Luwum), perhaps such avoidance was understandable! The conclusion at the end of the book is a useful summary of the main characteristics of the EAR. Because this book provides an inside view of the leadership of the EAR, it is helpful for both historical insight and for spiritual challenge.

880. Osei-Bonsu, Joseph

The Inculturation of Christianity in Africa: Antecedents and Guidelines from the New Testament and the Early Church

Frankfurt: Peter Lang, 2005. 132 pages, ISBN: 9783631537909.

Osei-Bonsu is a Roman Catholic bishop from Ghana who holds a PhD in NT studies from the University of Aberdeen. He was involved in teaching exegesis for many years prior to his transfer to the episcopate in 1995. He comes to this book, therefore, with a wealth of experience in both theological education and pastoral ministry in Africa. The present book is a worthy contribution to the study of inculturation and exegesis. Although most African biblical scholars approach the issue of inculturation by either applying the biblical text to some aspect of the African context, or by understanding the biblical text through some dimension of African tradition, Osei-Bonsu is interested in whether the idea of inculturation is itself a biblically-sanctioned idea. As one might imagine, his answer is a resounding "yes," and the book is therefore a sustained attempt to show how "the New Testament and the early church . . . articulate the Christian message in non-Jewish categories of thought." Many of the examples that Osei-Bonsu uses to demonstrate his thesis are rather obvious ones, for example the Jerusalem council in Acts 15 recognising the gospel imperative to include Gentiles in the church, or the problem of meat offered to idols in 1 Corinthians. It is surprising, however, that the author does not recognize just how pervasive is the issue of inculturation. The simple fact of the NT being written in Greek; the use of Greco-Roman rhetorical techniques; the use of Hellenistic epistolary structures; the context of Imperial Rome in the background of so many texts – all of these have to do with the translation of the gospel from its original Jewish matrix into the wider Greco-Roman context, but are aspects of the NT data which Osei-Bonsu does not discuss. On the other hand, Osei-Bonsu does helpfully carry the discussion of inculturation past the NT period into the early Patristic period, showing how Christians interacted with Stoic, Platonic and other Greco-Roman realities. The final chapter explores contemporary African issues and ways in which the NT and the early church provide an impetus to the church today to wisely and carefully interact with ethical, theological and liturgical issues. The book is brief, but it provides a good introduction to many of the complex missiological issues facing the African church as it seeks to live the gospel faithfully in the world today.

881. Osei-Mensah, Gottfried

Wanted: Servant Leaders: The Challenge of Christian Leadership in Africa Today

Achimota, Ghana: Africa Christian Press, 1990. 73 pages, ISBN: 9789964877972.

As a Ghanaian who has rich pastoral and administrative experience both in Africa and internationally, Osei-Mensah is well qualified to address the issue of leadership in the African church. He speaks from a biblical perspective on the challenge facing Christian leadership in Africa today. With characteristic simplicity, clarity, and persuasiveness, Osei-Mensah shows from Scripture that church leaders are appointed to serve those entrusted to their care. To be a *servant in leadership* is not a mark of weakness or insecurity but rather one of strength and dignity. Osei-Mensah discusses the prerequisites for effective church leaders, and skilfully uses Christ and other biblical examples to contrast leadership strengths and pitfalls. He concludes by emphasizing that "the African church has distinctive contributions to make for the renewal and enrichment of the universal church." However this can only be achieved, he says, as church leaders learn to act as servants in submission to the lordship of Christ. Because the principles expounded are so foundational for effective biblical leadership in Africa, this book has been widely used in theological schools throughout Africa.

882.   Oshagbemi, J. L.

The Christian Writer's Primer: An Introductory Manual for Aspiring Christian Writers

Lagos: Mercy Productions, 1993. 58 pages.

This manual is a brief introduction to the ministry of Christian literature from an African (and particularly Nigerian) perspective. The author was well qualified for the task. He holds a master's degree from Wheaton College (USA) in journalism and taught communications at ECWA Theological Seminary, Igbaja, Nigeria. Not a theoretical essay, this book is full of specific examples drawn from the author's own experience in writing for publication in Nigeria. Although "aspiring" writers are referenced in the subtitle, only one of the six chapters concerns the actual process of writing. Other topics addressed are: the purpose and place of writing in Christianity; different forms of print media; enterprises which support the writer (e.g. editorial services, production, distribution); professionalism in Christian literature; and the institutional environment conducive to Christian literature. The manual illustrates a realistic overview of the challenges and opportunities of a Christian literature ministry in Africa at the time of publication.

Ositelu II, Gabriel

see review 928

Ossom-Batsa, George

see review 365

Ostergard Jr., Robert

see review 686

883.   Otabil, Mensa

Beyond the Rivers of Ethiopia: A Biblical Revelation on God's Purpose for the Black Race

Bakersfield, CA: Pneuma Life Publishing, 1993. 114 pages, ISBN: 9781562294045.

Otabil is a leading Pentecostal in Ghana and West Africa, pastoring the many thousand members of the International Central Gospel Church in Accra, serving as Chancellor of Central University College, and frequently being used as speaker in international conferences. Back in the 1980s and early 1990s, Otabil developed a kind of "Afrocentric" theology, emphasizing God's special "purpose for the black race." The present book, published in 1993, is a major exposition of Otabil's theology. The book starts with a discussion of traditional, racial concepts of white superiority vs. black inferiority. In the author's perspective, such concepts – which to some extent have been legitimized by reference to the Bible – are now (1993) about to disappear; the mighty pillars of Apartheid are crumbling before our eyes, and the divine clock is ticking to signify a new time for the nations of the world. However, the fact that the Bible was misused to bind the people of Africa should not lead Africans to reject it. Rather, when someone is bitten by a snake, it takes an anti-snakebite serum prepared from the snake to bring healing and restoration. Otabil's book is apparently meant to function as such a serum, an anti-oppression serum, presenting God's special "purpose for the black race," against all kinds of political, cultural and mental oppression. This is done through a discussion of some central characters in the Bible and their ways with God, many of whom are argued to be black. The author argues that biblical history shows that "whenever the world has been in a crisis the black man has always appeared on the scene." The book is not a thorough discussion of African theology, or the African presence in the Bible. Its presentation is more in the pamphlet genre, presenting its case in capital letters. As such, it is a good introduction to central lines in the theology of this well-known Ghanaian church leader.

884. Ott, Martin

African Theology in Images

Blantyre: CLAIM, 2000. 604 pages, ISBN: 9789990816303.

This is a comprehensive study of the role of art in the process of inculturation in Africa, worked out in terms of developing a contextual theology for Malawi. Ott's overall objectives are ambitious. He intends for this book (1) to be the first systematic theology constructed in and from Malawi; (2) to establish a theology of symbolic expression in Africa, and (3) to serve as a substantial contribution toward a theology of inculturation in Africa. His contention is that a dialogue between African and biblical symbols can enrich the debate on contextualisation with unique forms of authentic Christian expression, faithful to the African and the Christian traditions. During the past thirty years, the KuNgoni Art Craft Centre in Malawi has been outstanding in its exploration of its local African and Christian identity and its development of new ways to express this. In paintings, carvings, and colourful liturgical celebrations the centre's artists have discovered and developed a unique mode of expression which is both African and Christian. The author believes that the approach to African art from the dual aspects of iconography and inculturation breaks new ground. This book brings the two domains together and thereby initiates a multi-disciplinary discussion involving theology, philosophy, religious studies, social anthropology, psychology, and aesthetics. The author proceeds in three stages. The fundamental principles laid down in Part One, and the contextualized background of KuNgoni presented in Part Two, are in Part Three integrated by means of the works of art themselves. In order to identify new directions for further progress in inculturation on the African continent and elsewhere, the findings are compared with similar discussions in scholarly literature. Among themes treated are: the myths of creation, the concept of God, African traditional themes that illuminate our understanding of Jesus Christ, community life based on a Trinitarian model, sacraments, and values and ethics. Underlying and shaping the whole is the basic quest to arrive at an authentic inculturation of the gospel message by means of the visual arts.

885. Otto, Eckart, and J. LeRoux, editors

A Critical Study of the Pentateuch: An Encounter Between Europe and Africa

Münster: LIT Verlag, 2005. 208 pages, ISBN: 9783825889821.

The background of this essay collection of eleven studies is "Pro Pent" (Project Pentateuch), a collaborative research project between South African and European (mainly German) OT scholars. The project was initiated in 2001 by the two editors, LeRoux of Pretoria and Otto of Munich. And it is still going on, with annual workshops, mainly in South Africa. The present volume includes papers from a 2004 workshop in Munich. Its subtitle, "an encounter between Europe and Africa," would probably lead some readers to expect contributions from various scholarly communities within the two continents. But whereas the European side is represented by scholars from Germany and Austria, the African side is represented by scholars all coming from the "white" scholarly community in South Africa. While "white" South African scholars need not be deemed somehow less "African" than their "black" or "coloured" colleagues, nevertheless this situation points to an interesting development in biblical studies in contemporary South Africa. In 2004 South Africa could be represented in a workshop on "an encounter between Europe and Africa" by members of one segment of its scholarly community, whereas the situation only a decade later would likely be quite different. The two communities encountering each other here share at least two important characteristics. One is that they have a predilection for historical/ diachronic approaches to OT studies, rather than a-historical/synchronic approaches. Another is that they perform their historical-critical studies of the Pentateuch in a post-Wellhausenian atmosphere; Wellhausen's source critical JEDP paradigm is here considered passé. Four of the essays should be mentioned in particular. One discusses South African approaches to the Pentateuch, from Bishop Colenso's mid- to late-nineteenth-century critical interpretation, acknowledging the interpretative experiences of his Zulu audience, through the dichotomy of the 1970s and 1980s between synchronic and diachronic approaches, to today's focus on the ethical consequences of the interpretation. Another discusses the theoretical background of the diachronic approach to the Pentateuch, arguing that African biblical scholarship must avoid working with the unhistorical tools of biblical fundamentalism. A third, "Africa in Need of an Exodus?!", makes a close analysis of Exodus 15:1–21, a key text in South African liberation theology. And a fourth offers some sociological perspectives to the question of poverty in Africa, and relates that to Deuteronomy 15:1–18, a key text in the Deuteronomistic handling of the poverty question. All in all, this essay collection is a useful contribution. Useful in the sense that it reflects the high standards of German and South African Pentateuchal scholarship, but also in that it demonstrates that its topic–how to read the OT in African contexts – is no longer a completely marginalized question within Western historical-critical scholarship.

Ouamba, Fabien

see reviews 51 and 282

886.   Overdulve, C. M.

A l'écoute de la parole: Une initiation à la prédication: théorie et pratique

Lomé: Éditions Haho, 2000. 393 pages, ISBN: 9782913746053.

"Preaching is an austere joy" – such is the opening declaration of the author. The student who reads through this homiletics textbook should be, by the end, in thorough agreement, having seen both the important responsibility incumbent on the preacher and the inherent joy in effectively communicating the Word of God. The author is a pastor from a Reformed Church background in the Netherlands, but this book represents the essence of his homiletics course given at the Protestant seminary in Butare, Rwanda, where he invested several years of his professional experience. The volume covers not only the task of preaching and how to accomplish it, but looks at the entire setting for preaching – the service and liturgy, the audience, the study of the Bible in preparation, and the question of Sabbath/Sunday. In the section on service and liturgy, the author stresses the importance of understanding the ambient culture (in his case, Rwanda). He strongly underscores the fact that preachers are never prepared to preach until they have themselves listened to the Word. Thus there is also a section concerning the preacher's view of his task. These different sections are complementary to what many would consider the "heart" of the book – approximately 100 pages on the homiletical process itself, from intention to act, and a further 40 pages on how to construct a sermon. Because the text represents what Overdulve actually used in his classroom lectures in training men and women to preach sermons, it is highly practical and clear in its presentation. One aspect of the work that may seem to be overly complicated to some practitioners (both students and pastors) is the emphasis on several different levels of Bible study, including historical-critical exegesis and semiotic analysis, before arriving at a clear understanding of the biblical text. The book would, nevertheless, be very useful for a classroom homiletics text at first-degree level, able to generate discussion in many dimensions.

887.   Overdulve, C. M.

Rwanda: Un peuple avec une histoire

Paris: l'Harmattan, 1997. 270 pages, ISBN: 9782738452924.

Overdulve is a former missionary to Rwanda (1961–1971; 1982–1994). He worked with the Presbyterian Church out in the countryside and in town, and later also taught practical theology at the theological college at Butare. His former publications include a book on the Kinyarwanda language and textbooks on practical theology published by the Protestant theological faculty at Butare. The more recent tragic events in Rwanda have often overshadowed public awareness of Rwanda's past; and where it was mentioned this was often done very superficially. This book is a remedy to that. It attempts to relate concisely Rwanda's social history through the different periods: pre-monarchic (till 1350), monarchic (till 1962), colonial (1895–1962) and republican (1962 to the present). The author shows the complexity of the social structures in the last century, and relates the life of the common people rather than that of the rulers. This comes out of his diaconal involvement in Rwanda. It is also a contribution to the analysis and interpretation of the recent past, sustained by a desire for reconciliation and justice. Overdulve shows that psycho-historical roots are an important factor for understanding Rwandan history. His description stops with the events in 1994. An extended annex offers historical documents not easily accessible, reflections by different people (e.g. Roger W. Bowen's J. C. Jones Lecture in 1995 on failures of the church), and a statement by Overdulve on the church's prophetic task. This book is important for anyone wishing to be informed about Rwanda and in particular for those who reflect on the role of the church in African contexts, be it church leaders in Africa or teachers of social ethics. An English translation would be welcome.

888.   Overhulser, Josephine Marie

They Called Him Mallam: The Biography of Joseph Ummel, a Pioneer Missionary to Northern Nigeria, West Africa

Carmel, IN: Cork Hill Press, 2005. 584 pages, ISBN: 9781594082849.

Overhulser is the daughter of Joseph Ummel, who served under the Mennonite Brethren in Christ Mission (later called the United Missionary Society) in the central-western area Nigeria (west of Zaria) from 1922 until his death from fever in 1943. Much of the text is taken from Ummel's very complete diaries, and the book is illustrated with a number of photographs, so it has a high proportion of primary source material. Ummel opened the Salka and Zuru stations, the first Protestant missions to the Kambari and Lelna people. The book is useful for illustrating the living conditions of both the missionaries and Nigerians during this time, and the type of spirituality that the missionaries had and promoted. There are also illustrations of the relations between missionaries and colonial officials. The book should be in collections of materials on the history of missions in northern Nigeria.

889.   Owusu, Robert Yaw

Kwame Nkrumah's Liberation Thought: A Paradigm for Religious Advocacy in Contemporary Ghana

Trenton, NJ: Africa World Press, 2006. 279 pages, ISBN: 9781592213122.

Owusu is a Ghanaian Baptist clergyman-scholar who holds a PhD from Baylor University. In this study he contrasts the pre-colonial culture of Ghana with the imposed Western culture and system of governance of the colonial and post-colonial eras. The author's assessment of pre-colonial Ghana, and one that echoes Nkrumah's, is of a well-ordered humanistic, communalistic, egalitarian, and just culture and system of governance. In contrast, colonial Ghana's governance by the British "imperialists" was self-serving, intentionally exploitative, individualistic, capitalistic, and rife with class discrimination. Independence did not end the failures, flaws, and injustices of colonialism; rather they continued in the post-colonial period, and continue in the current neo-colonial period. Hence, Nkrumah held, the citizens of Ghana (and Africa) need to be de-colonized and liberated from a culture that is the antithesis of the pre-colonial indigenous culture – a culture rejected by the British masters, and by missionaries as well, as being inferior. The liberation paradigm of Nkrumah was formulated from two converging streams of thought. One was Nkrumah's adapted version of Marxism that would employ for the common good the technology introduced in the colonial period, but exclude capitalism, individualism, the class system, and the foreign human and economic exploitation of that era. The other stream consisted of the values of the pre-colonial era, namely, African humanism, communalism, egalitarianism, and justice. Nkrumah maintained that the rehabilitation of the Ghanaian indigenous institutions would provide socio-human emancipation. Owusu, viewing the religions of foreign origin as social institutions, says that they, too, were in need of liberation. His proposed advocacy mission of the Ghanaian religious institutions would utilize numerous elements of Nkrumah's paradigm, combined with Owusu's understanding of the teachings on social justice of the OT prophet Ezekiel, and the liberation theology of ecofeminist Rosemary Ruether. The author does not advocate Ghana becoming a Christian state, or a religious state of any variety. He does advocate that the combined religious community hold the political leaders and others in places of power, including the religious institutions, accountable in seeing that justice and equality prevail for all people. Other than asserting that the solutions for Ghana and Africa must come from Africa and by Africans emancipated from the bondages of colonialism, Owusu fails to make any specific and concrete proposals on how to go about the advocacy he so eloquently proposes.

Ozodo, Moyo

see review 215

890. Paas, Steven

Beliefs and Practices of Muslims: The Religion of Our Neighbours

Blantyre: CLAIM, 2006. 182 pages, ISBN: 9789990890921.

This book might well become a popular textbook for theological institutions in Africa, with its goal of giving "objective information on Islam to Christian learners and workers in school and church." The thirty-one chapters guide the student from a biblical motivation for understanding Islam and Muslims, to a fairly comprehensive description of Islamic beliefs, theology and sects, to the final chapters on the history of Islam in Africa and in Malawi in particular. For better comprehension each chapter is enriched with a set of review questions. A significant set of appendices provides further insights into the challenge of Islam, the historical development of Islamic sects, assignments for witnessing among Muslims, a comparison of Christian and Muslim beliefs, the names of the Koranic Suras, and description of the interior of a mosque. Although the book is clearly intended to give only basic information on Islam, the observant reader will find fascinating details. For example, Paas describes the impact of the Mutazilites on the theological development of Islam; he explains the ideas of the fear and love of God prominent in the lives of Sufi saints such as Rabi'ah, al-Hallaj and al-Ghazali; he discusses the book by Sayyid Qutb, *Milestones* (1964), which "contributed much to the growth of fundamentalist radicalism in the world of Islam"; and he offers illuminating answers to the practical question: What makes Islam so attractive? Anyone not confident in such relevant issues will certainly benefit from working through this book. The author served for almost ten years in Malawi as a lecturer at Zomba Theological College, and has also contributed to many books in the Kachere series. He also spearheaded formation of a training and evangelism ministry among Muslims in partnership with the Synod of the Church of Central Africa Presbyterian (CCAP).

891. Paas, Steven

Digging out the Ancestral Church: Researching and Communicating Church History

Blantyre: CLAIM, 2000. 79 pages, ISBN: 9789990816334.

Paas was formerly a lecturer at Zomba Theological College in Malawi and a minister in the Church of Central Africa, Presbyterian (CCAP). Here he has written a very helpful summary of the nature, sources and methods of scholarly church history research. Reflecting his Dutch Calvinist background, Pass takes a strongly ecclesiastical and theological view of the subject. He is also not afraid to use a scholarly vocabulary and philosophical concepts, such as the "formal" and "material" characteristics of Church History, and the "material" and "instrumental" sciences, distinctions that would be a challenge to many post-graduate students, much less the first-degree students for whom the book is intended. Because the book is a short summary of the nature, sources, and methods of historical research, most of the discussion is presented in abstract terms. Furthermore, the research methodology presented is a general social science methodology. Most students will need a lecturer to explain terms and concepts and to provide concrete examples of how the principles and methods presented would be applied specifically to researching "African Church History." For this purpose, the teacher would find helpful two books that Paas relies upon heavily: J. E. Bradley and R. A. Müller's *Church History: An Introduction to Research Reference Works and Methods* (1995), and J. Mouton and H. C. Marais' *Basic Concepts in the Methodology of the Social Sciences* (1990). While the rigorous research methodology outlined in this book is suited for any scholarly research in Church History, its application to students in universities and theological schools would be most appropriate to large research projects like theses. Two features of the book make it particularly useful. The first is the lists of resources available for research in Church History, especially the list of websites that make primary sources and other resources available. The second is the appendix, which is an essay on working with oral sources. These two features alone make the book well worth using. The book is a competent guide to the nature, sources, and methods of Church History research in Africa that, if properly augmented by the teacher, would make a good basic textbook for historical research classes, or a guide to the writing of theses, especially since up to now there is nothing else equivalent on this topic that is written with particular focus for Africa.

892.   **Paas, Steven**

The Faith Moves South: A History of the Church in Africa

Blantyre: CLAIM, 2006. 288 pages, ISBN: 9789990876659.

The strength of this history text lies in its comprehensive coverage of the church in Africa, from its place among the earliest centres of the Christian faith, through a wealth of information on Nubian and Ethiopian Christianity, to the early Portuguese, Dutch and British impact, before finally covering its modern history in western, southern and eastern Africa. The author then turns to potentially controversial issues like missions and colonialism, church and mission in independent Africa, faith missions, and unity and cooperation, before giving a more detailed focus on modern mission in South-Central Africa. The text is far from mere facts and figures; it will stimulate the reader through substantial interaction with earlier books on African Christian history. Thus Kalu (2005), Sundkler and Steed (2000), Shaw (1996), Isichei (1995), Baur (1994), and Hastings (1994) all feature prominently. Although Paas gives a fair hearing to each, he also does not hide his personal standpoint. This becomes somewhat more apparent in the latter part of the book, where he deals with the specific issues of Pentecostalism and charismatics, conversion and even "the position of Africa's women." In discussing the biblical as well as cultural patterns of this latter topic he seems to have moved somewhat beyond the scope of a book on the historical aspects of the church in Africa. The many illustrations and substantial footnotes certainly add considerably to the usefulness of the text. Lecturers in African church history may want to get a copy either for possible use as a textbook or in aid of their own lectures.

893.   **Paas, Steven**

Johannes Rebmann: A Servant of God in Africa before the Rise of Western Colonialism

Nürnberg, Germany: VTR, 2011. 274 pages, ISBN: 9783941750487.

The traditional presentation of the early introduction of Christianity to the East African coast represents Johann Krapf as the visionary founder of the church, and the first to study the African languages in the region. In that telling Johannes Rebmann was the somewhat colourless junior partner, who had little to show for his years of dogged work at Rabai near Mombasa. In this important biography of Rebmann, Paas seeks to reverse that picture. It is his thesis that through patient evangelistic and linguistic work Rebmann was the true founder of the church in East Africa, rather than the flamboyant and inconstant Krapf. Paas details differences in personality, strategy, and theology between the two men, arguing that Krapf's flare for publicity won him the approval of the CMS committee in London to the detriment of Rebmann's work at Rabai, and eventually enabled Krapf to pass off Rebmann's linguistic work as his own. It was Rebmann's faithful and tenacious 29 years of service amid many obstacles and discouragements that finally resulted in the planting of a small African church that has grown to be the major faith in East Africa. Paas is a Dutch missionary scholar who worked formerly in Malawi. Assuming the legitimacy of the Christian evangelistic mission, he paints a vivid sketch of the difficulties of such pioneer mission work. Far from forcibly destroying the culture of the coastal Africans in an imperialistic venture, Rebmann found himself caught between his sympathy for and desire to help the African slaves, and the Arab and Swahili landowners and slave holders who dominated the region. On the one hand he had patiently to build relationships with the local African people who were indifferent to his presence and his message, and at the same time he had to fend off the efforts of the CMS to close the mission for lack of results or because he refused to follow Krapf's idealistic but impractical plan to plant a range of mission stations across Africa. Paas does not neglect the frustrations of Emma Kent, the CMS teacher Rebmann married in Cairo. Sometimes Paas burdens his narrative with too many German details for the English reader, and with occasional needless repetition, but these are minor flaws in this important treatment of pre-colonial mission work in East Africa, one that flies in the face of standard portrayals of the missionary "imperialist."

894.   Paden, John N.

Faith and Politics in Nigeria: Nigeria as a Pivotal State in the Muslim World

Washington DC: United States Institute of Peace Press, 2008. 180 pages, ISBN: 9781601270290.

Nigeria is certainly a pivotal country. It is the most populous country in Africa; it is the seventh largest oil producer in the world; and it has the sixth largest population of Muslims in the world. Since Nigeria is half Christian and half Muslim, it is a key player in Muslim-Christian relations. It is thus vital that Nigeria be a stable and influential country. This monograph commissioned by the United States Institute of Peace deals with these issues. The author, an American professor with long experience in Nigeria, identifies five challenges of nation building in Nigeria, namely: establishing a workable political system, consolidating rule of law, developing capacities for conflict resolution, facilitating economic development and stemming corruption at all levels. The overall goal is democratic federalism. Nigeria has an excellent constitution and a good tradition of power-sharing. But it is plagued by problems of corruption and regionalism. Paden contends that the future of Nigeria depends upon meeting the five challenges above. In particular, the success of the Nigerian enterprise depends largely on the place of Islam in the country. This book advocates even-handedness towards Islam, but it neglects the Muslim instigation of most religious conflicts in Nigeria in the last three decades. Apart from this shortcoming, this book is an excellent survey of the religious and political dynamics of this pivotal country.

Padwick, T. John

see review 97

895.   **Page, Hugh R., editor**

The Africana Bible: Reading Israel's Scriptures from Africa and the African Diaspora

Minneapolis: Fortress Press, 2009. 512 pages, ISBN: 9780800621254.

This multi-edited, multi-authored work (6 associate editors, 37 authors) compares with other contemporary publications linking biblical studies with Africa, namely *The Bible in Africa* (West and Dube, 2000), and the *Africa Bible Commentary* (Adeyemo, 2006). But whereas the former has a rather loosely organized, thematic profile, and the latter a more textual or exegetical profile, the present work combines the two, by offering a systematic and hermeneutically focused profile, going through book by book in the Hebrew Bible. The volume falls into five sections. The first offers a general discussion – in eight different essays – on what it means to read the Hebrew Bible in African and African Diaspora contexts. An illustrative example is the essay by David Adamo (Nigeria) on the Bible in twenty-first-century Africa, where he surveys in a systematic way different approaches to the Bible in contemporary Africa: Africa in the Bible, comparisons of Africa and the Bible, and the Bible as an item of power. The next four sections cover the three parts of the Hebrew Bible plus the deuterocanonical and pseudepigraphic writings. First comes a section on the Torah, with one essay on each of the five books, preceded by an essay on early Hebrew poetry and ancient pre-biblical sources. Second is a section on the Prophets, with introductory essays on prophetism and on the Deuteronomistic History, and then separate essays on the historical books from Joshua to Kings, and the three plus twelve prophetic books. The third section is devoted to the Writings, with an introductory essay, and then separate essays on the books from Psalms to Chronicles. Fourth is the section on the deuterocanonical and pseudepigraphic writings, again with an introductory essay and with separate essays on each book. The different authors seem to have been given quite some freedom to approach their material and express their concerns. Still, in most cases they offer a combination of isagogics (the what and when of the texts) and hermeneutics (the why of the texts). An illustrative example here is the essay by Makhosazana Nzimande (South Africa) on Isaiah: she gives a brief overview of the content and origin and historical context of the book, but her main focus is on contemporary issues: Isaiah and African identity politics, and Isaiah and black women's struggle for survival. Overall the book fills a gap in the current literature, demonstrating some of the interpretive potential of reading the Hebrew Bible from African and African Diaspora perspectives.

896.   **Pakenham, Thomas**

The Scramble for Africa, 1876–1912

London: Abacus, 1992. 768 pages, ISBN: 9780349104492.

While there are many historical accounts available on the "Scramble for Africa" in the last quarter of the nineteenth century, few are as comprehensive, carefully integrated and readable as Pakenham's fresh account. A skilled writer and accurate historian, Pakenham has produced a book that reads as easily as a novel, but simultaneously provides a sound historical basis for anyone seeking to understand the Scramble. Pakenham roots the Scramble in the legacy of Livingstone, but goes on to show how personal dreams, European rivalries, and shrewd African attempts to preserve local autonomy together fuelled the race to divide the continent, often flying in the face of apparent logic and self-interest. Pakenham is especially good at demonstrating the powerful influence an amazing cast of characters had in shaping the Scramble. Leopold, Rhodes, Stanley, de Brazza, Mwanga, Cetshwayo, Lobengula, Menelik and many others emerge as more than a list of names with their respective accomplishments; instead Pakenham skilfully develops each as a flesh-and-blood person whose personality, ambitions, and love-of-country changed the history of the continent. But though he gives careful attention to the role of individuals, this is no collection of unrelated biographies. Pakenham also shows how people and events in Europe and many parts of Africa interacted like falling dominoes, so that what would have seemed ridiculous in 1870 seemed inevitable by 1900: almost an entire continent ruled by Europeans. One of the book's most important contributions is its reminder of the atrocities committed during the Scramble, often in the name of civilisation, progress, and (though it sounds incredibly arrogant and hypocritical now) in the name of what was "best for Africa itself." This book is a must-read for all who try to reflect critically on the larger questions of the continent, especially as those questions have been affected by the history of European colonial expansion. Though Pakenham does not specifically focus on African Christian history during this period, he gives attention to how the Scramble affected missions and the emerging church, and how Christian opinion in Africa and Europe affected the Scramble. The author's rapid, back-and-forth style of presenting events makes the book less useful as a ready-reference work, but it would serve as an excellent background resource for a lecturer in African church history.

897.   Palmer, Timothy P.

Christian Theology in an African Context

Bukuru, Nigeria: Africa Christian Textbooks, 2015. 179 pages, ISBN: 9789789052653.

Together with a PhD from the University of Aberdeen, the author's thirty years of teaching at the Theological College of Northern Nigeria has well equipped him for the task of authoring this book. The title implies both a recognition of the historical and worldwide dimensions of theology, as well as the engagement with it of Christian thinking in the African context. The topics discussed are to a large extent the usual ones for any work of Christian systematic theology, though the chapter on 'The world of spirits' gives special room to this important African concern. It is to Palmer's credit that he includes in the unfolding discussion both the historically formative theologians of the past as well as the growing number of African theologians and thinkers. For example, the chapters on the Person and Work of Christ acknowledge the early debates and controversies leading up to the councils of Nicaea and Constantinople, and as well the contemporary African insights of Pobee, Kabasele, and Nyamiti. To attempt such an overview of complex issues ranging over two millennia in just 179 pages is a hugely challenging task. In some ways, the book's brevity is its attraction, because here in a very accessible and affordable paperback is a basic introduction to a vast subject, intended as a text for post-secondary theological and religious studies programs in Africa. The student setting out on theological studies has in his/her hands the broad strokes of the discipline. The very brevity of the book which is its attraction also inevitably limits the scope and depth of the enterprise. The huge topic of the Trinity, for example, is dealt with in just five short pages, that of the canon of Scripture just a couple of paragraphs. It can hardly be otherwise without expanding the book to become a weighty (and expensive) tome. In many places the reader will wish for a deeper, more nuanced discussion. Palmer helpfully ends each chapter with relevant questions for further study, and often suggests an essay title. A number of these relate specifically to the African context. Palmer deals equitably with historically divisive issues (e.g. grace and freewill, theories of the atonement, baptism and gifts of the Holy Spirit, eschatology) by distinguishing the alternatives while at the same time recognising that sometimes the answer may not be a simple yes/no but rather a combination of both/all. The book concludes with a concise overview of the historic development of Christian theology and doctrine from the 1st Century to the present day. Despite its brevity, this final summary, too, will be a helpful resource for those starting out in theological studies.

898.   **Palmer, Timothy P.**

A Theology of the New Testament

Bukuru, Nigeria: Africa Christian Textbooks, 2012. 160 pages.

The author has taught for the past 25 years at a theological college in Nigeria. This textbook undoubtedly represents material used in his lectures, and thus benefits from his many years of teaching experience. The preface states his evangelical presuppositions and his dependence on George Ladd's important work of the same title. In fact, Palmer has followed Ladd's basic structure (The Synoptic Gospels; The Gospel of John; The Early Church; The Theology of Paul; and Hebrews, General Epistles and Revelation), and the footnotes cite him frequently. Each of the 23 chapters ends with five or six study questions, based on the text but often prompting the student to elucidate the implications of the material. Another positive aspect of the book is its simplification of Ladd's presentation. First-degree students are often confused by Ladd's discussions of the positions against which he is arguing. Palmer eliminates the "opponents," opting to present a simple but solid evangelical position. This approach makes the theology clearer for the student, leaving the academic debates for the next level of studies. Another positive is that the book's bibliography, though brief, includes both classic (Cullmann, Jeremias) and more recent (Schreiner, Westerholm) offerings. The bibliography includes but one African author (Imasogie), and the text almost entirely avoids discussion of topics of cultural interest in Africa. (An exception would be the passing notice taken of Imasogie's view about the insufficiency of the European concept of demons). One might wish to find other African authors referenced, as well as study questions touching on African realities. Although the author probably makes such connections during classroom teaching, it would have been helpful to have provided some discussion-starters in this respect in the book itself. Palmer's treatment embodies two factors also present in the first edition of Ladd's *Theology*: no recognition that each of the Synoptic Gospels has its own theology, even as the three books overlap in many respects. Also, as with Ladd, Palmer does not develop in any detail the unity and diversity of NT theology, an important point for evangelicals. Nevertheless he has done a great service in providing a brief and reasonably-priced textbook, based on a clear understanding of an evangelical approach to NT theology. Those who teach NT theology at first-degree level in African theological colleges will want to consider the benefits of using this text, while also planning to flesh out the content with reference both to africanisation and to the two basic topics not included.

899.   **Palmer, Timothy P.**

A Theology of the Old Testament

Bukuru, Nigeria: Africa Christian Textbooks, 2011. 140 pages, ISBN: 9789789051175.

This book is a welcome addition to more than sixty books published and distributed by the well-regarded Nigerian Christian publisher ACTS. The author teaches at the Theological College of Northern Nigeria (TCNN). Both ACTS and the author are to be commended for their efforts to place reasonably-priced textbooks in the hands of African theological students. This book covers the common themes of OT theology, mainly drawing on Reformed writers in its footnotes. Chapters tend to consist of short topical paragraphs built around a single verse of Scripture. The text could suit both secondary and post-secondary levels. The single appendix is a brief excursus on JEDP theory and post-modernism. The book is basically a generic presentation on OT theology that would be suitable anywhere. While there are some illustrations and parallels from Africa mentioned in chapters where such might be helpful for African readers (as e.g. on the nature of God, spirits, worship, traditional wisdom), the text is not overtly attempting a specific engagement between its subject and the African context. Study questions at the end of each chapter are mostly based on the chapter's content rather than application of OT theology to African situations. Hence the book's usefulness is not particular to Africa; as it stands it could be suitable anywhere as a basic simplified introduction to OT Theology.

900. Paluku, Musuvaho

La théologie africaine face au syncrétisme

Ottignies-Louvain-la-Neuve, Belgium: NORAF, 1990. 150 pages.

Originally from Congo (DRC), Paluku has served as professor and dean of studies at the faculty of theology of the Université Libre des Pays des Grands Lacs at Goma in Congo (DRC). This is his doctoral dissertation, done in Brussels. The content treats successively: African theology, syncretism, and African theology facing syncretism. The author clarifies terms extensively, offers quotations from many different authors, informs well, and also presents his own careful view, which is evangelical. To root biblical revelation in the local culture, African theology must start with a sound exegesis of the Bible, and theological and anthropological reflections must follow. Assimilation and inculturation of the gospel are important and not inherently syncretistic; they can nevertheless become syncretistic if the revealed message is substantively altered in the hermeneutical process. General revelation, from which many traditional African views are drawn, finds its perfection in biblical revelation, and is therefore not sufficient as a basis on which to build an African Christian theology. Without a sound methodology, biblical and African traits are forced into premature concord, or the OT becomes displaced by ATR, or salvation is seen apart from Christ. Such outcomes are syncretistic. This book is an important reminder for theologians to use a sound methodology when creating an African theology. Both Protestant and Catholic theological libraries in francophone Africa ought to include this book in their collection. The numerous citations from French and from Catholic books on African theology would also make this a worthwhile resource to scholarship in anglophone Africa.

901. Paris, Peter J.

The Spirituality of African Peoples: The Search for a Common Moral Discourse

Minneapolis: Fortress Press, 1994. 208 pages, ISBN: 9780800628543.

In his search for basic elements characterising the perspective(s) of African Americans, Paris challenges traditional modes of academic scholarship by focusing not only on various dimensions of the African-American experience but also on African religious thought and practice. He underlines the necessity, both for Africans and for African Americans, of identifying and critically appropriating the theological understandings and moral virtues embedded in the sacred traditions of Africa. His purpose is to concentrate on the particular worldview of blacks in order to clarify a common basis for their religious and moral discourse. The contention is that the African-American experience cannot be fully understood apart from its ongoing connectedness with the religious and moral ethos of its African homeland. The basic presupposition underlying this volume is that historical experience shapes the nature of theology and ethics. Paris argues that the traditions of African peoples both on the continent and in the diaspora are diverse in cultural form yet united in their underlying spirituality; that the realities of cultural diversity and the unity of African spirituality both separate and unite African and African-American religious and moral traditions; and that a dynamic principle of unity permeates the diversity of African cultural traditions both on the continent and in the African diaspora. Paris concludes by clarifying the nature of theological and ethical perspectives that are grounded in and reflective of the spirituality of African peoples. The book would be useful for academic reflection on the issues addressed.

902.   Parker, Michael

Children of the Sun: Stories of the Christian Journey in Sudan

Nairobi: Paulines, 2000. 192 pages, ISBN: 9789966215154.

This is part of the "Faith in the Sudan" Series, which has produced ten volumes of substantial content documenting the theology and history of various aspects of Christianity in the Sudan, from a slim volume on Bible translation to a massive review of Sudanese church history. Other titles in the series have presented the story of Western missionary endeavours; the history of local Sudanese Christians; the stories of Christian women of the Sudan, and a discussion of Muslim-Christian relations. Most of these volumes are quite scholarly, including bibliographical resources, careful footnoting and much evidence of meticulous research. The present volume is in some ways an exception to this norm. It is a much more "popular" work, written at a level which can be of interest for readers who might struggle with the more academically oriented volumes. Parker has served for several years in the Sudan. Here he has made available for a wider audience a variety of stories about Christians and their struggles in the Sudan. The people presented represent a variety of Christian traditions and ethnic groups. Some are Christian leaders, but most are "ordinary" Christian people. All are stories from recent decades. These stories are not for the faint-hearted. They are stories of kidnapping, slavery, torture and murder. But there are stories of hope here as well – hope for those struggling under the power of witchcraft, for those whose families need reconciliation, hope even for Khartoum street children. Here is a tool which can help the wider Christian community become more familiar with the lives of ordinary fellow believers in such difficult times in Sudan.

903.   Parratt, John, editor

An Introduction to Third World Theologies

Cambridge: Cambridge University Press, 2004. 198 pages, ISBN: 9780521797399.

Parratt, professor of Third World Theologies at the University of Birmingham, UK, here gathers together six essays by different scholars presenting theologies of Latin America, India, East Asia (China, Korea, Japan), Africa (East and West), Southern Africa and the Caribbean. The guiding principle for the selection is contextuality. In the editor's opinion, the theologies of the "Third World" challenge the West with a new approach, questioning the universality of Western theology, and bringing the context to the forefront as a proper source of theology (and not merely as the background into which Western theology is to be "contextualized"). For purposes of this review the contributions on Africa are the most interesting. Diane Stinton, a Canadian then lecturing at Daystar University in Nairobi, presents African theologies as understanding and expressing the Christian faith in accordance with African needs and mentality. She highlights four key features: formal and informal expression, the importance of the community, the contextual nature of theologies, and the plurality of theologies. Based on the metaphor of an African cookpot, Stinton mentions three stones on which the pot of different theologies simmers: Life (Jesus as life, healer, victor), mediation (Jesus as ancestor) and community (Jesus as brother and mother). Contributions of major African scholars like Mbiti, Pobee, Bujo, Magesa, Mugambi and others are well presented and fairly discussed; Kato and Bediako as evangelicals are mentioned, but rather on the side. In Stinton's view, the holistic, communal and lived nature of the African theology is of special importance for the worldwide (and especially western) church. Isabel Phiri, professor of African Theology at the University of Natal, presents cultural theologies (Setiloane and others), black theology and women theologies (feminism). The essay is quite historical in its content and focused on liberation. Not addressed are the richness, diversity and problems of theology in the African Independent Churches with issues such as healing, demonology and ancestors. Most of the essays in this collection are consciously selective, with a slant towards a more liberal and liberationist position.

904. Parratt, John, editor

A Reader in African Christian Theology

London: SPCK, 1997. 216 pages, ISBN: 9780281049585.

Parratt prepared this slim but useful book with Majority World theological colleges in mind. It contains contributions from fifteen African authors, with introductory and concluding sections by Parratt himself. He arranges the material in three parts: the first concerns theological method, with essays by Harry Sawyerr, John Pobee, Tshibangu Tshishiku, and Desmond Tutu; the second relates to aspects of doctrine and has papers by Charles Nyamiti, Kofi Appiah-Kubi, Kwesi Dickson, and Manas Buthelezi; and the third is entitled "The Church and the World," with essays by Marc Ntetem, Ade Aina, Julius Nyerere, and Allan Boesak. The authors represent a broad spectrum of contribution, theological but also political, Catholic as well as Protestant. In the first edition of this collection, however, the feminine contribution was conspicuous by its absence; as was the absence of any representative evangelical voice. Both these lacunae have been filled in this new edition. Surprisingly, Mercy Oduyoye, probably the best-known woman theologian in Africa, does not feature (although Parratt refers to her in his preface). But there are chapters by Isabel Apawa Phiri and Irene John. Also included is an article by Tite Tiénou, one of Africa's leading evangelicals, in which he contends that an authentic African Christianity must steer between the rocks of westernisation on the one hand and of indigenous African authenticity on the other, and be guided by allegiance to God alone as revealed in Jesus Christ and Scripture. In this new edition Parratt also recognizes and welcomes the contribution of the *Africa Journal of Evangelical Theology*. The growing charismatic influence within much of Africa is sympathetically addressed by Irene John in a previously unpublished paper. Sadly, although Parratt regrets the meagre contribution of francophone writers in the first edition, he does little to correct it in the second. Conversely, it seems that the amount of space accorded to three apartheid-era articles (by Tutu, Buthelezi and Boesak), is disproportionate, given the extraordinary changes that South Africa has experienced subsequently. This book is to be welcomed for providing brief and ready access to a representative selection of principal proponents and perspectives of African Christian Theology in its earlier phases.

905.   **Parratt, John**

Reinventing Christianity: African Theology Today

Grand Rapids: Eerdmans, 1995. 227 pages, ISBN: 9780802841131.

In *Reinventing Christianity* Parratt attempts to chart the recent developmental flow of Christian theology in the African context. First published in German in 1991, the original presentation has been revised in light of more recent developments within African theology. The book covers a wide range of discussion, starting with a summary historical overview before surveying African work in theological methodology, revelation and theology, Christology, and political theologies. The conclusion encapsulates progress and prospects in the continual project of developing relevant theological reflection in Africa. Throughout the work, Parratt demonstrates competency with English, French, and German sources, and command of a broad range of scholarly works. Despite the depth of scholarship and the astute perceptions throughout the book, two major flaws impair its value. The first is the decision not to give recent writing the measure of reflection given to earlier works. The best analysis is devoted to works of the 1970s and early 1980s, with references to but little serious analysis of later works. Illustrating this, almost 70 percent of the footnotes refer to works written prior to 1980. This leaves the overall discussion unfortunately dated, especially given the 1995 publication date. More important, however, is a serious flaw of omission. In reading Parratt one is led to surmise that no evangelical theologising is taking place in Africa. With the exception of a two-page cursory (and misleading) dismissal of Kato's *Theological Pitfalls in Africa*, no evangelical work is presented. This is despite the fact that Parratt acknowledges that the conservative perspective is probably representative of the majority of African Christians. Evangelical theologians and academic institutions do not appear on Parratt's "theological map." While it does provide a useful survey of important segments of theological reflection in Africa, *Reinventing Christianity* cannot be commended as an entirely reliable overview of modern African theological thinking and development.

906.   **Partee, Charles**

Adventure in Africa: The Story of Don McClure–From Khartoum to Addis Ababa in Five Decades

Lanham, MD: University Press of America, 2000. 464 pages, ISBN: 9780761818090.

Partee has ably presented the life and ministry of his remarkable father-in-law, Dr Don McClure, who served for five decades (1928–1978) in Africa. The book is divided according to the six main locations of McClure's ministry: Khartoum, Doleib Hill, Akobo (all in Sudan), plus Pokwo, Gilo River, Addis Ababa and Gode (in Ethiopia). The bulk of the book is comprised of well-written and often humorous letters, full of human interest, written by McClure and skilfully woven together by Partee. The title of an earlier book on McClure's life, *Redheaded, Rash and Religious* (Fairman, 1954), hints at his zest for life. Thirty pages of fascinating endnotes add great value and interest regarding the wider context of McClure's ministry. McClure was a man full of pioneer spirit and wore many hats, among them teacher, agriculturalist, evangelist, administrator, reverend, and medical practitioner (though his "doctorate" was an honorary one). He served under the American Mission (Presbyterian). A missionary statesman and true servant of God, McClure was killed by a guerrilla's bullet and buried in the Ogaden of eastern Ethiopia.

907.   **Partrick, Theodore H.**

Traditional Egyptian Christianity: A History of the Coptic Orthodox Church

Greansboro, NC: Fisher Park Press, 1996. 226 pages, ISBN: 9780965239608.

This work is an attempt to document the history of one of the most ancient of Christian churches, the Coptic Orthodox Church of Egypt. The task is not without great difficulties. The scholar who would attempt to produce such a history must have a grasp of the ancient, medieval, and modern history of Egypt and its Mediterranean and African neighbours, and a knowledge of at least three primary languages (Greek, Coptic and Arabic). Even with these skills, the source materials for writing a history of Egyptian Christianity are less than plentiful. Partrick makes a valiant attempt to produce such a history, and his accomplishment is that he has in fact produced in one volume a continuous narrative of this fascinating African church. The book is not without problems: the use of source materials sometimes leaves the reader with the impression that the history of the church is the history of the Coptic Patriarchs and their relations with secular political authorities; the book sometimes reads more like a chronicle of events, than a social and religious history; there is little discussion of Coptic worship, art, or architecture, or of the social context of ordinary church members; the author does not always distinguish between Copts as an ethnic group and the Coptic Church as a religious society; although there is some discussion of the relationships between the churches of Egypt, Nubia and Ethiopia, there is little on the disappearance of Nubian Christianity or the distinctiveness of the Ethiopian church. On the other hand, Partrick has drawn together material which has hitherto been available only from a variety of sources, and he has provided a valuable bibliography. Until a more adequate history is written, this book merits inclusion in libraries intending a fulsome coverage for the history of Christianity in Africa.

908.   **Paternostro, Stefano, Lionel Demery, and Luc Christiaensen**

Growth, Distribution, and Poverty in Africa: Messages from the 1990s

Washington DC: World Bank Publications, 2002. 79 pages, ISBN: 9780821352137.

This book uses data from demographic and health surveys in several African countries to study the main factors behind documented poverty changes in eight countries: Ethiopia, Ghana, Madagascar, Mauritania, Nigeria, Uganda, Zambia and Zimbabwe. The countries chosen are those in which greatly improved household survey data has been collected and analysed during the past decade. The book presents research done by the World Bank in an effort to identify factors linking economic growth and poverty of the sort that result in some groups gaining from periods of economic growth while others are left behind. In other words, the book intends to identify successful ways to address poverty. Parts of the book use sophisticated statistical analyses which will not be easily understood by the non-specialist, but such analyses are then described and compared in readily comprehended language, supported by helpful graphs and charts. By identifying some of the micro-level issues that have a significant impact on household poverty in Africa, for example risk factors like illness and private endowments like education, this study provides helpful guidance to groups seeking effective ways to address household poverty, and to be a voice for the poor in policy making forums in their local context. The book will be most useful as a reference book in community development, both to those designing projects and also those teaching community development courses, and should be essential reading for anyone engaged directly in community development ministry. Also since theological colleges in Africa are being encouraged to increase their focus on community development and poverty alleviation, thereby preparing their graduates to give leadership in these areas when in ministry, this book would prove a helpful professional resource especially for the lecturer.

Pato, Luke

see review 490

909.   Patte, Daniel, editor

Global Bible Commentary

Nashville: Abingdon, 2004. 432 pages, ISBN: 9780687064038.

This relatively short one-volume commentary on the Bible is a self-conscious attempt to bring contextual insights to each book of the Bible. The contributors represent international scholars from North and South America, Europe, Africa, Asia and the Pacific. Although the volume is also ecumenical, the deutero-canonical books were not made a part of the project. Each book of the Bible was assigned to a scholar who was asked to describe their own interpretative situation, their own social, cultural and ecclesial location, the ancient context of the biblical book under discussion, some exegetical investigations in that biblical book (the volume is far too short to give a verse by verse analysis), and finally hermeneutical reflections based on the commentator's own location. In contrast to some other projects which have been hailed as international but have had very limited contributions from Africans, this volume has a good number of contributions from African scholars, and from various parts of the continent. Dora Mbuwayesango, a Zimbabwean who teaches in the USA, writes on Joshua; Fidèle Ugira Kwasi of the Congo (DRC) on Judges; Madipoane Masenya of South Africa on Ruth; Gerald West of South Africa on 1 and 2 Samuel; Benjamin Ntreh of Ghana on Job; David Adamo of Nigeria on Psalms; Victor Zinkuratire, a Uganda who teaches in Kenya, on Isaiah 1–39; Innocent Hambaza of Rwanda on Habakkuk; Justin Ukpong of Nigeria on Luke; Chris Ukachukwu Manus of Nigeria on 2 Corinthians; Teresa Okure of Nigeria on Colossians. The volume also contains some short essays on topics of special concern, several focusing on Africa: Anne Nasimiyu Wasike of Kenya on "Jesus: An African Perspective"; Musa Dube of Botswana (but teaching in the USA) on "Mark's Healing Stories in an AIDS Perspective"; and Teresa Okure on "Hebrews: Sacrifice in an African Perspective." Few of these scholars would describe themselves as "evangelical," and readers may therefore wish to compare the exegesis and contextual applications made in this volume with discussions found in *The Africa Bible Commentary*, edited by Tokunboh Adeyemo. The *Global Bible Commentary* should prove to be a valuable resource for presenting exegetical work being done not only by Africans, but in many other contexts around the world.

910.   Payne, Roland J.

A Miracle of God's Grace: A History of the Lutheran Church in Liberia

Monrovia: Lutheran Church in Liberia, 2000. 242 pages.

Liberia developed in the early nineteenth century on the western coast of Africa as an experiment in the resettlement of freed slaves returning to Africa from the New World. When American Lutherans began work here in 1860, they intended to reach out to the indigenous populations beyond these coastal settlements. The work proceeded with much difficulty and loss of life during its first decades, but gradually stations were established and work advanced into the interior. Nevertheless it was not until after World War II that the mission effort resulted in the formation of the Lutheran Church in Liberia (LCL). Here is the story of Liberia's Lutherans, from the earliest days to recent times, as told by Roland Payne, who served as the first Liberian bishop of the LCL from 1963 to 1984. The first part of the book covers the history of the Lutheran mission efforts from 1860 to 1940. While the account of this period is largely based on previously published studies, this re-telling is from an African perspective. Also the author was able to make use of a fresh search through archival resources, carried out by Margaret Miller, a retired missionary. Payne then surveys the Lutherans' evangelistic, educational, and medical work in Liberia from the beginnings to the present. Finally he addresses the events from 1940 onward, and especially the period when Lutheran life and work in Liberia was largely under his own direction. The presentation is full of interesting personal insights and evaluations. Payne's study was commissioned by his Church as an intentional step towards taking charge of its own history, and the present LCL bishop writes the foreword. Adrian Hastings references the LCL as the first church in Africa to permit baptism for believing polygamists, under certain strict specifications (such as that the marriage relationships had to have originated before the coming of the gospel to the area). Payne includes the text of that historic decision, taken in 1951, as well as some indication of its subsequent outworkings in the life of the Church. The book is equipped with multiple extended indices, plus a splendid collection of photographs derived from archives, all organized by Joyce Bowers, who has also been responsible for bringing the manuscript to publication following the untimely death of Bishop Payne in 1994 (while fleeing from rebel action during Liberia's civil wars). Payne's wife Priscilla adds a fascinating biographical appendix about her husband himself. Altogether this will prove a valued historical resource for the Lutherans of Liberia for years to come.

911. **Peel, J. D. Y.**

Religious Encounter and the Making of the Yoruba

Bloomington, IN: Indiana University Press, 2003. 440 pages. ISBN: 9780253215888.

The coming of Christianity to the Yoruba people is one of the great events in modern African Christian history. This book is an in-depth, definitive study of this event. A basic presupposition is that the conversion of the Yoruba to Christianity was and is a two-way street. Christianity impacted the Yoruba; and Yoruba culture influenced Yoruba Christianity. The deepest and richest source for such a study is the CMS archives, especially the journal entries of the missionaries and mission agents. Significantly, the bulk of these entries were written by Yoruba missionaries and mission workers. After discussing these sources, Peel explains traditional Yoruba religion, and Yoruba history immediately preceding the arrival of the first missionaries. The Christian (Anglican) mission to the Yoruba began properly in 1846. In Peel's telling, the CMS mission was a power among other political and social powers, but power of a different kind. Peel writes: "Like a charm . . . a white man was of ambivalent potential." Some Yoruba were drawn to this power; others took distance from it. At times there was communication between the preacher and the hearer; at times they were talking past each other. However, at the end of the nineteenth century there was a small but significant number of converts. Why did some Yoruba convert to Christianity? The author sees Yoruba conversion as a search for power, including the power of technology, healing and book knowledge. One of the most interesting results of this Christian mission enterprise is the creation of a unified identity among the Yoruba people. Before the coming of Christianity this ethnic group was fragmented; the Christian mission resulted in the concept of a single Yoruba people. While this book must be praised as a definitive study of the coming of Christianity to the Yoruba, two evaluative reservations may be raised. First, it is unfortunate that the Baptist mission among this ethnic group is totally ignored. The Southern Baptist mission began only four years after the Anglicans; and their impact in Yoruba culture is immense. A sister volume on this subject is needed. Secondly, one may wonder whether the primary reason for conversion among the Yoruba or any other people is solely a search for power. Might this be reductionistic? Surely people also converted for other reasons: a search for salvation, security, fellowship with God.

912.   **Persson, Janet**

In Our Own Languages: The Story of Bible Translation in Sudan

Nairobi: Paulines, 1997. 46 pages, ISBN: 9789966213495.

This booklet is a useful and concise review of Bible translation in Sudan. It offers its chronicle in terms of dates, organisations and individuals (including both Catholic and Protestant efforts), rather than the personal story of any community, translation or person. It is especially helpful since so little attention has been paid to this aspect of the story of Christianity in Africa during the era of modern missions. For the Sudan, the author has herself taken part in that story. One must hope that researchers in other parts of Africa will be able to offer similar studies on the history and status of Bible translation in their area, perhaps on a somewhat more fulsome scale than this one.

913.   **Petersen, Kirsten Holm, editor**

Religion, Development and African Identity

Uppsala: Nordic Africa Institute, 1988. 164 pages, ISBN: 9789171062635.

This is a collection of papers read by African and European scholars at a conference on "Religion, Development and African Identity," jointly arranged by the Scandinavian Institute of African Studies and the Nordic Institute of Missionary Research in August 1984 in Uppsala, Sweden. Approaching from various geographical, ideological and methodological angles, the papers focus on the interaction between religion and development in Africa, and the implications of this for the question of an African identity. The papers include regional studies of religion and politics in Zimbabwe (Ambrose Moyo, Terence Ranger), the Arab influence on Madagascar (Ludvig Munthe), religious change as transaction amongst the Zulus of South Africa (Jarle Simonsen), the identity of women in African development (Marja-Liisa Swants), and the role of Islam in development within West Africa (Peter Clarke). Of special interest is the paper by Emefie Ikenga-Methu of Nigeria, which analyses explanations of religious conversion in Africa. Having surveyed various previous explanations (by Trimingham, Horton, Fisher, and Ifeka-Moller), he argues that conversion in Africa is a multi-causal phenomenon, and that the academic study of this phenomenon is in need of more varied approaches and a more refined terminology. This is a book for specialists; it should be made accessible for scholars doing research on religious identity in Africa.

Petersen, Robin

see review 151

914. Petzer, J. H., and P. J. Hartin, editors

A South African Perspective on the New Testament: Essays by South African New Testament Scholars Presented to Bruce Manning Metzger during His Visit to South Africa in 1985

Leiden: BRILL, 1986. 274 pages, ISBN: 9789004077201.

As the over-long subtitle of this collection indicates, these essays were composed in honour of the international NT scholar Bruce Metzger and presented to him during his visit to various South African universities in 1985. The volume consists of twenty essays which, although presented in English, are representative of Afrikaans NT scholarship in the mid-1980s. The essays are grouped into three categories: methodology (two essays), Gospels (ten essays, including one essay on the *Protoevangelium of James*), and Epistles (eight essays). As one might expect in a Festschrift dedicated to Metzger, the volume contains a handful of essays on textual criticism and translation. Literary/narrative/rhetorical approaches form an unintentional unifying theme amongst most contributions to this collection, and these are discussed in H. J. B. Combrink's (inadvertently?) programmatic essay on "The Changing Scene of Biblical Interpretation." The wide range of topics addressed, however, means that the collection would only be of interest to scholars pursuing those specific questions. Aside from the scholarship, the collection is interesting because it offers a portrait of (mostly) Afrikaans NT scholarship as it existed during a crucial period in South African history. For the most part the uninformed reader would be unaware, however, that this was the case, since the book contains almost no hint of the crisis facing South Africa during this period. This silence is explained partially by the nature of these studies: historical-literary approaches provide far less occasion for discussion of current issues than theological ones might. Yet one cannot avoid wondering whether this historical focus allowed South African scholars the luxury of silence when a more costly decision would have been the right one.

915. Phillipart, Michael, editor

The African Church in the Communications Era: A Handbook of Source Texts for Christian Communication in Africa

Nairobi: Paulines, 1992. 160 pages, ISBN: 9789966210272.

This is a convenient handbook for Christian communicators in Africa. It makes a unique contribution by collecting together documents that thoughtfully address those issues relevant for training professionals in Africa in communications, including the production and use of media, government relations, and funding of media projects. The documents also address how to train those who receive the media to be discerning about content and cultural value. On the other hand, oral forms of communication such as preaching, storytelling, and drama are briefly mentioned but not emphasized. The orientation is Roman Catholic, with about half of the documents coming directly from meetings organized by Catholic bodies. Other texts come from ecumenical gatherings such as the World Association of Christian Communicators (WACC). Each document is introduced by helpful editorial comments which summarize the text and explain historical context. One strength of this handbook is the evident commitment to promoting the values of African culture. At the same time, some of the statements might seem to condone a careless assimilation or syncretism of cultural traditions without concern for biblical principles. Overall the various documents offer solid groundwork for the ministry of Christian communications in Africa, and will help to stimulate and guide thinking in this field. Because of its specialized content, the book would certainly be helpful for those pursuing advanced studies in the field, for those teaching Christian communications, and for those already professionally engaged in Christian communications in Africa.

916. Phillipson, David W.

Ancient Churches of Ethiopia: Fourth–Fourteenth Centuries

New Haven: Yale University Press, 2009. 288 pages, ISBN: 9780300141566.

Phillipson, former Professor of African Archaeology and Director of the Museum of Archaeology and Anthropology at the University of Cambridge, has produced an impressive, if unusual, study of early Christianity in Africa. The work has the size and feel of a coffee-table book, with scores of both colour and black and white photographs alongside a generous supply of sketches, maps and diagrams. These striking graphics simply add visual force to an extraordinarily learned piece of history. Both in popular perception and in the academy it has been commonly assumed that Christianity in Africa is essentially a modern phenomenon. More recently, works such as Thomas Oden's *How Africa Shaped the Christian Mind* have helped restore an understanding of the importance and influence of African Christian communities in the earliest centuries of the Christian movement. Phillipson's work continues that trend, but also significantly develops it by focusing on the Christian civilization that not only endured but flourished for more than a millennium in what is now northern Ethiopia and Eritrea, in a period when Christianity is widely thought to have been essentially absent from the continent. That perception of Christianity's absence from Africa may be attributable in part to the relative paucity of literary remains. However, Phillipson's careful attention to a growing body of archaeological data allows him to draw some significant conclusions. First, he substantiates the view that Christianity in the area initially began with the royal court; it did not begin, in other words, as a grassroots movement, as has often been the case with more recent Christian expansion in Africa. Second, this study emphatically asserts the essentially indigenous nature of the Christian tradition that developed in the region, especially after the decline of the Aksumite kingdom in the sixth century brought with it a growing isolation from outside influences. But even during the Aksumite period of the fourth to sixth centuries, Phillipson suggests that others have been too quick to assume that the Christian tradition which emerged there was simply borrowed. "Despite its geographical marginality, Aksum was at that time a member of an integrated international Christian community . . . and attempts to isolate a particular region – such as Syria – from which its Christianity derived have little relevance." The significance of this conclusion will not be lost on the growing number of people asserting the importance of the African Christian contribution to the shaping of contemporary Christianity.

917. Phipps, William E.

William Sheppard: Congo's African American Livingstone

Louisvillle: WJK, 2002. ISBN: 9780664502034.

The author is a Presbyterian professor of religion and philosophy in the US. The subtitle of his book certainly grabs attention, with its reference to the famous David Livingstone. William Sheppard (1865–1927) in contrast is relatively unknown, so how could a comparison with Livingstone be justified? Yet the author makes a strong case that Sheppard, an American with African roots, did indeed have much in common with the better-known

Scot who travelled in central Africa some fifty years earlier. Sheppard was born in 1865 and was educated at Hampton Institute, where much of the African art he collected is now housed. Sheppard was the first African-American missionary in central Africa. He and a white colleague, Samuel Lapsley, were pioneer missionaries in the Congo, serving under APCM (American Presbyterian Congo Mission). By all accounts they were close partners despite their racial difference. Lapsley died after only a few years, but Sheppard eventually spent almost twenty years there (1891–1910). He became especially known for his linguistic ability and his active defence of tribes in the Kasai region, where agents of Belgium's King Leopold oppressed the local people appallingly. Like Livingstone before him, Sheppard respected African culture and thus was often able to befriend chiefs when others had failed. Unlike Livingstone, Sheppard had many converts in Kasai. Certainly Sheppard's accomplishments are impressive, considering that in 1893 he was appointed a Fellow of the Royal Geographical Society at the age of 28, its first black member. He detailed Leopold's atrocities with such care that the colonial trading company sued him for libel, but he won the case. In the process of bringing such genocide to light, he was received by two American presidents. Yet he resigned soon after the end of the trial, partly because of several incidents of adultery in the Congo when his wife was in the US. After a year of suspension (he was openly repentant about his failures), he became a successful pastor at a church in Louisville until a stroke led to his death. Phipps' contribution may be compared with that of another recent study of William Sheppard, which also works with the Livingstone comparison: Pagan Kennedy's *Black Livingstone*. This carefully researched book is an important resource for the history of Christianity in the central part of the continent.

918. Phiri, Isabel Apawo, and Sarojini Nadar, editors

African Women, Religion, and Health: Essays in Honor of Mercy Amba Ewudziwa Oduyoye

Eugene, OR: Wipf & Stock, 2012. 302 pages. ISBN: 9781620320921.

Mercy Oduyoye deserves a book of essays in her honour. Born in Ghana, she grew up in a Methodist family and uses the image of "gentle tapping, not hammer and axe" to describe her style of persuasion as the veritable mother of African women theologians. Contributors to this book hail from South Africa, Nigeria, Ghana, Botswana, Congo, Malawi, Kenya, Zimbabwe and USA. All the writers are women with the exception of the final essay by the Nigerian scholar Ogbu Kalu. Part 1 celebrates Oduyoye's life and her founding of the Circle of Concerned African Women Theologians. Part 2 considers African women, the Bible and health, with case studies and Bible studies in Esther 2:1–8 and 2 Kings 4:1–7 from an oppressed woman's point of view. In Part 3, women as traditional healers in Africa are considered, and University of Botswana's professor Musa Dube presents a challenging chapter on HIV/AIDS in Africa where women are the majority of those affected. Her idea of exploring how woman healers in African traditional religions and community divination might be involved in bringing some healing and solutions to suffering communities will, no doubt, promote lively discussion. Sophia Chirongoma of Zimbabwe emphasizes how the church must be the support system in this situation which affects every dimension of women's lives. Both women are strongly and rightly committed to the fact that "spiritual" effort alone will not stem the tide nor bring shalom, defined by Oduyoye as "all that makes for fullness of life." Part 4 offers various chapters on African women's experiences of health and healing, endurance and peace-making, issues of justice, challenges to vows of non-violence, and a narrative theology of eschatological hope based on Romans 5:3. In the final essay, "Daughters of Ethiopia," Ogbu Kalu encourages greater dialogue between African American and continental African women theologians because of their common roots. Of special interest is Kalu's discussion of the impact of charismatic practice in the African churches today in regard to "womanist" theologies. Charismatic spirituality offers "more space" for women in such areas as the exercise of spiritual gifts, service, experience of freedom in Christ, creation of women's sodalities, women's spirituality when it comes to cultural and health issues, and matters of justice that affect women's lives. This book is a scholarly and engaging example of much more that one may expect to see from African women theologians.

919.   Phiri, Isabel Apawo, and Dietrich Werner, editors

Handbook of Theological Education in Africa

Oxford: Regnum, 2013. 1110 pages, ISBN: 9781908355195.

This is a massive volume, with rather massive intentions. The title, however, is somewhat misleading. A "handbook" would normally signal a handy reference work offering, in relatively compact form, overall essentials for a particular topic or field. This volume is not that. For one thing, at more than eleven hundred pages, this one is not exactly "handy." For another, the achievement here, for all its impressive bulk, does not rise to the level of a definitive reference resource. It is more of a sprawling compendium of articles by various individuals on assorted aspects of theological education in Africa. But in that character it is entirely unmatched, and will amply reward any patient researcher. Here one is offered 113 articles by just over a hundred contributors, covering history, regional surveys, denominational perspectives, issues, frontiers, plus selected models and case studies. That the sub-categories under "Key Issues and New Frontiers" embrace: biblical studies, mission and dialogue, gender, AIDS, justice, peace, ecology, practical theology, plus forms and models, suggests that the accumulation of submissions has sometimes escaped editorial controls. Amidst this huge collection one can assuredly find gems: narratives or analyses or data not previously available from any comparable source; and one can also find much that is not of this calibre. The project has also had an evident struggle with balance. For example, while contributors come from many parts of Africa, there is a markedly disproportionate representation from southern Africa compared to other parts of the continent; indeed up to a third are from South Africa alone. Also while the volume intends to represent the spectrum of Christian traditions on the continent, the mainline and ecumenical traditions clearly predominate. Perhaps this is to be expected; both of the editors hold WCC administrative appointments, and forewords are provided both by the WCC General Secretary and by the AACC General Secretary. On the other hand, hardly a tenth of the contributions derive from Africa's extensive evangelical community, while the pervasive presence of Roman Catholic theological education in Africa is, astonishingly enough, represented by even fewer numbers. While taking such limitations into account, the achievement does remain singular. The roster of contributors includes notable names such as: John Mbiti, Andrew Walls, Musa Dube, Jessie Mugabe, John de Gruchy, Kwabena Asamoah-Gyadu, Mercy Oduyoye, John Pobee, and Justin Ukpong. A representative cross-section of papers that readers could find useful might include: Christian theology in African universities (James Kombo); theological education in Ethiopia (Desta Heliso); the African Theological Fellowship as an innovative model (Gillian Bediako); a pan-African overview of Bible translation and theological education (Aloo Mojola); ethnicity in African theological education (Peter Nyende); Uganda Christian University (Stephen Noll); theological education in the African diaspora (Afe Adogame); and theological education in francophone Africa (Tharcisse Gatwa).

920. Phiri, Isabel Apawo, Betty Govinden, and Sarojini Nadar

Her-Stories: Hidden Histories of Women of Faith in Africa

Pietermaritzburg: Cluster, 2002. 428 pages, ISBN: 9781875053339.

With boldness, openness and honesty, this first product from the Circle of Concerned African Women Theologians serves as a powerful reminder that African Christian women and their experiences are an integral part of the story of the church in Africa. The purposes of the book are: to complement male-dominated African church history; to revise and retell women stories from women's perspectives; to shift women from being observers and victims to being participants and actors in history by telling their stories; and (since many of the stories are painful) to embark on a process of "narrative therapy." The book begins with a history of the Circle, which was founded in 1989 at Trinity College in Ghana, to serve as a "space for women of Africa to do communal theology." Following this is a survey of women who have been at the forefront of change in Christian history. Another section tells the stories of women's organisations in East Africa, Nigeria and South Africa, pointing out how women articulate their own spiritualities and address their needs. Also presented are the stories of various women pastors who have emerged to claim their roles as full heiresses of Christ's freedom, dignity and priesthood. Next are painful stories of women who continue to experience the effects of sexism and other forms of discrimination in the church. Finally the book recounts the story of an African Christian woman whose life journey spanned a period from pre-colonial days, to the time of colonisation and missionary influence, to the era of resistance and national liberation movements – the story of Mercy Dakwaa Yamoah, mother of the well-known African woman theologian Mercy Amba Oduyoye. The use of the storytelling technique, creatively interwoven with the academic style of writing, makes a powerful impact. Not only is the book an important contribution to African church historiography, and a motivation to hear more women's stories, but it also provides a sustained challenge to the male-dominated history of the church in Africa. This book will be important not least for all those engaged in understanding and teaching African church history.

921. Phiri, Isabel Apawo, Kenneth R. Ross, and James L. Cox, editors

The Role of Christianity in Development, Peace and Reconstruction

Nairobi: All Africa Conference of Churches, 1996. 302 pages, ISBN: 9789966886613.

This volume consists of sixteen essays presented at a conference in Zomba, Malawi, in 1993. The eponymous conference focused on southern Africa and this collection thus contains contributions from Botswana, Malawi, Mozambique, South Africa and Zimbabwe. Other essays come from England, Nigeria and Scotland, with the last-mentioned indicating the conference's link to the Centre for the Study of Christianity in the Non-Western World (University of Edinburgh). After two introductory chapters, the first major section of this collection focuses on "The Malawi Story" by means of historical essays. These papers all argue that the church had an important role to play in events that were unfolding in Malawi during the early 1990s, culminating with the dissolution of the Banda autocracy in 1993. A subsequent section contains "Selected Case Studies," which investigate the relationship between development and theology (usually by focussing on church-based activities) as it has developed in various sub-Saharan countries. In a short but instructive essay Gideon Thom argues that Reformed theology played a crucial role in the reconstruction of relationships between English and Afrikaner following the South Africa War (1899–1902). The "Fresh Perspectives" from which the fourth part of this collection takes its title are environmentalism, feminism and literature. These essays illustrate the diffuse nature of this collection which, as recognized by John Parratt in the book's concluding essay, contains a "bewildering number of issues." Important questions are raised in this collection, but one might have hoped for more constructive theological engagement in attempting to answer them. Readers with an interest in Malawian church history will benefit from several chapters; others can safely ignore this volume.

922. **Phiri, Isabel Apawo**

Women, Presbyterianism and Patriarchy: Religious Experience of Chewa Women in Central Malawi

Blantyre: CLAIM, 2007. 180 pages, ISBN: 9789990887280.

This is a recent publication of the productive Kachere Series, a line of books on religion and theology that is sponsored by the Department of Theology and Religious Studies of the University of Malawi. The author, herself a former member of this department, is currently Director of the Institute of Contextual Theology of the University of Durban-Westville (RSA). Since the issue of the status and ministry of women in the Christian church is becoming one of increasing importance, and frequently of controversy, in most denominations nowadays, Phiri's detailed historical and sociocultural study of the matter in the context of the Presbyterian Church of Malawi (CCAP) comes as a welcome introduction to many of the relevant aspects. The book begins with a survey of the important role that women played as spirit mediums and shrine leaders in the traditional religious practice of the Chewa people. The main body of the book then deals with the various struggles through which women attempted to have their voice heard and their talents utilized in a church that was initially characterized by a conservative "patriarchal theology" and male-dominated administrative practice. The author considers such crucial topics as female initiation, bride wealth, child marriages, husband desertion, a widow's property rights, and remarriage. Current attitudes towards women in the church are explored on the basis of personal field interviews, and various ecumenical efforts at promoting a greater awareness of women's issues are reported. Phiri concludes her study with a reflection on the ecclesiastical status of women in relation to several key Scripture passages that concern this subject. Here in particular is where the author expresses several potentially controversial opinions, and one wishes that her hermeneutical position had been somewhat more fully delineated. This book is written in the vigorous style that would be expected from one who has been an active participant in many of the stirring events about which she is reporting.

923. **Phiri, Khofi Arthur**

African Traditional Marriage: A Christian Theological Appraisal

Nairobi: Paulines, 2011. 104 pages, ISBN: 9789966085672.

The author, a Zambian Catholic priest, aims to demonstrate the common ground and some points of difference between African traditional marriage and Christian marriage as taught by the Catholic Church in Africa. He therefore begins by articulating some concepts of marriage generally, then focuses on specific concepts important in traditional marriage. He spends the majority of the book defining the church's current understanding of the sacramental nature of Christian marriage, and then in the later part of the book relates this to selected aspects of traditional marriage. He clearly states that this is not a guide to pastoral counselling in specific situations but rather an analysis of the pillar concepts of both traditional and Christian marriage. His goal is to highlight the "black spots" in traditional marriage that need to be "illuminated by [the] Christian message" to make married life truly Christian. One central concept common to both the traditional and the church conceptions is the importance of giving life through marriage. He identifies as a "black spot" in traditional marriage believing that the birth of children is essential to accepting a marriage as valid. He makes a clear case for the sacramental nature of childless marriages between Christians. He also defines Christian marriage as based on love between two equal partners, and points to pressure from the extended family and giving of bride-wealth as traditions that can undermine these Christian values. The book is written from a theological and philosophical perspective, and the author's writing style tends to be repetitive and even confusing at some points. It is therefore more useful to theologians and philosophers than to lay people or those seeking pastoral guidance for specific problems. While the author's frequent use of Catholic sources makes this a good articulation of insights into the nature of Christian marriage among Catholics in Africa today, it would also be a useful resource for those of any theological tradition dealing with the theology of marriage in Africa.

924.   Pierli, Francesco, Maria Teresa Ratti, and Andrew C. Wheeler, editors

Gateway to the Heart of Africa: Missionary Pioneers in Sudan

Nairobi: Paulines, 1998. 160 pages, ISBN: 9789966213747.

The Faith in Sudan series, to which this title belongs, originated from a major conference on "The Church in Sudan-Its Impact Past, Present and Future," held at Limuru in Kenya in 1997. This volume offers seven papers by different authors on missionary pioneers in the modern expansion of Christianity in Sudan. Those treated are: Daniel Comboni (1831–1881), with two supporting papers on the Comboni Brothers and Comboni Sisters; J. Kelly Giffen (1853–1932) and Thomas A. Lambie (d. 1954) of the United Presbyterian Church of North America among the Shilluk and Nuer; Archibald "Machuor" Shaw (1879–1956) and Kenneth Grant Fraser (1877–1935) of the Church Missionary Society, among Dinka and Moru respectively. These are preceded by an introductory paper providing a historical overview by Andrew Wheeler, the series General Editor. The book reinforces how influential personalities and a holistic witness have been for church growth in Africa.

925.   Pierli, Francesco

Missionary Ministry and Missiology in Africa Today

Nairobi: Paulines, 1994. 74 pages, ISBN: 9789966211323.

This first publication in the "Tangaza Occasional Papers" series coincided with the establishment of the Department of Mission Studies at Tangaza College, Kenya, and focuses on the contextualization of evangelism from a Roman Catholic perspective. As the first of a series, the booklet suffers somewhat from a lack of cohesion. The first article, by Pierli, basically strings together quotations from various Vatican documents. Okello's article on the relationship of expatriate and local clergy is a helpful analysis of areas such as liturgy, pastoral priorities and finances. Hearne investigates his speciality, mission as dialogue, and briefly notes that Catholics should try to learn from the recent popularity of "fundamentalism." Waruta, a Methodist, adds his own helpful perspective on mission as dialogue, along with his concern to balance the spiritual and physical elements of the gospel. He highlights specific causes for the weak prophetic stance of the churches in the face of great need (division, loss of influence on "Christian" politicians, ignorance of political matters, fear and the lack of a good model for problem-solving). The main weakness of this volume is the lack of careful editing. One may hope that future titles in the series will be found to have continued good analysis but without such distractions.

926. Pillay, G. J., and J. W. Hofmeyr, editors

Perspectives on Church History: An Introduction for South African Readers

Pretoria: Kagiso Publishers, 1991. 313 pages, ISBN: 9780798628358.

The contributors to this collection, all at various times lecturers at the Faculty of Theology, University of South Africa (UNISA), here set themselves the task of providing a condensed history of Christianity in a manner relevant to students from a wide range of church and social backgrounds in southern Africa. Chapters 1–18 give a general overview on the history of Christianity from the first to the nineteenth centuries. Of special importance in this section are two chapters on early African Christianity. Then chapters 19–23 concentrate on the history Christianity in South Africa during the last two centuries. These chapters are a useful introduction to students and scholars interested in better understanding the South African scene, and also provide essential information for understanding the development of Christianity in the rest of southern Africa. The authors attempt to understand Christian history from a modern trans-denominational perspective in order to understand the church free from cultural, social, theological and ideological divisions. The book is designed specifically for textbook use. Readers are assisted by special formatting and highlighting, and by helpful chapter summaries. Maps and chronological lists are used, and each chapter concludes with a recommended reading list. The text would now require some updating, but for the story up to the time of publication it would still be a very worthwhile resource and model.

927. Pobee, John S.

AD 2000 and After: The Future of God's Mission in Africa

Accra: Asempa Publishers, 1991. 94 pages, ISBN: 9789964782047.

Consisting of the Hale Lectures given in 1988 at Western-Seabury Seminary in the USA, *AD 2000 and After* is a reflection on the growth of the church in Africa by the Ghanaian-born and Geneva-based ecumenical leader John Pobee. The book is essentially a compilation of Pobee's thinking about Africa and the missionary enterprise there. In general, the book is a critique and analysis of past and present; while it gives general suggestions for a way to move forward, it lacks any sustained focus on the future as implied by the title. Early on Pobee notes that many proclaim that Africa has the fastest growing church in the world. He rightly questions whether we make too much of the growth rate and allow it to lull us into thinking that there are little or no corresponding problems. His concern throughout the book is to integrate his missiological outlook into historical analysis and contemporary theological reflection on the African scene. A central thesis is that missionaries followed an ideology of power. While he avoids some of the unnecessary "missionary-bashing" of more radical historical critics, he does state that "most missionaries were not colonialist or racist; but many were paternalists. They tended in most places to see the Africans as children." Running through the book is the theme of a battle against such an inappropriate ideology of power, whether wielded by missionary, African leader, or clergy. Pobee rightly argues for the involvement of all believers in the ministry. He maintains that the professional clergy have been paternalistic towards the laity. He calls for a spiritual formation which acknowledges both the gifting and the intended type of ministry of the one being equipped. Only multiple models of training can meet the needs of an increasingly pluralistic Africa. Unfortunately, Pobee does not address the danger that adopting such models uncritically may leave even wider open the door of class distinction in ministry, and thereby serve to strengthen the power ideology that Pobee wants to eliminate. This appears to compromise Pobee's proposed solution, leaving the reader to wonder what the alternatives might be.

928. Pobee, John S., and Gabriel Ositelu II

African Initiatives in Christianity: The Growth, Gifts and Diversities of African Churches–A Challenge to the Ecumenical Movement

Geneva: World Council of Churches, 1998. 74 pages, ISBN: 9782825412770.

This slender book is about "independent," "indigenous" or "break-away" churches in Africa, as distinguished from the "historic" or "mission-founded" churches. Four of these churches are members of the WCC. The attractiveness of such "African Initiatives in Christianity" (AICs) grows out of the attempt they make to express and live out their faith in genuinely African cultural forms and styles. In the general endeavour to contextualize the gospel, it can be worthwhile to look at what these churches developed in a practical way. At the same time, linking them with churches worldwide can be a help to them as well. Gabriel Ositelu II was primate of the Church of the Lord (Aladura), a Nigerian-based AIC which has been a member of the WCC since 1975. Pobee is an Anglican theologian from Ghana on the staff of the WCC's Programme on Ecumenical Theological Education. While their main focus in this book is on what the growth of AICs implies for the future of the ecumenical movement, they also examine some key teachings of the AICs, and trace the roots of the movement in African church history since the first century. In his foreword, Walter Hollenweger looks at various forms of organisation and communication of the faith in the AIC's, and indicates that the process of interpretation of the Bible in an ecumenical and cross-cultural way has only just begun. He sees a larger diversity in the Bible than is commonly perceived, and says that the encounter with AICs encourages us to study the biblical message afresh. Among topics addressed in the book are: how Christ arrived in Africa (first centuries), a description of the various types of AIC's, their ecumenical significance, the problems and promises of AICs, and the way ahead. This book could be a supplemental help to anyone needing to get oriented about the AICs, and for members of an AIC needing to know something about other churches of the same type and their possible ecumenical impact. While it does indicate points that need to be taken up in theological discussion relating to AICs, for addressing such issues this publication would be too superficial.

929. Pobee, John S., editor

Exploring Afro-Christology

Frankfurt: Peter Lang, 1992. 155 pages, ISBN: 9783631444689.

Pobee, a Ghanaian Anglican scholar working with the World Council of Churches, here collected thirteen papers which had been presented at a seminar of the WCC held in Bossey, Switzerland, in 1988. The contributors include two African American women, a theology professor from Barbados, as well as Africans from Ghana, Nigeria, Kenya and South Africa, with a wide denominational diversity (Catholic, Lutheran, Anglican, Reformed, Baptist, Pentecostal). Most papers have in common that Christology is constructed "from below," with a strong emphasis on or concern for anthropological data: Who are the people to whom Christ is being or should be presented, and how do they perceive the world? The four papers from South Africa and America focus on liberation Christology and theology. Others discuss African culture, worldview, and language problems as relevant to Christology, so that Christ is less a stranger in Africa and is not merely understood as saviour of Euro-American worldviews. Two papers describe the Christology of African Independent Churches (Kimbanguists, Legio Maria Church). In contrast to the rest, one paper advocates revelation and the divinity of Christ as the starting point for Christology, because God is all-present and powerful in African tradition. The word "Exploring" in the collection title is very apt; the different papers are very diverse, and there has been no attempt to unify or reach a conclusion. The papers are between ten and fifteen pages in length, which is very brief for elaborating effectively on a theme like ancestor Christology (Abraham Akrong) or the "unnamed Christ" in African religions (John Mbiti), or to assess carefully the Christology of an African Independent Church.

930.   Pobee, John S.

Kwame Nkrumah and the Church in Ghana 1949–1966

Accra: Asempa Publishers, 1988. 222 pages, ISBN: 9789964781682.

A Ghanaian Anglican scholar and theologian, Pobee here analyses those actions of Nkrumah and his Convention People's Party (CPP) that, during the period under review, invited pronouncements and reactions from the Church in Ghana. Nkrumah was reared and educated as a Roman Catholic, held a degree in theology, and as Ghana's president always identified himself as a "non-denominational Christian and a socialist Marxist." While he parroted Marxist views of religion, he seemed to blow hot and cold at the same time. In Pobee's estimation "it is difficult to ascertain whether there is any relation between the political theories Nkrumah put forward about religion and his personal convictions." Nkrumah, less brutal than other dictators, relentlessly sought total control of every aspect of life in Ghana – including religion – all to be used to accomplish his political agenda. Although the Church paid due respect to the State, the Church resisted when Nkrumah trespassed on the Church's turf. Ghana awarded education grants to Church schools, and in the process the Church lost exclusive control of the schools and their distinctly Christian influence. The Church recognized that, and let it pass. But when the government erected a 20-foot tall statue of Nkrumah with an inscription saying, "Seek ye first the political kingdom and all other things will be added to you," the Christian Council of Ghana asked for the inscription to be removed and substituted with a non-biblical one. The request was denied. When the Queen's representative came for the ceremony of handing over power, the Christian Council strongly objected to the pouring of a libation. The libation was poured. Nkrumah maintained it was simply projecting the African personality. When the government decreed that branches of the ruling party be established in all institutions including the Church, this was resisted. In this instance confrontation was avoided and the issue died a natural death. In efforts to deify Nkrumah, the title of *Asomdwehene*, or Messiah, was put in use. To this the Church objected, without effect. Increasingly it became apparent that the Nkrumah regime would brook no criticism. One would expect the author to have completely sided with the Church in his analysis. Surprisingly, he does not. While not an apologist for Nkrumah, Pobee rightfully gives him his due for good things accomplished, but treats him with a degree of lenient objectivity unexpected of a churchman. His assessment is that, for the most part, the Church chose the wrong battles to fight. Pobee asserts that the questionable morality of the Nkrumah regime, together with rampant graft and corruption, were areas scarcely addressed by the Church, and that while its resistance accomplished some good, it largely failed to tackle those greater issues.

931.   Pobee, John S., editor

Ministerial Formation for Mission Today

Accra: Asempa Publishers, 1993. 128 pages, ISBN: 9789964782146.

This is a collection of papers and responses from a consultation held in 1989 in Limuru, Kenya, in part under the auspices of the WCC Programme on Theological Education (WCC-PTE). The theme of the event is conveyed in the title of the book. The editor, John Pobee, is from Ghana, and at that time was on the executive staff of the WCC-PTE. He contributes an Introduction, and by way of conclusion and summary, also the Report and Recommendations. The other contributors are from India, Philippines, UK, Jamaica, Norway, Chile, Kenya, the Netherlands, and Aboriginal New Zealand. The papers contain the now-familiar calls for an alternation of praxis and reflection, for egalitarianism and listening, for the preferential option for the poor and the ministry of the laity (for which lay people also need formation), and for more use of methods of ministerial formation that take trainees outside the classroom. The Recommendations at the end include: more consultations of theological educators, more awareness by clergy of building and training laypeople for ministry, more use of non-residential methods of training (community theological training, TEE), and more attention to training women. Apart from the editor, the specific link of this book's content to Africa is minimal.

932.   Pobee, John S., and Bärbel von Wartenberg-Potter, editors

New Eyes for Reading: Biblical and Theological Reflections by Women from the Third World

Geneva: World Council of Churches, 1986. 112 pages, ISBN: 9780940989078.

One of the most important developments in African theology in recent years has been the emergence of theology by African women, especially those associated with the "Circle of Concerned African Women Theologians." About the same time that the Circle was beginning to come together, but before they had yet published any of their own volumes of essays, several publications began to assemble biblical and theological reflections of women from various parts of the non-western world. This slim volume was one of the first such books. Pobee is the well-known Ghanaian theologian; his co-editor van Wartenberg-Potter was director of the WCC sub-unit on Women in Church and Society (and wife of the then WCC General Secretary Philip Potter). The collection of eighteen short reflections is quite clear in its approach: each essay discusses a biblical text from the context in which the author lives. Giving privilege to the context of the reader, it is argued, has the advantage of recognizing that every theology has "limitations and biases," and that it is more honest to acknowledge this from the start. Several of the essays are by African women, some of whom have become very well known in the African theological scene. The very short (2 page) article by Elizabeth Amoah from Ghana is on Mark 5:25–29; Marie Assaad of Egypt writes on Luke 1:26–45; Grace Eneme of Cameroon on the biblical image of "living stones" (1 Peter 2:5); Mercy Oduyoye, one of the most prolific of African theologians, has contributed two essays, one on the biblical image of birth pains, and a longer essay on the significance of women for the church's mission; Kenyan theologian Bette Ekeya writes an essay arguing that church structures have often prevented the good news of Jesus' liberation of the oppressed from being experienced by women; Louise Tappa of Cameroon argues that Genesis 3:16 has often been used as justification for the domination of women by men. Each of the book's essays is clear and concise; most are also provocative and thoughtful. This was one of the very first works featuring essays by African women theologians.

933.   **Pobee, John S.**

Persecution and Martyrdom in the Theology of Paul

Sheffield: JSOT Press, 1985. 165 pages, ISBN: 9780905774527.

Pobee's study contends that Jewish martyr-theology, known to us through intertestamental literature, served as a vital shaping force upon Paul's theology and upon both his self-understanding and that of his churches. The argument proceeds through six chapters. The first examines forms of persecution mentioned in Paul's letter (e.g. imprisonment, stoning, etc.). The second briefly surveys martyr-theology in the intertestamental period. Chapters 3 and 4, perhaps the heart of the book, examine the influence of martyr-theology on Paul's understanding of Jesus' atoning work. The final two chapters explore Paul's and his churches' self-understanding in the face of persecution. The book has noticeable shortcomings. For example, Pobee claims that martyr-theology determines Paul's soteriology, Christology, eschatology, and ethics – a claim that certainly goes far beyond the evidence. In addition, while the book was published in 1985, the bibliography reflects research mostly done in the 1960s. Nevertheless, Pobee makes some valuable contributions. While his review of intertestamental literature is sketchy in places, he does establish that Jewish martyr-theology was not a single, unified entity. Furthermore, he rightly calls attention to an important, though often neglected, source for Paul's theological thinking. In his preface Pobee explains that the turmoil endured by his home country of Ghana while he was away studying at Cambridge first prompted him to focus on the subject of persecution and martyrdom; the volume thus reflects the spirit of one who does not come to the subject from a safe, academic distance. As an early contribution to NT studies by an African scholar, it could be included as a useful addition to theological libraries on the continent.

934.   **Pobee, John S.**

Religion and Politics in Ghana

Accra: Asempa Publishers, 1991. 150 pages, ISBN: 9789964781798.

In this book Pobee, the well-known Ghanaian theologian and church leader, gives a West African case study of a general problem: the role of religion/church in society; or to be more precise, the relationship between two sets of power structures: religion/church on the one hand, and state/politics/military on the other. The book describes and analyses how this general problem was experienced in Ghana throughout the 1960s and 1970s (the book was written in 1983, though not published until 1991). Even after the independence of Ghana in 1957, most historical churches (Catholics, mainline Protestants) continued to be led by expatriates, and when problems arose (school, health, marriage, etc.), progressive politicians could easily argue that these churches represented European colonialism and imperialism. This could not be said about what Pobee (at least in 1983!) calls "sects" (i.e. various prophetic, messianic and syncretistic movements). Several of these "sects" had a very positive relationship to leaders who came into power through a *coup d'état*, and Pobee argues that they were to some extent used to provide religious legitimacy for leaders that lacked democratic support. As a case study of a general problem for African Christianity, this is an important book. Researchers working with parallel cases in Africa will here find a helpful model and relevant approach.

935. Pobee, John S.

Skenosis: Christian Faith in an African Context

Gweru, Zimbabwe: Mambo Press, 1992. 174 pages, ISBN: 9780869225318.

In one of his earlier publications, *Towards an African Theology*, Pobee stated the need for an on-going "dialogue" between biblical Christianity and the African world. Now in this study he seeks to make Christian truths relevant to an African context. Although he is not the first to address the issue, his main contribution lies in his attempt to show that being wholly African is not incompatible with being a NT Christian. Using the Akan culture of his home country, Ghana, as representative of "the African culture," he highlights seven characteristics of African societies that reflect their worldview. His analysis is very helpful. According to Pobee, the Western concept of the world and of Christianity is highly intellectual. And for an African, whether in African traditional religions, Islam or Christianity: "to be is to be religious." Therefore his suggestions on how African Christians can integrate religious ontology and epistemology from an African Christian perspective are worth the price of the book. The "skenosis" in the title is taken from the affirmation in the Greek text of John 1:14 that the incarnate Word "tented" among us. Pobee wishes to point through and beyond this to the incarnation also intended for the Body of Christ within every context in which it takes up residence. Had the Greek word been translated instead of transliterated, more readers might have taken notice of this insightful study.

936. Pobee, John S., editor

Towards Viable Theological Education: Ecumenical Imperative, Catalyst of Renewal

Geneva: World Council of Churches, 1997. 164 pages, ISBN: 9782825412343.

This volume draws together proceedings from a 1996 consultation sponsored by the World Council of Churches entitled, "Ecumenical Theological Education: Its Viability Today." The fundamental question driving the meeting was "What sort of theological education and ministerial formation is needed to prepare Christian leaders who can inspire new life and renew and transform the church?" After an introductory essay explaining the consultation's rational, the volume includes a sermon, a series of Bible studies, a paper by Pobee, a series of five papers with responses, and a concluding summary essay. The writers form a truly international cast. Unfortunately, what results is a series of disjointed papers, each describing challenges faced in a particular contributor's corner of the world. Pobee's piece is the only one from an African, and he merely reviews and comments on what others have said. Apart from the fact that the editor is a well-known Ghanaian theologian, there is virtually nothing in this particular publication that directly relates to the African context.

937. Pobee, John S., and Carl F. Hallencreutz, editors

Variations in Christian Theology in Africa

Nairobi: Uzima Press, 1986. 113 pages.

Comprised of papers given at a symposium at Uppsala University in 1983, *Variations* unfortunately presents a very limited version of what the title implies. The primary disappointments are two: the papers effectively reflect the work of only four authors (and two are joint authors); and the papers effectively deal with only three countries on this vast continent. The contributing authors are John Pobee, Mercy Oduyoye, Stina Karltun and Lars Parkman. The latter two, writing jointly, were undergraduate students at Uppsala at the time of the symposium. The discussions centre on Ghana, South Africa, and in one chapter peripherally Nigeria. At least the topics show greater diversity; they include theological education, Black Theology in South Africa, feminism, gospel universals and symbolism. Pobee's contributions (four papers) are the strongest of the book. Though they suffer from being dated in terms of the actual events and geopolitical situations discussed, in fact similar situations continue to be found in Africa, and Pobee's analysis therefore remains relevant. Perhaps the best contribution in the book is his paper on symbolism, a still timely reflection on the need for finding appropriate indigenous symbols to use as vehicles for conveying biblical principles and truth. Readers who are interested in an African perspective on universal elements of the gospel will also appreciate his presentation on what he refers to as the *residuum evangelium*. Oduyoye's contribution focuses on the roots of feminist thinking in African settings. She appropriately discusses the differences in women's realities in Africa and the West, noting points of contact and similarities as well. Not unexpectedly the South African section suffers from being written before the overthrow of apartheid. It does, however, give a sweeping perspective on the history of certain theological developments within Black Theology in South Africa, at least from the perspective of two Scandinavian undergraduate students.

938.   Pobee, John S.

West Africa: Christ Would Be an African Too

Geneva: World Council of Churches, 1996. 52 pages, ISBN: 9782825411988.

In this booklet the Ghanaian Anglican theologian John Pobee tackles the ongoing task of relating the gospel to culture, asking specifically how Christianity can be Africanised. He seeks to encourage a "style of perceiving and discerning in African cultures the good on which to build and in which to couch an authentic African Christianity." The book consists of six short chapters, which in succession describe what Pobee regards as the task of authentic inculturation of the gospel, define the concept of "culture," explain what is meant by "African," relate the task of inculturation to ecumenism, provide examples of authentic gospel-culture encounters in Africa, and offer guidelines for further work on the task. Veterans of the gospel-culture debate in Africa will find well-trodden ground here. Yet that is no reason for overlooking this short work. Pobee has crafted a well-written, judicious overview of the subject. As one might expect in a WCC publication, his explanation of "gospel" is somewhat vague (though his treatment of the implications of the gospel is not). But his analysis of the Western cultural garb in which Christianity was brought to the continent, and his explanation of the need for meaningful African expressions of the faith, are straightforward and illuminating.

939.   Pobee, John S.

Who Are the Poor?: Beatitudes as a Call to Community

Geneva: World Council of Churches, 1987. 71 pages, ISBN: 9782825408841.

This slender volume contains five Bible studies (plus an introduction) originally presented by the author at a World Council of Churches seminar entitled, "Ministry with the Poor." Pobee is a Ghanaian who worked with the WCC in Switzerland and is well known for his numerous publications. While rooted in the list of beatitudes found in the gospels of Matthew and Luke, Pobee's studies also examine Jesus' teaching about and dealing with the poor. Also he draws parallels between Jesus' words and those found elsewhere in Scripture, especially Isaiah. On the whole these are balanced, thought-provoking studies. For example, Pobee takes Luke 6:27–45, a section immediately following the Beatitudes, as a "warning against activism in the name of religion when it is not rooted in a Christ-centered life" since "in a truly Christian context, social engagement and involvement should be rooted and anchored in a devotion to Christ the Lord." Many of Pobee's comments reflect his perspective as an African. Thus he interprets Jesus' words, "Blessed are the poor" in part as a call to community since, as an African, he knows that full blessedness can only be found in community. He also makes liberal use of Akan proverbs in order to illustrate his argument. These studies offer a useful resource for anyone teaching or preaching on the Beatitudes, particularly as they relate to matters of poverty, riches, suffering, and blessedness.

Pope-Levison, Priscilla

see review 639

940.　Posner, Daniel N.

Institutions and Ethnic Politics in Africa

Cambridge: Cambridge University Press, 2005. 337 pages, ISBN: 9780521541794.

When does ethnicity matter in politics? This is the critical question that the author (Professor of Political Science at UCLA in the United States) is trying to address in this book. Ethnicity is just one of the many fault lines in African societies. It is used and emphasized in certain political situations and downplayed in others. Using evidence primarily from Zambia, but also including widely divergent settings such as Los Angeles, Posner argues that ethnicity is all about coalition building. Voters in democratic states will change the aspect of their ethnic identity that they highlight (language, religion, region, etc.) in order to become members of a minimum winning political coalition. The key phrase here is the "minimum winning coalition," because Posner argues that when one is calculating the share of the spoils of political power, rational voters want to share with as few people as possible. Posner's argument is based on a set of strong assumptions: (1) that actors only care about their access to patronage resources and are not voting along ideological lines; (2) that contests over electoral power are won by the plurality group; and (3) that cross-group coalitions are not possible due to distrust or suspicion. While this is a technical book that will be of greatest interest to political scientists, and Posner's conclusions may seem debatable, the excellent detailed research on Zambia may be of interest to readers, as might be his argument that ethnic characteristics can be used and interpreted in a variety of ways depending on the political environment.

941.　Pottier, Johan

Re-Imagining Rwanda: Conflict, Survival and Disinformation in the Late Twentieth Century

Cambridge: Cambridge University Press, 2002. 272 pages, ISBN: 9780521528733.

Pottier has been Professor of Social Anthropology at the School of Oriental and African Studies in London, and has carried out considerable research in Central Africa. His argument here is that both the Western media and the post-1994 governments of Rwanda have misrepresented what took place in the Rwandan genocide and the subsequent conflict in Congo (1996–1997). Thus above all he aims "to reflect on how 'Rwanda' and 'eastern Congo (DRC)' came to be re-imagined in 1994–1996 through a synchronized production of knowledge . . . by which 'instant' journalists, diplomats, aid workers and academics accepted, formulated and spread images of Rwanda that chimed well with the RPF-led regime, now in power in Kigali." Pottier offers a substantial analysis and interpretation of the background to the conflicts in Africa's Great Lakes region during the 1990s, among other things rejecting, remarkably enough, the view that the genocide was caused by ethnicity: "Rwanda's bloodbath was not tribal. Rather it was a distinctly modern tragedy, a degenerated class conflict minutely prepared and callously executed." He critiques in some detail the narratives put forward by the press – especially the anglophone press – and the Rwandan Patriotic Front, the former tending to support that version of events favoured by the latter. A major element was "a discarded, idealised representation of Rwanda's pre-colonial past" which attributed the rise of Rwanda's ethnic divisions to the intervention of the European colonizers. Pottier argues that reconciliation can only take place on the basis of a careful and historically responsible analysis of Rwandan history, as opposed to an ideologically motivated account. Similarly he suggests that the present Rwandan government should not be immune from critical appraisal simply by virtue of its own "politically correct" construction of the events which brought it to power. Pottier's book is a significant and vigorous contribution to our understanding of the recent tragic history of this part of Africa, and perhaps a necessary reminder of the risks in hasty, simplistic and tendentious interpretations of often complex and conflicted events on the continent.

942.   **Poucouta, Paulin**

Lettres aux églises d'Afrique: Apocalypse 1–3

Paris: Éditions Karthala, 1997. 288 pages, ISBN: 9782865377695.

Many theological libraries may already have as part of their holdings on the final book of the NT both William Ramsay's archaeological classic *The Letters to the Seven Churches*, and Colin Hemer's more recent historical study, *The Letters to the Seven Churches of Asia in Their Local Settings*. For those seminaries in Africa where students or faculty readily use French, Poucouta's *Lettres aux églises d'Afrique* would be a good addition. Finding a scholarly study of the Apocalypse by a francophone African is a rare treat. Poucouta is a Cameroonian Catholic priest and professor. Although he acknowledges that the immediate impetus for the work came as a result of groundwork done for the 1994 All-Africa Synod of Bishops, it is obvious from its content that he has spent many years preparing himself for just such a commentary, a fact also demonstrated by his earlier articles and books centred on the theology of Revelation. Poucouta offers his readers a reasoned exegesis, strong on the literary aspects of Revelation 1–3, thus making the volume a good complement to Ramsay and Hemer. Poucouta begins the various sections of his work with a look first at Africa, then turns to the biblical text, and finally returns once again to Africa, following the hermeneutical spiral. In this way, while this volume might otherwise essentially be classified as a commentary, it also fits very nicely into that category of literature that addresses issues encountered by Christians living in modern Africa. The fact that Poucouta has chosen to continue living and ministering in francophone Africa lends credibility and poignancy to his analyses of the current situation.

943. Poucouta, Paulin

Quand la parole de Dieu visite l'Afrique: Lecture plurielle de la Bible

Paris: Éditions Karthala, 2011. 252 pages, ISBN: 9782811105402.

Poucouta's work in biblical studies is not sufficiently well known outside of francophone Africa. The fact that he has authored nearly twenty books and numerous articles in both OT and NT studies, mostly in the area of the Johannine literature, but also on Ezekiel, Daniel, Jonah, Paul, Acts, James and Matthew, should be sufficient to get our attention. Like many Roman Catholic scholars from francophone Africa, his work is characterized by careful methodological attention to the text, by a sensitivity to the African culture in which the text is being read, and by desire to be of use to the church. This publication covers a wide range of interpretative themes. Numerous scholars have noted that the Bible has been read and studied by African Christians from earliest times. Few African biblical scholars have actually made the attempt to read early exegetical works and explore their use for the church in Africa today. Poucouta's first chapter examines Egypt and the Bible, looking at Egypt in the OT, the Jewish community in Alexandria as the seedbed of the Egyptian church, and the Alexandrian catechetical school, and especially the contributions of Origen and Didymus to biblical studies. This is followed by a chapter on North African Christianity, which pays particular attention to Cyprian. The remaining five chapters concern exegetical method, the Bible according to Roman Catholic synodical statements (two synods on Africa, and the more recent synod on "The Word of God"), encouraging knowledge of the word of God among the laity, the Bible and liturgical worship, and women's theology. Poucouta's French throughout the work is clear and fluent, and wonderfully lacking in complex technical verbiage. He is well aware of anglophone African scholarship on the Bible, but his discussions and footnotes will also introduce the reader to the world of francophone African theological and biblical scholarship. It would be a shame if his scholarship were neglected by Protestant scholars, since his irenic and careful writing can teach even those who may have reason to disagree with some of his ecclesial commitments and presuppositions.

944. Pouwels, Randall L.

Horn and Crescent: Cultural Change and Traditional Islam on the East African Coast, 800–1900

Cambridge: Cambridge University Press, 2002. 288 pages, ISBN: 9780521523097.

A casual glance at this book's title might mislead many to assume that this is a study of the African "Horn," the region of Somalia/Eritrea/Ethiopia. However, the book is a synoptic history of traditional Islam along the East African Coast, with a major focus on the islands of Lamu and Zanzibar. Pouwels has done some brilliant research on the sociological and religious development along the Coast over a thousand year span, using a vast amount of oral and unpublished material, and penetrating the Swahili language and "soul" with unusual insights and perception. He maintains that present-day Swahili people of this coastal belt can only be understood if we know the shared history that connects these Afro-Asiatic people from the Lamu archipelago in the north to Pemba, Zanzibar, Mafia, and as far south as the Comoros Islands. Pouwels illustrates the effects which the early "Arabizing" phases had on culture and religion, followed by a discussion of the intellectual, social, and political *arrondissement*, which then serves as backdrop for the final section, covering the Zanzibar Sultanate of the nineteenth and twentieth centuries. Along the way are important insights for Christian awareness: the personality cult around Muhammad exemplified in ostentatious *mawlidi* [Muhammad's birthday] celebrations, which tend to elevate Muhammad from the classic "messenger" status to actually becoming the intercessor for the faithful; the Sufi influence through the significance of *nur*, "divine light" and *baraka* "blessedness, spiritual power." It is also quite revealing how a few influential Sunni "*ulama*" had such a broad and lasting impact on the spread of Islam during the colonial period. Zanzibari sheikh al-Farsi wrote triumphantly in 1972 about one of these Islamic scholars from the time of the UMCA missionaries, that "there has not been an '*alim* who has proven so effective in debating with the missionaries of Zanzibar as did Sh. Abdu'l-Aziz, for his arguments were the most strident . . . like the point of a gun: whatever stood before them could not escape destruction." In contrast was the Zanzibari Sultan Ali b. Hamud (1884–1918). Educated at Harrow (where he was nicknamed "Snowdrop") and thoroughly conditioned to Western culture and thought, yet proud and defensive about his Ibadi background, he liked to run his palace and household "on the lines of a royal court in Europe." This Sultan established the first Government school in Zanzibar in 1907 (in competition to the Mission schools), where next to traditional Arabic and Islamic sciences also "modern" subjects such as bookkeeping and various crafts were taught by a hired European teacher. Pouwel has admirably succeeded in giving us a deeper understanding how the past centuries have moulded the East African Coast from Lamu to Zanzibar into the multi-facetted, fascinating society we encounter today.

Pouwels, Randall L.

see also review 640

Powell, Eve Troutt

see review 491

945.   Presler, Titus Leonard

Transfigured Night: Mission and Culture in Zimbabwe's Vigil Movement

Pretoria: UNISA Press, 1999. 374 pages, ISBN: 9781868880515.

This thorough and thoughtful volume is one of the best examples available of a study of an African Christian phenomenon, a study which combines sympathy and personal involvement with an appropriate objectivity and analysis. The focus of Presler's study is the night vigil, or *pungwe*, in Shona society. The origin of the *pungwe* is traditional. In Shona society diviners, healers and spirit-mediums customarily met with their clientele in the night during which time various rituals took place including dream interpretation, sacrifices and trance-possessions, often accompanied by drums and dancing. The primary focus of these traditional *mapungwe* was to achieve communion with, appeasement of, and discernment from the ancestral spirits. Although churches began to hold night meetings before Zimbabwe's civil war in the 1980s, the war itself influenced the development and widespread popularity of the vigil movement. During the war, guerrilla fighters held their own *mapungwe* in order to raise the consciousness of the local population to the purpose of the war, and to recruit new fighters. These night-long meetings were often anti-Christian in nature and upheld the traditional Shona religion as the appropriate spirituality of the people, Christianity being seen as the white man's religion. These meetings differed from the traditional vigils in their focus on the political, and by emphasizing teaching. Political songs sung at these rallies often used hymn tunes known to local Christians and so had some continuity with local Christian culture. After the war night vigils have become increasingly popular among both mission-founded and African Initiated Churches. Presler shows how the continuity and discontinuity with both traditional Shona gatherings and with the wartime meetings have turned the church vigils into a powerful venue for evangelism, teaching (especially among the mission-founded churches), democratization, and liberation (both in terms of the greater freedom given to lay people, youth and women, and in terms of engagement with and liberation from evil spirits). This volume is to be commended not only for its contribution to understanding this particular phenomenon in African Christianity, but also for its careful methodology – a model of how good research should be done.

Pretorius, Hennie

see review 244

946.   Priest, Doug

Doing Theology with the Maasai

Pasadena: WCL, 1990. 240 pages, ISBN: 9780878084418.

Whatever one may feel about the conclusions of this inquiry, this is an excellent case study in the methodology of contextualizing theology in a local setting. Priest concentrates on developing a relevant understanding of Maasai sacrifice, in order to answer the question whether certain elements of that system may be viable for Maasai who have become Christian believers. His work is based on over seven years of close contact and research among the various Maa-speaking groups of Kenya and Tanzania. Throughout the text he carefully overviews the process used to gather his research material, and presents the material in a clear fashion which does not bog the reader down. The book combines introductory explanations of anthropological fieldwork, exegetical reflection and theological synthesis (following Charles Kraft's model of contextualization), and deals with a practical question in the real life of the people. While some of the sacrificial rites he describes could be explained in a sensationalistic manner, Priest is matter-of-fact in his tone, thereby avoiding unnecessary "demonization" of the people he studies. Not neglecting functional approaches, he focuses on understanding the symbolism of the Maasai sacrificial system and whether (as well as how) that integrates with biblical theology. Perhaps the greatest weakness of the study is that Priest does all the reflection; finding a way to incorporate the Maasai church into the deliberations would strengthen the development of an indigenous church which has its own resources to answer the questions it faces.

Probst, Peter

see review 271

947.   **Prunier, Gérard**

*From Genocide to Continental War: The 'Congolese' Conflict and the Crisis of
    Contemporary Africa*

London: Hurst, 2009. 576 pages, ISBN: 9781850656654.

Prunier is author of *The Rwanda Crisis*, a standard treatment of the events of 1994 and their origins. In this latest book he continues the story, showing how the Rwandan genocide led on to the wars in eastern Congo (DRC) in 1996–1997 and 1998–2002, which toppled Congo's dictator Mobutu, sought to remove his successor Laurent-Désiré Kabila, drew in several African nations from across the continent, and caused the deaths of close to four million Congolese, most of them civilians. It is an immensely complex story and Prunier displays a remarkable mastery of it. Readers may nevertheless struggle to keep up, and will certainly need to make repeated reference to the eleven-page list of acronyms, for political parties, rebel groups and so on. There is good material in the notes too, sadly relegated by the publisher to the end of the book. Prunier draws attention to the human rights abuses of the post-genocide Rwandan regime of Paul Kagamé, both within Rwanda and subsequently in Congo, as well as its exploitation of Western guilt following the genocide in order to further its political and economic aims and divert world attention from its own crimes. He argues that although the war has been described as "Africa's First World War," it might more readily be compared with the European Thirty Years War (1618–1648), since for most of the African countries involved it "took place purely because of the princes' ambitions, prejudices and security fears." At root, Prunier argues, it was a war between Rwanda and Congo, in which the Rwandese Patriotic Front sought a final solution of the Tutsi-Hutu conflict, and attempted "to vassalize its huge neighbour at the same time," drawn, as were others, by the allure of endless plunder. Elsewhere he describes Rwanda's invasion as "the first known instance of postcolonial imperial conquest in Africa by an African country." Along the way Prunier draws attention to the failures of the UN, and the inadequacy and naivety of Western responses, in terms both of diplomacy and of media attention. Prunier takes the story up as far as the Goma Roundtable Conference of January 2008, in which he sees a glimmer of hope. He doubts whether the war could be repeated elsewhere, since no other country "has the potential of creating such a continental upheaval." This book is a remarkable achievement and a core resource for anyone needing to better understand the recent events in the Great Lakes region of Africa and beyond.

948.   **Prunier, Gérard**

The Rwanda Crisis: History of a Genocide

New York: Columbia University Press, 1997. 389 pages, ISBN: 9780231104098.

The terrible events in Rwanda in 1994 must not be forgotten. The genocide that year has a long pre-history. Ideologies, myths, propaganda, and half-truths all played a role in what led to those gruesome events that shocked human understanding. Thus any book shedding light on these entanglements is welcome and necessary. And within the growing literature on the Rwanda crisis, this book stands out because of the range of informative detail it provides. Prunier is a well-known researcher on Africa. He uses critically the written and oral sources, places the conflict in its historical context and tries impartially to narrate the events. It is also evident that Prunier is a journalist: the book is well written. Nine chapters of this book were written by December 1994, the year of the genocide; the final chapter was added in 1997, at which time the earlier material was not touched, although by then the author might have put some accents differently. Prunier's contribution has been valued not least for its detailed discussion of the historical background to the 1994 events, which begins a century earlier. Then at the heart of the book come heart-wrenching sections on the 1994 genocide itself, answering successively: Who were the organizers? Who were the killers? Who were the victims? How long did it last? How many were killed? Prunier also discusses the patterns of the killing, the horrors, the complexities, the bystanders, and the unknown heroes. Rwanda presents an awful challenge to the Christian community in Africa as a whole. What are we to learn for the future? From reading Prunier it becomes clear that Christians must be taught not to execute orders that are against God's commandments. The church must also reflect on the prophetic role she should play in society, sometimes over against the state, so that state ideologies are examined critically, truth is upheld, and misinformation is not condoned. It does not always seem that the church in Rwanda nor in Africa in general has learned these lessons yet. Such reflections are necessary so that in future similar events might not happen so easily elsewhere on our continent. At the end of the book, when the whole situation seems rather dark, the big question that presses itself upon the reader is about ethnic reconciliation. How can it come about in Rwanda after 1994? This is an important book for any thinking, feeling Christian in Africa. Also theological colleges in Africa need to ensure that the Rwanda crisis is accorded fundamental reflection and assessment in their curriculum, for example in courses on Christian social ethics – and for such purposes this book would serve excellently as a resource.

Punt, Jeremy

see review 14

Authors
Q–T

949.   Quarcoopome, T. N. O.

West African Traditional Religion

Ibadan: African Universities Press, 1987. 200 pages, ISBN: 9789781482335.

When he wrote this book, Quarcoopome was teaching at a college of education in Nigeria. Earlier he taught in Cape Coast, Ghana, and wrote British "O" Level Bible Knowledge textbooks. This one is intended for the "A" Level student. As a text for students to pass exams, it has helpful features such as full chapter outlines and study questions. Quarcoopome relies heavily on Bolaji Idowu's 1979 book on African traditional religion (ATR) for his approach. In common with most early books on West African traditional religion, the examples chosen are practically all from the forest region of West Africa, leaving out the savannah and desert fringe peoples. Quarcoopome himself knows the Akan people of Ghana best, but there are numerous references to others like the Mende, Fon, Ashanti, Yoruba, Benin and Igbo. Topics include Idowu's critique of Western terms for ATR (e.g. pagan, primitive, heathen, fetish and animistic), which made all these terms "politically incorrect." Idowu's defence of the use of images, and his notion that ATR worships God in "diffused monotheism" are also followed. Later chapters examine the divinities, man, rites of passage, magic and medicine, traditional morality and secret societies. Quarcoopome writes as an advocate of reformed ATR. He consistently labels Christianity and Islam as "foreign" religions, and points out apparent evil effects they introduced. Overall, the book suffers from its inordinate deference towards what would now be commonly considered the interpretative idiosyncrasies and excesses of Idowu.

950.   Quinn, Charlotte A., and Frederick Quinn

Pride, Faith, and Fear: Islam in Sub-Saharan Africa

Oxford: Oxford University Press, 2003. 184 pages, ISBN: 9780195063868.

Among the host of issues facing the church in Africa, Islam represents one of the most pressing. Yet Islam in Africa remains seldom studied and little understood within the Christian community. This new volume by the Quinns is therefore most welcome. Charlotte Quinn, a lifelong student of Islam in Africa, completed the bulk of this book before her untimely death. The manuscript was finished by her husband, who for years served in the US foreign service in Africa. Written for a general audience, an opening chapter discusses key issues for the study of Islam on the continent, discussion that informs the treatment of Islam in particular locales throughout the book. The Quinns then examine Islam in five sub-Saharan countries: Nigeria, Sudan, Senegal, Kenya, and South Africa. A concluding chapter draws together the findings of these country-by-country studies. The book includes endnotes and a valuable bibliography. For each particular country the Quinns examine such issues as why Islam attracts converts and how it serves both as a stabilizing and as a destabilizing force in African societies. For example, they argue that Islam grows because it offers a sense of communal identity in a politically and socially changing environment. Thus, as respect for the state declines in many areas, the attraction of Islam correspondingly grows – a point that should cause Christian readers to take notice. In addition, the authors devote special attention to Islam's diversity in Africa, stating, "African Islam is first of all local Islam." This variety stems from factions within Islam itself, ethnic divisions among Muslims in any particular area, and a host of local circumstances in which Muslims must live out their faith. Although the target audience is the Western observer of Islam in Africa, this by no means diminishes the book's usefulness for readers in Africa. In their study of Islam in particular countries, the Quinns bring a sensitivity to local history, as well as an awareness of current political and social realities. The result is an informed, readable introduction to contemporary Islam in Africa.

951.   Quinn, Frederick

African Saints: Saints, Martyrs, and Holy People from the Continent of Africa

New York: Crossroad, 2002. 248 pages, ISBN: 9780824519711.

Quinn, an African-American who has served as an Episcopal priest, comes to this subject from his rich background of diplomatic service in several African nations. Through this book he wishes to make available – to individuals for their devotional meditation and to classes for their study of Africa – a wide variety of religious figures and groups who stand as significant representatives of spirituality in Africa. The major emphasis lies on Christianity (painted with broad strokes), from the early Church Fathers, such as Origen, to modern saints ("people of religious courage and virtue"), such as Festo Kivengere. Figures outside the Church are included, such as Hagar with her son Ishmael, as well as the Muslim Imam Abdullah Haron. Others fall more on the fringes of classic Christianity, such as Simon Kimbangu, or are not particularly known elsewhere for their Christian stand, such as Stephen Biko. Some come from outside the African continent (Mahatma Gandhi and Roland Allen) but had ties nevertheless to the history there. The book ends with two longer chapters: a ten-page extract from the author's diary of a visit to religious leaders in Africa in 1987, and a 13-page wide-ranging chapter entitled, "African Prayers, Proverbs, and Wise Sayings." Each of the 86 entries is brief (1–3 pages) and easily read. Each is also followed by a prayer or a relevant quotation. Since these short biographies are presented in alphabetical order, there is no sense of continuity, either geographical or chronological. Quinn has made a unique contribution, accenting a range of memorable individuals in the African story.

Quinn, Frederick

see also review 950

952.   Radelet, Steven

Emerging Africa: How 17 Countries Are Leading the Way

Washington DC: CGD, 2010. 169 pages, ISBN: 9781933286518.

Anyone remotely familiar with Africa knows that the international media can only hear bad news from the continent. It is not that there is no bad news. It is just that the media's focus on the sensational keeps it from seeing so much that is positive. In this book Radelet, formerly a senior fellow at the Center for Global Development (2002–2010) and economic advisor to the government of Liberia (2005–2009), documents changes at the macro-level in seventeen African countries over the years 1995–2010, changes that constitute overlooked good news. The book weaves together examples of statistical data, case studies, and a coherent narrative to produce an accessible account of both Africa's decline post-independence and its subsequent growth in recent years. Radelet sees five factors contributing to positive change on the continent. They include (1) democratization, which has contributed to government accountability; (2) better economic policies, that have limited harmful tax and regulatory regimes; (3) debt reduction, which has enabled greater funds to be used for education and health care; (4) technological developments such as the mobile phone; and (5) a new generation of leaders bringing fresh attitudes and ideas to the table. Examples of this last factor, what has been labelled the "cheetah generation" include: Patrick Awuah, who gave up a promising career in the US to found Ashesi University in his native Ghana; and John Githongo who has battled Kenya's culture of governmental corruption fearlessly and with great personal risk. Radelet divides African countries into three groups: the seventeen "emerging" countries that form the focus of the book, the "oil" countries, and "the rest." Radelet concludes with a chapter identifying what he sees as challenges and opportunities in the years ahead for emerging Africa. The challenges include such issues among others as, not surprisingly, deepening democracy, and managing the rise of China. Opportunities include first and foremost unleashing the power of girls and women. He also discusses the role of the international community in supporting the phenomenon of emerging countries, highlighting matters such as the need for emerging nations to take the lead in establishing priorities and designing programmes for development. In presenting a positive side of Africa, Radelet proves to be no pure "Afro-optimist." He recognizes that, like any other nations, the emerging countries he has profiled are flawed. Nevertheless, he seeks to present a balanced account that highlights the overlooked positive developments now ongoing across the continent. By its nature, then, the book is an overview of a sprawling, complicated subject. What it aims to do it does well.

953.   **Rader, Dick Allen**

Christian Ethics in an African Context: A Focus on Urban Zambia

Frankfurt: Peter Lang, 1991. 201 pages, ISBN: 9780820414539.

This revision of Rader's PhD dissertation at Southwestern Baptist Theological Seminary in the United States was shaped by ten years of missionary work in Zambia. Rader's goal is to facilitate Zambian development of ethical guidelines to face the realities of contemporary urban life. He does not want to try, as an outsider, to develop the ethical responses himself; rather he seeks to chart a path for the Zambian church to follow. In Part One he gives the background he considers necessary for approaching contextualized Christian ethics, including a survey of Zambia's historical demographic data, a sweeping overview of Zambian traditions (strangely split into "secular" and "sacred" traditions), a critique of early missionary efforts, and information on contemporary urbanization. In Part Two he discusses contextualization as ethnotheologizing, issues involved in developing an indigenous dynamic-equivalent Zambian church, and essentials for developing a Christian ethical system for the Zambian context. While laying a foundation, the book tends to give general parameters rather than to present pragmatic helps for ethical development. Perhaps this is asking more than the author intended, but the discussion would have been greatly strengthened by an extended case study of a particular issue in which the author's methodology was applied. Alternately, researching what Zambian church leaders see as the most pressing ethical issues they face would have put the book "on the ground" and significantly increased its relevancy. In parallel with Eitel's *Transforming Culture*, Rader's primary focus is building a foundation to deal with personal ethical issues. While he does mention social ethics and systemic realities in the last chapter of the book, daily realities such as corruption, bribery, and political oppression are not discussed. As an attempt to lay a foundation and develop a method for contextualizing ethics from a decidedly evangelical perspective, the book deserves consideration. However, while Rader's book will be helpful on a personal level of "ethno-ethical" thinking, it will be found wanting in relevance to the weighty social ethical matters being faced by today's African church.

954. Raharimanantsoa, Mamy

Mort et espérance selon la Bible hébraïque

Stockholm: Almqvist & Wiksell International, 2006. 529 pages, ISBN: 9789122021421.

The author, originally from Madagascar, has been teaching OT at the Faculté de Théologie Protestante de Brazzaville, Congo. The book is his doctoral dissertation for Uppsala University. It is a voluminous book, devoted to a complex topic: "death" and "hope" according to the Hebrew Bible. The book falls into two parts, each with three main chapters. The first part investigates a number of texts on death from three perspectives: biological, theological, and metaphorical concepts of death. Similarly, the second part investigates texts on hope from three perspectives: immortality, communion with God, and resurrection. Raharimanantsoa argues that there is a dialectic unity between the three perspectives of the first part and the three of the second: biological death corresponds with hope of resurrection, theological death corresponds with communion with God, and the metaphorical meaning of death corresponds with immortality. The book has a synchronic approach to its material, avoiding questions of dating the texts, at least in detail, and it is more of a theological than an exegetical investigation. The two theologically pregnant motifs, "death" and "hope," are argued to be of universal importance, and the analysis therefore includes comparative material also from other Ancient Near Eastern sources, such as from Babylon, Canaan and Egypt. This detailed study of two theologically important motifs, and not least the dialectic unity between the two, is a good example of theological sensitivity and skills in recent OT studies in Africa. No links are drawn between concepts of "death" and "hope" in the OT and its Ancient Near Eastern contexts on the one hand, and corresponding concepts in modern contexts (the Malagasy context for example) on the other hand. But after 500 pages the author is probably right in leaving that to another colleague.

955. Ranger, Terence, editor

Evangelical Christianity and Democracy in Africa

Oxford: Oxford University Press, 2008. 304 pages, ISBN: 9780195308020.

It is rare to see evangelicals acknowledged for playing any type of roles in developing and sustaining democracy in the Global South, let alone substantive analysis of those roles. And when evangelicals are acknowledged, they are usually the subject of sharp critique, especially for their apolitical orientation. This is the book on Africa in a four-book series "Evangelical Christianity and Democracy in the Global South." The fact that this series offers a more tempered set of perspectives on evangelicals and democracy should be encouraging. A fairly broad sense of who is evangelical is deployed. After the excellent introduction by Ranger, the wide variety of roles played by evangelicals in the development of democracy in Africa is explored in case studies of six nations: Nigeria, Kenya, Zambia, Zimbabwe, Mozambique, and South Africa. Ranger acknowledges the limitations of having only six case studies (e.g. no francophone countries are included). Also in at least two case studies the criteria used for determining who are evangelicals are stretched in ways that render them too plastic. In the Kenyan study literally all Protestant Christians are considered evangelical, so that the usefulness of the term is lost. Further, the author's clear disdain for the Evangelical Fellowship of Kenya ("a feeble Luo-Kalenjin alliance"), and in particular the dismissing of the Africa Inland Church (with a membership of 3 million – almost ten percent of Kenya's population), results in a less than balanced perspective. Likewise, in the Zimbabwe study the Masowe Apostles are included as evangelicals, even though the majority of evangelicals in Zimbabwe would not consider them such. This is nevertheless a groundbreaking book that deserves inclusion in theological libraries across the continent. Evangelical readers in Africa will benefit in particular from seeing the diversity of responses within their communities to significant political issues. At the very least, the authors have largely managed to portray evangelicals even-handedly, making it easier for evangelicals to understand themselves as others see them, and to gain a clearer picture of ways they can be more constructively engaged in the process of building their nations.

Ranger, Terence

see also review 1167

956. Rapold, Walter F.

"Der Gott, der abends heimkommt": Die Inkulturation des christlichen Gottesbegriffs in Rwanda durch Ernst Johanssen (1864–1934) anhand der Imana-Vorstellung

Volketswil, Switzerland: Verlagsgemeinschaft für Europäische Editionen, 1999. 642 pages, ISBN: 9783909093014.

This book on the inculturation of the Christian notion of God in Rwanda is Rapold's doctoral dissertation, accepted by the theological faculty of Fribourg University in Switzerland in 1997. Rapold taught at Butare Theological College in Rwanda from 1975 to 1979, and again from 1986 to 1992. This book is an impressive contribution to the controversial discussion on African concepts of God. Ernst Johanssen of Germany, the first Protestant missionary in Rwanda, did not use the Swahili term *Mungu* for God, as the Catholics had done, but instead used the local Kinyarwanda term *Imana*. The Catholic Church followed in this usage about 60 years later. This treatise profits from the fact that the author knows the source languages involved. This allows him to give an exposition that goes beyond what has been published before on Johanssen, to make use of all the existing published sources on *Imana*, and to include unpublished material as well. In this process he deals especially with the two extreme positions, namely that of Bernardin Muzungu, who in using scholastic theology retrospectively reads too many Christian elements into the traditional notion of *Imana*, and that of the linguist André Coupez, who reduces the traditional notion of *imana* to a diffuse impersonal force that can be translated in most cases by "chance." Rapold proposes that Johanssen did not translate Gott with *Imana*, but used *Imana* as a metaphor in the way described by Paul Ricoeur, thereby bringing the notion *Imana* into relation with the Christian notion of God. This allowed for a new interpretation and enrichment of this notion in a process that has been going on ever since. After detailed exposition and discussion of the sources, Rapold asks whether *Imana* was the right choice and shows this to be the case. However, notions of *Imana* as e.g. in the sense of inescapable fate have still retained force. On the other hand, Rapold deplores the fact that the dynamic aspect of *Imana* has not been sufficiently retained. This could have been done by use of the biblical notion of Ruach in the OT. Might it have been better to choose Rurema (creator, and not fully separated from *Imana*) as a metaphor for God-Father, and the life-force *Imana* for the Holy Spirit (instead of *umwuka wera*)? Even if it were so, this could not be changed now anyway. What needs to be done, however, is to find ways to give more appropriate place to the Holy Spirit in teaching and preaching. This is a remarkable book, and warmly recommended not least for those who would like to think more carefully about traditional African understandings of God and how to make better use of the possibilities these offer in expressing Christian truth.

957. **Rasmussen, Ane Marie Bak**

Modern African Spirituality: The Independent Holy Spirit Churches in East Africa, 1902–1976

London: I. B. Tauris, 1995. 208 pages, ISBN: 9781860640018.

This book is the fruit of the author's many years of participative research in East Africa from the mid-1970s to her untimely death in 1992. The four independent churches that are the focus of the book emerged from the Friends Africa Industrial Mission, itself created by American Quakers at the start of the twentieth century. The story is a fascinating account of how an American missionary enterprise in western Kenya that at first struggled to succeed suddenly ignited and swept forward in directions that were neither anticipated nor tolerated by the founders. One of the early Quaker missionaries was of Pentecostal experience, and his message calling for public confession of sin and the baptism with the Holy Spirit spread like fire among the African Christians in the far west of Kenya. The noisy and sometimes unruly manifestations incurred the public censure of the other missionary personnel and led, in 1929, to the breakaway Holy Spirit movement. Eventually this movement was to fragment further into four distinct Holy Spirit Churches. It is Rasmussen's contention that although each group had its minor distinctives, the splits were due more to personality, rival ambitions, and ethnic concerns. Certain common features such as hymns, purification rites, styles of prayer, patterns of Bible teaching, importance of dreams, as well as Pentecostal manifestations such as tongues, prophecy and healing, emphasize the similarities between the four groups. Unlike some of the Southern African Zionist movements, there is little in the way of sacred paraphernalia (water, staffs, etc.). Neither is there indication in any of the four churches of messianic claims on the part of their founders. Rasmussen links her research with wider scholarship, drawing on the findings of such well-known Africanists as Sundkler, Welbourn, Turner, McVeigh and Mbiti. She would be one of many that explain independency primarily in terms of protest movements, but actually her research would equally endorse Turner's insistence that these movements should also be allowed to be seen primarily as religious. Within their own Holy Spirit Churches these Africans discovered their emotional and spiritual needs being met in a way that had not been possible within the old mission-associated churches. It is an intriguing story and full of challenge for the ongoing story of the gospel in Africa.

958. **Rasmussen, Lissi**

Christian-Muslim Relations in Africa: The Cases of Northern Nigeria and Tanzania Compared

London: British Academic Press, 1993. 132 pages, ISBN: 9781850436416.

The stated aim of this book is "to analyse the relationship between Christians and Muslims in Northern Nigeria and Tanzania today and to describe those factors that determine the relationship." Nigeria and Tanzania were chosen because of their large populations of Christians and Muslims who live and work alongside one another in numerous communities, and because of the obvious contrast between their respective development tendencies and agendas as nations. In her study Rasmussen assumes that understanding Christian-Muslim relations is a holistic endeavour, not purely theological. Consequently, the author develops broad historical perspectives on the socio-cultural, economic, political and religious environment for each country and then factors these findings into her comparative analysis and conclusions. This historical approach to Christian-Muslim relations is reflected further in the outline of the book itself, which is divided into three sections. The first deals with the pre-colonial background of Islam in West and East Africa; the second relates to Christian-Muslim relations during the colonial era; the final section addresses developments since independence in the early 1960s. This book is based on the author's fieldwork conducted in Nigeria and Tanzania between 1977 and 1981, complemented by her experience and observations as a theologian and former lecturer on Islamic and African studies at the Theological College of Northern Nigeria (Bukuru). Although certainly not all will agree with her assumptions and conclusions, the study is a worthwhile exercise that will both challenge and provoke the reader interested in the perplexing issues of Christian-Muslim relations in Africa today.

Ratti, Maria Teresa

see review 924

959.   Reader, John

Africa: A Biography of the Continent

London: Penguin, 1998. 816 pages, ISBN: 9780140266757.

The subtitle of this book makes the rather dramatic claim to cover the biography of the African continent, so a person's immediate reaction might be one of scepticism. Nevertheless, the book has attracted such expressions of support as "The breadth of material is . . . awe-inspiring" and "the sheer range is impressive." The author, a writer and photojournalist who has spent much of the past forty years in Africa (especially Kenya and South Africa), has indeed done a remarkable job in bringing such a vast topic together into a single book (the bibliography itself fills 44 pages). He writes knowledgeably on a vast array of subjects, such as archaeology, palaeontology, geography and botany, as well as less scientific subjects. He is well acquainted with African political history, as can be seen most vividly in his case studies of the British South Africa Company's dealing with the King of the Lozi (in what is now Zambia), and in his analysis of the Ironsi coup soon after Nigeria's independence. Perhaps the most helpful section for the historian is his extended treatment (more than 100 pages) of the African slave trade, in which he thoroughly analyses all aspects of this horrific part of Africa's history – early Arab involvement, the provision of slaves by African chiefs, and the details of the Atlantic slave trade. The most disappointing aspect of the book from the perspective of anyone interested in African Christian history is the almost complete omission of any reference to the role of Christianity in Africa history. Missionaries seem to relate to Africa's biography only as they contribute to (or detract from) political life. Livingstone gets only a few passing comments. John Newton, the slave trader who converted to Christianity and wrote "Amazing Grace," gets as much attention. Ajayi Crowther is not mentioned at all. That is selective history at best, but still a fascinating read – perhaps more suitable for the lecturer's bookshelf (and bedtime or holiday reading) than for the theological college library.

Réamonn, Páraic

see review 805

960.   Reddie, Richard S.

Abolition!: The Struggle to Abolish Slavery in the British Colonies

Oxford: Lion, 2007. 264 pages, ISBN: 9780745952291.

This book, published to coincide with the bicentenary of the Slave Trade Act in 1807, is written by a British citizen with roots in Gambia and the Caribbean. His book is focused mainly on the UK and the Caribbean rather than on Africa, although there are useful sections on Africa as well. He prefers using the term "enslaved Africans" rather than "slaves" (who could be of another race or background), and he focuses on Africans as "agents of their own freedom." He assumes that most people (especially in the UK) know next to nothing about the Transatlantic Slave Trade. He is careful to distinguish between modern "people trafficking" (which is illegal and is considered despicable by most people) and slavery (which was acceptable and legal for centuries). He has researched his topic well (an example: the well-known former slave and abolitionist Olaudah Equiano's father owned many slaves, and the son did the same later!). The reader with a knowledge of slavery in Africa may be disappointed that the author tends to downplay indigenous African slavery as somehow less horrific than the transatlantic variety, whereas neither is remotely defensible. He does note that some African kings wept at the news of the passing of the 1807 bill because they would lose their main source of wealth. The treatment of British missionary activity in Africa is somewhat stereotypical, but he gives solid credit to the Quaker and Methodist leadership in the abolitionist movement in England. The 1792 return of freed slaves from Britain to Sierra Leone is seen as an attempt to rid the country of poor blacks, a kind of repatriation scheme that was run by whites who wanted to avoid setting up a welfare state for indigent freed slaves. As tempting as it must have been, Reddie does not deal with issues such as the economic impact on Africa or reparations. Although this book makes some contribution in understanding the Transatlantic Slave Trade and the Abolition Movement, probably only a third of the book deals with Africa itself.

961.   Reed, Colin

Pastors, Partners and Paternalists: African Church Leaders and Western Missionaries in the Anglican Church in Kenya, 1850–1900

Leiden: BRILL, 1997. 202 pages, ISBN: 9789004106390.

This superbly researched volume attempts to correct the predominant focus on Western missionaries in the telling of the history of the church in Kenya during the second half of the nineteenth century. Reed contends that it was capable Africans "who provided the consistent leadership" in the early Anglican church. Furthermore, he claims that the attitude of the Anglican church toward African leadership significantly shifted between 1850 and 1900. Originally, with only few missionaries on hand and prior to the onset of rapid colonialization, Africans were encouraged to take Christian leadership roles. But by 1900 colonialization was moving ahead full steam, and Africans were now expected to take positions under the authority of Europeans. Since it was the Europeans who told the story of the church in these days, Europeans dominated that story. Reed wants to tell the story of those who are thereby overlooked – the Africans. He does not intend to denigrate the efforts of early missionaries; rather he wants the African leaders to be accorded their proper place. The book draws on correspondence between personnel of the Church Missionary Society in Britain and Africa, as well as on the official reports of that organisation. Reed also canvassed the Kenya National Archives for information. This collection of material from not easily accessible sources, together with Reed's evaluation of its significance, deserves wide attention.

Reed, L.

see review 1186

962.   Reggy-Mamo, Mae Alice

Widows: The Challenges and the Choices

Charleston: Createspace Publishing Platform, 2014. 220 pages, ISBN: 9781497567702.

In writing this book Reggy-Mamo draws on her background as an African-American specialist in education and literacy, as well as on her life experience of being married to a Kenyan Luo, living in Kenya, and working extensively in cross-cultural communications. The book deals forthrightly with the many challenges facing African widows, including the grieving process, funeral and burial arrangements, settlement of the estate, pressure for traditional practices such as sexual cleansing and widow inheritance, helping children through their grief, and issues involved in remarriage of a widow in Africa. She moves smoothly from giving well-researched general information to illustrations from her own experience of dealing with the death of her husband while seeking to honour Luo customs as a committed Christian. Her husband's family worked with her toward the goal of a God-honouring blend of tradition with Christian faithfulness, and her section on how she used Scripture to guide her in this process is especially helpful. She also gives very practical suggestions on how churches can support widows in their time of need. This is an excellent book for sensitising pastors, church leaders, and theological educators to the ethical and social challenges that can face widows in contemporary African society, and the questions of appropriate response from within the Christian community to these needs – especially since there is so very little such literature specific for the African context currently available.

963.   Reijnaerts, Hubert, Ann Nielsen, and Matthew Schoffeleers

Montfortians in Malawi: Their Spirituality and Pastoral Approach

Blantyre: CLAIM, 1997. 496 pages, ISBN: 9789990816099.

The Montfortians (and the Sisters of Our Lady of Wisdom) are a Catholic missionary order which has been working since 1901 in the southern part of Malawi, and still has a considerable presence there. This book, written by insiders, is a careful historical inquiry into Montfortian spirituality, written at a time characterized by much success in missionary work, by a dwindling number of recruits for the order from Europe, by the first steps to include Malawians into the order, and by attempts to transmit Montfortian spirituality when some of its aspects (like the deep devotion to Mary) no longer go unquestioned. This book could be of interest for those who may want to study aspects of Catholic mission history and spirituality in Africa in close detail.

Renju, Peter M.

see review 1192

964.   Riamela, Daniel Odafetite

The Concept of Life after Death: African Tradition and Christianity in Dialogue (with Special Emphasis on the Urhobo Culture)

Ibadan: Claverianum Press, 1992. 130 pages, ISBN: 9789783218420.

This work is based on the author's master's thesis at the Catholic Institute of West Africa in Port Harcourt, Nigeria. After a brief literature review and short history of the Urhobo, Riamela outlines the Urhobo worldview with ideas about linear and cyclic time, and the soul's pre-incarnate choice of destiny. He then continues with attitudes to death and funeral rites. Next he explores biblical and Roman Catholic teachings about life after death. Finally he encourages dialogue between Urhobo belief and Christianity as an avenue for Africanisation of Christianity. Riamela finds traditional belief in many ways to be a preparation for the gospel, but Christianity needs to correct traditional views, such as: viewing violent death, or death of the young and childless (such as Jesus' death), as necessarily evidence of a cursed life; the Urhobo taboo on burials on the frequent traditional sacred days; and belief in reincarnation with absence of anticipation of the beatific vision. In other areas, such as veneration of the departed, there is compatibility with Catholic faith. The author recommends allowing the Christian children of Urhobo deceased to participate in burial and ancestor installation as part of honouring parents. The book is a clear and well-documented exposition of Urhobo and Catholic beliefs on the subject.

Rice, Chris

see review 557

Richards, Paul

see review 628

965.   Richburg, Keith

Out of America: A Black Man Confronts Africa

New York: The Perseus Books Group, 2009. 288 pages, ISBN: 9780465001880.

Richburg was the African bureau chief for the *Washington Post*, based in Nairobi from 1991 to 1994. Thus his book is similar to David Lamb's 1980s book, *The Africans*, and Blaine Harden's *Africa: Dispatches from a Fragile Continent* in 1990. But Richburg's journalistic experience in Africa was somewhat different from these predecessors because he is a black American. His African career coincided with the UN/American debacle in Somalia, the Rwanda massacres of 1994 and the Liberian civil war. Thus the material for his newspaper reports was tragic in the extreme, and he was particularly frustrated and disillusioned because he found that the gap between Africans and himself was too wide to cross, and that his blackness was often more of a liability than an asset. "In America, I may feel like an alien, but in Africa I am an alien." Richburg arrived in Africa determined to avoid the cynicism traditional to his journalist colleagues. But his initial idealism in returning to the continent of his ancestors was dealt a severe blow. He found himself quickly worn down by the bribery, red tape, corruption, starvation and the incredible slaughter he so often had to cover in his news dispatches. By the end of his tour of duty he admits to being "bitter, devoid of hope, drained of compassion." Angry that Africa's ills cannot be addressed by white journalists, lest they be accused of racism, he insists that "Africa's failings have been hidden behind a veil of excuses and apologies" – often, he says, by visiting black Americans who have no right to evaluate Africa unless they have lived here. This judgment is a healthy reminder that Christian analysis of Africa's problems must also be done from within the continent in order to have credibility, lest others continue to do our analysis for us. This is a secular book, but Christians need to hear in it a challenge toward greater involvement in – not withdrawal from – the socio-political crises facing modern Africa. One great sadness of Richburg's book is his isolation; his sources seemed to be limited to people who had as little hope as he, and this isolation left him in despair. Christians still have a message of hope to share in the midst of so much suffering and despair.

Richman, Amy

see review 638

966.   Richmond, Yale, and Phyllis Gestrin

Into Africa: A Guide to Sub-Saharan Culture and Diversity

London: Nicholas Brealey Publishing, 2010. 240 pages, ISBN: 9781931930918.

Richmond is a veteran of thirty years as a cultural officer in the US Foreign Service, and now writes and lectures extensively on cross-cultural communication; Gestrin has more than sixteen years of experience in African affairs. They intend this book "to ease the newcomer's entry into Africa." Written from a secular perspective, this is a highly readable book designed to introduce the "many factors (which) have shaped the character of (sub-Saharan) Africans, their values, and their institutions." Those who are interested in travelling to or within Africa, or living and working on the continent, will find this book especially helpful. Topics include the African community, communication with Africans, coping with customs, doing business in Africa, and tips for travellers. While the authors recognize similarities across Africa, regional differences are not neglected. Suggestions are given for planning and conducting training seminars for those desiring to work with development agencies. The book is not only helpful for non-Africans visiting the continent, but could be useful as well for Africans who may be travelling within the continent and who will therefore be involved with different cultures and customs.

967.   Rimmer, Douglas, and Anthony Kirk-Greene, editors

The British Intellectual Engagement with Africa in the Twentieth Century

London: Palgrave Macmillan, 2000. 288 pages, ISBN: 9780333695937.

This elegantly produced hardback was published to mark the centenary of the London-based Royal African Society, best known around the world through its highly-regarded quarterly journal, *African Affairs*. The academic interests of the Society rapidly expanded to become all-embracing. This breadth of concern is reflected in the ten chapters by different authors on representative subjects including history, politics, higher education, social anthropology, environment, literature and economic development. Within each specialist chapter we encounter often familiar names that represent contributions over the years towards an enhanced Western understanding of Africa: Roland Oliver, J. D. Fage, Terence Ranger and Basil Davidson (history); Frederick Lugard and Cecil Rhodes (administration); Evans-Pritchard and Radcliffe-Brown (ethnography and social anthropology); Joseph Conrad and C S Forester (literature); to mention just a few. This book makes it possible to situate each figure in the unfolding story of British engagement with Africa during the last century. The book rightly highlights not just people but institutions within both Africa and Britain which have been part of the "engagement" story: Fourah Bay College in Sierra Leone, Makerere University in Uganda, Legon University College in the Gold Coast/Ghana, Oxford and Cambridge with their courses for recruits to Colonial Service, London University's School of Oriental and African Studies with its specialist library and research facilities, and the Schools of Tropical Medicine in London and Liverpool – all these and others have been important in the interpenetration of Africa and Britain. The decades of the 1950s and 1960s were especially important as new university institutions were founded in Africa, staffed in the early years largely by British scholars. Special funding was also provided for British universities in the 1960s to promote "area studies" in the humanities and social sciences, which helped to raise the profile of Africa-related research. The book is fascinating and well researched. For those who are concerned to reflect on the historical and intellectual processes that have helped to shape the continent of Africa, and the understanding of Africa, this book will be of particular significance. For better or for worse the British engagement with Africa, intellectual or otherwise, has been sustained and far-reaching. This book indicates how.

Ringe, Sharon H.

see review 126

968. Rittner, Carol, John K. Roth, and Wendy Whitworth, editors

Genocide in Rwanda: Complicity of the Churches?

St. Paul, MN: Paragon House, 2004. 332 pages, ISBN: 9781557788375.

Genocide in Rwanda occurred in 1994 in a country that was nearly 90 percent Christian. Christian churches and clergy took part in the genocide in a way that demands explanation and reflection. This book begins to both document and reflect upon the role of churches and clergy as perpetrators and victims in the genocide and in the violence that continued in Rwanda in the aftermath of the genocide. The focus is predominantly and appropriately on the Catholic Church, as nearly 65 percent of Rwandans are Catholic. This edited volume is the result of a conference held in 2003 on the role of the churches in the genocide and begins helpfully with maps and a chronology of events. It is then divided into four sections discussing the church and power, the church and people, the church and responsibility, and the church and complicity. The essays vary considerably in nature. Some take an objective tone and note the alliance between certain churches and particular ethnic groups, for example the alliance between the Hutu and the Catholic and Anglican churches. Others discuss the role the churches played in affirming ethnic myths and contributing to a "genocidal mentality" or the role the church played in inadvertently reaffirming the ethnic divisions in Rwanda. There are additional essays delivering first person accounts by Westerners, many vowed religious, who observed parts of the genocide or its aftermath. These are fascinating accounts indeed, as some seem intended to justify the actions of particular individuals or religious communities, while others are clearly accusatory. This book takes on a tough topic, since the terrible complicity of the churches in the Rwandan genocide is not really a question – as the title of this book implies – but a fact. The *ad hoc* nature of the contributions makes some progress towards a serious reflection on Christianity and genocide in Rwanda, but far more needs to be done. The book raises questions regarding the depth of Christian commitment, the nature of church leadership and the role of theology that demand a more substantial analysis elsewhere.

Robert, Dana

see review 244

969.   **Roberts, J. Deotis**

Africentric Christianity: A Theological Appraisal for Ministry

Valley Forge, PA: Judson Press, 2000. 134 pages, ISBN: 9780817013219.

Whereas the title immediately suggests something closely engaged with Africa, the book is actually part of a North American discourse linked to the Black Theology movement there. Only one or two passing references occur to any theological discussion within Africa. Nevertheless, the book is relevant to African Christian reflection at least indirectly, in that it addresses issues that parallel core impulses of the African Theology movement on this continent, namely how to think out and live a Christianity that is centred on African identity. Along with James Cone, Roberts was one of the founding figures of the Black Theology movement in America. His long academic career has included teaching posts at the University of Virginia, Howard University, Duke University, and Eastern Baptist Theological Seminary. In this book he focuses on an energetic derivative of the black consciousness movement in America, namely "Africentrism." Africentrism has been characterized as an ideology, a scholarly project, and a social movement that, on behalf of those of African ancestry, seeks to counter the pervasive distortions of Eurocentricity by means of an accentuated affirmation of African heritage in all categories of thought and life. Curiously, in this pursuit of identity through heritage, Africentrism as a movement has tended to focus less on Africa's traditional culture (the focus of African Theology), and more on what Robert's terms "classical Africa," meaning the Africa of Mediterranean antiquity, or more specifically ancient Egyptian civilization. In the process the movement has not always avoided scholarly critique for historical eccentricities and distortions. Roberts is summarily dismissive of such criticism. He sets out to explore the ideological and practical implications of Africentrism for African-American Christians, and to advocate a constructive implementation of its agenda within the faith community. This he believes can serve to enrich and empower theology, culture, ministry, worship, and social witness. While the cultivation of a positive valuation and experience of one's heritage should be welcomed, one may wonder at Africentrism's commitment to deal with hegemonic European ethnocentricity by deploying an ethnocentric counter-narrative. Is one destructive ethnocentricity best addressed merely by promoting a rival ethnocentricity? Is Roberts wise in favouring this model as a credible and constructive option for Christian believers of African descent? On the other hand, some of the practical applications of Africentrism that Roberts proposes for Christian ministry and worship could prove of suggestive relevance in Africa.

970.   **Roberts, W. Dayton, editor**

Africa: A Season for Hope

Venture, CA: Regal Books, 1985. 125 pages, ISBN: 9780830711208.

This book is a collection of articles by African and American writers, Anglican, Catholic and Evangelical. Its focus is on relief and rehabilitation, and it seeks to answer the question, do you give a fish or a hook to those in need? The answer is to give both, but the stress here is on promoting sustainable grass-roots community development. Examples are mostly from World Vision endeavours, statistics are from a decade or more before the time of publication. The book considers the underlying causes of famine, such as drought, inadequate government policies, massive deforestation, and poor soil management. Food conditions in the main regions of Africa are outlined. Then the focus turns to conditions in some eighteen African countries. A whole chapter is given to the famine in Ethiopia and its deadly effect upon the population. Suggested ways and means for developing sustainable resources at the community level are presented. This is where the Church in Africa is called to a ministry of offering people hope – spiritual, physical, social, and economic.

971. Robinson, David

Muslim Societies in African History

Cambridge: Cambridge University Press, 2004. 242 pages, ISBN: 9780521533669.

Robinson, Distinguished Professor of History at Michigan State University, has produced an excellent and readable overview of the historical development of Islam in Africa. Although intended as a textbook for Western university students, it will be a valuable contribution to any African theological library, especially given the limited resources available on this subject. The first two chapters offer a brief survey of early Islamic history and the general features of Islamic practice, for the sake of students with little or no prior understanding of Islam in general. The heart of the book then focuses on the arrival and growth of Islam on the continent. The titles of chapters such as "The Islamization of Africa" and "The Africanization of Islam" point to the complex interplay between the vibrancy of Islam as imported from Arabia and the cultural vigour of traditional African society. Robinson then touches on the Muslim slave trade in Africa, and the faulty Western perspectives of both Islam and Africa. The final section is a welcome addition to any general survey: seven case studies of how Islam developed in specific places and time periods – Morocco, Ethiopia, the nineteenth-century states of Asante, Sokoto and Buganda (covering modern-day Ghana, northern Nigeria, and Uganda respectively), Sudan, and Senegal. Each of these sketches is valuable both as a representative survey, and as a resource for study in that particular region. Robinson ends with a fine conclusion, emphasizing both the unity and diversity of Islam as it has taken root on African soil. The author is to be commended for providing an accessible yet insightful introduction that will be serviceable for years to come.

972. Robinson, Paul W., editor

Choosing Hope: The Christian Response to the HIV/AIDS Epidemic: Curriculum Modules for Theological and Pastoral Training Institutions

Nairobi: MAP International, 1996. 114 pages.

Research at the time of publication found that while 97 percent of church leaders in one part of Africa recognized that AIDS was a pressing problem, and many confirmed that AIDS was now present within their own congregations, a clear majority also acknowledged that they have received no pastoral orientation for coping with this situation. While most theological colleges by then realized the urgent need to begin preparing their students for such challenges, most such colleges would have been hard-pressed to find materials easily at hand for setting up appropriate pastoral training courses relating to AIDS. This publication directly addressed this void. Putting it simply, *Choosing Hope* represents a major breakthrough. Released by the Africa branch of MAP International, the publication consists of 8 lesson modules, presented in a loose-leaf binder, which in combination offer a complete course of pastoral preparation for responding to the AIDS epidemic. The design also permits theological colleges to incorporate individual modules selectively into pastoral courses already in the curriculum, if that seems preferable. The modules include lesson plans, objectives, case studies, discussion materials, and suggested resources. The material is professionally prepared, reliable, and easy to use. Lesson plans are correlated with full-length supplementary manuals that come with the modules. These include: *Helpers for a Healing Community: A Pastoral Counseling Manual for AIDS*; *Learning about AIDS in Africa: A Guide for Community Trainers*; and *AIDS in Africa: The Church's Opportunity*. Also available is a video on the AIDS crisis in Africa, titled *Springs of Life*. Given the nature and extent of the crisis that has affected many parts of the continent, principals and academic deans at theological colleges should consider implementing at their colleges what such resources now make possible.

Roche, Margaret

see review 852

973.   Roland, Oliver

The African Experience: From Olduvai Gorge to the 21st Century

Boulder, CO: Westview Press, 2000. 368 pages, ISBN: 9780813390420.

This book represents the mature reflections of a retired British professor whose career has been spent teaching and writing about the continent of Africa. Although he clearly has a wealth of specific data at his command, Oliver here offers a uniquely broad overview, the sweep of history as the continent as a whole has developed and changed – from the time of the Garden of Eden (which the author believes was located in the highlands of East Africa) to the time of the post-Cold War struggles of the 1990s. This edition of the book comes some eight years after the first edition, and includes a new subtitle and a new chapter dealing with the decade of the 1990s in Africa. The themes of the book include: pastoralism and foodstuffs, the development of states and nations, slavery, African languages, and religion in Africa. Although Pharaonic Egyptian religion receives some coverage, other African traditional religions are mentioned only in passing. A discussion of Judaism along North African trade routes opens a chapter entitled, "People of the Book," which covers early Christianity in Egypt, Ethiopia, and northern African settlements, as well as the coming of Islam into the territories readily accessible to the Middle East. A later chapter, "The Things of God," deals more with modern Christian missionary efforts south of the Sahara. According to the author, Christianity made headway particularly because of its emphasis on general education and the willingness of missionaries to turn over responsibility to African leadership. The ability to compare (and/or contrast) one part of Africa with another enables the author to present a work that looks well beyond mere historical progression or individualized geo-political descriptions. The reader is left with the impression that what is common to all of Africa (and particularly sub-Saharan Africa) has been presented in a rare and thoughtful synthesis. Embracing this large scope of African history, all within 350 pages, necessarily means that specifics have to be filled in by other books. For example, the Rwanda crisis of 1994 is discussed in a cursory manner, while francophone Africa (with the exception of the Democratic Republic of Congo – still known as Zaïre at the time of the book's publication) receives somewhat less attention than anglophone Africa. Any devoted reader on Africa would find this learned, up-to-date yet easily accessible overview particularly rewarding.

974.   Ronzani, R., and Peter Onyango-Ajus, editors

What Christians Should Know about Islam

Nairobi: Paulines, 2010. 71 pages, ISBN: 9789966217585.

This book is meant as a companion volume to *What Muslims Should Know about Christianity?* by Thomas Michel. Basically it is offering a Roman Catholic understanding on Christian-Muslim relations, in order to "foster and encourage greater dialogue between Christians and Muslims." Surprisingly this book addressed to Christians is less than half the size as the other one directed to a Muslim readership. And the slenderness is in more than size. Although the editors confess that going into "all the many details of the Muslim faith" is beyond the scope of the book, the reader will still be disappointed and left with many questions. Why is one third of the content dedicated to Family Life and the role of Jesus and Mary in the Qur'an, but virtually not one page deals with apologetic issues? Did the editors actually live with and relate to Muslims? Or are they merely working from a rather selective and idealistic knowledge of Islam. The agenda seems to be to enable the reader's alignment with an official affirmation deriving from the Second Vatican Council, which concluded: "Muslims strive to submit themselves without reserve to the hidden decrees of God, just as Abraham submitted himself to God's plan . . . Although not acknowledging him as God, they worship Jesus as a prophet, his virgin Mother they also honour, and even at times devoutly invoke." Many Christians will not likely find such appraisals helpful in service of constructive dialogue.

975.   Ross, Andrew C.

Blantyre Mission and the Making of Modern Malawi

Blantyre: CLAIM, 1996. 216 pages, ISBN: 9789990816020.

Ross served with the Blantyre Synod of the Church in Central Africa Presbyterian from 1958 until 1965. Later he served as Principal of New College and Dean of the Faculty of Divinity at the University of Edinburgh. In this slightly revised publication of his PhD dissertation completed in the 1960s, he offers a full account of the foundation and early history of the Blantyre Mission of the Church of Scotland (later to become the Blantyre Synod of the Church in Central Africa Presbyterian), so that its impact on Malawian life up to the present day might be more fully appreciated. The story begins with the suggestion presented to the General Assembly of the Church of Scotland in 1881 that a mission should be initiated "among the natives of that part of Africa which has been hallowed by the last labours and death of Dr. Livingstone." Ross outlines both the subsequent foundation of that mission, and for various reasons, both locally and abroad, its initial failure. He then deals with the reconstitution of the mission under David Clement Scott, from 1881 until 1898. Attention is paid to the role of Scott, political factors influencing the Mission, and the growth of the young church. Next Ross treats the period from the time of Scott's departure in 1898 until the opening of the First World War, during which period Alexander Hetherwick led the Mission. A final chapter deals with the effects of the First World War, and the dawn of a fresh beginning for the young church. The publication of this authoritative study is an important contribution to the growing historiography of the church in Malawi.

976.   **Ross, Andrew C.**

David Livingstone: Mission and Empire

London: Bloomsbury, 2006. 288 pages, ISBN: 9781852855659.

Yes, yet another biography of David Livingstone – but this one may for now be the best of them all! The author is a Scot, an Honorary Fellow in the Faculty of Divinity at the University of Edinburgh, and well acquainted with southern African history. He makes clear at the beginning his reason for offering another book of the famous missionary: "David Livingstone did enough in his life to justify many descriptions. In some cases only a little can be challenged; in other cases later priorities and perceptions have imposed often unconscious distortions." Ross's careful assessment of the historical context and his generous use of Livingstone's own correspondence contrasts with other sometimes biased accounts of the same incidents. Thus Ross conclusively shows that Edwards did not save Livingstone's life after the lion incident at Mabotsa; Mebalwe should receive greater credit. Similarly, the Helmore party that died at Linyanti in 1860 had been told by Robert Moffat not to travel until they knew for certain that Livingstone was there; the author blames the LMS for the resulting tragedy, and dismisses the charge that Sekeletu poisoned the missionaries to steal their goods. Other debated areas are not avoided either – Livingstone's relationships with his family, with LMS directors and with fellow missionaries all come under scrutiny, and in doing so the author does not whitewash Livingstone's harsh words or other inadequacies. Throughout the book Ross stresses Livingstone's passionate defence of the rights of Africans, be they the Xhosa in South Africa who were abused by the Boers and the British, or various tribes in East Africa who were ravaged by Zanzibari slave traders. Yet many in British society followed the theory of "scientific racism" that taught the biological inferiority of Africans, and that policy (much to Livingstone's dismay) eventually carried the day when colonialism began in earnest. Ross says that Livingstone has been improperly proffered as a "hero of Protestantism" or an "icon of imperialism" (his trip across Africa in the mid-1850s was as a representative of Sekeletu, not as the leader of a British expedition), when he was more accurately a "patron saint of African nationalism."

977.   **Ross, Andrew C.**

John Philip (1775–1851): Missions, Race and Politics in South Africa

Aberdeen: Aberdeen University Press, 1986. 258 pages, ISBN: 9780080324579.

Dr John Philip, virtually unknown outside the South African context, was one of the truly outstanding early missionary leaders of Africa. The author of this book on Philip was a missionary in Malawi, and later lecturer in the history of missions in the Faculty of Divinity in Edinburgh and Principal of New College. His aim in this study is to understand John Philip, missionary of the London Missionary Society to South Africa during the first half of the nineteenth century, in the context of his own day. It attempts to see his work within the setting of a particular struggle within evangelical Christianity on the nature and role of the gospel in the world, and a conflict throughout the English-speaking world about race and "civilisation." Philip was the leader in South Africa of a worldwide movement among a minority stream of evangelicals committed to the achievement of racial and social justice, often in conflict with those evangelicals with a more pietistic interpretation of the demands of the gospel, and also in conflict with those for whom evangelicalism itself was unpopular. As product of the skilled artisan class when Scotland was enjoying the transformation of that society in its intellectual golden age, Philip's radical evangelism drove him to argue that the gospel had a bearing on all aspects of society – and also drove him in the mission field to expose a multitude of injustices. A man of deeply held convictions, of passionate feelings, and of untiring commitment to causes in which he believed, he provoked in some twentieth century commentators as sharp hostility as he did among his contemporaries. But he was a man capable of kindly tolerance not only within his family but with many others, not least the youth. Ross provides a striking portrait of a neglected but noteworthy man, an early missionary whose attitudes and arguments have continuing telling relevance for Africa today.

978.   Ross, Kenneth R., editor

Christianity in Malawi: A Source Book

Gweru, Zimbabwe: Mambo Press, 1996. 253 pages, ISBN: 9780869226414.

The book presents a selection of key primary sources reflecting the substance and inner logic of the religious consciousness which developed in Malawi as its people responded to the Christian message. In this way the book allows Malawian Christians to speak for themselves, so that church history might be formed by listening directly and critically to voices from the past. Drawing together under one cover these written documents and testimonies from different times and places, Protestant, Roman Catholic and African Initiated Churches, this book is unique in its comprehensiveness. It offers a composite picture of how Christianity in Malawi has evolved from the time of its introduction in the last quarter of the nineteenth century until its more recent interaction with the politics of transition to democratic rule. Not doubting that the writing of Malawi's church history will depend heavily on tapping oral sources, the present volume demonstrates that (as is likely elsewhere in Africa) Malawian church history is in fact rich in documentary sources, which can make an important contribution to the formation of a comprehensive church history. In this volume an attempt is made to make a selection of such documents readily accessible to the student of Malawi church history. Documents are grouped under four main headings: (1) Conversion to the Christian Faith, dealing with the questions why Malawians become Christians, and why the rapid church growth; (2) Faith, Culture and Gender, dealing with the attitude of Christian converts to traditional Malawian culture, the social impact of Christian witness, and how the Christian presence affected issues of gender; (3) the Rise of Independency, dealing with why some Malawians formed "independent" churches; and (4) Church and State, dealing with how the churches related to the political arena at the various stages of Malawian history. A selected bibliography supplying background material for a study of the texts collected in this book enhances its usefulness as source book. The book seeks to improve the teaching and learning of church history throughout the region, by enabling students to engage thoughtfully with their own church history. In addition the book serves as a resource for all readers seeking to understand Malawian society and the role Christianity has played in that setting. It is also a model of the sort of resource publication needed for Christian communities in many other African countries.

979.   **Ross, Kenneth R., editor**

Church, University and Theological Education in Malawi: A Model for Third World Theological Education

Blantyre: CLAIM, 1996. 84 pages, ISBN: 9789990843002.

The title of this useful booklet is taken from a report that constitutes its first major portion, namely a survey of higher theological education in Malawi. It overviews the way in which a cooperative arrangement has been established between several major theological institutions and the Department of Theology at the University of Malawi, in order both to capitalize upon the human, material, and scholarly resources available, and also to upgrade the overall standard of local theological training on several levels of expertise. This report presents an interesting summary of all the theological training schools in the country, those that are participating in the university-sponsored joint programme and the majority which are not. The report includes a comparison with the situation in neighbouring countries of south-central Africa and the universities of Oxford and Birmingham in the UK. The second half of this book is made up of a detailed presentation of the syllabus which governs each of the three theological programmes currently (1995) being offered by the University of Malawi: the Diploma in Theology, the BA in Theology, and Postgraduate Studies. The Malawian experience could be of special interest to theological educators elsewhere in Africa as a helpful model for establishing similar cooperative ventures among several theological schools, programmes that can maximize scarce resources and yet maintain individual theological distinctiveness.

980.   **Ross, Kenneth R., editor**

Faith at the Frontiers of Knowledge

Blantyre: CLAIM, 1998. 240 pages, ISBN: 9789990816112.

Ross was at one time Professor of Theology at Chancellor College in the University of Malawi, and subsequently Mission Secretary for the Church of Scotland. It was in the latter role that he coordinated the "Faith and Knowledge Seminar" on which this book is based. The challenge taken up in this book by scholars from a variety of disciplines is to wrestle with the relation of faith and science at the frontiers of knowledge. The contention is that unity of knowledge is not easily achieved in today's Africa, where often there is little conscious interaction between traditional beliefs, Christian faith and modern secularity. The papers are collected into two parts, the first devoted to Natural Sciences and the second to the Social Sciences. In the first grouping, an agriculturist delineates the causes and effects of environmental degradation in today's world, and argues that the Christian response would be a refusal to pass on the costs of exploitation of the environment to anyone else. A priest-scientist examines the anomaly of altruistic behaviour among animals supposedly conditioned by the "selfish gene." Drawing on a theology of grace perfecting nature, he offers a vision of an altruism surprisingly evident in the "old" creation that anticipates the "new" commandment of Christ. Next a mathematician draws on Christian faith to illuminate the role of creativity in mathematics, while a physicist explores the relativity of time and its implications for Christian beliefs. Finally, a specialist in the use of information technology in developing countries suggests that the new possibilities offered by computer technology raise very human questions concerning accountability. In part two, on the Social Sciences, a lawyer shows that the concept of social trust that forms the basis for the UN Convention on the Rights of the Child is supported by Christina teaching and practice. Another paper addresses perhaps the most critical frontier of knowledge in recent times:

that presented by the HIV/AIDS pandemic. A third paper offers a sharp critique of the civic education attempted in Malawi as it seeks authentic democracy. Finally a military historian offers a historical case study of one of the thorniest questions for Christian ethics: whether, if ever, is the Christian justified in using violent means to achieve laudable goals? This collection represents an altogether rare and remarkable attempt at multi-disciplinary Christian intellectual reflection in Africa, which merits both attention and also emulation.

981. Ross, Kenneth R., editor

God, People and Power in Malawi: Democratization in Theological Perspective

Blantyre: CLAIM, 1996. 272 pages, ISBN: 9789990816044.

This important collection presents studies by staff of the Department of Theology and Religious Studies at the University of Malawi which explore, from a religious perspective, various aspects of the then recent transition in Malawi from dictatorship to democracy (1992–1995). The central issue concerns the extent to which there has been operative a meaningful and God-pleasing transformation of power (in a theological sense), with special reference to the formerly disadvantaged (and often persecuted) segments of Malawian society, for example: Christian women, young people, Muslims, Jehovah's Witnesses, and people in prison. The book begins with a helpful historical overview by the editor, of the important role that was played by the Christian churches (Protestant and Catholic) in the dramatic series of events leading to what was assumed to be the "democratization" of the country. This is followed by a study of the distinct use of the Scriptures during this tense transitional period. The volume concludes with two essays of a more general nature, which summarize the current socio-political situation in Malawi, first of all with respect to the significant "power relations" within and among the different Christian churches in the country (K. Fiedler), and secondly in terms of a biblical evaluation of the relative effectiveness of the use of power on the part of both church and government leadership in the new age of democracy (K. Ross). These last two studies are models of critical analysis that will hopefully act as a mirror to reveal the extent to which "Church, state and society in Malawi [still] need a deep awareness that all exercise of power is accountable to God . . . [and that] God's politics has to do with the transformation of human politics" by means of forgiveness, love for all social groups, and humble service. All essays in this volume are interesting, well written, and extremely relevant to the Christian Church in Africa. The book provides a multifaceted, honestly critical perspective on the local manifestations of the "theology of power," both secular and religious, and thus stands as a case study which ought to be duplicated in other countries on the continent.

982. Ross, Kenneth R.

Gospel Ferment in Malawi: Theological Essays

Gweru, Zimbabwe: Mambo Press, 1995. 151 pages, ISBN: 9780869226155.

Ross, originally from Scotland, was a senior lecturer in theology and religious studies at the University of Malawi. This interesting collection of essays is part of a new series of texts intended to "advance understanding of religion and theology in Malawi." *Gospel Ferment* consists of eight conference papers and/or previously published articles which have been revised and edited for this volume. The principal question addressed in them all is: "What effect is the Gospel having today in Malawian religion, culture and society?" Ross aims to provide a historical perspective on the role of the church in nation-building (from a broad Presbyterian standpoint), with special reference to the dramatic socio-political as well as religious development, conflict, and change that took place in the years immediately prior and subsequent to the reform-oriented Pastoral Letter issued by the Catholic Bishops in 1992. In view of the length of this study, its treatment is quite selective in terms both of topic (the subjects treated) and of time (the historical period covered). But the book does give a good overview of some of the main issues that concerned the established main-line Christian churches, Protestant as well as Catholic, in relation to the Malawian society at large during a period of considerable trial, testing, and self-examination. Ross calls for a more active approach in "contextualizing" the gospel of Christ, so that it more fully engages the masses in both word and deed as they live out their lives during some very trying circumstances. This well-written "case study" of the role of the Church in the Malawian situation could readily serve a valuable comparative function for Christian communities in other geographical settings of Africa.

Ross, Kenneth R.

see also reviews 193, 831 and 921

Ross, Robert

see review 159

Roth, John K.

see review 968

983. **Rothchild, Donald**

Managing Ethnic Conflict in Africa: Pressures and Incentives for Cooperation

Washington DC: Brookings, 1997. 343 pages, ISBN: 9780815775935.

Churches in Africa have often played a vital role as peacemakers in the ethnic conflicts that have wracked the continent. Though this book is focused on the role of the state in conflict prevention and management, it nevertheless contains much that will profit those Christians involved in peace and reconciliation work in the African context. Rothchild, professor of political science at the University of California, Davis (USA), asks how states can use structural and policy incentives, both coercive and non-coercive, to encourage cooperation between leaders of ethnic groups in conflict. In the process, he argues three basic points. Those familiar with management theory will recognize these as a systems approach to conflict management. (1) The context in which the mediation is attempted demands close attention. In that context, one must ask what leverage a mediator can bring to bear on the situation in order to develop an effective "carrot and stick" approach. (2) Conflict management is a process that runs from pre-intervention preparation through implementation. All steps throughout the process are linked. (3) In certain situations, the management process can be moved along through the use of pressures and incentives. The opening chapter provides a historical overview of the ways conflict has been managed in Africa, beginning with the colonial era. The remainder of the book is divided into two large sections. The first deals with situations where the state political structures have remained intact and conflict is manageable. The second is concerned with situations where relationships between groups have dissolved and the state or an international organisation must intervene. Each chapter illustrates the principles that Rothchild recommends by using case studies of conflict in specific African nations. Two negatives about the book should be noted. First, the prose is decidedly unexciting; Rothchild is not out to capture his readers' attention. Unfortunately this textbook on conflict management in Africa too often reads like just that, a textbook. Secondly, Rothchild pays little attention to the role that church leaders and structures have played, or can play, in conflict management and resolution in Africa. The church occupies too important a position in most sub-Saharan societies to be so easily overlooked. Yet for those involved in peace-making ministry in Africa, and those who may need to be (including those in pastoral training), this volume offers much useful orientation that is not otherwise easily available.

Roux, A. P. J.

see review 218

984. Rowland, Stan

Multiplying Light and Truth through Community Health Evangelism

Mumbai: Gospel Literature Service, 2001. 325 pages, ISBN: 9789966850850.

For some years Campus Crusade operated a Community Health Evangelism (CHE) programme in East Africa. The programme was designed to enable communities to develop preventive health measures in a holistic way that includes addressing people's spiritual needs. This book presents a careful description of the methods, rationale, and results of the programme. The book focuses on the training of local "Community Health Evangelists." It acknowledges the difficulties associated with working with non-Christian community volunteers and with communities of other faiths. The author honestly presents both successful and failed projects, along with analysis of the factors contributing to such outcomes. This enables readers to learn from Campus Crusade's experiences, as well as from the many knowledgeable resources, both Christian and secular, referenced in the book. The book is particularly valuable for highlighting an ongoing practical example of holistic Christian social outreach in contemporary Africa. It would prove a useful resource for church and parachurch groups engaged in community ministries in Africa, or intending to implement such ministries, especially ministries addressing health issues.

985. Roy, Kevin

Zion City RSA: The Story of the Church in South Africa

Pretoria: South Africa Baptist Historical Society, 2000. 200 pages, ISBN: 9780620252270.

Roy has served on the staff of the Baptist Theological College, Cape Town. Here he sets down in an orderly and delightfully readable fashion the unique history of the church in South Africa. The story of the colourful, variegated and bewildering array of Christian churches in South Africa, from Calvinist to Catholic, from Charismatic to *Amazioni*, is told with sympathy, yet not omitting the failures and sins of its many participants. From an ecumenical evangelical perspective, and with an approach refreshingly free of any sectarian spirit, an accurate picture is presented of the whole Christian community. The book is divided into seven chapters: Overview; the Dutch Period; Arrival of the British; "Ethiopia shall stretch out her hands" (the establishment and growth of various churches during the nineteenth century); a "South African Pentecost" (revivals at the turn of the century, and the rise of the African Independent Churches and various forms of Pentecostalism in the first part of the twentieth century); the Growing Church Struggle; and Towards a New South Africa. This is a book worth noticing. It would make an excellent text for any course on the history of Christianity in South Africa. The presentation is sufficiently technical to be useful for final-year degree students, and sufficiently popular to be appropriate for first-year degree students.

Rubenson, Samuel

see review 379

986.   Rucyahana, John

The Bishop of Rwanda

Nashville: Thomas Nelson, 2008. 264 pages, ISBN: 9781595552372.

This volume is one of the growing number of first-hand accounts of the genocide in Rwanda and its aftermath. The strength of this book is its analysis of the causes and the aftermath of that horrific event. Rucyahana is a native Rwandese who is now an Anglican bishop in Rwanda (not "the" bishop, as the title mistakenly suggests; one realizes that authors rarely have control of the titles of their books). He is in a good position to discuss the ideological background to the genocide, having grown up in Rwanda. While in no way excusing the people of Rwanda who participated in genocide, Rucyahana places much blame for the creation of a racist society on Western powers, especially France. The United States and the UN also come under fire for their intolerably slow response to what is now widely seen to have been "genocide," a fact that the world was slow to acknowledge. Rucyahana is in an especially ideal position to discuss the present situation, and not least the situation of the church, which has had to do much soul-searching and has had to examine in great repentance the shallowness of its pre-genocide discipleship. The hope described in this book is hope in a God who raises the dead, a God who offers forgiveness and reconciliation. Trusting in this God, Rucyahana characterizes the emerging church in Rwanda as a church that has begun to rebuild, a church that is learning to serve, to forgive and to live together in peace. As the bishop says: "There cannot be any cruelty greater than the cruelty that was in Rwanda, and therefore there is no grace greater than the grace that is in Rwanda, . . . grace that comes from the cross of Jesus Christ."

987.   Rusesabagina, Paul

An Ordinary Man: The True Story behind Hotel Rwanda

London: Bloomsbury, 2007. 288 pages, ISBN: 9780747585589.

Many people have become familiar with the Rwandan genocide of 1994 principally through the film, "Hotel Rwanda." In this book the central figure depicted in that film, Paul Rusesabagina, the manager of the Hotel Mille Collines, tells his story from childhood up to his eventual departure from post-genocide Rwanda. It is clear that while the film took some liberties with the facts, it was nevertheless a reasonably faithful depiction. As a personal narrative by a Rwandan who lived through the period leading up to 1994, and through the genocide itself, the book offers insights into Rwandan culture and society, and some evaluation of the factors that produced the horrifying violence. There is strong censure of the role of the international community, especially the UN and USA, and criticism too of the government that emerged after the genocide. Rusesabagina refers also to the failure of the Rwandan churches, and the complicity in the genocide of many of those in church leadership. A major theme is the power of words, both in inciting hatred and murder through the Rwandan media of the early 1990s and, in his own case, in saving those who found refuge in the Mille Collines. "Today I am convinced that the only thing that saved those 1,268 people in my hotel was words. Not the liquor, not money, not the UN. Just ordinary words directed against the darkness." He explains the genocide in terms of a human "herd instinct," exploited by a political elite struggling to maintain its grip on power. However, despite his experiences, he retains a humanistic optimism – a belief in the "triumph of common decency." The genocide, he says, was an expression of human insanity, but "Human beings were designed to live sanely and sanity always returns. The world always rights itself in the long run." Before becoming a hotel manager Rusesabagina went to Cameroon to train for pastoral ministry in the Seventh Day Adventist Church, but there is very little theological reflection on the events he describes. He retains some faith in a "kind of Higher Power that is the origin of all we see around us," but "I felt that God left me on my own during the genocide . . . We don't talk much anymore, but I would like to think that we can one day reconcile, . . . and he will explain everything to me." *An Ordinary Man* is an easy and worthwhile read, but, as with all accounts of the genocide, it raises profound and perplexing questions for which Rusesabagina has no final answers.

988. Russell, Horace O.

The Missionary Outreach of the West Indian Church: Jamaican Baptist Missions to West Africa in the Nineteenth Century

Frankfurt: Peter Lang, 2000. 323 pages, ISBN: 9780820430638.

That those of African descent in the Caribbean actively participated in the nineteenth century Western missionary enterprise in sub-Saharan Africa is a phenomenon little known in mission studies or mission history. Between 1841 and 1897 five expeditions bearing over one hundred recruited black mission agents left the West Indies to participate in the project in Western Africa. These expeditions emerged from separate Christian communities in the British West Indies and represented a distinct West Indian desire in the mid-nineteenth century to contribute to the advancement of Africa through the agency of Christian mission. One of those missions was the Baptist Mission from Jamaica to the Cameroons. Horace Russell, a Jamaican Baptist churchman and scholar, has pioneered research interest in this subject. This study represents his doctoral dissertation at Oxford University in 1972. Russell points out that the origins of the Jamaican Baptist mission to western Africa occurred in the context of two important developments in the Jamaican society of the 1830s. One was the attempt by British Baptist missionaries in Jamaica to create a stereotypical black Christian identity for African slaves in Jamaica. The second was the Baptist missionaries' response to the opportunities to engage a new project following the final collapse of the British slave society in Jamaica in 1838. Their eagerness to capitalize on the opportunity for a big venture, especially in the circumstances of the absence of a clear plan for the reconstruction of the post-slave society, was well publicized in England by the Baptist missionaries in Jamaica in order to garner support. Russell argues that the Baptist initiative from Jamaica was a failure in Africa, in terms of its expectation and design. Yet, in his view, it had positive historical value both for the Baptist Union in Jamaica, as well as for the resultant Baptist churches of the Cameroon. The Africa Mission initiative helped to define the final shape and structure of the Union of Baptist Churches in Jamaica and at the same time leveraged Baptist witness in the Cameroon. It also laid the foundation for the eventual Baptist work in the Congo. Although he raises significant questions about the motive, authenticity and adaptation of the West Indians in Africa as participants in the Western missionary enterprise, nevertheless in his judgement this was "one of the finest stories of missionary endeavour." While Russell's work has opened interest in the subject, Caribbean historians for their part have yet to give full attention to this aspect of post-emancipation history of the British West Indies. His bibliographic introduction shows the extent of colonial neglect of the subject, as well as some post-colonial realities – both in the West Indies and in Africa – which have justified renewed interest in this historical phenomenon.

989.   Rwiza, Richard N.

Formation of Christian Conscience in Modern Africa

Nairobi: Paulines, 2001. 144 pages, ISBN: 9789966211934.

A Tanzanian Catholic priest, Rwiza penned this short monograph while pursuing doctoral studies at the University of Leuven. Three main subjects occupy Rwiza. The first is a sociological overview of urbanization in Africa and the ways in which the phenomena associated with this process influence the development of morals. Secondly the author offers theological reflections on the general issue of conscience – in Scripture, in terms of moral development theory, and in the formation of a Christian conscience. Thirdly Rwiza examines the problem of forming a Christian conscience specifically in an African context. The problem, according to Rwiza, is that many modern African Christians do not have a genuinely inculturated Christian conscience. Their experience as Africans and their experience as Christians are often dichotomized. In order to form such a conscience, the author contends that one must take into consideration the rural-urban continuum of experience that characterizes so much of life in Africa today. Only when these African realties are given full weight can Christian conscience become fully inculturated into the African setting. As one would expect in a work by a Catholic priest, the terms of discussion are largely formed by Catholic teaching. Thus, concepts like "inculturation" and natural law, and references to Vatican II abound. Rwiza is conversant with and makes use of theorists both of moral development and of ethics. Perhaps given the brevity of the book, the treatment of Piaget and Kohlberg, Aquinas and MacIntyre, can at times feel superficial. Yet the descriptions are generally clear, and Rwiza both critiques what he finds as faults and integrates into his own perspective what he finds of value. At times the text lapses into the use of generalizations that cloud rather than clarify the argument. For example, the author speaks of inter-tribal relations contributing to or deforming the "conscience," using the term in such a manner that one is left unsure of what effect he speaks. His description of "ethnicity" is fundamentally out of touch with modern discussions of the subject. This is a worthwhile exploration into an area not widely attended.

990.   Ryan, Colleen

Beyers Naudé: Pilgrimage of Faith

Grand Rapids: Eerdmans, 1990. 246 pages, ISBN: 9780802805317.

If anyone had any reason for confidence in Apartheid South Africa, it was Beyers Naudé: an Afrikaner of Afrikaners, a Stellenbosch-trained dominee of the Dutch Reformed Church (DRC), and a member of the Broederbond – a secret society set on advancing the cause of the Afrikaner. (Naudé's father had been the society's first president in 1918.) Yet in 1963 he left an influential pastorate to serve as head of the ecumenical and deliberately interracial Christian Institute (CI) that he had been instrumental in creating. The CI's vociferous critique of Apartheid and of DRC support of the government's racist policies was silenced in 1977 when Naudé and others were given banning orders (lasting, in Naudé's case, for seven years). Although this biography's narrative ends in the late 1980s, Naudé continued to play a significant public role in post-Apartheid South Africa until his death in 2004. Ryan, a journalist, has produced a very readable account of Naudé's life as it played itself out against the background of twentieth-century South African history. She draws on newspaper reports, archival material and personal interviews to paint a realistic portrait of Naudé. His leadership tended towards the autocratic, and his theological thinking lacked the profundity of some of his peers. Nevertheless, his life was guided by the unfaltering belief that the Bible is the authoritative word of God and that that word demands that people treat each other justly.

Ryan, Patrick

see review 700

991.   Saayman, W. A., and Jacques Kriel

AIDS: The Leprosy of Our Time?

Johannasburg: Orion, 1992. 83 pages, ISBN: 9780798706056.

The two authors aim to integrate perspectives from missiology and internal medicine (their individual specialisations) in promoting a Christian response to the AIDS epidemic that was looming at the time they wrote in 1992. Although their projections have been overtaken by events, some of the misconceptions they address are still with us. They contend that the modern biomedical model does not deal well with preventing a behaviourally-caused epidemic with strong social implications, but their solution – to integrate traditional African healers with the modern medical establishment – seems based more on pragmatic considerations of cost, availability and social acceptance than on either medical or spiritual considerations. Their defining of "closed sexual relations" as the only effective preventive to AIDS is designed to appeal to all religions as well as the non-religious. On the other hand, their appeal to Jesus' treatment of lepers as a metaphor for Christian response to AIDS sufferers is a well-argued and biblically based challenge to the church. The non-technical language used throughout would be easily understood by people with secondary-level education and above. Some of the positions taken, such as those relating to traditional healers and polygamy, may invite critical analysis by the reader.

992.   Saayman, W. A.

Christian Mission in South Africa: Political and Ecumenical

Pretoria: UNISA Press, 1993. 128 pages, ISBN: 9780869816974.

Saayman, at one time head of the Department of Missiology at the University of South Africa (UNISA), here attempts to redefine the mission of the Christian churches in South Africa on the basis of political and ecumenical factors. By examining three largely unknown black pioneers (Ntsikana, Tiyo Soga, Nehemiah Tile), three widely recognized white pioneers (John Philip, Bishop Colenso, Andrew Murray), and three ecumenical documents (Cottesloe, the Message to the People, Kairos), Saayman demonstrates how political and ecumenical persuasions are inseparably linked with doing mission. To separate them places the relevance of the church in serious jeopardy, as the crisis of Christian mission in South Africa bears out. "True spirituality grapples intensively with the historical" and therefore the church must "struggle to be liberated from the idols created by colonialism, racism and capitalism." Although Saayman writes primarily for the South African situation, the Christian church in the rest of Africa has also been impacted by similar influences. Saayman suggests a "decolonising" of the mind, and calls for honest and realistic assessment of both the limits and the potential of the church.

993.　Saayman, W. A.

A Man with a Shadow: The Life and Times of Professor Z K Matthews

Pretoria: UNISA Press, 1996. 130 pages, ISBN: 9780869819654.

Saayman here develops a brief historical assessment (rather than a complete biography) of the life of Zachariah Keodirelang Matthews (ZK) (1901–1968), the first African to obtain a BA degree in South Africa and the first black headmaster of a secondary school. Furthermore, ZK was the one to propose a congress to draw up a "Freedom Charter" which (according to Mandela) reshaped the liberation struggle for South Africa, was one of 156 people accused in the well-known "Treason Trial" of the late 1950s, became the first Africa Secretary in Geneva for the WCC's Division of InterChurch Aid, Refugee and World Service, and was "the first South African (black or white) to have been appointed specifically and exclusively as professor of missiology at any university." By considering the contexts which influenced ZK's life, and by undertaking a missiological interpretation of his contributions as an educator, political leader, and a Christian, Saayman seeks "to discover the role played by African Christians in the establishment and extension of Christianity during an important era of South African history." Saayman concludes that ZK's salutary "shadow" of influence and presence continues to be cast across the country. This study would appeal to historians and educators as well as missiologists.

994.　Saayman, W. A., and Klippies Kritzinger, editors

Mission in Bold Humility: David Bosch's Work Considered

Eugene, OR: Wipf & Stock, 2013. 192 pages, ISBN: 9781620328378.

This book is a tribute to David Bosch (1929–1992), the noted South African missiologist. Twelve writers present their particular understandings and assessments of the work and influence of Bosch. The two editors were colleagues of Bosch at the University of South Africa. The range of contributors says something about the influence of Bosch; for example, Roman Catholic, ecumenical and evangelical orientations are all represented, from Europe, Africa, Asia, and the Americas – thus underlining an impact that may have been increasing rather than decreasing since Bosch's death. Each writer says how he/she was influenced in some way by Bosch personally and/or by his writings. Each speaks of the fact that Bosch's influence will continue for many years to come, and that anyone involved in Christian mission must know something of Bosch's work. At the same time the assessments are not without honest criticism. Two may serve as samples. Especially in relation to Bosch's *magnum opus* (*Transforming Mission*), Chris Sugden suggests that there is more to be said about the theology, practice and mission of the church – particularly in the majority world – than Bosch allows. Sugden (who acknowledges the significance of Bosch's book by using it as a course text) says that Bosch needed to have more to say on such topics as the priority of the poor, the covenant and family, the integration of evangelism and social action, and the understanding of power in mission work. Frans Verstraelen, assessing the influence of Africa in Bosch's writings, asks whether Bosch's approach to missiology was essentially Western (i.e. approaching theology "from above" rather than "from below"). That is to say, Bosch tended to see an ideal and then compare and describe particular situations in relation to that ideal, rather than allow the particular situations themselves to determine the interpretation. Secondly, Verstraelen suggests that Bosch could have given more emphasis to the contribution of African theologians. He cites several Africans who he feels have made an impact on theological thinking worldwide but are omitted from Bosch's treatment. While this book focuses primarily on the theme of mission, other areas of Bosch's influence are also covered, for example his contribution to theology in general, his work for justice and peace, and his churchmanship. The essays also go beyond assessments of Bosch to make their own missiological contributions, thus advancing the discussion often beyond Bosch, which would have pleased him.

Saayman, W. A.

see also review 605

995.   Sachs, Jeffrey D.

The End of Poverty: How We Can Make It Happen in Our Lifetime

London: Penguin, 2005. 416 pages, ISBN: 9780141018669.

This book by Sachs is a very fascinating and accessible description of the challenges of global poverty, and the new and much-touted UN Millennium Development Goals. It is written from the perspective of a US economist who has a great deal of concern both for the poor around the globe, as well as for his own country's moral reputation. In eighteen chapters Sachs recounts his personal experiences in trying to bring about structural changes to several economies (Bolivia, Poland, Russia), as well as the success stories of Indian and Chinese development efforts. He then turns to an analysis of the economic and geographic challenges behind development, and focuses in on those people living in extreme poverty, those who Sachs argues have not yet made it to the lowest rung of the developmental ladder and therefore cannot yet benefit from globalization. By and large Sachs is talking about Africa. He argues that many East Asian and Latin American countries are on their way to addressing their own problems with poverty and are involved in the globalized economy. However, because of issues of health, education and geography, Africa is still largely outside of the globalized economy. The persistence of diseases such as malaria as well as HIV/AIDS make health concerns a burden for virtually all Africans living in the malaria belt. Rain-fed agriculture rather than irrigation means that livelihoods are unpredictable, and the remoteness of so many parts of sub-Saharan Africa due to a lack of infrastructure makes it unlikely that they would benefit from export processing zones that could take advantage of low labour costs. Sachs argues that pursuing the UN's Millennium Development Goals is one way to bring countries out of extreme poverty. He calls for all developed countries to commit to giving 0.7 percent of their GDP in foreign aid (a figure that developed countries committed to in 1970), and further argues that it would be in the national security interest of the US to do so, whereas presently that nation gives less per capita than almost any of the other developed countries. This book is optimistic and encouraging as well as being a good read. Sachs presents the economic arguments and figures in a way that will be understandable to most readers. While the author's assessments are based on the familiar assumption that outside intervention is required to rescue Africa from its current plight, Sachs believes that this is needed only to lift African people up to the bottom rung of the ladder, from which point he argues that globalization would begin to benefit them.

996.   Sahlberg, Carl-Erik

From Krapf to Rugambwa: A Church History of Tanzania

Nairobi: Evangel, 1987. 206 pages.

Why another church history book about Tanzania? Simply because you will find in this one many aspects which you will never find in any other church history resource. Johann Ludwig Krapf is certainly the better-known figure, remembered by Christians all over East Africa as the apostle to East Africa, while Laurian Rugambwa made Africans proud for being appointed by Pope John XXIII as the first African cardinal. The author was a Swedish missionary who during the 1980s taught church history at Makumira Lutheran Theological College in Tanzania (now Tumaini University Makumira). There he worked closely together with his international student body to develop this very readable book. Church history is treated in this volume in a very simple yet quite interesting way: some sixteen portraits demonstrate what an important role African evangelists played in the spread of the gospel; helpful, illustrations and photos provide special insights; diaries and personal notes from these missionaries take the reader right back into their time and setting; a good choice of statistical data lets you get the feel for the tremendous growth of Christianity in various stations across Tanzania and Kenya; and at the end of each of the six chapters revision questions assist the teacher in using this as a textbook. The author did an admirable job in describing a broad spectrum of denominational mission work both from the evangelical and Roman Catholic sides while acknowledging the progress of the major German Lutheran missions in a separate chapter. Unfortunately this book by now is showing its age, both in the rather basic layout and print quality, but also in the final chapter "Missio Dei in Tanzania," which gives a very brief look into the future as the author anticipated it more than a quarter century ago. It might be quite rewarding for some scholar at Makumira to rework and republish the book with an up-to-date ending.

997.   Saïdi, Farida

A Study of Current Leadership Styles in the North African Church

Carlisle, UK: Langham Monographs, 2013. 406 pages, ISBN: 9781907713804.

A recognized expert in Islamic issues, the author was born in North Africa, with much of her life and ministry in France spent working with North Africans. She observes that most of those in church leadership roles for the almost 100,000 known Christian believers in North Africa come from Muslim backgrounds. It is not surprising that leadership styles used by religious leaders can be affected by unique historical and cultural backgrounds. Saïdi seeks to identify how North African church leaders see their own leadership roles, and examines the extent to which these perceptions draw on cultural and historical perspectives reflecting both Islam and Christianity. It is her hope that understanding these unique leadership roles and styles within their contexts will better equip church leaders to nurture their congregations. This book is Saïdi's doctoral research at the School for Intercultural Studies at Fuller Theological Seminary in California. It contains a wealth of information on leadership within a culture about which few Christians elsewhere in Africa would know. To some extent her analysis draws on literature produced in (and for) the West, but it also looks closely at the sacred texts of both Islam and Christianity to identify characteristics and styles of leadership within the

North African context. She also examines the leadership qualities and styles of four important individuals, two of whom are Christian and two of whom are Muslim. Saïdi compares the literature and historical surveys with perceptions of leadership given her by respondents from the North African church. She did not want to colour the responses by asking people to choose qualities or leadership styles from lists developed from Western literature and theory. However, allowing respondents to create their own responses produced long lists of words and concepts that needed to be somewhat arbitrarily grouped into clusters for analysis in the light of history, the Koran and the Bible. What one learns from Saïdi's study is that the key leadership models within the North African context are those of a shepherd, a humble servant or a sheik. Family matters. Jesus is the chief Shepherd. Moses, Abraham, David and Paul are admired biblical models. What would have been useful is to have practical recommendations on how training programs could be (re)designed so as to develop biblically-grounded leadership models appropriate for the North African church. This book reads like a doctoral thesis. While most readers may not be interested in wading through the methodological details required by a thesis, Saïdi is in largely pioneer research territory, and publishing this thesis may be the only way for others to become aware of contemporary Christian presence in North Africa, and learn from what she has explored regarding Christian leadership styles in an African Muslim culture.

Sakenfeld, Katharine Doob

see review 126

998.   Salamon, Hagar

The Hyena People: Ethiopian Jews in Christian Ethiopia

Oakland, CA: University of California Press, 1999. 168 pages, ISBN: 9780520219014.

During the Ethiopian famine of 1984, Israel airlifted thousands of Ethiopian Jews (often known as Falashas) to safety in Israel. Salamon became interested in this ancient community while working during that time for the Israeli "Ministry of Absorption." To her astonishment Salamon noticed that "among the tattoos on their bodies" was to be seen "the symbol of the cross." These crosses challenged her ideas of Jewish and Israeli identity. This study examines Ethiopian Judaism in its relationship with the dominant Christian cultural context of Ethiopia, because the Falashas define themselves largely in relation to this Christian society. "The ethnography of Jewish life in Ethiopia *is* the ethnography of the Jews' relations with their Christian neighbours." The emerging picture of Ethiopian Jewish identity is highly ambiguous. On the one hand, the Falashas have been despised and dominated. They could own no land. They were relegated to professions on the periphery of life. The title of the book "Hyena People" comes from the image of the Jew as somehow other than human, on the wrong side of the divide between pure and impure. On the other hand, in their role as blacksmiths and potters their cultural products were essential and even valued. The image of the hyena is also a supernatural notion, some Christians believing that Jews disguised themselves as humans during the day, only to emerge at night in animal form. The ambivalence is expressed in the relationship that both communities have to the biblical texts: Ethiopian Christians and Jews respected each other for their high regard shown to the OT, but Christians worried that these blacksmiths might be descendants of the smiths who forged the nails of the crucifixion, and Jews considered the Ethiopian Christians to be idolaters. Still these communities participated (to a limited extent) in each other's festivals, and Christians would sometimes ask the Jewish clergy to pray for them, or even to offer sacrifice. For Salamon the existence of the Falashas as a "deviant" and racially "other" form of Judaism presents modern Judaism, especially in Israel, with an opportunity to re-think the meaning of "Jewishness." For Christians, Salamon's fascinating study provides an opportunity to reflect on the dangers of demonising those who differ from us, rather than reaching out to them in love – especially in those situations in which Christians find themselves as a majority culture.

999.   **Salisbury, Thayer**

God-Centred Bible Study: An Introduction to Bible Study

Nashville: African Christian Schools Foundation, 2004. 158 pages.

The author has taught at Bible Colleges in Nigeria, Swaziland, Zambia and Ghana. He is a member of the Churches of Christ, and his PhD is from Concordia Theological Seminary. In this useful book he introduces African diploma level Bible College students to the study of the Bible from an evangelical perspective. Section one focuses on the inspiration, text, and canon of the Bible before outlining its basic contents from topical and then chronological points of view. Section two focuses on knowing God through the laws he gives, his saving actions in history, and how he treats his friends, especially Noah, Abraham, Israel, David, and the Church. Section three deals with understanding and applying the Bible, touching on context, comparing translations, genre, word studies, background, cross references, and applying the Bible in Africa. Narratives set in Africa are an important part of how this book teaches, illustrating and reinforcing the lessons in ways that ordinary discourse cannot. As a simple introduction to studying the Bible in Africa, using basic English suitable for diploma level students and below, it is excellent. It does not cover everything a student needs to know, but it achieves its specific purpose with distinction. Institutions offering ministry training at such levels should consider securing a copy for textbook consideration.

1000.   **Salisbury, Thayer**

God's Mission Begins: A Study of the Pentateuch

Nashville: African Christian Schools Foundation, 2002. 139 pages.

This book is designed as an introductory study of the Pentateuch for diploma level African pastoral students. Obviously a 139-page book on the Pentateuch is not a verse-by-verse exposition. The author treats the Pentateuch as the first part of God's mission of salvation. Using selected passages from the Pentateuch, it attempts in sixteen lessons both to explain the major themes of the Pentateuch and to illustrate how this part of the Bible applies to modern African life. The lessons are meant to be studied after the related Bible passages are read. Inserted among the lessons are seven illustrative stories, intended to help African pastoral students think about how the Pentateuch applies in Africa today. The book accomplishes what it sets out to do. Pending availability of an African-authored text that would further contextualize the application of the Pentateuch to Africa for this level, this book would prove a useful classroom text for diploma-level students. The use of English is clear and simple, and the theological outlook is evangelical. A distinctively Churches of Christ outlook comes through in at least two places, on baptism and the Lord's Supper; these occasions will allow for classroom discussion of the ordinances, always an important aspect of teaching in Africa.

1001. **Sandblom, Alice**

La tradition et la Bible chez la femme de la CEZ: Influence de l'ancienne culture et de la pensée biblique dans le maintien d'une certaine conception de la femme au sein de la Communauté évangélique du Zaïre

Potchefstroom, South Africa: Potchefstroom University, 1993. 201 pages, ISBN: 9789155430931.

A former missionary with Svenska Missionforbundet, Sandblom has here made the Communauté Evangélique du Zaïre (now the Communauté Evangélique du Congo) the focal point for her doctoral dissertation. In her study she attempts to show how women are viewed in the context of this evangelical denomination. Specifically, Sandblom wanted to know why women were excluded from certain Christian and social functions during their menstrual periods. Was this physiological phenomenon seen as making them ritually impure and as highlighting an inherent inferiority? Why, she wondered, has this notion, which had disappeared for some years, reinserted itself in the CEZ churches? The reasons for the members' perception of women are sought in their traditional (i.e. pre-independence) culture, their understanding of certain biblical texts, and the "Zairian Authenticity" movement. The work is based almost exclusively on interviews (oral and written). The analysis is sociologically fascinating, explaining impurity interdictions practiced among certain Christian groups, marginal or otherwise, both in Congo (DRC) and elsewhere in Central Africa. Unfortunately, the author's interaction with the Bible is minimal. She gives no satisfying biblical response, preferring simply to describe the parameters of the situation, and merely hinting at her personal view that women are not inferior to men. One may hope that a theologian will now take up the challenge to respond, in a biblically informed manner, to the misconceptions expressed by those Christians interviewed. The specific content of this study may seem of limited value, addressing a situation in only one small part of the continent. But the findings illustrate issues that may arise in African Christian communities elsewhere, and the study can thus serve as an instigation for research that could be appropriately undertaken in other parts of Africa.

Sanders, Todd

see review 728

1002. **Sanneh, Lamin**

Abolitionists Abroad: American Blacks and the Making of Modern West Africa

Cambridge, MA: Harvard University Press, 2001. 320 pages, ISBN: 9780674007185.

It is commonly assumed that in the transatlantic slave trade the Europeans and Americans were the culprits and the Africans the victims. It is also usually assumed that the anti-slavery movement was primarily a European/American movement. But in this revolutionary book Sanneh demonstrates that both blacks and whites were implicated in the slave trade, and also that Africans also played a significant role in the anti-slavery movement. Sanneh shows that during the slave trade, there were two social orders. The old established order was that which supported slavery. Two categories of persons constitute this order: the European and American slave traders and slave holders; and the African chiefs for whom the slave trade was an essential part of their economy. But a new order arose which opposed slavery. This new order was driven largely by evangelical Christian convictions. It was also influenced by the democratic principles of the American Revolution. Significantly, evangelical

Africans played a key role in the anti-slavery movement. The old established order of African chiefs and Euro-American slave defenders opposed this new movement; but in the end it transformed America, Europe and Africa. Sanneh describes how the founding of Sierra Leone was central in this anti-slavery movement, and how the Christianity of the freed slaves in this settlement became a powerful driving force. From Sierra Leone, many mission efforts went out, most notably in the endeavours of Samuel Crowther in Nigeria. This groundbreaking book will upset some dominant secular presuppositions and give a new appreciation of the role that African evangelicals played in the anti-slavery movement.

1003.   Sanneh, Lamin, and Joel A. Carpenter, editors

The Changing Face of Christianity: Africa, the West, and the World

Oxford: Oxford University Press, 2005. 248 pages, ISBN: 9780195177282.

World Christianity in our day provides vast scope for descriptive study. Lamin Sanneh (of Yale Divinity School) and Joel Carpenter (of Calvin College) have here undertaken a collection of papers to further such an inquiry. Half the contributions were initially formulated for conferences on world Christianity held at Calvin College in 2000–2001. The importance of "Africa" in the book's title is obvious in Part 1, which includes essays on aspects of African Christianity such as: "Culture, Christianity, and Witchcraft in a West African Context" (Nigeria); "Shall They Till with Their Own Hoes? Baptists in Zimbabwe and New Patterns of Interdependence, 1950–2000"; and "The Role of Churches in the Peace Process in Africa: The Case of Mozambique Compared." Ghanaian Christianity is discussed in two papers: Paul Gifford's "A View of Ghana's New Christianity," and Kwame Bediako's "Christian Witness in the Public Sphere: Some Lessons and Residual Challenges from the Recent Political History of Ghana'. Bediako critiques Gifford's book *African Christianity: Its Public Role* for Gifford's "failure in perspective" to understand that Christianity in Africa is not just an extension of Western Christendom but thrives in a context of religious pluralism "where the Christendom model of Christianity's relation to society generally is not possible." Part 2 of the collection includes more "reflex impact" essays on the "World" part of the book's title, with emphasis on Asia. A rather long chapter deals with missionary thinking at the International Mission Council held at Tambaram in 1938, where Hendrik Kraemer held a prominent role in the debate regarding continuity and discontinuity between non-Christian religions and Christianity. Wilbert Shenk's chapter argues that contextual theology can only be authentically forged within local contexts, and he uses China as a twentieth century case study. Sanneh concludes the book by noting that the day has come when the Christian culture and thinking of the West may clash with the rest of the world, as is already happening in fact. He further comments that "to understand the changing face of Christianity today, we must forget our modern rationalism, our proud confidence in reason and science, our restless search after wealth and power and after an earthly kingdom." Perhaps all of us, in Africa and in the rest of the majority world, as well as in the West, have much to undo in terms of limited perspective, and much to learn freshly, of the way the face of Christianity is changing both in the majority world and in the West itself.

1004.   Sanneh, Lamin

The Crown and the Turban: Muslims and West African Pluralism

Boulder, CO: Westview Press, 1996. 304 pages, ISBN: 9780813330594.

A citizen of Gambia who converted from Islam to Christianity as a teenager, the author has been Professor of Missions and World Christianity at Yale Divinity School. In this book he builds up to a conclusion in which he advocates the idea that the state in West Africa should be neither secular nor religious. It should not be secular in the sense that the state arrogates to itself complete power and marginalizes religion merely to the private exercise thereof. It should not be religious in that the typical religious state compels its citizens to believe, and such compulsion is inherently corrupting for the nature of faith. Rather it should be a state in which all are conscious that their freedoms are derived from divine authority. In this way the individual is not required to accept any particular religion, but a suitable check on the powers of the state is also maintained. This would enable the co-existence of two substantially different religious blocs. In building up to this position Sanneh surveys the development of Islam in the hospitable pre-Islamic West Africa, and then looks at the encounter between Islam and colonialism. In a fascinating section he contrasts his own childhood in a Qur'anic school with attempts at modernising Islamic education in Freetown. Finally he addresses the relationship between Muslims and the secular national state. In all of this Sanneh shows his usual scholarly competence with a wide range of quotations, including extensive endnotes and bibliography covering English, French and Arabic sources. The book provides clarifying insight into the development of Islam, and into the structure of Islamic societies in West Africa. It also presents an irenic ideal of co-operation between Muslims and Christians – an ideal that in many West African contexts, especially Nigeria, is probably not possible. While Sanneh does refer to some of the Muslim-Christian constitutional conflicts that have dogged Nigeria, most of the book actually draws its inspiration and material from the Islamic communities in the far west of West Africa, in Senegal, Gambia, Guinea and Sierra Leone. One might see this as the book's major weakness, that it does not adequately explain the features and aims of the Nigerian Hausa-Fulani Islamic community – a community that is probably the largest Islamic grouping in West Africa. However, that acknowledged, what Sanneh does say is very valuable. Most informed Christian readers in Africa know to attend to anything Sanneh writes, while most advanced-level theological libraries by now expect to purchase anything Sanneh writes. This title should be no exception.

1005.   Sanneh, Lamin

Disciples of All Nations: Pillars of World Christianity

Oxford: Oxford University Press, 2007. 386 pages, ISBN: 9780195189612.

This book is the first in a new series on world Christianity, published by Oxford University Press and edited by Sanneh, the Gambian theologian and widely-read scholar of religion who serves as Professor of Missions and World Christianity at Yale Divinity School. In a prologue to the series, Sanneh points out how the church has moved from the north to the south, and argues that we are at present in the middle of massive shifts and realignments whose implications are only now beginning to become clear. This is the context of the new series, and this first book of the series provides a theological and historical introduction to this new context. The book has a loosely chronological structure, stretching from the apostles up to post-Mao China. It is not, however, another general history of the church. Instead the book offers some glimpses into the history of the church, glimpses from the perspective of *universality* as a major theological and historical characteristic of

Christianity. Sanneh first covers examples of the expansion of Christianity in the first millennium: in the Roman Empire, Arabia, India, England, and even up to Iceland. As in other of Sanneh's writings, the translatability of the faith into new languages and cultures is emphasized as a major resource for this expansive capacity. Next he discusses the interface between Christianity and Islam from the seventh to the sixteenth centuries. He argues that one reason for Islam's success in Arabia was the lack of an indigenous Arab church. The "great discoveries" of America and Africa allow for attention to the slave trade and the antislavery debate, followed by consideration of Christian mission under colonialism, up to post-WW II struggles for independence. After outlining some aspects of charismatic renewal movements, in particular in Africa, Sanneh analyses some West African prophetic figures and the cultural challenges they took up, and several Western missionary figures who contributed to the discussion of Western culture vis-à-vis African Christianity. China's encounter with Christianity also receives special consideration. Finally, Sanneh draws some statistical, strategic and theological conclusions, arguing that "Despite their role as allies of the empire, missions also developed the vernacular that inspired sentiments of national identity and thus undercut Christianity's identification with colonial rule." Sanneh's book offers a splendid discussion of the concept of the church as a universal entity. As expected in a book by Sanneh, African historical and theological experiences are highlighted, and the concept of translatability – both of the Bible and of the Christian message as a whole – is used as an interpretative entry to the historical and theological material. This focus makes the book an exciting reading experience, and it deserves a wide readership, by disciples of all nations.

1006.   Sanneh, Lamin

Encountering the West: Christianity and the Global Cultural Process

Maryknoll, NY: Orbis, 1993. 225 pages, ISBN: 9780883449295.

Sanneh is no stranger to the student of Christianity in Africa. His books have gained widespread attention, as have his numerous articles. A Gambian-born convert from Islam to Christianity, Sanneh previously taught at Harvard in the United States and more recently at Yale. In these essays the author reiterates his previously published thesis that the translation of the Bible into African languages strengthened those cultures, enabling them to resist and critique Western political and cultural imperialism. The fact that Bible translation enabled Christianity to be authentically expressed within the cultural idiom of the receptor people demonstrates that Christianity is not bound to Western culture. In this study Sanneh goes on to critique regnant Western understandings of culture, the relationship of religion and culture, and the moral and cultural relativism that undergird the typical critique of the missionary enterprise. In doing so, the author traverses ground far and wide. The breadth of Sanneh's research, the fact that he is one of those rare individuals at home in multiple cultural and religious settings, and the operation of a penetrating mind that draws all of this together, make this a book that will repay careful attention.

1007.   Sanneh, Lamin

Piety and Power: Muslims and Christians in West Africa

Eugene, OR: Wipf & Stock, 2015. 224 pages, ISBN: 9781498220453.

In this work Sanneh seeks to point a way forward for Muslim-Christian relations in Africa. After chapters which explore methodological and historical issues, he considers the question of religion and politics – perhaps the most public area of disagreement between Islam and Christianity in the modern world. Using examples from the African context throughout, Sanneh examines Islamic understandings of the integration of religion and politics, but also considers the inadequacy of the nation state to serve as an absolute moral arbiter of human relations. Religion may often get subsumed under nationalism, as the state seeks to exercise total authority, or religion may retreat into pietistic quietism. But Sanneh believes that religion in its critique of human nature has an essential public role to play in society. The modern Western ideal of the separation of church and state allows secularism and pluralism to thrive, whereas they are retarded when church and state are fused. Muslims have pushed relentlessly for religion to have a political role. Sanneh argues that the privatized notion of religion so common in the West blunts the ability to understand and handle this Islamic political agenda. He argues that religious freedom can really only be achieved through persuasion and personal conviction. This entails allowing religion a public role, in contrast to secularism's tendency to privatize it, but disallowing religion any theocratic status, which quickly leads to oppression and corruption. By providing the moral foundation for society to develop a true pluralism, theocentrism can become the basis for democratic liberalism in Africa – and thus also for effective interfaith relations. As with any of Sanneh's works, this one is full of copious footnotes and ample bibliographies. One may wonder if Sanneh's ideal of Islam is unduly influenced by the pacifist tradition of the Jakhanke clerics of Senegambia. In a more militant context, such as Nigeria, readers might justifiably remain somewhat unconvinced by Sanneh's arguments, albeit challenged by them. This characteristically probing study opens up fresh perspectives for any serious reflection on Muslim-Christian relations in Africa.

1008.   Sanneh, Lamin

Religion and the Variety of Culture: A Study in Origin and Practice

Valley Forge, PA: Trinity Press International, 1996. 96 pages, ISBN: 9781563381669.

This little book is one in a series entitled "Christian Mission and Modern Culture." Sanneh's contribution is a revised and expanded version of chapter one in his book *Encountering the West*. Sanneh gives a brief history of concepts of culture in the West, and critiques how the concepts of cultural relativism and physical/psychological determinism have been used to deny the validity of religion. Although cultural relativism has been seen as a remedy for cultural imperialism, because it recognizes no outside moral standard, it ends up accepting all manifestations of culture, including ethnocentrism and racism. Until cultures recognize responsibility to God and His standards of truth and right, and are willing to change parts of their culture that do not conform to this, we will continue to have the evils of ethnocentrism and oppressive sacralised nationalism. Although not specifically about Africa, these perceptive thoughts by a distinguished African academic do much to put the discussion on culture, nationalism and tribalism into a useful perspective.

1009.   Sanneh, Lamin

Summoned from the Margin: Homecoming of an African

Grand Rapids: Eerdmans, 2012. 299 pages, ISBN: 9780802867421.

Sanneh begins his memoir with a brief account of a visit in 2008 to the village of Georgetown on an island in the River Gambia in West Africa. This is where he was raised within an impoverished polygamous Muslim African family in a community wholly circumscribed by Islam. The beginning of the book creates the suspicion that the "homecoming" in the subtitle alludes to this return journey to Georgetown. But, in fact, the homecoming refers to his reception into the Roman Catholic Church some decades after his unlikely conversion from Islam to Christianity while still a young man in Gambia in 1961. Though the book opens selected windows onto Sanneh's life, there is a sense in which Sanneh's memoir is less personal than it is personal intellectual history. Those familiar with Sanneh's writings will profit from seeing the way in which the ideas for which he has become justly well known in his professional life emerge out of the extraordinary trajectory of his personal life. Those new to Sanneh will value the summaries of the major strands of his thought which have helped establish him as a major intellectual force in the study both of Islam and of what he prefers to call "world" (as opposed to "global") Christianity. Sanneh's early academic focus on Islam, together with his early life in Islam, helped make possible his later insights into the nature of world Christianity, Christian expansion and mission. Thus, for instance, did Sanneh intuitively resist the still common belief that Christian expansion in Africa advanced within conditions made conducive by colonialism. Instead, in contrast to the Islam of his early years, Sanneh was struck by Christianity's inherent embrace of the vernacular, and made this the explanation for Christian expansion. Thus did he then come to vest the significance of the Western missionary movement primarily in vernacular Bible translation. This insight also helped him see how, in contrast to the often destructive impact of Islamic expansion on local cultures, the rooting of Christian faith in vernacular languages has served the cause of cultural renewal. Students of comparative religion are not generally disposed to speak of false religion or false teachers, and Sanneh is no different. Alongside the ambivalence he often experienced from the Church, perhaps that scholarly disposition helps explain those seasons of his life in which he was more an observer than a participant in the Church. And perhaps these things, too, explain why there is very little indication that proclamation and persuasion play much of a role in his own sense of mission. But when he speaks, as he does in this book, of his own profound experience in leaving the religion of his birth to follow the resurrected Jesus, he is at times a powerful witness to the truth.

1010.   **Sanneh, Lamin**

Translating the Message: The Missionary Impact on Culture

Maryknoll, NY: Orbis, 2009. 288 pages, ISBN: 9781570758041.

True or false: Western missionaries were the conscious agents of imperial colonialism, and greatly retarded the development of the Christian church in Africa? False – at least according to this broadly argued book by Sanneh, the distinguished African scholar and professor of Missions and World Christianity at Yale Divinity School (USA). He traces the culture-specific contextualization of the gospel message (often included under the term "translation") from the apostolic age through its monolithic "Hellenistic phase," and its subsequent "break-out" into a succession of regionalized vernacular manifestations right up to the present day. Special attention is given to the growth of Christianity in West Africa, the author's specialty. Sanneh argues that missionaries, both Protestant and Catholic, have recognized by and large the urgent need to communicate with people in natural thought forms and via their mother tongue, particularly in relation to the Scriptures. They therefore relied upon translation and related activities (e.g. dictionary-making, anthropological studies, literacy) in order to convey God's message in the most effective way possible. This process of translation, whether done well or poorly, generally acted to set various indigenizing forces in motion which the missionaries themselves had not envisioned (much less desired) and which they often could not stifle or control, e.g. the development of ethnic pride and self-confidence, the move towards local leadership, a more independent, self-reliant attitude, and a broader, more nationalistic vision of the future. Sanneh concludes his study with an interesting and insightful comparison involving the policy of Bible translation in Christian missions in contrast to the practice of Islam with regard to its Koran. One problem with respect to Sanneh's view of mission "translation" is what appears to be an overly tolerant attitude towards virtually any type of local contextualization, including syncretism. However, his thesis is refreshingly different from what is normal in most contemporary studies of mission history and strategy. Thought-leaders in the African Christian community certainly need to be familiar with this classic.

1011. Sanneh, Lamin

Whose Religion Is Christianity?: The Gospel beyond the West

Grand Rapids: Eerdmans, 2003. 150 pages, ISBN: 9780802821645.

This slender volume examines the impact of the gospel in the non-Western world. The context here relates to the opposing trends of rapid decline for Christianity in the West, accompanied by its explosive growth in non-Western lands. The result, Sanneh contends, is "post-Western Christianity," involving the migration of the faith to a new context. Such a development generates profound transformations in how Christian faith becomes expressed, changes comparable to the Hellenization of the gospel in the early church. Sanneh emphasizes that this movement has not so much resulted from Western efforts (though he by no means discounts such labours), but by local response to and appropriation of the gospel in indigenous languages. For example, the remarkable growth of the church in Africa has largely taken place in the post-colonial era, after the heyday of the modern missionary movement. Two key concepts frame Sanneh's argument. On the one hand, "Global Christianity," refers to "the faithful replication of Christian forms and patterns developed in Europe." "World Christianity," on the other hand, speaks of "the movement of Christianity as it takes form and shape in societies that previously were not Christian," incorporating "a variety of indigenous responses through more or less effective local idioms." The bulk of the book explores the relationship of these new embodiments of the faith, their relationship to Western expressions of Christianity, and their relationship to contemporary social, economic, and political developments. This is carried out by a question and answer format, in which Sanneh engages an imaginary Western interlocutor regarding the nature and implications of Sanneh's argument. This approach allows Sanneh to discuss not only information and sources, but to grapple with attitudes as well. The result is an informative, engaging analysis of the momentous developments in Christian history over the last century. Readers should know that the bulk of Sanneh's observations regarding non-Western Christianity relate to Africa in particular, with immediate implications for assessing the significance, role and future of African Christianity. This is a book that warrants wide reading and careful reflection at senior levels of Christian leadership across the continent. It should especially be on the reading list of any theological educator who takes contextual awareness seriously. And of course, as with the entire Sanneh corpus, it merits inclusion in theological libraries throughout Africa.

1012. Sarah, Robert

Church Leaders and Christian Life in the Pastoral Letters

Nairobi: Paulines, 2001. 128 pages, ISBN: 9789966213730.

Archbishop Robert Sarah, who has had a distinguished career in the hierarchy of the Roman Catholic Church (Archbishop of Conakry, President of the Episcopal Conference of Bishops of Guinea, Secretary of the

Congregation for the Evangelization of Peoples) has produced a delightful study of Paul's *Pastoral Epistles*. The vast majority of published African exegetical work consists either of doctoral theses which are often extremely technical, or journal articles which tend to be brief and lean towards providing biblical insight into contextual issues. Sarah attempts to thread the needle between writing a scholarly study on the one hand, and exhorting the faithful on the other. He is a scholar who is also a pastor. He rightly speaks of the necessity of inculturation but also wisely warns that "every inculturation demands discernment, for it inevitably entails not only ambiguities but also the risk of mutilating the content of the revelation in order to make Christian doctrine more attractive by giving in to some demands of local culture." On the other hand, the book does not spend very much time discussing African issues. His concern is to discuss Paul's letters (and he is conservative enough to believe that Paul was the author of the Pastorals), with an eye to how they help Christian leaders to exercise their ministry. As such, his main audience is probably an educated Catholic priesthood (most lay people may not find useful the semi-technical footnotes to scholarly works in English, French and German, and the longish quotations from the church Fathers). Although Sarah's book does have some of the apparatus of a scholarly work, it is really devotional or spiritual in focus, and thus tends to use the biblical text as a springboard to speak of spiritual issues, rather than producing an exegetical or expositional study of the text itself.

1013.   Sauer, Christof

Reaching the Unreached Sudan Belt: Guinness, Kumm and the Sudan-Pioneer-Mission

Nürnberg, Germany: VTR, 2005. 454 pages, ISBN: 9783937965383.

The commendatory foreword by Professor Andrew Walls signals a book worthy of special notice. The "Sudan Belt" of the title is the area immediately south of the Sahara between Senegal and Ethiopia. In the late nineteenth century it had yet to be effectively penetrated by Christian missions. This is the story of one person who pioneered in that task. Karl Kumm (1874–1930) is best known as founder of the Sudan United Mission (SUM), which eventually established major work in Nigeria, as well as Cameroon, Chad, and Sudan (see BookNotes 03.38). But Sauer in this book sets out to explore a much less known story, namely that of Kumm before the founding of SUM. Of German nationality, Kumm began his missionary career in Egypt. There he met and married Lucy Guinness, of the wealthy Guinness family of distillery and missions fame in Britain. Feeling called to the unreached "Sudan belt," the couple organized the Sudan Pioneer Mission (SPM) in 1901, under the auspices of a board based largely in Germany. But misunderstandings and tensions quickly evolved between Kumm and the oversight body, mainly about how to reach the Muslim cultures of that day, resulting in Kumm's dismissal from SPM less than two years after its founding. (Kumm's critics said he was the "wrong person, pursuing the wrong goals, at the wrong time, with the wrong methods, in the wrong field, and from the wrong home base"!). The couple then founded the SUM in 1904, this time based mainly in Britain, where Kumm's father-in-law, Grattan Guinness, was a major figure in British missions. Sauer takes a missiological, not historical, approach, so he includes a helpful analysis of SPM and the reasons for Kumm's dismissal, which he believes can mainly be attributed to the tension over whether missionary direction should be "field-based" or "home-based." He also evaluates the main methods that SPM used in its attempt to reach what is now the Sahel region: Bible translation, schools, evangelism and colportage. A valuable side-benefit of Sauer's work is the details presented about the colportage ministry of Samuel Ali Hiseen (1863–1927), who may have been the first Nubian Christian to emerge since the collapse of Nubian Christianity in late medieval times. Although there is too much detail for the average reader (footnotes often fill more than half a page, and the appendices, bibliography and index take up 125 pages), the book will prove an excellent resource for scholars.

Sauer, Christof

see also review 76

1014. Sawyerr, Harry

The Practice of Presence: Shorter Writings of Harry Sawyerr

Grand Rapids: Eerdmans, 1959. 165 pages, ISBN: 9780802841155.

Harry Sawyerr was Canon of the Anglican Cathedral of the Sierra Leone Church as well as professor of theology and principal of Fourah Bay College, University of Sierra Leone. He belongs, along with Idowu, Mbiti, and others, to the earliest generation of modern African theological scholarship in the post-colonial era. As the subtitle indicates, *Practice of Presence* is a collection of Sawyerr's shorter writings. One of the nine articles, "Psyche in Conflict," appears here in print for the first time. Two articles, "Ancestor Worship" and "What is African Theology?" are seminal. They also represent the double foci of the collection and of Sawyerr's life-long interests, namely, African traditional religions and African Christian theology. Sawyerr is seen to be a penetrating thinker who sought critical understanding and engagement of the socio-religious context for African theological reflection. The discussion has moved on, and in that respect the book is dated. Still it offers invaluable insights for understanding significant currents and figures in that early generation of African theological formulation.

1015. Schaaf, Ype

On Their Way Rejoicing: The History and Role of the Bible in Africa

Oxford: Regnum, 2003. 252 pages, ISBN: 9781870345330.

This well-written text forms a useful, Africa-specific complement to Lamin Sanneh's important survey, *Translating the Message*. Schaaf's stated aim is to "describe how the Bible came to Africa, how it was translated and distributed, and how its message came to influence culture, politics, religion, education, and African society as a whole." Schaaf's broad experience as a former staff member of the Bible Societies (Cameroon and Gabon), his widespread travel on the continent (26 countries), and his extensive journalistic experience leaves a positive impression. The many short chapters, crisply and succinctly written, move the reader effortlessly along from one interesting topic to the next. The first part of the book (chapters 1–26) covers the 2000-year history of the use of the Scriptures in Africa, and its religious significance to the various peoples and churches concerned. The second part (chapters 27–38) is arranged topically to address such diverse issues as the Bible in relation to: literacy, colonialism, slavery, European influence, indigenization, and the contextualization of the message. Naturally in a survey of this type not a great deal of detail can be given, but Schaaf does provide a good overview of the main facts, coupled with many short human-interest accounts and insightful personal observations, which make for enjoyable reading. He recognizes his own Western perspective, and rightly sets forth this challenge for a follow-up to his work: "It goes without saying that it is for Africans themselves to write the history of the Bible in their continent." Kwame Bediako provides an epilogue on the larger theological significance of the translation of the Bible into African languages.

1016. Schalm, Gottfried

God's Pathways in Africa: Adventures of a Pioneering Family

Calgary: Gottfried Schalm, 2005. 146 pages, ISBN: 9780779501069.

It would seem that every missionary has a story to tell – many, in fact. And if they are of Africa they often seem to include stories of snakes, demon possession, primitive living conditions, tropical diseases, adverse travel conditions, perhaps romance and marriage, experiences on leave in the homeland and, of course, preaching the gospel and establishing churches, schools, and clinics. Schalm's narrative, of missionary work in north-central Nigeria, is no exception. Without discounting the potential value of such stores, those most interested in books of this genre are family, friends, and perhaps financial supporters. What sets Schalm's book apart is his keen grasp of cultural issues despite not being trained in anthropology, and the fact that his entire ministry was conducted within the parameters of a notably appreciative understanding of the host culture. It is one thing to know, another to do. Schalm both knew and did. The most valuable parts of this book are not the stories but those sections in which Schalm describes and analyses the culture of the ethnic groups among whom he and his wife worked. Some of those paragraphs border on the elegant. The rest of the book is just average. On the other hand, the man himself was hardly average. A German born of Christian parents in Poland, he was a member of the Hitler Youth movement and later joined the elite SS branch of the German Army. It was as a prisoner of war that he began reading the NT and embraced Christ. He writes: "I met God and realized that He had spared my life to live for Him and for others. It was the beginning of a journey with Christ, which eventually would lead me to Africa in His service." Schalm's culturally sensitive labour lasted for 25 years, and left notable outcome in believers, churches, clinics and educational institutions. When he later returned to his place of service in Nigeria, the local people honoured him by making him a chief.

1017. Schamp, Eike W., and Stefan Schmid, editors

Academic Cooperation with Africa: Lessons for Partnership in Higher Education

Münster: LIT Verlag, 2008. 256 pages, ISBN: 9783825813772.

This book's title is intriguing. It focuses on cooperation "with Africa" in the field of higher education, but Africa's counterpart in this cooperation is not identified. The editors – both teaching at Goethe University, Frankfurt am Main, Germany – seem to take for granted that potential readers intuitively will identify this counterpart as European or Western academia. And so it is. This is an essay collection presenting and discussing various experiences and challenges in the growing interaction between European (in this case, Germany, the Netherlands, France) and African (in this case, Nigeria, Benin, Guinea Bissau, Burkina Faso) academia. The editors open the essay collection with a brief but clear-cut presentation of the context of the book. Establishing universities in Africa is in most cases (numerically speaking) a postcolonial enterprise, and the institutions have mainly been modelled on "global" – that is Western – university traditions. Still, there are some major differences; one is less focus on research, another is a severe lack of funding. With these differences in mind, the question is how universities in Europe (now characterized by the Bologna process) and universities in Africa (where some countries attempt to apply the Bologna principles) can develop sustainable patterns for cooperation. Following the introductory essay are ten case studies, grouped into three parts. Part 1 discusses the social and cultural environmental conditions for academic cooperation between Africa and Europe (the impact of the traditional African knowledge systems and culture on contemporary educational achievements; a bibliometric assessment of patterns and trends in the African research landscape; patterns of academic communication at African universities, with bilingual Cameroon as a case). Part 2 discusses science at African universities and the role of international cooperation, i.e. from an organisational perspective (the African Studies Centre in Leiden as a case illustrating changing partnerships in African studies; some experiences of academic cooperation between Germany and Africa; the university and research landscape in lusophone Guinea Bissau). Part 3 discusses cooperation between academics, i.e. from an individual perspective (contemporary German research on Africa from an African perspective; research cooperation between Germany and Africa from the perspectives of partnership, patronage, and paternalism; museums in Africa as institutions for transfer of knowledge, with the Regional Museum of Northern Togo as a case; some "personal" reflection on research cooperation between two universities in Germany and Burkina Faso). The topics that are focused in this book seem relevant and illustrative for academic cooperation, generally speaking, between Europe and Africa. Also scholars in the fields of theology and religious studies will recognize many of the experiences and challenges that are highlighted, and they should be encouraged to reflect on the concerns of the book from their particular scholarly perspectives.

1018. Schineller, Peter

A Handbook on Inculturation

Mahweh, NJ: Paulist Press, 1990. 141 pages, ISBN: 9780809131242.

The author is an American Roman Catholic priest who served in West Africa as Superior for the Nigeria-Ghana Jesuit Mission. In this *Handbook* he shares his "search for ways in which the good news can be more deeply lived, celebrated and shared." In this basic, introductory-level textbook Schineller first traces the history of Christian inculturation, and then updates readers on the debate about contextualisation. Writing firmly within the Roman Catholic tradition, yet not afraid to be critical of that tradition, he traces the changes which have affected the Catholic community since Vatican II. These have included, not least, the use of vernacular languages in worship, followed by the questioning of the traditional adaptation method. Schineller uses Nigeria as a case study in a major chapter entitled "Toward Inculturation in Nigeria." However, he does not get down to many concrete issues, and thus the task of inculturation is still before the reader.

Schmid, Stefan

see review 1017

Schmidt, Heike

see review 271

1019. Schneider, Theo

The Sharpening of Wisdom: Old Testament Proverbs in Translation

Pretoria: Old Testament Society of South Africa, 1992. 260 pages, ISBN: 9780869817841.

A native of Switzerland, Schneider was a missionary for many years among the Tsonga people of southern Mozambique and northern Transvaal. The focus of his ministry was the Tsonga Bible translation project, which he directed as its Coordinator for over twenty years (completed 1989). This book stems from his doctoral dissertation, submitted to the Faculty of Theology at UNISA. It sets out in theoretical terms the philosophy of translation which he put into practice as a Bible translator for many years. It is based on solid experience and therefore worth careful attention. Schneider's principal aim is to promote a more "dynamic" translation of the book of Proverbs into the various languages of the world, a "functionally equivalent" rendering that effectively reproduces the "sharpness" of form and content that characterizes the original text. The first part of the book is primarily theoretical, as the author discusses some of the main textual, exegetical, literary and translational principles, tools, and approaches that modern translators of the biblical proverbs must consider. In part two Schneider applies his chosen methodology to a number of translation "case studies," with special reference to an African (Bantu) language and setting, coupled with the aim of achieving a vivid literary style that is designed to reproduce the rhetorical effect of Hebrew compactness and parallelism (in particular) as well as various other important poetic features, including also the sound (oral/aural) quality of the text. Schneider's first-rate scholarly study is not for the average reader, but anyone engaged at an advanced level in Bible translation or related work could certainly profit from this monograph.

1020.   Schoffeleers, Matthew

In Search of Truth and Justice: Confrontations between Church and State in Malawi 1960–1994

Blantyre: CLAIM, 2000. 388 pages, ISBN: 9789990816198.

Schoffeleers was formerly a missionary priest in Malawi and a lecturer in anthropology at the University of Malawi. Subsequently he has been professor of religious anthropology at the Free University of Amsterdam and the University of Utrecht. This book is a moving testimony of those who campaigned for freedom from fear in Malawi; who heightened international awareness of human rights abuses and the lack of freedom of speech; and who were detained, deported, imprisoned or exiled for challenging Banda's one party state. This diary of a Church discovering its mandate, and struggling to live it out, provides a chronicle of Africa speaking truth to power and of democracy hard earned. In telling this fascinating story from the 1960s until the emergence of the Public Affairs Committee and national elections in the 1990s, the author reveals the prophetic presence that has always existed hidden inside and outside the Malawian Church. Schoffeleers begins with the first major conflict between the Catholic Church and the Malawi Congress Party (MCP) of Kamuzu Banda in October 1960. The urge to speed up independence during 1961 and 1963 was accompanied by warning voices from the Christian Democratic Party (CDP) and its successor, the Christian Liberation Party (CLP), that things were getting out of control. In light of the growing unease and embarrassing silence of the churches after independence in 1964, the question is posed whether there was no one to protest against the increasing oppression. Schoffeleers shows that there were some courageous churchmen who gave witness within the narrow margins then available. While there was pressure on the churches from both without and within, there was little response as yet, due to the relative lack of interest in socio-political problems, combined with a lack of information and an all-pervasive climate of fear. Matters took a decisive change with the 1992 Lenten Pastoral Letter from Malawi's Roman Catholic bishops, which was followed by the inordinate reaction of the MCP government, and the intervention of the World Alliance of Reformed Churches. The subsequent formation of the Public Affairs Committee initiated by the local Presbyterian Church and embracing Catholics, Protestants and Muslims, played an important role in translating the bishops' letter into political action. A referendum on multiparty democracy then occurred in 1993, and events thereafter led to the General elections of 1994. These pages contain many eyewitness accounts, reports, statements, and letters, with the action vividly presented. The reader may be startled and shocked by some of the reports. This book deserves a wide reading by those concerned about the prophetic responsibility of the church in Africa.

1021. Schoffeleers, Matthew

Religion and the Dramatisation of Life: Spirit Beliefs and Rituals in Southern and Central Malawi

Oxford: Africa Books Collective, 2000. 168 pages, ISBN: 9789990816075.

The author is a long-serving Montfortian missionary priest, a former lecturer in social anthropology at the University of Malawi, and a renowned researcher in the traditional religion(s) of central Africa. The six essays contained in this book, written between 1967 and 1977, provide significant and detailed background information on several important facets of traditional religious belief and practice in Malawi. Schoffeleers first deals with the ancestral rain cults, which for centuries have played a central role in the religious and local political life of Malawi. He then treats the manifestation of territorial spirit mediumship, and the personal cults of spirit "affliction." These fascinating essays are preceded by an introduction in which the author helpfully sets them within a broader historical and socio-cultural context. Although "Christianity" has established itself as the predominant religion of this part of Africa, the great influence and impact of the indigenous religious heritage continues to be felt in all aspects of life. This monograph enables one to better understand one major area of such influence, namely that of the ancestral spirits. Though rather technical in places, the book is interesting and well written.

Schoffeleers, Matthew

see also review 963

1022. Schofield, Rodney

Mystery or Magic: Biblical Replies to the Heterodox

Blantyre: CLAIM, 2004. 136 pages, ISBN: 9789990816600.

Schofield was an Anglican missionary priest in Malawi, and Director of Research at the ecumenical Zomba Theological College. This book is a response to the high level of belief in witchcraft among African Christians. After a summary of witchcraft beliefs and Christian response through the history of Europe and America, and among Christians in South Africa and Malawi, the book surveys the OT and NT (including the Apocrypha) for what they have to say about divination, prophetic inspiration, dreams and visions, curses, the causes of sickness and suffering, beliefs about death and spiritual powers, and the place of ritual in combating these. The author highlights the NT theme of deliverance from evil in Christ. He doubts the personal nature of Satan and demons, preferring to talk of evil influences and psychological causes, but he agrees that some accommodation can be made to local beliefs (such as in the world of Jesus). Nevertheless, he condemns attempts at communicating with ancestors as necromancy, and the use of Christian rituals like baptism for spiritual "protection." He feels that the search for prosperity and protection is misguided for Christians, that they should instead be seeking personal transformation in Christ. This book's focus and intentions are worthy, but its conclusions may not prove entirely persuasive for African Christians in felt need of spiritual protection.

1023.   Schreiter, Robert J., editor

Faces of Jesus in Africa

Maryknoll, NY: Orbis, 1991. 200 pages, ISBN: 9780883447680.

Of the eleven essays that compose this volume, six come from the 1989 publication *Jesus Christ in African Christianity* (edited by Jesse Mugambi and Laurenti Magesa), and five others have been translated from the 1986 publication *Chemins de la christologie africaine* (edited by François Kabasele-Lumbala, *et al.*). The general orientation is Catholic, though at least one Protestant essayist is included, as is one woman. All the writers are resident in Africa. Unfortunately, all of the anglophone authors are located in Nairobi. The editor, from the Catholic Theological Union in Chicago, USA, has penned a helpful introduction to the collection. But his rather artificial division of the book ("Surveying African Christologies" and "Faces of Jesus in Africa") is not very useful. In theory, the first part has essays that deal with the nature of Christological thinking in Africa, and the second part has essays that deal with models through which the modern African can better understand Jesus. The essays themselves, however, refuse to remain in any one category. This work contributes interesting ideas to the discussion of Christology in an African context, but the essays are not all of equal importance, or quality or length (from 5 to 28 pages). Each essay is, however, undergirded by endnotes, some of which are good leads to other literature. As a survey of some Christological thinking in Africa in the 1980s, this compilation of essays can be useful. It can also be useful in giving English-only readers access to literature on the topic emanating from francophone Africa.

1024.   Schwab, Peter

Africa: A Continent Self-Destructs

London: Palgrave Macmillan, 2003. 224 pages, ISBN: 9781403960535.

Depressingly accurate, this book looks at the situation of sub-Saharan Africa from five perspectives: outside factors (foreign influences in African history); inside factors (wars and politics); human rights; poverty and HIV/AIDS; and globalisation. The sixth and final chapter then comments on what the future may hold for the continent. The author, a professor of political science in the State University of New York (SUNY) in North America, has spent some years previously in Africa, principally in Liberia and Ethiopia, and is primarily known for his writings in the area of human rights. Along those lines, he points out in this book that the Western view of human rights (as embodied in the UN Declaration) tends to be individual and political, whereas the African understanding runs more along collective and economic lines. Though the book is relatively brief, its scope is broad, covering both large and small nations as well as sub-Saharan Africa's major international language groups: English, French, and Portuguese. Very little about this volume is encouraging; indeed, the title sets the stage for what Schwab attempts to show. Those positive feelings generated at the time of independence, when the "giants" (such as Nkrumah, Kenyatta, and Senghor) took power, have been largely forced into feelings of despair in many quarters. Botswana is cited as a positive example, with a growing economy. South Africa, too, at time of writing had some positive aspects. But almost all other factors and statistics presented – whether dealing with the economy, health issues, human rights, or political stability – are on the negative side of the ledger for Schwab. (Schwab takes no notice whatsoever of at least one positive factor widespread throughout the continent, the growth of Christianity in Africa.) As for the future, the author expresses no optimism. Since the largest democracy and economic power in the world, the United States, has elected to maintain only negligible contact with the continent, Africa (according to Schwab) has little hope of better days to come. Indeed, it will simply continue to self-destruct. This book, while rather disturbing at times, presents what in Africa might be judged a generally realistic view in the areas examined, and does so with an evident sensitivity and concern for the continent. Readers in Africa, knowing all too well these painful scenarios from the inside, may therefore not have a great need for this book.

1025. Schwartz, Glenn J.

When Charity Destroys Dignity: Overcoming Unhealthy Dependency in the Christian Movement

Bloomington, IN: AuthorHouse, 2007. 412 pages, ISBN: 9781425993917.

This book attempts to address the unhealthy dependence that churches in majority world countries can develop towards outside funding and direction. The author's focus is largely on Africa, since his own missionary service was done in southern Africa, and the churches with whom he presently works are mostly in Africa. Schwartz's biographical prologue, in which he candidly describes his struggles with mission administration over issues of dependency, will help readers understand the evident slant in the book's analyses – including what may to some seem unexpectedly like an anti-missionary stance. Schwartz believes that the dependency that holds churches back from God's empowerment for ministry develops from a defective conversion, one that does not produce the gratitude to God that should result in healthy local giving. The causes of church dependency in Africa are identified as the disempowerment of the colonial experience and especially apartheid, combined with the paternalistic desire for control on the part of mission administrators. Conspicuously missing, however, is any reflection on how indigenous African cultures may also encourage dependency patterns. Both Africans who have experienced rural life, where dependence on the extended family and on the chief is required, and those who have read ethnographic studies of African culture, may feel that the assessment lacks essential balance in this respect. Also, while acknowledging that Christians in wealthy nations should help less resourced brothers and sisters in developing countries, Schwartz gives little direction for healthy forms of outside aid. Christian communities mired in dependency on outside funding, and the careless giving that can enable this, do indeed deserve attention. But this may not be the best place to seek an effective, judicious treatment of the issues involved and appropriate modes for resolution.

1026. Schwartz, Leslie

Culture and Mental Health: A Southern African View

Cape Town: Oxford University Press, 1998. 336 pages, ISBN: 9780195709810.

This is a thought-provoking volume of case studies and international research, written primarily for health workers and mental health professionals. Schwartz was professor of psychology at the University of Cape Town and has written extensively on cross-cultural issues in mental health diagnosis and treatment. One may rightly wonder what relevance this book has for informed Christian reflection in Africa. Yet who could question that pastors in Africa need to be equipped to understand and to provide effective counsel across a range of needs, including mental health needs. The book is not written from a Christian perspective, yet those in Christian ministry on the continent, as well as African Christian professionals in the field of mental health, will find much that is thought-provoking and relevant: psychiatry as a Western construction with its compartmentalization of mind and body, health and welfare; the interplay between Western biomedicine and traditional healing practices; what happens when counselling takes place through an interpreter; issues of power and powerlessness; issues of racism, justice and reconciliation (writing from South Africa, Schwartz discusses several times the mental health implications of the Truth and Reconciliation Commission); the interplay between mind and body in proneness or resistance to disease; escape from stressors through alcohol and drugs; post-traumatic stress disorder vs. living in a constant state of extreme stress in the ongoing struggle to survive; the myth of mental health work as dispassionate and value free. Schwartz makes this observation: "The job of a [health] professional is to alleviate suffering wherever it exists. My dilemma, though, demonstrated that mental health work is also about reproduction of a particular moral order." Can a clinician remain morally neutral? And can our Christian mandate to care for the whole person in the context of a church community ignore issues of justice and compassion in responding to the needs of those in Africa struggling in varying degrees with mental illness?

1027.   Scott Theological College

Africa Journal of Evangelical Theology, 1982–2002

Machakos, Kenya: Scott Theological College, 2004.

Offered here is one of those extraordinary resources now made possible for Africa by the information technology revolution – here on a single CD is the entire corpus of articles and reviews of the *Africa Journal of Evangelical Theology* (AJET) for its first twenty-one years of publication. AJET has long been African evangelicalism's premier publication of intellectual inquiry. And unlike so many journal ventures on the continent, this one has endured; indeed, it is now into its fourth decade of publication. This CD presents AJET's first 41 issues in PDF format. Since electronic copy did not exist for the majority of the earlier AJET volumes, all files have been created from direct scans of the AJET printed material. Easily searchable indices of authors, topics, and book reviews are also provided. Altogether this enormous compendium of material contains 174 AJET articles, contributed by many of the most familiar names of modern African evangelical thought, including: Tokunboh Adeyemo, Victor Cole, Scott Cunningham, Bulus Galadima, Richard Gehman, Osadolor Imasogie, David Kasali, Jacob Kibor, Titus Kivunzi, Samuel Kunhiyop, Yemi Ladipo, Scott Moreau, Samuel Ngewa, Paul Bowers, Cornelius Olowola, Watson Omulokoli, Gottfried Osei-Mensah, Mark Shaw, Tite Tiénou, Yusufu Turaki, Ernst Wendland, and Isaac Zokoué. The index of topics addressed shows 32 articles on aspects of theological education and church leadership in Africa; 30 on issues of contextualisation and the church in contemporary Africa; an additional 26 on social issues; a surprising 19 articles on topics of African church history; while only 16 relating to biblical studies; 13 on African Christian theology; and 11 articles on evangelism and mission. Also present are 204 AJET book reviews, including attention to many titles that have proven singular contributions to evangelical reflection in Africa, such as: Adeyemo's *Salvation in African Tradition*; Bediako's *Jesus in African Culture*; Bosch's *Transforming Mission*; Ferdinando's *The Triumph of Christ in African Perspective*; Gehman's *Doing African Christian Theology*; Kato's *Biblical Christianity in Africa*; Molyneux's *African Christian Theology*; and Tiénou's *The Theological Task of the Church in Africa*. The publisher of AJET is Scott Theological College/ Scott Christian University, located in Machakos, Kenya. Given the exceptional scope and convenience of this new resource, many lecturers, scholars and researchers will find it handy to secure their own personal copy. Holding all back issues of AJET has long been a way for any theological library in Africa to demonstrate its distinguished quality. Now all theological libraries in Africa, and overseas too, can attain that level of distinction – and should certainly do so!

1028. Scott, Joyce

Moving into African Music

Cape Town: Pretext, 2009. 136 pages, ISBN: 9780981422466.

South African born and educated, Scott has worked with the Africa Inland Mission (AIM) and other institutions in Africa for 50 years. She took training in ethnomusicology under Dr Andrew Tracey, the founder of the International Library of African Music at Rhodes University, South Africa, and is well connected to the International Council of Ethnodoxologists. Her first book, *Tuning in to a Different Song*, was published in 2000. This later book describes Scott's own journey into an increasing appreciation and understanding of the rich varieties of African music. She cleverly weaves her own story into a musical autobiography, beginning with early frustrations at the "sound" of African music, through an ensuing lifetime of learning experiences which have resulted in a fruitful musical career. Though not attempting to write a technical book, she does develop several important aspects of music study: types of music ranging from traditional rural to urban pop, a basic introduction to African musical instruments, a sense of what is involved in setting up song workshops, and several case studies in actual creation of spiritual and community songs. Scott seeks to encourage laypersons (whether African or expatriate) to realize that they do not have to be specifically trained to take an interest in indigenous music and/or to encourage the creation of culture-specific songs. Wanting the reader to have "ears to hear," she has enclosed with each book a one-hour CD offering sample snippets of music from about twelve African countries or islands of the Indian Ocean. Appendix A, an article by Dr Andrew Tracey on the basic values and dynamics found in African music, is most instructive. Other useful appendices include lists of internet resources and training courses, a specific catalyst's experience in song creation in Madagascar, accounts of music in the Bible, and thoughts on teaching theology through music. The book is very readable, informative and often charmingly humorous.

1029. Scott, Joyce

Tuning in to a Different Song: Using a Music Bridge to Cross Cultural Differences

Pietermaritzburg: Cluster, 2007. 144 pages, ISBN: 9781875053636.

Scott worked for nearly three decades in cross-cultural ministry in Kenya, serving there as Christian music developer with the Africa Inland Church. More recently she set up a curriculum for inter-cultural music ministry at a seminary in South Africa. The present book, developed from that programme, is designed to help those in ministry preparation learn how to understand and use music to maximum effectiveness in their ministry. Scott provides a holistic look at the ministry role of music and a guide for utilizing this lively art with cultural sensitivity, especially in the South Africa context. Scott has a special ability to simplify abstract concepts with concrete explanations, and this book is full of practical ideas for learning about culture and the role of music in sharing the gospel. Written in three parts, the text covers intercultural music in a global context, in cross-cultural missions, and in ministry training. Each part builds to prepare African leadership for ministry within growing interracial and interethnic congregations. Music, encoded with the values, beliefs, and behaviours of culture, provides a bridge into and across cultural barriers. While providing practical and traditional church ministry categories of worship, witness, and ministry, Scott has not shied away from the unique issues of Africa. She capably addresses issues of African and Western worldview differences; dance, processions, and drama; and differing worship styles. She further provides guidelines for the use of music in development and education projects. Each chapter is infused with examples and exercises. This book is highly recommended to theological colleges as a text for courses preparing students to understand and use music in contexts of multicultural ministry and outreach. It can also serve as a useful tool for the cross-cultural worker, as a helpful handbook for the thoughtful African pastor, and as a unique resource for students of African Christianity.

Sebahire, Mbonyinkebe

see review 275

Selvan, Sahaya G.

see review 614

1030.   Senator, David

For Use as Directed: A Missionary Pharmacist Takes Stock

Brisbane: BookPal, 2009. 372 pages, ISBN: 9781921681646.

This missionary autobiography begins with the author, the son of British non-observant Jews, nearly getting killed as a child during the London Blitz. The narrative moves through school days, exposure to Christianity and conversion, training as a pharmacist, required military service, marriage, and serving as a pharmacist in England and then in Australia. In Australia the couple eventually learned of needs in Africa, earned diplomas in theology at Melbourne Bible Institute, and headed off to Ethiopia with the international mission SIM. Describing their missionary career in Ethiopia and later in Liberia, Senator goes into considerable yet interesting detail about his work as a pharmacist, work that required persistent creativity and adaptability. Thus in Ethiopia his natural administrative and executive skills were unrecognized, and sharp critical treatment by a superior eventually reduced him to depression. Later in Liberia his native gifts were noticed, and his subsequent service as a hospital administrator was appreciated, affirmed and nurtured. In Liberia the couple also engaged in local outreach, which included a church planting ministry. Unlike some missionary biographies, Senator is commendably honest about his discouragements and weaknesses while keeping a positive attitude. In the course of his life he allowed such experiences to shape him into a better person and more effective missionary. The genre of missionary biography may seem somewhat dated by now in Africa, but such literature continues to appear. In this case little is added to the store of knowledge about the African nations where service was rendered, but what is added is renewed awareness of the behind-the-scenes joys and sorrows, disappointments and successes, of so many expatriate missionary lives given over the years in service in Africa.

1031. **Setiloane, Gabriel M.**

African Theology: An Introduction

Johannasburg: Skotaville Press, 1986. 50 pages, ISBN: 9780947009144.

A well-known South African theologian, Setiloane was formerly a professor at the University of Cape Town. In this brief volume he concisely charts a theological and philosophical approach to the development of theology built on an African understanding of the world. Setiloane argues that the Western incursion into Africa and consequent onslaught on African ways of life and thinking have resulted in a reactionary African theology which has had much of its focus on confronting the invaders. He intends to lay out a less reactionary foundation, preferring to go instead to the African traditional religious concepts to find anchors on which a theological paradigm may be built. Working from the framework of the sociology of myth, he portrays the African understanding of God, of the created order, and of people as the appropriate foundations for theological reflection in Africa. He discusses God as a type of dynamic force rather than a person, and suggests that pan-en-theism is an appropriate expression of the African experience of divinity. One of his central arguments is that it was the African's universal recognition of God which made possible the acceptance of the Christian message and thus the success in evangelisation of the continent. He presents the African view of humanity as an inclusive, collectivistic perspective which is not limited to the living but includes the ancestors. He notes the stark contrast of the African perspective to the isolating Western separation of people as autonomous individuals. In Africa "Being a human is attainable only in community," while the Western perspective is "I think, therefore I am." These foundational perceptions and the resulting ethics of life form the mythic structure out of which, Setiloane argues, African theology must operate. He seeks to establish a myth structure more relevant to the African than that brought by Western Christianity. Within that context he maintains that the African traditional religious foundations are on a par with the OT, since both embody a mythic approach to understanding the world from their respective contexts, and every context must work within its own myth to make sense of the world. Among the various streams of African theologians, Setiloane's thinking links most closely with those who would seek to forge an identity built on traditional orientations while accommodating the newer (Christian) traditions. As such this small book serves as an important early example of this genre of African theologies, and merits attention by those teaching or writing in the field of African theology.

1032. **Shank, David A., editor**

Ministry of Missions to African Independent Churches: Papers Presented at the Conference on Ministry to African Independent Churches, July 1986

Elkhart, IN: Mennonite Board of Missions, 1987. 291 pages, ISBN: 9781877736049.

This is a collection of edited papers presented at the "Conference on Ministry to African Independent Churches," held during 1986 in Abidjan, Côte d'Ivoire. The need for not only this text but others like it is obvious – the African Independent Churches (AICs) have often been the fastest growing segment of the African church, and Christian ministry workers and organisations from outside of Africa still exhibit confusion over how to relate with them. The vast bulk of the papers are case studies of collaborative efforts between mission agencies and AICs from a dozen countries spanning sub-Saharan Africa. The authors are willing to present the bumps and warts of the encounters, together with encouragement that many of the AICs are interested in contact and desire to participate more fully in the larger international body of Christ. The stories are generally framed in an empowerment dynamic, letting the AICs have the major share in initiating, defining, and maintaining the programmes which are reported. The major weakness of the conference is that the papers present only the missions' side – the voice of the AIC leaders themselves is notably lacking. The appendices are especially helpful in pulling back from the microscopic level of the case studies to the continental level, giving the text a relevancy that will fit anywhere on the continent.

1033.   Shank, David A.

Prophet Harris, The 'Black Elijah' of West Africa

Leiden: BRILL, 1994. 309 pages, ISBN: 9789004099807.

William Wadé Harris (c. 1860–1929) of Liberia led a remarkable mass movement to Christianity in neighbouring Côte d'Ivoire in the early part of the twentieth century. Framed out of doctoral research under the direction of Harold Turner, Andrew Walls and Adrian Hastings at Aberdeen, and including extensive bibliographic and ethnographic materials, Shank offers insightful commentary in this comprehensive study of Harris, which initially comprised over 800 pages in three volumes. Students of African church history and theology owe Jocelyn Murray a great debt for her editorial work in condensing the book down to its present more manageable size! The first section offers a tight, nuanced summary of the history (and controversies) of Harris from 1910 to 1929. The second section looks at Harris' life prior to 1910, and together these two sections lay the foundations for the third section, which is the most important in the book. In it Shank explores Harris' life, prophetic thought patterns, and spiritual dynamics in light of the missionary and colonial context against which he framed God's call on his life. The postscript places the ministry of Harris in the larger context of African Christianity. Richly interspersed with anecdotal pieces about the setting in which Harris ministered, the book sets out the prophetic worldview of this unique personality in the history of African Christianity, and makes him come alive to the contemporary reader, while satisfying the scholar's desire for extensive illustration and documentation from original sources. The condensation of the book at times makes for such a dense style that multiple readings may be necessary for solid comprehension – but the extra attention required is well rewarded in the end. This is an extremely important book, not only for understanding the African-initiated church movement, but also for understanding a crucial component of modern African church history.

Shattuck, Cynthia

see review 455

1034.   Shaw, Mark

Global Awakening: How 20th-Century Revivals Triggered a Christian Revolution

Downers Grove: IVP US, 2010. 221 pages, ISBN: 9780830838776.

Shaw has been Director of the World Christianity programme at Africa International University in Nairobi. Here he has produced a thought-provoking study of renewal movements which he calls "global revivals." Between an introductory chapter which explores the dynamics of global revival and a closing chapter which seeks to draw lessons from the study of revivals for understanding World Christianity, Shaw analyses eight instances of revival, all but one of which come from the global South. Each chapter focuses on a particular leader who served as a catalyst for such revival. Three of these focus on African revivals: "Joseph Babalola and the Aladura Revival of 1930"; "William Nagenda and the East African Revival in Uganda"; and "Mensa Otabil, African Pentecostalism and Reverse Mission." Shaw defines global revivals as "charismatic people movements that seek to change their world by translating Christian truth and transferring power." He positions his study as an attempt to understand the dramatic resurgence of Christianity in the twentieth century. Shaw does not deny the variety of factors which students of World Christianity have cited to explain this growth but wishes to highlight revival as one factor which has been overlooked. Although he regards key spiritual dynamics as "the most important ones in understanding revival," most readers will note that much of Shaw's attention falls on four other dynamics: cultural, historical, global, and group dynamics. This stands in noticeable contrast to the focus on the spiritual and theological in most other studies of revivals. The approach means that Shaw does not provide much theological critique of the movements he describes, such as the use in some of them of "the language of prosperity and material gain." Factors which others have cited in explaining the rise of World Christianity – local commitment to evangelism, missionary engagement, Bible translation, indigenization, contextualization, inculturation –feature prominently in the revivals that Shaw analyses as well. He acknowledges as much in his claim "that global revivals act as the delivery system for a variety of forces and factors that account for global Christian growth, vitality and diversity." It is thus important to note that the forces and factors which characterize these special movements of God's Spirit are the same forces and factors by which God ordinarily works. Not all will be satisfied with Shaw's understanding of revivals as movements which "seek to change their world by translating Christian truth and transferring power"; many of those who were part of them might say that they were seeking more simply and profoundly to turn to God out of a sense of brokenness. Nevertheless, Shaw's work should very certainly be read by anyone seeking to better understand the upsurge in Christianity over the last century, not least in Africa.

1035. Shaw, Mark

The Kingdom of God in Africa: A Short History of African Christianity

Grand Rapids: Baker, 1996. 328 pages, ISBN: 9780801020964.

Here we have a singularly successful attempt to portray the whole history of Christianity in Africa in one small, well-produced volume. Shaw uses the concept of witness to the Kingdom of God as the organising theme of his book, distinguishing three views: (1) the Kingdom as the providential and theocratic rule of God; (2) the Kingdom as the redemptive rule of Christ over hearts; and (3) the Kingdom as the promotion of justice. Shaw shows how these three vision "make" African church history, with the first predominant in the first 1800 years, the second dominant in the modern missionary movement, and the third becoming an important factor in the twentieth century. The concept of the (often broken, struggling and partial, but still real) witness to the Kingdom shows itself to be a useful tool to deal with the great diversity of African Christian history. Shaw is convinced that all such history has been a witness to the Kingdom, and that all three aspects are necessary for a full witness to that Kingdom. Shaw was the founding editor of the *Africa Journal of Evangelical Theology*, and has subsequently been a lecturer in church history at the Nairobi Evangelical Graduate School of Theology. He writes here from an evangelical perspective, without doing injustice to other positions. His treatment of evangelical African theology as one of the branches of current African theological discussion differs pleasantly from the frequent tendency to ignore it or brand it as "Western" or "fundamentalist." One problem remains with this book: space! 124 pages are allotted to the time up to the great missionary movement, whereas 82 pages are used for nineteenth century and 85 for the twentieth century. Much on the treatment of the early centuries can be read as a church history, but for the modern periods the book is much more a selective interpretation of African Christian history – although valuable as such. Overall this is a significant fresh contribution to the field of African Christian history.

Shaw, Mark

see also review 793

Shaw, R. Daniel

see review 464

1036.   Shaw, Rosalind

Memories of the Slave Trade: Ritual and the Historical Imagination in Sierra Leone

Chicago: University of Chicago Press, 2002. 304 pages, ISBN: 9780226751320.

Witchcraft discourses have histories. They are not immutable givens of static cultures but have developed over time. They have been shaped by the political and economic forces that have been at work in Africa since the era of the slave trade, and an attentive ear can still hear the echoes of this past history in contemporary talk about witches and their powers. This, at least, is what Shaw argues in this fascinating book based on her anthropological research in Sierra Leone. According to her analysis, contemporary discourses about mystical power ("the spirit landscape, techniques of divination, cosmologies of witchcraft, practices of witchfinding, colonial stories of "human leopards," and phantasmagoric rumours about malefic ties between diviners and postcolonial leaders"), carry in them cultural "memories" that go back as far as the slave trade. Shaw's perspective is very similar to and nicely complements that of Peter Geschiere in *The Modernity of Witchcraft*. She points out that the earliest ethnographic records, from the first moments of an incipient slave trade, say nothing about witchcraft as an aspect of African ritual practice. Ethnographic evidence from one hundred years later, however, suggests a radically different reality. Here accusations of witchcraft have become common, and seem to have an underlying economic motive: accusing someone of witchcraft was one way of reclassifying an individual as outside the pale of mutual social responsibility, thereby turning that person into a commodity that could be sold for a profit. At the same time, those who accumulated power by betraying their fellows to spiritually mysterious outsiders (white slave traders) began themselves to be viewed as participating in a dark world of the occult. This understanding of political power as implicated in and dependent upon occult forces has reappeared over and over in African history, down to the present. This is a significant contribution to the recent resurgence of attention to witchcraft discourse in contemporary Africa. As such it would be valuable for those seeking in pastoral terms to address the fears and rumours of witchcraft (sometimes leading to the ostracizing or execution of suspected "witches") in which too often even Christians may become involved.

1037.   Shenk, David W.

Justice, Reconciliation and Peace in Africa

Nairobi: Uzima Press, 1997. 181 pages, ISBN: 9789966855459.

Shenk was born of Mennonite missionary parents in Tanzania and on occasion recounts childhood experiences and influences from those days. He has also worked as an educator in both Somalia and Kenya, so he is well placed to write about the concerns he raises. Perhaps inevitably, the majority of his illustrations are from Kenya and Tanzania, so "African" culture in his book is more accurately East African culture. For example, it may be true that the stranger was always a special person among the traditional Gikuyu, so that racism was supposedly not a problem, but tribalism has certainly been a major problem in many African societies and is to this day. One sensed a bit of "political correctness" in an otherwise helpful section summarising the beliefs of traditional African culture, and Shenk eventually notes that the system is not working in modern Africa. He makes no apologies for insisting that the Christian gospel (and he explains exactly what he means) is a major factor in bringing justice, peace and reconciliation in Africa. He illustrates his point by using examples from the East African Revival, and independent churches such as the Kimbanguists from Congo. The common thread running through his examples is that the willingness to forgive can solve otherwise intractable problems, a message that needs continual emphasis in today's conflicts both in Africa and elsewhere. This book is a revision of the author's 1983 book, *Peace and Reconciliation in Africa*, but the reader may be disappointed at the rather brief references to the major crises in Africa since 1983. Also few of the books in the bibliography have publication dates later than the first edition. John Mbiti, in writing the foreword, complains that not enough is said about the evils of apartheid, although Christian influence in this era in South Africa is illustrated toward the end of the book. Similarly, the horrible 1994 genocide in Rwanda really merits greater coverage in a book of this title and with a revision date of 1997. In defence of the author, his concerns are not primarily political but personal and ecclesiastical, perhaps reflecting the focus of the East African Revival that was part of his own experience. The book would be an aid to anyone looking at the needed role of conflict resolution in Africa.

Shenk, David W.

see also review 551

1038.   Shields, Norman

Christian Ethics: Volume 1–The Biblical Basis; Volume 2–Contemporary Issues

Abak, Nigeria: Samuel Bill Theological College, 1996. 2 Volumes pages, ISBN: 9789782071101
9789782071118.

Shields has been teaching Christian Ethics for well over thirty years, at one time in Nigeria and more recently in northern Ireland. These two volumes have been revised and updated from booklets that he produced for Samuel Bill Theological College in southeastern Nigeria, where he was once a lecturer. They are written at a fairly basic level, using clear plain English and avoiding much theoretical or philosophical language. The first volume is a descriptive survey of laws and moral statements in the Bible from Genesis to Revelation. The Talmud is mentioned, but hardly any other extra-biblical writing is referenced. Morality is simply "read off" from the texts, and critical questions are never raised. The second volume discusses briefly but directly eighteen contemporary issues in Christian ethics. Shields addresses social as well as personal ethics (e.g. The Christian and Race, Acquiring Money, Censorship and Contraception). In areas where technology has presented new ethical questions (abortion, contraception, nuclear weapons) a bit of technical history helps to explain why there are problems. The author refrains from making many applications specifically to the African context, perhaps realising the limitations of a prolonged absence from Africa. He has also chosen not to mention authors and movements by name, he does not often footnote the few statistics that are quoted, and no bibliography is provided. Also there is very little interaction with African traditional religion or Islam. In general Shield's conclusions are moderate and sensible.

## 1039.	Shorter, Aylward

African Culture: An Overview (Social-Cultural Anthropology)

Nairobi: Paulines, 1998. 109 pages, ISBN: 9789966214126.

Virtually anything that Aylward Shorter writes about Africa is worth reading, and this brief introduction to social-cultural anthropology in an African setting is certainly no exception. The author, a Catholic priest and long-serving missionary educator in Africa, produced this volume as "a straightforward textbook, which aims to cover the whole subject within a relatively small compass." One might have doubted this could be done in a little more than a hundred pages, but Shorter has done it. As he takes us through his topic, Shorter gradually narrows the field, moving from Theoretical Premises; Society and Its Environment; Human Cultures; Socio-cultural Change; and Urbanisation (chapters 1–5) to Religion as a Cultural System; African Ethnic Religion; Symbolism and Culture; African Ritual Symbolism; Witchcraft, Spirit Possession and Divination; and Dreams, Prayer and Sacrifice (chapters 6–11); and finally to Marriage and Family in Africa; Community Values in African Culture; and Culture and Its Imagination in Africa (chapters 12–14). This is indeed an excellent survey of this important field of study. As one might expect, the book is quite concentrated content-wise, and it uses many technical terms. It may therefore require a certain amount of "unpacking" and elaboration or supplementation by lecturers who decide to use it as a class text. However, the discussion is relatively easy to follow, and it includes a sufficient number of examples selected from different parts of the continent (primarily eastern and southern Africa). On only a few issues do the author's particular theological affinities colour his perspective. There are relatively few references to books written in the 1990s (except for the author's own). But all in all this is a singularly valuable little text.

## 1040.	Shorter, Aylward

Celibacy and African Culture

Nairobi: Paulines, 1998. 48 pages, ISBN: 9789966213815.

The author is a well-known British Roman Catholic priest who has spent many years working in Africa. The early part of this slender book is a helpful summary of African marriage and culture, a topic on which Shorter is clearly an expert. Although his concern is to "contextualize" celibacy, the first half of the book hardly mentions celibacy, but rather builds a case for fidelity in sexual relationships (and sometimes the line between fidelity and celibacy is unclear). Then Shorter acknowledges that many African priests are in favour of "de-linking celibacy and the priesthood," but he says that such talk is "definitely not on the church's agenda," and therefore is unhelpful because it "undermines conviction and postpones real commitment." As it happens, the founder of his own order, Cardinal Lavigerie of the White Fathers, petitioned Rome in 1878 for permission to develop a married clergy in Africa, but this historical footnote goes unmentioned! The most fascinating part of the book is the development of a parallel between celibacy and initiation ceremonies, where initiates go through a kind of poverty (symbolized by nakedness), chastity (no sexual activity during the rite) and obedience (to the rite's authorities). Yet it must be noted that initiation rites are a preparation for normal sexual activity afterward, not a replacement for it. This well-written book will not convince Protestants of the necessity of celibacy for priestly life, but it is a sincere attempt to give Roman Catholic believers an African apologetic for the tradition of celibacy.

1041. **Shorter, Aylward**

Christianity and the African Imagination: After the African Synod: Resources for Inculturation

Nairobi: Paulines, 1996. 128 pages, ISBN: 9789966211675.

This book by Shorter is a response to the Special Assembly for Africa at the Synod of Bishops held in Rome in 1994. This took place during the Rwandan genocide and raised the issue of how such a horror could take place in a country that was "massively Christian," leading to the acknowledgment that an "evangelisation" was needed "that leads to an interiorisation of the gospel." The answer of the Synod was to encourage the process of inculturation through the use of the symbols found in the oral traditions of the people of Africa, which would appeal to their religious imagination. Following John Henry Newman, Shorter argues that faith is demonstrated through an act of the religious imagination. This imagination possesses a cultural "grammar" of symbols which is written into the very structure of language. These symbols are found in the stories, songs, riddles, and parables that comprise the oral traditions. It is through linking these cultural symbols with Christian truth that the faith of the people will become culturally rooted and effectively interiorised. Thus, for Shorter, oral tradition in Africa is the "great untapped resource" for the inculturation of Christianity. He argues that "for the mystery of Christ to become credible to contemporary Africa, it must appeal to the African religious imagination." He illustrates the relevance of the religious imagination to the process of inculturation through specific examples from African literature, the arts, and oral tradition. As a result, he stresses the importance of working in the vernacular, and emphasizes that the work of inculturation should not be done by outside experts but by the African believers themselves. While the author's primary application is to the liturgical and catechetical concerns of the Catholic Church, the concepts and insights he presents can be applied to the broader Christian context.

1042. **Shorter, Aylward**

The Church in the African City

London: Geoffrey Chapman, 1991. 152 pages, ISBN: 9780225666366.

Many will know and appreciate the author for his insights born of many years of experience and ministry as a Catholic priest in (mainly East) Africa. In this book Shorter, then president of the Missionary Institute, London, addresses the subject of Africa's urbanisation, the continent's "most important social reality." Writing graphically and often anecdotally, Shorter depicts the particular challenges that life in the rapidly growing cities of Africa poses for the Church: poverty, alienation, AIDS, social dislocation, crime. He describes all of this with the perception and eyewitness vividness of someone who year after year has lived the reality of the African urban scene. And in the midst of so much that is depressing, Shorter also details examples of solidarity, courage, self-help, and hope. The book issues a prophetic call to the Church which too readily in the past has favoured an anti-urban mind-set, creating instead "its own uncontaminated enclaves, its islands of holiness, away from the corruption, decadence, and worldliness of the city." Illustrating from actual examples what "basic Christian communities" and other initiatives can do in the urban and peri-urban contexts, Shorter challenges the Church to reach out in urban mission. The book's importance lies in the growing significance of urbanisation on the continent, "today's missionary reality in Africa." Its authority lies in the first-hand experience, sustained involvement and compassion of the author.

1043.   Shorter, Aylward

Cross and Flag in Africa: The 'White Fathers' during the Colonial Scramble (1892–1914)

Maryknoll, NY: Orbis, 2006. 288 pages, ISBN: 9781570756559.

Shorter is a well-known missionary anthropologist and author of many significant works on Africa. This one, based on substantial research into original archival sources, narrates the history of the Roman Catholic Society of Missionaries of Africa, popularly known as the "White Fathers." The society was founded by Cardinal Lavigerie at a time when the European "scramble for Africa" was at its height. By the time of Lavigerie's death the society was still in its infancy and facing an uncertain future. Among other issues, it had to cope with the violence surrounding the aftermath of the slave trade and the expansion of the colonial powers, as well as the challenge of anticlerical legislation in early twentieth-century France which threatened to undermine its existence. A principal hero of the story is Lavigerie's successor, Léon Livinhac, who overcame such difficulties to preside over a period of expansion and consolidation at the end of which the Society was firmly established, the number of its members and of its mission stations having each nearly quadrupled. Nevertheless Lavigerie's remarkable presence continues to be felt throughout the story, as so much of what took place flowed from his original visionary and creative leadership, and from the initiatives he set in motion. Successive chapters look at the White Fathers' often critical or ambivalent attitudes towards colonialism; their response to the slave trade and its continuing effects; their methods of evangelisation; their understanding of African culture; and their educational work. There is also consideration of their relationship with rival Protestant missions, and of developments in their understanding of Islam, including an anticipation of Rahner's notion of "anonymous Christianity," as well as some quite radical approaches to contextualization. The White Fathers were in the very forefront of ethnographic and linguistic studies in Africa, and through their seminaries laid the foundation of "an educated Catholic elite" which would eventually facilitate the transfer of authority to indigenous leadership. At various points the story is illuminated by brief biographies of some of the principal actors. *Cross and Flag* is a detailed, fascinating and sometimes surprising study of the White Fathers' pioneering years. It will undoubtedly be an essential resource for understanding the history of missions in Africa.

1044. Shorter, Aylward

Evangelization and Culture

London: Bloomsbury, 1994. 176 pages, ISBN: 9780225667233.

In the present book Shorter revisits some familiar themes. For the Church's task of communicating Christ effectively, Shorter appeals for a thorough-going inculturation (the author shares the general Catholic preference of this term over that of "contextualization" preferred by Protestant writers). This inculturation, or "new or second evangelization" goes beyond a mere "translation" of Western theology, liturgy and rituals, and promotes a creative, locally meaningful expression of the faith that can be lived out within the local culture. It is a process "from below" rather than from above. It situates the creative initiative within "basic communities" (i.e. the local church) rather than by imposition from outside, takes seriously traditional religious and spiritual perceptions, and underlines the role of the laity alongside the clergy. A considerable portion of the book examines conflicting dynamics within Catholicism: on the one hand the efforts to liberate Catholicism from its centralized, hierarchical, Vatican-centric structures of the past, on the other hand the measures that seek precisely to preserve all of that, and thus stifle the process of inculturation. These sections of the book will be less directly relevant to the non-Catholic reader, although certain meaningful parallels exist. As might be expected from one of his training, Shorter repeatedly urges that would-be evangelizers should have specialized equipping in social and cultural anthropology if they are to be effective in the process of inculturation. Finally, it is heart-warming that a book on this crucial subject is so robust in its insistence that the good news of Jesus Christ must be at the very heart of the inculturation process. This book will prove of relevance to all who are concerned with the effective communication and incarnation of the gospel.

1045. Shorter, Aylward, and Joseph N. Njiru

New Religious Movements in Africa

Nairobi: Paulines, 2001. 112 pages, ISBN: 9789966215703.

Shorter is a well-known Catholic scholar who was at one time Principal of Tangaza College in the Catholic University of Eastern Africa. Njiru is a graduate of Tangaza College, and subsequently served as a youth coordinator at a community centre in Nairobi. If Nairobi is in any way indicative of what is happening elsewhere in Africa, then here is an introduction to an important emerging trend in African Christianity. The authors direct attention to what they term the "new religious movements" (NRMs), which they define as essentially urban movements, such as open-air rallies, crusades, revival meetings, miracle centres, healing ministries and so on. Shorter and Njiru describe how NRMs are taking the place of African Instituted Churches (AICs), the differences between them, and how and why NRMs have proliferated in Kenya. AICs "helped people make the transition from the life of the ethnic homeland to that of the modern world." NRMs "already belong to the modern world, but it is a world full of problems, uncertainties and frustrations." The urban poor aspire to be wealthy, and an NRM offers such people "a problem-solving religion, even a problem-solving God." NRMs appeal to the trends towards secularism and individualism occurring in Nairobi today. The authors describe the role played by Pentecostalism in the genesis of NRMs, and also focus on the relationship between NRMs and neo-pentecostalism and the health-and-wealth "gospel." They then show how, from a Catholic perspective, these NRMs use the Bible and conceive of salvation, as well as their "fundamentalist" tendencies and their view of demons. A separate chapter considers the impact of the NRMs on the Catholic Church, why and to what extent Catholics join NRMs, and what the Catholic church can learn from NRMs, and then assesses the Catholic Charismatic Renewal. The final chapter discusses some Catholic NRMs, how NRMs become cults, and how NRMs may impact the future of Christianity in Africa. NRMs "are a religious short-cut to power, instant success and economic growth, which are the virtues of the secular world." Indeed, NRMs "represent a compromise, a step towards the secularization of Christianity, a secular aberration." What theology there is in the NRMs is often deeply flawed and even heretical from an evangelical as well as a Catholic point of view, but the preaching and practices are just what the itching ears of immature Christians want to hear and experience. Much reading and field research has gone into this book. The authors' theology and assessments are clearly Catholic, but thoughtful Christians of every theological tradition in Africa will benefit from what the books provides in bringing this emerging phenomenon into careful, reflected focus.

1046. Shorter, Aylward, and Edwin Onyancha, editors

Secularism in Africa: A Case Study–Nairobi City

Nairobi: Paulines, 1997. 144 pages, ISBN: 9789966213143.

John Mbiti once said "Africans are notoriously religious." This perspective is dominant in most of the research on the African mind-set and on the way to penetrate the African heart with the gospel. Yet Shorter and Onyancha show from their case study that in the city of Nairobi, and even in the rural areas surrounding it, secularism has become a profound force. The authors write from a Roman Catholic background, but do not limit themselves to their own church. Shorter from Britain brings to this study a long teaching and writing career in sociology, anthropology and missiology, spent mostly in East Africa. Onyancha from Kenya contributes his experience in social research, relating particularly to youth problems. Their sociological analysis in this volume provides disturbing information on the shallow Christian commitment and low church attendance in Nairobi, even more so among the urban poor. Even among those who would consider themselves to be Christian, their faith is not having a central place in their lives. The authors give an analysis of the influence of secularisation in relation to the affluent, the poor, the mass media, the youth, and the rural areas under urban influence. Their analysis shows that just the launching of more evangelistic campaigns will not provide a sufficient response. Both for the affluent and for the poor, Christianity as lived out at the moment lacks relevance for many sectors of urban life, particularly the public and the economic. The message of Christ needs to be related to a whole new set of questions and a whole new way of life. With the growing influence of urbanisation, Western mass media and Western economic and social values in Africa, there is no reason to suppose that this process will stop, or that Nairobi will be an exception among the cities of Africa, other than in degree or pace.

1047. Shorter, Aylward, and Edwin Onyancha

Street Children in Africa: A Nairobi Case Study

Nairobi: Paulines, 1999. 120 pages, ISBN: 9789966214488.

Any visitor to one of Africa's cities knows that the presence of street children presents a huge challenge to society and especially to the church. In this book, Shorter, a Catholic White Father with long and intensive experience in Africa, and Onyancha, a Kenyan teacher and social science researcher, present the results of their study of this issue in Nairobi, Kenya. The authors make use of data from a wide variety of authoritative sources including: earlier studies; data and statistics on the extent of the problem gathered by world bodies such as the UN, donor agencies and the media; organisations serving street children; government authorities with responsibility for children and juveniles; and above all former and current street children. Drawing on this data Shorter and Onyancha identify problems needing immediate action to alleviate the situation, but they also forthrightly address deeper issues in society that cause children to migrate to the streets. They warn that these children are growing into what they call "the alternative Africa," composed of urban itinerants who do not know or desire a stable existence in society. The authors identify five fundamental causes of the street children phenomenon as: cost of education; poverty; decline of the family; lack of public awareness; and lack of appropriate legislation. They further acknowledge the role played by urbanization generally, by the rise of individualism, by the lack of networking among voluntary organisations and by corruption. While they acknowledge that the high number of children born into poverty increases the problem, it appears that their theological links may prevent them from encouraging responsible fertility control as one way to alleviate the problem (especially in Kenya which has one of the highest fertility rates in the world). But overall, their suggestions for increasing the effectiveness of response to street children's problems are scientifically sound, compassionate, and above all biblically based and motivated by Christ's example. The authors also honestly address the difficulties faced by organisations seeking to help street children, such as families seeking to pass responsibility for their children to the organisations, street gangs guarding their members from contact with organisation personnel, lack of trained staff to deal with the children, and corruption (where unscrupulous individuals manipulate the assistance schemes for personal profit).

1048. Shorter, Aylward

Toward a Theology of Inculturation

Eugene, OR: Wipf & Stock, 2006. 304 pages, ISBN: 9781597525473.

Roughly speaking "inculturation" is in Roman Catholic discussion what "contextualization" has been in much Protestant discussion. This book is therefore about the relation of gospel and culture(s). It does not focus exclusively on African cultures, but most examples are from the African continent. Shorter is a widely-read Catholic scholar who has served for many years in eastern Africa, and his discussion in this book is primarily from within a Catholic frame of reference. He first discusses the nature and function of inculturation, clarifying terms (culture, acculturation, enculturation, inculturation), and reflecting on culture and religion as well as on cultural change in general. He then addresses a theology of inculturation. His Christological discussion includes a balanced critical treatment of incarnation and paschal mystery as models for inculturation. The soteriological section defends Rahner's thesis of anonymous Christians, and explicitly criticizes John Stott and the *Lausanne Covenant*. Shorter's chapters on the OT and NT are rather bland, emphasizing that faith is always lived within a culture, that God reveals himself in the process of dialoguing cultures, and that there is no conscious theory of inculturation. He then turns his focus to the Roman Catholic Church, considering the relation of mission and inculturation, the teaching of the Catholic Church on inculturation today (from Benedict XV to John Paul II), and the future of inculturation in the Catholic Church. Shorter's intent is twofold. In the first place, he wishes to welcome the paradigm shift in official Catholic teaching in the twentieth century on the relation of gospel and culture, moving from a monocultural view (since the fifth century) to a view of the universal church in cultural diversity. He tries to balance God's work in all cultures and God's overall salvific plan in human history, which have to be recognized and respected, with the irreducible content of Christianity as a historical religion (emphasizing the historical Jesus and the cultures of the Bible), which have to be transmitted. Such a balance avoids letting cultures swallow up the Christian faith, or letting one form of the Christian faith impose itself on other cultures. In the second place, Shorter wishes to reflect critically on the "Petrine office" (the Papacy) and the fact that the centre of the (catholic) Church lies in the West. He tries to show how this office can maintain its main function to unite the Church in its diversity, while at the same time participating in the process of inculturation, opening itself to a two-way-communication with the regional bishops synods and being a true listener as well as teacher. The book will prove useful as a concise example of Catholic thinking on this vital subject, worked out primarily within the African context.

1049.   Shorter, Aylward

Towards African Christian Maturity

Nairobi: St. Paul Publications, 1987. 170 pages.

The materials in this book were first given as monthly extension lectures at the Holy Family Cathedral in Nairobi by lecturers from the Catholic Higher-Institute of Eastern Africa (CHIEA). The main purpose of the nine-lecture series was to interact critically with social, cultural and theological issues in modern Africa from a Roman Catholic perspective. Some of these issues (such as new trends in canon law, liturgy, and ecumenism) may not be as significant for the non-Catholic reader. However, the presentations on ministering to the poor and disadvantaged are quite helpful and thought provoking, and the chapter on spirituality will prove stimulating for those who are interested in spiritual formation. Also dealt with are Bible reading, the doctrine of revelation, and the Catholic Church's present-day attitude toward African culture and religions. This book will be helpful for those interested in keeping up with current Catholic thinking in Africa. Also the lectures include issues with which the Protestant churches should be dealing as well. Though readers will not agree with all of the theology or conclusions reached, these reflections can provide a useful starting point from which to develop one's own perspectives.

Shorter, Aylward

see also reviews 586 and 870

1050.   Shyllon, Leslie E. T.

Two Centuries of Christianity in an African Province of Freedom: Sierra Leone: A Case Study of European Influence and Culture in Church Development

Freetown: Print Sundries and Stationers, 2008. 367 pages.

The author was for many years head of the Department of Theology at the University of Sierra Leone. His PhD dissertation, completed at Aberdeen in 1983 under the direction of Andrew Walls, was on the history of Methodism in Sierra Leone. The present publication, building on that research, seeks to offer a history of the entire Christian community in Sierra Leone from the late eighteenth century to the present. The story of the early Sierra Leone settlement at Freetown as a beachhead for Christian penetration throughout West Africa is well known; this is not the first attempt to present a history of Sierra Leone Christianity. The particular contribution of this work is rather in its depth of detail, and its attempt to cover the full spectrum of Christian communities in the country. Thus Shyllon devotes chapters to each mainline church and mission agency, while also exploring educational endeavours and various attempts at mission in the hinterland. He also brings the story up to recent times, describing the contemporary impact of Pentecostal and charismatic movements. Shyllon's overall evaluative assessments strive for and largely achieve an appropriate even-handedness. Nevertheless it is striking that, while the author has attempted comprehensive coverage, including the Catholic, Pentecostal, and AIC communities, the Evangelical Fellowship of Sierra Leone founded in 1959 is not presented, nor is its membership detailed. Shyllon makes the interesting point that in the case of Sierra Leone, mission did not precede church; the process was the reverse. Churches were established by the early settlers of African descent; then missions entered to consolidate and expand this Christian presence, and for a period to dominate it. Part of the author's interpretive scheme is the process by which the churches reclaimed their own direction. He recognizes challenges that contemporary Sierra Leone Christianity faces, such as frequent schism, secularisation of the educated class, syncretistic practices, and a lack of vibrancy and moral clarity. He feels that much could be put right by more thorough Africanisation in worship and theology. The presentation has not entirely escaped its origins in doctoral research. Much of the text is not so much narrative as a compilation of details on individual churches and missions, with dates, persons, places and even buildings listed back to their beginnings. The bibliography includes almost nothing published after the early 1980s. Nevertheless, much of the material in the book would not be easily found elsewhere, so that advanced-level libraries specialising in the history of African Christianity should hope to obtain a copy.

Sim, Ronald J.

see review 219

1051. Simon, Benjamin

From Migrants to Missionaries: Christians of African Origin in Germany

Frankfurt: Peter Lang, 2010. 262 pages, ISBN: 9783631598429.

A large number of African immigrants to Europe have in recent years established their own congregations there, and the present book is a case study of a segment of this development. There are more than 500 congregations of the label "African Initiated Churches" (AICs) in Germany alone. The author is a German theologian who has taught at universities in Tanzania, Congo (DRC), and Germany, and who has been working with the relationship of the Church of Baden to migrant churches. The book is organized in four parts. (1) A historical survey of African Christians in Germany is offered. In spite of an African presence dating back to the seventeenth century, the current presence is a result of post-WW II immigration (after Nazi racism which was also against Africans). (2) Also provided is a survey of various challenges facing the immigrants. The term "diaspora" is discussed and accepted; and a categorisation is made of three types of church initiatives: autochthonous (churches founded in Africa), diasporic (churches founded outside Africa), and transcultural (diasporic churches establishing congregations in Africa). (3) The major bulk of the investigation – nearly two-thirds of the book – is an analysis of three AICs in Germany, with special attention to their message/sermons: the Kimbanguist Church, with its background in Congo (DRC) and its particular Trinity theology; the Church of the Lord (Aladura), with its background in Nigeria and its rather classical AIC theology; and All Christian Believers' Fellowship, as an example of a more neo-Pentecostal AIC. This third part concludes with a more systematic discussion of the content of sample sermons in the three churches. (4) Finally, a brief discussion of the ecumenical orientation and practice of the three churches is offered. Simon's book is a valuable contribution to the study of religious developments in the African diaspora. In addition to its particular focus on three churches in Germany, it offers much more general information and reflection about the development of AICs in Europe. As such, the book can be used as a suitable general introduction to this phenomenon.

1052.   Simpson, Andrew, editor

Language and National Identity in Africa

Oxford: Oxford University Press, 2008. 367 pages, ISBN: 9780199286751.

Simpson is Professor of Linguistics at the University of Southern California. Here he has brought together a collection of essays that provide fascinating insight into the role of language in nineteen African countries, including fresh perspectives on the post-independence journeys of these countries as assessed through the lens of language. Yet somehow the book might seem to amount to less than the sum of its parts. This disappointment may be attributed in part to the scale of the book's ambition, for when language and national identity are in play, the goalposts are moving at both ends of the pitch. Some languages languish or die, whilst others are constantly evolving. Similarly, the concept of national identity is hard to pin down in a continent as ethnically diverse as Africa. Perhaps, however, the book's impact is handicapped more by the expectations its title can encourage, for anyone looking for some additional light on the role that language plays in the key issue of what it means to be African – and more importantly, what it means to be an African Christian. In fairness, however, Simpson's stated goal is somewhat broader and less focused than this. He aims, he says, to assist "everyone wishing to understand the dynamic interactions between language and politics in Africa." It is true that whenever we use a particular language (sometimes at the expense of another) we are making a powerful statement about how we see both ourselves and our listeners. Yet Simpson argues that there are also other important "indexes of identity" which can be more cohesive than language, including religious adherence, loyalty to ethnic group or clan, and a sense of belonging to a particular territory. It is sobering to realize that colonial languages have often proven the glue that holds ethnically diverse countries together, since for a government to favour one indigenous language over others (as the official language) would often be unpalatable to a majority of the population. It is hard to disagree, since (as he points out) Africa's monolingual countries – such as Rwanda, Burundi and Somalia – are amongst its most divided. Indeed the reader will come away with a heightened awareness that the issues of language and identity are complex. The book would merit attention from those concerned with the complicated identity issues of modern Africa.

1053.   Sindima, Harvey J.

Drums of Redemption: An Introduction to African Christianity

Santa Barbara, CA: Praeger, 1999. 232 pages, ISBN: 9780275965839.

Sindima is a Malawian who has served as associate professor of philosophy and religion at Colgate University in the United States. The publisher's blurb breathlessly rates this "the first book to cover the presence of Christianity in Africa from the first century in a continuous fashion, discussing all the contributions of Africans in the formulation of doctrine as well as covering contemporary issues." This is rather more than this book is able to deliver. It is divided into two parts. The first part consists of a brief survey of African church history. All the well-known names are here: from Tertullian and Augustine through to Harris and Kimbangu. The survey is far too brief, however, and the brush with which Sindima paints is sometimes too broad and not always accurate. (To imply that the Portuguese policy of *requerimiento* formed the basis of all missionary doctrine, for instance, is hardly correct.) The chapter on "The Diaspora and the Missionary Enterprise" will be of special interest to anyone whose idea of the missionary enterprise in Africa is confined to the work of the various Western mission societies. The second part of the book is concerned with theology. It starts with a discussion of "Missionary Thought and Practice" before moving on to investigate how African Christianity and African culture responded. In the final chapter Sindima looks at the origin of African Theology, and the various paths that have been followed since the mid-twentieth century. Here again the book suffers from a lack of detail and substantiation. That the "corruption" of African languages with compound words is a form of "genocide," for example, is a strong claim to make without substantial discussion. As the title indicates, the book is meant to be introductory. Those already familiar with the history of African Christianity and with African theology will probably not gain much from its reading. And as for the novice, other books may serve the need for initial familiarisation better.

1054. Sindima, Harvey J.

The Legacy of Scottish Missionaries in Malawi

Lewiston, NY: Edwin Mellen Press, 1992. 164 pages, ISBN: 9780773495746.

Sindima and Edwin Mellen Press present here a slender book on a worthy topic in hard cover at a very high price. In the first three chapters Sindima takes the reader through early Malawian mission history, then in three more chapters discusses issues like education, African leadership and colonialism. The book excels in hundreds of printing errors, words misplaced, and quotations wrongly copied. The author often refers to primary sources, but does not bring out much that is new, and either did not use or does not acknowledge the most important book on the subject (McCracken on the Livingstonia Mission) or the most fundamental dissertation (A.C. Ross on the Blantyre Mission). It is a pity that such a good topic has been covered in this way. The publisher certainly has something to answer for.

1055. Smit, Johannes A., and P. Pratap Kumar, editors

Study of Religion in Southern Africa: Essays in Honour of G. C. Oosthuizen

Leiden: BRILL, 2006. 298 pages, ISBN: 9789004143845.

Gerhardus Cornelis Oosthuizen has made significant long-term contributions in the study of religion in southern Africa extending back into the 1950s. This collection honouring him begins with a brief biographical sketch, which is followed by fourteen essays, ten of which were produced by scholars based in South Africa, with another two each from Botswana and Nigeria. The University of KwaZulu-Natal's students, graduates and professors contributed six of the South African essays. Very little, other than "the study of religion in southern Africa" holds this collection together. One essay, for example, is a Buddhist reading of Richard Bach's *Jonathan Livingstone Seagull*, while another discusses the Indian diaspora in South Africa. About half of the collection could be of direct interest to readers of these reviews. Three of these seem especially worth noting. Although A. O. Nkwoka's essay on "The Challenge of Nigerian Pentecostal Theology and the Perspicuity of Scripture" fails to resolve whether Pentecostal theology is meant to challenge or be challenged by the doctrine of the perspicuity of Scripture, it gives the uninitiated reader a fascinating glimpse of Nigerian Pentacostalism. In "The Prophetic Vocation of the African Scholar: A Celebration of Wholeness" M. S. Tshehla argues that

African Christian scholarship must be "scholastic," "contextual" and "ideological"; African biblical scholars cannot neglect the prophetic task they have been given to fulfil within their religious communities. Finally, in "Before Gandhi: Leo Tolstoy's Non-Violent Kingdom of God," J. A. Loubser considers Tolstoy's Christian pacifism which had a formative influence on Gandhi's *satyagraha* and on those, like Martin Luther King Jr. and Albert Luthuli, who followed him.

Smit, Johannes A.

see also review 754

1056.   **Smith, James Howard**

*Bewitching Development: Witchcraft and the Reinvention of Development in
    Neoliberal Kenya*

Chicago: University of Chicago Press, 2008. 272 pages, ISBN: 9780226764580.

In this fascinating ethnographic account of life in one particular region of Kenya, the author (Associate Professor of Anthropology at the University of California Davis), describes how local ideas about development (*maendeleo* in Swahili) and witchcraft play out in day-to-day social discourse. Having first encountered discussions about development in elite circles in Nairobi, he expected that the relatively remote rural area to which he then moved would be too taken up with local cultural discourses to be much interested in such modern notions. In fact, however, talk about *maendeleo* and how to achieve it was everywhere. Inseparably imbedded in such conversations, he quickly discovered, were ideas about the opposing power of various forms of black magic or witchcraft, inspired by jealous or selfish and overly ambitious neighbours, or by outsiders wielding terrible occult powers. Often rumour pointed to new rather than simply traditional types of witchcraft, which despite their newness were attributed to a dark past over against a brighter future that development should bring. Adding to the confusion and fear, these forces seemingly had the ability to insinuate themselves into the very public institutions that were supposed to ensure order and bring development. Smith describes various efforts made by local actors to capture the promises of development despite the opposition of the powers of witchcraft, but shows how at every turn such attempts were to one degree or another frustrated, and even ended up looking like new forms of witchcraft. Thus, in what is perhaps the most interesting chapter, Smith describes how local development committees voted to summon a well-known Tanzanian witch-hunter to cleanse their communities of the witches who were impeding development, only to conclude that this witch-hunter was himself nothing but an even greater witch. Smith sets this discussion in the larger context of pressures from the international community to adopt "structural adjustment," more transparent governance, and multiparty democracy – with all the economic and political turmoil and decline induced by these forced changes. Discussions about witchcraft and development, he suggests, should be understood in part as efforts to make sense of the growing hardships brought on by these poorly understood macro-level transformations. Smith's theoretical analysis is at times overly dense, but the ethnographic detail is rich and convincing. By describing in some detail how Africans in one particular contemporary context have interacted, for better or worse, with ideas about witchcraft and development, this book would prove useful to advanced levels of inquiry interested in the issues of contextualizing the gospel in light of contemporary discussions of witchcraft in many African settings.

1057. Smoker, Dorothy W.

Ambushed by Love: God's Triumph in Kenya's Terror

Fort Washington, PA: CLC USA, 1994. 284 pages, ISBN: 9780875087405.

The conflict for Kenyan Christians caught between legitimate concerns for political freedom and the anti-Christian position of the Mau Mau fighters in colonial Kenya of the 1950s is well known, but little has been published of the testimonies of Kenyan Christian believers during this difficult period of African history. Those who had been converted during the East African Revival of the 1930s and 1940s were suddenly faced with persecution from both sides of the political conflict. The Mau Mau fighters considered Christians to be supporters of colonialism for refusing to take blood oaths or renounce their Christian faith, while the colonial forces often arrested Christians who refused to report the Mau Mau to the authorities or to take up arms against them. Smoker, a long-term Mennonite missionary in Tanzania, has done us a great favour by relating the testimonies of some older Kenyan Christians who lived through this tense time – before these brothers and sisters would pass away with their stories untold. She begins with a helpful historical overview of the Mau Mau revolt during the 1950s, then divides the testimonies according to categories, such as those who died, Mau Mau fighters who became Christians, life in the detention camps, etc. In doing so, she has contributed to the welcome recent emphasis on researching oral history in Africa. Many of the testimonies relate the deep faith, courage and joy that Kikuyu believers showed when persecuted by practically everyone else in the society, and one Kenyan bishop (Obadiah Kariuki) insists that Revival Christians were a key factor in bringing peace and independence, partly because they were so willing to forgive atrocities by both sides in the conflict. The reader is also reminded of some of the weaknesses of the East African Revival, such as the strong Keswick emphasis on personal sin with little reference to social evil. The author compiled these testimonies to encourage persecuted Christians in similar situations, but she has also done historians a favour. Even though the book is written in a devotional tone, the issues it addresses remain important, making it a useful book for students of African church history. Perhaps enough years have now passed since African independence movements for such "politically incorrect" stories to be acknowledged and discussed more openly within the African Christian community.

1058. Snook, Stewart G.

Developing Leaders Through Theological Education by Extension: Case Studies from Africa

Wheaton, IL: Billy Graham Center Archives, 1992. 227 pages, ISBN: 9781879089099.

The central theme of this inquiry is: Why do some theological education by extension (TEE) programmes in Africa appear to succeed, while others seem to fail? The book is a major contribution to literature on the wellbeing of TEE in Africa. Using questionnaires sent to TEE administrators across Africa, as well as on-site visits to five leading African TEE programmes, in Gabon, Kenya, Nigeria, South Africa and Congo (DRC), Snook has usefully discerned the necessary component parts for successful TEE programmes. Snook served for many years in theological education in South Africa. This is a useful reference text on TEE in Africa for the time of writing.

Snyder, C. Arnold

see review 621

1059.   Soares, Benjamin F., editor

Muslim-Christian Encounters in Africa

Leiden: BRILL, 2006. 310 pages, ISBN: 9789004152649.

The editor holds a PhD from Northwestern University and is an anthropologist at the African Studies Centre in Leiden, Netherlands. The chapters in this volume focus on the actual encounters between Muslims and Christians as a means for better understanding the broader and extremely complex field of Muslim-Christian relations in Africa today. The various authors, mostly Western scholars of Islam in Africa, consider Muslims and Christians together "within a common analytical frame." The result is a series of essays dealing with a variety of fairly specific ways in which African Muslims and Christians have interacted in recent years, encounters which illustrate both tensions and opportunities in a given setting. Together these portray a multi-coloured fabric of contemporary African Muslim-Christian relations. Veteran author John Voll begins with a general historical survey of Muslim-Christian conflicts that have been labelled as religious, but which should rather be attributed primarily to cultural and political factors; Huntington's "clash of civilizations" thus becomes irrelevant in the African context. This is followed by chapters on: Muslim-Christian tensions in Ethiopia as reflected in their mutual prohibition of eating each other's meat; Muslim resistance to foreign Christian missionary activity in Egypt and Sudan; factors in the conversion of the Sereer-Safèn group in Senegal to Islam rather than to Catholicism; the irenic perspective on Christianity in the writings of the West African Muslim intellectual Amadou Hampâté Bâ; tensions from conservative evangelistic efforts by both Christians and Muslims in Kenya and Tanzania; and the decline of constructive Muslim-Christian relations in post-apartheid South Africa. Four other chapters focus on Nigeria: historical friction within and between Muslim and Christian communities; the 1976–1978 shari'a debate; the politicization of religion in contemporary Nigerian politics; and a biographical reflection on one man's journey of conversion from Islam to Christianity. Although much of the material deals with conflicts and competing interests between Muslims and Christians, the authors also highlight incidents of tolerance and cooperation. One may hope that lecturers and postgraduate students who wish to conduct research on any of the issues covered here will find a way to gain access to this valuable collection and will use it with profit.

1060.   Sogolo, Godwin

Foundations of African Philosophy: A Definitive Analysis of Conceptual Issues in African Thought

Ibadan: Ibadan University Press, 1993. 244 pages, ISBN: 9789781212376.

In philosophical and theological discussions in Africa nowadays it is essential to show the relevance of the discussion to Africa. There is no unanimous definition for "African Philosophy," but there are at least two main schools of thought on what it means. Some want to domesticate foreign (Western) philosophy. Usually they call themselves "Professional Philosophers." Others want to resuscitate the ancient wisdom of Africa. These are usually termed "ethno-philosophers." Sogolo's book is a blend of the two. A professor of philosophy in the

University of Ibadan, Sogolo was one of Africa's best-known philosophers. This book presents philosophical discussions in interaction with traditional African beliefs in such branches of philosophy as logic, epistemology, philosophy of religion, metaphysics, ethics, and social and political philosophy. Of most relevance to those engaged in theological reflection would be the section on religion and metaphysics. A startling example of the book's content is a comparative study of the ontological status of God and of witches. There are enough arguments to affirm and deny the existence of both. Although the author appears to be an agnostic, the book does usefully illustrate the various ways contextualization of knowledge is being done in the African academy today.

1061.   **Sparks, Allister**

The Mind of South Africa: The Story of the Rise and Fall of Apartheid

New York: Random House, 1991. 446 pages, ISBN: 9780749305987.

Veteran journalist Sparks has here attempted to write an intellectual history of South Africa, beginning with the semi-nomadic Khoi and San people, and the Nguni-speaking tribes that migrated south in the latter part of the first millennium AD, moving on to the arrival of Jan Van Riebeeck in 1652, and continuing through to the unbanning of the ANC in 1990. An epilogue, added in 1991 for this paperback edition of the book, discusses the release of Nelson Mandela. In the prologue Sparks introduces us to the Wild Almond hedge planted by Van Riebeeck to isolate what was initially meant to be a Dutch victualing station at the Cape of Good Hope from the rest of Africa. This hedge is carried through the rest of the book as a metaphor for the way in which white and black South Africans have been divided and separated from each other. The hedge took various shapes – ignorance, culture, greed – but was finally established in the twentieth century as Apartheid. Sparks' history is well researched, and his familiarity with some of the primary sources is commendable given that he is writing primarily as a journalist and not a historian. That background as a journalist also makes this a very readable book. A major shortcoming of this book is that it fails to give serious attention to black intellectual history, despite the author's desire to "encompass all those involved" and not simply white South Africans. The bulk of the book is devoted to tracking and explaining Afrikaner Nationalism and how it led to Apartheid. While Sparks realizes that this cannot be done in isolation from other developments in South Africa, these other are often glossed over. Very little is said of the ANC until the 1960s, for example. African Independent Churches are also treated superficially, and their considerable influence all but neglected. The author has made an attempt to explain the complicated relationship between the Dutch Reformed Church and Afrikaner Nationalism, but his treatment is unfortunately slanted. The influence that the church had on negative racist policies is emphasized, while any contrary examples are generally downplayed. Thus Christians who played positive roles in fighting Apartheid are highlighted as individuals, while those who made negative pronouncements are portrayed as representing the Church. While the complicity of many Christians in Apartheid is something that still needs to be dealt with by the Christian community in South Africa, from this book one would not learn of those individual Christians as well as churches that were involved in fighting against racism, and did so not primarily out of political or humanitarian convictions, but as part of their commitment to the gospel. Nevertheless Sparks has made a helpful contribution for anyone needing a basic, readable introduction to South Africa's intellectual history. Serious readers, especially those interested in Christian history and black intellectual history in South Africa, will need to supplement this with further reading elsewhere.

1062.   **Spartalis, Peter J.**

Karl Kumm: Last of the Livingstones

Bonn: Verlag für Kultur und Wissenschaft, 1994. 116 pages, ISBN: 9783926105189.

Although the roots of many African churches go back to evangelical missions in general, and to faith missions in particular, often these churches may know very little about their own origins and about their evangelical mission background. The missionary and academic communities may frequently be as badly informed. The China Inland Mission is known for its founder and hero of the faith, Hudson Taylor, but who knows anything about Karl Kumm and his first wife Lucy? Spartalis' book acquaints us with these great leaders of early faith missions in Africa, who founded the Sudan United Mission (SUM). Started in 1904 in the Middle Belt of Nigeria, SUM in due course became, together with the Sudan Interior Mission (SIM), most probably the principal factor in tilting the religious balance of Nigeria toward a Christian majority. The SUM expanded to Cameroon, Chad and Sudan (with Australian missionaries), and the various churches in Africa originating from SUM work now have well beyond a million members. Spartalis is an Australian mission historian who has taught at Nairobi Evangelical Graduate School of Theology (NEGST) in Kenya. His book is not a fully academic biography, but neither is it merely a pious story of a faith hero. It falls somewhat between, as a useful book for those interested in African evangelical mission history in general. It will be of particular interest for institutions in countries where the Kumms were active, namely: Nigeria, Cameroon, Sudan, Chad, South Africa, and Egypt. And for mission poets, Kumm's poem "Africa" will be of particular interest.

1063.   **Speckman, McGlory T.**

The Bible and Human Development in Africa

Nairobi: Acton Publishers, 2001. 311 pages, ISBN: 9789966888976.

Speckman has been a lecturer in NT at Grahamstown and at UNISA in South Africa. His motivation for this study, and that which guides the direction of his inquiry, is provided by his South African experience. He clearly feels deeply with the black people of his country as they work through the legacy of marginalisation and racism. His desire is to find guidance in the Bible for new directions in promoting healthy human development. To that end he focuses this study on the story of Peter and John healing the lame beggar in Acts 3. He uses what he calls "contextual exegesis" in his study of this passage, contending that conventional theological exegesis binds the African student into a foreign frame of reference that obscures points that would come naturally to mind for the untrained reader. He is meticulous in citing many sources to demonstrate that this "contextual exegesis" is as valid and scientific as the conventional model. This leads the author into some statements with which more evangelically oriented readers may disagree, especially when the author states that the meaning of the passage to the original author is not important for understanding it now. Rather, he appears to be convinced that applying Scripture directly to the current context is the way to proceed. He carefully studies concepts such as "beggar" and "charity" and "alms" in Greco-Roman, Judaeo-Christian, and medieval societies. He also gives a synopsis of the way the needy were treated in traditional African societies. Based on all this, Speckman notes that in Acts 3 the apostles empowered the beggar by treating him as fully human and giving him wholeness that enabled him to participate productively in the new society being created by the believers. This brought them into conflict with the restrictive rule of the religious elite of that day. The author's main principle derived from this passage is that the church's role is not to give alms or relief, but rather to empower the downtrodden to live as whole people, even if we need to oppose the current power structures in the process. Since the apartheid experience is still recent in South Africa, the effects of this on people's sense of identity and self-worth figure heavily in the argumentation. In other parts of Africa some readers may find this emphasis less suited to their context. This study is useful as an example of alternative interpretive models for the use of the Bible in Africa.

1064.   Spencer, Aída Besançon, editor

The Global God: Multicultural Evangelical Views of God

Grand Rapids: Baker, 1998. 282 pages, ISBN: 9780801021633.

The thrust of this book is a two-part question: (i) through what attribute is God most understood in your culture?, and (ii) what attribute of God needs to be more fully apprehended in your culture? The ten contributors are all evangelical Christians, but each looks at the God of the Bible from a different cultural perspective: American, Hispanic American, Caribbean, African, Chinese American, Chinese, Korean, and Korean American. The central message is that God has called all peoples into relationship with himself. In the process culture may have given some special insights into the nature of this God of the Bible, or it may have presented certain challenges to a true understanding. This needs to be sorted out. The contributors look at both the strengths and weaknesses of their cultural heritage in knowing and coming into relationship with the God of the Bible. Africa is represented with chapters by Nigerian theologian Tokunboh Adeyemo (Unapproachable God: The High God of African Traditional Religion) and Ghanaian pastor Edward John Osei-Bonsu (The God above Tradition Who Speaks to All Traditions). In addition, the Caribbean perspective (Transcendent but Not Remote) by theological educator Dieumème Noëlliste draws heavily on its heritage in African traditional religion ("The African religious presence in the Caribbean is pervasive.") All three wrestle with traditional belief in the inapproachability of the high god, his irrelevance in daily life. Noëlliste begins by reflecting on the relationship of theology to culture, recognizing the necessity of cultural mediation of theology, of "relevance without syncretism." He compares the traditional hierarchy of divinities with the God of the Bible, distinct from the world, divinely majestic, hidden and self-disclosed. Adeyemo first discusses the African worldview, the world of humanity and the world of the spirits; he then explains a number of ways Africans perceive God: through rational intuition, natural phenomena, oral tradition and history, providence and preservation, experience and cultural diffusion ("Revelation is God's initiative; perception is a human task"). Osei-Bonsu differentiates between traditional religion and "indigenous religion" that accepts the God of the Bible but in syncretistic ways. He ends with discussing ways biblical Christianity confronts both traditional and indigenous religion, and by recounting his personal faith journey. This should prove a valuable resource for pastors and theological educators both in Africa and in other parts of the world.

St. Clair, Raquel Annette

see review 1157

1065.   **Stakeman, Randolph**

The Cultural Politics of Religious Change: A Study of the Sanoyea Kpelle in Liberia

Lewiston, NY: Edwin Mellen Press, 1986. 264 pages, ISBN: 9780889461772.

Stakeman has served as professor of history and director of an African studies programme at a college in the United States. This book, based on field research conducted in 1977, represents his PhD dissertation for Stanford University. Stakeman sets out to demonstrate a methodology for tracking religious social change within the framework of historical inquiry. He does so by focusing on the encounter of Christianity with traditional Africa as seen among the Kpelle people of Liberia, specifically within the Sanoyea township, during the four decades following the founding of a Lutheran mission station in Sanoyea in 1917. He largely succeeds in what he attempts. In doing so, he clarifies aspects of religious change often opaque to conventional presentations of Christian expansion in Africa. For example, his fascinating final chapter sketches out the changes that have taken place within Kpelle traditional religion resulting from its encounter with Christianity. Stakeman makes good use of archival resources, and also effectively utilizes a range of local informants. A leading figure in his story, and one of the principal informants, is Peter Giddings, among the first to attend the mission school in Sanoyea, and later his father's successor as paramount chief in Sanoyea, in which role he was often in tension with the mission. While Stakeman makes effective use of his resources to represent the traditional religious situation of Sanoyea, when he comes to the mission he noticeably fails to achieve an inner understanding, with the treatment often ill-informed, at times even naïve, and a certain hostility barely concealed. More importantly, although the majority of his informants were Kpelle *Christians*, he used their input only for his study of traditional religion. When he comes to interpreting Kpelle Christianity, he retreats to extrapolating from sociological theory rather than letting these figures speak for themselves. By the time Giddings was interviewed in the later 1970s, he had in fact renounced traditional religion, returned to the Lutheran Church, and become a respected senior pastor. Had Stakeman allowed such Kpelle Christians to reflect their self-consciousness as Kpelle Christians, his overall history of religious change in Sanoyea would have been more authentic and complete. Much of benefit can nevertheless be gained from the methodological intentions of this study. Although a history of religious change worked out in terms of social cause and effect is by itself inevitably reductionistic, it could prove fruitfully illuminating for African Christianity in multiple contexts if used adjunctive to other approaches.

1066.   **Stanley, Brian**

The Bible and the Flag: Protestant Missions and British Imperialism in the Nineteenth and Twentieth Centuries

London: Apollos, 1990. 192 pages, ISBN: 9780851114125.

Stanley, with a PhD from Cambridge University, is director of the Centre for the Study of Christianity in the Non-Western World at the University of Edinburgh. In this scholarly work of eight chapters, Stanley addresses topics such as a definition of British imperialism, missions and the nationalist revolutions from 1895–1960, and Christianity and culture. The theology and worldviews of British evangelical missionaries (focusing mainly on Africa) are then considered. Missionaries have been both maligned and praised for their purported hand-in-glove compliance with imperialism. Stanley shows that the actual history was more complex. In some areas of Africa the British missionaries invited the British crown to bring peace and stability to sectors of the

African population preyed upon by slave-traders; but on the other hand they castigated land-hungry British settlers for their economic exploitation. Evidencing well-documented research, Stanley presents a corrective to the often misconstrued role of various missions which served within British colonies, including the Church Mission Society, London Missionary Society, Wesleyans, and Sudan United Mission. Stanley does not excuse the missionaries' failures in racial pride and display of arrogance; they often rode the bandwagon of the empire builders and succumbed to being used by British imperialism. He does affirm that the eventual demise of British imperialism in Africa resulted through mission schools in which nationalist leaders were educated. The majority of colonies that Stanley profiles are from former British East Africa and the Cape Colony. West African British colonies such as Nigeria, Ghana, and Sierra Leone are given limited coverage. In the final chapter pertinent questions with global application to contemporary mission are posed. Is such mission activity motivated by inward holiness? Is such missiology sensitively attuned to God's providence? Are we cognizant of the truth that both empires and missions are under God's divine judgment? And is Christianity an inherently "imperial" religion? One weakness of the book might be that Stanley does not sufficiently cover reasons why Africans were so attracted to the Christianity that the missionaries offered.

1067. Starcher, Richard L., and Enosh A. Anguandia, editors

Textbooks for Theological Education in Africa: An Annotated Bibliography

Bukuru, Nigeria: Africa Christian Textbooks, 2007. 213 pages.

Here we are offered an exceptionally useful new reference tool, one designed to respond directly to the common need of theological schools in Africa to find suitable textbooks written in and for Africa. Many such texts may already be available, but discovering their existence has often been the principal challenge. This new annotated bibliography lists and evaluates more than 700 books produced in and for Africa that might be put to use as relevant textbooks for theological institutions in Africa. No resource on this scale has ever been available before. Better yet, the entire text has been freely accessible on the web, all 213 pages, and may be downloaded in PDF format. The entries are sorted in terms of potential texts for the normal range of subjects and courses in theological schools in Africa. Indices allow one to search by author, academic department, subject, or key word. For each book the notes provide information on: availability, price, educational level, subject, and potential usefulness. The notes also rather bravely indicate "theological orientation," using designations such as: ecumenical, evangelical, liberal, Roman Catholic, secular, and undetermined. Some 70 percent of the entries include brief evaluative comments derived, with permission, from the reviews that have appeared in *BookNotes for Africa*. Starcher, presently on the faculty at Biola University in the US, has previously served at both the Faculté de Théologie Evangelique de Bangui (FATEB) and the Nairobi Evangelical Graduate School of Theology (NEGST). Anguandia holds an MTh from NEGST, and has been chair of the missions department at Shalom University in Congo (DRC). Here is certainly a resource that theological educators in Africa will want to explore and put to use. It also represents invaluable information for libraries and researchers both in Africa and abroad.

1068. **Stearns, Jason K.**

Dancing in the Glory of Monsters: The Collapse of the Congo and the Great War of Africa

New York: PublicAffairs, 2012. 416 pages, ISBN: 9781610391078.

Stearns brings a decade of research and personal involvement in Congo (DRC) to the writing of this powerfully moving and analytically solid account of the devastating wars that have been (and in some places continue to be) fought in the Democratic Republic of Congo since the final months of 1996. His experience in Congo includes involvement in a local human rights organisation, working for the UN peacekeeping operation in various capacities, and serving as an analyst for the International Crisis Group (ICG). While acknowledging that the horrors of these wars are "undeniable," he seeks to focus attention on "the perpetrators more than the victims," in an attempt to describe why the wars' protagonists made the choices they did. He argues that such personal decisions can only be understood in light of political realities that have taken shape over several centuries – through the slave trade, the brutal and racist colonial experience, and a continuing postcolonial exploitation of the vast majority of the population by privileged elites and their foreign trading partners, processes that have rendered violent conflict if not inevitable then at least explainable. His hope of course is that better understanding of this kind might lead to more effective policy, and pressures for systemic change both in the international community and in Congo itself. Woven into Stearns' account of the conflicts are a number of personal narratives of actors whom he has interviewed, whose stories provide striking examples of how particular kinds of decisions came to take on an air of inevitability given the context in which they were made. Stearns rightly traces the wars' origins to the 1994 genocide in Rwanda, and its aftermath of refugee camps established in Congo for Hutus fleeing the forces of the Rwandan Patriotic Front. Because these camps accommodated not only unarmed civilians, but also the retreating Rwandan army and Interahamwe *génocidaires*, they posed a serious threat to the new regime in Rwanda, one that the latter felt it could not ignore. The subsequent story of Rwanda's sponsorship of first one rebellion (led by Laurent Kabila), and then another (in an effort to overthrow the same Kabila); of variously motivated interventions by other African nations; and of the multiplication of rebel groups in a chaos of constantly shifting alliances; is too long and complex to describe here. But Stearns does an admirable job of providing insight into both the general course of events and some of the personal stories that form the detail of its tangled fabric. This book, then, comes highly recommended for anyone seeking to grasp the human realities of Congo's recent convoluted and tragic history, not just as wanton violence, but in terms of a political history that makes it "thinkable."

Steed, Christopher

see review 1079

1069.   Stenger, Fritz, Joseph Wandera, and Paul Hannon, editors

Christian-Muslim Co-existence in Eastern Africa: Papers Presented at the Joint Conference of Tangaza College, Nairobi and Radbound University, Nijmegen

Nairobi: Paulines, 2008. 296 pages, ISBN: 9789966083319.

Although there are numerous works on Islam in Africa, there are fewer that deal specifically with the important issue of Christian-Muslim relations in Africa. This work is the product of the conference mentioned in the title, which in turn resulted from several years of collaboration between the two institutions mentioned there, one in the Netherlands and the other in Kenya (the latter is a constituent institution of the Catholic University of Eastern Africa). The contributors, both Christian and Muslim, are either from Eastern Africa or have extensive experience there. They seek to address contemporary issues facing the two primary religious communities in the region, and succeed fairly well in addressing the need for greater respect and tolerance between the two faith communities. But most offer little regarding any direct application in the context of Eastern Africa. The first two chapters acknowledge the general tradition of peaceful co-existence in Eastern Africa, then focus on the breakdown of this tradition in Sudan and Somalia (Y. Tefsai), and in Kenya (O. Kinyua). F. Wijsen's chapter on Islamic reactions to modernity is set in the context of Eastern Africa, but his solution of a "trans-modern" perspective is more theoretical than practical. The next two chapters, by Kinyua and the al-Azhar scholar A. El-Ezabi, provide moderate Islamic views on co-existence and tolerance, but are bereft of any reference to Africa. The best chapter is the one by J. Wandera on "mihadhara," or Muslim public religious debates in Kenya and Tanzania, which tend to disparage Christians and their faith. He wisely advocates that Christians should respond in a restrained manner without equivalent counter-debate, although his pluralistic bent will not be accepted by every reader. This short book is thus mixed as to quality and benefit, but is nevertheless a worthwhile resource, especially given the general dearth of other material on Christian-Muslim relations in Africa.

1070.   Stenström, Arvid

L'Église et la mission au Congo

Uppsala: Swedish Institute of Mission Research, 2006. 269 pages, ISBN: 9789197428279.

The original volume (entitled *Mission blir kyrka*) appeared in Swedish in 1977, in celebration of the centenary of the Swedish mission Svenska Missionsförbundet. This French edition was published for the Congolese churches at the time of the 125th anniversary. Actually, the Svenska Missionsförbundet gave birth to two distinct church bodies based in the two Congos: l'Eglise Evangélique du Congo, Brazzaville, and la Communauté Evangélique du Congo, Kinshasa. This volume tells the story of their founding and growth, from the arrival of the first Swedish missionaries to the autonomy of the two church bodies. The history of the work of the mission in the Belgian and French Congos (with Kinshasa and Brazzaville, their respective capitals, being just across the river from each other) is told chronologically, with a theme for each period: Laying the Foundations (1881–1890), Growth and Maturity (1890–1930), The Outlines of a Church (1930–1957), The Idea of a Church Becomes a Reality (1958–1961). Although the history ends with the autonomy of the two churches in 1961, the opening pages of this French edition add some important details of the period from 1961 to 2006, with a new introduction and colour photographs of the past and contemporary leaders of the two Congolese denominations. This book represents a valuable contribution to understanding the history of these churches in their respective countries, and their ongoing relationship with the mission in Sweden. By providing this new edition, the mission has presented the two church bodies with a very readable resource, in a language accessible to their memberships, thus helping them better know their rich Christian heritage.

1071. Stephens, C. O.

Thinking Communally, Acting Personally: Rank and File Christians in an Age of Mega- and Macro-Institutions

White River, South Africa: C. O. Stephens, 1998. 196 pages, ISBN: 9780620228435.

Stephens' book is another contribution to the recent and welcome spate of publications which critique globalisation and bureaucracy and encourage Christian activism in development work. The author is an evangelical who was born and reared in Congo, has lived in four different African countries, and has travelled widely on the continent as a development consultant. He describes his book as "reflections" on his own experience which applaud recent trends away "from relief to development, and from interventions which perpetuate dependency to ones that are more sustainable." Stephens also argues for a transfer of both responsibility and resources to the grass roots. There are many good ideas, excellent quotations and bits of wise counsel in this book. The reader also certainly catches Stephens' enthusiasm and concern for both building community and for challenging individuals to take initiative and personal responsibility in meeting human needs. But unfortunately the organisation of the book and the writing style are notably self-defeating. The reader is presented with a collection of rather scattered ideas which lack organisation. One senses that this book may represent the author's treasury of diffuse notes from the nearly one hundred consultations and workshops he has attended. Many ideas are presented but left undeveloped, and too many disparate issues and problems are tackled without a thorough, satisfying discussion. Finally, many colloquialisms and off-hand remarks typical of informal oral communication distract attention (e.g. "no way, Jose," "desk jockeys," "bum rap"). For any second edition the author needs to submit to the disciplines of an editor.

Stichter, Sharon

see review 450

1072. Stine, Phillip C., and Ernst R. Wendland, editors

Bridging the Gap: African Traditional Religion and Bible Translation

Reading, UK: United Bible Society, 1990. 226 pages, ISBN: 9780826704542.

The gap between the biblical religious context and the African traditional religious context is the concern of all contextualisation – and the focus of this book. However, unlike many discussions, this book does not expound on the need, but is a serious attempt to analyse the gap, and to devote detailed attention to some specific problem areas. It is in two parts: the first three chapters by Wendland provide an overview of traditional religion in Central Africa, with repeated examples from the Chewa and Tonga cultures of south-central Africa. Wendland is a lecturer at a theological college in Zambia, holds a doctorate in African literature, and has long experience in translation projects of the Bible Societies. Wendland's three chapters could form a useful model for students to improve their own analyses of African traditional religion. Part II presents four case studies by four different authors, which explore the gap by examination of the terminological resources of each society/

language: the Turkana in Kenya (Krijn van der Jagt); the Luo in Kenya (Aloo Osotsi Mojola); the Godie in Côte d'Ivoire (Lynell Marchese Zogbo); and the Gbaya in Cameroon (Philip Noss). This monograph will repay consideration by all those engaged in understanding and communicating the biblical message in Africa, whether or not involved in Bible translation.

1073. **Stinton, Diane, editor**

African Theology on the Way: Current Conversations

London: SPCK, 2010. 208 pages, ISBN: 9780281062515.

The author has been based at Regent College in Canada, after having taught for many years in Kenya. Here she offers a reader in African theology, part of SPCK's *International Study Guides* series, which is aimed at those training for Christian ministry. This volume is heir to John Parratt's *A Reader in African Christian Theology*, first published in 1987 with a second edition in 1997. Following an introduction by the editor, there are sixteen rather brief contributions, seven of them originally published elsewhere. These are grouped in three sections: "Methodological Issues in African Theology," "Contemporary Issues in African Theology" and "The Church in the World." Each chapter begins with a helpful abstract and ends with study questions. The editor introduces the volume as a conversation or palaver among "representative men and women from various church traditions, geographical regions and linguistic zones." The notion of the palaver is a theme that emerges in two of the contributions, and the metaphor is certainly appealing, but in terms of form the book consists rather of sixteen monologues, with no actual "conversation" between the contributors. Moreover, despite the claim to be representative, apparently a characteristic of the African palaver, an unequivocally evangelical African contribution is largely absent from the "conversation," despite the manifest significance of evangelicalism across the continent, and its major contributions to an African theology "on the way." On the other hand, a number of chapters are variously shaped by commitments either to liberation theologies and the ideologies that underlie them, or to the beliefs and values of traditional African culture and religion. Nor is it always clear quite what the conversation is about. According to the editor the volume represents African theology "on the way, the way of Christ." However, Bujo's chapter, "Distinctives of African Ethics," while raising significant issues, focuses almost exclusively on a traditional African ethical approach with brief comparisons between that and his understanding of rationalistic Western ethics. Meanwhile, some other chapters, such as Dandala's "The challenges of ecumenism in African Christianity today," have little if any theological focus at all. As an introduction to the various ways in which some African scholars understand and approach theology this volume merits notice. Some individual articles are well worth reading, including Asamoah-Gyadu's on African Pentecostalism, Dau's comparison between traditional African and biblical approaches to suffering, and Mwaura's reflections on "Christian identity and ethnicity." However, too much in the volume is superficial, and the overall content rarely comes close to serious explication of the biblical meaning of the "way of Christ" for African churches and peoples.

1074. **Stinton, Diane**

Jesus of Africa: Voices of Contemporary African Christology

> Maryknoll, NY: Orbis, 2004. 320 pages, ISBN: 9781570755378.

Stinton's book represents a major contribution to the study of contemporary African Christologies. Stinton was professor of theology at Daystar University, Nairobi, and her book is the result of her doctoral work at the University of Edinburgh. Stinton combines a thorough understanding of published studies of African Christology over the past half-century with current ethnographic research in Kenya, Uganda, and Ghana. To this she has added a set of in-depth interviews with leading African Christological theologians (Bujo, Ela, Mugambi, Nasimiyu, Oduyoye, and Pobee). Inclusion of findings from focus groups and participant observation ensure that this is not simply a survey of what the professional theologians are saying; rather it is thorough study of what Africans of many social and educational contexts are thinking and saying about Jesus. Stinton begins her presentation with a historical survey of the development of Christologies in Africa. She then examines the sources of African Christology, which she identifies as the Bible and other Christian tradition, African culture, and African religions and culture. The heart of the book is her analysis of four over-arching images of how Jesus is understood by African Christians: as Life-giver (including Healer), Mediator (including Ancestor), Loved One (including Family Member and Friend), and Leader (including King or Chief). Her understanding and explanation of how Africans understand Jesus is clear and comprehensive, though occasionally her categorizations appear forced. Though she is primarily descriptive of how African Christians understand the person of Jesus Christ in their lives, she also provides a measure of evaluation, her primary criteria being whether or not Jesus is "significant to life in Africa today." Her evaluation might have been stronger had she taken more into consideration the degree to which the most widely held images of Jesus correspond to *biblical* images of Jesus, though she does emphasize the importance of Scripture controlling Christological images. Her own sympathies are clearly with a Christology of social engagement, and she emphasizes relevance and innovation as primary values in theological thinking. This book is recommended as essential reading for anyone wishing to become acquainted with the state of Christological perceptions in Africa.

Strauss, Scott

> see review 637

1075. **Stuart, John**

British Missionaries and the End of Empire: East, Central, and Southern Africa, 1939–64

> Grand Rapids: Eerdmans, 2011. 240 pages, ISBN: 9780802866332.

The author is a British academic historian who has specialized in Protestant church and mission history in Africa, especially during the critical transition of British Africa in the mid-twentieth century from colonial rule to national independence. He has already published a sequence of learned articles in this field, and here brings together the fruits of such research in a single study, illuminating the whole by focus on developments principally in Botswana, Zambia, Malawi and Kenya. Stuart intends to show how British church and mission agencies and personnel coped both with colonial powers and with nationalist political initiatives in the tumultuous transitions that played out in these countries. The largely simultaneous transition from expatriate mission endeavours to churches under African leadership is also not ignored. Stuart grounds his presentation in vast archival research, which lends singular authority to his findings, and will set a standard for all subsequent research in this field. Whereas popular discourse can often prove untroubled with sweeping generalisations about the role of Western missions in Africa, historians have been much more disciplined in clarifying the tangled complexity of the story. Stuart's contribution is a splendid example of the latter. Overall he demonstrates that British church and mission agencies, while generally intent on responding constructively within the chaotic decolonisation process, were often perplexed and overwhelmed amidst the heady events of the period, struggling to understand and to keep pace, and mostly unable to make any significant impact upon such developments. This was so whether they were dealing with the colonial governments or were responding to the emerging nationalist political movements. While they did often undertake to critique the colonial administrations, and to speak out for African rights, they were not always consistent in this, nor of one voice, nor markedly effective. While Stuart's documentation is satisfyingly fulsome, and his assessments judicious, the narrative thread of his presentations tends rather too easily to disappear within his dense reportage. This is the sort of book that only advanced libraries might need to own, and only advanced researchers need to read. For most others it will be both sufficient, but also important, to be aware of Stuart's particular contribution, and familiar with the direction of his findings.

1076. **Stuebing, Richard W.**

Training for Godliness in African Theological Education

Ndola: ACTEA, 1998. 81 pages.

A long-serving lecturer at the Theological College of Central Africa in Ndola, Zambia, Stuebing here provides a concise guide for the spiritual formation of students in Africa's theological colleges. This pioneering study is the outgrowth of Stuebing's 1994 DMin project at Gordon-Conwell (USA), and is supported by his experience of almost three decades of teaching in Africa. It is the kind of resource for which many of Africa's theological schools have long been searching. Stuebing first provides a brief, readable philosophical and biblical framework for the practice of spiritual formation within a programme of theological education. He then extensively reviews current discussion on the topic (primarily from a Protestant perspective), and offers an up-to-date guide for further reading on the subject through his bibliography (60 entries). In answer to the concern commonly expressed by seminary deans and principals ("We want to do it, but we don't know how"), many readers will find the chapter on "Selected Examples from Africa" particularly helpful. Here Stuebing describes how five selected theological colleges from different parts of the continent are successfully facilitating and evaluating the spiritual development of their students. This monograph provides the materials for informed reflection on a critical concern of many theological educators in Africa, a concern which thus far has rarely been addressed. As such it should prove a valuable resource for those directly involved with programs of spiritual formation at theological training institutions in Africa.

1077. Suberg, Olga Muriel

The Anglican Tradition in South Africa: A Historical Overview

Pretoria: UNISA Press, 1999. 134 pages, ISBN: 9781868880911.

This short study, one in a series of monographs examining the history of various denominations in South Africa, outlines the history of the Church of the Province of South Africa (CPSA) – the largest denomination within the Anglican tradition in that country. The author begins by narrating the arrival and initial period of Anglicanism in Cape Town in the early nineteenth century, and the division of the Anglican churches in southern Africa with the formal formation of the CPSA at a synod in 1870. In this discussion, the theological differences between the forceful Anglo-Catholic bishop of Cape Town, Robert Gray, and his opponents, such as John Colenso (the liberal bishop of Natal, who was eventually excommunicated for heresy), are often downplayed. The author suggests, rather, that at the heart of the conflict were Gray's desire for the necessary authority to bring about unity among the various churches, and his attempt to ensure that these churches did not become an established denomination like the Anglican Church in England. Subsequent chapters describe how the denomination developed in the interior of the land and in Natal. Until fairly recently, the church's historical links have been maintained through a clergy who were born and educated in Britain; the penultimate chapter therefore discusses the "indigenisation" of the CPSA, namely the attempt to move South African-born clergy, both black and white, into positions of leadership. Thus in 1986 Desmond Tutu became the first black South African-born archbishop of Cape Town. The final chapter highlights the contributions made by Tutu, Trevor Huddleston and others in the struggle against apartheid. Suberg's study lacks the narrative cohesion that one would expect from a work of this nature, and the author is often sidetracked by historical and legal minutiae that the intended audience (undergraduate students) would probably find unhelpful. While the history of Anglicanism in South Africa is increasingly relevant in light of developments within the Anglican Communion worldwide, interested readers may be better served by older works like Hinchliff's *The Anglican Church in South Africa* (1963).

Sugden, Christopher

see review 120

Sulayman, S. Nyang

see review 867

1078. Sumamo, Sorsa, and Brian Fargher

Bivocational Missionary-Evangelist: The Story of an Itinerant Preacher in Northern Sidama

Edmonton: Enterprise Publications, 2002. 178 pages.

Here former SIM missionary Brian Fargher, serving in the role of compiler, has enabled an Ethiopian Christian evangelist from the Kale Heywet Church to tell his own story. And the story Sorsa Sumamo tells illustrates the "missionary strategy" of a "bivocational missionary-evangelist," holding two jobs. "Six days a week he was a farmer; seven days a week he was a missionary-evangelist." Both this book and its companion volume by Mehari Choramo, also compiled by Fargher, would never have appeared without the committed efforts of Fargher. The subjects of both books were at time of publication about 80 years old, and both had been known by Fargher for about 40 years. The basis for both books is taped interviews. This one is the inspiring story of a twentieth-century Wolaitta apostle who crossed cultural boundaries within Ethiopia to bring the gospel to the Sidamo people. It was during a ten-month period while Sorsa was visiting his son residing in Edmonton, Alberta, that Brian Fargher did multiple interviews with Sorsa, and then compiled the interviews into a first-person account structured into three sections. Part One describes Sorsa's captivating vision to preach the Good News to the unevangelized for over 50 years. Initially he began preaching to his own family in Wolaitta, southwestern Ethiopia. Several years later his vision expanded to preaching in the area of a neighbouring tribe, the Sidamo, who had no love for the Wolaitta. Eventually through years of service, Sorsa saw some 400 churches established. Part Two elucidates four cardinal convictions which Sorsa put into practice: (1) The messenger must go and preach to everyone everywhere. (2) Believers would come together and form congregations. (3) God would provide spiritual leaders for these groups of believers. And (4) The Word of God has a supernatural quality to it when it is preached and taught. Part Three describes Sorsa's unwavering commitment. Early in his career Sorsa faced the temptation to take training as a medical assistant and thus assure himself of a guaranteed salary. Later in his ministry he languished in prison for over seven months on false charges. Rather than relinquishing his commitment, he asked the prison officials for an adjacent room where he could teach literacy and preach. It was "missionary-evangelists" like Sorsa who, through the impetus of the Holy Spirit and through personal sacrifice, changed the spiritual terrain of much of southern Ethiopia.

1079. Sundkler, Bengt, and Christopher Steed

A History of the Church in Africa

Cambridge: Cambridge University Press, 2000. 1252 pages, ISBN: 9780521583428.

The distinguished missionary statesman and scholar Bengt Sundkler was formerly a missionary in South Africa and Tanzania, and afterward professor of church history at the University of Uppsala. His later years were devoted to producing this massive, magisterial account of the history of African Christianity. But owing to Sundkler's death in 1995, the project was completed and prepared for publication by his former research assistant, Christopher Steed, who now teaches African history at Uppsala University. At the heart of Sundkler and Steed's presentation is the thesis that the well-known and well-documented missionary enterprise in Africa, essential as it was, constitutes only a small part of the full story of the Church in Africa. To understand African Christianity, it is crucial to view the whole picture, and that means taking fully into account the vital, creative role that Africans themselves played in the dynamic process of the continent's Christianisation. It is this particular perspective, one that "focuses not on Western partners but on African actors," that makes this such an especially worthwhile, indispensable contribution. That is not to say that the missionary contribution is underrated. The authors do not degenerate into "missionary-bashing," but regularly call attention to their considerable accomplishments. Despite the lengthy period of history and large geographical area that needed to be covered, the treatment is very complete and more balanced than one might have thought possible. Ironically, it is the most recent period that appears to be the most thinly discussed, with adequate coverage petering out rapidly for the final decade before publication (which is also reflected in the otherwise extensive bibliography). This is not a long, dry, fact-saturated historical report. On the contrary, the authors quickly engage the reader by their generally clear, interesting, and informative manner of writing. Their style is also lightened by periodic subtly humorous and ironic comments, and at the same time is often punctuated by important insights and penetrating observations. Several succinct topical studies of important subjects are also provided, such as on: African religions, missionary societies, David Livingstone, Church strategies, Islam, preaching, healing practices, African church music, and Independent churches. Also very detailed Name and Subject Indices enable the reader to quickly locate persons and topics of special interest. Sundkler and Steed's massive volume has now become one of the established, essential reference texts on African church history. It is keenly regrettable that the publisher never issued this immensely rich achievement in an affordable paperback edition for easy usage in Africa, not only for libraries but also for scholars, pastors, and academics on the continent.

1080. Swart, Morrell F.

The Call of Africa: The Reformed Church in America Mission in the Sub-Sahara, 1948–1998

Grand Rapids: Eerdmans, 1998. 552 pages, ISBN: 9780802846150.

The "Call of Africa" came to the Reformed Church in America (RCA) in 1946 as they declared their decision in a statement entitled "Our New Field – Africa." Bob and Morrie Swart served in Africa, mainly in Ethiopia, for forty of the fifty years of RCA's mission history covered in this substantial survey. But a look at the Index confirms that this is not just one family's story or even just the RCA story. Many other organisations and their personnel are included – perhaps because it has been a principal policy of RCA mission to cooperate with other groups, "not seeking to perpetuate its own organisation or constitutions but [helping] to build a church rooted in the land and suited to the culture of the people." There are three sections: The Sudan Years, The Ethiopia Years, and The Dispersion Years. In addition to the work in Sudan and Ethiopia, RCA's work in Malawi, Kenya, Tanzania, Zambia and Somalia is covered to varying degrees. Documentation is strong, using organisation archives, country-specific communications and personal correspondence. More dates could have been given to pinpoint events. One strength of the book is that the larger context of what was going on is regularly included: for example, details concerning the "Moratorium" issue, and quotations from newspapers about the Marxist revolution in Ethiopia. Colourful insights into the lives of many missionaries and African saints contribute to a fascinating read. For the church in eastern Africa, the book provides a slice of its own story, plus an illustration of the necessity of archives in enabling a reliable and personable church history.

Sybertz, Donald

see review 454

1081. Táíwò, Olúfémi

How Colonialism Preempted Modernity in Africa

Bloomington, IN: Indiana University Press, 2009. 368 pages, ISBN: 9780253221308.

The word "modernity" conjures up a variety of images, but mostly of a Western construct, forged through years of direct influence with the Western Enlightenment. With deft acuity Táíwò challenges such an assumption through a tantalizing tale filled with historical, socio-political, and legal arguments, which places African agency at the forefront of the discussion. His basic premise is that modernity began in Africa long before the colonial era, introduced into the continent by early missionaries and subsequently repackaged by Africans. This advanced wave of missionary presence (which the author locates at the beginning of the nineteenth century) carried not only modernity-related beliefs and artefacts, but also theological rationale, heightening its effectiveness. Táíwò cites such examples as the priesthood of believers, heterodoxy, individual conscience, and freedom of expression. As Africans received this heritage they subsequently altered it to fit their context, revealing distinct forms of modernity on the continent. However, years later, things began to change. Whereas early missionaries largely treated Africans as equals, affording them a fair measure of autonomy to receive the main ideas and artefacts of Western modernity and to reorganise such for themselves, subsequent Western agents dealt with Africans as inferiors, giving rise to what the author describes as dependency scenarios. Thus the author posits critical distinctions between colonialism and modernity, as well as between missionary and colonial administrator, challenging conventional assumptions. Táíwò marshals an extensive variety of evidence to demonstrate his thesis, looking at such as Henry Venn, as well as Samuel Ajayi Crowther, James Africanus Beale Horton, and Rev S. R. B. Attoh-Ahuma. He likewise works into political and legal discourses to show how modernity has been co-opted by colonial governance, and how the "aid model" has become subsumed within the African imagination, giving rise to dependency scenarios. At the end of the study, the author proposes a way forward, pleading with Africans to navigate the future with dexterity. He places the greatest hope in "ordinary Africans" who do not answer to Western agents, but craft their own forms of modernity through their own resources. Táíwò's book is highly readable, despite his propensity to labour through deeply intricate arguments. Anyone interested in retracing Africa's past engagement with missionaries and colonists, or looking ahead to the future of modernity, will find this book highly rewarding. The author dismisses those who want African modernity to embody a completely different nature than found within Western societies, as if anything truly "African" must be measured by its difference from the West. Instead, Táíwò anticipates something more dynamic, with active borrowing and alterations to existing forms. This book would make a valuable addition to the reading list of anyone interested in the variant contours of modern African intellectual life.

1082. Tarr, Del

Double Image: Biblical Insights from African Parables

Mahweh, NJ: Paulist Press, 1994. 209 pages, ISBN: 9780809134694.

Tarr was a missionary in West Africa for fifteen years, has a PhD in cross-cultural communication, and is former President of the Assemblies of God Theological Seminary in the USA. He puts all his scholarly and field-based experience to good use in this book, which offers an excellent anthropological and language-oriented introduction to the field of missiology in general and intercultural, inductive communication in particular. Tarr's seven major theses of cross-cultural communication may be summarized as follows: (1) the filter or point of view of an African culture can increase depth, perception and the concrete texture of Scripture understanding; (2) western society and culture, by its very nature, obscures certain biblical lessons; (3) western individualism, the desire for equality, the cult of youth, etc. may keep us from seeing some biblical truths; (4) we need to take a step back into the pre-scientific world of the Scriptures in order to better understand the supernatural realm; (5) a proper appreciation of "family" and its manifold extended inter-relationships is necessary for a proper biblical hermeneutic; (6) western "print literacy bias" can lead to a depreciation of the "oral/aural world" of biblical as well as African lifestyles and systems of communication; and (7) one should become sensitized to the Scripture-preferred mode of presenting a polarity of ideas that helps teach via contrast – as well as to Scripture's use of imagery, symbolism, life-experiences, folk literary forms, personal names, and certain dramatic rhetorical forms (e.g., irony, hyperbole, enigma, paradox). In addition to helping us develop a more balanced strategy of communication and method of biblical interpretation, Tarr also gently calls attention to blind spots that have hindered Western communication of the gospel in Africa: an over-emphasis on deductive logic, either/or categorical thought and "systematic" theology, the top-down (clergy-dominated) approach to problem-solving, "success"-achievement orientation; the ideal of openness and "democracy"; a desire to "control" nature and the environment; competition-driven capitalistic thinking and "goal"-centeredness; and a general secularisation and de-sacralisation of life. Tarr does not "preach" at the reader; rather he effectively teaches through his African parables, stories, and anecdotes. While it appears that Western missionaries are the primary intended readership, the methods of instruction and biblical applications would also be most helpful to any African reader wrestling with biblical interpretation and intercultural communication.

1083.   Tarrant, Ian

Anglican Swahili Prayer Books: Tanzania (1995) and Congo (1998)

Norwich: Canterbury Press, 2006. 56 pages, ISBN: 9781853118029.

Tarrant, a former CMS mission partner in the Congo (DRC), has provided a welcome study of Anglican liturgical revisions in two parts of Africa. As Tarrant points out, the Anglican prayer book revision in Kenya has received a lot of attention because it was compiled in English, whereas liturgical works done in Kiswahili have attracted much less discussion. Tarrant attempts to address this lacuna. The Anglican church in the Congo is relatively small, and strongest in the eastern part of the country. Tanzania's Anglican church was founded by two separate mission organisations, one evangelical and one Anglo-Catholic. This has complicated liturgical work, since issues like the significance of the elements in the Eucharist, whether there should be prayers for the departed, and the place of Mary and other saints are in dispute within the Tanzanian church. Tarrant describes the different processes used by the two churches to produce their recent prayer books, compares the various services (the Eucharist, Baptism, Marriage and others), notes the distinctive contributions of each book, compares the processes with that in Kenya, and notes the contribution of pan-African discussions. His conclusion is that the Tanzanian book was a rather modest revision of traditional Anglican formularies, but the revisers succeeded in producing a book that is recognizably Anglican and capable of being used by both traditions within that church. The Congolese church made somewhat more use of local African cultural traditions. For example at the end of the funeral service the Congolese book has this rubric: ". . . in Congo there are various customs at the time of death. Some are unacceptable to Christians, because they do not accord with the teaching of the Bible. But others may be performed in an attitude of prayer without sin and without shame." Still, says Tarrant, "it is clear that Kenya has taken on board more of local culture than Congo, which in turn was more inculturated than Tanzania."

Taylor, Rhena

see review 850

1084.   Teferra, Damtew, and Philip G. Altbach, editors

African Higher Education: An International Reference Handbook

Bloomington, IN: Indiana University Press, 2003. 728 pages, ISBN: 9780253341860.

This massive work of reference is the impressive fruit of the African Higher Education Project at the Center for International Higher Education at Boston College, USA. Both editors work as co-directors there. For this project they are joined by another 76 contributors. The first part presents separate chapters on such themes as the development of higher education in Africa, university governance and university–state relations, the economics of higher education in Africa, private higher education in Africa, future trends in African higher education, women in universities, tertiary distance education, the language predicament in African universities, student activism, scientific communication and research in African universities, and African higher education in relation to the world. The second part then goes through all 52 countries, discussing historical lines (a little) and contemporary challenges (much more). This volume will for years to come be an indispensable resource and discussion partner for anyone engaged in research on higher education in Africa. But also for the general practitioner – and that includes those who are responsible for the leading the theological institutions of Africa. There is much of serious usefulness here. Remarkably, the volume has a generally positive approach to private institutions of higher education. It is said repeatedly that the private institutions offer valuable additions to the study programmes of the state institutions, and that due to their relatively small size they may be able to catch new ideas and create new programmes more rapidly than are the state colossuses. The presence of theological institutions of higher education is hardly noticed in articles relating to francophone Africa, reflecting the general marginalization of theological and religious studies in the academia of the African francophone world. Not so for anglophone Africa. For example the Kenya chapter lists all thirteen private universities, including state-accredited ones like Daystar University and the Catholic University of Eastern Africa, as well as the ones not accredited by the Kenyan government, such as NEGST and St. Paul's. And all of these are included in the general discussion. This volume is an exceptional contribution to the understanding of higher education in Africa, and deserves to be familiar within the leadership circles of theological education in Africa. Also its challenges deserve to be met with more research on the role of theological and religious studies within society and academia in Africa. In spite of the impressive number of doctoral dissertations listed in the bibliography on questions related to higher education in Africa (302 of them!), there should be room for a few more addressing the particular issues of theological and religious studies in African higher education.

1085.   Tennent, Timothy C., editor

Theology in the Context of World Christianity: How the Global Church Is Influencing the Way We Think about and Discuss Theology

Grand Rapids: Zondervan, 2007. 320 pages, ISBN: 9780310275114.

With Christianity's centre of gravity now in the Majority World, and the faith being lived out in the heartlands of other major world religions, theological issues surface that have seldom if ever been considered in Western Christianity. So, for example, how should we evaluate the sacred texts of another religion? Because Christianity is unique in its translatability across culture, theology should also be translatable. Thus writes Tennent, who taught at Gordon-Conwell Theological Seminary in the USA, and at Luther W. New Jr. Theological College in India annually for two decades, and has more recently served as president of Asbury Theological Seminary in the USA. Tennent urges us to rethink systematic theology through a more comprehensive missional lens. Two chapters concern the Islamic world: Theology – "Is the Father of Jesus the God of Muhammad?"; and Ecclesiology – "Followers of Jesus in Islamic Mosques." Other chapters consider Bibliology – "Hindu Sacred Texts in Pre-Christian Past"; Soteriology – "Is 'Salvation by Grace through Faith' Unique to Christianity?"; Pneumatology – "The Holy Spirit in Latin American Pentecostalism"; and Eschatology – "Jonathan Edwards and the Chinese Back-to-Jerusalem Movement." The chapter on Christology – "Christ as Healer and Ancestor in Africa" will be of special interest to readers of this publication. As an example, the image of Christ as Ancestor raises challenges which Tennent evaluates according to Mbiti's four guidelines for theologizing, which are (1) a biblical exegetical standard; (2) a serious consideration of the creeds of the ancient churches; (3) the effectiveness of a view in response to the traditional African worldview; and (4) the connection to the living experience of African Christians. The author speaks of the challenges "peculiar to all contextual Christologies" and admonishes us of the necessity to be faithful to the biblical text, while at the same time acknowledging the gifts that are offered because Christianity has now exploded in many areas of the world simultaneously, thus creating more particular "centers of universality" (Mbiti). We must be committed to learning the best from each other. He offers wise advice for dialogue with non-Christian religions, and also considers various ramifications of an emerging "glocal" (global/local) theology. This book should become widely read and discussed among those concerned with appropriate and effective theology within African Christianity.

1086.   Tessier, Henri, editor

Histoire des chrétiens d'Afrique du Nord: Libye-Tunisie-Algérie-Maroc

Paris: Éditions Desclée de Brouwer, 1991. 313 pages, ISBN: 9782718905310.

Twelve individuals plus two religious communities have written chapters or parts thereof for this French-language history of Christianity in four countries of North Africa. The authors, themselves resident in North Africa, are Roman Catholic. With one exception, all are consecrated to (or preparing for) a full-time religious ministry. This background necessarily affects the book's perspective in that one finds nothing about the Protestant or Orthodox churches in the region. On the other hand, the final chapter discusses Catholic-Islamic cooperation. Each chapter has its own bibliography (in French mainly, none in English). There are no footnotes or endnotes. The five sections (fifteen chapters) are divided by historical era and then by country. Some interesting ideas are presented, such as the effect of the vacillating allegiances of North Africa to Europe (implantation of Christianity; colonialism) and to the Mideast (Muslim conquest; post-independence ties). If a francophone theological library does not already have a resource book on (Roman Catholic) Christianity in North Africa, this volume would be a good starting point, to be supplemented hopefully by one with a broader perspective and more documentation.

Thaba, Bitrus

see review 515

Theodosiou, Recah

see review 315

1087.   Theological Advisory Group

A Biblical Approach to Marriage and Family in Africa

Machakos, Kenya: Institute for Church Renewal, 1994. 233 pages, ISBN: 9789966860330.

Those looking for a well-balanced book on African Christian marriage and family will need to look no further. This study was produced by a research team of the Institute for Church Renewal at Scott Theological College in Kenya. The members of the team were all experienced, well-respected African Christian leaders, with a good grasp both of African culture and of Scripture. They cover virtually all relevant topics that come to mind on African Christian marriage and the family. The first chapter covers traditional marriage customs in Africa, followed by a chapter offering a biblical theology of Christian marriage considered within an African context. In the succeeding chapters the authors address specific issues in light both of African traditional marriage practices and biblical Christianity. A "dialogue" between the two becomes a major strength of the book. Fully recognising the value and validity of African culture, the authors do not forgot that, as with all human cultures, it too is fallen. Hence while offering seasoned Christian reflection, they do not cater for a careless compromise of biblical standards. Each of the nine chapters concludes with an extended set of practical discussion questions. The text and bibliography of this book indicate a competent awareness of previous publications on its topic. Although the book was written and published in Kenya, readers in other parts of Africa will actually find it very relevant and applicable.

1088.   Theological Advisory Group

'Come let us bow down...': Worship in the Christian Church in Africa

Kijabe, Kenya: Kesho Publications, 1991. 88 pages, ISBN: 9789966860170.

Produced by the Theological Advisory Group of the Africa Inland Church in Kenya, this is a twenty-session study guide on worship designed for leaders of small group Bible studies. A 56-page workbook for group participants is also available. The booklet offers lessons on: worship as a human response to God, the worth of God, things that spoil worship, how to worship by self-surrender, testimony, song, giving, prayer and obedience. This leaders' guide includes an aim and lesson instructions for each session, and suggests answers for each question in the workbook, ending with application questions and a suggested prayer. The lessons and workbook are written in accessible English and intended for use in local congregations. At points some particularly African concerns, such as fear of evil spirits, are addressed. The guide has an appendix discussing the words used for worship in African traditional religion in several languages of Kenya, and discusses various uses of the English term "worship." The publication is a relevant example of practical catechetical materials on an important topic produced by an evangelical African Christian denomination for use at parish level.

1089.   Theological Advisory Group

The Holy Spirit and the Church in Africa Today

Kijabe, Kenya: Theological Advisory Group, 2001. 449 pages, ISBN: 9789966860408.

Designed as a textbook for use in theological institutions, this book was produced by the Theological Advisory Group (TAG), a research team sponsored by Scott Theological College in Kenya, the same institution that publishes the *Africa Journal of Evangelical Theology*. Each of the main chapters is prefaced with a brief narrative or description drawn from the African context which serves as an introduction to the area under discussion, and each concludes with questions for review and further study, and a brief bibliography. The first chapter establishes the identity of the Holy Spirit, stressing his personality and divinity, and distinguishes him from evil spirits. The next two chapters survey the biblical teaching, and the fourth discusses the meanings of Pentecost, the baptism in the Holy Spirit and the initial sign of speaking in tongues. The fifth chapter explains the work of the Spirit in the life of the Christian, including conviction of sin, regeneration, securing believers, enabling them to grow, guiding them and finally resurrecting them. Chapter six discusses the place and importance of both the fruit and the gifts of the Spirit. The final – and longest – chapter examines what the authors term "those controversial gifts," namely healing, prophecy and tongues. This book thus provides a substantial treatment of the doctrine of the Spirit, presented with sensitivity to the African context. It also seeks to respond biblically to questions raised by the charismatic movement, which has had such considerable impact on contemporary African church life. In general, the most typical charismatic and Pentecostal distinctive interpretations are denied. And while the authors decline to affirm cessationism, it is viewed as true in practice. At the same time the tone of the discussion is conciliatory, and the writers seek to maintain a balance. They believe that miracles may still happen, and they cautiously accept the possibility that some believers may speak in tongues. In addition they note that the attraction of Pentecostal and charismatic Christianity is often a reaction to the cold, shallow formalism and nominalism of more traditional churches. This is a significant contribution to the discussion of the Holy Spirit within the African context. It will prove a useful tool for everyone seeking to understand the biblical teaching on the Holy Spirit in a way that is sensitive to the African setting, and especially so for those within non-charismatic Christian traditions.

1090.   Thiong'o, Ngugi wa

Dreams in a Time of War: A Childhood Memoir

New York: Random House, 2011. 272 pages, ISBN: 9780307476210.

While Ngugi's international fame can be attributed almost entirely to his novels and their insightful depictions of Kenya's colonial and post-colonial struggles, in *Dreams in a Time of War* he offers a significant and heart-warming autobiography. Covering his life from his earliest memories up to his admittance into Alliance High School (the most prestigious private school in Kenya at that time), it forms an illuminating complementary companion to Ngugi's novels. Ngugi was a precocious and perceptive child whose personal experiences shed light on the intense struggles endured by the Kikuyu tribe from which the Mau Mau (national freedom fighters) emerged. Ngugi succinctly analyses the situation: "People lived under a double fear: of government operations by day and the Mau Mau guerrilla activities by night." Members of his own extended family were on opposite sides of the conflict, and one of his half-brothers, Gitogo, a deaf mute, was shot to death by a British soldier because he could not hear the command to stop. This tragic incident is recaptured without alteration as an event recorded in *A Grain of Wheat*. *Dreams in a Time of War* sheds additional light on Ngugi's personal encounters with Christianity. His "most prized" book was a torn copy of the OT, and his familiarity with the Scriptures is evident in all of his novels. His personal spiritual journey, however, is characterized by ambivalence. Although influenced by his father's scepticism towards "the rituals of both tradition and Christianity," Ngugi found such rituals appealing. He underwent "the Christian rite of baptism by water" as well as adopting a biblical name, James, which he later relinquished, reverting to Ngugi wa Thiong'o in 1969. His announcement at the General

Assembly of the Presbyterian Church of East Africa in 1970 that he was no longer "a man of the Church; I am not even a Christian" is not completely surprising when viewed in the light of what he describes as "the irony" of his teen-age attempts to combine Sunday "worship and communion" with "a life of the mind" at school. Nevertheless, Ngugi's integration of biblical imagery and motifs, as well as his depictions of Moses and Christ as political liberationists, is a dominating feature of his novels. This autobiography shortens the distance between Ngugi the novelist and Ngugi the man.

1091. **Thompson, T. Jack**

Touching the Heart: Xhosa Missionaries to Malawi, 1876 – 1888

Pretoria: UNISA Press, 2000. 215 pages, ISBN: 9781868881406.

In this book Thompson focuses attention on the contribution of Africans to the planting of Christianity in Malawi during the latter part of the nineteenth century. The author meticulously reconstructs the stories of the first four Xhosa evangelists to Malawi from the Lovedale Institution in South Africa. Thompson combines painstaking historical research with deep insight into cultural and linguistic matters born of many years as a missionary in Malawi. He has left no stone unturned in his passion to rescue the Xhosa missionaries from historical obscurity, and to move African initiative in mission from the periphery to the centre of the narrative. These men sacrificed their health, families, and lives to plant the Presbyterian Church among the Ngoni. Multilingual and confident that the gospel was meant for African peoples, the Xhosa missionaries acted as cultural bridges between African and European worldviews. The reader is introduced to the four missionaries, the Lovedale Institution from which they graduated, and the events leading to their leaving in 1876 for Malawi to work with the newly formed Livingstonia Mission to Central Africa (Free Church of Scotland). In a moving account the reader is introduced to the life and ministry experiences of these first volunteers: William Koyi, Shadrach Mngunana, Isaac Williams Wauchope, and Mapassa Ntintille, plus William Isaacs who went to Malawi in 1883. Their contribution within the Livingstonia Mission at Cape Maclear, their support to the Blantyre Mission (Church of Scotland) and eventually their work at Bandawe in the northern part of Malawi are all described. This book reveals that indigenisation was not the tardy discovery of the post-colonial age, but a factor in the earliest days of the so-called "mission churches." It also uncovers the intimate struggles and trials of African missionaries operating under the European missionaries: they were essential to the success of the mission, yet subordinate to the Scottish missionaries. Thompson's work is a valuable addition to a much-neglected history of the contribution of Africans to the establishment of the Church in Africa.

Thomson, Dennis L.

see review 129

1092.   Thornton, John K.

The Kongolese Saint Anthony: Dona Beatriz Kimpa Vita and the Antonian Movement, 1684–1706

Cambridge: Cambridge University Press, 1998. 238 pages, ISBN: 9780521596497.

The author is an American professor of history who has taught at the University of Zambia. This book is based on his 1979 doctoral thesis, which apparently broke with the prevalent interpretation that a young Congolese woman of the early eighteenth century named Kimpa Vita (also known as Dona Beatriz), and the movement she inspired, were nationalist forerunners of the African independence movement. Thornton's objective is to fix the context of the movement more precisely and provide a narrative account in a way that is accessible to a non-academic audience. He does this well, using the diaries and letters of four Capuchin Fathers as his main sources; the book is well documented, considering the time and place in which Dona Beatriz lived. The historical context was not just tension with a colonial power (represented by the Capuchin Fathers) but that the Kongo kingdom (largely situated in what is now northern Angola) was on the brink of civil war. Dona Beatriz had already been a "nganga" (traditional spiritual leader) when she claimed to have died and been reborn in 1704 as St. Anthony, the patron saint of Portugal. It should be noted that the same word (nganga) was also used for the priests, because all such people were in contact with the Other World. Dona Beatriz claimed that Jesus and Mary were Kongolese, changed the words of Roman Catholic prayers and insisted that God saved people on the basis of their intentions, not the sacraments. St. Anthony even replaced Mary in the hierarchy, so it was no wonder that the Catholic fathers opposed her. Dona Beatriz herself preached chastity, but later tried to cover a pregnancy by hiding and claiming she had visited heaven. After she fled to have the baby, she was captured and executed, never renouncing her claim to be St. Anthony. The author notes the ambivalence of the Capuchins over Africans having visions when the fathers themselves supported apparitions of the Virgin Mary. Yet he does not make any judgment on whether Dona Beatriz was mad, demon-possessed or a church heretic (all of which were claimed at one time or another). Initiates such as Dona Beatriz were believed to have died, so their new bodies were not subject to the usual taboos such as incest, but the author seems ignorant that incest is still considered powerful magic among ngangas. In fact, he makes few moral judgments, even withholding his opinion over the Capuchins' support for slavery and their burning of Dona Beatriz as a heretic. Nevertheless, this remains a helpful source for a particular episode in African church history. Whether Dona Beatriz should be considered a forerunner of modern nationalist movements, in all events the evident parallels with the origins of some AIC movements cannot be ignored.

1093.   Thornton, Margaret, editor

Training TEE Leaders

Nairobi: Evangel, 1990. 108 pages, ISBN: 9789966850928.

This book grew out of a course offered at Daystar University in Nairobi, using papers presented by several men and women, both African and expatriate, involved in training leaders for theological education by extension (TEE) in Africa. The book is arranged in such a manner that one may use all or just certain units, depending on the knowledge and training already received and the time available for the training seminar. The book is most valuable if used in a group, so that appropriate practice takes place, but one could also greatly profit just from reading the book. The introduction gives some very helpful practical information on the organisation of a training seminar and the use of this book. While every unit in the book has value, among the most helpful are unit 3 (on the nature of the group), and unit 7 (on the preparation of appropriate discussion questions). Here is valuable information for all educators, not just TEE leaders. The book may give the impression that TEE is only used to train adults who have experience in ministry. Some TEE programmes include young people who have little experience, and the experience of the participants would greatly influence the nature of the discussion questions and the role of the TEE leader. Other helpful books of this nature are available in English, but this is possibly the only book of its kind also available in French.

1094.   Thorpe, S. A.

African Traditional Religions

Pretoria: UNISA Press, 1991. 129 pages, ISBN: 9780869817322.

This slender volume is designed as an introduction to African traditional religions (ATR) for first year university students. The author recognizes the value of continent-wide surveys on ATR (such as Mbiti's *Concepts of God in Africa*), but notes their tendency to overgeneralize what is in reality a mosaic of immense variety. The alternative to that is to focus on one ethnic group and to examine its religious dimensions in exhaustive detail (e.g. Daneel's three-volume study of South Shona independent churches). Thorpe attempts to steer a middle course. He selects just five examples: the San Bushmen of the Kalahari, the Zulu, the Shona, the Ituri Pygmies of Congo (DRC), and the Yoruba of Nigeria, looking in turn at historical, cultural, and especially religious distinctives of each. In doing so, the author leans heavily on the detailed work of others, but may be thanked for distilling their often voluminous findings into manageable proportions. In this way, due recognition of diversity is given, while a final chapter recognizes emphases and concerns common to all, which make it not inappropriate to speak of African traditional religion as a whole. An epilogue comments on African religions and the future. The tone here as throughout the book is sympathetic.

1095.   Thurow, Roger, and Scott Kilman

Enough: Why the World's Poorest Starve in an Age of Plenty

New York: PublicAffairs, 2010. 336 pages, ISBN: 9781586488185.

Thurow and Kilman, reporters with the *Wall Street Journal*, focus attention on hunger in Africa by telling the stories of people impacted by foreign aid policies in both positive and negative ways. Their book begins with an account of the work of Norman Borlaug, the architect of the Green Revolution. The Green Revolution was the combination of synthetic seeds and fertilizers which led to huge crop yields in Latin America and Asia, virtually eliminating hunger in both areas. Why Green Revolution technologies have not worked in Africa is discussed in the first part of the book, which tells stories of African farmers and their efforts to improve their yields and livelihoods. When African farmers cannot feed themselves they are sent humanitarian assistance in the form of grain and beans grown in the US and sent to Africa through government-subsidized shipping. Local markets in African beans and grains are crippled as "free" foreign food is sent in. The book is replete with examples and chastises US and European governments for agricultural policies which create hunger in Africa. These same governments then respond to hunger with humanitarian relief. The system of subsidies and humanitarian assistance has created an "Iron Triangle" of vested interests in the US: farmers, shippers and humanitarian aid groups – all of whom back the system of agricultural subsidies and food aid. The authors find the resulting programs and policies extremely harmful to Africans and helpful to US agricultural interests. *Enough* is by no means only about tragedy. In the second half of the book the authors recount what people are trying to do to change the nature of foreign assistance and humanitarian relief. They tell of a movement of people in churches and government who want something different and better.

1096.   Tibenderana, Peter

Islamic Fundamentalism: The Quest for the Right of Muslims in Uganda

Kampala: Fountain Publishers, 2006. 136 pages, ISBN: 9789970025725.

This is a distinctly uneasy book for Christians to read, but also a revealing one. Coming from a Christian background, the author spent years teaching at Ahmadu Bello University in Nigeria, at Makerere University in Uganda, and as a visiting lecturer at the Islamic University in Uganda, before his appointment as vice chancellor at Kampala International University. This is a scholarly book that reflects on Islam's struggle with modernity and cultural independence from the West ("We will be modern but won't be you"), the status of Islam within the Ugandan family of religions (1991 statistics), the various Islamic sects in Uganda (Sunni, Shia, Ismaelis and Ahmadiya), and the "Golden Era" of Islam under Idi Amin's rule from 1971 to 1979. Throughout the book the author seeks to express the convictions of Ugandan Muslims based on his own special research (out of 110 questionnaires sent out some two-thirds responded): "Many Muslims strongly believe that since the overthrow of Idi Amin's regime in 1979, they have been oppressed and marginalized by successive Ugandan governments." The reader gets a clear sense of the Muslim quest to move "from timidity to self-assertiveness." The author suggests ten rights which Muslims should seek to see implemented, such as "to be ruled by a fellow Muslim and in accordance with the sharia, to have a completely Islamic education, for a man to marry four wives, and for a man to divorce any of his wives whenever he chooses." Tibenderana also says it is essential for Islamic institutions of higher education to start programmes for the Islamisation of knowledge: this means to add Islamic principles to every normal non-religious subject of study. He advises the Ugandan government to drop its opposition to the formation of an Islamic political party, which he suggests is the only peaceful way forward. He does not conceal his own bias, e.g. when he comments on the Ugandan Muslim Supreme Council (UMSC) plan to solicit money from donor countries and NGOs to spread Islamic thought and knowledge: "This is a good idea which should be supported by all men of good will for the sake of advancing Islam in Uganda." It is not a surprise, therefore, that the Rector of the Islamic University in Uganda praises Prof. Tibenderana for having "tried his very best to write the book from a neutral position." It would serve Christian leaders well in many other parts of Africa to study the clarifying indications of this book about the Islamic religio-political agenda within countries of Africa.

1097.   Tiénou, Tite

The Theological Task of the Church in Africa

Achimota, Ghana: Africa Christian Press, 1990. 56 pages, ISBN: 9789964877965.

As former chairman of the association of evangelical theological colleges in Africa (ACTEA), later head of the Faculté de Théologie in Abidjan, and more recently dean of Trinity Deerfield in the USA, Tite Tiénou is eminently qualified to speak about the theological needs of the church in Africa today. This small but extremely important book deserves a most careful reading by any person seriously concerned about theological development in Africa. (For this second edition the author revised the text throughout, and contributed a completely new fourth chapter.) Tiénou sets forth the urgent need for an evangelical strategy to promote contextualized theological life at all levels in Africa. After first defining some basic terms, such as "evangelical" and "theology" as used in the African context, he proceeds to explain the reasons why such a strategy is so urgently needed. These reasons include the special (and mostly unaddressed) needs of African culture, the critical need to find concrete points of contact between biblical Christianity and African traditional religions, and the subtle dangers involved in the recent rise of "African theology." Tiénou warns that positive improvement in the situation will not automatically happen, due to a number of contrary factors in the African situation. However, he concludes by setting out a positive and workable strategy to overcome the present evangelical theological malaise, including a list of fourteen specific tasks which should be seriously addressed by evangelical leaders if the church in Africa is to achieve the growth and maturity that God intends for it in this generation. This is a widely read classic text of African evangelical theological reflection, with proposals that continue to deserve in-depth discussion and judicious implementation.

Tiénou, Tite

see also reviews 464 and 793

Tivnan, Edward

see review 143

1098. Tlhagale, Buti, and Itumeleng J. Mosala, editors

Hammering Swords into Ploughshares: Essays in Honor of Archbishop Mpilo Desmond Tutu

Grand Rapids: Eerdmans, 1987. 300 pages, ISBN: 9780802802699.

This Festschrift is an acknowledgement of the significant role Archbishop Desmond Tutu has played in modern African history and particularly the history of the Church's dealings with the apartheid regime in South Africa. The impetus for the collection of essays was the awarding of the Nobel Peace Prize to Tutu in 1984, and a desire to furnish the rest of the world with an *apologia* for a man too often misunderstood. Since the book pre-dates the end of apartheid, it provides a useful window on how South African Christians, both black and white, dealt with apartheid in their country at that time. This anachronism obviates some of the points made in some of the articles, but also permits fascinating insights into other aspects of life under the oppressive regime. Many of the authors address the apartheid issue, either directly or indirectly, and some articles attempt to prepare for a time when apartheid will no longer be an issue. The book is interesting as well in that the authors form a diverse group: men, women, black, white, differing educational levels, different career paths, and representing Europe, North America, and sub-Saharan Africa, as well as various segments of South African society. The work is particularly helpful when various essayists outline the theological foundations for some of Tutu's work. Maimela, for example, mentions Tutu's commitment to God as Lord of all life, and to an incarnational theology, as the theological basis for his involvement in politics. The practical interest in meeting human needs comes from Tutu's conviction that God is loving, compassionate and biased in favour of the oppressed. The Nobel Prize laureate's opposition to apartheid stems from a belief that, whereas apartheid separates and brings disunity, the Bible proclaims reconciliation, oneness and the inherent worth of each individual formed in the image of God. The book's essays cover variously: personal tributes, theological tributes, African theology, morality in African tradition, social ethics in South Africa, prophetic theology; the struggle in South Africa; and black theology in South Africa. For anyone studying the history of the Church's dealings with the apartheid regime in South Africa, this is a useful resource which through the footnotes will lead the researcher to other sources.

Tobler, Judy

see review 195

Toler, Michael

see review 686

1099.   Tolo, Arne

Sidama and Ethiopian: The Emergence of the Mekane Yesus Church in Sidama

Uppsala: Uppsala University, 1998. 312 pages, ISBN: 9789185424498.

Tolo served for a number of years as a missionary in the southern part of Ethiopia, and now lectures at an institute of higher learning in Bergen, Norway. His topic is the Sidama people of south-central Ethiopia, who during the last one hundred years have experienced continuous political, social and religious change. Politically the incorporation of the south into the Ethiopian empire by the end of the nineteenth century had severe consequences on the Sidama people. The *gabbar* system, a harsh form of economic oppression, broken by the presence of the Italians in 1936–1941, was not completely eradicated before the Ethiopian revolution in 1974. Also, as with other southern peoples of Ethiopia, the subjection of the Sidama within the Ethiopian empire brought with it the influence of the Ethiopian Orthodox Church. This in turn had already impacted the traditional beliefs that the first expatriate missionaries encountered when they entered the Sidama area in 1925. Tolo gives a good account for the cultural, political and historical background of the Sidama people and their place in the wider Ethiopian context. The main focus of the book, however, is to study why and how Sidama became one of the strongest evangelical areas of Ethiopia. The exiting story of the spread of the gospel in this area by means of national evangelists and overseas missionaries (the SIM and NLM) is foundational to the history of the two larger evangelical churches in Ethiopia, the Kale Heywet Church and the Ethiopian Evangelical Church Mekane Yesus, both of which have large followings among the Sidama people. Tolo's study is important for its survey of the struggles encountered by the Ethiopian Orthodox Church in a largely non-Orthodox area, for its account of the not-so-pleasant aspects of the Ethiopian empire, and especially for its exiting description of the growth and development of evangelical churches among the Sidama.

Tooke, John

see review 817

Tsala-Clémençon, Georgine

see review 368

1100. **Tshilenga, Emmanuel K.**

Collective Sins in Africa: A Missiological Approach to the African Crisis

Pretoria: UNISA Press, 2005. 220 pages, ISBN: 9781868883769.

Tshilenga is Congolese (DRC) by birth, but has also lived in the Central African Republic and now resides in South Africa. His wealth of pastoral experience is also evident in this work, which was originally his doctoral thesis for the University of Pretoria. After acknowledging original sin, individual sin and collective sin as separate categories, the author outlines three types of collective sins that have troubled the church in Africa, namely structural sin, cultural sin, and social sin. Every collectivity is subject to collective sins, but Tshilenga wants to address those which cause Africa to suffer, such as tribalism and apartheid. The illustrations throughout the book come (mainly) from the DRC, from RSA, and from church history throughout the centuries. Conscious that the topic could easily become mired in systematic theology or in various aspects of African culture or theology, the author keeps pursuing his basic focus: how can this information concerning collective sin be used by the church to further its mission in the world, and particularly in Africa? He emphasizes that the church is called to stand against those collective sins (such as tribal hatred) that it finds in the social groups within which it is embedded. Evangelism needs to be followed by discipleship that helps the new Christian to renounce collective sins. The final pages focus on specific things a church can do to fight against collective sin in the church. The church itself needs to work on contextualized services and especially music which would denounce collective sins and show a better way to live. The book is very readable, and its extensive research references will be helpful to anyone interested in pursuing the contributions of other African authors. The idea of collective sin is not one that is often pursued, and the insights offered could be helpful to those teaching and writing in theology, as well as those involved in Christian ministry anywhere in Africa.

1101. **Tshimika, Pakisa K., and Tim Lind**

Sharing Gifts in the Global Family of Faith: One Church's Experiment

Intercourse, PA: Good Books, 2003. 96 pages, ISBN: 9781561483877.

This book grew out of a mandate given in 1998 by the Mennonite World Conference to the authors, one American and one African, to visit each member conference in order to hold workshops to "teach and encourage the sharing of gifts in the church." The hope was that this would "encourage a new vision within the churches about the gifts God has given us and how we use them." The African delegate, Pakisa Tshimika, was from Congo (DRC), holds a doctorate in public health, and has served as Program Director in Africa for the Mennonite Brethren Mission. The purposes of the book include: first, to report on this experiment in identifying and encouraging Global Gift Sharing; second, to share what the authors learned through this experiment; and third, to make what has been learned available to local congregations in the global church through guidance for holding local workshops. The chapter titles illustrate the movement of the topics covered, from many gifts but one Spirit, through God as a sharing God, to the importance of being God's family and sharing gifts in the global family. They discuss what gifts are, how they are related to needs, what sharing is, and the biblical understanding of gifts, their origin and purpose, and God's intention of abundant life for all. The authors acknowledge obstacles to sharing gifts, with these including economic differences, lack of administrative capacity, fear of cultural and other differences, and greed. They end by describing what a gift-sharing church might look like. The authors acknowledge that Christians hold differing views on personal ownership, and differences in wealth, and that these views will affect how their book may be read. While they seek for balance, the authors do at some points reveal their disapproval of large disparity in wealth among churches of different countries. Also, some readers may wonder about the lack of emphasis on productivity to enable resources for sharing, and also on accountability to assess when sharing is not the biblical response. Cultural assumptions and how some of these may draw participants away from biblical guidelines on sharing could also have been addressed more clearly.

1102. Tuju, Raphael

AIDS: Understanding the Challenge

Nairobi: ACE Communications, 1996. 180 pages, ISBN: 9789966961105.

This book by the Nairobi-based journalist and broadcaster Tuju is a straightforward discussion of the challenge presented to Africa by the disease of AIDS. It is a book by an African for Africans, filled with medically accurate and culturally relevant material. Tuju skilfully deals with social issues such as the breakdown of the family and how pop-culture and local customs are changing and promoting the spread of AIDS. He also addresses some of the popular myths about the disease and how AIDS can be prevented. Although not written from an explicitly Christian viewpoint, Tuju does advocate abstinence, and faithfulness within a "monogamous sexual relationship as the best way to prevent the spread of the disease." Other valuable content includes information on sexually transmitted diseases and the particular issues that women and men face who have AIDS. Tuju also presents interviews with those who are infected with AIDS. The warnings from their experiences are quite powerful. A helpful section at the end of the book contains answers to commonly asked questions, as well as a glossary of terms. This book is a good, basic, credible discussion of the AIDS issue in Africa. It is well written and easily read. It could prove very helpful for use in AIDS-awareness programmes.

1103. Turaki, Yusufu

Christianity and African Gods: A Method in Theology

Potchefstroom, South Africa: Potchefstroom University, 1999. 359 pages, ISBN: 9781868223640.

This is a foundational study in methodology for African Christian theology, from within an avowed commitment to biblical revelation. The author is a theologian of considerable stature in Africa. He has previously been head of ECWA Theological Seminary Jos (JETS), and has held important leadership roles in his own denomination and in the continental Association of Evangelicals in Africa (AEA). Turaki starts from a recognition that the influence of African traditional religious thought and culture on the life of the church "is neither dormant nor docile, but has the power . . . to re-cast and transform [Christianity] into its own categories of thought and mentalities." Turaki shows a concern, almost an impatience, with purely comparative studies of various facets of Christianity and traditional religions. He argues for applying a more radically biblical critique, and a more fully Trinitarian theological methodology, in the assessment of traditional beliefs and the concomitant traditional practices. His purpose is to demonstrate a theological methodology suitable for a Christian approach to African traditional religions and cultures. In the process he first surveys some of the more prominent methodologies in the study of religions, in order to clarify "the theological and the functional meanings of traditional religions and how a Christian theology should approach them." The author then extensively sets out his understanding of the theological, philosophical, and ethical foundations of the traditional religious worldview, and proceeds to an in-depth examination of the nature and the theological basis of each of that system's specific components. He clearly believes that there are enough elements held in common by the various ethnic traditional religions of Africa for it to be possible to evaluate them as a whole. In the penultimate chapter the author then revisits each of the theological, philosophical, ethical and human foundations of African religious beliefs and practices, and analyses them in the light of a Christian theology. And finally he summarizes his theological method. The whole book is presented in the detailed and closely-argued style which one has come to associate with Professor Turaki. While it does not always make for easy reading, the book will amply reward careful study. As a basic analytical reference work, it stimulates a longing for the author's insights to be followed through into wider application in the life of the African Christian community.

1104. Turaki, Yusufu

An Introduction to the History of SIM/ECWA in Nigeria 1893–1993

Jos: Challenge Press, 1993. 310 pages, ISBN: 9789781373596.

In response to a request from the Evangelical Church of West Africa (ECWA) in Nigeria, and in preparation for the 1993 centennial celebration of SIM and ECWA in Nigeria, Turaki prepared a detailed history of SIM and ECWA during the first one hundred years of their presence in that country. As former head of ECWA Theological Seminary Jos, former ECWA General Secretary and thereafter ECWA Education Secretary, Turaki was an appropriate person to undertake this research. The book is presented as an introduction to its topic, but as such it turns out to be a surprisingly detailed and thorough reference to the forces, factors, people, policies, struggles and statistics that make up the history of one of the largest interdenominational missions and one of the largest Protestant churches in Nigeria. Especially informative and insightful is Turaki's analysis of the religious and political context in which SIM's work began a century ago. The book will be of particular interest to missionaries and missiologists who are concerned with the establishment of new work today in hard places, since pioneer missionary work often involves the same kinds of struggles and problems. It will also be useful reading to many in Africa and elsewhere who are concerned with church-mission relationships. And it especially deserves the notice of all who are interested in the history of Christian communities in modern Africa.

1105. Turaki, Yusufu

Tainted Legacy: Islam, Colonialism and Slavery in Northern Nigeria

McLean, VA: Isaac Publishing, 2010. 210 pages, ISBN: 9780982521830.

For more than three decades the author has been serving in public ecclesiastical and scholarly roles, including recently as Professor of Theology and Social Ethics at JETS, the seminary in Jos, Nigeria, of the Evangelical Church of West Africa (ECWA). His studies in the USA and South Africa, his roles as an official in ECWA, and as an executive in several inter-church associations, including the International Bible Society, give Turaki a depth of background that lends authority to his work. In this book Turaki comes back to his PhD research, building on his 1982 thesis, which was published in 1993 as *The British Colonial Legacy in Northern Nigeria.*

In this latest study the British legacy is reviewed, but the emphasis is now on the Sokoto Caliphate and its conquests and enslavement of non-Muslim peoples in Nigeria's Middle Belt region. Next, Turaki describes the use Muslims made of the positions of power that the British colonial authorities continued to allow the traditional rulers especially of Sokoto under indirect rule in Northern and Middle Belt Nigeria. Turaki tends to an analytic style of expression that can become numbing when used in sentence after sentence, and there is a fair amount of repetition. But, while the language is far from violent, the nails indicting the British and the Fulani-Hausa colonialists are hit solidly and relentlessly in every one of the fifteen chapters. The long-term consequences remain vividly evident in contemporary Nigeria. Turaki is not providing much new research here, although he provides an excellent bibliography. One would love to see specific examples from those connected with other early missions in the North additional to the SIM, such as the Church Missionary Society, the Sudan United Mission, and the United Missionary Society. Nevertheless, Turaki shows again that at least in Northern Nigeria missions were not tools in the hands of colonialists, as the stereotype has it. In a way, *Tainted Legacy* is a tract collecting the results of years of research and personal experience of Islamic exploitation in Northern and Middle Belt Nigeria. The final chapter draws conclusions for modern Nigeria. One conclusion seems to be that the offices of Fulani-Hausa traditional ruling families which were set up by the Caliphate or by the British over non-Muslim people groups must be abolished. Christian resentment at discriminatory practices must be reviewed with understanding of the theology of Islam toward slavery and toward conquest of non-Muslims. Muslims and Christians should re-examine their scriptures to awaken consciences to the evils of exploitation.

1106. Turaki, Yusufu

Tribal Gods of Africa: Ethnicity, Racism, Tribalism and the Gospel of Christ

Nairobi: AEA, 1997. 168 pages, ISBN: 9789783402560.

Coming close on the heels of the compendium edited by Buconyori on *Tribalism and Ethnicity*, this volume makes it clear that evangelicals in Africa have been awakened to the need to confront one of the most pressing challenges facing African Christian communities. Turaki is a leading Nigerian churchman. His typically well-researched and thoroughly documented study is very different from the Buconyori volume, since it develops an approach to the topic from sociological, cultural, historical and moral perspectives, and only then attempts to provide biblical foundations for peace and justice, and adumbrates possible solutions. Evangelicals in Africa will continue the search for an in-depth understanding of how the gospel speaks to the realities of ethnocentricity and tribalism. The book leads up to a challenge to both the church and the state in Africa to create a just and peaceful society in Africa. Stimulated by reflection on (amongst others) the ongoing crises in Rwanda and Burundi, the influences left over from the colonial period come in for the usual castigation, but are not deemed to be the sole or even the main cause of Africa's own deeply-rooted problems. "The failure of African states was not due to the lack of structural, constitutional, or social reforms, but rather the absence of universal moral and ethical values and principles" well sums up Turaki's thesis. The troubles of Africa are seen in terms of "tribal gods," and tribalism is seen as being intrinsically related to religion. The causes of tribalism's evil impact in African society are seen as deriving primarily from people mis-applying for their own ends the excellent cultural and traditional values found in Africa. This is the careful diagnosis; the cure is only hinted at. The author evidently finds that, as so often, it easier to expose and critique evils than to find ways to overcome them. So we must still look for further positive proposals from this important sector of the African Christian community. Turaki's depth of scholarly research and his style of writing will make this not an easily accessible book for the average reader, but this wide-ranging study will certainly reward careful perusal.

1107. Turner, Thomas

The Congo Wars: Conflict, Myth and Reality

London: Zed Books, 2007. 256 pages, ISBN: 9781842776896.

Turner, a lecturer at Virginia Commonwealth University in the United States, previously taught for extended periods in Congo, Rwanda, Kenya and Tunisia. The depth of his African experience is borne out by the rich detail of this nuanced account of the ongoing conflicts that have destabilized Congo since 1996. *The Congo Wars* is a forensic investigation of "one of the bloodiest yet least understood conflicts of recent times." Its stated aim is to "establish, first, what has happened in Congo, second, to sort out the explanations and, third, to offer some recommendations for the future." The first two goals are achieved admirably, but Turner seems to come up short in relation to his third objective. He points the finger at the (usual) suspects with conviction, but is less convincing when trying to point the way forward. Given the "indescribable cacophony" of the conflict he is trying to make sense of, this is not surprising, and perhaps the fault lies more with the extent of his ambition than the rigour of his analysis. The author is at his most compelling when unpacking the different myths of how Congo came to be in such a mess. There is little evidence of bias in his even-handed discussion of who is to blame, and he is cautious in singling out Belgium and Rwanda as the biggest contributors to the country's problems (as well as the most prolific exporters of its vast wealth). According to Turner, Belgium set the scene for what was to come by setting people groups against one another for profit, entrenching conflict through the imposition of an inappropriate European model of governance, and then setting independence up for failure by retaining proxy influence. For its part, Rwanda is judged to have had ideological and material motives for bringing about the downfall of Mobutu and then continuing to destabilize Congo. There is little room for the spiritual here. The (Catholic) Church is described as one third of the colonial "Trinity," alongside the state and foreign companies, but Turner never lapses into that simplistic scapegoating of Christianity to be found elsewhere. Essentially academic in approach and tone, this book would be a prudent read for anyone needing nuanced understanding of the persisting conflict it addresses.

1108. Tushima, Cephas

The Fate of Saul's Progeny in the Reign of David

Eugene, OR: Wipf & Stock, 2011. 372 pages, ISBN: 9781608999941.

The book is a revised version of a PhD thesis from Westminster Theological Seminary in the United States, supervised by Tremper Longman. The author has served as Acting Director of the PhD programme at Jos ECWA Theological Seminary, Nigeria. The book sets out to investigate the relationship between King David and the heirs of his predecessor Saul, according to 1–2 Samuel. The investigation shows that David, like other ancient Near Eastern usurpers, was in the most part unjust and calculating in his dealings with Saul's progeny. The book, divided into eight chapters, has the logical structure of a doctoral thesis: problem, research context, analysis, conclusion. Chapter one locates the investigation textually, demonstrating the author's preference for literary perspectives. Chapter two locates it in relation to the interpretive history of 1–2 Samuel, and chapter three locates it methodologically, with a presentation and discussion of narrative criticism. From chapter four on, the investigation goes into the key texts. Thus chapter four deals with the death of Saul and the contest for the succession to the throne. Chapter five deals with David's relationship to Michal, and chapter six with his relationship to Mephibosheth. Chapter seven offers an integrated reading of the research findings; first with an evaluation of David's interaction with the Saulides, studied in the light of Torah instruction, and then from a broader perspective, the biblical theological implications of the study. Chapter eight is mainly a summary of the investigation. Tushima's book is a welcome research contribution, offering a demonstration of the growing interest for narrative and literary approaches amongst the younger generation of African OT scholars.

1109.   **Tutu, Desmond**

An African Prayer Book

New York: Doubleday, 2006. 139 pages, ISBN: 9780385516495.

Here retired South African Archbishop Desmond Tutu has given us a window into the spirituality of Africa. In this collection of prayers, poems, litanies and hymns he has brought together the heart utterances of African Christians both ancient and modern, the saint and the sinner, the well-educated and the non-educated, the free and the oppressed, the young and the old, as well as the black and the white. Prayers are included from every geographical region as well as from many streams of Christianity: Anglican, Coptic, Ethiopian Orthodox, and Methodist to name a few. Even prayers of those of African descent such as African-Americans and those living in the Caribbean are included. Also included are prayers from non-Christian sources such as African traditional religion and a "Hymn to the Sun" by Pharaoh Ikhnaton. In these later cases the prayers help the reader gain an understanding into the general African belief in a universal creator God. The book is organized around the acrostic "ACTS," which in this case stands for: adoration, contrition, thanksgiving and supplication, with an additional section for daily life. Each section begins with a short helpful devotional introduction by Tutu. This book can serve as a source of spiritual inspiration. It will also be useful for those who may want to study and understand the soul of Africa in a poetic and meditative mode as distinct from a merely scholarly or analytical approach.

1110.   **Tutu, Desmond**

No Future without Forgiveness

London: Rider Books, 2000. 256 pages, ISBN: 9780712604857.

For many decades Tutu has been at the cutting edge of South African history. Upon his retirement as Anglican Archbishop of Cape Town, Tutu was appointed as Chairperson of the Truth and Reconciliation Commission (TRC), set up to examine human rights abuses committed during the apartheid era and to effect a process of reconciliation. In this moving book we have Tutu's reflections upon what he witnessed during the Commission's workings. The mandate given to the TRC was, in Tutu's words, to "balance the requirements of justice, accountability, stability, peace and reconciliation" in the new South Africa dispensation. Some said it would be an impossible task, and whilst debate continues as to the Commission's effectiveness, what can never have been in doubt are the spirituality, pastoral integrity and theological understanding of its chairperson. Tutu's book is profoundly disturbing, and yet he manages to convey a clear message of hope. It is disturbing insofar as it brings to light the terrible works of darkness perpetrated during the years of apartheid rule, exposing them for what they really were – evil. This in turn raises further questions, not least of which is: "Can it be right for someone who has committed the most gruesome atrocities to be allowed to get off scot-free simply by confessing what he or she has done?" It is with this issue that Tutu wrestles, and he refuses to offer trite solutions. Tutu's conclusion is as the title of this memorable book suggests. How he gets there involves narrative theology at its best. Tutu tells stories; harrowing stories, hopeful stories, stories that will bring tears to one's eyes, and stories that will make one smile, but always stories told against the backdrop of the greatest story ever told.

1111. **Tutu, Desmond**

The Rainbow People of God: South Africa's Victory over Apartheid

New York: Doubleday, 2000. 304 pages, ISBN: 9780385483742.

At a time when the credible black political leadership of South Africa was either in prison or in exile, it was left to Archbishop Desmond Tutu to speak on behalf of the oppressed in the name of the gospel. Few national figures were so systematically vilified by the South African media and so widely loathed by the white community as Tutu during those dark years. This book of sermons and speeches (including dramatic photographs) puts the record straight, by portraying a man of deep faith and commitment as well as great humanity. It reflects a man determined to interpret the gospel for the times of crisis through which his people and country were passing. Here we have the authentic prophetic voice of the church, biblical and contextual, passionate and uncompromising but never rude, speaking in the midst of encroaching darkness. For those seeking examples on how to speak the Word of God into situations of unfolding tragedy this book is an excellent resource. Each sermon/speech is placed in its context with a description of the situation in which it was spoken. For example, we have Tutu's righteous indignation at the funeral of Steve Biko. We have a polite yet firm rebuke of Prime Minister Vorster and President P. W. Botha. We have Tutu's measured but brilliant testimony before the Eloff Commission appointed by the apartheid government to look into the affairs of the South African Council of Churches. We have Tutu's unrestrained joy at the birth of democracy in South Africa. For those wanting to know more of the theology that underpinned Tutu's perspectives, this is an invaluable volume.

Authors
U–Z

1112.   **Udoekpo, Michael Ufok**

Re-thinking the Day of YHWH and Restoration of Fortunes in the Prophet Zephaniah: An Exegetical and Theological Study of 1:14–18; 3:14–20

Frankfurt: Peter Lang, 2010. 335 pages, ISBN: 9783034305105.

Originally from Nigeria, the author currently lectures at a seminary in the United States. This is a revised version of his doctoral thesis at the Pontifical University of St. Thomas Aquinas (Rome). The main point of the study is that the message of judgment, threats, punishment and justice related to the concept of a "day of YHWH" in Zephaniah 1:14–18 does not represent a negative end. Rather it expresses an anticipation of the joy, salvation, hope and restoration or reversal of fortunes that are evident in a subsequent Zephaniah text, 3:14–20. Seeing the two texts together, the book also has a message for our own time: an invitation to all people, irrespective of culture and nationality, to repentance and reassurance of God's love and promises. Still, the book is first and foremost an exegetical study, with six main chapters. Chapter one surveys the research history of the concept of a "day of YHWH" and of the book of Zephaniah. Chapter two focuses on Zephaniah's understanding and use of a "day of YHWH." Chapter three turns to the second text under investigation, the restoration and salvation focus of Zephaniah 3:14–20. Chapter four goes to the concept of a "day of YHWH" within the wider prophetic canon. Chapter five relates the two Zephaniah texts to other texts and traditions in the OT. Finally, chapter six proposes an "ecumenical-interreligious" interpretation of the two texts, relating them: (a) to the NT and the church; (b) to African traditional religion and Islam; and (c) to challenges of contemporary culture. The main dialogue partners of this chapter are found within the Roman Catholic tradition. In spite of the attempts in chapter six to point out the relevance of the texts in contemporary cultural and religious contexts, the strength of the book lies in its exegetical analysis of the concept of a "day of YHWH," both within the book of Zephaniah and in the OT as a whole.

1113.   **Udoh, Enyi Ben**

Guest Christology: An Interpretative View of the Christological Problem in Africa

Frankfurt: Peter Lang, 1988. 296 pages, ISBN: 9783631407172.

Udoh writes from within the context of the Presbyterian Church in Nigeria. He repeats what many before and since have asserted, that the numerically impressive response to the Christian message in Africa masks an underlying malaise. Like others, he traces that malaise to the presentation of missionary Christianity that accompanied the colonial political and economic scramble for Africa. Christ entered the African scene as a forceful, impatient and unfriendly tyrant, and those Africans who chose to follow him were doubly disinherited, both from their traditional past and by the white-dominated colonial society by which they sought to be accepted. The result has been a widespread unthinking acceptance of values that (in the author's specific context) owe more to Knox and Calvin and their worlds than to the African or even biblical world. Much here is familiar territory to those aware of the debates surrounding Christianity in Africa. Udoh's particular contribution is in narrowing the malaise to the realm of Christology. He argues that while there is a general congruity between African and biblical notions of God, it is the notion of Christ that is alien. In his view, since the problem is Christological, the solution must be too. Udoh evaluates three attempts at meaningful, contextual christologies in Africa: Christ as *bongaka* or healer (e.g. Setiloane); Christ as liberator (e.g. Mugambi, Tutu, Boesak); and Christ as kin (Mbiti). The author concludes that if all three models are flawed, at least together they sound the alarm that it is in the area of Christology that the search for a remedy needs to be concentrated. Udoh's proposal is that Christ should be encountered first as Guest; the One who is admitted, welcomed in from outside, not as dogma but as person. African Christology "must seek to reinstate the human face of Jesus Christ." Only when Christ is discovered (through the gospel stories rather than through the dogmatic creeds of the early Christian centuries) and admitted as a member of the community can he become acknowledged as leader or Lord. Through this dynamic Christology that moves from Christ-as-Guest to Christ-as-Kin and eventually to Christ-as-Lord, Udoh seeks to provide Africa with a more human "from below" Christology. For those readers who may be uneasy with the vagueness of his proposal, Udoh freely acknowledges that his Guest Christology is imprecise; it is deliberately vague, because it is concerned more with relational encounter than with creedal propositional statements. The author believes that when the Church embraces such a Christology it will itself in turn be released to act as guest and servant, rather than as an imperialistic institution. The book is one example of the ongoing complex discussion of Christology in the African context.

1114. Uka, Emele Mba

Missionaries Go Home?: A Sociological Interpretation of an African Response to Christian Mission

Frankfurt: Peter Lang, 1989. 315 pages, ISBN: 9783261038746.

The author has been a lecturer in sociology of religion at the University of Calabar in Nigeria. In this study he focuses especially on why the moratorium call of the 1970s, "missionary go home," was made, as distinct from whether that call was needed or not needed, right or wrong. To this end Uka attempts a sociological interpretation, applying the principles from Karl Mannheim's "Sociology of Knowledge," with special emphasis on the concepts of "ideology" and "utopian," in order to analyse the social, economic, political and historical contexts. It is out of such contexts that ideas and beliefs emerged which determined relationships between the dominant (Western Missions) and the dominated (African Church). At the heart of the conflict were two groups shaped by different socio-historical factors. On the one hand there is the "ideological" group, the West with its political and economic power and its missionary organisations, which want to maintain the *status quo* both in their missionary endeavour and their economic and political dominance. On the other hand there is the "utopian" group, Africa and its churches, who want to be set free from continued economic and political subservience to world powers and missionary organisations. Thus, rather than interpreting the call for moratorium as anti-mission or anti-West, Uka proposes that it should be understood as dramatizing the need for a more prophetic, holistic, authentic and contextualized missionary endeavour of the world-wide church, one that demonstrates its relevance through preparedness to suffer. In this way it can demonstrate that the gospel is capable of challenging and transforming both the powers that oppress and dehumanize and as well the victims of oppression and dehumanisation. Uka thus resumes an inquiry that seems to have been set aside since the moratorium call of the 1970s, but may be pressing again even more strongly to the fore in the context of increased globalisation.

1115.   **Ukpong, Justin**

Proclaiming the Kingdom: Essays in Contextual New Testament Studies

Port Harcourt: Catholic Institute of West Africa, 1993. 158 pages, ISBN: 9789782728036.

One of the sad realities of African biblical studies, and of much of African theology in general, is that so often it is published either by expensive Western academic presses, thus making such materials difficult to obtain for African scholars and libraries, or else by local African publishers with very limited resources to do quality production, publicity and distribution. The one sort becomes widely known in Africa but not easily accessible, while the other sort becomes locally accessible in Africa but not widely known. This slim volume of essays fits into the latter category. Being locally produced in Africa, it may be hard to find beyond its original place of publication, and therefore easily missed. Ukpong is one of the most accomplished, careful and insightful of African biblical scholars in recent years. He is among the few whose work has become known not only across the continent but around the world. This volume brings together essays addressing a number of texts (mostly from the Synoptic Gospels and Paul) on various theological and cultural issues. Three of these essays ("Jesus' Prophetic Ministry and Its Challenge to Christian Ministry"; "Biblical Perspectives on Human Work and Creation"; "Proclaiming the Kingdom of God in Africa Today") had not been previously published. Of special note is the article, "The Letter to the Galatians and the Problem of Cultural Pluralism in Christianity" in which Ukpong exegetes Galatians 3:1–29 with a view to the way that Paul's theology of grace, which embraces both Jew and Gentile, has missiological implications: "In the first century AD it was a matter of Law observant Christianity and a gentile Christianity without observance of the Law. Today it is a matter of alternative forms of Christianity and theology based on a diversity of cultures in which Christianity finds itself." In each of the essays Ukpong seeks to marry careful exegesis done within a broad confessional framework (he is a Roman Catholic, and his exegesis is done within a context of canonical, not merely historical questions), with sensitivity to the African culture for which he writes. In sum, he says, "particularly in the Third World, biblical studies is witnessing a departure from the model of detached analysis of the biblical text to that of contextual engagement with the text."

1116.   **Ukpong, Justin, Musa W. Dube, and Gerald O. West, editors**

Reading the Bible in the Global Village: Cape Town

Atlanta: SBL, 2002. 224 pages, ISBN: 9781589830257.

This volume is a collection of papers given in 2000 at a meeting of the Society of Biblical Literature in Cape Town, South Africa. There is no single editor, and the clarity and accuracy of some of the contributions might have benefited from one. Most of the eight contributors teach in Africa; half are resident in South Africa. They actually engage in very little "reading" of the Bible, nor do they address a single theme, although the South African context of the meeting and certain hermeneutical and political assumptions run through many of the essays. The opening plenary address was given by Ukpong, "Reading the Bible in a Global Village: Issues and Challenges from African Readings." He refers to a range of African approaches to reading the Bible and focuses on what he terms "inculturation hermeneutics," which aims at popular participation and relevance, as opposed to the often abstract and intellectualist concerns of the academy. He goes on to argue that if there is to be a truly "global village" then all voices need to be acknowledged, such that there is a decentring of biblical scholarship. A basic assumption here, and one that is echoed by several contributors, is that of the essential subjectivity of "readings" of the Bible. Musa Dube's reply to Ukpong, "Villagizing, Globalizing, and Biblical Studies," takes him to task for a lack of commitment to issues of race, class and gender, thereby introducing a second significant emphasis of the volume, namely a concern for generally liberationist, socio-political readings. Masoga brings the two themes together: the Bible is a terrain of struggles and must be read from the perspective of liberation if it is not to become an instrument of exploitation. Gottwald, however, questions whether the Bible – more specifically the OT – can be used to support liberationist agendas at all: "we are in a new situation and on our own"; "we have come to the end of naïve trust in the innocence of the biblical text." Moving in the opposite direction, Punt attempts to remedy the neglect of Paul in discussions of liberation, and to demonstrate Paul's significance for socio-political issues. The fundamental question raised by the volume, but not addressed, is whether the Bible can speak with its own authentic and authoritative voice, or whether "readings" simply depend on the philosophical stance of the reader. Is it judge or victim of "readings"? Indeed, if readers interpret the Bible on the basis of ethical criteria drawn from the various non-biblical socio-political ideologies that they espouse, why use the Bible at all to advance their positions (a question that Tinyiko too briefly raises)?

Ukpong, Justin

see also review 382

1117. Umar, Muhammad S.

Islam and Colonialism: Intellectual Responses of Muslims of Northern Nigeria to British Colonial Rule

Leiden: BRILL, 2005. 298 pages, ISBN: 9789004139466.

The author holds a PhD from Northwestern University. In this book he surveys the responses of the Muslim Emirs, the religious leaders, and the Western educated elite to British colonialism in their homeland, Northern Nigeria, in the years between 1900 and 1945. He does so by examining original documents written by members of these groups. He finds that the Emirs looked for ways to excuse their surrender to and co-operation with a non-Islamic government, which was contrary to Islamic law. They found the answer in the law's leniency in situations of duress and the need to preserve Muslim lives. The religious leaders were concerned about the way British "Christian" influence and rule corrupted the morals and lifestyle of Muslims, and strove to keep people's loyalty to Islam intact. Western educated Muslims absorbed the colonial claim that things were better under British rule, but they also upheld the superiority of Islam. Because the British needed these three classes of Nigerian Muslims in order to carry out their necessary policy of indirect rule, they made many concessions to Islam. But contrary to claims of some (e.g. M. Crowder) that the British promoted Islam in Northern Nigeria, Umar sees a British policy of appropriation (commandeering Islamic institutions as instruments of British rule), containment (modifying Islamic law and custom to suit British norms) and surveillance (spying on those suspected of being able to use Islam to foment revolt). Although in theory the British did not support the spread of Islam to non-Muslim tribes, in practice they never considered the "pagans" to be as "advanced" as the Muslims, and at times allowed Islamic law and custom to affect "pagans." The colonial government realized that their educational efforts would fail if linked to Christian missions, so they set up "secular" schools to impart Western education to the youth they were grooming to take over eventual rule. Because the British allowed practically no contact between Northern Nigeria's Muslims and those who wished to convert them to Christianity, Umar has very little to say in his book about missions. He presents the British as in no way concerned to see the Muslims converted to Christianity, only to rule successfully, and notes that the British preferred to be referred to as "Europeans" rather than "Christians." Those who are familiar with the viewpoint of the non-Muslim peoples of Northern Nigeria will recognize in this book a distinctly different point of view. The colonialists' view of non-Muslims as less civilized than the Muslims is presented without comment, and pre-colonial slave raiding of pagan areas is downplayed. However, the attitude of Muslim leaders (we must wait out this calamity to Islam; we will be able to revive our Muslim hegemony and full Sharia law someday), speaks directly and eloquently to the situation in Northern Nigeria today.

1118.   Umoren, Anthony Iffen

Paul and Power Christology: Exegesis and Theology of Romans 1:3–4 in Relation to Popular Power Christology in an African Context

Frankfurt: Peter Lang, 2008. 207 pages, ISBN: 9783631575543.

Originally a doctoral thesis, Umoren's study combines a solid NT exegesis of Romans 1:1–3 with a theologically perceptive analysis of the language of power in Nigerian church life. Until recently almost all doctoral degrees earned by Africans were granted by European or North American institutions. There are now a number of places within the continent that have the expertise and the resources which have allowed the establishment of doctoral programmes. Teresa Okure, a very accomplished biblical scholar, supervised this dissertation. Umoren did spend a year in Rome doing research, but the degree was granted by the Catholic Institute of West Africa. In fact, it is doubtful whether this study could have been written in Europe or North America, since so much of the author's work focuses on a careful analysis of Nigerian church life. His major conclusion with regard to context is as follows: "In Nigeria, as a whole, . . . there is emerging a popular affirmation of Jesus as power, and use of his name as a source of power for prosperity, miracles, healing and other spiritual benefits." Umoren does not deny that Jesus' name is powerful or that he does miracles, but Umoren does find the rather different emphasis on the meaning of power associated with Jesus in the NT. In the text which is the focus of his study Umoren discovers that "power" is "a central affirmation" about Jesus Christ. As one would expect, Umoren finds that the theme of Jesus as power in Paul's opening greeting signals a theme which is found "in the entire book of Romans" – the power of God for salvation to all who believe on the basis of the cross of Christ. He finds that the NT does not use the name of Jesus as a "magical incantation" to solve all of life's problems. Yes, God is opposed to all of those things, occult powers, poverty, abuse of civil authority, sickness, which dehumanize and which oppose life, but Jesus' power comes through the cross. Therefore although Christians should not seek suffering, they cannot always avoid it, and God's saving power works through suffering. The power of Jesus is also meant to give glory to God alone, rather than to some special "man of God," a Christian version of a diviner. Umoren concludes by appealing for a more holistic understanding of power, and for clearer teaching of multi-dimensionality of power issues in the Nigerian churches. This book is a wonderful model of a creative, pastorally sensitive, and exegetically sound piece of African scholarship.

1119.   Ungar, Sanford J.

Africa: The People and Politics of an Emerging Continent

London: Simon & Schuster, 1989. 571 pages, ISBN: 9780671675653.

This is a popular North American text intended to "introduce the general reader to the complexity, the fascination, and the tragedy of Africa." As such it succeeds – if not any longer, then at least for its time of publication in 1989. Ungar was formerly Dean of the School of Communication at American University in Washington DC, and managing editor of the influential journal *Foreign Affairs*. Although his presentation is usually not only readable but also refreshingly realistic, judicious, and informed, it does not escape a noticeable unevenness. Nearly half the book is devoted to detailed (and instructive) chapters on Liberia, Nigeria, Kenya, and South Africa, while the remaining countries are then surveyed in groups, with mostly only a few pages devoted to each country. The presentation can thus become at times fairly skimpy, not least for the francophone countries. Surveying country by country also means that overall thematic interpretation of the continent is not this book's strength. One can also not help noticing that religion in Africa – whether Christianity, Islam or traditional religion – receives only very incidental passing reference. A distinguishing feature of the book is the American interpretive perspective that is sustained throughout. In the process Ungar provides an informative overview of American attitude and foreign policy towards Africa for the past two centuries. Yet this controlling transAtlantic perspective also means that America's role in Africa (or at times its lack of role) is accorded greater significance than might seem justifiable, and this slant can distract. The reader cannot help noticing how much of consequence has changed for Africa in the period since its publication. When Ungar wrote, Mengistu of Ethiopia was still in place, as were Barre of Somalia, Doe of Liberia, and Mobutu of Congo (DRC). The presentation is thus unavoidably dated. For this third edition Ungar did manage to append ten brief pages on the then emerging AIDS plague, but Rwanda is still future, and Mandela too. This unintended reminder of all that has consequentially changed for Africa in such a comparatively short period may feel striking to the reader of today. It is equally striking, and sobering, to find how little may require adjustment in Ungar's 1989 prognosis for Africa's future. Ungar's commitment to Africa and its people is evident throughout his book; he cares about what is happening, and he lauds all the heady achievements of the past century. But he is no romantic. His concluding summary of Africa's prospects is in keeping with the candour of his detailed treatment throughout. In 1989 he found the outlook for the continent's immediate future painfully bleak. The thoughtful reader of today is left reflecting whether this prognosis is now to be considered dated.

1120.   Utuk, Efiong

From New York to Ibadan: The Impact of African Questions on the Making of Ecumenical Mission Mandates, 1900–1958

Frankfurt: Peter Lang, 1991. 352 pages, ISBN: 9780820414010.

Utuk is originally a Presbyterian from southeastern Nigeria. This book is based on his dissertation at Princeton Theological Seminary. Many people think that the mission ideas of the influential International Missionary Council in the first half of the twentieth century had no input from Africa, because these ideas were shaped by Western missionaries. This, says Utuk, is simply not true. The Council developed the policies it did mainly as a response to the conditions that missionaries met in Africa. African social conditions dictated a heavier emphasis on education, health care, and economic and political action. The few Africans who participated directly in making recommendations (e.g. James Aggrey) helped move the IMC in that direction. To trace how the ideas developed, Utuk searched the archival records of sixteen ecumenical mission conferences from New York in 1900 to Ibadan in 1958, looking for evidence of the impact of African social and political conditions, traditional religion, non-mission-related churches, and race relations, on the issues addressed and policies made. He also notes how it was especially the situation in Africa that made ecumenical unity imperative. The book includes documents from four of the conferences, an index, and a seventeen-page annotated bibliography. It represents an important corrective to common assumptions regarding the place of Africa in the sequence of historic international mission consultations in the first half of the twentieth century.

1121.   Uzukwu, E. Elochukwu

Worship as Body Language: Introduction to Christian Worship: An African Orientation

Collegeville, PA: Liturgical Press, 1997. 384 pages, ISBN: 9780814661512.

Uzukwu lectures at the Spiritan International School in Enugu, Nigeria and has also been a visiting lecturer in Paris and at the Catholic Institute of West Africa. He has written other books: Liturgy: *Truly African, Truly Christian*, and *A Listening Church*. Uzukwu's special interest in this book is the development of African rituals and their use in Christian communities and liturgies. He first deals with human gestural behaviour and how we make ritual-symbolic actions. He then discusses the Greco-Roman concept of spirit and body, aspects of Jewish-Christian ritual, myth and symbol as they are related to ritual, and some of the specific attitudes and ritual displays of Africans. Uzukwu goes on to describe various creative emerging liturgies in Africa, giving examples from West, Central and Eastern Africa. If from the title and subtitle one were to expect a wider coverage than Catholic churches, one would be disappointed. For example, only very brief mention is made of the Ethiopian Orthodox Church, a prime and ancient example of the subject being discussed. A main premise in Uzukwu's writing is "Africa's right to be different," and this book is all about how liturgy can be developed to be culture specific. With his extensive knowledge of church rites, and of Christian liturgical practice and history, Uzukwu has written a very scholarly tome which would be of more interest to those from liturgical traditions, but scholars of other traditions may also find a new appreciation for worship as body language.

1122.   Vahakangas, Mika, and Andrew A. Kyomo, editors

Charismatic Renewal in Africa: A Challenge for African Christianity

Nairobi: Acton Publishers, 2003. 197 pages, ISBN: 9789966888990.

This collection of nine articles plus an introduction derives from something called the Tanzania Theological Colloquium. Apart from the fact that the contributing scholars belong to the older churches (Lutheran, Roman Catholic, Moravian, Anglican and Presbyterian), very little additional background information is provided. Most of the contributors apparently have Tanzanian connections, though Ghana and Kenya are also represented, and Finland. Internet searching reveals that the editors and two others lecture at Makumira University College in Tanzania. Most contributors do not seem to be charismatics themselves, though according to the introduction some are. The articles range from those that speak consistently negatively about charismatic churches, through those that see some helpful aspects in these newer churches, to one that is uncritically positive towards them. The issue of the rapid rise and influence of the Pentecostal and charismatic churches, and many of the African Initiated Churches, has challenged Africa's mainline, mission-founded churches for years. The challenges mentioned in this book include the penetration of the older churches by charismatic/Pentecostal theology and practices; the movement of people (especially younger people) from the older churches to the charismatic churches; members of the older churches visiting the younger churches (especially for healing services); an overly simplistic theology that impoverishes all those affected by it, whether in the newer or older churches; the need for mainline churches to learn whatever seems good from these charismatic churches through a critical dialogue with them; the non-African origin of Pentecostal and other charismatic churches and organisations; and how to view the gifts of the Holy Spirit. Of special interest is a long article by J. N. K. Mugambi on "Evangelistic and Charismatic Initiatives in Post-Colonial Africa," since Mugambi persistently lumps evangelicals and charismatics together in ways that neither group would consider fair or true. While this book is a useful collection of viewpoints and opinions, it suffers from serious grammatical, editorial, and proofreading deficiencies, which affects its usability. Despite such blemishes, the topic is of wide relevance in Africa, and the book will prove of interest not least for surfacing viewpoints on these matters not so commonly available in print.

1123. Vahakangas, Mika

In Search of Foundations for African Catholicism: Charles Nyamiti's Theological Methodology

Leiden: BRILL, 1999. 326 pages, ISBN: 9789004113282.

Nyamiti is one of the leading African theologians of our time. This study of his theological methodology by a Finnish Lutheran is welcome, despite the fact that it appeared before Nyamiti's multi-volume systematic theology. Nyamiti is known for his theology of ancestorship. So what was Nyamiti's methodology? The author states that Nyamiti believes in the inculturation of the gospel into the African context, and is primarily interested in doing inculturated systematic theology. So what are the sources of his African systematic theology? Nyamiti believes in both special and general revelation. Following the Roman Catholic tradition, he says that God reveals himself both in the Bible and in tradition. According to Vähäkangas, "Tradition holds an unlimited authority in Nyamiti's eyes. . . The Bible and the later infallible teaching of the church . . . are thus absolutely infallibile." Nyamiti believes that truth is absolute. God is truth. Theology is a human reflection on truth. Theology "is an attempt to translate divine wisdom to human language." But God also reveals himself in creation. African traditional religions "contain a considerable amount of valuable genuine revelation," but the resulting theology is not infallible or absolute. Yet he uses the African concept of ancestor to form his theology. In the Trinity, the Father is an ancestor; in salvation history Jesus Christ is an ancestor; and supposed ancestor values like communality, hierarchy and fullness of life should qualify church and society. However, Nyamiti modifies the traditional African concept of ancestorship to fit his Catholic theology. This modification is so strong that "not much of its content seems to be left intact . . . The ancestral category appears thus more like a root metaphor or a paradigm." The conclusion is that Nyamiti's basic theological and philosophical foundations are Roman Catholic (neo-Thomist) but his theology is genuinely African. This book is a superb study on an important African theologian.

van Beek, Walter E. A.

see review 129

1124.   **van de Walle, Nicolas**

African Economies and the Politics of Permanent Crisis, 1979–1999

Cambridge: Cambridge University Press, 2001. 306 pages, ISBN: 9780521008365.

Why do Africa's economic woes persist despite decades of international efforts to spark growth? With this volume, van de Walle, a veteran writer on African political and economic affairs and professor of political science at Michigan State University, adds his contribution to this vexing debate. The author faults studies that inform the policies of Western lending institutions for their almost exclusive focus on economic issues to the neglect of the political sector. As a result, they fail to consider the *ability* and *willingness* of African governments to implement reforms. In contrast, van de Walle directly examines political realities. With regard to the *ability* to reform, he contends that donors have consistently overestimated the capacity of African states to carry out reform programs. Typically, adjustment packages emphasize privatisation and civil service reductions. Yet, structural factors essential for successful implementation such as accountability, judicial reform, and transparency are relegated to secondary phases of reform. With regard to *willingness*, van de Walle contends that African leaders have been more concerned with preserving their hold on political power and opportunities for financial gain than with economic development. Thus, opposition to reform comes not from outside the state in the form of pressure groups or societal opposition (as usually proposed), but from within the governments supposedly implementing the reforms. Political institutions, therefore, hold the key to the African crisis. Political reform must precede economic reform. The blame for the African crisis lies, according to van de Walle, both with African governments and with international lending institutions whose faulty analytical tools (economic-focused studies) perpetuate ill-advised policies. Consequently, the way forward lies with policies that take Africa's political realities seriously. Backed by thorough documentation, this important work suggests more realistic assessments of entrenched challenges presently affecting the African continent.

1125.   **van der Walt, B. J.**

Leaders with a Vision: How Christian Leadership Can Tackle the African Crisis

Potchefstroom, South Africa: Potchefstroom University, 1995. 101 pages, ISBN: 9781868221899.

This book presents the text of lectures delivered at the Pan African Leadership Assembly II, held in Nairobi in 1994. The author has been a professor in Christian philosophy at Potchefstroom University in South Africa, and director of the Institute for Reformational Studies there. His lectures are based on the premise that Africa's present crisis is precipitated in major part by a failure of leadership at all levels: educational, social, political, economic, religious, and in family life. Five leadership styles or traditions familiar to Africa are critiqued: (1) the paternalistic elder tradition, (2) the sage tradition of the leader as the ultimate teacher, (3) the warrior tradition of liberation fighters and military rulers, (4) the charismatic style of the leader as inspiring personality, (5) a monarchical tendency, which results in a personality cult and the glorification and even sacralisation of authority. This book argues that leaders cannot be real leaders without a biblical view of the following: (1) what office, authority, power and responsibility entail; (2) how society at large should be structured (3) and if necessary, be changed; (4) what, in the case of the state, the responsibilities of governments and citizens should be. The book is probably most provocative in its critique of a dualistic Christian worldview which drives a wedge between the sacred and the secular, and which thereby disempowers Christians in Africa from bringing about meaningful change particularly in this area of leadership. Anyone involved in Christian leadership in Africa, or in the training of such leadership, would benefit from interacting with this book, as would anyone seeking to think carefully about church-state relations or Christian social responsibility in Africa.

1126.   van der Walt, B. J.

The Liberating Message: A Christian Worldview for Africa

Potchefstroom, South Africa: Potchefstroom University, 1994. 625 pages, ISBN: 9781868221400.

The author's contention is that the basic need in Africa is for an integral, encompassing and powerful Christian worldview, a Christian perspective on all facets of human life, without which Africa will perish. The author maintains that the traditional African worldview was holistic and all-embracing, integrating the whole of the African's life and giving it clear direction. African cultural values and structures were profoundly affected by the introduction of Christianity, Western education, and Western political and economic institutions. A correct choice for Africa after colonialism, post-colonialism and independence (with all its own challenges to the African worldview) – and even after post-Christianity – would be the choice for a pre-scientific biblical worldview, which would lie at the basis of man's scientific thought. The crisis brought about by the transformation of Africa is basically a worldview crisis. More than the approaches of indigenisation, Africanisation, the developing of African theology or contextualization, is the need for a Christian worldview approach, because it penetrates deeper and also offers a wider perspective. Only by developing such a radical Christian worldview, contends the author, can the African situation be adequately and effectively addressed. A radical, integral Christian worldview can really liberate Africa. Although lengthy, the book makes for easy reading and is well worth attention among those involved with African theological reflection.

1127.   van der Walt, B. J.

Transformed by the Renewing of Your Mind: Shaping a Biblical Worldview and a Christian Perspective on Scholarship

Potchefstroom, South Africa: Institute for Contemporary Christianity in Africa, 2001. 198 pages, ISBN: 9781868223824.

Van der Walt is a Christian philosopher-theologian teaching at the University of Potchefstroom in South Africa. His interest is Christianity on the African continent, especially its impact on social, economic, political and educational life. This book discusses a variety of topics: historical developments in Christianity as well as present trends in African Christianity; the cultural reasons for the dismal failure of development projects on the continent; the need for Christian education; the challenge of Christian scholarship and more. A central message runs through all topics – the vital importance of a biblical worldview, and Christian education inspired by this vision. The first chapter indicates the disastrous results of all kinds of dualistic Christian worldviews, emphasising the urgent need for the development of a holistic, integrated Christian worldview based on the correct interpretation of Scripture. The second chapter analyses the issue of development from the perspective of such a biblically-informed worldview. The third to sixth chapters explain the implications of this radical, genuine Christian worldview for Christian scholarship and Christian higher education. Renewal or transformation in our worldview and in tertiary education are contended to be two urgent needs in contemporary Africa. It is proposed that if this ideal could be achieved, the rebirth of a new Christianity on this continent at the dawn of the twenty-first century will be possible.

1128.   van der Walt, B. J.

Transforming Power: Challenging Contemporary Secular Society

Potchefstroom, South Africa: Institute for Contemporary Christianity in Africa, 2007. 441 pages, ISBN: 9781868225118.

The South African author of this book, a prolific philosopher from Potchefstroom University for Christian Higher Education (part of North-West University since 2004), issues a call for Christians to reject the increasing secularisation of the twenty-first-century world (defined in terms of the growing divide between public/non-religious and private/religious spheres of life) through a commitment to a Christian social philosophy that entails engagement with, and transformation of, the world in place of accommodation or isolation. The transformation called for by the author is developed from a neo-Calvinist "philosophical worldview" stance (over which the shadows of Kuyper, Vollenhoven and Dooyeweerd constantly fall), and is carefully applied within a South African context. In fifteen chapters the author addresses topics that include family life, friendship, mission, non-Christian religions, Christian scholarship, sports and human sexuality. These chapters are all translations of Afrikaans essays published elsewhere, and the author is to be thanked for making them available to the English-speaking world. However, the text would have benefited from the attention of a careful editor: the book suffers from a fair amount of repetition and lacks a literary skeleton. While the concise nature of the individual chapters and their discussion of social issues allow them to be used fruitfully as an introduction to Christian social analysis from within this particular philosophical system, readers outside of the particular South African context discussed by van der Walt will need to work out how these ideas might be transposed to address different contexts.

1129.   van der Walt, B. J.

Understanding and Rebuilding Africa: From Desperation Today Towards Expectation for Tomorrow

Potchefstroom, South Africa: Institute for Contemporary Christianity in Africa, 2003. 564 pages, ISBN: 9781868224197.

This book began life as a textbook for van der Walt's course on "Philosophy in Africa" at the Potchefstroom University for Christian Higher Education (now North-West University) in South Africa. Despite its title, the focus of this volume is primarily on "understanding Africa" by focusing on its religions, cultures and worldviews, in order to illuminate the continent's social, economic and political situation. The piecemeal nature of this collection is illustrated by the fact that sixteen of the book's twenty chapters have been published elsewhere in one form or another. Not only does this inevitably lead to repetition, it also means that the topics of each chapter are generally dealt with in a cursory fashion. The titles of the chapters give an indication of the range of subject matter, from "The impact of slavery, colonialism, neo-colonialism and Christianity on Africa" to "Different schools of philosophy in Africa," and "Development of the African continent." There are, inter alia, also chapters on corruption, ecology, reconciliation, religion and politics, economy and the African renaissance. The concluding chapter reveals the reason for the author's wide-ranging concerns. Working within an explicit philosophical-theological paradigm instructed largely by the Dutch Neo-Calvinism of Kuyper and Bavinck, van der Walt insists that every aspect of life in Africa must be informed by this form of Christianity in order for Christ to transform culture. All other aberrant types of Christian engagement are considered forms of "dualism" which have "weakened, crippled, and paralysed Christianity for two thousand years." Despite his misgivings in this regard, one would have liked the author to engage other African theologies of reconstruction in order to enrich his vision for "understanding and rebuilding Africa."

1130.   van der Walt, B. J.

When African and Western Cultures Meet: From Confrontation to Appreciation

Potchefstroom, South Africa: Institute for Contemporary Christianity in Africa, 2006. 324 pages, ISBN: 9781868225101.

The author for many years directed the Institute for Reformational Studies at Potchefstroom University, and in that capacity produced numerous articles, books and pamphlets. This contribution to a Christian understanding of cultures and adaptations is similar to his earlier ones in that it is eminently readable. His references to other scholars indicate a breadth of interaction, but the reader is not overwhelmed by heavy academic language. Thus the book is an accessible sort of introduction to the problems facing Africa, and possible paths toward solutions, from a Christian perspective. The author stresses "creational ordinances" that transcend cultural boundaries and the idea that truth is communicated in creation, in the Scriptures and in Christ. His vision is one where both ethnocentrism and relativism are seen as inadequate, where each person can appreciate the culture of the other, different though it may be. The introductory chapter communicates the Christian perspective from which the author will examine different areas of concern. The topics he has selected are readily recognized in the current African setting: poverty, development, globalization, leadership models, shame versus guilt as the main element of cultural values, cultural thought processes (Western, Eastern, African), women in Africa, agricultural concerns. Surprisingly, there is no separate treatment of the HIV/AIDS crisis. The chapters are complete in themselves and could be read separately. Some chapters seem to flow together naturally, but others are independent. There is no concluding summary to the work. The book remains a pointer toward discovering solutions rather than attempting to have definitive answers for these diverse and thorny problems.

van Lin, Jan

see review 295

van Thiel, Paul

see review 858

van't Spijker, Gérard

see review 194

1131.   **Vavrus, Frances**

Desire and Decline: Schooling Amid Crisis in Tanzania

Frankfurt: Peter Lang, 2003. 168 pages, ISBN: 9780820463117.

The author draws on her fieldwork in the Old Moshi area on the slopes of Mt. Kilimanjaro to document changes in the role of and expectations for education in modern Tanzania. She began her work in 1992, and repeated visits to the area allowed her to make longitudinal assessments of the issues she deals with in this book. She focuses especially on the interplay of what she calls the "feminist modern" viewpoint, that women empowered with education should become the driving force in development for their communities, and indeed their nation, and the perspectives on the place of education represented by the post-colonial condition, neo-Marxism, developmentalism and postmodernism. She warns that education is being seen as the "panacea" which is expected to bring about social change, reduce poverty and overcome social problems, without addressing policy issues and governmental decisions that are strongly influencing the society's welfare. Her data is drawn from secondary school students, their parents, and community organisations in the Old Moshi area, and she notes people's continuing reliance on education to improve their lives even as social and economic conditions deteriorate around them. Many of her subjects are professing Christians and the secondary school is a mission school, so the influence of Christianity is also included, especially the interplay between church and school teaching on family planning and condom use to prevent the spread of AIDS. While being careful not to give "cookie cutter" answers, she concludes with descriptions of several indigenous organisations that are effectively dealing with specific areas of need in the community. This is a well-written analysis that highlights the need and benefit of accessing professional specialist literature for informed contextual understanding in Africa, not least for those engaged in Christian ministry in such contexts, and especially for those who prepare them for such a role.

1132.   **Venter, Dawid, editor**

*Engaging Modernity: Methods and Cases for Studying African Independent
    Churches in South Africa*

Santa Barbara, CA: Praeger, 2004. 248 pages, ISBN: 9780275969035.

As the title suggests, this edited collection deals with various methodological approaches to the study of African Independent Churches (AICs) in South Africa, focusing in particular upon the broader theme of modernity. The contributors use a wide array of methods and perspectives for investigating the thoughts and "voices" of AICs, each valuable for what it contributes to the broader understanding. Hence the goal of the book is an expansive panorama of patterns and models, as researchers explore how Africanness and modernity "relate to each other in a complex solidarity." Underlying each of the presentations are the central affirmations that the extensive diversity of the AICs opposes monolithic descriptions, and that dichotomised caricatures between tradition and modernity need to be eschewed in favour of more flexible and interdependent models of the relationship. Whereas spiritual power remains foundational to this relationship; the tendency seen in the book is to define traditions exclusively within the "older" traditions (ancestral worship, orality and magic) rather than recognising some of the "newer" traditions that have taken form from the years of contact with Christianity. All of the authors are notable scholars of Christianity in South Africa, and a few demonstrate how their faith affirmations contribute to the validity and relevancy of their findings. This self-awareness (reflexivity), as seen in one of Robert Garner's contributions, provides a healthy insight into the methodology of research in religion, where the researcher is both objective and subjective, simultaneously insider and outsider. Thus Garner speaks openly about the strengths and weaknesses of his evangelical convictions, rather than trying to hide behind some myth of researcher neutrality. This book would be very useful for in-depth reflection on appropriate methodology for the study of Christianity in Africa, as well as study of global patterns in understanding modernity. Of course it is also helpful for better understanding the independent churches of South Africa. South African readers would particularly benefit from this collection, but researchers elsewhere on the continent, as well as overseas, can easily profit from extrapolating the methodology and findings for understanding and analysing constructions of global Christianity upon broader societal flows.

1133. Verstraelen-Gilhuis, Gerdien

A New Look at Christianity in Africa: Essays on Apartheid, African Education, and a New History

Gweru, Zimbabwe: Mambo Press, 1992. 109 pages, ISBN: 9780869225189.

Verstraelen-Gilhuis lectured for years in the Department of Religious Studies, Classics and Philosophy at the University of Zimbabwe. This book derives from four of her papers previously published in Dutch, which eventually became the principal chapters of this book. In the first chapter the author describes and analyses Apartheid Theology and Back Theology in South Africa. She does so by looking at how the South Africa Council of Churches and the Roman Catholic Church wrestled with these politically oriented theologies which dominated the South African theological scene for several decades. In her second chapter, "African Education as seen from Le Zoute, 1926," Verstraelen-Gilhuis looks back at the history and influence of Christian missions in Africa, especially in Central Africa. Her historical data and documentation are very useful to any student of African church history in the colonial period. However, her criticism of Christian missions of that day could have been more nuanced if she were to appreciate the fact that pioneer missionaries were not cultural anthropologists. Chapter three focuses on the Majority World's perspective on mission history, while the last chapter calls for re-writing the history of Christianity in Africa. The author provides case studies to demonstrate her point that in historiography of Christianity in Africa the important role of the African agents in that story is essential in understanding the development of Christianity in this vast continent. Any student of African church history will find the book especially stimulating.

1134. Verstraelen, F. J.

Christianity in a New Key

Gweru, Zimbabwe: Mambo Press, 1996. 322 pages, ISBN: 9780869226483.

This volume highlights the role played in enriching global Christianity by what the author refers to as the "Third Church," by which he means Christians and their respective cultural churches in Africa, Asia, Latin

America, and the Pacific. As a result of the shift of the centre of Christianity from North to South, new voices can now be heard which contribute to a "polyphonous" Christianity that sounds more cross-cultural, attractive and compelling than the "monophonous" Christianity formerly voiced by only the North (that is, Europe and North America.) The new voices indicate also new alternative ways of expressing the Christian faith in places of worship, in day-to-day living, and in evangelistic outreach. In each cultural setting there is, therefore, a need for the gospel message to be explained, heard, and understood contextually by those who are yet to turn to Christianity. There can be no substitute to relevance. Before assuming a professorship in religious studies at the University of Zimbabwe, Verstraelen had spent over thirty years in different intercontinental mission experiences and in research of new developments in global Christianity. It must be acknowledged that he is more of an anthropologist than a theologian. While he is strong in philosophical and cultural analyses, his presentation is not only weak in biblical exegesis, but seems to pay very little attention to Scripture. Nevertheless his volume can prove a mind-stretching resource for reflection for practitioners like theologians, cross-cultural church planters, and students of the history of the expression of the Christian faith in different cultural settings. There is an African proverb that says, "If you have not travelled, you think that your mother is the best cook." Cross-culturally, Christians who have knowledge only of their own type and practice of the Christian faith would be much tempted to consider others less "perfect," and thus unacceptable. Verstraelen's contribution will help the reader learn to appreciate a rich variety of responses to and experiences with the Christian gospel when incarnated or enculturated in different contexts and social groups.

1135.   Verstraelen, F. J.

History of Christianity in Africa in the Context of African History: An Assessment

Gweru, Zimbabwe: Mambo Press, 2002. 60 pages, ISBN: 9780869227695.

This slim but fascinating booklet, written by a Professor of Religious Studies at the University of Zimbabwe from 1989 to 1998, compares and contrasts four major textbooks used for teaching African church history, namely: John Baur's *Two Thousand Years of Christianity in Africa*, Adrian Hastings' *The Church in Africa, 1450–1950*, Elizabeth Isichei's *A History of Christianity in Africa*, and Bengt Sundkler and Christopher Steed's *Africa: A Church History*. It is unfortunate that Mark Shaw's *The Kingdom of God in Africa* (1996) was not included in the assessment. Verstraelen's main concern is to assess how well his selected authors combine "archival" (mainly missionary) history with "oral" (mainly African) history in their books, because "African Christian historiography has . . . moved beyond a missionary (often hagiographical) or nationalist (excluding the foreign factors, or judging them only in a negative way) to a holistic approach." The author is particularly supportive of Hastings' work because he feels the others are still reacting to "reproaches made by nationalist historians." Hastings is the most self-reliant, seeing no need to express "special indebtedness to Africans"; and he has the best bibliography because he uses only books from the last thirty years (might another factor be that Hastings was at one time also on the faculty at the University of Zimbabwe?). Verstraelen accepts Baur's admittedly Roman Catholic bias because the book was written for such an audience. He feels that parts of Sundkler's book are somewhat dated because it was written over such a long period of time, and that the length of the book makes it read more like an encyclopaedia. He complains that there are virtually no illustrations in any of the books, save the front covers. Finally, he challenges African historians to take up the task of writing African church history because such history is otherwise often seen as "an appendix at the periphery" rather than a "contributing partner." However one may wish to adjust some of Verstraelen's assessments, it is helpful to have evaluative surveys of this sort, and not least as a resource for those lecturing or writing on this important subject in Africa and elsewhere.

1136. Verstraelen, F. J.

Zimbabwean Realities and Christian Responses: Contemporary Aspects of Christianity in Zimbabwe

Gweru, Zimbabwe: Mambo Press, 1998. 164 pages, ISBN: 9780869227299.

Published in 1998, this book by the former Professor of Religious Studies at the University of Zimbabwe could lay claim to being the best study of the role of Christianity in post-Independent Zimbabwe. Verstraelen has done a first-class job in gathering and mastering a diverse range of material, and presenting his readership with an overview of Christian perspectives to issues in recent Zimbabwean history. In a country with "a bewildering diversity of Christianity" Verstraelen argues that (citing an observation of a Ugandan theologian): "Time has come when we should minimize quarrels on doctrinal statements because so far they have not served a positive purpose, at least in Africa" (surely an ice-breaker for a theological seminar if ever there was one!). He underscores the need for "authentic religion" as against the mere increase in religion. What is needful is authentic religion that expresses itself in "Biblical radicalism." This, in Verstraelen's view, is a summons to the church in Zimbabwe to engage more seriously and creatively with its African context, a context that embraces both the socio-economic and cultural-religious environments. The main streams of Christianity within Zimbabwe (including the role of the Evangelical Fellowship of Zimbabwe or EFZ) are evaluated in this light. Most of Verstraelen's accolades are reserved for the Catholic Church in Zimbabwe whose "more pastoral approach," he argues, "meets people where they are, and from there brings them with their culture and religion to the fullness of salvation in Christ." The author's perspectives on the contentious issues of land, the involvement of Mugabe's Fifth Brigade in the ruthless suppression of dissent in Matabeleland, African traditional religions and the role of the prophetess and spirit-medium Mbuya Nehanda, as well as former President Rev Canaan Banana's controversial proposal to rewrite the Bible, are all salutary contributions to ongoing debates. Not everything Verstraelen says will elicit hearty "Amens!" On the whole, however, he is even-handed, and there can be little doubt that the author understands his subject and has important things to say. This book is a valuable addition to the subject of Christianity in Africa, and Zimbabwe in particular. It certainly deserves greater profile than it has actually enjoyed.

Verstraelen, F. J.

see also review 757

1137. Villa-Vicencio, C., and John W. de Gruchy, editors

Doing Ethics in Context: South African Perspectives

Maryknoll, NY: Orbis, 1994. 221 pages, ISBN: 9780883449905.

Attending to theology and praxis in Africa requires that the student of ethics be exposed to a vast range of ethical models, methods and ways of doing ethics. Just such exposure is provided for in this volume. Here twenty-two South African theologians, from a wide range of traditions and perspectives, offer reflection on themes introductory to the study of Christian ethics, various ethical theories, contextual ethics, and several specific ethical issues. The book is divided into four main parts. The first deals with ethics in theological context, philosophical ethics, and the Bible and ethics. The second covers ethical theories like natural law ethics, law and grace, ethics of responsibility, ethics of character and community, Marx and beyond. Part Three concentrates on ethics in context, with essays on ethics in Liberation Theology, ethics in Black Theology, ethics in African Theology, and ethics in Feminist Theology. In Part Four some ethical issues are given consideration, including medical ethics, abortion, AIDS, euthanasia, political ethics, war, violence and revolution, human rights, economic justice, ecology, reparation and land. The format of the book makes it most useful for teaching, and the diversity of theological approaches ensures a generous class discussion. This book is recommended for thoughtful Christians, especially in southern Africa, who are seeking to understand the Christian faith and relate it to issues facing individuals, churches, and society in their context.

1138.   Villa-Vicencio, C., and C. Niehaus, editors

Many Cultures, One Nation: A Festschrift for Beyers Naudé

Cape Town: Human & Rousseau, 1995. 183 pages, ISBN: 9780798134125.

In this splendid volume of essays presented to Beyers Naudé (or Oom Bey as he is affectionately known), South African theologians pay tribute to this extraordinary minister of the gospel. At one time a rising star in the Afrikaner establishment, Naudé underwent a remarkable conversion that turned him into an opponent of the apartheid system that had nurtured and earmarked him for future leadership. After a foreword by Nelson Mandela, the book is divided into three sections: (1) The Witness of Oom Bey; (2). Theology and Culture; and (3) Towards a Rainbow Nation. Amongst the thirteen essays that go to make up this important book, several may be selected as perhaps worthy of particular notice. Villa-Vicencio gives an illuminating account of Beyers Naudé's life in his essay "An Afrikaner of the Afrikaners." Kistner's essay on Naudé's witness engages the Apostle Paul on how, in a situation of social conflict, we can discern the will of God such that we are willing to follow Christ though it means losing face and being despised by those who are close to us. Father Albert Nolan, a key theological figure in the church's struggle against apartheid, has a helpful essay on gospel and culture. And the ever-disturbing African Christian theologian, Itumeleng Mosala, contributes a thought-provoking essay in which he accuses the liberation movements, black theologians and those churches active in the political struggles during the turbulent apartheid years, of "failing to serve as representatives and defenders of the culture of the African people." Mosala calls for a theology of mission which "presupposes a genuine conversion to black and African people and not simply to their causes," and he points to the black Christians of the African Independent Churches ("the only truly black working-class Christian form") as the custodians of that cultural spirit of resistance to missionary teaching. This faith, Mosala concludes, "constitutes the basis of a powerful new theology of mission out of which can emerge a radically prophetic vision of Spirit as Power." Mosala makes some telling points and his essay demands a response. Villa-Vicencio's second essay, on a theology of reconciliation, and Shun Govender's "Life between the Times: The South African Renaissance," give further weight to this impressive Festschrift. This book is a fitting tribute to a courageous soldier of Jesus Christ and a true hero of the Faith. Those wishing better to understand Christian reflection in the mid-1990s in South Africa will certainly find much to ponder in this collection.

1139. **Villa-Vicencio, C., editor**

Theology and Violence: The South African Debate

Grand Rapids: Eerdmans, 1988. 309 pages, ISBN: 9780802803597.

By the late 1980s the political struggle in South Africa had reached critical intensity, with state repression and military build-up from the side of the Apartheid government, and with an intensification of the armed struggle under leadership of the ANC in exile. The violence inherent in the prevailing ideologies reflected itself more and more in the daily life of ordinary South Africans. In this context this important study was published, edited by Villa-Vicencio, then Associate Professor at the Department of Religious Studies at the University of Cape Town. Twenty-four contributors address the issue of violence, including professional theologians, clergymen and women, and representing a variety of denominations. This is done from the perspective of the victim in the human struggle for life – with the judgement of the gospel echoing through the pages. The major issue confronting concerned churches (and Christians) in South Africa during this period was that whilst historically Christianity has frequently been appealed to in a variety of situations to legitimate violence in the interest of maintaining law and order (and so also in South Africa), what should be said about the freedom of those suffering under sustained oppression and imposed servitude because of state violence? Is there a theological legitimisation for revolutionary struggle and violence? The essays in this volume contribute to a quest for a responsible Christianity in a violent society. Basic to that inquiry is also the question of how the fundamental causes of political violence in South Africa can be eliminated. The essays are largely of a historical nature, each seeking to uncover the ways in which past generations have wrestled theologically with the question of violence. The discussion is inclusive of the classic teaching of the church on violence, just war theory, pacifism, women and violence, the ecumenical debate on violent revolution and military disarmament. This is all carried out through the hermeneutical lens of the South African context – and done so without apology, because when a society (and the church within that society) clings to self-affirming and legitimating myths about the past, refusing to become self-critical in its historical consciousness, it is unlikely to be able to control its present or creatively to shape its future. This book remains fundamentally relevant because, while the setting has now changed, the causes of political violence throughout a greater part of contemporary Africa need to be addressed concretely by the Christian community. Too often the church in Africa has been reluctant to take up a committed quest for responsible Christianity within a violent society. For such a quest this volume may give substantive guidance.

1140. **Vingborg, Elisabeth**

Nigerians Engaged in Mission Work Today

Jos: Grace Foundation, 2001. 105 pages, ISBN: 9789783530263.

The subtitle of this book is: "Glimpses of the Manifold Mission Activities and Achievements of Some of the Churches/Mission Agencies Currently Working in Northern Nigeria." Vingborg is a Danish Lutheran missionary who worked in Nigeria for some four decades. In the later years she was helping Nigerian missionaries of the Lutheran Church of Christ in Nigeria pioneer in cross-cultural church planting. In the early part of 2001 she collected the information for this book by interviewing over 40 Nigerian mission leaders. Vingborg writes for two main audiences, namely for expatriate missionaries in Nigeria, and for the overseas supporters of missions to Nigeria, both of whom need to know what Nigerians themselves are doing in mission. This will inspire these two audiences in their own efforts and enable them better to recognize where their supportive input could be most useful. She also writes to publicize the work of Nigerian missions to Nigerians themselves to enlist their help. Vingborg treats four types of indigenous Nigerian organisations involved in mission work: (1) mission departments of church bodies planted by overseas missions (e.g. Lutherans, Anglicans, Roman Catholics, Baptists, ECWA, Assemblies of God); (2) the independent churches (e.g. Deeper Life, Church of God Mission, Redeemed Christian Church of God); (3) organisations founded specifically to do mission work (e.g. Harvesters for Christ, Missionary Crusaders, Global Outreach Ministries); and (4) network organisations (e.g. Nigeria Evangelical Missions Association – NEMA, African Missions Summit, Agape Network). She also mentions TV, film and radio ministries, and missionary training facilities. Other chapters describe various facets of Nigerian missions such as missionary qualifications, providing for MKs, funding, church-mission relations, and partnership with foreign missions. Vingborg says that overseas missions working in Nigeria should recognize and support the work of Nigerian missions by prayer, visits, training and finances. This should include assistance to local missions to which the overseas mission bodies have no historic tie, since new Nigerian missions are often closer in ethos to the overseas bodies than are the church denominations in Nigeria that those overseas missions originally birthed. The treatment is fairly brief and written in easy English. Also this is not an in-depth, comprehensive study; Vingborg's material concentrates mostly on pioneer work in Northern Nigeria, and a number of groups doing mission work are overlooked. However, the presentation covers the important points and major players, and given the paucity of published material on Nigerian cross-cultural missions, this is an invaluable resource on this remarkable phenomenon of contemporary African Christianity.

Vogel, Marianne

see review 645

1141.   Volz, Stephen C.

African Teachers on the Colonial Frontier: Tswana Evangelists and Their Communities during the Nineteenth Century

Frankfurt: Peter Lang, 2011. 293 pages, ISBN: 9781433109492.

The author offers an examination of nineteenth-century Christianity in what today is central southern Africa, in the time frame and area where Robert Moffatt and David Livingston worked. The book focuses not on such missionary figures but on the Tswana evangelists and teachers who interpreted Africa to the missionaries, and interpreted Christianity to Africa. Volz did his doctoral studies on these evangelists, based on a trove of correspondence originating from educated Tswana of that era that he encountered in the course of his research. What impresses Volz from the study of this material is how "the development of African churches over the centuries . . . has demonstrated the . . . enduring capacity of Africans to make God their own." The earliest Tswana evangelists were generally members of ruling families for whom the gospel was a supplemental source of politico-religious authority. By the mid-nineteenth-century evangelists were diplomats, traders and itinerant religious specialists, including "rain-makers." Towards the end of the century, evangelists "became members of a nascent African bourgeoisie, utilizing their literacy and knowledge of European ways to secure gainful employment . . . As such they became agents, less for the Tswana-isation of Christianity, and more for the European-isation of Batswana." And yet Volz notes, "Tswana evangelists were driven more by their own desires to reconcile personal faith with social obligations than by the ambitions of European missionaries." We see this as Tswana evangelists taught in terms that made sense to themselves and fellow Batswana. Volz provides valuable insights into the impact of language, theological training, and ordination in this close study of an African-directed contextualization of Christianity. In the process he manages to assess with remarkable even-handedness. It is to be expected that there were differences between missionaries and evangelists over initiation rites, *lobolo*, polygamy and many other traditional African issues. Volz neither ridicules the African beliefs, nor the basics of biblical teaching. As such he has contributed an excellent localized case study for inquiries in African theology, in African church history or in mission strategies. This is a fascinating and well-documented contribution.

Wa Kasonga, Kasonga

see review 625

1142. Wachege, P. N., editor

Jesus Christ Our Muthamaki (Ideal Elder): An African Christological Study Based on the Agikuyu Understanding of Elder

Nairobi: Phoenix Publishers, 1992. 271 pages, ISBN: 9789966471871.

Wachege's study represents a very thorough and insightful attempt to inculturate biblical theology in an African setting. The author, a respected Kenyan university professor and local Catholic parish priest, divides his presentation into two major parts. In the first he makes a detailed and well-written anthropological survey of the traditional Agikuyu social and religious way of life, with a particular focus on their notion of "elderhood" (*uthamaki*). In part two, Wachege utilizes this African concept of "elderhood" as a means for better understanding the person and work of Christ from an African (Gikuyu) viewpoint. He then applies this perspective in presenting what he feels is a more contextualized Christology, together with its contemporary spiritual, catechetical, and pastoral relevance. Wachege's approach is generally balanced, and in many respects his treatment provides a helpful model for similar studies needed in other ethnic settings. At times his Roman Catholic ecclesiastical framework intrudes, or he can appear rather uncritical in his acceptance of certain "African Christologies" in contemporary literature (which, while they may be "African," are not always "Christian"). But on the whole, Wachege's book is a useful contribution.

1143. Wafawanaka, Robert

Am I Still My Brother's Keeper?: Biblical Perspectives on Poverty

Lanham, MD: University Press of America, 2012. 242 pages, ISBN: 9780761857013.

The author originally comes from Zimbabwe, but has been teaching in the USA since he completed his doctoral thesis at Boston University in 1997. The present work is a revised version of the major parts of his thesis (some of the thesis material excluded here has in the meantime been published as articles). The book is a critical analysis of biblical perspectives on poverty, structured in three main sections. Section I offers a general introduction, discussing the research context and some methodological and hermeneutical questions. Section II looks at the phenomenon of poverty within the three major parts of the OT: the Law, the Prophets, and the Writings. Section III then concludes, and offers some perspectives on the relevance of these texts in today's world. Of these three sections, Section II is the major contribution, with more than two thirds of the total number of pages. The author here demonstrates a cross-cultural concern, aiming to use traditional African societal values – like family, kinship circles, religious value systems, communal obligations, and social responsibilities – in order to illuminate OT discourse on poverty: the Law, with its attempts at organising a society built on justice; the Prophets, railing against injustice and oppression of the poor; and the Writings, discussing poverty from various perspectives of theology and experience. The African comparative material (which unfortunately is somewhat reduced compared to what was included in the original thesis) enables the author to go beyond a mere historical investigation. The African experience also lies beneath the book's political agenda: even in our time we have something to learn from the biblical texts with regard to the question of poverty. Wafawanaka's welcome study should find many readers.

Wagner, Shari Miller

see review 719

1144.   Waliggo, John M., editor

Inculturation: Its Meaning and Urgency

Kampala: St. Paul Publications, 1986. 83 pages.

This brief collection of essays, dealing with the inculturation of Christianity in Africa, is a call to take seriously the statement of Pope Paul VI when he said, "You may and you must have an African Christianity." To encourage this, Waliggo and his fellow contributors discuss the definition and scope of inculturation. They deal with the present state of African Christianity and its struggle to move beyond a mere dependence on Western forms, worship and theology, to a truly African expression of its faith. This is done in a balanced manner, as it is recognized that Christianity was birthed in a specific historical and cultural context. The starting point for a consideration of the inculturation of Christianity should not be the abstract separation between Christianity and Western culture. This is because "Christianity cannot divest itself fully of its European historical destiny, without running the risk of denying its very essence." Inculturation can begin to take place as efforts are made by African Christians "to proclaim Christ and the values he stood for, as found in the Scriptures, by embodying them in expressions and symbols taken from the life experiences of the people." These expressions will take unique forms as they are shaped by different cultures responding to the concrete specificity of Christ. By relating back to the objective reality of the historic Christ, subjective inculturations will be avoided. The last essay deals with practical applications of these ideas, and points the way to making these suggestions a reality in the areas of catechesis, liturgy, liberation and the development of a "truly authentic African local church." Waliggo is a Ugandan with a doctorate in history from the University of Cambridge. At the time of writing he was a lecturer at the Catholic University of Eastern Africa in Nairobi, and he subsequently served as a lecturer at Uganda Martyrs University in Kampala. The other contributors, all impressively credentialed, are from Kenya, Rwanda, and the Netherlands. The book is intended for a wider readership than just the Roman Catholic tradition represented by its contributors. It will prove helpful for those who are wrestling with issue surrounding the relationship between Christianity and culture, and the inevitable conflicts, opportunities and challenges that arise as they interact.

Waliggo, John M.

see also review 583

1145.   **Walker, David S.**

Challenging Evangelicalism: Prophetic Witness and Theological Renewal

Pietermaritzburg: Cluster, 1993. 228 pages, ISBN: 9780958314121.

This publication is based on doctoral work completed at the University of KwaZulu-Natal in South Africa in 1990, hence taking form during the period when South Africa was emerging from the Apartheid era and moving toward a more democratic dispensation. As the ambiguous title indicates, the author means both to challenge conservative evangelicals and to present an argument in favour of a more positive form of evangelicalism comprised of "radical evangelicals." Within his dualistic system, "radical evangelicals" are defined as those who are found "challenging structures of social evil . . . and standing in uncompromising opposition to evil systems of power and authority"; all other evangelicals presumably form part of the alternative group that Walker wishes to challenge. The putative lack of concern for social issues amongst the "other evangelicals" Walker traces back to "Protestant Scholasticism" (embodied primarily in the Princetonian theology of Charles Hodge) and "Fundamentalism." However, the genealogical relationship between these two movements and late twentieth-century South African evangelicalism is never shown. Walker also mentions the rise of "neo-evangelicalism" as a response to fundamentalism, but does not give any indication what difference this significant movement makes to his analysis. The author argues that evangelicalism should be characterized by a theology that prioritizes the poor, a contextualized methodology and holistic mission. In making this case he draws heavily on the work of Orlando Costas, Vinay Samuel, Chris Sugden and René Padilla. With the exception of a handful of South African thinkers, African voices are largely absent from this discussion. This is especially unfortunate in a book that includes a chapter entitled "Taking Context Seriously." Although Walker claims that Western evangelicalism suffers from being too abstract, one of the major weaknesses of the book itself consists in its failure to provide concrete examples or suggestions of what theological renewal along these proposed lines might look like. The social issues facing the church are generally far more complex than Walker's analysis allows. Does concern for the poor trump justice? How would a theology contextualized to this one dimension address cultural or racial situations that pit the poor against the poor? Walker's concern for the poor is laudable, yet his critique is not careful enough to be truly prophetic, nor is his construction substantive enough for true theological renewal.

1146.   **Wallis, Jim, and Joyce Hollyday, editors**

Crucible of Fire: The Church Confronts Apartheid: Essays by Leading South African Christians 1980–1990

Eugene, OR: Wipf & Stock, 2005. 192 pages, ISBN: 9781597523301.

During the latter half of the 1980s the political tensions within South Africa were rapidly escalating. When it seemed that neither national nor international concern against apartheid was being adequately voiced, it was the churches within South Africa that took up the burden. Since white churches and denominations were largely ignorant, indoctrinated or apathetic to the situation, the perspectives to be heard were predominantly those of the black church leadership. It is these perspectives, then, that are reflected in *Crucible of Fire*, edited respectively by the editor and by the associate editor of *Sojourners* magazine. The book contains a sermon each by Allan Boesak (president of the World Alliance of Reformed Churches) and Desmond Tutu (Anglican archbishop of Cape Town). The editors' interviews with both men are also included, as are interviews with Frank Chikane (general secretary of the South African Council of Churches), Charles Villa-Vicencio (head of the Department of Religious Studies, University of Cape Town), Motlalepula Chabaku (pastor in exile from South Africa), and Beyers Naudé (former Dutch Reformed pastor). An appendix reprints five letters between the then State President, P. W. Botha, and church leaders. The original intention of the book was to summon the support of Christians worldwide to act immediately against apartheid. The situation in South Africa has of course evolved dramatically since 1989. This book will nevertheless prove a useful resource for anyone studying the Christian response to apartheid in South Africa.

1147. **Walls, Andrew F.**

The Cross-Cultural Process in Christian History: Studies in the Transmission and Reception of Faith

Maryknoll, NY: Orbis, 2002. 288 pages, ISBN: 9781570753732.

Walls is the well-known former director of the Centre for the Study of Christianity in the Non-Western World at the University of Edinburgh. A core contribution of this new study is that, while attending to a wider frame of reference, Walls usefully places some of the most interesting African Christians and aspects of African Christianity within a global and historical perspective, and provides an optimistic view of Africa's place in and contribution to world Christianity. The three parts of the book – the Transmission of Christian Faith, Africa in Christian History, and Vignettes of the Missionary Movement from the West – work together in that the latter two sections illustrate the themes of the first section. Of several themes running through the book, three may be mentioned. First, along with Latourette, Walls notices that Christianity expands serially, moving across cultural borders from one heartland to form another, while eventually receding in the former heartland some time after the cross-cultural transmission is achieved. Thus the great increase in the number of Christians in Africa and elsewhere in the non-Western world as a result of the missionary movement from the West is being matched by the decrease in Christianity in the West itself. Secondly, Christendom – the notion that "Christianity was essentially linked to territory and the possession of territory" – was the result of moulding the gospel to European realities before Europe knew that much of the rest of the world existed. Through the modern missionary movement, Christendom has given way to a wide variety of forms of Christianity throughout the world, including Christianity in Africa. Third, all the forms of Christianity need one another in order to be complete as the Church was meant to be, namely one body made up of many members who are very different from one another and yet beneficially interdependent. Walls rejects mono-cultural Christianity and post-modern egalitarian pluralism in favour of the Ephesian vision, or as Walls puts it: "the translation of the life of Jesus into the lifeways of all the world's cultures and subcultures through history." He goes on to say: "None of us can reach Christ's completeness on our own. We need each other's vision to correct, enlarge, and focus our own; only together are we complete in Christ." Therefore African Christianity is vital to the health of the whole worldwide church. Walls' consequential vision of African Christianity's place in and contribution to world Christianity merits widespread critical evaluation and appropriation within African Christianity.

This is the sort of book that thoughtful Christian leaders on the continent would do well to read and ponder during their next holiday break!

1148. Walls, Andrew F.

The Missionary Movement in Christianity: Studies in the Transmission of Faith

Maryknoll, NY: Orbis, 2006. 250 pages, ISBN: 9781570750595.

As a renowned historian of world Christianity, Walls here fulfils the desire of many by bringing together in one book a large number of his previously published articles. The articles span a period of over twenty years, and are divided into three sections. Part 1 presents some of Wall's notable essays on how Christianity is transmitted from one culture to another, what factors affect that transmission, and how Christianity is thereby reshaped. Part 2 is titled "Africa's Place in Christian History." Walls was among the earliest visionaries to herald the shift of Christianity's "centre of gravity" from the Western world to the non-western world. In the process, he has also argued that Africa has now become a significant base for Christianity and thereby a key player in its spread. This second part also examines the Western context out of which Christianity came to Africa, the role of Africans in the dissemination of the new faith, and the nature of Africa's response. Part 3 examines the missionary movement in some detail. It talks about what ought to be the nature of mission studies, the changing image of the missionary, as well as the missions scholar and the missionary movement. Walls was at one time a missionary to Sierra Leone and Nigeria. In this collection he has eminently demonstrated his special insights about Africa and about Christian presence in Africa. Lecturers and students in Christian history, missions, and theology in Africa will find this a richly stimulating book, enabling them better to understand the past and thereby better to know how to participate in "The Transmission of Faith" in the future.

Walls, Andrew F.

see also review 356

1149. Wambutda, Daniel Nimcir

A Study of Conversion among the Angas of Plateau State of Nigeria with Emphasis on Christianity

Frankfurt: Peter Lang, 1991. 238 pages, ISBN: 9783820497809.

The Ngas (or Angas) are a medium-sized but significant ethnic group in the Middle Belt of Nigeria. The former Nigerian head of state, General Yakubu Gowon, is Ngas. This PhD dissertation, by the former professor in religious studies at the University of Jos, outlines the initial events of the conversion to Christianity of a large part of the Ngas. The study was completed in 1978 at the University of Ife but was only published in 1991. The first three chapters look at the social and religious background of the Ngas before and during the advent of Christianity. These detailed and informative chapters evidence a man who knows his own culture. Following this is a description of how Christianity came to the Ngas. In 1910 the Cambridge University Missionary Party (CUMP) began to work among the Ngas. They were active among the Ngas until 1930, when the work was handed over to the British branch of the Sudan United Mission. The CUMP were Anglican by persuasion. Wambutda believes that the people responded because of the holistic approach of the mission: "the CUMP had always believed in the development of the whole man." The mission had a strong emphasis on education, while medicine and agriculture were also important. So why did the people convert? In the author's estimation, most people converted because they thought Christianity was "a better way" in comparison to traditional religion or Islam. In terms of conversion theories, while missiologists tend towards "numinous" theories that emphasize the working of the Holy Spirit, and sociologists opt for "naturalistic" theories, the author commendably concludes that we have to recognize that both the divine and human factors are at play in the conversion of a people. This book is a valuable study about conversion to Christianity in Africa, while also providing primary information on the Ngas.

1150.   Wamue, Grace, and Mary N. Getui, editors

Violence against Women: Reflections by Kenyan Women Theologians

Nairobi: Acton Publishers, 1996. 85 pages, ISBN: 9789966888488.

This book focuses on various forms of violence against women in society and the church as encountered and experienced by the Kenyan women contributors, who write in anticipation of a time when there will be no gender-related violence. The various writers highlight the following topics: the mission, obstacles and future dreams of African women theologians; the violence against women present in oral literature and especially proverbs; the hurt experienced by childless women and co-wives in polygamous marriages; the exclusion of mothers from the naming of their children; and the traumas of widowhood, rape and economic exploitation of women. The silence of the church in the face of these issues, even when they occur within the church, leads to a call for justice for all Christians, women as well as men. The final chapter is a reappraisal of a traditional method of moral education among the Gikuyu of Kenya, presented in an effort to incorporate effective principles to help the church in Africa address the need for greater mutual sensitivity between men and women. The contributors are all theologians in departments of religion and mission in Kenyan universities or international church bodies and their theological perspectives reflect this diversity. While some critique early missionary responses to indigenous culture, all acknowledge that naming oppressive aspects of indigenous culture involves breaking strong cultural taboos that have silenced women for centuries. This is an edited compilation of papers given in different settings, some based primarily on interview data and others citing a variety of published sources. As a whole the book furnishes broad-based insight on the current views among informed African women on the subject of gender violence. The chapters generally conclude with suggestions or recommendations on how churches and women themselves can seek solutions to the problems being described. By presenting women's voices and thoughts on the various aspects of violence affecting women, this book will be valuable to the wider church and especially to men, whether in the church or in society.

1151.   Wan-Tatah, Victor

Emancipation in African Theology: An Inquiry on the Relevance of Latin American Liberation Theology to Africa

Frankfurt: Peter Lang, 1989. 225 pages, ISBN: 9780820402840.

The author, originally from Cameroon, was professor of religious studies at an American university. This book is an attempt to apply Latin American liberation theology to the African context. The particular context of

Wan Tatah's theological reflection, as treated in his opening chapters, concerns pre-colonial Cameroon, Western missionary contacts and the colonial legacy. He stresses the positive aspects of his traditional African culture, stating that "the God of the missionaries was already working his way in African religion." He examines the role of the white missionaries in his country, noting that at times they opposed the colonial policies. He then looks at the largely negative impact of colonialism on Cameroon. The capitalistic cash economy forced many people out of their villages into cities and into impoverishment. The role of missionaries in this situation was ambivalent. The author then summarizes Latin American liberation theology, which focuses on the liberation of the poor and oppressed. But this theology must be contextualized for Africa. Wan-Tatah claims that three sources are needed for African Christian theology: the African culture, the socio-political context and the biblical sources. The last chapter finally sets forth Wan-Tatah's own theology: a Christology of the refugee. There are refugees in Africa from war but also from oppressive military governments. Theologically, Jesus should be considered a refugee who fought for the rights of the oppressed and refugees. Likewise, the African church should be a "refugee church" since it has different values from the world and it struggles for the poor. Apart from the question of the refugees, this book is in many respects predictable liberation theology. Theology and salvation are primarily social or horizontal.

Wandera, Joseph

see review 1069

Ward, Honor

see review 88

1152. **Ward, Kevin, and Emma Wild-Wood, editors**

The East African Revival: History and Legacies

Abingdon, UK: Routledge, 2012. ISBN: 9781138111103.

In 2008 a conference was convened in Cambridge, England, to celebrate the donation to the Henry Martyn Centre for the Study of Mission and World Christianity in Cambridge of special archives relating to the East African Revival (EAR). This book emerged from that conference. Edited by two leading scholars of African Christianity, Kevin Ward and Emma Wild-Wood, the essays in this collection boast an impressive array of themes dealing with the EAR. Although the origins of the revival date back to the 1930s and to a small corner in south-west Uganda, the effects of the EAR have significantly shaped the expression of Christianity throughout that part of Africa. The book begins with a historical overview of the revival by Ward, and then engages the reader with first-hand accounts of key figures in the region. Following sections cover principal historical dimensions, cultural dynamics, and broader summary chapters dealing with the revival. As with most edited books, not all the contributions are created equal. One finds an excellent essay by Derek Peterson dealing with the nature of revival and dissent in East Africa. The more recent Routledge edition includes two insightful concluding essays, one by Ward and one by Wild-Wood, that reflect on the revival's influence upon African Christianity and its place in the study of African Christianity. This book celebrates the gift of Joe Church's papers to the archives in Cambridge, so the reader should be prepared to see his influence interspersed throughout the chapters, influential as he was in the origins of the revival. This is perhaps the best treatment of the EAR to date. While the hardback version is too costly to mention, Routledge has just released a paperback version that is not prohibitively expensive. This volume will function as essential for all scholarly study of the East African Revival going forward, and as an important addition to any library intending a credible collection on Christianity in Africa.

Wartenberg-Potter, Bärbel von

see review 932

1153. Waruta, Douglas W., editor

African Church in the 21st Century: Challenges and Promises

Nairobi: All Africa Conference of Churches, 1995. 155 pages, ISBN: 9789966886019.

Waruta has been a professor in the Department of Religious Studies at the University of Nairobi and secretary for the Association of Theological Institutions in Eastern Africa (ATIEA). Here he provides an edited collection of papers and responses delivered at ATIEA's 1993 Annual Staff Institute in Dar es Salaam, Tanzania. The collection also includes Bible studies given at the conference. The four primary papers, addressing the church of the future in Africa, were authored by members of the All Africa Conference of Churches (AACC). Respondents and Bible study leaders represented various universities and theological colleges of mostly mainline denominations from Tanzania, Kenya, Uganda, and Ethiopia. The primary challenges presented for the future church in Africa were wrapped around the themes of church and denominational unity, the strength and accuracy of its witness, the establishment of its selfhood and identity, and the religious pluralism it faces – all within the African context. Some related challenges mentioned were superstition, the interpretation and application of God's Word to both head and heart, individual and societal character, poverty and disease, drought and famine, and the role of religion in ethnically and religiously inspired conflict.

1154. Waruta, Douglas W., editor

Caring and Sharing: Pastoral Counselling in the African Perspective

Nairobi: Uzima Press, 1995. 278 pages, ISBN: 9789966855367.

This text contains fifteen papers presented by professors from East African theological institutions and university departments of religion. These were given as part of a staff institute of the Association of Theological Institutions in East Africa (ATIEA) which was held in Nairobi in 1992. The editor, who was also Secretary of the Association, begins the book with an excellent chapter providing a broad perspective on pastoral counselling in Africa. He gives an overview of the kinds of healing that have been used in traditional Africa, a review of Western approaches to counselling, and the contributions and weaknesses of the approach used by many churches. He proposes the need for an integrated approach. The other fourteen chapters focus on a variety of subjects within the general sphere of pastoral care and counselling. The book is strong on elaborating the many issues of concern to the church and the pastor in modern Africa, such as urbanisation, corruption, poverty and drugs. There are several chapters dealing with the pastoral care of the ageing and of the dying along with their families. There are several chapters focusing on alcohol and drug abuse. The book is weak in the area of counselling theory, whether African, Western, biblical or integrative. The reader will have to go elsewhere for this. The book is both readable and represents a good quality of scholarship. *Caring and Sharing* should certainly be read by anyone in Africa teaching in the field of pastoral care and counselling, and those already in pastoral ministry should find it helpful for better understanding the tough issues that their members are facing.

1155.   Waruta, Douglas W., and Hannah W. Kinoti, editors

Pastoral Care in African Christianity: Challenging Essays in Pastoral Theology

Nairobi: Acton Publishers, 1994. 242 pages, ISBN: 9789966888129.

The eleven essays in this collection seek to promote contextual theological reflection on the pastoral counselling ministry in Africa. Approaching from an ecumenical perspective, the contributors wish to challenge the church to equip its pastors with an awareness of the context in which Christian truth needs to be applied, so that it may be relevant in the African situation. The introduction presents the essence of pastoral counselling as a ministry of restoring the wholeness of God's people as they encounter suffering. Two essays treat domestic violence against women, and violence against women in general. The church is challenged to take a clear protective stance by confronting attitudes that tolerate domestic wife-beating, and to raise consciousness on this problem in the wider society. Other contributors call attention to the recent plight of street children, discussing the Kenyan experience and calling the church to include them as beneficiaries of the Good News. One writer urges the church to attend to pastoral care for students and youth. He argues that this group has been neglected by the church and has consequently received ministry from the West, which has created a gap between the youth and their parents. Another essay considers pastoral care for the elderly, and proposes that African culture can teach us something about caring for our elderly. Research done in Tanzania among Catholic clergy leads Laurenti Magesa to give some suggestions for the care of this group. The last essay presents a study of problems among clergy from nine denominations in Kenya, and clearly underlines the need for pastoral care of pastors. The book is not so much a text on pastoral counselling as a series of theological reflections on pastoral care, in which the church is urged to think through specific pastoral issues facing the African church. This is a very helpful contribution to have, especially since so little has been written in this field specifically for Africa. Those in pastoral ministry in Africa, as well as those preparing others for such ministry, should find the various essays both stimulating and instructive.

Waruta, Douglas W.

see also review 777

1156.   Waters, John

David Livingstone: Trail Blazer

London: IVP-UK, 1996. 256 pages, ISBN: 9780851111704.

Written by a literature consultant with the Church Mission Society (CMS), this book is yet another in the legion of books about the best-known missionary explorer of Africa. The author's approach is to allow the well-known story to flow freely without unnecessary details. For example, Livingstone's boyhood is almost completely omitted, for readers presumably want to know about trailblazing in Africa, not Scotland. He uses original sources effectively, especially the well-known works of Schapera, carefully documenting opinions when they differ. Waters sticks to his two "frequent motifs" throughout, namely: Livingstone's dedication to Christ, and his determination to end slavery. It soon becomes obvious that the author agrees with the importance of these motifs, and gives them principal focus. As a result, one must look elsewhere for details on Livingstone's concerns with plants and animals, and the famous lion incident at Mabotsa receives only a quick mention, for Waters is far more concerned with the missionary explorer's impact on people. He is balanced in his judgment that the man had far more problems relating to Europeans than to Africans, although he gives little attention to the harsh attitudes that Livingstone had toward some fellow missionaries. His final chapter, entitled "The Fruit," makes plain his reasons for writing yet another book on Livingstone. Unlike another recent biographer, who curiously ended his book by comparing Livingstone to a well-known modern faith healer, Waters instead calls attention to several of Livingstone's key perceptions: that Africans could benefit from commerce (especially to replace the slave trade); that good relationships with Africans were essential to the missionary cause; that preaching could be done widely as a preparation for others who followed; that contextualising the gospel was important, rather than Europeanising the African and causing dependence. Waters even claims that Livingstone would encourage theological educators in Africa, including extension programmes, noting his burden that Christians be well taught. This book is a welcome addition to the literature, as a relatively non-technical, but carefully accurate, account of one of the most controversial Christians in African history.

1157. Watley, William A., and Raquel Annette St. Clair

The African Presence in the Bible: Gospel Sermons Rooted in History

Valley Forge, PA: Judson Press, 2000. 118 pages, ISBN: 9780817013493.

The principal author is senior pastor of St James African Methodist Episcopal Church in Newark NJ, USA. His co-author is on the staff of the church. Their chief concern is their congregants' ignorance of the place of Africans in Scripture, so this book addresses the main biblical passages where Africans played a role. Since the Scriptures have been misused to denigrate blacks, both in Africa and elsewhere, the authors seek to change the perception that Africans were cursed. The overall aims are twofold: to establish the African presence in the Scriptures, and to address contemporary issues. Since good sermons should establish the context before making application, the authors are to be commended for attempting to do this. The eighteen sermons that follow, of mixed quality, cover the main texts associated with Africans (Moses' Cushite wife, the Cushite messenger in 2 Samuel 18, the lovers in the Song of Solomon, lifting Jeremiah out of the well, Simon of Cyrene and the Ethiopian eunuch), along with a few others that have a more limited connection. The style, especially the sermonic material by St. Clair, is more inspirational than academic. The material contributed by Watley generally goes deeper into the various passages that are used and the historical background. This book could be a resource for those who may share an ignorance of African presence in the Scriptures. The very first sermon ("We Are Included") is the foundation for the whole.

1158. Webb, Pauline, editor

A Long Struggle: The Involvement of the World Council of Churches in South Africa

Geneva: World Council of Churches, 1994. 133 pages, ISBN: 9782825411353.

This book traces the history of the World Council of Churches' struggle against the apartheid system of South Africa, through its Programme to Combat Racism (PCR), which was launched at the WCC Uppsala

Assembly in 1968. Eight persons who were closely involved with the PCR tell the story of its controversial and costly engagement in the struggle to overcome apartheid. Despite a lack of self-criticism in the majority of chapters, each contains valuable information on different aspects of that struggle. Thus Baldwin Sjollema, the first director of the PCR, shows how an ecumenical theology opposing racism was being formulated even in the years before the establishment of the WCC. Sjollema also shows how the debate initiated by the PCR's action-oriented programme affected the whole life of the WCC itself. Following chapters take up how these developments also affected regions of the world outside South Africa, especially in Europe and North America. For example, David Haslam, director of the Office for Racial Justice of the Council of Churches in Britain and Ireland emphasizes how the controversy surrounding the PCR became itself an effective means of education and awareness-building in the UK and northern Europe. From within South Africa, former PCR director Barney Pityana offers a theological analysis of the reaction of South African churches, and draws out lessons on church/state relations, methods of doing theology and the need for a renewed understanding of the nature of the church. Charles Villa-Vicencio of the Department of Religious Studies in the University of Cape Town goes to the nub of the debate about violence, as it was understood by many churches at the height of the controversy over the PCR financial grants to the liberation movements. He suggests that the nature of the violence still prevalent in South Africa has increased the urgency of finding non-violent ways of Christian involvement in the cause of racial justice. The book concludes with a paper by Philip Potter, general secretary of the WCC from 1972 to 1984. He assesses the continuing role of the ecumenical community in giving support to the churches in South Africa as they enable people to participate in the democratic process. He also stresses that all kinds of injustices in the world need active combating by all Christians. Whether one agrees with the methods used by the PCR or not, this book offers an effective overview of the WCC program.

1159. Weber, Charles W.

International Influences and Baptist Mission in West Cameroon: German-American Missionary Endeavor under International Mandate and British Colonialism

Leiden: BRILL, 1993. 176 pages, ISBN: 9789004097650.

Weber has been Professor of History at Wheaton College, USA. This historical text concentrates on the development of Baptist ministry in the former German colony of Kamerun during the period from 1922 to 1945, when the British and French had mandates from the League of Nations to govern sections of the country. The British sector was known as Cameroon Province and it is this region that is Weber's focus. The book has just five chapters. The first is a very detailed account of the development of Baptist ministry during the period mentioned, and is primarily a collection of names, dates and places. The second chapter is dedicated to a review of the ministry impact of three particular missionaries: Carl Bender, Paul Gebauer and George Dunger. These three men were not only important as Baptist missionaries, but were also significant missiologists of their day. Bender was a man who practiced contextualisation long before the term had been invented. He made it a priority to become fluent in the local language through living as closely with the people as possible, and employed every anthropological skill he knew to understand the mind and culture of the people. From this research he sought to share the gospel in as contextualized a way as possible. He wrote many books on the culture and mind of the people, and these were used by Gebauer and Dunger. Gebauer majored on developing culturally appropriate teaching methods for the Baptist churches and for the many schools they established. Dunger sought to develop the three-self principles for the churches – self-governing, self-funding and self-propagating. He also espoused a philosophy of ministry that saw mission as engaging cultures in all aspects of their development. Chapters 3 to 5 consider the specific educational and mission policies of the Baptists, and how they were applied within the historical and political realities of the Cameroon Province. This is not a book for the popular market, but it would be of interest to those engaged in advanced research on the Christian mission in Africa.

1160.   **Welsby, Derek A.**

The Medieval Kingdoms of Nubia: Pagans, Christians and Muslims along the Middle Nile

London: British Museum, 2002. 296 pages, ISBN: 9780714119472.

This work provides a comprehensive and authoritative update on research relating to the ancient Christian communities of northern Sudan. These little-noticed Christian kingdoms in Africa's interior lasted a thousand years, from about the fifth century AD until early in the sixteenth century, and covered an area along the Nile from Aswan to well south of Khartoum. Little was commonly known about these communities until major archaeological discoveries began from the 1960s onward. The author, on the research staff of the British Museum, has been closely involved with archaeological excavations in Sudan since 1982. Whereas the most productive source for fresh information on Christian Nubia has been archaeology, no overall survey of such findings has been attempted in recent years. In tracing out the social life and history of this part of Africa during the Nubian Christian era, Welsby references the entire scope of modern published reports and discussion, archaeological and otherwise, and attempts a synthesis, thereby rendering an invaluable service. The presentation throughout is accompanied by detailed notes, extensive bibliography, and splendid maps and photographs. An enhanced awareness of the altogether remarkable and until recently poorly noted Nubian Christian communities of medieval Sudan can reinforce African Christianity's sense of its own indigenous heritage. Whereas most of the archaeological work has focused on the northern parts of Nubia, Welsby himself has worked in the southern area around Khartoum, and he introduces new findings from that area, including foundations of a major Nubian Christian cathedral just east of modern Khartoum. He also references remains of medieval Nubian churches up to 200 kilometres south of Khartoum. Regarding Nubian Christian cultural influence westward into central Africa, he lists all possible evidence, but concludes that earlier reported remains as far west as Darfur and Chad have not been confirmed. Welsby also offers detailed discussion of the disappearance of Nubian Christianity by the early sixteenth century, with full academic apparatus. For the serious researcher in this field of inquiry this volume will prove indispensable. Informed African Christianity will also want increasingly to take into account the implications of such findings in understanding its own heritage and identity on the continent.

Wendl, Tobias

see review 853

1161. **Wendland, Ernst R., editor**

Biblical Texts and African Audiences

Nairobi: Acton Publishers, 2004. 204 pages, ISBN: 9789966888419.

This collection of essays represents the work of translation consultants within the United Bible Societies in Africa. The essays are grouped in three sections. The first deals with Bible translation in relation to the work of African intellectuals. Thus one essay discusses the Kenyan writer Ngugi wa Thiongo in relation to the enterprise of translating the Bible in Africa, while a second essay considers the literary skill of Julius Nyerere, the first President of Tanzania, who translated the Gospels and Acts in the form of traditional Kiswahili *tenzi* verses. The next section of essays deals with Bible translation in relation to specific social contexts: inculturation theology as it has been developed in the Catholic Faculty in Kinshasa since the 1960s; the image of God and its implications for the image of African women suffering from HIV/AIDS; and a project in Senegal that involved Muslims in reading the Bible. Finally, the third section of essays deals with Bible translation and multicultural complexities. This includes: challenges of producing a study Bible in Chechewa; some sociolinguistic challenges of publishing Christian scriptures in Africa; and the relationship between Bible translation and interfaith relations in Africa. This collection of essays is matched by a companion volume on related themes, titled: *Bible Translation and African Languages* (edited by Yorke and Renju).

1162. **Wendland, Ernst R.**

Buku Loyera: An Introduction to the New Chichewa Bible Translation

Blantyre: CLAIM, 1998. 224 pages, ISBN: 9789990816082.

A Protestant translation of the Bible into the Chinyanja language of Malawi first appeared in 1922 under the title *Buku Lopatulika* (Sacred Book). This was followed by a Catholic translation, called *Malembo Oyera* (Holy Letters/Writings), in 1966. This is a study of the third Chichewa Bible, published in 1998, an inter-confessional translation called *Buku Loyera* (Holy Book). Wendland, theologian, linguist and a member of the translation team, begins with a brief historical overview, and an outline of the general rationale and organisation of this inter-church, popular-language project. He then provides a detailed summary of the main principles and procedures for meaning-oriented Bible translation, as exemplified by the new text in comparison with the older Protestant and Catholic versions. Wendland offers detailed illustrations of how and why the *Buku Loyera* translation differs from its predecessors, first in relation to a number of key biblical words considered individually, and then with respect to several longer, mainly poetic passages, where the effects of the two basically different translational techniques may be compared in terms of general intelligibility, emotive impact, and aesthetic appeal. Wendland concludes with thoughts on assessing the quality of a given translation both on its own terms and also in relation to other versions, and the historical and socio-cultural implications of Bible translation for the growth and vitality of the Church in both theology and praxis. Besides being a tribute to the work of successive translators in the Chichewa/Chinyanja language over a period of more than a century, this book will prove a useful tool and reference resource for those concerned with the ongoing task of Bible translation in Africa and elsewhere.

1163.   **Wendland, Ernst R.**

Comparative Discourse Analysis and the Translation of Psalm 22 in Chichewa, a Bantu Language of South-Central Africa

Lewiston, NY: Edwin Mellen Press, 1993. 260 pages, ISBN: 9780773492899.

This distinguished scholar and theologian has served for many years at the Lutheran Seminary in Lusaka, and also since 1999 as a visiting professor at Stellenbosch University in South Africa. He is particularly well known as a widely published translation consultant with the United Bible Societies in Africa. Here he has provided us with a rare product: a full-length text analysing a single poem in the source language, a comparative analysis of lyric structure in the receptor language, a translation of the poem and an evaluation of the exercise. We have few such full discussions of poetic translation available to us, especially a composite discussion of the constraints imposed by dealing with a complete piece of sacred text; an original context distanced from us in time, space, culture and thought-form; and a Bantu community in which traditional oral discourse is alive and well, and which also employs the written medium. The translation is the result of work by a class of third-year seminary students who undertook a study of ndakatulo (a Chichewa lyric form) alongside a study of Hebrew lyric poetry from Psalms. Translations of Psalms published in old and new versions of the Chichewa Bible were evaluated and the students were then set to work to try their hand. Their own efforts were critically discussed, improved, and evaluated with the help of Wendland's consultancy experience, and a single final version was tested with other Chewa speakers. The present book is built around the resulting translation. Anyone concerned with effective communication of the biblical message in African culture would do well to read this book.

1164.   **Wendland, Ernst R.**

The Cultural Factor in Bible Translation: A Study of Communicating the Word of God in a Central African Cultural Context

Reading, UK: United Bible Society, 1987. 233 pages, ISBN: 9789999601191.

This study is concerned with the cultural mismatch between biblical culture and receptor cultures, and the ensuing problems for Bible translation. It is copiously illustrated by examples from Chichewa (Malawi) and Chitonga (Zambia). A quotation from the Song of Songs 1:2: "Oh that you would kiss me with the kisses of your mouth, for your love is better than wine" (RSV), provides a dramatic opening example of the book's theme. In Tonga culture, kissing is not a cultural expression of love, and the words seem to allude to prostitutes and alcohol. Whether one prefers to read the Song of Songs as an allegorical poem of Christ's love for the Church, or as a song exalting a deep, romantic expression of human love, if its opening words conjure up associations of promiscuity in a bar, then "the cultural factor" cannot be ignored. Chapter 1 briefly covers the way that culture can impose on interpretation, and gives a very brief introduction to worldview approaches. This is followed by a discussion of communication models, and a general introduction to ATR in Central Africa. Chapters 4 to 6 form the core, with attention to translation problems and the contribution the receptor culture makes. Discussion covers biblical concepts unfamiliar to receptor cultures, figurative language, and direct speech quotations. Chapter 7 goes through the Book of Ruth, with a running commentary of Tonga/Chewa cultural contrasts which could lead to difficulty in a clear interpretation. This is a fascinating technical study for those who must wrestle with the task of faithful biblical translation and interpretation in the African context.

1165. **Wendland, Ernst R.**

Preaching That Grips the Heart: A Rhetorical-Stylistic Study of the Chichewa Revival Sermons of Shadrack Wame

Blantyre: CLAIM, 2000. 108 pages, ISBN: 9789990816297.

Central to the Christian movement in Africa today is preaching. In this pioneering study Wendland investigates in some detail the principal stylistic resources and rhetorical strategies of popular preachers in Malawi, as they seek to stimulate or encourage a spiritual renewal (revival) and religious reinforcement among specific audiences on particular occasions. The major question is: from the point of view of language, what is it that grabs the hearts of these audiences? From an analysis of over 125 recorded Chewa sermons, ten principal stylistic features pertaining to rhetorical strategy are identified. These are: narrative preference, dramatic delivery, personal exemplification, affective appeal, traditional allusion, strategic reiteration, verbal intensification, idiomatic figuration, evocative description and audience involvement. These stylistic-rhetorical devices are described and illustrated in Wendland's text almost exclusively with reference to the sermons of Shadrack Wame (aged 58 and not a trained theologian), from Salima on the shores of Lake Malawi. (In an appendix Wendland provides Evangelist Wame's biographical testimony about his personal life history and religious pilgrimage.) Wendland begins with a brief overview of the Chewa sermon corpus, and then situates the ten critical stylistic features within a broad classical (Greco-Roman) framework of rhetoric. This is followed by an introduction to the inductive approach to literary composition, in comparison with a deductive method in basic homiletical composition. The major portion of the monograph offers a selective, paradigmatic description of the ten stylistic forms (form-oriented) and rhetorical devices (function-oriented). This is then extensively illustrated with three complete sermons by Wame (in English translation). The dynamic (south central) African homiletical style is briefly evaluated from a wider functional perspective with regard to its overall communicative effectiveness, and also in comparison with a traditional Western deductive homiletical model. Wendland concludes with comments concerning the significance of this and related studies that seek to elucidate the rhetorical potency of preaching within the context of contemporary African society. Wendland, lecturing at the Lutheran Seminary in Lusaka since 1968, consultant for the Bible Societies of Malawi and Zambia, and Visiting Professor at the University of Stellenbosch, has set a singularly exemplary standard for research into the nature and character of preaching in the African Christian context.

1166. **Wendland, Ernst R.**

Sewero!: Christian Drama and the Drama of Christianity in Africa

Blantyre: CLAIM, 2005. 296 pages, ISBN: 9789990876260.

This book's further subtitle clearly grounds it in Africa, specifically in Malawi: "the genesis and genius of Chinyanja [vernacular language] radio plays in Malawi with special reference to Trans World Radio and African Traditional Religion." The author draws on feedback from his seminary students in Lusaka, Zambia, and on close collaboration with the local actors in Malawi who recorded radio plays on contemporary issues for Trans World Radio. The plays are intended to attract a mass audience to a typical interaction on a current social issue, and deliver a biblical lesson that deals with the issue. The issues are drawn from the daily lives of the actors and the people they live with, and attention is given to all contextual details, things like appropriate background sounds and accents, that will make the drama believable to the hearers. The book offers broad and detailed insights and instructions on techniques needed for the production of quality radio plays that will capture and hold the attention of a wide and varied listening audience. The one word title, *Sewero*, means "the play," and that is clearly the primary focus of the book. As the subtitle indicates, however, the content of these plays is intertwined with the techniques throughout the book. The insights given by the local actors as they address current issues, which usually include aspects of African traditional religion, are extremely enlightening to all seeking to build Christ's kingdom in Africa today. Even readers who are not especially interested in producing radio plays will benefit greatly from the emphasis on this "drama of Christianity in Africa." Drama is a traditionally acceptable way to deal with secret and sensitive material in Africa, and the actors use this liberty to address subjects as sensitive as the requirement for incest in order to activate powerful magic purchased from sorcerers as a means to acquiring riches. Local versions of various biblical parables, and examples of Christians addressing social issues, are also presented effectively in the plays. Wendland includes the scripts of several dramas to illustrate his points with good effect. His study of anthropological principles enriches his insights on the relationship between scripture and African traditional religion, and also guides him in presenting biblical material in relevant and convincing ways within the African context.

Wendland, Ernst R.

see also reviews 647 and 1072

1167.   Werbner, Richard, and Terence Ranger, editors

Postcolonial Identities in Africa

London: Zed Books, 1996. 304 pages, ISBN: 9781856494168.

This volume originated with a colloquium held at the University of Manchester in England. It consists of papers presented at that time, and others commissioned for this book. The contributors are anthropologists, political scientists and social historians drawn from Africa, Europe and America. The essays focus on questions related to the multiple identities of African peoples in the postcolonial period. By "multiple identities" the authors refer to the fact that individuals in postcolonial Africa must function within several social spheres, each with its own "rules" and context. Therefore, ethnic "identity" alone serves as too narrow a concept accurately to describe the realities in which Africans must now function. The theme that seems to unify the essays is that the entire idea of "postcolonial" identity is a "Eurocentric" concept produced by Western scholars that seeks to continue Western hegemony on the African continent. Regrettably, much of the material in this collection is characterized by impenetrable prose. Unless one is already deeply conversant with post-modern discourse on identity politics, these essays may prove slow going or even defeat comprehension. This is unfortunate, for the issue of identity in modern Africa is a critically important one, both in terms of practical social dynamics and in terms of intellectual trends. Perhaps the most serious problem with this book lies in the conceptual categories put forth to examine identity issues in Africa. The essays propose to argue that the very idea of "postcolonial" identity conceals the continued dependence of African countries on Eurocentric Western scholarly categories. But where then did the conceptuality of "post-modernity" come from that so infuses the outlook of the contributors? Whose tools are now being used? And to whom then does the concept of "identity" belong, and whose intentions does it conceal? Such assessments can begin to turn in on themselves. These essays do include valuable critical reflection, on a topic that merits careful attention, but much is provided here in a mode of discourse and with a particular agenda that, for most readers, will serve to conceal rather than illuminate.

Werner, Dietrich

see review 919

1168. Werner, Roland

Das Christentum in Nubien: Geschichte und Gestalt einer afrikanischen Kirche

Münster: LIT Verlag, 2013. 520 pages, ISBN: 9783643121967.

This is the fruit of the German linguist and theologian Roland Werner's longstanding work with Nubian languages and history. It is indeed an impressive result; in the years (and probably decades) ahead, this book will be a key resource for anyone working with the history of a church that has often been ignored among church historians. The term 'Nubia' is here used in its medieval sense, the area along the Nile, between Aswan and where the Blue Nile and White Nile meet, namely southern Egypt and northern Sudan. For a millennium or so, approximately from the fifth to the fifteenth centuries, this area hosted the "third" church of northeastern Africa, in addition to the Coptic and Ethiopian ones, and shared many of their challenges and characteristics. The archaeological excavations of the Nile valley south of Aswan precipitated by the construction of the Aswan Dam in the 1960s caused a renewed interest in Nubian history, and resulted in unprecedented access to sources of Nubian Christianity. Werner is familiar with this archaeological and epigraphic material, which he approaches from two perspectives. The first part of the book deals with the material from a chronological perspective, presenting the history of Christian Nubia from the first examples of Christian influence (fourth century), through a process of Byzantine mission (sixth century) where Christianity become the state religion, and eventually a discussion century by century. The second part of the book deals with the material from a more systematic perspective, discussing key characteristics of the church, such as Bible translation, liturgy, and ministry, plus the role of the king and of the monasteries, also theological concepts and practices of baptism, piety, faith in Jesus, understanding of the cross, and veneration of Mary. This is a most welcome study of a church about which most African and Western historians and theologians have only a rather vague knowledge. The Nubian church is an example of an early African church that, in contrast to its sister churches in northeastern Africa, the Coptic and Ethiopian ones, did not survive. This raises important historical and missiological questions that deserve further attention.

1169. Werner, Roland, William Anderson, and Andrew C. Wheeler, editors

Day of Devastation, Day of Contentment: The History of the Sudanese Church across 2000 Years

Nairobi: Paulines, 2000. 704 pages, ISBN: 9789966215291.

This is an amazingly comprehensive history of Sudanese Christianity, with a warmly ecumenical approach to the story of the church in that land, and one that never loses sight of the individual personalities who played a part in that story. The presentation is well supplied with maps, photographs, and shaded panels that summarize major dates or that offer fascinating digressions into parts of the story that should not be forgotten. This massive treatment is likely to become the standard text on its subject for years to come. Within Africa the Muslim community has been at pains to develop an apologetic for Islam as an African religion, and to present Christianity as a foreign, intrusive, latecomer. This apologetic has not been the less dangerous for simply being untrue. The story of the presence of earliest Christianity in Africa needs to be told and re-told. This lengthy volume devotes over a hundred pages to the story of early Nubian Christianity, which was located in northern Sudan. Christian witness first penetrated this part of Africa in the first century (i.e. Acts 8 – hence the reference to "2000 years" in the title). Christianity then became the established faith for Nubia from the fifth century onward, and the Christian community lasted here for an entire millennium, before eventually succumbing to the encroachments of Islam. Part 2 of this volume tells the story of the replanting of Christianity in Sudan in the nineteenth century. Part 3 recounts the Sudanese response until 1964, and Part 4 presents the history of the independent Sudanese church from 1964 until 2000. A poignant note is supplied on the translation in the Septuagint of the Hebrew *Kush* by the Greek *Aithiops*, which reveals the longing of both Nubia (Sudan) and Ethiopia to be identified with the biblical promises of blessing. The book's title is taken from a contemporary Dinka hymn, and catches the spirit of the people, who continually find inner peace in an environment seemingly hostile to their very existence. This is one of very few paperbacks that one could wish had been published in hard covers! It will assuredly become an established reference work, and given its size the publishers would do well to ensure that part of an (inevitable) reprint is furnished with the durable covers worthy of such an indispensable resource in African Christian history.

Wessels, W. H.

see review 872

1170.   West, Gerald O.

The Academy of the Poor: Towards a Dialogical Reading of the Bible

London: Bloomsbury, 1999. 181 pages, ISBN: 9781850757580.

West lectures at the University of Natal in South Africa, and is the Director of the Institute for the Study of the Bible. Through the Institute he has been active in forging links between the academic world of biblical scholarship and the day-to-day world of ordinary Bible readers in South Africa, especially those whom West refers to as "poor and marginalized communities." The book is actually an extended hermeneutical reflection on the problems and dangers, joys and gains, of a critical interaction between (socially engaged) scholars and ordinary readers of the Bible in the South African context. Much of this material has appeared in oral form at conferences and in written form in journal articles. Here West has brought together some of the fruit of his reflections. Readers may raise their eyebrows at West's tendency to speak of reading the Bible against itself. Along with a number of others (Elisabeth Schussler Fiorenza and Itumeleng Mosala, for example), West believes that the "ideological nature of interpretation, and indeed of all texts, including biblical texts" means that the Bible can be used to oppress, not only because of the oppressive interpreter but because of the oppressive nature of some of the texts themselves. Therefore he advocates a hermeneutic of suspicion as well as trust. This aside, there is still much for theologically sensitive scholars to learn here. West is at his best and most useful when he is dealing with a text and with how that text is understood and received by ordinary African readers. The book contains interesting reports of studies on the Joseph story, the healings of Jairus' daughter and the woman with the flow of blood (Mark 5:21–6:1), and the story of Rizpah (2 Sam 21:1–14). Most important is the call which West's book embodies for scholars to engage in dialogue and humility with African communities. These groups already have resources for understanding the text's significance, but need the help of trained Bible readers in order to hear the message and its application with greater discernment. At the same time, scholars need the insights of the ordinary reader if their scholarship is going to be anything more than an ivory tower exercise. The book is a witness (sometimes in spite of itself) to the transformative potential of the Bible.

1171. West, Gerald O., and Musa W. Dube, editors

The Bible in Africa: Transactions, Trajectories, and Trends

Leiden: BRILL, 2001. 828 pages, ISBN: 9780391041110.

This massive, diverse, and informative volume of essays is edited by two senior African scholars, Gerald West of the University of Natal and Musa Dube of the University of Botswana. The stated aim of their collaborative, interdisciplinary effort is "to present . . . as wide a sense of the presence of the Bible in Africa as possible . . . [and] to give a sense of the breadth and richness of what African biblical scholars are up to." The book contains a far-ranging set of essays on a variety of topics written in depth from many different perspectives, and thereby admirably accomplishes its major objectives. Since a review of all 38 essays is impossible here, perhaps a selective listing of titles will at least give a sense of the content. The articles are grouped into four major sections. Part 1 – Historical and Hermeneutical Perspectives: "Developments in Biblical Interpretation in Africa: Historical and Hermeneutical Directions" (Ukpong); "Mapping African Biblical Interpretation: A Tentative Sketch" (West); "Old Testament Scholarship in Sub-Saharan Africa North of the Limpopo River" (Holter); "New Testament Exegesis in (Modern) Africa" (LeMarquand). Part 2 – Particular Encounters with Particular Texts: "The Role of the Bible in the Rise of African Instituted Churches" (Ndung'u); "Contextual Balancing of Scripture with Scripture: Scripture Union in Nigeria and Ghana" (Igenoza); "The Role of the Bible in the Igbo Christianity of Nigeria" (Nkwoka); "Biblical Interpretation in Contemporary Hymns from Tanzania" (King); "The Impact of the Bible on Traditional Rain-making Institutions in Western Zimbabwe" (Mafu). Part 3 – Comparison and Translation as Transaction: "Corporate Personality in Botswana and Ancient Israel" (Letlhare); "The Biblical God of the Fathers and the African Ancestors" (Mafico); "The Swahili Bible in East Africa from 1844 to 1996" (Mojola). Part 4 – Redrawing the Boundaries of the Bible in Africa: "Africa in the Old Testament" (Holter); "Popular Reading of the Bible in Africa and Implications for Academic Readings" (Ukpong); "To Pray the Lord's Prayer in the Global Economic Era" (Dube). The volume concludes with an extraordinary contribution in its own right, Grant LeMarquand's comprehensive and definitive "A Bibliography of the Bible in Africa," exceeding 160 pages! Generally speaking, the essays are well written and will serve as a good entry point for surveying the expanse of biblically-related studies in Africa. Readers will surely not agree with everything that has been written here, whether in terms of content, method, interpretation or conclusion. Some serious follow-up research will undoubtedly include a significant amount of critical response. But the standard for engagement has now been set by this immensely valuable multi-purpose study text in and for Africa.

1172. West, Gerald O.

Contextual Bible Study

Pietermaritzburg: Cluster, 1993. 95 pages, ISBN: 9780958380744.

West is a white South African and Professor of Biblical Studies at the University of Natal. He has written extensively on the use of the Bible in Africa, and with Musa Dube edited the massive volume, *The Bible in Africa*. Here he offers a detailed analysis of the different ways in which South African Christians, both black and white, theologically trained and untrained, can read and interpret the Bible together, hearing God speaking to them in their specific context, and effecting individual and social transformation. West identifies four commitments that enable such "contextual" Bible study: (1) to read the Bible from the perspective of the South African context, particularly from the perspective of the poor and oppressed; (2) to read the Bible in community with others, particularly with those from contexts different from our own; (3) to read the Bible critically (though West approaches the Bible with liberal and liberationist assumptions, "critical" here includes asking tough "why?" questions); (4) to pursue individual and social transformation through contextual Bible study. West goes on to describe how this can be achieved in group settings by combining one or more modes of reading the Bible critically: (1) reading behind the text (using Western historical-critical methods and sociological analysis); (2) reading the text itself (using literary methods); and (3) reading in front of the text (using a form of reader-response methodology). West next demonstrates how to do such contextual Bible reading process using 1 Timothy 2:8–12, Mark 10:17–22 and the book of Job. It is here that his liberal and liberationist assumptions and conclusions come out very clearly; readers may not find themselves in agreement with all that he says. This is nevertheless an important book in that it attempts to facilitate a necessary change in the way the Church in Africa studies the Bible. Whereas thoughtful readers may rightly dissent from many of the interpretive conclusions West presents, they can also learn much from reflecting critically on his methodological suggestions. For example, trained Christian leaders do need to read the Bible in community with ordinary church members. Furthermore, the Bible does need to be read in ways that more deliberately make for not only individual and but also social transformation. Social transformation towards biblical ideals of justice is not happening to the extent that it should throughout Africa. If a liberationist hermeneutic like the one espoused in this book is not the answer, alternative approaches have evidently also not been enough to make a difference either.

1173.   **West, Gerald O., and Musa W. Dube, editors**

"Reading With": Africa Overtures

Atlanta: Scholars Press, 1996. 228 pages.

This is a special issue of the academic journal *Semeia* (#73). The full subtitle is: "An Exploration of the Interface between Critical and Ordinary Readings of the Bible." It represents an effort by African and Africa-based biblical scholars (the "critics") to promote more life-related and need-oriented interpretations of the Scriptures by "ordinary," "pre-critical" lay Christians without unwanted influence or interference from the theological biases of the scholarly and clerical establishments. On offer are a collection of eleven essays on the subject of "reading with" (promoting, facilitating, enabling) various lay-constituted Bible study groups, located mainly in South Africa, including members of African Independent Churches, Botswana women, Marian communities, peasant farmers, and urban workers. The book concludes with four generally positive evaluations by selected respondents (somewhat strangely, only one of these comes from Africa). This composite text offers a number of good suggestions as to how pastors, teachers, and other church leaders might promote more involved, inductive, and interactive community-based and locally-contextualized Bible studies, especially among people who are non-literate but no less interested in learning more about the Scriptures and their contemporary application. Unfortunately, in a number of these essays, which are written from the perspective of "liberation theology," socio-political ideology appears to get in the way of responsible exegesis. Thus, the preferred critical method of biblical interpretation, namely, "reader response criticism" (in which every individual receptor of the text becomes as it were "a maker of meaning in the act of reading [or hearing]") is all too often allowed to degenerate into a subjective "postmodern" approach that permits interpreters, whether professional or lay, "to abandon their quest for the certainty of 'the right' reading in favour of more humane concerns for useful reading and resources." The result is a fatal "fusion" of hermeneutical "horizons," as a concern for the original text and context of Scripture tends to get eclipsed in the shadow of present-day issues and causes that all too often have little or nothing to do with the particular biblical text under consideration. An over-emphasis on interpretative creativity and current relevance thereby reduces a corresponding concern for fidelity to the original communication event. A focus on the here-and-now also diminishes the desire to put forth the necessary effort to determine first what these passages were trying to say in their own words and socio-cultural settings. This collection of essays is a good exemplification of some current hermeneutical trends and developments in biblical studies, which for better or for worse are gaining in their influence all over the continent.

West, Gerald O.

see also reviews 216 and 1116

1174.   **Westerlund, David, and Eva Evers Rosander, editors**

African Islam and Islam in Africa: Encounters between Sufis and Islamists

Athens, OH: Ohio University Press, 1997. 357 pages, ISBN: 9780821412145.

The title of this extensive collection of essays provides an excellent summary of its contributions. On the one hand, the expression "African Islam" is used to denote various forms of contextualized or localized Islam in Africa; these are usually associated with Sufi orientations. On the other hand, the expression "Islam in Africa" is used to denote various forms of Islamism; these usually seek to purify the religion, partly from Western influence, but partly also from indigenous African ideas and practices. Some of the essays focus on expressions respectively of "African Islam" or of "Islam in Africa," while others focus on the interaction between these two "forms" of Islam. A brief survey of the essays will demonstrate the broad approach of this collection: Rosander (Sweden) introduces the collection, discussing Islamization from the perspectives of tradition and modernity; Hunwick (USA) discusses Islam in Sub-Saharan Africa in relation to the wider world of Islam; Joffé (UK) presents a case study parallel to the project of the whole book: Maghribi Islam and Islam in the Maghrib; An-Na'im (USA) discusses the relationship between Islam and human rights in Sahelian Africa; Lacunza-Balda (Italy) discusses problems and challenges of translating the Qur'an into Swahili; Gerholm (Sweden) discusses the Islamization of contemporary Egypt; Mahmoud (USA) discusses the relationship between Sufism and Islamism in Sudan; Andezian (France) discusses the role of Sufi women in an Algerian pilgrimage ritual; Lake (USA) presents a mahdi ("guide," "messiah") in Senegal; Holtedahl (Norway) and Djingui (Cameroon) present an Islamic judge in Cameroon; Loimeier (Germany) discusses the Yan Izala movement in Nigeria; and Westerlund (Sweden) concludes the collection with a discussion of possible causes for the rise of Islamism. This brief listing should indicate that the book will prove a valuable and thought-provoking resource for lecturers and researchers working with Islam in Africa. At the same time a number of the essays should also be of interest to scholars of Christian presence in Africa. One example is An-Na'im's discussion of the relationship between Islam and human rights in Sahelian Africa. Scholars working with the encounter between Christianity and Islam should notice how this essay argues that the potential for promoting human rights is to be found in a contextualized "African Islam" and not in an Islamist and sharia-oriented "Islam in Africa." Another example is

Lacunza-Balda's discussion of problems and challenges of translating the Qur'an into Swahili. Bible translators and lecturers will here find interesting parallels as well as principal differences.

1175.   **Westerlund, David**

African Religion in African Scholarship: A Preliminary Study of the Religious and Political Background

Stockholm: Almqvist & Wiksell International, 1986. 104 pages, ISBN: 9789171463449.

Westerlund is a Swedish scholar of comparative religion who has studied the works of a number of scholars writing on African traditional religion in anglophone East and West Africa, and to some extent also francophone Central Africa. His aim in this study is to demonstrate how religious and political outlooks and interests have influenced their scholarship. First, with regard to their religious background, Westerlund points out how the Christian and ecclesiastical commitment of important scholars like Mbiti influenced their scholarly work. An *interpretatio Christiana* of African traditional religions results (i) in a structure that corresponds to that of Christian systematic theology, and (ii) in a development of the concept of God, from a previously dominating *deus otiosus* to a God that is more active. Secondly, with regard to the political background, Westerlund points out how the nationalistic interests of some scholars such as Idowu influenced their concepts of continuity between African traditional religions and Christianity, and also how certain theistic representations of African traditional religions could be regarded as politically opportune in young nations attempting to unite diverse peoples (e.g. Nigeria). This is an important critical study – for specialists. Lecturers on African traditional religions, as well as students of contemporary African Theology, will gain from exposure to its source critical methodology and its sensitivity to the ideological contexts of African scholarship on African religion. They will certainly also need to reckon with the possibly significant implications of its findings for their fields of study.

1176.   **Wetmore, Hugh**

Why Christians Disagree When They Interpret the Bible: Finding Unity in Our Loyalty to Scripture

Cape Town: Struik Christian Media, 2001. 232 pages, ISBN: 9781868234448.

This is not a book to satisfy our curiosity about the obvious disunity among Christians who nevertheless together profess a high view of Scripture. Its intention is rather in highlight the factors that influence the different ways we interpret Scripture, and to move beyond that awareness to grasp basic principles of Bible interpretation. Wetmore was at one time national coordinator of the Evangelical Alliance of South Africa. The book is an invitation to examine and interpret Scripture more accurately, hold firmly and obediently to that which is fundamental, live more charitably with those who share our faith but differ with us on debatable non-essentials, and focus especially on what unites us. This book is not just a plea for Christian unity; it is a book on hermeneutics. It also seeks to address the real biases that tend to divide us. The book will not remove all our differences, but it calls us to re-examine the principles of interpreting the Bible, to look again at those things we hold in common, and humbly to accept that none of us has a monopoly on truth. One may hope that such an approach will lead us not only to be better interpreters of Scripture, but also to display in a practical way the unity that our Lord prayed for. This would be a useful book in basic hermeneutics as well as a tool for evangelical self-understanding. It is made very relevant by the applications it offers to a number of "hot potatoes" that superficial unity sometimes avoids discussing. Contributions from participants in the National Hermeneutics Workshops in South Africa help to make this book applied rather than theoretical.

1177.   Wheeler, Andrew C., editor

Announcing the Light: Sudanese Witnesses to the Gospel

Nairobi: Paulines, 1998. 288 pages, ISBN: 9789966214188.

This book offers an ecumenical cross-section of the lives and ministries of Christian Sudanese witnesses from the mid-1800s to the present. Writers include several Sudanese Christians, the series editors themselves – Andrew Wheeler (CMS) and Bill Anderson (Presbyterian), both long-term missionary scholars, plus others, notably from the Comboni Missionaries and Episcopal Church. Several chapters offer a collection of brief biographical sketches, but more than a dozen biographies are chapter-long, four of them about women. The material is divided into three major sections: Early Sudanese Christians, Evangelists and Teachers, and Martyrs and Prophets. The whole is enhanced by maps, photos and a thorough index. The European and Catholic influences in Sudan are, of course, major factors in the lives of the early Christians. Many of the early believers were freed slaves, and their biographies contribute tellingly to a social history of that era. Evangelists and teachers represent a wide geographical and cultural range within Sudan and impress one with the depth of commitment in many different kinds of situations. Martyrs and prophets remind the world of the ongoing suffering of the church in Sudan, and provide a rich biographical repository on the lives of its saints. The entire series of which this book is a part is impressive not least because it deals with the history of mission and church in Sudan through a sequence of small, topical books rather than by means of a massive one-volume history. It thus represents a commendable model for Christians in other African countries wishing to capture their histories in writing, presented in a very attractive and readable style, and offered at affordable price, so that these materials can be easily accessible not only to scholars and theological libraries but also to the local Christian communities.

1178.   Wheeler, Andrew C., editor

Land of Promise: Church Growth in a Sudan at War

Nairobi: Paulines, 1997. 152 pages, ISBN: 9789966213266.

This monograph offers seven papers on culturally sensitive approaches to Christian faith among different people groups in the Sudan, and specifically among the Mayo, Jieng Bor (Dinka), Uduk, Murle, and Nuer. Particularly eye-catching are those which reflect on cattle as a symbol of salvation, the cross as a symbol of regeneration, religious aspects of reconciliation, and Christian faith as a new lineage. This booklet is part of a series which furnishes, at an affordable price, a wide range of fresh reflection on Christian presence in Sudan, and deserves to be widely available in African theological libraries.

1179.   Wheeler, Andrew C., editor

Voices from Africa: Transforming Mission in a Context of Marginalization

London: Church House Publishing, 2002. 160 pages, ISBN: 9780715155523.

This fine collection of 38 very short essays brings to print the lives of marginalized African Christians whose stories might not otherwise be heard. Especially highlighted are the testimonies of refugees, women, children and young people, people living with HIV/AIDS, and those threatened by militant Islam. There are some helpful contributions from African bishops and theologians, but for the most part these are the stories of ordinary African Christians and the realities of their day-to-day struggles. Every section of sub-Saharan Africa is represented (East, West, South, Central) and the authors are both men and women. All of the authors are Anglicans. The book is published in the UK and the editor is British (a long-term missionary in Africa), so the intended readership is evidently British. The book will be especially useful for laypeople there who have little knowledge of the African church. African readers will also benefit from hearing the voices of other ordinary believers from across the continent.

Wheeler, Andrew C.

see also reviews 560, 924 and 1169

Whiteside, Alan

see review 96

Whitworth, Wendy

see review 968

1180.   Wijsen, Frans Jozef Servaas, and Bernardin Mfumbusa

Seeds of Conflict: Religious Tensions in Tanzania

Nairobi: Paulines, 2004. 88 pages, ISBN: 9789966219473.

This booklet presents both research and reflection on the Islamic fundamentalist crisis in Tanzania in recent decades, in an attempt to explain the prevailing situation from a historical, political and religious point of view. Special attention is given to the mainland population centres of Mwanza, Dodoma, Kondoa, and Dar es Salaam, and to Zanzibar island. Exploring some missionary and expansionist trends in Islam both past and present then leads to a final evaluation and recommendations for the future. To pack all this into seventeen brief chapters, within the space of less than 70 pages, demands a high level of condensation. One is impressed by the vivid description of various eruptions of religious intolerance during the 1990s, which reached its tragic peak during the 2001 demonstrations on Zanzibar island, when 29 people were killed in clashes between police and rioters. One of nine strategies listed for promoting Islam is the use of the media, not surprisingly. Another is "Influencing Manners," meaning the propagation of Islam through socio-cultural means such as promotion of wearing hijab (face covering) for women, or banning pork and alcohol being sold in areas where the majority is Muslim. The description of Islamic organisations and movements, although brief, is quite useful for understanding the dynamics of Islam in Tanzania, whereas the chapter on "Revivalism and Modernization in Islam" attempts too much in trying to describe the pluralist or secularist movements in Indonesia, Tunisia and Turkey. The two Catholic authors amiably try to show fairness to Muslims' complaints and grievances, while pointing out the dire consequences of denied justice, whether real or imagined. One appreciates the call for a "better understanding among Christians for the basic principles that underlie the Muslim attitude towards Christians." However, the authors' hope "to move beyond a Christian perspective by real empathy and sympathy with Islamic concerns" results in some less than realistic recommendations, such as: "affirmative action in favour of Muslims should be taken"; "a comparative theology should be constructed, both from a Christian and a Muslim point of view"; or "promoting common ideals and practices by praying and fasting together." It seems unlikely that either Catholic or Protestant Christians directly coping with aggressive Islamic initiatives will prove eager to heed such recommendations as realistically useful.

Wild-Wood, Emma

see review 1152

1181. Wilhite, David E.

Tertullian the African: An Anthropological Reading of Tertullian's Context and Identities

Berlin: De Gruyter, 2007. 232 pages, ISBN: 9783110194531.

Wilhite is an American lecturing at Baylor University. This book is a revision of his doctoral thesis at the University of St. Andrews in Scotland. Not much is known about the life of Tertullian, except that he was a Christian who lived in Carthage, North Africa, in the later second century, and wrote a number of theological works. His writings show that Tertullian was well educated in the Greco-Roman tradition, yet he was critical of the Roman Empire and the Roman Church. This book looks for evidence that Tertullian considered himself an "African" and rejected his probable former status as a "new elite" (a person from a colony who took on Roman ways and became wealthy). This was probably due to his conversion to Christianity. Tertullian's identity is researched from his writings, using the insights of kinship theory, class theory, ethnicity theory, and the anthropology of religion. The final chapter briefly relates Tertullian to African theologians and theology of today, noting the differences and the shared situation of a colonized Christian interacting with the Christian and pagan aspects of the beliefs of the colonizers. In the process Wilhite mentions Mulago, Tshibangu, Muzorewa, Nyamiti, and Dickson. Bediako is cited in a footnote (but not Thomas Oden, whose *How Africa Shaped the Christian Mind* appeared the same year as Wilhite's study. This is a valuable contribution toward tracing the Christian heritage in Africa and showing the African side of an early church father.

1182. Willcox, Sandy

Cut Flowers: Female Genital Mutilation and a Biblical Response

Addis Ababa: SIM Press, 2005. 135 pages.

Willcox was born in South Africa and has taught anthropology at the Evangelical Theological College in Ethiopia. She has written this accessible volume to apply biblical principles to the practice of female genital mutilation (FGM), and to encourage an informed and compassionate response by the church. Although the book includes medical descriptions of the various levels of FGM (levels defined by WHO), and a glossary of medical terms, the author's emphasis lies elsewhere. Willcox includes case studies that provide an overview of FGM practices among a number of people groups mostly in Ethiopia and Kenya. These case studies illustrate the variation in the practice as well as many of the cultural reasons for FGM. The author reminds us that this practice is not (usually) done to hurt or maim women, but rather to fulfil some need in the culture – but, she would add, any level of FGM alters a body that God has created and can create great hardship for women. Some reasons for FGM are based on a faulty understanding of a woman's body and/or Scripture, and Willcox deals with these. Although she firmly believes that "the gospel should impact culture," she wisely emphasizes the need to understand both the form and function of culture – lasting change will not occur unless both aspects are addressed. The book also includes a lengthy chapter on counselling "victims" of FGM and those who perpetrate it. Willcox acknowledges that some of the material in the book (especially the case studies) is outdated and further research is needed; she includes a comprehensive bibliography to encourage such. The book is well researched and clearly written, making it a useful resource for Christian reflection on this complex issue.

Williams, David T.

see review 14

1183.   Williams, Pat, and Toyin Falola

Religious Impact on the Nation State: The Nigerian Predicament

London: Ashgate, 1995. 378 pages, ISBN: 9781859720738.

Williams from Ogun State University in Nigeria, and Falola from the University of Texas in the USA, write on the impact of religion on the Nigerian state. It was assumed at its independence that Nigeria would be a country of good relations between Christians and Muslims. But by the 1980s Nigeria had become a "dangerous zone." This book is a detailed study of the relation between religion and politics in Nigeria. The ideal for the authors is secularism or a secular state. By secularism they mean the non-interference of religion in politics. They observe that at independence Nigeria was largely a secular state. The political parties, for example, were originally not formed along religious lines. The various national constitutions held to secularism. Nigerian international relations often followed secular principles. But this secularism broke down as both Christian and Muslim religious groups got involved in the national and political life. Radical Muslim and Christian groups contributed to the breakdown of secularism. The authors conclude by renewing their plea for a secular state. But their secular presuppositions are problematic and deserve challenge. Secularism really means the exclusion of God and religion from society. From a Christian perspective, can the Sovereign Lord of heaven and earth really be excluded from political life? And in traditional African perspective, is not all of life religious? Muslims rightly call for a multi-religious state. It can be argued that Christians should avoid using secularism as an ideal since this contradicts fundamental Christian commitments. The confusion is increased by the authors' appalling definition of the "Christian World" as "the whole of Western Europe" plus other places like the United States and Latin America and parts of Africa and Asia. The book also has a confusing and unfortunate chapter on dangerous radical religious groups like the Maitatsine – *and* Scripture Union! How can SU be joined with the Maitatsine, a militant Islamic group that preceded Boko Haram of today? Perhaps the fundamental problem of this book is the profoundly secular (non-religious) approach of the authors themselves.

Wilson-Hartgrove, Jonathan

see review 556

Wondji, Christophe

see review 687

1184. **Wooding, Nick**

There's a Snake in My Cupboard!: The Continuing Story of Kiwoko Hospital, Luwero, Uganda

Chichester, UK: New Wine Press, 2005. 157 pages, ISBN: 9781903725542.

The subtitle for this book is an accurate description. Wooding built upon and continued the medical ministry begun by Dr Ian Clarke that was ably described in Clarke's own book, *The Man with the Key Has Gone!*. As a medical student at Oxford, Wooding did an elective in rural Uganda. Then after completing his General Practice education, he attended All Nations Christian College in the UK for two years, and then departed for service in Uganda, ultimately ending up at Kiwoko Hospital as the medical superintendent. As was the case with Clarke, Wooding was immediately and of necessity pressed into being a surgeon. He gives due credit to his Ugandan surgical assistant, who not only assisted, but very diplomatically taught him. The experiences of Wooding and his family run the gamut: handling the frustrations of dealing with petty bureaucrats, the heartache of treating so many HIV/AIDS patients only eventually to see them die, and the ever-present need to raise funds and to communicate effectively with donors. The main difference between Clarke's and Wooding's experiences is that Clarke faced the challenge of founding and building Kiwoko Hospital, while Wooding faced the less glamorous but possibly more daunting challenge of both maintaining and expanding the hospital and bringing it to new plateaus of excellence. Those expecting snake stories from missionaries to Africa will not be disappointed, as the title of this book suggests. The most harrowing encounter was when Wooding's wife saw one in their cupboard that then disappeared. They lived for two weeks not knowing where in their house it was still hiding, or if it was venomous. Comparing Clarke's and Wooding's books, Clarke is the better writer by far, but Wooding's book has more variety, and overall is better balanced. While he does not ignore the HIV/AIDS scourge, he deals with other health issues as well, especially the ones that affect Africa's most vulnerable, the children; among these, Wooding identifies as the four M's: malaria, measles, malnutrition, and meningitis. Both Clarke's and Wooding's books convey some realistic examples of contemporary Christian medical outreach in Africa.

Wratten, Darrel

see review 195

1185.   **Wrong, Michela**

In the Footsteps of Mr Kurtz: Living on the Brink of Disaster in the Congo

London: Fourth Estate, 2000. 336 pages, ISBN: 9781841154213.

Negotiations concerning the future of Congo (DRC) seem repeatedly "in process" in recent decades. The 1990s were especially turbulent times for this tortured country: a huge influx of refugees from Rwanda in 1994 was followed a few years later by civil war that is yet to be resolved. Michela Wrong is a journalist who spent six years during this period writing about Africa for various major news organisations. Her book describes the role that Mobutu Sese Seko and his regime played in Congo from independence until his death in 1997. The deleterious influence of Western countries and organisations like the World Bank and IMF is also examined. Wrong's approach is not chronological; rather the narrative is carried forward by means of a number of vignettes. She talks to a taxi driver in his dilapidated car, a doctor who holds patients hostage until they pay him for his services, the manager of Congo's nuclear power plant which had lost a uranium fuel cell, and many others. While the story is often tragic, Wrong manages to convey the humour that she finds active in many of Mobutu's citizens. One might think of this as a sequel to *King Leopold's Ghost*, since it picks up where Hochschild's book left off. Wrong has a similar easy-to-read style in which the history of Congo is described from her vantage point in Kinshasa during the 1990s. The book will offer the non-specialist a usable introduction to post-colonial Congo (DRC).

Yahya, Saad S.

see review 87

1186.   **Yamamori, Tetsunao, Bryant L. Myers, Kwame Bediako, and L. Reed, editors**

Serving with the Poor in Africa

Monrovia, CA: MARC, 1996. 230 pages, ISBN: 9780912552989.

This book illustrates a recent trend of using case studies as starting points for discussion of mission issues. The first section presents eight African projects involving six organisations in five countries (Ethiopia, Ghana, Mozambique, Uganda, and Zimbabwe). They range from large-scale relief and resettlement efforts, and AIDS education and care, to a small-scale loan cooperative, community health, and a cattle project. The cases all follow the same format: an introduction to the project's context, an explanation of the project, the results of the project, the process of sharing Christ during the project, and an evaluation of the project. The second section is the meat of the book. It consists of five reflections on the cases from the perspectives of development, management, anthropology, theology, and missiology, with the last two providing the most challenging insights. The development chapter examines the significance of community participation and how to engage that participation. The management chapter is an attempt to present management principles drawn from Genesis 1–3 and illustrated in the case studies. One wonders how many readers will have previously encountered management principles taken out of the Creation account! The anthropological reflection presents generalized African cultural themes as seen in the case studies. Bediako, in the theological section, penetratingly reflects on conversion and the theological construct of holism. The missiological chapter defines mission and examines the case studies in light of the missiological practices resulting from the definition. These last two reflections are the only ones really to critique the projects. In a concluding chapter, Myers ties the case studies and reflections together, raising questions for future exploration. One significant contribution of the book is the concern to integrate evangelism and social action in practical mission projects. A second is seen more in absence than in presence – in none of the case studies are structural issues faced. While this was noted in two of the reflections, there was no follow-up discussion. It could appear from this that an emphasis on "holism" may not in actual practice always include addressing structural justice concerns.

1187.   Yamauchi, Edwin M., editor

Africa and Africans in Antiquity

East Lansing, MI: Michigan State University Press, 2001. 324 pages, ISBN: 9780870135071.

This essay collection goes back to a conference on "Africa and Africans in Antiquity" held in 1991 at Miami University in Ohio. The conference brought together scholars (mainly US) from various disciplines to re-examine textual and archaeological material from northeastern Africa, an area that for antiquity is well documented by texts, monuments, and archaeological excavations. The broad approach of the book is best indicated by a listing of the essays: Hodge (linguist) examines the linguistic relations of northeastern Africa; Yurko (Egyptologist) analyses the relationship between Egypt and Nubia; Russmann (art historian) reviews the ascendance of the Kushites to dominance over Egypt (716–656 BC, the so-called Kushite dynasty); Burstein (historian) describes the history of the kingdom of Meroe; Adams (anthropologist) analyses the Ballaña kingdom; Bullard (geologist and archaeologist) examines the Berbers of the Maghreb and ancient Carthage; White (archaeologist) surveys the archaeology of the Cyrenaican and Marmarican regions of northeastern Africa; Snowden (classicist) analyses attitudes towards blacks in the Greek and Roman world; Bard and Fattovich (archaeologists) compare parallel developments of state formation in ancient Egypt and Ethiopia; and Swanson (historian) discusses various attempts to explain the ruins of Great Zimbabwe. In his interesting analysis of attitudes towards blacks in the Greek and Roman worlds, Snowden points out that Greek and Roman sources use the word "Ethiopian" ("sun-burnt face") when referring to dark- and black-skinned people south of Egypt, and that their literary and artistic representations include not only references to skin colour, but also to physical characteristics such as woolly hair, broad noses, and thicker lips. Whereas earlier scholarship tended to see these characteristics as reflecting colour prejudice, Snowden (here, as well as in his well-known 1970 monograph on the same topic) argues that the Greeks and Romans regarded black and white skin as accidents without any necessary stigma attached to them. This includes early Christian writers such as Augustine and Origen. Another very interesting essay is Swanson's discussion of attempts at explaining the ruins of Great Zimbabwe. After the Western discovery of the ruins in 1871, various kinds of "outside" influence were suggested, stretching from OT Israelites to ancient Phoenicians and Arabs. Swanson is then able to demonstrate how these "outside" perspectives in reality reflect late nineteenth century European colonizing interests: Great Zimbabwe was interpreted as an example of how Africa even in ancient times benefited culturally and economically from "outside" influence! The book is a handy and useful introduction. Most of the contributors are well-known specialists in their respective fields, able to provide balanced discussions.

1188.   Yamauchi, Edwin M.

Africa and the Bible

Grand Rapids: Baker, 2006. 298 pages, ISBN: 9780801031199.

Yamauchi has been professor of history at Miami University in the United States. His vast publishing list includes an edited essay collection on *Africa and Africans in Antiquity* (2001). The eight chapters of the present volume give the impression of a collection of independent essays rather than a monograph, yet with an underlying textual focus throughout the book. The relationship between Africa and the Bible is approached from three distinct but closely related perspectives: (i) the historical and archaeological background of biblical texts that deal with Africa and the Bible; (ii) the traditional Western exegesis of these texts; and (iii) the ramifications of later interpretations and misinterpretations of these texts. The first half of the book discusses OT-related questions, such as the so-called curse of Ham, the Cushite wife of Moses, Solomon and Africa, and Tirhakah and other Cushites. The latter half then turns to the NT, with discussions of Rome and Meroe, the Ethiopian Eunuch, and Cyrene in Libya. A final chapter then offers a most interesting discussion of Afrocentric biblical interpretation, including an appendix on Martin Bernal's *Black Athena*. The two first chapters usefully illustrate the different approaches of the book. On the one hand, the approach of the first chapter is analysis of the reception history of a text, in this case Genesis 9:25, the so-called curse of Ham (actually a curse of Canaan!). No other text has been more misused throughout centuries to legitimate exploitation of Africans and African Americans, and Yamauchi is able to outline this ugly reception history. The approach of the second chapter, on the other hand, is analysis of the historical context of a text, in this case Numbers 12:1, about Moses' Cushite wife. This chapter gives a broad survey of Cushite history, and concludes that we should not doubt the possibility of Moses' marriage to a Cushite woman. On the whole, Yamauchi is able to combine throughout the book an extraordinarily wide historical scholarship with a conscious and sensitive approach to contemporary concepts of "Africa." His balanced interpretation of the ancient sources, fair assessment of previous scholarship, and vast bibliography make the book not only an important research contribution but also a most valuable handbook for students and scholars in the field.

1189.   Yekonda Lofoli, Bosekaetunga

L'humanité de Jésus-Christ à travers l'ontologie Bantu

Bangui: FATEB, 2000. 158 pages.

Jesus is God. That much is clearly understood by Bantu Christians of Africa's central regions. But the doctrine that Jesus is both divine and human encounters major difficulties. Yekonda Lofoli's master's thesis, the first in a series published by the Faculté de Théologie Évangélique de Bangui (FATEB) in the Central African Republic, attempts to discover the reasons for this resistance and to suggest ways to get beyond the current impasse. What is actually taught in Bantu churches, and what do the people really understand of the doctrine of the humanity of Jesus Christ? The author, currently a pastor in the Congo (DRC), used interviews, questionnaires, and her personal observations as the basis of the descriptive part of the thesis, supplementing it with insights from African theologians. Having identified a weakness in recognising Jesus as truly human, the author then shows that the basic problem lies in the way in which the Bantu peoples are accustomed to viewing the world. Bantu ontology (like many other ontologies past and present) has no category for understanding a God-Man. It is thus not surprising that Bantu Christians understand Jesus' divinity but are puzzled by the doctrine of his humanity. The result is an impoverished Christology that can never truly explain the salvific work of Christ. In the author's estimation, the only way this weakness can be effectively overcome will be by clear and patient teaching. To be effective, such teaching must first help Bantu Christians understand the biblical worldview and the Bantu worldview, and the similarities and differences between them. Since Bantu ontology centres on God, Yekonda Lofoli proposes that the study of Christology *per se* needs to come at the end of a "pluri-doctrinal" approach that begins with the doctrine of God and creation. It should then proceed through biblical anthropology, soteriology and ethics, eschatology, before finally arriving at Christology. It is in this way, says the author, that the humanity of Jesus can best be explained to the Bantu people. Having understood the other doctrines, they will then be able to grasp the biblical idea of the dual nature of Jesus Christ. Yekonda Lofoli highlights particularly the idea of Jesus as the Mediator between God and humankind as a potent image for helping Bantu peoples understand the humanity of Christ. Once having understood that image, they will also be able to find in Jesus an ethical model for their own lives. This study well represents that much-needed type of theological inquiry that is deliberately sensitive to the realities of the African believing community, and therefore can assist in practical ways in securing appropriate theological foundations. Any theological libraries which include French titles among their acquisitions would profit from having access to this material. It could also be valuable for use in pastoral conferences, to help pastors see why their message about Jesus may not communicate clearly, and to suggest ways to overcome that difficulty.

1190.   Yesehaq Mandefro,

The Ethiopian Tewahedo Church: An Integrally African Church

Nashville: Winston-Derek Publishing, 1997. 244 pages, ISBN: 9781555237394.

Archbishop Yesehaq presents an insider's view of the Ethiopian Orthodox Church (EOC), but no explanation or evidence of how it is "integrally African." The EOC claims to be the oldest church in Africa, after the Coptic Church in Egypt. This book can thus serve as a reference source on one important and ancient form of African Christianity. "Tewahedo" in the title means "united," reflecting the monophysite non-Chalcedonian doctrine of Christ having a single nature, uniting divine and human. The author presents a clear statement of monophysitism, clarifying and correcting what he perceives as Western misunderstandings. He explains the historic controversy within the EOC regarding Christ's two or three "births." He offers important original material in his first-person account of the EOC's interaction with the Rastafarians in Jamaica, a unique event in church history. Rastafarians contacted EOC, wanting to join, but EOC maintained a stand against a messianic belief in Haile Selassie. The book helps outsiders understand some reasons (historical and theological) why EOC deeply resents outside evangelists. The author's application of Scripture is an example of a hermeneutic that is not meaning-based.

1191.   **Yinda, Hélène, and Kä Mana**

Pour la nouvelle théologie des femmes africaines: Repenser la différence sexuelle, promouvoir les droits des femmes et libérer leurs énergies créatives

Oxford: Regnum, 2001. 192 pages, ISBN: 9782723501446.

Yinda heads the Africa and Middle East regional department for the YWCA, while Kä Mana directs a research centre in Benin. These two contemporary African theologians have combined their efforts to present this rarity, a volume on African Christian feminism produced in French. The chapters are grouped under three major headings: Part I, dealing with the relevance of Christianity to African women; Part II, examining the precarious position of women in the economic crisis of Africa; and Part III, on the sexual domination of women by men in African society. Though grouped in this way and intended to be read in order, the chapters can profitably be studied separately. One of the riches of this volume is the reference to other African writers. Although the bibliography is limited in scope, the endnotes reference these writers for further study. Not only has this book been the joint effort of an African man and an African woman who view the situation of the African women from different standpoints, but their combined experience has also been strengthened by their research undertaken in sixteen different African nations, primarily in the French-speaking sector. While their research has enabled the authors to note progress in different areas, they are insistent that much more needs to be done to liberate African women, and that the church has a definite role to play, first by providing spiritual and ethical training, with the expectation that those women who are trained will also train others; and secondly by providing women with economic empowerment and helping them claim all their social, cultural and political rights, through whatever different forms of pressure and propaganda are necessary. This may be accomplished not least by making the church-family and its small groups the focus for action (rather than awaiting action from the State or the NGOs); and by encouraging the church not to be merely a critic of society but itself an innovative force in the fight against poverty. A final section deals with male social and sexual domination in Africa, and the issue of AIDS is part of that discussion. Throughout the book the authors address problems that, while especially pertinent to African women, relate to all Africans. The volume is definitely one that can be read profitably by both sexes.

1192.   **Yorke, Gosnell L. O. R., and Peter M. Renju, editors**

Bible Translation and African Languages

Nairobi: Acton Publishers, 2004. 225 pages, ISBN: 9789966888297.

Growing out of the collaboration of translation consultants within the United Bible Societies in Africa, this set of essays falls into three parts. The first offers some historical perspectives: an outline of the whole history of Bible translation in Africa, followed by separate presentations for Ethiopia, Zulu, Portuguese-speaking Africa, and Spanish-speaking Africa. The second part of the collection attends to certain regional contexts, including: the Swahili Bible in relation to post-colonial translation theory; cultural and political aspects of Bible translation in Ethiopia; NT hermeneutics and translation in francophone Africa; and how to render the "passover lamb" in East African translations. Finally, the third set of essays presents some general challenges, such as: the role of the Bible in African Christian theology; some changes in translation theory and the consequences for Bible translation in Africa; and the relationship between interpretation and contextualization in African translation projects. Such collections as this vividly demonstrate that international organisations devoted to the translation and distribution of the Bible, such as Wycliffe/SIL and the United Bible Societies, are employing scholars with high academic standards in linguistics, exegesis, etc. as translation consultants. One also takes heart from the knowledge that several academic institutions throughout the African continent have established study and research programmes related to Bible translation in Africa that will carry forward work of this calibre. This volume, together with its companion volume, *Biblical Texts & African Audiences* (edited by Wendland), deserve a wide readership in African theological circles, as examples of this scholarly development, and as glimpses into the workshop of Bible translation in Africa.

1193. Young, John

The Quiet Wise Spirit: Edwin W. Smith (1876–1957) and Africa

Norwich: Epworth Press, 2002. 300 pages, ISBN: 9780716205531.

When so distinguished a scholar of African Christian history as Adrian Hastings refers to 1925–1950 as "the age of Edwin Smith," it is surprising that so few people have ever heard of the man. Young (who served in the Methodist ministry in Zambia) has done Africa a great service in researching the life of this remarkable missionary linguist and anthropologist. In 1920 Smith wrote *Ila-speaking Peoples of Northern Rhodesia*, which is described as "one of the great classics of African ethnography." Born in South Africa to Primitive Methodist missionary parents, Smith went to the UK for his education. There he met various important people from Central Africa, such as Chief Khama and Francois Coillard; he was also influenced by the writings of David Livingstone. In 1898 he returned to Africa as a missionary to Lesotho, and later to what is now Zambia. His approach to local people was distinctive from the beginning. He extolled the ability of Africans when others were calling them "savages"; he gave both of his children African names; he contextualized his preaching by using African proverbs; he attacked apartheid long before it became entrenched in South Africa; and he learned local languages quickly. He stressed that missionaries were temporary, so Africans would determine the form that Christianity would take on their own continent. Through years of careful observation he became an amateur anthropologist who "distanced himself from those anthropologists who regarded Africans as a living cultural archive, needing to be preserved but with no right to change or develop." Yet he was accepted in academic circles to the extent that he was an external examiner for theses written by Geoffrey Parrinder and by Isaac Schapera (who edited Livingstone's journals). In many ways he was a man ahead of his time, and he eventually split from his mission society over differences in strategy – he wanted to establish an African training school along the lines of Lovedale and Livingstonia, but the mission refused. In 1915 he returned to the UK and after World War I began a long career with the British and Foreign Bible Society. He was a prolific writer; among his best-known works are *The Golden Stool*, a biography of the Ghanaian churchman J. E. K. Aggrey, and a theological handbook for African pastors, *African Beliefs and Christian Faith*. It is ironic that Smith, with all his knowledge of African culture, believed that there was no reality in witchcraft and expected African religion to vanish through contact with Western civilization. He is said to have paid little attention to prayer, preferring "consecrated human effort," and he expressed discomfort with healing and exorcism that were part of both the NT and African cultures.

1194.   Young, Josiah Ulysses

African Theology: A Critical Analysis and Annotated Bibliography

Santa Barbara, CA: ABC-CLIO, 1993. 288 pages, ISBN: 9780313264870.

Written by an African American seminary professor who found himself "drawn to the continent of his ancestors," this book attempts to cover developments in African theology by summarising a monumental 609 books and articles written between 1955 and 1992. He notes that he has chosen only those sources that exemplify "the import of social and religio-cultural analyses" and the "types" of African theology, claiming that the works cited "adequately represent the various voices of African theology." Evangelicals might question the balance of his selection when they discover that among such well-known writers as Adeyemo, Bediako, Kato and Tiénou, only Kato is cited, and that only once. Similarly, in his chapter on black South African theology, the author cites himself four times and the African American James Cone thirteen times, while omitting white South Africans David Bosch (one citation elsewhere) and Michael Cassidy. The brief introductory chapters define the categories that are used for the later bibliographical sections. There he contrasts the "old guard" (Idowu, Mbiti, Sawyerr, *et al.*) who did not sufficiently address African liberation in their theology, with the "new guard" (Adoukonou, Mveng, Oduyoye, *et al.*). The first bibliographical section on history and social analysis is not strictly African theology; its emphasis is shown by the multiple citations from former African presidents Kaunda (5), Nkrumah (6) and Nyerere (5). Among the book's most helpful aspects may be the cross-referencing in the annotations, where Young notes where one author has interacted with another in print. For example, if a reader wants to find reactions to Mbiti's many books and articles, responses from various perspectives are cited. For this reason, this book is a useful reference tool for those interested in comparing the theological contributions of modern African writers.

1195.   Young, Josiah Ulysses

Black and African Theologies: Siblings or Distant Cousins?

Maryknoll, NY: Orbis, 1986. 146 pages, ISBN: 9780883442524.

This book highlights a debate that took place in the 1970s as black theologians and church leaders from Africa and the USA met together in several consultations to explore the issues that were common to them and the perspectives that divided them. A paper given by Desmond Tutu at one of those consultations, held in Ghana in 1974, was entitled: "Black Theology/African Theology: Soul Mates or Antagonists?" As the title intimates, already by that time there was a difference of opinion as to the closeness or distance between the two approaches, with Mbiti stressing the distance and Tutu the closeness. Young's doctoral dissertation pursues the question with the care and rigour of a detective case. In the course of his historical and contemporary investigation, Young gives major consideration to selected representatives of the two theologies and their perception of each other. Many other contributors, anglophone and francophone, female and male, African and Afro-American, are drawn into the debate, so that the discussion has considerable breadth to it. The widely acknowledged "weighting" of black theology towards liberation and of African theology towards cultural and socio-religious concerns is recognized, and indeed the sections of the book are structured to reflect this fact. But if Young clarifies the differences, he also identifies the similarities. The verdict Young comes to at the last is consistent with the analogy he uses in his subtitle. Siblings can choose to maximize the relationship they undoubtedly have, or they can choose to go their own separate ways. Young suggests that a "Pan-African theology" which works towards the uplifting of the black poor of both Africa and the US, and beyond them the poor and oppressed everywhere, could draw the two closer in response to a common challenge. At the time of publication, Young was a lecturer in philosophy and religion at Colgate University in New York. The strength of his book may lie more in its analysis than in its conclusions, but this is still a basic resource for tracing one important phase of modern theological development on the African continent.

1196. Young, Josiah Ulysses

A Pan-African Theology: Providence and the Legacies of the Ancestors

Trenton, NJ: Africa World Press, 1992. 310 pages, ISBN: 9780865432772.

Young is an African American who has served as professor of systematic theology at Wesley Theological Seminary in Washington, DC. In this sweeping, densely written work, Young offers his reflections on Pan-Africanism as "an indispensable orientation for blacks who reject the alienation wrought by white supremacy and desire to grow in Afrocentric commitments to the black poor of Africa and Diaspora." As this statement suggests, the author works within the framework of liberation theology, pitting white, imperialistic, Eurocentric values against African mores and norms. Young wishes to articulate an African spirituality or praxis directed toward liberation from these debilitating structures and oppressive consciousness for Africans both on the continent and among the diaspora. After an opening chapter identifying elements of a Pan-African theology (Part 1), Young examines and critiques the theology of two African "ancestors," Alexander Crummell and Edward Blyden (Part 2). On the basis of these critiques, Young then identifies key issues that he subsequently incorporates into his positive theological proposal for a Pan-African theology (Part 3). The book provides a useful analysis of African religion in its social context in both its African and North American manifestations. Yet the framework within which Young conducts his investigation cannot help but raise questions. Liberation theology begins with human experience and proceeds from that basis to articulate a theological praxis. Is this a wise and sufficient way for truly Christian thinking to proceed, in Africa or anywhere? In all events, the influence of liberation theology has waned considerably since this work was written. As such, the theological framework shaping the book has lost much of its traction in the Christian world, thereby rendering Young's proposals less persuasive. In summary, useful analysis of Pan-African (as Young defines the term) experience and religion can be found here, but the liberationist framework for both the analysis and the constructive proposals limits the book's value.

1197. Zimmermann, Armin, editor

Voices from Kumba: Theological Reflections for Cameroon, Africa, and the World. Celebrating 50 Years Presbyterian Theological Seminary, Kumba

Kumba, Cameroon: Presbyterian Theological Seminary, 2002. 167 pages.

This essay collection is published as part of the 50th anniversary celebration of the Presbyterian Theological Seminary in Kumba, Cameroon. Its eleven essays are grouped in three concentric circles. The first circle of three essays describes the institution in Kumba being celebrated. One contributor reflects on his days as a student and later as lecturer and administrator, another discusses how to combine academic excellence and spiritual commitment, and the third describes the academic development of the seminary during the years 1999–2002, when it moved into a degree-giving institution (which involved extending the new BTh program from three to four years, developing the content and structure of the studies, addressing the grading question, and not least keeping the academic standards high). This essay is of particular interest in that not only does the Kumba experience correspond with that of many other seminaries throughout Africa, but also this essay now valuably documents this common concrete experience in African theological education. The second circle of six essays moves to the broader Cameroonian and African context. This includes essays on traditional rituals, the situation of women in traditional and modern Cameroon, witchcraft beliefs in Cameroon, Tanzania and the Central African Republic, ethical implications of the concept of God's wrath, and reading the eighth commandment ("you shall not steal") from an African perspective. In this last essay the author argues that the traditional (western) focus on the commandment as a means of protecting individual private property ought to be balanced by a more (African) communal approach: "You shall not steal the goods of the community." Finally, in the third circle two essays move to more global perspectives, one relating the fragmentation of postmodern life to the concerns of systematic theology, and the other offering some missiological reflections on the biblical narratives about Babel and Pentecost. Here the contributor notes that both narratives favour a diversity in languages and cultures: the Babel narrative tells how the people are sent to the ends of the earth to live in linguistic and cultural diversity, and the Pentecost narrative tells how the church, too, is sent to the ends of the earth, in linguistic and cultural diversity. This, according to the contributor, provides a paradigm for "mission as translation" rather than "mission as diffusion."

Zinkuratire, Victor

see review 383

Zo'o Zo'o, Daniel

see review 282

1198.   Zokoué, Issac

Jésus-Christ: Le mystère des deux natures

Yaoundé: Éditions Clé, 2004. 224 pages, ISBN: 9789956090143.

The author was for many years principal of the Bangui Evangelical School of Theology (BEST/FATEB) in the Central African Republic. His concern in this book is to identify an approach to Christology which faithfully communicates the biblical testimony to Christ's divinity and humanity, and yet expresses it in language that is appropriate to an African context. Zokoué argues specifically that terms such as "nature" and "hypostasis," which characterize Western creedal definitions, have no equivalents in African languages, which reflect rather different assumptions about human beings. Initially he develops his theme through substantial and informed discussion of both the Chalcedonian definition and the Christological thought of Karl Barth, giving brief critiques of both of them. He moves on to his own proposal in the final section of the book, where he rejects the philosophical categories and abstractions which, he argues, are typical of Western theology, in favour of a more relational, symbolic and concrete approach. He argues that this would reflect biblical thinking more closely than Western theology manages to do, as well as being much closer to African modes of thought. At the same time he is concerned that Christian faith in Africa should not be "diluted in ancestral beliefs," and shows awareness of the danger of allowing cultural considerations to dictate theological content. Indeed, throughout the work he displays a high view of the Scriptures and offers solid evangelical critiques of his chosen interlocutors, especially Barth. This is a valuable contribution to ongoing attempts to articulate a biblical Christology in the African context. Possibly the discussion of Barth takes up a disproportionate amount of space given the book's explicit purpose, and especially when compared with the relatively brief third section, "The Two Natures of Christ in an African Perspective." An English translation would be a welcome development.

1199.   Zulu, Princess Kasune, and Belinda A. Collins

Warrior Princess: Fighting for Life with Courage and Hope

Downers Grove: IVP US, 2009. 272 pages, ISBN: 9780830833146.

The author is a Zambian woman who lost both her parents as well as other family members to AIDS when she was a teenager. As her mother's oldest child, she was responsible for the younger children, dropped out of school, and resorted to befriending older men who could pay for her junior siblings' education. At 17 she married a man almost 25 years her senior, who had already lost two wives to AIDS, a disease she could not yet name. When she was 21 she found out that she was HIV positive. She began a life of AIDS activism, at first by herself trying to educate others and help orphans, and later under the umbrella of World Vision. Her husband did not support her AIDS activism, and this led eventually to divorce. He himself died of AIDS in 2007. There were two daughters from this marriage, neither of whom is infected with HIV. Through her work with World Vision and other international agencies, Princess has become a celebrity in the USA, including a visit to the White House. She has remarried and lives in the United States. This book tells her life story as a case study of what HIV/AIDS does to African families. The book is an appeal for readers to be active in education about the disease and in support of those who live with it. It could also be read as a testimony to God's help and guidance for a person who is willing to dedicate herself to a call from God despite obstacles. Although the book seems pitched primarily to a Western audience, readers in Africa will readily find inspiration in the author's courage and faith, as she has lived with AIDS and tried to help others.

1200.   Zvobgo, C. J. M.

History of Christian Missions in Zimbabwe 1890–1939

Gweru, Zimbabwe: Mambo Press, 1997. 412 pages, ISBN: 9780869226285.

This is a comprehensive study of the work of early missionaries in Zimbabwe, set within the broader context of Christian missionary activities in Africa. Unlike other studies on the subject, this volume focuses on the efforts of pioneer missionaries of various denominations in all parts of Zimbabwe. The description and analysis of missionary activities centre on three components: evangelism, education and medical services. Zvobgo was a senior lecturer in the Department of History at the University of Zimbabwe. His contribution is unique in blending African history and missions history in an objective and positive way. He does not overlook the inevitable mistakes associated with the missionary work, but he also articulates the undeniable contributions Christian missionaries made in Zimbabwe and in Africa as a whole. The author gives us insight into methods and tools by which evangelism, church planting and education were effectively done. It was missionary efforts that resulted in "African advancement." The sacrificial work of the early missionaries was not focused on gaining personal fame but was intended to benefit Africans educationally, spiritually and physically. The author also offers valuable information on how African peoples perceived both the missionaries and the Christian message. The book is monumental in scope, and also offers a bibliography on the topic that is unequalled. A special attraction are the photographs of key historical figures in the narrative, both of missionaries and of African converts and leaders. This is a work of serious academic quality, and a must for any student of the history of Christian missions in Zimbabwe.

Author Index

Note: The numbers attached to each author entry below indicate the reference numbers of the relevant reviews, *not* page numbers.

A

Abarry, Abu S., 72

Abba, Joe-Barth Chiemeka, 1

Abe, Gabriel Oyedele, 2–3

Aben, Tersur A., 4

Aboagye-Mensah, Robert K., 5

Abogunrin, Samuel O., 6–12

Abraham, Emmanuel, 13

Abrahams, Samuel P., 14

Abubakre, R. D., 15

Achermann, Eduard, 16

Ackerman, Denise, 17

ACTEA, 18

Adadevoh, Delanyo, 19

Adamo, David Tuesday, 20–24

Addai-Mensah, Peter, 25

Addo, Ebenezer Obiri, 26

Adebo, Tarakegn, 607

Adei, Georgina, 27

Adei, Stephen, 27

Adeleye, Femi B., 28

Adeso, P., 29

Adewuya, J. Ayodeji, 30–31

Adeyemi, E. A., 32

Adeyemi, Femi, 33

Adeyemo, Tokunboh, 34–38

Adogame, Afe, 377

African Rights, 39

Agang, Sunday Bobai, 40–41

Agbede Afolabi, Ghislain, 42

Agbeti, J. Kofi, 43–44

Ahoua, Raymond, 45

Ajayi, J. F. Ade, 46

Ajayi, Joel A. A., 47

Ajulu, Deborah, 48, 386

Akallo, Grace, 699

Akanmidu, R. A., 15

Akao, J. O., 10

Akinade, Akintunde E., 49

Akintunde, Dorcas Ola, 10, 50–51

Akpunonu, Peter Damian, 52–53

Alana, E. O., 15

Alazar Abraha, MCCJ, 54

Alkali, Nura, 55

Altbach, Philip G., 1084

Altschul, Paisius, 56

An-Na'im, Abdullahi Ahmed, 57

Ande, Titre, 58

Anderson, Allan, 59–61

Anderson, David M., 62

Anderson, Richard, 63

Anderson, William, 1169

Anglican Church of Kenya, 64

Anguandia, Enosh A., 1067

Anonby, John A., 65

Appiah, Kwame Anthony, 66

Arén, Gustav, 67

Arenas, Fernando, 68

Asamoah-Gyadu, J. Kwabena, 69–71, 652

Asante, Molefi Kete, 72

Aseka, Eric M., 73

Ashforth, Adam, 74

Association of Evangelicals in Africa, 75

August, Karel T., 76

Ault, James, 77
Autesserre, Séverine, 78
Awoonor, Kofi Nyidevu, 79
Ayanga, Hazel, 380, 471
Ayegboyin, Deji, 80, 506
Ayittey, George B. N., 81–82
Ayuso Guixot, Miguel A., 99

B

Backeberg, Werner, 85
Bakare, Sebastian, 86
Bakari, Mohamed, 87
Baker, Kristina, 88
Bakke, Johnny, 89
Balisky, E. Paul, 90
Balisky, Lila, 91
Banana, Canaan S., 92
Banerjee, Abhijit V., 93
Bangsund, James C., 94–95
Barnett, Tony, 96
Barrett, David, 97
Barry, Hallen, 98
Barsella, Gino, 99
Bascom, Kay, 100
Bassey, Michael Edet, 101
Bates, Robert H., 102–103
Battle, Michael, 104
Bauckham, Richard J., 105
Baudena, Peter, 106
Baur, John, 107–108
Bayart, Jean-François, 109–110
Bayley, Anne, 111
Bediako, Kwame, 112–115, 1186
Bediwegi, Etienne Ung'eyowun, 116
Behrend, Heike, 117–118
Bekele, Girma, 119
Belshaw, Deryke, 120
Benson, G. Patrick, 407
Berinyuu, Abraham Adu, 121–122
Bertsche, Jim, 123
Biko, Hlumelo, 124
Bilinda, Lesley, 125
Bird, Phyllis, 126
Bissainthe, Gérard, 581
Bissu, Emmanuel, 127
Bitrus, Daniel, 128

Blakely, Thomas D., 129
Blaschke, Robert C., 130
Bloomberg, Charles, 131
Blum, William, 132
Blyth, Mike, 362
Bodunrin, P. O., 133
Boer, Jan H., 134–140
Boesak, Willa, 141
Boge, Paul H., 142
Bok, Francis, 143
Bond, Bruce, 144
Bond, Norene, 144
Bone, David S., 145
Bonnah, George Kwame Agyei, 146
Boraine, Alex, 147
Borer, Tristan Anne, 148
Bosch, David J., 149–150
Botman, H. Russel, 151
Bouba Mbima, Timothée, 152
Bourdanné, Daniel K., 153–154
Bourdillon, M. F. C., 155
Bowen, John, 156
Bowers, Paul, 157
Brain, Joy, 158
Brazelton, T. Berry, 638
Bredekamp, Henry, 159
Breman, Christina M., 160
Brockman, Norbert C., 161
Brown, Stuart E., 162
Brubaker, G, 163
Bryan, Steven M., 164
Buconyori, Elie A., 165–166
Bujo, Bénézet, 167–172, 360
Bukasa, Kabongo J., 529
Bunza, Mukhtar Umar, 173
Burgess, Richard, 174–175
Burney, Robert S., 176
Burns Jr., J. Patout, 177
Burrows, William R., 178
Burton, Keith Augustus, 179
Butler, Carolyn, 180
Byamungu, Gosbert, 181
Byaruhanga, Christopher, 182

C

Calderisi, Robert, 120

Callaghy, Thomas, 183
Campbell, Mavis C., 184
Carmody, Brendan, 185
Carpenter, Joel A., 1003
Carr, Stephen, 186
Cassidy, Michael, 187–190
Chabal, Patrick, 191
Chaillot, Christine, 192
Chakanza, J. C., 193
Chesworth, John, 689
Cheza, Maurice, 194
Chidester, David, 195
Chikane, Frank, 196
Chilver, Alan, 197
Chipenda, Jose B., 198
Chitando, Ezra, 199
Choramo, Mehari, 200
Christiaensen, Luc, 908
Christian History Magazine, 201
Chuba, Bwalya S., 202
Chukwulozie, Victor, 203
Chukwuocha, A. C., 204
Chung, Meehyun, 205
Church of the Province of Kenya, 206
Church, Henry G., 207
Clarence-Smith, William Gervase, 208
Clark, Phil, 209
Clarke, Clifton R., 210
Clarke, Donald S., 211
Clarke, Ian, 212
Clarke, Peter B., 213–214
Clement, Atchenemou Hlama, 215
Cochrane, J. R., 216–217
Coetzee, P. H., 218
Cole, Victor Babajide, 219
Collier, Paul, 220
Collins, Barbara, 221
Collins, Belinda A., 1200
Colson, Elizabeth, 222
Comaroff, Jean, 223
Comaroff, John L., 223
Concerned Evangelicals, 224
Connor, Bernard F., 225
Conradie, Ernst M., 226
Cook, David, 227
Coomes, Anne, 228–229

Cooper, Barbara M., 230
Cooper, Frederick, 231
Coquery-Vidrovitch, Catherine, 232
Corbitt, J. Nathan, 233
Corten, André, 234
Coulon, Paul, 235
Cowley, Roger W., 236
Cox, James L., 237–238, 757, 921
Craig Harris, Lillian, 239–240
Croegaert, Luc, 241
Cross, K. E., 476
Cummings, Mary Lou, 242
Cunningham, Scott, 243
Cuthbertson, Greg, 244
Cutter, Charles H., 245

D

Dali, Rebecca Samuel, 246
Daloz, Jean-Pascal, 191
Damap, Justina Karimu, 247
Daneel, M. L., 248–252
Dau, Isaiah Majok, 253
Davenport, Rodney, 307
Davidson, Basil, 254
de Gruchy, John W., 217, 255–260, 1137
de Jong, Albert, 261–262
de la Haye, Sophie, 263
de Visser, Arjan J., 264
de Waal, Alex, 265
Debela, Birri, 266
Decorvet, Jeanne, 267
Decret, François, 268
Dedji, Valentin, 269
Delgado, Mariano, 597
Demery, Lionel, 908
Denis, Philippe, 158
Detago, Misgana Mathewos, 270
Deutsch, Jan-George, 271
Dickson, Kwesi A., 272
Dietrich, Walter, 273
Dike, Eugene Ebere, 274
Dikirr, Patrick M., 686
Dimandja, Eluy'a Kondo, 275
Dixon, Suzanne, 638
Djoeandy, Omar, 276
Donders, Joseph G., 277

Dong, Peter Marubitoba, 278
Donham, Donald L., 279
Doré, Joseph, 529
Dortzbach, Deborah, 280–281
Dossou, Marcelin S., 51, 282
Draper, Jonathan, 17, 283
Dube, Jimmy G., 284
Dube, Musa W., 285–287, 1116, 1171, 1173
Dube, S. W. D., 873
Dubow, Saul, 131
Duflo, Esther, 93
Dunn, D. Elwood, 288
Dyrness, William A., 289–290

E
Eber, Jochen, 291
Eboussi Boulaga, Fabien, 292
Edwards, S. D., 872
Eide, Oyvind M., 293–294
Eijk, Ryan van, 295
Eitel, Keith E., 296
Ejeh, Theophilus Ugbedeojo, 297
Ekem, John David Kwamena, 298
Ekwunife, Anthony N. O., 299
Ela, Jean-Marc, 300–303
Ellis, Stephen, 109, 304–306
Elphick, Richard, 307
Engelke, Matthew, 308
Englebert, Pierre, 309
Englund, Harri, 310
Eric, Walter, 786
Erlich, Haggai, 311
Erwin, Steve, 499
Esack, Farid, 312–313
Eshete, Tibebe, 314
Etue, Kate, 315
Evers Rosander, Eva, 1174
Eze, Emmanuel Chukwudi, 316
Ezeh, Uchenna A., 317
Ezigbo, Victor I., 318

F
Falk, Peter, 319
Falola, Toyin, 320–321, 1183
Fape, Michael D., 322
Fargher, Brian, 200, 323, 1078

Fasokun, T. O., 324
Fatokun, Samson Adetunji, 325
Fendall, Lon, 718
Ferdinando, Keith, 326
Ferguson, James, 327
Fiedler, Klaus, 328–330
Finneran, Niall, 331
Fish, Burnette C., 332–333
Fish, Gerald W., 332–333
Fisher, Humphrey J., 334
Folarin, George O., 335–336
Fon, Wilfred, 418
Forslund, Eskil, 337
Foulkes, James, 338
Fowler, Stuart, 339
Fraser, Eileen, 340
Fredericks, Charl E., 226
French, Howard, 341–342
Freston, Paul, 343
Froise, Marjorie, 344–347
Fuller, Clare, 348
Fuller, Lois, 349–354
Fulljames, Peter, 355
Fyfe, Christopher, 356

G
Gachiri, Ephigenia W., 357
Gaidzanwa, Rudo B., 358
Gaiya, Musa A. B., 359, 482
Galgalo, Joseph D., 635
Galvan, Maria, 360
Gamley, Anthony M., 361
Garland, Jean, 362
Gaskin, Ross F., 219
Gaskiyane, I., 363
Gates Jr., Henry Louis, 66, 364
Gatti, Nicoletta, 365
Gatumu, Kabiro wa, 366
Gatwa, Tharcisse, 367–368
Gaudeul, Jean-Marie, 369
Gbade, Niyi, 370
Gehman, Richard J., 371–375
Gelfand, Michael, 376
Gerloff, Roswith, 377
Geschiere, Peter, 378
Gestrin, Phyllis, 966

Getachew, Haile, 379
Getui, Mary N., 380–385, 1151
Gibbs, Sara, 386
Gibellini, Rosino, 387
Gibson, James L., 388
Gichinga, Emmy M., 389
Gichuhi, John, 106
Gichure, Peter Ignatius, 390
Gifford, Paul, 391–397
Gilbert, Lela, 674
Gilbert, Marvin, 840
Gilbreath, Edward, 521
Gilchrist, John, 398–399
Gillespie, Carol, 442
Gilliland, Dean S., 400
Gilmore, Alec, 401
Gitari, David, 402–407
Gitau, Samson K., 408
Gittins, Anthony J., 409
GMI, 410
Gofwen, Rotgaf, 411
Golka, Friedemann W., 412
Goma, Lameck K. H., 46
Gordon, April A., 413
Gordon, Donald L., 413
Gordon, Murray, 414
Gornik, Mark R., 178
Gourevitch, Philip, 415
Govinden, Betty, 920
Gray, Richard, 416, 445
Graybill, Lyn S., 417
Grebe, Karl, 418
Grenstedt, Steffan, 419
Grignon, François, 787
Groves, Jonathan D., 420
Guest, Emma, 421
Guest, Robert, 422
Guillebaud, Meg, 423–424
Guma, Mongezi, 425
Gunda, Masiiwa Ragies, 426
Guy, Michael R., 748
Gwamna, Je'adayibe Dogara, 427
Gyekye, Kwame, 428

H
Haar, Gerrie ter, 238, 306, 429–434

Hackett, Rosalind I. J., 435
Haile, Ahmed Ali, 436
Halbert, Jim, 437
Halbert, Viola, 437
Hallencreutz, Carl F., 937
Hamlin, Catherine, 438
Hanciles, Jehu, 439
Hannon, Paul, 1069
Hansen, Len D., 440
Harden, Blaine, 441
Hardwick, Lorna, 442
Harries, Patrick, 443
Hartin, P. J., 914
Harvey, Charles H., 444
Hasan, Yusuf Fadi, 445
Hasenhüttl, Gotthold, 446
Hassan, Raymond, 215
Hassett, Miranda K., 447
Hastings, Adrian, 448–449
Hay, Margaret J., 450
Haynes, Jeffrey, 451
Hays, J. Daniel, 452
Healey, Joseph, 453–454
Hebga, Meinrad, 581
Hefling, Charles, 455
Hege, Nathan B., 456
Hegeman, Benjamin L., 457
Helgesson, Alf, 458
Henderson, I. W., 216
Henderson, Lawrence, 459
Hendriks, H. Jurgens, 460
Henkel, Reinhard, 461
Henry, Helga Bender, 462
Herbst, Jeffrey, 463
Hexham, Irving, 872, 874
Hibou, Béatrice, 109
Hiebert, Paul G., 464
Hildebrandt, Jonathan, 465
Hill, Graham, 466
Hilliard, Constance B., 467
Hillman, Eugene, 468
Himbaza, Innocent, 469–470
Hinga, T. M., 471
Hinton, Mark, 472
Hiskett, Mervyn, 473
Hochschild, Adam, 474

Hock, Klaus, 377
Hoekstra, Harvey Thomas, 475
Hofmeyr, J. W., 476, 926
Hogendorn, Jan S., 650
Holland, Grace, 163, 477, 783
Holland, Scott, 718
Hollyday, Joyce, 1147
Holmes, Peter, 592
Holter, Knut, 383, 478–481
Hopkins, Mark, 482
Horton, Robin, 483
Hostetler, Marian, 484
Howell, Allison M., 485–487
Hudson, John, 488
Hull, Richard, 489
Hulley, Leonard, 490
Hunwick, John, 491
Hydén, Göran, 492
Hylson-Smith, Kenneth, 493

I

IAPCHE, 494
Ibewuike, Victoria Oluomachukwu, 495
Ijatuyi-Morphé, Randee, 496
Ijezie, Luke Emehiele, 497
Ikenga-Metuh, Imefie, 498
Ilibagiza, Immaculée, 499
Iliffe, John, 500–501
Imasogie, Osadolor, 502
Imberg, Rune, 503
Insoll, Timothy, 504
International Association of Universities, 505
Ishola, S. Ademola, 80, 506
Isichei, Elizabeth, 507–508
Iwe, John Chijioke, 509
Izekwe, Augustus Chukwuma, 510

J

Jacobs, Donald, 657
Jaeschke, Ernst, 511
James, Wendy, 512
Janvier, George, 513–515
Jeal, Tim, 516
Jenkins, Paul, 517
Jenkins, Philip, 518–519
Jennings, Christian, 320

Johnson, Dean, 718
Johnson, Douglas H., 62
Johnson, G. Ampah, 46
Joinet, Bernard, 520
Jones, Howard O., 521
Jones, L. Gregory, 522
Jung, Albert de, 523

K

Kabasele Mukenge, André, 524–526
Kabasele-Lumbala, François, 527–530
Kafang, Zamani B., 531
Kahl, Werner, 532
Kalilombe, Patrick A., 533
Kalu, Ogbu U., 534–538
Kalu, Wilhelmina, 678
Kane, Thomas A., 539
Kanyadago, Peter M., 381, 540
Kanyoro, Musimbi R. A., 541, 846
Kapolyo, Joe M., 542
Kapteina, Detlef, 543
Karamaga, André, 544–545
Karanja, John, 546
Kariuki, Obadiah, 547
Kassimir, Ronald, 183
Kastfelt, Niels, 548–550
Katahoire, Anne, 324
Kateregga, Badru D., 551
Kato, Byang H., 552–553
Katongole, Emmanuel M., 554–558
Kaufman, Zachary, 209
Kauta, John, 559
Kayanga, Samuel F., 560
Kebede, Messay, 561
Keefer, Constance, 638
Keese, Alexander, 562
Kelley, Robin D. G., 636
Kelly, Robert, 563
Kemdirim, Protus O., 564
Kennedy, Pagan, 565
Kiaziku, Vicente Carlos, 566
Kibor, Jacob, 567
Kidula, Jean N., 577
Kiel, Christel, 568
Kiiru, MacMillan, 569
Kiki, Célestin Gb., 570

Kilby, Stella E., 571
Kilman, Scott, 1095
Kim, Caleb Chul-Soo, 572
Kimaro, Lucy R., 573
Kimilike, Lechion Peter, 574
Kimuhu, Johnson M., 575
King, Noel Q., 576
King, Roberta R., 577–578
Kings, Graham, 579
Kinkupu, Léonard Santedi, 580–581
Kinoti, George, 582
Kinoti, Hannah W., 583, 1155
Kinyua, Johnson Kiriaku, 584
Kirk-Greene, Anthony, 967
Kirwen, Michael C., 585
Kisangani, Emizet F., 787
Kisembo, Benezeri, 586
Kitoko-Nsiku, Edouward, 759
Kitshoff, M. C., 587, 873
Kivuti, N. A., 588
Knibb, Michael A., 589
Knighton, Ben, 590
Kobia, Samuel, 591
Kolini, Emmanuel M., 592
Kombo, James Henry Owino, 593
Komolafe, Sunday Jide, 594
Kore, Danfulani, 595–596
Kornfield, Bill, 215
Koschorke, Klaus, 597
Koudouguéret, David, 598
Koulagna, Jean, 599–600
Krabill, James R., 577, 601
Krätli, Graziano, 602
Kretzschmar, Louise, 490, 603–604
Kriel, Jacques, 991
Kritzinger, J. N. J., 605–606
Kritzinger, Klippies, 994
Kubai, A. N., 471, 607
Kukah, Matthew Hassan, 608
Kumar, P. Pratap, 1056
Kunhiyop, Samuel Waje, 609–611
Kuperus, Tracy, 612
Kurewa, John Wesley Zwomunondiita, 613
Kyomo, Andrew A., 614, 1122
Kyomya, Michael, 615

L
Lacy, Joe, 338
Lademann-Priemer, Gabriele, 616
Lagerwerf, Leny, 617
Lamle, Elias Nankap, 618
Landau, Paul Stuart, 619
Lande, Aasulv, 379
Langworthy, Harry, 620
Lapp, John, 621
Larom, Margaret S., 622
Larom, Peter, 623
Larsson, Brigitta, 624
Lartey, Emmanuel Y., 625–627
Last, Murray, 628
Latham, Robert, 183
Laukkanen, Pauli, 629
Launhardt, Johannes, 630
Lawrence, Carl, 631
Lawrie, Ingrid, 685
Lefkowitz, Mary, 632
Leiderman, P. Herbert, 638
Lemarchand, René, 633
LeMarquand, Grant, 634–635, 802
Lemelle, Sidney J., 636
Leonard, David K., 637
LeRoux, J., 885
LeVine, Robert A., 638
LeVine, Sarah, 638
Levison, John R., 639
Levtzion, Nehemia, 640
Lewis, Damien, 779
Lewis, Donald M., 641
Leys, Colin, 642
Libawing, Benjamin L., 771
Lierop, Peter van, 643, 644
Lind, Tim, 1101
Linn, Stella, 645
Linz, Johanna, 646
Little, John, 438
Lo, Jim, 783
Loba-Mkole, Jean-Claude, 647, 759
Logan, Willis H., 648
Long, Meredith W., 280, 649
Lovejoy, Paul E., 650–651
Low, Alaine, 537
Ludwig, Frieder, 597, 652

Luig, Ute, 118
Lund, Gregory, 653
Luneau, René, 529
Lutz, Lorry, 654
Luz, Ulrich, 273
Lydon, Ghislaine, 602

M
Mabuntana, Phillipina, 655
Macharia, Paul, 686
Mackenzie, Rob, 656
MacMaster, Richard, 657
Magesa, Laurenti, 586, 658–661, 746, 752
Maier, Karl, 662
Maillu, David G., 663
Makower, Katharine, 664
Maluleke, Tynyiko, 382
Mamdani, Mahmood, 665–666
Mana, Kä, 667–668, 1191
Manaranche, André, 669
Manning, Patrick, 670
Manus, Ukachukwu, 671–672
Maranz, David, 673
Marshall-Fratani, Ruth, 234
Marshall, Paul, 674
Marshall, Ruth, 675
Martey, Emmanuel, 676
Martin, Stephen, 217
Masamba ma Mpolo, Jean, 677–679
Mashinini, Emma, 17
Masolo, Dismas A., 680
Matadi, Ghislain Tshikendwa, 681
Mawanzi Ndombe, César, 682
Maxey, Gary S., 683
Maxwell, David, 443, 684–685
Mazrui, Ali A., 686–687
Mbanda, Laurent, 688
Mbilah, Johnson A., 689
Mbiti, John S., 690–691
Mbugguss, Martha, 692
Mbugua, Judy, 693
Mbuy-Beya, Marie-Bernadette, 694
McCain, Danny, 695–696
McCracken, John, 697
McCullum, Hugh, 698
McDonald, Huibrecht, 655

McDonnell, Faith J. H., 699
McGarry, Cecil, 700
McKenna, Joseph C., 701
McLean, Janice A., 178
McLellan, Dick, 702
Meier, Inge, 703
Meinardus, Otto F. A., 704
Meiring, Piet, 705
Meja, Markina, 706
Mejia, Rodrigo, 707
Melady, Margaret Badum, 708
Melady, Thomas Patrick, 708
Melvern, Linda R., 709
Meredith, Martin, 710
Messi Metogo, Éloi, 711
Meyer, Gabriel, 712
Mfumbusa, Bernardin, 1180
Michael, Matthew, 713
Michel, Thomas S. J., 714
Middleton, John, 715
Mijoga, Hilary B. P., 716
Millard, J. A., 717
Miller, Donald, 718
Miller, Gerald L., 719
Miller, Helen, 720
Miller, James C., 721
Miller, Joseph C., 715
Miller, Norman, 722
Mills, DiAnn, 794
Milton, Leslie, 425
Mkandawire, Orison Ian, 723
Mogensen, Mogens S., 724
Mojola, Aloo Osotsi, 725
Molyneux, K. Gordon, 726
Moon, W. Jay, 727
Moore, Henrietta L., 728
Moreau, A. Scott, 729
Morgan, Geoff, 579
Morrison, Philip E., 730
Mosala, Itumeleng J., 731, 1098
Mossai, Sanguma T., 732
Mous, Maarten, 645
Moyo, Ambrose, 733
Moyo, Dambisa, 734
Mpindi, Paul Mbunga, 735
Msiska, Stephen Kauta, 736

Muchimba, Felix, 737
Mudenge, S. I. G., 738
Mudimbe, V. Y., 102, 739–741
Mugambi, Jesse N. K., 588, 742–754
Mukendi, Félix Mutombo, 755–756
Mukonyora, Isabel, 757
Mulenga, Kampamba, 758
Mulholland, Dewey, 759
Mullen, Roderic L., 760
Mundele, Albert Ngengi, 761
Mungazi, Dickson A., 762
Munro-Hay, Stuart, 763
Murphy, Conor, 764
Murphy, Edward J., 765
Musekura, Célestin, 522
Museveni, Yoweri K., 766
Musolo W'Isuka, Kamuha, 767
Musopole, Augustine C., 768
Muya, Juvénal Ilunga, 169
Muzorewa, Gwinyai Henry, 769
Mveng, Engelbert, 770–771
Mvumbi, Frederic Ntedika, 772–773
Mwakimako, Hassan, 774
Mwaura, P., 471
Mwiti, Gladys, 775
Myers, Bryant L., 1187

N
Nadar, Sarojini, 918, 920
Nankuni, I, 163
Naré, L., 29
Nash, Peter T., 776
Nasimiyu-Wasike, Anne, 753, 777
Naudé, Jacobus A., 778
Nazer, Mende, 779
Ncozana, Silas S., 780
Ndjérareou, Abel, 781
Ndletyana, Mcebisi, 782
Ndlovu, Danisa, 783
Ndubuisi, Luke, 784
Neckebrouck, Valeer, 785
Nehls, Gerhard, 786
Nest, Michael, 787
Neuhaus, Richard John, 788
Ngara, Emmanuel, 789
Ngewa, Samuel, 790–793

Nhial, Abraham, 794
Niang, Aliou Cissé, 795
Niccum, Curt, 796
Nicolson, Ron, 797–798
Niehaus, C., 1138
Nielsen, Ann, 963
Niemeyer, Larry L., 799
Nihinlola, Emiola, 800
Nikkel, Marc R., 801–802
Niringiye, David Zac, 803
Njiru, Joseph N., 1045
Njoroge, J., 29
Njoroge, Lawrence M., 804
Njoroge, Nyambura J., 805
Nkemnkia, Martin Nkafu, 806
Nkurunziza, Deusdedit R. K., 807
Nolan, Albert, 808
Nolen, Stephanie, 809
Noll, Mark A., 810
Norlén, Gunnar, 811
Northrup, David, 812
Ntamushobora, Faustin, 813
Nthamburi, Zablon, 661, 814–815
Ntlha, Moss, 603Nupanga, Weanzana wa, 816
Nürnberger, Klaus, 817–819
Nussbaum, Stan, 820–821
Nuttall, Michael, 822
Nwachuku, Daisy, 625, 677
Nwachukwu, Mary Sylvia C., 823
Nwafor, John Chidi, 824
Nyamiti, Charles, 825–828
Nyirongo, Lenard, 829–830
Nzunda, Matembo S., 831

O
O'Barr, Jean F., 102
O'Donovan, Wilber, 832
O'Donovan, Wilbur, 833
Obeng, Emmanuel A., 385
Obinwa, Ignatius M. C., 834
Ochieng'-Odhiambo, Frederick, 835
Oden, Thomas C., 836–839
Oduaran, Akpovire B., 324
Odunze, Don, 840
Oduro, Thomas A., 577
Oduyoye, Mercy Amba, 564, 841–846

Oduyoye, Modupe, 847–849
Oehrig, Robert J., 850
Ogbannaya, A. Okechukwu, 851
Ogola, Margaret, 852
Oguejiofor, Josephat Obi, 853
Ojo, Matthews A., 854
Okenimkpe, Michael, 227
Okorocha, Cyril C., 855
Okoye, James Chukwuma, 856
Okuma, Peter Chidi, 857
Okure, Teresa, 858–859
Oladipo, Caleb Oluremi, 860
Olang', Festo, 861
Olaniyan, Mojisola, 800
Olowola, Cornelius, 862–863
Olupona, Jacob K., 864–867
Omondi, Diane, 850
Omoyajowo, Joseph Akinyele, 868
Ondeng, Pete, 869
Onyancha, Edwin, 870, 1046–1047
Onyango-Ajus, Peter, 974
Onyinah, Opoku, 871
Oosthuizen, Gerhardus C., 872–875
Orgu, Cletus C., 876
Orobator, Agbonkhianmeghe E., 877
Osborn, H. H., 878–879
Osei-Bonsu, Joseph, 880
Osei-Mensah, Gottfried, 881
Oshagbemi, J. L., 882
Ositelu II, Gabriel, 928
Ossom-Batsa, George, 365
Ostergard Jr., Robert, 686
Otabil, Mensa, 883
Ott, Martin, 884
Otto, Eckart, 885
Ouamba, Fabien, 51, 282
Overdulve, C. M., 886–887
Overhulser, Josephine Marie, 888
Owusu, Robert Yaw, 889
Ozodo, Moyo, 215

P

Paas, Steven, 890–893
Paden, John N., 894
Padwick, T. John, 97
Page Jr., Hugh R., 895

Pakenham, Thomas, 896
Palmer, Timothy P., 897–899
Paluku, Musuvaho, 900
Paris, Peter J., 901
Parker, Michael, 902
Parratt, John, 903–905, 1014
Partee, Charles, 906
Partrick, Theodore H., 907
Paternostro, Stefano, 908
Pato, Luke, 490
Patte, Daniel, 909
Payne, Roland J., 910
Peel, J. D. Y., 911
Persson, Janet, 912
Petersen, Kirsten Holm, 913
Petersen, Robin, 151
Petzer, J. H., 914
Phillipart, Michael, 915
Phillipson, David W., 916
Phipps, William E., 917
Phiri, Isabel Apawo, 918–922
Phiri, Khofi Arthur, 923
Pierli, Francesco, 924–925
Pillay, G. J., 926
Pobee, John S., 927–939
Pope-Levison, Priscilla, 639
Posner, Daniel N., 940
Pottier, Johan, 941
Poucouta, Paulin, 942–943
Pouwels, Randall L., 640, 944
Powell, Eve Troutt, 491
Presler, Titus Leonard, 945
Pretorius, Hennie, 244
Priest, Doug, 946
Probst, Peter, 271
Prunier, Gérard, 947–948
Punt, Jeremy, 14

Q

Quarcoopome, T. N. O., 949
Quinn, Charlotte A., 950
Quinn, Frederick, 950–951

R

Radelet, Steven, 952
Rader, Dick Allen, 953

Raharimanantsoa, Mamy, 954
Ranger, Terence, 955, 1167
Rapold, Walter F., 956
Rasmussen, Ane Marie Bak, 957
Rasmussen, Lissi, 958
Ratti, Maria Teresa, 924
Reader, John, 959
Réamonn, Páraic, 805
Reddie, Richard S., 960
Reed, Colin, 961
Reed, L., 1187
Reggy-Mamo, Mae Alice, 962
Reijnaerts, Hubert, 963
Renju, Peter M., 1193
Riamela, Daniel Odafetite, 964
Rice, Chris, 557
Richards, Paul, 628
Richburg, Keith, 965
Richman, Amy, 638
Richmond, Yale, 966
Rimmer, Douglas, 967
Ringe, Sharon H., 126
Rittner, Carol, 968
Robert, Dana, 244
Roberts, J. Deotis, 969
Roberts, W. Dayton, 970
Robinson, David, 971
Robinson, Paul W., 972
Roche, Margaret, 852
Roland, Oliver, 973
Ronzani, R., 974
Ross, Andrew C., 975–977
Ross, Kenneth R., 193, 831, 921, 978–982
Ross, Robert, 159
Roth, John K., 968
Rothchild, Donald, 983
Roux, A. P. J., 218
Rowland, Stan, 984
Roy, Kevin, 985
Rubenson, Samuel, 379
Rucyahana, John, 986
Rusesabagina, Paul, 987
Russell, Horace O., 988
Rwiza, Richard N., 989
Ryan, Colleen, 990
Ryan, Patrick, 700

S
Saayman, W. A., 605, 991–994
Sachs, Jeffrey D., 995
Sahlberg, Carl-Erik, 996
Saïdi, Farida, 997
Sakenfeld, Katharine Doob, 126
Salamon, Hagar, 998
Salisbury, Thayer, 999–1000
Sandblom, Alice, 1001
Sanders, Todd, 728
Sanneh, Lamin, 1002–1011
Sarah, Robert, 1012
Sauer, Christof, 76, 1013
Sawyerr, Harry, 1014
Schaaf, Ype, 1015
Schalm, Gottfried, 1016
Schamp, Eike W., 1017
Schineller, Peter, 1018
Schmid, Stefan, 1017
Schmidt, Heike, 271
Schneider, Theo, 1019
Schoffeleers, Matthew, 963, 1020–1021
Schofield, Rodney, 1022
Schreiter, Robert J., 1023
Schwab, Peter, 1024
Schwartz, Glenn J., 1025
Schwartz, Leslie, 1026
Scott Theological College, 1027
Scott, Joyce, 1028–1029
Sebahire, Mbonyinkebe, 275
Selvan, Sahaya G., 614
Senator, David, 1030
Setiloane, Gabriel M., 1031
Shank, David A., 1032–1033
Shattuck, Cynthia, 455
Shaw, Mark, 793, 1034–1035
Shaw, R. Daniel, 464
Shaw, Rosalind, 1036
Shenk, David W., 551, 1037
Shields, Norman, 1038
Shorter, Aylward, 586, 870, 1039–1049
Shyllon, Leslie E. T., 1050
Sim, Ronald J., 219
Simon, Benjamin, 1051
Simpson, Andrew, 1052
Sindima, Harvey J., 1053–1054

Smit, Johannes A., 754, 1055
Smith, James Howard, 1056
Smoker, Dorothy W., 1057
Snook, Stewart G., 1058
Snyder, C. Arnold, 621
Soares, Benjamin F., 1059
Sogolo, Godwin, 1060
Sparks, Allister, 1061
Spartalis, Peter J., 1062
Speckman, McGlory T., 1063
Spencer, Aída Besançon, 1064
St. Clair, Raquel Annette, 1157
Stakeman, Randolph, 1065
Stanley, Brian, 1066
Starcher, Richard L., 1067
Stearns, Jason K., 1068
Steed, Christopher, 1079
Stenger, Fritz, 1069
Stenström, Arvid, 1070
Stephens, C. O., 1071
Stichter, Sharon, 450
Stine, Phillip C., 1072
Stinton, Diane, 1073–1074
Strauss, Scott, 637
Stuart, John, 1075
Stuebing, Richard W., 1076
Suberg, Olga Muriel, 1077
Sugden, Christopher, 120
Sulayman, S. Nyang, 867
Sumamo, Sorsa, 1078
Sundkler, Bengt, 1079
Swart, Morrell F., 1080
Sybertz, Donald, 454

T
Táíwò, Olúfémi, 1081
Tarr, Del, 1082
Tarrant, Ian, 1083
Taylor, Rhena, 850
Teferra, Damtew, 1084
Tennent, Timothy C., 1085
Tessier, Henri, 1086
Thaba, Bitrus, 515
Theodosiou, Recah, 315
Theological Advisory Group, 1087–1089
Thiong'o, Ngugi wa, 1090

Thompson, T. Jack, 1091
Thomson, Dennis L., 129
Thornton, John K., 1092
Thornton, Margaret, 1093
Thorpe, S. A., 1094
Thurow, Roger, 1095
Tibenderana, Peter, 1096
Tiénou, Tite, 464, 793, 1097
Tivnan, Edward, 143
Tlhagale, Buti, 1098
Tobler, Judy, 195
Toler, Michael, 686
Tolo, Arne, 1099
Tooke, John, 817
Tsala-Clémençon, Georgine, 368
Tshilenga, Emmanuel K., 1100
Tshimika, Pakisa K., 1101
Tuju, Raphael, 1102
Turaki, Yusufu, 1103–1106
Turner, Thomas, 1107
Tushima, Cephas, 1108
Tutu, Desmond, 1109–1111

U
Udoekpo, Michael Ufok, 1112
Udoh, Enyi Ben, 1113
Uka, Emele Mba, 1114
Ukpong, Justin, 382, 1115–1116
Umar, Muhammad S., 1117
Umoren, Anthony Iffen, 1118
Ungar, Sanford J., 1119
Utuk, Efiong, 1120
Uzukwu, E. Elochukwu, 1121

V
Vahakangas, Mika, 1122–1123
van Beek, Walter E. A., 129
van de Walle, Nicolas, 1124
van der Walt, B. J., 1125–1130
van Lin, Jan, 295
van Thiel, Paul, 858
van't Spijker, Gérard, 194
Vavrus, Frances, 1131
Venter, Dawid, 1132
Verstraelen-Gilhuis, Gerdien, 1133
Verstraelen, F. J., 757, 1134–1136

Villa-Vicencio, C., 1137–1139
Vingborg, Elisabeth, 1140
Vogel, Marianne, 645
Volz, Stephen C., 1141

W
Wa Kasonga, Kasonga, 625
Wachege, P. N., 1142
Wafawanaka, Robert, 1143
Wagner, Shari Miller, 719
Waliggo, John M., 583, 1144
Walker, David S., 1145
Wallis, Jim, 1146
Walls, Andrew F., 356, 1147–1148
Wambutda, Daniel Nimcir, 1149
Wamue, Grace, 1150
Wan-Tatah, Victor, 1151
Wandera, Joseph, 1069
Ward, Honor, 88
Ward, Kevin, 1152
Wartenberg-Potter, Bärbel von, 932
Waruta, Douglas W., 777, 1153–1155
Waters, John, 1156
Watley, William A., 1157
Webb, Pauline, 1158
Weber, Charles W., 1159
Welsby, Derek A., 1160
Wendl, Tobias, 853
Wendland, Ernst R., 647, 1072, 1161–1166
Werbner, Richard, 1167
Werner, Dietrich, 919
Werner, Roland, 1168–1169
Wessels, W. H., 872
West, Gerald O., 216, 1116, 1170–1173
Westerlund, David, 1174–1175

Wetmore, Hugh, 1176
Wheeler, Andrew C., 560, 924, 1169, 1177–1179
Whiteside, Alan, 96
Whitworth, Wendy, 968
Wijsen, Frans Jozef Servaas, 1180
Wild-Wood, Emma, 1152
Wilhite, David E., 1181
Willcox, Sandy, 1182
Williams, David T., 14
Williams, Pat, 1183
Wilson-Hartgrove, Jonathan, 556
Wondji, Christophe, 687
Wooding, Nick, 1184
Wratten, Darrel, 195
Wrong, Michela, 1185

Y
Yahya, Saad S., 87
Yamamori, Tetsunao, 1186
Yamauchi, Edwin M., 1187–1188
Yekonda Lofoli, Bosekaetunga, 1189
Yesehaq Mandefro, Abuna, 1190
Yinda, Hélène, 1191
Yorke, Gosnell L. O. R., 1192
Young, John, 1193
Young, Josiah Ulysses, 1194–1196

Z
Zimmermann, Armin, 1197
Zinkuratire, Victor, 383
Zo'o Zo'o, Daniel, 282
Zokoué, Issac, 1198
Zulu, Princess Kasune, 1199
Zvobgo, C. J. M., 1200

Title Index

Note: The numbers attached to each title entry below indicate the reference numbers of the relevant reviews, *not* page numbers.

790	1 & 2 Timothy and Titus
725	150 Years of Bible Translation in Kenya, 1844-1994: An Overview and Appraisal
107	2000 Years of Christianity in Africa: An African Church History
809	28 Stories of AIDS in Africa
960	Abolition!: The Struggle to Abolish Slavery in the British Colonies
1002	Abolitionists Abroad: American Blacks and the Making of Modern West Africa
1017	Academic Cooperation with Africa: Lessons for Partnership in Higher Education
1170	Academy of the Poor, The: Towards a Dialogical Reading of the Bible
927	AD 2000 and After: The Future of God's Mission in Africa
906	Adventure in Africa: The Story of Don McClure–From Khartoum to Addis Ababa in Five Decades
79	Africa: The Marginalized Continent
309	Africa: Unity, Sovereignty and Sorrow
441	Africa: Dispatches from a Fragile Continent
959	Africa: A Biography of the Continent
1119	Africa: The People and Politics of an Emerging Continent
1024	Africa: A Continent Self-Destructs
970	Africa: A Season for Hope
245	Africa 2002: World Today Series
1187	Africa and Africans in Antiquity
20	Africa and Africans in the New Testament
21	Africa and the Africans in the Old Testament
1188	Africa and the Bible
102	Africa and the Disciplines: The Contributions of Research in Africa to the Social Sciences and Humanities
81	Africa Betrayed
34	Africa Bible Commentary: A One-Volume Commentary Written by 70 African Scholars
620	Africa for the African: The Life of Joseph Booth
82	Africa in Chaos
73	Africa in the 21st Century

1027   Africa Journal of Evangelical Theology, 1982–2002

304   Africa Now: People, Policies and Institutions

285   Africa Praying: A Handbook on HIV/AIDS Sensitive Sermon Guidelines and Liturgy

231   Africa since 1940: The Past of the Present

191   Africa Works: Disorder as Political Instrument

812   Africa's Discovery of Europe 1450-1850

686   Africa's Islamic Experience: History, Culture and Politics

869   Africa's Moment

561   Africa's Quest for a Philosophy of Decolonization

496   Africa's Social and Religious Quest

637   Africa's Stalled Development: International Causes and Cures

500   African AIDS Epidemic: A History , The: A History

201   African Apostles, The

161   African Biographical Dictionary, An

448   African Catholicism: Essays in Discovery

425   African Challenge to the Church in the Twenty-first Century, An

69   African Charismatics: Current Developments within Independent Indigenous Pentecostalism in Ghana

609   African Christian Ethics

586   African Christian Marriage

167   African Christian Morality at the Age of Inculturation

652   African Christian Presence in the West: New Immigrant Congregations and Transnational Networks in North America and Europe

4   African Christian Theology: Illusion and Reality

726   African Christian Theology: The Quest for Selfhood

742   African Christian Theology: An Introduction

610   African Christian Theology

391   African Christianity: Its Public Role

534   African Christianity: An African Story

77   African Christianity Rising

429   African Christians in Europe

210   African Christology: Jesus in Post-Missionary African Christianity

814   African Church at the Crossroads, The: A Strategy for Indigenization

1153   African Church in the 21st Century: Challenges and Promises

915   African Church in the Communications Era, The: A Handbook of Source Texts for Christian Communication in Africa

241   African Continent, The: An Insight into Its Earliest History

185   African Conversion

576   African Cosmos: An Introduction to Religion in Africa

300   African Cry

1039 African Culture: An Overview (Social-Cultural Anthropology)

50 African Culture and the Quest for Women's Rights

491 African Diaspora in the Mediterranean Lands of Islam, The

248 African Earthkeepers: Volume 1 Interfaith Mission in Earth-Care; Volume 2 Environmental Mission and Liberation in Christian Perspective

1124 African Economies and the Politics of Permanent Crisis, 1979–1999

973 African Experience, The: From Olduvai Gorge to the 21st Century

46 African Experience with Higher Education, The

673 African Friends and Money Matters: Observations from Africa

684 African Gifts of the Spirit: Pentecostalism and the Rise of a Zimbabwean Transnational Religious Movement

228 African Harvest: The Captivating Story of Michael Cassidy and African Enterprise

743 African Heritage and Contemporary Christianity

1084 African Higher Education: An International Reference Handbook

587 African Independent Churches Today: Kaleidoscope of Afro-Christianity

80 African Indigenous Churches: An Historical Perspective

928 African Initiatives in Christianity: The Growth, Gifts and Diversities of African Churches–A Challenge to the Ecumenical Movement

72 African Intellectual Heritage: A Book of Sources

782 African Intellectuals in 19th and Early 20th Century South Africa

1174 African Islam and Islam in Africa: Encounters between Sufis and Islamists

360 African Journey through Mark's Gospel, An: A Tool for Small Christian Communities

836 African Memory of Mark, The: Reassessing Early Church Tradition

271 African Modernities: Entangled Meanings in Current Debate

535 African Pentecostalism: An Introduction

316 African Philosophy: An Anthology

680 African Philosophy in Search of Identity

218 African Philosophy Reader, The

492 African Politics in Comparative Perspective

1109 African Prayer Book, An

1157 African Presence in the Bible, The: Gospel Sermons Rooted in History

820 African Proverbs Project, The

727 African Proverbs Reveal Christianity in Culture: A Narrative Portrayal of Builsa Proverbs Contextualizing Christianity in Ghana

59 African Reformation: African Initiated Christianity in the Twentieth Century

658 African Religion: The Moral Traditions of Abundant Life

1175 African Religion in African Scholarship: A Preliminary Study of the Religious and Political Background

659 African Religion in the Dialogue Debate: From Intolerance to Coexistence

400 African Religion Meets Islam: Religious Change in Northern Nigeria

498   African Religions in Western Conceptual Schemes: The Problem of Interpretation. Studies in Igbo Religion

951   African Saints: Saints, Martyrs, and Holy People from the Continent of Africa

864   African Spirituality: Forms, Meanings and Expressions

453   African Stories for Preachers and Teachers

1141 African Teachers on the Colonial Frontier: Tswana Evangelists and Their Communities during the Nineteenth Century

676   African Theology: Inculturation and Liberation

1194 African Theology: A Critical Analysis and Annotated Bibliography

1031 African Theology: An Introduction

884   African Theology in Images

168   African Theology in Its Social Context

169   African Theology in the 21st Century: The Contribution of the Pioneers (Volume 1)

769   African Theology of Mission, An

1073 African Theology on the Way: Current Conversations

554   African Theology Today

923   African Traditional Marriage: A Christian Theological Appraisal

418   African Traditional Religion and Christian Counseling

862   African Traditional Religion and the Christian Faith

371   African Traditional Religion in Biblical Perspective

372   African Traditional Religion in the Light of the Bible

1094 African Traditional Religions

865   African Traditional Religions in Contemporary Society

806   African Vitalogy: A Step Forward in African Thinking

232   African Women: A Modern History

495   African Women and Religious Change: A Study of the Western Igbo of Nigeria, with a Special Focus on Asaba Town

450   African Women South of the Sahara

918   African Women, Religion, and Health: Essays in Honor of Mercy Amba Ewudziwa Oduyoye

895   Africana Bible, The: Reading Israel's Scriptures from Africa and the African Diaspora

320   Africanizing Knowledge: African Studies across the Disciplines

501   Africans: The History of a Continent

295   Africans Reconstructing Africa

969   Africentric Christianity: A Theological Appraisal for Ministry

543   Afrikanische Evangelikale Theologie: Plädoyer für das ganze Evangelium im Kontext Afrikas

872   Afro-Christian Religion and Healing in Southern Africa

873   Afro-Christianity at the Grassroots

209   After Genocide: Transitional Justice, Post-Conflict Reconstruction and Reconciliation in Rwanda and Beyond

423   After the Locusts: How Costly Forgiveness Is Restoring Rwanda's Stolen Years

991   AIDS: The Leprosy of Our Time?

1102   AIDS: Understanding the Challenge

280   AIDS Crisis, The: What We Can Do

281   AIDS in Africa: The Church's Opportunity

96   AIDS in the Twenty-First Century: Disease and Globalization

362   AIDS Is Real and It's in Our Church

88   AIDS, Sex and Family Planning: A Christian View

211   AIDS: The Biblical Solution

117   Alice Lakwena and the Holy Spirits: War in Northern Uganda, 1986-1997

249   All Things Hold Together: Holistic Theologies at the African Grassroots. Selected Essays by M. L. Daneel

527   Alliances avec le Christ en Afrique: Inculturation des rites religieux au Zaïre

848   Alphabetical Psalms, The: Systematic Instruction for a Life of Faith and Trust

1143   Am I Still My Brother's Keeper?: Biblical Perspectives on Poverty

419   Ambaricho and Shonkolla: From Local Independent Church to the Evangelical Mainstream in Ethiopia: The Origins of the Mekane Yesus Church in Kambata Hadiya

1057   Ambushed by Love: God's Triumph in Kenya's Terror

621   Anabaptist Songs in African Hearts

559   Analysis and Assessment of the Concept of Revelation in Karl Rahner's Theology: Its Application and Relationship to African Traditional Religions

660   Anatomy of Inculturation: Transforming the Church in Africa

599   Ancien Testament, pour commencer, L'

916   Ancient Churches of Ethiopia: Fourth–Fourteenth Centuries

698   Angels Have Left Us, The: The Rwanda Tragedy and the Churches

447   Anglican Communion in Crisis: How Episcopal Dissidents and Their African Allies Are Reshaping Anglicanism

402   Anglican Liturgical Inculturation in Africa: The Kanamai Statement with Introduction, Papers from Kanamai and a First Response

1083   Anglican Swahili Prayer Books: Tanzania (1995) and Congo (1998)

1077   Anglican Tradition in South Africa, The: A Historical Overview

1177   Announcing the Light: Sudanese Witnesses to the Gospel

331   Archaeology of Christianity in Africa, The

504   Archaeology of Islam in Sub-Saharan Africa, The

490   Archbishop Tutu: Prophetic Witness in South Africa

435   Art and Religion in Africa

160   Association of Evangelicals in Africa, The: Its History, Organization, Members, Projects, External Relations and Message

184   Back to Africa, George Ross and the Maroons: From Nova Scotia to Sierra Leone

348   Banfield, Nupe, and the UMCA

807   Bantu Philosophy of Life in the Light of the Christian Message: A Basis for an African Vitalistic Theology

389 Basic Counselling Skills

841 Beads and Strands: Reflections of an African Woman on Christianity in Africa

221 Becoming a Trans-Cultural Woman

255 Being Human: Confessions of a Christian Humanist

768 Being Human in Africa: Toward an African Christian Anthropology

890 Beliefs and Practices of Muslims: The Religion of Our Neighbours

149 Believing in the Future: Toward a Missiology of Western Culture

234 Between Babel and Pentecost: Transnational Pentecostalism in Africa and Latin America

457 Between Glory and Shame: A Historical and Systematic Study of Education and Leadership Training Models among the Baatonu in North Benin

1056 Bewitching Development: Witchcraft and the Reinvention of Development in Neoliberal Kenya

990 Beyers Naudé: Pilgrimage of Faith

456 Beyond Our Prayers: Anabaptist Church Growth in Ethiopia, 1948-1998

866 Beyond Primitivism: Indigenous Religious Traditions and Modernity

883 Beyond the Rivers of Ethiopia: A Biblical Revelation on God's Purpose for the Black Race

1063 Bible and Human Development in Africa, The

778 Bible and its Translations: Colonial and Postcolonial Encounters with the Indigenous, The: Colonial and Postcolonial Encounters with the Indigenous

105 Bible and Mission: Christian Witness in a Postmodern World

1066 Bible and the flag, The: Protestant Missions and British Imperialism in the Nineteenth and Twentieth Centuries

690 Bible and Theology in African Christianity

273 Bible in a World Context, The: An Experiment in Contextual Hermeneutics

1171 Bible in Africa, The: Transactions, Trajectories, and Trends

583 Bible in African Christianity, The: Essays in Biblical Theology

1192 Bible Translation and African Languages

1088 Biblical Approach to Marriage and Family in Africa, A

744 Biblical Basis for Evangelization, The: Theological Reflections Based on an African Experience

552 Biblical Christianity in Africa

832 Biblical Christianity in African Perspective

833 Biblical Christianity in Modern Africa

6 Biblical Healing in African Context

731 Biblical Hermeneutics and Black Theology in South Africa

22 Biblical Interpretation in African Perspective

513 Biblical Preaching in Africa: A Textbook for Christian Preachers

7 Biblical Studies and Corruption in Africa

8 Biblical Studies and Women Issues in Africa

1161 Biblical Texts and African Audiences

47 Biblical Theology of Gerassapience, A

9   Biblical View of Sex and Sexuality from African Perspective

216   Bibliography in Contextual Theology in Africa: Volume 1

246   Biography of Rev. Dr. Musa D. Gotom, A: A Pastor of Pastors and a Man Seeking after God's Heart

182   Bishop Alfred Robert Tucker and the Establishment of the African Anglican Church

547   Bishop Facing Mount Kenya, A: An Autobiography, 1902-1978

986   Bishop of Rwanda, The

1078   Bivocational Missionary-Evangelist: The Story of an Itinerant Preacher in Northern Sidama

1195   Black and African Theologies: Siblings or Distant Cousins?

416   Black Christians and White Missionaries

797   Black Future? Jesus and Salvation in South Africa , A

565   Black Livingstone: A True Tale of Adventure in the Nineteenth-Century Congo

254   Black Man's Burden, The: Africa and the Curse of the Nation-State

975   Blantyre Mission and the Making of Modern Malawi

179   Blessing of Africa, The: The Bible and African Christianity

758   Blood on Their Hands

176   Book of Revelation, The: African Bible Commentaries

220   Bottom Billion, The: Why the Poorest Countries Are Failing and What Can Be Done About It

1072   Bridging the Gap: African Traditional Religion and Bible Translation

967   British Intellectual Engagement with Africa in the Twentieth Century, The

1075   British Missionaries and the End of Empire: East, Central, and Southern Africa, 1939-64

511   Bruno Gutmann: His Life, His Thoughts, and His Work: An Early Attempt at a Theology in an African Context

1162   Buku Loyera: An Introduction to the New Chichewa Bible Translation

560   "But God Is Not Defeated": Celebrating the Centenary of the Episcopal Church of the Sudan 1899-1999

263   Byang Kato: Ambassador for Christ

1080   Call of Africa, The: The Reformed Church in America Mission in the Sub-Sahara, 1948-1998

369   Called from Islam to Christ: Why Muslims Become Christians

563   Calming the Storm: Christian Reflections on AIDS

462   Cameroon on a Clear Day: A Pioneer Missionary in Colonial Africa

683   Capturing a Lost Vision: Can Nigeria's Greatest Revival Live Again?

852   Cardinal Otunga: A Gift of Grace

1154   Caring and Sharing: Pastoral Counselling in the African Perspective

158   Catholic Church in Comtemporary Southern Africa, The

108   Catholic Church in Kenya, The: A Centenary History

528   Celebrating Jesus Christ in Africa: Liturgy and Inculturation

1040   Celibacy and African Culture

804   Century of Catholic Endeavour, A: Holy Ghost and Consolata Missions in Kenya

520   Challenge of Modernity in Africa, The

27   Challenge of Parenting, The: Principles and Practice of Raising Children

261   Challenge of Vatican II in East Africa: The Contribution of Dutch Missionaries to the Implementation of Vatican II in Tanzania, Kenya, Uganda and Malawi 1965-1975, The: The Contribution of Dutch Missionaries to the Implementation of Vatican II in Tanzania, Kenya, Uganda and Malawi 1965-1975

1145   Challenging Evangelicalism: Prophetic Witness and Theological Renewal

148   Challenging the State: Churches as Political Actors in South Africa, 1980–1994

1003   Changing Face of Christianity, The: Africa, the West, and the World

1122   Charismatic Renewal in Africa: A Challenge for African Christianity

529   Chemins de la christologie africaine

638   Child Care and Culture: Lessons from Africa

421   Children of AIDS: Africa's Orphan Crisis

902   Children of the Sun: Stories of the Christian Journey in Sudan

341   China's Second Continent: How a Million Migrants Are Building a New Empire in Africa

723   Chiswakhata Mkandawire of Livingstonia

972   Choosing Hope: The Christian Response to the HIV/AIDS Epidemic: Curriculum Modules for Theological and Pastoral Training Institutions

816   Chrétien et la Politique, Le: Actes du Colloque Interdisciplinaire 06-10 janvier

825   Christ as Our Ancestor

671   Christ, the African King: New Testament Christology

392   Christian Churches and the Democratisation of Africa, The

611   Christian Conversion in Africa: The Bajju Experience

643   Christian Education: Principles and Practice

738   Christian Education at the Mutapa Court: A Portuguese Strategy to Influence Events in the Empire of Munhumutapa

494   Christian Education in the African Context: Proceedings of the African Regional Conference of IAPCHE, Harare, 4-9 March 1991

1038   Christian Ethics: Volume 1–The Biblical Basis; Volume 2–Contemporary Issues

953   Christian Ethics in an African Context: A Focus on Urban Zambia

789   Christian Leadership: A Challenge to the African Church

35   Christian Mind in a Changing Africa, A

89   Christian Ministry: Patterns and Functions within the Evangelical Church Mekane Yesus

992   Christian Mission in South Africa: Political and Ecumenical

173   Christian Missions among Muslims: Sokoto Province, Nigeria, 1935-1990

461   Christian Missions in Africa: A Social Geographical Study of the Impact of Their Activities in Zambia

863   Christian Pilgrims in Nigeria

567   Christian Response to Female Circumcision

713   Christian Theology and African Traditions

745   Christian Theology and Social Reconstruction

897   Christian Theology in an African Context

882   Christian Writer's Primer, The: An Introductory Manual for Aspiring Christian Writers

1069   Christian-Muslim Co-existence in Eastern Africa: Papers Presented at the Joint Conference of Tangaza
        College, Nairobi and Radbound University, Nijmegen

76   Christian-Muslim Encounter in Africa

958   Christian-Muslim Relations in Africa: The Cases of Northern Nigeria and Tanzania Compared

131   Christian-Nationalism and the Rise of the Afrikaner Broederbond in South Africa, 1918–48

235   Christianisme et humanisme en Afrique: Mélanges en hommage au cardinal Bernadin Gantin

530   Christianisme et l'Afrique, Le: Une chance réciproque

328   Christianity and African Culture: Conservative German Protestant Missionaries in Tanzania, 1900-1940

1103   Christianity and African Gods: A Method in Theology

256   Christianity and Democracy: A Theology for a Just World Order

393   Christianity and Politics in Doe's Liberia

310   Christianity and Public Culture in Africa

685   Christianity and the African Imagination: Essays in Honour of Adrian Hastings

1041   Christianity and the African Imagination: After the African Synod: Resources for Inculturation

299   Christianity and the Challenges of Witchcraft in Contemporary Africa

1134   Christianity in a New Key

112   Christianity in Africa: The Renewal of a Non-Western Religion

377   Christianity in Africa and the African Diaspora: The Appropriation of a Scattered Heritage

356   Christianity in Africa in the 1990s

978   Christianity in Malawi: A Source Book

177   Christianity in Roman Africa: The Development of Its Practices and Beliefs

195   Christianity in South Africa: An Annotated Bibliography

307   Christianity in South Africa: A Political, Social and Cultural History

641   Christianity Reborn: The Global Expansion of Evangelicalism in the Twentieth Century

292   Christianity without Fetishes: An African Critique and Recapture of Christianity

394   Christianity, Politics and Public Life in Kenya

667   Christians and Churches of Africa Envisioning the Future: Salvation in Jesus Christ and the Building of a
        New African Society

134   Christians and Muslims: Parameters for Living Together: Studies in Christian-Muslim Relations, Volume 8

568   Christians in Máasailand: A Study of the History of Mission among the Máasai in the North Eastern
        Diocese of the Evangelical Lutheran Church in Tanzania

135   Christians: Why this Muslim Violence?: Studies in Christian-Muslim Relations, Volume 3

136   Christians: Why We Reject Muslim Law: Studies in Christian-Muslim Relations, Volume 4

170   Christmas: God Becomes Man in Black Africa

755   Christologie des pères apostoliques, La

10   Christology in African Context

870   Church and AIDS in Africa , The: A Case Study: Nairobi City

625   Church and Healing, , The: Echoes from Africa

824   Church and State: The Nigerian Experience

588   Church Come of Age, A: Fifty Years of Revival in the CPK Diocese of Embu 1942-1992

163   Church History, part 2: Lessons from the Church in Africa

449   Church in Africa, 1450-1950, The

198   Church in Africa, Towards a Theology of Reconstruction , The

746   Church in African Christianity, The: Innovative Essays in Ecclesiology

459   Church in Angola, The: A River of Many Currents

1042 Church in the African City, The

803   Church in the World, The: A Historical-Ecclesiological Study of the Church of Uganda with Particular Reference to Post-Independence Uganda, 1962-1992

1012 Church Leaders and Christian Life in the Pastoral Letters

831   Church, Law and Political Transition in Malawi 1992-1994

458   Church, State and People in Mozambique: A Historical Study with Special Emphasis on Developments in the Inhambane Region

979   Church, University and Theological Education in Malawi: A Model for Third World Theological Education

367   Churches and Ethnic Ideology in the Rwandan Crises 1900–1994, The

482   Churches in Fellowship: The Story of TEKAN

847   Churches' Responsibility for Understanding Islam and the Muslims in Africa, The: A Short Bibliography

123   CIM/AIMM: A Story of Vision, Commitment and Grace

665   Citizen and Subject: Contemporary Africa and the Legacy of Late Colonialism

622   Claiming the Promise: African Churches Speak

442   Classics in Post-Colonial Worlds

810   Clouds of Witnesses: Christian Voices from Africa and Asia

1100 Collective Sins in Africa: A Missiological Approach to the African Crisis

125   Colour Of Darkness, The: A Personal Story of Tragedy and Hope in Rwanda

92   Come and Share: An Introduction to Christian Theology

1088 'Come let us bow down...': Worship in the Christian Church in Africa

664   Coming of the Rain, The: The Biography of a Pioneering Missionary in Rwanda

30   Commentary on 1 and 2 Corinthians, A

688   Committed to Conflict: The Destruction of the Church in Rwanda

1163 Comparative Discourse Analysis and the Translation of Psalm 22 in Chichewa, a Bantu Language of South-Central Africa

747   Comparative Study of Religions, A

964   Concept of Life After Death, The: African Tradition and Christianity in Dialogue (with Special Emphasis on the Urhobo Culture)

380   Conflicts in Africa: A Women Response

1107 Congo Wars, The: Conflict, Myth and Reality

707   Conscience of Society, The

70   Contemporary Pentecostal Christianity: Interpretations from an African Context

1172 Contextual Bible Study

390   Contextual Theology: Its Meaning, Scope and Urgency

205   Contextual Theology: Voices of West African Women

748   Contextual Theology across Cultures

342   Continent for the Taking, A: The Tragedy and Hope of Africa

624   Conversion to Greater Freedom?: Women, Church and Social Change in North-Western Tanzania under
        Colonial Rule

817   Cost of Reconciliation in South Africa, The

147   Country Unmasked, A: Inside South Africa's Truth and Reconciliation Commission

591   Courage to Hope: A Challenge for Churches in Africa, The: A Challenge for Churches in Africa

473   Course of Islam in Africa, The

823   Creation-Covenant Scheme and Justification by Faith: A Canonical Study of the God-Human Drama in
        the Pentateuch and the Letter to the Romans

109   Criminalization of the State in Africa, The

885   Critical Study of the Pentateuch, A: An Encounter Between Europe and Africa

749   Critiques of Christianity in African Literature, with Particular Reference to the East African Context

1043   Cross and Flag in Africa: The 'White Fathers' during the Colonial Scramble (1892-1914)

215   Cross-Cultural Christianity: A Textbook on Cross-Cultural Communication

1147   Cross-Cultural Process in Christian History, The: Studies in the Transmission and Reception of Faith

850   Crossing Cultures for Christ

1004   Crown and the Turban, The: Muslims and West African Pluralism

1146   Crucible of Fire: The Church Confronts Apartheid: Essays by Leading South African Christians 1980–
        1990

16   Cry, Beloved Africa!

1164   Cultural Factor in Bible Translation, The: A Study of Communicating the Word of God in a Central
        African Cultural Context

1065   Cultural Politics of Religious Change, The: A Study of the Sanoyea Kpelle in Liberia

618   Cultural Revival and Church Planting: A Nigerian Case Study

566   Culture and Inculturation: A Bantu Viewpoint

1026   Culture and Mental Health: A Southern African View

595   Culture and the Christian Home: Evaluating Cultural Marriage and Family in the Light of Scripture

1182   Cut Flowers: Female Genital Mutilation and a Biblical Response

485   Daily Guide for Culture and Language Learning, A

539   Dancing Church Around the World

1068   Dancing in the Glory of Monsters: The Collapse of the Congo and the Great War of Africa

1168   Das Christentum in Nubien: Geschichte und Gestalt einer afrikanischen Kirche

682   Das symbolische Denken als Schlüssel zum Verständnis der negro-afrikanischen (Bantu-) Weltanschauung:
        eine religionsphilosophische Deutung im Anschluss an die Kulturphilosophie Ernst Cassirers

842   Daughters of Anowa: African Women and Patriarchy

656   David Livingstone: The Truth behind the Legend

1156   David Livingstone: Trail Blazer

976   David Livingstone: Mission and Empire

1169   Day of Devastation, Day of Contentment: The History of the Sudanese Church across 2000 Years

781   De quelle tribu es-tu?

734   Dead Aid: Why Aid Is Not Working and How There Is a Better Way for Africa

829   Dealing with Darkness: A Christian Novel on the Confrontation with African Witchcraft

469   Décalogue et l'histoire du texte, Le: Etudes des formes textuelles du Décalogue et leur implications dans l'histoire du texte de l'Ancien Testament

11   Decolonization of Biblical Interpretation in Africa

580   défis de l'évangélisation dans l'Afrique contemporaine, Les

750   Democracy and Development in Africa: The Role of Churches

661   Democracy and Reconciliation: A Challenge for African Christianity

787   Democratic Republic of Congo: Economic Dimensions of War and Peace, The: Economic Dimensions of War and Peace

818   Democratic Vision for South Africa, A: Political Realism and Christian Responsibility

361   Denis Hurley: A Portrait by Friends

956   "Der Gott, der abends heimkommt": Die Inkulturation des christlichen Gottesbegriffs in Rwanda durch Ernst Johanssen (1864-1934) anhand der Imana-Vorstellung

581   Des prêtres noirs s'interrogent cinquante ans après

1131   Desire and Decline: Schooling Amid Crisis in Tanzania

1058   Developing Leaders Through Theological Education by Extension: Case Studies from Africa

860   Development of the Doctrine of the Holy Spirit in the Yoruba (African) Indigenous Christian Movement, The

368   Dictionnaire des personnalités célèbres du monde négro-africain

711   Dieu peut-il mourir en Afrique?: Essai sur l'indifférence religieuse et l'incroyance en Afrique noire

225   Difficult Traverse from Amnesty to Reconciliation, The

891   Digging out the Ancestral Church: Researching and Communicating Church History

801   Dinka Christianity: The Origins and Development of Christianity among the Dinka of Sudan with Special Reference to the Songs of Dinka Christians.

600   Dire l'histoire dans la bible hébraïque: Perspectives exégétiques et herméneutiques

18   Directory of TEE Programmes in Africa

1005   Disciples of All Nations: Pillars of World Christianity

799   Discipling: A Kingdom Necessity in the African City.

800   Discovering the Other Side: Challenges of Other Religions

788   Dispensations: The Future of South Africa as South Africans See It

266   Divine Plan Unfolding: The Story of Ethiopian Evangelical Church Bethel

340   Doctor Comes to Lui, The: A Story of Beginnings in the Sudan

593   Doctrine of God in African Christian Thought: The Holy Trinity, Theological Hermeneutics, and the African Intellectual Culture, The: The Holy Trinity, Theological Hermeneutics, and the African Intellectual Culture

373 Doing African Christian Theology: An Evangelical Perspective

1137 Doing Ethics in Context: South African Perspectives

533 Doing Theology at the Grassroots: Theological Essays from Malawi.

946 Doing Theology with the Maasai

503 Door Opened by the Lord: The History of the Evangelical Lutheran Church in Kenya, A: The History of the Evangelical Lutheran Church in Kenya

1082 Double Image: Biblical Insights from African Parables

1090 Dreams in a Time of War: A Childhood Memoir

86 Drumbeat of Life, The: Jubilee in an African Context

1053 Drums of Redemption: An Introduction to African Christianity

633 Dynamics of Violence in Central Africa: National and Ethnic Conflict in the 21st Century, The: National and Ethnic Conflict in the 21st Century

268 Early Christianity in North Africa

837 Early Libyan Christianity: Uncovering a North African Tradition

298 Early Scriptures of the Gold Coast (Ghana): The Historical, Linguistic, and Theological Settings of the Gã, Twi, Mfantse, and Ewe Bibles

1152 East African Revival, The: History and Legacies

165 Educational Task of the Church, The

270 Efficacy of Parental Blessing, The: A Narrative Critical Study of Gen 27:1–28:9 in Its Context of Gen 25:19–33:20

1070 Église et la mission au Congo, L'

465 Eldoret Missionary College: From Vision to Reality, The First Ten Years

1151 Emancipation in African Theology: An Inquiry on the Relevance of Latin American Liberation Theology to Africa

536 Embattled Gods: Christianization of Igboland, 1841-1991, The: Christianization of Igboland, 1841-1991

952 Emerging Africa: How 17 Countries Are Leading the Way

289 Emerging Voices in Global Christian Theology

874 Empirical Studies of African Independent/Indigenous Churches

767 En mission comme le Seigneur

66 Encarta Africana

1006 Encountering the West: Christianity and the Global Cultural Process

722 Encounters with Witchcraft: Field Notes from Africa

995 End of Poverty, The: How We Can Make It Happen in Our Lifetime

854 End-Time Army, The: Charismatic Movements in Modern Nigeria

1132 Engaging Modernity: Methods and Cases for Studying African Independent Churches in South Africa

1095 Enough: Why the World's Poorest Starve in an Age of Plenty

408 Environmental Crisis, The: A Challenge for African Christianity

67 Envoys of the Gospel in Ethiopia: In the Steps of the Evangelical Pioneers 1898-1936

783 Ephesians and Philippians

143   Escape from Slavery: The True Story of My Ten Years in Slavery—and My Journey to Freedom in America

171   Ethical Dimension of Community, The

236   Ethiopian Biblical Interpretation: A Study in Exegetical Tradition and Hermeneutics

192   Ethiopian Orthodox Tewahedo Church Tradition, The: A Brief Introduction to Its Life and Spirituality

200   Ethiopian Revivalist: Autobiography of Evangelist Mehari Choramo

1190   Ethiopian Tewahedo Church, The: An Integrally African Church

523   Ethnicity: Blessing or Curse?

562   Ethnicity and the Long-Term Perspective: The African Experience

439   Euthanasia of a Mission: African Church Autonomy in a Colonial Context

955   Evangelical Christianity and Democracy in Africa

230   Evangelical Christians in the Muslim Sahel

314   Evangelical Movement in Ethiopia, The: Resistance and Resilience

157   Evangelical Theological Education: An International Agenda

224   Evangelical Witness in South Africa: South African Evangelicals Critique Their Own Theology and Practice

343   Evangelicals and Politics in Asia, Africa and Latin America

630   Evangelicals in Addis Ababa (1919-1991): With Special Reference to the Ethiopian Evangelical Church Mekane Yesus and the Addis Ababa Synod

540   Evangelising Polygamous Families: Canonical and African Approaches

514   Evangelism and Discipleship: Training for Africa

1044   Evangelization and Culture

544   Evangile en Afrique, L': Ruptures et Continuité

760   Expansion of Christianity: A Gazetteer of Its First Three Centuries, The: A Gazetteer of Its First Three Centuries

23   Explorations in African Biblical Studies

929   Exploring Afro-Christology

853   Exploring the Occult and Paranormal in West Africa

237   Expressing the Sacred: An Introduction to the Phenomenology of Religion

128   Extended Family, The: An African Christian Perspective

283   Eye of the Storm, The: Bishop John William Colenso and the Crisis of Biblical Inspiration

1023   Faces of Jesus in Africa

398   Facing the Muslim Challenge: A Handbook of Christian-Muslim Apologetics

217   Facing the Truth: South African Faith Communities and the Truth & Reconciliation Commission

795   Faith and Freedom in Galatia and Senegal: The Apostle Paul, Colonists and Sending Gods

894   Faith and Politics in Nigeria: Nigeria as a Pivotal State in the Muslim World

980   Faith at the Frontiers of Knowledge

257   Faith for a Time Like This: South African Sermons

120   Faith in Development: Partnership Between the World Bank and the Churches of Africa

892   Faith Moves South, The: A History of the Church in Africa

349   Faith of our Fathers: Life Stories of Some UMCA Elders

250	Fambidzano: Ecumenical Movement of Zimbabwean Independent Churches
1108	Fate of Saul's Progeny in the Reign of David, The
142	Father to the Fatherless: The Charles Mulli Story
357	Female Circumcision
229	Festo Kivengere: The Authorised Biography
861	Festo Olang': An Autobiography
370	Final Harvest, The: Mobilizing Indigenous Missions
701	Finding a Social Voice: The Church and Marxism in Africa
878	Fire in the Hills
12	First Letter of Paul to the Corinthians, The: African Bible Commentaries
668	Foi chrétienne, crise africaine et reconstruction de l'Afrique: Sens et enjeux des théologies africaines contemporaines
1030	For Use as Directed: A Missionary Pharmacist Takes Stock
522	Forgiving as We've Been Forgiven: Community Practices for Making Peace
989	Formation of Christian Conscience in Modern Africa
132	Forms of Marriage: Monogamy Reconsidered
1060	Foundations of African Philosophy: A Definitive Analysis of Conceptual Issues in African Thought
172	Foundations of an African Ethic: Beyond the Universal Claim of Western Morality
546	Founding an African Faith: Kikuyu Anglican Christianity 1900-1945
452	From Every People and Nation: A Biblical Theology of Race
947	From Genocide to Continental War: The 'Congolese' Conflict and the Crisis of Contemporary Africa
996	From Krapf to Rugambwa: A Church History of Tanzania
751	From Liberation to Reconstruction: Christian Theology in Africa after the Cold War
1051	From Migrants to Missionaries: Christians of African Origin in Germany
815	From Mission to Church: A Handbook of Christianity in East Africa
1120	From New York to Ibadan: The Impact of African Questions on the Making of Ecumenical Mission Mandates, 1900-1958
32	From Seven to Seven Thousand: The Story of the Birth and Growth of SIM/ECWA Church in Ilorin
426	From Text to Practice: The Role of the Bible in Daily Living of African People Today
689	From the Cross to the Crescent
813	From Trials to Triumphs: The Voice of Habakkuk to the Suffering African Christian
381	From Violence to Peace: A Challenge for African Christianity
244	Frontiers of African Christianity: Essays in Honour of Inus Daneel
724	Fulbe Muslims Encounter Christ: Contextual Communication of the Gospel to Pastoral Fulbe in Northern Nigeria
85	Fundamentalism: Muslims Differ Widely from Evangelicals
555	Future for Africa: Critical Essays in Christian Social Imagination, A: Critical Essays in Christian Social Imagination
791	Galatians

924   Gateway to the Heart of Africa: Missionary Pioneers in Sudan

687   General History of Africa: Africa since 1935 (Volume 8)

968   Genocide in Rwanda: Complicity of the Churches?

657   Gentle Wind of God: The Influence of the East African Revival, A: The Influence of the East African Revival

395   Ghana's New Christianity: Pentecostalism in a Globalizing African Economy

699   Girl Soldier: A Story of Hope for Northern Uganda's Children

1034   Global Awakening: How 20th-Century Revivals Triggered a Christian Revolution

909   Global Bible Commentary

466   Global Church: Reshaping Our Conversations, Renewing Our Mission, Revitalizing Our Churches

1064   Global God, The: Multicultural Evangelical Views of God

327   Global Shadows: Africa in the Neoliberal World Order

355   God and Creation in Intercultural Perspective: Dialogue between the Theologies of Barth, Dickson, Pobee, Nyamiti, and Pannenberg

798   God in AIDS?: A Theological Enquiry

808   God in South Africa: The Challenge of the Gospel

999   God-Centred Bible Study: An Introduction to Bible Study

981   God, People and Power in Malawi: Democratization in Theological Perspective

1000   God's Mission Begins: A Study of the Pentateuch

1016   God's Pathways in Africa: Adventures of a Pioneering Family

141   God's Wrathful Children: Political Oppression and Christian Ethics

376   Godly Medicine in Zimbabwe: A History of Its Medical Missions

830   Gods of Africa or the God of the Bible, The: The Snares of African Traditional Religion in Biblical Perspective

350   Going to the Nations: An Introduction to Cross-Cultural Missions

736   Golden Buttons: Christianity and Traditional Religion among the Tumbuka

982   Gospel Ferment in Malawi: Theological Essays

335   Gospel of John in African Perspective, The

792   Gospel of John: A Commentary for Pastors, Teachers and Preachers, The: A Commentary for Pastors, Teachers and Preachers

521   Gospel Trailblazer: An African-American Preacher's Historic Journey across Racial Lines

124   Great African Society, The: A Plan for a Nation Gone Astray

319   Growth of the Church in Africa, The

908   Growth, Distribution, and Poverty in Africa: Messages from the 1990s

1113   Guest Christology: An Interpretative View of the Christological Problem in Africa

505   Guide to Higher Education in Africa

615   Guide to Interpreting Scripture, A: Context, Harmony, and Application

502   Guidelines for Christian Theology in Africa

430   Halfway to Paradise: African Christians in Europe

1098	Hammering Swords into Ploughshares: Essays in Honor of Archbishop Mpilo Desmond Tutu
761	Handbook of African Approaches to Biblical Interpretation, A
919	Handbook of Theological Education in Africa
1018	Handbook on Inculturation, A
720	Hardest Place: The Biography of Warren and Dorothy Modricker, The: The Biography of Warren and Dorothy Modricker
187	Heal the Land: A National Initiative for Reconciliation in South Africa
875	Healer-Prophet in Afro-Christian Churches, The
649	Health, Healing and God's Kingdom: New Pathways to Christian Health Ministry in Africa
843	Hearing and Knowing: Theological Reflections on Christianity in Africa
655	Helping People to Good Health
920	Her-Stories: Hidden Histories of Women of Faith in Africa
756	Herméneutique athée et exégèses modernes. A propos d'un thème capital de la foi chrétienne: Le Fils de l'Homme
100	Hidden Triumph in Ethiopia
1086	Histoire des chrétiens d'Afrique du Nord: Libye-Tunisie-Algérie-Maroc
2	History and Theology of Sacrifice in the Old Testament
1200	History of Christian Missions in Zimbabwe 1890-1939
507	History of Christianity in Africa, A: From Antiquity to the Present
1135	History of Christianity in Africa in the Context of African History: An Assessment
597	History of Christianity in Asia, Africa, and Latin America, 1450-1990, A: A Documentary Sourcebook
640	History of Islam in Africa, The
1079	History of the Church in Africa, A
476	History of the Church in Southern Africa: A Select Bibliography of Published Material to 1980
288	History of the Episcopal Church in Liberia, 1821–1980, A
765	History of the Jesuits in Zambia, A
278	History of the United Methodist Church in Nigeria, The
31	Holiness and Community in 2 Cor 6:14–7:1: Paul's View of Communal Holiness in the Corinthian Correspondence
48	Holism in Development: An African Perspective on Empowering Communities
146	Holy Spirit, The: A Narrative Factor in the Acts of the Apostles
1089	Holy Spirit and the Church in Africa Today, The
475	Honey, We're Going to Africa!
762	Honoured Crusade, The: Ralph Dodge's Theology of Liberation and Initiative for Social Change in Zimbabwe
582	Hope for Africa and What the Christians Can Do
944	Horn and Crescent: Cultural Change and Traditional Islam on the East African Coast, 800–1900
438	Hospital by the River, The
838	How Africa Shaped the Christian Mind: Rediscovering the African Seedbed of Western Christianity

1081	How Colonialism Preempted Modernity in Africa
431	How God Became African: African Spirituality and Western Secular Thought
569	How to Develop Resources for Christian Ministries
542	Human Condition, The: Christian Perspectives Through African Eyes
1189	humanité de Jésus-Christ à travers l'ontologie Bantu, L'
719	Hundred Camels, A: A Mission Doctor's Sojourn and Murder Trial in Somalia
998	Hyena People, The: Ethiopian Jews in Christian Ethiopia
739	Idea of Africa, The
772	Identity of Christ in Islam: From the Perspective of Thomas Aquinas, The: From the Perspective of Thomas Aquinas
358	Images of Women in Zimbabwean Literature
432	Imagining Evil: Witchcraft Beliefs and Accusations in Contemporary Africa
636	Imagining Home: Class, Culture and Nationalism in the African Diaspora
40	Impact of Ethnic, Political, and Religious Violence on Northern Nigeria, and a Theological Reflection on Its Healing, The
239	In Joy and in Sorrow: Travels among Sudanese Christians, Faith in Sudan, Volume 8
626	In Living Colour: An Intercultural Approach to Pastoral Care and Counselling
912	In Our Own Languages: The Story of Bible Translation in Sudan
1123	In Search of Foundations for African Catholicism: Charles Nyamiti's Theological Methodology
1020	In Search of Truth and Justice: Confrontations between Church and State in Malawi 1960-1994
403	In Season and Out of Season: Sermons to a Nation
1185	In the Footsteps of Mr Kurtz: Living on the Brink of Disaster in the Congo
119	In-Between People, The: A Reading of David Bosch through the Lens of Mission History and Contemporary Challenges In Ethiopia
700	Inculturating the Church in Africa: Theological and Practical Perspectives
1144	Inculturation: Its Meaning and Urgency
880	Inculturation of Christianity in Africa, The: Antecedents and Guidelines from the New Testament and the Early Church
858	Inculturation of Christianity in Africa
940	Institutions and Ethnic Politics in Africa
467	Intellectual Traditions of Pre-Colonial Africa
647	Interacting with Scriptures in Africa
672	Intercultural Hermeneutics in Africa: Methods and Approaches
401	International Directory of Theological Colleges 1997, An
1159	International Influences and Baptist Mission in West Cameroon: German-American Missionary Endeavor under International Mandate and British Colonialism
497	Interpretation of the Hebrew Word 'am (People) in Samuel-Kings, The
537	Interpreting Contemporary Christianity: Global Processes and Local Identities
382	Interpreting the New Testament in Africa

383   Interpreting the Old Testament in Africa

183   Intervention and Transnationalism in Africa: Global-Local Networks of Power

966   Into Africa: A Guide to Sub-Saharan Culture and Diversity

662   Into the House of the Ancestors: Inside the New Africa

844   Introducing African Women's Theology

541   Introducing Feminist Cultural Hermeneutics: An African Perspective

584   Introducing Ordinary African Readers' Hermeneutics: A Case Study of the Agikuyu Encounter with the
         Bible

282   Introduction à la théologie systématique, Volume 1: Dogmatique

51   Introduction à la Théologie Sytématique, Volume 2: Ethique

691   Introduction to African Religion

1104   Introduction to the History of SIM/ECWA in Nigeria 1893-1993, An

903   Introduction to Third World Theologies, An

740   Invention of Africa, The: Gnosis, Philosophy, and the Order of Knowledge

36   Is Africa Cursed?: A Vision for the Radical Transformation of an Ailing Continent

786   Islam: As It Sees Itself, as Others See It, as It Is (Volume 1)

572   Islam among the Swahili in East Africa

1117   Islam and Colonialism: Intellectual Responses of Muslims of Northern Nigeria to British Colonial Rule

811   Islam and Its World

208   Islam and the Abolition of Slavery

55   Islam in Africa: Proceedings of the Islam in Africa Conference

87   Islam in Kenya: Proceedings of the National Seminar on Contemporary Islam in Kenya

1096   Islamic Fundamentalism: The Quest for the Right of Muslims in Uganda

265   Islamism and Its Enemies in the Horn of Africa

856   Israel and the Nations: A Mission Theology of the Old Testament

634   Issue of Relevance, An: A Comparative Study of the Story of the Bleeding Woman (Mk 5: 25-34; Mt 9:20-
         22; Lk 8:43-48) in North Atlantic and African Contexts

793   Issues in African Christian Theology

437   Ivory in Our Hearts: The Special Work of God in Our Lives

532   Jesus als Lebensretter: Westafrikanische Bibelinterpretationen und ihre Relevanz für die neutestamentliche
         Wissenschaft

164   Jesus and Israel's Traditions of Judgement and Restoration

752   Jesus Christ in African Christianity: Experimentation and Diversity in African Christology

1142   Jesus Christ Our Muthamaki (Ideal Elder): An African Christological Study Based on the Agikuyu
         Understanding of Elder

317   Jesus Christ the Ancestor: An African Contextual Christology in the Light of the Major Dogmatic
         Christological Definitions of the Church from the Council of Nicea (325) to Chalcedon (451)

113   Jesus in Africa: The Christian Gospel in African History and Experience

114   Jesus in African Culture: A Ghanaian Perspective

509 Jesus in the Synagogue of Capernaum: The Pericope and Its Programmatic Character for the Gospel of Mark. An Exegetico-Theological Study of Mk 1:21-28

1074 Jesus of Africa: Voices of Contemporary African Christology

1198 Jésus-Christ: Le mystère des deux natures

489 Jews and Judaism in African History

291 Johann Ludwig Krapf: Ein schwäbischer Pionier in Ostafrika

893 Johannes Rebmann: A Servant of God in Africa before the Rise of Western Colonialism

859 Johannine Approach to Mission, The: A Contextual Study of John 4:1-42

977 John Philip (1775-1851): Missions, Race and Politics in South Africa

773 Journey into Islam: An Attempt to Awaken Christians in Africa

365 Journeying with the Old Testament

1037 Justice, Reconciliation and Peace in Africa

648 Kairos Covenant, The: Standing with South African Christians

332 Kalenjiin Heritage, The: Traditional Religious and Social Practices

1062 Karl Kumm: Last of the Livingstones

240 Keeping the Faith: Travels with Sudanese Women. Faith in Sudan, Volume 7

65 Kenyan Epic Novelist Ngugi, The: His Secular Reconfiguration of Biblical Themes

474 King Leopold's Ghost: A Story of Greed, Terror, and Heroism in Colonial Africa

1035 Kingdom of God in Africa, The: A Short History of African Christianity

29 Kingdom of God in the Synoptics: Conversion, Justice and Peace in Africa

646 Kirchen und Demokratisierung in Afrika: Neuere Entwicklungen im afrikanischen Christentum

1092 Kongolese Saint Anthony, The: Dona Beatriz Kimpa Vita and the Antonian Movement, 1684-1706

26 Kwame Nkrumah: A Case Study of Religion and Politics in Ghana

930 Kwame Nkrumah and the Church in Ghana 1949-1966

889 Kwame Nkrumah's Liberation Thought: A Paradigm for Religious Advocacy in Contemporary Ghana

264 Kyrios and Morena: The Lordship of Christ and African Township Christianity

886 l'écoute de la parole, A: Une initiation à la prédication: théorie et pratique

1178 Land of Promise: Church Growth in a Sudan at War

1052 Language and National Identity in Africa

1125 Leaders with a Vision: How Christian Leadership Can Tackle the African Crisis

58 Leadership and Authority: Bula Matari and Life - Community Ecclesiology in Congo

290 Learning about Theology from the Third World

374 Learning to Lead: The Making of a Christian Leader in Africa

499 Left to Tell: Discovering God amidst the Rwandan Holocaust

83 Legacy of Arab-Islam in Africa, The: A Quest for Inter-religious Dialogue

440 Legacy of Beyers Naudé, The

1054 Legacy of Scottish Missionaries in Malawi, The

848 Le-mah sabach-tha-niy?: Lament and Entreaty in the Psalms

412 Leopard's Spots, The: Biblical and African Wisdom in Proverbs

478 Let My People Stay!: Researching the Old Testament in Africa. Report from a Research Project on Africanization of Old Testament Studies

404 Let the Bishop Speak

942 Lettres aux églises d'Afrique: Apocalypse 1-3

575 Leviticus: The Priestly Laws and Prohibitions from the Perspective of Ancient Near East and Africa

1126 Liberating Message, The: A Christian Worldview for Africa

258 Liberating Reformed Theology: A South African Contribution to an Ecumenical Debate

737 Liberating the African Soul: Comparing African and Western Christian Music and Worship Styles

409 Life and Death Matters: The Practice of Inculturation in Africa

524 Lire la Bible dans une société en crise: Etudes d'herméneutique interculturelle

512 Listening Ebony, The: Moral Knowledge, Religion, and Power among the Uduk of Sudan

1158 Long Struggle, A: The Involvement of the World Council of Churches in South Africa

848 Longest Psalm, The: The Prayers of a Student of Moral Instruction

603 Looking Back, Moving Forward: Reflections by South African Evangelicals

794 Lost Boy No More: A True Story of Survival and Salvation

518 Lost History of Christianity: The Thousand-Year Golden Age of the Church in the Middle East, Africa, and Asia–and How It Died, The: The Thousand-Year Golden Age of the Church in the Middle East, Africa, and Asia–and How It Died

68 Lusophone Africa: Beyond Independence

728 Magical Interpretations, Material Realities: Modernity, Witchcraft and the Occult in Postcolonial Africa

868 Makers of the Church in Nigeria

819 Making Ends Meet: Personal Money Management in a Christian Perspective

37 Making of a Servant of God, The

145 Malawi's Muslims: Historical Perspectives

717 Malihambe: Let the Word Spread

993 Man with a Shadow, A: The Life and Times of Professor Z K Matthews

212 Man With the Key Has Gone!, The

983 Managing Ethnic Conflict in Africa: Pressures and Incentives for Cooperation

735 Manuel de morale chrétienne en Afrique: Vivre la foi chrétienne au quotidien

1138 Many Cultures, One Nation: A Festschrift for Beyers Naudé

226 Mapping Systematic Theology in Africa: An Indexed Bibliography

614 Marriage and Family in African Christianity

279 Marxist Modern: An Ethnographic History of the Ethiopian Revolution

305 Mask of Anarchy, The: The Destruction of Liberia and the Religious Dimension of an African Civil War

202 Mbeleshi in a History of the London Missionary Society

855 Meaning of Religious Conversion in Africa, The: The Case of the Igbo of Nigeria

1160 Medieval Kingdoms of Nubia, The: Pagans, Christians and Muslims along the Middle Nile

1036 Memories of the Slave Trade: Ritual and the Historical Imagination in Sierra Leone

301 Message de Jean-Baptiste, Le

1061   Mind of South Africa, The: The Story of the Rise and Fall of Apartheid

931   Ministerial Formation for Mission Today

472   Ministering among Muslims in Africa: An Annotated List of Practical Materials

1032   Ministry of Missions to African Independent Churches: Papers Presented at the Conference on Ministry to African Independent Churches, July 1986

910   Miracle of God's Grace, A: A History of the Lutheran Church in Liberia

556   Mirror to the Church: Resurrecting Faith after Genocide in Rwanda

5   Mission and Democracy in Africa: The Role of the Church

262   Mission and Politics in Eastern Africa: Dutch Missionaries and African Nationalism in Kenya, Tanzania and Malawi, 1945–1965

777   Mission in African Christianity: Critical Essays in Missiology

994   Mission in Bold Humility: David Bosch's Work Considered

605   Mission in Creative Tension: A Dialogue with David Bosch

25   Mission, Communion and Relationship: A Roman Catholic Response to the Crisis of Male Youths in Africa

315   Mission: Africa: A Field Guide

1114   Missionaries Go Home?: A Sociological Interpretation of an African Response to Christian Mission

351   Missionary and His Work, The

585   Missionary and the Diviner, The: Contending Theologies of Christian and African Religions

379   Missionary Factor in Ethiopia, The

352   Missionary Handbook on African Traditional Religion, A

156   Missionary Letters of Vincent Donovan, The: 1957–1973

925   Missionary Ministry and Missiology in Africa Today

1148   Missionary Movement in Christianity, The: Studies in the Transmission of Faith

988   Missionary Outreach of the West Indian Church, The: Jamaican Baptist Missions to West Africa in the Nineteenth Century

159   Missions and Christianity in South African History

957   Modern African Spirituality: The Independent Holy Spirit Churches in East Africa, 1902-1976

223   Modernity and Its Malcontents: Ritual and Power in Postcolonial Africa

378   Modernity of Witchcraft, The: Politics and the Occult in Postcolonial Africa

669   monothéisme chrétien, Le

963   Montfortians in Malawi: Their Spirituality and Pastoral Approach

753   Moral and Ethical Issues in African Christianity

954   Mort et espérance selon la Bible hébraïque

774   Mosques in Kenya: Muslim Opinions on Religion, Politics and Development

1028   Moving into African Music

60   Moya: The Holy Spirit in an African Context

730   Multi-Church Pastor, The: A Manual for Training Leadership in a Multi-Church Setting

984   Multiplying Light and Truth through Community Health Evangelism

577   Music in the Life of the African Church

551   Muslim and a Christian in Dialogue, A

971   Muslim Societies in African History

203   Muslim-Christian Dialogue in Nigeria

1059   Muslim-Christian Encounters in Africa

137   Muslims: Why Muslim Sharia Law: Studies in Christian-Mulsim Relations, Volume 6

138   Muslims: Why the Violence?: Studies in Christian-Muslim Relations, Volume 2

139   Muslims: Why We Rejected Secularism

302   My Faith as an African

84   My Neighbour's Faith: Islam Explained for Christians

1022   Mystery or Magic: Biblical Replies to the Heterodox

321   Nationalism and African Intellectuals

444   Ndoki: Trapped in the Web of Witchcraft

33   New Covenant Torah in Jeremiah and the Law of Christ in Paul, The

396   New Crusaders, The: Christianity and the New Right in Southern Africa

49   New Day, A: Essays on World Christianity in Honor of Lamin Sanneh

397   New Dimensions in African Christianity

715   New Encyclopedia of Africa: 5 Volume Set

932   New Eyes for Reading: Biblical and Theological Reflections by Women from the Third World

519   New Faces of Christianity, The: Believing the Bible in the Global South

1133   New Look at Christianity in Africa, A: Essays on Apartheid, African Education, and a New History

1045   New Religious Movements in Africa

764   New Testament, The: The African Bible

213   New Trends and Developments in African Religions

227   Ngugi wa Thiong'o: An Exploration of His Writings

174   Nigeria's Christian Revolution: The Civil War Revival and Its Pentecostal Progeny (1967–2006)

140   Nigeria's Decades of Blood 1980–2002: Studies in Christian-Muslim Relations, Volume 1

1140   Nigerians Engaged in Mission Work Today

571   No Cross Marks the Spot

1110   No Future without Forgiveness

196   No Life of My Own: An Autobiography

606   No Quick Fixes: The Challenge of Mission in a Changing South Africa

277   Non-Bourgeois Theology: An African Experience of Jesus

601   Nos Racines Racontées: Récits historiques sur l'Eglise en Afrique de l'Ouest

632   Not Out of Africa: How Afrocentrism Became an Excuse to Teach Myth as History

127   Nouveau Testament: Introduction, texte et contexte

822   Number Two to Tutu: A Memoir

721   Obedience of Faith, the Eschatological People of God, and the Purpose of Romans, The

579   Offerings from Kenya to Anglicanism: Liturgical Texts and Contexts Including 'A Kenyan Service of Holy Communion'

251   Old and New in Southern Shona Independent Churches

479   Old Testament Research for Africa: A Critical Analysis and Annotated Bibliography of African Old Testament Dissertations, 1967–2000

312   On Being a Muslim: Finding a Religious Path in the World Today

851   On Communitarian Divinity: An African Interpretation of the Trinity

1015   On Their Way Rejoicing: The History and Role of the Bible in Africa

111   One New Humanity: The Challenge of AIDS

339   Oppression and Liberation of Modern Africa, The

987   Ordinary Man, An: The True Story behind Hotel Rwanda

323   Origins of the New Churches Movement in Southern Ethiopia, 1927-1944, The

286   Other Ways of Reading: African Women and the Bible

663   Our Kind of Polygamy

64   Our Modern Services: Anglican Church of Kenya 2002

693   Our Time Has Come: African Christian Women Address the Issues of Today

965   Out of America: A Black Man Confronts Africa

388   Overcoming Apartheid: Can Truth Reconcile a Divided Nation?

52   Overture of the Book of Consolations (Isaiah 40:1–11), The

455   Oxford Guide to the Book of Common Prayer: A Worldwide Survey, The: A Worldwide Survey

1196   Pan-African Theology, A: Providence and the Legacies of the Ancestors

741   Parables and Fables: Exegesis, Textuality, and Politics in Central Africa

525   Parole se fait chair et sang, La: Lectures de la Bible dans le contexte africain

805   Partnership in God's Mission in Africa Today: The Papers and Reports of the Consultation of African Women and Men of Reformed Tradition, 9-15 March 1994, Limuru, Kenya

188   Passing Summer, The: A South African Pilgrimage in the Politics of Love

623   Pastor: A Practical Guide for Church Leaders

677   Pastoral Care and Counseling in Africa Today

1155   Pastoral Care in African Christianity: Challenging Essays in Pastoral Theology

121   Pastoral Care to the Sick in Africa: An Approach to Transcultural Pastoral Theology

644   Pastoral Counseling: A Comprehensive Text for Pastors, Counselors, Teachers

627   Pastoral Counseling in Inter-Cultural Perspective: A Study of Some African (Ghanaian) and Anglo-American Views on Human Existence and Counseling

961   Pastors, Partners and Paternalists: African Church Leaders and Western Missionaries in the Anglican Church in Kenya, 1850-1900

387   Paths of African Theology

483   Patterns of Thought in Africa and the West: Essays on Magic, Religion and Science

1118   Paul and Power Christology: Exegesis and Theology of Romans 1:3-4 in Relation to Popular Power Christology in an African Context

784   Paul's Concept of Charisma in 1 Corinthians 12: With Emphasis on Nigerian Charismatic Movement

366   Pauline Concept of Supernatural Powers, The: A Reading from the African Worldview

353   Pentateuch, The: Foundation of God's Message to the World

871   Pentecostal Exorcism: Witchcraft and Demonology in Ghana

709   People Betrayed, A: The Role of the West in Rwanda's Genocide

933   Persecution and Martyrdom in the Theology of Paul

427   Perspectives in African Theology

553   Perspectives of an African Theologian: The Writings of Byang H. Kato Th.D.

926   Perspectives on Church History: An Introduction for South African Readers

219   Perspectives on Leadership Training

759   Philemon: Fellowship in God's Family

133   Philosophy in Africa: Trends and Perspectives

1007   Piety and Power: Muslims and Christians in West Africa

879   Pioneers in the East African Revival

333   Place of Songs, The: A History of the World Gospel Mission and the Africa Gospel Church in Kenya

598   Poétique et traduction biblique: Les récits de la Genèse dans le système littéraire sango

675   Political Spiritualities: The Pentecostal Revolution in Nigeria

697   Politics and Christianity in Malawi: 1875-1940: The Impact of the Livingstonia Mission in the Northern Province

189   Politics of Love, The: Choosing the Christian Way in a Changing South Africa

363   Polygamy: A Cultural and Biblical Perspective

93   Poor Economics: A Radical Rethinking of the Way to Fight Global Poverty

359   Portrait of a Saint, A: The Life and Times of Pa Yohanna Gowon (d. 1973)

287   Postcolonial Feminist Interpretation of the Bible

1167   Postcolonial Identities in Africa

1191   Pour la nouvelle théologie des femmes africaines: Repenser la différence sexuelle, promouvoir les droits des femmes et libérer leurs énergies créatives

574   Poverty in the Book of Proverbs: An African Transformational Hermeneutic of Proverbs on Poverty

538   Power, Poverty and Prayer: The Challenges of Poverty and Pluralism in African Christianity, 1960-1996

322   Powers in Encounter With Power: Spiritual Warfare in Pagan Cultures

1014   Practice of Presence, The: Shorter Writings of Harry Sawyerr

106   Prayer in an African Context

28   Preachers of a Different Gospel: A Pilgrim's Reflections on Contemporary Trends in Christianity

613   Preaching & Cultural Identity: Proclaiming the Gospel in Africa

1165   Preaching That Grips the Heart: A Rhetorical-Stylistic Study of the Chichewa Revival Sermons of Shadrack Wame

950   Pride, Faith, and Fear: Islam in Sub-Saharan Africa

308   Problem of Presence, A: Beyond Scripture in an African Church

545   Problems and Promises of Africa: Towards and Beyond the Year 2000: A summary of the proceedings of the symposium convened by the AACC in Mombasa in November, 1991: A proposal for reflection

1115 Proclaiming the Kingdom: Essays in Contextual New Testament Studies

1033 Prophet Harris, The 'Black Elijah' of West Africa

876 Prophets as Social Critics: The Role of Prophets in Nation Building

57 Proselytization and Communal Self-Determination in Africa

531 Psalms: An Introduction to Their Poetry, The: An Introduction to Their Poetry

848 Psalms of Satan, The

324 Psychology of Adult Learning in Africa, The

703 Quand Dieu a parlé... au Nigeria: Une traductrice de la Bible raconte

943 Quand la parole de Dieu visite l'Afrique: Lecture plurielle de la Bible

252 Quest for Belonging: Introduction to a Study of African Independent Churches

130 Quest for Power: Guidelines for Communicating the Gospel to Animists

763 Quest for the Ark of the Covenant: The True History of the Tablets of Moses, The: The True History of the Tablets of Moses

1193 Quiet Wise Spirit, The: Edwin W. Smith (1876-1957) and Africa

313 Qur'an, The: A Short Introduction

206 Rabai to Mumias: A Short History of the Church of the Province of Kenya, 1844-1994

1111 Rainbow People of God, The: South Africa's Victory over Apartheid

318 Re-imagining African Christologies: Conversing with the Interpretations and Appropriations of Jesus in Contemporary African Christianity

941 Re-Imagining Rwanda: Conflict, Survival and Disinformation in the Late Twentieth Century

1112 Re-thinking the Day of YHWH and Restoration of Fortunes in the Prophet Zephaniah: An Exegetical and Theological Study of 1:14-18; 3:14-20

1013 Reaching the Unreached Sudan Belt: Guinness, Kumm and the Sudan-Pioneer-Mission

904 Reader in African Christian Theology, A

24 Reading and Interpreting the Bible in African Indigenous Churches

94 Reading Biblical Hebrew: A Grammar and Basic Lexicon

776 Reading Race, Reading the Bible

420 Reading Romans at Ground Level: A Contemporary Rural African Perspective

1116 Reading the Bible in the Global Village: Cape Town

1173 "Reading With": Africa Overtures

619 Realm of the Word, The: Language, Gender and Christianity in a Southern African Kingdom

839 Rebirth of African Orthodoxy, The: Return to Foundations

104 Reconciliation: The Ubuntu Theology of Desmond Tutu

259 Reconciliation: Restoring Justice

732 Réconciliation: Gage pour la reconstruction

557 Reconciling All Things: A Christian Vision for Justice, Peace and Healing

269 Reconstruction and Renewal in African Christian Theology

517 Recovery of the West African Past: , The: African Pastors and African History in the Nineteenth Century, C.C. Reindorf & Samuel Johnson

276	Redefining Success: Exchanging Bondage for Blessings
506	Rediscovering and Fostering Unity in the Body of Christ: The Nigerian Experience
570	Réforme du Culte, La: Une nécessité pour les églises d'Afrique
905	Reinventing Christianity: African Theology Today
19	Religion & Government in Africa: A Christian Response
548	Religion and African Civil Wars
445	Religion and Conflict in Sudan: Papers from an International Conference at Yale, May 1999
451	Religion and Politics in Africa
934	Religion and Politics in Ghana
590	Religion and Politics in Kenya: Essays in Honor of a Meddlesome Priest
549	Religion and Politics in Nigeria: A Study in Middle Belt Christianity
15	Religion and Politics in Nigeria
155	Religion and Society: A Textbook for Africa
1021	Religion and the Dramatisation of Life: Spirit Beliefs and Rituals in Southern and Central Malawi
1008	Religion and the Variety of Culture: A Study in Origin and Practice
129	Religion in Africa: Experience and Expression
193	Religion in Malawi: An Annotated Bibliography
3	Religion of the Exile, The
913	Religion, Development and African Identity
608	Religion, Politics and Power in Northern Nigeria
433	Religious Communities in the Diaspora
411	Religious Conflicts in Northern Nigeria and Nation Building: The Throes of Two Decades 1980-2000
911	Religious Encounter and the Making of the Yoruba
1183	Religious Impact on the Nation State: The Nigerian Predicament
486	Religious Itinerary of a Ghanaian People, The: The Kasena and the Christian Gospel
867	Religious Plurality in Africa: Essays in Honour of John S. Mbiti
508	Religious Traditions of Africa: A History, The: A History
13	Reminiscences of My Life
303	Repenser la théologie africaine: Le Dieu qui libère
785	Resistant Peoples: The Case of the Pastoral Maasai of East Africa
405	Responsible Church Leadership
293	Restoring Life in Christ: Dialogues of Care in Christian Communities: An African Perspective
592	Rethinking Life: What the Church Can Learn from Africa
639	Return to Babel: Global Perspectives on the Bible
62	Revealing Prophets: Prophecy in Eastern African History
294	Revolution and Religion in Ethiopia: The Growth and Persecution of the Mekane Yesus Church, 1974-1985
757	Rewriting the Bible: The Real Issues
642	Rise and Fall of Development Theory, The

97   Rise Up and Walk!: Conciliarism and the African Indigenous Churches, 1815-1987

678   Risks of Growth, The: Counselling and Pastoral Theology in the African Context

921   Role of Christianity in Development, Peace and Reconstruction, The

274   Role of Mass Media for the Pastoral Development of the Catholic Church in Nigeria, The

573   Role of Religious Education in Promoting Christian-Muslim Dialogue in Africa, The

386   Role of the Church in Advocacy, The: Case Studies from Southern and Eastern Africa

629   Rough Road to Dynamism: Bible Translating in Northern Namibia, 1954-1987: Kwanyama, Kwangali and Ngonga

39   Rwanda: Death, Despair, and Defiance

424   Rwanda: The Land God Forgot? Revival, Genocide and Hope

631   Rwanda: A Walk through Darkness into Light

887   Rwanda: Un peuple avec une histoire

948   Rwanda Crisis, The: History of a Genocide

558   Sacrifice of Africa: A Political Theology for Africa, The: A Political Theology for Africa

54   Saint Justin de Jacobis: His Missionary Methodology in Eritrea and Ethiopia

679   Saint-Esprit interroge les esprits, Le: Essai de relecture et pistes psychopastorales de la spiritualité en Afrique: Cas de la République Démocratique du Congo

38   Salvation in African Tradition

692   Same Gender Unions: A Critical Analysis

267   Samuel Ajayi Crowther: Un père de l'Église en Afrique noire

780   Sangaya: A Leader in the Synod of Blantyre Church of Central Africa Presbyterian

311   Saudi Arabia and Ethiopia: Islam, Christianity, and Politics Entwined

446   Schwarz Bin Ich und Schön

896   Scramble for Africa, 1876-1912, The

550   Scriptural Politics: The Bible and the Koran as Political Models in the Middle East and Africa

1046 Secularism in Africa: A Case Study–Nairobi City

1180 Seeds of Conflict: Religious Tensions in Tanzania

162   Seeking an Open Society: Inter-Faith Relations and Dialogue in Sudan Today

718   Seeking Peace in Africa: Stories from African Peacemakers

126   Semeia 78: Reading the Bible as Women: Perspectives from Africa, Asia, and Latin America

716   Separate but the Same Gospel: Preaching in African Instituted Churches in Southern Malawi

297   Servant of Yahweh in Isaiah 52:13-53:12:, The: A Historical Critical and Afro-Cultural Hermeneutical Analysis with the Igalas of Nigeria in View.

1186 Serving with the Poor in Africa

1166 Sewero!: Christian Drama and the Drama of Christianity in Africa

422   Shackled Continent, The: Africa's Past, Present and Future

1101 Sharing Gifts in the Global Family of Faith: One Church's Experiment

399   Sharing the Gospel with Muslims: A Handbook for Bible-Based Muslim Evangelism

849   Shariy'ah Debate in Nigeria, The: October 1999–October 2000

1019   Sharpening of Wisdom, The: Old Testament Proverbs in Translation

98   Short History of African Philosophy, A

1099   Sidama and Ethiopian: The Emergence of the Mekane Yesus Church in Sidama

628   Sierra Leone 1787–1987: Two Centuries of Intellectual Life

71   Sighs and Signs of the Spirit: Ghanaian Perspectives on Pentecostalism and Renewal in Africa

199   Singing Culture: A Study of Gospel Music in Zimbabwe

935   Skenosis: Christian Faith in an African Context

779   Slave: My True Story

487   Slave Trade and Reconciliation, The: A Northern Ghanaian Perspective

670   Slavery and African Life: Occidental, Oriental, and African Slave Trades

414   Slavery in the Arab World

334   Slavery in the History of Muslim Black Africa

650   Slow Death for Slavery: The Course of Abolition in Northern Nigeria, 1897–1936

284   Socio-Political Agenda for the Twenty-First Century Zimbabwe Church, A: Empowering the Excluded

826   Some Contemporary Models of African Ecclesiology: A Critical Assessment in the Light of Biblical and Church Teaching

91   Songs of Tesfaye Gabbiso

325   Soteriology: An African Outlook

233   Sound of the Harvest, The: Music's Mission in Church and Culture

344   South African Christian Handbook 1999-2000

914   South African Perspective on the New Testament, A: Essays by South African New Testament Scholars Presented to Bruce Manning Metzger during His Visit to South Africa in 1985

1   Special Pastoral Formation for Youths in Africa in the 21st Century: The Nigerian Perspective: With Extra Focus on the Socio-Anthropological, Ethical, Theological, Psychological and Societal Problems of Today's Youngsters

434   Spirit of Africa: The Healing Ministry of Archbishop Milingo of Zambia

118   Spirit Possession: Modernity and Power in Africa

443   Spiritual in the Secular: Missionaries and Knowledge about Africa, The: Missionaries and Knowledge about Africa

770   Spiritualité et libération en Afrique

901   Spirituality of African Peoples, The: The Search for a Common Moral Discourse

516   Stanley: The Impossible Life of Africa's Greatest Explorer

110   State in Africa, The: The Politics of the Belly

710   State of Africa: A History of Fifty Years of Independence , The: A History of Fifty Years of Independence

612   State, Civil Society and Apartheid in South Africa: An Examination of Dutch Reformed Church-State Relations

463   States and Power in Africa: Comparative Lessons in Authority and Control

329   Story of Faith Missions, The: From Hudson Taylor to Present Day Africa

1047   Street Children in Africa: A Nairobi Case Study

607   Striving in Faith: Christians and Muslims in Africa

181 Stronger than Death: Reading David's Rise for Third Millennium

99 Struggling to be Heard: The Christian Voice in Independent Sudan 1956-1996

827 Studies in African Christian Theology, Volume 1: Jesus Christ, the Ancestor of Humankind: Methodological and Trinitarian Foundations

828 Studies in African Christian Theology, Volume 2: Jesus Christ, the Ancestor of Humankind: An Essay on African Christology

336 Studies in Old Testament Prophecy

1149 Study of Conversion among the Angas of Plateau State of Nigeria with Emphasis on Christianity, A

997 Study of Current Leadership Styles in the North African Church, A

1055 Study of Religion in Southern Africa: Essays in Honour of G. C. Oosthuizen

460 Studying Congregations in Africa

840 Successful Family Living

253 Suffering and God: A Theological Reflection on the War in Sudan, Faith in Sudan series, 13

681 Suffering, Belief and Hope: The Wisdom of Job in an AIDS-Stricken Africa

1009 Summoned from the Margin: Homecoming of an African

186 Surprised by Laughter: Some Good News out of Africa

242 Surviving Without Romance: African Women Tell Their Stories

345 Swaziland Christian Handbook 1994

654 Sword and Scalpel: A Surgeon's Story of Faith and Courage

477 T.E.E. Study Materials—Which Way for a Changing Africa?

1105 Tainted Legacy: Islam, Colonialism and Slavery in Northern Nigeria

436 Teatime in Mogadishu: My Journey as a Peace Ambassador in the World of Islam

708 Ten African Heroes: The Sweep of Independence in Black Africa

1181 Tertullian the African: An Anthropological Reading of Tertullian's Context and Identities

754 Text and Context in New Testament Hermeneutics

1067 Textbooks for Theological Education in Africa: An Annotated Bibliography

796 The Bible in Ethiopia: The Book of Acts

510 The Future of Christian Marriage among the Igbo vis-à-vis Childlessness: A Canonical cum Pastoral Study of Canon 1055 par.1

674 Their Blood Cries Out: The Untold Story of Persecution against Christians in the Modern World

653 Theological Education in Africa: An Annotated Bibliography

635 Theological Education in Contemporary Africa

207 Theological Education That Makes a Difference: Church Growth in the Free Methodist Church in Malawi and Zimbabwe

384 Theological Method and Aspects of Worship in African Christianity

1097 Theological Task of the Church in Africa, The

900 théologie africaine face au syncrétisme, La

275 Théologie et cultures: Mélanges offerts à Mgr Alfred Vanneste

152 théologie pratique en milieu africain, La: Ouvrage d'enseignement dans les Facultés et Instituts de théologie

771   Théologie, Libération et Culture africaines: Dialogue sur l'anthropologie négro-africaine

194   Théologiens et théologiennes dans l'Afrique d'aujourd'hui

115   Theology and Identity: The Impact of Culture upon Christian Thought in the Second Century and in
       Modern Africa

260   Theology and Ministry in Context and Crisis: A South African Perspective

1139   Theology and Violence: The South African Debate

877   Theology Brewed in an African Pot

330   Theology Cooked in an African Pot

1085   Theology in the Context of World Christianity: How the Global Church Is Influencing the Way We Think
       about and Discuss Theology

385   Theology of Reconstruction: Exploratory Essays

898   Theology of the New Testament, A

899   Theology of the Old Testament, A

14   Theology on the Tyume

1184   There's a Snake in My Cupboard!: The Continuing Story of Kiwoko Hospital, Luwero, Uganda

888   They Called Him Mallam: The Biography of Joseph Ummel, a Pioneer Missionary to Northern Nigeria,
       West Africa

484   They Loved Their Enemies: True Stories of African Christians

1071   Thinking Communally, Acting Personally: Rank and File Christians in an Age of Mega- and Macro-
       Institutions

243   'Through Many Tribulations': The Theology of Persecution in Luke-Acts

488   Time to Mourn, A: A Personal Account of the 1964 Lumpa Church Revolt in Zambia

578   Time to Sing, A: A Manual for the African Church

175   Times of Refreshing: Revival and the History of Christianity in Africa

338   To Africa with Love: A Bush Doc's Story

151   To Remember and to Heal: Theological and Psychological Reflections on Truth and Reconciliation

493   To the Ends of the Earth: The Globalization of Christianity

222   Tonga Religious Life in the Twentieth Century

1091   Touching the Heart: Xhosa Missionaries to Malawi, 1876 – 1888

695   Tough Tests for Top Leaders: God's Strategy for Preparing Africans to Lead Global Christianity

1048   Toward a Theology of Inculturation

1049   Towards African Christian Maturity

468   Towards an African Christianity: Inculturation Applied

454   Towards an African Narrative Theology

857   Towards an African Theology: The Igbo Context in Nigeria

122   Towards Theory and Practice of Pastoral Counseling in Africa

936   Towards Viable Theological Education: Ecumenical Imperative, Catalyst of Renewal

428   Tradition and Modernity: Philosophical Reflections on the African Experience

1001   tradition et la Bible chez la femme de la CEZ , La: Influence de l'ancienne culture et de la pensée biblique dans le maintien d'une certaine conception de la femme au sein de la Communauté évangélique du Zaïre

907   Traditional Egyptian Christianity: A History of the Coptic Orthodox Church

616   Traditionelle Religion und christlicher Glaube: Widerspruch und Wandel

1076   Training for Godliness in African Theological Education

75   Training God's Servants: A Compendium

1093   Training TEE Leaders

602   Trans-Saharan Book Trade: Manuscript Culture, Arabic Literacy and Intellectual History in Muslim Africa, The: Manuscript Culture, Arabic Literacy and Intellectual History in Muslim Africa

45   Transference of the Three Mediating Institutions of Salvation from Caiaphas to Jesus, The: A Study of Jn 11:45-54 in the Light of the Akan Myth of the Crossing of a River

945   Transfigured Night: Mission and Culture in Zimbabwe's Vigil Movement

594   Transformation of African Christianity, The: Development and Change in the Nigerian Church

651   Transformations in Slavery: A History of Slavery in Africa

1127   Transformed by the Renewing of Your Mind: Shaping a Biblical Worldview and a Christian Perspective on Scholarship

296   Transforming Culture: Developing a Biblical Ethic in an African Context

150   Transforming Mission: Paradigm Shifts in Theology of Mission

1128   Transforming Power: Challenging Contemporary Secular Society

589   Translating the Bible: The Ethiopic Version of the Old Testament

1010   Translating the Message: The Missionary Impact on Culture

645   Translation and Interculturality: Africa and the West

470   Transmettre la Bible: Une critique exégétique de la traduction de l'AT: le cas du Rwanda

835   Trends and Issues in African Philosophy

1106   Tribal Gods of Africa: Ethnicity, Racism, Tribalism and the Gospel of Christ

166   Tribalism and Ethnicity / Tribalisme et Ethnicité

153   Tribalisme en Afrique , Le: et si on en parlait?

326   Triumph of Christ in African Perspective, The: A Study of Demonology and Redemption in the African Context

154   Trois mariages pour un couple

480   Tropical Africa and the Old Testament: A Select and Annotated Bibliography

78   Trouble with the Congo, The: Local Violence and the Failure of International Peacebuilding

406   Troubled but Not Destroyed: The Autobiography of Archbishop David Gitari, Retired Archbishop of the Anglican Church of Kenya

417   Truth and Reconciliation in South Africa: Miracle or Model?

596   Truths for Healthy Churches

1029   Tuning in to a Different Song: Using a Music Bridge to Cross Cultural Differences

821   Turner Collection on Religious Movements 1492-1992: Index to the Microfiche, Volume 2: Africa

1050   Two Centuries of Christianity in an African Province of Freedom: Sierra Leone: A Case Study of European Influence and Culture in Church Development.

704   Two Thousand Years of Coptic Christianity

56   Unbroken Circle, The: Linking Ancient African Christianity to the African-American Experience

706   Unbroken Covenant with God

272   Uncompleted Mission: Christianity and Exclusivism

180   Under African Skies: Reflections on Advent and Christmas

1129   Understanding and Rebuilding Africa: From Desperation Today Towards Expectation for Tomorrow

413   Understanding Contemporary Africa

464   Understanding Folk Religion: A Christian Response to Popular Beliefs and Practices

515   Understanding Leadership: An African Christian Model

95   Understanding the Old Testament: An Introduction and Theological Overview

178   Understanding World Christianity: The Vision and Work of Andrew F. Walls

238   Uniquely African?: African Christian Identity from Cultural and Historical Perspectives

526   unité littéraire du livre de Baruch, L'

937   Variations in Christian Theology in Africa

42   Vers une doctrine biblique et évangélique sur Marie

53   Vine, Israel and the Church, The

1150   Violence against Women: Reflections by Kenyan Women Theologians

116   vocation du prophete des nations, La: Une lecture africaine de Jr 1,4-19

604   Voice of Black Theology in South Africa, The

1179   Voices from Africa: Transforming Mission in a Context of Marginalization

1197   Voices from Kumba: Theological Reflections for Cameroon, Africa, and the World. Celebrating 50 Years Presbyterian Theological Seminary, Kumba

881   Wanted: Servant Leaders: The Challenge of Christian Leadership in Africa Today

712   War and Faith in Sudan

204   War Within, The: Christians and Inner Conflicts

1199   Warrior Princess: Fighting for Life with Courage and Hope

702   Warriors of Ethiopia: Ethiopian National Missionaries: Heroes of the Gospel in the Omo River Valley

696   We Believe: An Introduction to Christian Doctrine (Volume 2)

63   We Felt Like Grasshoppers

415   We Wish to Inform You That Tomorrow We Will Be Killed with Our Families: Stories from Rwanda

938   West Africa: Christ Would Be an African Too

214   West Africa and Christianity

43   West African Church History, Volume 1: Christian Missions and Church Foundations 1482-1919

44   West African Church History, Volume 2: Christian Missions and Theological Training 1842-1970

949   West African Traditional Religion

974   What Christians Should Know about Islam

766   What Is Africa's Problem?

714   What Muslims Should Know about Christianity

1130   When African and Western Cultures Meet: From Confrontation to Appreciation

1025   When Charity Destroys Dignity: Overcoming Unhealthy Dependency in the Christian Movement

41   When Evil Strikes: Faith and the Politics of Human Hostility

144   When Spider Webs Unite They Can Tie Up A Lion

103   When Things Fell Apart: State Failure in Late-Century Africa

666   When Victims Become Killers: Colonialism, Nativism, and the Genocide in Rwanda

375   Who Are the Living Dead?

939   Who Are the Poor?: Beatitudes as a Call to Community

845   Who Will Roll the Stone Away?: The Ecumenical Decade of the Churches in Solidarity with Women

1011   Whose Religion Is Christianity?: The Gospel beyond the West

1176   Why Christians Disagree When They Interpret the Bible: Finding Unity in Our Loyalty to Scripture

802   Why Haven't You Left?: Letters from the Sudan

247   Widowhood: A Challenge to the Church

962   Widows: The Challenges and the Choices

846   Will to Arise, The: Women, Tradition, and the Church in Africa

917   William Sheppard: Congo's African American Livingstone

617   Witchcraft, Sorcery and Spirit Possession: Pastoral Responses in Africa

74   Witchcraft, Violence, and Democracy in South Africa

190   Witness Forever, A: The Dawning of Democracy in South Africa: Stories Behind the Story

101   Witnessing in the Acts of the Apostles: A Study of the Communication Strategies and Their Relevance to the Evangelization of Africans Today with Particular Reference to the Efik/Ibibio People of Nigeria

407   Witnessing to the Living God in Contemporary Africa

90   Wolaitta Evangelists: A Study of Religious Innovation in Southern Ethiopia, 1937–1975

694   Woman, Who Are You?: A Challenge

17   Women Hold Up Half the Sky: Women in the Church in Southern Africa

564   Women, Culture and Theological Education

922   Women, Presbyterianism and Patriarchy: Religious Experience of Chewa Women in Central Malawi

471   Women, Religion and HIV/AIDS in Africa: Responding to Ethical and Theological Challenges

197   Women's Ministry in the Church: An African Perspective

364   Wonders of the African World

337   Word of God in Ethiopian Tongues, The: Rhetorical Features in the Preaching of the Ethiopian Evangelical Church Mekane Yesus

346   World Christianity: South Central Africa

347   World Christianity: Southern Africa: A Factual Portrait of the Christian Church in South Africa, Botswana, Lesotho, Namibia and Swaziland

410   World of Islam, The: Resources for Understanding

705   World of Religions, A: A South African Perspective

729   World of the Spirits, The: A Biblical Study in the African Context

306   Worlds of Power: Religious Thought and Political Practice in Africa

1121   Worship as Body Language: Introduction to Christian Worship: An African Orientation

481   Yahweh in Africa: Essays on Africa and the Old Testament

834   Yahweh My Refuge: A Critical Analysis of Psalm 71

354   You Can Learn New Testament Greek

775   Young Lives at Risk

733   Zimbabwe: The Risk of Incarnation

1136   Zimbabwean Realities and Christian Responses: Contemporary Aspects of Christianity in Zimbabwe

61   Zion and Pentecost: The Spirituality and Experience of Pentecostal and Zionist/Apostolic Churches in South Africa

985   Zion City RSA: The Story of the Church in South Africa

Subject Index

Note: The numbers attached to each subject entry below indicate the reference numbers of the relevant reviews, *not* page numbers.

A

AACC, 198, 544–545, 750, 1153

Adeyemo, Tokunboh, 19, 160, 219, 1064

AEA, 75, 197, 263, 543, 552–553, 693

Africa and the West, 16, 73, 79, 170, 238, 254, 271, 339, 416, 429–431, 433, 447, 466, 520, 592, 645, 709, 748, 812, 896, 967, 1017, 1046

Africa Inland Church, 221, 465, 955, 1088

Africa Inland Mission, 63, 1028

Africa, academic study of, 102, 320, 443, 483, 967

Africa, and global Christianity, 178, 273, 289–290, 466, 639, 909, 1003, 1005, 1085, 1120, 1134, 1147

Africa, general reference, 66, 245, 364, 368, 410, 413, 715, 1084

Africa, in the Bible, 20–21, 23, 481, 1188

Africa, modern, assessment, 73, 79, 81–82, 103, 109–110, 124, 183, 191, 220, 231, 254, 271, 304, 306, 309, 327, 341–342, 413, 422, 441, 463, 538, 544, 582, 637, 662, 665, 710, 766, 869, 908, 952, 965, 1024, 1119, 1124, 1129–1130, 1153, 1185

Africa, modern, politics, 81–82, 109–110, 191, 306, 309, 492, 661, 665, 710, 1052, 1124

African archaeology, 1187

African archaeology, Christian, 331, 1160

African archaeology, Islamic, 504

African Christianity, modern, 997

African diaspora, 72, 491, 636, 901, 969, 1196

African diaspora, Christian, 56, 377, 429–430, 433, 1051, 1157

African Enterprise, 187, 228, 423

African identity, 36, 179, 238, 561, 632, 636, 680, 726, 739–741, 771, 806, 913, 969, 1052, 1167

African Initiated/Independent/Indigenous Churches, 24, 59–61, 69, 80, 210, 244, 248–252, 264, 308, 330, 397, 488, 512, 587, 616, 641, 684, 716, 746, 758, 821, 872–875, 883, 928, 957, 1032, 1034, 1064, 1132

African intellectual life, 72, 321, 467, 561, 602, 680, 726, 739, 740–741, 749, 980, 1081, 1161, 1167

African literature, 65, 227, 358, 749

African literature, oral, 453–454, 1041

African Theology, 4, 104, 112–113, 168–169, 194, 216, 226, 269, 275, 286–287, 290, 292, 317–318, 355, 385, 387, 502, 530, 554, 581, 667–668, 676, 726, 742, 745, 768, 814, 826–828, 830, 841, 851, 900, 903–905, 1014, 1031, 1053, 1073, 1113, 1123, 1151, 1175, 1194–1195

African Traditional Religion, 38, 62, 92, 112–114, 117–118, 130, 185, 222, 244, 248, 299, 305–306, 326, 330, 332, 352, 366, 371–372, 378, 400, 418, 444, 464, 483, 498, 559, 576, 585, 592–593, 658–659, 669, 682, 691, 729, 747, 768, 827–830, 851, 862, 865, 901, 946, 949, 1014, 1021, 1031, 1039, 1064, 1072, 1094, 1103, 1166, 1175. *See also* culture, African traditional

Afrocentrism, 20–21, 632, 969

afterlife, death. *See* death, afterlife

aid, development. *See* development aid

AIDS in Africa, 88, 96, 111, 211, 280–281, 285, 362, 421, 500, 563, 681, 809, 972, 991, 1102, 1199

AIDS, Christian response to, 88, 111, 211, 280–281, 285, 362, 471, 563, 798, 870, 972, 991, 1199 ancestor veneration, 112, 317, 330, 375, 814, 825, 827–828, 860, 1021, 1123

Anglicanism, 58, 64, 182, 206, 283, 402–403, 405–406, 447, 455, 546–547, 560, 579, 588, 623, 692, 802–803, 822, 861, 911, 961, 1014, 1077, 1083, 1179

Angola, 68, 444, 459, 566, 654, 1092

anthropology. *See* ethnology *and also* humanity, in theological perspective

Apartheid, South African, 131, 187–188, 190, 217, 255, 258, 289, 425, 440, 612, 648, 788, 808, 818, 1061, 1098, 1110–1111, 1133, 1138–1139, 1146, 1159. *See also* South Africa

Aquinas, Thomas, 171–172, 772

art, African, 68, 435, 884, 1166

B

Balokole Revival Movement. *See* East African Revival

Baptist, 462, 988, 1159

Bediako, Kwame, 77, 269, 289, 1015

Benin, 457

Bible study, group, 360, 1088, 1170, 1173

Bible translation, 298, 469, 589, 598, 629, 645, 647, 703, 725, 764, 778, 796, 912, 1006, 1010, 1015, 1019, 1072, 1161–1164, 1192

Bible, in Africa, 22, 24, 47, 105, 179, 286–287, 298, 308, 322, 335–336, 382, 426–427, 478–481, 519, 583–584, 647, 672, 690, 731, 757, 761, 764, 796, 880, 895, 943, 999, 1010, 1015, 1063, 1171, 1188, 1192

Bible, interpretation, 22–24, 126, 236, 273, 382–383, 524–525, 532, 583, 615, 634, 639, 672, 754, 761, 776, 813, 909, 932, 939, 999, 1063, 1082, 1170–1173, 1176, 1188. *See also* hermeneutics

biblical languages, Greek, 354

biblical languages, Hebrew, 94

biblical studies, 33–34, 452, 1157. *See also* OT studies *and* NT studies

bibliography, 193, 195, 216, 226, 244, 472, 476, 479–480, 653, 820–821, 847, 867, 1067, 1171, 1194

biography, 161, 184, 283, 368, 499, 516, 708, 879, 951, 987, 1090

biography, African Christian, 13, 100, 104, 142–143, 196, 200, 228–229, 246, 263, 267, 349, 359, 361, 406, 436, 440, 547, 706, 717, 723, 780, 782, 810,

852, 861, 867–868, 951, 990, 992–994, 996, 1009, 1033, 1078, 1177, 1179, 1199

biography, missionary, 144, 182, 186, 291, 338, 340, 348, 424, 437–438, 462, 475, 511, 521, 565, 571, 620, 654, 656, 664, 703, 719–720, 762, 802, 888, 893, 906, 917, 924, 976–977, 1013, 1016, 1030, 1062, 1156, 1177, 1184, 1193

Black Theology (South African), 604, 731, 937, 1133, 1194–1195

Bosch, David, 119, 605, 994

Botswana, 619

Bujo, Benezet, 317

Burundi, 633

C

Cameroon, 300, 302–303, 418, 462, 1159, 1197

Cassidy, Michael, 228

celibacy, 1040

Central African Republic, 598

charismatic Christianity, 60, 69, 174–175, 234, 377, 395, 397, 784, 854, 957, 1045, 1089, 1122. *See also* Pentecostalism

Chikane, Frank, 196

child abuse, 775

child care, 27, 638

children, 510, 638, 699

children, street, 1047

China, 341

Christian Education, 165, 643. *See also* discipling, discipleship

Christian life, 204, 276, 735, 829

Christianity and culture, 35, 92, 113–114, 154, 170, 178, 194, 277, 290, 292, 296, 310, 363, 371–372, 387, 444, 446, 464, 468, 485, 496, 533, 545, 566–567, 577, 585, 592, 618, 624, 626, 659–660, 682, 700, 733, 736, 742, 743, 771, 807, 814, 858, 862, 880, 884, 911, 938, 945, 964, 1010, 1022, 1041, 1044, 1053, 1103, 1121, 1129, 1144, 1164, 1166, 1178, 1182, 1191, 1197. *See also* contextualization

Christianity and Islam, 40–41, 49, 57, 76, 83–84, 99, 134–140, 145, 162, 173, 203, 311–312, 369, 399, 411, 445, 472, 550–551, 573, 607–608, 689, 714, 773, 786, 847, 849, 890, 958, 974, 1007, 1059, 1069, 1180, 1183

Christianity, in Africa, 49, 80, 119, 195, 344–347, 356, 493, 535, 545, 622, 646, 690, 748–749, 902, 919, 1003, 1005, 1011, 1086, 1134, 1148

Christianity, post-western, 1011

Christology, 10, 210, 264, 317–318, 326, 529, 671, 752, 755, 772, 825, 827–828, 929, 1023, 1074, 1113, 1118, 1142, 1189–1190, 1198

church history. *See* history, African Christianity

Church Missionary Society, 206, 267, 439, 878, 893, 911

church-mission relationships, 261, 1104, 1114

church-state relationships, 36, 148, 404–405, 458, 612, 619, 816, 824, 930, 968, 1020

church, doctrine of the. *See* ecclesiology

civil war, 78, 253, 305, 548, 633, 787, 794, 947, 1068, 1107

colonialism, 254, 339, 416, 474, 488, 516, 650, 665–666, 758, 896, 1057, 1066, 1075, 1081, 1105, 1117

commentary, 34, 909

communications, religious, 101, 274, 521, 882, 915, 1082

community vs individualism, 1071

comparative religions, 705, 747, 800

conflict, 380–381, 548, 947, 1037, 1107

conflict resolution, 78, 522, 607, 689, 718, 732, 787, 983, 1037

conflict, ethnic. *See* ethnic conflict

conflict, religious. *See* religious conflict

Congo (Brazzaville), 1070

Congo (DRC), 58, 78, 474, 527–528, 633, 679, 694, 726, 732, 787, 917, 947, 1068, 1070, 1083, 1107, 1185

conscience, 989

contextualization, 10, 45, 61, 64, 112, 167, 172, 216, 261, 273, 326, 330, 360, 366, 373, 384, 390, 402, 409, 453–455, 525, 528, 530, 552–553, 570, 578–579, 581, 593, 610, 634, 639, 646, 660, 667, 677–678, 690, 727, 737, 752, 754, 761, 825, 855, 857–858, 877, 909, 932, 935, 956, 1018, 1023, 1048, 1141, 1144, 1172, 1189, 1198. *See also* Christianity and culture

conversion, 185, 369, 611, 785, 855, 1149

Coptic Orthodox Church, Egypt, 704, 907

corruption, 7, 309, 342, 394

counselling, 121, 389, 626, 644

counselling, pastoral, 121–122, 293, 389, 418, 617, 625–627, 644, 677–678, 775, 1026, 1154–1155

Creation, theology of, 355

cross-cultural adjustment, 315, 673, 966

Crowther, Samuel, 267, 685, 868

culture, African modern, 154, 310, 420, 614, 833, 966, 1042, 1049

culture, African traditional, 50, 247, 279, 332, 357–358, 363, 418, 428, 446, 453, 468, 541–542, 567, 591, 627, 658–660, 663, 665, 667, 681, 713, 733, 735–736, 743, 753, 806–807, 832, 841–844, 846, 935, 945, 962, 964, 1001, 1039, 1041, 1065, 1082, 1106, 1132, 1143, 1150, 1164, 1182

D

dance, liturgical, 539. *See also* worship, Christian

Daneel, Inus, 244

death, afterlife, 375, 954, 964

decolonization, 11

democracy, 5, 189, 256, 392, 661, 750, 818, 955, 981

demonic forces, 299, 322, 326, 366, 679, 871

dependency syndrome, 1025

development aid, 48, 93, 120, 341, 637, 734, 869, 970, 1025, 1071, 1095, 1186

development, economic, 16, 79, 93, 220, 304, 327, 422, 492, 637, 642, 710, 734, 750, 908, 913, 995, 1056, 1071, 1124, 1129, 1131

discipling, discipleship, 374, 514, 618, 799

drama, African Christian, 647, 1166

dreams, 679

E

East African Revival, 424, 592, 657, 815, 878–879, 1034, 1152

eastern Africa, 62, 261, 572, 749, 785, 815, 944, 1069, 1152–1153

ecclesiology, 53, 460, 557, 594, 700, 746, 826

ecology. *See* environment, care for

economics, 183, 787. *See also* development, economic

economics, practical, 673, 819

ecumenism, 250, 506, 746, 845, 928, 1120, 1153, 1158

ECWA, 32, 1104

education, adult, 324

education, Christian, 494

education, general, 1131

EECMY, 13, 67, 266, 294, 337, 419, 630, 1099

EKHC, 89–90, 323, 706, 1078

Ela, Jean-Marc, 269, 387, 558

environment, care for, 244, 248, 408

Episcopal, 288

Eritrea, 54

ethics, African Christian, 51, 167, 172, 226, 296, 555, 609, 735, 753, 953, 1038, 1137

Ethiopia, 13, 54, 67, 89–91, 100, 119, 144, 192, 200, 236, 266, 279, 294, 311, 314, 323, 337, 379, 419, 438, 456, 475, 589, 630, 702, 706, 763, 796, 906, 916, 998, 1030, 1078, 1099

Ethiopian Orthodox Church, 192, 236, 763, 1190

ethnic conflict, 78, 153, 166, 171, 367, 523, 556, 562, 732, 781, 983

ethnicity, 523, 562, 781, 940, 1106

ethnology, 638, 776, 872, 946, 1036, 1039, 1142, 1181

ethnology and religion, 74, 222–223, 308, 409, 444, 464, 483, 486, 512, 576, 728

ethnomusicology, 91, 199, 233, 577–578, 1028–1029

evangelicalism, in Africa, 85, 160, 224, 314, 329, 343, 371–373, 375, 407, 496, 543, 552–553, 593, 603, 609–610, 641, 693, 735, 793, 830, 832–833, 897, 955, 1027, 1097, 1103, 1145, 1176, 1198

evangelism, 57, 90, 101, 130, 200, 369, 514, 580, 1044

exorcism, Christian, 871

F

family, 27, 128, 614, 638, 840, 1087

female genital mutilation (FGM), 357, 567, 1182

feminism, 126, 286–287, 541, 844, 846, 937, 1191

fiction, African Christian, 829

financial management, 569, 817, 819

forgiveness, 522, 1110

fundamentalism, Christian, 524

fundamentalism, Islamic, 85

genocide, Rwandan, 39, 125, 209, 367, 415, 423–424, 499, 522, 556, 631, 666, 688, 698, 709, 941, 948, 968, 986–987. *See also* Rwanda

G

Ghana, 5, 25–26, 69, 71, 77, 114, 210, 395, 486–487, 532, 627, 727, 871, 883, 889, 930, 934

gifts, sharing, 1101

globalization, 537

God, doctrine of, 593, 669, 851, 956, 1064

H

healers, traditional, 434, 649, 875, 1092

health services, 96, 212, 338, 340, 376, 438, 984, 1184

health, healing, 6, 434, 625, 649, 655, 872, 918, 984, 1026, 1154–1155

hermeneutics, 11, 273, 382, 524–525, 532, 584, 600, 615, 639, 672, 731, 754, 756, 1170–1173, 1176. *See also* Bible, interpretation

higher education, African, 46, 321, 494, 505, 1017, 1084

higher education, Christian, 1127

history, African, 184, 320, 473, 489, 501, 507, 517, 602, 640, 812, 886, 959, 971, 973

history, African Christianity, 43–44, 67, 97, 107, 159, 163, 201, 266, 288, 307, 314, 319, 323, 333, 367, 377, 379, 439, 449, 459, 461, 476, 482, 495, 508, 534, 536, 546, 560, 597, 601, 621, 685, 704, 725, 738, 763, 801, 815, 891–892, 907, 910–911, 920–921, 926, 978, 985, 996, 1015, 1035, 1050, 1053, 1077, 1079, 1091, 1099, 1104, 1135, 1141, 1169

history, African Christianity, early, 56, 115, 177, 268, 518, 589, 760, 796, 836–839, 916, 943, 1092, 1160, 1168, 1181

history, African Christianity, modern, 59, 89–90, 158, 160, 169, 174–175, 239, 240, 278, 294, 356, 419, 447, 456, 488, 588, 630, 641, 683, 758, 803, 822, 919, 997, 1034, 1122, 1136

history, African, early, 241, 467, 1187

history, African, modern, 231–232, 254, 265, 305, 321, 339, 474, 516, 628, 633, 687, 708, 710, 766, 788, 889, 896, 948, 1002, 1059, 1068, 1081, 1090

Holy Spirit, 60, 146, 204, 860, 1089

homosexuality, 9, 692

human rights, 50, 57, 386, 824, 1096, 1110

humanity, in theological perspective, 542

hunger, famine, 1095

I

identity, African. *See* African identity

identity, African Christian, 115, 238, 452, 537, 613, 836–838, 883, 1006, 1147–1148, 1157, 1181

Idowu, Bolaji, 115, 483, 851, 1175

illness, the ill, 122, 655

immigrant churches, African, 429–430, 433, 652, 1051

inclusivism, 272

inculturation. *See* contextualization

indigenous agency, in African Christianity, 537, 685, 961, 996, 1079, 1133, 1141

indigenous church principles, 323, 439

initiation rites, 384, 527, 1040

intertestamental studies. *See* Second Temple Judaism

Islam, 145, 203, 208, 311–313, 400, 602, 811

Islam and Christianity. *See* Christianity and Islam

Islam, in Africa, 55, 76, 83–85, 87, 265, 410, 473, 504, 572, 640, 686, 772–774, 786, 847, 890, 944, 950, 971, 974, 1004, 1096, 1105, 1117, 1174, 1180

Islamic fundamentalism. *See* fundamentalism, Islamic

Ivory Coast, 437

J

Jesus, 114, 210, 318, 772, 1023, 1074, 1118, 1189

Judaism, in Africa, 489, 998

justice, 259, 386, 817, 1143

K

Kä Mana, 269, 295

Kato, Byang, 115, 160, 263, 437, 810

Kenya, 64, 87, 108, 206, 291, 332–333, 360, 394, 402–406, 437, 465, 503, 546–547, 567, 579, 584, 588, 590, 638, 692, 725, 774, 804, 852, 861, 870, 893, 946, 961, 1046–1047, 1056–1057, 1090, 1142

Kivengere, Festo, 229

L

Lakwena, Alice, 117

languages, African, 956, 1052

leadership, 19, 368, 789

leadership, Christian, 37, 58, 219, 246, 260, 301, 349, 374, 395, 405, 515, 695, 881, 997, 1125

liberation theology, 126, 198, 300, 302–303, 387, 554, 676, 731, 742, 744–745, 751–752, 770–771, 905, 929, 1073, 1116, 1151, 1196

Liberia, 288, 305, 393, 521, 910, 1030, 1065

literature ministry, 882

literature, African. *See* African literature

Livingstone, David, 656, 976, 1156

London Missionary Society, 202, 571, 619, 976

Lord's Resistance Army, Uganda, 699

Lutheranism, 13, 337, 503, 549, 568, 630, 910, 1065

M

Malawi, 145, 193, 207, 533, 620, 697, 716, 723, 736, 780, 831, 884, 890, 921–922, 963, 975, 978–979, 981–982, 1020–1021, 1054, 1091, 1162

Mandela, Nelson, 417

Mariology, 42

marriage, Christian, 132, 154, 510, 540, 586, 595, 614, 923, 1087

marriage, gay, 692

marriage, traditional African, 540, 586, 595, 923, 1040, 1087

Marxism, in Africa, 279, 701

Mbiti, John, 115, 387, 561, 743, 768, 851, 867, 1085, 1175, 1194

Mennonites, 123, 456, 621, 657, 1101

Methodism, 207, 278, 458, 762

missiology, 149, 150, 511, 568, 605, 724, 777, 925, 1147–1148, 1186

missions, 119, 130, 159, 173, 606, 611, 767

missions, African indigenous, 75, 350–351, 370, 465, 485, 652, 702, 850, 1078, 1091, 1140

missions, history, 54, 63, 67, 123, 178, 182, 202, 214, 283, 288, 314, 319, 328–329, 333, 379, 416, 443, 458, 461, 475, 482, 503, 512, 549, 568, 571, 618–619, 656, 697, 744, 765, 927, 961, 975, 985, 988, 1013, 1043, 1054, 1066, 1070, 1075, 1080, 1120, 1133, 1147–1149, 1159, 1200

missions, medical, 212, 338, 340, 376, 438, 654, 719, 984, 1184

missions, Protestant, 230, 279

missions, Roman Catholic, 54, 156, 261, 262, 804

missions, theology of, 105, 149–150, 272, 350–351, 605, 769, 856

missions, western, 777, 1032

modernity, African, 68, 103, 183, 186, 223, 378, 428, 520, 537, 728, 739, 740–741, 865, 1081, 1132

monotheism, 669

Moratorium, 1114

Mozambique, 68, 458

Mugambi, Jesse, 269, 1122

music, in Christian worship, 91, 199, 233, 577–578, 737, 801, 1028–1029

Muslims, Christian witness to, 398–399, 472, 724, 786

N

Namibia, 629

Naudé, Beyers, 1138, 1146

neo-colonialism, 81, 1167

Ngugi wa Thiong'o, 65, 227, 1090

Niger Republic, 230

Nigeria, 1, 15, 32, 40, 41, 134–140, 173–174, 203, 246, 263, 267, 274, 278, 348–349, 359, 370, 400, 411, 427, 482, 495, 498, 506, 510, 536, 549, 594, 596, 608, 611, 618, 650, 675, 683, 696, 703, 724, 784, 800, 824, 849, 854–855, 857, 860, 863, 868, 876, 888, 894, 911, 958, 964, 1016, 1018, 1104–1105, 1117, 1140, 1149, 1183

Nkrumah, Kwame, 26, 889, 930

North Africa, 177, 268, 837, 997, 1086

northern Africa, 997

NT studies, 12, 20, 29–31, 45, 53, 101, 127, 146, 164, 176, 243, 322, 335–366, 420, 509, 532, 634, 671, 721, 754, 756, 759, 783–784, 790–792, 795, 823, 859, 880, 898, 914, 933, 942, 1012, 1115, 1118

Nubian Christianity, 331, 364, 892, 1160, 1168–1169

Nyamiti, Charles, 317, 746, 1123

O

orphans, 421, 794

OT studies, 2–3, 21, 47, 52–53, 95, 116, 181, 270, 297, 336, 353, 365, 383, 412, 469–470, 478–481, 497, 531, 574–575, 589, 598–600, 681, 813, 834, 848, 856, 876, 885, 895, 899, 954, 1000, 1019, 1108, 1112, 1143, 1163–1164

P

Pan-Africanism, 321, 636, 1196

pastoral theology, 122, 152, 260, 293, 299, 301, 374, 460, 514–515, 586, 623, 677–679, 695, 881, 1154–1155

pastors, African, 301, 457, 515, 623, 730, 1165

Patristics, 755

peace, 381

peace, peace-making, 41, 718, 983, 1037

Pentecostalism, 59–61, 69–71, 234, 264, 314, 335, 397, 493, 535, 641, 675, 684, 1122. *See also* charismatic Christianity

persecution, of Christians, 100, 239–240, 253, 294, 484, 674, 712, 1057

philosophy, African, 98, 133, 218, 316, 428, 446, 561, 680, 682, 806–807, 835, 1060

Pneumatology. *See* Holy Spirit

politics and religion, 15, 26, 92, 378, 451, 548, 550, 590, 608, 612, 708, 849, 889, 894, 913, 934, 940, 1004, 1007–1008, 1096, 1117, 1183

politics, African Christianity and, 5, 19, 259, 262, 284, 307, 343, 391–393, 396, 404, 451, 549, 554, 590, 648, 661, 675, 688, 803, 816, 831, 921, 930, 934, 955, 981–982, 1020

polygamy, 132, 296, 363, 540, 663

postcolonialism, 286–287, 442, 584, 739, 740–741, 1167

poverty, the poor, 93, 120, 220, 386, 407, 422, 538, 574, 734, 808, 908, 995, 1095, 1143, 1186

power, 1118

prayer, 106, 1109

preaching, 257, 337, 420, 453, 513, 613, 887, 1165

Presbyterianism, 266, 780, 917, 922, 975, 1054, 1113, 1197

prophets, African traditional, 62, 875

proselytism, 57, 379

Prosperity Gospel, 28, 70–71, 276, 325, 395, 646, 675, 684, 855, 1045, 1118

proverbs, African, 412, 574, 727, 820

R

race, 452, 776

Rahner, Karl, 559, 1043

reconciliation, 259, 388, 522, 557, 732, 817

reconstruction, theology of. *See* theology of reconstruction

Reformed, 131, 612, 805, 1080

religions, comparative. *See* comparative religions

religions, in Africa, 57, 129, 155, 193, 213, 222, 237, 435, 489, 498, 507, 576, 705, 747, 800, 864, 867, 1004, 1055

religions, primal, 821, 866

religious conflict, 99, 411, 445, 607–608, 689, 1007, 1183

religious education, 573

religious indifference, in Africa, 711. *See also* secularism

religious life and customs, Christian, 177, 180, 242, 310, 426, 519, 596, 945, 1001

religious orders, Roman Catholic, 527, 765, 804, 963, 1043

revelation, theology of, 559

revival, renewal, 174, 175, 493, 683, 1034

Roman Catholicism, in Africa, 29, 42, 108, 158, 169, 225, 235, 274–275, 277, 300, 302–303, 361, 390, 409, 448, 495, 528–529, 533, 566, 580, 617, 694, 700–701, 707, 773, 784, 824, 858, 877, 925, 963, 1018, 1040, 1048–1049, 1086

Rwanda, 367, 423, 469, 633–664, 878, 886, 956. *See also* genocide, Rwandan

S

sacrifice, 2, 946

salvation. *See* soteriology

Sanneh, Lamin, 49, 129, 1009

Second Temple Judaism, 526

secularism, 431, 711, 816, 1046, 1128, 1183

Senegal, 795

sermons, African Christian, 337, 403–404, 513, 716, 1111, 1165

sex, sexuality, 9

Sharia, Islamic, 84, 134–140, 550, 689, 849, 1096, 1117, 1174

Sierra Leone, 184, 439, 628, 1014, 1036, 1050

SIM, 32, 144, 230, 279, 323, 457, 611, 1104

sin, collective, 1100

slavery, 56, 208, 1036

slavery, abolition of, 208, 960, 1002

slavery, African, 334, 650–651, 670, 1105

slavery, Islamic, 83, 334, 414, 491, 650, 670

slavery, modern, 143, 779

slavery, slave trade, 487, 491, 651

slavery, trans-Atlantic, 670

Smith, Edwin, 251, 1193

social responsibility, Christian, 35, 48, 86, 120, 141, 148, 151, 153, 166, 167, 171, 187–190, 198, 217, 224–225, 230, 247, 255–258, 284, 295, 307, 380–381, 385–386, 391–394, 405, 408, 425–426, 474, 496, 520, 523–524, 538, 544–555, 558, 582, 591, 603, 606, 624, 631, 648–649, 651, 668, 701, 707, 750–751, 762, 781, 808, 818, 831, 876, 962, 970, 982, 986, 992, 1049, 1061, 1100, 1125, 1128, 1138, 1145, 1186, 1191

sociology of religion, 117–118, 155, 185, 213, 234, 310, 394, 397, 464, 534, 575, 587, 747, 785, 1046, 1065, 1106, 1114, 1128

Somalia, 265, 436, 719–720

soteriology, 38, 45, 325, 797

South Africa, 14, 17, 61, 74, 76, 124, 141, 147–148, 151, 159, 189, 195–196, 224, 228, 256–257, 260, 264, 283, 307, 312–313, 344, 361, 388, 490, 603, 606, 616, 705, 782, 822, 914, 977, 985, 990, 992–994, 1077, 1098, 1128, 1132, 1137, 1139, 1145–1146, 1172. *See also* Apartheid, South African

southern Africa, 249, 346–347, 396, 476, 717, 778, 872–875, 926, 1055, 1141, 1163, 1173

spirit-possession, 118, 617, 729

spirit-world, 117, 305–306, 322, 326, 366, 378, 434, 572, 585, 679, 729, 1021

spiritual formation, 1076

spirituality, 204, 431, 770, 1109

Sudan/South Sudan, 99, 143, 162, 239–240, 253, 265, 340, 445, 475, 512, 560, 712, 779, 794, 801–802, 902, 906, 912, 924, 1160, 1169, 1177–1178

suffering, 100, 239, 294, 407, 484, 712, 813

Swaziland, 345

syncretism, 213, 222, 330, 769, 860, 900

T

Tanzania, 156, 328, 511, 568, 573, 624, 946, 958, 996, 1083, 1131, 1180

Tertullian, 115, 268, 1181

theological education, 14, 18, 43–44, 75, 157, 207, 219, 401, 457, 477, 635, 653, 730, 738, 919, 931, 936, 972, 979, 1067, 1076, 1197

Theological Education by Extension, 18, 163, 324, 477, 783, 1058, 1093

theology, 253, 255–256, 259, 390, 559, 748. *See also* God, doctrine of

theology of reconstruction, 198, 269, 295, 385, 668, 745, 751

theology, Christian, 177, 585, 696, 830, 980

theology, ecumenical, 777, 1073

theology, in Africa, 10, 194, 289, 318, 325, 373, 375, 407, 427, 454, 496, 502, 533, 543, 593, 609–610, 713, 793, 839, 843–844, 846, 857, 877, 897, 904–905, 929, 937, 1027, 1064, 1074, 1085, 1097, 1103, 1126, 1198. *See also* African Theology

theology, practical, 152, 276, 460, 594, 596, 713, 729–730, 832–833, 863, 989, 1022, 1049, 1089, 1130

theology, Reformed, 258, 264

theology, systematic, 226, 610, 897

Tiénou, Tite, 552, 904

traditional healers, 74, 625

translation, 645

translation, Bible. *See* Bible translation

trauma healing, 423, 487, 1154–1155

TRC South Africa, 147, 217, 225, 388, 417, 1110

tribalism, problem of, 153, 166, 781, 983, 1106. *See also* ethnicity

Trinity, the, 669, 851

Tutu, Desmond, 104, 417, 490, 822, 1098, 1146, 1195

U

Uganda, 117, 182, 212, 229, 803, 1184

universities, in Africa. *See* higher education, African

urbanization, cities, 799, 833, 953, 989, 1042, 1047

V

Vatican II, 261

violence, 633, 699, 947, 1107, 1139

violence, Christian response to, 40–41, 253, 380, 432, 484, 1139, 1146, 1150, 1158

W

Walls, Andrew, 49, 77, 178, 652

WCC, 86, 285, 591, 845, 938, 1158

West Africa, 44, 214, 517, 601–602, 853, 949, 1002

West Indies, missions from the, 988

western missions in Africa, 272, 767, 769, 1010

westernization. *See* Africa and the West

widows, 247, 962

witchcraft accusation, 432

witchcraft, occult, 74, 223, 299, 378, 432, 444, 617, 722, 728, 829, 853, 871, 1022, 1036, 1056

witness, cross-cultural, 156, 215, 221, 350–352, 370, 400, 465, 485–486, 850, 1091, 1140, 1178

women in ministry, 194, 197, 221, 564, 693, 770, 805, 922

women, role of, 8, 17, 50, 126, 197, 205, 232, 240, 242, 286–287, 358, 377, 380, 450, 471, 495, 527, 541, 564, 624, 663, 693–694, 841–846, 918, 920, 922, 932, 1001, 1150, 1191

worldview, Christian, 1126–1127

worship, Christian, 64, 384, 402, 455, 528, 539, 570, 579, 1083, 1088, 1121. *See also* dance, liturgical *and* music, in Christian worship

Y

youth, ministry to, 1, 25, 315, 746

Z

Zambia, 202, 222, 338, 434, 461, 488, 654, 737, 758, 765, 953

Zimbabwe, 77, 86, 199, 250–252, 284, 308, 358, 376, 684, 733, 738, 762, 945, 1136, 1200

Contributors

Those who have contributed reviews to the journal *BookNotes for Africa* through the years are in almost every case either from Africa or have served at length in Africa. Nearly all have been involved to one degree or another in theological education on the continent. Most have had earned doctorates. Below is a selective listing of such reviewers to the journal from the first issue in 1996 through to the present. The list includes geographical designations to identify where each person is from and/or has principally served in Africa.

Alan Chilver (Nigeria)
Andy Wildsmith (Nigeria, Kenya)
Ann Miller (Kenya)
Anne Nguku (Kenya)
Barbara York (Kenya)
Benno van den Toren (Central African Republic)
Bill McCall (Togo)
Bill O'Donovan (Nigeria, Kenya)
Bitrus Sarma (Nigeria)
Bruce Dipple (Niger)
Bulus Galadima (Nigeria)
Chris Beetham (Ethiopia)
Clare Fuller (Nigeria)
Danny McCain (Nigeria)
Dave Rousseau (Zimbabwe)
David Langford (Congo)
Debra Bowers (Kenya)
Delbert Chinchen (Malawi, Liberia)
Don Hall (Ghana, Nigeria)
Dorothy Bowen (Kenya)
Douglas Carew (Sierra Leone, Kenya)
Ed Klotz (Nigeria, Eritrea)
Ernst Wendland (Zambia)
Esther Spurrier (Zambia)
Frew Tamrat (Ethiopia)
George Folarin (Nigeria)
George Foxall (Nigeria)
Gordon Molyneux (Congo)
Grant LeMarquand (Kenya, Ethiopia)
Gregg Okesson (Kenya)

Israel Simbaya (Zambia)
Jacob Kibor (Kenya)
Jacob Rodriguez (Ethiopia)
James Gray (South Africa)
Janet Wildsmith (Nigeria, Kenya)
Jim Miller (Kenya)
Joe Simfukwe (Zambia)
John Anonby (Kenya)
Johnny Bakke (Ethiopia)
Jonathan More (South Africa)
José Nzuiki Phuela (Congo)
Judy Hill (Nigeria, Central African Republic)
Jurie van Wyk (Zambia)
Kathy Stuebing (Zambia)
Keith Ferdinando (Congo)
Kenneth Ross (Malawi)
Klaus Fiedler (Malawi)
Knut Holter (Norway)
Las Newman (Jamaica)
Lila Balisky (Ethiopia)
Lois Fuller Dow (Nigeria)
Mabiala Kenzo (Congo)
Mark Hinton (Kenya, Sudan)
Musa Gaiya (Nigeria)
Olusegun Olawoyin (Nigeria)
Onesimus Ngundu (Zimbabwe)
Paul Balisky (Ethiopia)
Paul Bowers (Nigeria, Kenya)
Paul Kleiner (Angola)
Paul Mpindi (Congo)

Paul Todd (Nigeria)
Peter Ford (Ethiopia, Kenya)
Peter Unseth (Ethiopia)
Phil Morrison (Kenya)
Rich Stuebing (Zambia)
Richard Gehman (Kenya)
Richardson Oyediran (Nigeria)
Roger Kemp (Zambia)
Ron Sim (Kenya)
Sam Folarin (Nigeria)
Sam Olarewaju (Nigeria)
Sam Kunhiyop (Nigeria)
Sandra Joireman (USA, Ethiopia)
Scott Cunningham (Nigeria)

Scott Moreau (Kenya)
Sid Garland (Nigeria)
Steve Bryan (Ethiopia)
Steve Hardy (Mozambique)
Steve Morad (Kenya)
Steve Strauss (Ethiopia)
Tim Palmer (Nigeria)
Tim Stabell (Congo)
Tom Kopp (South Africa)
Walter Gschwandtner (Kenya)
Walter Rapold (Rwanda)
Weanzana wa Nupanga (Congo, Central African Republic)

Book Notes
FOR AFRICA
A R E V I E W J O U R N A L

REVIEWS OF RECENT AFRICA-RELATED PUBLICATIONS
RELEVANT FOR INFORMED CHRISTIAN REFLECTION IN AFRICA

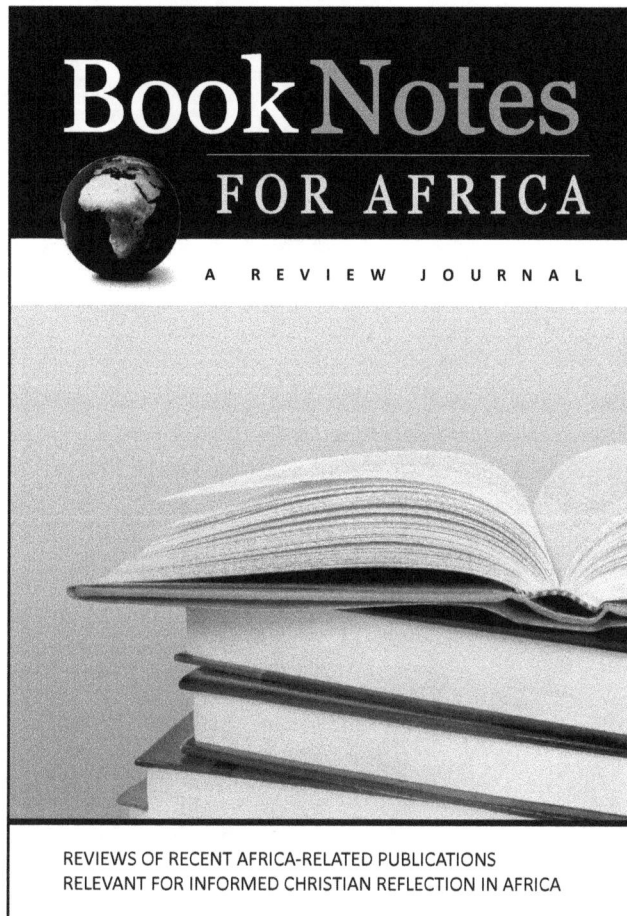

BookNotes for Africa is an occasional publication (usually twice yearly) offering one-paragraph evaluative reviews of recent Africa-related publications relevant for informed Christian reflection in and about Africa. Titles are selected especially for potential interest to theological educators, libraries, ministry leaders, scholars and researchers in Africa and overseas.

For further information contact: booknotesforafrica@langham.org

Langham

PARTNERSHIP

Langham Literature and its imprints are a ministry of Langham Partnership.

Langham Partnership is a global fellowship working in pursuit of the vision God entrusted to its founder John Stott –

to facilitate the growth of the church in maturity and Christ-likeness through raising the standards of biblical preaching and teaching.

Our vision is to see churches in the majority world equipped for mission and growing to maturity in Christ through the ministry of pastors and leaders who believe, teach and live by the Word of God.

Our mission is to strengthen the ministry of the Word of God through:
- nurturing national movements for biblical preaching
- fostering the creation and distribution of evangelical literature
- enhancing evangelical theological education

especially in countries where churches are under-resourced.

Our ministry

Langham Preaching partners with national leaders to nurture indigenous biblical preaching movements for pastors and lay preachers all around the world. With the support of a team of trainers from many countries, a multi-level programme of seminars provides practical training, and is followed by a programme for training local facilitators. Local preachers' groups and national and regional networks ensure continuity and ongoing development, seeking to build vigorous movements committed to Bible exposition.

Langham Literature provides majority world preachers, scholars and seminary libraries with evangelical books and electronic resources through publishing and distribution, grants and discounts. The programme also fosters the creation of indigenous evangelical books in many languages, through writer's grants, strengthening local evangelical publishing houses, and investment in major regional literature projects, such as one volume Bible commentaries like *The Africa Bible Commentary* and *The South Asia Bible Commentary*.

Langham Scholars provides financial support for evangelical doctoral students from the majority world so that, when they return home, they may train pastors and other Christian leaders with sound, biblical and theological teaching. This programme equips those who equip others. Langham Scholars also works in partnership with majority world seminaries in strengthening evangelical theological education. A growing number of Langham Scholars study in high quality doctoral programmes in the majority world itself. As well as teaching the next generation of pastors, graduated Langham Scholars exercise significant influence through their writing and leadership.

To learn more about Langham Partnership and the work we do visit **langham.org**

www.ingramcontent.com/pod-product-compliance
Lightning Source LLC
Chambersburg PA
CBHW062015090426
42811CB00005B/861